50th ANNIVERSARY OF WORLD WAR II

Beaver County Times

50th ANNIVERSARY OF WORLD WAR II
Beaver PA

We gratefully acknowledge the help of the **Laughlin Memorial Free Library**, Ambridge; **B.F. Jones Memorial Library**, Aliquippa; **Carnegie Free Library**, Beaver Falls; and the Dominick Curtaccio family. Our thanks also go to Beaver County Times employees Connie Fields, Jack Mitchell and Joe Tronzo, who led the effort in preparing this book.

F. W. Gordon, Publisher
Beaver County Times, Allegheny Times

Developed under agreement with **Historical Briefs, Inc.**
Box 629, Sixth Street & Madalyn Ave., Verplank NY 10596

Printed by:
Monument Printers & Lithographer, Inc.
Sixth Street & Madalyn Ave., Verplank NY 10596

Foreword

In reflecting upon the 50th anniversary of World War II, the editors of the Beaver County Times and Allegheny Times have chronicled in this book those fateful years between 1939 and 1945 that shaped the history of this country.

In the pages that follow, you will read about the victories and defeats, the sorrow and joy, the sacrifices and dedication that accompanied this "war to end all wars" as reported so faithfully in your hometown newspapers a half-century ago.

These newspapers were the predecessors of the Beaver County Times — Aliquippa Gazette, Aliquippa News, Aliquippa Evening Times, Ambridge Citizen, Beaver Daily Times and The News Tribune of Beaver Falls.

Their pages tell a story of how a community reacted to the cataclysmic events of far-off battles; how it sent thousands of its sons and daughters to war, hundreds never to return; how it hunkered down at home to mold one of the strongest industrial bastions in the world — one that contributed mightily to winning the war.

Between the reports of the Nazis' blitzkrieg of Poland and the signing of the Japanese surrender terms on the U.S.S. Missouri in Tokyo Bay, the pages that follow weave a fabric of Smalltown U.S.A. during The War Years. It is a fascinating story.

For nearly six years, readers of our hometown papers demanded and were fed a daily dose of war news on page 1. In the absence of television, it was devoured. News of the war was paramount. But life went on at home, as reflected on other pages of the newspapers of the day.

Item: June 18, 1941 (from the Beaver Daily Times) — Hitler and Mussolini met in Munich to map the fate of France, while in Beaver County coffee was selling for 13 cents a pound and bacon for 17 cents a pound; the Snyder Garage Inc. advertised a new Special 6 Pontiac Sedan for $838 and Blondie and Dagwood, as usual, drew chuckles on the comic page.

Those who were around here during The War Years — perhaps one in three of our residents of today — may recall, fondly or otherwise, the rationing of gasoline and sugar, the weekly scrap drives, the air raid "blackout" drills, the highly successful War Bond efforts and the hard work in the mills.

Especially the hard work in the mills. Before the war Beaver County, as most of Western Pennsylvania, suffered dearly in the throes of the Great Depression. It emerged from World War II as the seventh largest industrial area in the nation.

The Aliquippa Works of Jones and Laughlin Steel Corp. set world records for production. The Curtiss-Wright plant in Vanport (now Westinghouse) employed 4,600 and produced 150,000 airplane propeller blades. The American Bridge Division plant of U.S. Steel in Ambridge built tank landing barges; Dravo Inc. on Neville Island turned out LSTs. Koppers Co.'s Kobuta plant became a prime producer of synthetic rubber components.

Indeed, World War II changed dramatically the face and fiber of our community. But the war took its toll on many families and in many ways. A paragraph in the V-J edition of the Beaver Daily Times of Sept. 3, 1945 summed it up:

"It is good to live again in a world which, once gone mad with greed and bloodshed, has returned to peace and sanity."

We hope you enjoy reliving a unique chapter in the history of this country through the pages of this book.

The editors of The Times

From the pages of the . . .

Ambridge Citizen, Aliquippa Gazette, Aliquippa News, Aliquippa News Gazette, Aliquippa Evening Times, Beaver Daily Times and the Beaver Falls News Tribune.

Bargain Offerings Plentiful in Three-Hour Sale of Merchants Here

TEN PAGES

The Aliquippa Gazette

SERVING AN INDUSTRIAL COMMUNITY OF 50,000

WEATHER — Fair and slightly colder tonight. Saturday fair and warmer. Sunday rain with mild temperature.

VOL. XVII. No. 174 | SERVED BY UNITED PRESS MEMBER OF P. N. P. A. | ALIQUIPPA, PA., FRIDAY, JANUARY 6, 1939 | PHONE 981-935 | 3 CENTS; BY CARRIER, 15 CENTS A WEEK

Leg Shortened In Crash, Claimed In Suit

RELIEF GIFTS HIT $1,000

Betty Grable Off To Ma; Jackie With Uncle

Betty Grable, the actress-wife [illegible] is living with an [illegible] settlement of his suit against his family for an accounting of his earnings.

$100 DAMAGES ASSESSED BOYS

Two Logstown youths, charged with malicious mischief and having destroyed to the extent of nearly $100 a vacant house owned by Itskovitz and Co., were free today pending restitution of damages within a week.

At a hearing last night before Peace Justice Ivor L. Jones the two were assessed costs and ordered to pay damages to the property.

According to Patrolman Phillip Pastine, head of the juvenile bureau of the department here, a group of boys have been playing in the building. Damage included the dismantling of electric light switches and the complete destruction of the walls in several of the rooms.

The pair were found guilty of the mischief charge after testimony of some four other boys revealed they had entered the building with saws and hammers. The razing was first heard by neighbors in the vicinity of the 105 Miller street building.

If complete restitution is not made within the specified time more serious prosecution will be followed, Jones said.

CLASH ON CZECH FRONTIER; 15 DIE

BUDAPEST, Hungary (UP)—Czechoslovak soldiers, using machine guns and artillery, battled Hungarian troops at the frontier town of Munkacs today in a clash officially reported to have cost at least 15 lives. The engagement was still going on this afternoon.

The fighting, considered an outgrowth of the recent dispute over the Czechoslovak-Hungarian frontier, began at 3:40 a. m., the government announced. Officials asserted that Czech troops and a unit of the Ukrainian Free Corps attacked Oroszrev with machine guns and three tanks.

(In Prague, the government admitted that a "frontier incident" had occurred on the Hungarian border but details were lacking. The Ukrainian Free Corps mentioned in dispatches from Budapest apparently was connected with recent agitation for creation of an independent Ukrainian state in territory now within the frontiers of Poland, Rumania, Soviet Russia and Czechoslovakia. The Ukrainians also seek a very thin slice of territory on the Hungarian frontier.)

MANY BARGAINS LISTED HERE IN 3-HOUR SALE

Dozen Leading Firms Are Co-operating In New Movement

Bargain offerings galore feature a three-hour community sale, sponsored by a dozen progressive Aliquippa business concerns, here tomorrow afternoon.

The sale, something new in cooperative, community merchandising activity will continue from 2 p. m. until 5 p. m. only in participating stores of Aliquippa.

Each participating business house is offering from one to four outstanding values during the period marked down to below ordinary clearance prices. Men's wear, women's wear, drug store merchandise, white goods and kitchen ware are included in the score of offerings.

Sponsors of the bargain carnival pointed out the prices listed would hold only during the hours the sale continues and that before and after that period regular prices will prevail.

In some instances stocks of the [illegible] shoppers are urged to come early since a "first come, first served" policy will prevail in each of the participating shops.

For additional details turn to advertisements on page 6 of today's Gazette.

$10,000 Suit Is Filed By Man Here

A $10,000 damage suit was filed at Beaver today by counsel for Gust Skuda of Aliquippa against James Mancini, owner of the Mancini Baking company of Pittsburgh, to recover for injuries allegedly suffered by the plaintiff when struck by the defendant's truck.

Skuda claims his right leg was shortened and his earning powers lessened as a result of the accident.

It is charged the plaintiff was crossing Franklin avenue here July 15, 1938, at 11 a. m., when a truck belonging to Mancini and operated by Ovidio DeClemente, hit him.

The plaintiff avers he was confined at Beaver Valley hospital until Sept. 3, receiving treatment and also was under care of a doctor at his home.

Curtis Brown Dies; Veteran Of The War With Spain In 1898

Curtis Brown, 67, father of Loyal [illegible] here, died today at his home in Wampum. He was a veteran of the Spanish-American war.

In addition to his son here, he leaves the following children: Elmer, William, Charles, Raymond and Mrs. Regis Arnold, of Wampum.

The body is at the Marshall funeral home in Wampum. Funeral service will be there Sunday at 2:30 p. m.

Dues Inspection At Donora Plant Leads To Clash; Police Out

DONORA, Pa. — (UP) — Pickets for the Steel Workers Organizing Committee and employes of the American Steel and Wire Co. plant here, skirmished in front of the main gate last night in what was described as a controversy over union membership and payment of dues.

The pickets lined up at the Sixth and Meldon street gates and tried to prevent non-union workers and union members who are delinquent in their dues from entering the plant.

The resultant skirmish became so serious that a detachment of state motor police was called to help local officers restore order at the midnight change of working shifts.

Funeral Services Tomorrow At 10 a.m. For Mrs. Plodinec

Funeral service for Mrs. N. S. Plodinec, Sr., prominent Aliquippa woman, who died yesterday, will be tomorrow at 10 a. m. at St. Titus R. C. church here. The Rev. Fr. Edward Zauner will officiate and burial will be in Mt. Olivet cemetery.

The Aliquippa W. B. A., of which lodge Mrs. Plodinec was a member, will hold services at the Plodinec residence this evening, starting at 7 p. m. All members of the W. B. A. are requested to attend the rites.

Beauty Parlor on the Beach

Barbara Sysle is pictured giving Irmagard Dietel a hasty pedicure on the sands at Tahiti Beach, Miami, Fla., after having "set up shop" for the convenience of hurried bathers.

3 Reactions to Presidential Message

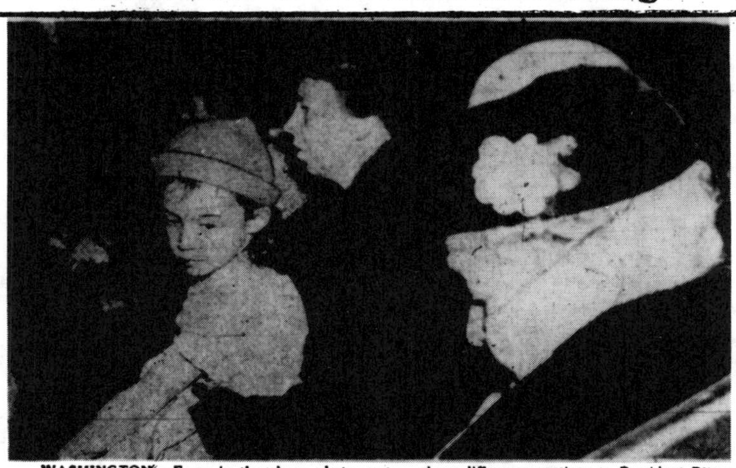

WASHINGTON.—Faces in the above photo portray three different reactions to President Roosevelt's message to Congress. Mrs. Roosevelt, left, portrays intentness; Commerce Secretary Hopkins' daughter, Diana, on Mrs. Roosevelt's lap, portrays indifference; and Mrs. Sara Delano Roosevelt, right, shows deep study. Almost obscured in between the two women is Frederick Delano, the President's uncle. (Acme Photo)

"Desert Rat", on Visit Here, Hears the Call of the Yukon

By Vernon Langille

When a "desert rat" hits a steel town like Aliquippa his nostrils plug, he hears the clink of nuggets on the washing pans; the strike of the pick; pure air and the steady thunder of the rapids in the Yukon call him; his feet itch and his visit is over.

He's off on another prospecting trip.

That, briefly, is the story of Mike Dawson, who for 45 years has followed the paydirt.

He is here visiting his brother, Joseph F. Dawson, Hall street, New Sheffield. He came due to the death of another brother, James Dawson, in a Veteran's hospital.

Few gold rushes in the latter half of the 19th century and early 20th have passed without the Dawson claim. Mike Dawson, who is known by prospectors in Death Valley, the Yukon, in Alaska, Montana, Nevada, the Klondike, Skagway, and a dozen other gold mining spots, has hit every one of them.

"You have to have that certain disposition to stick to prospecting," Dawson told the Gazette reporter. "The nervous type man will blow up. There's something to pecking around for gold that is fascinating. When that something gets under your hide you're a prospector."

Prospector Dawson was introduced to Aliquippa's mixologist, Henry Loud. The two had a heart-to-heart talk on gold, the backbone of the U. S. Mint.

Henry has 11 claims.

Dawson, a Pennsylvanian, left the state in the spring of 1897 and landed among the painted ladies, wholesale gambling and a rough crowd of old miners in the copper mining town of Butte, Montana.

According to Dawson, every gambling device on the face of the globe made its way into Butte.

"The town boasted the fastest race track in the country," he said, "the prettiest women and the best copper."

After some 20 months, the Alaska gold rush attracted the Pennsylvanian.

"In 1898 every man in Montana caught the "gold fever," he explained. "I, like hundreds of others, assumed the grass grew greener farther on. Within the next few months hardly a prospector was left in Montana."

When he arrived at the Yukon, he was branded a chechocker, meaning newcomer, by the Indians. He traveled over the Chillocute Pass by the way of Diea, through Forks and landed in Dawson.

Dawson revealed that in the Yukon payment for work to the miners was made with gold dust. [illegible] of 1, [illegible] and 10-dollar denominations were used [illegible]. Every [illegible] had its [illegible].

In Dawson, Mike went to work on Bonanza creek.

Mr. Dawson told of the Indians, "packers," who took contracts on carrying provisions to the top of Chillecote, Alaska, a treacherous pass three miles straight up. The Indian packers worked for seven cents per pound.

"When the packing was over," Dawson said, "there was enough provisions such as bedding, food, powder, tents, etc., to load a 50-car freight train."

"It was surprising the load that the 'packers', especially Indians, could carry over the narrow, rough

(Continued on Page Four)

COUNTY PILOTS FLY TO RACES

Four Beaver county pilots flew their airplanes to Miami, Fla., yesterday to participate in the All-American air races there this week-end.

The county planes are among more than 500 that will take part in what will be the greatest concentration of aircraft in history of the U. S.

Aviators who hedge-hopped to the southern city from the nearby airports included:

John Pollinger, Conway, Aeronca plane; A. J. Moore, Conway, Craft plane; Russ Kerr and Walter Zundle, both of Patterson Heights airport, flying cub planes.

SPIKE SMUGGLING RING

NEW YORK.—(UP)—Policemen, disguised as criminals and aided by coast guardsmen and customs agents, sprang a trap on a smuggling mob early today, captured three men and seized $150,000 worth of opium after a gun battle on the Brooklyn waterfront.

One policeman was wounded.

The opium was brought here on the S. S. Ida, from Italy, and was transferred in the harbor to a launch at midnight during a rain storm. The smugglers thought their own men were aboard the launch but it was manned by policemen in disguise.

The climax came an hour later when the policemen took the cans of opium to the pier and kept the rendezvous with the smugglers' shore gang there to receive it. In setting the trap, the whole area had been surrounded with federal and city agents in cutters, launches and automobiles. Fifteen authorities took part in the gun battle and more than 100 shots were fired.

The Ida meanwhile had proceeded to dock in Hoboken, N. J., and it was reported that federal agents had boarded her and taken off three more prisoners. This was not confirmed immediately, nor was the Ida identified.

Nominated to Highest Court

WASHINGTON.—"Hot Dog!" could well have been the ejaculation uttered by Prof. Felix Frankfurter when he was notified that he had been nominated to the United States Supreme Court by President Roosevelt. Frankfurter, a Jewish scholar of 56, is shown above in his office at Harvard University Law School. (Acme Photo)

RELIEF DRIVE AT HALF-WAY MARK IN BORO

Kiefer Again Elected To Head Local Aid Group

Aliquippa Central Relief association officials revealed today, following their annual organization meeting, a $383.22 balance was left from 1938 in the organization's treasury.

At a joint session in the council chambers in the borough building last night, election of officers, committee reports and disposition of routine business took place.

Robert Crawford, chairman of the solicitation committee in charge of the association's fund drive, reported more than $756 collected thus far.

"If all that have pledged donations and other collections were received, we would have well over $1,000," he said.

The quota is set at $2,200.

Those unanimously named to serve as officers of the relief agency included the same officers as for 1938.

They are Burgess George L. Kiefer, president, who is taking office for the second year; Dr. J. L. Miller, vice president; T. C. [illegible]

Vice President Miller presided at the meeting of the relief board.

New donations to the relief fund as announced last night by Chairman Crawford included $35 by the Junior Woman's club; Eastern Star, $10; Ladies' Aid Society of the Presbyterian church, $25; Willing Workers class of the Mt. Carmel U. P. church, $4; and $316 donated by Aliquippa school teachers.

It is expected that the fund will increase more rapidly now, after the Christmas holidays, Crawford said.

It is especially stressed that individuals who wish to donate not wait until they have been contacted by committee members. They are requested to make their donations to the particular organizations to which they belong or leave their deposit at the Woodlawn Trust Co. here.

"It is rather impossible for us to contact individually," Chairman Crawford said. "We receive donations from organizations in which we hope the individual's donation is included.

"The drive for funds to alleviate conditions of the poor here," he continued, "will continue through this month and longer if necessary."

Many bridge clubs are sponsoring benefit bridges to assist in the drive.

Organizations that can are especially urged to do this, fund committeemen explained.

The next meeting of the Board of Directors has been set for Feb. 2.

Nick Zernik Visits At Home Of Parents

Nick Zernik, first class private in the U. S. Marines and stationed at New Port, Rhode Island, was visiting today with his parents, Mr. and Mrs. Marko Zernik, 186 Shaffer street.

He has been enlisted in the Marines three years and last year was stationed in China.

He is at the Naval Torpedo station in New Port at the present time.

Beaver And Ohio Valley Hospitals

Pearl Cameron, Rochester, entered Rochester General hospital yesterday for treatment.

Discharged from the hospital were Frances Fiejdafz, Aliquippa, and Mrs. Pearl Andrews, Freedom.

Mrs. Michael Nurgem, West Aliquippa, and Mrs. Ernest Grosglass and John Morgan, both of Beaver Falls, were new admissions to Providence hospital for treatment yesterday.

Admitted to Beaver Valley hospital during the last 24 hours were Cornelius Dodds, New Galilee; Mrs. Riley Carr, Beaver Falls, and James Suplir, Beaver.

Leaving the institution were Helen Frishkorn, New Brighton; Paul Siktar, Beaver, and Nellie Pieri, New Galilee.

FILES DIVORCE SUIT

Mrs. Louise A. Nos of Aliquippa today had filed a divorce suit at Beaver against Carl Rudolph Nos, charging cruelty. They were married Feb. 25, 1927.

Coach Lippe To Alter Quip Lineup Tonight

Galento Knocks Out Brescia In 1 Round

NEWARK, N. J. (UP) - Two-ton Galento, of Orange, N. J., knocked out Jorge Brescia, heavyweight champion of Argentina, in 1:41 minutes of the first round of their scheduled ten-rounder last night before more than 10,000 fans here.

Brescia, who had lasted nearly three rounds with Joe Louis in 1936, took the full count after he had gone to the floor for the second time. Galento tore at Brescia at the opening gong, using his left hand like a broadsword. Brescia did not land a hard blow to Tony's face.

LAST NIGHT'S FIGHTS
By United Press

NEWARK.—Tony Galento, 236, Orange, N. J., kayoed Jorge Brescia, Argentine, 216 (1).

BOSTON.—Bob Pastor, 182½, New York, outpointed Tiger Warrington, 176½, Nova Scotia (10).

DENVER.—Tony Canzoneri, 139, outpointed Wally Hally, 136½, Los Angeles (10).

PATRONIZE OUR ADVERTISERS

Tickets Going Fast For Ambridge-Quip Game Next Tuesday

Tickets were going fast today for the annual Aliquippa-Ambridge basketball game at the hilltop gym here next Tuesday night.

A. H. S. officials said their supply of reserved seats, being sold at the high school, is almost exhausted. Reserved ducats also are available at Dudley's News Stand, Young's Drug Store, Joe, the Barber on Plan 12, and Roma's Billiard parlor, Plan 11.

Ski Trails Opened In Park Near Kane

KANE, Pa. — (UP) — Allegheny National park, the only federal forest in the eastern United States to offer 12-month recreational facilities, has opened five miles of ski trails at Twin Lakes, seven miles south of here.

Skiing facilities complete equipment for play throughout the year. Previously there had been bathing in the summer, camping and fishing in the spring, and hiking trails for summer use.

The new skiing course includes a two and one-half mile racing bank which will be used for competition as well as for general skiing.

GAMES TONIGHT

Aliquippa at New Brighton.
Ellwood City at Ambridge.
Beaver Falls at Butler
Beaver at Freedom.
Monaca at Zelienople.
Evans City at Midland.
Alumni at New Castle.
Leetsdale at Neville.
Sewickley at West View.

THREE RESERVES READY TO FILL VARSITY POSTS

Team Makeup Uncertain; New Brighton Host To Aliquippa

New names will grace Aliquippa High's starting lineup tonight for its Section III encounter against New Brighton on the down-river floor.

Dissatisfied with the performance of his charges in the Butler clash here Tuesday, Coach Nate Lippe has groomed three Reserves for varsity duty. He is determined to uncover a winning combination.

"If my regulars want to fiddle while Rome burns, it's O. K. by me," the Quip mentor said today. "I'll put boys in there who want to play basketball."

Lippe will not decide upon his first-string crew until this evening but indicated he would shift Capt. Bobby Hanshew to the center slot, replacing Hank Walsh.

Undergraduates Blicha, Volitich and Hodovanich are ready to supplant such regulars as Nick Vincich, Tom Branchetti and George Woodward. Paul Bar, who has alternated as a varsity man and substitute all season, likely will start at forward, the coach declared.

New Brighton has won only one game in four starts, that being at the expense of Butler on the latter team's floor. It has the poorest scoring team in the section, with the work of Emery, Panner, Klutka, Dwyer and Nagy standing out thus far.

Tonight's game will start at 8 p. m., following a prelim between Reserves of both schools.

Aliquippa Junior High travels to Rochester this afternoon for a non-league game with the future Rams.

St. Veronica Cagers Wallop St. Casimir

The Crusader floormen of St. Veronica High ran roughshod over St. Casimir's cagers at Pittsburgh last night and won by the lop-sided score of 51 to 20.

Skrzpek, Hricik and Atkinson accounted for 33 points between them to lead the Crusaders' drive. Gerdauskis was best man for the home pack. Lineup:

St. Veronica—51	G	F	Pts.
Skrzpek, f	4	4	10
Persuitti, f	1	0	2
Casl, c	2	0	4
[illegible], g	6	1	13
[illegible]	[illegible]	[illegible]	[illegible]
[illegible]	2	0	4
[illegible], f	2	0	4
Amato, g	1	0	2
Battles, f	0	1	1
Deeb, c	0	1	1
Totals	23	5	51

St. Casimir—20	G	F	Pts.
Sasinas, f	0	0	0
Slanceauskis, f	0	1	1
Kinutis, c	2	2	6
Camulis, g	1	0	2
Moeceka, g	1	1	3
Gerdauskis	4	0	8
Totals	8	4	20

FRANKLIN PIN LEAGUE

	W	L.	Pct.
Bucs	22	8	.733
Bontempo's	25	11	.694
Athletic Club	15	18	.455
State Store	12	15	.444
Pete's S. S.	6	9	.400
Plodinec's	10	20	.333

GENEVA MASTERS BETHANY BISONS

Geneva's Covenanters mastered the Bethany Bisons again, 49, to 35, in their return contest at Beaver Falls last night. The Covies forged into a 27-13 lead at halftime and preserved the margin until the end.

John Billie, Geneva's freshman center, paced the cagers with 15 points to his credit. Cullison was main performer for Bethany. Lineup:

Geneva—49	G	F	Pts.
Winters, f	2	1	5
Kidder, f	1	4	6
Billie, c	7	1	15
Roselli, g	2	0	4
Hartshorn, g	4	0	8
Harbowicz, f	1	0	2
Milanovich, g	1	0	2
Meskola, g	2	1	5
Stasko, f	0	2	2
Totals	20	9	49

Bethany—35	G	F	Pts.
Petroff, f	3	4	10
Kuhns, f	0	1	1
Taylor, c	0	2	2
Jackson, g	2	3	7
Cullison, g	5	1	11
Gordon, g	1	0	2
Conghaner, g	1	0	2
Totals	12	11	35

Bucs Boost Lead In Franklin Pin League

Victorious over B[illegible]empo's by a 1-2 score, the Aliqu[illegible] Bucs padded their hold on le[illegible]hip of the Franklin Community league here last night.

Pete's S. S. won the odd game from Plodinec's while State Store took three from the Athletic club via the forfeit route. A. Skiba of the Bucs won gross honors with a 537 total and his brother had high single game score, 214. Summaries:

Bucs—2319

	1st.	2nd	3rd	Tot.
H. Skiba	214	127	132	473
C. Gnarra	93	...	...	93
Laurito	161	162	66	389
S. Maravich	121	...	...	121
A. Skiba	154	195	188	537
Klyeyk	...	167	146	313
Westman	...	155	138	293
Totals	743	806	670	2319

Bontempo's—2067

Jack Villa	119	110	76	305
Piccirrilli	127	139	118	384
Fusco	183	145	170	498
Beaner	128	157	153	438
Anthony	135	134	170	439
Totals	692	685	687	2067

Pete's S. S.—[illegible]

Deferrie	119	144	145	408
Shantik	139	140	148	427
Gaural	89	122	144	355
Trbovich	126	106	87	370
Jack Stalla	189	155	129	473
Totals	712	667	653	2032

Plodinecs—2072

Druzinsky	129	130	160	419
Petkovich	122	...	141	263
Thomas	146	86	160	392
Filligan	165	122	156	443
Greco	141	124	113	378
Plevel	...	77	...	77
Totals	703	539	730	2072

State Store—1931

S. Hacko	99	126	135	360
Trbovich	141	90	95	326
Zuccaro	109	122	134	365
Howell	140	107	125	372
Hartman	142	145	121	408
Totals	631	590	610	1931

PATRONIZE OUR ADVERTISERS

YANKEE STALWART TESTS STRENGTH

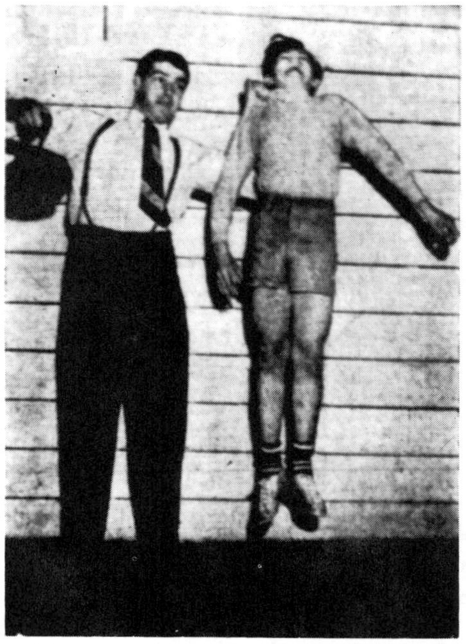

Joe DiMaggio, member of the Yankee powerhouse, limbers up with a bit of weight lifting, using Donald O'Connor to balance the weight in his right hand, during a visit to a Hollywood studio.

FLOOR RESULTS

SCHOLASTIC

Wilmerding 26, E. McKeesport 25.
Har-Breck 26, Springdale 19.
Youngwood 28, Derry Twp. 23.
Redstone 41, N. B. Vernon 24.
St. Veronica 51, St. Casimir 20.
St. Joseph 33, Duke Preps 22.
St. Mary Mount 36, St. Luke's 27.
Dunbar 34, Montgomery 23.
Elkview 49, Clay 32.

COLLEGIATE

Geneva 49, Bethany 35.
Geneva Res. 25, Bloom 34.
Fairmont 52, W. Va. Wesleyans 45.
Edinboro 64, California 44.
Duq. Frosh 40, St. Vincent Prep 38.
Blue Ridge 43, Shenandoah 23.
Western Union 40, Wartburg 29.
Kent State 30, Ashland 27.
Findlay 45, Lawrence Tech 43.
Marietta 54, Otterbein 40.
Susquehanna 58, Bucknell 39.
Villanova 37, Catholic U. 26.

Bowman, Berres Sign New Pirate Contracts

PITTSBURGH, (UP) - The signed contract of Joe Bowman, right-handed hurler from Kansas City, Mo., was received today by the Pittsburgh Pirates' Baseball club. It will be Bowman's third year with the Pirates.

At the same time, it was revealed that Catcher Ray Berres, who will serve as relief man for Ray Mueller, had mailed in his signed contract from his home in Kenosha, Wis. It will be his second year with the Pirates.

COCHRAN CAGERS GRAB THRILLERS

The Cochran A. C. cagers of Aliquippa won two games this week by the narrow margin of one point, defeating Burgettstown, 51-50, at Burgettstown, and nosing out the Plan 12 All Stars, 27-26, at Franklin gym here.

Two fouls by Kaye Batchelor in the fading seconds of play earned the Cochrans their win at Burgettstown. Paul Ward and [illegible] Bailey were scoring stars for the Aliquippans, the former getting 24 points and the latter 16.

Batchelor sparked the team to its victory over the All Stars with 19 points. His goal in the last minute of play decided the contest. Lineups:

COCHRANS—51	G.	F.	Pts.
Ward, f.	12	0	24
Shannon, f.	1	0	2
Bailey, c.	5	6	16
Peoples, g.	0	0	0
Batchelor, g.	1	7	9
Totals	19	13	51

Non-scoring sub—Schuck.

BURGETTST'N—50	G.	F.	Pts.
Canning, f.	3	1	7
Hall, f.	5	0	10
Butch, c.	5	0	10
Power, g.	4	0	8
Critchlow, g.	0	1	1
Harris, f.	3	2	8
Merush, c.	1	0	2
Miller, g.	1	0	2
Tennyson, g.	1	0	2
Totals	23	4	50

Halftime score, 19-15, Burgettstown. Referee—Power.

COCHRANS—27	G.	F.	Pts.
Shannon, f.	1	0	2
Morris, f.	2	0	4
Turney, c.	0	0	0
Peoples, g.	0	0	0
Batchelor, g.	8	3	19
Thomas, g.	1	0	2
Totals	12	3	27

ALL-STARS—26	G.	F.	Pts.
Evans, f.	1	1	3
Cribbs, f.	2	2	6
Johnson, c.	3	1	7
Pezzelle, g.	1	0	2
Hobbs, g.	3	2	8
Totals	10	6	26

Non-scoring subs: Dudash, Gray.
Halftime score, 13-10, All Stars.
Referee—Rebich.

PATRONIZE OUR ADVERTISERS

Two Men, Woman Hurt In Beaver County Accidents

TEN PAGES

The Aliquippa Gazette

SERVING AN INDUSTRIAL COMMUNITY OF 50,000

WEATHER — Rain changing to snow. Colder tonight. Colder in west portion Saturday. Partly cloudy and colder with snow flurries

VOL. XVII. No. 204 | SERVED BY UNITED PRESS MEMBER OF P. N. P. A. | ALIQUIPPA, PA., FRIDAY, FEBRUARY 10, 1939 | PHONE 934-935 | 3 CENTS; BY CARRIER, 15 CENTS A WEEK

POPE DIES; WORLD CONCLAVE CALLED TO NAME SUCCESSOR

Valiant Spiritual Leader Passes Away With 'Peace' Murmured As Farewell Word

POPE
PIUS
XI

Pope Pius XI, the 261st leader of the Catholics, who died Thursday night at Vatican City, Rome. The Holy Father succumbed after a valiant fight against an illness that attacked him in 1936. Despite his illness the Pope carried on a constant diplomatic battle for peace among nations of the world. He was the most modern of any ruler of the Vatican. All civilization united today in mourning the loss to Christianity.

NATIONS UNITE TO MOURN LOSS; MASSES ORDERED

Final Illness Strikes As Father Nears 82nd Birthday

VATICAN CITY (UP) — **Eugenio, Cardinal Pacilli, as- [illegible] voked a world [illegible] dinals today to elect a pope in succession to Pius XI.**

Pope Pius died at 5:31 a. m. (11:31 p. m. Thursday, EST) after successive attacks of cardiac asthma and other complications following upon the rapid development of influenza.

His last word, murmured as he entered his death agony, was "Peace." A few minutes before, as he fought for breath, he had said: "We still have so many things to do."

The bells of St. Peter's and other churches began to toll, and special editions of the newspapers informed the people that a beloved spiritual

(Continued on Page Five)

Aliquippa Holding Special Services

Proclaiming the death of His Holiness, Pope Pius XI, the death knell was sounded shortly after midnight in Aliquippa. Today services and prayers for the repose of the soul of the aged Pontiff who died at dawn, were held this morning in religious institutions as subjects here joined in mourning with some 400,000,000 persons over the world.

At noon today, four churches including the St. Joseph R. C., and St. George's Greek Catholic, West Aliquippa; St. Titus R. C. and the S. S. Peter and Paul Ukrainian, awaited notice from heads of their respective diocese regarding mourning services.

Tributes already completed here included a Requiem High Mass in the St. Joseph church this morning by Rev. Fr. Joseph Altany who also announced that a catafalque had been placed in the church and will remain there until after the burial of the Pope.

Rev. Fr. Schmoniuk of the S. S. Peter and Paul announced a special service for the Pope to be held tomorrow following regular mass. The ringing of church bells three times each day for three successive days is also a part of the tribute to the Holy Father.

Both the St. Titus and the West Aliquippa St. George's church, controlled by different diocese heads, will hold special services and prayers upon notification from their respective Bishops.

The Most Rev. Hugh C. Boyle, bishop of the Pittsburgh Diocese, in calling upon all Catholics to pray for the repose of the soul of the Pope, announced that a date would be set for a pontifical Requiem High Mass in St. Paul's Cathedral.

It also was understood the Bishop was considering plans for a simultaneous Requiem High Mass in the 368 churches in the Pittsburgh Diocese which comprises a 10-county area.

The St. Titus and the St. Joseph's R. C. churches are under this jurisdiction.

CAVE-IN TRAPS ONE; PASSENGER IN BUS INJURED

Fall Down Stairs May Mean Fractured Skull For Third

Vehicular, industrial and home accidents in Beaver county during the last 24 hours brought injury to two men and a woman, all of whom were taken to Rochester General hospital for treatment.

The casualties are:

Phillip Juhn, 40, of Ohioview avenue, Ambridge; suffering from back injuries.

Adam Cocco, Pacific avenue, Monaca; possible fractured skull.

Mrs. Ruth Hickinbottom, Rhode Island avenue, Rochester; suffering from shock, bruises of head and hands.

Juhn was hurt late yesterday afternoon when dirt caved-in upon him while he was digging in a hole at Ambridge. He is employed by the Austin Co., of Pittsburgh, which is building a new office building for the H. H. Robertson Co., Ambridge.

Cocco lost his footing and plunged down the cellar steps at his home last evening. His condition was described as fair at the hospital today.

Mrs. Hickinbottom was a passenger on a bus which is reported to have made a sudden halt under the culvert between Beaver and Bridgewater. She was thrown from her seat to the floor, according to the report given hospital attaches.

Crew Fights Threat Of Highway Slide

State highway department employes were battling this afternoon to keep the main highway between Aliquippa and Monaca open for travel, [illegible], a quarter of a mile below [illegible] Aliquippa. The highway was partly blocked at one o'clock by earth, rock and trees, while the movement extended several hundred feet above the roadway.

The Aliquippa-Monaca road has been the scene of severe landslides in previous yaers, during similar weather conditions.

PUC Closes Ambridge Water Rate Probe

HARRISBURG.—(UP)—The public utility commission today officially closed its investigation into justness of the Ambridge borough, Beaver county, water service rates and charges.

The inquiry really ended last month when the PUC sustained complaint of Harmony township supervisors that the borough's proposed rate increase would be too high.

BUSINESS DROPS

PITTSBURGH.—(UP)— Business activity in the Pittsburgh district dropped 1.3 points in the week that ended Feb. 4, the Bureau of Business Research, University of Pittsburgh, reported today, leaving the adjusted index approximately 16 per cent higher than it was in the corresponding week of 1938.

Lawyer-Police Chief Clash In Court

Police Chief W. L. Ambrose of the Aliquippa department and Attorney A. G. Helbling, Ambridge, clashed at a hearing yesterday before Peace Justice Ivor L. Jones when an Ambridge physician, Dr. Herbert Flemming, was named defendant in the airing of an alleged traffic-light violation.

Despite accusations by Defense Attorney Helbling in which he flared and said the Aliquippa department "had an old grudge to settle," Squire Jones found the physician guilty of having driven through a red traffic signal at Main street and Franklin avenue Jan. 23.

According to Helbling, Flemming was key witness in a court case at Beaver last year in which an officer of the local department was charged with assault and battery in connection with an arrest.

In the presence of several witnesses, school children who testified the Ambridge doctor ran through the light, and Burgess George L. Kiefer, disinterested in either the prosecution [illegible] ming accused arresting [illegible] Pastine with neglect [illegible] and said the traffic lights were not burning when he approached them from upper Franklin avenue.

A heated argument followed between Chief Ambrose and Helbling in which the department head here flayed the defense attorney on the subject of good ethics in his profession by bringing up personal matters before a court.

"Only, in one case out of 5,999 would such a charge have been made against a man," the attorney reiterated. "It is absolutely absurd."

According to Flemming, he stopped for the signal momentarily and drove on thinking the signal was not burning and that the traffic was being directed by Patrolman Pastine who stood at the curb.

It is not known whether the case will be appealed. Dr. Flemming was released on bond.

MEETING CALLED

All employees of the shipping, labor and butt weld departments of the welded tube plant of the J. and L. Steel corporation have been requested to attend a special departmental meeting in Aliquippa SWOC headquarters tomorrow at 2:30 p. m. Presiding will be Grievance Committeeman Domenic Delturco.

SENATORS FEAR SLASH IN STATE SCHOOL SUBSIDY

Hospitals, Homes Also May Get Cut Under Economy Move

HARRISBURG (UP)—Legislative leaders were uneasy today over the prospect that a sharp slash must be made in state subsidies to schools, hospitals and homes if the anticipated $204,000,000 relief load for the next two years is to be carried without additional taxation.

Some majority legislators were hesitant to discuss the fiscal situation publicly prior to receiving Gov. Arthur H. James budget message, but private expressions of misgivings over the implications of such a move were handed out freely.

The Governor has faced the issue frankly, disclosing to newspapermen [illegible] the annual convention of school directors "we must adjust our wants to our ability to pay."

The flood of hospital and school appropriation bills started this year, as in the past, immediately after announcement of committees, and while checked by resolution in the house has been unabated in the Senate. Organized demands for increasing amounts of state-aid for the welfare and educational institutions have pushed Pennsylvania's subsidy cost up to a top rank among states and made their reduction synonomous with "dangerous politics."

ROOSEVELT ILL, ORDERED TO BED

WASHINGTON (UP)—President Roosevelt was suffering from a slight attack of [illegible] and all White House engagements were cancelled.

Dr. Ross T. McIntyre, White House physician, said Mr. Roosevelt's temperature was 99.6—one degree of fever. He instructed the chief executive to remain in bed today.

White House Secretary Stephen T. Early said Mr. Roosevelt likely would be confined to bed over the weekend. All engagements, including the usual Friday morning press conference, were cancelled.

"He has a light touch of grippe," Early said.

The President's indisposition set in yesterday when he was confined to his room by a slight head cold but saw several callers.

Nods At Wheel, Crashes; Gets Arrested

A New Brighton man fell asleep at the wheel of his automobile early today, causing the machine to run wild and damage a mail box, highway marker and another car.

The motorist, J. F. Shane, of 301 Eleventh street, was arrested on a charge of reckless driving.

Arraigned before Burgess Tom Bishop this morning he was assessed a fine and ordered to pay all damages caused by his auto.

Shane was travelling north on Third avenue when he fell asleep at 2:15 a. m., police said. The car knocked down a mail box and highway marker and then shot across the street, crashing into a parked machine belonging to William Gordon, 1324 Third avenue.

14 Of 25 Are Freed In WPA Graft Case

ALBUQUERQUE, N. M.—(UP)— **A federal court jury today acquitted 14 of the 25 men and women charged with trafficking in Works Progress Administration jobs in what the government alleged was a conspiracy to aid the state Democrat faction led by U. S. Sen. Dennis Chavez.**

Beaver Oil Men Draft Three Point Legislative Program Designed To Aid Motorists

Oil men of Beaver county, meeting last night at Brodhead hotel in Beaver Falls, unanimously endorsed a three-point legislative program designed to aid motorists of Pennsylvania.

The county's division of the Associated Petroleum Industries of Pennsylvania firmly pledged to support these specific types of legislation:

1. To secure license plates on the first of April instead of the first of January, when family finances are at a low ebb due to seasonal demands.

2. To obtain a reduction of the state gasoline tax from four cents to three cents and the elimination of the federal gasoline tax of one cent.

3. To ask legislators to support a constitutional amendment which will prohibit the use of motor taxes for any purpose other than legitimate highway expenditures.

J. G. McCaw, county chairman, who presided over the meeting, stressed the far-reaching benefits that would accrue to motorists, the petroleum industry and the commonwealth on the attainment of the association's objectives. He said divisions similar to the Beaver county unit have been organized in every county of the state and, in cooperation with motorists and other organized groups, were actively working in behalf of the legislative program.

Other speakers were W. R. Leih Monaca, county vice-chairman, and Harry L. Wisner, Freedom, county secretary. Committees appointed by Chairman McCaw to serve during the new year include:

Legislative—Frank E. Garvin, Bea-

(Continued on Page Four)

Three Aliquippans Feel Axe Of State

Three Aliquippa men were among 226 persons dismissed yesterday by the Public Utility commission at Harrisburg in line with its enforced economy campaign. Aliquippans dismissed included:

Thomas P. Connelly, assistant examiner, $1,860; John Todora, investigator, $1,860, and Tony L. Riccitelli, messenger, $1,020.

U. I. S. W. CALLS MEET

Members of the United Iron and Steel Workers Union of Aliquippa will assemble at 110 Wykes street tonight for a business meeting, officers announced. The session will start at 8 p. m.

Local IOOF Members Expected At Monaca

A delegation of members of the Aliquippa I. O. O. F. Lodge 1065 are expected to accompany the first degree team to Monaca tomorrow night when the degree of Friendship will be conferred on a class of candidates. All local Odd Fellows wishing to attend are requested to meet at the order's social rooms here at 7 p. m. today. Transportation will be furnished.

FISH FRY TONIGHT

The Croatian-American Social club will hold a fish fry tonight in its Plodinec Annex club rooms. The action will start at seven o'clock. The public is invited.

Monaca's Tax Rate To Remain Unchanged

Monaca borough's tax levy for 1939 will remain unchanged at 16 mills, council decided last night after approving the new budget which calls for an outlay of $85,000.

Of the budget total, $58,000 will be applied to the general fund and $27,000 for the water department.

Council re-elected William A. Eberle as health commissioner for a new, five-year term.

It was voted to send delegates to the annual convention of the State Association of Boroughs at Harrisburg Feb. 23 to 25.

The burgess and police department reported 18 arrests in the borough last month and collection of $24.50 in fines.

Beaver And Ohio Valley Hospitals

Admitted to Providence hospital for treatment during the last 24 hours were Mrs. Anton Zeldevich, Aliquippa; Mrs. Harold Greer, Ellwood City, and Mrs. Lyle Brewer, Beaver, R. D.

Paul Motz, Jr., Mohaca, entered Beaver Valley hospital for treatment.

New admissions to Rochester General hospital yesterday included: Amy Zehner, Zelienople; Lois Eiffler, Sr., Freedom; Mrs. Frank Anderson, Aliquippa; Catherine Anthony, Rochester; Mrs. S. C. Holland, Bridgewater.

A daughter was born to Mr. and Mrs. Nicholas Radovic, of Freedom, at the hospital yesterday.

Persons leaving the institutions were Mrs. John Mann and infant son, Aliquippa, and Roy Chamberlain, Rochester.

SEEK GUNMAN

OIL CITY, Pa.—(UP)—More than a dozen state motor police searched today for a paroled convict who escaped after a gun battle with a patrolman who sought to question him in connection with a holdup. Patrolman Paul A. Longo suffered a flesh wound on the forehead during the fight with Harry Lodan Rossey, 31, in the home of Rossey's brother-in-law, William Houser.

MOONEY PLAYS GALLANT

Tom Mooney, awaiting an operation in California, is shown above as he assisted wealthy Mrs. Gardiner Hammond down the front steps of her estate at B[illegible]ymede, where he is convalescing. Mrs. Hammond was one of Mooney's staunchest backers during his fight for pardon. (Acme Photo)

Firemen To Report At Meet Thursday

A special committee of the Aliquippa Volunteer Firemen was preparing a report today outlining local participation in the Beaver county "Fire School." It will be entered and discussed at a special meeting of the Volunteer group in the borough building tomorrow night.

Committeemen who attended a session of the County Fire Chiefs' Association last week and gathered [illegible] plans of other valley departments, are Reese Maiden, Elmer Sankey and William Walthers.

The "Fire School" is under the sponsorship of the County Fire Chiefs' Association and according to present plans will be open to firemen of all Beaver county fire departments. Representatives of the assistance departments will be given a full course on fire fighting, committeemen said.

SUFFERS INJURED HAND

Glen Irwin, Aliquippa High school student, living near Kennedy's Corners, suffered a badly crushed left thumb yesterday afternoon. A young woman who travels to and from school with the youth was unaware the latter had his thumb in the crack of the front door and slammed the door on it. The thumb, almost severed, was stitched and placed in a cast b yDr. H. S. McMillin.

FOOT INJURED

F. C. Kimmell, of [illegible] employee of the Pennsylvania [illegible] road, suffered lacerations of the [illegible] foot last night while at work in [illegible]chester. He was taken to [illegible] General hospital for treatment.

The Beaver county courthouse was closed today because of the observance of George Washington's 207th birthday anniversary.

DEATHS

MRS. MARY E. WHISLER

Mrs. Mary E. Whisler, widow of Dr. A. M. Whistler, formerly of New Brighton, died last evening at Pittsburgh. Funeral service will be tomorrow at 7:30 p. m. at the home of her daughter, Mrs. H. C. Fry, Jr., 3000 Iowa street, Pittsburgh. Private burial will be Friday in Beaver cemetery.

MOROHOVIC FUNERAL

Funeral service for Mrs. Mary Morohovic, 62, who died suddenly yesterday morning, will be Friday at 9 a. m. at the home, 109 Waugaman street, followed by requiem high mass at 9:30 in St. Titus R. C. church here. The Rev. Fr. Edward Zauner will officiate. Burial will be in Mt. Olivet cemetery.

A resident of Aliquippa 30 years, Mrs. Morohovic was a member of the Altar and Rosary society of [illegible] church. She leaves the [illegible] children: Mrs. Mary Dudash, [illegible] Anna Dudash, Mrs. Emma Zanker and Nicholas, Paul, Alexander and Margaret, all of Aliquippa, and Michael Morohovic, Cleveland, O. Twenty-four grandchildren also survive.

TOADAR PARJA

Toadar Parja, 63, former employe of the J. & L. Steel Corp. here, dropped dead from an acute heart attack at 7 p. m. yesterday at his home along Brodhead road in Center township. He had been retired ten years.

He leaves two children, Nick and Veronica, both in Roumania. The body is at the Pearce funeral home here awaiting completion of funeral arrangements.

DR. ROBERT WATTERSON

Dr. Robert Watterson, 78, widely known Darlington physician, died at 11 p. m. Monday at his home following a prolonged illness.

A Beaver county native, he attended Peirsol's Academy at Bridgewater, Beaver Seminary and graduated from Pitt university in 1889. He had practiced medicine at Darlington since 1891.

He leaves his wife, Jennie; two sons, Dr. R. Wayne Watterson and Glenn H. Watterson, of Darlington; six grandchildren and one sister. Funeral service will be tomorrow at 2 p. m. at the home. Burial in Beaver Falls cemetery.

MRS. MARY S. BAZORI

Mrs. Mary Solomon Bazori, 49, wife of Samuel Bazori, died at 8:45 a. m. today at her home, 529 Cass street, Rochester.

She leaves her husband, two sons and one daughter. Funeral service will be Friday at 2 p. m. at the home. Burial in Beaver cemetery.

ANDREW MEITER

Andrew Meiter, 66, former resident of New Sheffield here, died at 6:45 a. m. today at the Beaver county home, where she had resided five years.

The body is at the Milo Prosser funeral home here awaiting the completion of funeral arrangements.

Alleged Child Stealer Held In California

PASADENA, Cal. (UP) — Townsend Davis, 40, lanky church organist, faced life imprisonment today for the abduction of eight-year-old Anne Louise Sweitzer and several other moral crimes to which police said he had confessed.

The child stealing charge which the parents of Anne Louise filed yesterday, when she and Davis were brought back from a flight across state, could, police said, also contain a morals count, to which he has confessed.

Attacker Clubs Film Actress; Girl Believed Dying

Aliquippa Relief Chiseler Given Six Months

Socialite Lost On River

Hope Brewster, 24, Memphis, Tenn., socialite, was being hunted today somewhere adrift in a small boat that she rented on the Mississippi bound for New Orleans. (Acme Photo)

The campaign is on to give the "Little Philosopher" a decent burial. Give him the honors due. Story on Page One.

The Aliquippa Gazette

SERVING AN INDUSTRIAL COMMUNITY OF 50,000

WEATHER—Rain and warmer tonight and Thursday.

SERVED BY UNITED PRESS — PHONE 934-935 — MEMBER OF P. N. P. A.

VOL. XVII. No. 244 — ALIQUIPPA, PA., WEDNESDAY, MARCH 29, 1939 — 3 CENTS; BY CARRIER, 15 CENTS A WEEK

England Drafting New Plans For Front To Halt Germany

BULLETIN

LONDON (UP) — Great Britain ordered her territorial army increased to war-time basis of 340,000 men today as diplomatic gestures against Europe's dictators gave way to military precautions.

LONDON (UP) — Great Britain was reported today to have abandoned plans for a public "stop Hitler" declaration and to be seeking a secret agreement among key nations to aid each other if they were menaced by German expansionism.

The cabinet held its weekly meeting today, and was reported to be discussing the following diplomatic program:

1—Close co-ordination of British and French military plans for any eventuality, including any threat to Holland, Belgium, Denmark or Switzerland.

2—Joint British-French effort to induce Poland, Rumania and Jugoslavia to agree to go to each other's assistance if Germany threatened any one of them.

3—A British-French promise to aid these nations if they banded together for self protection.

4—To maintain the most friendly relations with Russia but to leave her out of "official" agreements.

SPAIN KEY CITIES FALL TO FRANCO

MADRID. (UP) Nationalists, swiftly following up the surrender of Madrid, captured key cities throughout Republican Spain today while Generalissimo Francisco Franco sent columns of food trucks into the starving capital.

Valencia, third largest city of Spain, fell to the Nationalists, 24 hours after the fall of Madrid.

Men of the "Fifth Column" of Nationalist supporters in Republican territory seized control of Ciudad Real, Cuenca, Murcia and Almeria.

NEW RELIEF LAW TO START APR. 1

HARRISBURG. (UP) — Pennsylvanians applying for any type of public assistance other than blind pensions will be required after April 1 to sign confessing judgment against real or personal property which may be owned or later acquired, as an acknowledgment of the state's claim to repayment of tendered assistance, public assistance secretary, Howard L. Russell announced today.

Finances Discussed At Forum Meeting

Stressing the importance of government loaning rather than outright spending, Manuel Wood, Aliquippa SWOC district organizer, addressed the Aliquippa Community Forum club in the absence of scheduled speaker Harold J. Ruttenburg, SWOC research director.

Mr. Thompson, combining his topic with Ruttenburg's subject, "Technicological Unemployment," explained how the housing authority has contributed largely to relieving of unemployment.

"The government should concentrate a little more on loaning rather than spending," he said, "which would open the sales market and stimulate the 'work' problem."

Wood, in his address, advocated the support of all bond issues as a helpful means of creating new construction.

"Bond issues aimed at creation of public and private work can be of great assistance in solving technicological unemployment," he said.

Mr. Ruttenburg, who was called from his Pittsburgh office on urgent business, will be invited to address the forum group at a future date, Ralph Rudd, educational committee chairman, said.

Townsend Club Adds Fifteen New Members

The Aliquippa Townsend club today had increased its membership by 15 and executive members of the newly-formed club had definite plans to organize two more such units here.

At a regular meeting of the organization in the borough building last night, Vice President Edw. Farland outlined plans for the institution of similar clubs in West Aliquippa and Plan 11.

F.D.R. TO BEGIN SOUTHERN TRIP

WASHINGTON. (UP)—President Roosevelt leaves the capital this afternoon for a 10-day vacation at his southern home in Warm Springs, Ga.

Mr. Roosevelt completed unfinished, pending business and received routine reports of legislative and international situations before boarding his special train at 2:30 p. m.

He will deliver two brief addresses tomorrow.

Mr. Roosevelt and his party will arrive at Tuskegee, Ala., tomorrow morning where he will address the students of Tuskegee Institute extemporaneously. He will motor to Auburn, Ala., in the afternoon to speak briefly to the student body of Alabama Polytechnic Institute.

Last Of Big Shot Gangsters On Trial

Johnny Torrio, first, most powerful and last of the big shot gangsters, goes to trial today charged with federal income tax evasion.

He was the man who tutored Scarface Al Capone and installed him in Chicago to rule the south side war on Dion O'Banion, who was known and dreaded by racketeers in a dozen cities as "the big fellow," and who has enjoyed 20 years of immunity from the law and the gang wars.

He was charged with having evaded $86,000 in taxes between 1933 and 1935. He reported $10,000 income in that period. The government said he made $322,000.

BOY HURT

Robert Mitchell, 8, of 1528 Eighth avenue, Beaver Falls, was discharged from the Providence hospital there today where he received treatment for deep lacerations of the hands and arms suffered when he fell upon broken glass. The boy was admitted last night following the accident. He was ordered confined to his home today.

YOUNG ACTRESS BELIEVED DYING AFTER SLUGGING

Hollywood Police Link Crime With Slaying Last Month

HOLLYWOOD (UP) — Adelia Bogart, young actress who played the pig-tailed role of Tomboy Taylor in the old "Mickey Maguire" comedies, was slugged with a club and perhaps fatally injured on a Hollywood street early today.

The 17-year-old actress, currently cast in a picture with Jackie Cooper, was waylaid as she walked home from a late motion picture show. Her assailant leaped from the shadow of a building and beat her over the head with a section of 2x4 scantling. He made no attempt to criminally attack her, police said.

Her screams were heard by Olive and Bess Johnston, sisters, and they ran from their home to find her sitting on the lawn, blood streaming from her head.

She was removed to the General hospital where surgeons said she had only a slight chance to survive.

An examination established that her skull had been fractured.

Mrs. Laura Lee, whose home is near the scene of the attack, also heard the screams.

She snatched a club from her husband's golf bag in the hallway and rushed to Miss Bogart's aid. She said she flogged and drove away, a "tall man in a gray topcoat" who was stooping over his victim.

Police believed the assailant may have been the same man who killed Anya Sosoyevn, beautiful Russian dancer, on the City College campus last month.

CALL FOR HELP

LONDON.—(UP) — Lloyd's shipping agency said today that the radio station at Niton, in the Isle of Wight, had picked up a message from the French steamship Ploubazlanec appealing for assistance at a point about 40 miles east of Valencia, and asserting "we have been overhauled by a war vessel which is compelling us to accompany her."

STEEL WORKERS MEET

All members of the United Iron and Steel Workers of Aliquippa are requested to attend a regular meeting of the local tomorrow at 8 p. m. at 110 Wykes street. Important business relative to unionism will be discussed.

Just a few hours before her divorce case was to be heard in Hollywood, Calif., Joan Crawford, of movie fame, and her husband, Franchot Tone, movie star, had dinner together and then went night-clubbing. In the above photo the two are shown dancing in a New York night club shortly after midnight. Joan explained that she thought "all divorces should be friendly." (Acme Photo)

POLAND'S KEY MEN

Col. Josef Beck, foreign minister, and President Ignatz Moscicki are two of Poland's key men in the present crisis of threatened German invasion as troops mass in Corridor. (Acme Photos)

England's King, Queen Due In U. S. June 8

WASHINGTON. (UP) Washingtonians today were promised an unusual spectacle June 8 when King George and Queen Elizabeth arrive for a two day visit at the White House.

President and Mrs. Roosevelt will meet them at the railway station and accompany them to the White House.

EMERGENCY TAX BILLS IN HOUSE

HARRISBURG. (UP)—Bills Gov. Arthur H. James urged to extend for two years $163,000,000 worth of emergency relief taxes went to the the Senate today from the House.

Greatest opposition was directed against the 4-mill state levy on intangible personal property, including investments yielding no returns to their owners, but it cleared the House with a comfortable margin, 159 to 30, late yesterday.

Four to seven votes were cast against extension of the other seven emergency levies originally imposed by the preceding Democratic administration of George H. Earle.

The personal levy, amended to exclude ground rents, clarify and limit exemptions, was listed for $24,000,000 of revenue during the biennium opening June 1. An additional four mills is collected on intangible personal property by the counties.

The other emergency taxes, their rates, estimated biennium yields and the vote by which they cleared the House:

Cigaret tax, one cent for each 10 smokes, $22,300,000, vote 192 to 7; corporate net income, 7 per cent, $52,660,000, 195 to 5; gasoline, 1 cent a gallon extra, $28,640,000, 197 to 5; utilities gross receipts, 13 mills, $9,750,000, 194 to 4; liquor sold at state stores, quarter per cent, $15,000,000, 187 to 7; bank and trust company shares, 4 mills, $4,250,000, 192 to 4; corporate loans, 4 mills, $6,400,000, 196 to 3.

CUT WPA BILL

WASHINGTON. — (UP) — The full house appropriations committee, calling for economies in WPA administration, today reported an additional $100,000,000 relief bill, $50,000,000 below the appropriation urgently requested by President Roosevelt.

RELIEF CHISELER JAILED; ADMITS THREE INCOMES

Court To Cut Term If Prisoner Returns Excess

Paul Cocos, 45, of 128 Iron street, was given a six-month jail term at Beaver today for being a "relief chisler."

Appearing before Judge Frank Reader, Cocos pleaded guilty to the "chiseling" charge and admitted receiving a $7 weekly relief check in addition to employment insurance amounting to $15, and $12 disability insurance received from the Jones and Laughlin Steel plant.

Cocos, who was indicted on charges of receiving money under false pretenses a week ago, was ordered to pay costs, a $1 fine and serve six months in the county jail.

Judge Reader said the sentence would be cut in half if the defendant repaid the $94 he chiseled.

TWO OTHERS

The Aliquippa man, who began serving his sentence today, entered his plea of guilty with two others, one, a Beaver Falls man, sentenced to from one to three and one-half years in the Allegheny county workhouse.

Terming the case the "most flagrant I have ever heard," Judge Reader pronounced sentence on Isaac Veon, 28, a Beaver Falls W.P.A. worker for involuntary manslaughter in connection with the death Dec. 23 of Leslie Graham, 73, a fellow worker.

According to testimony, Veon and four others left work on a near-Darlington W.P.A. project to go on a "spree." The defendant's automobile plunged over an embankment and Graham was killed instantly.

ESCAPES CHARGE

Sentence on a charge of "driving while drunk" as returned by the Grand Jury was suspended. Veon was assessed costs and a $1 fine in addition to his prison term.

Testimony to determine the degree of guilt in the case of Virgil Reynolds, 31, New Brighton, who has pleaded guilty to participating in the killing of Tony Spitale, Monaca beer truck driver, got underway this morning.

Entering testimony for Reynolds who turned "state's evidence" was County Detective Charlie O'Loughlin, Sergeant Frank Milligan and Private J. J. Henecheck of the State Motor Police.

ASKS PROTECTION

According to witnesses, Reynold's only request was that in the event he turned witness for the commonwealth, "my three children and wife in Rochester be protected."

"Louie the Carpenter" Tolento recently was acquitted of a murder charge in the Spitale killing. Tolento was accused by Reynolds of being the "trigger man" in the slaying.

Reynolds is under a sentence in New York for the murder of Tony Massaro, of Rochester.

Gus Vargas, formerly of Massilon, Ohio, pleaded guilty to conducting a lottery and was fined $250. The defendant was arrested in Hopewell township. He was placed on probation for one year and must leave the state.

Aid Comes As Citizens Begin Final Gesture To "Philosopher"

Two $5 contributions from donors who asked their names not be made public today boosted the Mario Ezzo monument fund in Aliquippa to $20 and forecast early completion of the campaign to move the body of Aliquippa's "Little Philosopher" to a decent resting place and erect a modest monument to his memory.

Ezza, the immigrant who died of burns in the county home last week, was the man who brought nation-wide attention to Aliquippa by his determination to perform voluntary public work in the borough in payment for relief assistance he was receiving. The object of the campaign for $150 is to remove the body from the potter's field where it lies to a decent resting place and appropriately mark the grave.

Aliquippa Gazette officials, behind the drive, emphasized today that any Aliquippa person who wishes may contribute to the fund and that no donation, no matter how small, will be rejected. Contributions thus far include:

The Aliquippa Gazette	$10.00
Gazette Reader	5.00
An Aliquippan	5.00
Total	$20.00

FIREMEN GIVEN APPARATUS DRILL

"Chemical extinguishers and their use and how to employ nozzles and play pipes to combat fires," was the subject of last night's second meeting of the class enrolled in the Beaver County Fire School.

More than 30 firemen representing Central station here, West Aliquippa, Plan 12 No. 2 company, Ambridge, South Heights, Baden, Harmony and Economy townships, were in attendance.

The second class enrolled under the supervision of Captain William K. Fulham of No. 16 engine company, Pittsburgh, will convene at 7:30 tomorrow in the borough building.

Forgery Case Suspects Fail To Give Bonds

Eddie Zdancevich and Rudolph Morrone, defendants in a forgery case before Peace Justice R. J. McLanahan, were committed to the Beaver county jail today in default of $1,000 bond each.

An alleged accomplice in the forgery of the $145 check, Antonio Galzerano, also of Aliquippa, posted bond to assure his appearance for court hearing and was released.

The trio, it is alleged, forged the check dated Jan. 13, making it payable to Zdancevich and using the signature of E. Morrone, Rudolph's father.

REPORT TROUBLE

BUCHAREST.—(UP) — Serious Separatist incidents were reported today in Cluj and other Transylvanian towns, where Hungarian minorities form a large percentage of the population. The reports indicated high tension, which political circles here feared might lead to international complications.

DINSMORE HEADS ALIQUIPPA B.P.O.E.

Election of Norman Dinsmore as new Exalted Ruler and voting unanimously to purge passage of the "alien registration" bill highlighted the annual organization meeting of the Aliquippa B. P. O. E.

Also named to fill executive posts of the order for this year were Carl Weible, leading knight; Joseph Allen, loyal knight; Clyde Hayward, lecturing knight; D. P. Smith, secretary; Harry Drake, treasurer, and W. L. Roberts, tiler.

Christian Henderson and John Gross were named trustees. Appointed as delegates to the state convention was J. P. Walsh, present exalted ruler; Fred Mac Gribble and John Bowden. Alternate delegates will be W. N. Dinsmore, J. H. Miller and Clyde Hayward.

With 72 members in attendance, the order went on record as favoring House Bill No. 6 calling for the registration of all aliens 18 years of age or over who have lived in this country and have shown no intentions of becoming citizens.

The measure was passed unanimously and Secretary Smith was authorized to contact the county's three state government representatives and one senator asking support of the new bill.

Speakers at last night's session included District Deputy Fred Mac Gribble and Michael Kane. A dinner was served following the meeting.

Installation of officers will be made at a meeting April 11 when executive members of the Rochester Elks will be in charge of the exercise. The following day, officers here will install at the Rochester order.

BOND ISSUE APPROVED

Beaver county's bond issue was given approval of the State Department of Internal Affairs, county officials announced today. The bonds have already been sold.

In The World Of RADIO

THURSDAY, APRIL 6

KDKA

4:30—Afternoon Varieties.
5:00—Erskine Hawkins' Orchestra.
5:15—Sheriff Bob.
5:30—Don Winslow of the Navy.
5:45—Melody Time.
6:00—News, Temp.
6:08—Movie Magazine of the Air.
6:15—Manuel Contrares' Orchestra.
6:30—Chet Smith.
6:45—Lowell Thomas.
7:00—Easy Aces.
7:15—Mr. Keen.
7:30—Chasing Shadows.
7:45—Merry Music.
8:00—Parade of Progress
8:30—Eastman School of Music.
9:15—Whispering Choir
9:30—America's Town Meeting.
10:30—Fu Manchu.
10:45—The Curtain Rises.
10:53—AAA Weekly Tour.
11:00—News.
11:05—Jack Hollister; Temp, Weather.
11:15—The Music You Want.
12:00—Al Marsico's Orchestra.
12:15—Buddy Fisher's Orchestra.
12:30—Lee Shelley's Orchestra.

WJAS

5:00—Questions Before the House.
5:15—Howie Wing.
5:30—Today's Programs.
5:35—Baron Elliott's Orchestra.
6:05—Judge Smith.
6:08—Rhythm Roundup.
6:15—News of the World.
6:30—Today with Bob Trout.
6:45—National Radio Association.
7:00—Amos 'n' Andy.
7:15—History Speaks.
7:30—Joe E. Brown.
8:00—Kate Smith.
9:00—Major Bowes' Amateur Hour.
10:00—Tune-Up Time.
10:45—American Viewpoints.
11:00—News, Ken Mildebrand.
11:15—Henry Busse's Orchestra.
11:30—Cab Calloway's Orchestra.
12:00—Sammy Kaye's Orchestra.

KQV

5:00—Charlie Cook Series.
5:45—Headline News.
6:00—Music of Today.
6:15—Bess Saunders.
6:30—Modernaires.
7:00—Pittsburgh Star Italian Hour.
7:30—Nite Club of the Air.
8:00—Toni Carroll.
8:15—Fireside Chats.
8:30—McGill Choral Singers.
9:00—Robert Mitchell.
9:15—15 Minutes in Hollywood.
9:30—Munroe and Nolte.
9:45—7th Ave. Vocalettes.
10:00—Scooping the News.
10:10—Music.
10:15—Wrestling Matches.
11:00—Freddie Berren's Orchestra.
11:15—Doc Sellars Stories.
11:30—Ave Maria Hour.
12:00—Pittsburgh Dances.

WWSW

5:00—Surf Riders.
5:15—Radio Stars on Parade.
5:30—Talking Drums.
5:45—Italian Airs.
6:00—News.
6:15—Entertainment Time.
6:30—Bill Leroy Orchestra.
7:00—Dance Music.
7:30—B. C. Sports Slants.
7:45—Dinner Dance Music.
8:00—Conti and Prietsch.
8:15—Hobby Hall.
8:30—Dr. Clausen Round Table.
9:00—Parade of Melody.
9:45—Hi-Jinks in Strings.
10:00—Grotto Orchestra.
10:15—Sherdina Walker Orchestra.
10:30—Ed Kroen—News.
10:45—Seger Ellis Orchestra.
11:00—Interlude at Eleven.
11:15—Al Fremont Orchestra.
11:30—Sherdina Walker Orchestra.
11:45—House of Peter MacGregor.

EARLY FRIDAY PROGRAMS

KDKA

6:30—Milton's Barnyard Rustlers.
6:45—Farm Markets.
7:00—Musical Clock.
7:15—Western Trails.
7:30—Musical Clock.
7:45—Ma Perkins.
8:00—News.
8:30—Musical Clock.
8:15—Dr. Sunshine.
9:30—Musical Clock.
9:00—Shopping Circle.
9:15—Linda's First Love.
9:30—The Editor's Daughter.
9:45—On the Mall.
10:00—Melody Time.
10:15—Jane Arden.
10:30—The Gospel Singer.
10:45—Houseboat Hannah.
11:00—Mary Marlin.
11:15—Vic and Sade.
11:30—Pepper Young's Family.
11:45—Getting Most Out of Life.
12:00—News, Music, Weather, Temp.
12:15—Voice of the Farm.

12:30—National Farm and Home Hour.
1:15—Farm Radio News
1:30—Women and the News.

WCAE

7:00—Morning Express.
8:00—Morning News.
8:15—Today's Almanac.
8:30—Garden Talk.
8:35—Do You Remember?
8:45—Hits and Encores.
9:00—Lillian Malone.
9:15—Band Goes To Town.
9:30—Gems of Melody.
9:45—Secret Diary.
10:00—Central City.
10:15—John's Other Wife.
10:30—Just Plain Bill.
10:45—Woman in White.
11:00—David Harum.
11:15—Lorenzo Jones.
11:30—Widder Brown.
11:45—Road of Life
12:00—Noon News
12:10—Melodies
12:15—The O'Neills.
12:30—Elm St. Carters.
12:45—Singin' Sam.
1:00—Musical Caravan.
1:15—Sophisticated Ladies.
1:30—Bernie Cummins' Band.
1:45—Voice of Experience.

WJAS

7:30—Musicale.
8:00—Morning Headline News.
8:15—Time Again.
8:30—Musical Revue.
8:45—Cheerie Melodies.
8:55—Today's Programs.
9:00—Lutheran Inner-Mission.
9:15—Manhattan Mother.
9:30—Joyce Jordan.
9:45—Bachelor's Children.
10:00—Young Doctor Malone.
10:15—Myrt and Marge.
10:30—Hilltop House.
10:45—The Stepmother.
11:00—It Happened in Hollywood.
11:15—Scattergood Baines.
11:30—Big Sister.
11:45—Aunt Jenny's Life Stories.
12:00—Mary Margaret McBride.
12:15—Her Honor, Nancy James.
12:30—News of the World.
12:45—Our Gal Sunday.
1:00—The Goldbergs.
1:15—Life Can Be Beautiful.
1:30—Road of Life.

POPE ON RADIO EASTER SUNDAY

ROME. (UP)—Pope Pius XII will broadcast to the world on Easter Sunday an important speech on international affairs, the Giornale Ditalia said today

The speech will be broadcast by the Vatican City radio at 10 a. m.—4 a. m. E. S. T.—the newspaper said.

Pope Pius, famed as a diplomat and a student of international affairs, has given the closest attention to the European situation since his election last month. There have been repeated indications that his first important address would be devoted to international problems.

PATRONIZE OUR ADVERTISERS

Beaver And Ohio Valley Hospitals

Admitted to Rochester General hospital during the last 24 hours for treatment were Vivian Dennis and Carl Beharka, both of Monaca, and Charles Green and Mrs. Mary Rich, of Midland.

Discharged from the institution were Mrs. Geneva Schmidley, Rochester, and Mrs. Edna Cribbs, Baden.

Charles Kyler, of Beaver Falls, R. D., Philip Diaello of Beaver Falls, and Mrs Henry Cordes, Freedom, entered Providence hospital yesterday for treatment.

Charles Lowry, New Brighton, was discharged from Beaver Valley hospital yesterday.

ASKS WALLY HONOR

LONDON (UP)—The Daily Express urged editorially today that the title of royal highness be granted the Duchess of Windsor so the Duke could return with her to England.

LITTLE MARY MIXUP

WELL, MARY--THIS IS YOUR FIRST LOOK AT THE PACIFIC OCEAN-
IT TASTES JUST LIKE THE ATLANTIC-
NOW-LET'S JUST SIT HERE AND REALIZE WHAT WE ARE SEEING--YOU KNOW--THE PACIFIC IS MUCH BIGGER THAN THE ATLANTIC-
R. M. BRINKERHOFF
YES-I SEE IT IS-
4-6

THE CAPTAIN AND THE KIDS

RAJAH—YOU AND ME HAVE BEEN CHUMS FOR YEARS—BUT YOU GOTTA QUIT TURNING MAMA'S HEAD WIT' YOUR WILES!! I DON'T WANNA HEAR ANY MORE ABOUT IT!!
VERY WELL LITTLE BROTHER! YOU SHALL HEAR NO MORE ABOUT IT!!
HE SHALL HEAR NO MORE ABOUT IT! HEH HEH!
A FEW MILES OFF THE COAST, THE PIGEON SIGHTS A MYSTERIOUS CRAFT!
PEEP!
HERE COMES ACHMED, THE MASTER'S CARRIER PIGEON!!
EXCELLENT! NO DOUBT HIS HIGHNESS DESIRES SOME INFIDELS LIQUIDATED!

BRONCHO BILL

THE LAST GUARD TO MEET THE ESCAPING PRISONERS, REPORTS—
THEY'RE HIDIN' IN THE RAVINE, BOSS—JES' JUMPED ME AND TOOK MY RIFLE
FETCH THE BOYS AND TELL 'EM TO SURROUND THE PLACE—
IN HIDING, JONES SEES THE BOSS RIDING WITHIN RIFLE RANGE—
I'M GONNA PLUG THAT ORNERY COYOTE, RIGHT NOW!
PLEASE DON'T SHOOT! AFTER ALL—HE IS MY UNCLE
IN HIS ANXIETY, BOSS HARVEY FAILS TO NOTICE A BULL CHARGING FROM THE REAR— 4/6

FRANKIE DOODLE

SH—!! ORDER IN THE COURT!!
MEDDLER'S LAWYER IS ADDRESSING THE JURY—HE'S BEEN TALKING MORE THAN FIVE HOURS, BUT—HE'LL SOON HAVE TO SHUT UP OR FALL DOWN—
SO LET'S PEEK IN AND SEE WHAT HAPPENS—
—AND NOW, GENTLEMEN, I ASK YOU TO LOOK AT THIS POOR, UNHAPPY WOMAN WHO HAS NEVER HAD CHICK NOR CHILD TO COMFORT HER—ALL SHE HAD TO CUDDLE TO HER BOSOM WAS A PET CAT!—IMAGINE, IF YOU CAN, THIS CHILDLESS WOMAN HABITUALLY PLACING A PAN OF MILK UNDER THE KITCHEN TABLE—THEN, SUDDENLY REMEMBERING—
—THAT THIS BRUTE HAD ROBBED HER OF THE ONLY COMFORT SHE HAD IN LIFE!!—ISN'T $10,000. A SMALL RECOMPENSE FOR A LOSS SO OVERWHELMING!!!
NOW IT'S OSCAR'S LAWYER'S TURN—
GENTLEMEN OF THE JURY, YOU HAVE HEARD A LONG AND IMPASSIONED PLEA FOR MONEY—BUT I AM WILLING TO TRUST YOU TO RENDER A JUST VERDICT WITHOUT FURTHER ADVICE FROM ME—I THANK YOU, GENTLEMEN—

TROOPERS RUSHED TO COUNTY MINE

EUROPE'S "HEAD MAN" CELEBRATES 50TH BIRTHDAY WITH BIG REVIEW

Durr Named 'Mayor' Of Ohio Valley

TEN PAGES

The Aliquippa Gazette

SERVING AN INDUSTRIAL COMMUNITY OF 50,000

WEATHER — Partly cloudy. Slightly warmer in west portion. Friday mostly cloudy and somewhat warmer.

SERVED BY UNITED PRESS — PHONE 934-935 — MEMBER OF P. N. P. A.

VOL. XVII. No. 263 — ALIQUIPPA, PA., THURSDAY, APRIL 20, 1939 — 3 CENTS; BY CARRIER, 15 CENTS A WEEK

Adolf Hitler, German Fuehrer, celebrates his 50th birthday today, April 20, and above is the photo especially posed by Hitler in connection with the anniversary. Picture arrived in the United States aboard the Bremen. (Acme Photo)

Nazis Parade Military Might; Il Duce Rejects FDR's Plans

BERLIN.—(UP)—The entire 1920 conscript class and about half of the 1919 class were called up for medical examination today as Germany's armed forces, parading in honor of Adolf Hitler's 50th birthday, displayed anti-aircraft guns believed to be larger than any seen before in public.

Men called up for examination will go into the labor corps for the customary six months' labor service, and then will serve two years in the army.

Men of the classes of 1918, 1919 and 1920—those born in the years named—of the Sudetenland which Germany obtained from Czechoslovakia last September were included.

Nazis said that today's call was a routine one.

It came simultaneously, however, with the greatest display ever of Germany's new military might.

Military attaches of foreign embassies and legations were early at the birthday parade, expecting a Nazi "surprise." Last year's was a new mobile gun of formidable range.

MUSSOLINI SAYS AXIS WANTS PEACE

ROME.—(UP) — Premier Benito Mussolini replied to President Roosevelt's peace appeal today by asserting that Italy and Germany wanted peace, that Italy distrusted "arch-conferences" such as the president suggested, and that Italy would not permit itself to be oppressed by "Messiah-like messages."

He denounced as absurd "the system of reciprocal ten year guarantees as well as the pyramidal errors of geography incurred by individuals who lack a rudimentary knowledge of European affairs."

The president had suggested a 10 year, or if possible a 25 year, guarantee by Italy and Germany against aggression.

Thus parenthetically Mussolini disclosed that he and Adolf Hitler, his axis partner, had not yet decided whether to reply formally to the president's message or to ignore it so far as formal diplomatic channels were concerned.

At least, he had anticipated his partner Hitler in a verbal reply. Hitler had called a meeting of the Nazi Reichstag for April 28 to make his own reply.

BRITAIN, FRANCE READY FOR RUSSIA

PARIS—(UP)—Great Britain and France have informed Russia that they are prepared to conclude a three-power military assistance treaty with her, it was understood today.

MEMORIAL DAY RITES PLANNED

A meeting open to all Aliquippa veteran, civic, educational and fraternal organizations for the purpose of arranging for a community-wide Memorial Day service here will be held in Moose Temple next Thursday at 8 p. m. The service, under the auspices of the "Americanism Federation" and co-operating committees of representative organizations, is hoped to be the biggest ever held here. Ladies' Auxiliary of the various lodges have also been asked to participate.

Marchetti To Speak At Art Conference

Joseph Marchetti, head of Aliquippa High school's art department, will be featured speaker at an art conference to be held in conjunction with the 50th anniversary celebration at Slippery Rock State Teachers college next Friday and Saturday, April 28-29.

Speakers at the general sessions will be Dr. Lester K. Ade, state superintendent of public instruction, and Dr. Henry W. Homes, graduate school dean of Harvard university. At the art conference Saturday morning, Mr. Marchetti will speak on "Stone Carving in High School."

Police Seek Thief Who Rifled Clothes

Aliquippa police were on the lookout today for the "small fry" thief who believes in doing things in a spectacular way.

Wednesday night, while more than a score of persons were taking "gym" training in the auditorium of the Franklin Junior High school, the building was suddenly thrown into darkness.

An instructor went to the switch in the corridor of the auditorium and turned on the lights.

An hour later when students changed clothes to go home, one of the group found his clothes had been searched and a wallet with a few dollars in it was missing from his pocket.

SON IS BORN

A son was born to Mr. and Mrs. Harry Schmidt, R. D. No. 2, Aliquippa, early this week. The baby was born at the home. Both mother and child were doing nicely today.

COLORED VOTERS SELECT H. D. DURR AS VALLEY MAYOR

Local Undertaker Wins Honorary Post From 12 Entrants

Polling more than 149,000 votes in an election conducted by a newspaper, Howard D. Durr, prominent Aliquippa funeral director, today was elected mayor of all colored persons of the Ohio Valley.

He defeated 12 other candidates, including John Thornton, the C.I.O. organizer of Midland, in spirited balloting underway during the last several weeks. Colored folk from all sections of the valley participated in the election.

Mr. Durr will hold an office identical to that held by Bill Robinson, nationally known dancer, who is mayor of Harlem in New York.

He will be inducted into office at inauguration ceremonies at Junction park, New Brighton, next Friday, April 28. Burgess George L. Kiefer, of Aliquippa, will administer the oath of office at the ceremony.

The five candidates trailing Mr. Durr in the balloting will serve as members of his cabinet.

Explaining the purpose of electing mayors of colored folk in all sections of the country, Mr. Durr today said:

"It is our sincere hope that by the formation of such administrations that we will be able to do something for the colored people."

Candidates besides Thornton whom he defeated included: Arthur D. Hays, Beaver Falls; L. E. Stanton, New Brighton; Parker J. Key, Coraopolis; Louis Pate, Sewickley; William D. Mason, Midland; Leroy House, Rochester; William Miller, Aliquippa; William F. Butler, Beaver; H. W. Patterson, Sewickley; H. F. Garrett, Ambridge, and J. Edward Johnson, West Bridgewater.

Beaver Co. I.O.O.F. Plans Birthday Meet

Odd Fellows of Beaver and nine other western Pennsylvania counties will gather at Sherodd temple in Sheridan Saturday, April 29, to celebrate the 120th anniversary of the founding of the order. Rebekahs will hold a similar meeting at Hazel-Glenn lodge hall in Hazelwood the same day. Grand lodge officers of Pennsylvania, West Virginia and Ohio will attend the celebration, which will be climaxed by a banquet at Fort Pitt hotel, Pittsburgh.

The following day, Sunday, will be given over to a sight-seeing tour of Pittsburgh, visits to the orphanage and home for aged Rebekahs, maintained by the order, and memorial services at North Side Carnegie Music hall.

Beaver County Women Open Drama Festival

Seventh annual drama festival sponsored by the Beaver County Federation of Women's clubs opened last night at Beaver High school and will continue tonight and tomorrow. The Monaca Juniors and Beaver Woman's club presented last night's plays while tonight the Baden Woman's club and the Frill and Dagger society of Geneva college will be featured. The Aliquippa Woman's club will present a play, titled "The Purple Door Knob," tomorrow evening.

Board Of Trade Men Call Friday Meet

Members of the retail trade committee of the Aliquippa Board of Trade will meet Friday at 8 p. m. in the Aliquippa Gazette office to formulate final plans on the World's Fair trip contest here this summer, Chairman Louis Young announced today. All members of the committee are urged to be present.

Widow Files Suit In Mate's Death; Demands $25,000

Mrs. Anna Turchik of Harmony township, widowed mother of three children, today filed a $25,000 damage suit at Beaver against Anthony Fabbio, Beaver Falls, driver of a hit-and-run car which snuffed out her husband's life near Legionville bridge two months ago.

The plaintiff, who charges Fabbio with negligence, claims she was deprived of her support and her husband's companionship. The victim, Andrew Turchik, was employed by the H. H. Robertson Co. at Ambridge and earned $125 monthly, she said.

RAID ON STILL NETS 4 ARRESTS

Three Plus 11 colored men were being held by police here for arraignment today for violation of the state liquor laws and a woman had been fined as a result of a raid in which Aliquippa officers confiscated a 50-gallon still.

Officers pulled the surprise blow shortly after 10 p. m., yesterday and rounded up three alleged operators of the still and placed a woman inmate, Eula Mae Colquit, 23, of 152 Fourth avenue, under arrest.

Held for hearing tonight before Justice Ivor L. Jones were Leroy Gray, William Booker and John Clark. The latter, who allegedly ran from the place when police entered, was taken into custody five hours later.

Two hundred gallons of fermenting mash and several gallons of whiskey were also confiscated, police reported.

Choir To Make First Appearance Thursday

One of the most recent additions to the music department of the Aliquippa High school, the Madrigal Choir, will take a limelight part in the "Senior Night" program of the school's twelfth annual Music Festival next Thursday.

The special choral group, made up of selected singers of the Bach choir, will appear on the program under the direction of Mrs. Grace Mansell. It will mark their first concern appearance.

They will sing "In These Delightful Pleasant Groves," a seventeenth century Madrigal; and "The Silver Swan," a Gibbons composition. Appearing on the same program will be the school's noted Bach choir of 125 voices. They will sing "Down the Street a Violin is Playing," and "Spirit ob de Lord," by Cain.

FR. HENSLER TO SPEAK

The entire membership of the S.W.O.C. Contract committee which numbers 59 persons have been requested to be present for Monday's meeting of the Aliquippa Community Forum at the high school. Father A. Hensler will speak on "An Economic Program for America."

New Kroger Self-Serve Store Opens In Aliquippa Tomorrow

The Kroger Self-Serve Market, Aliquippa's newest and one of the most modern business houses in the borough, opens its doors to the public at 9 a. m. tomorrow.

With a $15,000 frontage at 475 Franklin avenue and a deeply set interior boasting every convenience known to merchandising for aiding the shopper, the store makes its bow with new stock and equipment under the management of H. F. Hetrick, who has had direction of the older store across the street.

The grand opening tomorrow comes as the climax to weeks of work during which the new building was entirely remodeled and reenforced with the latest girder construction methods.

The store has five times the serving capacity of the former Kroger Market building with a total of 5,000 feet floor space.

It will be a modern "serve yourself" style with every item in the thousands of dollars of new equipment especially designed to lighten the burden of the thrifty shopper. Every piece of merchandise in the store has been price marked, every shelf and float labeled for the convenience of the purchaser. Customers will use the latest type "buggy shopper," in which patrons wheel their own choice of produce from the shelves of the store to the cashier.

In addition to the new lighting system, a 12 by 10-foot refrigerator, fully equipped with the most modern dairy department cooling systems, all-metal counters and cases have been installed for sanitary purposes.

Also featured are the new cash registers having half-cent keys. The customer will pay 12½ cents for goods of that price and not 13 cents, Manager Hetrick pointed out.

The new "self-service" store will be open daily except Sundays from 9 a. m. until 10 p. m. From 30 to 40 clerks and other attendants will be employed.

COMPLETE MINE TIEUP ORDERED

Coal Union Threatens Closing Unless Pact Is Signed

NEW YORK (UP) — The United Mine Workers of America today ordered a strike in all soft coal mines in the country May 4 unless operators have granted them a new working contract before then.

The order affected 130,000 miners in mining districts of 21 states. Since April 1, the 340,000 miners of the Appalachian eight-state area in the east have been idle, while negotiations among the union and the operators have continued in deadlock and a coal shortage has been developing.

It has been estimated that 1,000,000 men already have been idled in the railroad and other industries by the lack of coal shipments and shortages of fuel. Negotiations have been deadlocked by the union's demand for the elimination of so-called penalty clauses from the proposed new working contract. The clauses impose fines of $1 to $2 a day for each miner who strikes.

Unemployment Checks Distributed In Area

More than 600 Unemployment Compensation checks valued at $7,122 were distributed during the week ending April 7 to workers here registered with the Aliquippa District No. 5 headquarters.

One hundred and eighty-seven original claims are still on file, Manager Kenneth Morris said, with 1,655 continued claims. Distribution from seven offices in the entire district amounted to well over $65,000.

Local Men To Attend B'nai B'rith Session

Attorney John C. Stern and Drs. B. Greenberger, J. Weinberger and Charles Aliskovitz, all of Aliquippa, will attend the annual spring meeting of the Western Pennsylvania Council of B'nai B'rith lodges at Oil City Sunday. The session and banquet, which will climax the day's activities, will be in the K. of C. auditorium. Rabbi Rothschild, Pittsburgh, will be featured speaker.

Pittsburgh Plant Gets Coal From Local J-L

J. and L. plant officials said today that shipment of coal by barge from the stock yards of the mill here to the South Side Pittsburgh branch of the corporation has been underway this week. The thousands of tons of fuel were stocked here in preparation for the recent mine strike. Some of the stock is now being moved via the Ohio river to the smaller yards of the Pittsburgh plant.

Miss Dorothea Watkins To Handle Assembly

Miss Dorothea Watkins, Franklin Junior High school teacher, will be in charge of the school's May Day assembly this year. May pole dancing and other program rehearsals are underway in the junior high gymnasium this week. A detailed account of the program will be published before the presentation at assembly period next Wednesday.

District Attorney, Iron, Steel Workers Aid Ezzo Memorial

Two new contributions swelled the Mario Ezzo fund in Aliquippa and today $8 more had been added to the total which will move the body of the Italian immigrant here from the potter's field and place it in a decently marked resting place.

Executive committeemen of the United Iron & Steel Workers of Aliquippa dug down in their treasury last evening to assist the fund by $3. Today from Philadelphia where District Attorney R. E. McCreary is vacationing came a check for $5 from him, a half page of comment and an editorial cartoon on the Ezzo campaign from the Philadelphia Inquirer, and this letter:

"I am enclosing herewith a drawing and an editorial which appeared this morning in the Philadelphia Inquirer. You may want to reprint it. I am also enclosing my check for $5 to help defray the expense of perpetuating in marble the philosophy of Mario Ezzo—'My bread it tastes sweet, and I feel like a man because I work.

"Congratulations to your paper for giving Mario Ezzo his niche in the hall of fame."

Today the total stood at $128.50, rapidly nearing the $150 needed to pay Aliquippa's final tribute to the man who swept the streets here in payment for his relief check and so attracted nation-wide commendations.

(Continued on Page Four)

BATTLE FEARED AS 250 PICKETS SURROUND MINE

Guards Carrying Shot Guns Patrol Area; Showdown Seen

Fearful of violence at Beaver county's largest coal stripping plant, in operation continually since the general cessation of activities in the bituminous field, Sheriff William V. Kennedy and state motor police today summoned reinforcements to the Shirley Gas Coal Corp. property near Zelienople.

The extra officers were called after 250 union miners of Culmerville, near Butler, appeared on the scene this morning for picket duty. Union leaders said their ranks would be swelled to between 800 and 1,000 before nightfall.

Although there was no trouble until early this afternoon, police and company officials feared that a showdown was imminent. The situation at the plant, observers reported to the Gazette, is "exceedingly tense."

A spokesman for the firm said the night shift was slated to start work at 3 p. m. He hinted that attempts may be made by the pickets to prevent the men from going to work.

TROOPERS GATHER

About 25 state troopers from Beaver, Butler, Perrysville, New Castle and Pittsburgh were on the scene, together with the sheriff and a staff of deputies and company guards.

The company guards, it was learned, were patrolling around B. & O. freight cars loaded with coal, while the motor police were standing by, armed with tear gas guns, ready for any emergency.

The stripping plant, it was said, has been shipping between 800 and 1,000 tons of coal daily, supplying special government orders and coal for county schools and hospitals. The concern employs 82 men.

REFUSE UNION

Operations were at a standstill today at the Old Furnace and Cunningham Coal plans nearby, reports indicated.

No attempt was made to stop the Shirley workmen from entering the plant this morning but leaders of the union pickets went into conference with corporation officials in an effort to get them to curb operations.

Shirley employes shunned pleas for them to align with the U. M. W. A., it was reported.

Shortly before noon, several leaders of the pickets rushed to Pittsburgh to confer with U. M. W. A. officials.

The pickets, except for booing truck drivers leaving the scene with loads of coal, were said to be orderly. Police were keeping them on the highway paralleling the plant, located in Franklin township.

Funeral Rites Held For William Roberts

The Rev. E. C. Poole, pastor of the Aliquippa First Baptist church, officiated at the funeral service held for William D. Roberts this afternoon. Members of the B. P. O. E., of which Mr. Roberts was a charter member, participated in the burial service.

CHANGE STATIONS

Center township's popular radio entertainers, the Prairie Wranglers, will transfer from Station WKSD, New Castle, to Station WWSW at Wheeling, W. Va., effective May 1.

The Manteer Trio, composed of James, Emmett and Mary Mateer, brothers and sister, appeared before the Exchange club here Tuesday night and presented a program of hill-billy songs.

FIREMEN TO MEET

Members of the Aliquippa volunteer fire department will meet in regular session at 8 p. m. today in Central station. President Ed Smith will preside over the meeting. Routine business matters will be taken up.

TWENTY QUARANTINED

Twenty cases of contagious disease were reported today by the Aliquippa Board of Health. Placed under quarantine by Health Officer James Tanner were 11 chickenpox and nine mumps cases. Three pneumonia cases were also reported.

EX-FIRE CHIEF PRAISES ALIQUIPPA'S DEPARTMENT

"It's the best equipped and cleanest department I have ever seen. The chief surely knows his stuff."

That was the comment of Captain William Fulham of the East Liberty fire department, Pittsburgh, when he was escorted through the Central Fire station of Aliquippa.

Captain Fulham, a veteran of 23 years service and former chief of Pittsburgh's departments, is now one of selected men conducting Beaver county's "fire school" classes.

"Fire Chief C. B. Ransom is one fellow whom I can't stick," he said. "He deals with chemistry and gases like an expert. In fact, I think so much of what he has done here that I am going to report an account of his work to Harrisburg."

Since becoming acquainted through instructing the Aliquippa district, Captain Fulham has brought several Pittsburgh firemen here to show them the Aliquippa station. "Captain Joseph Fay," he said, "was amazed at the fine setup for a town of this size."

"Aside from good general equipment, which I see is kept in perfect operating condition, Chief Ransom has tools known only to large city departments."

Among incidentals seldom seen in departments of this size and to many unheard of, are foamite generators for oil fires, fog nozzles and cellar pipes which give access to smoky burning basements by drilling through the floor.

"The service truck and ladder truck would be a credit to any department, large or small," he said, "and the alarm system is the best that can be had."

Captain Fulham took great interest in the fact that despite fire hazards here, a threatening geographical condition, mills and refineries which might be potential threats, "the chief has set a fine record of cutting fire loss."

"The fire classes here are well received and the Aliquippa district enrollees are the best I have," Fulham credited. He lauded the volunteers and said, "they are all a smart group of boys."

At the class last night Captain Fulham told members that in the near future, as soon as weather conditions permit, outside classes will be held. The boys will be drilled in every phase of fire-fighting and every piece of equipment available will be used. They will lay hose and stand ladders like in actual fighting, he explained. It is expected the closing nine weeks of the 15-week course will be devoted to this type of instruction.

The county fire chiefs' class will convene at Beaver municipal building Sunday night.

Verbal Clashes Mark Inauguration Of "Mayor"

Woman Burned In $6,500 Freedom Fire

TEN PAGES

The Aliquippa Gazette

SERVING AN INDUSTRIAL COMMUNITY OF 50,000

WEATHER — Fair with light frost tonight. Sunday fair and slightly warmer

VOL. XVII. No. 271 | SERVED BY UNITED PRESS MEMBER OF P. N. P. A. | ALIQUIPPA, PA., SATURDAY, APRIL 29, 1939 | PHONE [illegible] | 3 CENTS; BY CARRIER, 15 CENTS A WEEK

WOMAN BURNED AS FIRE RAZES FREEDOM HOUSE

Aliquippa Department Fights Two Brush Blazes

A Freedom woman was burned painfully last evening during a $6,500 fire which swept through the building in which she resided and 100 week-old chicks were cremated in another blaze at North Rochester later in the night. Aliquippa firemen stamped out two brush fires here during the last 18 hours.

Mrs. William Sacoulas, 45, suffered burns of the hands and forearms shortly after 7 p. m. when flames shot from an empty storage room in her home on the second floor of the J. B. Hetche building at 868-872 Third avenue, Freedom. She was treated by a doctor.

ORIGIN UNKNOWN

The fire, of unknown origin, was discovered by Irene, seven-year-old daughter of Mrs. Sacoulas, who observed smoke pouring from the upstairs. She notified her mother and the latter was seared seconds later.

Traffic was paralyzed for three hours and two westbound tracks of the P.R.R. were blocked during the blaze. Trains were re-routed over an eastbound track.

Flames virtually gutted the building and damaged a pool room, on the first floor, operated by Benny Faber and [illegible] of [illegible], along with a refrigeration storage plant owned by the Jurich Electric company.

Damage to the building was estimated at $5,000, the Saçoulas family said their loss was $800, the stor-

(Continued on Page Six)

River Victim's Body Remains Unidentified

Body of the middle-aged man found floating in the Ohio river near Vanport Thursday remained unidentified today at the Anderson funeral home in Beaver.

Additional persons viewed the body during the last 24 hours but could not identify the victim. Neither were police able to take fingerprints of the man due to the badly decomposed condition of his body.

Publishers' Chief

John S. McCarrens, above, is the new president of the American Newspapers Publishers' Association. The vice-president and general manager of the Cleveland Plain Dealer was elected at the recent convention of that body at New York. (Acme Photo).

CROWTHER TO BE EXCHANGE GUEST

Guest speaker at next Tuesday evening's dinner-meeting of the Aliquippa Exchange club at Woodlawn Presbyterian church will be Ernest C. Crowther, dean emeritus of the Pittsburgh School of Accountancy.

Mr. Crowther, past president of the Pennsylvania Institute of Certified Public Accountants, also is operator of amateur radio station W8QWB.

Hayward Is Appointed Health Staff Member

Clyde Hayward, former Aliquippa Justice of the Peace, received notice from Harrisburg this week of his appointment to the health officer's staff of Beaver county. In an interview at the state seat with Dr. I. Campbell, state health department official, the Aliquippa appointee was favorably received, and expects to fill his new post early in May.

NEW PROPOSALS MAY BRING HALT TO COAL CRISIS

Break Seen As Lewis Summons Policy Group

NEW YORK (UP) — An early break in the Appalachian soft coal deadlock appeared possible today.

Overnight developments aroused hope that the month-long suspension of mining in the eight-state area might be ended soon and a national emergency averted.

Wage-hour negotiators for 2,000 Appalachian coal operators were understood to have prepared a new recognition formula designed to meet demands of the United Mine Workers of America for protection against rival unions.

Whether or not the compromise proposal would be acceptable to John L. Lewis, UMWA president, and the other union negotiators remained to be seen.

It was evident, however, that the miners believed an agreement might be in prospect. Union leaders sent out instructions for members of the miners' policy committee, who must ratify any proposed contract, to return to New York on Tuesday.

Woman Posts Bond For Second Hearing

Over-riding a decision handed down by Burgess George L. Kiefer at a morning sitting of his court this week, Lillian Stowski, 430 Merchant street, Ambridge, who was discharged before the burgess on an assault and battery charge, had posted bond of $500 today to assure her appearance at court hearing upon the order of Justice Ivor L. Jones.

The Ambridge woman, whose case came under the jurisdiction of the burgess as a borough ordinance violation, was recalled for hearing upon an information filed before Jones by Pauline Mullen, West Aliquippa. The latter claimed she was attacked by Miss Stowski and appealed to the squire for collection of a doctor's bill.

Girl And Two Men Hurt In Auto Crash

A New Brighton girl and two men were injured today in a collision of two automobiles and a truck on Ohio river boulevard.

A truck driven by George Brklacih, 55, of McKees Rocks, crashed into a machine driven by Christy Summerfield, 25, Beaver Falls, and a machine driven by Chief of Police M. Omohundro, Ben Avon.

Summerfield suffered cuts and bruises. Mildred Stein, 20, New Brighton, was cut on the head, legs and suffered possible fracture of the right foot. Brklacih suffered minor injuries. The police chief was not injured.

Four Aliquippans At Rotary Meeting

Four Aliquippa Rotarians attended the second annual conference of the 176th District International at the Brodhead Hotel, Beaver Falls, yesterday. They were: James Keifer, W. R. Troxel, Dr. H. C. Thel and E. J. Tilton.

G. Rees Carroll, R. H. Schaller, R. B. Reeves, S. C. Moore, C. P. Sims, E. Laughner, Mr. Keifer, Mr. Troxel and Dr. Thel attended the banquet in the evening.

Beaver County IOOF At Sheridan Meeting

Odd Fellows of Beaver county, including members of Aliquippa's Russell Lodge, will participate in an anniversary rally at Sherodd temple, Sheridan, tonight with representation from nine other Western Pennsylvania counties in commemoration of the 120th birthday of I. O. O. F. The order here will also celebrate the anniversary at an installation ceremony and entertainment program Monday.

County 4-H Clubs Are Reorganized

Reorganization of all 4-H clubs in Beaver county was underway today as the girls met in their respective communities to elect officers, select projects for the new year and plan their club calendars for the summer months.

Queens of May Rule Again Monday

Geoffrey Chaucer, the father of English poetry who lived in the fourteenth century, gave this simple explanation of May Day which is still celebrated but has undergone a number of changes.

"Forth goeth all the court, both most and least, to fetch the flowers."

Thirty-eight years ago while in prison for reactionary activities, Nicolai Lenin, father of Russian Communism, said in a secret petition to more than 2,000 St. Petersburg factory workers:

"It is time that we Russian workers smash the chains that the bosses and government have placed upon us."

According to authoritative historians, May Day, now a day of labor and demonstrations by many workers, began originally as a function in Europe and reached peak festivity at about the sixteenth century.

A day of adoration of beauty, dancing around the may pole, the common assessory of every village commons. The Hawthorne bloom was named the May. At sunrise the entire population turned out to go "A Maying." Maidens requested:

"Wake me early, dear mother, for I must dance at the May."

The King and Queen and entire court chose this day to mingle with their subjects and crown the "May Queen." Centuries before that, Romans observed May 1 by worshipping

(Continued on Page Six)

Europe In Brief

LONDON—[illegible] may [illegible] Hitler non-aggression pact as reply to encirclement charges and test of German offer to guarantee any nation in President Roosevelt's peace appeal program.

PARIS—Britain may approach France for joint offer of security guarantees to Germany, diplomatic quarters report.

ROME—Mussolini orders additional military precautions as answer to British conscription plan.

MILAN—Mussolini's newspaper calls Roosevelt "hippopotamus in a crystal shop" for message to him and Hitler.

BUCHAREST — Rumania proposes immediate negotiations to settle government and private debts to United States.

BERLIN—Nazis hail "utter defeat" of Roosevelt as Hitler studies reaction to Reichstag address; to make another speech Monday.

WARSAW—Poland to answer Germany's denunciation of nonaggression treaty; maintains full military precautions on frontier.

VERBAL CLASHES FEATURE FIRST 'MAYOR' MEETING

District Attorney And Labor Leader Stage Debate

John Thornton, colored labor leader of Midland, today stood banished from the cabinet of Mayor Howard D. Durr of Ohio Valley's colored populace after he had made District Attorney Robert E. McCreary the target of disparaging remarks during induction ceremonies for the "mayor" at Junction Park last night.

Thornton was loudly booed from the speakers' platform and threatened with ejection from the hall for a time following his unexpected verbal attack against the county's D. A., which supplanted what was scheduled to have been a speech in line with the evening's program.

1,700 PRESENT

Seventeen hundred persons, who crowded into the building, heard Thornton in his one-man demonstration in the presence of Mr. McCreary.

Thornton charged that "the district attorney and his stooges failed to prosecute two very famous cases under the equal rights law of Pennsylvania."

Mr. McCreary was permitted to return to the platform after order had been restored in the crowd and apologies were offered by Mayor Durr.

The district attorney asserted Thornton "is a bad colored man." He charged that Thornton is a Communist and one who should not be allowed in society. He added:

"I know the colored people do not approve of his actions. Last year he stood outside my offices and said 'we are going to clean out this bunch.'

CITES CASES

"The two civil rights cases which I handled in Beaver county were the only ones in the state, since the enactment of the civil rights law, to reach the jury."

Earlier Mr. McCreary had paid tribute to Mr. Durr and said all men, whether black, white or yellow, are equal under the law and should uphold the constitution.

"Mayor" Durr, after taking office and being installed by Burgess George L. Kiefer of Aliquippa, said in part:

"There are certain conditions existing among our people that I do not blame on the others (white folk) and which our people place on their shoulders. It is our responsibility to correct them as we are solely re-

(Continued on Page Six)

J. & L. Schedules Aliquippa Works

Hot Mills 1 through 12 will be idle during the week of April 30th, 1939.

WIRE BUNDLING ROOM OPERATIONS
Week of May 2, 1939

Tuesday, May 2, 1939, 3:00 p. m. to 11:00 p. m., 2 gangs; Wednesday, May 3, 1939, 7:00 a. m. to 3:00 p. m., 2 gangs.

Special bundling as lined up.

GALVANIZED BUNDLING OPERATIONS

Sunday, May 1, 1939, 11:00 p. m to 7:00 a. m., 2 bundlers; Monday, May 2, 1939, 7:00 a. m. to 3:00 p. m., 2 bundlers; 3:00 p. m. to 11:00 p. m., 2 bundlers.

STRAIGHTENING AND CUTTING OPERATIONS

Tuesday, May 2, 1939, 7:00 a. m. to 3:00 p. m., 3 and 4 machines; 3:00 p. m. to 11:00 p. m., 3 and 4 machines; Wednesday, May 3, 1939, 7:00 a. m. to 3:00 p. m., 3 and 4 machines.

No. 1 operators to call in Wednesday.

WIRE DEPARTMENT OPERATIONS

No. 1 Rod Mill, on at 7:00 a. m., Tuesday, May 2; No. 2 Rod Mill, on at 7:00 a. m., Wednesday, May 3; Wire Mill, on at 7:00 a. m., Monday, May 1; Nail Mill, on at 7:00 a. m., Tuesday, May 2; Galv. Dept. (No. 4 frame) on at 11:00 p. m., Sunday, April 30; (No. 5 frame) continuous operation; Pat. Annlrs. (No. 2 frame) not scheduled; (Nos. 1-3 frames) on at 7:00 a. m., Tuesday, May 2; Field Fence, on at 7:00 a. m., Tuesday, May 2; Barb Fence, on at 7:00 a. m., Tuesday, May 2.

The following departments of the Welded Tube department will resume operations Monday, May 1, 1939, as follows:

No. 7 Lapweld Furnace—7 to 3:30 turn, Al Zihmer's crew; 3:30 to 12:00 turn, Mike Kovich's crew.

No. 4 Seamless Mill—Starting at 8:00 a. m., May 1. 8 to 4 turn, Johnson's crew; 4 to 12 turn, Morgan's crew; 12 to 8 turn, Hallisey's crew.

14" ROLLING MILL

Will resume operations at 8:00 a. m. Monday, May 1, 1939.

Roll crews reporting as follows:

Mr. Malley's crew at 8:00 a. m., Monday; Mr. Hennessy's crew at 4:00 p. m. Monday.

Finishing end crews reporting as follows:

Mr. Baker's crew at 8:00 a. m. Monday; Mr. Barton's crew at 4:00 p. m. Monday; Mr. Young crew at 12:00 o'clock Monday night (Tuesday a. m.)

10" SKELP MILL

No starting time available at this date—watch for notice later.

Mate Dies In Strike Fight

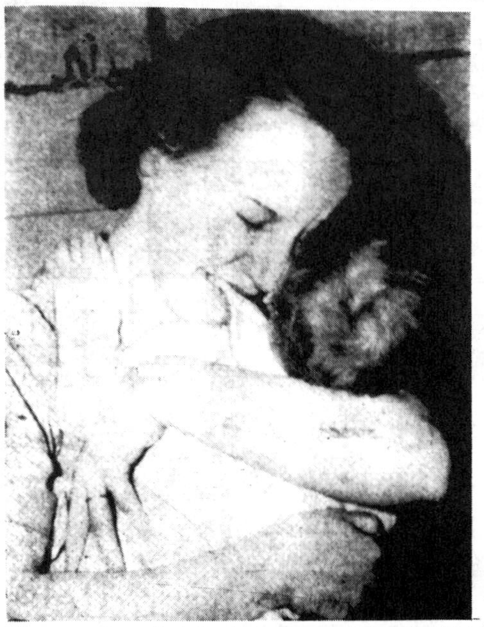

Great was the grief of Mrs. Marie Abhrom of New Philadelphia, O., when this picture was taken. Her husband, John, had just been killed in a strike battle at a coal mine near Otsego, where he was picketing. Mrs. Abhrom, bites on the dress of her one-year-old daughter as she tries to hold back tears. (Acme Photo).

Two Score Aliquippa Scouts Pass Tests For Merit Badges

At the final board of review before Honor Court next month, more than two score Boy Scouts from seven Aliquippa troops last night passed tests for merit badges and first and second class ratings.

Harry Hartley served as chairman of the board, assisted by Robert McPhilimy and Scouters Dean Larabee, Al Harvey, Michael Bires, V. R. Mrozoski and Lee A. Wadding.

The board met at Aliquippa High school. Opening the meeting was the pledge of allegiance to the flag and Scout oath, led by Michael Bires of Troop 452. Tests were taken by the following Scouts and Scouters:

TROOP 430

Second class—Perry Smith, Kasimere Barkovich and Joseph Ribar. First class—Paul Ribar. Merit badges—Joseph Branchetti, John Kerlin, Louis Salvati and Mike Lis, firemanship; Nick T. Kerlin, poultry keeping; George Trombulac, reading; Mike Belsky, printing and journalism; Julian Miazgovicz, plumbing; Edward Kwolik, leathercraft and handicraft; Paul Ribar, carpentry and art; Edward Gnup, athletics and scholarship; John Zajac, plumbing; John Ruby, leathercraft, leatherwork, art, personal health and carpentry; Fred Kofler, firemanship, civics; V. R. Mrozoski, plumbing, printing and jouralism.

TROOP 436

Second class—Thomas Belan.

TROOP 438

Second class—Donald Cummings, George Holden, Ralph Cochran, Samuel Wright, William Jenkins and James Rowley. First class—Robert Whitehill, William Snow and Robert Risher. Merit badges—Robert Whitehill—Bugling and music; George Bull, dramatics and public speaking; Courtney Kronk, book-binding.

TROOP 441

Lee A. Wadding merit badges in camping, cooking, pathfinding, masonry, plumbing and public health.

TROOP 452

First class—John Zeigler. Merit badges—handicraft by Robert Lasto.

TROOP 456

Second class—Bert Smith and Don Nelson. Merit badges—leatherwork by James Marshall.

TROOP 476

Second class—Harry McFarland, Thomas White, James Hudson and Wallis Davis. First class—Arnold and Eugene Springer. Merit badges—Metalwork by Arnold Springer.

Star Scout—Jack Turner of Troop 438. Life Scout—Lee A. Wadding, scoutmaster of Troop 441. Eagle Palm—V. R. Mrozoski, scoutmaster of Troop 430, going up for his fourth eagle palm.

BANQUET TONIGHT

Between 50 and 60 reservations have been made for the annual banquet of the Aliquippa Veterans of Foreign Wars' which will take place at 8 p. m. today in Hotel Woodlawn. A short speaking program will highlight the dinner.

Soviet Fliers Crash; 1 Hurt; Await Rescue

MISCOU PLAINS, N. B. (UP)—Two Russian fliers who crashed their monoplane on rocky Miscou island after completing 4,000 miles of a projected non-stop flight from Moscow to New York, waited disconsolately beside the wreckage today for rescuers coming by airplane from Boston.

In a strange country, surrounded by fishermen and farmers whose language they could not understand, neither flier would leave the plane although one, believed to be the pilot, Brig. Gen. Vladimir Kokkinaki, had suffered several broken ribs in the crash.

Creator of Muggs and Skeeter Finds Inspiration as He Sails

When Wally Bishop isn't creating refreshing antics and hilarious situation sfor MUGGS AND SKEETER on the comic page, he usually is navigating on the high seas. Here you see "Skipper" Bishop studying the course of the recent Havana-St. Petersburg ninth annual race in which he captured the Bacardi trophy, winning first place in the schooner division sailing the 40-foot Aloha, also pictured.

Muggs and Skeeter will be found each day on the comic page of the Aliquippa Gazette beginning Monday. Don't miss a chapter.

HOUSECLEANING TIME IS CLASSIFIED AD TIME

Gazette Classified Advertising

No charge less than 25c.
Copy for classified advertising must be in by 11 a. m. on days of publication to insure insertion on desired date.

When sending advertising by mail, write plainly and give complete instructions as to number of insertions.

Right is reserved to edit or reject all copy.

Now 3 three-line advertisements for 50c for three days. Count 5 average words to the line.

Announcements

Monuments 4

Rome Monumental Work
Lowest Prices in Valley
Come down . . . save sales commission
499 Delaware Avenue, Rochester

Personals 5

MEN OLD AT 40! GET PEP. New Ostrex Tonic Tablets contain raw oyster invigorators and other stimulants. One dose starts new pep. Value $1.00. Special price 89c. Call, write Eckerd's Drug Store.

Lost and Found 7

Lost or strayed: Male Fox Terrier, white with black markings. Return to 357 Franklin Avenue or phone 70-R. REWARD.

Lost: Lady's Bulova wrist watch on Franklin avenue or Church street. Reward. Call 1278-J.

Employment

Male Help Wanted 9

Wanted: EXPERIENCED PAPER HANGER. Must be reasonable. Inquire 600 Sheffield Avenue.

Employment Wanted 12

Walls washed and wallpaper cleaned. Grass cut at reasonable prices. Phone Aliquippa 250-W.

Merchandise

For Sale Miscellaneous 16

SMALL BABY GRAND
DELIVERED 60 DAYS AGO
IN ALIQUIPPA. WILL TRANSFER
BALANCE DUE ON TERMS TO
RELIABLE PARTY.
DRAKE-KAPPHAN
702 LIBERTY AVENUE,
PITTSBURGH, PA.

Building Materials 18

CONCRETE BLOCKS
Marcello Manufacturing Co.
14th St., Monaca. Phone Roch. 3479

Garden Supplies 20-A

Farm & Garden Supplies. Feed, Seed, Lime, Fertilizer. Free Delivery. Phone Mrs. J. H. Figley, 459-R.

Good Things to Eat 22

Let's have lunch at Guy's. Sandwiches, 5c and 10c. Real Italian Spaghetti. Tudor Building.

Soft Drinks and Confections 22-A

Refreshing & delicious. We carry a complete line of soft drinks. Apollo Soda Water Co. Tudor Building.

Pep Up with "Wake Up"
Yaky and Sons
143 Main Avenue, Phone 71

Household Goods 23

For Sale: Olive gas range, like new, $15; three piece living room suite, $8; studio couch, $7; three piece bedroom suite, $20; porcelain top kitchen table, $2; American Beauty iron, $1; two single beds, $20. Very reasonable for quick sale. Inquire Josephine Ritz, 536 Merchant Street, Ambridge.

Jewelry and Repairing 24

Eye Glass Frames Soldered,
Jewelry and Watch Repairs
HARTSTEIN'S, 377 Franklin Ave.

Seeds, Plants and Flowers 27

We invite you to see our fine selection of flowers for MOTHER'S DAY. Sheffield Greenhouse, Brodhead Rd.

Landscaping 27-A

Call Fred Schulthels, experienced landscaper, lawns trimmed. 137 Spring Street, phone 1165.

Specials at the Stores 28

"The Perfect Dessert" . . . . is ice cream. We carry all flavors, 29c qt. New Sheffield-Pettibon Dairy.

If Harry Babiak of Main Street will call at the Gazette Office he will receive a free ticket to the Strand Theatre to see "The Westerner."

FREE!
Look for Your
Name
in the
Classified Ads
for
Free Tickets
to the
STATE
TEMPLE
STRAND
THEATERS

Merchandise

2½ pounds QUEEN ANNE Candy with framed reproduction of Whistler's Mother. Dudley News, Phone 1.

Wearing Apparel 29

For Sale: $200 Hudson Seal Coat, Fitch collar. Size 16. Sacrifice price, excellent condition. Phone 1150.

Business Service

Wanted to Buy 30

WE PAY 5c a pound for large white rags. No silks or rayons. Aliquippa Gazette.

Business Service Offered 36

Wall Paper Removed by Modern Steam machinery. No dirt, no mess. Call 934 for details.

Royal Typewriters Sales & Service. All makes repaired. Phone C. F. Brown, Beaver Falls 3379. Federal Title and Trust Bldg.

Fires . . . are caused by DEFECTIVE wiring. Call us for estimates. Atkinson Electric Co. Phone 592.

Trucks Sprayed and Lettered
Guaranteed complete.
Phone Ross Adams, 1389-R.

If Mrs. Robert O'Connor of Hopewell Avenue will call at the Gazette Office she will receive a free ticket to the State Theatre to see "Dodge City."

Beauty Parlors 37

Be smart . . . be well groomed.
Steam Oil Permanents, $3.95 up.
Phone 2040. Phil's Beauty Shop

Your hair is your crowning glory!
Keep it lovely.
Chickie's Beauty Shop. Phone 2218

Cleaning-Pressing 39

LOOK YOUR BEST FOR LESS FAME Beaver Valley Laundry will do 11 lbs. family laundry bundle, washed and ironed, any day in week for 98c. Approved by Good Housekeeping. Phone Aliquippa 2011. We call for and deliver.
FAME Beaver Valley Laundry Co.

Winter garments cleaned & stored in MOTH PROOF BAGS for next year's wearing. Delivery service. Franklin Cleaning Co., Rear 340 Franklin Avenue. Phone 1150.

Transfer-Storage 44

LIGHTNING LOCAL EXPRESS CO. Daily pick-up & delivery between Pittsburgh & Aliquippa. Calls taken until 11 a. m. with delivery same day. Phones Atlantic 5434, Sewickley 1697 and New Brighton 1113.

Hammel's Express
Local and Pittsburgh Express
Phone Walnut 3768

Where to Go 49-A

Come and bring your friends.
Dine & Dance—Delicious Sandwiches
Zernich Ballroom, 143 Hopewell Ave.

California State Teachers College Alumni are holding their first annual dance, Friday, May 5, at Herron Hall. Featuring Bob McGowan's Orchestra.

Rooms For Rent

Walls Cleaned 50-A

Estimates gladly given on wall paper cleaning - wall washings. Inquire 319 Park Street. Phone 1778-R.

Housekeeping Rooms 52

For Rent: Two completely furnished rooms. Adults only. Inquire 115 Orchard Street.

For Rent: Three rooms, bath, garage. Kitchen and bedroom furnished. $25. 306 Larimer Street or phone Rochester 6132-R-3.

For Rent: Two adjoining rooms, furnished or unfurnished. Columbia Hotel. Reasonable rent. Call 1875-J.

Rooms For Rent

For Rent: Two furnished rooms for light housekeeping. Only Americans need apply. Inquire 139 Spring Street.

Unfurnished Rooms 55

For Rent: Three unfurnished rooms, excellent location. Inquire 1719 Irwin Street.

For Rent: Two unfurnished rooms, close to bus. Excellent location. Also one furnished room suitable for young man. Inquire 1807 Jackson Street.

For Rent: Two unfurnished rooms, sink in kitchen, garage. Inquire 119 Waugaman Street.

For Rent: Four unfurnished rooms, bath. Inquire 68 George Street on First Floor.

If Mrs. Mary E. Hart of 212 Franklin Avenue will call at the Gazette Office she will receive a free ticket to the Temple Theatre to see "Ride a Crooked Mile."

Apartments and Flats 56

Modern convenient apartments. 2 or 3 rooms. Apply Young's 5 and 10c Store. 360 Franklin Avenue.

Business Places 57

For Rent: Storeroom suitable for drugstore, confectionery, grocery store, barber shop, pool room. Inquire 378 Franklin Avenue.

Real Estate For Sale

Houses for Sale 66

For Sale: Six room dwelling, bath. 3 furnished attic rooms, garage. Price $4000. Terms. Write Box 110, Gazette.

Lots for Sale 68

For Sale: Bargain for quick buyer! Three lots, 50x150, Sheffield Terrace. A. Shemer, Phone 991.

Financial

Business Opportunities 71

Make savings work for you. 5% interest means $50 per year on $1000. Workingmen's Building & Loan Assn. 536 Franklin Avenue, Phone 619.

Money to Loan 73

AUTO LOANS
Borrow on your car. Easiest, quickest way to get cash.
Confidential—No endorsers.
AUTOMOBILE LOAN ASS'N
Prince Theatre Bldg. Amb. 1500

Classified Display

Automotive

Automobile Agencies 75

1936 Plymouth, 2 door deluxe. Black, large trunk $325
Snyder Garage, Inc.
337 Franklin Ave.

1939 Plymouth, 2 door Sedan Demonstrator, reduced price.
OHIO VALLEY MOTOR COMPANY
126 & 255 Station Street

Bargains in Used Cars for May

1937 Ford Tudor, 60 h.p.,	$365.00
1937 Ford Coupe, radio	395.00
1937 Ford Tudor, trunk,	$395.00
1935 Ford Standard Coupe, heater	250.00
1937 DeSota Coupe, radio, heater	$485.00
1936 Chevrolet Tudor	$365.00
1931 Chevrolet Fordor Sedan	80.00

Others To Choose From
SIMS MOTOR SALES
167 Franklin Ave. Phone 603

Classified Display

Automobiles for Sale 76

2 Ford A Models, 1930-1931
YOUR CHOICE, $50
Todd Motor Sales, 1725 McMinn St.

1937 Ford "60" Sedan, $325.
1934 Packard Sedan, $325.
1933 Ford Coach, $100.
1932 Auburn Cabriolet, $65.
1935 Plymouth 4 door Sedan, $249
1930 Chevrolet Sedan, $25.
Todd Motor Sales, 1725 McMinn St.

Auto Supplies 78

Automobile Mufflers; Guaranteed against blowout, they're leak proof, too. Abe's & Sons, Auto Wreckers, Phone 9572.

Service Stations 79

Triple Play for Spring. White Flash, change oil, lubrication service . . . ATLANTIC. Pete Cost Service, Phone 4.

ROCHESTER MOTOR COACH CO.
From Rochester to Aliquippa
Via Brodhead Road
Effective February 27th. 1939

WEEK DAYS Roch.	WEEK DAYS Aliq.	SUNDAYS Roch.	SUNDAYS Aliq.
A.M.	A.M.	A.M.	A.M.
6:00	6:45	6:00	
6:45	7:30	6:45	8:15
7:30	8:20	9:30	10:15
8:15	9:05	11:05	
9:05	10:05	P.M.	P.M.
*10:05	*11:05		12:05
11:05		1:05	2:05
P.M.	P.M.	1:45	3:15
*12:05	12:05	2:45	4:15
1:05	*1:05	4:05	5:05
1:45	1:45	5:05	6:05
2:30	2:30	6:05	7:05
3:15	3:25	7:05	8:05
4:05	4:15	8:05	9:05
4:45	4:45	9:10	10:05
5:30	5:40	10:05	10:45
6:15	6:15	10:45	11:30
7:05	7:05	11:30	12:30
8:05	8:05		
9:10	9:05		
10:05	10:05		
10:45	10:45		
11:30	11:30		
	12:30		

ZONES AND FARE RATES
Zone No. 1—Rochester to Sweltzer's Service Station.
Zone No. 2—Sweltzer's Service Station to Mihalek's Store.
Zone No. 3—Mihalek's Store to Aliquippa Terminal.

For any ride entirely within one zone, the fare is 10c. For any ride extending into any two zones, the fare is 15c. For any ride extending into three zones, the fare is 20c.

This schedule is subject to change without notice.

*J. & L. Pay Day and Saturdays Only.

Passengers are requested to remain seated until the coach comes to a complete stop.

DEATHS

ALBERT D. EMERICK

Albert D. Emerick, 77, Rochester, died Saturday at Rochester General hospital from a foot infection. Funeral service was this afternoon, with burial following in Irvin cemetery.

He leaves his wife, Catherine, and six children.

MELVIN S. HOLLAND

Melvin Slater Holland, 16, son of Mr. and Mrs. Enoch Holland of Baden, died Saturday at his home from pneumonia. Funeral service was today, followed by burial in Beaver cemetery.

Lightning's Course Shown

Most lightning flashes pass from top to bottom of the thunder cloud but occasionally the bottom of the cloud sparks to the ground and a tree or barn or a transmission line is "struck by lightning."

South Heights, Glenwillard, Wireton, Bon Meade, Carnot News

Ladies' Guild Holds Meeting

The April meeting of the Ladies' Guild of St. Catherine's church, South Heights, was held in the church parlors last week. Mrs. L. B. Eberle conducted the business session, at which plans were discussed for a celebration to be held in June in honor of the guild's sixth anniversary. Arrangements will be completed at next month's meeting.

The sick committee reported on the condition of a member, Mrs. A. D. McKallip, Bon Meade, who is recuperating at her home following several months' confinement at Valley hospital, Sewickley.

Prizes for five hundred games, played during the social period preceding the business session, were awarded to Mrs. N. J. Frey and Mrs. L. B. Eberle. Lunch was served at a long table which had decorations of spring flowers.

The next meeting will be held on Thursday evening, May 18.

Ladies' Aid Meets Thursday

The monthly meeting of the Ladies' Aid society of the Riverdale Presbyterian church, Glenwillard, will be held on Thursday afternoon at the home of Mrs. Harry Porter.

Members of the society sponsored a successful covered dish dinner in the church parlors last week.

On behalf of the members, Mrs. W. T. Russell, president of the society, presented Mrs. David Owens with a purse in appreciation of her 13 years service as secretary of the Ladies' Aid.

Hi-Y Club Is Entertained

Mrs. Philip Hineman, South Heights, was hostess at the weekly meeting of the Hi-Y club at her home last week. Prizes for high scores were awarded to Mrs. Harry Burkhart and Mrs. Charles Wright, McCoy Heights. Mrs. Burkhart was also awarded the draw prize. Following the games, lunch was served by the hostess.

The next meeting will be held at the home of Mrs. Charles Barnhart, of South Heights.

School Directors Direct Collections

At an executive meeting of the South Heights board of school directors on Friday evening, Tax Collector Frank D. Springer was fully authorized to collect all 1937 delinquent school per capita taxes.

Ten day notices, as required by law, will be mailed to all delinquent tax payers within a short time. If payments are still not forthcoming, the board plans to carry out its previously announced intention of legally collecting taxes. One of several drastic methods will be applied in an effort to collect the funds, which are sorely needed.

The next regular meeting of the school board will be held on Thursday evening, May 11.

The South Heights Athletic club will sponsor a benefit dance at Brodhead park this evening. Round and square dancing will be featured at the event which is open to the public.

Mr. and Mrs. George Stringer and infant son, Robert, Wireton, and Mrs. Stringer's brother and sister-in-law, Mr. and Mrs. Charles Shoemaker, Aliquippa, were called to Lewistown, Pa., on Friday by the death of their brother-in-law, Charles Collins.

The last in a series of card parties was held Friday evening at Crescent Gardens, Brodhead road, by Mrs. G. E. McKinley and Paul Keim, Bon Meade. A door prize and high score awards for five hundred were featured.

Members of the Crescent Township Girl Reserves and their councillors will be guests of the Ambridge Girl Reserves at a reciprocity meeting to be held in the Ambridge Senior High school on Thursday evening.

The local girls will sponsor a benefit treasure hunt on Friday evening which will begin and end at the Glenwillard Methodist church parlors. The event is being held to raise funds for the annual camping trip.

Ronald Schofield, eight-year-old son of Mr. and Mrs. Clifford Schofield, Wireton, underwent an operation at the Ohio Valley hospital, McKees Rocks, last week for a head injury sustained while at play several weeks ago. During his stay at the hospital, the lad's tonsils and adenoids were removed.

Ray Eberle, local boxer, has returned to Hamburg, N. Y., after a six weeks' visit at the home of his parents, Mr. and Mrs. Harry R. Eberle, Wireton.

Miss Evelyn Henning has returned to her home in Glenwillard after spending some weeks in Monaca at the home of Mr. and Mrs. Arthur Laughner.

Mr. and Mrs. Louis Onora, Wireton, are parents of a baby girl born Friday morning at Valley hospital, Sewickley.

Mr. and Mrs. Ernest Hogue, South Heights, observed their 22nd wedding anniversary yesterday. Mr. Hogue is still being treated at the South Side hospital, Pittsburgh, for burns to the face sustained while at work several weeks ago.

The annual senior prom was held in the auditorium of Moon Township High school on Friday evening. Miss Norma Kern was chairman of the committee in charge of arrangements.

May devotions will be observed this month at St. Catherine's R. C. church, South Heights, with special services each Wednesday morning and evening at 7:30 o'clock. Devotions will be in honor of the Virgin Mary.

The Feast of St. Catherine of Seana, patron saint of the church, was observed Sunday, when Father Filipcic offered the high mass for members of the parish.

Charles Werme of Glenwillard observed his birthday on Saturday.

26 QUARANTINED

Twenty-six cases of contagious disease were reported today by James Tanner, health officer. They included 13 chicken pox, three scarlet fever, nine mumps and one whooping cough case.

GRANGE TO MEET

Regular meeting of Center Township Grange will be held this Friday at 8 p. m. in the grange social rooms. Routine business and committee reports are expected to take up a greater part of the session. All grangers of the lodge are requested to be present.

HARVEY ILL

Edward Harvey, 504 Church street, well-known Aliquippa man, was seriously ill today in Conneautville hospital, Conneautville, Ohio. He is suffering an attack of pneumonia and complications.

The GIRL in the TRAILER
by
SYLVIA
CARSON

Jerry Crandon, young Indiana novelist parks his home-made trailer near a Kentucky town and finds everyone suspicious of a stranger. Especially so is elderly Judge Weatherford, owner of a nearby estate who has a vivacious granddaughter Mercedes, blonde and 17. One night she visits Jerry's trailer. They hear a radio broadcast which suggests that Jerry a foundling, might be the missing heir to the Crandon estate in eastern Kentucky. They go to see Judge Weatherford, who knows the Crandons but at that moment Blake Feaster supposed fiance of Mercedes blusters in to accuse Jerry of hiding Mercedes while her grandfather hunted for her.

CHAPTER VII

THEY all turned in a little group to confront Blake Feaster as he dashed through the door He stopped just inside, glaring vindictively at Jerry.

"So you didn't know where Mercy was eh?" Blake burst out. "I suppose you didn't lie about it when I talked to you at your trailer"

Jerry shrugged his shoulders. "I didn't lie" he said softly

"You told me you hadn't seen Mercy"

"Now you're lying." Jerry told him "If you received that impression you simply jumped to a groundless conclusion"

"That's right" Mercedes gurgled. "I was hiding under a mattress all the time you were there Blake and I heard everything Jerry said If you hadn't been so scared you would have realized he didn't say anything definite about me."

"There you are Judge." Blake scowled and turned to Judge Weatherford "Mercy admits being in the trailer with him Hiding under the mattress—she says."

The judge's eyes twinkled as he glanced from Blake Feaster to Jerry. "You know how Mercy is." he said mildly. "A man would have to use a gun to drive her away if she was determined to stay."

"And Mr. Feaster seems to be the handiest with a gun around here." Jerry said, adding ironically: "Did you bring your shotgun with you this time, Mr Feaster?"

Blake licked his lips and backed away a step. "I never thought the day'd come when I'd hear the judge taking up for a Yankee."

Mercedes confronted her suitor. "Jerry Crandon is no more Yankee than you are. He didn't know it before, but he's actually the heir, to the Crandon estate up near Ashton."

JERRY cleared his throat and said mildly: "That is—I may be. There isn't any definite proof."

"What's that, young man? I thought Mercy said Gerald Crandon was your daddy." Judge Weatherford bristled up.

"Look." said Jerry wearily, "can't we all sit down and discuss this thing quietly? I'm a human being, whether I was born in Kentucky or north of the Mason and Dixon line."

"But you were born on the Crandon estate near Ashton." Mercedes asserted positively, clinging to his arm.

Jerry smiled down at her, led her to a chair. "Perhaps," he conceded. "We'll have to see about it."

"It's nothing but a frameup for him to sneak into your house and get next to Mercy," Blake Feaster told the old judge hotly.

Jerry walked over to Blake. "Do you want your teeth knocked down your throat?" he asked quietly.

"Now see here—" Blake backed away but Jerry followed him implacably

"You've been mixing into my affairs too persistently" Jerry told him without raising his voice "First you lied to the judge about seeing Miss Weatherford and me together Then you came to my trailer and threatened me with a shotgun Now with no knowledge of the facts whatever you take it upon yourself to deny my paternity Don't you think you've said quite enough for one time?"

"Mr Crandon is right," Judge Weatherford said severely "If Mercy was at his trailer she went there of her own free will and accord without his knowledge or consent. I'll ring for juleps."

"NO!" Blake Feaster said from the doorway his face livid with rage "I'm not drinking with scoundrels I'm going to protect Mercedes She's engaged to me and it's my right to—"

"I'm *not* engaged to you Blake Feaster" Mercedes was out of her chair in a flash "I never have been I wouldn't marry you if—if you were the last man on earth"

"You didn't talk that way until this fellow came along" Blake sneered "I suppose he's been making love to you"

Mercedes turned to look at Jerry with a smile "He hasn't but I wish he would And I bet he does before I'm through with him".

"Mercedes!" Judge Weatherford spoke in shocked reproof

"What's wrong with that?" Mercedes asked defiantly "Why shouldn't I tell him the way I feel?"

"I," said Blake haughtily "am going home I think I know quite a number of people in this vicinity who would like nothing better than to ride you out of the state on a rail Crandon We won't stand for anybody like you laying claim to a Kentucky estate and making love to our women."

Jerry faced him quietly "I'll be waiting," he promised. "And I've definitely decided to claim the estate at Ashton I won't be driven away with threats."

"All right." Blake Feaster cast a final glowering look about the room, then departed muttering to himself

"I seem to be the focal point of trouble." Jerry said with a wry smile "If I get out of the way—"

"You can't do that." Mercedes exclaimed fiercely clinging to his arm "Tell him he musn't run, Grandpa."

Judge Weatherford glanced at the younger man and shook his head. "I wouldn't worry about that, Mercedes. Not if he's a Kentucky Crandon."

Mercedes' hand quivered on his arm. "You wouldn't!"

"No," said Jerry slowly "I guess I wouldn't. But what do you think about my claiming the estate?" he asked the judge.

"What proof have you that you are Gerald Crandon's son?"

"None."

"Well then, how can you expect to press your claim successfully?"

"I REALLY don't know. You see, I know nothing about my parents, except that they left me in a foundling home when I was very young."

Judge Weatherford was shaking his head. "You'll have to have proof, young man I can't support the claim of an impostor Go back to your trailer and don't enter my house again under any such false pretences."

(To be continued)
(The characters in this serial are fictitious).

NEW MIDGET CAR SEATS FOUR

Operated by a two cylinder engine, the new midget automobile built by Powell Crosley, Jr., to sell for around $300, is shown above. Ten feet long, five feet high, and weighing less than 925 pounds, the car is said to be capable of speeds up to 50 m. p. h. and get more than 50 miles to a gallon of gasoline. (Acme Photo).

"Art" Works Disappear From Cement Subway

West Aliquippa's outdoor art gallery, the walls of the cement subway leading to the town beneath the completely destroyed today but not by vandals.

Street Commissioner Ray Eberle and a crew of borough workmen spent a half-day washing the subway "art center" this weekend. The borough's pressure generating machine with plenty of steam and washing fluid was used to erase last year's football, basketball, and baseball scores from the walls.

It took more than three hours to remove a large painted "Yes" and "No" from a section of the retaining wall at the outer entrance not to mention art work and public notices

Aliquippa Boy Scout NEWS

Scoutmasters Meet Here This Evening

Scoutmasters' monthly round table meeting in Borough Scout room at 8:15 p. m. today.

Harold N. Seylor, Beaver Falls commissioner, will be present to discuss a patrol leader's course.

All scoutmasters are urged to attend or have their troop represented by assistants. Important business will be discussed, according to V. R. Mrozoski, secretary.

TROOP 438

Scoutmaster, Al. Harvey; Assistant Scoutmaster, George Peters; Scribe, James Rowley.

A board of review was held last Friday. Bob Whitehill, Bob Risher and Bill Snow were up for first class.

For second class there were Donald Cummings, Ralph Cochran, Bill Jenkins, Fred Kelsey, George Holden, Sam Wright and Jim Rowley.

We all got universal badges last night.

Jim Rowley was awaredd the plaque for the last point contest with a score of 52.

Come on, boys, let's get those planes in to Mr. Dudley. We want that new flag for the Memorial day parade.

Thanks to the budget system, we will be getting our community strips in a couple of weeks. What about a perfect attendance next week?

TROOP 430

V. R. Mrozoski, Scoutmaster; John Zajac and Nick T. Kerlin, assistants.

Wednesday being the first meeting of the month, we held our business meeting and discussed going to church the second Sunday with the Holy Name society, out-door meetings, camping trips, patrol and troop good turns, scouting in general and our present patrol contest.

Assistant Scoutmaster Nick Kerlin had a special meeting of our Bird Club, to which we all belong. Some time near the end of this month, we will be going on a field trip to see how many different birds we can see in one day. For the best painted or colored bird pictures turned in next week, Nick is giving three bird books as prizes. All scouts are eligible. They will be judged by some of our local scouters.

The Flying Eagles did their patrol good turn during the week by helping put out a brush fire. This patrol already has the framework of its log cabin erected. Considerable work has been done by working after school hours.

Before leaving Camp Umbsteatter last week, the scouts swept and cleaned the lodge, for which they were complimented by the care-taker. He said it was the first time that any troop did this.

Scout Edward Kwolik, now working on his pigeon - raising merit badge, reports that a strange pigeon came in with his brood and upon examination, the metal tag on its leg read "S. F. World's Fair—1939." A few days later it was gone.

The Stamp club will meet at two. Bring your collections. The catalog will be given to an up-to-date member and the New York Fair block of six will be given away.

We again had the "match Box" relay and the Wood-Pgieons came out on top—copping the red ribbon award. For next week, each patrol is to turn in a "Hike Stick." The Wood-Pigeons are leading in the contest to date. The scoutmaster's benediction ended the meeting.

Lost—A pitcher's glove, fitting the right hand. If found, please get in touch with troop leaders or Howard Vogel.

TROOP 401

Scoutmaster, Mr. Reed; assistant, Mr. Hauck; junior assistant, G. Krnvonic; scribe, Jim McGinnis; senior patrol leader, C. Catley; reporter, B. Suhayda.

We met in Franklin Junior High school and opened our meeting with a song led by the Flying Eagle patrol. The scribe took points and good turns. We had initiation of new members, including B. Suhayda, R. Kelley, J. Thomas, D. Carl, N. Campbell, B. Marshall. We then closed the meeting and discussed our trip this Saturday to Cook's Forest. We are to meet in front of the library at 6:30 a. m. and return Sunday night. Mr. Reed, Mr. Hauck, Mr. VanBlarcom, C. Catley, B. Suhayda, Jim McGinnis, of the Flying Eagle patrol; R. Kelly, H. Hauck, J. Thomas, of the Flying Arrow patrol, and G. Krnvonic, Sam Capperis, F. Telespis, of the Seneca patrol, are the officers and scouts planning to go on the trip.

TROOP 456

James Marshall, Scoutmaster.

Our meeting was opened with the scout oath, led by Scout Bert Smith, and followed by roll call and dues collection. Our business meeting followed and we made plans for future activities, and arrangements for our overnight hike, which will be held tonight at Camp Annie Good. Following the business meeting we had a patrol period in which the boys studied various test requirements. Our bird house contest, held over from last week, was won by Scout Dick Mortland, with Edward Diewalt giving him plenty of competition.

The Rev. H. P. Smith, our pastor, was a visitor and gave a short talk on wren houses. Mr. Mrozoski judged the contest, and we thank him for his cooperation. The meeting was closed with the pledge to the flag and the scoutmaster's benediction.

Don't forget the hike to Annie Good tonight. All out, Scouts!

TROOP 441

Lee O. Wadding, scoutmaster; Dan Carl and Bud Wadding, assistants; Ben L. Oaks, troop reporters.

Exercises and marching preceded our April 24 meeting, which opened with the Scout oath and law, led by John Connelly. The troop heard a report on a week-end hike made by David Keefer, George H., and Bud Wadding. After business had concluded, patrols held meetings. Leaders of Beaver patrol are John Connelly and Art Sleith with Bob Baker as scribe; the Pine Patrol leaders are Paul Short and Bob Wykes, and the Eagle Patrol is headed by George H. and Ben Oaks.

At our May 1 meeting, we also marched to music at the outset. Paul Short led the oath and law, followed by roll call and reports on good turns. Bud Lynn had the best one.

Two weeks from tonight is parents' night in our troop. We will have movies, in line with plans made at our meeting. Patrol periods followed and Bud Wadding showed pictures of their hike.

Beaver patrol reported it will have a handicraft display for mothers and fathers. We sang songs. Lee Wadding demonstrated first aid.

Bishops Consecrated

A split that divided Methodists 111 years ago was finally healed at the conference of the United Methodist church at Kansas City when that meeting resulted in the consecration of two bishops from former Protestant division. They are Bishop John Calvin Broomfield, left, of Fairmont, W. Va., and Bishop James H. Straughn, right, of Baltimore. (Acme Photo)

MR. AND MRS. PARNES HOSTS

Mr. and Mrs. A. Parnes, 1152 Franklin avenue, entertained at a dinner recently announcing the engagement of Mrs. Parnes' niece, Miss Lillian Thelma Seewald and Rudy Goldstein, both of Pittsburgh.

Senior Baseball Pilots Meet Here Tonight

HOLLYWOOD TEAM WALLOPS C. C. C., PLAN 12 EAGLES

Bulldogs Display Power Attacks To Win By Large Scores

Hollywood's Bulldogs of the Gazette Softball league walloped the C. C. C.-V. F. W. team of Frankfort Springs, 16-4, in a return game on Newell field here yesterday afternoon and won handily over the Plan 12 Eagles, 14-5, in another week-end tilt at the swimming pool field.

Heavy hitting marked yesterday's game, with the stick work of J. Raffle, Maeder, Mendenhall, Michael standing out for the winners and that of Baird, Kaney and McCabe for the losers. Pitzer, G. Mossholder, Ertz and Lang, of Hollywood, clouted homers.

Micheal and L. Mossholder handled mound duties for Hollywood against the Eagles and gave up only four hits. L. Mossholder, J. Raffle and Lang starred for the Bulldogs and Walker for the Eagles at the plate. Box scores:

HOLLYWOOD

	AB	R	H	P	A	E
Lang, 1b	1	1	1	1	0	1
A. Diewald, 1b	3	1	0	0	0	1
R. Rattle, 2b	2	1	1	3	0	1
C. Mossholder, 2b	2	1	1	2	0	2
Ertz, 3b	5	1	1	3	1	1
Morrow, ss	5	0	1	1	4	1
F. Mossholder, rs	2	0	0	0	0	0
Rorick, rs	3	2	2	3	0	0
Finks, rs	2	1	1	0	0	0
J. Raffle, lf	3	3	3	1	0	0
D.Mossholder, cf	2	1	0	0	0	0
Maeder, cf	2	2	2	1	0	0
Swan, rf	2	0	1	0	0	0
Mendenhall, rf	3	1	0	0	0	0
Schuster, c	1	0	1	6	0	0
Pitzer, c	3	1	1	5	0	0
Kirkwood, p	1	0	0	0	0	0
Michael, p	3	0	2	1	0	0
TOTALS	45	16	20	27	5	7

C. C. C.

	AB	R	H	P	A	E
Billochick, lf	4	0	1	1	0	0
Davis, 1b	5	0	1	6	0	1
Mustard, 3b	5	0	0	4	1	0
Myers, ss	5	2	1	3	3	1
Baird, rs	4	2	2	1	0	0
Meniece, rf	2	0	0	0	0	0
Cross, rf	2	0	0	0	0	0
Serdensky, cf	4	0	1	5	0	0
Kaney, p	4	0	2	0	1	1
R[illegible]sell, c	4	0	0	2	0	0
McCabe, 2b	4	0	2	2	0	0
TOTALS	43	4	10	27	5	3

C.C.C.-V.F.W.	010	001	020	— 4
Hollywood	020	634	10x	—16

Home runs—Pitzer, C. Mossholder, Ertz, Lang. Two base hits—Bairds 2, J. Raffle, Michael, Rorick, Mendenhall 2, Maeder. Base on balls—Off Michael 1, off Kirkwood 1, off Kaney 3. Struck out by—Michael 4, Kirkwood 4, Kaney 1. Umpire—Cooky.

EAGLES

	AB	R	H	P	A	E
Dudash, 2b	3	2	1	3	0	1
Cribbs, p	4	0	0	0	1	0
Pezzelle, 1b	4	0	0	5	0	0
Walker, c	3	0	2	7	0	1
Smith, rf	4	0	0	1	0	0
Kirkwood, cf	4	1	1	2	0	1
Ertz, lf	4	0	0	4	0	0
Orr, rs	3	1	0	3	0	0
Gibb, 3b	4	1	0	1	1	3
Caldwell, ss	3	0	0	1	1	1
TOTALS	36	5	4	27	3	7

BULLDOGS

	AB	R	H	P	A	E
Lang, 1b	2	1	1	2	0	1
A. Diewald, 1b	3	1	0	2	0	3
Swan, lf	2	1	1	0	0	0
J. Raffle, lf	3	2	2	1	0	0
D.Mossholder, rs	4	2	0	3	0	0
Hutton, 2b	2	0	0	1	0	0
G.Mossholder, 2b	3	1	0	2	1	0
Schuster, c	2	1	1	1	0	0
Pitzer, c	3	1	1	0	0	0
L.Mossholder, cf-p	5	1	3	1	1	0
C.Mendenhall, rf	5	0	1	2	0	1
R. Morrow, ss	4	0	0	1	1	0
J. Evans, 3b	4	1	0	2	0	0
J. Micheal, p	2	1	0	0	2	0
Maeder, cf	1	1	1	3	0	0
TOTALS	45	14	11	27	5	5

Hollywood	440	100	033	—14
Plan 12 Eagles	110	020	010	— 5

Home runs—J. Raffle, Lang. Two-base hit—Walker. Base on balls—off Cribbs 2, off Micheal 2, off L. Mossholder 2. Struck out by—Cribbs 2, Micheal 5, L. Mossholder 2. Umpire—G. Swan.

Waynesburg College Track Star Brother Of Aliquippa Man

Raymond (Bud) Long, one of the stars on Waynesburg college's current track team, is a brother of Floyd Long, Jr., an employe at the J. & L. plant in Aliquippa. He also is a brother-in-law of Sam Faddis, of Crafton, formerly in the chemical department at the local mill.

Long, a dash man and jumper, rates next to Henry Wilkins, colored flash of Coraopolis, who is No. 1 performer on the Yellow Jacket squad this spring.

KENTUCKY DERBY WINNER IS PREAKNESS FAVORITE

Here's Johnstown, big bay colt owned by William Woodward, which won the Kentucky Derby Saturday in the third fastest time in the 65-year history of the Churchill Downs classic at Louisville. Today, as Johnstown arrived for the Preakness this Saturday, he was being ranked with War Admiral for greatness. He's eligible for every three-year-old stake of importance, including the Belmont and Withers. Johnstown won at Louisville by six lengths, with Challedon second and Heather Broom third.

Jockey Stout, who rode William Woodward's two-year-old across the finish line, is up. "Sunny Jim" Fitzsimmons, Johnstown's trainer, with hat, is standing before the horse.—"Acme Telephoto."

THE STANDINGS

NATIONAL LEAGUE

Yesterday's Results

Pittsburgh	9	Boston	2
New York	10	Chicago	3
Cincinnati	13	Philadelphia	4
Brooklyn	2	St. Louis	1

Standing of the Clubs

	W.	L.	Pct.	G.B.
Cincinnati	9	5	.643	
Brooklyn	8	6	.571	1
Boston	8	7	.533	1½
St. Louis	7	7	.500	2
New York	8	8	.500	2
Philadelphia	7	9	.437	3
Chicago	7	9	.437	3
Pittsburgh	6	9	.400	3½

Games Today—Pitching Selections

Pittsburgh at Boston — Tobin (0-2) vs. Macfayden (2-1); Cincinnati at Philadelphia—Vander Meer (0-0) vs. Butcher (1-3); St. Louis at Brooklyn—Weiland (1-1) vs. Poffenberger (0-0) or Evans (0-2); Chicago at New York—Lee (2-3) vs. Schumacher (0-2).

AMERICAN LEAGUE

Yesterday's Results

Philadelphia	10	Detroit	3
New York	15	Chicago	4
St. Louis	6	Boston	3
*Cleveland	8	Washington	7

Standing of the Clubs

	W.	L.	Pct.	G.B.
New York	10	4	.714	..
Boston	9	4	.692	½
Chicago	10	6	.625	1
Washington	7	8	.467	3½
St. Louis	7	8	.467	3½
Cleveland	6	9	.400	4½
Detroit	6	11	.353	5½
Philadelphia	5	10	.333	5½

Games Today—Pitching Selections

New York at Chicago—Ferrell (0-0) vs. E. Smith (0-0); Boston at St. Louis—Bagby (2-1) vs. Kramer (20-); Philadelphia at Detroit—Ross (0-2) vs. Harris (1-0); Washington at Cleveland—Chase (1-2) vs. Hudlin (1-2).

INVENTOR OF CATCHER'S GLOVE

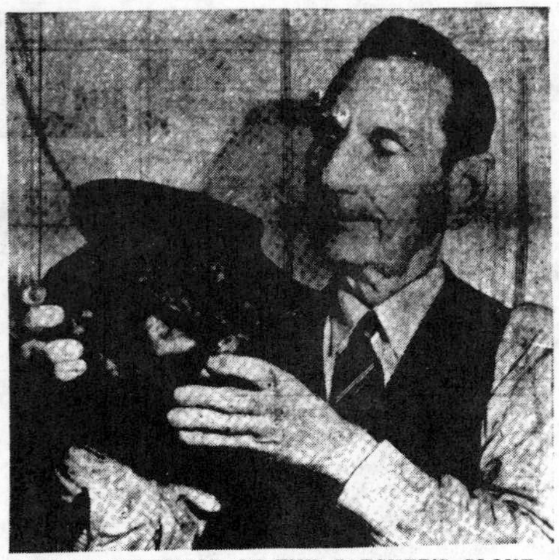

CALLED INVENTOR OF THE CATCHER'S GLOVE—Joseph Gunson, 76, of Philadelphia, Pa., holds what he claims is the first catcher's mitt, designed by him in 1888, when he was a player for the Kansas City Blues. He says he got little from it.

Around The Majors

NATIONAL LEAGUE

Pittsburgh	000	003	015	—9	14	1
Boston	001	000	001	—2	6	1

Klinger and Berres; Posedel, Shoffner, Earley and Lopez.

Chicago	001	100	100	— 3	6	2
New York	010	141	03x	—10	16	2

Bryant and Hartnett; Melton and Danning.

Cincinnati	452	020	000	—13	10	1
Philadelphia	000	030	001	— 4	9	3

Derringer and Lombardi; Mulcahy, Hollingsworth, Henry and Davis.

St. Louis	000	000	010	—1	6	0
Brooklyn	000	200	00x	—2	4	1

Bowman, Warneke and Owen; Tamulis and Todd.

AMERICAN LEAGUE

New York	010	623	201	—15	19	0
Chicago	000	022	000	— 4	9	3

Ruffing and Dickey; Whitehead, Knott, Dietrich and Tresh.

Boston	000	010	020	—3	7	1
St. Louis	013	000	20x	—6	11	3

Auker, Galehouse and Peacock; Newsom and Sullivan.

Geneva Track Squad Meets Tartans Today

Geneva college's track team was scheduled to meet Carnegie Tech in at dual meet this afternoon at Tarton bowl in Pittsburgh, with weather conditions favorable. The meet was postponed from April 22.

The Geneva golfers defeated Grove City, 10-8, in a match Saturday, while the Covenanter tennis pack bowed before the Grover team, 5-4.

Philadelphia	000	141	022	—10	14	0
Detroit	101	001	000	— 3	9	1

Caster and Brucker; Benton, McKain, Coffman, Lynn and York.

Washington	120	001	020	1	—7	13	3
Cleveland	001	201	200	2	—8	13	3

Leonard, Welaj, Appleton, Thomas and Giuliani; Allen, Humphries, Feller and Pytlak.

COMPLETE WORK OF FORMING NEW GAZETTE LEAGUE

Jr. League Managers Assemble Tomorrow To Form Loop

The finishing touches will be applied tonight to organization of the Aliquippa Gazette's Senior Baseball league at a conference of managers and representatives in the Gazette office.

The league, scheduled to play on Sunday, May 28, will have at least six and possibly eight clubs for the 1939 race, since the charter will not be closed until after tonight's parley.

Already in the fold are the Aliquippa Celtics, Whitesox, Bucs, the Plan 12 A. C., and Newell club. Also expected to enroll are the Manhattans, fast local colored aggregation.

Two additional teams of the Aliquippa community will be admitted to membership in the event they make application at today's meeting, which starts at 7:30 p. m.

Adoption of more rules and an official league baseball and selection of umpires will occupy attention of the pilots at the meeting.

A new call was issued today for teams desiring to join the Gazette's Junior Baseball circuit. Another meeting for the purpose of forming a junior alliance is called for tomorrow at 7:30 p. m.

To prevent any further dispute over the age limit, sponsors of the proposed league announced today that only teams in the 17-year-old bracket will be admitted to membership in the loop.

Players who will reach their eighteenth birthday before July 1, 1939, will not be eligible to play in the league. Wrangling over the age question caused the first meeting of managers Friday to break up without any progress being made.

Indoor Polo Returns To Pitt This Week

PITTSBURGH—Indoor polo, absent from the sport picture of greater Pittsburgh for years, will return tomorrow when the Western Pennsylvania Polo Association stages its first annual championships at Duquesne Garden. The tournament will run for five nights.

Fox Chapel, the Four Horsemen and the Pittsburgh Polo Club have already sent in entries for the matches, according to Col. C. C. McGovern, president of the association. The winner of the Western Pennsylvania Indoor title will play the championship team from Salem, O., Saturday night as the feature of a doubleheader.

AMERICAN ASSOCIATION

Minneapolis 17, Indianapolis 2.
Minneapolis 8, Indianapolis 4.
St. Paul 6, Louisville 3.
St. Paul 5, Louisville 1.
Toledo 17, Milwaukee 10.
Milwaukee 6, Toledo 5.
Kansas City-Columbus, rain.

INTERNATIONAL LEAGUE

Newark 1, Montreal 0.
Newark 6, Montreal 5.
Rochester 7, Baltimore 3.
Baltimore 5, Rochester 2.
Jersey City 9, Syracuse 2.
Syracuse 4, Jersey City 1.
Toronto 17, Buffalo 2.

TACKLES HALL

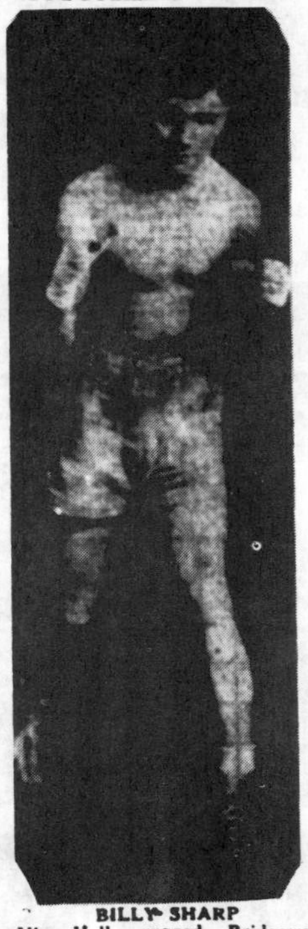

BILLY SHARP

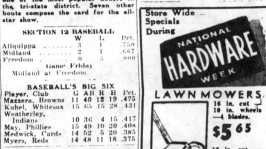

Vic Hall, rugged Bridgewater boxer who has been piling up an impressive string of victories, is expected to meet tough opposition in Billy Sharp, Weirton, W. Va., in one of the feature bouts of the Rochester Young Republicans Club boxing show to be staged this evening in the Rochester opera house. Sharp is West Virginia open champion and one of the most popular boxers in the tri-state district. Seven other bouts compose the card for the all-star show.

SECTION 12 BASEBALL

	W	L	Pct.
Aliquippa	3	1	.750
Midland	2	1	.667
Freedom	0	3	.000

Game Friday

Midland at Freedom.

BASEBALL'S BIG SIX

Player, Club	G	AB	R	H	Pct.
Mazzera, Browns	11	40	12	19	.475
Kuhel, Whitesox	15	65	15	28	.431
Weatherley, Indians	10	36	4	15	.417
May, Phillies	15	49	10	20	.408
Medwick, Cards	14	52	5	20	.385
Myers, Reds	14	48	11	18	.375

WHITESOX DROP GAME TO GREEN GARDEN OUTFIT

Behind the two-hit hurling of Frank Caler and Syers, the Green Garden Baseball team conquered the Aliquippa Whitesox, 8 to 3, on the Green Garden diamond yesterday afternoon. The game was ragged, a double of eight errors having been committed.

Feature of the fray was a home run by Vespazaini, who also socked two singles. Brown hit a double and single to help spark Green Garden. Hudak and Palsa accounted for the Whitesox hits.

Green Garden meets Shippingport this Thursday evening in a return engagement on the Garden field. Box score:

Green Garden—8

	AB	R	H	PO	A	E
Green, 1st	5	[illegible]	1	6	1	0
Holland, 2b-c	2	0	0	0	3	0
McClure, 3rd	4	0	0	5	1	2
Pfeifer, 3rd	0	0	0	0	0	0
Brown, c	3	2	2	15	0	0
Hysong, cf	3	1	0	1	0	1
Chambers, l	3	1	1	0	0	0
S. Lukitich, rf	4	1	1	0	0	1
Vespazaini, ss	4	2	3	0	0	1
F. Caler, p	1	0	0	0	1	0
Syers, p	1	1	1	0	1	0
L. Barker, p	0	0	0	0	0	0
I. Lukitich	0	0	0	0	0	0
Totals	30	8	9	27	7	5

Whitesox—3

	AB	R	H	PO	A	E
Fennych, l	3	1	0	0	0	0
Arnick, r	3	1	0	1	0	0
Petrelli, s	4	0	0	0	0	0
Hudak, 1st	4	0	1	5	0	0
Paladina, c	4	0	0	16	0	1
Palsa, 2nd	3	0	1	0	0	0
Likovich, 3rd	3	0	0	1	1	1
Keron, cf	3	0	0	0	0	0
Penar, p	4	1	0	1	0	1
Totals	31	3	2	24	1	3

Barker batted for Caler.

Home runs, Vespazaini. Two base hits, Brown. Base on balls, off F. Caler 2; Syers 1; off Penar 3. Struck out by F. Caler 6, Syers 12; by Penar 14.

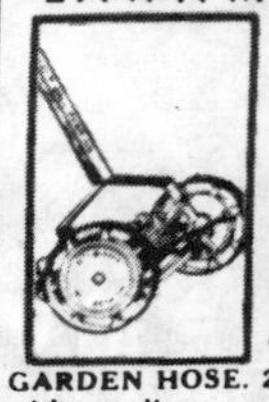

1,302 Home Loans Made In State In Three Months

FIRST QUARTER SHOWS BIG GAIN OVER YEAR AGO

[illegible]

... Such savings are protected against loss up to $5,000 per investor by the Insurance Corporation, a $218,000,000 federal government instrumentality.

As of April 1, these associations had assets of $69,752,000, a rise of $2,500,000 in a year. The figures ... by Mr. Fallon were based on reports received from the associations and Ralph H. Richards, president of the Federal Home Loan Bank of Pittsburgh, the regional home mortgage credit reserve bank serving thrift and home-financing institutions in Pennsylvania.

Small But Charming

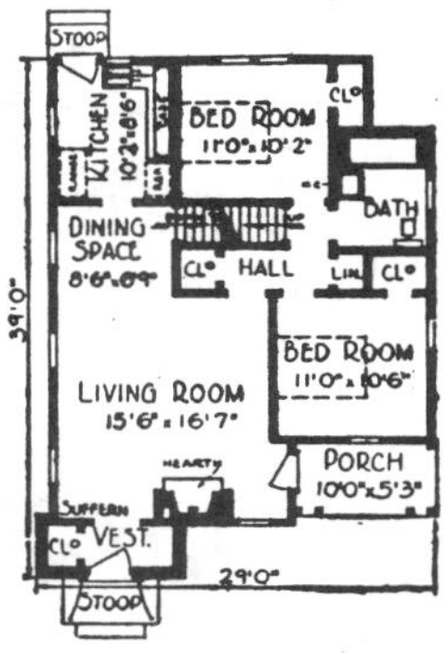
STOOP
KITCHEN 10'2"x8'6"
BED ROOM 11'0"x10'2"
CL
BATH
DINING SPACE 8'6"x6'9"
CL
HALL
LIN
CL
BED ROOM 11'0"x10'6"
LIVING ROOM 15'6"x16'7"
PORCH 10'0"x5'3"
HEARTH
CL
VEST.
STOOP
39'0"
29'0"

FOR THOSE who prefer a small home, this charming English bungalow is suggested. It not only has a pleasing exterior, but a compact and practical interior.

The four rooms are well arranged, and really are equal to five rooms in efficiency. The attic space may be utilized for rooms in the future.

The floor plan is so designed that the space allotted for dining might well be made a part of the living room when not in use at mealtime.

STOKER SALES UP

Sales of modern bituminous coal stokers have increased faster during the past four years than have the sales of any other type of heating equipment.

SHORT LOANS DISCOURAGED

By discouraging the short-term unamortized low-[illegible] mortgage with its attend[illegible]nd mortgage, the governme[illegible] [illegible] additional steps to prot[illegible] [illegible]erienced builders.

The essence of [illegible] is that home buyers shou[illegible] their homes through on[illegible] loan, amortized over a [illegible]iently long to make the pa[illegible] [illegible]tively low. Thereby, [illegible] costs and renewal [illegible] avoided, and recurre[illegible] liquidations can be pre[illegible].

Among the importan[illegible] between the old system a[illegible] sured mortgage system t[illegible] National Housing Act g[illegible] the fact that the home bu[illegible] ters upon a deal based upo[illegible] common sense instead of u[illegible] ent fallacies. The emphasi[illegible] shifted from the fiction [illegible] trinsic and immutable val[illegible] real estate to the soundn[illegible] transaction as a whole, se[illegible] distinct from the security [illegible] the collateral.

In other words, instead [illegible] lating foreclosure, it is in[illegible] the transaction first ju[illegible] apart from that unfortuna[illegible] ity.

REMOTE HEAT CONTROL

Modern automatic coal burners, or stokers, eliminate personal attention to the furnace. They may be controlled from the living room easy chair.

Heavy Traffic May Cut Property Value

Properties facing residential streets which bear a heavy traffic load tend to decrease in valu[illegible] despite the popular belief to t[illegible]ontrary, according to building experts.

Traffic congestion is detrimental to any land use, be it residential or commercial, they point out. Commercial structures should be concentrated at suitable centers, with adequate parking facilities, adjoining major thoroughfares and accessible by way of local connecting streets to nearby neighborhoods.

Elimination of fast through travel in residential areas by controlling street widths and alinement is rapidly becoming standard practice. Considerable economies are effected by reason of lighter pavement requirements, narrower streets, and a larger percentage of the land remaining for subdivision.

When local streets [illegible] designed adequately to serve the needs of a neighborhood and to discourage the circulation of through traffic, a neighborhood will develop in an orderly fashion and provide protection from the encroachment of adverse land use.

COPPER FINDING MANY NEW USES IN MODERN HOME

Although more than 6,000 years have elapsed since it was first discovered and utilized by man, copper continues to find new outlets for its usefulness in modern industry.

Immune to rust, copper and its alloys, brass and bronze, today play an increasingly important part in the building of American homes, according to the Copper and Brass Research Association. Its many products are almost universally specified in the construction of better-built homes, and indorsed by federal agencies and financing institutions identified with housing.

Because of its durability and comfort-giving qualities, copper is favored by home builders for flashings, gutters and downspouts, and in recent years has found widespread use for whole roofs. Brass pipe and copper tube are in general use for hot and cold water lines, while solid brass or bronze hardware and lighting fixtures are virtually indispensable in the construction of high quality dwellings.

As an insulating material, copper has been adopted for both weather-proofing and damp-proofing the home. This type of insulation provides a protective barrier against infiltration of cold or warm air through the joints and pores of building materials, and when embodied in the construction of the home represents an infinitesimal part of the building dollar. Such methods of insulation pay for themselves many times over in savings in fuel bills and in added comforts.

Copper insect screens for windows, doors and porches long have been recognized by the house building industry as an indispensable part of the better built home. Bronze insect screen cloth cannot rust, and therefore the danger of a break through which insects might enter is minimized.

Many other uses have been devised for copper and its alloys in the modern home. Bronze windows, like bronze screens, are neat and trim, cannot rust and never require painting. Weatherstripping with bronze is a vital point in installing windows and doors.

Adding to the spaciousness of rooms and enhancing their appearance, copper, with its high heat conductivity, is finding steadily wider use in the construction of radiators, enabling the utilization of much smaller units.

Competent Architects Listed As Necessity

The expense of retaining competent architectural and engineering service in the design and supervision of construction is a sound investment, points out Myron L. Matthews, writing in the Dow Service Daily Building Reports.

Too often, Mr. Matthews points out, the owner who tries to economize by dispensing with such service finds that this saving of a small fraction of the total cost of building turns out to be false economy, and the owner discovers flaws in construction or layout which interfere with renting, refinancing or sale of the property.

The lending agencies today are placing growing emphasis on this point and generally will not advance funds unless competent architects and contracts are employed, Mr. Matthews added.

NEED STEADY HEAT

Continuous heating, rather than intermittent supply characteristic of some heating plants, is essential to adequate operation of winter air conditioning apparatus, according to experts.

Replacing Outmoded Hardware Suggested

Home owners who have been tolerating faulty door locks, loose or broken hinges, and other inefficient or outmoded hardware may this Spring eliminate this source of annoyance by installing new hardware under the Property Improvement Credit Plan of the Federal Housing Administration.

New hardware not only makes the home a more pleasant place to live in by correcting loose-fitting doors but can improve both the interior and exterior appearance as well. Door hinges, knobs, letter slots, and knockers may accentuate the original architectural style of the home, while new knobs throughout the interior may add a note of freshness that will go far to making a Spring paint or wallpaper job more satisfactory.

PLYWOOD SHEATHING

Douglas fir plywood has been accepted because of structural, insulating and wind-proofing properties as a preferred material for sheathing. Its rigidity was demonstrated in tests at the U. S. Forest Products Laboratory at Madison, Wis., and it has been approved by the Federal Housing Administration.

Aliquippa Gazette Magazine Page

Camp Is Boy Builder!

Ideal Time for Youth, Parents To Bury the "Emotional Bottle"

By GARRY C. MYERS, Ph.D.

WE WISH all children living in crowded places might have the opportunity to spend several weeks annually in a summer camp. The time may come, by and by, when they will. Even now a few of these children enjoy this privilege, thanks to certain thoughtful, generous groups and individuals.

Most children whose parents can afford to send them to a private summer camp do not live in crowded homes and crowded communities. These "privileged" children usually are sent in order that they might learn to get along better with other children their age and acquire more independence, self-reliance and responsibility.

But many a child, especially an only-child, who most needs to attend a summer camp doesn't do so because he can't break away emotionally or his parents can't bear to have him out of their sight. Yet, going to camp is about the best way for this child and his parents to bury the emotional bottle. The parents must, of course, take the initiative, for which an enormous amount of self-discipline may be required.

Send Him to Camp

Suppose you have a boy or girl over 12 or 14 who does not mix well with others of his age and who, you realize, is too dependent on his parents. Plan, if at all possible, to send him or her to a camp for several weeks this coming summer.

But suppose this child doesn't want to go. Begin now to prepare him to want to go and be ready to go. Have him now and then spend a night or week-end with some friends away from home. Attract more boys and girls of his age to your home. Set the stage so he will meet some new friends and mingle with them. Plan a program to exercise him gradually in more independence, self-reliance and responsibility right now at home.

In the meanwhile, assemble literature on the best available camps, inducing your child to study this literature with you. Invite a camp director in whom you have confidence to call to see your child; also some other youths who have attended summer camps.

Investigate Camp

Consider only those camps which you know to have perfect sanitation and are run under the best physical and moral health conditions. If possible, visit the camp site. By all means meet the camp director and have reliable assurance of his ability, personality and character.

All set, announce the date when your child will leave for camp. From then on take his going for granted.

And when, at last, he goes, leave him in the care of the camp director. Manage your emotions. Wean yourself. Don't write too often nor childishly. Stay away from the camp, at least for several weeks. Don't expect the child to make visits home. Put him on his own and yourself on yours. Be grown-up about it.

Glamor Shadows

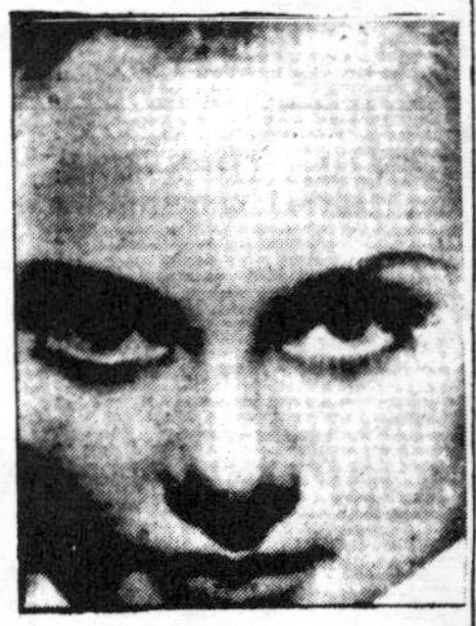

SONJA HENIE . . . *applies eye shadows carefully and expertly.*

* * *

They're Cream On Beauty Cake

By HELEN FOLLETT

YE SHADOWS are the cream the beauty cake. If you can get ay with them you'll look divinely ... Remember, a little

Marginal Straight

Spread the creamy pigment on close to the lashes, sweeping outward from the inner corner of the eye, stopping on a line with the end of the eyebrow. Continue until the lid is tinted, always spreading on the coloring in the same direction. Do a fadeaway where the lid sinks in under the eye socket.

One must be tricky and subtle, know when to stop. Blues, mauves, purples, greens and bronze tones can be had. You pays your money and takes your choice.

HAVE YOU any beauty problems? Let the Beauty Box Editor help you solve them. Address all inquiries regarding beauty to the Editor of the Beauty Box, care of this newspaper. Be sure to enclose an addressed, stamped (three cents) envelope for reply.

The Stars Say

For Saturday, May 20

By GENEVIEVE KEMBLE

AN EVENTFUL, stirring and productive day is forecast, with affairs moving at high tension, despite certain depressing and menacing lunar aspects. If the mind is alert to fraud, duplicity and subtle "boring from within," even audacious propositions may have conspicuous success. A change of plans or location may bring benefit.

Those whose birthday it is may expect a year of important accomplishment in productive lines in spite of menacing, depressing and undermining conditions. With alertness to sinister situations, treachery, fraud and peculiar pitfalls which may involve mental and nervous reactions, major programs may be successfully launched. Reorganized plans or new environs would prove of benefit.

A child born on this day, although versatile, original and audacious, may also have peculiar or deep-seated undercurrents which may undermine its success. Intrigue, expediency, craftiness and sensationalism may prove detrimental unless early direction be exercised and high principle inculcated.

TODAY'S MENU

By BETSY NEWMAN

Fruit Juice
Stuffed Mushrooms a la Astor
Asparagus Tips Beet Pickles
Rolls Jam
Fresh Strawberries Cookies
Coffee

STUFFED MUSHROOMS — Ingredients: One jar or three and one-half ounces dried beef, cut in small pieces; butter, 12 large mushrooms, two teaspoons finely-minced onion, one cup fine, soft breadcrumbs, two teaspoons finely-minced parsley (may be omitted), a little black pepper, one-fourth cup milk, one-half cup buttered breadcrumbs; one cup light cream. Sauté dried beef in one tablespoon butter until crisp and lightly browned. Wash mushrooms, dry (if skin is thick and coarse, peel), remove stems, and sauté caps in one tablespoon butter three or four minutes. Place, inverted, in shallow buttered baking dish. Chop stems fine and sauté with onions in one tablespoon butter. Add 1 cup breadcrumbs, dried beef, parsley and pepper; blend. Add milk slowly, tossing all lightly with a fork. Stuff into mushroom caps and sprinkle with buttered breadcrumbs. Pour cream around them. Bake in moderately hot oven (370° F.) 20 to 30 minutes. Serves six. Sauté means fry, you know.

Cape Cod Molasses Cookies—Ingredients: One-third cup shortening, one-half cup sugar, one egg, one-fourth cup milk, one-third cup molasses, one-half cup bran, one and one-half cups flour, one-fourth teaspoon soda, one teaspoon baking powder, one-fourth teaspoon salt, one-half teaspoon nutmeg, one-half teaspoon cinnamon, one-fourth teaspoon cloves. Cream shortening and sugar thoroughly. Add egg; beat until creamy. Add milk, molasses and bran. Add flour which has been sifted with soda, baking powder, salt, nutmeg, cinnamon and cloves, and mix well. Spread batter very thin in greased large jelly roll pan with heavy waxed paper in the bottom. Bake in slow oven (300° F.) about 25 minutes. Cut diagonally into diamond shapes as soon as cookies are removed from oven. Let cool slightly before removing from pan.

Enter, the Large Hat

Pliant, natural color straw, right, coaxed into a rippling crown with dark green leaves growing out of the odd little crown.

By PRUNELLA WOOD

LITERALLY, we're getting our money's worth in hats. Smart restaurant diners of Paris are due part of the credit for rebelling, somewhat suddenly, from bits of flowers and froth and insisting on larger and sim-

...r costume complements ...ils, when present, match hat ...raws, which are frequently ...ight, and are neat rather than ...ttery.

Allergy May Start In Childhood

By DR. HERMAN N. BUNDESEN
President, Chicago Board of Health

IT HAS been found that more than half the people who are allergic (over-sensitive) to food or some other substance, had the disorder during childhood. Persons eating certain foods or breathing pollens from certain plants or certain kinds of dust may develop asthma, eczema, hay-fever or hives. These are forms of allergy.

In a study of 250 children with allergy or over-sensitiveness, Doctor B. Ratner, of New York, found that more than half had symptoms during their first year of life. By the fifth year, 80 per cent of them had shown symptoms; by the eighth to the tenth year, the allergy was present in all.

FASHION SHOW TONIGHT

Women's fashions ranging from the low-cut, silvery evening dress to the common every-day house garment and children's clothes of all designs will be on parade at 8 o'clock in the Polish Hall, when 75 models o fthe Plan Eleven "50 and 12" present their annual spring fashion show.

Marriage Meddlers • A Sequel to "Married Comrades" • By ADELE GARRISON

Trying to Delay Entry of Men Into Apartment, Madge Hears Them Threaten to Break Down Door

SYNOPSIS: Experiencing more adventure than she anticipated when she set out from the Hotel Lansfield with Lillian Underwood to investigate the source of a letter purportedly sent by her father, Madge Graham now finds herself in a really dangerous position. Left to guard the apartment of Gus, the superintendent of Lillian's secret hide-away, while Lillian and Gus leave for another part of the building, Madge is forced to assume the role of a frightened little girl when two men seek to gain entrance in the apartment. Coached by Lillian through a speaking tube to keep the men out as long as she can, Madge engages the men in conversation until she realizes they are about to lose their patience, and then informs them that she has thought of a way to be sure they are friends of Gus, as they contend.

FOR A second or two after my announcement that I had just thought of a way to make sure that they were friends of Gus, the superintendent, the men outside the door were so silent that I could almost hear the traditional pin drop. Then one of them broke loose into vicious—if subdued—objurgations, while the second tried to quiet him.

"You damned fool!" the second man said, not violently, but as one states a fact. "You'll ruin everything and scare her to death in the bargain. Let me handle this."

"You've been handling it, haven't you?" the first man asked. "And see how far it's got you."

Second Man Angry

"Farther than you'd have got in a thousand years," the second man retorted. "Now, will you shut up before I slam you one?"

"You and how many others of your mob," the first man sneered, but his protest was as futile as it sounded, and the second man addressed himself to me.

"All right, Baby," he said. "Let's hear your scheme!"

"It isn't mine," I said, frantically playing for time, knowing that every second I could keep this conversation going would aid Lillian's plan to have these two looked over by the trusted men of my father's organization for whom I was sure she had sent.

Gus Planned It

"Whose is it then?" he asked after a pause during which I had remained stubbornly silent.

"Gus planned it out," I said. "You know Gus, you said, didn't you?"

"Yes, we know Gus," he returned grimly, "and we're sure going to know him better. But where do you come in anyway?"

"I'm Mamie's niece," I told them quaveringly. "Mamie's Gus' wife, you know."

I paused as if for an answer, and the first man appealed to his Maker again.

List Somewhere

"Yes, yes, we know," the second man said quickly. "And now tell us what is this thing Gus planned?"

"Why, he has a list here somewhere," I said, "with all the names written out, and if they come I'm to let them in. There aren't very many, but each one has written out his name—sometimes it's her name—" I gave an affected little giggle—"in their own handwriting, so me and Mamie can tell if the people asking are really the ones."

"Look here!" the first man interrupted fiercely. "Are you going to waste time listening to this rot?"

"Shut up!" the other commanded as fiercely. Then he spoke to me again. "Well! where's your list? We're on it. You may be sure."

"I'm going to hunt for it right now," I said eagerly. "It isn't in the place where Gus usually keeps it, for I've looked, but I'll look in all the places, and I'm sure I'll find it right away."

Suspects She's Stalling

"Can't you see she's stalling?" the first man growled. "And I don't believe she's what she's pretending to be either. She's probably one of those other dames that were on the other street tonight."

My pulses beat faster. Here was proof for Lillian when she needed it. But the second man was speaking again, slowly, malevolently.

"You've sure smeared it if she is," he said. "And I'll remember it when I wring your —— neck for speaking out of turn. But there's something in your chatter at that. Listen you—in there. If you don't open that door this minute we're going to break it down. We're officers of the law, see, and we want Gus."

(Continued tomorrow)

Odd Fact

Muslim pilgrim, Mohamed Jalil, so devout that he must say a prayer after walking every five steps, has walked for three years in wrong direction for Mecca. He must now retrace his steps and start again.

Household Hint

Heating some vinegar and water in the tea kettle is one way to soften the hard mineral scale that frequently collects on the bottom and sides of the kettle. The vinegar should be rinsed out thoroughly afterward.

RUFFNER, MOORE HONORED BY FIRM

J. A. C. Ruffner and Stewart C. Moore, well known insurance men of Aliquippa, members of the insurance firm of Ruffner and Moore, and who represent the Continental Insurance company, a member company of the America Fire Insurance and Indemnity Group, have just been presented with electric clocks by Continental, in token of more than twenty-five years' representation.

On the back of their individual clocks their names are engraved on gold plates.

The clocks were given by Special Agent C. R. Van Wickle, field man for the Continental, and accompanied by a letter from Bernard M. Culver, which said:

"It is with great pleasure that I and my associates welcome you into the "Old Guard"—that association of local agents and company employees who have been connected with the companies of the America Fire Group for over twenty-five years.

"Our company has grown and prospered greatly during the period of your association with us, and we wish to acknowledge your contribution to this success.

"We thank you for your loyalty, and sincerely trust that your splendid representation of this company will continue for many years to come."

Aliquippa Girl Making Record

Miss Henrietta Ulatoski, of Aliquippa, one of the members of this year's graduating class at Geneva college, is graduating June 6 with highest honors. She is one of 15 who graduate with honors of varying degrees and one of the 11 who receive highest honors, which means that along with her regular studies she acquired 24 reading points and had an average of above 2.4 credit points a semester hour during her junior and senior years.

HENRIETTA VLATOWSKI

Must Keep Gallows in Repair

Since 1676 a clause in the lease of Eastwich Farm, in Hampshire county, England, has required each successive occupant to keep in repair a gallows that stands on the land and has never been used since the execution for which it was erected more than two and a half centuries ago. Furthermore, says Collier's Weekly, it must be rebuilt when necessary, and the present one is the third on the site.

Thirteen Birds Named Carolina

There are 13 birds which have as their specific name Carolina or its derivatives.

BRITAIN TO FIGHT

Six-page supplement in today's Gazette heralds approach of the new school term in Aliquippa.

The Aliquippa Gazette

WEATHER: Generally fair tonight and Saturday. Little change in temperature.

SERVING AN INDUSTRIAL COMMUNITY OF 50,000

VOL. XVIII. No. 105 | SERVED BY UNITED PRESS MEMBER OF P. N. P. A | ALIQUIPPA, PA., FRIDAY, SEPTEMBER 1, 1939 | PHONE 904-905 | 3 CENTS; BY CARRIER, 15 CENTS A WEEK

"STATE OF WAR" IN POLAND

★ ★

NAZI - POLISH WARFARE FLARES

Fighting Begins On Polish Frontier; Six Cities Hit In Early Morning Air Raid

WARSAW. — (UP) — President Ignacy Moscicki proclaimed a state of war in Poland today after German airplanes had bombed Polish cities, including Warsaw, and German troops had smashed across the frontier from Slovakia to the Baltic. The state of war proclamation was in nowise a declaration of war.

[illegible] proclamation declared as anti-aircraft around the capital burst into action for the fourth time since dawn.

The state of war proclaimed by the President was a domestic measure designed to put war-time regulations into effect. Poland probably will seek to avoid an outright declaration of war in order to avoid handicaps which might then be imposed on the nation by the United States neutrality law.

The proclamation issued by the President was required by the Polish constitution in order to put the nation fully on a war time basis. Political sources said that the sejm (parliament) might be summoned shortly.

An official announcement said three men and two women had been wounded in the bombardments of Warsaw. No fatalities were mentioned.

WARSAW. — (UP) — German airplanes bombed the Polish capital at 9 a. m. (4 a. m. EDT) today, it was announced officially, within an hour after German bombardments had been reported in five other cities in Poland.

The foreign office immediately charged Germany with aggression, announcing:

"Shortly after 7 a. m. Germans started military action at different points on the frontier. This undoubtedly is German against Poland. Military action now is developing.'

The foreign office did not name the places of action.

It was reported that the German bombing squadrons had not been large. The government announced that they had not bombed among other places, the railway station at Czew, the town of Rynpic and the town of Putzk, near Czew.

Private sources here said heavy fighting was underway at Chojnice, on the northwestern border.

The bombardment at Warsaw began with heavy detonations outside the city. Apparently most of them were anti-aircraft barrages but some possibly were bombs.

The explosions were almost continuous. Then the drone of big planes was heard.

(Continued on Page Three)

AMBROSE ABIDES BY SOLICITOR'S RULING IN TIFF

Will Keep Sergt. Bloom At Headquarters' Desk Here

Chief of Police W. L. Ambrose is going to abide by the rulings of the borough solicitor in the controversy with Burgess George Kiefer over the removal or retention of Sergeant Clair Bloom on the desk at the Aliquippa police station.

That was revealed today as word came that the Burgess had informed Chief Ambrose he (the chief) would be held responsible for enforcement of the original Kiefer order to remove Sergeant Bloom from the desk.

The Chief is between two conflicting orders.

One from the Burgess commanding him to remove the Sergeant from the desk and one from council's police committee, instructing him to keep the Sergeant at his present post.

Explaining he can't obey instructions from both parties, Chief Ambrose yesterday asked Borough Solicitor W. D. Craig for a ruling as to whose authority — council's or Burgess'—shall prevail. And on the basis of that ruling he will determine his policy, he indicated today.

Young Man Nabbed On "Numbers" Count

Peter Benderkovic, 21, of New Brighton, was being held today under $1,000 bond pending court trial on a "numbers" writing charge.

State motor police arrested the youth yesterday afternoon along the P. & L. E. railroad at Fallston, near the Townsend company plant. He was selling "numbers" to employes, they said.

At a hearing before Thomas Bishop, of New Brighton, Officers Privates Henecheck and McCullough said Benderkovic hid two "policy" racket pads and a small sum of money under a stone when he saw them coming. They were recovered and presented as evidence.

When questioned in Burgess Bishop's office, the defendant said: "I'll sit it out before I'll tell on my boss." He was doing that today pending court airing of the case.

CARD PARTY TONIGHT

Sons of the Veterans of Foreign Wars here will sponsor a card party at the V. F. W. hall, 1803 Main street, starting at 8 p. m. today. Proceeds will be used for the organization of a local drum and bugle corps.

F.R. Has Hopes U.S. Can Stay Out Of War

WASHINGTON (UP) — President Roosevelt said today that he hopes and believes the United States can stay out of war.

He told his press conference that the administration will make every effort to preserve the neutrality of this country in the grave European crisis.

Mr. Roosevelt announced that Hugh R. Wilson, U. S. Ambassador to Germany who was recalled last year for "report and consultation," resigned today and his resignation was accepted.

With Secretary of State Cordell Hull sitting beside him, the President authorized a direct quotation of his belief that this country can avoid war.

Speaking in measured and sober phrases in response to a question as to whether he had anything to say about the United States remaining neutral, Mr. Roosevelt said:

"On this—that I not only sincerely hope so, but I believe we can and that every effort will be made by the administration so to do."

PLANS FOR DRUM CORPS DROPPED

Officials of the V. F. W. and the recently-formed Sons of V. F. W. here today announced that plans for a drum and bugle corps have been scrapped and their fullest support will be offered in the organization of a community band.

This is a complete reversal of opinion as stated by Ray Lester, chairman of junior activities of the Waugaman post and senior vice-commander of the senior organization, who recently said:

"We inaugurated a campaign for the organization of a junior drum and bugle corps, and it is our intention to go through with the idea."

Expense in organizing and maintaining the corps, and its narrow field of activities, were reasons for the change of policy, officials explained. It is felt that a community band would meet with greater approval and support from the community, and concerts and other activities of such a band would appeal more to the average Aliquippan.

TO OCCUPY PULPIT

In the absence of the minister, who is on vacation, the pulpit of the Raccoon U. P. church will be occupied this Sunday by M. C. Gilchrist, president of the Beaver County Sabbath School association. The unified service will start at 10:30 a. m.

POLES STRIKE BACK; PARIS EVACUATION STARTS; WAR RAGES

BULLETIN!

WARSAW.—(UP)—An official communique tonight charged that Germany was bombarding open cities, including Warsaw, and that many civilians were dead and wounded.

The communique charged Fuehrer Adolf Hitler with violation of his pledge to spare civilians. The communique asserted that Polish defenders brought down three German bombers at Cracow and shot down four German planes in the Gdynia district. The Poles said they disabled and captured a German armored train near Chojnice in the Polish Corridor.

[illegible] The House of Commons tonight approved a war credit of 500,000,000 pounds (approximately $2,[illegible]).

BERLIN.—(UP)—Air raid sirens shrieked throughout Berlin at seven o'clock tonight.

The alarm, possibly heralding the approach of raiding Polish airplanes, broke an amazing calm throughout the day which had made the Polish-German conflict seem remote from Berlin.

Thousands in the street scurried to the nearest refuges as the sirens sounded for minutes at a time. Amidst the monotonous wailing of the alarm, troops manned anti-aircraft batteries on the ground and on rooftops, preparing for action.

BERLIN—(UP)—An army communique tonight said German troops were advancing on all fronts against Poland. The communique said there were hostilities near Graudenz, 18 miles southwest of Marienwerder, on the East Prussian frontier below Danzig. The German troops on the south front have advanced to a line reaching from Neumarkt to Sucha, the communique said.

PARIS.—(UP)—A new order for evacuation of Paris was issued by the government tonight.

The order insisted that all those who are not obliged to remain must leave Paris at once.

LONDON (UP)—Prime Minister Neville Chamberlain told the House of Commons today that Great Britain would fulfill its obligations to Poland without hesitation. Unless Germany withdraws her troops from Polish soil, he said, the British ambassador to Berlin is under instructions to "ask for his passport."

Chamberlain said that, if a general war comes, the responsibility for it must rest with one man—Adolf Hitler.

The way had been open to settlement of the European crisis up to the middle of this week, he added, and he had believed that Germany at least until that time was willing to reach a solution.

Now, he said, it is time for action rather than words.

The Nazi Fuehrer "has not hesitated to plunge the world into misery to serve his senseless ambitions," said Chamberlain.

Great Britain could not have done more to find an equitable settlement between Germany and Poland, nor could she have warned the German government more forcefully of her intention to oppose force with force.

Chamberlain said that the desire of Great Britain to aid negotiations between Germany and Poland had been made perfectly clear in the white paper which the British government published tonight, and which contained the messages exchanged between London and Berlin.

One of these messages, the Prime Minister asserted, showed that a final showdown might have been avoided if there had been a desire on the part of Hitler to reach a solution.

This message had been sent by the British government to Germany and to Poland, urging them both to promise that no aggressive military action would be taken during the course of the negotiations then in progress. The Polish government, Chamberlain said, offered on August 31 to make such a promise if Germany also agreed.

Chamberlain said that he feared that Germany would not heed the protest of Great Britain, which he described as "a last warning."

The Prime Minister asserted that Germany had never definitely replied to the British proposal.

He said that the 16-point program published in Berlin last night as having been advanced by Hitler as the basis for negotiations with

(Continued on Page Six)

HOLD TWO MORE IN THEFT HERE

John (Jack) Doyle, 27, of 827 Franklin avenue, gave himself up to police here last night and confessed to the part he took with two other men in conducting a $58 "whiskey" robbery of the Slovak club social rooms, July 21.

Local officers already had arrested, arraigned and held for court under $1,000 bond, Thomas Ward, also of Aliquippa, for having taken a leading part in the forced entry and looting of the Sheffield avenue club rooms.

After listening to a voluntary confession from Doyle, Sergeant "Whitie" Crosskopf of the Aliquippa force, accompanied by Ward and Pittsburgh city police, arrested Charles Ford, 32, in a North Side beer dive.

Ford, a resident of Pittsburgh, was implicated by the two local men in their confessions. Police said they put the finger on Ford as being the "ring leader."

QUEEN FUNERAL

Dr. Crawford L. Queen, D.D., M.D., LL.D., of Aliquippa, aged 65, who died at Rochester General hospital Wednesday, will be buried in Woodlawn cemetery tomorrow.

H was born at Grafton, W. Va., March 3, 1874, coming here 18 years ago. Queen was active in the Methodist church. He preached occasionally at the Temple Heights mission, Glenwillard, South Heights and West Aliquippa.

Surviving him are two sons, Col. Clyde L., and Paul, both of San Francisco, Cal.; and a daughter, Mrs. Bessie Ulrich, of Adrian, Michigan.

Friends will be received at the Douds' funeral home here, where funeral service will be tomorrow at 2:30 p. m., in charge of the Rev. Arthur Sellers, Methodist minister of West Aliquippa. Burial will follow in Woodlawn cemetery.

Mrs. Lewis, Former Resident Here, Dies

Mrs. James G. Lewis, 55, former well known resident of Aliquippa, died at Long Beach, Cal., after an operation Wednesday, relatives and friends here were advised yesterday.

Accompanied by her husband, she had gone to California two months ago in the interests of her health. Before coming to Aliquippa the family resided in New Castle.

In addition to her husband she leaves a son, John (Jack) Lewis, of Boundary street, Aliquippa, and a niece, Mrs. Philip H. Jones, Highland avenue.

Word was expected here today as to whether the body will be shipped to Aliquippa or New Castle for funeral rites and burial.

Man Jailed, Another Fined On Firearms Charge In Borough

Two Plan 11 colored men, one of whom is being held in borough jail facing a 30-day jail sentence to Beaver in default of fine, were arraigned before Justice Ivor L. Jones today on charges of violating the firearms ordinance.

James Hairston, 38, of 322 Fifth avenue, was fined heavily and released. Confined to jail is John Alexander, 30, of the same address. According to officers, the two were fighting over a pistol. Neither would claim ownership of the weapon when questioned.

State Revenue Secretary Pleads For Safety In Advance Of Labor Day Week-End; Suggests Ways To Save Lives, Prevent Auto Accidents

Motorists in Pennsylvania can save 26 lives and prevent 800 persons from being injured over the Labor Day week-end if they exercise caution and especial care in the operation of their automobiles, Secretary of Revenue William J. Hamilton, Jr., warned today.

"It's a thought to consider from the selfish viewpoint," he said, "because one of those 26 lives may be yours, or the life of a member of your own family.

"The Labor Day week-end death toll in Pennsylvania last year was 26 persons, 800 were injured. The life of every man, woman and child lost in that slaughter might have been spared if someone had not been careless or reckless or indifferent to the hazards and dangers of automobile driving.

CHECK BRAKES

"These accidents cannot be blamed on automobiles. It isn't enough to say that the brakes failed or the lights of the car blinded the driver of the other machine. The car cannot be held responsible. But the person at the wheel has the power and the duty to make sure that those parts of the automobile on which safety depend are in good working order.

"Brakes should be checked. Do

(Continued on Page Six)

The Editors Believe:

The [illegible] column of [illegible] occurrences . . . [illegible] to the people of Aliquippa and the Beaver valley. The column below, however, is reserved for the OPINIONS of the editors of the Aliquippa Gazette. Usually right, sometimes wrong, they are at all times honest convictions. Letters to the editor, agreeing or disagreeing with the opinions voiced here, are welcome and will be published subject only to the limitations of space and the postal laws.

"If you work in a town, in Heaven's name work for it. If you live in a town, live for it, give for it. Help advance your neighborhood. Respect the great power that protects you, that surrounds you with the advantages of advanced civilization, and that makes it possible for you to achieve results. Speak well of it. Stand by it. Stand for its civic and commercial supremacy. If you must obstruct or decry those who strive to help, why—quit the town. But as long as you are a part of a locality, do not belittle it. If you do, you are loosening the tendrils that hold you to the community and with the first high wind that comes along you will be uprooted and blown away. And probably you will never know why."

Charles G. Dawes.

Aliquippa, Pa., Thursday, September 7, 1939

Gazette Program For Aliquippa

1. Provision of adequate, Free Parking Space for Shoppers.
2. Resurfacing of Franklin Avenue from the Stone Arch to the Wye.
3. Repair and Resurfacing of the Aliquippa-Monaca River Road.

WHAT'S THE MATTER WITH ALIQUIPPA

"You must first sell Aliquippa on Aliquippa before you can hope to make progress."

That statement by R. J. "Denney" Schill, dynamic Ellwood City Chamber of Commerce official, before the Aliquippa Board of Trade the other night is well worth the consideration of every man, woman and child in Aliquippa.

What is needed, he declared, is the conviction on the part of every Aliquippa person that Aliquippa is the nation's finest community—and their determination to make it even better.

Is that pretty moralizing? We don't think so. In Schill's case, he has pretty direct and important evidence to prove that attitude pays big dividends.

When the business man can submerge his own personal interests to the community interest; when municipal officials can drop their political feuds to work together and advance the welfare of the town; when industrial and labor leaders can put their community first and their own disputes second; when townsfolk square away when some critic begins pouring abuse on their community—when that time comes, there'll be a major change in this community, a change all to the good.

What's the matter with Aliquippa, after all? It has an immense industrial establishment with an annual payroll of some $27,000,000. It has a cooperative group of industrial and labor leaders. It has some splendid residential sections, yet with the need for more homes evident on every hand. It boasts the finest school system in western Pennsylvania, good churches, two swimming pools, playgrounds and baseball fields by the hundreds, plenty of [illegible], beautiful, shaded streets. It is ad-[illegible] waiting only to be tapped. It's a "one industry town" but that one industry is itself diversified so there is always work in some department.

What's the matter with Aliquippa? We suspect the difficulty is ours—yours and everyone else's. We're a bit blind to what we have. We've listened too long to the critics without eyes to see our possibilities. It takes an outsider, one with an impressive record of achievement in his own community, to emphasize our possibilities.

Library Here Gets Additional Books

Books added to the B. F. Jones Memorial library during the week of September 2, as announced by Susan B. Himmelwright, head librarian, include:

Fiction

"Death of the Heart," Bowen; "You Can't Get Away by Running," Chambers; "Off With Her Head," Cole; "Mystery of the Stolen Hats," Jeffries; "Midas Touch," Kennedy.

General

327 H68b, "Background of International Relations," Hodges.

330.1 J35e, "Everyday Economics," Janzen.

330.9 B62v, "Visualized Economic Geography," Bischof.

q330.9 K65i, "Introductory Economic Geography," Klimm.

330.9 W57w, "The Working World," Whitbeck.

338.2 P49, "Hot Oil," Pettengill.

347.94 T12, "Witnesses in Court," Taft.

370.1 B66p, "Progressive Education at the Crossroads," Bode.

374.1 C13r, "Reading in High Gear," Cage.

522.2 P39m, "Men, Mirrors, and Stars," Pendray.

709 S43a, "Art in the Life of Mankind," 4 v., Seaby.

747 P88a, "The Attractive Home,' Powel.

796 B21g2, "Games," Bancroft.

q796.34 M56, "Lawn Tennis Manual," Merrihew.

799.12 W96, "Lee Wulff's Handbook of Freshwater Fishing," Wulff.

808.6 F66, "Post Haste," Foley.

808.85 R33, "Reference Shelf," "Chain Stores and Legislation," Bloomfield, "U. S. and War," Johnsen.

POSTPONE HEARINGS

Hearings on two Labor Day auto accidents, one a hit and run case, were deferred to later dates, local squires reported today. The case of J. R. Hlopek, Ambridge, charged with failing to stop after colliding with a car driven by Irvin L. Alger, 1920 Irwin street, was deferred until Sept. 13. Action taken against W. F. Jones, 204 Superior avenue, who was picked up by police after he had smashed into two parked cars on Franklin avenue, will be aired Sept. 11. Louis P. Ladish, 1905 Irwin street, and William R. Strader, 6347 Marshand street, Pittsburgh, will press charges.

"REVIEW OF THE WEEK"

YOU'D BETTER GO OVER IT AGAIN JUST TO MAKE SURE THAT YOU HAVEN'T FORGOTTEN
WORLD WAR
COST
LIVES
MONEY
LESSONS
U.S.

Unites Canada

Dr. Robert J. Manion

Dr. Robert J. Manion, leader of the Conservative opposition party in the Canadian House of Commons, announced his party would cooperate with Britain in the war on Germany, and Prime Minister Mackenzie King is believed likely to form a union government for duration of the conflict.

The Aliquippa Gazette

Founded March, 1922
Published Every Afternoon Except Sunday
By the Franklin Publishing Company
Rear 384 Franklin Avenue
At Aliquippa, Pa.

E. J. Tilton, President
J. H. Sherrard, Vice President
Walter Catterall, Secretary-Treasurer

Entered at the Postoffice at Aliquippa, Pa., as Second-Class Matter

BELL TELEPHONES
934 — 935

E. J. Tilton.........Editor and Publisher
Donald O. McCann.........City Editor
Richard L. Amper.........Sports Editor
Lewis L. Luster, Advertising Manager
Charles McRobbie.........Circulation Manager

SUBSCRIPTION RATES

By mail within first Three Zones, postage paid strictly in advance.

One year	$6.00
Six months	3.00
Four months	2.20
Two months	1.10
One month	.55
Per week, 1 or 2 weeks	.18

The Gazette is delivered by carrier in Aliquippa and suburbs for 15c a week; $7.50 per year, payable in advance. Single copy three cents.

Advertising Rates Furnished on Application

Member Pennsylvania Newspaper Publishers Association
Central Press Association
World-Wide Service of United Press

NATIONAL REPRESENTATIVES
Paul de Guzman
Test Market Newspapers
480 Lexington Avenue
New York, N. Y.

Beaver County Newsetts

Being A Compilation of Interesting Bits of News Gathered Here And There Throughout Beaver County—Fact, Gossip and Neighborly Chatter From Every Section of the Beaver Valley.

With the primary election scheduled next Tuesday, the board of control of the Beaver County Young Republicans has gone on record as not being in favor of any candidate or ticket. The board is made up of delegates from each Young G.O.P. club in the county. It intends to leave each member follow his own likes and dislikes in the ballot booths. The board has called a special meeting for Tuesday evening, Sept. 26, when nominees will be invited to attend and express their feelings toward the Young Republican organization.

Darlington's new consolidated school will be dedicated next Friday night. Pupils from Darlington township and borough are attending classes at the school, which is two stories high and has a dozen rooms.

The Youth Temperance council of New Brighton, composed of numerous boys and girls of the community, have banded together for the purpose of making an appeal to voters there concerning the local option. Mrs. O. C. Caughey is directress of the Youth movvement. Members have been provided with arm bands and they will visit New Brighton homes in pairs delivering their temperance message.

Ole Larson, who served as assistant to Lewis Vincent, former resident engineer inspector for the PWA on the College Hill and county home infirmary projects, is now in charge of the government's supervision on those jobs. Vincent resigned after the Hatch bill became effective in order to devote his entire time to running for Beaver county commissioner.

Pythian Knights and their families of the Beaver valley will attend the annual home-coming of the Pythian Home association of Pennsylvania at Harmony this Sunday. Grand officers, including Grand Chancellor J. W. Rawson of Pennsylvania, will be in attendance. Ambridge Lodge 504 will exemplify "The Lesson of Friendship."

The County Return Board will meet at noon Friday, Sept. 15, in Courtroom No. 3 at Beaver, to make an official tabulation of votes to be cast at the primary election next Tuesday.

Big Knob Grange's annual fair will continue through today and tomorrow. It is free to the public. Fruits, flowers, fancywork and quilts are displayed in the hall and more than 100 head of cattle, horses and hogs are on display at Grange grounds, near Unionville. A display of poultry, pets, cattle and hogs by the 4-H club also is a feature attraction. John D. Cole is general chairman of the fair.

Beaver county banks, which are members of the Federal Reserve System, will be required to pay unemployment compensation tax in Pennsylvania, in line with a ruling handed down by the Dauphin County court.

Organ Listener Is Craftsman

HONOLULU. (UP)—An organ-listener and a shower-clocker are among the unusual "craftsmen" supplied by the territorial employment service.

Hand Washing Fatal

GALION, O. (UP)—V. D. Carlin died as the result of burns received when naphtha, in which he was washing his hands, exploded.

The Aliquippa Gazeteer

By DEAN C. MILLER

HE OF FORESIGHT.—Deep-set, piercing eyes overshadowed by shaggy eyebrows similar to those of John L. Lewis . . . He awed us somewhat today when we tested his vaunted prescience. Ramus the Second, currently playing at the State theater, is the man we're talking about.

Right away we wanted to know how the present European slugfest would bow out in a yet-unwritten chapter of history. Three years ago he said he prophesied guns would bark along the Rhine and bomb-spewing planes would cast ominous shadows over cowering civilians this year.

"This war won't last longer than six months," he predicted. "And if it should go over that length of time, it won't be settled in less than five years of bloody futility." Along the same vein he said "Hitler will be a raving maniac by 1941."

Located in Hollywood for many years, Ramus has auditioned half the film colony. "From Wallace Beery and Tyrone Power to Shirley Temple I found them to be humans, just as you and I, interested in their careers and proud of their homes," he revealed. "They're not the glamad people publicity makes them out to be."

Three years ago Tyrone Power asked Ramus whether he'd live to see his name in lights. The prophecy was "yes" in a year and a half. And so he did. The late Jean Harlow was interested in her marital future. Ramus predicted three vows at the altar. Jean protested, but it came to pass. Shirley Temple's mother laughed when he told her 11 years ago she'd give birth to a girl. But she did as cinema-goers will vouch.

In a quick round-up of national problems and personalities, the psychic says that: Roosevelt will not run for a third time . . . The country will go Democratic, and the new president will be one of the present cabinet members (he hesitates at naming any one individual just yet) . . . The Townsend bill will never pass . . . There will be a general upward trend in business by spring and it will last for several years.

All in all, we learned a great deal in a five-minute chat.

* * * *

JOLLY GOOD FELLOW.—At the recent plant shin-dig held in honor of the original Gazetteer's leaving for college, one man stood out above the crowd. Physically he wasn't a giant, but he had a heart of gold. Many a coke did he set up that night. And to top things off correctly and prepare us for the coming winter, he presented each member of the party with a bottle of white shoe polish and a pack of shoe strings. The name, Charles P. Cascio, Jr., of 6206 Broad street, Pittsburgh.

* * * *

JUST PLAIN ROSE.—She wouldn't tell us her last name. "Just call me Rose," was the answer to our snooping. But she'll fight at the least whisper of criticism hurled at the Pittsburgh Pirates. She, like Rosey Rowswell, calls them "my Bucs." Wonder if they permit baseball broadcasts in a convent, 'cause that's where she's going next spring? All the breakfast club members down at Sophia's confectionery on Franklin avenue will miss her.

* * * *

ODD NAMES DEPT.—A Franklin avenue barber has all his mail addressed to DICK SHINGLER.

The Wishing Well

2	6	3	5	4	7	6	2	3	5	4	8	3
Y	A	A	T	N	S	P	O	S	A	E	N	W
5	3	8	4	6	2	3	5	7	4	6	3	5
K	E	E	W	R	U	E	E	A	T	E	T	O
3	4	2	7	5	3	6	8	4	6	5	2	3
O	O	W	V	A	L	S	W	G	E	R	I	D
6	3	5	4	2	6	8	3	5	4	2	3	7
N	L	E	S	L	T	P	A	O	A	L	D	E
2	5	3	6	4	7	3	6	2	5	4	8	3
D	F	Y	F	R	N	G	O	O	A	E	A	U
6	3	4	2	5	3	8	6	4	7	3	5	2
R	I	D	N	C	D	L	Y	U	O	E	O	A
3	2	8	5	3	6	4	7	3	2	5	6	3
S	T	S	L	Y	O	E	W	O	E	D	U	U

98

HERE is a pleasant little game that will give you a message every day. It is a numerical puzzle designed to spell out your fortune. Count the letters in your first name. If the number of letters is 6 or more, subtract 4. If the number is less than 6, add 3. The result is your key number. Start at the upper left-hand corner of the rectangle and check every one of your key numbers, left to right. Then read the message the letters under the checked figures give you

WARSAW FALLS TO GERMANS

Fate Of Eastern Europe Hanging In Balance

The Aliquippa Gazette

SERVING AN INDUSTRIAL COMMUNITY OF 50,000

WEATHER—Generally fair tonight and Thursday. Slightly cooler tonight in west portion. Warmer Thursday. Friday showers and cooler.

SERVED BY UNITED PRESS — PHONE 934-935 — MEMBER OF P. N. P. A.

VOL. XVIII. No. 126 — ALIQUIPPA, PA., WEDNESDAY, SEPTEMBER 27, 1939 — 3 CENTS; BY CARRIER, 15 CENTS A WEEK

POLISH CAPITAL FINALLY FALLS AFTER LONG SIEGE; ARMISTICE AGREED UPON; EASTERN EUROPE'S FATE IN BALANCE

BERLIN—(UP)—An official announcement tonight said Warsaw had unconditionally capitulated on the 20th day of siege.

LONDON—(UP)—An Exchange Telegraph dispatch from Warsaw today said that an armistice was agreed upon at noon and that conditions for capitulation of the Polish capital were being discussed.

WASHINGTON—(UP)—The German embassy said today it received official information that Warsaw had capitulated this morning.

The message said that the capitulation was unconditional. No other details were available immediately.

LONDON—(UP)—The Warsaw radio has been silent since 11:20 o'clock last night, the ministry of information said today.

At that time the Warsaw station reported that the city was under such terrific bombardment that people were burrowing into debris and in some sections it was impossible to circulate in the streets to distribute food.

Since then radio listeners here have heard Berlin radio stations broadcasting that the Warsaw military commander has offered to surrender the city and that the German army high command has designated Gen. Blaikowitz to negotiate the city's surrender.

MOSCOW — (UP) — Nazi Foreign Minister Joachim Von Ribbentrop arrived today to participate in a series of conferences expected to affect eastern Europe from the Baltic to the Dardenelles.

Flying from Berlin with a group of 35 German experts, Ribbentrop arrived at 10:40 a. m. (EST) as the Soviet capital was lavishly entertaining Turkish Foreign Minister Sukru Saracoglu and preparing for further conversations with Esthonian Minister Karl Selter. The Esthonian ministers invited here by Soviet For- accompanied by several high officials, this evening.

Official sources were reticent regarding the full scope of the conversations which may be direct or indirect among the various foreign ministers invited here by Soviety Foreign Commissar Viacheslav Molotov, but diplomatic circles believed that there would be a general discussion of international problems affecting the Baltic states, Poland and the Balkans.

German troops today retired to the [illegible] fall in the Soviet sphere of influence and the Balkans, including Rumania, in the Nazi sphere.

TALLINN, Esthonia. (UP) — The government vigorously protested to Moscow today against "repeated" violations of Esthonian neutrality by Russian military planes. The government asserted that Russian military planes flew over Esthonian territory yesterday and today in repeated violation of Esthonian neutrality.

By UNITED PRESS

The Nazi aerial armada claimed a smashing victory today over Great Britain's battle fleet.

Perhaps answering the question of whether warships are vulnerable to air assault, German planes attacked a fleet of British battleships, cruisers, destroyers and an aircraft carrier blockading the North Sea lanes and reported the sinking of an aircraft carrier and the damaging of a battleship. Nazi planes returned safely, the High Command announced.

The victory claimed by Nazis, if confirmed, might indicate that Germany's reported 10,000 first line airplanes would be in a position to fight the blockade by which Britain is seeking the economic strangulation of the Nazi war machine. The fact that only one warship—the second British aircraft carrier lost in the war—was reported sunk appeared certain, however, to leave the final question of naval or air superiority open to future battles.

While the sea war was reaching its most dramatic climax, the political fate of eastern Europe appeared to be at stake in Moscow, where for-

(Continued on Page Eight)

Red Cross Workers Here Map Plans For November Roll Call

Plans for the annual roll call of the Beaver County Chapter, American Red Cross, from November 11 to 30, will be completed at a special meeting here next Tuesday afternoon—so far as Aliquippa is concerned.

The meeting, of directors of the county organizations living in Aliquippa, will be at 4:30 p. m. in the Woodlawn Building & Loan office.

That was the conclusion of an initial gathering of directors under Aliquippa Chairman T. C. Swarts last evening that heard E. L. Freeland, Beaver newspaperman and county roll call chairman, outline the objectives of this year's annual membership campaign.

Discussion of the most effective procedure to follow to insure the fullest contribution on the part of [illegible] to the nationwide drive [illegible]

TEACHERS LOSE FIGHT IN COURT

Judge Henry H. Wilson today quashed the attempt of two school teachers to force the Darlington township and borough school boards to re-employ them.

The teachers, Florence Davis and Louisa Mae Stein, lost their jobs when the Darlington township and borough school districts were combined.

They sought to invoke provisions of the state teachers' tenure act and asked for a writ of mandamus to compel the school board to reinstate them.

Miss Davis, who taught elementary grades for 19 years, and Miss Stein, who taught since Sept. 1932, claimed seniority rights to the jobs. Judge Wilson ruled that the tenure act did not apply to joint school districts until after the initial hiring of teachers.

Three teachers had been employed by the borough and seven by the township, but only eight were retained when the two merged.

Install Dr. Risher As Elks' Secretary

Dr. R. R. Risher, 406 Franklin avenue, was installed as secretary of the B. P. O. E. lodge here at a meeting in the Elks hall last night. Dr. Risher will fill the vacancy caused by the death of D. P. Smith, former grand exalted ruler, secretary for 20 years and oldest lodge member in Aliquippa. Benjamin Lewis presided at the installation.

Plans for a program of entertainment, to be inaugurated this fall, were also laid at the meeting. Next meeting will be held October 10.

PUC TOSSES OUT POLLUTION CASE FROM BEAVER CO.

Rules Problem Beyond Its Jurisdiction; U. S. Gets Case

HARRISBURG — (UP) — The Public Utility commission said today that the problem of stream pollution is beyond its jurisdiction and therefore a matter for state and federal control.

That decision was reached by the PUC after terminating an inquiry into quality of water furnished by the Beaver Valley Water company, finding that pollution of the utility's supply from the Beaver river originated in vicinity of Youngstown, O. [illegible] a major source of industrial waste pollution, is currently and for years has been the principal reason for complaints against the Beaver Valley water company, the company and its customers must suffer until some correction is made in pollution from that source," the commission said.

In view of the interstate complications, the PUC ruled it lacked power to prevent "both industrial and municipal" stream pollution and claimed "relief lies with the commonwealth and the state of Ohio." A copy of its order was forwarded to Health Secretary John J. Shaw.

"Authority for interstate compacts and effective federal legislation," the order said, "seem to be highly desirable to protect domestic water supplies from costly effects of uncontrolled stream pollution.

"The instant case is a good example of increased operating costs forced upon water companies to deliver a palatable and pure supply of water to their customers, both domestic and industrial, which, paradoxically, are causes of pollution of the raw water supply."

Indications are that the desired quality of water "probably cannot" be achieved by treatment alone, the PUC said in regard to the Beaver Valley company's attempt to purify its supply. Abatement to a "considerable degree" of pollution of the Beaver river and its tributaries appears necessary, the commission said, inferring the state should take some action to curb it.

Legion Post Here To Elect New Officers

Nomination and election of officers will feature a meeting of Aliquippa Legion Post 225 at 8:30 p. m. tomorrow in Plodinec's annex here.

Save Woman From Gas Death

Soviets "Black Sea Pact" May Stop Hitler

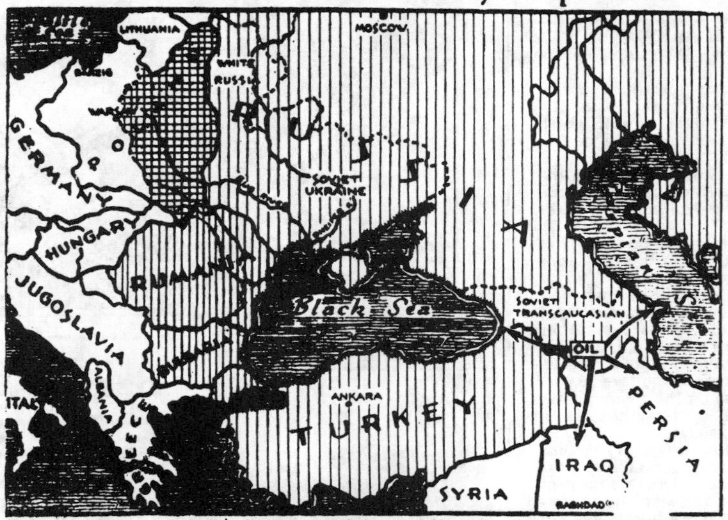

LITHUANIA
MOSCOW
WHITE RUSSIA
GERMANY
P O
SOVIET UKRAINE
R U S S I A
HUNGARY
RUMANIA
JUGOSLAVIA
ALBANIA
Black Sea
SOVIET TRANSCAUCASIAN
OIL
ANKARA
TURKEY
PERSIA
IRAQ
SYRIA
BAGHDAD

Soviet Russia summoned Turkey, Rumania and Bulgaria to Moscow to discuss a "Black . . . Pact," to prevent "others" from encroaching on their zone of influence. Such a move would halt Hitler's drive to the East and keep him from the coveted oil fields of Rumania, Persia and Iraq. Vertical lines show the conference nations. Russia's share of Poland, cutting Germany off from Rumania, is cross-hatched.

OVERCOME IN BED, MISS CORA SMITH IS REVIVED HERE

Quick Work Of Police, Firemen Saves Her At Residence

A young Aliquippa colored woman, who last night fell asleep with a small oil stove burning in her bedroom, today was rescued from death by carbon monoxide poisoning.

Quick action of Aliquippa policemen, one of whom administered artificial respiration, and the fire department here, which rushed an inhalator to the gas filled room, saved the life of Cora Smith, 20, of 153 Baker street.

According to Lena Powell, in whose home the Smith woman resides, she heard a strange noise in the bedroom where she was sleeping. Investigating, Mrs. Powell discovered the sleeper unconscious and the room filled with smoke and carbon monoxide gas.

When police and firemen arrived in the bedroom the young woman was rigid. With the aid of an inhalator and prone pressure artificial respiration, she regained consciousness in one-half hour.

The attending doctor pronounced her "out of danger," [illegible]

OFFICIAL COUNT OF PRIMARY VOTE ENDS AT BEAVER

The Beaver county election board's official count of votes cast in the September primary showed today that Zella Fleming Jones of Aliquippa, won the Republican nomination for county clerk of courts by 80 votes.

She polled 6,450 to 6,370 for her opponent, Mrs. Loree Emrick, of Beaver Falls, in one of the primary's closest races.

The official tabulation varied slightly, if at all, with the unofficial count.

The official returns for the county follow:

REPUBLICAN

County Treasurer—Prosser, 3740; Galton, 3232; Bentel, 4623; Kennedy, 6991; Moore, 4295.

District Attorney—McCreary, 10,243; deCastrique, 6,866.

(Continued on Page Four)

Itinerant Handed 15 Day Jail Sentence

A Los Angeles colored man, looking for employment in Aliquippa, was arrested yesterday on a charge of larceny from the person and sentenced to 15 days in Beaver jail after a hearing before Squire Ivor L. Jones.

George King, barber, of 100 Sheffield avenue, made complaint, testifying that Jerry Thornton, 42, approached him yesterday morning, asked "can you stand a shake-down, buddy?" and proceeded to rob him of 55 cents.

The National Whirligig

(News Behind the News)

WASHINGTON

By Ray Tucker

SIGNAL—The feverish spurt in business and industrial activity resulting from creation of a war-time psychology deeply disturbs federal and private economists. Unless closely policed, they fear it may produce a mild economic crackup in midwinter or spring. They prefer a more orderly forward movement.

The economic index figure leaped from 92 in May to 102 for August, and will probably touch 110 for the present month a sensational rise. At a recent session here between the ablest economic experts of the government, industry and finance, the opinion was almost unanimous that no basic factors justify such runaway conditions. They regard it as "wholly speculative" a duplication on a large-scale of the housewives' rush to make advance purchases of sugar and other pantry supplies at the outbreak of the war.

It was also agreed that this fast pace can be maintained and a collapse avoided only through a sharp increase in exports or heavy investment of new capital in expansion and repair of existing plants. Though divided, inside sentiment is dubious on both prospects.

* * * *

HEADACHE The problem of slowing down the advance, however, is extremely difficult, according to hard-headed spokesmen for commercial and industrial establish-

(Continued on Page Four)

REGISTRARS SIT HERE NEXT WEEK

The Beaver County registration committee composed of Commissioners Arthur W. Coombs, Paul H. Baldwin and Edward J. Schleiter, today announced registrars will sit at the Aliquippa municipal building next Tuesday and Wednesday, October 3 and 4, to enable electors of this district to register, change party enrollment or file removal notices for the general election November 7.

The registrars will serve electors of the ten precincts in Aliquippa, three precincts in Hopewell township, Raccoon township, Independence township and the borough of South Heights.

Hours the registrars will sit each day will be from 10 a. m. to 3 p. m. and from 7 p. m. to 10 p. m. (EST).

5 Abandoned Puppies Found In Beaver Co.

Five puppies, left to starve in a wooded section along the Ellwood City-Beaver Falls road, are being cared for today by Fred L. St. John of North Sewickley township, official of the Western Pennsylvania Humane society.

The pups, believed to be about six weeks old, are described as being of good hound stock. An effort is being made to trace their ownership.

Coop Raided Here, $5 In Fowl Stolen

Three roosters and a hen, valued at $5, were stolen early today from the coop of Mrs. Frank Di Gennero, 405 Washington street.

Mrs. DiGennero reported to police that a neighbor's dog awakened her at 3 a. m., and when she investigated she discovered the theft.

Applications Being Received In County For C. C. C. Camps

Applications from boys who desire to enroll in C. C. C. camps next month are being received by the State Department of Public Assistance, 115 Shields street, Rochester, Director Paul Heffley announced today.

Young men, whose parents are receiving assistance from the state, are being encouraged to enlist in the corps. They will be given priority over all other applicants, Mr. Heffley said.

Beaver county's quota for October is 130 enrollees.

Pleads To Drunken Driving, Fined $25

Judge Frank E. Reader today placed William H. Wharton of 531 Sycamore street, Glen Osborne, on probation for three years and fined him $25 and costs after he pleaded guilty to operating an auto while intoxicated.

Wharton was charged with crowding a bus on the Ambridge-Aliquippa bridge Sept. 10. Aliquippa police pursued him to Glenwillard, where he was arrested.

Car Upsets, Ambridge Man Escapes Injury

Lawrence Bobby, 30, of 242 Park road, Ambridge, escaped injury early today when his automobile overturned in a collision on Beaver road in Edgeworth.

His car and one driven by John M. Cannon, 55, of Pittsburgh, collided at an intersection. Bobby's automobile skidded 100 yards, struck a curb and was overturned. Neither of the two was hurt.

A 100-year-old locust tree, 75 feet high and two feet in diameter on the Patterson estate nearby was uprooted when auto wreckers tried to right Bobby's machine by pulling on a chain attached to the car and drawn around the tree.

LEAVES ON VACATION

Attorney Harry Richardson, 530 Franklin avenue, left this week on a vacation jaunt which will take him to Philadelphia and then to New Hampshire, where he will visit relatives.

CHILD CUT IN FALL

Two stitches were required to close a badly lacerated cut on the forehead sustained yesterday by Edward DiCicco, 4, of 433 Beaver avenue, West Aliquippa. The youth, playing at home in the backyard, fell and struck his head on a brick paving.

LACERATED BY KNIFE

Alfred Johnson, 11, colored, of 166 Baker street, suffered a deep gash on the back of his right hand yesterday when a knife thrown by a playmate missed its mark and hit him. Two stitches were required to close the laceration.

ALIQUIPPA BOOMING BUT---

Shortage Of Housing Facilities Here Costing Merchants Millions In Retail Trade Annually, Survey Shows Today

By DEAN C. MILLER

Aliquippa is booming.

But a lack of housing facilities is diverting $11,000,000 retail trade from butchers, insurance companies, automobile dealers, etc., here. This figure is one and one-half times more than the actual yearly retail trade of approximately $7,000,000 as shown by an official survey of Aliquippa in 1936.

A survey among real estate agents today revealed the following conditions:

The first office reported not one house for rent and only 11 vacant apartments, as compared with six weeks ago, when three houses and 16 apartments were available.

Another reported not a single empty home and 18 apartments. The same office six weeks ago offered five homes and 28 apartments for rent.

The official in charge there said of the situation: "We could rent 200 homes within three weeks if they were available."

A private realty concern reported no vacant apartments or homes.

The Woodlawn Land company showed a long "waiting list" but suggested that a similar situation has existed for years.

Just what does it all mean, then?

Surveys show that there are 5,000 homes and dwelling places in Aliquippa. Of these, 313 are occupied by retailers, 175 by professional men and their employes and approximately 500 by employes of industries other than the Jones & Laughlin Steel corporation.

In prosperous eras, Jones & Laughlin mills here employ between 9,000 and 11,000 men and women. Subtracting all the homes occupied by families other than those dependent on steel work here it is shown that, roughly, there are only 4,500 of the 10,000 employes of Jones & Laughlin mills living in the town in which they earn their money!

Surveys to determine the average spending power of each employe at Jones & Laughlin reveal that each

(Continued on Page Eight)

Dinner-Meeting Opens 13th Annual Mazda Lamp Campaign In Beaver County; Electrical Dealers, Storekeepers Will Be Guests Of Light Company

Electrical dealers and other storekeepers who sell Mazda lamps in Beaver county will be guests of the Duquesne Light company at a dinner-meeting at Penn Beaver hotel, Rochester, at 6:30 p. m. tomorrow.

At that time complete details will be outlined concerning the 13th annual Mazda lamp campaign inaugurated by the utility company.

Representatives of leading manufacturers of electric light bulbs will explain the part of their companies in the activity. Executives of Duquesne Light's sales organization will show the complete 100 percent dealer arrangement, in which all orders taken by employes of the utility will in turn be placed with local dealers for immediate delivery.

All Duquesne Light employes in Beaver and Allegheny counties are qualified to participate in the annual campaign for the sale of Mazda lamps. Valuable prizes will be awarded those showing the greatest sales volume. Dealers will be given the opportunity to take part in the movement to show the users of electric current the greater benefits through proper lighting.

One of the largest advertising campaigns of its kind ever undertaken by the Duquesne Light company has already been started and will be continued until December 15. Representatives of district newspapers will be guests at Thursday night's meeting.

Sutherlands Play For Soccer Lead Tomorrow

The Armchair Athlete

By RICHARD AMPER

The column goes to bed, as we say in the patois of the press room, long before the day's football games are started.

So, I have no chance of hearing by radio the first few minutes of play to obtain a clue to which team will win. In other words, my selection of winners now would be no different from what they would have been if I had picked them yesterday except a day late.

So here is how the games will go:

Aliquippa over Rochester. And it's about time.

Beaver Falls over Sharon. But no money on it.

Johnstown over Jeannette. But I'm willing to be pleasantly surprised.

Tulane over Columbia. The Bayou boys Beat the Broadwayites easily.

Cornell over Dartmouth.

Pittsburgh over Nebraska. Missouri showed 'em how.

Penn State over Army. Because Dean Miller, the Gazeteer, went to Penn State.

Missouri over Oklahoma. It's Christman time in the Midwest.

Aliquippa over Rochester. Mr. Quips says goodbye to football this year with a triumph.

Tennessee over Vanderbilt. Any questions?

Iowa over Minnesota. The corn's still growing taller.

Aliquippa over Rochester. Now if I can only convince the Quip players.

Ohio State over Illinois.

Princeton over Yale.

Sutherlands over Dunwicks. That's soccer, but what's the difference? See the rule books if you really want to find out.

Oregon State over California.

Yankees over Cincinnati. Those Yanks'll win the pennant this year.

Purdue over Wisconsin.

[illegible]

Villanova over Temple.

One Egg over lightly.

Aliquippa over Rochester. Just to make sure.

Duke over North Carolina.

And Aliquippa over Rochester.

* * *

Johnny Francona, that dapper entrepreneur and inveterate impresario, has found something new and different to promote. He wants Aliquippa fans to see native Zulus play basketball.

So he is dickering with the Zulu Kings from Chicago to play some good team here. The Zulus haven't showed me their birth certificates to prove they're the real McCoy wild men, but we've seen a picture of them, and they play in grass skirts.

They troop onto the court with war paint and full tribal attire. This game ought to be interesting if Johnny completes arrangements for it.

* * *

Aliquippa over Rochester.

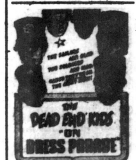

Battle Dunwicks For Allegheny Valley Loop's Top Position

There'll be a showdown between Aliquippa and the Dunwicks tomorrow in the Allegheny Valley soccer league.

The local Sutherlands will play at the Dunwicks' in an attempt to unseat them from the top position in the standings.

The Aliquippans are riding high in second place, tied for the runner-up spot with the Hornings, each showing five triumphs, a loss, and a tie for 11 points. Two points are scored for a victory, one for a tie.

The Dunwicks hold the lead with four triumphs and four ties for 12 points.

The Duns are one of the toughest teams in the loop. If they tie with the Sutherlands, the standings will remain unchanged for both teams will be credited with one point. The Dairymen need a triumph to take the loop lead, and they'll be dead set on getting it.

The Sutherlands beat the sixth place Acme booters here last Sunday. They won despite some of their most lackluster play of the season, but team members said they were playing "off-day" ball and probably would be a fine fettle to play the league pace-setters.

The Aliquippa lineup probably will have Ujevich at goal, J. Haber, right back; Juscak, left back; J. Cantwell, right half; M. Haber, center half; Mastich, left half; Brooks, outside right; Cantwell, inside right; M. Sella, center forward, and Tabinowski, outside left.

The Hornings can tie the loop lead without playing either Aliquippa or Dunwicks if the latter two tie and the Hornings beat Coraopolis. The triumph will give them two points. Coraopolis is in next to last place in the standings, and the Hornings are favored to win.

A victory by Aliquippa and the Hornings would put them in a deadlock for the loop.

Indianola and Bairdford trail the first three teams by only a slight margin and the league race still belongs to anybody.

Weekly play in the league may be halted so that the teams may compete in the West Penn Soccer Cup elimination to be held in Pittsburgh. Dates for games will be drawn.

The Allegheny Valley Loop standings follow:

	W	L	T	Pts.
Dunwicks	4	0	4	12
Aliquippa	5	1	1	11
Hornings	5	1	1	11
Indianola	4	1	2	10
Bairdford	4	2	1	9
Thistles	3	2	3	9
Acme	2	2	3	7
Russellton	2	5	0	4
Curry	2	4	0	4
Coraopolis	1	6	0	2
Scotties	0	7	0	0

Games Sunday

Aliquippa at Dunwick.
Indianola at Acme.
Scotties at Russellton.
Curry at Bairdford.
Coraopolis at Horning.
Thistles idle.

TWO TEAMS SHARE A. & S. LOOP LEAD

Leadership of the A. & S. Duckpin league here today was being shared by the Coke Racks and Dumps.

Last night's round of matches saw the Racks take the odd game from the Box Cars while the Dumps were making a clean sweep at the expense of the Hoppers.

The Flats dominated their match with the Gondolas, winning two games. Dragan of the Coke Racks topped 491 sticks to capture scoring honors for the night. Summaries:

COKE RACKS—1944

DeSantis	165	182	117—	414
Duchene	84	71	113—	278
Butteri	110	106	115—	331
Lias	149	125	149—	414
Dragan	133	184	174—	491
Yetso	86	81	127—	294
Totals	634	628	682—	1944

BOX CARS—1732

Berger	82	133	101—	316
Tomb	79	93	102—	274
Radkte	79	95	105—	279
Bealman	101	132	134—	367
Cravener	117	139	98—	354
McKenna	123	147	142—	412
Totals	502	646	584—	1732

FLATS—1823

Johnston	128	155	120—	408
Warner	84	123	129—	333
Hainley	99	86	136—	321
Deaknick	144	132	116—	392
Tovey	96	104	131—	331
Yoho	93	117	88—	298
Totals	560	631	632—	1823

GONDOLAS—1774

Grats	102	103	136—	341
Osborne	90	135	145—	370
Wissinger	112	129	141—	382
Zabic	111	115	185—	411
Dummy	90	90	90—	270
Totals	505	572	697—	1774

HOPPERS—1552

Sayre	78	90	99—	267
Kinkead	157	169	124—	450
Anderson	142	102	95—	343
Hasting	77	85	64—	226
Dummy	90	90	90—	270
Totals	544	536	472—	1552

DUMPS—1841

Ellis	118	140	119—	377
Young	60	120	102—	282
Hughes	163	140	150—	453
Rauscher	140	129	190—	459
Dummy	90	90	90—	270
Totals	571	619	651—	1841

GUS PROVES A PUSHOVER FOR BILLY CONN

Champion Easily Licks Lesnevich But Billy Still Lacks Weight

The Pittsburgh kid retained his title at Madison Square Garden last night in 15 heart-stopping rounds, 15 rounds of flawless boxing against a tought and rugged guy named Gus Lesnevich. But the victory only showed again that Conn can't punch hard enough to go against heavyweights. Like a new and shiny automobile, he is a perfect piece of fighting machinery if he only had the gas to give him a punch.

Lesnevich looked good for the first three rounds, but after that he was a novice taking a boxing lesson from a boy with the swiftest, surest left hand that has shown around these parts in five years. There have been stories that Conn would grow bigger, would pick up power as he grew, but last night he weighed only 171-¼ and in the thirteenth round he hit Lesnevich with everything except the microphones that hung above his head. Gus took it and come on for more.

The victory leaves Billy sort of suspended in mid air. He has whipped all the good middle weights and light heavyweights in sight. He has proved that he has a fighting Irish heart, and in the 10th round last night he proved that he would take one on the button and stay in the fight. Lesnevich put across a hard right that rattled Conn's teeth and sent him back on his heels, but Billy came out stabbing with that picture book left and courageously fought his way out of danger.

The sign post points to an invasion of the heavyweight ranks for Conn, but there are not many who want to see Billy in there against Joe Louis unless some more weight is added to that graceful, lanky form. For one thing, Conn is a slow starter and three or four of Louis' jabs and rights wouldn't add anything to Billy's speed. He probably would be fogged up before he could get under way with his dazzling footwork and his waspy left.

It was a great show that Conn and Lesnevich staged. Gus is one of those solid, plodding boys who hits hard with either hand and who is willing to take three to land one. Last night it was a stinging left hook which came flashing at him from all angles that brought about his downfall. That left hook is a comparatively new weapon in the Conn arsenal. Up until now he has been a jabber—and what a jab it is!—standing up straight and fighting like somebody out of one of those old time boxing prints. Last night he threw hooks, leaping through the air half the time to do it, and then came through with a short, chopping right to the head.

Only a person with an adding machine could tell how many times Conn hit Lesnevich in that mad 13th round. But Gus shook 'em off and came wading in and the only answer to that is that Conn hasn't any steam behind his punches.

Conn must be an irritating fellow to fight. Every time Lesnevich looked up last night, that soggy, red leather glove in Conn's left hand was in his face. Sometimes it was jabbing him on the nose; other times it was smacking him on the right side of the head—but always it was there. Giving away too many inches in height and reach, Lesnevich just had to stand there and take it and hope that luck would give him a shot for the button. Luck conspired with Conn to see that that never happened.

For in addition to being a flashy boxer, Conn is a great defensive fighter. He stands dead in his tracks at times and flicks away blows with both gloves. Other times he shifts a couple of inches and makes his opponent miss so badly that it looks silly.

Fate has been lavish in the things she has given Conn, but fate is a fickle dame and she withheld from him the thing he needs most in his business—a right hand punch that whistles a lullaby as it explodes on the button.

BLAST FURNACE DUCK LOOP
Standings

	Won	Lost	Pct.
Tuyers	17	10	.630
Coolers	17	10	.630
Blowpipes	12	15	.444
Pigs	8	19	.296

A. & S. DUCKPIN LEAGUE
Standing Of Teams

	W.	L.	Pct.
Coke Racks	10	2	.833
Dumps	10	2	.833
Flats	7	5	.583
Box Cars	4	8	.333
Gondolas	3	9	.250
Hoppers	2	10	.167

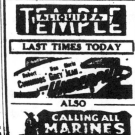

GIANT KILLER - - - - By Jack Sords
AND YOU THOUGHT YOU WERE TOUGH!
LITTLE JIMMY WAS THE CHIEF REASON ILLINOIS RUINED MICHIGAN'S BIG TEN TITLE HOPES
JIMMY SMITH
LATE-SEASON SENSATION OF THE UNIVERSITY OF ILLINOIS
HE STREAKED 82 YARDS THROUGH THE WHOLE WISCONSIN TEAM FOR A 7 TO 0 VICTORY

Pirate Pros' Next Opponent Boasts Some Of Grid "Great"

The Philadelphia Eagles, who meet the Pittsburgh Pirates at Forbes Field Nov. 26, have Davey O'Brien on their roster, but they also have a number of other collegiate "greats" hidden behind publicity heaped on the famed Davey.

Nevertheless, these players have been doing their work in fine style and on any other club where there was no O'Brien would be the feature headliner.

Take Franny Murray, former Pennsylvania University halfback, for example. In college he captained both the football and basketball teams and was one of the greatest athletes at Pennsylvania U. He is equally good at running, passing, kicking and blocking. As a junior at Penn he averaged 56 yards in punting in the Yale game, getting off one kick for 73 yards. In his senior year he converted 22 of 25 placement tries for points after touchdowns.

Another star on the team is Joe Carter, veteran end, playing his seventh season with the Eagles. Carter was an all-Southwestern conference selection for two seasons while playing with Southern Methodist University. In 1934 he led the National League is pass receiving, and he has always been near the top in this department of play. Last season he was surpassed in scoring only by Clark Hinkle and Don Hutson of Green Bay.

Bill Hewitt needs no introduction to professional football fans. He is recognized as greatest end in football and one of the greatest performers ever to play football. He has been selected All-Pro end four times, 1933, '34, '36, and '37.

Other stars include Dick Riffle from Albright, and George Somers from LaSalle College, both of whom were members of the Little All-American Bree Cuppoletti, guard from Oregon U., and an All-Pro selection in 1936, and Clem Woltman, All-Big Ten tackle from Purdue.

CARTWRIGHTS TO BOWL AGAINST FEDERALS TONIGHT

The Steubenville Federals will be the Aliquippa 'Cartwrights' bowling opponents tonight at Orpheum alleys.

Walter Butza, captain of the Cartwrights, has asked his pinmen to appear at 7:30 p. m.

GRID RESULTS

Apollo 21, Bell Township 6.
Allegheny 12, Perry 0.
Oliver 26, South Hills 0.
German 6, Monongahela 0.
Clearfield 33, State College 0.
Ferndale 18, Nanty-Glo 0.
Hazelton 21, Pottsville 6.

COLLEGIATE

Pitt Frosh 18, Kiski 12.
Muskingum 26, Georgetown C. 0.
W. Va. Wesleyan 14, Salem 7.
Temple Frosh 14, Albright Frosh 0
Dubuque 15, Penn, Ia., 7.
Cornell 20, Carleton 6.

Gauls Seek Games

The Aliquippa Gauls are looking for opponents for practice games. Teams interested in playing them were asked to communicate with Coach Milo Tatalovich.

SNYDERS TO ENTER GREATER PITTSBURGH BASKETBALL LEAGUE

The Aliquippa Snyders will compete this year in the Greater Pittsburgh Basketball loop.

The Snyders played independent ball last year.

Three new cagers have joined the squad. They are Russ Robinson, Bernard Bailey and Carl Pezzuli.

Boys Scout Mosquitoes

OPELIKA, Ala. (UP)—A 10-day mosquito survey has just been completed by Apelika boy scouts. The boys canvassed every home in the town, reporting their findings to county health authorities.

"Lafayette, here we are and here we mean to stay." Signed, Your Uncle Samuel.

DRY AS SAHARA - - -

Christmas And New Year's Eves, Falling On Sundays, Will Find State Laws Enforced To Letter

By RICHARD AMPER

What the governor of North Carolina said to the governor of South Carolina is history.

But what the governor of Pennsylvania said to the State Liquor Control board about the sale of liquor this New Year's Eve was—according to Gov. Arthur H. James today — absolutely nothing.

And celebrants who want to wear paper caps, blow horns and consider it no celebration at all if the liquor is missing will observe —like the governors of the Carolinas—"it's a long time between drinks."

For New Year's Eve this year falls on Sunday. This means that saloons, beer gardens, tap rooms, cocktail lounges and night clubs - in fact any dispensary of the cup that cheers— will be closed from midnight, Saturday, Dec. 30, to 7 a. m. Monday, Jan. 1.

But more than that—as a double blow to the glass tilters—Christmas eve also falls on Sunday.

Those folk entertaining the idea that state liquor law enforcement agents may be touched by the plight of New Year's Eve whoopee-makers and might be inclined to be considerate and look the other way when the night club set tries to dispense drinks were advised today by the governor and Walter H. Hitchler, chairman of the Liquor Control board, to forget it.

Speaking by telephone to his Harrisburg office from Texas, where he is vacationing, Gov. James denied reports that he told the liquor board either to "go easy or hard" on enforcement of the law keeping bars closed on Sundays.

Hitchler said that the governor "had not communicated with the chairman or any other member or officer of the board by telephone or otherwise, relative to sale of liquor on Christmas or New Year's Eve."

"Days and hours during which liquor may be sold lawfully are fixed by legislation and not by regulation of the board or order of the governor," Hitchler said. "The legislature has not given anyone the power to suspend the law. I received no instructions nor orders . . . as to manner or method of enforcing the law."

Since Mr. Hitchler is also dean of the Dickinson law school, there was little chance of his slipping up on the statutes.

He said the liquor board's staff would enforce the law with the "usual co-operation" of local police.

Even if the board wanted to give the drinkers a "break," it couldn't, said Clyde E. Smith, chief enforcement officer of the control board.

"The law's the law on the subject, and the board can't do anything about it."

There is one "out," however, for celebrators.

Licensed clubs are excepted from the ban on Sunday liquor sale.

So anyone who belongs to a club, or has a friend who belongs to a club, or wants to join a club before New Year's Eve, will be able to usher in 1940, and sing "Auld Lang Syne" with a drink in hand.

Lippe must build new Aliquippa High basketball team this season around one veteran. Read story on Page 5 today.

The Aliquippa Gazette

SERVING AN INDUSTRIAL COMMUNITY OF 50,000

WEATHER — Fair tonight and Wednesday. Somewhat warmer Wednesday.

VOL. XVIII. No. 177 | SERVED BY UNITED PRESS MEMBER OF P. N. P. A. | ALIQUIPPA, PA., TUESDAY, NOVEMBER 28, 1939 | PHONE 934-935 | 3 CENTS; BY CARRIER, 15 CENTS A WEEK

10th BRITISH SHIP SUNK; 1,762 DEAD

Social Security Act To Benefit 912,000 In 1940

YOUNG NAZI HERO COMMANDS SUB WHICH SANK SHIP

Russia Will Denounce Treaty With Finns, Molotov Says

BERLIN—(UP) — An official announcement tonight said that a 10,000-ton British cruiser—10th British warship lost in furious sea warfare—had been sunk by a U-boat commanded by the youthful German [illegible] whose submarine sank the Battleship Royal Oak in ScapaFlow, Lieut. Commander Guenther Prien.

The sinking as announced by the Germans brought the death toll in the 10 sea victories to at least 1,782 British.

LONDON.—(UP) — Naval circles said tonight that there was no confirmation of German claims that a U-boat sank a British heavy cruiser of the London type.

MOSCOW. — (UP) — Soviet Premier - Foreign Commissar Viacheslav M. Molotov informed the Finnish minister today that the Soviet Union will denounce the Soviet-Finnish non-aggression pact.

Molotov said that Russia denounces the pact because of Finland's anti-Soviet policy, which he said was inconsistent with the treaty.

Molotov replied to the Finnish note of yesterday and rejected the Finnish explanation of the frontier incident in which four Russian troops

(Continued on Page Eight)

Terrace Boy Hurt Playing Football

Eight stitches were required to close a head laceration suffered by Steve Marcus, 11, of Sheffield Terrace, in a football game in the basement of his home. The lad struck his head on a section of the chimney when tackled by a playmate.

They Seek Her Immortality

Here is Baby Jean, the five-months-old baby adopted by James B. Schafer, master metaphysician, who predicts that if plans work out Jean will live forever. Plans call for Baby Jean to refrain from meats (including eggs, milk and butter) and never to hear the words "sickness" or "death." Forty master metaphysicians, whose headquarters are in Oakdale, L. I., are cooperating in the "eternal life" program.

2 Beaver County Men Named Members Of Legion Committees

Michael J. Kane, prominent Aliquippa Legionnaire, has been appointed by National Commander Raymond J. Kelly as a member of the Distinguished Guest committee of the American Legion. Also named to a national Legion committee is Frank A. (Bridgie) Weber, Beaver Falls, who is a member of the Veterans' Preference committee.

Twins Born To Green Garden Road Couple

Twins—a boy and a girl—were born late last night to Mr. and Mrs. Thomas Rogish, of Green Garden road. The boy weighs nine pounds while his sister tipped the scales at 9¼ pounds.

Early last year twins were born to the couple but one of them died this year.

F. Watson, Storekeeper For Duquesne Light Co., Dies At Bridgewater

Fred Watson, storekeeper at Bridgewater headquarters of the Duquesne Light company and highly respected resident of Bridgewater, died at his home, 627 Market street, shortly before 2 p. m. yesterday.

Confined to his home four weeks ago with a severe cold, he developed a heart ailment and had been in critical condition three weeks.

Born at Brosley, Eng., a son of Benjamin and Harriet Watson, he was attracted to the opportunities existing in the United States through letters written by an elder sister living in Bridgewater. He came to America when he was 17.

The sister, Mrs. Jeremiah Shaw, has been seriously ill for a period of months and was unable to visit her brother during his fatal illness, although a resident of the im-

(Continued on Page Eight)

Advice On Bulb Culture Given Rotarians By Horticulturist

Holland has a virtual monopoly on fine tulip bulbs because of a happy combination of climate and soil. For the Dutch, tulip culture is big business but it's a business perennially threatened by politics, war and scientific advances in plant production.

So declared R. F. Elliott of Evans City, widely known expert on horticulture, in an address before the Aliquippa Rotary club last night.

The address was an interesting combination of technical discussion, shrewd observation and keen good humor and it touched everything from the history of the "bulb industry" to the political and economic factors that affect it.

Drawing on two score years of experience, the speaker explained how the long, cold springs of Holland and a perfect growing soil had given that country an unchallenged leadership in tulip production and built an industry running into tens of millions of dollars per year.

He explained how political factors had threatened Dutch imports of tulip bulbs into the United States, how tulip fanciers had defeated

(Continued on Page Eight)

MANY CHILDREN ARE INOCULATED AT CLINIC HERE

Toxoid Treatments To Be Given 3 More Days This Week

More than 300 Aliquippa children have been inoculated since the start of the fourteenth annual diphtheria clinic [illegible] yesterday under sponsorship of the Aliquippa school district.

West Aliquippa, 161 children were treated yesterday with the toxoid, seven of them being of pre-school age. Pupils of St. Joseph Parochial school as well as Washington building children were inoculated.

Drs. J. L. Miller and D. F. Sennett, in charge of the clinic at Franklin Junior High school today, reported that more than 200 children were inoculated. Of this number 35 were less than six years of age.

Schools Superintendent L. M. Wilson today reiterated his appeal to mothers of pre-school children to cooperate in this attempt to stamp out diphtheria in this community.

"This is the time in life when diphtheria is most fatal," he said, "and if all parents will co-operate in making this clinic the most successful in Aliquippa's history the scourge will be wiped out."

Mothers are urged to take their children to the building nearest their homes. Future clinics will be held at the following buildings between the hours of 9 and 11 a. m.

Jones building, tomorrow; Logstown, Thursday; and New Sheffield, Friday.

Consent slips are being distributed throughout the school system for children of school age, Mr. Wilson said.

Dozen Air-Minded Persons Enroll In New Aviation Class

Two women were among a dozen aviation enthusiasts who attended the first class in the "ground school" for flying instruction organized last night at the home of Hartley Neal at Conway airport.

Miss Doris Eppers, of Beaver, and Miss Katherine Moore, of Baden, enrolled for the 50-hour course, of which Everett Hart, New Brighton High school teacher, will be instructor.

The classes, to be conducted two hours each Monday and Friday evenings, are designed to prepare flyers for written examinations they must take before they are granted a private, limited or commercial license by the government.

Hart is one of 500 federally licensed aviation instructors. The school is managed by Neal and A. C. (Slim) Harting of Freedom.

BREAKS COLLARBONE

Lucille Petro, about 4, of 242 Beaver avenue, West Aliquippa, today was reported recovering from a fractured collarbone suffered when she fell off a chair in her home.

MARRIAGE APPLICATION

Joseph [illegible] of Superior avenue, Aliquippa, and Maud Daniels, Pittsburgh, applied today at Beaver for a license to marry.

BOY FOR DINELLOS

An eight-pound son was born at 4 a. m. today to Mr. and Mrs. Carl DiNello, of 523 Fifth street, West Aliquippa.

George D. Hayden, Veteran J. & L. Foreman, Succumbs

Active Church, Lodge Worker; Carpenter Foreman Here Since 1910

George Djokn Hayden, 68, veteran carpenter foreman at the J. & L. Steel Corp. plant here, died at 5:30 p. m. yesterday at his home, 204 Kiehl street. He was stricken ill with pneumonia last Wednesday. Mr. Hayden was one of the organizers of St. Elijah Serbian church, Aliquippa, and at the time

He had served as a deacon for years. He was financial secretary of the German Beneficial Union of Aliquippa; a member of C. F. U. No. 428 here and Zora Serbian Lodge No. 92 of Aliquippa. He also was a member of the J. & L. Veteran Employes' association of Aliquippa.

He was first employed at the J. & L. plant on the South Side, being transferred to Aliquippa in 1910. He married Miss Martha Vujnovich in 1909.

In addition to his wife he leaves four children: Mrs. Nedelle Ciganovich, Youngwood, and George, Jr., Lilye and Robert Hayden, all at home.

Funeral service will be Thursday at 2 p. m. at St. Elijah church. Burial will be in the church cemetery.

Central Relief Group Here Meets Dec. 7 At Municipal Building

Annual meeting of the Aliquippa Central Relief association is scheduled Thursday, Dec. 7, starting at 8 p. m. in council chambers of the municipal building here, Mrs. Ida C. Wright, secretary, disclosed today.

Election of a new board of directors for the ensuing year will transpire and local, county and state officials will be present to answer all questions pertaining to relief work in the community.

Three representatives of all organizations affiliated with the relief association are invited to attend the important meeting.

Aliquippa Elks To Initiate Members

Initiation of candidates will feature a meeting of the Aliquippa B. P. O. E. lodge in the Franklin avenue club rooms at 8:30 p. m. today. Luncheon will follow the business session.

Final arrangements for the memorial service to be held jointly with Coraopolis, Rochester and Ambridge at Rochester Sunday, Dec. 3, will also be completed. Since this date is the date of the next R. A. C. A. meeting, it was decided to combine the two affairs.

Large delegations from here and throughout the valley are expected to attend.

Beaver Falls Child Injured By Machine

A 12-year-old girl was injured when she dashed across Beaver Falls' main thoroughfare yesterday afternoon into the path of an auto driven by a woman.

The victim, Geraldine Stewart, 1625 Second avenue, was hit by a car driven by Mrs. Gifford Patterson of 616 Twelfth street. The girl was treated at Providence hospital for a cut knee.

The National Whirligig

(News Behind the News)

PRACTICAL — A gentlemen's agreement over the shipment of foodstuffs, involving the United Kingdom, Germany and Denmark, has recently fallen into official hands here under cover of confidence. It illustrates vividly what a phoney sort of war Europe is waging at the present moment.

Germany, as the party of the first part, has agreed not to sink British ships carrying animal feedstuffs to Denmark, although the vessels must traverse waters easily strewn with mines or guarded by submarines. In return for this favor, Great Britain has agreed to permit Denmark to ship to Germany certain food supplies in larger quantity than the Danes did throughout the peacetime year of 1938. The pro-German commodities include such vitally important supplies as cattle, live pigs, lard and various meat products.

There may be some method in this seeming British madness, however. Denmark raises no feedstuffs and must import them to fatten its stock. Denmark also supplies Great Britain with cattle, pigs, poultry, eggs and butter to the disadvantage of American producers and exporters. On these shipments to the British, however, there is no guarantee of immunity from German submarines or mines. Who was it that said chivalry —commercial, of course—was dead?

* * *

STRATEGY—Republican National Chairman Hamilton has served quiet notice—although Rival James A. Farley may have missed its significance —that the G. O. P. will play a waiting game in nominating its Presidential ticket next year. The canny Kansas red-head, for the first time, has tipped his hand as to 1940 strategy.

Mr. Hamilton recently issued a call for a meeting of the executive committee of the National Committee December 7. Ordinarily the larger body assembles about that time—the first week in December—and fixes the date for the national convention in June. The Democrats then hold their powwow, and take advantage of the obliging Republicans by arranging to hold their quadrennial circus after the G. O. P. has given its performance.

What Jim may have missed is the fact that the executive committee has no authority to select either a date or a site for the national convention. They will discuss routine matters such as shaping of the platform at their December 7 gathering. Some time later—perhaps after Mr. Farley's merry men have met and ar-

(Continued on Page Six)

Hopewell Twp. School Board Meets Tonight

The granting of contracts for school picnics and discussion of a teachers' group hospitalization program will highlight a meeting of faculty members and directors of the Hopewell Township school district at 7:45 p. m. today in the high school building.

FIRST PAYMENTS UNDER INSURANCE PLAN TO BE MADE

Old-Age System Will Become Effective On January 1

WASHINGTON — (UP) — Social Security board officials estimated today that approximately 912,000 persons will receive benefits [illegible] made under the old-age insurance [illegible]

The old-age insurance system in which workers and employers in covered industries have been contributing for three years becomes effective Jan. 1, 1940. Officials estimate that between 45,000,000 and 50,000,000 wage earners are covered by that plan.

Jan. 1 will be the date when the first monthly benefits become payable to those who can qualify. In that category the board believes there will be 912,000 persons before the end of 1940. That estimate is based on the assumption that there will be 485,000 primary old-age beneficiaries—that is, persons 65 years of age or older— who are fully insured in their own right; 125,000 wives and 20,000 widows over 65; 78,000 young widows with dependent children; 194,000 dependent children; and 10,000 dependent parents.

The benefits will vary from $10 a month to a maximum of $85 a month. The amount of the benefit will depend on the previous monthly average wage and the length of time employed before applying for the pension.

Last year, Congress amended the original act passed in 1935, to "liberalize" benefits of the act and include more than 1,000,000 workers not previously covered by its provisions.

Among the changes made by Congress were advancement of the date for payment of old-age benefits from 1942 to Jan. 1, 1940; additional benefits to wage-earners for dependents,

(Continued on Page Eight)

Recount Of Ballots Cast In Ambridge Precinct Ordered

Three Democrats in Ambridge asked the county court today for a recount of ballots cast in the fifth precinct of the third ward in the Nov. 7 general election.

They charge "fraud or error" in the computation of the ballots.

The petitioners for the recheck are Louise Quail, Dean W. Maley and Walter Wojcik.

Judge H. H. Wilson set tomorrow at 9 a. m. for a recount by County Commissioner Paul Baldwin, Pauline Ruckert and Elizabeth Johnston, all of Rochester.

21
SHOPPING DAYS TILL
Christmas

Junior Bucktails To Run District Fox Hunt

Arranging Chase With District Game Warden

Record Crowd Of 400 Attends Joint Meeting Of Junior And Senior Sportsmen's Groups; Hussey Names Committees For 1940

Tally ho!

The Junior Bucktails announced today that they would call district sportsmen to horse and hounds for their first fox hunt over woodlands surrounding Aliquippa.

The fox hunt, an innovation in the district sporting scene, was decided upon last night at a joint meeting of the junior and senior Bucktail clubs.

More than 400 persons attended the meeting last night at the sportsmen's club house on the Brodhead road. This was the largest turnout for any meeting of the Bucktails since they organized.

The fox hunt, date of which will be set later, will be staged with the help of Jack Brezendine of Ambridge, deputy game warden.

Brezendine will plan the hunt and will furnish hounds. Wardens George Crothers and Bradley McGregor will co-operate in the hunt.

Several members of the senior club will accompany the Junior Bucktails on the hunt.

Brezendine, an expert fox hunter, who has caught four of the animals this season, said that a low bounty of $4 on the grey fox does not encourage his capture or a decrease in the number of foxes in surrounding woods.

"There is now more fox in Beaver county than any time before," Brezendine said. "The hunt will make local woods safe for rabbit breeding and give young sportsmen a chance to enter the woods and learn outdoor life under the trained supervision of the three district game wardens."

A narrated color movie on activities of fowl, animals and reptiles was screened as a feature of the meeting.

Bob Ford of Homestead, naturalist and outdoor enthusiast, screened and discussed the film. The film included pictures of game at Pymatuning Lake.

R. M. Hussey, president of the Bucktails, appointed the following committees for the year:

Finance—Chairman, Marshall Davies; vice chairmen, John Davey, Floyd King and Robert Crawford.

Grounds—Chairman, Harry Shumate, Charles Crissman, Stanley Beggs, junior representative.

House—Chairman, Herbert Dentywiller, R. N. Maples and Forrest Campbell.

Publicity—Chairman, F. J. King, Stanley Beggs and J. L. Brougher.

[illegible] Mile Prosser, C. Ciche and W. Vance.

Membership—Chairman, C. Wyngant, M. Beggs, M. Prosser, C. L. Martin.

Skeet Trap—Chairman, W. Kirk. Skeet Division, chairman, C. Crissman. Trap Division, chairman, G. Slezak and T. Klavack.

Farm Game Program—Chairman, C. L. Martin, Ed Douds, E. Haas, George Crothers and W. Gaw.

Prizes were awarded George Hoffman, W. C. Acheson, George Dixon and Harry Rice.

Among guests at the meeting were McGregor, Beaver county warden, and Deputies Crothers and Brezendine, Alex Pearson, Rochester burgess, and others from Ambridge and Monaca Bucktail groups.

The next meeting of the Bucktails will be Feb. 8.

3 TEAMS SWEEP DUCKPIN GAMES

Second-half race in the Community Duckpin league here got under way at Orpheum alleys last night with three teams, Drinkmore, Eagles and Apollo, making clean sweeps of their matches.

Drinkmore walloped Egers's, the Eagles dusted off the Bucs and Apollo conquered Jacobson's, while Sergi's was winning the odd game from P. M. Co.

Leading rollers of the night were Myers, 554; Shaffalo, 544; Springston, 536, and Fisher, 524. Summaries:

SERGI'S—2237				
Sergi	158	130	183—	471
Marrone	155	130	148—	433
Montine	137	144	177—	458
Palidora	156	127	127—	410
Deep	133		—	133
Gulley		124	122—	246
Stalla	163	146	119—	428
Darkin	128	159	129—	416
Totals	769	709	759—	2237
P. M. CO.—2153				
Laing	134	182	132—	448
Blasic	179	122	76—	377
Herbert	164	122	143—	429
Brown	117	126	96—	339
Isles	109	113	86—	308
Twaddle	107	170	162—	439
Merges	121	115	183—	419
Totals	715	722	716—	2153
EGERS—2149				
Waterman	92	159	175—	426
Sisson	109	114	159—	382
Swan	111	141	129—	381
Hamilton	123	156	—	279
Matz	165	131	114—	410
Westlake	118	130	140—	388
Randle			132—	132
Browne	156	154	114—	424
Totals	673	741	735—	2149
DRINKMORE—2415				
Bingham	131	116	186—	433
Moreno	124	147	119—	390
Morgan	90		118—	208
Fouse	165	167	146—	478
Coulson	121	107	—	228
Myers	125	227	201—	553
Fisher	171	161	192—	524
Buchanan		153	118—	271
Totals	716	855	844—	2415
BUCS—2223				
Skiba	117	139	191—	447
Calabro	147	171	148—	466
Augustine	113	157	135—	405
Westman	142	110	96—	348
Silkroski	156	118	115—	389
Carbone	145	135	110—	390
Kulcyk	164	120	158—	442
Totals	754	722	747—	2223
EAGLES—2493				
Joseph	147	81	190—	418
Carl	188	120	205—	513
Andy	141	166	171—	478
Opsatnik	157	148	156—	461
Shaffalo	163	187	194—	544
Kaletz		160	118—	278
Totals	796	781	916—	2493
APOLLO—2302				
King	112	132	120—	364
Springston	194	167	175—	536
Yoho	138	136	166—	440
Dunbaugh	132	187	179—	498
Sterbutcel	145	147	172—	464
Totals	721	769	812—	2302
JACOBSON—2236				
Emert	150	103	158—	411
Shannon	118	101	—	219
Miller	137	127	155—	419
Pritchard	152	140	123—	415
Dyer	134	157	207—	498
Rosico		124	100—	224
Povelitis	117		112—	229
Malovich	135	204	133—	472
Totals	708	752	776—	2236

Greenies Lose Close One To Pittsburghers

The St. Stan quint of Pittsburgh licked the Aliquippa Greenies, 46-41 in a game at Goodwill gym, Pittsburgh, yesterday.

H. Zisnon led the losers' scoring with 12 points, while Flowers of the Pittsburgh aggregation counted 12.

The lineups:

St. Stan	FG	F	TP
Mezzee, f	4	2	10
Dynibels, f	2	0	4
Flowers, c	5	2	12
Grominski, g	2	1	5
Crick, g	3	0	6
Walshor, c	3	3	9
Totals	19	8	46
Greenies			
L. Cerneskie, f	1	2	4
A. Arniak, g	1	1	3
F. Japic, c	2	1	5
Smith, g	1	2	4
Zisnon, g	6	0	12
Cycholl, f	1	0	2
Domitrovich, c	2	0	4
Westlake, f	1	2	4
Rock, g	1	1	3
Totals	16	9	41

THE GAZETTE—FAMILY PAPER

STILL A CHAMP - - - By Jack Sords

LEE GRISSOM
NEW SOUTHPAW FOR THE NEW YORK YANKEES ACQUIRED FROM CINCINNATI BY THE WAIVER ROUTE
WHAT DO I CARE — I'M STILL WITH THE CHAMPS
GRISSOM IS A SPEED-BALL ARTIST WHO SHOULD GO GOOD WITH THE YANKS
AMERICAN LEAGUE CHAMPS
NATIONAL LEAGUE CHAMPS
SORDS

Grimes Advances To Mitt Tourney Finals

Johnny (Jack) Grimes, rated as Aliquippa's leading amateur boxer, battled his way to the final round of the 160-pound open division in the annual Diamond Belt tournament at Palisades rink in McKeesport last night.

Fighting under colors of the Monaca A. C., Grimes first decisioned Steve Kulick, of the Barto A. C., in three rounds, and then went three additional rounds before eliminating Sam Whetstone, Hill Top A. C., from the tourney.

Whetstone had reached the semi-finals [illegible] over Tony Sarkins, Mitchell A. C.

Grimes will battle it out with Ray Harris, St. John's Lyceum, at Duquesne Garden next Monday night, when survivors in the eight classes in both the open and novice divisions clash for the championships of 1940.

Harris won his way to the final round in the 160-pound open class after winning the nod over Junior Hill, Slater A. C., in a quarter-final bout, and Joe Provident, Lewis club, via the decision, in the other semi-final.

Paired for the title in the 160-pound novice division are Arthur Hardy, Superior A. C., and Art Authors, Pittsburgh Lyceum.

PHALANX WINS AT PING PONG

Formal ping pong competition got underway at Cappy's Recreational Center yesterday when the Phalanx club licked Cappy's All Stars, 10 games to 5.

Harold Evans starred with the paddle, copping the three games he played against Bud Orr. Ed Freese and Gordon Evans won two of their three games.

Ertz won two of three games against Marley McQueen while Dakis copped the best of three with Matajasic.

GAZETTE—A PAPER WITH NEWS

Quips Buck Castlers Here Tonight

Bridgers Host To New Brighton, Butler Plays Ellwood In Loop Tilts

Aliquippa goes to court with New Castle at the high school gym at 8:30 p. m. today in one of three games in Sec. 3 of the Western Pennsylvania Interscholastic Athletic league.

With a .500 average—one triumph, one loss—the Quips buck the Castles, who have won two and lost one.

The Quips licked Ellwood City as badly as New Castle did but lost to Beaver Falls by two points. New Castle tripped New Brighton and lost to Ambridge by six points.

The Red and Black will have the advantage of playing on a familiar court on which Coach Nate Lippe was expected to use a zone defense for the second time this season.

The lineup that started the previous games will probably open against the Castlers with the possible exception of Catroppa, a guard, who may be kept on the bench until later in the game.

Bar, Blicha, Fuderich and Belas will probably start the action.

Ambridge, only undefeated team in the section, plays host to New Brighton, and the odds favored the Bridgers to make it four straight, for the Bridgers showed power in licking not only New Castle but also Butler, defending section champions.

Butler plays at Ellwood City, and although the 1939 titlists are by no means as strong as they were last season, Ellwood is considerably weaker and will probably go into the game the underdog in the odds.

The Aliquippa Reserves will play a preliminary game with the New Castle subs starting at 7:15 p. m.

Cooper in Germany

"The Prairie," one of Fenimore Cooper's most American stories, was written at Bad Duerkheim, Germany; and today there is a small museum there in his memory.

Eagles Win WARC Tilt With Panthers, 22-16

In the only game played last evening at the West Aliquippa Recreational Center, the floundering Flying Eagles upset the Black Panthers of the Intermediate basketball league, 22-16.

Forfeit triumphs went to the Gym All-Stars of the Senior circuit over the Waner's A. C. and to the Redwing Juniors, pace-setters in the Junior division, over the Black Aces.

After being held on fairly even terms by the Panthers in the opening half, the Eagles, led by high-scoring A. Smerigan, edged ahead in the second semester and won going away. Smerigan tallied as many points as the entire losing team on seven field goals and two out of three free throws.

Flying Eagles	F.G.	F.	Pts.
Martin, f.	1	1	3
Hanich, f.	0	0	0
Ondeyka, f.	0	0	0
Glomb, c.	1	0	2
DiNardo, c.	0	0	0
Smerigan, g.	7	2	16
Haber, g.	0	1	1
Totals	9	4	22

Black Panthers	F.G.	F.	Pts.
Dzugan, f.	2	1	5
Vince, f.	1	1	3
Pinkosky, c.	1	0	2
DiNardo, g.	0	0	0
Tonyk, g.	2	1	5
Crivelli, g.	0	1	1
Totals	6	4	16

Referee—A. Donavan.

More Sports Page 8

Beggs Signs Red Contract

Says He Is "Pleased With Terms;" Goes To Camp In Feb.

Joe Beggs of Aliquippa said today that he has signed a contract to play with the Cincinnati Reds this year and that he was "very much pleased with the terms."

Beggs, a righthanded pitcher, was traded by the New York Yankees to the Reds last week for Lee Grissom, southpaw hurler.

The Aliquippa ball player, who has been spending his winter ice skating, chopping wood and hiking and hunting to keep in shape, said he would report to the Reds' training camp at Tampa, Fla., the middle of next month, two weeks before the rest of the squad arrives.

This will be the third year Joe will have worked out in a major league training camp. He worked with the Yankees twice when they brought him from the Newark farm in the International league.

W. A. R. C. BASKETBALL Standings

Senior League	W.	L.	Pct.
Mustangs	10	2	.800
Gym All-Stars	6	4	.600
Waner's A.C.	4	6	.400
Toth's Artillery	2	8	.200
Intermediate	**W.**	**L.**	**Pct.**
Black Panthers	10	2	.833
Redwings	[illegible]	[illegible]	.583
Flying Eagles	6	6	.500
Tiger	1	14	.083
Junior League	**W.**	**L.**	**Pct.**
Redwing Juniors	9	0	1.000
Dead End Kids	5	3	.625
Black Aces	3	6	.333
Pirates	0	8	.000

Games Tonight

Dead End Kids vs. Pirates
Flying Eagles vs. Redwings
Waner's A.C. vs. Mustangs

Games Tomorrow

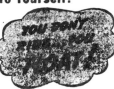

Redwing Juniors vs. Pirates
Dead End Kids vs. Black Aces

Weather Forecast
Snow flurries tonight and Sunday; continued cold tonight; slowly rising temperature Sunday and Monday.

THE DAILY TIMES

ROCHESTER-BEAVER-MONACA
FREEDOM—BRIDGEWATER—CONWAY—VANPORT—MIDLAND

Local History,
Log schoolhouses were the first local educational institutions and greased paper was used to admit light at the windows.

EST. APRIL 2, 1874 | BEAVER AND ROCHESTER, PA., SATURDAY, JANUARY 27, 1940. | BY CARRIER 15 CENTS A WEEK—3 CENTS PER COPY

ALIQUIPPA FIRE CAUSES $30,000 DAMAGE

ATTEMPTED PAYROLL ROBBERY FAILS

ADVERSE REPORT MADE ON CANAL

LAKE ERIE-OHIO RIVER CANAL IS OPPOSED BY ICC

Canal Would Cause $35,000,000 Loss Annually To Railroads, Report Declares

Proposed Waterway Would Affect At Least 56,000,000 Tons Of Traffic Yearly

President Roosevelt was told by the Interstate Commerce Commission that railroads would suffer a loss of $35,000,000 annually in their gross revenue if the proposed $240,000,000 Lake Erie-Ohio river canal is constructed.

An Army board of engineers had declared that if railroads would permanently reduce their rates by an average of 29 cents per ton, construction of the canal would not be justified. The President had asked the ICC for its opinion as to whether the rate reductions suggested by the Army engineers would be economically justified.

In making its report yesterday to the President, the ICC stated the rate reductions specified by the engineers would not be economically justified prior to the construction of the canal because—on the information now available, these reductions could not be confined to the traffic of those roads which would be expected to benefit by construction of the waterway.

RAILROADS AMPLE

The commission, however, made no recommendation as to the economic justification of the canal,

(Continued on Page Ten)

Borah's Successor Named By Governor

By the United Press

BOISE, Ida., Jan. 27 — John Thomas, 65, a Republican and a banker, prepared today to assume the Senate seat of William E. Borah.

Unlike Borah he is an old-guard Republican, but he is an isolationist. "I pledge myself to an undying fight in behalf of Senator Borah's aften expressed determination to keep our nation out of war," he said. "I dedicate my services to those ideals of good government for which he so courageously and valiantly fought."

Gov. C. A. Bottolfsen appointed Thomas yesterday. It was the second time in 15 years that Thomas had been named to the seat of a deceased Senator.

He went to the Senate first in 1926 after the death of Frank R. Gooding. He was elected to the seat in the next general election, and served until defeated in the Democratic landslide of 1932. Borah's term expires Jan. 1, 1943, but under Idaho law Thomas can serve by appointment only until this fall's general election.

Attack On WPA Is Resumed By James

By the United Press

PHILADELPHIA, Jan. 27—Pennsylvania faces a "thinly veiled" threat of loss of its federal funds for relief and unemployment compensation, Gov. Arthur H. James told the Philadelphia Chamber of Commerce.

The "threat" he said in an address last night, came from "certain employes" of the federal social security board who interpreted social security amendments by Congress last year as giving the board arbitrary power to withhold these federal funds if in its opinion state enabling legislation, especially with regard to personnel, is faulty.

James' attack was his second on a New Deal agency in two months. In December he charged Republican states were being forced by the New Deal to "bear the brunt of WPA reductions."

Rochester Merchants Opposed To Parking Meters, Plan Meeting

Rochester merchants who are opposed to the installation of parking meters in the Junction City will meet at a luncheon in the Penn Beaver hotel Wednesday, January 31, at 12:30 o'clock.

Firemen Injured Fighting Flames

Two firemen were overcome by smoke, several others were injured and 25 persons were forced to flee into the sub-freezing cold Thursday afternoon when fire swept the Harrison building, Franklin and Hopewell avenues, Aliquippa, causing damage estimated unofficially at $30,000.

Other nearby buildings in the heart of the Aliquippa business district were threatened and traffic was delayed for hours by the fire.

Three fire companies were called and fifty firemen battled the flames three and a half hours before bringing the fire under control. Traffic was blocked and motorists were forced to detour over the hills for many miles.

George Opsatnic, a member of the regular fire company, and Paul Barton, a volunteer fireman, were overcome by smoke and were given first-aid treatment by a physician. Later, they returned to the fire.

Mary Batis, four-year-old daughter of Mr. and Mrs. Mike Batis, 144 Franklin avenue, who lives in an apartment in the building adjoining the Harrison building, has been ill for some time and was carried from her home when the fire started. She was removed to Rochester hospital where she is confined today.

CAUSE UNDETERMINED

The source of the fire had not been determined today. It is believed to have been caused by hot ashes from the furnace igniting rubbish in the cellar or by an overheated furnace.

The alarm was turned in at 3:54 o'clock and flames were breaking through the first floor from the cellar when the first firemen arrived. Three storerooms on the first floor, a tavern, shoe shop and a combination barber shop and poolroom were swept by the flames.

Following an airshaft to the second and third floors, the fire caused slight damage to one room on each floor but firemen prevented it spreading. The eight apartments on the two upper floors were considerably damaged by smoke and water.

TRAFFIC TIED UP

The firemen were handicapped by dense smoke and were forced to don gas masks to get to the source of the blaze. Although the fire was under control at 7:30 o'clock, the fire companies did not leave until two hours later as they "wet down" the charred first floor and cellar.

Employes of the Jones and Laughlin Steel Corporation were coming off duty as the fire broke out and many immediately began to aid the firemen. Other steel workers from out of town who drive to work were unable to leave when they came off duty at four o'clock as the street was blocked outside the tunnnel entrance to the mill property. The drivers were three hours in leaving the mill.

FIREMEN INJURED

Fire Chief C. B. Ransom was descending the basement stairs after the fire was extinguished, but slipped on the ice on them and fell into four feet of water in the cellar. He went to the fire station, changed clothes and returned to the scene to continue his investigation. A number of other firemen were also

(Continued on Page Ten)

Personal Property Taxes Are To Be Collected By State

Tax Examiner To Be Stationed At Court House To Aid County Residents

The annual campaign for collection of taxes due the state on Personal Property has been started by the Department of Revenue. E. B. Reed, tax examiner for the department, will be located at the Beaver County Court House, Beaver, Monday, Tuesday, and Wednesday of each week until February 15, which is the last day, under the law, for filing returns and also the 1 st day for payment of state tax without penalty.

All personal holding stocks, bonds, mortgages, notes, annuities or other evidences of debt must file a return and pay the tax due the Commonwealth. In case of his failure to file such a return, the law provides that the Department of Revenue may make an arbitrary assessment with added penalties.

TAX BASIS CHANGED

Certain stocks and bonds that were exempt for previous years are taxable for 1940. As protection, the taxpayer should ascertain the taxable status of his stocks and bonds before filing a return. This information may be procured from the tax examiner.

Return forms already have been distributed by the Commonwealth to persons known to have had taxable property in the past. The state four-mill personal property tax is identical with the personal property tax collected by the counties.

ICE GORGES RIVER

By the United Press

AURORA, Ind., Jan. 27. — Ice gorged the Ohio river today, choking off the Cincinnati watershed and city officials said they feared heavy flood damage in Southern Indiana if a thaw started the gorge moving on a rising river.

FOUR BURN TO DEATH

By the United Press

MACOMB, Ill., Jan. 27—A 21-year-old mother, her two small children and her young sister were burned to death today when the small frame house in which they were sleeping caught fire and burned to the ground.

Great Game Of Politics

— By Frank R. Kent —

(Copyright, 1939)

THOSE BRITISH NOTES

Washington, Jan. 27.

UNQUESTIONABLY the State Department is on sound ground in sharply calling the British attention to the holding up of American ships in the Mediterranean and in the opening of and diversion of mail. It is necessary that the protest be made and it is better that the State Department make it voluntarily than that complaints should pile up and a demand for action arise.

—o—

NEVERTHELESS, there is no reason for any public feeling on the subject and nothing like the indignation is felt inside the State Department that the sternness of its protesting language would indicate. Actually, it is recognized that the British are within their legal rights in delaying and searching American ships bound for neutral ports with mail and cargo. The only real grievance is not what they have done, but the way in which they have done it.

—o—

ASIDE from the chronic British baiters in Congress, no one here is inflamed against England because of these happenings. Nor do informed persons take them seriously. The

(Continued on Page Four)

Rochester Woman Is Fatally Stricken

Mrs. Anna Margaret Graff, 58, wife of Herman Fred Graff, 389 Vermont avenue, Rochester, and highly esteemed resident of the Junction City, died at 8:35 o'clock this morning in the home of her daughter, Mrs. George V. White, 523 Cross street, Rochester, where she had lived for some time.

The body was removed to her home in Vermont avenue. Funeral services will be held Tuesday evening, January 30, at 10 o'clock in St. Cecilia Roman Catholic church. Burial will be in St. Cecilia cemetery. She was a member of St. Cecilia church and Christian Mothers of the Church.

Surviving are: her husband, two sons, Herman J. Graff and Howard M. Graff, Rochester; four daughters, Mrs. White, Rochester; Mrs. Richard P. Steward, New Brighton, and Misses Marie H. and Viola E. Graff, at home; one brother, Philip Goedeker, Rochester; two sisters, Mrs. John S. Gremer, Tampa, Fla., and Mrs. Frank H. Kubler, Coraopolis, and four grandchildren.

Rochester Couple Well-Known Here

—Photo by Graule Studios

MR. AND MRS. FRANK W. WHITE

Among the prominent residents of the valley are Mr. and Mrs. Frank W. White, 364 Virginia avenue, Rochester, well-known and life-long residents of Beaver County. Mr White celebrated his 82nd birthday anniversary last September. He was formerly employed by the old Rochester Tumbler Works and later by the H. C. Fry Glass Company.

Mrs. White will be 80 years of age in April. She was formerly Miss Emma Shanor, daughter of the late John E. and Belinda Cable Shanor, Rochester. She was born in Unionville, the oldest of 16 children, and six of her brothers and two sisters are still living.

Mr. and Mrs. White are members of the Methodist church, Rochester. They have two sons and a daughter: William, Sunflower road; Charles, Rochester, and Mrs. Walter Darling, Rochester. The Whites celebrated their sixtieth wedding anniversary on December 26, 1939.

PWA Projects Here Cost $2,000,000 In 1939, Report Shows

Schools And Other Public Buildings Constructed Under Program In Past Year

P. W. A. projects in Beaver County in 1939 cost a total of two million dollars, according to figures recently released.

The projects include: Addition to elementary school, Harmony Township; addition to water system, Ambridge; street improvement, Ambridge; new elementary school, Aliquippa; two elementary schools, Hopewell Township; new elementary school, Center Township; new highway maintenance building, East Rochester; new fire station, College Hill, Beaver Falls; new elementary school, Darlington, and new infirmary, Beaver County Home, Potter Township. The last project is now nearing completion and is to be opened in the Spring.

CONSTRUCTION HEAVY

The year 1939 brought the largest heavy public construction boom in a decade to the State of Pennsyl-

(Continued on Page Ten)

Relief Payments Increase Slightly

Relief recipients of Beaver County received a total of $12,021.10 for the week ending today. This is a slight increase over the preceding week. A decrease of $17,533.90 is noted by comparison to the same week of last year, and 2,104 fewer checks were written.

This report on the changing relief picture was made today by State Treasurer F. Clair Ross in his weekly summary of disbursements made through the Bureau of Assistance Disbursements in the Treasury Department.

Disbursements for the current week were $12,021.10, made with 1,944 checks; disbursements last week were $11,446.40, made with 1,877 checks, disbursements a year ago were $29,555, made with 4,048 checks.

Lambskin Club Will Have First Event Of 1940 Next Week

Family Party To Be Held By Masonic Group Jan. 31 In Beaver High School

Wednesday evening, January 31, has been selected as the date of the first of the 1940 events of the Lambskin Club of Beaver County. The affair will be held at Beaver high school auditorium and there will be a two and one-half hour vaudeville entertainment. Later dancing will be enjoyed in the gymnasium. The event will be for members and their families.

Steve Forester, well known Pittsburgh musical and stage director, is bringing a large number of high-class acts to the county seat for the occasion and will provide an orchestra for dancing. The program

(Continued on Page Ten)

Miners' Union Turns To CIO's Campaign

By the United Press

COLUMBUS, Ohio, Jan. 27 — United Mine Workers union officials turned their attention to the C. I. O's steel organizing drive today as the Miners' Golden Jubilee Convention adjourned until Monday.

A mass meeting of Ohio Steel workers and other Congress of Industrial Organizations adherents was called for two p. m. and Philip Murray, UMW vice president and chairman of the Steel Workers' Organizing Committee, will be the principal speaker.

President John L. Lewis awaited national reaction to the speech yesterday of his favorite Democratic presidential candidate, Sen. Burton K. Wheeler, D., Mont.

The 2,400 delegates gave him a rising vote of confidence after he had proposed a National Conference of Industrial, Agricultural and Labor Leaders to solve unemployment and other basic problems which he said had not been solved in the seven years of the New Deal.

STATE DEMOCRATS SPLIT IN DISPUTE REGARDING GUFFEY

Party Leaders To Meet Next Saturday In Capital To Name Primary Slate

Only Treasurer Candidate Remains To Be Selected By Republican Organization

By the United Press

HARRISBURG, Jan. 27. — The Pennsylvania Democratic organization, still suffering effects of its 1938 factional blow-up, will meet here a week from today to select its April primary candidates for the U. S. Senate, State Treasurer, Auditor General and Delegates at Large to the National Presidential Convention.

State Chairman David L. Lawrence announced that Pennsylvania's four at-large votes at the National Convention again will be cast by 16 persons, each with a quarter vote, as was done in 1936. Seventy district delegates with a full vote each also will be elected in April.

Temper of party county leaders, who blame their superiors to a large degree for the complete Republican sweep in the last gubernatorial election, was admittedly disturbing to state leaders who feel another bad primary fight would be heaping disaster on disaster.

OPINION DIVIDED

Opinion was divided, however, on how vigorous a protest the faction opposed to U. S. Senator Joseph F. Guffey's bid for another term will register.

Lawrence said his canvas of the State found no strong candidate against the present Democratic Senator but has not yet said he is for Guffey.

So far former Pittsburgh Mayor William N. McNair is the only announced Democratic Senatorial candidate besides Guffey. Congressman Robert G. Allen, D., Westmoreland, and Francis E. Walker, D., Northampton, have expressed a willingness to run if the party wants them.

OTHERS MENTIONED

One of the most outspoken members of the anti-Guffey faction is Luzerne County Leader, State Senator Leo C. Mundy. He is also opposed for renomination by Arthur Colegrove, former Secretary of Property and Supplies and former Erie County Democratic chairman. Colegrove is publisher of the Corry Journal.

The names of U. S. Ambassador to France William C. Bullitt and former Internal Affairs Secretary Thomas A. Logue have been suggested as compromise candidates.

Republican State Chairman James F. Torrance said today no definite agreement had yet been reached on the party's only unfilled primary ticket opposition, candidate for State Treasurer, but that he expected a decision within a week.

The selection, according to plans of State leaders who met several weeks ago at the capital to select a primary ticket, is to be a Western Pennsylvanian. Actual selection was left to Western County leaders and Young Republicans, with Torrance's approval.

Harmony Twp. Man Sentenced Today

John Koczera, Harmony township, who was convicted during the December term of court on two charges of felonious assault and battery in connection with the shooting and wounding of Mr. and Mrs. John Wolaszyn, his neighbors last October, was before Judge Henry H. Wilson today for sentence.

In each of the two cases Judge Wilson sentenced Koczera to pay the costs, a fine of $1,000 and serve from one to three years in jail. The court's order contained a provision that upon properly executed adjustment of the damage to Mr. and Mrs. Wolaszyn within 30 days, remission of both the fine and costs would be considered, otherwise the fine would be certified for collection. Mr. and Mrs. Wolaszyn have filed civil damage suits against Koczera.

Koczera, it was charged at the trial, climaxed a wordy argument by going into his house and returning to Wolaszyn's back yard and shooting both Mr. and Mrs. Wolaszyn. Mrs. Wolaszyn lost an eye and her husband's jaw was shattered, it was said.

George Stephens, 19, of Hopewell township, entered a plea in court today to a charge of arson. It was alleged he set fire to a small cottage owned by Ernest Cleric, of East Carnegie, on the Reed Farm in Hopewell township. He was committed to the Industrial Reformatory at Huntingdon.

Bandits Thwarted By Women Clerks At Local Pottery

Quick thinking on the part of two women employes saved the payroll of the Sherwood Brothers Pottery Company, Block House Run, New Brighton, Friday afternoon when two men entered the office of the company with drawn guns.

The bandits were told the payroll had been distributed, although it was in an adjoining office. Taking about $40 from the seven employes in the office, the two men fled in an automobile which an accomplice had waiting.

The two men, one masked, entered the office at 3:55 o'clock yesterday afternoon and demanded the payroll. Mrs. Mary Carey Secy and Miss Geneva Clinton, two of the office force, told them the payroll had been brought in at 1:30 o'clock and had been distributed an hour later.

In reality, the entire amount was in the next office, but was not found by the bandits. They asked the employes for the money they had and then ordered all seven into the vault at the point of their guns. The men did not shut the door, but warned the office workers not to raise an alarm for ten minutes.

RUN FROM OFFICE

Both men then ran from the office and leaped into a waiting automobile driven by a third man. They fled up Marion Hill before the victims of the hold-up could see the license number of the car. New Brighton police were immediately notified and are investigating today.

According to the description given police, one of the men was about six feet tall and wore a handkerchief across the lower part of his face and the other about five feet eight inches and did not wear a mask.

Two Persons Are In Hospitals Today As Result Of Cold Wave

Aliquippa Woman Almost Frozen To Death; Beaver Falls Man's Feet Frozen

Two persons are in local hospitals today suffering from effects of the prolonged cold weather which continues to grip Beaver County today in sub-freezing temperatures.

Slight relief is promised over the week-end as the Pittsburgh office of the Weather Bureau states there will be a slight rise in temperature.

WOMAN NEAR DEATH

Mrs. Mollie Meholick, 319 Park street, Aliquippa, was admitted to Rochester hospital at 7:15 o'clock Friday evening after having been found in her home almost frozen to death. Her condition is critical today, it was reported. No details were available this morning.

WORKMAN IN HOSPITAL

Zisaro Garrett, 2223 East avenue, Beaver Falls, is in Beaver Valley hospital today suffering from frozen feet received while at work Friday. He is a plasterer by trade and worked in a house under construction in Beaver Falls all day yesterday. In the evening he went to the hospital when his feet began to pain him and discovered the members were frozen.

SOUTH STILL SUFFERS

Sub-zero temperatures extended far into the South, today adding to the suffering and damage caused by a week-long cold wave.

A record low of nine below zero was recorded at 5:30 a. m. at the Birmingham, Ala., airport. Nearly all of Tennessee and the north portions of Mississippi, Alabama and Georgia recorded sub-zero temperatures.

It was one below at Jackson, in central Mississippi, and in Atlanta the mercury had dropped three degrees in an hour to four above and was still falling.

Florida, where orange growers had

(Continued on Page Ten)

FLASHES :

By the United Press

COLLEGE HEADS ELECT

HARRISBURG, Jan. 27—Clement C. Williams of Lehigh University today headed the Pennsylvania Association of College Presidents, succeeding G. Morris Smith of Susquehanna University. Fred Pierce Corson of Dickinson College was elected vice-president, William P. Tolley of Allegheny College, secretary, and Norman E. McClure of Ursinus, treasurer.

APPROVE APPOINTMENT

NEW YORK, Jan. 27—The Federal Council of Churches of Christ in America, has approved, with reservations, President Roosevelt's appointment of Myron C. Taylor as his personal representative at the Vatican to work for world peace.

JACK CHAUCER WINS

LEOPARDSTOWN, Eire, Jan. 27—H. L. Egan's Jack Chaucer, third among the favorites, today won the Red Cross steeplechase, run under the auspices of the Irish hospital sweepstakes. Sir Alexander Maguire's Sterling Duke was second and Miss B. Kearns' Knockadroleen ran third.

BLAST FURNACE DOWN

PITTSBURGH, Jan. 27. — Carnegie-Illinois Steel Corporation's blast furnace operations were reduced to 20 out of a total of 28 in the Pittsburgh district today with the banking of one furnace in its Duquesne Works. It was the first change in blast furnace production of the U. S. Steel Corp. subsidiary since Oct. 21, 1939.

Insurance Men Meet For Monthly Dinner

The Beaver County Association of Insurance Agents held its monthly dinner meeting Friday evening at the Nicholas Grill, Ambridge, with James W. Doncaster, Rochester, president, presiding.

The group discussed the insurance contract the Home Owners' Loan Corporation has with the Stock Company's Association, which will expire in the near future. It is understood that with the cancellation of this contract, the H. O. L. C. will place its insurance on mortgaged property.

Plans for a proposed "safety campaign" for Beaver county also were discussed. Information regarding such plans will be presented at the next meeting of the association, Friday, February 16.

Mr. Doncaster spoke briefly of his recent trip to Europe, particularly regarding insurance. At the invitation of Beaver agents, the February meeting will be held in Beaver.

County Man Heads Memorial Craftsmen

Fred O. Schleiter, Beaver, of O. Schleiter's Sons, Freedom, was elected president of the Pennsylvania Cemetery Memorial Craftsmen, at the annual meeting of the organization held this week in Harrisburg. George R. White, Claysville, was chosen secretary - treasurer. They are elected for one-year terms.

Mr. Schleiter for the past several years has served as secretary of the Pittsburgh Memorial Art Club, a group of Cemetery Memorial dealers in the Pittsburgh district.

Bar Committees Are Named By Court

Judges Frank E. Reader and Henry H. Wilson today announced the appointment of two committees of the Bar Association for 1940. The committees are:

Law Library—Attorneys Harold F. Reed, Beaver; Thompson Bradshaw, New Brighton; Leonard L. Ewing, Beaver Falls; Robert E. McCreary, Monaca, and Thomas C. Buchanan, Beaver.

Board of Law Examiners—Attorneys Forest G. Moorhead, Beaver; Charles R. Eckert, Beaver; Lawrence M. Sebring, Beaver; Myron E. Rowley, Aliquippa, and E. E. Autenreith, New Brighton.

Weather Forecast
Fair and continued cold tonight; slightly warmer Friday, with light snow by night

THE DAILY TIMES

ROCHESTER-BEAVER-MONACA
FREEDOM—BRIDGEWATER—CONWAY—VANPORT—MIDLAND

Local History
Scudder Hart Peirsol, grandson of an early local pioneer, was one of the outstanding educators of Western Pennsylvania 60 years ago.

ESTABLISHED APRIL 2, 1874 | BEAVER AND ROCHESTER, PA., THURSDAY, FEBRUARY 15, 1940 | BY CARRIER 15 CENTS A WEEK—3 CENTS PER COPY

MONACA TAX LEVY FOR 1940 UNCHANGED

COUNTY DIGS OUT OF RECORD SNOW

IONACA COUNCIL FIXES BORO TAX, APPROVES BUDGET

ifteen-Mill Levy Unchanged; Budget For 1940 Fixed At $101,793

Budget Provides $70,893 For General Borough Purposes, $30,900 For Water Dept.

Final adoption of the budget for 940 and passage of an ordinance ixing the millage for the year featured a regular session of Monaca Council, Wednesday night.

The budget is in the sum of $70,893 or general borough operations and 30,900 for the municipal water department.

Ordinance No. 389, fixing the tax or the year at 15 mills, the same s last year, was passed on final eading.

The report of Burgess Elmer E. Ricks and the Police Department or January showed three arrests nd fines amounting to $12.50.

Progress was reported on all W. P. A. projects in the borough. A. Howard Brown, president, presided

Girl Held For Murder In Aliquippa Death

Shirley Moore, 20, colored, 1604 Cliff street, Pittsburgh, is held today in Beaver County jail on charges of murder according to Coroner H. C. McCarter. The charges were preferred Wednesday following a coroner's inquest held in Aliquippa on the death of Mrs. Lula Mae Clark 30, colored, 307 Park street, Aliquippa, who was stabbed to ... Saturday night in a brawl in an Aliquippa tavern.

The young Pittsburgh girl and a companion, Clifford Myers, colored, same address, were taken into custody by Aliquippa police, but Myers was released after questioning.

Monaca Workers To Seek New Contract

Union employes of the U. S. Sanitary Manufacturing Company, Monaca, will meet tonight to consider action on the company's refusal to grant a wage increase and union shop, Joseph Timko, sub-regional director of the Steel Workers Organizing Committee, said today.

Timko said that in all probability a strike vote would be taken or arrangements made for conducting a strike vote.

He charged that the company refused to grant any concessions in a new contract. The present contract expires February 28. He said that although the company has agreed to renew the present document, the union's position is that if the contract is not replaced with an improved contract the union will call a strike.

SNOW CLOSES SCHOOLS

SCRANTON, Feb. 15—All schools in Lackawanna County, except those in the borough of Troop, were closed today because of the heavy snow storm. The snowfall on Scranton measured 14 inches, and another light snow began falling today.

Great Game Of Politics

— By Frank R. Kent —
(Copyright, 1939)

HER JUDGMENT POOR

Washington, Feb. 15.

BEFORE the meeting of the American Youth Congress in Washington last week wholly fades from the public mind it seems worthwhile, for the sake of the record, to sum up some of the undisputed facts. This is the organization practically mothered by Mrs. Roosevelt. She took it in her arms, constituted herself its chief defender, publicly proclaimed her fondness for its leaders, attended every session, talked to it at length.

—o—

NO one quarrels with Mrs. Roosevelt about that. She is a very good woman and deeply sympathetic with a great many causes and things. Once in response to some rather mild criticism she pleaded that she and her children be "allowed to lead our normal lives." No one has any objection to them doing that and ordinarily her taste in organizations, causes and people would be her own affair and nobody's business.

—o—

BUT when as wife of the President of the United States she puts the stamp of the White House upon an organization which has been criticized by a committee of Congress and is engaged in trying to get through legislation which will appropriate half a billion dollars of the public money, it would seem

(Continued on Page Four)

Monaca Youngsters Popular In Town

—Photo by Graule Studios

FRANCIS, ERNEST AND JOSEPH PERRI

Among the well-known youngsters of Monaca are the three sons of Mrs. Stella M. Perri and the late Dr. E. L. Perri, prominent physician. They are: Francis Regis, 14; Ernest Lawrence, 10, and Joseph Richard, 3. Francis, a member of the Freshman class at Monaca high school, was awarded the American Legion medal last year for the outstanding Eighth grade boy, an award presented annually by Monacatootha Post, No. 580, American Legion. Ernest, a student in the Fifth grade, First Ward building, stands high scholastically.

MONACA POPULARITY CONTEST ATTRACTS 58 GIRL ENTRANTS

Earle W. Timmons, chairman of the Popularity Committee for the Monaca Centennial, today announced the list of contestants who have been entered in the contest.

The contest will be in full swing Monday, February 19, when Monaca merchants, most of whom are participating, will give coupons for cash sales. Each 25 cent purchase entitles the purchaser to one coupon. A complete list of merchants participating will be announced later.

The most popular young lady will receive the title of "Miss Monaca" and $50; the second most popular will have the honor of being "Queen of the Centennial" and $35; third award, $25; fourth award, $15; fifth award, $10, and sixth award, $5. There also will be several other smaller awards.

TO DEPOSIT SLIPS

One large deposite box will be placed in front of the Monaca municipal building, where tickets are to be deposited and will be collected once a week by the committee.

The contest will run from February 19 through May 4. All tickets

(Continued on Page Seven)

Rochester Council President Selects Committee Members

Standing Committees For Boro Council Are Appointed By J. Warren Ganoe

J. Warren Ganoe, president of Rochester Borough Council, has named the various standing committees. The other members of Council are: Cornelius E. Mellon, Paul E. Perkins, William Graff, Gilbert Sohn, J. Oren Carpenter, Ernest F. Dentzer, George A. Bentel, William J. White, Robert J. Cloughley, James C. Wilson and Clifford H. Betz. The committees are:

Street—Carpenter, chairman; Perkins, Cloughley, White.

Finance—Dentzer, chairman; Sohn, Graff, Betz.

Sewer—Wilson, chairman; Carpenter, Mellon, Dentzer.

Fire and Water—Cloughley, chairman; Sohn, Perkins, White.

Light—Bentel, chairman; Wilson, Graff, Carpenter.

Health and Sanitary — Mellon, chairman; Betz, Dentzer, Sohn.

Building and Grounds — White, chairman; Carpenter, Cloughley, Graff.

Public Safety — Betz, chairman; Bentel, Sohn, Mellon.

Purchasing—Sohn, chairman; Betz, Perkins, Dentzer.

Ordinance — Perkins, chairman; Wilson, Carpenter, Bentel.

Litigation — Wilson, chairman; Mellon, Sohn, White.

Wharf—Graff, chairman; Bentel, Cloughley, Carpenter.

County Milk Producers' Group To Have Meeting

The secretary of the State Milk Producers Association is to speak at the meeting of the Beaver County branch, scheduled Saturday evening in the assembly room of the court house.

Triennial Court Of Appeals From Tax Assessments Opens

Commissioners And Assessors Sit As Board Of Revision On Tax Assessments

Beaver County Commissioners Art W. Coombs, Joseph S. Edwards and E. H. Markey were in session as the county board of tax assessment revision today as the triennial Court of Appeals opened at the court house.

The Court of Appeals will continue until March 6. A schedule has been prepared by the commissioners and property owners in the various boroughs and townships have been advised as to the date on which their complaints, if any, will be heard. The assessors of the various townships and boroughs attend.

CONTINUES NEXT WEEK

Appeals of residents of Ambridge borough and Harmony township

(Continued on Page Seven)

COUNTY FARMERS CHOOSE OFFICERS AT ANNUAL MEET

E. E. Duncan, Brighton Twp., Re-elected President Of Agricultural Extension Ass'n.

Secretary Of State Grange Speaks At All-Day Meeting In Chippewa Grange Hall

Fifty farmers and their wives attended the annual meeting of the Beaver County Agricultural Extension Association at Chippewa Grange hall Wednesday. Heavy snow prevented many people living off main roads from attending the meeting.

Miles Horst, secretary of the Pennsylvania State Grange, spoke in the afternoon. Mr. Horst stressed the importance of sound management in farming endeavor. He said that lower prices for the things that farmers must buy, rather than higher prices for the commodities they sell, is one of the farmers' important needs at the present time.

E. E. Duncan, Brighton Township, was re-elected president of the Association. Harvey Fogel, Marion Township, was elected vice-president, east side; Ralph Stewart, Green Township, vice-president, south side; John Braun, Chippewa Township, vice-president, west side; and John Elder, Chippewa Township, secretary-treasurer.

REPORTS ARE GIVEN

At the morning session projects reports were given on "Steer Feeding and Management," by R. W. Hartenbach, Center Township; "Producing Plants that Succeed," by Paul Arnold, Chippewa Township; "Remodeling Clothing, a 4-H Project," by Isabelle Searight, Raccoon Township; "Hybrid Corn," by T. N. Gillespie, North Sewickley Township; "Furniture Slip Covers," by Mrs. Martin Koehler, New Sewickley Township; "Strip Farming," by Kenneth Brenner, New Sewickley Township; "4-H Club Work," by C. D. Morley, Asst. County Agent.

At the afternoon session County Farm Agent R. M. Gridley gave a report of his work throughout the year. Miss Lois M. Laughlin reported on home economics extension activities, and J. M. Fry, State College, discussed briefly extension work from an administrative standpoint.

Dog Quarantine Imposed In County

Due to the increased number of rabies cases in the county within the past few months, a 100-day quarantine on dogs has been imposed in the county, effective today, according to Dr. H. J. McLaren, County Medical Director.

All police, peace and special officers have been requested to cooperate in the enforcement of the quarantine and to eliminate the large number of unlicensed dogs and dogs running at large throughout the county.

Dog owners have been requested to comply with the quarantine and to keep their dogs tied, as well as procure licenses for them. It is believed this will result in the reduction of the number of rabies cases.

Don't Forget To Feed Your Bird And Animal Friends During Snow

Don't forget your bird and animal friends! With deep snow blanketing the county, birds—along with rabbits, squirrels and other game—are unable to obtain food from the ground. So, clear a spot in your yard and scatter bread crumbs, suet, green vegetables, grain and other foods so that the birds and animals can eat until they can forage for themselves again.

Heads GOP Committee

SHERIFF C. J. O'LOUGHLIN

Sheriff Charles J. O'Loughlin has been elected chairman of the Central Republican Committee of Aliquippa, succeeding the late Attorney Harry W. Leonard, who died several weeks ago. William J. Fowler has been re-elected treasurer.

A new leader for Precinct No. 8, West Aliquippa, will be named later. Albert K. Weigel, No. 8 precinct leader several years, plans to move from the West Side to Franklin avenue. Other precinct leaders in the borough are: No. 1, Paul Smith; No. 2, William Williams; No. 3, Louis A. Smith; No. 4, Edward Mooney; No. 5, Charles W. Lucas; No. 6, Robert McIlvain; No. 7, Bruce Weitzel; No. 9, W. J. Fowler; No. 10, Arthur Tracy.

Two Contracts Let By Rochester Boro School Authorities

Emergency Lighting Plant To Be Installed In High School Building

The monthly meeting of the Rochester Board of Education, postponed from last Monday, was held Wednesday evening in the high school building.

The Reno Electric Company, Ambridge, was awarded the contract for the installation of a 3,000-watt emergency lighting plant in the high school building to replace the present unit. This company, whose bid of $820 was the lowest, will install a Kohler lighting plant.

Authorization was made for a survey of the new school property adjoining the present athletic field. A cross-section will be made preparatory to seeking a project for the installation of a drainage system on that portion to be used for athletic purposes.

The secretary was instructed to seek approval at Harrisburg of the

(Continued on Page Seven)

Minor Judiciary Group To Meet This Evening

Plans for the banquet to be held Thursday evening, February 29, in the Penn Beaver Hotel, Rochester, are to be discussed this evening at the special meeting of the Beaver County Minor Judiciary Association to be held this evening at 8 o'clock in the assembly room of the court house. All members have been urged to attend this special session.

FIREMEN BATTLE SNOW DRIFTS TO GET SICK MAN TO HOSPITAL

After fighting their way through deep snow drifts and aided by the Pennsylvania Department of Highways "bulldozer," the Rochester Volunteer Fire Department First-Aid unit, after 2½ hours of hard labor, Wednesday evening succeeded in removing Joseph Ineman, who is ill, from his home in Allendale to Rochester hospital.

The call for the fire department ambulance was received at 8 o'clock. Warren D. Miller, Kenneth Haney and Charles St. Clair promptly responded. When within three-fourths of a mile of the Ineman home, the ambulance was unable to proceed further because of the bad road conditions.

HIGHWAY WORKERS AID

Taking the cot from the ambulance, the ambulance crew tramped through snowdrifts, hip deep at some places, toward the Ineman home, leaving the ambulance at the intersection near the Catholic cemetery, where they were forced to return.

The "bulldozer" operated by "Joe" Uzmack, of Library, Pa., and his helper, Ernest Traylor, Vanport, joined the ambulance unit and ploughing through the snowdrifts succeeded in towing a light truck to the Ineman home and back to the ambulance where the crew awaited the patient and removed him to the hospital for treatment, arriving there at 10:30 o'clock.

The Rochester Volunteer Fire Department ambulance service is given free to all persons in need of the service.

EASTERN SEABOARD BATTERED TODAY BY GALES, SNOW

No Immediate Danger Of Flood Seen In Pennsylvania Despite Snow

Storm Leaves Trail Of Dead, Widespread Damage In Several Eastern States

The record blanket of snow covering every one of Pennsylvania's 45,126 square miles does not in itself constitute a serious flood threat, L. F. Conover of the federal-state flood forecasting service said today.

Conover, chief of the United States Weather Bureau at Harrisburg, explained that over-flows of the state's water sheds usually are caused when a number of conditions, such as heavy rain, snow followed by a sudden thaw and serious ice-jams, occur closely together.

He pointed out that the snow, although it ranges to more than 20 inches in some sections and is generally heavy throughout the state, will not raise the present below-normal river levels seriously unless it is followed by a sudden thaw and prolonged rains or other adverse conditions.

SEVEN PERSONS DIE

At least seven deaths were attributed directly or indirectly to the storm and a number of persons were injured in automobile accidents and falls on icy pavements.

Meanwhile, the highways department had 14,000 men on the job clearing roads of high drifts and sub-snow ice, which made highway travel extremely dangerous and in many cases halted traffic completely. The department had all its own equipment in operation and rented 868 trucks and plow to meet the emergency. Ashing of slippery stretches will follow snow removal.

Hundreds of motorists were stranded on highways and rural routes, and several instances were reported in which rural school pupils were forced to remain away from home overnight and had to stay with volunteer hosts.

VILLAGES ISOLATED

A number of small communities were marooned with huge snow drifts covering roads leading to them for miles. Communication and electric lines were down.

Thousands of children in various parts of the state had a vacation from school yesterday and many of them probably will remain away from class rooms until Monday.

The tri-state section of Eastern Pennsylvania, Delaware and Southern New Jersey experienced belated relief from the blizzard which continued today. Traffic generally was halted and schools were closed in rural districts and at Harrisburg, Scranton, Wilkes-Barre and other large communities. Fourteen school children were marooned in a bus for seven hours at Lewes, Del.

Hundreds of Pennsylvania and New Jersey homes were darkened when power lines went down.

SEABOARD BATTERED

A storm which for almost 24 hours battered the eastern seaboard from North Carolina to Ontario and left most of it buried under three to 20 inches of snow moved ocean-

(Continued on Page Seven)

B. & W. Tube Firm Agrees To Election Demanded By SWOC

Company Approves Election To Be Conducted By Labor Board At Beaver Falls

The Babcock and Wilcox Tube Company today agreed to a National Labor Relations Board election among the 1,899 employes at its Beaver Falls plant.

The agreement was made today at a hearing before Examiner Charles Persons, with company counsel John E. McLaughlin, Jr., announcing that the company had no objection to an election and will cooperate fully with the Board.

The election would determine whether Local 1082 of the Steel Workers Organizing Committee has a majority of employes at the plant.

UNION CLAIMS 1,031

Homer McClain, Beaver Falls, financial secretary of the Local, testified that the union has 1,031 members at the plant. At present the SWOC has a contract with the company covering only its own members. Foremen, assistant foremen, supervisors and salaried employes would be excluded under the proposal of the SWOC. It was agreed that the February 11 payroll would be the basis for determining eligibility to vote.

The company operates a plant at Barberton, O., but bargaining rights there are held by the American Federation of Labor through a Federal labor union.

Workmen Struggle To Clear Highways Of Deep Drifts

Beaver County residents continued today to dig out of nearly twenty inches of snow which fell during a twenty-six-hour blizzard, the worst snow storm in the history of the county.

Although the snow ended Wednesday night after falling steadily since Tuesday afternoon, automobile traffic and transportation facilities were still demoralized today, numerous rural schools remained closed and homes in outlying farm districts were completely isolated because of deep drifts blocking highways.

It was estimated that slightly less than twenty inches of snow fell in the county, eclipsing the previous record of nearly sixteen inches set in 1902.

Scores of employes of the State Highway Department, the county Road and Bridge Department and borough and township workers struggled frantically to clear the heavy snow from highways and streets and re-open closed roads to traffic.

In addition to being late for work Wednesday morning, many residents of outlying districts were forced to leave their automobiles along the highways and walk into town and walk home again last night. Many rural residents were unable to reach town at all and rural students attending Valley schools were unable to get to classes.

AUTOS ABANDONED

Scores of automobiles were abandoned, both on rural highways and in borough streets when they became stalled in the deep drifts. School buses were unable to operate over the clogged roads and buses and trains were unable to maintain their schedules.

Many motorists were unable to take their cars from their garages yesterday, or having once removed them, were unable to return them there.

Attendance at all county schools was disrupted because many pupils were unable to reach the school buildings from their homes.

SCHOOLS REMAIN CLOSED

Schools in Brighton township, it was reported, will not re-open until Monday. Hopewell township schools will be closed until Monday and at least two schools, Boggs and Romigh were closed in New Sewickley township, roads being blocked by drifts several feet deep. Center township schools were closed today but will re-open Friday, it was said.

St. Felix school, Freedom parochial school, is closed today due to weather conditions. Many of the students were unable to attend classes Wednesday, but those who did, including a number from rural sections, remained. Classes will be resumed Friday, however, according to Rev. Fr. Stephen Bieneman, pastor of the Freedom parish.

OPENING HIGHWAYS

Crews of the county division of the State Highway Department are being staggered today to keep men constantly at work battling the drifts and opening roads clogged by snow. More than 200 men are

(Continued on Page Seven)

Two Killed, Woman Wounded In Isolated Washington Co. Home

Police, Doctor Battle Snow Drifts In Attempt To Reach Scene Of Killings

By the United Press

WASHINGTON, Pa., Feb. 15—An automobile carrying two state policemen and a physician today battled waist-deep snow drifts to reach an isolated farm house east of here where a man was reported slain and another committed suicide last night.

The physician went along to treat the wife of the slain man, who was wounded in both arms as she tried to shield her husband, whose assailant forced her to pull the trigger that sent a fatal shotgun charge into the slayer's own chest.

Police authorities here were informed of the murder-suicide in a telephone call by Charles Owens, a farmer, who lives near the scene of the tragedy, about seven miles east of here.

The slain men, Owens said, were Ralph Caldwell, 35, and Glenn Plants, 28, neighboring farmers. Mrs. Caldwell was wounded.

BROKE INTO HOUSE

Owens said Phillips told him Plants appeared at the Caldwell house about 8 o'clock last night. Caldwell answered a knock at the door, but slammed it shut when he saw Plants was armed with a shotgun.

Undeterred, Plants walked around the house and peered in a kitchen window. Seeing Plants, Mrs. Caldwell threw her arms around her

(Continued on Page Seven)

Malone Endorsed By Governor, Torrance

By the United Press

HARRISBURG, Feb. 15.—James F. Malone, Jr., Allegheny County co-leader of Gov. Arthur H. James' campaign for election, was assured today of a place on the Republican primary ticket. James announced that Malone was his choice for the nomination of GOP candidate for State Treasurer and James F. Torrance, state Republican chairman, said he was satisfied that "Jim Malone's candidacy will have the approval of the voters in the 67 counties."

Railroaders Aid Man Who Lost Leg Four Years Ago In Mishap

A Conway man whose leg was amputated following a traffic accident four years ago, looked to the future with confidence today, thanks to the 300 members of Lodge No. 345, Brotherhood of Railroad Trainmen.

Hearing of the plight of Paul Van Moos, a former trainman and conductor in the Conway yard of the Pennsylvania Railroad, the Brotherhood members "chipped in" and bought him an artificial limb, and have assured him of a better job. Since the accident, Van Moos had been selling household articles from door-to-door in an effort to make a living.

Girls Reopen Court House Restaurant

The Court House restaurant, recently closed by illness of Mrs. Minnie McMinn, has been reopened by three young women, including two sisters. They are Betty Irons, Peggy and Delia Renner. They serve lunches, noon meals and evening dinners.

Former Beaver Man Dies In Texas Home

William Brandon Carlon, 60, former well-known resident of Beaver, died in the family home, 1648 Richmond road, Houston, Tex., Wednesday morning, according to word received today in the Valley by relatives.

Mr. Carlon, employed for many years by the Pure Oil Company, had resided in Texas the past 10 years. He was a member of the Houston Methodist church and the New Castle Consistory. When he resided in Beaver he was a member of the Beaver Methodist church and St. James Lodge, No. 457, F. and A. M.

Surviving are his widow, Mrs. Mary Frew Carlon, a former Baden resident; one son, William Brandon Carlon, Houston; and five daughters, Mrs. George J. Lack and Mrs. Milton Andrews, Houston; Frances, Elizabeth and Lola Ann, at home, and the following brothers and sisters: F. C. Carlon, Oil City; G. M. Carlon, Washington, D. C.; Sumner S. Carlon, Beaver; J. E. Carlon, Syracuse, N. Y.; Mrs. Walter A. Gordon, Rochester, and Mrs. Margaret Givler, Cleveland, O. Three aunts also survive. They are: Mrs. Carrie Bovard, Mrs. Mary Bolton and Mrs. Jessie Anderson, Beaver.

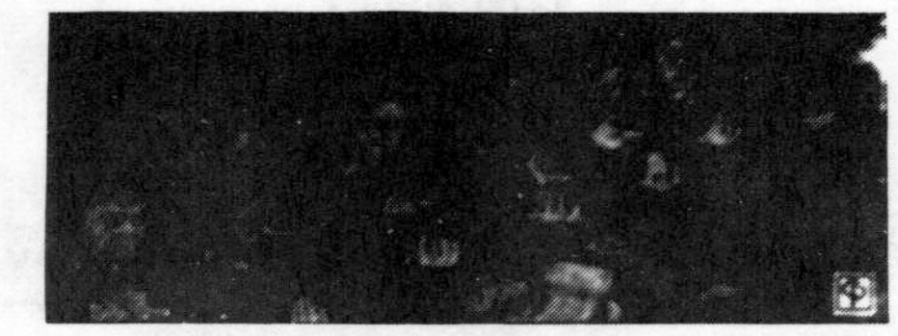

BANG! BANG! BANG!—Sharpshooters of Drexel Institute in Philadelphia line up for a "shot" in the school gym.

THE DAILY TIMES

NEWS OF SPORTING EVENTS

BILL ANDERSON, Sports Editor — BEAVER AND ROCHESTER, PA., — MONDAY, FEBRUARY 19, 1940

SAILS IN THE WIND—Yachts in Miami-Nassau race make a pretty picture against the cloudy sky.

GENEVA COLLEGE QUINT TOPS WAYNESBURG IN CLOSE GAME

Covenanters Passers Tackle Duquesne Five at Pittsburgh Tonight; Billie and Winters Are Scoring Stars

The Geneva College basketball team, with two successive upset victories over favored district foes on the record book, moves into Pittsburgh tonight to tackle the powerful Duquesne University quintet in the Bluffites' gym. In their previous clash with the Dukes the Genevans came out on the short end of a 24 to 33 score.

Saturday night before a crowd of about 1,000 wild-eyed fans the Covenanter passers achieved their second unexpected victory in three days by downing the favored Waynesburg College team, 40 to 37, in a game that was packed with excitement from start to finish.

Leading the Covenanters in scoring were John Billie, crack sophomore, and Ray Winters, dependable senior. Between them they accounted for all but five of the points scored by the Genevans, Billie getting 20 on eight field goals and four fouls, and Winters cutting the cords for seven fielders and one foul for 15 points. Taggart and Kidder each made a foul and Hartshorn got one basket and one foul.

Bob Simmers, the Jackets' classy center, was off on his shooting and was held to a total of five points, while scoring honors for the Wolfpack were claimed by Jack Beisler, forward, who hit for seven twoplyers and two fouls for 16 points.

Winters, whose shooting from the side and corners aided the Covenanters greatly in penetrating the zone-defense thrown up by the Jackets, dropped in the first field goal from the side. Pasquale followed suit for Waynesburg, and Billie converted a free throw. Pasquale again tied the score with a foul, but Hartshorn took a pass from Billie to ring up a fielder that sent the Genevans off to a lead that mounted to 11-6 at the quarter.

That was the widest margin separating the two clubs during the game. By the halftime intermission the Wolfpack, led by Beisler, had whittled the Gold and White's advantage to two points at 20-18.

Only once during the game was Waynesburg able to gain the lead. That was in the third period when two consecutive goals and a foul by Beisler brought the score to 25-24 in favor of the Jackets, but Kidder's foul and Billie's sixth bucket of the evening made it 29 to 27, Geneva, as the final quarter began.

The game was finished amid the wildest excitement the Tiger gym has seen for sometime. A one-handed heave by Brady, Jacket substitute, knotted the score at 37-37 with 2 minutes left to play, and with both teams fighting for the ball Simmers fouled Billie, who promptly converted. A moment later the clever forward took a pass under the hoop and dropped it through the cords. There was no more scoring although the final minute of play saw the Jackets fighting desperately for possession of the ball. Red Hartshorn was fouled but missed the free throw. After that the Covenanters froze the ball until time ran out.

While Billie and Winters carried off scoring honors, other members of the Geneva team turned in sterling performances. Taggart, freshman center, rendered valuable aid in penetrating Waynesburg's zone defense, and Kidder and Hartshorn starred on defense and also set up many shots for Billie and Winters. The lineups:

GENEVA

	G.	F.	Pts.
Winters, f	7	1-2	15
Billie, f	8	4-6	20
Taggart, c	0	1-1	1
Kidder, g	0	1-1	1
Hartshorn, g	1	1-4	3
Zillian, g	0	0-0	0
Milanovich, c	0	0-0	0
Totals	16	8-14	40

WAYNESBURG

	G.	F.	Pts.
Pasquale, f	2	1-1	5
Beisler, f	7	2-3	16
R. Simmers, c	2	2-3	6
Anthony, g	1	0-2	2
Byers, g	1	0-0	2
Coulson, c	0	0-0	0
Brady, g	1	0-0	2
Varnak, f	2	0-0	4
Totals	16	5-9	37

Score by periods:

Geneva	11	9	9	11—40
Waynesburg	6	12	9	10—37

Referee, Hetra. Umpire, Allison.

Alston And Gennock Hold Scoring Leads

The pace-setters in both Section 11 and Section 3 maintained their leads in the local scholastic cage games Friday evening as Dave Alston, Midland, advanced his total beyond the 200 mark while Gennock, New Castle, held his lead as his team was idle.

Bill Supak, Freedom forward, set a new scoring record for Section 11 as he poured 25 points through the nets against Beaver topping the old record for the year of 23 held jointly by Mel Leonard of Rochester and Alston.

The leaders:

SECTION 11

D. Alston, Midland, 204; Supak, Freedom, 133; Beeken, Beaver, 123; Swink, Monaca, 113; Hunter, Midland, 108.

SECTION 3

Gennock, New Castle, 107; Bar, Aliquippa, 103; Murphy, Ellwood City, 87; Thomas, New Brighton, 86; Sentak, New Brighton, 82; Rays, Beaver Falls, 82.

SPORT SLANTS

By BILL ANDERSON
SPORTS EDITOR

Last week the Geneva College basketball team played three games, two at home and one away, and is booked for three more contests this week, but all of them will take place on opponents' floors. Tonight Coach Smiley Weltner will take his club to Pittsburgh for a battle with the sensational Duquesne University five which already holds a 33 to 24 victory over the Covenanters. Thursday night the gold and white meets Grove City at Grove City, and on Saturday night will oppose Westminster's Titans at New Wilmington.

Geneva and Duquesne opened basketball relations back in 1914, and since then the two schools have engaged in 33 hardwood encounters, the Dukes winning 25 and Geneva eight. While the record of games won and lost would seem to show the series had been one-sided, such has not been the case for many of the 25 games won by the Dukes were exceedingly close affairs and were won by margins of three to five points. The first game this year was an exciting one and the Covenanters were in it right down to the finish.

Three of Beaver Valley's numerous sportsmen's clubs are scheduled to hold meetings this week. The Ambridge district Sportsmen's Association meets tonight at the American Legion hall, 310 Third street, Ambridge, at eight o'clock. The Beaver Falls Sportsmen's Association meets Thursday evening at eight o'clock in the Legion rooms in the city building with Rollin Heffelfinger as the principal speaker, and on Friday night at eight o'clock the Rochester Sportsmen's club at the municipal building, the program will include speakers, movies and door prizes.

Mr. Chick Davies, Duquesne University coach, was an interested spectator at the Geneva-Waynesburg basketball game at Beaver Falls, Saturday night. The Duke mentor, whose team boasts a record of 11 straight wins and a total of 13 wins in 14 starts, was on hand to get a line on both the Geneva and Waynesburg teams, since his passers will face both this week, meeting the Covenanters at the Duke gym tonight, and Waynesburg on the Jackets' court on Wednesday evening. Because the Covenanters appear to have belatedly hit their best stride as tonight's game looms as a more serious test for the Dukes than it did a week ago. In their last two games the Genevans upset both Pitt and Waynesburg and a victory over the strong Duquesne team would just about make the season an outstanding success.

BRIEFS Moe Rubenstein is pointing his Ambridge high school passers for the WPIAL Class A eliminations in Pitt Stadium, but we bet he won't want to lose Tuesday's clash with Aliquippa although the game cannot effect the Section 3 championship. Saturday night Rubenstein and his varsity players were geusts at the Geneva-Waynesburg game. The Kinsley House Pittsburgh, will sponsor the Junior A. M. A. boxing championship on Feb. 29, March 1, 2 and 3.

The Senior A. M. A. championships are scheduled at the Pittsburgh Athletic Association, March 28, 29 and 30, and the winners will be eligible to compete in the National Senior A. A. U. tourney in Boston, April 8, 9 and 10. A movement is on foot among Allegheny Mountain Association officials and supporters to perpetuate the memory of the late John T. Taylor, organizer and secretary, by inaugurating an annual award to be known as the "John T. Taylor" award, to the outstanding A. A. U. athlete of the district. It's doubtful if any man handicapped by an artifical leg could be a successful big league pitcher, but you can't have anything but good wishes for Monte Stratton, the Whitesox twirler who lost a leg in a hunting accident in 1938, as plans to have a try for a berth. Stratton has a job with the Whitesox as coach, but he thinks he can pitch again, although he admits the fielding part may be more than a little difficult. Benny Andy, Aliquippa boxer, is about ready to return to the ring wars after recovering from an appendectomy. Phillipi, W. Va. high school boasts a basketball player, Darl Wilmoth, who has scored 366 points in 13 games for a 28.1 average.

They Lead Indiana to Bid for Big Ten Basketball Crown

Marv Huffman
Guard
Bill Menke
Center
Paul Armstrong
Forward
Bob Dro
Guard

Indiana university's cage squad, coached by Branch McCracken, is making a strong bid for the Big Ten basketball crown won last year by Ohio State. The four players pictured above are leading the Hoosier attack.

Pirate Vanguard To Leave On Saturday

PITTSBURGH, Feb. 19. — Add signs of spring: The first party of players and officials of the Pittsburgh Pirate Baseball Club will leave here Saturday for the Pirate training site at San Bernardino, California.

Pirate President William E. Benswanger and 12 others will board a Pennsylvania Railroad train to get the annual spring training trek underway. Manager Frankie Frisch, who will leave from Chicago, expects to be awaiting the arrival of the first party of players upon their arrival in California. Actual training is expected to start Wednesday of next week.

PROS WIN THREE

The Pros won three games from the Nips as the girls of the Pittsburgh Screw and Bolt Company staged another bowling session at the Monaca alleys. Total pins were 1170 to 1068 and M. Pukanich, with a single game of 126 and a total of 311 for three games, was the individual star. Team scores:

Pros	382	384	404—1170
Nips	326	366	376—1088

Monaca Saxons Eliminated By New Castle As Contender For Eastern Division Title

Floor Calendar

TONIGHT
College
Geneva at Duquesne.
Grove City at Slippery Rock.

TUESDAY
High School, Section 11
Midland at Monaca.
Rochester at Freedom.
Zelienople at Beaver.
Mars at Evans City.
High School, Section 3
Ambridge at Aliquippa.
New Brighton at Beaver Falls.
Butler at New Caste.
Junior High
Monaca at Midland.
Beaver at College Hill.
Ambridge at Highland, Harmony Township.
College
West Virginia at Pitt.
St. Francis at Youngstown.
Thiel at Allegheny.
California T. at Frostburg.
Bethany at W. Va. Wesleyan.
St. Vincent at Mt. St. Marys.

WEDNESDAY
College
Duquesne at Waynesburg.
Penn State at Georgetown.
Bethany at Fairmont.
St. Vincent at Catholic U.
High School
West View at St. Veronica.

THURSDAY
College
Geneva at Grove City.
Penn State at Temple.

FRIDAY
College
Allegheny at Hobart.
Junior High
Monaca at Conway.
Leetsdale at Ambridge.
Beaver at Freedom.

SATURDAY
College
Pitt at Carnegie Tech.
Waynesburg at Fairmont.
West Virginia at Wash-Jeff.
Allegheny at Hamilton.
St. Vincent at Youngstown.
Geneva at Westminster.
West Liberty at California T.

Prize Under Milk Bottle

NILES, O. (UP)—Miss Bernice Burrows looked under the milk bottle on her front porch for a bill and found—a free ticket to the New York World Fair. It was the winning prize in a contest sponsored by a milk company.

New Castle Saxons Hand Monaca Club Second Defeat Of Season In Fast Game On Monaca High School Floor; Monaca Girls Win

The Monaca Saxons lost their last chance to claim the Eastern Division championship of the District Saxon Basketball League when they bowed to the New Castle Saxons, 47 to 56, in a fast game on the Monaca high school court Saturday night. The defeat was the second suffered by the Monaca team this season.

Both Monaca's defeats were at the hands of the New Castle quintet which clinched the eastern division title again for the third straight year. The New Castle team is undefeated this year in league competition.

New Castle built up a 16 to 11 lead in the first period of Saturday's game, and led 29 to 23 at the half. Monaca rallied in the final chapter but was unable to overtake the Lawrence Countians.

Greaf of New Castle claimed scoring honors with 23 points and Charles Sowash of Monaca followed with 19.

In the preliminary game the Monaca Girls' team defeated the Homestead, Pa., girls, 37 to 12, with J. Schuller and Fuller leading the attack with 11 points apiece.

Next Saturday the Monaca Saxons have an open date and will close their season on March 2, meeting the Salem, O., team at Salem. The lineups:

NEW CASTLE

	G.	F.	Pts.
Lang, f	4	2-4	10
Greaf, f	11	1-2	23
G. Binder, c	4	1-2	9
J. Binder, g	0	1-3	1
Snyder, g	5	1-2	11
Leinert, g	1	0-0	2
Totals	25	6-13	56

MONACA

	G.	F.	Pts.
Sowash, f	8	3-7	19
Schuller, f	2	0-0	4
M. Fuller, c	3	0-1	6
Kloos, g	2	1-2	5
Soppelt, g	2	1-1	5
Robitz, f	2	2-2	6
Theil, f	1	0-0	2
F. Fuller, c	0	0-0	0
Totals	20	7-13	47

Score by periods:

New Castle	16	13	13	14—56
Monaca	11	12	6	18—47

Referee—Zigerell.

MONACA GIRLS

	G.	F.	Pts.
Theil, f	3	1-3	7
J. Schuller, f	5	1-3	11
Fuller, c	5	1-3	11
Fenser, g	2	0-0	4
E. Schuller, g	2	0-0	4
Totals	17	3-9	37

HOMESTEAD GIRLS

	G.	F.	Pts.
Theil, f	0	0-0	0
Kraft, f	0	0-0	0
Schlett, c	0	1-2	1
Weprech, g	1	2-6	4
Leprech, g	1	1-5	3
Weber, f	1	0-4	2
Kramer, c	1	0-0	2
Totals	4	4-17	12

Spring IS Here! Dodgers Open Training Season

Proving that spring is here, the Brooklyn Dodgers open their training spiel at Clearwater, Fla., with Manager Leo Durocher showing mound recruits how the new pitching stance rule will work. The Dodgers are the first major league club to begin the long grind.

Connellsville Claims W. P. I. A. L. Swim Title

By the United Press

PITTSBURGH, Feb. 19—Connellsville High School held the WPIAL swimming championship today, having downed seven opponents and set three league records to gain the title for the third year in succession. The Corkers stroked up 48 points in the Carnegie Tech pool Saturday to become the first school since 1934 to win three years in a row.

Green Hornets Win Over Scout Cagers

The Green Hornets defeated the Bridgewater Boy Scouts, in a double header at the K. of P. Hall in Bridgewater Saturday morning. The Hornets won 38 to 32 and 12 to 11. The lineups:

Hornets	G.	F.	P.
J. Wilson, f	0	0	0
J. Deeley, f	9	0	18
M. Patterson, c	1	0	2
B. Yost, g	1	1	3
B. Gridley, g	6	1	13
Beeken, c	0	2	2
Totals	17	4	38

Boy Scouts	G.	F.	P.
L. Miller, f	1	0	2
W. Woodman, f	4	0	8
S. Holland, c	3	0	6
B. Truschel, g	5	0	10
B. Behanna, g	3	0	6
Totals	16	0	32

Monaca, Freedom Win In Catholic Men's Floor Loop

Phil Predo Counts 28 Points As Monaca Entry Crushes Beaver, 85 To 39

Monaca and Freedom emerged victorious Friday evening in the games played in the Catholic Men's Cage League on the Monaca High school floor. Monaca, loop leaders, crushed the Beaver team beneath an avalanche of points as Phil Predo paced the winners to an 85 to 39 victory. Predo tallied 28 points while Zigerelli had 21. The winners had a 21 to 9 advantage at the quarter and lengthened it to 38 to 15 at the half. As the last period opened the count stood at 65 to 25 and the winners added to their advantage in the last eight minutes.

North Rochester and Freedom staged a hard fought battle with Freedom having a slight edge in the first two periods. The winners led 15 to 11 at the quarter and 28 to 21 at the half-time intermission. In the third period Freedom scored 10 points to one for North Rochester but the losers rallied in the closing minutes but could not close the gap.

The lineups:

Monaca	G.	F.	P.
Predo, f	13	2	28
Marotti, f	2	0	4
Glass, c	8	0	16
Barco, g	8	0	16
Zigerelli, g	9	3	21
Totals	40	5	85

Beaver	G.	F.	P.
Cascio, f	3	1	7
Leary, f	5	0	10
Farelly, c	5	0	10
Haugh, g	1	1	3
Knott, g	1	1	3
Coughlin, g	0	0	0
Tompkins, g	3	0	6
Totals	18	3	39

Score by periods:

Monaca	21	17	27	20—85
Beaver	9	6	10	14—39

North Rochester	G.	F.	P.
Miganelli, f	1	0	2
Fusco, f	4	1	9
Fedele, c	1	1	3
Lombardi, g	0	0	0
Liberatore, g	0	1	1
Pinchotti, f	3	0	6
Piscione, c	3	0	6
Silipgne, f	1	0	2
Totals	13	3	29

Freedom	G.	F.	P.
Spagnolia, f	4	1	9
Ciani, f	2	0	4
B. Miller, c	5	1	11
Golletti, g	1	1	3
Bilotto, g	3	0	6
W. DeCanio, g	2	0	4
T. Miller, g	3	0	6
F. DeCanio, g	0	0	0
Totals	20	3	43

Score by periods:

North Roch.	11	10	1	7—29
Freedom	15	13	10	5—43

HIGH SCHOOL FLOOR TEAMS TO CLOSE SEASON TUESDAY

Monaca-Midland Clash Heads Program; Rochester Invades Freedom; Beaver Meets Zelienople

Members of the Monaca and Midland High school cage teams are having their final drills today in preparation for "Der Tag", Tuesday, when their game is to decide the championship of Section 11 or will throw the standing into a deadlock at the end of the season. In case of the latter, a playoff later this week or early next week will be necessary to determine the standard-bearer in the Class B eliminations for the WPIAL crown.

Both teams have swept through the season undefeated with the exception of their meeting in the first half of the schedule when Monaca emerged the victor by a 27 to 24 count in a close, hard-fought battle on the Midland floor. Tomorrow night the Monaca floor will be the scene of the second and perhaps final meeting of the two teams.

Any attempt to pit one team against the other on paper results only in confusion. Both have downed the same teams during the past season and most of them by sizeable margins.

Monaca has scored 570 points in 13 games to date for an average of 43.85 points per game. Their opponents record for the same length of time totals 322 points or 24.77 per game.

The Leopards have a slightly higher record for the same period as they have tallied 622 points, averaging 47.85 counters per game while their opponents have an average of 25.61 points.

Swink, Karcis, Linkovich and Figley are the sharpshooters for the defending Class B champs while Dave Alston, Hunter and DiCiccio are the leading scorers for the high-geared Leopard machine.

Local fans are not forgetting the thrilling game which ended the 1939 season as Midland downed the Southsiders to tie for the section toga. They also remember the Monacans won the playoff and went on to take the WPIAL Class B title. Tickets for the game have been on sale for several days in Monaca and Midland and have been selling fast.

The final game of the 1940 season also finds a number of other rivals of long standing meeting in this locality. Rochester journeys to Freedom and will attempt to avenge an early season defeat at the hands of the Bulldogs who have apparently found themselves and are a worthy opponent for any local five.

The Beaver high cagers will close a disasterous season by meeting the Zelienople high team on the Beaver court, and in the other section 11 game pits Mars against Evans City on the latter's court.

The Section 3 race lost some of its glamor when Ambridge claimed the championship last week but the well-founded rivalry between the teams scheduled for action Tuesday will probably revive interest. Ambridge plays at Aliquippa and the Steelers' followers still believe the Lippemen have the better team as they came within a minute of beating the champions in their first meeting.

Beaver Falls is to be host to New Brighton on the Tiger's floor and Butler travels to New Castle in the remaining game.

Freedom Gains In Monaca Dux League

The Freedom Nationals moved into second place in the Monaca Community Bowling league last week by taking three games from Silver Bar while the Franks dropped three to Phoenix Glass.

High individual scores this week were: One game—J. Hiltz, 219; F. Galdony, 212; J. Smith, 213; J. Battaglia, 209; A. Zemany, 209; Three games.N. Tuccinard, 539; A. Zemany, 538; F. Galdony, 537; F. Lyons, 503; J. Battaglia, 523.

TEAM SCORES

Freedom	784	769	784—2327
Silxer Bar	761	738	768—2267
Phoenix	825	730	787—2342
Franks	688	692	666—2046
Sons of Italy	716	828	736—2280
Graters	699	806	—724—2229
Monaca Nat'ls.	684	555	571—1710
Saxon	Forfeit		

TEAM STANDING

	Won	Lost
Sons of Italy	50	16
Freedom	45	21
Franks	43	23
Silver Bar	42	24
Phoenix Glass	39	27
Monaca Nat'ls.	34	32
Graters	30	36
Saxons	12	54

Schedule for This Week

Wednesday—Early
Graters vs. Monaca Nat'ls.
Franks vs. Freedom.
Wednesday—Late
Phoenix Glass vs. Silver Bar.
Sons of Italy vs. Saxons.

Riding High

WISCONS

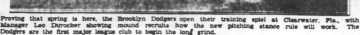

Chuck Fenske

Outstanding performer in the indoor track season this year, Chuck, former Wisconsin mile king, is being hailed as the coming world mile champion. Fenske has beaten Glenn Cunningham several times this winter.

Armstrong-Garcia Bout Is Postponed

By the United Press

LOS ANGELES, Feb. 19.—Cries of "running out" threaded through boxing circles today after the announcement that the 10-round middleweight championship fight between Henry Armstrong, Los Angeles negro and Ceferino Garcia, bolo-punching titleholder, had been postponed to March 1 because of a rope burn on Garcia's leg. The fight was scheduled for Thursday.

Beach Styles Tested

FAIRFIELD, Conn. (UP)—The question whether men should wear tops to their bathing suits became such an issue that the Park Commission this year decided on an experiment. In past years men had been required to cover their chests. The ban was lifted for this summer to study the reaction.

ADDITIONAL SPORT NEWS
ON PAGE NINE

Two of These Ten Film Stars Will Win "Oscars"

Greta Garbo
Robert Donat
Bette Davis
Clark Gable
Greer Garson
Mickey Rooney
Irene Dunne
The Academy award
Laurence Olivier
Vivien Leigh
James Stewart

Ten motion picture stars—five men and five women—have been nominated by the Academy of Motion Picture Arts and Sciences for consideration for the annual gold awards for best performances in 1939 motion pictures. The 10 eligible for the awards, gold statuets known to film folk as "Oscars," are shown above. The awards will be made in Hollywood, Feb. 29. Approximately 12,000 persons in the industry will choose the winners—an actor and an actress—from among the 10 nominees.

New Brighton News

Wedding Anniversary Celebrated Here By New Brighton Couple

Mr. And Mrs. Steven Blaho, Second Street, Observe Thirty-Fourth Anniversary

Mr. and Mrs. Steven Blaho, Second street, observed their thirty-fourth wedding anniversary Sunday with a family dinner. Covers for 14 were arranged at a nicely-decorated table. An informal social period was enjoyed following the dinner. Mr. and Mrs. Blaho were married 34 years ago Saturday, February 17.

Word has been received from Michael F. Winkler, son of Mr. and Mrs. M. Winkler, Eleventh avenue, of his transfer to the United States Army Signal School, Fort Monmouth, N. J. Winkler received the appointment in competition with other enlisted men.

The semi-monthly meeting of The Dial is to be held this evening in the Y.M.C.A.

New members are to be honored at the reception and tea to be held Wednesday afternoon by the New Brighton Woman's Club in the Fifth Avenue Methodist church.

Plans are being completed for the turkey dinner to be enjoyed Thursday evening by the Anderson-Adkins American Legion Post.

Rev. Berthold Jacksteit, Twelfth avenue, is one of the 228 students who received degrees at the University of Pittsburgh this month. Rev. Jacksteit received his Master of Arts degree.

Members of the Thelma Hardy Harris Society will meet Tuesday evening at the home of Mrs. Archie Blankenbicker in Sixth street.

The Statue of Liberty weighs 450,000 pounds (225 tons).

RADIO PROGRAMS

6 p. m.
KDKA, News, Movie Magazine; Melody Time
WCAE, Law for the Layman; News, Music
WJAS, Edwin C. Hill, News of the World

6:30 p. m.
KDKA, Music; Jack Hollister; Lowell Thomas.
WCAE, Reggie Childs Music Hits and Encores.
WJAS, Baron Elliott Music; Life Can Be Beautiful.

7 p. m.
KDKA, Easy Aces; Mr. Keen.
WCAE, Pleasure Time; I Love a Mystery.
WJAS, Amos 'n' Andy; Jimmy Fidler.

7:30 p. m.
KDKA, Tap Time.
WCAE, Let's Dance, Inside of Sports.
WJAS, Helen Mencken.

8 p. m.
KDKA, The Aldrich Family.
WCAE, Johnny Presents.
WJAS, Big Town; Edward G. Robinson.

8:30 p. m.
KDKA, Information, Please.
WCAE, Pot of Gold.
WJAS, Court of Missing Heirs.

9 p. m.
KDKA, Cavalcade of America.
WCAE, Battle of Sexes.
WJAS, We, the People.

9:30 p. m.
KDKA, Explorer's Club; G-Men and Crime.
WCAE, Fibber McGee and Molly.
WJAS, Concert in Rhythm.

10 p. m.
KDKA, WPA Symphony.
WCAE, Bob Hope.
WJAS, Glenn Miller Music; Americans at Work.

10:30 p. m.
KDKA, Music As You Like It.
WCAE, Uncle Walter's Doghouse.
WJAS, Americans at Work (ctd.); Four Clubmen.

11 p. m.
KDKA, News; Johnny Messner Orchestra.
WCAE, News Parade; Benny Burton Orchestra.
WJAS, News; Dick Stabile Orchestra.

11:30 p. m.
KDKA, Lou Breeze Orchestra.
WCAE, Blue Barron Orchestra.
WJAS, Bob Crosby Orchestra.

12 Midnight
KDKA, Al Marsico; 12:15, Herman Middleman; 12:30, Charles Barnet.
WCAE, Frankie Masters; 12:30, Lang Thompson; 1:00, Leonard Keller.
WJAS, Dance Orchestra.

SAFETY PIN REMOVED

McKEESPORT, Feb. 20 — An esophagoscope, one of medical science's latest aides, was credited today with saving the life of a Belle Vernon, Pa., child who swallowed a safety pin. McKeesport Hospital physicians used the delicate instrument to remove the pin from the throat of 20-months-old Carol Steele.

BEAVER THEATRE

The new Paul Muni starring picture "We Are Not Alone," adapted from the best-selling novel by James Hilton, author of "Goodbye, Mr. Chips," concludes tonight at the Beaver Theatre. "We Are Not Alone" has received unanimous acclaim from all the critics who previewed it in Hollywood.

Muni's role is a complete departure from the historical biographies he has done in the past several years. In "We Are Not Alone" he plays a modern, fictional character, a small town English doctor, who serves his patients with compassion and skill but is completely unable to remedy the pain in his own life. The film tells the story of his neither happy nor melancholy life in a little cathedral town, and of how the pattern of that life was shattered by his summons to attend a little Austrian dancer in a down-at-the-heel stock company. The story of the linked fates of these two is one of love, jealousy, passion and enduring faith.

When a Chicago gangster becomes an English Earl by inheritance, it develops into one of the most unusual motion picture situations ever filmed, and with Robert Montgomery departing from his customary genial playboy roles to give a startlingly realistics performance as the gangster, "The Earl of Chicago," opens tomorrow starring Robert Montgomery.

GRANADA THEATRE

"Wake Up and Cheer," Broadway's newest hit road show concludes its stage appearance at the Granada tonight. Headliners include Nat Nazarro, Jr., outstanding star of the famous New York Winter Garden show, with Carl Nixon and Carmen Sans from the Street of Paris revue; Naomi Ray and Eddie Harrison from the Radio City Music Hall; Idylle and Billy Shaw from the London Crazy Show; Marjorie Nelson delineator of the "oomph" in songs, and all their stooges which are sure-fire insurance against the blues, while the glamour girls contest winner beauty chorus selected from the various Miss Americas of 1939 contests and the Musi-Maniacs swing band complete one of the strangest casts of entertainers to take to the road in a popular price musical show in a decade.

The vivid story of Maximilian and Carlota is told dramatically by Medea Novara, Austrian-born star, Conrad Nagel and Lionel Atwill in "The Mad Empress," the screen offering in connection with the above stage show.

By special agreement with the producers, the management of the Granada Theatre has been able to arrange an early engagement of the new Warner Bros. film, "The Fighting 69th," co-starring James Cagney, Pat O'Brien and George Brent, which has excited so much favorable comment from critics who previewed it at the West Coast. It will open at the Granada on Wednesday.

Of the 28 men on Warner Bros. list of contract players, 18 have featured roles in "The Fighting 69th," a complete cast list issued from the Strand Theatre revealed today.

This figure sets a new Hollywood high for number of stars and important featured players under contract to one studio set for the same picture.

Perfect!

Winning a contest to find "the perfect photographic figure," in which 300 girls competed, Yvonne Duval was rewarded with a Hollywood screen ... Yvonne is a war baby, ...sace-Lorraine in 1918.

RIALTO THEATRE

That matchless producer-director combination of Darryl F. Zanuck and Henry King which gave to the screen such unforgettable productions as "In Old Chicago," "Alexander's Ragtime Band," "Stanley and Livingstone" and "Jesse James," offers its most spectacular film to date in Zanuck's production of "Little Old New York," now playing at the Rialto in Beaver Falls.

The superb cast is headed by such popular character artists as Alice Faye in her most colorful role as the fiery belle of the waterfront who falls headlong for handsome Robert Fulton; Fred MacMurray is seen as the burly shipbuilder engaged to build the Clermont, after Fulton's mode for the first steamboat; Richard Greene is seen as the dashing inventor himsef; and blonde Brenda Joyce has the role of the lovely girl who loved him, helped him to attain his dream in the face of ridicule, and who later became his wife.

"Little Old New York" is a robust, romantic drama of the good old days when the Astors and the Roosevelts were just starting on their way and vividly portrays the story of a fiery belle of the waterfront who fought for the love of handsome Robert Fulton, while the boisterous little old town cheered her on!

A large portion of the New York waterfront of the period was reconstructed for the film, including a flotilla of ocean-going sailing craft and river boats. The scene is a veritable forest of masts, crossyards and rigging and is one of the most realistic settings Hollywood has ever seen.

"Little Old New York" is augmented by a special laugh treat! Leon Errol in "Truth-Aches" and the latest in front page news. Here is one program you should place on your "must see" list.

Evening screenings are scheduled for 7:00 and 9:10.

MOTION PICTURES
Are Your Best
Entertainment

ORIENTAL THEATRE

A story of a great Broadway love affair is set to the music of some of America's best-loved melodies in "The Great Victor Herbert," the tuneful romance which concludes tonight at the Oriental Theatre, with Allan Jones, Mary Martin and Walter Connolly heading a large cast of popular players.

Victor Herbert, the great Irish-American composer and producer of some of the biggest hits in Broadway history, appears in the picture not as a member of the love team, but as the lasting friend of the two sweethearts, Jones and Miss Martin, the man who makes them the king and queen of the show world and helps them find happiness together. He is played by Connolly, whose resemblance to the late maestro is said to be amazing.

Against the fascinating background of gas-lit Broadway at the turn of the century—the world of Rector's and bustles, of Luchow's and hansom cabs, of the diamond horseshoe and Tony Pastor's— "The Great Victor Herbert" tells of the romance between a lovely, wide-eyed young girl determined to become a star and the handsome matinee idol of the day.

The picture traces the career of the two young stars, their rise to the heights of fame in Victor Herbert's great operettas, their struggle for marital happiness in the gilded, and mad-paced world of the theatre and their efforts to make another star out of their gifted daughter.

James Cagney's newest starring picture "The Fighting 69th," will be the next attraction opening tomorrow for the balance of the week. In "The Fighting 69th," he shares starring honors with Pat O'Brien and George Brent, with a featured cast including Jeffrey Lynn, Alan Hale, Frank McHugh and dozens of others.

MAJESTIC THEATRE

The greatest double horror show on earth concludes tonight at the Majestic. The titles of these sensational twin-thrillers are "The Return of the Frog" and "The Demon Barber of Fleet Street." You'll have to have a strong heart and a sturdy constitution to see this mammoth show . . . but, you'll have the grandest time ever and you'll experience sensations you've never had while viewing any other pictures you've ever seen.

Starring Jack Holt as a humanitarian research scientist, "Hidden Power," new Columbia drama due to open Wednesday, is said to provide a terrifying glance at the destructive power which can be generated in a science laboratory. The demonstration of the explosives which are developed in the film promises a dramatic indication of the role that science will play in the next great conflict.

According to his legion of fans, Holt has never had a better role than that of Stephen Garfield, the chemist whose accidental discovery arouses the enthusiasm of the munitions magnates. He is tempted with the prospect of wealth, intimidated with the threat of force, harassed by a nagging wife and faced with the break-up of his home, but he stubbornly clings to his ideals, refusing to become a party to mass-murder. This thrilling impasse is skillfully developed into a smashing climax in which Holt gambles the life of his eleven-year-old son against the skepticism of the medical profession.

"Jim Hanvey, Detective," starring Guy Kibbee, is the added feature for Wednesday and Thursday.

Circus Head Back

John Ringling North

John Ringling North, head of the Ringling Brothers and Barnum and Bailey combined circus, is pictured above as he arrived in New York on the liner Rex from a European tour on which he shopped for new oddities and attractions for his circus.

Star Model at 16

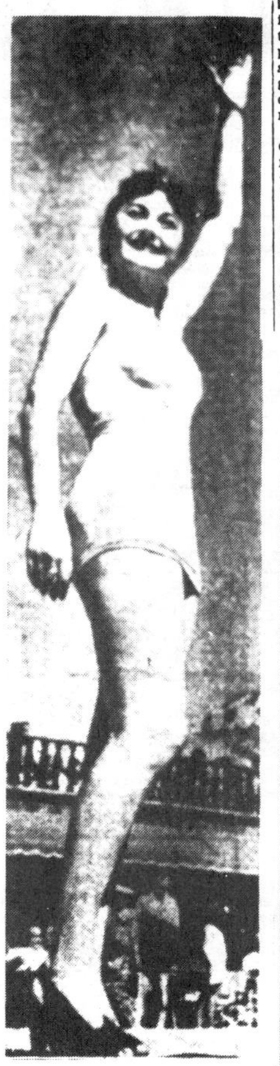

Miss Shirley Swede

Miss Shirley Swede, 16, is one of the most sought-after models now wintering at Miami, Fla.

URGES "YOUTH" MEETING

PITTSBURGH, Feb. 20—Reiterating his demand for a national youth conference to ascertain the "real aims" of American youth, U. S. Sen. James J. Davis, R., Pa., today offered a sponsor such a gathering.

YOU SAVE MONEY EVERY TIME YOU READ THE WANT ADS

CLASSIFIED ADVERTISING

This classified advertising department is for the convenience of the public. To insure publication the same day orders should be received by 10 a. m. Orders not received in time will be published the following day. All copy received subject to being edited or rejected by us. When sending advertisements by mail care should be used to write plainly giving complete instructions so that we may give efficient service in the preparation and publication of the advertisements. When possible, payment should accompany the order. This will be expected with orders from strangers. Cash with order, one cent a word for each publication. No advertisement published for less than 25 cents for each publication. Six consecutive publications for price of four. Extra charge will be made for use of large type. Classified advertisements not accompanied by cash will be charged at two cents per word with a minimum of 50 cents for each publication. This is absolutely necessary on account of the clerical work involved. Fifty per cent discount will be allowed on charge classified advertisements if paid for before expiration date. Usual cash rates will apply to advertisers having other running open accounts with us. The above is a local schedule applying only within Beaver County

Office Telephones

Beaver 1800 Rochester 2300

Political Announcements

For Congress
LOUIS E. GRAHAM
Beaver, Pa.
26TH DISTRICT
REPUBLICAN PRIMARIES
APRIL 23, 1940

Wanted

WANTED: Curtains to launder, medium size 25c, large size 35c a pair, handwork. Phone Beaver 2468-R. 2|26

WANTED: All kinds of typing to do at home, all work confidential and reasonable rates; will call for and deliver work. Inquire Maddalean Robinson, Freedom, or call Roch. 3317-M. 2|26-3|2 inc

WANTED: Parties interested in securing fill dirt. Can have dirt for hauling it away. Gas shovel will load trucks. 200 loads. Inquire 830 East Rochester Blvd., at once. Phone Roch. 9141. 2|26-3 2 inc

WANTED: Moving and hauling. Equipment for moving refrigerators. Inquire at Store, 830 East Rochester - Freedom Boulevard, next to Oscar's Cafe. Phone Rochester 9141. 2|24-3|1 inc

WANTED: Paper hanging and painting. Also paper removed by steam system. William Schmidt & Son, 338 Deer Lane. Phone Roch. 1908-W. 1940 wallpaper furnished reasonable. 2|22-28 inc

WANTED: Typewriting work to do at home by experienced young man; rates very reasonable. Call Roch. 3207 or inquire 626 Third Ave., Freedom. 2|21-27 inc

WANTED: Paper to remove by steam, no dirt or muss; prices very reasonable. Fred Hamilton, Vanport. Phone Beaver 2155-W. 2|20-26 inc

Wanted—To Buy

WANTED: To buy a small coal cook stove. Write "C. C." c/o DAILY TIMES, Beaver. 2|26

WANTED: To buy a farm for cash in Beaver County on improved road. Write, giving full details. Address "Farm," c/o DAILY TIMES, Beaver. 2|26-3|2 inc

WANTED: Good 1938 or 1939 car, preferably from individual who cannot meet payments and stands to lose it. Will assume payments. Confidential. No Dealers. Write "A-35" c/o DAILY TIMES, Beaver. 2|26

WANTED: To buy second hand living room suite (not mohair), fair condition. Also mahogany or maple dresser. Call Roch. 1230. 2|26

Wanted—To Rent

WANTED TO RENT: 3-4-5-room house with or without garden, or will buy on monthly payments. Write H. D., 1922 Beaver Road, Ambridge, Pa. 2|26

Help Wanted—Female

WANTED: Woman for general housework, family of one. Apply at 441 Turnpike street, Beaver. 2|26

WANTED: For temporary position, experienced typist, must be good at figures. Write S. C. E. c/o DAILY TIMES OFFICE, Rochester. 2|26-28 inc

A MOST UNUSUAL OPPORTUNITY with a legitimate corporation. The finest of references must be given. This is a permanent life position for a woman who can qualify. Personal interview only, 10 a. m. Sylvania Hills Memorial Park, John C. Campbell, president. 212 Brodhead Hotel, Beaver Falls. 2|24-27 inc

WANTED: An experienced woman for day work. Write "A-100" c/o THE TIMES, Beaver. 2|24-3|1 inc

WANTED: Experienced girl for general housework; references required. Call Rochester 1511. 2|23-26 inc

Help Wanted—Male

STEADY WORK—GOOD PAY RELIABLE MAN WANTED to call on farmers in South Beaver County. No experience or capital required. Make up to $10 a day. Write McNESS CO., Chandler Bldg., Baltimore, Md. 2|26

Wanted—Situations

WANTED: By white girl position doing housework or as mother's helper. Reliable, can furnish reference. Write Miss Frances Showalter, R. D. 1, Darlington. 2|21-27 inc

For Sale

FOR SALE: Cheap, child's bed (drop side), in good condition. Inquire 384 Laura street, Beaver, or call Beaver 853. 2|26-27

NOTICE—Apple Sale No. 5 continued; fine large Golden Delicious apples delivered to your door for 50c per bushel. Exceptionally good eating or cooking. Order by phone, Beaver 6103-J-1. S. H. Warren. 2|22-28 inc

AT LOHRY'S
FOR SALE—APPLES
You may get our apples at the same price at Munson's Grocery Store, 453 Third St., Beaver. And also at the Farm Storage. The small apples are 3 bushel for $1.00. We also have butters, jellies, jams and fresh eggs.
WE DELIVER
Call Beaver 1433-W. 2|10*

Jersey's Corner, Rochester. Special! Turtle soup daily. Bring your container to take soup home. Live chickens 20c lb.; fully dressed 26c lb. 2|20-26 inc

FOR SALE: Store equipment, or purchaser to take over place of business; equipment includes cooler, meat case, 2 scales, etc. Write "Store," c/o DAILY TIMES, Rochester. 2|24-3|1 inc

BIG WALLPAPER SALE: ½ off thousands of rolls, fine new Spring papers, 5c to $2.00 roll. Room lot $1.52. WILLIAM HELMICK, 390 Brighton avenue, Rochester. 2|24-3|1 inc

FOR SALE: Two rare antique grapevine gate leg tables opens 48x69½, solid cherry. No prices quoted over phone. Inquire L. H. Stitt, 1016 Washington avenue, Monaca. 2|21-27 inc

For Sale—Used Cars

1939 Chevrolet town sedan in fine condition; fully equipped with radio, heater, defroster, fog lights, spotlight, two-door, with trunk, $675; 1936 Chevrolet two-door, trunk, $295.
Ralph D. Ewing, Olds.
Beaver, Pa. 2|26-3|2 inc

Dependable Used Car Bargains
1938 Ford Deluxe Coupe
1938 Ford Tudor Sedan
1937 Studebaker 4-door Sedan Dictator
1937 Ford Tudor Sedan
1937 Ford Fordor Sedan
1937 Ford Coupe
1936 Terraplane Deluxe 2-door Sedan
1936 Lafayette 2-door Sedan
1935 Ford Fordor Sedan
1934 Ford Chevrolet Master Deluxe Sedan
1936 Chevrolet Stake Body Truck
1936 Ford Panel
1932 Dodge Chassis and Cab
MANY OTHERS
STUMP'S
Ford Sales & Service
Harmony Ave., Rochester
Phone 173
2|24-3|1 inc.

1939 Olds Light Six 4-door sedan, perfect condition. Also the same in a business coupe. These cars have had one owner, and are priced for quick sale to any one wanting a late model, light used car $675 and $695.
Ralph D. Ewing, Olds
Beaver, Pa. 2|26-3|2 inc

FOR SALE: Best bargains in town—1937 Chevrolet Deluxe sedan, a lot of extras; 1937 Studebaker Deluxe coupe, fully equipped; 1937 Graham Light Six sedan, repossessed, $195. Inquire 451 Deer Lane, Rochester. Phone 1493-R. 2|26

FOR SALE: 1935 Chevrolet Deluxe coupe, paint, tires, upholstery excellent. One owner. Phone Beaver 6137-R-2. 2|23-29 inc

USED CARS
1935 Chev. Std. Coach, New Tires, Reconditioned $195
1935 Chev. Std. Coach, Radio and Heater, only - - $215
1934 Chev. Deluxe Coach, Knee Action, only - - $175
1933 Chev. Deluxe Coupe, Radio and Heater - $145
BAKER CHEVROLET CO.
Beaver, Pa. 444 Third St.
29 yrs. in Beaver
2|21-27 inc.

For Sale—Livestock

FOR SALE: Fresh Jersey cow with heifer calf at side, $65. Route 856, near Knob Store. O. A. Baker. 2|20-26 inc

FOR SALE: Two farm horses, weight 1500 and 1600 respectively, price reasonable. Inquire Manuel Steinacker, Rochester, Pa., R. D. No. 1. 2|19-3|2 inc

For Sale—Houses

BEAVER HOMES
A selected list of good homes in Beaver and vicinity—$2600 to $12,000. Financing arranged. A house to meet every demand.
Also a wide choice in building lots with all Beaver Borough conveniences and several attractive building sites in Brighton Township.
Tell me what you want and I will try to meet your requirements.
ROBT. F. GARVIN
Real Estate Broker
682 Third St., Phone Beaver 424 2|26-3|2 inc

"OWN A HOME IN BEAVER"
7-room frame on Fourth street, $4500.
6-room frame, garage attached, $4000. Terms.
5-room bungalow and garage in Westview, $2600.
5-room brick, 1-car garage, on paved street, easy terms.
Other bargains—see our listings.
BOVARD-ANDERSON CO.
Real Estate, Insurance, Rentals
617 Third St. BEAVER 1121 2|26-28-3|1

MONACA—Modern frame duplex, first floor has 5 rooms and bath; second floor has six rooms and bath. Fine location. Price $6900. Write "B-20" c/o DAILY TIMES, Beaver. 2|26-3|2 inc

FOR SALE: 100-acre farm with large orchard, 8-room bungalow house, new, with all modern improvements, on improved road. Price $14,000. J. L. Holmes, Beaver, Pa. 2|23-29 inc

FOR SALE: Four-room bungalow with bath, one acre ground. Cemented cellar, furnace, stationary tubs, running water, electric pump. House in excellent condition. Located Harvey Run Road, Freedom. Phone Roch. 3317-M. 2|22-28 inc

SMALL HOUSE for Sale: Allola Park, 3 rooms and bath, front and rear porches. Insulated with rock wool and nicely finished. A bargain, $600. Call Roch. 725. 2|22-28 inc

FOR SALE: Five-room house; all conveniences, double lot, double garage, small chicken-house. Inquire G. H. Thornburg, 308 Nimick Ave., Monaca. 2|20-26 inc

For Sale—Coal

SPECIAL: Zelienople Coal—Lump $3, egg $3. Delivered anywhere. Also manure and loam. For details, call Baden 5071. C. R. McCoy. 2|26-3|2 inc

CLINTON COAL: Pittsburgh vein lump $4.25; ¾ lump $4.00; Zelienople coal, lump $3.50; egg $3.50. 25c ton extra on 1-ton orders. Phone New Brighton 1863. Thurman Stewart. 2|26-3|2 inc

ZELIENOPLE COAL—Lump $3.25, and $3.50; egg $3.00; Shirley lump $3.75, egg $3.25. These prices 2 ton or over. We deliver anywhere. Call Beaver 490. Gulla Bros. 2|24-3|1 inc

Ask for PORT Coal, more heat and less ash. PRICES REDUCED on orders for two tons or more. Prompt deliver. Call Beaver 2564. Kiernan-Courtney Coal Co. 1|6*

Special Zelienople Coal—4-in. lump $3.00; 1¼x2 inch nut $2.85; 1x1¼ Stoker $2.85, 1-in. Slack $2.40. Shirley Coal—5-in. lump $3.70, 2-in. lump $3.50, egg $3.20, Stoker $3.15, nut $3.10. All orders C.O.D. These prices 2 tons or over. Call Bowmann's, Rochester 6132-J-2. 2|6-12 inc*

For Sale—Farms

FOR SALE: 60-acre farm in New Sewickley township, ¼ mile off improved road; sell reasonable to settle estate. Inquire Albert Spratley, R. D. 1, Rochester. 2|22-28 inc

FOR SALE: 100 acres with 6-room house, good barn, and other buildings, fruit and lots of water. Three miles from Beaver on improved road. Write P. O. Box 177, New Brighton. 2|22-28 inc

Business Opportunities

FOR SALE: Modern Beauty Shoppe, complete in every detail. Call Rochester 134-W. 2|23-29 inc

For Rent

FOR RENT: Store room at 136 Brighton Ave., Rochester, available March 1st. Inquire Wm. F. Brehm, 350 Jefferson St., Rochester. Phone 686-J. 2|21-27 inc

For Rent—Houses

FOR RENT: 7-room modern house with bath, large lot and garage at 711 Indiana avenue, Monaca. Inquire 905 Atlantic avenue, Monaca, or call Rochester 439-W. 2|26-3|2 inc

For Rent—Rooms

FOR RENT: Three nicely furnished rooms for light housekeeping with bath in Rochester. Inquire 195 Clay street, Rochester. 2|24-3|1 inc

One or two large front rooms furnished complete for housekeeping. Running water both rooms, light and heat. Park location. 804 Turnpike street, Beaver 9052. 2|24-3|1 inc

FOR RENT: Furnished room for gentleman. Inquire 600 River Road, Beaver. Phone Beaver 1226-J. 2|23-29 inc

FOR RENT: Two nicely furnished rooms for light housekeeping, sink and range in kitchen, all electrical appliances, adults. Inquire 318 Pennsylvania Ave., Rochester. 2|23-29 inc

For Rent—Rooms

FOR RENT: Two or three unfurnished rooms, private entrance, first floor; also furnished bedroom suitable for gentleman. Call Rochester 712-R. 2|26-3|2 inc

FOR RENT: Two completely furnished rooms for light housekeeping. Sink and range. $5.00 week. Adults. 1528 Seventh Ave., New Brighton. 2|26

FOR RENT: Furnished room with kitchenette, very reasonable. Inquire 1601 Virginia Ave., Monaca. 2|26

FOR RENT: To two roomers, willing to share same room, board if desired in modern home and conveniently located. Inquire rear 287 Pinney street, Rochester. 2|26-3|2 inc

FOR RENT: Three large rooms furnished for light housekeeping, on first floor, with private bath and entrance. Inquire 488 Hull street, Rochester. 2|26-3|2 inc

FOR RENT: Two furnished rooms with private bath and entrance. Inquire 514 Adams street, Rochester. 2|23-29 inc

FOR RENT: Two unfurnished rooms in Rochester; newly painted; adults only. Phone Rochester 1565-R. 2|22-28 inc

FOR RENT: Two light housekeeping rooms, all new furniture. Inquire 176 West Madison street, Rochester. Phone Roch. 1745-R. 2|21-27 inc

FOR RENT: Two clean furnished rooms, $20 per month. Inquire 284 Buffalo street, Beaver. 2|20-26 inc

FOR RENT: Nicely furnished rooms, suitable for one or two gentlemen; modern conveniences. Inquire 220 Fifth avenue, Freedom. Phone Rochester 2302-W. 2|20-26 inc

Miscellaneous

Balza's Wallpaper Shop, 411 Third St., Beaver. Slogan Contest Awards: Mrs. Springer, Vanport; Mrs. Knox, Beaver; Mrs. Tomilsons, Vanport; Mrs. Catanese, Beaver. See our new line of wallpaper, curtains, etc. 2|26

PATTERSON TOWNSHIP FIREMEN—Penny Carnival every Friday Night. A good place to play your favorite pastime. Patterson Township Firemen, Darlington Road, Beaver Falls, Pa. 2|6*

Carnival Every Thursday—9 P. M.—50c for all evening. 3 cards $1.00, $10.00 door award. $1.50 single award. Old School House, Marion Hill. Benefit Pulaski Firemen. 2|1-3|6 inc*

FOR FLOOR SANDING call E. J. Cochran, Rochester 6108-J-2. Hardwood floors layed, sanded and finished. Old floors finished like new. 2|1*

INDOOR CARNIVAL
New Legion Home
Adams St., Rochester
TUES. & FRI. NITES
8:30 P. M.
33 Games 50c—Prizes $1, $2, $3, $5 in Merchandise

Beauty Culture

Mrs. Gillen wishes to introduce her new assistant—Miss Taylor, a stylist and expert permanent waver. Pre-Easter Rush Special. Call Beaver 1225. 2|20-26 inc

Repairs—Service

REX & BOBISH RADIO SHOP. Dependable service on home or auto radios. Work guaranteed, prices reasonable. Tubes tested free. Phone Beaver 991-J. 985 Fifth St., Beaver. 2|26-3|2 inc

With our many years of experience at painting, graining and paper-hanging, we guarantee workmanship and material to be the best. George J. Dean. W. Bridgewater. Phone Beaver 2308-J. 2|22-28 inc

For Dependable Maytag service, call Beaver County Maytag Store, New Brighton—2484. We have some good bargains in used ironing and washing machines. 6|9*

RADIO SERVICE: Guaranteed on all makes of home radios; price right. Call Roy Huysman, Roch. 428-W or inquire 378 New York avenue, Rochester. 2|16-29 inc*

Furniture Refinishing and Repairing. Expert on refinishing antique furniture and repairing; work guaranteed. Can furnish reference on work already done in Beaver. Phone Beaver Falls 1964-J. 2|20-3|4 inc

Coal chutes made to order of heavy Armco iron. If your roof leaks, your furnace smokes, we can stop it. Prompt, efficient service. Phone Roch. 1567. 1|13*

PLUMBING & HEATING
Repairs and installations at minimum prices. Satisfaction guaranteed.
RUUD WATER HEATERS
With a 20 year guaranteed tank.
W. A. ZUBAUGH
Rear City Bldg. - Beaver
Phone 2723 Day or Nite
1|17 - 2|13 inc.*

The Hospitals

Rochester hospital: Total patients—81. Admitted—Enoch Engle, James Pacitti, Mrs. Steve Skolnekovich, Jr., and Turl Delp, Monaca; Robert Graham, Uniontown, and Mrs. Fred Schleiter, Beaver. Discharged—Mrs. Meryle McConnell, Mrs. Samuel Urich, Mrs. Ellsworth Law and son, Mrs. John Swartz and Mrs. Elizabeth Caldwell, Aliquippa; Mrs. David Smith, Mrs. John McLaughlin and son and Mrs. Minnie McMinn, Beaver; Emma Havranek, Conway; William Milnes, Rochester, and Mike Schuller, Monaca.

LOANS
Check our 5 point plan
✓$25 to $300.
✓On your signature
✓Immediate service
✓No red tape
✓Small payments to suit you
Guardian FINANCIAL CORP.
1400 Seventh Av.
Beaver Falls
Telephone Beaver Falls 968
Only You need sign

USED CAR HEADQUARTERS
1939 Nash LaFayette 4-dr. Sedan $765
Radio, Cond. Air, New Tires
1938 Dodge 4-dr. Sdn. $575
Deluxe, Heater, Defroster, New Tires
1934 Terraplane 4-dr. Sedan $195
Heater, Deluxe
1931 Plymouth Coupe . $ 65
Good Tires, Heater
Why Don't you trade your car in on a New Nash?
VOLLMER'S
Nash & LaFayette
Rochester Phone 603

SINCLAIR Super-Flame KEROSENE BURNS CLEAN
Agent Sinclair Refining Company (Inc.)
L. G. REITZEL
Phone 1615-J, Beaver Falls

FOR INCUBATORS — Poultrymen find Sinclair Super-Flame Kerosene an ideal fuel for incubators and brooders. Since it burns clean and clear, there is no danger that it will give off objectionable odors or poisonous gases that might penetrate the shell of the eggs and kill the hatch. Its even-burning quality assures steady, even temperature without the need for constant adjustment of the wicks.

PROMPT TANK TRUCK DELIVERY AT WHOLESALE PRICE

Still Down on Farm

MANHATTAN, Kas. (UP)—Despite all the talk about modern youth deserting the farm, the agricultural population of the United States on Jan. 1, 1939, was only 18,000 short of the record high set 29 years earlier, W. E. Grimes, Kansas State College economist and sociologist, discloses.

QUICK CASH LOANS!
You Can Borrow Up to $300 Here On Your Auto or Furniture.
No Signers or Endorsers. Up to 18 Months to Repay.
Inquire About The "Union" Repayment Plan.
Reliable—34 Years in Beaver Falls
UNION LOAN CO.
Rooms 2 & 4—2nd Floor
Benson Bldg.
Cor. 12th St. & 7th Ave.
Beaver Falls—PHONE 244
QUICK SERVICE

INVESTIGATE
OUR NEW PLAN
It offers all that is best for the saver and the investor
ROCHESTER BLDG. & LOAN ASS'N.
361 Brighton Ave. - Rochester

THE NEW CHIROPRACTIC
PAINLESS METHODS
DEFINITE CORRECTION
CHARLES F. SHIELDS, D. C.
Beaver Trust Building

NOTARIES PUBLIC
Office of Bovard-Anderson Co., 617 Third St., Beaver
INCOME TAX BLANKS
ALL KINDS AUTO BLANKS

CHAMPION COAL
6 in. lump or furnace.
Lowest prices — Prompt delivery.
SAM CUTRONA
Phone 123 or 824 Rochester

YOU CAN SEW THESE YOURSELF

EASY-TO-MAKE, CHEERY APRONS

Marian Martin
PATTERN 9326

Of course you want your "kitchen-duty" costume simple to make. But it can be crisply pretty at the same time. Here's proof in Marian Martin's Pattern 9326. See the well-fitting front lines, with the smartly curved side bodice sections that form one piece with the shoulders. In back the shoulder straps are joined together to stay up. Best news of all, the front and back are cut in just THREE PIECES each, excluding the sash and the optional pockets. Take your choice of two gay versions: one with contrast; the other with a colorful, easy flower applique.

Pattern 9326 may be ordered only in sizes small, medium and large. Small size, view A, requires 1½ yards 35 inch fabric and ⅝ yard contrast; view B 2¼ yards 35 inch.

Send FIFTEEN CENTS in coins for this MARIAN MARTIN pattern. Be sure to write plainly your SIZE, NAME, ADDRESS, and STYLE NUMBER.

Our NEW MARIAN MARTIN PATTERN BOOK brings the world of fashion right into your home! Without stirring from your arm-chair you can plan your whole Spring wardrobe—on inexpensive, easy-to-sew terms. There's evening drama, followed by a complete trousseau for the Spring bride. Gay school and play modes for tots, teens, and twenties—plus slim-line matron frocks, home chic, vivacious cottons, prints and travel wear. Order a copy NOW! BOOK FIFTEEN CENTS. PATTERN FIFTEEN CENTS. BOOK AND PATTERN TOGETHER, TWENY-FIVE CENTS.

9326
A
B

Address all orders to THE DAILY TIMES, Pattern Dept., Beaver, Pa. Marian Martin New Chart Complete Diagrammed Included

COUPON

Name ....
Town ....
Street No. ....
Pattern Size ....
Pattern Number ....

The New Maytag Master Washer

IT'S A BEAUTY!

Streamlined throughout with a gleaming baked enamel finish. It is the finest looking washer we have ever seen. Same washing action and performance as the old well-known Maytag Washer — dressed up and beautified for you. Its performance in the home makes happy wash days.

Call us for a demonstration. Liberal allowance for your old washer. Low carrying charge.

"NOW IS THE TIME TO TRADE"

Beaver County Maytag Store
John W. Young, Proprietor
9th St. & 10th. Ave., Phone 2484 New Brighton
Near High School—Open Evenings By Appointment

To the Man with a Job ... who needs CASH

You can get up to $300 here quickly. The main requirement is your ability to repay in small, regular amounts.

You Ask No Favors

When you get a loan here you ask no favor of anyone. We do not require endorsers, and do not take wage or salary assignments. Employer or friends are not notified.

Know Exact Cost

Come in, tell us how much you need, and pick the monthly repayment most convenient for you. We state our charges plainly, you get the *full* amount of your loan in cash without deductions; and there are *no extras, no fees,* and *no fines.*

Personal FINANCE CO.

Ground floor Masonic Temple Assn. Bldg. 728 12th St. Beaver Falls, Phone 2540

THAT'S WHERE WE COME IN, WITH QUALITY COAL THAT "Makes Warm Friends"
CAMPBELL BROS.
PHONE BEAVER 2330

COAL
Running
Low?

Your Automotive Center —
HERMAN ACON
EXPERT REPAIRING ON ALL MAKES OF CARS
Auto Body Rebuilding
C. W. WAGNER, JR.
NEW AND USED CARS PRICED TO SELL
Opposite First Nat'l Bank
Rochester - Phone 9054

NOTARY PUBLIC
Maude F. McBrier
DAILY TIMES Office, Beaver
Income Tax Blanks

ROYAL TYPEWRITERS
Allen Wales Adding Machines
Sales - Service - Supplies
All Makes Repaired
C. F. BROWN
218 Federal Title and Trust Building.
Phone 2379 Beaver Falls

MOVING
TRANSFER and PIANO MOVING GENERAL HAULING
S. E. WALTON
BEAVER
Phone Beaver 168
500 Corporation Street

TILE BATH ROOMS — MANTELS — SHOWERS
Estimates—No Obligations
FRANK H. GRIMM
1006 Tenth Street, New Brighton, Pa.
Phone N. B. 2610

Read THE TIMES Classified Ads.

SHANE BROS.
3/4 LUMP COAL
Screened to eliminate all slack and nut smaller than 2 inches. By analysis—more heat and less ash.
ORDER NOW FOR PROMPT DELIVERY
Phone Rochester 1444

Let Hudson's Give Your Washer A Special Spring Check-Up!
For A Limited Time Only—
Change Oil In Gear Box
Oil Motor
Check Wringer Rolls
Repack Wringer Gear Box
Oil Casters
ALL FOR ONLY $1.75
Hudson's Appliance Shop
136 Brighton Avenue — Rochester — Phone 300

Read THE TIMES Classified Ads for Bargains

Weather Forecast
Saturday fair, with little change in temperature; snow or rain Sunday, with slowly rising temperature.

THE DAILY TIMES

ROCHESTER-BEAVER-MONACA
FREEDOM—BRIDGEWATER—CONWAY—VANPORT—MIDLAND

Local History
Dr. John McMillan was one of the earliest of the Presbyterian missionaries in Beaver County.

ESTABLISHED APRIL 2, 1874 | BEAVER AND ROCHESTER, PA., FRIDAY, MARCH 8, 1940 | BY CARRIER 15 CENTS A WEEK—3 CENTS PER COPY

WORKMAN KILLED IN BLAST AT PLANT

REPORTED RUSSIAN PEACE TERMS ARE OPPOSED BY FINNS

Soviet Demands On Besieged Nation Termed Inacceptable By Finnish Leaders

Numerous Conferences Reported In Progress Regarding Possibility Of Peace

By the United Press
HELSINKI, Finland, March 8—Finland is prepared to fight to a finish rather than accept peace terms dictated by Russia, it was indicated today.

Finns looked to their Scandinavian neighbors and to the Allies to give them the aid which would enable them to hold off the Red army. They commented bitterly that the Russian terms were harsher than those the rejection of which last Fall brought on the war. The government's position was that it had always sought an honorable peace but that the peace "offered" by Russia was not an honorable one. If Russia cared to make proposals that a free country could accept, it was said, Finland would welcome them.

TERMS REPORTED

Reports that Russia had demanded Hango on the southwest coast; the Karelian Isthmus and the Lake Ladoga region were received here from abroad and were declared to be inacceptable. Hango is more than 200 miles from the Russian frontier. To turn it over to Russia, it was held, would be to make a puppet state of Finland.

It was realized that the Russians now had the initiative in the war and that Viipuri must fall. But it was said that the Finns were holding the Russians on all fronts except the Viipuri one and that the Viipuri offensive was taking a terrible toll of Russian lives.

There were many imponderable factors: What attitude Great Britain, France and Germany had taken in the last few days; What help Finnish leaders thought they might get from abroad; What guarantees Germany or other nations might be willing to give; The final attitude of Sweden and Norway toward direct assistance and toward the passage of foreign troops and materials across their territory.

Many Finns believed that Germany had actually been the initiator of the peace proposals. It was reliably reported that the German minister, Wipert von Bluecher, had sounded out Finnish leaders on the possibility of peace after his return from a recent visit to Berlin.

LEADERS CONFER

BERLIN, Mar. 8.—Well-informed
(Continued on Page 8)

Monaca High Floor Team Reaches Championship Finals

—Photo by Graule Studios

Pictured above is the Monaca high school basketball squad, Section 11 title holders, and defending W.P.I.A.L. Class B champions, who last night reached the finals in the annual championship tournament as the result of a 38 to 32 victory over North Belle Vernon high school on the Pitt Stadium court. The Southsiders, who are coached by Stanley J. Berkman, former Thiel College star athlete, will meet Point Marion high of Fayette County at the Washington, Pa., high school gymnasium next Tuesday night in the Class B championship contest.

Members of the Monaca squad are: left to right— Front Row — Managers Arthur Renner, Richard Eberle, Eugene Buccini, William Ruckman, Calvin Swink; Second Row—Glenn Swink, Henry Flati, Frank Walters, Matthew Fronko, Eugene Zigerelli, Furman Massey, Adam Karcis, Steve Predo; Third Row—Albert Vlasic, Edward Ofcharka, Merle Taormina, William Zoph, Mike Linkovich, Edwin Figley, Joseph Cronin, David Sinclair; Fourth Row—Joseph Trella, Anthony Scussa, Joseph Antoline, Joseph Seery, Daniel Sabella, Steve Ogrizek, Albert Kermiet, Gerard Schachern.

Starting this season where they left off in 1939, the Monaca floormen romped through 14 straight league games to claim the Section 11 crown for the second year in a row and the fourth time in the last six years.

The Southsiders were unbeaten in Section 11 competition this season and prior to last night's game with North Belle Vernon defeated Apollo, 28 to 18, and East Washington, 13 to 28, in W. P. I. A. L. Class B play-off contests.

Lobbying By NLRB Officials Probed By Agents Of FBI

By the United Press
WASHINGTON, March 8. — The Federal Bureau of Investigation is investigating charges today that National Labor Relations Board officials violated federal statutes by lobbying against proposed amendments to the Wagner Act.

Attorney General Robert H. Jackson, it was learned, ordered the investigation last month before he declined to advise Chairman Howard W. Smith of the special House Committee investigating the board whether alleged activities of board officials were illegal.

The FBI's investigation was revealed as battle lines formed in the House over drastic changes proposed in the board and the labor act by a majority of Smith's committee. Those amendments — including ones to abolish the present board and substitute a judicial board to hear cases prosecuted by a new labor act administrator — were sent to the House Labor Committee which will meet next Wednesday to consider them.

OPINION DIFFERS

The proposed changes were assailed as "emasculatory" by defenders of the Wagner Act and praised as "a step in the right direction" by its critics. Spokesmen for the United States Chamber of commerce, which is sponsoring a series of amendments of its own, said it was "a pretty good bill." Sen. Robert F. Wagner, D., N. Y., author of the Labor act, said he would make an extensive statement soon.

The FBI's investigation of alleged Labor Board lobbying followed several days of controbersy at Smith Committee hearings when committee counsel Edmund M. Toland read letters and communications indicating that board officials had sought to stimulate opposition to proposed changes in the act. Toland, asserting that these efforts were carried on during working hours and through official labor board channels, called attention to a "rider" in a 1919 appropriation bill prohibiting use of federal funds for efforts to influence congress.

TO BLOCK DELAY

Advocates of Wagner act revision contend any attempt by the committee to pigeon-hole the amendments will result in one of two retaliatory moves: 1. A dicharge petition, requiring 218 names, for removing the bill from the Labor Committee after 30 days; 2. A rule from the Rules Committee ordering it to the floor for debate.

Chairman Mary T. Norton, D., N. J., of the House Labor Committee, who predicted that the Smith amendments would be defeated in the House, reasserted her previous stand that action on Wagner Act changes should await a final report of the Smith Committee which plans to continue its investigation.

Mrs. Norton's committee has held extensive hearings on several sets of Wagner Act amendments. Action was delayed at the last session when the House ordered its investigation of the Labor Board.

VAT FILLED WITH BOILING GREASE EXPLODES TODAY

New Brighton Man Dies In Hospital After Accident This Morning

Explosion Occurs At Plant Of New Brighton By-Products Company

One man was fatally injured and another escaped unharmed when a seven-foot vat exploded at three o'clock this morning at the plant of the Brighton By-Products Company, Block House Run, New Brighton, and poured boiling grease over an employe standing nearby. The company renders dead animals.

Michael Terek, 49, New England Hill, New Brighton, received lacerations of the lips and head, fractured ribs, possible puncture of a lung and a back injury, as well as burns about the body, face and arms. The vat was filled with a boiling mass of meat which was being cooked when excess pressure blew off the door, company officials stated today.

DIES IN HOSPITAL

Terek was knocked down by the force of the explosion and coated from head to foot with the boiling mixture. John Boyer, New Brighton, a fellow-employe, was also standing near the tank when the explosion occurred, but was not injured.

Efforts to save Terek at Beaver Valley hospital where he was taken after the accident proved futile and he died at 8 o'clock this morning.

He was a member of SS. Cyril and Methodius Roman Catholic church, New Brighton. Surviving are his widow, Mrs. Anna Terek; three daughters, Agnes and Margaret Terek, at home, and Mrs. Emile Slovak, Beaver Falls, and two sons, Michael Terek, Jr., at home, and Steve Terek, in the United States Navy.

Man Kills Wife, Daughter, Self

By the United Press
UNIONTOWN, Mar. 8—A penefled note blaming an "unhappy married life" was a clue to the motive which drove a farmer to fatally shoot, bludgeon and mutilate his wife and 16-year-old step-daughter and then take his own life today in the barnyard of their home.

A shotgun, butcher knife and two pistols were used, police believed, to take the lives of Charles Blasic, 40, Spillway Lake; his wife, Mary, 38, and Florence Blasic, 16.

The Blasic family occupied half of a double house on the farm of Mrs. James Hazen, situated ten miles northwest of Uniontown on Route 51. Carrying a feed bucket in each hand, a son, John, discovered his father's body, a pistol clutched in his hand, as he started for the barn.

Inside the barn, the boy discovered the body of his mother. Apparently, she had been shot outside and later dragged into the building. The body of Florence was discovered in a wash shed, nearby.

The Blasics had four other children besides Florence and John, two of them boys.

County Students On Honor Roll At Tech

Five students from Beaver County were named on the honor roll at the Carnegie Institute of Technology for the first semester, Registrar Alan Bright has announced.

Ruth M. Rotzler, Beaver, led the Sophomore class with a factor of 4.00 indicating a "straight A" record, and her brother, Ross William Rotzler, a Senior in chemical engineering, achieved a factor of 3.95. Miss Rotzler is enrolled in the nurses' training course in Margaret Morrison Carnegie College. Their parents are Rev. and Mrs. W. F. Rotzler, Beaver street.

Millard Freeman Gordon, Rochester, and Melvin W. Green, Midland, both Freshmen in electrical engineering, were also named on the honor roll. Gordon is the son of Mr. and Mrs. James W. Gordon, Connecticut avenue, and Green's parents are Mr. and Mrs. Aaron Green, Beaver avenue. Both hold scholarships at Tech this year. Sarabelle Pearlman, daughter of Mr. and Mrs. Morris Pearlman, Midland, was also mentioned.

Great Game Of Politics

— By Frank R. Kent —
(Copyright, 1939)

TOWARD THE LOWER LEVELS

Washington, March 8

AS THE present state of national affairs is viewed it is impossible to avoid the conclusion that campaigns for the Presidential nomination are now being waged on a level considerably lower than ever before.

—o—

THE pretense that the office should seek the man largely has been abandoned. In both parties the aspirants are engaged in what seems a scramble. Dignity has been thrown to the winds and no holds are barred. This reflects not only upon the candidates but upon the people. It marks a deterioration in political standards
(Continued on Page Nine)

BABSON SAYS U. S. STANDING AT POLITICAL CROSSROADS

By ROGER BABSON

ST. PETERSBURG, Fla., March 8 – Eight million idle workers and sixteen billion idle dollars is 1940's strange paradox. It's the result of a ten year battle between those who want government control of all credit (State Capitalism) and those who want a free hand for private employers and capital. Captains of industry can afford to fight. So can the princes of politics. But you and I and our unemployed neighbors can't. We have reached the crossroads and we must choose either "the high road or the low".

Eight million unemployed must be put back to work. Under State Capitalism they could have army or other compulsory jobs within several years. Under Free Enterprise they could have voluntary jobs in a similar length of time. But under today's half-way system, the best hope is that only a million or two will be absorbed in public or private hands within the next few years. Meanwhile, sixteen billion dollars, greatest hoard of cash ever assembled, strains the nation's bank vaults. This fund could create twice the amount of credit necessary to
(Continued on Page Seven)

DEPUTY COUNTY PROTHONOTARY OBSERVES HIS 75TH BIRTHDAY

—Photo by Graule Studios
JAMES McLAREN

James McLaren, Beaver, deputy prothonotary of Beaver County for the past fourteen years, celebrated his seventy-fifth birthday today by going about his duties at the court house as usual.

While Mr. McLaren declined to vary his usual routine, his associates in the office of Prothonotary Edwin C. Wallover presented him a birthday cake and a greeting card shower when he came out of the court room at noon today. A huge vase of flowers, from the Beaver County Bar Association, was delivered at the Prothonotary's office this morning.

DINNER TONIGHT

Mr. McLaren first became deputy prothonotary on January 1, 1926. He was admitted to the Beaver County Bar in 1928, but had been a member of the Bar in Allegheny county before moving to the Valley. He was admitted in Allegheny County in 1889, slightly over fifty years ago.

This evening Mr. McLaren will be honored at a family dinner to be held at Snapp's tea room, Beaver.

Beaver Tot Appears In Pensive Mood

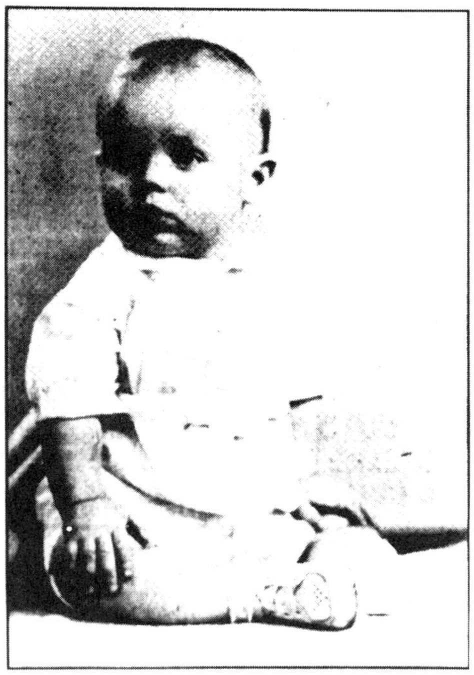

—Photo by Graule Studios

ROBERT LANCE DAVIES

Here's little Robert Lance ("Lanny") Davies, son of Mr. and Mrs. R. Clifford Davies, 169 College avenue, Beaver, just looking around in pensive mood while his busy little brain concocts some new mischief. "Lanny" has sandy hair and blue eyes.

Union, Company Fail To Agree On Monaca Contract Dispute

Conferences Opened Thursday To Be Continued On U. S. Sanitary Contract

Representatives of the SWOC, officials of the United States Sanitary Manufacturing Company, Monaca, and mediators of the Federal and state labor departments met Thursday afternoon in the offices of the company, but failed to reach an agreement on the strike which has closed the plant since midnight, February 28.

Another conference was to be held at one o'clock this afternoon and they are to be continued until some definite settlement is reached, it was said.

OFFICIALS CONFER

The union representatives were led by Joseph J. Timko, regional director, and A. J. Marsh, field rep-
(Continued on Page Eight)

Rochester Parking Rules Unchanged

Although Rochester borough council has taken initial action to modify the present parking meter ordinance to permit free parking after 6 p. m. on Saturdays, the present parking regulations will be in effect until the amended ordinance is passed finally, borough officials warned today.

The amendment was passed on first reading last Monday evening. Until final passage, the meters will be in operation daily from 8 a. m. to 6 p. m. (9 p. m. on Saturdays) but will not be used Sundays.

TRADE PROGRAM APPROVED

By the United Press
WASHINGTON, Mar. 8. — The Senate finance committee today approved a three-year extension of the administration's reciprocal trade agreement program. It rejected an amendment to subject the agreements to Senate ratification.

COUNTY MAN HAS NOTED PLACE IN MUSIC AND GOLFING WORLDS

By FRANCES GIBBONS DOHERR

Beaver Valley may well be proud of the association brought about by the residence here of a man who won fame in musical circles and in the sports and newspaper world in many larger communities.

E. Ellsworth Giles and his wife, Florence James Giles, reside in Ohioview and carry on a busy schedule to promote greater interest in these professions. They work tirelessly and unselfishly toward this goal. Mr. Giles is director of the Beaver Methodist church choir and maintains vocal studios in Beaver and East Liverpool, O. He was for years teacher of voice in Beaver College when it was located here. Mrs. Giles is organist and director of the East Liverpool Episcopal church choir.

Mr. Giles and his augmented choir of solo voices present many special services of oratorio and other fine music. Mrs. Giles plays most of the accompaniments. Mr. Giles also conducts a golf course in Ohioview and does his share of golfing.

While listening to reminiscences
(Continued on Page Six)

—Photo by Graule Studios
E. ELLSWORTH GILES

Mrs. Olive M. Mahan Dies At Rochester

Mrs. Olive M. Mahan, 86, wife of Stanley H. Mahan, 490 Connecticut avenue, Rochester, died at 8:30 o'clock Thursday evening in Rochester hospital, where she was admitted last Saturday suffering from injuries received in a fall Thursday of last week. She had been in failing health several years and the shock resulting from the fall hastened her death. The body was removed to the Coleman funeral home, Rochester, pending funeral arrangements.

Mrs. Mahan was born in Locust Grove, O. She had been a resident of Rochester the past 45 years and was held in high esteem by a wide circle of friends. She was a member of the Free Methodist church and for many years was teacher of the Woman's Bible class of that church. Surviving are her husband, two daughters, Miss Anna S. Mahan, at home, and Mrs. Virginia M. Mason, Gary, Ind., and one grandchild, Virginia Ann Mason.

Funeral services will be held Sunday afternoon at 2:30 o'clock in the Coleman funeral home, Rochester. Burial will be in Nessley chapel cemetery, Arroyo, W. Va.

FIVE BURNED TO DEATH

By the United Press
MOUNT PLEASANT, Tenn., Mar. 8—Mrs. Gilliam Mosley, 39, and four of her childrden burned to death Thursday when fire of unknown origin destroyed their three-room house.

HITLER LEADS NAZI MIGHT AGAINST HOLLAND, BELGIUM; ALLIES RUSH AID

EXTRA

The Aliquippa Gazette

SERVING AN INDUSTRIAL COMMUNITY OF 50,000

WEATHER—Increasing cloudiness followed by light showers late tonight or early Saturday. Slightly cooler Saturday.

SERVED BY UNITED PRESS — PHONE 934-935-936 — MEMBER OF P. N. P. A.

VOL. XIX—No. 9 — ALIQUIPPA, PA., FRIDAY, MAY 10, 1940 — 3 CENTS; BY CARRIER, 15 CENTS A WEEK

CHAMBERLAIN RESIGNS

CLAIMS JUSTICES TRYING CASES OUT OF JURISDICTION

McCreary Informs Two Local Squires Of Illegal Acts

District Attorney Robért E. McCreary warned Aliquippa's justices of the peace today that punishing gamblers and "numbers" writers was none of their business.

In letters to Justices Ivor L. Jones and R. J. McLanahan, McCreary said the squires bit off more than they were legally allowed to chew and that in the future they were to turn over the prosecution of gambling and lottery law violations to the county court.

McLanahan told a Gazette reporter, "I have nothing to say," but Squire Jones said he did not understand why the district attorney was making a "fuss."

* * *

Said Jones: "I have always understood our jurisdiction was established by borough ordinance. It (disposition of numbers cases)

(Continued on Page Four)

The National Whirligig

(News Behind the News)

BACKGROUND — Great Britain's menacing moves against Italy—the shift of Naval strength to the Eastern Mediterranean, withdrawal of merchantment from the sea, the ultimatum to Il Duce—were not part of a great game of psychological bluff. They were precipitated by happenings at Rome which shocked the Vatican, the White House and 10 Downing Street.

Mussolini's warlike thrill over Hitler's attack on Norway has already been recounted here. The Roman referred to it in glowing terms as "the greatest feat of arms in hundreds of years." He was, of course, even then receiving assurances from Berlin that there was no chance of dislodgment by the British. Now, according to confidential advices here, Mussolini was so assured of eventual German victory that he laid papers before the King for the latter to sign—official proclamations that Italy was entering the war on the side of Hitler.

The King, with the backing of the Vatican, refused to sign. Then—and this explains the present tense strategy—Il Duce launched a publicity blitzkrieg through his newspapers and official statements to mobilize the Italian public's mind against his distinguished and beloved blockers. It was then, too, that President Roosevelt directly intervened to prevent "a spread of the war in other directions." But the outcome still hangs in tragic balance.

* * *

DEMPSEY—President Roosevelt sideswiped two major and two minor Presidential rivals with his second and more buglelike demand for enactment of the Hatch Act. The quartet consisted of such eminent bigwigs as Vice President Garner, National Chairman Farley, Speaker Bankhead and House Leader Rayburn.

F. D. R. had previously expressed a rather mild desire for favorable action on the "clean politics" bill, but his Capitol Hill aides apparently did not believe him. The four men listed above persisted in their opposition. Even after the Presidential utterance, a topheavy House Judiciary Committee ordered a secret vote

(Continued on Page Twelve)

As War Spread Into Peaceful Netherlands

Thousands of men like the pair shown at left are manning Holland's defenses as the Netherlands dig in to repel invasion by the Nazis. At right a Dutch army anti-tank gun commands the main street of a Dutch village on the German border.

4,000 AT COUNTY GYM EXHIBITION

Four thousand citizens of the Beaver Valley jammed Reeves stadium in Beaver Falls last night to watch the first annual county play day festival.

Ten county schools sent 640 students to participate in mass gymnastic exercises supervised by athletic coaches of each school.

Easily the most outstanding drill of the program was a mass flag waving drill in which all the students participated. The meet was sponsored by the Beaver County Principal association.

Coaches Elizabeth Carver and Nathan M. Lippe supervised the Aliquippa entries.

Graham's Stand On "Clean Politics" Bill Is Uncertain

Representative Louis E. Graham of Beaver is on the political "pan" today.

Beaver county voters eyed him with mild bewilderment as the Republican representative and member of the House Judiciary committee continued to hedge his stand on jimmying loose the new Hatch clean politics bill out of that committee and onto the floor where Congressmen will have a chance to put themselves on record by a vote.

* * *

Last week his constituents thought him for the bill when he favored it in a vote of his committee colleagues. He preserved remnants of the voting strip of the secret ballot to prove his stand.

But early this week Graham voted unsuccessfully with his committee not to reconsider a tabling motion. Political observers interpreted this as a definite anti-Hatch bill stand.

Bucktails' Meeting Draws 100 Sportsmen

Approximately 100 sportsmen enjoyed a roast pig dinner at the Aliquippa Bucktails' meeting last night at their clubhouse on Broadhead road. The meal was prepared by A. D. Murphy.

District Fish Warden Cliff Inman spoke on fish laws and regulations governing fish licenses. Five reels of fishing pictures were screened.

The club will meet again June 13.

Polish Benefit!

"Mother's" Program To Realize Funds

A Mother's Day program for the benefit of suffering mothers and children in Poland will be held here Sunday.

Sponsored by the Polish Women's Alliance, Group 345 of Aliquippa, the program is to be presented by club members at Polish hall, starting at 2:30 p. m. Proceeds will be dispatched to Poland.

Carnations will be sold at St. Titus church on Mother's Day, following each Mass, by the Polish Young Women's club. Proceeds also will be sent to Polish refugees.

James' Relief Bill May Cost Aliquippa $17,000 In Refunds

Aliquippa borough stands to lose approximately $17,000 if Gov. James' proposed relief bill passes the present extraordinary session of the state legislature.

The governor's budget calls for milching boroughs and cities of liquor license tax refunds to provide $7,000,000 for relief purposes.

Council this year budgeted $17,000 in anticipated revenues from such licenses. Last year's collection totalled $19,000.

SPEED TRAP AT LEETSDALE 'DUD'

Leetsdale's auto speed trap—third laid in the district—proved a "dud" today because motorists had been "tipped off."

Leetsdale police used the same telephone setup to trap speeders as Baden and Freedom police employed, but autoists were warned of the trap either by bus drivers or drivers posted at the entrance of the trap.

Police cars were stationed an eighth of a mile apart in Leetsdale. The first car was on the north side of the road a half mile in borough limits, while an eighth of a mile further down the highway toward Ambridge another car was stationed. Policemen wore plainclothes, communicated by phone lines connected to light poles and their cars were parked off the highway.

Police Chief A. W. Noland waited below the eighth of a mile sped trap and waved down speeders he had been advised by phone to stop.

But bus rivers got "hep" early today and passed the word around and four cars parked near Edgeworth signalled motorists approaching the trap. One driver, speeding toward the trap, got the signal, shifted into low gear, and tipped his hat to police as he moved slowly past them.

West Aliquippa Tot Lacerates Forehead

Three-year-old Patricia Hallisey fell from a chair at her 232 Beaver avenue home yesterday and suffered a deep cut of the forehead. Dr. J. L. Miller closed the cut with five clips.

National Convention Of Greek Societies Slated Here In July

Aliquippa once again will be host to a national convention.

President George Gerasimon, of the Pan-Rhodian Society, Apollo Lodge 5 here, announced today that the Aliquippa lodge will entertain 20 other Greek orders from all over the United States, starting July 4 and lasting four days.

Two thousand delegates are expected for this 14th annual convention according to Secretary Theodore Nishes. They will come from as far as Washington state. Three other Pennsylvania lodges Farrell, Canonsburg and McKeesport will also be represented.

* * *

President Gerasimon has requested the Board of Trade here to solicit merchants to arrange patriotic decorations during the four day convention and the cooperation of business firms in the preparation of a souvenir album book.

Details of the convention have not yet been completed but the local president said that a banquet and dance would highlight the confab.

N. CHAMBERLAIN RESIGNS POST AS PRIME MINISTER

Britain Prepares For Expected Arrival Of Nazi Push

BULLETIN!

LONDON, (UP) — Prime Minister Neville Chamberlain resigned tonight and Winston Churchill agreed to form a new government.

The new government—it was agreed without exception—shall be one of national unity in which Labor, Liberals and Conservatives alike will join to meet the threat of the dread German blitzkreig.

LONDON — (UP) — Prime Minister Neville Chamberlain is scheduled to broadcast to the nation tonight at 9:15 p. m.—(4:15 p.m. EDT)—announcing his resignation and appealing to all factions to unite behind a government headed by Winston Churchill.

1. Utmost military aid—chiefly by the British air force and land forces in northeastern France—was rushed to the Netherlands and Belgium.

2. Britain prepared against the expected arrival of the dread German air attacks in force on the British Isles.

3. First German bombs dropped on a British town near Canterbury.

4. Emergency stand-by orders

(Continued on Page Five)

LEGION-SPONSORED SHOWS HERE WILL BEGIN TOMORROW

Hurry . . . hurry. Right this way for the pink lemonade and pop corn!

Once again Aliquippans — young and old—can thrill to the barker's cry at the American Legion's carnival which starts at Newell field here tomorrow and runs for one week.

McPherson Shows, Inc., of Buffalo, N. Y., has been engaged for the seven-day stand and will bring five rides and five shows here.

Commander Joseph Kleber of Post 225 assured the public that the Legion was proud to offer such an attraction suitable for "all members of the family."

4 More Aliquippans To Tie Marital Knots

Four Aliquippa residents were among six valley couples who applied at Beaver today for marriage licenses.

Applicants were William R. Stanko, Monaca, and Margaret W. Westerg, Irwin street, Aliquippa; Joseph R. Summers, Franklin avenue, Aliquippa, and Rita Fett, Beaver Falls; William Sestilli, Ambridge, and Jennie B. Kubera, Third ave., Aliquippa; Henry Anderson, rear Fifth ave., Mattie Jeter, Griffith street, Aliquippa, colored; Martin Mild and Edna Smith, Monaca; Joseph Laase and Gladys Powers, Ambridge.

Four Aliquippa Men Appointed To Survey Slum Conditions Here

The Beaver County Housing Authority disclosed today the names of four Aliquippans picked to survey slum conditions in the borough prior to filing a request to the U. S. government for a low-cost housing program here. They include Angelo Romo, George Radulovich, Fred Warren and Wheatley Cobb. The survey will be inaugurated next week.

DUTCH, BELGIAN TROOPS DIG IN; NAZIS DRIVE ON

BULLETIN!

BERLIN—(UP)—German armed forces tonight were reported to have driven 15 to 20 miles into Dutch and Belgian territory and completed the occupation of Luxembourg in a blitzkreig campaign for victory in the European war.

German troops smashing across the Low countries frontiers were reported to have reached the Dutch town of Maastricht and to have seized several bridges on the Albert canal, chief Belgian defense line.

German sources also claimed that the Belgian city of Malmedy had been captured.

BRUSSELS—(UP)—A defense ministry communique said today that Belgian armed forces, now under command of King Leopold, had halted invading German troops at the frontier.

The German forces were halted by the destruction of communication lines, dynamiting of bridges and resistance of Belgian troops, it was asserted.

A terrific aerial battle was reported from the Mons area, where Allied planes joined with Belgian fighting craft to challenge the Germans. About 20 persons were killed and many houses were destroyed or set afire by German bombardment of the Brussels area.

Foreign Minister Henri Spaak rejected the demand of the German Ambassador that the government order the Belgian army and population to cease resistance to the invasion and, following in the footsteps of his father, King Leopold took command of the army to wage war against the Germans.

The defense ministry said that the German invasion was being checked on all fronts. (British and French forces were reported sweeping rapidly into Belgium to aid the fight against the German advance.)

BERLIN—(UP) — Germany's armed forces, under personal direction of Adolf Hitler, struck into Holland, Belgium and Luxembourg at "the hour of decisive combat" today and reported sweeping successes on all fronts.

The Germans claimed that:

1—The Dutch capital, The Hague, had been occupied.

2—Three French airdromes, including the important base at Metz, had been "totally destroyed" and many others badly damaged.

3—All important Dutch and Belgian airports and surrounding districts captured.

4—The airports of Antwerp and Brussesl "successfully" bombed and a Belgian fort captured.

5—A broad attack successfully launched across the western frontiers of Germany.

Hitler, at field headquarters, was directing the vast operations of land, sea and air forces which swept across the low country frontiers, attacked by air and landed along the coast. The Germans were reported using flat bottomed naval craft to operate in areas which the Dutch flooded by blasting their dykes.

The German move to take the low countries under Nazi "protection" was described by Hitler and Foreign Minister Joachim von Ribbentrop as necessary to block an alleged Allied plot for immediate occupation of those states. Hitler, in a proclamation, told the German troops that the "hour for decisive combat for the future of the German nation is now at hand."

The High Command announced that operations were proceeding successfully and the official news agency claimed sweeping triumphs for the German forces.

A communique of the Dutch high command said that defense forces were resisting "desperately" against German troops along the Ijsel and Maas rivers, and on the northeast coast opposite Emden.

The Germans, landing aerial troops at scattered strategic points, were fighting to occupy Rotterdam, where defense barricades were thrown up in the heart of the city and gunfire echoed through the streets.

Belgian troops, under command of King Leopold, were reported fighting strongly in the Aachen district, on the German-Belgian frontier near Holland and the defense ministry at Brussels said that the German advance had been checked at all points while British and French troops rushed to the aid of the low countries.

Air battles were fought over many cities and towns in Holland, Belgium, France and Switzerland, where German planes bombed a railroad near Baule.

WASHINGTON.—(UP)—President Roosevelt met today with the secretaries of state, treasury and justice and the chiefs of the army and navy to consider pressing problems of United States neutrality.

Secretary of Treasury Henry Morgenthau, Jr., originally not scheduled to participate in the extraordinary conference, arrived at the White House unexpectedly.

Serious and showing indications of a sleepless night were Secretary of State Cordell Hull, Undersecretary of State Sumner Welles, Attorney General Robert H. Jackson, Gen. George C. Marshall, chief of staff, and Admiral Harold R. Stark, chief of naval operations.

The full cabinet will hold a regular meeting at 2 p. m.

BERLIN.—(UP)—Belgium, through her ambassador, today delivered a note to Germany declaring a state of war and asserting that history would judge the innocence of Belgium in the conflict with Germany.

LONDON.—(UP)—The Netherlands radio broadcast a Dutch communique this afternoon reporting that the Dutch were strongly resisting the Germans along the line of the Maas and Yssel and were maintaining their positions at Delfzijl opposite Emden.

(Continued on Page Eight)

MONACA CENTENNIAL EDITION

THE DAILY TIMES

ROCHESTER-BEAVER-MONACA

FREEDOM—BRIDGEWATER—CONWAY—VANPORT—MIDLAND

Weather Forecast

Continued cool tonight and Sunday.

Local History

Phillipsburg, later to become Monaca, was incorporated as a borough by the Act of March 6, 1840.

ESTABLISHED APRIL 2, 1874 — BEAVER AND ROCHESTER, PA., SATURDAY, MAY 25, 1940 — BY CARRIER 15 CENTS A WEEK—3 CENTS PER COPY

1840 - MONACA - 1940

Monaca And The Broad Curve Of The Ohio River As Seen From The Air

Monaca Founded On Land Grant

The plot of land which now is known as the First, Second, and Third wards of Monaca, is approximately the same as was originally covered in a Pennsylvania Land Grant to Ephriam Blaine in the year 1787, in pursurance of an application of the land grant dated July 25, 1769, by William A. Lungen, who in the same year granted to Ephriam Blaine all his rights in the application for the grant. The plot of land contained about 330 acres of land and was named in the grant "Appetite."

In 1801 this tract of land was conveyed from Ephriam Blaine to James Blaine. During the same year the tract was transferred from James Blaine to Robert Callender. In 1802 Robert Callender died and in his will bequeathed the land to John Wilkins, George Wallace and Alexander Addison, they to act as trustees and divide the property as set forth in the will of Callender.

In July, 1813, the trustees above named sold the tract of land to John Niblow and in the same year the land was again sold by Niblow to Francis Helveti. In 1821 through a judgment of Frederick Rapp against Helveti, the land was sold by the Sheriff and purchased by Frederick Rapp.

INCORPORATED IN 1840

In 1822 Frederick Rapp sold the tract to Stephen Phillips and John Graham, and in 1834 these men transferred the land to Adam Schule and Anthony Knapper. At

(Continued on Page Twenty-Nine)

Graule Studios

Most of the photos appearing in this Monaca Centennial section of THE TIMES today are from the well known Graule Studios in Rochester. Many of them were printed without identification. Some photos were contributed by the owners, some were taken by TIMES reporters, and still others were obtained from other sources. There are many other prominent, active and worthy men and women of the town whose photos we had hoped to print in this edition. We regret we were unable to get these, although repeated efforts were made. Our sincere thanks are hereby expressed to all who did cooperate with us in furnishing and procuring photos for this edition.—
THE DAILY TIMES.

CHAIRMAN OF CENTENNIAL IS ACTIVE IN TOWN'S AFFAIRS

GLEN F. WILSON

Serving as General Chairman for the Monaca Centennial celebration, Borough Secretary Glen F. Wilson has worked tirelessly and with unbounded energy directing arrangements for the week-long observance.

During the past year Mr. Wilson has devoted most of his leisure time to committee meetings, conferences and other gatherings — many of them continuing until late in the night—pertaining to the celebration. Headquarters for the Centennial is located in the municipal building and there he has been actively and directly in charge of a myriad of details in connection with the week-long observance.

Mr. Wilson, one of the better-known residents of the Southside, has always taken an active part in church, community and civic affairs. A member of the Men's Bible class and the Unit Men of the Monaca Methodist church, he served as first president of the Monaca Men's Club, of which he was one of the organizers; served as president of the old Isaak Walton Lea-

(Continued on Page Thirty-One)

HIGHLIGHTS OF CENTENNIAL CELEBRATION AT MONACA

SUNDAY, MAY 26

11:00 a. m. *Special Morning Services* in all the churches.

2:30 p. m. *Free Band Concert*, Monaca Stadium, Col. Joseph H. Thompson Post No. 261, American Legion.

7:30 p. m. *Community Church Services*, Monaca Stadium. In case of rain, transferred to High School Auditorium.

MONDAY, MAY 27

12:00 Noon *Official Opening* Monaca Centennial, Airplane bombardment.

7:00 p. m. *Streets of the World* and Carnival attractions open.

8:00 p. m. *Mass Band Concert*—Monaca Stadium. Five High School Bands and the Celebrated J. & L. Chorus.

All Day Relic Displays. Manufacturers' Exhibits. Wild Life Displays of the Monaca Sportsmen.

TUESDAY, MAY 28

10 a. m. to 8 p. m. *Special Centennial Attraction—P. & L. E. R. R. and Railway Express Display, Including Modern Train Display.*

1:00 p. m. *Horse Show*—showing the best saddle horses in this section. Monaca Stadium.

7:30 p. m. *Acknowledgement* and reception of Monaca Old Timers.

9:00 p. m. *"Thru the Years."* First showing of Pageant spectacle. Cast of 600—Monaca Stadium.

All Day Relic Displays. Manufacturers' Exhibits. Wild Life Display. Streets of the World, Carnival Attractions.

WEDNESDAY, MAY 29

10:30 a. m. *Children's Parade.* Pets, floats and gaily decorated vehicles.

1:30 p. m. *Children's Events.* Races, etc., Monaca Stadium. Special attraction, Mann School of Dancing.

(Continued on Page Twenty-Nine)

"MISS MONACA"

MISS MARIAN GAERTNER

"MISS CENTENNIAL"

MISS HELEN HEIDEL

Plans Complete For Celebration

Monaca will play host next week to thousands of residents of the tri-state district who will throng the town to join with Southside folk in celebrating the Centennial anniversary of the Ohio river community. All arrangements for the week-long program have been completed and the hundreds of Centennial committee members, tired but happy over the success of their efforts, today awaited fulfillment of their dream.

Gayety and merry-making will prevail throughout the week as crowds swarm through the streets of the thriving borough which is the outgrowth of the tiny village of Phillipsburg.

Many former residents of Monaca now scattered over the eastern United States, relatives and friends of Southside folk and Monaca college and university students home for their summer vacations will swell the throng.

An intensive program has been arranged for the mammoth celebration, one of the most elaborate ever planned in Beaver County. Starting with an entertainment sponsored by Monaca Croatian people this evening in the high school auditorium, the Centennial events will continue throughout the week, with some feature scheduled every day.

Flags, bunting and other gay decorations will adorn the streets, homes and buildings of the town during the celebration and Monacans will don their best bibs and tuckers for the observance. Displays of relics and antiques of the early days of the community, arranged in store windows, are expected to attract much attention.

Band concerts, church services, a parade and contests for children, a horse show, a spectacular historical pageant, athletic contests, an all-nations' festival, a Memorial Day parade and out-board boat regatta, an "old timers' night" program, fire-fighting and first-aid exhibitions, wild life exhibits, manufacturers' and railroad displays, and a "Streets of the World" exhibit are among the highlights of the celebration, which will be climaxed by a huge parade next Saturday afternoon, followed by a boxing show in the evening.

Historical spots about the community and its environs will come in for their full share of attention from the visitors, along with quaint old homes and public buildings.

All municipal officials, church, civic, fraternal and community organizations are co-operating wholeheartedly in sponsoring the program and the celebration is expected to be one of the best ever staged in this district.

CONGRATULATIONS TO MONACA

Today, THE TIMES joins with everybody else in extending congratulations and best wishes to Monaca and all her people. The occasion is the centennial celebration. It will begin tomorrow and continue through next week.

Thirty-two pages of today's TIMES are devoted to an effort to picture the progress, achievements and changes that have taken place in one hundred years in Monaca and her predecessor Phillipsburg. The record herein presented, we know, is incomplete. Many more newspaper pages would be required; much more time and energy would need be expended to show a complete record of advancement in the town and vicinity since the first settlers located there.

However, it is our hope that the word and picture record herein presented will, in a measure, serve the purpose for which it was intended. It will advertise to the general reading public the many features of the centennial celebration; it will mirror to the public at

(Continued on Page Twenty-Nine)

Qualifier Starts Today At Golf Club

Linksmen To Compete In June Match-Play Event

Qualifying rounds for the June match play tournament were scheduled to start today at Aliquippa Golf club.

But threat of rain and wet grounds may delay the golfing until tomorrow. The qualifying play will continue, however, until next Thursday, Decoration Day.

The June matched tourney will be the first links event at the club this season.

Golf Pro John Capebianco said the number of flights for the tournament would be determined by the number of entries in the qualifier. But two flights of 16 linksmen each were expected to compete next month.

The first women's golfing event was slated for June 4—a blind bogey competition.

The women golfers will gather at the club for each Tuesday for a golf lesson and then compete in a special tournament.

Among the events on the club's calendar season will be a special pro-amateur event late this season, possibly in August. Numerous tri-state district professional golfers said they intended to participate.

GLASSES BUOY BUD PARMALEE FOR COMEBACK

Ex-Giant Will Start With Louisville, Red Sox Farm

NEW YORK (UP)—More than one major league baseball player has slipped into minor league oblivion because of poor eyesight but today LeRoy (Bud) Parmelee, former New York Giant pitcher, is trying to reverse that procedure.

Only one fault — wildness — has kept Parmelee from becoming one of the National League's greatest pitchers. He's had trials with three senior loop and had his last opportunity with the Philadelphia Athletics, but he never found the answer to his chief problem.

But now, Parmelee, who's still young enough to make good—he'll be 33 soon—will try for a comeback with the Louisville Colonels of the American Association, wearing glasses.

Dogged by Ill-Luck

Typical of the ill-luck that dogged his footsteps when he was with the New York Giants, St. Louis Cardinals, Chicago Cubs and finally with the Athletics, was his first pitch after donning spectacles.

Pitching in a spring training game at the Colonels' base in Arcadia, Fla., he hit the first batter to face him on the side of the head with a fast ball. The batter was taken to a hospital but was not seriously injured.

Since then Parmelee has consistently improved and observers believe he might regain a major league berth. He pitched three innings against Newark of the International League in his first assignment and was always ahead of the batter—a strange feeling for him. He didn't walk a man, fanned two and allowed two hits.

May Go to Red Sox

If the blasses continue to exercise their magic, Parmelee may get another crack at the big time in the uniform of the Boston Red Sox, who own part of the Louisville club. Manager Joe Cronin would welcome the addition of the big right-hander whose fast ball hasn't lost any of its zing.

All the managers who had Parmelee under their wing realized the enormous talents he possessed but were unable to solve the secret of his apparently incurable wildness. Even cunning old Connie Mack, dean of major league managers, failed to effect a cure, although Parmelee was with him for a shorter time than any of the other pilots.

Even today, Mack shakes his head when asked about Parmelee.

"He's got just as much stuff as ever and if something can be done about that wildness, he might make the grade," said Mack.

PENN STATE ASSOCIATION

Yesterday's Results

Washington 6, Johnston 3.
Other games postponed, rain.

Standing Of The Clubs Today

	W.	L.	Pct.
Johnstown	9	4	.692
Beaver Falls	6	5	.545
Warren	5	5	.500
Washington	6	7	.462
Butler	5	6	.455
McKeesport	3	8	.275

Games Today

Washington at McKeesport.
Johnstown at Butler.
Warren at Beaver Falls.

Games Sunday

Washington at McKeesport.
Johnstown at Butler.
Warren at Beaver Falls.

ARMSTRONG WINS FROM ZANNELLI IN FIFTH ROUND

BOSTON, Mass. (UP) — World Welterweight Champion Henry Armstrong last night defended his title for the seventeenth time when he scored a technical knockout over Ralph (Ripper) Zamelli of Providence, R. I., in the fifth round of a scheduled 15-round bout at Boston Garden.

Armstrong, who at $140\frac{1}{2}$ conceded five pounds to the challenger, punched with machine-like precision

HENRY ARMSTRONG

to drop Zannelli four times for the count of nine before Referee Johnny Martin stopped the bout at one minute 30 seconds of the fifth round.

A crowd of 9,230 fans, who paid $17,336 at the gate, stood in their seats most of the battle.

Armstrong started with a rush and his experience gave him a tremendous advantage over the 25-year-old Italian who previously never had been stopped in 55 fights. Zannelli tried gamely to stick close to the champion but after the first round had only one hope, to land a wild-swinging crusher.

Armstrong was credited with four rounds on the United Press score sheet. The first round was even.

Zannelli attempted to force the fighting in the first round but Armstrong tied him up. In the second, Armstrong floored the Italian for a count of nine. Armstrong floored Zannelli in the third for a count of nine and continued to batter him in the fourth.

Armstrong rushed from his corner at the start of the fifth and sent Zannelli to the canvas for another count of nine. The challenger staggered to his feet and promptly was dropped again.

As the Providence boy rose mechanically to his feet, Martin stopped the fight.

INTERNATIONAL LEAGUE

Newark 17, Baltimore 7; Buffalo 9, Montreal 6; Buffalo 8, Montreal 3. Only games played.

Grimes Fights 1st Pro Bout Monday

Promoters Keep Eye On Jack As Up-And-Comer; Grow So Interested They Even Change His Name

Aliquippa's Jack Grimes will make his debut as a professional fighter Monday night at Hickey Park Bowl, Millvale, in a four-round bout with Lou Pitts of Homewood.

And when Jack Grimes climbs through the ropes in the second step up the fistic ladder, the promoters will regard him as a ring "career man" of vast potentiality, a 160-pounder who has shown every earmark of reaching the top.

Promoter Jake Mintz, who matched Grimes for his first pro battle, said:

"The promoters and managers have heard a lot of good things about Grimes. Johnny Ray, Billy Conn's manager, predicts big things for him. And Art Rooney is very much interested in the boy."

Rooney is the promoter who helped stage the Dorazio-Boyd battle this week at Forbes Field.

"Grimes is going to get every opportunity to make good," Mintz said.

Just how great has been the promoters' interest in Grimes is indicated by the fact that it extends even to his name. Mintz said it would be changed to "Pat," and this is doubly significant.

For although "Pat" may seem a better-ring "tag" to the promoters, it is also the name of Grimes' father, who once fought as a professional himself, and the appropriation of his name is all the more appropriate since in his son, Pat sees his own aspirations. And also because he has trained Jack

Simantiras Photo.
JACK GRIMES
Now He's "Pat"

and taught him boxing from an early age, so it will largely be Pat's knowledge and energy transmuted to his boy.

Pat pronounced Jack in "good shape," completely recovered from the rib injury that kept him inactive for a month.

And he said he hoped Jack would have as much success in the pro ranks as in the amateur ring in which the Aliquippa boy swept the 160-pound diamond belt championship and cleaned up almost every honor available. He fought a score of bouts, losing only three, and evened all but one of them in return frays.

Jack will encounter no pushover in Pitts, who has been a professional for two months. But in that time he has won five straight bouts. Moreover, he did as creditably as Grimes while an amateur, copping the junior and senior welterweight titles in 1939.

The Mintz card will include two four rounders, a six, an eight, and a ten. The main event will be between Irish Jimmy Webb, who fought John Kapovich Tuesday in the Forbes Field show, and Vic Sarlin, the "Beltzhoover bad boy."

In the second 4-rounder, Art Canter of Pittsburgh will be making his debut as a pro. He has won the amateur middleweight championship. He will take on Steve Walters of Sewickley.

Red Dorgan, 138, of Duquesne University, will battle Jesse Glenn of the Pittsburgh Hill district in the six-round set-to. And Johnny Rucker, 135, of Pittsburgh, was slated to go eight rounds with Mike Camieri of Cleveland, a classy lightweight who has licked Wes Ramey and Ray Sharkey.

Umpire Urges 'Back To Farm' Movement For Young Players

SEYMOUR, Ind.—(UP)—Harry Geisel of Indianapolis advises that athletic youth go back to the farm where flies, hickory and popcorn flourish—the baseball farm.

In an address before a crowd of Hoosier baseball fans here Geisel, a big league umpire for 25 years, asserted that prospects for success in professional baseball "are better than ever before."

He said that both leagues are in dire need of good players.

Crashing into the big league is not the primary benefit in joining a farm, he said. Physical culture and experience, he said, are more important and at the same time more certain.

Help Declared Lasting

"Not everyone can hope to be a Bob Feller," added the veteran umpire. "But if the youth doesn't make good in the training camp he has had a fine experience and a background for future life."

Geisel pointed out that pecuniary returns for a rookie were not as good as wages in industrial occupations, but he countered with the statement that there is always a chance to break into the big money of the higher brackets.

Reminiscing, Geisel told of how in the "old days" the crowds regarded the umpire about as impartial as a doting mother-in-law.

"Street car companies refused to let us ride on their cars," he recalled. "They said the hostile fans would hurl stones at the windows of the trolley."

No Taxis Either

He said that even the cabs wouldn't haul an official to or from the ball park for the same reason.

"We just walked and thought nothing of it," he said.

Geisel saw his first world series from the stands last year. Previously he had worked the games.

"An ump doesn't get much kick out of watching the game after you've spent a quarter of a century on the lot learning to be impartial," he said. "It takes something out of the game if you can't be partial."

The veteran official will work out in the Detroit Tiger camp in Miami until the spring circuits open. He declared that physical fitness is important to the umpire in calling balls and strikes.

Baseball Standing

NATIONAL LEAGUE

Yesterday's Results

New York, 8; Boston 1.

Pittsburgh-Chicago, postponed, wet grounds.

Brooklyn-Philadelphia, postponed, rain.

Only games scheduled.

Standing Of The Clubs Today

1939		W.	L.	Pct.	G.B.
2	Cincinnati	18	8	.692	
6	Brooklyn	18	8	.692	
7	New York	16	11	.593	$2\frac{1}{2}$
3	Chicago	17	13	.567	3
8	Philadelphia	11	13	.458	6
1	St. Louis	10	17	.370	$8\frac{1}{2}$
5	Boston	8	16	.333	9
4	Pittsburgh	6	18	.250	11

Games Today—Pitching Selections

Chicago at Forbes Field—French (5-2) vs. Bowman (1-2).

St. Louis at Cincinnati (2) — Warneke (1-4) and McGee (3-2) vs. Walters (6-0) and Thompson (5-2).

Brooklyn at Philadelphia—Hamlin (2-2) vs. Higbe (3-3).

Boston at New York— Sullivan (1-4) vs. Lohrman (2-0).

Games Sunday

Chicago at Forbes Field, 3 p. m.
Brooklyn at Philadelphia.
St. Louis Cincinnati.
Boston at New York.

AMERICAN LEAGUE

Yesterday's Results

Chicago 2; Detroit 1.
Only games scheduled.

Standing Of The Clubs Today

1939		W.	L.	Pct.	G.B.
2	Boston	19	8	.704	
4	Cleveland	18	10	.643	$1\frac{1}{2}$
7	Detroit	15	14	.517	5
3	Chicago	14	16	.467	$6\frac{1}{2}$
5	Washington	13	17	.433	$7\frac{1}{2}$
6	Philadelphia	12	16	.429	$7\frac{1}{2}$
8	St. Louis	11	15	.423	$7\frac{1}{2}$
1	New York	11	17	.393	$8\frac{1}{2}$

Games Today—Pitching Selections

New York at Boston (2)—Pearson (3-2) and Chandler (1-3) vs. Dickman (4-2) and Harris (2-1).

Detroit at Chicago—Trout (0-1) vs. Knott (2-0).

Cleveland at St. Louis—Harder (1-1) or Milnar (4-1) vs. Bildilli (1-2).

Philadelphia at Washington—Dean (4-1) vs. Leonard (4-3).

Games Sunday

Philadelphia at Washington.
Cleveland at St. Louis.
New York at Boston.
Detroit at Chicago.

Farewell To Arms, But Just To Enter Race At Indianapolis

AL PONTE DI PASSEGGIATA
TO PROMENADE DECK

Rene Le Begue (left) and Rene Dreyfus, French soldiers, arrive in New York aboard the Italian *Conte di Savoia* en route to Indianapolis, Ind., for the annual 500-mile Memorial Day automobile race. They were given special leave from the army so they could drive in the race.

BORO'S VALLEY LOOPERS IDLE OVER WEEK END

The P. C. club's baseball contest with Chippewa at Franklin field was rained out yesterday.

And unless last-minute arrangements are made for Sunday games, the Celtic-Reds and the P. C.'ers, the borough's entries in the Beaver Valley baseball league, will remain idle until next week.

But they'll have a full schedule then.

The Celts go to bat Monday at Ambridge, Wednesday Chippewa plays here and Friday the Celts will travel to Freedom. Manager John Ayoob, however, was reported to be trying to line up an opponent for Fireman's field tomorrow.

The P. C. team will play at Rochester Tuesday, and meet East Rochester here Wednesday. The Hilltoppers of Coach Fred Milanovich will travel to Darlington next Friday.

Light Favorite To Cop Altoona Race Thursday

ALTOONA, PA.—Mark Light of Lebanon, the east's second ranking A.A.A. driver of 1939 and current leader in the running for 1940 individual honors, looms as a pre-pace favorite to win major awards in the automobile events at the Altoona speedway Memorial Day.

The Lebanon veteran faces competition from a star-studded field that includes Texan Buddy Rusch, winner of the 1939 feature race, but twice this spring he has served notice that he is championship bound.

Light took first place in the 20-lap feature event at Reading in the eastern inaugural last month. After turning in the fastest qualifying lap to win the pole position he finished third in a 10-lap sprint.

Light finished second in one 8-lap race and was leading the pack in another when a broken connecting rod forced his withdrawal and enabled Buster Warke to capture first place.

Susnjer's Chances To Cop Shot Put Title At State Meet Today Look Good

But To Break State Record For Event Is Tougher

Nick Susnjer of Aliquippa High will have to better his shot put by a good four feet if he is to break the record for the event today in the Pennsylvania Interscholastic Athletic league track and field meet at State College, Pa.

But indications were that a heave slightly better than 50 feet, possibly 51, would cinch the title this year.

Susnjer, who left yesterday for the event with Coach Roger Jones, had tossed the shot 49 feet $4\frac{1}{2}$ inches, but the hottest contenders in the **meet, a few boys from Erie, have done only slightly better with heaves** of about 50 feet.

The 53 foot, 7 inch state record has stood since 1936 when Smith of Ridley Park set the mark.

Preliminary heats in the track contest and field trials were slated for this morning with the finals this afternoon. The meet is being held in conjunction with a dual meet between Penn State's varsity and Navy's unbeaten track stars.

The best of the schoolboy track and field athletes will compete. District champions all. District 7 is defending its team championship won last year.

BEGGS TO PLAY HERE NEXT WEEK

Reds Come To Forbes Field For Three-Day Stand

The first double-header in a new baseball season always is a magnet that draws the fans to the park in large numbers. Next Monday afternoon, is the time set for the initial bargain bill of 1940 at Forbes Field, **and the card carries additional appeal because the club appearing** against the Pirates will be the champion Cincinnati Reds.

District fans have not had a previous chance to see the Reds in action this year, as when Bill McKechnie's champions first visited Pittsburgh to play what was scheduled as the opening series of the Forbes Field season, all three of the slated games were postponed on account of rain, cold and wet grounds. The extra game in Monday's twin card is one carried over from April 20.

* * *

McKechnie's champs are admittedly stronger than in 1939, when they won their first pennant since 1919. One of the prize rookies of the year, Mike McCormick, has come up from Indianapolis to bolster the outfield; Eddie Joost has given the infield some new and helpful blood; the pitching staff has been augmented and improved by the acquisition of Jim Turner, from the Bees, Joe Beggs, from the Yankees, and others, and there is additional new timber, including Johnny Rizzo, former Pirate outfielder and power hitter.

Joe Beggs is from Aliquippa, and a host of local friends will be at Forbes Field to do him honor during the four-game series on Monday, Tuesday and Wednesday. Monday's double-header will start at 1:45 o'clock Eastern Daylight Saving Time. The Reds will remain over for single contests on Tuesday and Wednesday, starting at 3:15 p. m. They will be followed on Thursday, Memorial Day, by the St. Louis Cardinals for a big holiday doubleheader, starting at 1:45 p. m., Eastern Daylight Saving Time.

PHILS SIGN BLANTON

PHILADELPHIA, (UP) The Philadelphia Phillies today announced the signing of Darrell (Cy) Blanton, curve ball pitcher recently set free from the Pittsburgh Pirates. Blanton, a native of Waureka, Okla., is 31. He joined Pittsburgh late in 1934.

Southside Boasts Of Many Fine Farms

Many fine farms are found in the rural area immediately surrounding Monaca. In Center and Potter townships and other sections of the Southside are some of the finest dairy, fruit and crop farms in the county. Numerous Southside farmers have won prizes with their products at fairs and other competitions.

Monaca Man Pursues Photographic Hobby

A prominent Monaca resident, F. E. Garvin, makes photography his hobby and has attained an enviable reputation for his work in that field. Possessing numerous cameras, including a large portrait outfit, he has a fully-equipped darkroom in the basement of his home where he develops and prints his pictures.

Old Houses In Monaca Stand As Landmarks

Numerous houses erected in the early days at Monaca still stand as landmarks of a bygone era. With their quaint style of architecture, and some of them built out flush with the sidewalk, the old structures arouse much interest among visitors.

Monaca's Only Triplets Pride Of Community

Romischer Triplets Today

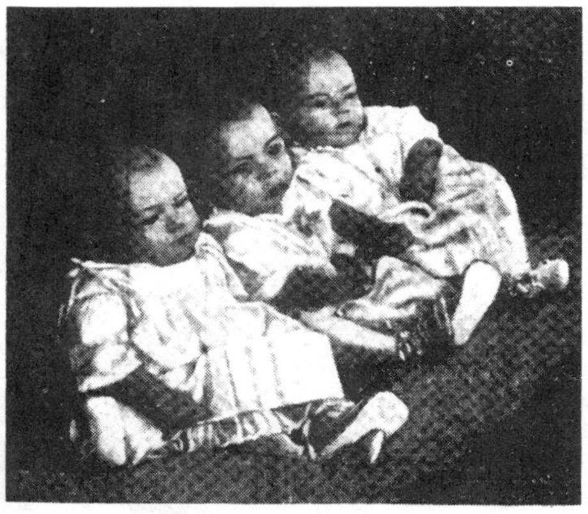

Romischer Tripl ets As Babies

Danella, Dean and Danciel Romischer, three smiling-faced blondes, Monaca's only triplets and first triplets to be born in Rochester hospital, are the children of Mr. and Mrs. Daniel Romischer, 499 Fourteenth street, Monaca. They were born October 25, 1937.

The trio, all perfect specimens of health, have sunny dispositions. Their splendid health is attributed to a careful diet planned by Dr. John H. Trumpeter, Monaca, for the first year. They converse freely and are especially fond of each other.

The Romischers have three other daughters—Ella Mae, 9; Mary Sue, 7, and Marlan Lee 6. They assume much of the responsibility of entertaining and caring for their younger sisters and brother while their mother carries on her household duties.

Sportsmen's Club Aided By Auxiliary

The Ladies' Auxiliary to the Beaver Valley Sportsmen's Club, Monaca, organized in 1933, is one of the active women's groups of Monaca. The organization, comprising fifty members, meets semi-monthly in the sportsmen's clubhouse.

Women who were instrumental in organizing the auxiliary are: Mrs. Louis G. Smith, Mrs. Earl Davis, Mrs. Elizabeth Davis, Mrs. William Volhardt and Mrs. Harry Lavery.

MRS. DENNIS CRONIN

The first group of officers elected included: President, Mrs. Lavery; vice-president, Mrs. Earl Davis; secretary, Mrs. Volhardt; treasurer, Mrs. Elizabeth Davis. Officers now serving are: President, Mrs. Dennis Cronin; vice-president, Mrs. McKinley Sinclair; secretary, Mrs. William Riddle; treasurer, Mrs. George P. Elmer.

Monaca String Orchestra Aids In Centennial

The Liberty String Orchestra, (above) Monaca, composed entirely of Croation young folk, gave benefit performances to aid in promoting the "All-Nations Festival" and "Streets of the World," to be a part of the Monaca Centennial celebration.

The orchestra, organized four years ago, is made up entirely of residents of the Fifth Ward, Monaca, and directed by Prof. Rosgay, Ambridge. Jacob Jancio, Monaca, is the manager.

Members of the orchestra are: Julia Turbish, George Susie, Prof. Rosgay, George Cindrich, Barbara Susie, Matthew Zupsic, Matthew Frenchic, John Shaban, Matthew Rebrovic and Steve Turbish.

MONACA SENIOR WOMAN'S CLUB ORGANIZED AT MEETING IN 1921

Having caught the vision of existing problems and conditions awaiting the "touch of a woman's hand," and sensing the expediency of an organization in Monaca that would unite the influence and the enterprise of women, a number of women answered the call of Mrs. D. J. Mitchell (now deceased), and Mrs. D. C. Locke, to meet the afternoon of January 19, 1921, in the old Presbyterian church, with Mrs. Lillian C. Hurst, Rochester, president of the Beaver County Federation of Women's clubs.

Mrs. Locke was made chairman of the meeting, with Mrs. J. H. Martsolf (now deceased), as secretary. Out of this embryo meeting, emerged the present Woman's Club of Monaca.

An organization was effected on that day with thirty-eight members. Following is a list of the first officers elected: President, Mrs. D. C. Locke; first vice-president, Mrs. D. J. Mitchell; second vice-president, Mrs. Mary Jenkins (deceased); recording secretary, Mrs. C. M. Wagner; corresponding secretary, Mrs. J. H. Martsolf (deceased), treasurer, Mrs. Charles Houston; delegates to the county Federation, Mrs. E. M. Callaghan and Mrs. E. H. McMahon.

The following Thursday, the club was received into the Beaver County Federation of Women's clubs at the county's first annual meeting in Beaver Falls, and on April 7, 1921, the club became a member of the Pensylvania State Federation of Women's clubs.

CIVIC ORGANIZATION

Although the club cannot be credited with any spectacular accomplishments, still it has striven "to touch and to know the great common heart of us all" by reaching out into many philanthropic and civic fields such as the American Red Cross, Salvation Army, Disable Veterans, Rochester General Hospital, Passavant Memorial Homes, Beaver County Children's Home, New Brighton; Beaver County Home for the Aged, New Brighton, Beaver County Sanatorium, Monaca; Students' Fund, school and town libraries, assisted with the Girl Scout movement, the work of the blind, and sponsored other civic projects.

The club also sponsored the Mitchell Memorial essay contest, a community Christmas tree, toy mission and other enterprises.

The club has a swimming pool fund and a club house fund awaiting the town's co-operation in making these dreams realities.

In the fall of 1933, the club endorsed the organization of a Junior Woman's club, and, in January 1940 a Garden committee was appointed which eventually will become the Garden Club of Monaca.

PRESENT OFFICERS

The president of the Beaver County Federation of Women's club is Mrs. William J. Miller, one of Monaca's own club members. The club's representative on the Centennial Board is Mrs. O. H. Locke.

The club officers are: President, Mrs. E. E. Groth, first vice-president, Mrs. John M. Dunn, second vice-president, Miss Edna Langer, recording secretary, Mrs. Gilbert Trumpeter, corresponding secretary, Mrs. John A. Swanson, treasurer, Mrs. Lee R. Boezer. Mrs. Frank T. Dindinger and Mrs. Harry I. Johnston, are the club delegates.

MRS. E. E. GROTH

The club continued to meet in the old Presbyterian church until the church was razed in 1931 and since then has been meeting in the Methodist church.

Monaca Noted For Its Unexcelled Gardens

Monaca has long been noted as one of the "garden spots" of Beaver Valley. Scores of residents of the town take great pride in their fine gardens, both vegetable and flower, and much of the vacant land in the borough is utilized for that purpose in the Spring and Summer. Many Monacans have enviable reputations as vegetable and flower growers.

Mary Campbell Ferry Landing, Monaca, Before Bridges Were Built

Here is pictured the landing at the old Monaca wharf which was long used by the historic old ferryboat "Mary Campbell," plying the Ohio river between Monaca and Rochester. When a bridge was built between the two communities the ferryboat no longer was needed.

Heads School Board, Library Directors

Hugh C. Johnston, (above) prominent Monaca citizen, who was named first president of the Monaca Library Board when the board organized recently, has served as a member of the Monaca Board of Education the past five years.

Associated with the Pittsburgh-Fairmont Coal Company at Pittsburgh, as traffic manager, Mr. Johnston, at the general session of the Interstate Commerce Commission in its offices at Washington, D. C., in 1936, was enrolled as a practicioner, which permits him to present traffic cases to the Interstate Commerce Commission. He is one of the few traffic experts in Western Pennsylvania holding a practicioner's certificate.

Born in Freedom, a son of Mrs. Sara Johnston, Beaver, and the late Hugh C. Johnston, he has spent his entire life in the lower Valley and the past 26 years has been a resident of Monaca.

Two Monaca Banks Were Organized And Chartered In 1901

National And Citizen Banks Merged As First National Bank In 1937

In the year 1901, the need of banking facilities in Monaca was keenly felt, especially as a result of the establishment of the plants of the United States Sanitary Manufacturing Company and the Colonial Steel Company with the resultant increase in population. Responding to this demand, two groups of civic-minded men met and organized the Monaca National Bank and the Citizens National Bank of Monaca. The charter of the Monaca National Bank was issued on April 4, 1901, while the charter of the Citizens National Bank of Monaca was issued June 25, 1901.

The Monaca National Bank was capitalized at $25,000. Its first Board of Directors were: George Lay, Martin Carey, Harry C. Glasser, Charles Houston, James R. Gormley, Henry J. Eckert, and Robert L. Hood. Its first officers consisted of George Lay, president; James R. Gormley, vice president, and Robert L. Hood, cashier.

The Citizens National Bank of Monaca was capitalized at $50,000. The first Board of Directors of this bank were: John T. Taylor, James H. Welch, John J. Allen, Henry C. Fry, Edward Kaye, Christian Will, Frederick Bechtel, J. C. Martin, and A. M. Jolley. Its first officers were: John T. Taylor, president; John J. Allen, vice president, and Thomas C. Fry, cashier.

BOTH SOUND BANKS

The two banks served the community well and under careful and capable management played a prominent role in the development of the town. The strength of the two banks were never in doubt, and, at the conclusion of the bank holiday in 1933, both banks were reopened, proving their stability.

In order to better serve the people of Monaca, on January 2, 1937, the two institutions were consolidated, forming the First National Bank of Monaca with a capitalization of $100,000. The first officers elected were: George W. Weinman, president; Alonzo S. Batchelor, vice president; and Charles W. Weinman cashier. The death of George W. Weinman occurred in January, 1937, after which Alonzo S. Batchelor succeeded to the presidency, and F. A. LeGoullon and Dr. D. C. Moore were elected vice presidents.

The present members of the board of directors of the bank are; Alonzo S. Batchelor, D. C. Moore, F. A. LeGoullon, Charles W. Weinman, R. E. McCreary, J. H. E. McMillan, Frank M. Batchelor, Thomas H. Howard, W. R. Jeffreys, Morgan H. Sohn, and C. F. Arrott. The present officers are: Alonzo S. Batchelor, president; Dr. D. C. Moore, vice president; F. A. LeGoullon, vice president; Charles W. Weinman, cashier; Fred H. Brobeck, assistant cashier; J. Renwick Gormley, assistant cashier, and Mont D. Youtes, Jr., assistant cashier.

First National Bank of Monaca

A. S. BATCHELOR

Many Families Were Among Pioneers Of Early Phillipsburg

Numerous Names Connected With Early History Of Community On Southside

The signing of the Greenville Treaty in 1795 made safe the settlement of the Northwest Territory. One of the last acts of the old Continental Congress was the passage of the "Ordinance of 1787" which defined the manner and form of land grants in this territory. Much of those lands were already possessed by those who were able to purchase large tracts for exploitation, when the first wave of settlers came, and the questions of ownership soon became the leading one.

Again, the soldiers who had served in the Revolutionary armies were largely paid in land. Portions of these grants were usually sold to others to enable the original owner to consolidate the remainder. When these large tracts were held undivided, the settlers were often compelled to go back further into the interior to secure lands.

For these, and many other reasons, the pioneer families were widely-scattered in this vicinity. Many of our prominent citizens of today are descendants of these hardy pioneers. In this first group are found the names of Blaine, Baker, Bruce, Quinn, Temple, Tod, Srodes, Phillips, Graham, McConnell, Potter, LeGoullon and others. These were largely of Scotch-Irish descent.

The purchase of the holdings of Phillips and Graham by Maximilian brought in the Germanic group from Economy some 30 years later. In this wave are the names of Autenreith, Frank, Fath, Trumpeter, Lay, Lais, Schaefer, Knapper, Davis, Shule, Erb, Hahn, Heydl, Fischer, Schmidt, Zutle and others. While many of these spread over the farm lands of the rural sections, the majority settled in Phillipsburg, which they dominated for the next 50 years, or until the coming of the industries.

To these must be added another group of those who were recruited from Economy or came directly from Germany. In this last wave we find the names of the Botts, Blatts, Bimbers, Bechtels, Erbecks, Ackers, Huffs, Merkels, Markeys, Bickerstaffs, Vollhardts, Muellers (Millers), and others. Limited space will not permit mention of many whose vigor and leadership were an asset to this community.

Monaca Sportsmen's Club Is Affiliated With County League

Recently Formed Organization Now Embraces Membership Of More Than 100

The Monaca Sportsmen's club, organized November 15, 1939, is affiliated with the Beaver County Sportsmen's League, also the Pennsylvania Federation of Sportsmen.

Officers of other Valley sportsmen's clubs were in attendance for the organizations meeting when officers were elected. The officers include: President, Ralph Aumack; vice-president, Frank Sephton; secretary - treasurer, Arthur H. Brown. The board of directors, including the above officers, are: Councilman A. Howard Brown, Henry H. Grosshans, John Miller and James Arbogast.

When the club organized there were about 50 members enrolled and the present membership is 115. Meetings are held once a month in the Monaca Polish-Alliance hall.

RALPH AUMACK

Among the most active sportsmen of the Valley is Ralph Aumack.

Monaca Not Dependent On Any One Industry

Monaca, unlike so many small towns, is not a "one industry" community, but instead boasts a diversity of industrial enterprises.

In a dozen or more plants a great variety of products are manufactured, ranging from glass to bathroom fixtures. Hundreds of persons are employed in Monaca industries and the community is a thriving manufacturing center.

Dr. Huber Wagner Once Monaca Star

Dr. J. Huber Wagner, now a prominent physician and surgeon in Pittsburgh, was perhaps the greatest of all Monaca's early football stars.

During his career Dr. Wagner played every position in football except that of quarterback, but it was at end that he achieved lasting fame. University of Pittsburgh men of 25 years or more ago still regard him as one of the greatest ends to ever perform for the Panthers.

Wagner, according to best available records, began his football career in Monaca high school during the seasons of 1906, 1907 and 1908. In 1909 he went to Geneva, but transferred to Pitt the following year and starred for the Panther elevens for four seasons.

Following his graduation from Pitt Dr. Wagner played professional football three years. Today, although his fame as a doctor and surgeon has overshadowed his fame as a football player, older Monaca residents still regard him as one of the greatest of the Southside community's many great athletes.

Monaca Women Completed Red Cro ss Course In Hygiene, Care Of Sick

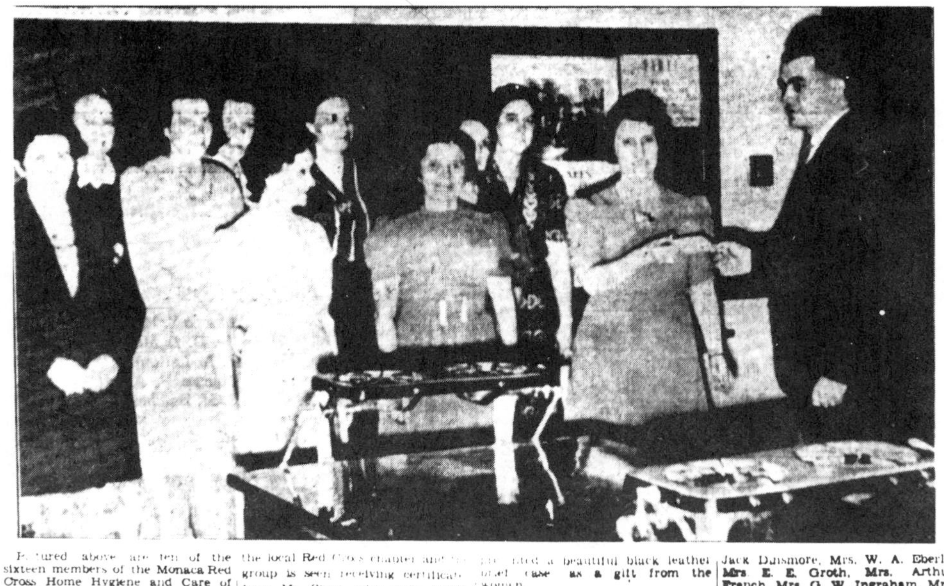

Pictured above are ten of the sixteen members of the Monaca Red Cross Home Hygiene and Care of the Sick class, and Robert C. Stout of Beaver, chairman of the Beaver County Chapter of the American Red Cross.

The class completed its course, conducted under the supervision of the local Red Cross chapter and the group is seen receiving certificates from Mr. Stout, who spoke briefly of the Red Cross, its work, activities and accomplishments.

The class was taught by Mrs. Helen Schupay, R. N., of Monaca, the Monaca school nurse. She was presented a beautiful black leather brief case as a gift from the women.

Following is a list of members of the class: Mrs. A. W. Anderson, Mrs. Helen Aumack, Mrs. James Barnett, Mary Bucsko, Esther Dinsmore, Mrs. F. B. Dinsmore, Mrs. Jack Dinsmore, Mrs. W. A. Eberle, Mrs. E. E. Groth, Mrs. Arthur French, Mrs. G. W. Ingraham, Mrs. Maude Kuhn, Mrs. O. H. Locke, Mrs. L. G. Moslener, Mrs. I. H. Todd, Mrs. J. A. Swanson.

All are residents of Monaca with the exception of Mrs. Kuhn, who lives in Rochester.

First Woolen Mill in Monaca

SCENES FROM MONACA'S BIG CENTENNIAL CELEBRATION

"Miss Monaca" (Marian Gaertner) and "Miss Centennial" (Helen Heidel), winner and runner-up, respectively, in the Centennial popularity contest, viewing the spectacular Centennial historical pageant, "Thru the Years." Seated around them are their attendants and members of their court.

Photo by Graule Studios

Polish folk-dance presented by lower valley young people as part of "All-Nations Festival".

Photo by Graule Studios

Czecho-Slovakian group from Ambridge presenting native dance at "All-Nations Festival".

Awarded first prize in the Centennial parade, the crack drum and bugle corps of Walter S. Roth Post, No. 498, American Legion, Rochester, is shown parading past the reviewing stand.

Photo by Graule Studios

The covered-wagon used in the Monaca pageant depicting the means of transportation used by early settlers of the county.

Monaca borough officials, undaunted by the rain, marching past parade reviewing stand. Red Cross first-aid trailer shown in background.

County Commissioner E. H. Markey, Monaca, parade marshal, and his chief-of-staff, leading the Centennial parade on motorcycle.

NEW BRIGHTON
N B

Prize-winning New Brighton Borough float bearing "birthday cake" topped with 100 candles, and inscription reading: "Happy Birthday Monaca."

Prize-winning Crescent Township Drum and Bugle Corps executing drill in front of parade reviewing stand.

Thousands View

(Continued from Page 1)

were: Judges for the various divisions; older members of the American Legion Auxiliary to Monacatootha Post, No. 580; Mrs. G. W. Winkle, Monaca's only Gold Star Mother; Beaver County officials and guests; other prominent county folk and newspaper reporters.

Headed by County Commissioner E. H. Markey, Chief Marshal; O. H. Locke, Chief of Staff; John J. Hanlon and Clare R. Sowash, aides to the Chief of Staff, the parade formed at Sixth street and Indiana avenue, moved up Indiana avenue to Sixteenth street, thence to Pennsylvania avenue and past the reviewing stand to Sixth street.

PARTICIPATING UNITS

Included in the parade were: Massed colors, Col. Joseph T. Thompson Band, Co. B 110th Infantry, Rochester Legion Drum and Bugle Corps, Beaver County Legion Posts, New Castle Cadet Band and New Castle American Legion Band, Veterans of Foreign Wars and Sons of Veterans, British War Veterans and Sons of Veterans, New Brighton High School Band, American Legion Auxiliary to Monacatootha Post No. 580, Ambridge Sons of Legion, Beaver County Chapter No. 14, Military Order of the Purple Heart.

Monaca Council and Monaca Board of Education, Aliquippa Woman's Benefit Association, Monaca Woman's Benefit Association, Ambridge Community Band, Czecho-Slovak Society, Croatian Fraternal Union, Monaca Polish Society, United Polish Society, Ambridge Band, Monaca Z. N. P. No. 841, West Aliquippa Sons of Italy, Monaca Sons of Italy, Crescent Township Band.

Aliquippa Troop No. 430, Aliquippa American Legion Troop No. 401, Aliquippa Troop No. 401, Aliquippa Troop No. 436, Ambridge Troop No. 403, Beaver Falls Rotary Troop No. 411, Beaver Falls Troop No. 437, Crescent Township Troop No. 415, Freedom High School Band, New Brighton Troop No. 480, Bridgewater Troop No. 448, Rochester Cub Pack No. 7, Patterson Heights Cub Pack No. 51, West Mayfield Girl Scout Troop and Midland Troops No. 1 and 2, Campfire Girls, Midland High School Band.

Beaver High School Band, New Brighton Fire Department, Freedom, Center Township, Conway, Sewickley and Ambridge Fire Departments, Sharpsburg Girls' Drum and Bugle Corps, Sharpsburg Cadets, Patterson Township Fire Department, Baden, Fallston, East Rochester and Vanport- Fire Departments, Rochester High School Band, Rochester, Aliquippa and Beaver Falls Fire Departments, Beaver Falls High School Band, Millvale Fire truck, Millvale Fire Department, Beaver Fire Department, Midland Fire Department, Rochester Township Fire Department, White Township Fire Department and Auxiliary, Ellwood City Fire Department, J. Wilbur Randolph American Legion Post, No. 157, Ellwood City, Ellwood City fire trucks, New Galilee squad car, Monaca fire trucks.

Butchelor Brothers ambulance, Pettibon Dairy Company, Christy Antoline ("The Man From Mars"), "Chief Monacatootha" and "Queen Aliquippa," Monaca First Ward School, "May Queen", Monaca Fourth Ward School, Marshall Road School, Dolores Garvin, little Beaver girl riding her own pony; George E. Dietrich, Monaca, bathroom display, Koehler and Weigle outfit, Balamut Electric, Junior Order United American Mechanics, Monaca Girl Scouts, Rochester Eagles, Sloboda Croatian orchestra, Sons and Daughters of Liberty, Monaca Saxon Society, Miller Market, Morris Service Station, Frank E. Garvin, Monaca, and old car, Vanport Auto parts, Beaver Valley Service Company, Monaca Men's club, Dalzell's Clover Farm store, Derringer Service station, Beaver County ambulance service.

Monaca High School Band, Monaca Borough float, New Brighton Borough float, Charles H. Haney Lumber Company, Freedom, Fezell's Super Service, Hartzel Brothers, Rochester, Rochester Rotary club, Martin M. Meiter farm tractor, Monaca Senior Woman's club ("Indians"), Frick's Service station, Railway Express, delivery truck, United States Sanitary bathroom display, Aliquippa W. B. A. drill team, Louis Horvatin Croatian Society, Beaver Falls Rotary Scout Troop 411, Italian Society and Band, Crescent Township Drum and Bugle corps, Boy Scout troop No. 495, Aliquippa; Chippewa Township Boy Scouts, Monaca Body Shop, Freedom High School Band, Funk Dairy, Beaver County Chapter, American Red Cross, Coleman ambulance.

New Brighton firemen (marching), Freedom firemen (marching), Freedom Fire Department pumper, Center Township Forest Fire Company, Center Township firemen (marching), Center Township light pump, Conway Fire Department pump, Sewickley Fire Department pump, Ambridge Fire Department ladder truck, Vanport chemical truck, Patterson Township Auxiliary, firemen, truck and pumper, Fallston, East Rochester chemical and hose trucks, Rochester firemen (marching) and service truck, Aliquippa Indians and service truck, Beaver Falls firemen (marching) pump and ladder, Patterson Heights light pump, Millvale squad car, Beaver Fire Department, pumper and ladder truck, Bridgewater's combination pump and hose wagon, Midland Service car and ladder truck, Rochester Township Fire Department (marching) pump and service car, White Township chemical truck, White Township auxiliary to the Fire Department, Koppel Fire Department and pump, Ellwood City Drum Corps, firemen (marching) and pumper and squad, New Galilee squad car, Monaca Volunteer Fire Department and aerial truck, Rochester hospital nurses.

BOROUGH OFFICIALS IN LINE

Burgess Elmer E. Hicks, Monaca police, Monaca Borough Council and Glen F. Wilson, borough secretary and general chairman of the Centennial Committee, and Monaca Board of Education were among the first in line.

There were approximately forty-

(Continued on Page Five)

Miss Betty White Of Rochester Marries Woodrow W. Smith

Couple Married In Wellsburg, W. Va.; To Reside In Bridgewater

Mr. and Mrs. Charles I. White, Rochester, announce the marriage of their youngest daughter, Betty, to Woodrow W. Smith, youngest son of Mrs. Elizabeth Smith of Beaver.

The ceremony was performed on April 26, in Wellsburg, W. Va., and kept a secret until the bride, a member of the 1940 class of Rochester high school, was graduated. The bridegroom is a graduate of the Avella high school, class of 1938, and is manager of the A. B. Patsch service station, Conway's Corner, Rochester.

Mr. Smith sustained three broken bones in his right foot in an accident the latter part of last week and after he recovers the couple will make their home in Market street, Bridgewater.

Commencement To

(Continued from Page One)

auditorium, both on the main floor and in the gallery was occupied, with some extra chairs near the entrance to the lower floor. He chose for his text Hebrews 8:5, God's admonition to Moses when he was about to make the tabernacle: "See that thou make all things according to the pattern showed to them in the mount." Using these words as a Scriptural basis, he urged the members of the class to build their lives on a solid foundation, with a noble purpose, strengthened with integrity, and with a constant look upward.

Practically all the members of this year's classes in both the June and August divisions were present to hear the sermon, as well as numerous alumni from various sections of the country who are here for tonight's alumni reunion and banquet, the commencement exercises tomorrow and the reunion of certain classes following the exercises. Among those are some from as far west at Arizona and as far east as New York and New Jersey, and south to Kentucky.

The usual "class day" exercises were held at 10 a. m. today and drew a large crowd, filling the auditorium.

Weather Forecast
Local showers and thunderstorms tonight and Tuesday; not much change in temperature.
Pollen count: Trees, 3; grasses, 164.

THE DAILY TIMES

ROCHESTER-BEAVER-MONACA

FREEDOM—BRIDGEWATER—CONWAY—VANPORT—MIDLAND

Local History
On September 23, 1836 Beaver Council took a subscription for a new fire-engine and collected $130; the engine cost $125.

ESTABLISHED APRIL 2, 1874 | BEAVER AND ROCHESTER, PA., MONDAY, JUNE 10, 1940 | BY CARRIER 15 CENTS A WEEK—3 CENTS PER COPY

ITALY ENTERS WAR TODAY

WORK STARTED ON PASSAVANT HOMES RECREATION HALL

Impressive Ground-Breaking Ceremony Held Sunday At Institution In Rochester

Forty-Fifth Anniversary Of Homes Also Observed At Service Held Yesterday

Attended by friends of the institution from Beaver county and the Pittsburgh district, impressive ceremonies marking the forty-fifth anniversary of the Passavant Memorial Homes for the Care of Epileptics, Rochester, and the breaking of ground for the proposed new $53,000 recreation hall were held Sunday afternoon at 3 o'clock.

The anniversary service was held in the beautiful stone chapel, which was well filled with interested visitors, while the 133 patients and staff of attendants, seated comfortably under the trees on the lawn adjoining the chapel, heard the entire service by means of a loud speaker.

The service opened with an organ prelude—(a) "Aria" (Buxtehude) (b) Choral Prelude on "He Leadeth Me" (Matthews) by E. Franklin Bentel, Rochester; hymn, "Spirit of Mercy, Truth and Love"; responsive service and Psalm 125, led by Rev. H. R. Browne, Shields, member of the Board of Trustees; anthem, "When I See the King," Men's Choir, Presbyterian church, Beaver, Mrs. Alfred H. Hutchinson, New Brighton, organist.

MINISTERS SPEAK

Rev. Louis H. Evans, D. D., pastor Third Presbyterian church, Pittsburg, and member of the Board of Trustees, was the first speaker. He gave an inspiring talk on works of mercy with impressive illustrations. An anthem, "He Will Not Let Me Fall,'" by the Men's Choir, was followed by an address by Rev. Louis A. Sittler, D. D., pastor of Trinity Lutheran church, Northside, Pittsburgh.

Dr. Sittler spoke chiefly of the life and works of the late Rev. W. A. Passavant, D. D., founder of the "Homes" and other institutions which since their inception have

(Continued on Page Ten)

Local Youths Given Degrees At College

President Ralph D. Hetzel today presented baccalaureate and advanced degrees to a record high graduating class of 1,160 students—including eight from Beaver County—at the June commencement exercises of the Pennsylvania State College.

Included in the procession of graduates were 100 who had qualified for the advanced degrees of doctor of education, master of arts, master of science, and master of education. The others received bachelor of science and bachelor of arts degrees.

In number of doctor of philosophy degrees awarded, today's exercises set an all-time high of 16. Graduates included:

Aliquippa—Eleanor H. Connelly, commerce and finance; Ambridge—Richard B. Steele, electrical engineering, with honors; Beaver Falls—Donald E. Rhodes, industrial engineering; Midland—Elmer D. Longfellow, metallurgy, with honors; Leo C. Wysocki metallurgy; Monaca—Jacob K. Brown, forestry; William J. Massey, agricultural economics; Rochester—Duane W. Swager, commerce and finance.

County Students To Get Penn Degrees

Three local persons will be among the more than 1,700 to receive degress Thursday morning at the annual Commencement exercises of the University of Pennsylvania to be held in municipal auditorium, Philadelphia. The university is also observing its bicentennial anniversary this year.

Jessie W. Warden, Rochester, is to receive the master of science degree in education; Edward E. McKee, Rochester, is to receive the doctor of medicine degree, and Ferd E. Blowers, Monaca, the bachelor of science degree in economics.

Dr. Thomas S. Gates, president of the university, will preside at the exercises and the Commencement address is to be delivered by Dr. William E. Leingelbach, professor of modern European history and dean of the College of Arts and Sciences at the University.

Beaver Scout Committee Meets Tuesday Evening

The Beaver District Committee, Boy Scouts of America, will hold its monthly meeting at the Fort McIntosh school building on Tuesday evening, June 11, at eight o'clock, Chairman Charles E. Cole announced today.

To Leave Rochester

REV. JAMES F. MERRIFIELD

Rev. James F. Merrifield, who the past four years has been pastor of the Wesleyan Methodist church in Rochester, was appointed to the pastorate of the Wesleyan Methodist church in Akron, O., at the annual conference of the Wesleyan Methodist Church held Wednesday, June 5, through Sunday, June 9, on the Wesleyan camp ground at Stoneboro.

Rev. Merrifield will succeed Rev. T. McCracken as pastor of the Akron, O., Wesleyan Methodist church and Rev. McCracken will be Rev. Merrifield's successor as pastor of the Rochester church. Rev. and Mrs. Merrifield and family will leave this week for Akron and Rev. and Mrs. McCracken and family will arrive in Rochester Wednesday.

Midland Groups Aid In Red Cross Drive For Refugee Funds

Numerous Benefit Affairs Are Held By Organizations To Obtain Relief Money

Response to the Red Cross war relief campaign in Midland has been marked by the complete cooperation of every civic group, members of foreign societies and other organizations, to the extent that predictions were made today that a total of fully $1,500—nearly double the original quota for the borough—would be raised.

Under the capable leadership of Mrs. P. A. Fernsler, Midland chairman, numerous benefits and other events have been held or have been arranged, to continue until the end of June.

The outstanding money-raising affair will be a benefit card party at the high school at 8:30 o'clock Tuesday evening. Mrs. Fernsler and members of her general Red Cross committee will have the assistance of various groups.

Fire Chief Edward J. Barrett will conduct a carnival feature; Mrs. Marshall Ungetheum, Miss Mae Sherman and Hugh Dillon will handle the refreshments; Miss Ruth Kissinger and a group of Girl Scouts will prepare tallies; Boy Scouts will arrange tables and other details. Mrs. Meyer Silverman, chairman of the ticket committee, reported today that hundreds of tickets have been sold.

Attracted by the unusual and successful methods adopted by Mrs. Fernsler in her campaign, Red Cross workers from many of the Beaver Valley towns plan to attend Tuesday night's card party and obtain first-hand information. A contribution of considerable proportions was realized as a result of benefit shows conducted last week at the Midland theater.

Freedom Youth To Receive His Degree

Robert Fleming Carothers, only son of Mr. and Mrs. Walter D. Carothers, West Fifth avenue, Freedom, will be graduated with the class of 1940 at the annual commencement exercises at Muskingum College, New Concord, O., on Tuesday morning. He was home over the weekend and this morning accompanied his father and Rev. and Mrs. J. R. Mohr of the Freedom Presbyterian manse, to New Concord.

They will attend the commencement and visit friends there, returning home Tuesday evening. Mrs. Carothers, who became suddenly ill on Saturday, is confined

(Continued on Page Two)

Conway Borough's Population 1,862

The population of Conway as shown by a preliminary count of the returns of the Sixteenth Census, taken as of April 1, 1940, is 1,862. These figures are preliminary and subject to correction. The population of this area was not shown separately in 1930.

YOUNG PEOPLE OF PRESBYTERY HAVE CONVENTION HERE

Spring Meeting of Young People's Christian Union Held In Beaver Church

Officers Elected For Ensuing Year; Interesting Program, Banquet Feature

The annual Spring convention of the Young People's Christian Union of the Beaver Valley Presbytery of the United Presbyterian church was held Saturday, June 8, in the United Presbyterian church, Beaver. About 400 young people from the churches of the Presbytery attended the afternoon and evening sessions.

The afternoon session convened at 3 o'clock with Miss Jean Gardner of the Bethel church presiding. She first introduced Robert A. Duff, choirmaster of the Highland United Presbyterian church, New Castle, who led the convention in the singing of several songs. Mr. Duff also had charge of all singing during the day. Miss Louise Grine of the host church then extended greetings to the convention. Howard Douds, Beaver Falls, sang a baritone solo, accompanied at the organ by Miss Myrta Jean Todd, Beaver, who was also the organist for all the group singing.

Officers were elected during the business session. The officers are: President, Miss Edna McConnell, New Castle, re-elected; vice-president, Clyde Byers, Ambridge; secretary, Margaret Battersby, New Castle, and treasurer, Anna Grace McCoy, near Aliquippa. A new constitution was also approved during the business session.

AWARDS PRESENTED

A number of announcements were made as follows: New Wilmington Missionary conference, presented by Robert Ralston, business manager; Estes Park national convention, by Ruth Stewart; Pittsburgh train party to Estes Park, by Charles A. Colgate, Mt. Lebanon; Camp Ar-Co-Ho, by James Van Gorder and the oratorical contest by Rev. Vance Yarnelle, secretary of the contest.

Awards were made to the Ellwood City society for the highest membership during the past year and to the Bethel society for the highest attendance at the convention.

The afternoon speaker was Dr. W. W. Hickman, a professor at Assuit College, Assuit, Egypt, who spoke about his work in Egypt, as well as the work of Rev. Neal McClanahan, missionary supported wholly by young people of the Beaver Valley Presbytery.

At the close of the afternoon session the group inspected the publicity exhibit containing posters made by the societies during the last year.

DINNER ENJOYED

At 6 o'clock dinner was served in Guild Hall by the Miss McKee Bible class of the host church. About 350 were served. Rev. Vance Yarnell of the Four-Mile United Presbyterian church was toastmaster. During the banquet new Presbyterial officers were introduced, among whom was Miss Louise Grine, of the Beaver Society, who is to be publicity and Look-Out Secretary for the next two years.

At 8 o'clock the convention reopened with Miss Maurine Smith presiding. Miss Smith is editor of

(Continued on Page Two)

Patrol Car, Bicycle Involved In Mishap

Two boys narrowly escaped serious injury shortly after noon Sunday when the bicycle on which they were riding struck the side of a state police automobile at the intersection of the Rochester-Freedom boulevard and Stewart avenue, East Rochester.

Donald Davis, 12, 371 Fifth avenue, Freedom, received a minor laceration of the left knee in the mishap. Edward Stewart, 12, near New Brighton, escaped uninjured.

The boys were riding along the boulevard and apparently did not see the car turn into Stewart avenue. They turned into Stewart and struck the side of the car operated by Private C. E. Mullen. Both lads were taken to Rochester hospital for treatment and then removed to their homes.

Army, Navy Officers To Visit Plant Here

The Jones and Laughlin Steel Corporation plant, Aliquippa, is included in the itinerary of 69 United States Army and Navy officers who are to make a three-day inspection tour of district industrial plants. The officers, members of the class to graduate June 19 from the Army Industrial College, Washington, D. C., are making the tour as part of a post-graduate course in problems of military supply.

Aged Guests At County Reunion

Above are pictured the three oldest guests attending the Householder reunion at Wises Grove Saturday. They are Mrs. Caroline H. Householder, 86, wife of George Householder, Oak Hill, New Brighton; Mrs. Amelia Householder, wife of Philip Householder, Butler county; and Jacob H. Householder, Marian township, Beaver county. Group photo of guests at reunion on page two.

The annual Householder reunion, held Saturday afternoon in Wises Grove, drew a large crowd of relatives and friends. The clan gathered early in the day. One hundred guests were present for the noon feast, and one hundred and five were counted at the evening meal.

(Continued on Page Two)

LETTER FROM WAR REFUGEE RECEIVED BY LOCAL FAMILY

While the Beaver County Chapter, American Red Cross, presses an intensive county-wide campaign for funds to aid the suffering refugees of war-town Europe, a Rochester family has received first-hand information from a Belgian relative regarding the tragic plight of refugees from the horrible war raging in France and Belgium.

By air mail from France, via Portugal, a tragic letter was received by Mr. and Mrs. Alphonse Coune and Mr. Coune's mother, Mrs. Marguerite Coune, 511 Harmony avenue, from Mr. Coune's cousin, Elisa Derouaux, who lived in Brussels, Belgium, prior to the invasion by the German army.

Miss Derouaux, a stenographer, with her mother and father, Mr. and Mrs. Joseph Derouaux, who lived in Vaux-Sous-Chevremont, near Liege, Belgium, have fled to Finistere, France. As yet, they have not located a son and daughter-in-law of the elder Derouaux and the young Derouaux' daughter. Also missing are a brother and sister-in-law of the elder Mrs. Coune, Mr. and Mrs. Thomas Balthasart, and a sister, Mrs. Laurantine Ancion, who also lived in Vaux-Sous-Chevremont.

WRITTEN IN FRENCH

Miss Derouaux spent her last few francs to mail the letter, written May 31. Translated from French to English by Mr. Coune, the letter read as follows:

"Dear Everyone: I am sending you a letter by air mail to give you an idea of the terrible things that are happening to us over here.

"We had already gone through the war of 1914 to 1918 and thought that it was the worst thing that could ever happen to any one, but it was nothing compared to this.

"Everyone will have a different story to tell of their terrible experiences later on.

"What was the beautiful and peaceful little country of Belgium is now nothing but ruins. Never again will we see our homes.

"The war of 1940 is a war which no one understands. Hitler obtained everything that he desired. We believed that he would be content with what he had already taken in other countries and that Belgium, being so well fortified, he would not attempt to attack. But, we find that his object is not to only occupy the territories, but to totally destroy the population.

"The amazing thing is that Hitler's armies arrived in France before us. Not expecting to be attacked in the least, at 4:30 a. m. on May 10, German planes bombed Brussels incessantly, causing the residents, young and old, to leave their homes in haste. A sad procession of old people, little children, partly clothed and mostly barefooted, carrying enormous bundles. They traveled night and day.

"I always told my family to come to Brussels at the least alarm.

"I went to the Brussels railroad station which had been bombed that morning, expecting to see my people come on a refugee train. Not finding them, I managed to return to Liege. I found every one ready

(Continued on Page Two)

Blue-Eyed Blonde

Photo by Graule Studios

GERTRUDE TEICHMAN

"Trudy" to her friends, Gertrude Teichman is the three-year-old daughter of Mrs. Clair R. Teichman, 503 Eleventh avenue, New Brighton. She has blonde hair and blue eyes. Mrs. Teichman was formerly Gertrude Weaton, Beaver.

Nineteen Students From County To Be Given Pitt Degrees

Annual Commencement Exercises To Be Held Wednesday, June 12 In Stadium

Among the 1,326 students who will receive degrees at the University of Pittsburgh commencement in the Pitt Stadium on Wednesday morning, June 12, nineteen are from Beaver County.

Largest group of candidates is in the Graduate School, with 226 seeking advanced degrees. Other candidates are: College, 300; School of Education, 191; Engineering and Mines, 152; Business Administration, 145; Medicine, 46; Law, 41; Pharmacy, 40; Social Work, 38; Dentistry, 33; Retail Training, 25; and Nursing, four.

Dr. Franklyn B. Snyder, president

(Continued on Page Two)

PRESIDENT WILL MAKE IMPORTANT ADDRESS TONIGHT

Roosevelt Expected To Give Important Pronouncement On International Affairs

House Committee Votes To Increase Size Of Regular Army To 400,000

By the United Press

WASHINGTON, June 10 — The House military affairs committee was reported authoritatively to have approved a bill increasing the authorized strength of the regular army to 400,000 men. This new action today on the defense program was reported as President Roosevelt prepared to deliver a "very important pronouncement" on the international situation this evening.

It was reported the President's address might deal with proposals for compulsory military training.

The House committee action came on a bill by Rep. Overton Brooks, Dem., La., which called for an increase from the authorized strength of 280,000 to 375,000. The committee changed the bill to make the army's strength 400,000 and then voted to approve it.

TO ADDRESS SENIORS

Late this afternoon (6:15 P. M., EST) the President will speak at the graduating exercises of the University of Virginia at Charlottesville, Va., where his son, Franklin D. Jr., receives a law degree.

Mr. Roosevelt had planned to attend the exercises if the international situation allowed, but his decision to speak was made suddenly to a surprised capital late last night. It was announced by his secretary, Stephen Early, in an unusual telephone call to the press associations a few minutes before midnight. The presidential party had returned earlier from a week-end cruise on the Potomic.

In some quarters there was speculation that Mr. Roosevelt might have something to say about increasing the manpower of the armed forces to man the greatest, mechanized army, navy and air force in this country's history. Observers pointed out that most of the President's defense program—for machines and materials—is nearing completion in congress.

Likewise, legislation to help pay for the $5,000,000,000 program will be brought up in the House this week in the form of a bill to add more than $1,000,000,000 to the annual tax bill.

TO BROADCAST SPEECH

Early said that arrangements have

(Continued on Page Two)

Memorial Rites Are Held By Grangers At County Meeting

Pomona Grange Pays Tribute To Deceased Members At Service In Hookstown

The annual memorial service and a address by Rev. Edwin Shoemaker, Mahoningtown, were features of the quarterly meeting of Beaver County Pomona Grange, No. 66, in the Hookstown Presbyterian church, Saturday afternoon. Hookstown Grange was the host group.

The afternoon session was presided over by O. Walker Shannon, Hookstown, Pomona Master, and the memorial service was conducted by Mrs. A. J. Todd, North Sewickley Township, Pomona chaplain. She was assisted by Rev. J. R. Rutledge, North Sewickley, who gave the memorial address.

Deceased members for whom the service was held included: Cummings Weigle, Mrs. Julia Todd and Clarence Coyle, Center; S. H. Todd, Brighton; Mr. Harbison, Economy; Lawrence Hartung, Big Knob; Mrs. Margaret Boyer and Howard Hazen, North Sewickley.

PLAN "HUSKING BEE"

Musical selections presented during the afternoon included: Violin duet, Miss Melva Brooks and Miss Myrna Carothers; vocal solo, Eileen Brooks; selections—quartet, Samuel Fair, Ray Sands, Melva and Eileen Brooks; duet, Miss Ruth Caven and Samuel Fair.

During the business period, plans were discussed for the annual "corn husking bee" and the following committee was named to complete arrangements: Dan Brenner, Brighton Grange, chairman; Calvin Creighton and Frank Wagoner, Chippewa; W. Frank Elliott, Center and Armour Mullen, Big Knob.

At the evening session, Rev. Shoemaker's address featured. James Musgrave, 86, a member of Economy Grange, entertained with several humorous readings memorized 65 years ago.

Women of the host Grange served dinner to more than one hundred Grangers.

The September meeting will be held at Brighton Grange hall, with members of Allegheny County Pomona Grange as guests. The fifth degree will be conferred on a class of candidates at that meeting.

War Declared On Allies By Duce's Order

By the United Press

ROME, June 10—Premier Benito Mussolini took Italy into the European war today on the side of Germany.

The declaration of war against Great Britain and France was announced by the Premier in a speech from the balcony of Venice Palace to a loudly-cheering crowd.

"The hour of destiny has arrived for our fatherland," Mussolini said. "We are going to war against the decrepit democracies, to break the chains that tie us in the Mediterranean."

Italian troops were stationed close to the United States Embassy today as hundreds of black-shirted infantrymen were marched to Venice Square and other strategic points to handle throngs already gathering in the streets. The British Embassy instructed all Britons to say off the streets and it was expected that the few remaining British would leave today.

Significance of the celebration was to emphasize the strength of the Italian navy which Foreign Minister Galeazzo Ciano's newspaper Leghorn Telegrafo said would "settle" Italy's Mediterranean problem. The most important ceremony was at the monument to the late King Victor Emmanel II in Venice Square.

Meanwhile, Italy's war preparations were pushed to the limit. Thousands of new recruits poured out of Rome and other large cities en route to southern ports from where they were expected to proceed to Africa.

Relations between Italy and Russia, Germany's non-aggression partner, appeared to be improving. It was announced that Augusto Rosso was returning to his post as Italian Ambassador to Russia and that Nicholas Gorelkin would assume his duties as Soviet Ambassador here. Gorelkin came to Rome last fall to take over the post but returned to Moscow when Italian newspapers criticised Russia's invasion of Finland.

WASHINGTON, June 10—Ambassador William C. Bullitt telephoned President Roosevelt from Paris at 11:53 a. m. (EST) that Italy had declared war on France.

German Tanks Are Only 25 Miles Away From Paris

By the United Press

PARIS, June 10—Germany, bringing 1,500,000 men and 4,000 tanks into the battle of France, today was reported to have broken through defense lines of the Seine, the Oise and the Aisne, moved on toward the Marne and thrust a spearhead within 25 or 30 miles of Paris.

German tank colums were operating south of Beauvais, apparently within 25 or 30 miles of the capital.

Across France from the English Channel to the Argonne forest, ever closer to Paris, the Germany army, its reserves now thrown into battle, smashed at the French line with the terrific force of a war machine that the Nazis had been building for seven years against "the day."

Gen. Maxime Weygand, studying battle maps at his headquarters, waiting for some opportunity to strike back, urged every officer and man to stand at his post.

The war office communique this morning, No. 561 of the war, was eloquently brief "From the sea to the Argonne the battle continues more and more violently."

SERIOUS SITUATION

Military quarters described the situation as extremely serious but not desperate. French troops were reported to be fighting with the greatest determination and to be making the Germans pay a terrible price for every mile they gained.

On the main fronts, where German infantry sought to consolidate the positions that its tanks had reached, military experts said that the Germans were fighting almost elbow to elbow, in massed formation, and that Allied artillery and machine guns were cutting them down by thousands. "A veritable slaughter," one expert called it.

GOLF OFFICIAL DIES

By the United Press

PITTSBURGH, June 10. George A. Ormiston, 66, long-time secretary of the Western Pennsylvania Golf Association, and one of the guiding lights in the development of golf in this district, died at his home yesterday following an illness of several weeks.

Raccoon Citizens To Vote On Bond Issue

Citizens of Raccoon township will vote on a proposed bond issue of $15,000 at a special election to be held on Wednesday, June 26.

The proposed increase in indebtedness, if approved by the voters, will be used to purchase land and help defray the cost of erecting a new public school building for the township.

Nazis Claim Army Gaining Steadily In French Advance

By the United Press

BERLIN, June 10.—Germany's offensive was officially reported rolling forward on a 210-mile front into France today after Nazi tanks and airplanes had smashed the Allied main defenses, broken up rear line positions and smashed all counter blows.

At some points, the high command said, the German advance turned into a "pursuit" of the enemy. The official press said that the Germans were smashing nearer to Paris, Rouen and LeHavre and had taken huge quantities of food, ammunition and arms. Allied staff headquarters near Rheims were reported heavily bombed from the air.

A "battle of movement" such as is best suited to the German mechanized forces is now in progress and has "reached a peak on the English channel, on the front south of the River Somme and south of Soissons.

PLANES AID ADVANCE

German airplanes supported the advance of the army on the Lower Seine (in the Rouen sector and presumably to cut off Le Havre) and in the Champaigne area, the communique said.

Allied counter-attacks were made with tanks, but failed, it added.

The German air force "heavily" bombed the harbor and quays at the important French ports of Cherbourg and Le Havre, according to the communique. Numerous ships in both ports as well as on the Lower Seine river were reported hit and damaged.

One 5,000 ton Allied troop ship was set afire and destroyed, it said. (The British announced today that additional fresh British troops had been landed in France.)

NAZIS CONTROL NORWAY

The end of the "Battle of Norway" gave German control of almost the entire European coast from the Petsamo frontier, at the extreme northern tip of Norway, to a point south of Abbeville, France.

Berlin sources said that hostilities with Norway had ceased at midnight Sunday. Aside from the moral effect of the Norwegian victory, coming at a time when details of specific victories in the Western Front fighting were scarce, it was of considerable economic and strategic significance here.

TWO DIE IN PLANE

By the United Press

BERWICK, Pa., June 10.— An investigation was conducted today to determine the cause of an airplane crash near Berwick airport in which two sportsmen pilots were killed. The victims were Lee Fahringer, 34, a lumber dealer, and Luther Young, 27, owner of the plane and operator of a food business.

P. C.'ers End 1st Half By Beating Conway, 6-5

WANERS LOSE 2ND TIME TO NEW BRIGHTON

The New Brighton Baker's Service softball club ascertained their superiority over the Waner A. C. when they defeated that club for the second time, 7-4, last evening, at the River avenue field.

Although badly outhit, 13 to 5, the Waners' defeat could be traced to sloppy fielding and poor base running.

The victors shelled the offerings of Joe Krnyevich for five runs in the first inning to take a lead which they never relinquished.

Jerry with three hits and MacKeage with a double and a single, paced the Brighton club at the plate, while Valiga's two-base clout was the longest smash for the losers.

New Brighton

	AB	R	H	PO	A	E
Miller, 1b	5	1	1	11	1	1
Lecker, ss	4	1	1	1	4	0
Horstman, cf	4	1	1	0	0	0
MacKeage, 3b	4	1	2	1	5	1
Jerry, c	4	2	3	9	0	1
Baker, 2b	4	0	0	0	3	1
Tuffy, rs	4	1	1	1	0	0
Hall, rf	4	0	2	1	0	0
White, lf	4	0	2	1	0	0
Haddox, p	4	0	0	2	3	0
Totals	41	7	13	27	16	4

Waner's A. C.

	AB	R	H	PO	A	E
J. Ondeyka, 1b	4	0	1	5	0	1
J. Seech, 3b	4	2	1	0	3	1
J. Reszetylo, 2b	4	0	1	2	1	1
P. Huey, lf	4	1	1	5	0	0
W. Ludwico, ss	3	0	0	3	1	1
P. Zovath, c	4	0	0	2	0	0
J. Krnyevich, p	4	0	0	0	1	0
M. Susnjar, rf	4	0	0	2	0	3
M. Valiga, cf	3	1	1	1	0	0
W. Paulibinski, rs	3	0	0	4	0	1
J. Manditty	1	0	0	0	0	0
Totals	38	4	5	24	6	8

J. Manditty batted for W. Paulibinski in the ninth.

Two-base hits, MacKeage, M. Valiga. Base on balls, off J. Krnyevich 1; off Haddox 2. Struck out by J. Krnyevich 1, by Maddox 8.

Double plays, J. Krnyevich to J. Ondeyka to J. Seech.

Umpires, J. Hodovanich and G. Ondeyka.

Hopewell Trounces Ramblers Here, 19-5

The Hopewell Tigers romped to a 19-5 triumph over the Ramblers in a softball game at the high school field here yesterday. Paluzzi and Kendrick starred for the victors at the plate, the former socking a homer, triple and single, and Kendrick getting a home run and single.

D. Albert socked a four-bagger, J. Telepis had two singles, Matz a double and single to feature the losers' offensive. D. Bonomi, winning hurler, fanned four and walked six while A. Citara fanned seven and allowed four walks. Line score:

Hopewell	903	0205—	19	21	1
Ramblers	050	0000—	5	8	4

D. Bonomi and C. Bonomi; A. Citara and J. Albert. Umpire—Piroli.

NATIONAL LEAGUE

Yesterday's Results

Cincinnati, 5; Pittsburgh, 4.
New York, 15; Philadelphia, 2.
Chicago, 11; St. Louis, 5.
* Brooklyn, 6; Boston, 2.
*20 innings.

Standing Of The Clubs Today

1939		W.	L.	Pct.	G.B.
5	Brooklyn	44	21	.677	
1	Cincinnati	44	23	.657	1
2	New York	39	26	.600	5
4	Chicago	38	35	.521	10
3	St. Louis	27	36	.429	16
6	Pittsburgh	25	39	.391	18½
8	Boston	23	38	.377	19
7	Philadelphia	22	44	.333	22½

Games Today—Pitching Selections

Pittsburgh at St. Louis (2) — Heintzelman (1-1) and Sewell (4-1) vs. McGee (6-5) and Warneke (5-6).

Cincinnati at Chicago — Derringer (9-7) vs. Mooty (5-0).

Brooklyn at Boston - Pressnell (4-2) vs. Errickson (5-2).

Philadelphia at New York—Beck (2-5) or Pearson (1-0) vs. Schumacher (5-7) or P. Dean (2-2).

Games Sunday

Pittsburgh at St. Louis (2).
Cincinnati at Chicago.
Philadelphia at New York (2).
Brooklyn at Boston.

AMERICAN LEAGUE

Yesterday's Results

Chicago, 10; St. Louis, 8.
Boston, 9; Washington, 4.
Philadelphia, 6; New York 3.
Only games scheduled.

Standing Of The Clubs Today

1939		W.	L.	Pct.	G.B.
3	Cleveland	44	28	.611	
1	Detroit	41	27	.603	1
2	Boston	39	30	.565	3½
1	New York	36	32	.529	6
5	Chicago	31	36	.463	10½
8	St. Louis	33	41	.446	12
7	Washington	29	44	.397	15½
6	Philadelphia	27	42	.391	15½

Games Today—Pitching Selections

St Louis at Detroit (2) - Kennedy (6-7) and Harris (2-5) vs. Gorsica (3-3) and Newsom (11-1).

Chicago at Cleveland — Dietrich (4-1) vs. Harder (3-5).

Boston at Washington — Grove (4-2) vs. Chase (5-10).

New York at Philadelphia—Breuer (6-3) vs. Ross (4-1).

Games Sunday

New York at Philadelphia (2).
Boston at Washington (2).
Chicago at Cleveland.
St. Louis at Detroit (2).

Svedock Hurls Another Triumph; Hilltoppers Open 2nd Half Monday

The Aliquippa P. C. club ended its first half schedule in the Beaver Valley league by setting back Conway, 6 to 5, yesterday at Franklin Field.

It was the second defeat for Conway this week at the hands of a local team. The Celtic-Reds deposed Conway from second place.

Tommy Svedock turned in another first rate mound job, fanning 13 batters, walking four, allowing six hits to the P. C.'s nine off P. Celia.

While Svedock kept the Conwayites in check, the Hilltoppers piled up a 4-0 lead until the fifth when Conway tallied twice. The visitors tried to come from behind in the seventh, but could get only one run, while the P. C. nine upped their total with two more. Conway added a brace of tallies in the ninth, missing a tie by a run.

Sammy Milanovich had a perfect day at bat, four hits in four trips, one a triple, one a double. Hodovanich tripled in getting two hits in four attempts.

The P. C.'ers play East Rochester at Franklin Field Monday in the first game of the second half.

Conway	000	020	102—	5
P. C.	110	200	20x—	6

Three base hits, S. Milanovich, Hodovanich. First base hits, S. Milanovich. Base on balls, off Svedock 4, off Celio 6. Struck out by Svedock 13, by Celio 5. Stolen bases, Hendricks 2, S. Milanovich 1. Umpire, Bianchi.

TENNIS WORLD MAY ACCLAIM WESTERN BOY

CORONADO, Cal. (UP)—Bobby Carruthers has red hair and he is at that fiery, uncertain age of 18, so when his coach says he is pointing for the National Junior tennis championships at Culver City, Ind., Aug. 2, rivals had better watch out.

Regarded as one of the finest young tennis players in the West, he was eliminated in the quarter-finals of the National Junior championships at Culver City last year by the same Ted Schroeder who went on to win the title.

Carruthers' coach, Pat O'Hara, the genial Hotel del Coronado professional who has been Bobby's friend and adviser ever since the youthful performer decided to take his first lesson in 1935 at the age of 13, says his charge is pointing for the Culver City event this year.

And it wouldn't surprise O'Hara to see the Coronado high school senior come home with the title.

To Enter Six Tourneys

In fact, it wouldn't surprise him if Bobby brought home a couple or three old "brass mugs" as the result of his current eastern and mid-western tour that will see him take in six tournaments throughout the country (including the National Junior championships).

Carruthers was scheduled to compete in the Minnesota state championships at St. Paul the last week in June, but reports here indicated that the tourney was rained out temporarily.

The next tourney on the youth's schedule is the National Interscholastic in Haverford, Pa., July 1. Bobby, who won the Southern California Interscholastic championship at Los Angeles early this year, would like to add the National title to his record.

His next stop is the Indiana state tourney in Indianapolis, July 8, and from there he jumps to the Central Michigan championship tournament in Grand Rapids, on July 15.

Goes To Minnesota

Then Bobby reverses his field and scoots back to Minneapolis, Minn., to compete in a tournament on July 22. The National Junior championship at Culver City, Ind., Aug. 2, completes his itinerary.

Carruthers' younger brother, Jack, a 15-year-old "comer," who is a better doubles player than he is at singles, also will be in Culver City Aug. 2 to play in the National Boys' Tournament, which will be held in conjunction with the older boys' event.

Coronado fans are watching the progress of Caruthers on this barnstorming trip, for the lad who held the National Boys championship in 1937, the Western Canadian Men's Championship in 1938 and the Missouri Valley Men's championship in 1939 may be due to "tuck away" a big-time tournament title this year.

PIGS LIKE BETTER SERVICE

STATE COLLEGE, Pa. (UP)—Giving pigs more "eblow room" and better service at meals results in more rapid fattening at less cost, two members of the agricultural experiment station at Pennsylvania State College have discovered.

HOLLYWOOD A. C. NIPS FAIR OAKS

A five run splurge in the third inning and a tally in the fourth held up for the Hollywood Aces for five innings as they took Fair Oaks, 6 to 5, in a B. & A. softball league game yesterday at Newell field.

The losers scored twice in the fourth, and one run each in the fifth, sixth and eighth, but were unable to knot the tally.

The Fair Oaks club outhit Hollywood, 8 to 6, Opriska and Nitkulinich homering for the losers. Delong pitched the triumph.

Hollywood

	AB	R	H	PO	A	E
Conwell, 2b	3	1	1	2	0	0
B. McCafferty, rs	3	1	1	3	0	0
Catroppa, ss	3	1	1	2	2	0
McMullen, c	3	1	1	0	2	0
Ujevich, 1b	3	0	0	10	0	0
Baer, 3b	3	0	0	1	4	0
Raffle, lf	3	1	1	3	0	1
McConnel, cf	2	1	1	4	0	1
R. McCafferty, rf	2	0	0	2	0	0
Delong, p	2	0	0	0	0	0
Totals	27	6	6	27	8	2

Fair Oaks

	AB	R	H	PO	A	E
Opriska, cf	2	2	1	1	1	1
Nitkulinich, ss	4	1	1	2	4	0
Sieminski, 3b	4	1	0	0	2	0
Dragovich, 1b	4	0	0	9	0	0
Wrobleski, rs	4	0	3	2	0	0
Melenchick, c	4	0	0	4	0	0
Opperman, lf	3	0	1	3	0	0
Gearer, 2b	4	1	1	2	1	1
Kostyk, rf	3	0	0	1	0	0
Steebner, p	3	0	1	0	2	0
Totals	35	5	8	24	10	2

Home runs, Opriska, Nitkulinich. Three base hits, McConnel. Two-base hits, Wrobleski, McMullen.

Base on balls, off Delong 3, off Steebner 3. Sacrifice hits, B. McCafferty. Umpire, Robison.

WHITNEY FARM TAXED TO KEEP PROUD RECORD

LEXINGTON, Ky.—(UP)—Whenever a Whitney horse races across **the finish line out front, chalk up one more mark for "the farm."**

Probably more consistent money winners have come from the 916 acres of blue grass owned by C. V. Whitney just outside Lexington than from any other racing stable.

A combination of scientific breeding, sportsmanship and good business seems to be the answer, but each year the competition gets tougher. The more winners turned out by the Whitney stud, the harder it is for its owner to carry on his self-imposed job of upholding the reputation of the string.

One thing is certain. Whitney's heavy burdens as board chairman of several large corporations have not altered his devotion to the farm, but instead have been an aid to him in injecting business methods into the farm.

Since its establishment at Lexington as the only Whitney breeding farm, Whitney horses have included such names as Equipoise, Top Flight and Whichone.

The Whitneys — C. V. and his father, the late Harry Payne Whitney—have won every one of the historic American stakes at least once, some of them several times. The farm has led American breeding establishments 10 times in the annual summaries of "leading breeders in money won."

The stud actually was founded by C. V. Whitney's grandfather, William C. Whitney, secretary of the navy under President Cleveland.

AMERICAN ASSOCIATION

Columbus 6, Toledo 4; Louisville 5, Indianapolis 3.

Steel was the third samest industry last year, according to the National Safety Council. Only tobacco and cement industries reported better records.

WESTERN CHAMPION - By Jack Sords

BABE DIDRIKSON ZAHARIAS
WOMEN'S WESTERN OPEN GOLF CHAMPION
MRS. ZAHARIAS SET AN ALL-TIME WISCONSIN RECORD OF 72 IN ONE OF HER MATCHES.
SHE WAS THE GIRL STAR OF THE 1932 OLYMPICS
SORDS

Grimes Fights 2nd Pro Battle Monday

Tangles With Walter Montini In Zivic-Harris Prelim

Pat (Jack) Grimes will take on Walter Montini of Pittsburgh Monday in a four round preliminary to the Fritzie Zivic-Ossie Harris ten rounder at Hickey Park Bowl, Millvale.

PAT (JACK) GRIMES

Grimes, who went to work for a month after dropping a decision in his professional debut against Lou Pitts, was reported in first rate shape, his timing improved over that of his first pro battle.

Montini, his opponent Monday, appeared in a preliminary to the Teddy Yarosz-Bud Mignault fight last week in East Liverpool, O.

PENN STATE ASSOCIATION

Yesterday's Results

Johnstown 7, Warren 0.

Standing of the Clubs Today

	W.	L.	Pct.
Butler	30	10	.612
Johnstown	30	20	.600
Washington	24	24	.500
McKeesport	24	24	.500
Beaver Falls	23	27	.460
Warren	16	31	.340

Games Today

McKeesport at Butler
Beaver Falls at Washington.
Johnstown at Warren.

Games Sunday

McKeesport at Butler.
Beaver Falls at Washington.
Johnstown at Warren.

S. Of I. Bows To Thorn Run In Loop Fray

The West Aliquippa Sons of Italy, pace setters in Section 2 of the B. and A. softball loop, suffered their third league defeat and the second straight when Thorn Run tripped them up in a ten-inning game, 7-6, last evening, at the River avenue field.

Regotti singled home Swagger in the tenth with the winning marker after the S. O. I. had knotted the count at 6-all with a run in their half of the ninth.

Billy Cercone with a perfect performance, three hits in three trips to the platter, and Chuck Leonard and John Merendo hit often enough to win most ball games, but the distance clouting of Regotti and Swogger offset this advantage.

West Aliquippa S. O. I.

	AB	R	H	PO	A	E
D. Casoli, rs	5	1	1	5	0	0
E. Casoli, lf	2	0	0	1	0	0
B. Cercone, rf	3	2	3	4	0	0
C. Leonard, cf-lf	4	0	2	0	0	0
M.Yacopino, rf-cf	3	1	0	0	0	0
J. Merendo, 2b	4	0	2	0	1	1
A. Ciccone, 1b	2	0	0	4	1	0
A. Tony, 3b	3	2	1	1	2	2
P. Dinello, ss	3	0	0	3	0	1
J. Belcastro, c	2	0	0	5	0	0
J. Carlini, c	2	0	0	2	0	0
F. Letteri, p	4	0	0	5	0	0
Totals	37	6	9	30	4	4

Thorn Run

	AB	R	H	PO	A	E
Regotti, rs	4	2	2	2	0	0
Val, 2b	4	2	1	3	1	0
Bossetti, c	4	1	0	6	0	0
Buggo, 3b	3	0	1	4	3	1
D. B., ss	4	0	1	0	0	2
Grafa, cf	3	0	0	1	0	0
Lesh, 1b	4	0	0	8	0	1
Willard, rf	3	0	0	3	0	0
Swagger, lf	3	2	2	2	0	0
Grogan, p	4	0	1	1	1	0
Totals	36	7	8	30	5	4

Three base hits, D. Casoli, A. Tony, Regotti, Grogan. Two base hits, Swogger. Base on balls, off F. Letteri 2, off Grogan 7. Struck out by F. Letteri 5, by Grogan 4.

Double plays, Buggo to Lesh to Bossetti; A. Tony to A. Ciccone to A. Tony. Umpire, Feroni.

Mrs. Shoaf Introduces Easy Type Of Skeet Shoot For Beginning Marksmen

Mrs. Lillian Shoaf, of 1741 Grant street, Aliquippa, will introduce today a new type of trap shooting designed for women, children and persons anxious to learn to use a rifle.

On the theory that women and young people in the borough lack facilities for developing rifle marksmanship, Mrs. Shoaf will set up at the Bucktails' skeet field a small trap shooting apparatus. It will vary from conventional trap shooting in that the .22 rifle loaded with bird shot is used.

The usual blue rock, or clay pigeon will be released as a target.

Because the .22 rifle has none of the recoil of the shot gun usually employed in skeet shooting, Mrs. Shoaf's apparatus is particularly adapted to women and young boys and girls.

The apparatus, available to anyone anxious to shoot, will be set up at 2:30 p. m. today and tomorrow at the Bucktails recreational tract off the Brodhead road. The regular Bucktails' skeet field also will be open.

The Old Rivals Meet

P. C. Nine And Celtic-Reds To Play Here Tomorrow

The Aliquippa Celtic-Reds and the P.C. Club, those diamond enemies from away back, clash tomorrow for the third time this season.

The game is slated for Fireman's field at 2:30 p. m.

And if there's anything to the third-time's-a-charm stuff, then the P.C. nine is due to win, for twice before they ventured against the combine and got licked.

The game is not a Beaver Valley league affair. Donald Dukovich is the probable Celtic-Red hurler although Branchetti, Paul Bar and DiAddigo will be on hand if needed.

Either Petey Stamos or Tommy Svedock or Dave Palfi will handle the hurling for the P.C. Club.

TERRACE TIGERS NIP SPAULDINGS

Musulin hurled and helped bat the Terrace Tigers to a 6-4 win over the Spaulding A. C. in a Junior League game at Linmar park yesterday afternoon. He allowed only seven hits while he and his mates were nicking Babich for ten safe blows.

Castrique, Morrison and Musulin each clouted two hits, the latter getting a double. Young hit a triple and Campbell, Lynch and Yates had singles to their credit for the winners.

Radvinski and Moskola connected for two-baggers. S. Kospender and Babich each had a brace of hits and D. Kospender hit a single for the opposition. Musulin fanned 12 and walked six. Babich had six strikeouts and allowed two walks. Line score:

Spaulding	001	210	000—	4	7	3
Terrace	001	000	23x—	6	10	3

Babich and Moskola; Musulin and Yates. Umpires—Jones and Casp.

Indians Claim Two By Forfeit, Third Place

The Beaver Indians of the W.A. R.C. National Mushball League claimed twin, forfeit victories over the Sluggers and the Green Hornets.

The victories shoved the Indians into sole possession of third place, a half game behind the runner-up Knights.

BASEBALL'S BIG SIX

	G	AB	R	H	Pct.
Wright, White.	66	261	43	94	.3601
Radcliff, Browns	69	264	40	95	.3599
Finney, Reds	61	288	47	101	.351
Danning, Giants	62	239	38	84	.351
May, Phillies	58	203	27	68	.335
Walker, Dodgers	57	225	34	75	.333

INTERNATIONAL LEAGUE

Toronto 7, Rochester 4; Baltimore 7, Syracuse 6; Newark 4, Jersey City 2.

Junior Eagles Take Duchesses, 14 To 11

The West Aliquippa Junior Eagles continued their victorious march against the local feminine mushball clubs when they dumped the Duchesses, 14-11, in an extra inning encounter, last evening, at Plan 11 field.

Three runs in the tenth spelled doom for the home team in a game which saw the lead see-saw continually.

Murgen, aided by her battery mate, Shomsky, again was the big noise for the victors, clubbing four hits and twirling fine ball in the clutche[s]. Zdranik got five for five, one a triple, to feature for the losers.

Junior Eagles	012	040	130	3	14
Duchesses	021	310	211	0	11

Murgen and Shomsky, Walsh and Popps.

White Sox Defeat Leetsdale, 7-3

The Aliquippa Whitesox invaded Leetsdale and came out with a 7 to 3 Beaver and Allegheny Counties' baseball league triumph.

Grago hurled the victory, fanning four, allowing five hits. His mates reached Kasarda for eight, one a homer by Thomas. Neely hit for the circuit for the losers.

Aliq. White Sox	110	008	101—	7	8	3
Leetsdale	100	002	000—	3	5	1

Home runs, Thomas, Neely.

W. A. R. C. NATIONAL MUSHBALL LEAGUE

Standings

Team	W	L	Pct.
Redwings	6	0	1.000
Knights	4	2	.667
Beaver Indians	4	3	.571
Green Hornets	2	4	.333
Black Panthers	1	2	.333
Sluggers	0	6	.000

No Games Today

Games Monday

Redwings vs. Sluggers (double-header) 10:30 a. m.

The Editors Believe:

The news columns of the Aliquippa Gazette strive to portray impartially and without bias the facts of daily occurrences . . . interesting to the people of Aliquippa and the Beaver valley. The column below, however, is reserved for the OPINIONS of the editors of the Aliquippa Gazette. Usually right, sometimes wrong, they are at all times honest convictions. Letters to the editor, agreeing or disagreeing with the opinions voiced here, are welcome and will be published subject only to the limitations of space and the postal laws.

"If you work in a town, in Heaven's name work for it. If you live in a town, live for it, give for it. Help advance your neighborhood. Respect the great power that protects you, that surrounds you with the advantages of advanced civilization, and that makes it possible for you to achieve results. Speak well of it. Stand by it. Stand for its civic and commercial supremacy. If you must obstruct or decry those who strive to help, why—quit the town. But as long as you are a part of a locality, do not belittle it. If you do, you are loosening the tendrils that hold you to the community and with the first high wind that comes along you will be uprooted and blown away. And probably you will never know why."

Charles G. Dawes.

Aliquippa, Pa., Friday, July 12, 1940

Gazette Program For Aliquippa

1. Provision of adequate, Free Parking Space for Shoppers.
2. Resurfacing of Franklin Avenue from the Stone Arch to the Wye.
3. Repair and Resurfacing of the Aliquippa-Monaca River Road.

"NON-PROFESSIONAL" COMPETITION

An Aliquippa school teacher uses his summer's vacation to start selling insurance—promptly incurring the enmity of a score of business men who have made insurance their life's work.

An Aliquippa mill worker takes advantage of his day off to sell appliances and appliance dealers register a protest. One of his associates employs his free day as an electrical repairman and union leaders object emphatically. Still another works after mill hours, hauling coal from nearby custom mines.

A student, taking an undergraduate printing course, buys a small job press and a font of type and goes into business, printing tickets and broadsides. College students, seeking funds for next year's tuition, go about hawking hosiery, clothing and aluminum ware.

So it goes—men seeking to capitalize on idle time and other men, with whom such activities compete, objecting to competition from such sources.

The situation is a never-ending source of controversy. As always, there are two sides to the question. One can't blame men for declining to sit about idly when they can swell their incomes and be of service during vacation periods. And one can't blame business men with heavy investments and heavy responsibilities, tied by a host of governmental regulations and tax obligations, from objecting to competition by those who escape such restrictions.

Yet we have an idea such matters work themselves out. If the legitimate print shop, with its wide experience and its improved equipment, cannot compete with the "basement printer," then it should go out of business. If the legitimate insurance firm, with years of experience and a reputation for responsibility, cannot compete against the "part time" salesman with inferior companies, then it deserves the same fate.

If the electrical repairman, skilled and responsible, cannot hold his own with a part time worker, then he ought to find other employment. In the long run responsible services and responsible business men aren't hurt much—though the temporary affect may be painful.

About the only thing this perennial problem proves is that attempts to freeze employment conditions by artificial means are futile. We can register insurance men, professionalize electricians, establish unions for craftsmen of all types. Yet we can't prevent a man with an especial ability in some line of work from employing that ability for his own benefit.

The only injustice is the constantly increasing restrictions on responsible business establishments that place them at a disadvantage with such competition . . . which prevent them from giving still better service . . . which hamstring them with labor, tax and operations requirements determined by law and drawn by some young visionary in Washington without experience or a practical understanding of the fluid nature of business life.

Only Two Grievance Committee Posts To Be Contested Here

Only two of the seven grievance committee posts will be contested at an election in S.W.O.C. headquarters here next Tuesday, President Joseph Krivan announced today.

In zone No. 7 at the mechanical department Peter P. Haubner, incumbent, and Thomas Johns will fight it out for the position. Three mill workers aspire for the committeeman's spot in the seamless division of the J. & L. plant here. They are Louis Fairbanks, Anthony Kubick and William J. Lanahan.

Unopposed candidates include: Eli Uzelac, blast furnace; James Downing, open hearth; Domenic Del Turko, welded tube; Earl Stipe, tin plate department; and Richard Munro, of the rod and wire mill.

CRAWFORDS ON VACATION

Mr. and Mrs. Robert M. Crawford and daughter, Vivian, today were vacationing at Mr. Crawford's home town, Pemberville, O. Mr. Crawford, principal of Aliquippa High school, will be away for a month, during which time he will fish in Michigan.

WISHING WELL

Registered U. S. Patent Office

2 S	5 T	8 D	3 A	6 O	4 D	7 L	5 A	6 L	2 W	8 A	6 D	4 A
5 K	6 L	4 T	7 O	5 E	8 A	2 E	8 N	7 V	3 N	6 D	4 E	5 C
4 O	7 E	2 E	5 A	6 Y	3 O	8 G	6 C	4 F	5 R	7 F	2 T	6 A
5 E	3 T	6 R	8 E	4 C	7 I	6 E	2 N	8 R	6 L	5 O	6 E	7 N
2 E	5 F	7 D	4 H	6 S	8 S	3 E	8 A	5 O	6 S	7 S	8 R	5 L
6 W	7 A	5 D	6 I	8 R	7 W	4 E	6 T	8 I	2 W	7 A	5 L	6 H
5 A	4 E	6 F	8 V	2 S	6 I	5 D	7 Y	6 R	8 E	4 R	6 E	5 Y

HERE is a pleasant little game that will give you a message every day. It is a numerical puzzle designed to spell out your fortune. Count the letters in your first name. If the number of letters is 6 or more, subtract 4. If the number is less than 6, add 3. The result is your key number. Start at the upper left-hand corner of the rectangle and check every one of your key numbers, left to right. Then read the message the letters under the checked figures give you. 7-12

THE BOOKMAKER

1940 PRESIDENTIAL RACE
Third Term Tradition
OLD MAN HISTORY
?

Beaver And Ohio Valley Hospitals

Iola Battalini, of Aliquippa, was admitted to Rochester hospital in addition to Mrs. John Babish, Monaca; and Joseph Johnson, Midland. Discharged were Fred Anderson and Margaret Malesh, Aliquippa; Hugh Johnson, Monaca; Mrs. R. E. Forseman, Beaver; and Mrs. Henry Camp, Rochester.

* * *

Admitted to Beaver Valley hospital were Mrs. Harold L. Panner, Beaver; Donald Snowberger and Angeline Amygdalos, New Brighton; Elmer Anderson and Thomas and Theodore Moore, Jr., Beaver Falls. Florence Lincoln of Aliquippa, and Mrs. Harmon Hawk, Sr., of Monaca, were discharged.

Entering Providence hospital were Margaret Lightfoot, Darlington; and Carol Ganelin and James March, Beaver Falls. Discharged: Mrs. Patrick Adduci and daughter, Aliquippa, R. D.; Mrs. O. H. Dunmire and daughter, Beaver; Mrs. Eleanor Pluna, Mrs. George Whitslar and Mrs. Mollie Davidson, Beaver Falls.

Local Altercation Is Aired By Squire

Sam Grazulis, 24, and Marko Maslich, 52, who live together at 112 Brushton avenue, paid a doctor bill and a fine and costs before Squire R. J. McLanahan today for chasing each other around their home with a baseball bat and a chair.

During the altercation, in which Grazulis charged that Maslich chased him with a baseball bat, Maslich suffered a black eye and small cuts about the face.

The Aliquippa Gazette
Founded March, 1922
Published Every Afternoon Except Sunday
By the Franklin Publishing Company
Rear 384 Franklin Avenue
At Aliquippa, Pa.

E. J. Tilton, President
J. H. Sherrard, Vice President
Walter Catterall, Secretary-Treasurer

Entered at the Postoffice at Aliquippa, Pa., as Second-Class Matter

BELL TELEPHONES
934 — 935 — 936

E. J. Tilton .... Editor and Publisher
Donald O. McCann .... City Editor
Richard L. Amper .... Sports Editor
Lewis L. Luster, Advertising Manager
Chas. McRobbie, Circulation Manager
Elizabeth Collins, Classified Ad. Mgr.

SUBSCRIPTION RATES
By mail within first Three Zones, postage paid strictly in advance.

One year	$6.00
Six months	3.00
Four months	2.20
Two months	1.10
One month	.55
Per week, 1 or 2 weeks	.18

The Gazette is delivered by carrier in Aliquippa and suburbs for 15c a week; $7.50 per year, payable in advance. Single copy, three cents. Advertising Rates Furnished on Application

Member Pennsylvania Newspaper Publishers Association
Central Press Association
World-Wide Service of United Press

NATIONAL REPRESENTATIVES
Paul de Guzman
Test Market Newspapers
110 East 42nd St.
New York, N. Y.

Beaver County Newsetts

Being a Compilation of Interesting Bits of News Gathered Here and There Throughout Beaver County—Fact, Gossip and Neighborly Chatter From Every Section of the Beaver Valley.

Interest in the forthcoming presidential election has speeded up activity at the Beaver county registration office. The present registration period ends Oct. 5. During the first ten days of July, 99 persons registered for the first time, including 54 Republicans, 38 Democrats, two Prohibitionists, four Non-Partisans and one Independent.

Rochester General hospital's indebtedness was reduced more than $10,000 during the last year. A mortgage on the nurses' home has been satisfied in full and all bonds redeemed.

Srgt. L. M. (Luke) Kelly of the Midland police force has been offered the position of superintendent of police at Indiana, Pa. Former member of the State Highway patrol, he has been with the Midland force since 1933.

Monaca residents have been directed by council there to cut down certain poplar trees, the roots of which are a menace to sewers in the borough. At present the order may only apply to sidewalk trees, later to private property in the event the condition still exists.

Numerous valley men and their families will attend the 20th annual picnic of the Pennsylvania System Veteran Employes' association, to be held this Saturday at Meyers Lake, Canton, O.

Phillips Schmertz and Co., investment brokers of Pittsburgh, purchased Baden borough's $10,000 bond issue this week. Its bid was 2½ per cent on a premium of $90.

Runs GOP Campaign

Joseph W. Martin, Jr.

House Minority Leader Joseph W. Martin, Jr., of Massachusetts, is shown as he held his first press conference after being named chairman of the Republican national committee. He predicted President Roosevelt would be nominated for a third term and that he would go down in defeat at the hands of Wendell L. Willkie.

Cars Collide Here, Causing $20 Damage

Cars driven by Ernest L. Gray, of 1119 Wade street, and L. B. Casida of Aliquippa, R. D. 1, collided last night on Main street near Nineteenth street, causing damage estimated at $20. According to police, the Gray car pulled out from a parking stall on Main street into the path of the Casida car.

Be Thankful You Are An American

New Act Will Ban Thousands In State From 1940 Politics

HARRISBURG, (UP) — Several thousand employes of Pennsylvania state government agencies will be removed from participation in the 1940 presidential campaign by the new federal "clean politics" act awaiting President Roosevelt's signature.

The measure, finally approved by Congress yesterday, will affect employes of four governmental subdivisions, the Turnpike commission building the Harrisburg-Pittsburgh super highway, the Department of Public Assistance, the Division of Unemployment Compensation and the Highway department.

The Aliquippa Gazetteer

By DEAN C. MILLER

JOTS AND DASHES—Our nomination for the world's meanest man (at least we don't think a woman would do a skunky trick like this one): The person who stole four tickets to a boat ride sponsored by the West Aliquippa Musical club for the benefit of paralyzed Angelo (Angel) Conti. As if it weren't enough for the club to lose $55.76 on the excursion.

* * * *

In case you gals at the Aliquippa golf course wonder where Mrs. Jane Moore Nordstrohm has been while you tourneyed sans her professional club over your heads—it's this way.

La Moore has been thespianing at the Fox Chapel Play House for several weeks. Yes, the feminine scourge of the fairways has foresaken her favorite No. 2 iron for grease paint.

She's doing quite well, too. This week Jane managed props for the "Last of Mrs. Cheney" show which featured Polly Rowles Snyder, who forsook Hollywood a while back when Cupid tugged a little harder than Goldwyn.

When she's not busy hunting for moose heads and owls and period furniture she's worrying whether Henrietta, a kid sister, is muffing a line. Henrietta is wrapped up with the theater and plays "Lady Mary Sindley" in the Rowles vehicle.

* * * *

If you haven't noticed it (but we know you have) the Gazette daily carries a feature column entitled "National Whirligig." If you want to be the life of the party, the man who knows and sees all, the individual friends turn to when Junior swallows dad's collar button—you simply can't afford to miss a single installment of the feature.

Seriously, it has been uniquely correct in forecasting coming events—big coming events. F'rinstance: More than a year ago, 6 28 39 to be exact, the column told readers that Willkie would be the GOP nominee.

* * * *

Sight One Can't Afford to Miss: Anne, the big brown-eyed waitress at the Tritt Drug store here, in her bright red blouse. Makes all the boys whistle.

* * * *

We admired the frankness and utter disregard for conventional niceties exhibited by the colored woman who sent a postcard to her husband in town here, demanding a divorce. No beating around the bush for her; she didn't care if his whole rooming house knew that she no longer cared. They did. No, we didn't peek over shoulders. It was only told to us.

* * * *

WISHFUL THINKING or STORIES WE'D LOVE TO WRITE

BERLIN, July 12 (DNB) — A hate crazed assassin rid the world of a skunk today. Hitler is dead. A dawn to sunset survey disclosed three persons visited his bier—all just making sure.

READ GAZETTE FOR ALIQUIPPA NEWS

Weather Forecast
Generally fair tonight and Saturday; slightly warmer tonight; continued warm Saturday and Sunday.
Pollen count: Grasses, 13.

THE DAILY TIMES

ROCHESTER-BEAVER-MONACA
FREEDOM—BRIDGEWATER—CONWAY—VANPORT—MIDLAND

Local History
The first Beaver Presbyterian church was erected in 1825 on a grant of land on the public square for this purpose.

ESTABLISHED APRIL 2, 1874 | BEAVER AND ROCHESTER, PA., FRIDAY, JULY 19, 1940 | BY CARRIER 15 CENTS A WEEK—3 CENTS PER COPY

ROOSEVELT LAUNCHES HIS CAMPAIGN

BRITAIN URGED BY HITLER TODAY TO END DESTRUCTION

German Fuehrer Makes "Appeal To Reason" To British In Reichstag Address

Air Raids, Sea Warfare Continue On All Fronts Of European Warfare

By the United Press

BERLIN, July 19 — Adolf Hitler today addressed an "appeal to reason" to Great Britain to avert "destruction of a great world empire" but he made it clear that rejection would mean an attack with all of the forces at the command of the axis powers.

"In this hour and before this body," the Nazi Reichsfuehrer told the German Reichstag in the presence of Italian Foreign Minister Count Ciano, "I feel myself obliged to make one more appeal to reason to England.

"I do this not as a victory, but for the triumph of common sense."

Without delivering any ultimatum, Hitler said that it had never been his desire or his aim to destroy the British empire. Hitler said that his two cardinal aims in foreign policies had been friendship with Britain and Italy.

NAZIS MAKE CLAIMS

A German submarine has returned to its base to report the sinking of another 31,30 0tons of shipping, the German high command said in a communique today. Another submarine, it was said, "shot up" a large armed merchantman from a "strongly protected convoy."

The high command said that yesterday German bombers again "successfully attacked" airfields, harbors and barracks in England as well as shipping off the north Scottish and English channel coasts.

It claimed that German aviation sank four Merchant ships totalling 12,000 to 14,00 tons and damaged 12 merchantmen and two naval patrol boats.

The high command's communique said that on July 17 an enemy submarine was bombed and sunk and it claimed that last night German anti-aircraft defense prevented serious enemy bombing of northwestern Germany.

British air losses yesterday were 12 airplanes and two barrage balloons, the communique said, including seven British planes shot down in air battles. It was admitted that two German planes were missing.

AIR RAIDS CONTINUE

LONDON, July 19—Sporadic German air raids on British towns and shipping continued today with seven or eight bombers and one fighter reported shot down.

Air Ministry communiques reported that British fighters had shot down a German bomber into the sea off the southeast coast of England. Meanwhile, the coastal command of the Royal Air Force said that its reconnaissance planes had battled four German fighters which were attacking trawlers. One of these planes was shot down.

Shortly after dawn a raider dropped two salvos of bombs, starting a fire near a town in southeast England.

Near mid-day another German plane bombed a number of areas in southwest Scotland. A bomb struck a building and workers still were searching for victims there shortly after noon.

OTHER PLANES DOWNED

The Ministry of Home Security announced that last night German

(Continued on Page Eight)

Democrats Break, 'Draft' Farley

By the United Press

CHICAGO, July 19.—James A. Farley reportedly was re-elected chairman of the Democratic National Committee by acclamation today. Farley was said to have agreed to serve only until August 17 because his own personal financial position requires him to quit politics. This information came from a member of the National Committee, who would not be quoted directly because the full committee still was in executive session.

Convictions Of Democrats Upheld

By the United Press

PHILADELPHIA, July 19 — The State Superior Court today upheld the conviction of three men on various charges resulting from the investigation into the administration of former Gov. George H. Earle.

The triubunal upheld the conviction of Roy E. Brownmiller, Pottsville; James P. Kirk, Allegheny county Democratic leader, and Victor Skok, an insurance business associate of Kirk.

Brownmiller, Highway Secretary in the Earle cabinet, was found guilty of misusing motor funds and was sentenced to a year in county prisons and fined $3,000. He was the first of twelve Democrats indicted in the grand jury probe which followed the bitter 1938 primary, to be tried. He was sentenced on two counts in connection with payroll padding in Luzerne County during the 1938 Democratic campaign.

Kirk and Skok were found guilty of conspiracy to monopolize state bonding contracts.

County Sea Scouts to Cruise on Chesapeake Bay For Two Days

Photo by Graule Studios

Beaver County's Sea Scouts and several Scout leaders packed their duffel bags today and left this afternoon by automobile for the Severn river in Maryland preparatory to embarking Saturday morning on the Scouts' "big adventure"—a two-day cruise on Chesapeake Bay aboard an 85-foot schooner with auxiliary motor.

Included in the party, pictured above, are: Front row, left to right—Charles Darner, Jacque Beyer, Charles Droz, Earl Fox, Richard Rogers and Billy Moore, Ambridge; Glenn Sheets and Peter Okupski, Beaver Falls; Second row—R. A. Beyer, Ambridge, Beaver-Ohio Valley Division chairman of Organization and Extension; Ray R. Wiegand, Beaver, Division Executive; Walter Rich, Beaver Falls; William Hartling, Ambridge; Robert Beyer, "Skipper" of Ambridge Ship, No. 527; Clyde Miller, "Skipper" of Beaver Falls Ship, No. 546; Darrell Sheets and Carl Crawford, Beaver Falls,; Jack Malone, Rochester, who will cover the cruise for THE TIMES; Dawn Snair, Beaver Falls; Back row—George H. Merrin, Ohioview, division chairman of Health and Safety; Glenn Miller, John Shoe, Albert Claple, Beaver Falls; Robert Droz, Ambridge; Robert Shaffer, Beaver Falls; Harry Heyslerman and W. B. McBride, Ohioview, division Commissioner.

Others not pictured who planned

(Continued on Page Eleven)

PICKETS BAR WORKERS FROM ENTERING PLANT AT MONACA

Employes of the United States Sanitary Manufacturing plant, Monaca, who were not members of the CIO or were members and were far in arrears in their dues were not permitted to enter the plant to work this morning, according to the Monaca office of the Steel Workers Organizing Committee. Union members with paid up dues were permitted to go to work as usual.

The men were stopped by pickets at the entrance to the plant and approximately twenty percent of the morning shift, about 40 men, were not permitted to work as they were either non-union or in arrears in dues, union officials stated.

According to the agreement reached early this year by the CIO and the company following a strike, the company was to urge the employes to affiliate themselves with the union, but the plant was not a closed shop. The CIO was not seeking a closed shop, Joseph Timko, regional director of the CIO, reported today. The action taken this morning was not a violation of the contract existing between the union and the company, Mr. Timko stated.

PICKETING TO CONTINUE

Officials at the Monaca SWOC headquarters reported the employes who were not permitted to work today would be permitted to return to work when they had joined the union or when they had paid their dues.

Approximately 80 per cent of the morning shift, about 160 men, went to work this morning as they were paid-up members of the union, SWOC headquarters reported.

Officials of the company could not be contacted for statements this morning and information was refused at the office of the Monaca plant.

FLASHES:

By the United Press

CAR STOLEN, STRIPPED

PITTSBURGH, July 19.—Jack H. Schaum, Sewickley, reported the theft of his automobile to police and when they located it last night, the machine had been stripped of five tires and wheels, a radio, two watches and a set of golf clubs.

NEW CASTLE MAN DROWNS

NEW CASTLE, July 19. — Lloyd Ramsey, 26-year-old New Castle postal clerk, drowned yesterday in Slippery Rock creek at McConnells Mills near Portersville. Two young women companions with him were unable to reach him. The body was recovered.

No One Injured When Gotham Bomb Explodes

NEW YORK, July 19.— An explosion which police believed was caused by a "scare bomb" ripped through the stone wall on the Fifth avenue side of Central Park in midtown Manhattan Thursday.

The blast threw a shower of metal fragments into the avenue but no one was injured.

Annual Industrial Outing To Attract Record Attendance

Special Trains To Carry Picnickers To Kennywood Park, Pittsburgh, Saturday

Hundreds of persons throughout the county are planning to attend the annual Beaver County Industrial Picnic, to be held Saturday at Kennywood Park, Pittsburgh. Most of the picnickers will make the trip on the special trains being run over the Pennsylvania Railroad from the county to the park, although many will go in private automobiles.

Favors are to be distributed to persons attending and free entertainment and dancing will also be enjoyed. Special ticket prices have been in effect for some time. This rate is only good through this evening.

The committee in charge is to hold its final meeting this evening in the Townsend Club, New Brighton.

A number of awards are also to be made at the park. According to the advance ticket sale, there will be a record crowd.

The picnic is sponsored by a number of the industrial companies in Beaver county and is for the employes, their families and friends.

Following is the train schedule:

Leave Homewood Junction, 9:05 (DST); Morado, 9:10; Beaver Falls, 9:15; New Brighton, 9:19; Rochester, 9:25; Freedom, 9:29; returning —7:45 and 11:25 p. m. Returning

(Continued on Page Eleven)

Relief Recipients May Attend School

The Beaver County Board of Assistance is pointing out to employable relief recipients the opportunity being offered to them by the school boards in the county who are co-operating with the national defense program by sponsoring vocational courses to train and retrain men for industry. The Beaver Falls, Ambridge, Aliquippa and Midland schools are making available their vocational departments.

The County Assistance Board, it is announced, will permit relief recipients who are accepted for training by the school authorities, to earn their grants by attending school regularly and proving satisfactory.

Hopes To Be Farmer

JAMES FRANK LAUGHNER

Young James Frank Laughner, three-year-old son of Mr. and Mrs. Arthur F. Laughner, Potter Township, member of a well-known Southside family, plans to be a real agriculturist if his parents plans are realized. His eyes are blue and his hair is light brown. He is especially fond of playing ball.

TO RELEASE PRISONERS

BERLIN, July 19—Adolf Hitler today ordered release of all Belgian prisoners of war, except officers and non-commissioned officers. Transportation of Belgians to their homes already has begun.

TWO COUNTY PHYSICIANS HAVE PRACTICED FOR HALF-CENTURY

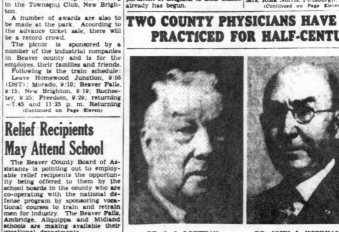

DR. J. S. LOUTHAN

DR. JOHN J. WICKHAM

Two widely-known Beaver County physicians—Dr. John J. Wickham, Rochester, and Dr. J. S. Louthan, Beaver Falls—are among the forty-six Western Pennsylvania physicians who have practiced medicine fifty years or more who were awarded certificates of appreciation at the annual meeting of the Tenth Coun-

(Continued on Page Two)

FIVE HUNDRED ATTEND 4-H CLUBS' PICNIC HELD HERE

Five hundred 4H Club members, parents and friends attended the fourth annual county-wide picnic at Huber's Beach, North Sewickley Township, Thursday.

The day's program started at 10 a. m. with a mushball tournament in charge of Joe Parks, Brush Creek Club; Robert Cowan, Blackhawk Club; Earl Cooper, Patter Club; Lawrence Searight, Raccoon Club; Ralph Hartenbach, Center Club; and Marion Buckley, Brighton Club. Boys' clubs participating in the tournament were Brighton, Potter, Blackhawk, Center-Raccoon, North Sewickley, and Brush Creek. Girls' clubs having teams in the tournament were Brighton, Chippewa, and New Sewickley.

The final play-off between the winners was the last event of the afternoon. This game was played between the Blackhawk boys' club and the Brighton girls' club. The boys' team won the tournament and received a watermelon as a prize.

Those not participating in the mushball tournament played games and relay races under the direction of Isabelle Searight, Beatrice Caler, and Virginia Searight, of Raccoon Club. Volley ball was played during the day.

CONTEST CONDUCTED

Following a picnic lunch at noon, an amateur hour was conducted. Those participating were Frank

(Continued on Page Eleven)

Installation Held By State Lodge At Convention Session

Grand Chapter Of Colored Eastern Star Closes Annual Meeting At Rochester

Installation of officers for the ensuing year, featured the closing session of the annual convention of Deborah Grand Chapter of Pennsylvania, Order of Eastern Star, Thursday evening in the American Legion Home, Rochester, where the convention had been in session since Monday evening.

The officers, elected at the Thursday afternoon session, were installed by Worshipful Grand Master Thomas D. Lowe, Rochester. They are: Worthy Grand Matron, Mrs. Dorothy Williams, Harrisburg; Worthy Grand Patron, Harry P. Smith, Harrisburg; Worthy Grand Associate Matron, Mrs. Anna Washington, Williamsport; Worthy Grand Associate Patron, Charles Allen, Philadelphia; Grand Secretary, Mrs. Ella S. Moore, Philadelphia; Grand Treasurer, Mrs. Roberta C. Lisle, Pittsburgh; Grand Conductress, Mrs. Rosa Norris, Pittsburgh; Grand

(Continued on Page Eleven)

Street And Sidewalk Improvements Were Discussed By Solons

Improvements Under WPA Projects Discussed At Meet Of Rochester Council

Street and sidewalk improvements, under WPA projects in progress, were discussed at a special meeting of Rochester Council, Thursday night. Joseph Bontempo, in charge of WPA activities in Beaver county, was present.

A number of streets already have been improved and others are in progress. Council decided the next street to be improved shall be Webster street, from New York avenue to Harmony avenue, a distance of three blocks. Work on this street will be started Tuesday, July 23.

The sidewalk project also was discussed. Property owners desiring to avail themselves of the opportunity to have sidewalks laid are to make application at once at the office of the borough secretary, where complete information may be had.

Council agreed to build satisfactory retaining walls for properties in East Washington street, provided the property owners sign release for damages.

Warren J. Ganoe, president, presided. Ben F. Ellis, borough controller, was acting secretary in the absence of J. W. Duncaster, who is on vacation.

Democrats Meet To Name Leader

By the United Press

CHICAGO, July 19—Franklin Delano Roosevelt today ordered the New Deal-Democratic party into an immediate offensive against Wendell L. Willkie, the Republican presidential candidate. He had accepted a tradition-shattering third term nomination which, he said, he had hoped earnestly to avoid.

Secretary of Agriculture Henry A. Wallace, an Iowa New Dealer, was nominated for vice president by Mr. Roosevelt's order. That was the second demonstration of Mr. Roosevelt's power over the Democratic National Convention which convened here at noon Monday and adjourned sine die at 2:05 a. m. (EDT) today.

The party purge was almost completed early today when Wallace was substituted for Vice President John N. Garner who ran with the winning ticket in 1932 and 1936. It will be finished within a few hours when the New Deal drops the pilot, Chairman James A. Farley of the Democratic National Committee. The committee meets today to reorganize and Farley is stepping down.

It was a rowdy wind-up to four days of "stop-and-go" politics in which Farley and a scattering of anti-third term conservatives sought to make a river flow uphill. They lost. The galleries clamored and there were shouts and boos from the floor last night and today as the constricting pressure of White House influence forced the convention steadily toward Wallace, a former Republican, for vice-president.

The campaign is on between the Roosevelt - Wallace ticket ratified here and the Republican presidential candidate Wendell L. Willkie and his running mate, Sen. Charles L. McNary, Ore. It is New Deal vs. the most articulate and adverse critic of the Roosevelt administration that business has produced.

"STAGE MANAGING" CHARGED

Whether this convention "drafted" Mr. Roosevelt or was "stage managed" into nominating him is a matter of some dispute. There are conservatives here who hold the latter to have been the fact.

"Had this been a free and open convention . . ." said Sen. Scott Lucas, D., Ill., last night in asking that his name be withdrawn from the list of vice-presidential contestants. There were others who felt that way about it. But the returns are in, the old line Democrats are out and the 1940 presidential contest is moving toward November.

Conference room and platform rebellions blazed through the afternoon and early evening. But Wallace would not stay down. Mr. Roosevelt sent word that he would address the convention at 9 p. m., and then that he would not—unless he got his man. He got him after a wrangling roll call in which big delegations had to poll and came up with tenths and fifths of votes cast in protest against the administration organization.

ROOSEVELT SPEAKS

And then a silence fell upon the assembly. At 12:20 a. m. the President began to speak—just as eight years ago he spoke from the platform here in the Chicago Stadium to accept his first nomination.

But this time he was not there. His voice came, smooth and reassuring as a benediction, from a bluster of loud speakers overhead as he said—"I will."

No campaigning will he do this year, he told the convention, but he will talk to the press and over the radio from time to time to report to the people on the crisis he says exists and to refute "deliberate or unwitting falsification of fact, which are sometimes made by political candidates."

He was loathe to continue in the White House and would rather retire. But for the developments after Europe's September declarations of war, Mr. Roosevelt said,

(Continued on Page 15)

Wins Nomination

Henry A. Wallace

Personal choice of President Roosevelt and backed by the New Deal administration, Secretary of Agriculture Henry A. Wallace was nominated by a slim margin as the Democratic candidate for vice-president just before the party's national convention closed early today at Chicago. A former Republican, Wallace was nominated by virtue of the vote of delegates from four large states — Pennsylvania, New York, New Jersey and Illinois—after every mention of his name previously had been repeatedly booed while the names of other candidates were cheered.

Two Workmen Burned At Aliquippa Plant

Two open hearth workers at the Aliquippa plant of the Jones & Laughlin Steel Corporation received severe burns Thursday night when molten iron splashed on them while they were pouring an ingot.

The victims are Joseph Vokovich, 34, 2215 Front street, Monaca Heights, injured on the left leg, and George Malanovich, 46, 251 Superior avenue, Aliquippa, burned about the arms and left hip. They were taken to Southside hospital, Pittsburgh.

Hemphill Improving Following Operation

George R. Hemphill, Beaver Falls, Beaver County's chief probation officer, is convalescing at Providence hospital following a minor operation performed Wednesday morning. Mr. Hemphill was taken ill Monday and entered the hospital last Tuesday He is expected to be about again in a few days.

State Delegation Casts 68 Votes To Aid Wallace Drive

Division Of Delegates Manifested At Caucus Held Prior To Administration Signal

CHICAGO, July 19. — Pennsylvania cast 68 of its 72 votes for Secretary of Agriculture Henry A. Wallace for vice-president on the first ballot after word was received that he was the choice of President Roosevelt.

Philip Murray of Pittsburgh, SWOC chairman and a delegate-at-large, seconded Wallace's nomination at the convention.

Despite a division in the delegation between Wallace and the other potential candidates, manifested at a caucus meeting early Thursday — the 84 delegates indicated a desire to support whoever the President wants.

SHOWDOWN AVERTED

Word from Washington before the balloting was to begin, averted what threatened to be a showdown fight among Pennsylvania Democrats over the vice presidency.

Former State Chairman David L. Lawrence, backed by leading labor delegates from the state, joined Guffey forces early Thursday in advocating a solid first-ballot vote for Wallace.

He told the caucus meeting in the Congress Hotel that "it will be playing smart politics by leading

(Continued on Page 15)

Aged Resident Of Vanport Is Dead

Chris Aeschbacher, 76, Ferry avenue, Vanport, died at 12:10 o'clock this morning in Rochester hospital.

Friends are to be received at the home of the son, Chris F. Aeschbacher, Vanport, until two o'clock Sunday afternoon. Private funeral services are to be held at 3 30 o'clock Sunday afternoon in the home. Interment will be in Oak Grove cemetery, Industry Township.

Mr. Aeschbacher was born in Switzerland, but had resided in this country for many years. Surviving are the widow, Mrs. Elizabeth Aeschbacher, the son, three daughters, Mrs. Eliza Wolf, Vanport, Mrs. Freda Casey, Rochester, and Mrs. Charles Willison, Baltimore, Md., and one brother, Ollie Aeschbacher, East Liverpool.

Serious Shortage Of Housing Facilities For Workers In National Defense Program, Reports Show; USHA 'Stymied' Through Lack Of Funds

(Continued from Page One)

President Roosevelt proposed the defense program and workers immediately began trooping in large numbers to industrial areas to find jobs. Some of the major requests included:

YOUNGSTOWN, O. — The steel center has a housing shortage "so serious that many families now are building shacks out of store-box materials as squatters on land skirting the city."

VALLEJO, Calif. — Site of the Mare Island Navy yard, estimated need for 3,400 homes for enlisted personnel and civilian workers who will be brought to the area.

LOS ANGELES.—Estimated need for $2,100,000 for homes for increased Navy and industrial personnels.

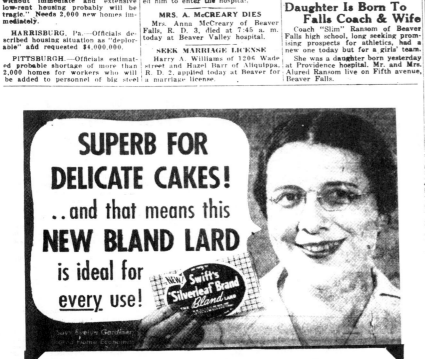

CAMDEN, N. J.—Large shipbuilding center during the first World War, officials said "further expansion of defense program activities without immediate and extensive low-rent housing probably will be tragic." Needs 2,000 new homes immediately.

HARRISBURG, Pa.—Officials described housing situation as "deplorable" and requested $4,000,000.

PITTSBURGH.—Officials estimated probable shortage of more than 2,000 homes for workers who will be added to personnel of big steel and other industrial plants.

KNOXVILLE, Tenn. — Heart of Tennessee Valley Authority and proposed site of defense industries, reported "no surplus housing . . . and expansion of nearby plant of American Aluminum company will create serious shortage."

Meanwhile, the USHA is studying housing situations in Detroit, Cleveland, Dayton, O., Peoria, Ill., Washington, New York, Rochester, N. Y., Binghamton, N. Y., and other industrial centers.

Judge J. H. Wilson Of Butler County Ill

BUTLER, Pa. (INS)—Ordered to seek a complete rest, Judge John H. Wilson of Butler county was a patient in Butler County Memorial hospital today.

Taken ill unexpectedly while speaking a week ago during Zelienople's centennial celebration, he recovered sufficiently to attend court Monday. His physician finally urged him to enter the hospital.

MRS. A. McCREARY DIES

Mrs. Anna McCreary of Beaver Falls, R. D. 3, died at 7:45 a. m. today at Beaver Valley hospital.

SEEK MARRIAGE LICENSE

Harry A. Williams of 1206 Wade street and Hazel Barr of Aliquippa, R. D. 2, applied today at Beaver for a marriage license.

S. S. Association's Officers To Attend Spruce Creek Confab

M. C. Gilchrist, president of the Beaver county Sabbath School association, and Treasurer E. N. Hogue will attend the organization's state convention for presidents and secretaries at Camp Kanesatake, Spruce Creek, Pa., tomorrow and Sunday.

At the August meeting of the association in New Brighton, Gilchrist urged more temperance education, better Sabbath observance and more leadership training, daily vacation schools and "100 per cent visitation of church schools in the county.

He announced the annual state convention would be in Wilkes-Barre, Pa., Oct. 8 to 11.

Plans for the association's work in the county next year were formulated. M. C. Baker conducted devotions and led group singing, with Miss Mary Ann Miller of Aliquippa as piano accompanist.

A pamphlet, "Six Studies of the Day," in which Sabbath observance is discussed, is available at the office of the secretary of the association.

Daughter Is Born To Falls Coach & Wife

Coach "Slim" Ransom of Beaver Falls high school, long seeking promising prospects for athletics, had a new one today but for a girls' team.

She was a daughter born yesterday at Providence hospital. Mr. and Mrs. Alured Ransom live on Fifth avenue, Beaver Falls.

Weather Forecast
Cloudy with showers tonight; showers and slightly warmer Sunday

THE DAILY TIMES

ROCHESTER-BEAVER-MONACA
FREEDOM—BRIDGEWATER—CONWAY—VANPORT—MIDLAND

Local History
The first steps toward the erection of a Roman Catholic church in Beaver were taken in 1835

ESTABLISHED APRIL 2, 1874 — BEAVER AND ROCHESTER, PA., SATURDAY, AUGUST 17, 1940 — BY CARRIER 15 CENTS A WEEK—3 CENTS PER COPY

Willkie Formally Accepts GOP Nomination

BRITISH PLANES RAID GERMAN AREAS

WILLKIE GREETED BY HUGE CROWDS TODAY AT ELWOOD

Republican Presidential Candidate Delivers Long-Awaited Acceptance Speech

Little Indiana Town Thronged By Thousands of Visitors For Colorful Ceremony

ELWOOD, Ind., Aug. 17—Wendell Lewis Willkie, the corn belt Tom Sawyer who made good, returns to the town of his birth today to accept the leadership of the Republican party as its presidential nominee and to reveal to the nation his stand on major issues of state.

He was scheduled to leave Rushville, Ind., home town of his wife, Mrs. Edith Wilk Willkie, by special train at 10:30 a. m. to deliver the long-awaited acceptance speech in which he will declare his policies on foreign affairs, conscription, national administration and agriculture. The address was to be broadcast by three national networks (NBC, CBS and MBS) from Callaway Park where an estimated 200,000 Republicans from all states will be assembled.

The town was in festival mood for the occasion with bunting and decorations and pictures of the candidate hung everywhere. Special trains arrived at the little Elwood stations and poured out the thousands of spectators who jammed the streets of this town and almost crowded out its 11,000 citizens. Highways were lined with automobiles bringing more spectators.

SEEK FARM VOTE

This is an attempt to rally the agricultural middle west around the Republican standard and away from President Roosevelt and the New Deal.

It was the first major political occasion here since William Jennings Bryan spoke during one of his campaigns for the presidency. That time it rained inches. But today

(Continued on Page Two)

Rev. Fr. P. A. Brady To Be Buried Monday

Solemn high mass of requiem will be celebrated Monday morning in St. Veronica's Church, Ambridge, for the Very Reverend P. A. Brady, V. F., pastor of the church and dean of the Ambridge district, who died Thursday night in St. Joseph's Hospital following a long illness.

Father Brady, born in 1870 in Ireland, came to the United States in 1894. He studied at St. Vincent's Seminary in Latrobe and was ordained to the priesthood on October 29, 1897. His first appointment was to St. John the Baptist's Church in Pittsburgh. On May 1, 1925, Father Brady assumed the pastorate in Ambridge.

Surviving are a sister, Mrs. James Rilley, Ireland; a niece, Mrs. Andrew Neumann, Union City, N. J., and two nephews, Hugh McGivney, Woodridge, N. J., and Francis McGivney, Union City, N. J. The body will lie in state at the parish house, 725 Glenwood avenue, Ambridge, until Sunday afternoon at 3:30 o'clock, when it will be moved to the church to await the mass Monday morning at 9:30 o'clock.

THE GREAT GAME OF POLITICS

By Frank R. Kent

ELECTION YEAR AND WPA

Washington, Aug. 17.

IT IS a strange thing that the number of distressed unemployed on the WPA relief rolls should show a consistent increase in the election years and just as consistent decrease in the years free from elections. But that is the indisputable record.

—o—

IT HAPPENED exactly that way under the fantastic partisan Mr. Harry Hopkins, expounder of the political virtues of spending, and it seems about to happen in the same way under Mr. Hopkins' successor, Col. F. C. Harrington, who is not politically minded at all. In 1934, 1936 and 1938 the Federal relief rolls began to swell early in September, increased daily through October and reached their peak just about election day.

—o—

THERE are unmistakable evidences that this performance will be approximately duplicated in 1940. Chiefly, this assertion is based on

(Continued on Page Two)

Lost and Found

ROCHESTER MEN LAUNCH BOAT BUILT IN GARAGE

TIMES photo, by Russell D. Porter

George and Elmer dropped "Omar" (shown above) in the Ohio river at Freedom Friday evening about eight o'clock, thus climaxing one of the most talked-about and highly speculative projects to be undertaken in the Junction City in years and years. In case you are not acquainted with these personalities, George and Elmer are Messrs. Marshall and Otto, respectively. Both are amateur wood craftsmen and are better known as members of the Rochester Board of Education.

GEORGE G. MARSHALL

Their mutual creation of "Omar," however, has entirely removed the stigma of amateur rating and advanced them to the foremost position of professionals in their favorite hobby.

"Omar," their pride and joy, is a trim 17-foot deluxe cabin cruiser of the trunk type and weighs approximately 800 pounds.

The idea for "Omar" was conceived way back in March of 1938 when George and Elmer, both loyal followers of Izaak Walton, happened to be looking through a magazine. Having had nothing to bring home from their semi-annual fishing trips to Canada, it occurred to them that at least they could bring home a boat. And thus Omar became a "project."

In justice to the creators, it can be said that although actual work on "Omar" was begun in 1938, approximately six months of the actual working time was expended on the construction.

(Continued on Page Two)

C. ELMER OTTO

Legion Convention In Reading To Close With Election Today

Action On 56 Resolutions Scheduled Today; Altoona Gets 1941 Convention

READING, Aug. 17—The Pennsylvania Department of the American Legion ends its 22nd annual convention today with election of a state commander, action on important resolutions and a gigantic street parade in which more than 30,000 persons will participate.

Nominees for state commander were Tom E. Williams, Wilkes-Barre, and Charles S. Cook of Pittston. Cook is a Pennsylvania Motor Police lieutenant and Williams is director of the State Bureau of Vital Statistics at Harrisburg.

Legionnaires were scheduled to pass upon 56 resolutions yesterday but deferred action until today. Important pending motions would: demand immediate adoption of the Burke-Wadsworth conscription bill; demand jobs or pensions for veterans; outlaw the Communist party; pledge the state's 76,000 veterans to service in any emergency; guarantee continued efforts of Legionnaires in ferreting out subversive elements in the state.

JAMES GIVES SPEECH

Altoona was selected during the sessions as the site of the 1941 convention. There was no opposition.

Gov. Arthur H. James, in an address warned that America "must not follow France's example of fatal complacency."

William J. Rhoads, or Norwood, Delaware County, was elected eastern vice-commander; James P. Murray, Forest City, central vice-commander, and Daniel C. Hartbauer, Pittsburgh, western vice-commander.

Rev. Willis Hall, Johnstown, was named state chaplain and J. Guy Griffith of New Kensington was re-elected as national committeeman. Griffith defeated former State Commander Frank E. Gwynn, Allentown, 545 to 485. Harry K. Stinger, Philadelphia, was named alternate national committeeman.

U. S. ORDERS PLANES

WASHINGTON, Aug. 17—A $15,899,642 order with two manufacturers for 156 bombing and training planes was announced today by the war department.

County Payments For Relief Drop

Direct relief payments made to needy Beaver Countains during the week ended today show a decrease of $164 from those of the previous week, and 88 fewer checks were required to make the payments, according to State Treasurer F. Clair Ross.

Payments for the week totaled $9,221, which was $12,731 lower than those of the comparable week of last year. Current payments required 1,664 fewer checks than those of a year ago.

Payments by the Bureau of Assistance Disbursements in the Treasury Department follow:

Current week—$9,221, made with 1,592 checks; previous week—$9,385, made with 1,630 checks; comparable week 1939—$21,951, made with 3,256 checks.

Cadet Corps Holds First Maneuver In Gypsy Glen Today

Cadets "Surround Enemy" And Find Tables Spread For Outdoor Feet

The recently-organized Cadet Corps of Company B, 110th Infantry, Pennsylvania National Guard, held its first field maneuvers today in the Gypsy Glen area near Beaver. About 75 boys, aged 14 to 18, participated in the games which were under the direction of R. O. T. C. Lieut. Col. L. A. M. Corkan, New Brighton.

The Cadets assembled at the court house and marched to the Beaver Recreation Park in Gypsy Glen to begin their maneuvers. The problem was designed to teach the boys to take advantage of natural cover and topography in surrounding and surprising an "enemy."

JUDGED BY REFEREES

For this purpose the corps was divided into three troops. Rev. M. S. Ashton, Harold Hazlett and Herbert Lawrence, acted as referees, watching and judging the maneuveds from vantage points on the Gypsy Glen road.

The "enemy" was a pleasant surprise to the cadets. When the three units had completed their pincer-

(Continued on Page Two)

County Elks' Lodges To Picnic Sunday At Log Cabin Park

Ellwood City and Coraopolis Lodges Also to Participate In Annual Outing

Members of Elks lodges in Beaver County, Coraopolis and Ellwood City numbering several hundred will be in attendance at the annual Elks' picnic Sunday at Log Cabin Park, near Aliquippa.

C. C. Weigle, Aliquippa, general chairman, has as his assistants J. Shorts, Rochester; William Wells and Earl Connors, Coraopolis.

The amusement committee in-

(Continued on Page Two)

ROOSEVELT MEETS CANADIAN PRIME MINISTER TODAY

Defense of Western Hemisphere to Be Discussed at Conference Today

Roosevelt to Witness War Games Enroute to Meeting With MacKenzie King

By the United Press

ABOARD PRESIDENTIAL SPECIAL EN ROUTE TO NORWOOD, N. Y., Aug. 17—President Roosevelt meets the Canadian Prime Minister, W. L. MacKenzie King, tonight for a conference which may result in an understanding on problems of defending the Western Hemisphere.

Mr. Roosevelt had already announced that conversations are in progress with Canada on defense of the Western Hemisphere and negotiations are proceeding with Great Britain for western hemisphere defenses against aggression from overseas.

King will board Mr. Roosevelt's train at Ogdensburg, N. Y., after the President has inspected the war games of the First Army in progress there. In approximately 100 square miles in the Ogdensburg region bordering on the Canadian border, 91,000 regulars and National Guardsmen are simulating the conditions of actual warfare.

TO REMAIN OVERNIGHT

In Mr. Roosevelt's private car, the President and King will have dinner together and spend the evening talking. The Prime Minister will spend the night aboard Mr. Roosevelt's train and Sunday morning will accompany the President to military religious services conducted in the field for the troops.

Sometime around noon Sunday, King will go back to Canada and Mr. Roosevelt will leave for his home at Hyde Park, N. Y.

Mr. Roosevelt, in his Friday press conference statement, already has served notice that he is seeking to implement the Monroe Doctrine by acquiring naval and air bases on Britain's Western Hemisphere possessions. His conference tonight, it appeared, may result in an understanding on mutual problems and new world defense with Britain's western hemisphere dominion. Mr. Roosevelt, in 1938 in an address at Kingston, Ont., declared that the United States would never stand idly by should Canada be subjected to invasion by an aggressor from beyond the seas.

MAY JOIN AMERICAS

Authoritative sources said today that Canada may be invited to assume full partnership with the 21 American republics in the defense of the Western Hemisphere.

Some authorities expressed doubt that the President is seeking American naval and air bases in Canada, but thought he probably was encouraging the Canadian government to strengthen its fortifications and, possibly, establish new bases with United States financial assistance. It was believed that some provision could be made for use of these bases by the armed forces of all the nations of this hemisphere.

Inclusion of Canada in the hemisphere defense union might obviate the need for a cash payment for island bases, some officials believed

(Continued on Page Two)

HELD IN FAKE HOLDUP SHOOTING

Pennsylvania police hold Mrs. Otis Cumberledge, 36, left, and Mrs. Elizabeth Pettit, 25, for the murder of Ada Headley, a resident of Waynesburg, Pa., of whom it is claimed they were jealous. Police added that it was the most cleverly arranged slaying in that county. The women donned men's clothing and shot their victim in a fake holdup, and in this manner they disguised the motives and put investigating authorities on the wrong trail, police said.

Youthful Dancers

Bernadine Deveney, Monaca, and Eleanor Sherwood, Beaver, (above) both 11 years of age, are among Beaver Valley's outstanding young dancers. They have appeared as a team on numerous benefit programs in the Valley in the past few years in tap, acrobatic and solo dances. They are students of the Barth School of Dance, Rochester and are the daughters of Mr. and Mrs. Joseph Deveney and Mr. and Mrs. John Sherwood, respectively.

Ford Gears Plant To Manufacture Motors For Fighting Planes

Negotiations Being Made With War Department For Making 4,000 Motors

By the United Press

DETROIT, Aug. 17—Henry Ford today geared his industrial organization to national defense ready to build airplane motors at once and it was understood that powerful fighting airplanes might be put into production soon.

Ford Motor Company officials announced that a contract was being negotiated with the War Department for the manufacture of 4,000 airplane motors of the Pratt and Whitney design. Ford engineers have designed a plane powered with two liquid-cooled motors, similar to the U. S. Army's new twin-motored Lockheed P-38 pursuit planes, said to be the deadliest of fighters.

REFUSED PREVIOUS CONTRACT

Two months ago, Ford announced that he could build 1,000 planes daily without taxing the capacity of his vast River Rouge plant, largest industrial unit in the world.

Later, Ford refused to accept a contract to make 3,000 Rolls Royce motors for the United States and 6,000 for Great Britain because he didn't want to devote American plants to foreign war orders, though his Canadian and English factories are assisting the British war efforts. The new contract is for motors for United State use only.

A representative of William S. Knudsen, production chief of the National Defense Commission was on hand to discuss the contract.

Opening Of Turnpike Again Is Postponed

The Pennsylvania Turnpike Commission again has changed the date for the dedication of the "dream highway" as the tentative date, September 15, has been cancelled and the dedicatory ceremonies are to be held later.

Originally scheduled to be opened July 4, the completion of the $70,050,000 "all-weather" highway was delayed by heavy spring rains and the opening was set for Labor Day. Recently that date was changed to September 15.

The newest date for the formal opening of the 160-mile ribbon of concrete and steel is to be set Wednesday when the commission is scheduled to meet.

Large Income Gain Reported By P. R. R.

Pennsylvania Railroad reports for six months ended June 30, 1940 net income of $11,296,274, equal to 86 cents per share, against revised net income of $4,175,100, or 32 cents per share in the first six months of 1939.

Nazis Blockade British Coast

Civilian Areas Of Germany Reported Bombed By Nazis

BERLIN, Aug. 17—Germany proclaimed a complete blockade of the British Isles today and in formal notes to neutral governments which have not forbidden their ships to enter British waters said that "in the future every neutral ship approaching the British coast subjects itself to the danger of destruction."

Notes were not sent to the United States and Argentina, which have banned their vessels from British waters.

Denouncing the British blockade of Germany as in controvention of international law, the German government said that it had "decided to retaliate with an 'eye for an eye' and act with the same ruthlessness" as the British "around the British coast."

GERMAN AREAS BOMBED

The German high command disclosed today that British bombing planes had raided Germany last night, apparently in retaliation for the German air force's mass assault on London's industrial suburbs.

British planes attacked several German towns, causing "moderate material damage" and "killing two civilians and wounding several others," the high command said.

The British raids followed furious German attacks which, German sources claimed, left parts of East London in smoking ruin and reduced Britain's most important harbors and war industries to rubble.

Nazi sources charged that the British raided Weimar, shrine of German poets and musicians, and dropped bombs in Goethe Park near the house where the poet lived and on a Red Cross station.

VICTORIES CLAIMED

The High Command, claiming destruction of British Airdomes, Harbors, Anti-Aircraft Batteries, and other widely separated objectives in raids yesterday and last night, listed British losses at 89 planes, including 59 shot down and 30 destroyed on the ground, 22 barrage balloons, armed merchantmen totaling 25,000 tons, and a destroyer.

German war planes followed up yesterday's raids with forays last night in which "other suburbs of London," arms factories in the midlands, harbors and docks at Cardiff, Newport and Bristol, and air fields and gun emplacements in Southern England were "successfully bombed," the Communique added.

British Retaliate On Germans After Bombing Of London

By the United Press

LONDON, Aug. 17—British bombers smashed deep into Germany last night and early today as aerial warfare continued over the British Isles with little respite.

German bombers began the seventh consecutive day of mass air raids over England today as British anger mounted over what was described officially as an "unwarranted" bombing of civilians yesterday when raiding planes flew up the Thames and bombed London's suburbs.

One raider dropped 16 incendiary bombs on a southeast coast town this morning. Fourteen more bombs were dropped near a golf course on the southeast coast, but there was little damage.

Britain was prepared for another day of massed plane attacks on harbors, airports, railroads and industrial areas.

CASUALTIES SAID HIGH

The new raid began as air raid protection workers dug into the debris of London's southwest suburbs which had been battered by German bombs. It was believed the casualty list from yesterday's attacks would run high.

The rescue workers were hampered by delayed action bombs which the Germans had dropped yesterday and which had been exploding throughout the night and early morning hours. Authorities said the workers knew the locations of the bombs and had warned all persons to stay away from them.

Londoners were angered by the attack on the suburbs and many suggested that British planes strike at thickly populated industrial districts in Germany. The British have bombed military objectives around Essen and Munich. British planes also have flown over Berlin, but have never dropped bombs on the German capital.

The British fought back stubbornly, counting an official "bag" of 71 German planes while admitting the loss of 18. Pilots of 10 of the lost British planes were reported safe and uninjured.

RAIDS CONTINUE

Swarms of German bombers and fighters—some estimates placed the number at 2,500—swept out of leaden skies from dawn to dusk and blasted England, Scotland and Wales, and some broke through the defenses to reach London, the heart of Britain's far-flung empire.

The Germans continued sporadic raids over the English countryside during the night, but it appeared that the force of the attack had been spent. British raiders again spread out over German-occupied portions of the continent in an effort to paralyze Adolf Hitler's aerial blitzkrieg at the source.

(Dispatches from Switzerland again reported that "foreign planes" had passed over Swiss territory during the night. British planes have bombed industrial areas in southern Germany and northern Italy twice this week.)

Munich, a major city, only a few miles from Hitler's Bavarian retreat at Berchtesgaden, was reported raided during the night, but Germans minimized the damage.

Rochester Corps Second In State

The crack bugle and drum corps of Walter S. Roth Post, No. 498, American Legion, captured second place in the Class B state championship competition held Friday evening in Albright College Stadium, Reading, before 13,000 people. The contest was held in conjunction with the annual state convention of the Legion. The local corps finished second to the Blue Devils corps of the Johnstown Post.

Class B competition is for bugle and drum corps not composed entirely of Legionnaires. Class A is competition for all-Legionnaire corps.

Windsors Arrive At Bahamas Post

By the United Press

NASSAU, BAHAMAS, Aug. 17—A flag was hoisted over ancient Fort Fincastle today heralding the arrival of the Duke and Duchess of Windsor. More than 12,000 persons including many American tourists and Bahaman natives were on hand to welcome the Duke when he stepped ashore on these islands which he will rule as governor and commander-in-chief.

The Windsors were to disembark at 9 A. M. from the ship which is bearing them from Hamilton, Bermuda, where they landed Aug. 8 after a voyage from Lisbon, Portugal, aboard the American export liner Excalibur.

The ship, completing a 1,000-mile voyage from Hamilton, tied up at St. George's wharf and the ceremony of swearing the Duke into his new post will follow immediately.

The government proclaimed a public holiday to give everyone a chance to see and welcome the Windsors. Natives from all parts of these far flung islands had come to Nassau.

Local Girl To Be In Oratory Contest

Miss Ruth Gullyes, daughter of Mr. and Mrs. R. J. W. Gullyes, Baden, accompanied by Miss Edna McConnell, New Sheffield, Glenn Woods, New Brighton, and Rev. Vance Yarnell, pastor of Four Mile United Presbyterian church, left recently on a two-weeks motor tour through Colorado, South Dakota and Yellowstone National Park. On August 22, Miss Gullyes will compete in the national Y. P. C. U. oratorical contest at Estes Park, Colo. Miss Gullyes is one of two national finalists in the junior girls competition.

Local Men Attending Acceptance Ceremony

Thompson Bradshaw, New Brighton, district delegate to the national Republican convention in June, and O. Scott McFarland, Ambridge, are attending the formal acceptance of the GOP nominee, Wendell L. Willkie, today in his home town, Elwood, Ind.

THE DAILY TIMES

NEWS OF SPORTING EVENTS

BILL ANDERSON, Sports Editor — BEAVER AND ROCHESTER, PA., WEDNESDAY, AUGUST 28, 1940.

EIGHT LETTERMEN TO FORM NUCLEUS FOR BEAVER TEAM

Maroon and Gray Squad Drilling Hard at Camp Near Edinboro Lake; Opening Game With Midland

Beaver High school's football squad, including 33 players, coaches and manager, is in the midst of pre-season drills at Camp Tecumseh near Edinboro Lake, Erie county, in preparation for a ten game schedule. The county-seaters will remain in camp until the end of the week, then return home to complete training for the opening game with Midland on September 11.

The Maroon and Gray's training camp was made possible this year through the efforts of the Beaver Boosters Club which contributed a large part of the cost. The boys themselves and the school board supplied the balance.

Head Coach Arthur F. Detzel planned to put his candidates through two stiff practice sessions each day, and finish the day with a chalk talk in the evening. He hoped to accomplish a great deal more at the camp than could be accomplished by training at home since the boys will be free of outside diversions.

While it is too early to hazard a guess as to how strong the county seaters will be this year it is known that Coach Detzel will be able to field a heavy line, with a backfield composed principally of experienced veterans.

Of the eight lettermen on the squad, three — Fred Knott, Pete Bunish and Gilbert Flocker—were regulars last season. Vic Morevec, a halfback, missed the latter part of the 1939 campaign because of a leg injury, but is expected to render real service this Fall.

The returning lettermen on the line are Reed Campbell, an end; Dean Berry and Charles Eaton, tackles, and Dan Smith, tackle and guard. Three other lettermen did not return to school. They were Russell Swank, center, who will attend Kiski Prep, Lee Koett and Ira Bradford. One of Detzel's biggest tasks will be to develop a capable center, a couple of guards and an end for regular duty, as well as replacements for nearly every position.

Lettermen lost by graduation last June included: Lyle Bayliss, Howard Braun, William Cramer, Albert Farance, Roy Jackson, John Knott, Peter Cullen, Harry Lopes, Ralph McLaughlin, George Meier, Charles Romigh, Bill Steele and Jim Stroeter.

To the 1940 Maroon eleven will go the honor of inaugurating two innovations at Beaver this year. This season will be marked by the first night grid games in the history of the school according to present plans, and this year's eleven will be the first to play on the new athletic field in Recreation Park.

Through efforts of the Boosters Club contracts have been executed for the use of a portable lighting system for the game with Avalon on September 19 and the game with Zelienople high on October 11.

Construction of the new concrete stadium at the football field has been partially completed, and school officials have been promised that about two-thirds of the structure will be ready for use by September 19, date of the first home game.

This will also be the first Beaver campaign that has terminated before Thanksgiving Day. The Beaver-Rochester contest, which has been a Turkey Day fixture for many years, has been moved forward this season and will be played on Saturday afternoon, November 16, at Beaver. In between the Midland and Rochester games the Maroon and Gray eleven will meet Avalon, Evans City, Monaca, Zelienople, Leetsdale, New Brighton, Avonworth and Freedom in the order named.

Tom Board Is Third In State Horseshoe Tourney Aug. 24-25

Board Only Contestant To Beat State Champion At Fayette City

Tom Board of Rochester, a member of the Beaver Valley Horse Shoe Club, placed third in the State Horse Shoe Tournament held in Fayette City, Saturday and Sunday, August 24 and 25.

On Saturday "Tom" threw 37 ringers out of 50 shoes to qualify. On Sunday he played 11 games in the round robin, winning 8 of them. His highlight game was a 95 per cent one when he tossed 31 ringers out of 32 shoes. He participated in the three best games of the tournament.

"Tom" was the only contestant to beat the State Champion, George Curry. The score was 48-50 "Board" threw 79 ringers and Curry 78 ringers. It was the champs only defeat of the tournament.

"Tom" will be in an exhibition with the Beaver Valley Horse Shoe Club against the Pittsburgh All Stars on Saturday, August 31 at South Park, Pittsburgh.

"Bert" Miller, New Brighton, Class A; Elmer Emerick, East Rochester, Class B, and "Bud" Mitch, New Brighton, Class B, all members of the Beaver Valley Horse Shoe Club took part in the State Tournament held at Fayette City.

Miller won two games and lost nine in the round robin play, while Emerick and Mitch were defeated in the second round of the Class B eliminations.

National Rifle And Pistol Matches To Start On Sept. 1

Three Weeks Of Firing To Decide Coveted Shooting Titles At Camp Perry

WASHINGTON, D. C., Aug. 28 — With the opening gun only a few days off, thousands of American men and women will soon start their annual battle for the most coveted shooting titles in the world, to be settled in three weeks of almost continuous firing at Camp Perry, Ohio. This greatest peacetime gun battle will fill the period from September 1 through 21, with practically every top-notch rifle and pistol marksman of the nation competing.

The first contingent heading for the Ohio National Guard Camp on the shores of Lake Erie, where the National Rifle and Pistol Matches will be held, is well on its way from far off Hawaii, and numbers more than twenty-five members of the National Guard and Civilian rifle teams of the Pacific possession. Teams from Alaska and Puerto Rico will start this week to meet more than 5,000 marksmen from every state in the Union, including all branches of the American armed forces, police and civilians, to again make the National Matches the largest shooting event in the world and one of the greatest sporting spectacles in this country.

In all, 105 separate matches will be fired in small .22 caliber, the large .30 caliber military rifles and in pistols, with all individual and team championships at stake. Older by two years than the famous Kentucky Derby, the National Matches stand as America's most venerable sports event, with two of the country's oldest trophies, the Leech Trophy and the Wimbledon Cup, in competition.

Baseball Summary

NATIONAL LEAGUE

Yesterday's Results

Chicago 3, New York 1.
St. Louis 4, Boston 3.
Brooklyn-Pittsburgh, postponed, rain.
Philadelphia-Cincinnati, postponed, rain.

STANDING OF THE CLUBS

	Won	Lost	Pct.
Cincinnati	75	44	.630
Brooklyn	67	51	.568
St. Louis	62	55	.530
New York	61	56	.521
Pittsburgh	59	58	.504
Chicago	62	61	.504
Boston	47	72	.395
Philadelphia	39	75	.342

Games Today

Philadelphia at Pittsburgh (2).
Brooklyn at Cincinnati.
New York at St. Louis.
Boston at Chicago.

Games Thursday

Philadelphia at Pittsburgh
Brooklyn at Cincinnati.
New York at St. Louis.
Boston at Chicago.

AMERICAN LEAGUE

Yesterday's Results

*New York 5, Chicago 4.
Cleveland-Washington, postponed, rain.
Detroit-Philadelphia, postponed, rain.
Only games scheduled.
*10 innings.

STANDING OF THE CLUBS

	Won	Lost	Pct.
Cleveland	72	50	.590
Detroit	69	53	.566
New York	65	54	.546
Boston	66	57	.537
Chicago	62	57	.521
Washington	52	68	433
St. Louis	51	73	411
Philadelphia	46	71	.393

Games Today

St. Louis at New York.
Chicago at Boston
Cleveland at Philadelphia.
Detroit at Washington

Games Thursday

St. Louis at New York.
Chicago at Boston.
Cleveland at Philadelphia.
Detroit at Washington.

BEAVER COUNTY BASEBALL LEAGUE

TEAM STANDING

	Won	Lost
Aliq. Celtic-Reds	16	4
Baden	16	4
East Rochester	15	5
Freedom	13	5
Roch. Pirates	10	8
Conway A. C.	10	8
Fallston	7	12
Aliquippa P. C.	5	10
Chippewa	5	12
Ambridge	3	16
Beaver Grays	1	18

Games Tonight

Roch. Pirates at Freedom.

MONACA SOFTBALL LEAGUE

Results Tuesday

G. O. P. 8, Saxons 4.

TEAM STANDING

	Won	Lost
Ramblers	10	2
G. O. P.	10	2
Sportsmen	8	4
Stone Quarry	8	4
Cubans	2	9
F. O. E.	2	9
Saxons	0	12

Playoff Game Friday

G. O. P. vs. Ramblers.

AUTOS DAMAGE ENGINES

EL PASO, Tex. — The Southern Pacific railroad says it spent $37,297 last year for repairs to locomotives, other equipment and right-of-way damaged in crossing collisions with trucks and autos.

Monaca Gridders Prepare For Season's Opener Next Week

TIMES photo, by Russell D. Porter

The members of the Monaca high school football squad now going through pre-season drills daily are pictured above. Reading left to right, they are: Sitting — Eugene Knopp, Elmer Petrello, Adam Karcis, Joe Trella, Joe Antoline, Stanley Wyworth, Paul Stanik, John Yarosz and Marshall Olshanski; Kneeling—Dan Sabella, Willard LeGoullon, Mike Fedeles, John Deveney, George Matascik, Frank Walter, George Jurkovac, Tony Battaglia and Thomas Namadden, and Standing—Gerald Fleischer, Frank Crawford, Stewart Shields, Paul Glancy, Edward Fronko, Ralph Aumack, Edwin Wiblin, William Milne and Tony Bobish.

G. O. P. Beats Saxons To Tie Ramblers For Second Half Honors

G. O. P. Team Can Clinch Monaca League Title By Winning Playoff Game Fri.

Scoring an 8 to 4 victory over the Saxons Tuesday evening, the G. O. P. softball team deadlocked the Ramblers for first place in the Monaca Softball League, necessitating a playoff for the second half championship.

The two teams will clash in a single game on Friday evening on the Monaca high school field. The winner will be the second half champion and since the G. O. P. outfit claimed first half honors, it can clinch the league title by beating the Ramblers. A close, hard-fought game is in prospect.

The G. O. P. club staged a five-run rally in the eighth inning of last night's game to beat the Saxons. The G. O. P. took a 3 run lead in the third, but the Saxons tallied three in the sixth to tie the score and went ahead on a single run in the seventh.

Galdony pitched for the winners and allowed six hits, while Thomas, Saxon pitcher, was nicked for 12.

The scores:

Saxons	AB	R	H	PO	A	E
Dietrich, lf.	3	1	1	1	0	0
Soppelt, ss.	3	0	0	4	0	0
Schuller, 3b.	3	1	2	3	3	0
Jaros, 1b.	4	0	1	9	1	0
Schmuck, c.	4	0	1	4	0	1
Alexander, rov.	4	0	0	0	0	0
Ogrezik, rf.	3	0	0	0	0	0
Herman, 2b.	2	1	1	0	2	1
Schmidt, cf.	3	0	0	2	0	0
Thomas, p.	2	1	0	1	7	0
Total	31	4	6	24	13	2

G. O. P.	AB	R	H	PO	A	E
Setting, lf.	4	1	1	0	0	0
Pigza, 3b.	3	1	0	0	3	0
Kermiet, ss.	4	1	2	4	5	0
Snyder, cf.	3	0	2	2	0	0
Barco, c.	3	0	0	5	2	0
Rudish, 1b.	3	1	1	10	0	0
Zigerelli, 2b.	4	1	2	1	1	0
Doyle, rov.	3	1	1	2	0	0
Linkovich, rf.	4	1	2	2	0	0
Galdony, p.	4	1	1	1	3	0
Total	35	8	12	27	14	0

Saxons ..... 0 0 0 0 0 3 1 0 0—4
G. O. P. ..... 0 0 3 0 0 0 0 5 *—8

Two-base hits—Snyder, Dietrich, Schuller.
Three-base hit—Herman.
Home run—Galdony.

Metz Takes Medal In PGA Qualifying Round

Dick Metz, Oak Park, Ill., golfer, copped the medal in the 36-hole qualifying round of the Professional Golfers Association Tournament Tuesday at Hershey, Pa., with a total of 140 strokes for the two rounds six strokes under par. Match play begins today and will reduce the field of 64 to only 16 this evening.

SPORT SLANTS

By BILL ANDERSON
SPORTS EDITOR

John Peasenelli, former Rochester high football player, who later starred on the Stamford, Conn. high school eleven, is visiting relatives in Rochester for a few days before going to South Bend to try for a berth on the Notre Dame varsity squad. Peasenelli will be a sophomore at Notre Dame this fall and make his first bid for a varsity berth. During the summer Peasenelli worked as a playground supervisor in Stamford. He came on here to visit his folks and to attend the wedding of his brother Joe.

From Peasenelli's conversation we surmised that playing football at Notre Dame is almost a full time job. Any candidate for Coach Elmer Layden's varsity who reports for fall practice in anything but tip-top condition stands a very slim chance of making the grade for the competition for every position is most intense. There will be about 200 candidates for the varsity squad, and it's a continual fight throughout the season for every berth. Peasenelli said he was given detailed instructions on how to keep in condition during the summer vacation. Advice as to diet was also included. While visiting at the home of his parents in Rochester, Peasenelli has been working out with Charles McNeil of Midland, who will be a junior at Notre Dame this year. Both Peasenelli and McNeil will be backfield candidates. Peasenelli now scales 179 pounds.

The former Rochester boy expects to leave Sunday for South Bend Unless present plans are cancelled four other Irish candidates from Stamford and vicinity will stop off in Rochester enroute to camp to pick him up. This group includes Milt Piepul of Thomasville, Conn., who will captain the Irish eleven this year; and Buddy O'Mera, Thomas Callahan and George Rassas, all of Stamford. Rassas is slated for a regular end job this season.

Byron Morgan, ex-Geneva college fullback, is the latest to be offered the position of assistant football coach at New Brighton high school. Earlier in the year Bob Bingham and Mel Miller were named to assist Grid Coach Joe Gibson and Floor Coach Ollie Molter. Bingham preferred an assistant coaching post at Grove City, and Herman Keppen was elected to fill the vacancy, but it is understood that he will continue to work at the American Bridge Company. Morgan is expected to accept.

Art Grahame is holding nightly drills for his Beaver Valley Giants to get his team in the best possible condition for the game with the Pittsburgh Steelers at Reeves Field next Monday night. Some new players have been enrolled by the Giants this year including Dale Fesler, former Ohio State star and Earl Boyde a fullback. Both played with the Akron Awnings last season. Others among the new men are: Eddie Cottage, ex-Ambridge high star; Bill Walkowitz, Ambridge; Charley Turzan, former Geneva center; Harry Smith, and Wayne Groom of Beaver Falls. Among the holdovers are: Tom Groom, Harry Fairman, Joe Tachick, Tommy Tachick, Willie Walker, Cappy Armstrong, Amie Marconda, Tommy Jeros, Bill Young and Joe Trn.

Leonard Krouse, ex-football star at Rochester high and a luminary on the surprising Penn State eleven last fall, has received a pair of football shoes from Coach Bob Higgins, Penn State grid coach. Krouse was instructed to wear them and to have them broken in before he reports early in September. Higgins claims sore feet cause many players to miss early practice sessions and mails out shoes to all outstanding players before the practice sessions begin.

Krouse claims the difference between high school and college football is remarkable for the collegians go deep into detail to rectify errors. He states motion pictures are taken of each game and are developed and returned to the coaching staff on the Sunday following. The pictures are run and re-run as the coaches watch each player throughout the game. Each coach watches one man all through the game and takes notes on his mistakes. On Monday each man is told of his mistakes, where he failed to block, where he failed to take out his man and the like and if he wants to dispute the point, the pictures carry the proof. It is no wonder the Penn State team is making its name known in the gridiron world.

Butler-Johnstown Game To Be Played Tonight

Rain Tuesday evening forced postponement of the playoff game between Butler and Johnstown for the Penn State League championship. The contest has been re-scheduled for this evening at Johnstown, which will delay the start of the Schaughnessy playoff series until Thursday evening.

The Beaver Falls Browns will play the winner of the Butler-Johnstown game in the first round of the Schaughnessy playoff series. The first game will be played on the field of the league champion, and the second at Beaver Falls, probably Friday evening.

AGES IN CYCLE

YUBA CITY, Cal.—On a recent evening the ages of all prisoners arrested at the city jail appeared to run in a cycle of decades. They were respectively 73, 63, 53, 43, and 33 years of age. Police Judge Hugh D. Moncur completed the cycle for most of them the next morning by ordering "23 skidoo."

Winners Announced By Foremen's Club

Prize winners for the golf tournament sponsored by the Beaver County Foremen's Club last Saturday at the Blackhawk golf course, are announced by officials of the Foremen's Club. The event, the second of its kind held during the current season, again proved very popular, with nearly forty men from 17 different valley plants participating. It was held in the form of a blind bogey, with each man choosing his own handicap, and seeking to make a net score of 70 to 80.

Prize winners were as follows: Dividing first prize with a net score of 74 were J. Schauberger, St. Jos. Lead; J. A. Almore of Mid-West Abrasive; J. B. Patterson of Union Drawn Steel and H. A. Wilson of Pittsburgh Bridge Co.

Second Prize—Score 75; E. J. McClain, of Pittsburgh Screw and Bolt, W. J. Teichman of B. & W., and Ray Snyder of Beaver Falls Steel.

Third prize with a score of 77 was won by T. W. Morris of B. & W.

Fourth prize was won by H. L. Lawrence of Duquesne Light, Geo. Cornelius and R. J. Wick of Pgh. Screw and Bolt, H. J. Arnot of Pgh. Tube and V. T. Pate of National Supply.

An extra contest to see who should drive from the tee and get closest the pin on the ninth hole was won by W. Morris of B. & W. whose first shot carried him only 10 feet 2 inches from the hole.

This is the second year for these golf events and club officials are well pleased with the response among the local industries. Other athletic activities are expected to be sponsored during the coming winter months.

SYSTEM BAFFLES INDIAN

ALBANY, N. Y.—Peter Labillois, 22-year-old Iroquois Indian, is skeptical of the American profit system. He and seven companions from the Eel River Bar reservation in Canada were hired to work in an Adirondack lumber camp. After a month's work the paymaster said the Indians owed the company $20. Labillois told immigration authorities.

RAIN ANSWERS AD

FAIRBURY, Neb.—Harold Acker wanted rain. He inserted an ad in the paper asking for a downpour, with one stipulation: The moisture must not interfere with a picnic in nearby Steele City. Result: The picnic ended on a Saturday night and the following day 2.03 inches of rain fell.

SPEEDY ON LICENSES

RENO, Nev. — The Reno marriage license bureau on a single Saturday issued 106 licenses in three hours, or one license in each minute and 12 seconds. It takes a minute to get the names, write them down, get the signature, but the 12 seconds extra delayed the rhythm of romance.

SMALL SQUAD DRILLING DAILY AT MONACA HIGH SCHOOL FIELD

Twenty Seven Players Preparing For First Game Next Week; Only Three Lettermen Return

By BILL HEYMAN

Twenty-seven candidates for the Monaca High school football team, 1940 edition, are drilling twice daily this week at the high school athletic field in preparation for the first game of the season to be played Friday, September 7, against the Ambridge High team on the Monaca field.

The practice sessions began Monday morning and will continue two each day the remainder of this week with the exception of Saturday when Coach Leland Schachern stated he only expected to have one session. The drills will be resumed next Tuesday evening after school as conditioning of the various players and practicing of plays for the inauguration of the session will be rushed.

The gigantic task of replacing most of the 1939 team is facing Schachern as only three lettermen from last year's squad are among the players drilling daily. Stewart Shields, an end, Paul Glancy, a lineman, and Adam Karcis, a back, are the only veterans returning so far this week.

Mike "Bull" Yuran, hard-hitting fullback of the 1939 team, and Henry Flati, shifty halfback, both lettermen last year, have not yet reported for practice. Three other members of last year's squad also have not reported. They are Edward Petres, Edwin Figley and Dale Anderson, the last named having transfered to Beaver High school where he is a member of the grid squad. With the exception of Anderson, the others are expected to report later.

Schachern at present, faces the job of constructing a team around two veteran linesmen and an experienced back in ten days and drilling that team to clash with the Bridgers, co-county champions and runner-up for the Class AA WPIAL title last season, Saturday of next week.

If Flati, a halfback, and Yuran, fullback, join the squad later, the Monaca mentor's backfield worries will be alleviated to some extent.

The Southsiders, despite a small squad, must play as tough a schedule as any school in the Valley this year. Following the Ambridge game Monaca's gridders will meet Beaver Falls, New Brighton, Midland, Beaver, Ellwood City, Chester, W. Va., and Freedom, on successive weekends. The schedule permits an open date on November 2, a week before the final game of the year with Rochester.

Six District Golfers Qualify For 'Amateur'

By the United Press

PITTSBURGH, Aug. 28—Three Western Pennsylvania golfers and three from the Ohio Valley in the district won the six places open to Pittsburgh district golfers in the National Amateur tournament to be held at Winged Foot, Mamaroneck, N. Y., Sept. 9-14.

The golfers are: Toby Lyons, Cambridge Springs, 149; Steve Kovach, Brackenridge Heights, 150; Fred Brand, Jr., Pittsburgh Field Club, 152; J. C. Watson, of Weirton, W. Va., 153; Tom Bloch, Wheeling, 154; and Henry Pabian, Steubenville, O., 154.

Modern Jesse James?

James Horan

Considered by the Federal Bureau of Investigation to be the most notorious desperado in the United States, James Horan, above, is the object of an extensive search as the 1940 Jesse James who engineered the recent mail train holdup in New York City.

Vanport News

Vanport School To Begin 1940-41 Term Tuesday, September 3

Miss Adda M. Yohe, Beaver, Succeeds Mrs. Clifford Reed On Faculty

Vanport Public School will open Tuesday, September 3. All first grade children and new entrants must present a vaccination certificate. Children must be six years old before February 1, 1941 to be eligible for first grade. Miss Adda M. Yohe, Beaver, has been elected to fill the vacancy caused by the resignation of Mrs. Clifford Reed.

Mr. and Mrs. Alex George of Aliquippa have named their son, born last Thursday, Alex George. Mrs. George was Miss Lois Pitcher before her marriage.

Steve Ostridge is spending a ten-day furlough from the U. S. Navy with his father, George Ostridge, Sr.

Mr. and Mrs. Merle Guthrie, Rimersburg, spent the past weekend with friends here.

War Gets Business, Agricultural Boom On Island Of Eire

Sharp Rises Shown In Production As Irishmen Fear Involvement In Conflict

By the United Press

DUBLIN, Aug. 28. — Eire today presents a strange paradox.

On the one hand, Irishmen fear involvement in the war and are arming their nation against invasion.

On the other, they rejoice in an almost unprecedented business and agricultural boom which the war has brought to their nation.

Always an agricultural country, Eire today is near the record highs in production of grains, root crops, and livestock. Simultaneously, industry levels are rising sharply, under impetus of demand from Britain.

Everything points to very definite improvement of the Irish economic situation with each passing month the war continues—always provided Eire can stay out of the conflict.

This Irishmen are determined to do. Today more than 200,000 men are enrolled either in the army or the local security corps—more than one quarter of the entire male population between the ages of 18 and 64—and most of these are in the regular army.

Women Shape Plans For Pop Concert

Members of The Beaver County Council of Republican Women are busy completing plans for the Pop Concert to be held at Windyghoul Estates, Beaver, on Thursday evening, August 29, at eight o'clock.

Members of the Ways and Means Committee, of which Mrs. Harry Garman, New Brighton, is chairman, are in charge of ticket sales in various towns throughout the county. The ticket sale is under the direction of Mrs. George Shaw, Beaver, and her committee is made up of the following women: Mrs. William Freiler, Beaver Falls; Mrs. John Sclagel, Rochester; Mrs. Graham Shaddick, East Rochester; Mrs. Harry Garman, New Brighton; Mrs. Zenobia Jurkowski, Ambridge; Mrs. Charles Lucas, Aliquippa; Mrs. Fred High, Midland; Mrs. Frank Nick, Monaca; Mrs. H. B. Hill, Vanport; and Mrs. Morris Wise, Bridgewater. This committee is being assisted by officers and Directors of the Council and a large group of Republican women.

A program of music, dancing, and impersonations will be presented. The Purple Heart Band, The Clef Singers of Midland, a program of impersonations by John Brandt of New Brighton, and novelty numbers by Betty Brown of Rochester, are part of the entertainment being arranged.

Mrs. Isaac James, president of the Beaver County Council of Republican Women, has announced that in case of inclement weather the concert will be held the following evening.

FIRE BOX TRAPS TARS

OAKLAND, Cal. — Eric Moultrie and Fred Wood, British sailors, had mail for home. So they did just what you do in London. They went to the red box and pulled the handle. They were still waiting for the slot to open and let them drop their mail in when the fire department arrived. They apologized.

GOLD-RINGED PENNEY

ORIDLEY, Cal.—Postmaster C. R. Pierce found in his day's receipts a penny with a gold wedding ring about it. The presumption is that some woman had the wedding ring loose in her purse and that it circled the penny without being noticed.

FIREMEN TO RESCUE

DELANO, Cal. — S. Flores, Jr., knew how to get help in a hurry when he needed it. Unable to extract his arm which caught in a washing wringer, he turned in a fire alarm. Three city and two county trucks roared to the rescue.

Beaver High Squad In Training Camp At Edinboro

Pictured above is the Beaver high school football squad, coaches and managers. The photo was taken by Ross M. Gridley, Beaver, at the first practice held Monday at Camp Tecumseh near Edinboro Lake, Erie County. Members of the party are: Front row, left to right: Delos Linzey, manager, Bill McClarey, Herman Schmid, Bob Brown, Bob Gridley, Tom Cochran, Dick Bundy, Bud Grove, Jack Morgan, Don Parsons, Dick Knott, Gail Perault, and Ralph Donaldson, senior manager; middle row, left to right: Warren Beeken, Allen Stitler, Bill Emmerich, Fred Knott, Otto Schoeppler, Dean Berry, Gilbert Flocker, Charles Eaton, Dale (Anderson) Kidd, Claire Holt, Andy Boyde, Pete Bunish, and Charles S. Linn, faculty manager; back row, left to right: Assistant Coach Edward Young, Assistant Coach Gene Moffett, Dick Hume, Bob Behanna, Reed Campbell, Vince Morevec, Bill Wachter, Ralph Farrelly, Smith Hayward, Bob Pinkerton, Jack Deeley, Don Carlon, Dan Smith and Head Coach Arthur Detzel.

Read the editorial, "Delay In Conscription," appearing on Page 4 of today's Gazette.

The Aliquippa Gazette

SERVING AN INDUSTRIAL COMMUNITY OF 50,000

WEATHER—Showers tonight and Tuesday. Considerably cooler Tuesday and Tuesday night.

VOL. XIX—No. 110 | SERVED BY INTERNATIONAL NEWS SERVICE MEMBER OF P. N. P. A. | ALIQUIPPA, PA., MONDAY, SEPTEMBER 9, 1940 | PHONE 934-935-936 | 3 CENTS; BY CARRIER, 15 CENTS A WEEK

F. D. R. SIGNS 'TOTAL DEFENSE' BILL

★ ★

Nazi Bombs Kill 600, Wound 2,500 In London

BRITISH CAPITAL STARTS DIGGING OUT AFTER RAIDS

3 Hospitals, 2 Museums Hit; Many Blazes Under Control

LONDON, (INS)—With 600 already counted dead and 2,500 inured in two days of incessant raids, German planes renewed their onslaught against London areas this evening.

A few minutes after the air raid sirens sounded at 5 p. m., sending London's millions to shelter for the third night in a row, bombs began dropping in the London area. Two separate formations of planes passed over the city at a tremendous altitude.

LONDON, (INS)—Granted a temporary daylight respite from crippling German air raids, London attempted today to dig itself out of the debris of last night's violent attack which cost an estimated 300 lives and irreparable damage to the heart of the capital.

The extra-heavy "super-bombs" [illegible] largest aerial "battle- [illegible]

(Continued on Page Five)

AL[illegible]PPA HIT BY FLAS[illegible]LOOD

Borough workmen today dug Aliquippa out from tons of mud washed onto Franklin avenue last evening when the second flash flood in two weeks clogged the town's inadequate sewer system.

Street Commissioner **Michael Wallace** could not be reached for a statement, but a survey of stores near the McLon street high water point of the flood failed to reveal any damage.

WPA projects on Highland and Sheffield avenues were not damaged, Resident Engineer G. V. Gustafson announced.

Merchants in the retail section of town hurriedly threw up flood gates and kept water from flooding cellars. At some points the water gushed over the curb.

The National Whirligig

(News Behind the News)

By Ray Tucker

SUGGESTION — The non-political nature of President Roosevelt's "national defense inspection trips" can be best assayed by the newspapermen and the unprejudiced officials who have accompanied him on these sorties. Frankly, in their opinion, the President's pilgrimages contribute nothing to the nation's preparation for war, and they appear to be a serious drain on his strength.

When the President visits a shipyard engaged in building naval vessels, he simply rides around the skeleton of the ship. He does not inspect the craft or talk with the laborers engaged in actual construction. When he "inspected" the small naval ordnance arsenal at Charleston, West Virginia, he merely promenaded about the place in his automobile. His tour of the Northern New York area during the Regular Army National Guard maneuvers actually disrupted the military operations. The troops spent two days in shining guns, shoes and buttons so that they would make a full-dress showing when the Commander-in-Chief arrived on the scene.

It is admitted that the President's visits pep up both officers and men at these national defense centers. But if he really wants to ascertain what progress they are making in

(Continued on Page Six)

'BOSS' KIEFER ISSUES WARNING

LETTERS! LETTERS! LETTERS!
Dear Chief Trevor: Just reminding you that I'm boss of our Police Department Etc-Etc-Etc-
Your boss, Burgess Kiefer
BURGESS KIEFER
ALIQUIPPA POLICE HEADQUARTERS
I'M BOSS
I'M BOSS KIEFER
BOSS
SHEVCHIK

REGISTER 17% OF ALIENS HERE

Seventeen per cent of Aliquippa's estimated 3,000 aliens will be registered by 5 p. m. today, Assistant Postmaster Earl S. Cummings reported.

Headquarters in the borough building for the registering and finger printing of non-citizens here was jammed again today.

Workers there estimated that the daily average of 50 applicants would be handled, bringing the total to 500.

"We'll have to average 50 a day," Cummings said, "to get all the non-citizens registered here by the Dec. 28 deadline."

Valley Woman, Who Lived 2 Weeks With Dead Husband, Dies

The death of Mrs. Louis A. Strobridge relegated today to New Brighton's most macabre lore the story of how she lived two weeks with the body of her husband without knowing he was dead.

Enfeebled by her 85 years, she died Saturday at Beaver Valley hospital of natural causes and became the subject of a story so strange and incredible that future generations might scoff at it as pure legend were it not confirmed by official county documents.

For the records of the health department tell how last October

(Continued on Page Five)

A WATCH FOR A NICKNAME

☆ ☆ ☆

Gazette, Eger's Will Make Award To Person Naming Hopewell Team

Hopewell Township High school wants a nickname for its athletic teams.

So the Aliquippa Gazette and Eger's Jewelry store will award a handsome wrist watch to the person whose choice of a name for the athletes is considered best by judges of the contest.

This is Hopewell township's first high school football team and it has not yet been dubbed. The contest is open to men, women and children in Aliquippa, South Heights, Glenwillard, Monaca, Shippingport, Center township and contiguous districts.

The contest is simple. Merely suggest a name corresponding to the "Panthers" of Pitt, Beaver Falls "Tigers," Rochester "Rams," Ambridge "Bridgers," Freedom "Oilers," Midland "Leopards," etc.

Print your choice of a nickname and your name and address on the blank appearing in the Gazette. Send it to the Gazette or to Eger's. All entries must be submitted by Sept. 18.

Judges of the contest, their decisions being final, will be **Mason J.** Bodkin, supervising principal of Hopewell schools; Executive Secretary Rudy Beyer of the Aliquippa Board of Trade, and Richard Auper, Gazette sports editor.

J. & L. BUYS TIN PLATE DIVISION AT McKEESPORT PLANT

The McKeesport Tin Plate corporation today announced the sale of fixed assets and good will of its tin plate division at McKeesport to the Jones and Laughlin Steel Corp.

The McKeesport corporation, the announcement reported, will concentrate on the operation and expansion of the National Can Division with manufacturing plants at Maspeth, N. Y., Baltimore, Md., Hamilton, O., and Boston, Mass. It will also continue operating its lithographing division located at McKeesport.

Aliquippa Man Sues I.W.O. Here For $375

The International Workers' Order, insurance and welfare group, was sued today by an Aliquippa man for $375 in sick benefits.

Joseph Mrovich, 41, charged in the county court that the I. W. O. had insured him against illness but that it failed to pay him $10 a week for 15 weeks to which he said he was entitled. The suit includes $75 for an appendicitis operation.

Mrovich said he was ill from July 1 to July 12, 1939, from Dec. 15, 1939 to Jan. 23, 1940, from March 7 to April 6, 1940, and underwent an operation March 12 but had not received any money on his insurance policy.

School Strike Ends In Daugherty Twp.

A week-old strike of pupils in the one-room Brookdale school in Daugherty township was over today. Virtually all of the 30 pupils were at their desks today, with Mrs. Grace McDonald, a substitute teacher, in charge.

The strike was attributed to objections on the part of some of the parents that Daniel C. Smith, 60, was too old for the children. Smith resigned to accept another teaching job, thereby ending the controversy.

TRAFFIC ACCIDENTS INJURE SIX IN AREA

1 DEAD, 2 BURNED IN MISHAPS AT J. & L. PLANTS

One man died and two were burned severely in accidents at Jones & Laughlin steel plants over the week-end, the company reported today.

A post mortem was scheduled today into the death of a 20-year-old Hazelwood youth, William Calhoun, found unconscious last night on the floor of No. 18 mill in the South Side plant. He died enroute to South Side hospital. Physicians said he probably died of electrocution.

Intense heat and flames from an overturned mixer of 50 tons of iron at an Aliquippa blast furnace burned two men late Saturday afternoon. One of them is still confined at South Side hospital today. He is Steve Crevar, 32, 488 Penn avenue, who operates a crane at the blast furnace. Crevar sustained "painful" burns of the hands, face and neck. His condition is not considered serious.

The other victim, Robert Eadie, 37, 185 Spring street, mixer-man, was discharged yesterday from the hospital. He suffered burns on [illegible] mouth and throat.

Plant employes said the mixer stuck and that during repairs the mold upset, pouring white-hot metal on the floor. The metal did not reach the two injured employes.

Two young women were injured seriously in district weekend traffic accidents involving 11 persons, four of them Aliquippa residents.

Miss Bernice Hart, 20, of 1021 Third avenue, Beaver Falls, was in fair condition in Providence hospital today. She suffered a fractured pelvis, possible brain concussion and multiple cuts and bruises when a car in which she and five others were riding bounded out of control and crashed into a tree and pole in Beaver Falls yesterday morning.

Gertrude Donnelly, 26, Mt. Washington, a passenger in the car also suffered a fractured pelvis, bruises and cuts. Four others riding with them were John Gross, 24, Beaver Falls, the driver; Fred Dunlop, 316 Ninth avenue, dislocated left shoulder; Ann Beercok, Beaver Falls, cut on the temple; Lenora Ward, owner of the car, minor wounds.

Gross said the car got out of control, bounded across fourth avenue at 36th street, hit a tree, knocked down a pole and was spun around.

Angelo Ricci, 35, 112 Economy street, Aliquippa, and Dominic Cerilli of 163 Fifth avenue, Aliquippa, and his two children escaped injury when Ricci, blinded by automobile lights, crashed into a pole Saturday night on Green Garden road, two miles east of Kennedy's Corners.

The crash knocked down a [illegible] nearby homes. State police estimated damage to the car at $200.

Joseph W. Mrosek, 23, of Industry, R. D., reported that the front wheel of his motorcycle was locked suddenly Sunday, causing him to run into a viaduct in Vanport. The extent of his injuries have not been determined.

A green coupe sideswiped a car driven by Roland Elliott of Jordan street, South Heights, yesterday near the Stone Arch here and then drove away without stopping. Aliquippa police patrol cars are searching for the hit and run driver.

An unknown motorist smacked into Charles Cunningham's car parked last night in front of his home at 1615 Main street here. Cunningham said that he would not press charges if damage to a fender is paid.

Police Banished!

★ ★ ★

Skunk Cause Of It All At Beaver

Privates C. C. Yaughner and J. V. Dorsey were kicked out of the state police barracks at Beaver today.

They became personae non grata, ousted by state police for doing a "smelly" job in a gun battle when they answered a call at 11:30 a. m. at the home of H. J. Hartley of 197 College avenue, Beaver.

They arrived to find a prowler on the premises. They cornered the invader, drew pistols and shot him, but not before he "shot" them.

The object of their hunt was a skunk.

Fellow officers ran Yaughner and Dorsey out of the barracks and told them to burn their clothes.

Only One Contagious Disease Case Here

Only one case of contagious disease was reported today by the Aliquippa Board of Health.

Henry Chester, 18, colored of 706 Grove street, was under quarantine for para-typhoid. He has been ill several weeks, despite the average seven-day duration of such a case.

Plan Merchandising Campaign For Boro Retail Merchants

Retail members of the Aliquippa Board of Trade were scheduled to meet in Plodinec's Annex at 8:30 p. m. today to plan a merchandising campaign extending until 1941, Secretary R. A. Beyer announced.

All retail members are urged to attend and participate in discussion which will center about Hallowe'en, Thanksgiving and Christmas sales campaigns. Chairman L. L. Bowman invites ideas from any and all merchants.

ANDREW HEDWIG

Andrew Hedwig of Beaver Falls died at 4:58 p. m. yesterday at Beaver Valley hospital.

Features Of Aliquippa Night Program Wednesday At Center Grange's Annual Fair Listed

The Aliquippa Board of Trade will pack fun, frolic, music and clowning in Aliquippa's night to howl—Wednesday—at the Center Grange Fair.

Borough merchants and other residents will attend the Aliquippa night program, which will include such features as Dr. A. D. Davenport, head of the high school music department, and his "Hay Seed" band, and musical selections by other talented Aliquippans.

Trade Board Secretary Rudy Beyer announced special efforts were being made to bring Dr. Allan Roy Dafoe and the Dionne Quintuplets, or a reasonably accurate facsimile thereof, to the fair.

The program of Aliquippa performers:

Victor Herbert's "Italian Street Song," sung by Natheleen Murphy Vaughan, coloratura soprano; "Lover Come Back To Me," Sigmond Romberg, to be sung by Mrs. Vaughan, accompanied by Flutist Henry Mancini. Bishop's "Lo, Hear the Gentle Lark," with Miss Betty Bowman, accompanying Mrs. Vaughan.

The Hartstein musical store will provide accordions for a solo by Milo Musulin, a duet by the Frey Brothers and the trio of Edward Winters, Shirley De Corlo and William De Martines.

A milking contest will be another feature. The program starts at 8 p. m.

BILL ASSURES U.S. OF 2-OCEAN NAVY, 18,000 AIRPLANES

Army Of 1,200,000 Men Included In Giant Program

HYDE PARK, N. Y., (INS)—As reports from besieged England grew grimmer, President Roosevelt today signed the $5,246,000,000 "total defense" bill which will give the U. S. a two-ocean Navy, enable the raising and equipping of an army of 1,200,000 men, and start the construction of more than 18,000 additional airplanes.

Refuting opposition criticism of the Administration's slowness in putting the defense program into actual effect, Presidential Secretary Stephen T. Early announced that simultaneously with signing of the huge supply measure, the Navy department was prepared to "allocate to navy yards and award —private—contracts for the construction of all combatant vessels" included in the bill — which increases the strength of the sea arm by 70 per cent

Undersecretary of the Navy James Forrestal advised the President that the Navy department would at once put into effect contracts totalling more than $[illegible]

[illegible] retary of War Robert P. Patterson sent word to Hyde Park that the War department was ready to let contracts at once totalling $[illegible]000,000 for ordnance, guns, ammunition, public works, propulsion machinery, etc.

Mr. Roosevelt put his signature on the bill which raises America's defense appropriation to over $11,000,000,000 at 10 a. m. (E.D.T.). Word of the signing was flashed simultaneously from the presidential study to the press, to Undersecretary Forrestal for the Navy, and to Col. James H. Burns, executive officer in the office of Assistant Secretary of War Patterson.

Within half an hour, Secretary Early returned to temporary executive offices at Poughkeepsie to outline the manner in which the military establishment had "taken time by the forelock" in working out contracts in advance of actual approval of the bill.

Early read a memorandum from Forrestal which said that exhaustive surveys of all shipbuilding facilities, both private and in navy yards, had been completed and "preliminary negotiations have been entered into for every combatant vessel."

WASHINGTON.—(INS) — Rep. Vinson (D.-Ga.), chairman of the House Naval Affairs committee, announced that the Navy department today will announce award of contracts for approximately 200 warships under the $4,[illegible] two-ocean Navy bill. The awards will mark the largest single contract-letting in history.

SCHOOL TEACHER ILL

Miss Jean Force, home economics teacher at Aliquippa high school, today was unable to attend classes because of illness.

Editors Believe:

The news columns of the Aliquippa Gazette strive to portray impartially and without bias the facts of daily occurrences . . . interesting to the people of Aliquippa and the Beaver valley. The column below, however, is reserved for the OPINIONS of the editors of the Aliquippa Gazette. Usually right, sometimes wrong, they are at all times honest convictions. Letters to the editor, agreeing or disagreeing with the opinions voiced here, are welcome and will be published subject only to the limitations of space and the postal laws.

"If you work in a town, in Heaven's name work for it. If you live in a town, live for it, give for it. Help advance your neighborhood. Respect the great power that protects you, that surrounds you with the advantages of advanced civilization, and that makes it possible for you to achieve results. Speak well of it. Stand by it. Stand for its civic and commercial supremacy. If you must obstruct or decry those who strive to help, why—quit the town. But as long as you are a part of a locality, do not belittle it. If you do, you are loosening the tendrils that hold you to the community and with the first high wind that comes along you will be uprooted and blown away. And probably you will never know why."

Charles G. Dawes.

Aliquippa, Pa., Friday, October 4, 1940

Gazette Program For Aliquippa

1. Provision of adequate, Free Parking Space for Shoppers.
2. Resurfacing of Franklin Avenue from the Stone Arch to the Wye.
3. Repair and Resurfacing of the Aliquippa-Monaca River Road.

LET'S MAKE IT WORK

(Continued from Page One)

whose sincerity can't be questioned but whose enthusiasm sometimes carries away their judgment.

There are indications these last few weeks that type of man has been dominating S. W. O. C. activity. Proof is the way minor strikes are bubbling up here and there—almost every hour, keeping union representatives running, racing here and there, day and night trying to get work started again. No one seems to know what the grievance is or what the union's policy is. Strike at the drop of the hat seems to be the watchword.

We submit that kind of situation is good for no one. Like the measles, when one case is settled another breaks out. A great many people are being hurt—through loss of work, loss of production, loss of income—by a thousand petty disputes that could quickly be settled over a conference table.

Two things, quite obviously, are needed—a definite union policy and then an iron clad authority on the part of union leadership.

This newspaper has made it a point never to meddle in union affairs. But the public interest is involved here—as well as the larger interests of the union itself.

In the next few days a meeting of the union membership has been called to determine upon a policy. We'd like to see every member of the Aliquippa local on hand. We'd like to see out of that meeting come a policy truly representative of all the membership—of all the army of men who work in the mill. We'd like to see authority centered in union leadership so there can be some control, some order, some united effort. Then disputes could be settled over the council table. Then there could come peace and work activity once more for the people of Aliquippa.

THE LIGHT THAT NEVER FAILS AMERICANS

TRUTH
COMICS
WINSOR McCAY JR.

Today you know more of world affairs and the affairs of your own country than any other people. For there are no gags on INS, AP and [illegible] newspapers. Everywhere, they have Americans waiting, watching, observing, interviewing, reporting, writing, cabling and telegraphing the news—obliterating time and space to make Americans the best informed people on earth. Nobody is big enough or strong enough to deny the press of this country. The American press, with its rights firm in the basic structures of our government, is big enough, and strong enough, and good enough—so it doesn't have to [illegible], pro-[illegible] or [illegible]; it doesn't have to protect anybody's interest but YOURS—the Reader of the American Newspaper.

Hands Off Europe, Jap Minister Warns

(Continued from Page One)

Axis powers. Matsuoka displayed marked impatience with the attitude of the United States and with the new American embargoes "which threaten the peace of the Pacific."

* * *

(Editor's note: President Roosevelt has declared an embargo on export of scrap iron to Japan, effective Oct. 16.)

He then threw down the challenge that the United States "must recognize the new order in the Far East or face responsibility for war in the Pacific and in the entire world."

"I have always considered America my second home land," Matsuoka, who was educated at the Oregon Law college, declared.

* * *

"I have always known the American people as a good and decent people, so it grieves me to realize that today America is the most unprogressive nation on earth, clinging to old conceptions and attempting to impede those who desire a swift change to the better.

* * *

"Japan can no longer be strangled in her desires to establish a new order of mutual prosperity in her sphere in East Asia, and has taken a place with the major powers of the world which desire to establish and maintain a new order of mankind."

Dramatically the one-time bus boy and Oregon university graduate who has become foreign minister of this Far Eastern empire accused the United States of responsibility for the trouble in Europe today. He said:

"The United States and Great Britain, it is clear to me, have forced the Axis Powers into the use of force in Europe.

"Germany and Italy are not to blame for what they are doing. The United States must once and forever understand that the new order is here, otherwise there is no use in looking forward to a peaceful settlement.

"Naturally the United States desires talks and discussions for other methods of settlement, even over a period of several years, because the United States can wait. They are in no hurry.

"It is nice for the United States to say that we must settle everything peacefully, but if we wait for America, we must perish in the years of waiting.

"So I say to America: 'Now is the time for action, and Japan will not hesitate when its hour arrives'."

Matsuoka hinted time and again in the course of the interview that he would broadcast an appeal direct to the American people "at the psychological moment" in an effort to give them a true picture of the current Far Eastern situation.

"Whether or not the European war [illegible] world war [illegible] United [illegible]

Americans must see clearly [illegible] spirit of the tri-partite pact which is candidly aimed at them [illegible]

* * *

"We in Japan would welcome changes with full understanding and broad-mindedness with a view toward peace. But if the United States continues such measures as tightening the embargo, she will only further anger the Japanese nation.

* * *

"You must admit we have been bearing all this pressure with remarkable patience. I wonder, were the situation reversed, if the American people would stand for it so long. They would already be at war."

Matsuoka closed the interview by expressing a wish for peace and improved Japanese-American relations "from the bottom of my heart and with all human sincerity."

Georgetown Schools Get $330 Payment

HARRISBURG. (INS) — Auditor General Warren R. Roberts today authorized the payment in state aid of $330.49 to the Georgetown borough school district in Beaver county.

The Aliquippa Gazetteer

By DEAN C. MILLER

AT THE COUNTY COURTHOUSE

Attorney James B. Ceris, who tucks in for the night at Edgeworth on the Boulevard, recently plunked a large sparkler on the finger of attractive Mary Simone, Beaver Falls worker in the treasurer's office. She's a comely brunette.

* * * *

Thomas E. (Tim) Poe, Jr., ex-assistant D. A. and Beaver lawyer who calls Judge Henry H. Wilson boss and uncle, is holding up well since his return from a transcontinental honeymoon. He hasn't even talked about the wife, our informant said.

* * * *

Jim Griffith, court stenographer, is back from a Florida vacation and looking quite well, thank you.

* * * *

Mike Robbe, ex-Westminster footballer and now employed to dig up scoops for an Ambridge daily, made his debut with the county press guys and gals this week.

* * * *

Echoes of the recent Babock & Wilcox picketing: The eyes of 100 pickets fell on a car driven by Sheriff C. J. O'Loughlin as he went past the B. & W. picketers for a quick glance to see whether all was peace and order. Not one boo or catcall marred the inspection.

* * * *

Luther Cornwall, Beaver Falls newspaper photog, angling for pictures on the B. & W. story and plenty burned up because it was interfering with fishing plans. The biting was worse than if he had been working a noisy stream. There just wasn't any action. In fact, the pickets turned tables on the newshawks by asking some rather technical questions on how the cameras were operated. For a short time it looked like the pickets would put "Corny" on the line and snap shots of him.

* * *

IT WAS A BREEZE

Stanley N. Novakovich, the Aliquippa man who claims he has figured out a way to keep a person breathing and healthy for just as long as he wants to live, yesterday ran from Station street to the Ambridge-Aliquippa boulevard bridge just for the exercise. He said he legged it that distance (5450 feet) in 15 minutes. Stanley is quite a versatile man, he claims. He dances like a Nijinsky, plays the violin on a par with Kreisler, can give you the formula for eternal life at a moment's notice and sings like a Caruso . . . well maybe not exactly but almost.

WISHING WELL

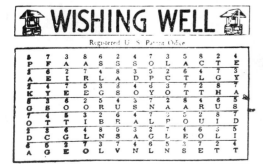

Registered U. S. Patent Office

6	7	3	8	6	2	4	7	3	5	8	2	4
P	F	A	A	S	S	S	O	L	A	C	T	E
3	6	2	7	4	8	3	5	2	6	4	7	3
A	E	I	R	L	A	D	P	C	T	L	G	Y
2	4	7	5	3	8	4	6	3	7	2	8	7
K	Y	E	E	G	S	O	Y	O	T	T	H	A
6	3	6	2	5	4	3	7	2	8	4	6	5
G	S	O	O	R	U	S	N	A	A	R	U	S
7	4	5	3	2	6	4	7	3	5	2	8	7
O	T	T	I	B	R	A	L	P	O	U	I	D
2	3	6	4	8	5	3	2	7	4	6	3	5
D	C	G	L	N	S	A	C	L	E	O	L	I
6	5	2	7	3	7	4	6	5	3	7	2	4
A	G	E	O	L	V	N	L	N	S	E	T	T

HERE is a pleasant little game that will give you a message every day. It is a numerical puzzle designed to spell out your fortune. Count the letters in your first name. If the number of letters is 6 or more, subtract 4. If the number is less than 6, add 3. The result is your key number. Start at the upper left-hand corner of the rectangle and check every one of your key numbers, left to right. Then read the message the letters under the checked figures give you.

10-4

The Aliquippa Gazette

Founded March, 1922
Published Every Afternoon Except Sunday
By the Franklin Publishing Company
Rear 384 Franklin Avenue
At Aliquippa, Pa.

F. J. Tilton, President
T. F. McDonald, Vice President
Walter Catterall, Secretary-Treasurer

Entered at the Postoffice at Aliquippa, Pa., as Second-Class Matter

BELL TELEPHONES
934 — 935 — 936

F. J. Tilton ..... Editor and Publisher
Charles P. Vorhes Business Manager
Donald O. McCann ..... City Editor
Richard L. Amper ..... Sports Editor
Lewis L. Luster, Advertising Manager
Chas. McRobbie, Circulation Manager
Elizabeth Collins, Classified Ad. Mgr.

SUBSCRIPTION RATES

By mail within first Three Zones, postage paid strictly in advance.

One year	$6.00
Six months	3.00
Four months	2.20
Two months	1.10
One month	.55
Per week, 1 or 2 weeks	.18

The Gazette is delivered by carrier in Aliquippa and suburbs for 15c a week; $7.50 per year, payable in advance. Single copy, three cents.

Advertising Rates Furnished on Application.

Member Pennsylvania Newspaper Publishers Association
Central Press Association
World-Wide Service of International News Service

NATIONAL REPRESENTATIVES
Paul de Guzman
Test Market Newspapers
110 East 42nd St.
New York N. Y.

Beaver County Newsetts

Being a Compilation of Interesting Bits of News Gathered Here and There Throughout Beaver County—Fact, Gossip and Neighborly Chatter From Every Section of the Beaver Valley.

Work on East Rochester borough's $83,000 sanitary sewer project will begin October 15. Employment will be provided 50 men for a year.

* * *

George F. Mengel, 67, lifelong resident of Freedom, died yesterday at his Mengle Heights home of a sun stroke suffered in August. He was an active member of St. John's Lutheran church.

* * *

Alvin (Mote) Bergmann, Ambridge's marathoner, has arrived at Elkins, W. Va., where he hiked to take part in the Mountain State Forest Festival this week-end.

* * *

Beaver Falls' third annual Community Chest drive today had passed the half way mark in the $25,000 goal. The drive will conclude this evening.

* * *

Enrollment at the Freedom school this term shows an increase of 25 students, Supervising Principal Ada Jackson has announced. There are 35 additional high school pupils this year, while enrollment in the grades shows nine less than a year ago.

Beaver And Ohio Valley Hospitals

A son was born yesterday at Beaver Valley hospital to Mr. and Mrs. Ervin Hetzler of Beaver.

A son was born at Rochester hospital to Mr. and Mrs. H. D. Meyers of Baden. Admitted were Dominic Cozzucoli, Aliquippa; Calvin Benton, Monaca; Dorothy Goehring, Rochester; and Mrs. Amelia Weinman, West Bridgewater. Mrs. Wayne Hounker of Aliquippa, Betty Koenig of Ambridge and Mrs. Charles McCourt of Rochester were discharged.

The potential energy contained in one year's supply of gasoline for U. S. motorists is greater than the available horsepower in 13 Niagara Falls if all water were used for power.

READ GAZETTE FOR ALIQUIPPA NEWS

ROOSEVELT WINS, TAKES 37 STATES; DEMOS SWEEP BORO, COUNTY, PENNA.

Tables showing how Aliquippa and Ambridge voted yesterday appear on Page 8 of today's Gazette.

The Aliquippa Gazette

SERVING AN INDUSTRIAL COMMUNITY OF 50,000

WEATHER — Cloudy with occasional snow flurries tonight and slightly colder in north portion. Thursday fair and warmer in south portion.

SERVED BY INTERNATIONAL NEWS SERVICE — PHONE 934-935-936 — MEMBER OF P. N. P. A.

VOL. XIX—No. 160 — ALIQUIPPA, PA., WEDNESDAY, NOVEMBER 6, 1940 — 3 CENTS; BY CARRIER, 15 CENTS A WEEK

BEAVER COUNTY'S VOTERS SUPPORT NEW DEAL TICKET

Congressman Graham Loses County But Is Re-Elected

Supported heavily by labor's vote, the New Deal ticket headed by President Roosevelt swept through victorious in Beaver county yesterday and routed three incumbent Republican assemblymen — Harry E. Goll, Everett Y. Calvin and Floyd Marr.

Congressman Louis E. Graham was re-elected to office, although badly beaten in his home county of Beaver. Pluralities accorded him in Butler and Lawrence counties, which help comprise the 26th Congressional district, enabled him to emerge triumphant.

Totals, by counties, in the Congressional race, were as follows:

	Reising (D)	Graham (R)
Beaver	31,904	26,159
Lawrence	17,598	19,649
Butler	12,859	19,693
Total	62,361	65,501

J. K. McQuiddy, Democrat, was elected state senator from the Beaver-Lawrence senatorial district by defeating W. Sharpe Fullerton. He piled up a plurality of nearly 5,000 votes.

Totals, by counties, in the state senatorial race, follows:

	McQuiddy (D)	Fullerton (R)
Beaver	31,626	24,953
Lawrence	17,418	19,442
Total	49,044	44,395

President Roosevelt was given a great "vote of confidence" by Beaver countians, 33,718 favoring a third [illegible] 24,322 backed Wendell L. Willkie.

(Continued on Page Eight)

15 Volunteer Here For Army Service

Hail The 'Champ of Champs'

[illegible] 150 years of American tradition today [illegible] by an astounding victory over Wendell Willkie. Here the Chief Executive is pictured yesterday after casting his vote at Hyde Park, N. Y., along with his mother and his wife, left.

ONLY TWO WILL BE ACCEPTED FOR 1ST UNIT FROM COUNTY

Joseph F. Patuc Initial Volunteer; Draftees Depart Nov. 26

Draft board officials here announced today that enough Aliquippa young men had volunteered for Army service to fill Beaver county's initial quota.

Only two of the 15 volunteers here will be accepted, however. The quota for Beaver county has been set at 14. Two from each of the seven county draft boards will be chosen, provided they pass questionnaire and physical requirements.

First two volunteers here were Joseph F. Patuc, 22, of 1512 Liberty avenue, employe at the Fricano-Flam Co., and Howard W. Smith, 21, of 1116 Wade street, single.

Patuc, also single, volunteered one day after his serial number was drawn 894th in the draft lottery. Two days later Smith volunteered.

These two will be Aliquippa's representatives in the state quota of 770 taken from 422 draft boards if they pass physical examinations conducted locally by Dr. C. W. Smith. Draft officials reported that both volunteers have "hounded" the office to get into the Army.

No favoritism in enlistments will be shown by the local draft board, men being chosen in the order of their appearance to volunteer. Other volunteers here include:

Steve E. Zurowicz, 22, of 628 Sixth street, drawn 1153rd in the lottery; Arbeno J. Frank, 22, unemployed, 118 Riverview avenue; Leonard DeMarco, 21, of 416 Sarah street; Edmund C. Bialick, 26, of 225 Fourth avenue.

Aliquippa draftees will leave Nov. 26 for induction at the Pittsburgh Station. All draftees from Area E—Allegheny, Armstrong, Beaver, But-

(Continued on Page Four)

Newest Victim Of New Deal

[illegible] L. Willkie, the Republican nominee for President, [illegible] Willkie [illegible] cast their votes in New York City [illegible]. There's no question who they voted for! He still held high hopes until early today but finally was forced to concede defeat.

FDR BIDDING FOR 4 MORE STATES IN IMPRESSIVE WIN

Willkie Assured Of But 7 States In Bowing Before 'Champ'

NEW YORK — (INS)—Incomplete and unofficial returns indicated this afternoon President Franklin Roosevelt would have a plurality of less than 6,000,000 votes compared to the 10,000,000 he polled in 1936. With about two-thirds of the nation's votes counted, tabulations showed:

Roosevelt	19,347,272
Willkie	15,936,596

The President definitely had taken 37 states with a total electoral vote of 437, leaving Willkie with only 45 electoral votes.

NEW YORK—(INS)—President Roosevelt today was swept into the White House for a precedent-shattering third successive term on the crest of a tidal wave of ballots that swamped the vigorous effort made by Wendell Willkie to oust the New Deal from office.

Late returns had given the President such a resounding vote of confidence that the Republican nominee, after hours of apparent disbelief, conceded he had been vanquished and dispatched a telegram of congratulations to Mr. Roosevelt.

Meanwhile, as states [illegible] doubtful overnight [illegible] the Roosevelt victory [illegible] finitely had taken [illegible] states with a total electoral vote of 437, wrested an early lead in New Jersey, [illegible] and Indiana from Willkie, and was bidding tenaciously for North Dakota and Wisconsin, where Willkie's lead still held.

Should the latter four states swing definitely to the President, he would have a total electoral vote of 486, far beyond private

(Continued on Page Four)

Rochester Board Of Trade Plans Dinner

Need of full cooperation upon the part of every organization of the community toward the advancement of Rochester and vicinity will be stressed at a Board of Trade dinner to be held in the First Baptist church in Rochester tomorrow evening.

President James W. Doncaster of the trade body stated today that the various civic groups of the district are solidly behind the meeting, which will be in the nature of an open forum to discuss possible means to regain the once proud place held by the Junction City as one of the chief industrial and mercantile centers of the Ohio Valley.

LEWIS TO ABANDON C.I.O. PRESIDENCY

WASHINGTON—(INS)— John L. Lewis is determined to carry out his promise to abandon the presidency of the CIO in the light of President Roosevelt's overwhelming re-election to office, it was learned today.

Lewis, according to authoritative quarters, regards his declaration of Oct. 25 that he would leave the CIO leadership if President Roosevelt was re-elected, as a bond. He intends to resist against any efforts that might be made to draft him into another term of service as head of the union.

Trade Board Here To Hold Confab Tonight

Monthly meeting of the Aliquippa Board of Trade is scheduled tonight, starting at 8:30 p. m., at Plodinec's hall. Items of importance will be considered, Secretary R. A. Beyer announced.

SPAIN CALLS RESERVES

NEW YORK — (INS)—Spain today called five classes of reserves to the colors, according to a BBC report picked up here by the National Broadcasting company.

RE-ELECTED

LOUIS E. GRAHAM

Beaten in his own county of Beaver, Congressman Graham was accorded heavy support in Butler and Lawrence counties yesterday and won re-election as Representative from the 26th Congressional district over Peter P. Reising, Democratic standard-bearer.

The National Whirligig

(News Behind the News)

By Ray Tucker

AMERICA Washington has witnessed a curious but fortunate phenomenon in the closing hours of the most bitter Presidential campaign since the Hoover-Smith clash of 1928. Both Republicans and Democrats—New Dealers and Old Dealers—came closer to friendship and understanding as the hours for closing the polls approached. They indulged in the good old American custom of kissing and making up after making faces at each other for several months.

Hard-boiled G. O. P.-ers conceded the sincerity and honesty of their opponents, from the President down. They recognized his right to defend the reforms he has inaugurated, and to insist upon their preservation. Despite surface squabbling and differences, the political handshakers ex-nominees agreed on certain fundamentals. Both Mr. Roosevelt and Mr. Willkie were not far apart on future domestic and foreign policies. It is probable that they will co-operate if the occasion should offer in the future.

The behavior of the two 1928 contestants epitomized the belief that no irreparable damage was done the American way of life in this battle. Forgetting all bitternesses, Herbert Hoover and Al Smith gave an inspiring demonstration of how men can fight—and forget. The former President delivered calm and philosophic speeches for Mr. Willkie. Mr. Smith's humorous, good-natured remarks showed his true stature, and were the delight of millions. In view of this closing of ranks, it would have surprised no onlooker if the candidates had stood up, wrapped their

(Continued on Page Six)

ALIQUIPPA GIVES ROOSEVELT SLATE 2 TO 1 MAJORITY

Borough's Voters Join Nation In Favoring Third Term

For detailed tabulation of the vote in Aliquippa see box on Page

In a record turnout at the polls Aliquippa's electorate chose the tradition-shattering president by more than a 2 to 1 majority.

But amid the Democratic triumph, Aliquippa's Justice of the Peace R. J. Mc Lanahan, candidate for state representative, polled 41 fewer votes that his running mate, a New Galilee farmer, Reuben Nagel.

Republican Presidential Candidate Wendell Willkie fared in the borough about as well as Alfred M. Landon, the 1936 Roosevelt rival who lost 2 to 1, but the third term triumph in the borough was even greater because it was achieved in a record local vote.

More than 80 per cent, or 9,834 persons of the 11,743 registered in the borough, balloted yesterday, and approximately 70 per cent of the voters picked Roosevelt, or 6,621 compared to 3,213 for Willkie.

It was about the same ratio as in the 1936 presidential election when Roosevelt took 6131 borough votes to Landon's 2971.

And Democratic candidates for state and federal offices beat their GOP rivals in the borough by Roosevelt's 2 to 1 strength.

All the way down the ballot, the ratio of victory was about the same with U. S. Senator Joseph Guffey winning over Jay Cooke, 6292 to 3336; G. Harold Wagner leading for the state treasurership over James F. Malone, 6319 to 3320; F. Clair

(Continued on Page Two)

PHILADELPHIA ACCORDS F.D.R. BIG WIN OVER WILLKIE

PHILADELPHIA — (INS)—Traditionally Republican Philadelphia today accorded President Roosevelt a smashing victory in his precedent-shattering re-election to a third term.

By a smaller plurality than in 1936, but a majority of landslide proportions nevertheless, this one-time stronghold of the GOP handed the nation's Chief Executive 580,527 votes against 355,632 compiled by Wendell Willkie.

Midland Labor Vote Chooses FDR 2 To 1

Midland, with a strong labor vote, picked Roosevelt over Willkie for President by more than a 2 to 1 majority, tabulation of election returns showed today.

Other Democratic candidates won by approximately the same majorities. The returns:

President—Roosevelt 1652, Willkie 779. U. S. Senator (for which the first precinct did not vote)—Guffey 1406, Cooke 432. State Treasurer—Wagner 1406, Malone 432. Auditor General—Ross 1592, Gelder 785.

Congressman—Reising 1608, Graham 796. State Senator—McQuiddy 1583, Fullerton 803. Assemblyman—Nagel 1591, McLanahan 1538, Goll 593, Calvin 780.

UNOFFICIAL VOTE IN BEAVER COUNTY

(110 Precincts)

PRESIDENT	
Roosevelt (D)	33,718
Willkie (R)	24,322
U. S. SENATOR	
Guffey (D)	31,071
Cooke (R)	24,442
STATE TREASURER	
Wagner (D)	31,885
Malone (R)	24,690
AUDITOR GENERAL	
Ross (D)	32,175
Gelder (R)	24,353
CONGRESS	
Reising (D)	31,904
Graham (R)	26,159
STATE SENATE	
McQuiddy (D)	31,626
Fullerton (R)	24,953
STATE ASSEMBLY	
(Second District, Two Elected)	
Nagel (D)	19,439
McLanahan (D)	18,701
Goll (R)	15,727
Calvin (R)	15,758
(First District, One Elected)	
Hamilton (D)	11,900
Marr (R)	9,028

Germans May Dispatch Troops Against Greece

BUDAPEST — (INS) — Germany soon may send troops against Greece, according to news dispatches received in Budapest today from Berlin.

SON FOR TODDS

A son was born yesterday at Rochester hospital to Mr. and Mrs. Wayman Todd of Aliquippa.

NEW DEAL MAKES SWEEP IN STATE

HARRISBURG — (INS) — Riding the crest of a nationwide victory, Pennsylvania Democrats gained three seats in Congress and today threatened to capture a majority in the 34-member delegation on the basis of incomplete returns.

With only six districts yet to be tabulated, 14 seats were in the Democratic camp—a similar number being held by the Republicans.

The Democrats smashed their way to a commanding lead in the Pennsylvania House of Representatives, gaining at least 42 new seats and overturning a 50-member Republican majority.

By a curious trend, however, the Democrats lost five seats in the state senate, increasing the Republican lead in the upper chamber for the 1941 session from 31 to 19.

Thus, for the third time in 84

(Continued on Page Two)

ASSEMBLYMAN

R. J. McLANAHAN

Squire McLanahan of Aliquippa won on a Democratic candidacy for representative to the state assembly but failed to poll more votes in his home community than his running mate, a New Galilee farmer, Reuben Nagel. They won in the borough, 6314 and 6273, over Incumbents Harry E. Goll, 3339, and E. Y. Calvin, 3280. It will be McLanahan's first public office other than justice of the peace.

AMBRIDGE BACKS NEW DEAL SLATE

Voters of Ambridge responded overwhelmingly to the third term plea of President Franklin D. Roosevelt in yesterday's election—giving the Chief Executive a two to one majority over Wendell Willkie, his Republican opponent.

Roosevelt polled 4,201 votes, Willkie 1,821.

As was the case throughout the nation, the President led his entire ticket but Democratic candidates, with one exception, polled more than two to one over their opponents. The lone exception was Congressman Louis Graham of Beaver who led the Republican ticket throughout the borough. Reising counted 3,499 votes—Graham 1,957.

A hard working, smoothly functioning Democratic organization carried all but one of the voting dis-

(Continued on Page Two)

SWOC Threatens Fight Over State Jobless Pay

Aliquippa SWOC officials vowed today they would go to court if necessary to determine once and for all whether 100 J. & L. workers thrown out of work by a recent unauthorized strike here had a right to compensation which they say the State Unemployment Compensation office has denied.

Sore spot in the dispute is whether an employe dependent on a strike-bound department for work is entitled to compensation for hours lost or whether, as the compensation office claims, that employe is also involved in a "labor dispute" and therefore not legally entitled to a check.

Manuel Wood, international SWOC representative, claims a "labor dispute" involves only employes actually quibbling with the employer and not workers indirectly affected by the dispute.

He has advised employes claiming compensation to appeal their cases to a referee and promised that the union would "stand behind the appeals ready to give any necessary assistance, including legal

(Continued on Page Eight)

Local order numbers of more Aliquippa registrants appear on Page 2 of today's Gazette.

The Aliquippa Gazette

SERVING AN INDUSTRIAL COMMUNITY OF 50,000

WEATHER — Cloudy with mild temperature. Occasional rain Friday and in extreme north portion tonight.

VOL. XIX—No. 172 | SERVED BY INTERNATIONAL NEWS SERVICE MEMBER OF P. N. P. A. | ALIQUIPPA, PA., THURSDAY, NOVEMBER 21, 1940 | PHONE 934-935-936 | 3 CENTS; BY CARRIER, 15 CENTS A WEEK

Hopewell Township To Organize Fire Department

3 INJURED IN FREEDOM EXPLOSION

Bulgaria, Rumania Expected To Join Axis Alliance

MEETING CALLED AT SCHOOL NEXT MONDAY EVENING

Township Supervisors Backing Movement To Form Company

Hopewell township is expected to soon boast a volunteer fire department.

A movement to organize a new department — which would be the first in the township's history — was launched today.

And plans will be advanced at a meeting in the Five Points school building next Monday at 7:30 p. m. All residents of the township interested in a fire department are invited to attend.

"There is urgent need for a fire company in our township due to the great increase in the number of homes and the rapidly increasing population," [illegible] the township commissioners said today.

There are quite a few men, who formerly were volunteer firemen in Aliquippa, who now reside in Hopewell township.

The three supervisors, John D. Shannon, Charles L. Martin and Alfred S. Warren, are behind the movement to form a fire company.

Greeks Had A Word For It

OH ADOLF!
I DIDN'T KNOW MY STRENGTH UNTIL I MET UP WITH YOU!
THE GREEKS
SHEVCHIK

'I'm Confident Of Victory,' King Of Britain Declares

'White Paper' Out

★ ★ ★

Dies Issues 413-Page Document Today

WASHINGTON. (INS)—The Dies committee today issued a 413 page "white paper," replete with reprints of documents, describing widespread Nazi propaganda in the United States and South America together with a program for reorganization of German-controlled industry in the United States after the World War.

The document contains the names of high Nazi consular officials and agents, and discloses that large sums of money are being spent in propaganda activities in the Western hemisphere countries.

The "white paper" includes purported letter from Hans Thomsen, charge d' affaires in Washington congratulating Mannfred Zapp upon his appointment to what the Dies committee describes as a vital German propaganda organization in the United States—Transocean News Service.

A letter announcing a meeting of secret agents of the Rome-Berlin Axis in a New York apartment house Dec. 6, 1939—less than a year ago—is also included.

WASHINGTON — (INS) — The Dies "white paper" contains, among its many disclosures, an intriguing document with plans of organization of German industry in the United States after the war, establishment of a $5,000,000 German bank in New York and methods of proposing trade with Germany.

The program is described in documents which, the committee said, were taken from files of the Chemical Marketing company, an American firm, headed by Dr. Ferdinand A. Kertess, a native German who recently became an American citizen.

STARRS HAVE SON

Mr. and Mrs. Philip Starr of Main street, Aliquippa, are parents of a son, born last night at Sewickley Valley hospital.

Praises United States For Furnishing Aid In Address To Parliament

LONDON. (INS)—With increased American war assistance, King George told Parliament today, "I am confident of victory."

As Nazi raiders were being beaten off from London, the King spoke at the ceremonial opening of a new session of Parliament.

"Relations of my government with that of the United States could not be more cordial," he said. "I learn with the utmost satisfaction of the ever-increasing volume of the munitions of war which is arriving from that country."

The King and Queen drove in state to the houses of Parliament, and all ceremonial was observed, but public pageantry of former years, when thousands thronged the Mall and Whitehall, was eliminated.

"My people and my allies are united in their resolve to continue the fight against the aggressor nations until freedom is secure," the King

(Continued on Page Two)

Evening School Pupils Here To Attend Social At High School Tonite

The men and women who go to school in the evening here will take time off tonight to frolic.

E. W. Devitt, supervisor of Aliquippa evening school courses, announced that a social will be held in the high school gymnasium immediately following a speech by Melvin K. Whiteleather, noted press correspondent. Evening school classes will be dismissed early to permit students to attend the lecture.

HUNT FOR MISSING BOYS

Police in Beaver county were asked to look out today for two 14-year-old Beaver Falls high school boys missing from home. They are William Binder of 2303 Eleventh avenue, and Edward Jones of R. D. 3, Steffin Hill. They were last seen after high school yesterday.

The National Whirligig

(News Behind the News)

By RAY TUCKER

CONFLICT—Alfred P. Sloan Jr.'s proposal for relaxation of laws governing wages and hours struck no responsive chord among labor or liberal members of the Administration. It simply stiffened them in their movement to prevent the foreign crisis from striking down the gains won in the last eight years.

The General Motors Chairman's suggestion came at a particularly unfortunate moment. It coincided with word that Marshall Petain, under pressure from the Nazis, has abolished labor and employer organizations, and taken over the key industries of France. It also jibed with official concern over strikes in several factories engaged in the manufacture of defense weapons. Labor spokesmen regard it as a forerunner of growing demands for longer hours, abolition of overtime and freezing of wages without any visible check on a possible price rise.

New Dealers recognize it as a distinct threat that may become sharper with increasing employment and further demands for aid to England. They also realize that Mr. Sloan's ideas are shared by numerous hard-boiled Army, Navy and National Defense Commission officials, and powerful bloc within Congress. In short, they believe that the automobile maker—William S. Knudsen's former boss—has sounded the keynote of a conflict that will become increasingly serious.

* * *

ALIGNED—The reaction of Willkie businessmen to President Roosevelt's re-election is tempered by improved economic conditions arising from the defense program and the conviction that he will subject them to no disturbing shocks on the domestic front. In private powwows here and elsewhere they have concluded that they can stand four more New Deal years after surviving the first and furious eight.

Businessmen do NOT believe that

(Continued on Page Six)

MILITARY ACTION BY NAZIS IN S. E. EUROPE EXPECTED

Birmingham Pounded By Raiders; Turks Issue Warning

BUDAPEST — (INS)—Diplomatic quarters today expressed the view that Bulgaria and Rumania, following the lead of Hungary, would join the Axis alliance this week.

Inclusion of these two countries within the totalitarian orbit, it was pointed out, will force Yugoslavia to choose between the Axis and her present "on-the-fence" foreign policy.

Hungary's move in joining the German-Italian-Japanese bloc at Vienna yesterday led to a flood of reports in Budapest today that German military action is south-east Europe is imminent.

Meanwhile, it was rumored that Bulgaria may [illegible] Greece, [illegible] of Thracian and Macedonian territory to provide a corridor to the Aegean sea.

BERLIN. (INS)—Rumanian Pre-

(Continued on Page Two)

Thanksgiving Day Observed In 32 States

By International News Service

Americans by the millions in 32 states observed Thanksgiving Day with prayers and feasting for the peace which is still theirs in a war-torn world.

The holiday, instituted by the pilgrims with their first bountiful harvest in 1621, will be observed in the other 16 states next Thursday.

President Roosevelt, who instituted the innovation of observing Thanksgiving a week earlier than previous custom, returned to his home at Hyde Park, N. Y., for the day. There he gave thanks that this country has thus far been spared the holocaust that has overtaken Europe and prayed that it continue to remain at peace.

As usual, turkey was the predominant menu throughout the feasting states today. And also as usual, hundreds of charitable and religious organizations made certain that there was turkey also for the poor.

New England, where the tradition for the "old-fashioned" Thanksgiving Day of next week is still strong, was the principal section not observing the holiday today. In addition to the New England states, Pennsylvania, Kansas, Iowa, Florida, Tennessee, North Carolina, Florida, Arkansas, Oklahoma, South Dakota and Nevada also deferred the holiday until next week.

Last year a total of 26 states had observed the later date. Mr. Roosevelt advanced the date at the request of business men who sought a longer Christmas buying season.

Union Thanksgiving Service At Lutheran Church Here Nov. 27

The Rev. H. Parker Smith of the United Presbyterian church, will deliver the sermon at the annual Thanksgiving service next Wednesday at 8 p. m. at the House of Prayer Evangelical Lutheran church here.

The Rev. Harman F. Miller, pastor of the House of Prayer, announced today that leaders in civic, church, education and industrial activities would join in the service.

The choir of the host church, with Organist Lois C. Wilt will lead the service and render special religious music.

The service will be under auspices of the Aliquippa Ministerial association, which has requested that the Lutheran Rituals and Collects be used, Mr. Miller said. There will be an offering for the Central Relief committee.

"The trustees of the host church meet all expenses incident to the service," Mr. Miller said, and the worshippers are asked to make a generous response in support of the cause for which the offering is taken."

100 Boy Scouts Here To Enjoy Camping Trip

Approximately 100 local Boy Scouts are expected to make their first camping trip [illegible] National park near [illegible] Springs.

The trip will be made during the Thanksgiving school vacation Nov. 29, 30 and Dec. 1.

Transportation will be provided to and from the park to Scouts wishing to make the trip. They are to contact troop leaders and arrange to obtian food and blankets. Cots will be provided. Heavy clothing and high top shoes and boots will be needed in event of snow and cold weather.

Auto Rams Parked Car Here; $150 In Damages

It cost Joseph R. Summers almost $100 to park his car on Franklin avenue last night.

Summers, 150 Franklin avenue, told police he parked his car near Kiehl street when a coupe driven by John Matijascic, 646 Franklin avenue, crashed into it.

The police report estimated damage at $150.

Cars driven by Raymond J. Skiba, 182 Franklin avenue, and John R. Eppinger, Harmony, Pa., collided yesterday at the Wye. Skiba said Eppinger ran into his car as he (Skiba) started to pull away from the curb. Damage was not reported.

Pittsburgh Quartet Here Today, Friday

The Royal T male quartet of Pittsburgh will present concerts at the Emmanuel A. M. E. Zion church here today and tomorrow, starting at 8 p. m. There will be no admission fee but a silver offering is to be collected, the Rev. R. J. Tipp, pastor, announced. The quartet will present spiritual numbers. The stewards' board of the church is sponsoring the program.

Mrs. H. I. Knepp, Sister Of Aliquippa Funeral Director, Succumbs

Mrs. Harold I. Knepp, 27, sister of Funeral Director Charles Marsden of Aliquippa, died yesterday at Pontiac, Mich., after a lingering illness. A heart condition caused death.

The body will be shipped to Clearfield, Pa., for funeral service and burial.

Doctor's Son Here Named In $87,500 Damage Suit

John (Jack) A. Stevens, Jr., 909 Franklin avenue, had damage suits totalling $87,500 dumped in his lap today.

One action for $51,500 was filed by his father, Dr. J. A. Stevens. The other was brought in Columbiana county court, Lisbon, by Mrs. Maryellen Koeh of Philadelphia, for $36,000 for injuries.

Dr. Stevens charges that his car was sideswiped by a truck near East Palestine, O., Nov. 24, 1938, and that a car following his and driven by his son, crashed into him when he pulled off the road to check the damages.

Dr. Stevens contends that he formerly was a doctor here earning approximately $15,000 per year and that injuries received in the wreck had permanently and wholly incapacitated him.

War Correspondent To Speak Here Tonight

M. K. WHITELEATHER

Melvin K. Whiteleather will give an eye-witness account of recent European history and the dictators who are making it when he speaks tonight at Aliquippa High school.

Whiteleather, for 13 years a correspondent for the Associated Press, has "covered" European news and will relate his experiences in the gymnasium at a lecture sponsored by the Aliquippa Education association. The public is invited to hear him.

Whiteleather has worked in Italy, Germany and France and has interviewed Hitler, Stalin and Mussolini.

Smith, Stauffer Named To VFW Offices Here; Five Turkeys Awarded

Waugaman Post No. 3577 of the V. F. W., meeting last night at the the municipal building here, elected Srgt. John Smith as alternate delegate to the County V. F. W. Council and George Stauffer as new post adjutant. Fred Good was reinstated as trustee.

Smith replaces Attorney A. D. deCastrique, who is ill, while Stauffer fills the vacancy created recently by the resignation of John Serdencky.

The veterans furthered plans for the grand military ball to be held at Moose hall here Friday, Dec. 20, for benefit of disabled veterans at Aspinwall hospital. Henry M. Loud, committee member, outlined details of the proposed event.

It was decided to distribute Christmas baskets to needy veterans and their families in the Aliquippa community. The joint committee of the V. F. W. and Legion posts, which is arranging for the military ball, will handle distribution of the baskets.

The post awarded turkeys to C. J. Malloy, 1211 Boundary street; Steve Zuonor, Aliquippa, R. D.; C. Faris, 358 Merchant street, Ambridge; R. C. McCacovy, 169 College avenue, Beaver, and John Jenkins, 1815 Pierce street here.

Twenty-two members attended the meeting, which was climaxed with the serving of a turkey dinner.

HARBOR WORKERS TO STRIKE

LOS ANGELES.—(INS)—**As an agreement appeared imminent in the six-day-old Vultee Aircraft strike at the Downey plant today, another strike within the national defense industries was called for Monday by** Los Angeles harbor shipyard workers.

BOROUGH JARRED AS OIL EXPLODES IN R. R. TANK CAR

One Man Badly Burned —Sabotage Theory Is Discounted

Oil being loaded from a railroad tank car into a truck exploded today at the Freedom Oil works, seriously burning one man and injuring two others.

A plant official flatly discounted a theory of sabotage.

The blast, a terrific detonation that sent flames spurting high in the air, was heard throughout Freedom.

Most seriously injured was Thomas B. Lowe, 56, colored, of Rochester, employe of the company, who suffered burns of the face and hands, a broken right arm and possible [illegible] back. Dr. [illegible] said Lowe [illegible] company employe, and David [illegible], New Castle, driver of the truck into which the oil was being loaded, suffered minor burns of the face and hands. Lowe was standing on the truck.

The victims are being treated at Sewickley hospital.

The explosion occurred about 10:15 a. m. while the men were loading the oil into the truck owned by the C. M. Marshall company of Rossville, Pa.

Joseph McCall, oil company's safety director, refused to disclose any details of the blast. He would not confirm or deny a report that gas had been in the tank truck before the oil was poured in and that this might have contributed to the explosion.

The Freedom fire department was called immediately after the oil was ignited, but the flames had died.

McCall would not say how much oil was in the tank car nor would he estimate the extent of damage.

Inoculate 130 More Children Here Today

One hundred thirty children were inoculated at the free diphtheria prevention clinic at Logstown school here today. They included 58 from the Logstown building, 54 from McDonald school, and 18 of pre-school age.

Dr. J. L. Miller was in charge of today's clinic, assisted by school nurses. The clinic will close at the New Sheffield building tomorrow morning.

NEED FOR MORE HOMES IN AREA CITED

★ ★

Beyer, Trade Board Secretary Here, Leaves Jan. 15

The Aliquippa Gazette

SERVING AN INDUSTRIAL COMMUNITY OF 50,000

WEATHER — Mostly cloudy and slightly colder tonight and Saturday with snow flurries in north portion.

SERVED BY INTERNATIONAL NEWS SERVICE PHONE 934-935-936 MEMBER OF P. N. P. A.

VOL. XIX—No. 206 ALIQUIPPA, PA., FRIDAY, JANUARY 3, 1941 3 CENTS; BY CARRIER, 15 CENTS A WEEK

BOARD TO RETAIN OFFICE; WILL NOT CURTAIL PROGRAM

Anticipated Financial Support Not Given, President Says

R. A. "Rudy" Beyer, widely known executive secretary of the Aliquippa Board of Trade will terminate his connection with that organization January 15, it was announced today.

That decision was reached by the board of trustees of the organization last evening.

"Failure of the Aliquippa community to give the board anticipated financial support," according to E. J. Tilton, board of trade president, made the move necessary.

Office of the board will be retained with Miss Cathérine Dufalo, Mr. Beyer's secretary, in charge. Committees of the board will carry on the work into the new year and no curtailment of the program is anticipated.

Selection of a new executive secretary, it was said, is dependent on the decision of the trustees and membership.

Mr. Beyer came to Aliquippa early last summer as the spearhead of an enlarged Board of Trade program. Previously the personnel director of the Central Tube Co. in Ambridge, he is widely known as public speaker, dramatist and for his work with fraternal organizations. His plans for the future are indefinite.

Leaves Post Here

R. A. BEYER

R. A. (Rudy) Beyer, executive secretary of the Aliquippa Board of Trade since last summer, will relinquish his position effective January 14.

U. S. TO BUILD 200 NEW SHIPS

WASHINGTON — (INS) — Taking cognizance of terrific shipping losses as a result of the war, President Roosevelt today announced a new merchant ship construction program which contemplates turning out approximately 200 vessels at a cost of around $300,000,000.

The ships, which will average about 7,500 tons each, can be turned out in a year's time and will be constructed in a number of new plants, the President says.

Mr. Roosevelt disclosed he had allocated $36,000,000 from his special contract authorization fund to start construction of these new plants.

Godshalls' Baby Still Leads Derby

All was quiet along the "Stork Derby" front here today as communiques from county hospitals and doctors in districts near Aliquippa recorded no new births to threaten the lead taken 5 hours and 21 minutes after New Year's by Mr. and Mrs. Louis Godshall's new-born son.

Runner-up in the merchant-sponsored "Stork Derby" thus far is the nine-pound daughter born to Mr. and Mrs. Matt Fatur, West Aliquippa, at 2:15 p. m. Jan. 1.

The Godshall son, born at Magee hospital, Pittsburgh, will call 2012 McMinn street home.

Twelve merchants have contributed prizes for the first child born on New Year's. One donated a prize to the second born.

The contest officially closes Jan. 8. Entries after that date will not be considered in the selection.

Fired Relief Worker Here Does Not Report

The tacit feud between borough council and the relief worker it fired Wednesday ended today when she did not report for work.

Yesterday Mrs. F. J. Ley explained that she was still sticking to her office because the council president had not notified her of the dismissal. That, she said, was why she ignored the order and had reported for work as usual.

SWOC OFFICERS TO MEET

Lodge officers and the resolution committee of the SWOC here will meet in union headquarters on Franklin avenue at 7 p. m. tomorrow, President Joseph Krivan announced today.

PETAIN CABINET IS REORGANIZED

VICHY, France. (INS)—Chief of State Marshall Henri Philippe Petain today reorganized his cabinet, concentrating major powers in three of his strongest men to fill the gap left by dismissal of former Vice Premier Pierre Laval.

The triumvirate is composed of Admiral Jean Darlan, Navy Minister, Pierre-Etienne Flandin, Foreign Minister, and General Charles L. C. Huntziger, war minister.

They will operate together, but will enjoy various graduations of power. Darlan stands next to Petain in prerogatives, followed by Flandin and then Huntziger.

Petain remains as chief of the government, with full powers. But he is expected to delegate numerous duties to the triumvirate, particularly as regards negotiations with Germany.

Fernand de Brinon, ambassador to occupied France, is returning to Vichy shortly.

Relations between France and Germany were still characterized as "delicate." But there is nothing alarming in prospect, well-informed sources said.

GREGOR IN HOSPITAL

Fred Gregor, 619 Franklin avenue, conductor on the A. & S. here, today was convalescing at Veterans' hospital in Aspinwall. He was admitted New Year's day.

The National Whirligig

(News Behind the News)

By Ray Tucker

REFLEXES—New Dealers have reluctantly surrendered to the realization that the war's impact will strip off at least temporarily many economic gains of the last eight years. Their only hope is that they can preserve and even extend certain advances on the social welfare front.

Under the pressure of labor shortages, it is believed that the Walsh-Healey and Wage-Hours Laws will have to be modified or administered more charitably. The National Defense Commission has awarded contracts to Ford, despite his clashes with the N. L. R. B. Labor may still bargain, but the President has asked it to scabbard its supreme weapon—the strike. Under the dictum that consumers' goods must make way for war stuff in any production clash, dreams of an expanding and more abundant economy based on higher purchasing power have been packed away with New Year resolutions. De

(Continued on Page Two)

Judge Assails Liquor Law

GREEKS WIPE OUT SKI TROOPS; MANY HUNDREDS KILLED

R. A. F. Bombers Raid Bremen & Emden On Big Scale

ATHENS — (INS) — Italy's first attempt to use ski-troops on a large scale in Albania today resulted in one of the Fascists's worst defeats as the Greeks continued to push forward slowly on all fronts.

Gliding down steep snow-covered mountainsides, the Italian skiers sped straight into Greek machine-gun fire on the Tepelini front and were mowed down by the hundreds.

Desperate attempts by the Italians to maintain their hold on heights along the Tepelini-Klisura front failed, and the Fascists were dislodged from several strategic positions, according to latest advices from the battle zones.

Aided by a heavy R. A. F. raid on Elbasan, the Greeks resumed their offensive on the northern front, and advance guards were reported only five miles from Elbasan, highway key to Tirana, the capital.

LONDON. (INS) While Nazi raiders concentrated on a south Wales town, R. A. F. bombers last night hammered German shipyards and factories at Bremen for the second successive time and plastered Emden with high explosives.

Authoritative London quarters said today that the latest R. A. F. attacks were carried out on a "very heavy scale."

In addition, it apeared that the British raids were lengthly ones. The Deutschland radio remained off the air for more than four hours during the night.

BERLIN. (INS) Authoritative quarters today declined to offer clarification of many new rumors regarding the situation at Vichy but they endorsed, at least partially the view that trouble is in store for France unless its attitude is changed.

The newspaper Voelkischer Beobachter, organ of Chancellor Hitler, came out flatly with a suggestion that a dark year lies ahead of France and added:

"Many Frenchmen apparently have not yet understood developments."

LONDON.—(INS) — Authoritative British circles today accused Germany of responsibility for recent bombings of Eire.

"Many" such attacks have occurred, it was said. German planes involved in raids on the British Isles are equipped with adequate flying

(Continued on Page Eight)

DEMO CLUB TO MEET

The Aliquippa Democratic social club will meet at 7:30 p. m. Sunday, Recording Secretary A. W. George announced today.

Quits Allied Aid Helm

William Allen White, above, 72-year-old publisher of Emporia, Kan., has resigned his post as chairman of the Committee to Defend America by Aiding the Allies. White, who had been one of the first of prominent U. S. citizens to advocate full war aid to Great Britain, claimed that the chairmanship demanded the full-time energies of a younger man.

Customs Of Eastern Rite Churches Still Prevail In Nation

By MICHAEL PINKOSKY

(Editor's note: This is the first of several articles to appear in The Gazette concerning customs still practiced by Eastern Rite churches in America. Many folk do not understand the reason why Christmas is being observed on January 7 by the Russians, Ukrainians, Serbians, Carpatho-Russians, Greeks, Syrians, Hungarians and Macadonians of Orthodox and Greek Catholic Rites and a small number of Croatians and Italians belonging to those rites. Keeping the Julian calendar, which is 13 days from the Gregorian, is the reason for the coming observance).

Eastern Rite church members, have been approached many times by the puzzled folk as to why they celebrate Christmas in January instead of December. Some have simply answered that it was their custom and thereby

(Continued on Page Seven)

Staman's Store To Be Remodeled Here Within Near Future

Aliquipap's business session will be made brighter soon by the streamlining of one of its oldest business houses.

On Page three of today's Gazette Staman's announces the opening of their "Remodeling Sale" preparatory to a complete renovation of the store, located at 378 Franklin avenue.

Work on remodeling plans will commence as soon as sufficient stock has been moved out to lessen the confusion when carpenters, electricians and others go to work, M Staman announced today.

Man Faces Court For Theft Of Watch, Cash

Squire R. H. Davis last night ordered Frank Fioravanti, 23, of Conway, jailed *in default of $500 bond* after a hearing on charges of larceny of the person and receiving stolen goods.

Fioravanti was accused of taking home an intoxicated man Dec. 23 and "rolling" him for his watch and between $5 and $10.

HANDED SIX-DAY TERM

Julius Rayfort, colored, 721 Sheffield avenue, today started a six-day term at Beaver jail after he failed to pay a fine and costs assessed by Squire Ivor L. Jones on a drunk and disorderly conduct charge. Aliquippa police arrested Rayfort, who said he was unemployed, on Franklin avenue.

LIQUOR BOARD IS 'NO GOOD,' JUDGE WAYCHOFF AVERS

West Bridgewater Man Handed Term In Workhouse

Visiting Judge Challen W. Waychoff of Greene county today assailed the state liquor law as "the most abominable law we ever had" and accused the Liquor Control Board of "laxity."

"The liquor board is no good," Judge Waychoff charged, "and the liquor law is no good . . . It is the most abominable law we ever had . . . It will stay that way so long as the state seeks to encourage the sale of liquor."

The Greene county jurist leveled his salvo at the liquor statute as he imposed an unusually severe sentence on Nick Hodnick, 54, of Brady's Run, West Bridgewater, convicted last June on a disorderly house charge.

Judge Waychoff fined him $25, assessed him costs and sentenced him to three months in Allegheny county workhouse. Usually liquor law violators in the county are not imprisoned.

The denunciation of the law came after a character witness for Hodnick declared that the defendant's beer and whisky establishment was

(Continued on Page Seven)

Housing Authority Seeking Viewers To Determine Damages

The Beaver County Housing Authority today asked for the appointment of viewers to determine damages to five properties the Authority has condemned in seeking a site for a housing project in Beaver Falls.

The suits named the property owners and the county commissioners. The viewers would appraise the damages the housing project would cause to the property.

Named in the five suits were the Pennsylvania and Pittsburgh-Fort Wayne and Chicago railroads; Frank R. and Julia H. Resier; Mary Bloom, Sarah M. Houston and Milton H. Bell, heirs of Harry Bloom; Irene Moses, Hilda and Jacob Fleishman, Earl Stauffer, heirs of Mrs. Annie Stauffer; Charles F. Moses and Marion and James Moses, the latter two minors, and all heirs of Wilford Stauffer.

The court named Jacob Fleishman guardian of the minors.

Bartholomous Hedwig also was named in the suits.

FDR Sending Hopkins To England Pending Selection Of Envoy

WASHINGTON.—(INS)—President Roosevelt today disclosed that he is sending his trusted friend and adviser, Harry Hopkins, to London as his personal representative pending announcement of the appointment of a new U. S. ambassador to England.

Long Voyage Home

Axel G. Anderson

Caught in the German blitzkrieg of Norway last spring, five-year-old Axel G. Anderson of Queens, New York, finally comes back home after being forced to travel through several countries, including Germany. He departed from Europe at Lisbon, Portugal

$45 Damage In Two Traffic Accidents

Damage estimated at $35 resulted yesterday when cars driven by John Ranich, 1 Hopewell avenue, and George Yakin, 133 Kiehl street, collided near the Aliquippa-Ambridge bridge. Ranich told police he stopped quickly while driving in a funeral procession and was rammed by the car driven by Yakin.

Robert Mihalik, 2102 Oakwood avenue, told police yesterday he hit a car driven by Earl Ross, 490 Franklin avenue, near Engle street. Damage was estimated at $10.

Bus Driver, Injured In Wreck, Improving

Beaver Valley hospital attendants reported today that Edward Frasinelli, injured this week when a bus he was driving crashed through guard cables on Constitution boulevard onto P. & L. E. railroad tracks below, was "very much improved and doing nicely."

The unidentified driver of the car which forced Frasinelli to drive his bus through the cables has not been apprehended.

CONCLUDES VISIT HERE

Kenelm Winslow, senior at Bowling Green State college, Ohio, today returned to school after a visit with his uncle, Robert M. Crawford of 2023 McMinn street here.

Roosevelt Will Request Broad Powers For Lease-Lend Program

WASHINGTON. (INS) President Roosevelt will ask the new Congress to give the executive branch broad discretionary powers for administration of his proposed lease-lend program to aid Great Britain, White House sources disclosed today.

In advance of his appearance Monday before a joint session of the 77th Congress, convening today, the President is sounding out Democratic leaders on the prospect of obtaining speedy approval of the new policy under which he hopes to make still more planes, freighters, tanks, guns and munition immediately available to the hard pressed British.

Senate Majority Leader Barkley, Sen. Harrison (D) Miss., Chairman of the Senate Finance committee, and Sen. Byrnes (D) S. C., were summoned to the White House this morning. Mr. Roosevelt discussed his message yesterday with Speaker Rayburn and House Majority Leader McCormack.

The Chief Executive is represented as feeling that approving legislation

(Continued on Page Seven)

Draft Board Explodes Popular Myth Concerning Married Men

The Aliquippa draft board exploded a popular myth today.

Generally speaking, the public has believed that men married after the draft law went into effect would be treated as single men and subject to all regulations governing an unmarried registrant.

This is not true, it was announced locally today following receipt of Bulletin 23 from Harrisburg headquarters. To quote the bulletin:

"Whether a man was married at the time he registered or has been married since, the same yardstick should be applied in determining his classification."

Conceding that sole jurisdiction in classifying registrant rested with the local board the state office cautioned that "all Class 3 deferments should be determined with sympathetic regard for the registrant and his dependents."

The following rules for determining whether a registrant is put in an "immediately available" class or deferred were outlined in the bulletin:

1. A sympathetic regard for the

(Continued on Page Eight)

HUNDREDS OF NEW HOMES NEEDED AT ONCE, ROARK SAYS

Valley May Lose Many Defense Orders, Audience Told

Beaver county needs hundreds of new homes "immediately" for laborers if its industries are to get war orders and keep from "obstructing" U. S. defense, Clemons Roark declared last night.

Roark, Federal housing official, told the Beaver County People's Housing Council at Monaca that there were only 140 vacant homes in the county or a ratio of a third of one per cent compared to a three per cent ratio which he said was the minimum for adequate housing in any community.

"Five thousand workers in the county are forced to live outside the county because of the lack of available homes for sale or rent," Roark said.

Industrial production is expanding in the valley, he declared, and army procurement officials consider the housing supply second only to labor in the national defense program.

The council, composed of public officials, realtors, architects and labor representatives met to discuss a plan for the construction of 1,600 dwelling units as a part of the defense housing program.

Roark pointed out that the Commission for Industrial Expansion in the county is enlisting all available plants, space and other unused production capacities in the defense effort and that the army procurement division considers adequate housing for laborers a vital factor is assigning war orders.

"If we are not to obstruct the program here, immediate steps must be taken to [illegible] new homes," Roark said.

Roark added the construction job was up to private builders but that the housing authority would co-operate and that if private building "fell short," the government would do the job

Six hundred of the contemplated 1600 new homes for rent or sale would be built by private capital," Roark said.

He has been named on a committee of three who will represent Pennsylvania and confer with national defense commission representatives next Tuesday in Washington on defense housing in the state. The committee has picked Aliquippa, Ambridge, Freedom, Monaca, Midland and Beaver Falls as towns needing more homes.

County Controller Ralph C. Bennett was elected temporary chairman of a committee to arrange a conference at which the report on next week's housing conference will be heard and to plan the local program.

Religious Fanatic Slashes Himself At Beaver County Jail

Andrew Hritsick, 25, of Ambridge, alleged religious fanatic who thinks the "world ought to be cleaned up," started his campaign last night by cutting himself with a razor.

The act of self-immolation was committed in Beaver jail where he has been confined for mental observation. Ambridge police said he recently threatened to "hurt" his father and was arrested.

The county warden said Hritsick was a "model" prisoner. He was taken to Rochester hospital for treatment.

Walkers Split

Mrs. Betty Walker

James J. Walker

Mrs. Betty Compton Walker, former musical comedy star, has filed suit for divorce in Key West, Fla., against James J. Walker, one-time mayor of New York. She charges "extreme cruelty."

LOCKHEED PLANT WHERE HUDSON BOMBERS ARE BUILT

The assembly line at the Lockheed Aircraft company plant in Burbank, Cal., is shown above. Here is where the Hudson bombers are turned out for the Royal Air Force to use in the bombing of German-held "invasion" ports along the French channel coast.

To Prevent Disease

1732—George Washington—1799

Kidnap Victim

Dirk Van de Geer

Holland's 78-year-old former premier, Dirk Van de Geer, condemned recently by the Dutch government-in-exile because he reportedly had returned to his native land from London, now may be a hero instead of a traitor, according to a story revealed by a London newspaper. The paper said that Van de Geer was the victim of an aerial kidnaping by the Nazis in a plot closely resembling one in the American film, "Foreign Correspondent." This account said that the ex-premier, kidnaped from Lisbon, Portugal, is in Stuttgart prison because he has refused to divulge British secrets.

"Ice Follies" Star

Beautiful Bess Ehrhardt heads the big cast of skating stars in "Ice Follies of 1941" which will play a return engagement at The Gardens in Pittsburgh, March 3 through March 8.

Panamanian Envoy

Ambassador Brin

Carlos N. Brin, new ambassador to the United States from Panama, is shown above as he entered the White House in Washington to present his credentials to President Roosevelt. He succeeds Don Jorge E. Boyd.

A Taft Visits F. D. R.

Charles P. Taft

On the way to a conference with President Roosevelt, Charles P. Taft, brother of Senator Robert A. Taft of Ohio, is pictured at the door of the White House in Washington. **He recently was appointed assistant co-ordinator of public health activities related to national defense.**

Drives Ambulance

Mrs. Juanita Pagella

American-born Mrs. Juanita Pagella, above, is one of the two American women with the American ambulance corps in Great Britain. Mrs. Pagella is the former Juanita Bruton of Palo Alto, Cal. **The corps is a voluntary outfit, supported by funds raised in the United States.**

Countess Sakhnoffsky

Countess Ethleene Sakhnoffsky, above, is seeking separate maintenance of $1,000 a month from Count Alexis de Sakhnoffsky, magazine illustrator. In her suit being heard in Los Angeles, she charges cruelty.

He Tomatoed Hitler

Back in the days when Adolf Hitler was an obscure rabble rouser in Munich, John Leisl, a native of the city, was one of a group which frequently pelted the future fuehrer with overripe tomatoes, eggs and apples. Now those days are gone forever, and Leisl is shown with his wife at Philadelphia federal district court after taking the oath as a United States citizen.

CHAMP IN 1940, SPANIEL AGAIN IS BEST-IN-SHOW

My Own Brucie and trophy

Winner of the best-in-show laurels in the 1940 Westminster Kennel club dog show in New York, My Own Brucie, a cocker spaniel owned by Herman E. Mellenthin of Poughkeepsie, N. Y., again is adjudged the champion dog in the Westminster show, just concluded.

Canada's "Adopted Sons"

Two young Americans now ready for overseas service are leading aircraftmen T. R. Maguire (left), of East Orange, N. J., and G. C. Daniel, of Strong City, Kansas. They recently received their wings in the Royal Canadian Air Force at a presentation ceremony at the Uplands Air Station near Ottawa.

WHISTLES WAY TO MOVIE CHANCE

Miss Mauricette Melbourne

The role of Rima in the film version of W. H. Hudson's classic romance, "Green Mansions," goes to Miss Mauricette Melbourne, above, daughter of an Australian physician, partly because of her extraordinary gift for whistling. Noel Coward, producer-actor-playwright, described Miss Melbourne's whistling as "the most exquisite thing I have ever heard."

BRITISH GUARD CONVOY FOR GREECE PASSING 'ROCK'

There have been many reports of Axis plans for capturing it, but the famous British fortress of Gibraltar still guards the western entrance to the Mediterranean. The British warships shown above in the straits in front of the "Rock" are guarding a convoy loaded with war material destined for Greece. Left to right, they are the aircraft carrier Ark Royal, an unidentified battleship and the battleship Renown, units of the British Mediterranean force which has been active against Italy.

12-YEAR-OLD GIRL BEARS SON

Mrs. Wilmer Munn and baby

Mrs. Wilmer Munn, who was 12 last December, is shown above with the six-pound son to whom she gave birth in Union, Miss. Mrs. Munn and the infant's 17-year-old father were married last April.

ALIQUIPPA GETS DIAL 'PHONES IN '43

The Aliquippa Gazette

SERVING AN INDUSTRIAL COMMUNITY OF 50,000

WEATHER — Snow flurries and slightly colder tonight. Thursday cloudy and colder in east portion.

SERVED BY INTERNATIONAL NEWS SERVICE | PHONE 934-935-936 | MEMBER OF P. N. P. A.

VOL. XIX—No. 228 | ALIQUIPPA, PA., WEDNESDAY, JANUARY 29, 1941 | 3 CENTS; BY CARRIER, 15 CENTS A WEEK

PREMIER METAXAS DIES

★ ★ ★ ★ ★ ★ ★ ★ ★ ★ ★ ★ ★ ★ ★ ★ ★ ★ ★ ★

Mystery Fire Hits Store Here

GERMAN AIRMEN IN ITALIAN CITY

—Central Press Radiophoto

This radiophoto from Berlin shows members of the German Luftwaffe marching through an unnamed Italian city, substantiating reports that the German airforce is assisting the Italians in their war efforts. It is unusual to note that the Italian populace in the picture shows no evidences of cheering the supporting German flyers.

SWOC, 'BIG STEEL' TO RENEW SALARY PARLEY ON FRIDAY

Union Leaders To Map Plans For Size Of Raise Wanted

PITTSBURGH — (INS) — The Steel Workers Organizing Committee will complete the preliminary phases of its informal wage discussions with the biggest of the "Big Steel" companies this Friday, it was learned today.

Twenty-four hours later, Philip Murray, chairman of the SWOC and president of the CIO, will sit down at a conference table with his board of strategy—three of the SWOC's top leaders—and make a full report on the conferences he has been holding with United States Steel corporation.

Then, it was learned from an authoritative source, these four men—Murray, Clinton S. Golden, of Pittsburgh; Van A. Bittner, of Chicago, and William Mitch, of Birmingham, Ala.—will decide on the issues to be presented to U. S. Steel, including

(Continued on Page Four)

Blooming Mill Credit Union Here Declares 5 Per Cent Dividend

Members of the Jones & Laughlin Blooming Mill Credit union here last night approved a five per cent dividend on all outstanding shares at a banquet meeting attended by 70 in Hotel Woodlawn.

The financial report by Treasurer Ronald Davies outlined total assets of the union today as $22,000, compared with $1,800 in 1937 when it was organized. Membership today is 739. In 1937 it was 125.

Present officers of the union are H. J. Berny, president; Joseph Hennessy, vice-president; and Davies, treasurer. New officers will be elected next week at a joint meeting of incumbent officers and the board of directors.

Man Awarded $1,374 For Death Of His Son

A jury of five women and seven men debated three hours yesterday and then gave Carl Gray, New Galilee, $1,374.50 for the death of his son, Wayne, 18, run over by a Bea-Falls truck last July.

The father had asked Beaver court for $20,000. The young man was hit by a truck driven by Pete Frederick of Beaver Falls as he cycled home from a jaunt to Darlington Lake. He died two days later in Providence hospital of a fractured skull.

January term of civil court ended today without calling the third week panel of veniremen to action. Next term of court will be in March when criminal cases will be aired.

Dozen Aliquippa High Students Appear On Greenville Program

Twelve Aliquippa High School students sang today on the Mid-western Chorus Festival program in Greenville. They are:

Norma Jean Barrett, Ruth Miller, Louise Kozina, Maggie Calabro, Eleanor Davies, Eleanor Marocco, Marjorie Kronk, Betty Miller, John Orsag, Robert Chaimovitz, Lonzie Rinker and Joseph Cristini.

Large Shipment Of War Relief Articles Sent By Red Cross

Mrs. Robert Garvin of Beaver, chairman of Red Cross Volunteers in Beaver county, today announced that the fifth and largest shipment of war relief production articles left local Red Cross headquarters yesterday for New York ready for shipment to European refugees.

Throughout the county more than 500 Red Cross Volunteers have been knitting and sewing to complete the articles for this shipment. The quota given by National headquarters was met and exceeded.

Mrs. H. W. Douglass, New Brighton, chairman of war relief production, and Mrs. Frank Darragh, New Brighton, chairman of shipping and packing, report that the following articles were included in the shipment:

30 caps, 15 mittens, 105 scarfs,

(Continued on Page Four)

U. S. Photographers Will Snap Pictures Of Valley Industries

Two crack government photographers—John Vashon and Jack Delano—will train cameras on Beaver county industrial plants and housing (or the lack of it) all next week, it was announced today.

In communications to officials of the Beaver County Housing Authority and Committee for Industrial Expansion, Morris L. Cook, secretary of the National Defense Commission, said that the photographers would snap pictures of industrial plants here—possibly with lush orders in mind.

No photographs of actual plant operations will be made, the announcement said.

Install Officers Of McKinley GOP Club

President Carmine Molinari and other officers of the McKinley Republican club of Aliquippa were installed at the organization's January meeting. Others inducted include:

Angelo Cardis, vice president; Victor Ferri, corresponding secretary; Joseph Donina, financial secretary; Anastasio Petitta, treasurer.

Trustees—Leo Andreozzi, Frank Rossi, Phil Cervi and Alfred Cafrelli. Orators—Pete DelGreco, Lawrence Colonna and Lowe Sugar. Masters of ceremony—Angelo Ricci, Nick Ferri, Lowe Sugar and Lawrence Colonna. Sentinel—Virginio Bianchi.

PLAN 11 GROCERY HIT SECOND TIME IN 39-DAY PERIOD

Four Persons Forced To Flee Early Morning Blaze Here

A mysterious fire, which Fire Chief August Thomas said "may have been started by rats chewing matches," struck a Plan 11 grocery store today for the second time in six weeks. Damage was estimated at $160.

Grocer Alex Sachs told firemen he had heard "noises" in the basement of his store just as the night of Dec. 19. Fire hit the cellar that night, also.

Starting behind a cellar door at the rear of the basement, the fire ate through the store floor before firemen confined it with a booster tank.

A young man walking past the store at 906 Davis street at 12:55 a. m. pulled the alarm which brought out Central station firemen.

Chief Thomas said that matches were strewn in the basement behind the door.

Mrs. Sachs and her two children fled to the Woodlawn hotel. Damage to the building was set at $125; to the contents, $35.

Non-Firemen Barred From Riding Borough Trucks, Chief Warns

Aliquippans who are not regular firemen or volunteers will just have to curb that desire to "ride a fire-truck" from now on, Fire Chief Thomas warned today.

"While we appreciate any help residents may want to give," Thomas said, "we cannot and will not allow citizens to ride to or from fires in borough trucks."

The borough, he explained, would be responsible for injuries received under such circumstances. Reason for Thomas' warning was that two spectators last night hopped on a fire truck as it started out for a Plan 11 fire.

ELKS, LEGION TO FETE DRAFTEES

The Elks and American Legion will stage a party for Aliquippa's next group of draftees Saturday, Feb. 15.

Carl Weible, exalted ruler of the B. P. O. E. lodge here, last night appointed ten lodge members to assist M. J. Kane, chairman of the entertainment committee, in completing banquet details.

A prominent speaker will be engaged and a dinner served in honor of the Aliquippa young men who will leave Feb. 19 for a year of Army life. Wives of Elk and American Legion members will attend.

$102,181,321 Profit For U.S. Steel In '40, $8.84 Dividend

NEW YORK. (INS) The steel industry, operating at virtual capacity, faced a rosy future today with unfilled orders on the books of one firm alone amounting to approximately 4,600,000 net tons of finished products which is equivalent to three months shipments at current rates of delivery.

These unfilled orders are possessed by United States Steel Corp., which during 1940 enjoyed the highest annual earnings in a decade. Big Steel's net profit for last year was $102,181,321, equivalent after preferred dividends to $8.84 a share on common stock. This compared with a $41,119,984 profit in 1939 and a 1930 net profit of $104,421,572.

Although somewhat below the levels of last December, the final month of the best fourth quarter Big Steel has recorded since World War days, the demand for steel still continues to exceed the rate of shipment, Irving S. Olds, Big Steel's board chairman, reported.

WEST ALIQUIPPA SWIMMING POOL GETS WPA O.K.

WPA heads in Washington today approved a $62,000 swimming pool project for West Aliquippa.

This was the last official red-tape facing project sponsors before contracts are let and actual construction begun.

The Federal government will foot $31,175 of the bill. Aliquippa borough will put up approximately $31,015

Joseph Mundo, WPA engineer in charge of the project, has not yet announced when actual construction will start.

Bids must be advertised and contracts let by borough council after it mulls over details of the swimming pool in open and caucus sessions.

Several informed observers said they "doubted" work could be started before spring. If so, there is small chance that the project will be completed in time for summer swimming this year.

Outlined in the communication okaying the project were the following units to be constructed:

A bath house and pool with walks fringing it, a water recirculation system, fences and a filtration plant.

Mundo will meet with borough council in the near future to complete arrangements for materials and equipment to be used in the project and set a date for the groundbreaking ceremony.

Aliquippa, Ambridge Being Surveyed For Steel Workers' Rooms

Fifteen Defense Commission survey workers scoured Aliquippa and Ambridge today to determine whether transient steel workers converging on this district because of a steel production boom would have rooms in which to sleep.

Survey findings will be correlated with unemployment figures for the district. Proprietors of rooming and boarding houses will be included in the survey.

One worker reported that more than 300 mill workers are sleeping in one church building in Midland, location of the Crucible Steel plant.

U. S. To Acquire Naval Base On Martinique

WASHINGTON. (INS)—The United States will acquire a naval base on the French island of Martinique, in the Caribbean sea, when France regains her fredom, Rear Admiral John W. Greenslade, head of the U. S. Navy mission to select military bases on British Western Hemisphere possessions, declared today.

SHOW GETS RECORD

NEW YORK. — (INS) — Sonja Henie's ice show hung up new records for Madison Square Garden, it was announced today. The skating star's eight performances with her troupe drew 134,000 persons and a net gate of $280,000.

ULTRADRAMATIC FDR--

Took Pains To Make Halifax Welcome To U. S. Historic, Spectacular Event

(THE NATIONAL WHIRLIGIG)
By Ray Tucker

President Roosevelt excelled his usual ultradramatic self to make his personal welcome to Lord Halifax an impressive, historic and spectacular event. It was another gesture to tell the world that Yankee weapons—if not men—are coming.

It was the President who broke the first news that Britain's Ambassador was arriving on a battleship named after the King. For speed and safety, most foreign dignitaries have traveled by Clipper since the war. When asked the position of the warship, Mr. Roosevelt frowned on premature publicity. He warned that any premature announcement would subject the King George VI to sub, surface and air attack, although it was then well within American waters and amply convoyed. The President notified the press early in the morning that he would greet the Viscount in person, but would not let them "flash" the news until he was about to depart for Annapolis. He had his eye on big, black headlines in before supper editions—also

(Continued on Page Four)

Expecting Stork

Lili Damita

Errol Flynn, dashing movie hero, and his wife, Lili Damita, are expecting the birth of a baby in May, Lili has told Hollywood friends. The couple was married six years ago.

Local Bus Firm Will Get PUC Hearing For Alleged Violations

HARRISBURG. (INS)—The Public Utility Commission has instituted a complaint upon its own motion against Stanley and Frank Ference, doing business as the Ohio River Motor Coach Co., alleging approximately 68 violations of their certificate of public convenience, it was nounced today.

The company is directed to answer the complaint within 15 days of service and a hearing has been scheduled for Feb. 14.

The Ohio River Motor Coach company is authorized to operate between Aliquippa, Beaver county and Pittsburgh, but no right is granted to transport persons between Aliquippa and Ambridge, between Ambridge and Sewickley, and between the western boundary of Emsworth and the Pittsburgh terminus, and between intermediate points in each of these restricted zones, the commission declared.

"STRONG MAN" OF GREECE SUCCUMBS AFTER OPERATION

Nation, Stricken With Grief, Determined To 'Carry On'

ATHENS — (INS)—Premier Gen. John Metaxas of Greece, who smashed the legend of Fascist invincibility by turning back the Italian invasion, died today after undergoing an operation for a throat ailment.

The nation, grief-stricken by its loss, made clear its determination to carry on the war against Italy to a victorious conclusion.

Flags were flown at half-staff everywhere throughout Athens and in every town and village of the country. Many persons in the streets wept without restraint when announcement came over loud-speakers that the man who had successfully led Greece against the Fascist invasion had passed away.

There was complete calm, however, and every indication that all of Greece would persist in its determination to preserve liberty and independence at all costs.

King George II lost no time in choosing a successor to Metaxas in the person of Alexanderhos Korizis, governor of the National Bank of Greece.

(Editor's Note: A German official news agency (DNB) dispatch from Athens said Metaxas died of heart failure.

(This same agency reported from Sofia that telephone connection between that city and Athens was suspended by the Greeks this morning.)

Born in Cephalonia in 1871, Me

(Continued on Page Eight)

Nabbed On Burglary Charge, Man, 32, Tries Suicide By Hanging

Rochester police last night thwarted a 32-year-old man's suicide attempt and then sent him to Beaver jail on a burglary charge.

Officers picked up the defendant, John L. McIlveen, at his home in Beaver for allegedly breaking in and stealing change from the Weiss grocery store in Rochester Sunday.

Clue to the arrest was given police by Regina Weiss, proprietor, who said she heard the tinkle of glass and then caught a glimpse of the burglar, whom she identified as McIlveen.

McIlveen was jailed. Shortly after his confinement police found him with his shirt, ripped into rope-like sections, tied around his neck. McIlveen pleaded guilty before Squire William Brown of Rochester and was taken to Beaver jail to await court action.

Outlay For Assistance In Beaver County Last Year Dropped $504,916

The Beaver County Board of Public Assistance expended $1,073,030.29 last year — $504,916.43 less than the 1939 outlay—for all types of assistance in the county, Executive Director Paul Heffley announced today in issuing a report on the board's activities.

An enormous decrease in the case load, directly attributable to the current employment trend, also was revealed by the director. A total of 41,191 cases, representing 93,829 persons, was handled in the county during 1940, compared to 38,527 cases, or 146,070 persons, in 1939.

General assistance topped the 1940 outlay, a total of $527,579.44 having been expended. A total of $219,469.99 went for aid to dependent children; $255,842.56 for old age assistance and $69,138.30 for pensions to the blind. Burial and medical expenses were not included in the expenditures, Mr. Heffley pointed out.

A gradual decrease in expenditures

(Continued on Page Four)

BELL FIRM PLANS TO BUILD CENTRAL BUILDING IN BORO

Manual Switchboard Will Give Way To Dial System

Dial telephone service is coming to Aliquippa in 1943, it was announced formally today by George M. Koontz, manager for the Bell Telephone company.

The official said plans for replacement of the present manual switchboard here with the dial system are now being formulated.

After installation of the dial system, members of the operating force in Aliquippa will be given an opportunity to qualify for positions elsewhere in the company, Mr. Koontz declared.

Bell plans to establish a new central office in the borough, according to the official.

"The new office will provide for continued telephone development in this community," he said.

Its location was not disclosed by Mr. Koontz, who said announcement to that effect will be made later

(Realty transactions this week at the Beaver county courthouse showed the Bell Telephone Co. of Pennsylvania purchased the property of Dr. J. A. Stevens at Franklin avenue and Main streets here for consideration of $16,000.)

The manager for Bell said there are now 3,744 telephones in the Aliquippa exchange. This is an increase of 1,204 over the number in service five years ago, he pointed out.

The official said an enormous amount of work is entailed in replacing a manual switchboard with the dial system, which Bell plans to have ready for operation here in two years hence.

Midland and Baden have dial telephone systems.

PLASTER FALLS IN AMBRIDGE P.O.

A scare report came out of Ambridge today that the roof of the postoffice there had fallen in.

But Postmaster Charles W. Goerman said "there's nothing to be alarmed about" and reported that "a little" plaster fell off the ceiling onto the main working floor at 10:30 a. m.

Goerman said the fall of plaster was gradual, starting as a trickle. Postal employes moved out and then went back with brooms to clear away the dust.

The building is a new one, being erected in 1936. But Goerman poohpoohed a suggestion that there may be structural defects by saying that "it was just a little plaster."

Willkie Indicates He Favors All-Out Aid

LONDON. (INS) After meeting the entire British cabinet at dinner last night and attending a vital British labor meeting today, Wendell L. Willkie strongly hinted that he favors all-out American aid to Great Britain.

In the middle of a rapid-fire round of conferences, the former Republican presidential candidate indicated without directly saying so that he is prepared to return to the United States and urge heavy financial and other aid to the British war effort.

Bridgers Expect Full House For Quips Tonight

Aliquippa Sports Gazette

TUESDAY, FEBRUARY 25, 1941 ★ ★ ★ PAGE FIVE

Oakdale Finishes Hopewell, 40-22

COUNTY COURT TEAMS FINISH LEAGUE CARDS

Aliquippa high's courtmen put the finishing touch on the 1941 Section 3 cage picture tonight at Ambridge, threatening to set a precedent. A full house was expected.

If Coach Nate Lippe's boys extend their winning streak to 10 games with the season finale, they will be the first squad ever to sweep Section 3 undefeated.

The Red and Black squad was pronounced fit and ready, and Coach Moe Rubenstein reported his quint, runner-up to the Quips, in first rate shape.

Renewals of the school's traditional rivalry always attract capacity crowds, and a packed gym was expected at Ambridge high.

The Reserve quints of both schools will clash in a preliminary starting at 7 p. m.

The next hottest district battle was expected in the reckoning between Monaca and Midland on the latter's court.

Midland is only a game in front of Monaca in the Section 11 race, and Coach Stan Berkman said his runners-up have "a pretty fair chance with some sophomores and a couple of juniors" replacing the three veterans the team lost last week.

Figley and Karcis, two crack cagers, quit the squad because, "I guess they resented sitting on the bench when I used sophomores and juniors in order to give them playing experience," Berkman said.

Linkovich, first string forward and one of the squad's mainstays in winning the Class B title was ineligible to play.

But Berkman said he expected his boys to make a hot scrap of tonight's encounter.

The Junior Quips make it a three-way Aliquippa day at Ambridge by playing the Juniors there this afternoon.

Other teams in Section 3 will try to resolve the three way tie for third place. Beaver Falls, New Brighton and New Castle are deadlocked. The Falls and Brighton quints, natural rivals, clash at New Brighton, while New Castle seemed a sure thing against last place always beaten Ellwood.

In other Section 11, Class B, game, Freedom goes to Rochester, Evans City plays at Mars and Beaver at Zelienople.

In Section 10, the main show will be put on by Robinson at Neville. Robinson is unbeaten in sectional wars and Neville ranks third. Neville, incidentally, was the only team besides Oakdale that Hopewell beat.

Whitesox To Meet

The Aliquippa Whitesox baseball club will meet Saturday at 6:30 p. m. at the Green street clubhouse. All members and candidates for the teams were urged to attend.

BEARS OPTION BERGMANN

NEWARK, N. J. (INS) The Newark Bears of the International League today announced that Shortstop Russ Bergmann, former Duke University athlete, had been optioned to Atlanta in the Southern Association. Bergmann played with Binghamton last season.

ELECTRIC DEPT. DUX LEAGUE

Motors				
McIlvain	130	171	144	445
Fouse	102	107	154	363
Havey	85	145	117	347
Erenstein	97	94	133	324
Davidson	159	145	111	415
Pezzelle		125	154	279
Totals	573	695	702	1970
Cables				
Kibler	149	102	82	332
Hill	112	106	109	327
Snyder	142	106	112	360
Ciper	88	103	133	324
McKenzie	114	125	103	342
Gillooly	157	173	153	483
Cavender	118	118	98	334
Totals	680	628	610	1918
Terminals				
Miller	142	160	115	417
Jenkins	101	116	73	290
J. Stewart	66	69		135
Palmer	110	135	107	352
Carlson	105	133	135	373
Vest	139	159	186	484
Holeman	102	130	124	356
Totals	598	716	667	1981
Controls				
Morgan	144	153	194	391
Young	127	124	85	336
Cable	83	99	129	311
Fowler	107	160	104	371
Kotun	162	116	171	499
J. Stewart			97	97
S. Palmer			144	144
Totals	623	698	742	2063

ELECTRIC DEPT. DUX LEAGUE
Standing

	W.	L.	Pct.
Cables	36	30	.545
Motors	35	31	.530
Terminals	32	34	.485
Control	29	37	.439

Advertise Goods You Have To Sell!

B-O-W-L-I-N-G

BLAST FURNACE LEAGUE

Blow Pipes				
H. Brittain	118	85	90	293
Mayberry	111	123	142	376
Puckett	125	113	110	348
McConnell	110	153	173	436
Queener	140	151	128	419
Fisher	172	151	124	447
Totals	666	701	677	2044
Tuyers				
Hetrick	131	120	112	363
Barlett	208	129	154	491
Leviseue	116	104	95	315
Myers	154	146	175	475
Totals	709	599	636	1944
Pigs				
Ross	140	136	123	399
Whitehill	132	146	98	376
Floyd	122	121	111	354
Albaugh	71	113	119	303
Kramer	152	188	171	511
Creager	116	141	149	406
Totals	662	732	673	2067
Coolers				
Parahus	100	136	98	334
McFarland	117	99	212	428
Watson	98	162	130	390
Thomas	109	115	115	339
Seaman	94	145	108	347
McCormik	101	97	96	294
Totals	525	657	663	1845

BLAST FURNACE LEAGUE
Standing

	W.	L.	Pct.
Tuyers	33	15	.688
Blow Pipes	27	21	.563
Pigs	21	27	.553
Coolers	15	33	.395

MOOSE DUX LEAGUE

All American				
Kleber	117	105	141	363
J. Ragona	115	171	145	431
Elliott	100	104	140	344
Jarrett	114	99	88	301
Jim Ragona	134	109	171	414
Villa	153	168	127	448
Totals	633	657	724	2014
Superior				
Kuhl	132	148	93	373
McHaffie	124	134	140	398
Taylor	137	112	149	398
Totals	573	574	562	1709
All Stars				
Neish	129	100	127	356
Calabro	169	140	143	452
Todora	134	161	129	424
Totals	607	581	599	1787
Rinky Dinks				
Knapp	109	127	124	360
L. Kontos	92	148	113	353
Liptak	124	152	105	381
Dushac	111	151	205	467
Totals	326	668	637	1831
Crackers				
C. Essey	104	115	106	325
Plonka	118	140	111	369
Palazzi	117	205	90	412
Einstein	91	149	106	346
Raznak	97	80	92	269
Bransteter	119	105	90	314
Totals	555	714	505	1774
Blue Ribbon				
Lucas	102	143	111	356
Gural	160	150	168	478
Arnick	201	124	149	474
Basco	152	180	142	474
Wallace	116	103	91	310
Smallwood	84	129	132	345
Totals	731	726	702	2159

MOOSE DUX LEAGUE
Standing

	W.	L.	Pct.
Blue Ribbon	18	3	.857
All American	14	7	.667
Superior	12	9	.571
All Stars	11	10	.524
Rinky Dinks	6	15	.286
Crackers	2	19	.086

A & S DUX LEAGUE

Accounting				
Pietsch	149	95	133	377
Ellis	105	142	128	375
Tovey	91	139	86	316
Johnson	122	120	147	389
McKenna	115	134	130	379
Lais	136	158	109	403
Totals	627	701	647	1975
M. OF W.				
Radtke	101	91	81	273
Osborne	78	80	114	272
Rockwell	100	131	91	322
Barto	94	122	141	357
Wissinger	144	140	125	409
Geist	153	125	114	392
Huges	172	171	175	518
Totals	670	689	669	2028
M. P. No. 1				
DeSantis	100	141	148	389
Hainley	146	98	114	358
Sayre	71	107	109	287
Yetso	160	126	160	444
Peoples	115	133	134	382
Zebic	100	150	100	350
Totals	621	657	665	1943
M. P. No. 2				
Berger	120	156	127	403
Crossland	99	87	114	300
Warner	128	131	133	392
Holland	128	117	106	351
Cravener	156	105	133	394
Totals	631	596	613	1840
Engineers				
Barnhart	129	135	119	383
F. Johnston	100	120	102	322
Backus	105	109	118	332
Barto	137	201	164	502
Dragan	147	105	139	391
Totals	618	670	642	1930
Transportation				
Bealman	136	105	137	378
Yoho	110	124	213	447
Tomb	126	121	105	352
Padgett	169	125	141	435
Greksa	148	142	131	421
Totals	689	617	733	2039

A & S DUX LEAGUE
Standing

	W	L	Pct.
M. of W.	11	4	.733
M. P. No. 2	11	4	.733
M. P. No. 1	9	6	.600
Accounting	5	10	.333
Engineers	5	10	.333
Transportation	4	11	.267

VIKINGS BOW IN LAST LOOP TILT, TIE FOR CELLAR

Oakdale pulled down Hopewell high's cagers into a deadlock for last place in Section 10 of the WPIAL last night at Oakdale, with a 40-22 triumph to avenge the Vikings 37-24 conquest last Friday.

It was the last game for the Vikings, and complaining repeatedly against the referee's decision, they were unable to handle the Oakdale quint as easily as they had last week.

The game was a playoff of a first half tilt postponed because of the flu epidemic at Hopewell. The game left both quints in the cellar with 10 defeats compared to two victories each.

The home club stepped to a 7 to 3 lead in the first period and ran it to 19-11 by halftime. The Vikings offense bogged down in the protested referee's ruling as the Oakdaler's moved to a 23-15 advantage the third stanza in which the Vikings worked hard to hold down the home club scoring to four points. But Oakdale spurted ahead easily in the final quarter.

Andy Palsa shared scoring honors with Beaumont of Oakdale, each tallying 15 points.

The Vikings next play St. Veronica at Ambridge high floor Friday night. Last night's was the final home league game.

In a preliminary, Oakdale's Reserves nosed out Hopewell's Subs, 13-12.

Hopewell	FG	F	TP
Machak, f	3	0	6
Vignovich, f	0	0	0
Clere, c	0	0	0
Palsa, g	6	3	15
Gill, g	0	1	1
Milich, f	0	0	0
Totals	9	4	22
Oakdale	**FG**	**F**	**TP**
Lisbon, f	4	0	8
Teets, f	2	3	7
B. Stiles, c	2	2	6
H. Stiles, g	2	0	4
Beaumont, g	7	1	15
Totals	17	6	40

Referee—McCarthy.

PIPE SHOP DUX LEAGUE

Steam				
Klacik	130	96	108	334
Davis	95	112	138	345
Deamico	99	81	90	270
Kramer	109	77	84	270
Altvater	95	100	154	349
Shaffalo	163	154	150	467
Totals	596	553	640	1789
Driox				
Kaletz	135	108	114	357
Miller	150	122	101	373
Ambrose	85	75	137	297
S. Lechman	180	140	114	434
L. Lechman	148	129	141	418
McCormick	117	153	176	436
Totals	730	652	682	2064
Water				
Kleber	117	145	146	408
Kotun	130	158	165	493
Pinkosky	115	126	153	394
Miller	92	104	113	309
Ross	143	128	152	423
Yoko	116	93	115	324
Totals	621	661	731	2013
Hydraulic				
Buff	115	135	119	369
Fetchen	121	115	170	406
Minor	89	91	98	278
Smerigan	92	168	166	426
Cope	108	91	92	291
Yarosz	132	186	106	424
Totals	568	695	659	1922
Air				
Williams	158	145	181	484
Matzger	155	76	131	462
Bolombi	111	87	111	309
Danjanic	167	123	121	411
Totals	667	517	628	1812
Gas				
Sol	76	98	84	258
Dudash	142	100	123	365
Jimmy	128	86	105	319
Buffy	192	165	126	483
Ray	112	96	103	321
Totals	650	545	541	1736

WEST SIDERS PUT OFF PING PONG FINALS

The conclusion of the W. A. R. C. annual senior ping pong tournament was put off until Wednesday night, as Chester Manasterski and Al Wasel, leading contenders for the crown, could not be present, last evening.

Wasel still has a quarter-finals match to play with William Shaffalo, while Manasterski was to battle John Ondeyka in a semi-finals contest. Anthony Dercole awaits the winner of the Wasel-Shaffalo match in the other semi-final setto.

SWEDEN'S CHAMP DROPS DEAD IN CHICAGO FIGHT

CHICAGO.—(INS)—Arne Anderson, 22-year-old heavyweight boxing champion of Sweden, dropped dead last night before 1,800 horrified fight fans in Chicago's Marigold Gardens as he was exchanging blows with Lou Thomas, Indianapolis fighter, in the seventh round.

Anderson, whose home was in St. Paul, was felled in 2 minutes and 33 seconds of the round and was counted out in routine fashion. It was not until his handlers could not revive him that officials at the ringside were aware anything was wrong.

The knockout occurred at 10:49 p. m., and within ten minutes a fire department pulmotor squad was working over Anderson. The firemen labored without avail for more than an hour before the fighter was pronounced dead.

Neither Anderson nor Thomas had taken much punishment up to the seventh round of the scheduled 10-round fight, and judges' and the referee's tallies showed the fight was a draw up to the time of the knockdown.

TIGERS MAUL ACES, 55-26

The Tigers' basketball team snowed under the Washington Aces, 55-26, last evening, at the West Aliquippa Recreational Center.

Their vaunted offensive checked by the Aces in the opening half, the Tigers got up steam in the final semester and proceeded to steamroll the hapless Washingtonians. John Durkin, Tony Giannetti and John Maly scored 40 points between themselves to pace the devastating attack.

The defensive play of George Glomb, losers' pivot-man, and Mike Vince's scoring efforts stood out in the Aces' showing.

Aces	F.G.	F.	Pts.
N. Ciccone, f.	0	0	0
M. Vince, f.	5	2	12
G. Glomb, c.	3	1	7
R. Ciccone, g.	1	1	3
M. Dzugan, g.	1	0	2
N. Perza, g.	1	0	2
Totals	11	4	26
Tigers	**F.G.**	**F.**	**Pts.**
T. Giannetti, f.	6	1	13
J. Durkin, f.	7	1	15
J. Maly, f.	6	0	12
M. Petrick, c.	0	2	2
M. Modrak, g.	1	1	3
M. Ondovchik, g.	4	0	8
G. Pinkosky, g.	1	0	2
Totals	25	5	55

Tigers	3	12	23	17—55
Wash. Aces	1	3	8	14—26

Referee—L. Zagar.

FRANKLIN INTRAMURAL BASKETBALL

Elites 33, Indians 22.

BADGERS HEAD FOR TITLE

CHICAGO. (INS) Already assured of at least a tie for the Big Ten basketball championship, Wisconsin's amazing Badgers today looked ahead eagerly to Saturday night, when they will take on Minnesota in their closing game with the chance to clinch their first undisputed conference court crown since 1918.

WARC To Start Junior Court Tourney March 5

The West Aliquippa Recreational Center will sponsor a Junior basketball tournament, beginning March 5, Howard "Sarge" Alberts, supervisor at the Center, said today.

Any team in Aliquippa or West Aliquippa, sporting a roster composed of boys 16 years of age and under, is eligible to compete. Entries must be accompanied by players' names and ages.

All those desiring to join may mail their entry not later than March 3, to Howard Alberts, West Aliquippa Recreational Center, West Aliquippa.

Pros Head For Florida Golf Tournament

ST. PETERSBURG, Fla. (INS) – Professional Golfdom's winter tournament parade turned toward Florida today for the opening of the $5,000 St. Petersburg open tomorrow following Harold "Jug" McSpaden's victory last Sunday in the $3,000 Thomasville, Ga., open.

Although McSpaden pocketed the $750 top money in the Thomasville event, Ben Hogan, the White Plains, N. Y., sharpshooter, continued to lead the pro's in total winnings for the winter circuit. The smallish young native Texan received a check for $360 for a second place tie at Thomasville, thereby boosting his earnings to a total of $4,510 for the year.

YANKS ORDER DIMAGGIO TO TRAINING CAMP

SAN FRANCISCO. (INS) The New York Yankees have ordered hold-out Joe DiMaggio to report for dut at St. Petersburg, Fla., training camp by March 2, brother Tom DiMaggio reported today.

The American League's champion slugger is insisting on a salary raise which will boost him into the $40,000 a year bracket.

LOUIS WANTS TO JOIN ARMY

Expects Draft Call In Next 90 Days

CHICAGO — (INS) — Joe Louis, world's heavyweight boxing champion, expects to be drafted within 90 days, is ready and willing to enter the Army and, in fact, wants to be a soldier!

Home from two months of fight training camps and ring campaigning, the Brown Bomber, relaxed in his Chicago apartment, became almost loquacious today as he discussed the prospects oftraining for Uncle Sam instead of just for Joe Louis.

"My draft number was 2611," he said. "That placed me 378th on the list of my local board. I returned my questionnaire Jan. 7 and expect to be called for physical examination any day.

"Sure, I want to be a soldier. I'll be a good one, too. I've taken orders for years from my trainer, so I won't have any trouble taking orders in the Army."

Bobo Kayos Delaney

Another knockout was written into the record books today for Harry Bobo, Pittsburgh's leading Negro heavyweight. Bobo, weighing in at 203¼, switched to a body attack in the seventh round of his fight last night with Al Delaney, 189½, and salted him away in the eighth with a solid left hook. The time was one minute and 15 seconds.

BLONDIE

By Chic Young

BLONDIE, WHERE ARE MY PANTS?
DOWN HERE, DEAR--I BROUGHT THEM DOWN TO GET SOME CHANGE OUT OF THEM WHEN THAT C.O.D. PACKAGE CAME
WELL, WHERE ARE THEY?
I HUNG THEM ON THE FRONT DOOR KNOB
I THOUGHT THEY WERE TO GO TO THE CLEANER-- I GAVE THEM TO THE MAN WHEN HE CALLED
ARE YOU MAD AT US, DEAR?
OH, NO--- I'VE BEEN MARRIED LONG ENOUGH TO BE PHILOSOPHICAL ABOUT THESE THINGS
3-3
CHIC YOUNG

MUGGS AND SKEETER

By WALLY BISHOP

YOO-HOO, SISTER!! WE'RE HOME! WE'RE HOME FROM SCHOOL!!
OH HELLO!! YOUR KIND SISTER HAS RETIRED TO HER BOUDOIR TO FRESHEN UP A BIT AND CHANGE HER FROCK!
HUH ?
WHO ARE YOU?
I'M "REGGIE"-H. REGINALD BULWARK!! I ASSUME YOU ARE MY HOSTS... THE McGINNIS CHAPS?
YOUR WHAT ?
MY HOSTS! I'M HERE FOR THE DURATION, Y'KNOW! SO DECENT OF YOU TO HAVE ME - I HOPE WE'LL BE FAST FRIENDS!!
SURE! SURE! SAY, MUGGS, WHO IS THIS GUY?
SEARCH ME! LET'S FIND SISTER!
3-3
Wally Bishop

BIG SISTER

Registered U S Patent Office

By LES FORGRAVE

YESSIR! BONES! HUMAN BONES STACKED UP THERE INSIDE THE CAVE!
H'M! AFTER ALL THAT'S HAPPENED UP IN THOSE WOODS I'M READY TO BELIEVE ANYTHING!
AND THIS CASE CALLS FOR ACTION!
YOU'RE NOT GOING UP THERE BY YOURSELF, ARE YOU?
NOT BY A LONG SHOT! THINGS HAVE REACHED A STATE NOW WHERE THE LAW MUST STEP IN!
3-3
FORGRAVE

BRICK BRADFORD—On the Throne of Titania

By WILLIAM RITT and CLARENCE GRAY

I'VE GOT TO REACH BUCKO BEFORE THAT WAVE STRIKES!
JUST AS BRICK REACHES HIS FRIEND HE IS DELUGED BY THE WAVE—
CLUTCHING BUCKO, HE FIGHTS AGAINST THE SURGING WATER
I CAN'T HOLD ON MUCH LONGER!
3-3
CLARENCE GRAY

ETTA KETT

Registered U S Patent Office

By PAUL ROBINSON

GUESS I'M WACKY -- BUT I WAS SURE I SAW ETTA AND NANCY HERE!
YEAH! ME, TOO! THEY SAID THEY WERE COMING DOWN TO CAMP TODAY TO VISIT US!
RICKY AND BEEZY DON'T KNOW TWO OTHER FELLAS HAVE CUT IN AND ARE SHOWING THE GIRLS AROUND--
COME ON, LET'S GET OUT OF THIS TANK!
THINK FAST, BUDDY RICKY AND BEEZY ARE PARKED OUT THERE - IF WE LET THE GALS LEAVE NOW, THEY'LL SEE THEM SURE!
PIPE DOWN A MINUTE! THOUGHT I HEARD VOICES IN THAT TANK!
COULD BE!
??
WATCH YOUR STEP!
CIVILIAN GAS MASK DRILL!! NEVER HEARD OF IT!
3-3
Paul Robinson

INSPECTOR WADE

By Edgar Wallace

JIM! YOU WENT INTO THE JUNGLE AND GOT 'EM!
GET ME A TOWEL AND AN INTERPRETER--- I WANT TO GET THIS GOO OFF MY FACE --AND I WANT TO HEAR WHO SENT THESE LITTLE PLAYMATES
TAPU, YOU KNOW THEIR LINGO?
YES, BWANA THEY ARE SWAHILI --- I WILL ASK WHERE THEY COME FROM...
SWAHILI COME FROM THERE, BWANA. WHITE MAN SEND THEM.
DON, I KNOW THEIR LANGUAGE! TAPU IS LYING!
3-3

DONALD DUCK

By Walt Disney

OUCH!
OH, HEAVENS! DID NANKI POO BITE YOU?
BITE ME? SHE ALMOST TOOK MY ARM OFF!
DAISY DUCK
DRUGS
GARGLE
Distributed by King Features Syndicate, Inc.

JUST KIDS

By Ad Carter

HAS BEEN BLAMED FOR GIVING MUSH TWO BLACK EYES —
HAVE BEEN STOLEN
HAS BEEN ACCUSED OF THAT! — THERE IS NEVER A DULL MOMENT IN BARNESVILLE!
I WONDER WHERE HE CAME FROM?— HE'S A STRANGER IN TOWN--
AD CARTER
I THINK I'LL KEEP AN EYE ON HIM
3-3

THE OLD HOME TOWN

Registered U S Patent Office

By STANLEY

HANK'S HAMBURGER PALACE
HOT DOGS 5¢
HAMBURGER ON BUN 10¢
IT'S SAM SLUMPS HAT, IF ANY BUBBLES COME UP FLAVORED WITH ONION- WE'LL KNOW SAM'S UNDER THE HAT---HE JUST HAD A HAMBURGER ON A BUN!
THAT MUD HOLE ON LOWER MAIN STREET—
3-3

SCOTT'S SCRAP BOOK

Registered U S Patent Office

By R. J. SCOTT

3-3
FRED W. JENSEN, NEW YORK JEWELER, HAS A CLOCK THAT WALKS AROUND IN A SIX-INCH CIRCLE
THIS HUGE RED CEDAR, 62 FEET 8 INCHES IN CIRCUMFERENCE, IS PROBABLY THE NATION'S LARGEST OF ITS KIND — IT GROWS IN THE OLYMPIC NATIONAL PARK, WASHINGTON
FELT HATS ARE BEING MADE PARTIALLY FROM MILK - THE CASEIN IS PROCESSED INTO FIBER

SALLY'S SALLIES

Registered U. S. Patent Office

THIS MILK IS SOUR
ARE YOU SURE, MISTER JONES?
3-3
Distributed by King Features Syndicate, Inc.

One way of keeping milk from going sour is to leave it in the cow.

BOROUGH TO GET 200 PARKOMETERS

Mike Lucas, Aliquippa's new pro fighter, chalks up triumph in his debut. Read story on Page 7.

The Aliquippa Gazette

SERVING AN INDUSTRIAL COMMUNITY OF 50,000

WEATHER — Snow flurries tonight and Wednesday. Colder tonight.

SERVED BY INTERNATIONAL NEWS SERVICE — PHONE 004-005-000 — MEMBER OF P. N. P. A.

VOL. XIX—No. 263 — ALIQUIPPA, PA., TUESDAY, MARCH 11, 1941 — CENTS: BY CARRIER, 15 CENTS A WEEK

SLAIN IN SLEEP

—Central Press Phonephoto

Police of Kansas City, Mo., sought an "undoubted maniac," believed the murderer of Miss Leila Welsh, 24, above, killed in her boudoir with a stone mason's hammer and a butcher knife. The body was mutilated. Miss Welsh was the daughter of a prominent real estate broker.

Envoy's Heir

Mme. Procope and Johann

Madame Hjalmar Procope, wife of the Finnish minister to the United States, is pictured with her son, Johann Fredrik Procope, at his christening in Washington. The ceremony was performed by the Reverend Jokl of the Finnish Evangelical Lutheran church in Brooklyn, N. Y.

To Succeed George?

Prince Paul

Prince Paul of Greece, younger brother of King George, may succeed his brother on the Grecian throne, according to reports from German-controlled Sofia, Bulgaria. King George, it is said, has indicated his willingness to abdicate.

Lawyers Clash At Holdup Trial

Peace Predicted If British Hold Out

QUARTERS IN U. S. BELIEVE BRITAIN CANNOT WIN WAR

Predict A Negotiated Compromise Peace Later In Year

By KINGSBURY SMITH (Copyright, 1941, by International News Service)

WASHINGTON — (INS)— There is a rising tide of opinion in officials quarters today that Great Britain alone cannot defeat Germany and that, if the British manage to hold out this summer, the European conflict eventually will end in a negotiated compromise peace.

Some of the highest authoritative sources in Washington in close touch with the Euro ean situation are convinced it will be impossible for the British to defeat the German army on the European continent even with all the help President Roosevelt plans to give Britain under the lease-lend bill.

These sources hope American aid will enable the British to hold out against Germany until the German people realize it is impossible to defeat Britain and are willing to conclude a reasonable and honorable peace.

Unless American aid to Britain should be extended to include manpower as well as materials, it is felt this country's help will not be sufficient to assure a decisive British military victory.

On the question of manpower, there does not appear to be the (Continued on Page Six)

FOUR MEN CRASH CIO PICKET LINE

Four men fought their way today through a dues inspection line of about 200 men set up by the SWOC at the American Bridge works in Ambridge.

Another dues inspection line of about 50 CIO members was thrown around the Pittsburgh Crucible steel company plant at Midland.

No other violence was reported and plant operations were not stopped.

Joseph Timko, sub-regional director of the CIO, said about 150 men were turned back at the main gate of the Ambridge plant because they lacked paid up union dues cards.

"Some may have gotten in through other gates," Timko said, claiming that all but about 150 of the plant's 2800 workers were union members.

One newspaper reporter said a (Continued on Page Six)

F.D.R. Finds Wallace One Obliging Man

(THE NATIONAL WHIRLIGIG)
By Ray Tucker

President Roosevelt has begun already to cash in on having such an old and faithful servant as Henry Wallace in the vice-presidential chair. Democrats and Republicans now realize why the White House sidetracked John N. Garner for the former Secretary of Agriculture.

Few weeks ago Mr. Wallace had the appointment of a committee to investigate the possibility of an automatically balanced budget in ordinary times. Sponsor was anti-New Dealer Tydings, who has lambasted the Administration for extravagance. F. D. R. did not want a majority of hostiles on this committee. He laid the problem before Henry, and instructed him to get in touch with G. O. P. Leader McNary about the Republican member.

Now, long before Mr. Wallace came to the Capital he had been palsy-walsy with "Mac" in 20-year-old movements for the farmers. The good-natured "Mac", who has received many favors from the White House, hearkened to Henry and named as G. O. P. member his colleague from Oregon, the inexperi- (Continued on Page Ten)

No Evidence Kiefer Attempted To Conceal Or Alter Records, District Attorney Discloses

Three Aliquippa gambling house proprietors, arrested in a pay day raid a month or more ago, paid fines and costs at hearings before Burgess George Kiefer.

That was revealed today by District Attorney Robert E. McCreary who declared the Gazette had misinterpreted a previous statement he had issued on the gambling cases conveying the impression the names in question were not properly accounted for.

Mr. McCreary said there was no evidence the Burgess was attempting to conceal his records or alter them in any way. At the time the Gazette story appeared, he said, his men had checked the Kiefer records . . . they did not at that time know the names of the most recent victims of Aliquippa police raids . . . and that they had just gone back to check them further at the time his last statement was issued.

He said today his investigators later discovered records of the hearings of the four on the "arrest slips" at the police station and from the burgess' files.

The three are: Polly Gordon, Fred Campbell and August Rossi. Each paid $27.50, including $25 fine and $2.50 costs. A fourth, Robert Huey, was assessed a similar fine and cost Feb. 10.

The district attorney said he would ask the court to reverse the action of the burgess, refund the fines and bring the defendants into county court to answer gambling charges—where the cases should have been handled in the first place.

For a number of weeks the district attorney has insisted gambling comes under the jurisdiction of the county court . . . that the burgess must either release such prisoners or hold them for court at Beaver and that he (the burgess) is without authority to dispose of such cases under borough ordinance where the county's authority takes precedence.

PAY BOOST FOR UMW DEMANDED

NEW YORK—(INS)—Wage increases, in some instances amounting to $1 a day, were demanded today by John L. Lewis, president of the United Mine Workers of America (CIO) in submitting to the nation's soft coal operators proposals for a new contract affecting 450,000 miners.

Lewis presented the miners' demands at the Appalachian joint wage conference attended by about 100 soft coal producers and 150 members of the Union's International policy committee.

The present contract expires March 31 and Lewis suggested the agreement be extended two years. (Continued on Page Five)

St. Barnabas Brothers Will Attend Service Here Tomorrow Night

The Brothers of St. Barnabas will attend mid-week Lenten services at All Saints' Episcopal church here tomorrow, starting at 7:45 p. m. Gov. P. Hance, S.B.B., founder and manager of St. Barnabas' Free Home at Gibsonia, will speak.

St. Barnabas' home is a home for incurable men and boys which the Brothers have maintained for more than 40 years. It is a "free" home in every sense of the word because it (Continued on Page Two)

West Aliquippa Man Suffers Cut Hand In Quarrel With Huckster

Steve Mihalic, 617 River Ave., West Aliquippa, suffered a cut hand last night in a quarrel with an unidentified Pittsburgh huckster over the price of potatoes and apples.

Mihalic allegedly became angry when the huckster quoted a price and a fight resulted. He was treated by Dr. J. L. Miller.

Rep. Powers Urges Defense Studies In State Institutions

HARRISBURG. — (INS) — Rep. John L. Powers (D), Allegheny, today urged adoption of his bill asking military training for all boys and nursing training for all girls in the state's industrial and correctional institutions. The bill directs the Department of Welfare to provide the necessary courses.

Program For Observance Of Good Friday Here Completed

The Aliquippa Ministerial association today announced completion of plans for the Good Friday observance here April 11.

An invitation to hold the three-hour service from 12 noon to 3 p. m. at All Saints Episcopal church, extended by Vicar Frederick P. Hurd at the association's March meeting, has been accepted.

As a nucleus for the service, the ministers agreed to make use of the program distributed by The Church World Press. The program calls for a series of seven meditations on Our Saviour's last words from The Cross.

The following ministers will be invited to conduct the meditations with the co-operation of other members of the Ministerial:

The Rev. Milo Milanovich of the Raccoon U. P. church; the Rev. Harman F. Miller, of the House of Prayer Evangelical Lutheran church; the Rev. Ernest Anderton, of the Logstown Presbyterian Mission; the Rev. Samuel E. Brown, of the Aliquippa Methodist church; the Rev. John R. Thomson, of the Mt. Carmel Presbyterian church; the Rev. T. J. Tipp, of the Emmanuel A. M. E. Zion church, and Vicar Frederick Hurd of the Episcopal church.

William Neville, choir master of the host church, will have charge of the musical part of the program. Under his direction a roster of organists will be supplied and a composite choir to lead in a worshipful rendition of the hymns incorporated in the program.

MAN INJURED BY HIT & RUN AUTO

A hit-and-run driver knocked over Frank Zabich, 315 Cooper St., Aliquippa, yesterday as he walked on Sixth avenue here. Zabich told police the car was a black sedan but gave no further description. He suffered slight hip injuries.

A car driven by John Yager, Jr., 1738 Pierce St., Aliquippa, was damaged slightly on Franklin avenue yesterday when hit in a slow line of traffic near Jones library.

Sister Of Aliquippa Woman Dies In Crash

Funeral services will be conducted tomorrow for Mrs. John Brallier, Latrobe, sister of Mrs. H. M. Fair of Aliquippa, who was killed in an automobile accident.

Mrs. Brallier was enroute to the home of a daughter, Mrs. Harold Allison, Pittsburgh, formerly of Aliquippa, when her car collided head-on with another machine near the Westinghouse bridge.

Mrs. Brallier was the wife of a Latrobe dentist, who with his sister, and assistant, Dr. Jack Kelly, also were injured in the crash. Burial will be in Indiana, Pa.

Lenten Reminder

Lord, who shall abide in Thy tabernacle? who shall dwell in Thy holy hill? He that walketh uprightly, and worketh righteousness, and speaketh the truth in his heart.—Psalm 15:1, 2.

"Tillie the Toiler"

Kay Harris

A former secretary employed by a Cincinnati radio station, Kay Harris, above, has been selected to play the title role in the movie version of Russ Westover's famed comic strip, "Tillie the Toiler." Miss Harris was discovered by Producer Robert Sparks while honeymooning in Cincinnati with his bride, Penny Singleton, who plays the title role of Blondie, film version of Chic Young's popular comic strip.

PRICE HEARING ON MILK CALLED

Petitioned by three producer organizations representing practically all dairymen of the Pittsburgh milk marketing area, the Milk Control Commission today scheduled a general price hearing for that area to be held in the Gold Room of the Roosevelt hotel, Pittsburgh, March 18, at 9 a. m.

Unanimous in their request that the present producer prices be continued through the summer months, the producer groups who petitioned the Commission were the Dairymen's Cooperative Sales association, Pittsburgh, the United Farmers of America, Latrobe, and the Keystone Milk Producers, Freeport.

Under the existing price order, the Class 1 (milk, bottled and bulk, for human consumption) producer price (Continued on Page Two)

Water Service Sought For Figley Plan Here

E. L. Tardy, R. D. 1, Aliquippa, has filed an application with the Public Utility Commission for permission to furnish water to approximately 15 families of the Figley plan, Hopewell township, the P. U. C. announced today.

According to information given the commission, the system consists of a 160-foot well and a 1000-gallon storage tank. Tardy said the plan has neither water for drinking purposes nor fire protection.

M'CORMICK CASE HANDED TO JURY AT BEAVER TODAY

Defense Lawyer Claims State Police Forced Man To Confess

BULLETIN!

After deliberating 2¾ hours, a jury at Beaver today acquitted James McCormick, Aliquippa, of holding up a couple in Hopewell Twp. The verdict was returned at 2:45 p. m.

District Attorney Robert E. McCreary and Defense Counsel Lawrence Sebring of Beaver bandied arguments about the honesty of "foreigners" in the state police as the robbery trial of James McCormick, Aliquippa, neared an end today.

McCormick pleaded he was drunk and knew nothing about the holdup of an Aliquippa couple in [illegible] in Hopewell township. Against him was the testimony that Private George Mazza found McCormick with the loot in a car described by Sam Muzolin, 2108 McLean st., Aliquippa, as the one in which the holdup man escaped after robbing him.

Impugning the integrity of the state policemen, and charging they forced McCormick to make statements about the holdup damaging to his case, Sebring, alluding to Privates Michael Zerbe and Mazza, said:

"Listen to those names. They're foreign.

"My name's McCreary," the prosecutor retaliated. "My ancestors just came over three generations ago. McCormick's probably a foreigner, too. His ancestors probably came over not long ago. If that makes them liars then McCormick's a liar, and I'm a liar, and we're all liars."

Answering charges that he sat in a car 50 feet from where Joe Wiles, Aliquippa, who admitted the holdup, took money and jewelry from Muzolin and Mary Shaffer as they sat in a stalled auto, McCormick said he (Continued on Page Six)

Brother Of Two Folk Here Injured Fatally In Traffic Accident

Sidney F. Martin, 48, of Lockport, N. Y., brother of Albert Martin and Mrs. Joshua Llewellyn of Aliquippa, was injured fatally in an automobile accident last week-end. He died Saturday in a Lockport hospital.

He leaves his wife, Lillian, and six children, Sidney, Jr., Mary Jane, Richard, Jack, Beth Ann and Thelma, all at home.

Yearbook Committee Of Aliquippa High To Sell Subscriptions

Twenty-five members of the staff of Aliquippa High school's yearbook, "The Quippian," tomorrow will start a house-to-house canvass for subscribers for the 1941 edition.

1940 Best Year For J. & L. Steel Corp. Since 1929

PITTSBURGH. — (INS) — The Jones & Laughlin Steel corporation, in its annual report for the year 1940, reported today that it had netted a profit of $10,277,029 for the 12 months ending last Dec. 31.

This, the statement showed, compared with a profit of $3,276,256 for the year 1939.

"The better showing in the last half of the year was due principally to the increased volume of business with resultant low costs and to some improvement in prices realized from certain products," the financial report said.

"The results from operations in the year 1940 were the best for any year since 1929."

COUNCIL ORDERS CONTRACT DRAWN FOR PARKOMETERS

New Truck Purchased At Special Meeting Of Councilmen Here

Borough Solicitor Louis Klein today drew up a contract which, if accepted by council and the Auto Park Service Co. of Pittsburgh, will pave the way for the installation of at least 200 parkometers in Aliquippa.

An ordinance authorizing execution of the contract had been approved earlier by council, which met in special session last night, with only Councilmen John J. Todora, Dr. J. L. Miller, M. J. O'Connor and George Haas in attendance.

In addition to instructing Klein to draw up the contract, council purchased a Ford truck for W. P. A. work from the C. P. Sims Co. of Aliquippa.

Points which Solicitor Klein was instructed to incorporate into the parking meter contract and submit to council for approval include:

Minimum purchase of 200 Miller-Pioneer meters on a rent-with-option-to-buy basis, 65 per cent of revenues going to the company and the remainder to the borough.

They will be installed on a six-month trial basis before the expiration of which time council can vote to retain them on a rent or purchase basis or reject them.

If the machines are retained revenues taken in during the trial period can be applied to the purchase price, which Solicitor Klein said was $65 per machine. Company representatives claim the machines average 25 cents per machine per day.

The borough also is requesting that the meter concern pay for the training and hire of an employe to service the machines. If approved this man will be hired at a salary of $100 per month by the borough to be paid by the borough with a kick back from the meter company. This [illegible] would stand during the life of the contract [illegible]

Council will also stipulate, Klein said, that the company paint traffic lines, keep the meters in repair and replace out-moded machines with improved meters when such improvements are marketed.

Solicitor Klein pointed out that either council or the meter company can reject this contract which he will present next Monday at regular session of council.

Four other bids on another truck the borough desires to purchase for general use were rejected and referred back to the street committee with power to act on Councilman O'Connor's motion, seconded by Councilman Miller.

No reason was given at the meeting for rejecting the bids which were: Ford, $985; General Motors Co., $1515; International, $1525.65; and Dodge, $1527.

Urling Opens Office On Linmar Place Here

Walter C. Urling, manager of the Linmar Place plan of lots here, today announced the opening of a new office at Elgin, Sharon and Upland Streets. Construction of the office was completed several days ago, he said.

Improvements to the streets and erection of signs on every street on Linmar Place is progressing, the manager announced. His office phone number is Aliquippa 2160.

SOCIETY

Daughters Of The American Revolution Has Luncheon To Celebrate 36th Anniversary

Fort McIntosh Chapter, Daughters of the American Revolution, observed the thirty-sixth anniversary of the founding of the Chapter with a luncheon in Beaver, Tuesday afternoon.

New members received during the past year were guests. A patriotic color scheme in red, white and blue, was carried out in flowers used for table decorations. Corsages were given to new members and guests. Miss Leonora Ashton of New Brighton, voiced the invocation.

Following the luncheon, a short business session was conducted by the Regent, Miss Evelyn Patterson, Beaver. Mrs. C. M. Merrick, chairman of the music committee, introduced Mrs. Carolyn Wallace Craven of New Brighton, who sang a group of songs, accompanied at the piano by Mrs. Lucile Wilson Hutchinson, also of New Brighton. Miss Patterson introduced Mrs. Lawrence M. Sebring, Beaver, who read the story of "White Cliffs of Dover," by Alice Deurr Miller. In closing, Mrs. Craven sang another group of songs.

Mary Kathryn Hall Is Wed To Ohio Man

Mr. and Mrs. Harry Raisley, New Brighton, announce the surprise marriage of their daughter, Mary Kathryn Hall, to Chester Sinclair, Youngstown, O., which took place March 8 in Georgetown, O.

Mr. and Mrs. Sinclair are making their home in Youngstown, where the groom is employed. Mrs. Sinclair attended Freedom high school.

Miss Diana Milligan Presents Report To Rochester Auxiliary

Hospital Aid Group Discusses Plans For General Fund at Meeting

The Woman's Auxiliary to Rocheseter hospital held its monthly meeting Monday evening in the Nurses' Dining room, when discussion of projects followed the routine business session. Miss Diana Milligan superintendent of the hospital, presented the hospital report. Mrs. William Moritz and Mrs. Harry Headland were appointed on the hospital committee for April.

A plan was evolved by which contributions produced by the efforts of small groups would be disposed of for their monetary value—these groups meeting on successive Saturdays of each month. The funds will be added to the general fund, designated for the purchase of rugs for the Nurses home. Lunch was served by the hospital dietician, Miss Betty McGovern.

Dramatic Series By Freedom Woman On Air Starting Tonight

A dramatic series, entitled, "Howdy Stone," from the pen of Pearl Bucklen Bentel, Freedom, will be broadcast from Pittsburgh during a fifteen-minute period, from 5:45 to 6 o'clock, each evening, Monday through Friday, beginning tonight.

The scene of the story is laid in a small steel town and centers about a boy and a girl who become involved in a sabotage scheme and other exciting experiences. Pittsburgh talent is being used in portraying the characters.

Next Monday evening, March 17, also from Pittsburgh, the "Wayside Theatre" will present from 8:30 to 9 o'clock, a one-act drama, "Blind Corridor" also written by Mrs. Bentel.

NAVY BASE OPENED

By the United Press

CORPUS CHRISTI, Tex., March 12—The Navy commissions today its newest and largest air base and training station, a $44,000,000 project covering 10,000 acres.

Republican Wins In Congressional Vote

NEW YORK, March 12. —Joseph Clark Baldwin, Republican city councilman who had the active barking of Wendell L. Willkie, was elected to Congress from Manhattan's Seventeenth district by a three to one majority to fill the vacancy created by the death of Representative Kenneth Simpson.

Baldwin outdistanced his Democratic opponent, Dean Alfange, Greek-born attarney, whose candidacy was wished success by President Roosevelt. The third candidate Eugene P. Connolly, representing the left-wing faction of the American Labor party, ran far behind.

MEETING POSTPONED

The monthly meeting of the Conway Board of Education, scheduled for Tuesday evening, was postponed.

Operations To Be

(Continued from Page One)

ject to provide living quarters for the employes for that reason.

TO MAKE ONLY BLADES

Only propellor blades will be manufactured here, he said, as under the Curtiss-Wright system of production each of four plants operated by the company make only parts for propellors. Blades manufactured here will be assembled in Indianapolis, Ind., where the company also is erecting a new plant.

Eventually, operations now conducted at the Neville Island plant probably will be transferred to the local plant, Mr. McKee declared. Over 960 persons are now employed at the Neville Island plant, which is working 24 hours daily. That plant, which is leased, was started in 1930 with only seven men. Last month, 767 propellors were produced there, according to Mr. McKee.

The Curtiss-Wright Corporation was founded in 1922, Mr. McKee said, expressing the opinion that by the end of this year 100,000 persons will be employed by the company. Except for a few propellors manufactured for use in China, only controllable - pitch propellors are produced by the company, and Curtiss-Wright propellors are used on all outstanding Army and Navy fighting planes, he declared.

There is only one other large manufacturer of metal propellors in the United States, according to Mr. McKee, that concern being a manufacturer of aluminum propellors. It is located in Hartford, Conn. Curtiss-Wright is getting 60 per cent of the propellor business in the United States, he said.

RAILROAD DISCUSSED

P. L. Howard, Philadelphia, traffic manager for the Sun Oil Company—controlled by the Pews—spoke briefly regarding transportation arrangements for the new plant. He said that about two cars daily, or approximately 600 cars a year, will be moved in and out of the plant.

Mr. Howard also said that the Pews proposed to sell the Vanport section of the Beaver Valley Connecting Railroad which will serve the plant—between Vanport and College avenue—to the Pennsylvania Railroad, and abandon the section from College avenue to the Pittsburgh and Lake Erie Railroad tracks in Bridgewater. Permission for that action must be granted, however, by the Inter-State Commerce Commission.

The Rotarians voted to jointly sponsor, with the Rochester Lions Club, an essay contest for Rochester high school students to be conducted in connection with the forthcoming Rochester "clean-up, fix-up, paint-up" campaign, April 27 to May 3. Cash prizes will be awarded the winners.

Axis Assails U. S.

(Continued from Page One)

planning parachutist and anti-parachutist exercises this week.

The Germans were reported to have made stronger demands upon Jugoslavia after negotiations for —Jugoslav signature of a non-aggression pact virtually had been completed.

The Foreign Affairs address to the to the Turkish Parliament by Premier Dr. Refik Saydam, scheduled for today, was indefinitely postponed.

The Greeks were prepared for eventualities in Thrace. A new military governor was sent to take charge of the area.

Germany reported that sinkings of British shipping totalled 2,037,000 tons from Nov. 1 to March 1 of which 1,524,000 tons was credited to naval attacks and 513,000 to air attacks.

London revealed that more German bombs have fallen on Buckingham palace, damaging a garden wall and a porter's lodge.

At Saigon, the French Colonials charged that Japan had cheated them "shamelessly." The "peace" settlement was roundly denounced and the French warned that it would shortly become clear that Japan has gained from her "mediation."

The Vichy government denied that German bases had been established in North Africa.

Beaver Schools

(Continued from Page 1)

building needs for next year due to the establishment of the Curtiss-Wright plant in the community was discussed. This problem was left for further study, but from all indications the immediate concern of the school district is the possible increase in senior high school enrollment.

The Secretary was instructed to advertise for general school supplies. The benefit basketball game between the Curtiss-Wright team and Geneva College was announced and the Board members were urged to be present at this affair on March 13.

Labor, Agricultural

(Continued from Page One)

liberalize benefits under the Unemployment Compensation Law was ready for introduction.

Considerable interest was evidenced in a first reading bill to repeal an 1878 act prohibiting employment of women in places serving intoxicants. It was reported favorably to the floor by the liquor control committee which has a sub-group investigating suspected variations between the state liquor control board regulations and the legislative enactments underlying them.

DEFENSE BILL UP

Senate leaders indicated the House-approved bill to set up state and local defense councils would be reported favorably with minor amendments, and that the Walker-Cavalcante bill barring "subversive" parties from election ballots would be held for "further study" by the judiciary general until next week.

It appeared likely the local government commission bills to appropriate $7,500,000 to counties and $15,000,000 to other municipalities from the motor fund for road work would be recommitted to the appropriations committee today after second reading. The proposed $15,000,000 grant represents a wide departure from custom and, since it would divert to political subdivisions money that would otherwise be spent by the State Highways Department, the Governor may be expected to veto the bill if the "home rule" crowd succeeds in forcing it through the House and Senate.

Important hearings scheduled by the Senate include one March 26 by the agriculture committee for testimony on the House-approved Moul-Woodring bill to establish statewide uniform inspection standards for milk and dairy products.

President's Request

(Continued from Page One)

amount for labor, and the remaining one-fifth for overhead, which would include profits. The amount spent for labor would include the outlay at the production or construction sites and for employment in the output of raw materials.

These experts said that for every dollar of expenditure there would be a corresponding hour of employment, direct or indirect. Put another way, the $7,000,000,000 would provide a little more than one years' work for 3,000,000 men on a 40-hour work week.

ESTIMATED COST

In the 1942 budget submitted to Congress by the President in January, Mr. Roosevelt estimated that the U. S. defense program totaled $28,480,000,000. This figure, he said, was based on appropriations and authorizations enacted from June, 1940, up to January, the supplementary appropriations and authorizations for 1941 fiscal year, and the $10,800,000,000 defense recommendations for the 1942 fiscal year beginning Next July 1.

During the World War, Congress appropriated $10,000,000,000 for foreign loans. Of this, $3,000,000,000 was included in the first liberty bond act of April 1917. The following September, the second liberty bond act appropriated $4,000,000,000 for that purpose. Subsequently, there were two appropriations of $1,500,000,000 each for foreign loans.

The largest single defense appropriation measure ever enacted was a World War Army Bill, approved July 9, 1918, calling for $10,225,000,000 cash and $1,858,000,000 contract authorizations.

Horse Racing, Gambling Bills Believed Doomed

By the United Press

HARRISBURG, March 12—Bills by Sen. John J. Haluska, D., Cambria, to legalize and regulate horse racing, bingo games, slot machines and pin ball games and appropriate the proceeds received by the state for pensions and welfare work seemed doomed today.

Haluska, who has tried every week since the bills were introduced February 4 to have them reported out of the judiciary general committee, interrogated Sen. John M. Walker, R., Allegheny, on action by the committee on the bills at its meeting yesterday.

Strike In Aluminum Plant Disrupts Work

Workers at the Edgewater, N. J., plant of the Aluminum Company of America went on strike today, disrupting production of sheet aluminum essential to the manufacture of airplanes for the nation's defense program.

The strike brought to 31 the number of industrial plants and projects involved in the national defense program which were affected today by labor disputes.

Beaver News

Bessie Brooks Study Group Does Work For Missions At Meeting

Methodist Church Group Is Entertained By Mrs. Robert Toussaint, Jr.

Members of the Bessie Brooks Study Group of the Women's Society of Christian Service of the Methodist church were entertained in the home of Mrs. Robert Toussaint, Jr., Corporation street, Monday evening. Mrs. Andrew W. Culley, in an interesting manner, reviewed the last two chapters of the book, "Dangerous Opportunities in China" and Mrs. Charles A. Bukey gave a report on the Bradley Home. Mrs. Charles R. Wolf conducted the devotions and Mrs. Robert O. Davis, president, presided over a business session. During the evening, some of the group sewed, making dresser scarfs for home mission fields, while others cut and prepared Christmas cards to be sent to Miss Mary Boyde, formerly of Beaver, who is a missionary at Meerut, India, to be used in her work among the natives. "The Birthday Offering" was received also. There were about twenty in attendance. During a social hour, the hostess and her associate hostess, Mrs. Melvin E. Toussaint, served a lunch of pretty St. Patrick's Day appointments in green and white. On Monday evening, April 14, Mrs. Thomas V. Morgan, Jr., will be hostess to the group at her home in Wayne street. Misses Velma Rees and Eleanor Pusch will be the assistant hostesses.

Rev. Dr. E. V. H. Condron of Springdale, a United Presbyterian minister, will be the speaker at the monthly meeting of the Beaver Junior Woman's Club, Thursday evening, March 13, at 7:45 o'clock in the Presbyterian church. His subject will be "Roommates." Gayle Chaffin of Midland, with Mrs. Frank O. Hand, also of Midland as his accompanist, will sing. Mothers of the clubmembers will be guests on this occasion. Hostesses will be officers and directors of the club and members of the Braille committee. During a business session, officers for the ensuing year will be elected.

The Josephine White Missionary Society of the United Presbyterian church will hold its monthly meeting in the Memorial room of the church Thursday evening, March 13, at eight o'clock.

Mrs. Walter A. Zubaugh will entertain her two-table bridge club at her home in Third street, Friday evening, March 14.

The Official Board of the Methodist church will meet this evening at the close of the mid-week Lenten service. Rev. Charles R. Wolf, pastor, will speak on the subject "What Rejects Christ" at the Lenten service at 7:45 o'clock.

Miss Dorothy Jean Eakin, daughter of Mr. and Mrs. Howard M. Eakin, Canal street, left Tuesday for Denver, Col., to spend the remainder of the winter. She accompanied her uncle and aunt, Mr. and Mrs. Stephen J. Millard, and her aunt, Mrs. C. G. Pritchard, who were called here by the death of Mrs. George F. Retzer, Rochester, a sister-in-law of Mrs. Millard and Mrs. Pritchard. Mrs. Millard and Mrs. Pritchard are daughters of Mr. and Mrs. Charles W. Retzer, Rochester.

Mrs. Glenn Isenberg, Colonial apartments, underwent an emergency operation Monday night in the Beaver Valley hospital, New Brighton, and her condition is reported to be satisfactory.

At the meeting of the Mission Study class in the United Presbyterian church Youth hall, Monday evening, the Y.P.C.U. president, Miss Louise Grine, and Miss Ida Burton, who has been in charge of the study class, reviewed the sixth and final chapter of the mission study book, "Stand By for China." Miss Burton was also leader for the evening. Fifteen young folk were in attendance and after the study a recreational period and refreshments were enjoyed The class was sponsored by the Y. P. C. U.

Magee Hospital Head To Address Alumni

A special meeting will be held by the Rochester Hospital Nurses' Alumni Association Friday evening, March 14, at 8 o'clock in the Nurses' home. The topic will be "Eight-Hour Private Duty." Miss Jessie Turnbull, superintendent of the Elizabeth Steele Magee hospital, Pittsburgh, will be the speaker.

Aliquippa Man Is Acquitted By Jury In Robbery Trial

Midland Junk Dealer Sentenced Today For Buying Junk From Minors

James McCormick, 29, Aliquippa, who testified he was so drunk he had no recollection of driving a companion, Joe Giles, Aliquippa, to the Green Garden Road, or of Giles robbing Sam Muselin and Miss Mary Schaeffer, was acquitted of a robbery charge by a jury in Judge Henry H. Wilson's court Tuesday afternoon.

The Commonwealth had accused McCormick of participating in the robbery to which Giles pleaded guilty. The prosecution contended McCormick drove his car from Aliquippa to the scene of the alleged hold-up and back to Aliquippa by way of Monaca, and that he and Giles were sitting in the car dividing the loot when taken into custody by State and Aliquippa police. McCormick declared he had been drinking all evening and has no recollection of the trip to the Green Garden Road or the hold-up.

Aubrey Thornton, Aliquippa, was acquitted of charges of robbery and assault and battery, but Judge Henry H. Wilson ordered him to post bond in the sum of $1,000 to keep the peace. Sava Tepich, Aliquippa barber, alleged Thornton broke into his home via a cellar window, and hit him with a hammer. Thornton declared Tepich was injured in a fight that climaxed a poker game. Judge Wilson directed the jury to return a verdict of not guilty in the case charging robbery, and the jury acquitted Thornton on the assault charge.

OTHERS SENTENCED

William Booker, colored, Aliquippa, was found guilty today on a charge of felonious assault and battery preferred by Eula Mae Colquit, Aliquippa.

Charles Vollmer, New Brighton, was acquitted by direction of Judge Frank E. Reader, on aggravated assault and battery charges preferred by O. C. Cunningham on account of an automobile collision. The jury divided the costs.

George Cooks, Aliquippa, entered a plea to illegal possession of liquor and was sentenced by Judge Wilson to pay the costs and a fine of $100 or serve three months in jail.

John Radella, Midland, entered a plea before Judge Reader today to buying junk from minors. He was sentenced to pay the costs, a fine of $100 and serve three months in jail.

William Gray, Jr., Beaver Falls, tried yesterday before Judge Reader on a charge of snatching a purse from Mrs. Olive Shillito, Beaver Falls, was found not guilty by the jury.

President Makes

(Continued from Page One)

less than two hours after it was completed by the House. And today Congress prepared to match him.

House leaders scheduled hearings for tomorrow on the British-Aid appropriation, and promised to have the bill ready for floor consideration by next Tuesday.

There was possibility that final Congressional approval might come the following week, although a few Senate isolationists have said they would go over the request with extreme care—a procedure which might consume some time.

Sen. Gerald P. Nye, R., N. D., an opposition leader, was considering an amendment for a $7,000,000,000 tax program to put British aid on a "pay-as-you-go" basis. Other members said Sen. Robert M. La Follette, Prog., Wis., was considering a similar plan.

SPEED PLEDGED

New pledges of speed were not confined to Mr. Roosevelt and the Congressional majority. Defense officials, already working overtime to convert American industry from peacetime levels to war production highs, predicted that their agencies would be tripling their activities to administer the mounting rearmament program.

The reminder by Sens. Nye and La Follette that taxes must be enacted to pay for some of the aid program, won support from Sen. Burton K. Wheeler, D., Mont., opposition leader, who said the $7,000,000,000 was only the beginning of what would be asked.

The note of national unity was echoed in the Senate and House yesterday. During two hours of debate in the House on acceptance of Senate changes in the aid bill, Republican leader Joseph W. Martin, Jr., of Massachusette spoke for harmony. Sen Guy Gillette, D., Ia., who voted against the bill in his chamber struck a similar note in a statement to reporters.

Zelienople Motorist Is Held For Court

Edward McClure, near Zelienople, was arraigned Tuesday afternoon before Justice William A. Wehr, Rochester, on a charge of operating a motor vehicle while under the influence of liquor and entered a plea of not guilty. He posted bond of $500 to assure his appearance in court.

McClure was arrested Monday evening after his automobile collided with a car owned by Victor Hall, Bridgewater, parked in Virginia avenue, Rochester.

Aliquippa May Get 200 Parking Meters

Steps are being taken in Aliquippa for the installation of 200 parking meters in the borough if the contract being prepared by Borough Solicitor Louis Klein is approved Monday evening by Aliquippa Council and the Auto Park Service Company, Pittsburgh.

The ordinance authorizing the execution of the contract was passed some time ago. The meters are to be installed on a six-month trial basis and 65 per cent of the revenue during that period is to go to the company and the remainder to the borough.

If the machines are to be retained after the trial period, all revenues taken in during the trial can be applied to the purchase price of $65 per machine, according to Solicitor Klein.

SWOC Seeks To Open

(Continued from Page One)

of a majority. (The SWOC now is recognized only as agent for its members.)

2. 10 cent-an-hour increase in wages. (The present basic rate is 62 1-2 cents an hour.)

3. Hours of work to provide 48-hour weekly rest periods. (Hours now limited to 40 per calendar week, or five days followed by a 48-hour rest period, at discretion of the company.)

4. One week vacation for employes with one to five years experience; two weeks for those with five or more years. (One week now provided for five years or more only.)

5. Seniority to be based on length of service only. (Physical fitness, skill, family status and residence are now factors.)

6. Acceleration of grievance machinery. (Five distinct steps of appeal now provided without time limits, except in case of discharge.)

7. Establishment of a joint commission for equalization of labor classification rates. (Present agreement provides settlement by local plant adjustment "on a mutually satisfactory basis.")

8. Re-instatement of military draftees. (No provision now.)

9. Establishment of machinery for dues collections. (No existing provision other than prohibition of membership solicitation on company time or property.)

Deaths

PETER McBENNETT

Peter McBennett, 63, Chippewa Township, died at 4:10 o'clock this morning in the Beaver County hospital. Friends are to be received at the Scott funeral home, Beaver Falls.

ROBERT V. NIEDBALA

Robert V. Niedbala, 7, son of Mr and Mrs. John Niedbala, died at the home, 1404 rear Sixth avenue, Beaver Falls, Tuesday evening, from pneumonia. Surviving are the parents and one brother, John, at home. The boy was a pupil in the Second grade at the Fifth avenue school. Private funeral services will be held in the home Friday morning at 9 o'clock. Burial will be in St. Mary's cemetery.

MRS. JOHN BRALLIER

Funeral services were to be held today for Mrs. John Brallier, wife of a Latrobe dentist and mother of a former Beaver woman, who was killed in an automobile accident.

En route to the home of her daughter, Mrs. Harold Allison, Pittsburgh, formerly of Beaver, Mrs. Brallier was killed when the car in which she was riding and another car collided near Wilkinsburg. Dr. Brallier, his sister and his assistant, Dr. Jack Kelly, were injured in the crash.

Mrs. Brallier was the sister of Mrs. H. M. Fair, Aliquippa. Burial took place in Indiana.

Hudson Convertibles Herald Spring

A colorful display of Hudson Convertible models will officially herald the approach of spring this week in Hudson showrooms over the country, it was announced today by the Hudson Motor Car Company. Shown above in a spring setting is a Hudson Eight Convertible of 128-horsepower mounted on 121-inch wheelbase. Tops which raise or lower automatically at the touch of a button are standard equipment.

Monaca High's Prospects Are Brighter For Next Season

THIRTEEN VETERAN PLAYERS AVAILABLE AT MONACA IN 1942

Albert Vlasic Led Southsiders in Scoring During Past Season; Red and Blue Won 15 Out of 22 Games

By BILL HEYMAN

Although the opening of the 1941-42 basketball season is still more than nine months away, the flame of enthusiasm is burning brightly in Monaca when the Southside cage fans consider their prospects for next season.

With the entire squad which finished the past season returning next year, the Blue and Red looms as one of the outstanding Class B quintets of the district as Coach Stan Berkman will be working with thirteen lads with varsity experience garnered this year, and that number, in this case, should be good fortune instead of bad.

During the past season, the Southsiders finished on the long end of the score fifteen times in 22 starts, winning three and losing five non-sectional games and copping twelve of fourteen Section 11 games. The Berkman - coached outfit finished the Section 11 race in second place, losing only a pair of decisions to the sectional champions, Midland.

In the season's finale, the Monacans dropped a 41 to 42 game to the Midlanders in a thrill-packed battle when the Blue and Red was without the services of three veterans.

The Southsiders recorded their first victory over the Ambridge high team in years and forced the Aliquippa team, Section 3 champion, to the utmost before losing 30 to 31 in another warm-up game.

Individual scoring honors went to Albert Vlasic who tallied 119 points during the season, 96 of them in the last seven games. He was followed by Adam Karcis with 117 and Edwin Figley with 106 points.

The Southsiders scored 760 points during the season, an average of 34.55 points per game while their opponents counted 560 points, an average of 25.05 points per game.

In the sectional race, Monaca tallied 572 points, averaging 40.86 per game, while allowing a total of 339 or 24.07 points each contest. This total would have been more lop-sided had Coach Berkman not substituted liberally when far out in front.

At the beginning of the past season, Berkman had three veterans from the 1940 season, Mike Linkovich, Adam Karcis and Edwin Figley. Linkovich was ineligible during much of the second half schedule, while Karcis and Figley did not finish the season with the squad.

Returning next year will be Albert Vlasic, Joe Trella, Edward Ofcharka, and Steve Ogrisek, all juniors now, and Anthony Scassa, John Dietrich, John Hlebo, Dave Sinclair, Tony Battaglia, Stanley Wywrot, Eugene Knopp, Bill Holic and Bob Pickrell, sophomores.

The individual scoring for the season is as follows: Vlasic, 119 points; Karcis, 117; Figley, 106; Ofcharka, 102; Linkovich, 96; Trella, 82; Scassa, 47; Dietrich, 33; Sinclair, 22; Battaglia, seven; Pickrell, six; Knopp, three, and Holic, Hlebo, Wywrot and Ogrisek, two points each.

The record for the past season was:

NON-LEAGUE GAMES

Monaca 26	E. Liverpool, O.	36.
Monaca 15	Ambridge	14.
Monaca 30	Aliquippa	31.
Monaca 26	Chester, W. Va.	25.
Monaca 27	New Brighton	28.
Monaca 5	St. Jos., Oil City	17.
Monaca 22	Chester, W. Va.,	38.
Monaca 37	St. Jos., Oil City	32.
188		221

LEAGUE GAMES

Monaca 39	Mars	17
Monaca 37	Rochester	21.
Monaca 42	Evans City	19.
Monaca 39	Beaver	15.
Monaca 46	Freedom	25.
Monaca 41	Zelienople	25.
Monaca 30	Midland	34.
Monaca 34	Mars	27.
Monaca 47	Rochester	21.
Monaca 54	Evans City	29.
Monaca 37	Beaver	24.
Monaca 46	Freedom	12.
Monaca 39	Zelienople	28.
Monaca 41	Midland	42.
572		339

Vendex Leads Court House League By One Game Margin

Only one game separated the Vendex and Mandamus teams in the Court House Bowling league today, after Vendex, the leader, had absorbed a three game defeat at the hands of the Mandamus outfit. In other matches Caveat won two games from Habeas Corpus, and Capias lost all three to Talesmen, while Certiorari took three from Decedents by forfeit.

Cliff Holland rolled 167 for the high single game for the men, while Marion Hogsett had 439 for the best three game total. Mary Engle rolled 139 and 333 for the women.

The Mandamus had the high single team score of 702 and put together 576, 616 and 702 for the three game score of 1894.

Bill Detrick, Habeas Corpus, had 159 and 390; K. Carroll, 109 and 276; Ralph Bennett, Caveat 148 and Frank Suffoletta and Bennett shared 393 for the three game score, Edith Cadley had 94 and 252; Bob Orr, Vendex, 157 and 375, Mary Winterburn, 119 and 331; Frank Kelker 165 and Hogsett, 439, Mary Engle, 139 and 333; Wilson, Talesmen, 156 and 431; Eberle, Capias, 145 and 338 and Alberta Todd, 113 and 272; Cliff Holland, 167 and 421, Kathleen Ray 103 and Loretta Gerber 247.

TEAM SCORES

Habeas Corpus	505	671	581—1757
Caveat	526	584	596—1706
Vendex	553	600	518—1671
Mandamus	576	616	702—1894
Talesmen	482	500	539—1521
Capias	405	429	404—1238

TEAM STANDING

	Won	Lost
Vendex	41	19
Mandamus	40	20
Caveat	37	23
Certiorari	32	28
Talesmen	31	29
Habeas Corpus	26	34
Capias	25	35
Decedants	8	52

Schedule, March 14.
Talesmen vs. Mandamus.
Vendex vs. Capias.
Habeas Corpus vs. Certiorari.
Decedents vs. Caveat.

Figure Skating Star To Appear At Garden

Megan Taylor, present world's figure skating champion, will appear at the Gardens, Pittsburgh, with her father, Phil Taylor, the famous stilt skater, this evening at the Cleveland - Pittsburgh hockey game.

This English girl finished second to Sonja Henie in the world's championship competitions in 1934, 1935 and 1936, and won the title in 1938 and 1939. At her American debut at the St. Paul Ice Carnival, eight thousand spectators were present on opening night, February 5, and the two remaining performances were sold out in advance. Never before in the history of skating in St. Paul has any show attracted so many people.

WPIAL TOURNEY

CLASS A
Playoff Results
Section 4—Monessen 28, Charleroi 24.
Section 8—Coraopolis 31, McKees Rocks 29.
First Round Result
Avalon (2) 30, Springdale (5) 17.
Quarter-Final Results
Ford City (1) 32, Avalon (2) 25.
Duquesne (6) 41, Braddock (7) 28.
Aliquippa (3) 43, Coraopolis (8) 35.
Monessen 40, Connellsville 34.
Semi-Finals
Tuesday—Ford City (1) vs. Duquesne (6), 8 p. m.
Wednesday — Aliquippa (3) vs. Monessen (4), 8 p. m
FINAL
SATURDAY. MARCH 15.
CLASS B
Playoff Results
Section 14
Burgettstown 27, Trinity 24.
Burgettstown 45, Cecil 24.
Section 15
Bentleyville 34, N. Belle Vernon 16.
Preliminary Result
Peters Twp. (25) 25, Claysville (19) 17.
First Round Results
Sharpsburg (18) 31, Glassport (16) 17.
Bridgeville (12) 36, Robinson (10) 34.
Ligonier (13) 31, Eld. Ridge (21) 24.
Midland (11) 55, Wampum (20) 15.
So. Union (22) 25, W. Newton (24) 20.
Carmichaels (23) 42, Peters Twp. (25) 28.
Bentleyville (15) 27, Rostraver (17) 23.
Quarter-Final Results
Sharpsburg 33, Bridgeville 22.
Ligonier 36, South Union 28.
Burgettstown (14) 26, Carmichaels (23) 24.
Bentleyville 38, Midland 36.
Semi-Finals
Thursday, March 13—Sharpsburg (18) vs. Ligonier (13) 7:30 p. m. Burgettstown (14) vs. Bentleyville (15), 8:30 p. m.—Pitt Stadium floor
FINAL
Site and date to be announced later.

Colt, Filly Favored For Hambletonian

By the United Press

GOSHEN, N. Y., March 12. —Bill Gallon, a colt, and Flormel, a filly, stand one-two in the spring books here at 2-1 and 3-1 respectively to win the 1941 Hambletonian Stakes, richest purse in Harness racing.

Bill Gallon, owned by R. H. Johnston, was purchased in 1939 for $1,800 and his name changed from Ashley Hanover. He earned $14,145 last year as the top money-winning colt of the season and Lee Smith now is training him at Charlotte, N. C.

Flormel, owned by E. Roland Harriman, is being trained at Longwood, Fla., by Billy Dickerson and Harry Pownall. This bay filly, by Spencer, winner of the 1928 Hambletonian and sire of last year's winner, Spencer Scott, was timed in 2:03 1-2 last year in the Kentucky Futurity, fastest mile by a two-year-old in 1940.

COMEBACK—After being beaten in the rich Handicap, Mioland comes back to win the San Juan Capistrano race at Santa Anita.

GRID TO COCKPIT—Former members of the Argonauts' football club of Toronto, these youths are now Canadian pilots.

THE DAILY TIMES
NEWS OF SPORTING EVENTS
BILL ANDERSON, Sports Editor BEAVER AND ROCHESTER, PA., WEDNESDAY, MARCH 12, 1941.

CURTISS-WRIGHT TEAM TO MEET GENEVA THURSDAY

TIMES photo, by Russell D. Porter

The above photo shows members of the Curtiss-Wright Propeller Division basketball team that will clash with the Geneva College cagers on Thursday evening at the Beaver high school gym. Coaches, trainer, manager and some of the plant officials are also shown in the picture.

They are: Standing, left to right —Nordy Hoffman, coach; W. O. Lehew, plant personnel manager; Jack Rosfeld, forward; Eddie Wilhelmy, guard; Jim McQuilken, business manager; J. H. McKee, works manager; Vinnie Dwyer, forward; Curt Stone, forward; Mike Rosso, guard and captain; Johnny Schleder, trainer; seated—left to right—Walt Baldinger, center; Eddie Hensler, forward; Finis Boyce, center; Johnny Burby, center, and Bud Squires, forward.

Nordy Hoffman, the Curtiss-Wright coach, is a former All-American football guard in 1931. He was a roommate of Frank Leahy, newly-appointed Notre Dame coach.

Mike Rosso captain of the team, is a former Washington and Jefferson College star, and played against the Geneva College team a few years ago. Hensler, Squires, Stone, Rosfeld and Baldinger are all former Pittsburgh Municipal League stars, and the others are all independent players of considerable experience.

To date the Curtis-Wright passers have won 24 games and lost seven. They are leading the Coraopolis - Neville Island Industrial League in the second half of play after losing the first half championship in a playoff game with the Neville Coke Company team.

ST. VERONICA CAGERS EDGE MONACA HIGH IN CLOSE GAME

A field goal from the corner in the last five seconds of play by Popps, crack center of the St. Veronica High school quintet, Ambridge, gave the Crusaders a 24 to 23 decision over the Monaca High cagers for 1942 Tuesday evening on the Ambridge High school floor.

The Southsiders will be seeking revenge when they clash again Friday evening with the St. Veronica team on the Monaca floor in a benefit game for 'Chick' Holy, former Monaca cager, who recently had a leg amputated following an infection.

Last night, the Monaca team jumped away to a 11 to 4 lead in the first period but was out-scored in the last three periods. The Saints cut two points from the Monacans' margin in the second period but still trailed 10 to 15 at the half.

A rally in the third period knotted the count at 18-all as the last canto got underway. Monaca was leading 23 to 22 with less than 30 seconds to play when the victors worked the ball down-floor, passed to Popps in the corner and that worthy tossed in the tying and winning points.

The scoring for the winners was all credited to Popps and Kasper, Popps collecting 15 points while his mate had the remaining nine. Ed Ofcharka and Joe Trella divided scoring honors for Monaca with six points each.

Dave Sinclair started at forward for the Southsiders but received an ankle injury on the opening tipoff and was forced to leave the game.

The lineups:

Monaca.	G.	F.	Pts.
Vlasic, f	1	0-0	2
Sinclair, f	0	0-0	0
Ofcharka, c	3	0-0	6
Trella, g	2	2-5	6
Dietrich, g	2	0-0	4
Scassa, f	1	0-1	2
Pickrell, f	0	3-4	3
Totals	9	5-10	23

Substitutions: Ogrisek, Holic, Knopp, Battaglia.

St. Veronica.	G.	F.	Pts.
Battles, f	0	0-0	0
Planneky, f	0	0-0	0
Popps, c	6	3-4	15
Kasper, g	4	1-3	9
Kearns, g	0	0-0	0
Totals	10	4-7	24

Score by periods:

Monaca	11	4	3	5—23
St. Veronica	4	6	8	6—24

Referee—Moll.
Umpire—Riggs.

CAGE TOURNEY PLANNED

The first Ohio Valley Independent basketball tournament is scheduled for March 20, 21, 22, 28 and 29, at the Croatian Hall, Ambridge, it was announced today by John Zivic, director. Competition will be in two classes, Junior class for players under 18 years of age, and the Senior class, no age limit. Managers interested can write John Zivic, 433 Maplewood avenue, Ambridge.

Titans Meet Long Island Blackbirds

NEW WILMINGTON, Pa., Mar. 12—Westminster College drew the Long Island U. Blackbirds as their first opponent in the Metropolitan intercollegiate basketball tournament in Madison Square Garden, Wednesday night, March 19, in the second game of a double-header. Rhode Island State and Seton Hill will be opponents in the initial game of the evening.

Last year, Long Island beat the Titans 47-42, by coming from behind in the final five minutes of play after Westminster had led the blackbirds during the first three quarters.

Coach Washabaugh of Westminster will take ten Titan players with him on the New York trip, and will leave from New Castle Sunday, March 16.

Monaca Ex-High Squad To Drill

Former Monaca high basketball players who will make up the Ex-High team that will oppose the Boris Five of New Brighton in the first half of the Carl Holy benefit program at the Monaca high auditorium on Friday night, will hold a practice session on Thursday evening at 8:30 o'clock.

Chick Alexander will serve as coach of the Ex-High team and desires the following players to report for practice Thursday evening: Bill Vongray, Richard Thomas, Frank Busang, Eugene Zigerelli, Bill Zopf, Phil Predo, Glenn Swink, Matthew Fronko, Tommy Yarosz, Furman Massey, Mike Linkovich, Adam Karcis and Edwin Figley.

Greenberg Flat-Footed U.S. Army Exam Reveals

LAKELAND, Fla., March 12. — Hank Greenberg, the Detroit Tiger slugging outfielder, has flat feet. Dr. Grover C. Freeman, retired U. S. Navy Lieutenant Commander, gave Greenberg a physical examination for Selective Service yesterday and reported the ball player passed the test in "fine shape" except for second degree flat feet. Whether the feet will keep Hank out of the Draft Army remains to be seen. Meanwhile, he participates today in the Tigers' first intra-squad game of the spring training season.

Game Protector, Fish Warden Give Reports At Sportsmen's Meet

Motion Pictures of 200-Mile Boat Trip in British Columbia Shown Sportsmen

Reports by Clifford Iman, district fish warden; Bradley McGregor, county game protector, and president Ray H. Fischer, and movies shown by Andy Stiveson, Pittsburgh, featured the annual spring rally of the Beaver Sportsmen's Club at the Odd Fellows Hall Tuesday evening.

About 130 men were in attendance at the rally and about twenty-five new club members were enrolled.

President Fischer opened the meeting with a brief review of club activities. Fish Warden Iman gave a highly informative report on the stocking of Beaver County fishing streams during the last few months, and distributed posters showing native Pennsylvania fish in their natural colors, intended for use in schools for nature study.

Game Protector McGregor told of the progress made in restocking county woodlands with rabbits and pheasants. The rabbit stocking program is practically completed he said and the liberation of ringneck pheasants for breeding purposes will be started soon. Birds are being procured this year from Wisconsin and Ohio. McGregor reported that 576 rabbits had been trapped this winter in boroughs of the county and released in the open country.

A resolution putting the club on record as opposed to any legislation that would place a restriction on the ownership of sporting firearms by United States citizens, was adapted.

Visitors were presented from Midland, Aliquippa, Freedom, Rochester, Beaver Falls, Monaca and Ambridge and several of them spoke briefly.

The color motion pictures shown by Stiveson, taken on a 200-mile boat trip in the vicinity of Tweedsmuir Park, British Columbia, Canada, last summer proved highly interesting.

Harry Eberle, Glenwillard, brought to the rally a mounted albino raccoon, which he caught last year in Hanover Township. The animal was pure white, a perfect albino, and the first that many sportsmen had ever seen.

Club officials announced that Brady's Run will be stocked Friday with about 2,000 legal size rainbow and brook trout. The fish are scheduled to arrive at the Rochester Post Office about 11:30 Friday morning. Later the truck will stop at Market and Fourth streets, Beaver, and any sportsmen who wish to help place the fish in the stream will be welcome.

Three door prizes were awarded, and lunch was served by the committee in charge.

The average acres of farms in Oklahoma is placed at 165.5.

Basketball Scores

COLLEGE
National College Tourney
Superior T. 51, Morningside 42.
Austin 64, Simpson 50.
Murray State 68, Oregon Col. 46.
Santa Barbara 32, Wayne 26.
Baltimore 52, Omaha U. 35.
Remidji 35, Kansas State 33.
West Virginia Tourney
Salem 70, Fairmont 64.
Glenville 85, Shepherd 39.
Concord 65, W. Va. Wesleyan 64.
Alder-Broaddus 64, W. Liberty 42.
High School
W. P. I. A. L. Tourney
Duquesne 38, Ford City 14.
Junior W. P. I. A. L. Tourney
Monessen 30, Bentleyville 25
Swissvale 24, Parnassus 20.
P.I.A.A. Tourney
Sharpsville 32, Erie East 29.
Lower Merion 29, Coatesville 28.
Williamsport 44, Shamokin 25.
Franklin 35, Johnstown 26.
Bradford 45, Mt. Jewett 31.
Everett 38, Boswell 35.

Interstate Loop Now Five State Circuit

By the United Press

PHILADELPHIA, March 12.—The Interstate Baseball League became a five-state wheel with transfer of the York, Pa., franchies to Bridgeport, Conn.

The Boston Bees, owners of the franchise, said at a meeting yesterday that the transfer was being made for economic purposes.

Bridgeport and Hagerstown, Md., thereby become two new teams this year, taking over Pennsylvania franchises. Other loop clubs are Harrisburg, Reading, Allentown and Lancaster, all of Pennsylvania; Wilmington, Del., and Trenton, N. J.

Tom Harmon To Sign For Lead In Movie

By the United Press

ANN ARBOR, Mich., March 12.—All-American halfback Tommy Harmon of the University of Michigan said today he would go to New York Friday to sign a contract for a starring role in a motion picture.

Harmon said that under terms of a contract with Bing Crosby's agency he would receive $13,500, and that the agency would receive an option for his services in a second film for which he would get $17,500.

GET RECOGNITION

TULSA, Okla. (UP) — "Jitterbugging" has been classified as a "sport" at the University of Tulsa. The Independent Men's Association at the University included a jitterbugging exhibition on the program at its recent sports carnival.

ADDRESS FAILS TO PASS

GADSDEN, Ala. (UP) — The city commission turned down an application to renew a beer and whisky permit for the Royal Palm Cafe, a Negro eating place. The owner's address was given as "Federal Penitentiary, Atlanta, Ga.

Ross L. Leffler Of Game Commission To Speak At Sportsmen's Banquet On Friday

Annual County-Wide Sportsmen's Banquet at Rochester Methodist Church Friday Evening; Extensive Program of Entertainment Is Arranged

Ross L. Leffler, McKeesport, president of the Pennsylvania State Game Commission, will be the principal speaker at the annual county-wide banquet of Beaver County sportsmen at the Rochester Methodist Church Friday evening at 6:30 o'clock.

Leffler will discuss the work of the game commission and perhaps proposed legislation effecting sportsmen. His message is sure to be interesting, and a large attendance is expected. Sportsmen, whether members of any sportsmen's club or not, and their wives and friends, will be welcome, but reservations for the banquet must be made no later than noon Thursday. Tickets can be procured through officials of any of the eleven sportsment's clubs in the county, or from Gordon Camp, Rochester, or the Sahli Motor Company in Beaver Falls and Rochester.

An extensive program of entertainment is planned for the banquet. Each of the eleven Sportsman's organizations affiliated with the Beaver County League, has been made responsible for a portion of the entertainment. The program will include vaudeville acts, both vocal and instrumental music and other presentations.

Several representatives of the Game and Fish Commission in addition to Commissioner Leffler, are expected to attend the banquet. President F. W. Crawford of the County Sportsmen's League, will preside. Ralph Aumack, Monaca, is the league secretary.

Bill Lee Baffled By Tactics Of Cubs In Salary Dispute

Big Bill Thinks Cubs Aren't Being Fair; Has Made No Plans to Join Cubs

By the United Press

PLAQUEMINE, La., March 12. — The biggest holdout story in baseball is in this little Louisiana town.

It concerns Big Bill Lee, of the National League's top pitching hands, and the Chicago Cubs. Lee, bewildered and baffled by the Cubs squeeze play tactics, told the story and it was evident he thinks there is some skulduggery going on.

"In two years the Cubs have slashed my salary from $20,000 to $10,000," Lee said. "I should be cut but not the way the Cubs are slashing me. I was the league's top pitcher in percentage and earned runs in 1938, winning 22 games. I made $20,000 and Mr. Wrigley gave me a $5,000 bonus at the end of the season.

"I won only 19 games in 1939 and they cut me $2,500. Last season I had a miserable year and I expected to be cut some more. The cut was $5,000 but when I started to dicker with them they threatened me with another $2,500 cut unless I reported at Catalina Island on time.

"Not only that, but they told me they had obtained waivers on me. That's what I don't understand. I wrote them I'd buy my release for the $7,500 waiver price and they ignored my offer. Do you honestly think that every club the majors has waived on me? Well, I don't and I don't understand that kind of treatment."

Lee attributes his decline last season to physical ailments. Since the season ended he's had his tonsils removed and had a major posterior operation performed. Altogether, he was layed up five weeks.

"I know I wasn't a winning pitcher last year," Lee said. "I wasn't in shape. My ailments prevented me from running and keeping in condition. Of course, I have to prove I can still win but the Cubs are trying to whip me in line by making me think nobody wants me."

Lee, who donned spectacles last year in mid-season, got up from his easy chair and went to his trophy case where he picked up half a dozen balls at random.

"Look at these scores," Lee said, reading off 1-0, 3-2, and 2-1 games. "I don't know how many of them I've pitched. I was looking at my scrap book the other night and I read a story in 1937 where my record in July was 11 won and 9 lost. In those nine games the Cubs made a total of five runs for me. They never got me any runs. I'm not crying but the Cubs' management isn't being fair with me."

Lee's family, his wife, two young children and father and mother, listened to their son tell about his predicament. Then his father said. "I'm a man of the woods. I know I wouldn't let Bill come out there and tell me how to run my business. But he's been up there in that baseball game seven years and he ought to know what he's talking about. If they don't like him why don't they get rid of him?"

The strapping righthander has made no plans to join the Cubs. But he's working out daily, getting in shape for the day when he joins the Cubs or some other club. He weighs 198 now as compared with 215 last spring.

"I thought I might go to San Antonio when the Cubs come through there to talk things over but I see that they aren't playing there this year. I might go to Chicago when they get there April 11, then I might not. I've even been thinking of working down here and pitching for a semi-pro oil team. I can't make $20,000 but I can save just as much and besides I'd be at home with my family. I've done enough traveling. I'm a home man at heart and sure wouldn't [illegible] to death around here. [illegible] let's go to breakfast."

SPORT SLANTS

By BILL ANDERSON

A dispatch from Southern California quotes Connie Mack, venerable manager of the Philadelphia Athletics as saying of Pete Suder, Aliquippa resident:

"He's the best third baseman we've had in years. He's going to be a great player."

The words of praise came after the Aliquippa product had singled twice in five times at bat, and drove in one run as the A's beat San Diego, 3 to 2.

Most of the bowlers who were among the leading prize winners in the annual Pennsylvania and Ohio Duckpin Tournament at Meadville last week, are scheduled to compete in the Beaver County open tourney at New Brighton, March 22 to March 29. The local venture, started last year, promises to be a big success this year. Pete Furman and George Remington of Pittsburgh, doubles winners at Meadville with a 1158 score, are entered, and so is Joe Leister, of Carrick, the all-events winner in the Penn-Ohio affair, with a total of 1671 pins in nine games. The Servand All-Stars of Monessen, winners of the five-man team event, are also enrolled in the local tournament. The Monessen team won at Meadville with a score of 2646, and Wilkinsburg, also entered in the county event, was second with a 2608 score.

Aliquippa's Serbian basketball team, with Press Maravich, Davis-Elkins College star in the lineup, is looking forward to the National Serbian basketball tournament at Detroit starting March 31, with high hopes of winning the championship. Last Saturday night Maravich led the Aliquippa Serbs to a 58-31 victory over the Johnstown Serbs, also entered in the National tourney, at the Aliquippa high school gym. Maravich, one of the highest scoring college players in the country this year, contributed 21 points toward Aliquippa's total. Other members of the Aliquippa team are Fred Milanovich, former Geneva star; Sammy Milanovich, Pitt guard this season; Mike Vukitich of Edinboro Teachers and Mitch Philipovich of Geneva. Since Pitt has accepted a bid to play in the NCAA tournament at Madison, Wis., Sammy Milanovich may be lost to the Serbs.

John E. Dreshar, newly elected football coach at Beaver Falls high school has compiled an enviable record at Tarentum high school over the last four years. After playing three years at Kiski Prep and four at Carnegie Tech and captaining the Tartans two years in a row, Dreshar began his coaching career as an assistant at Western Reserve in Cleveland in 1931. He took post-graduate work at Pitt in 1932, and took over the coaching reins at Tarentum in the fall of 1933. All his Tarentum teams have been good ones, but in the last four seasons, 1937, 1938, 1939 and 1940, Tarentum lost only three out of 40 games, and climaxed an undefeated season last fall by defeating Rampey high, 14 to 12 for the WPIAL Class A championship. Dreshar will sign a three-year coaching contract at Beaver Falls. His salary is $2,800, including $1,800 for teaching and $800 for coaching the football team.

Aliquippa To Play In Class A Tourney Semi-Final Tonight

Steelers Play Monessen For Right to Enter Title Game With Duquesne High

Aliquippa and Monessen meet tonight in a semi-final Class "A" match at the Pitt Stadium to decide which team will meet Duquesne High School basketball team in the finals of the WPIAL Saturday night.

Duquesne, the only repeating sectional winner in the WPIAL, which is District 7 in the PIAA, rolled into the finals last night by overwhelming Ford City by a 38-14 score. Ford City could score only one field goal in the last three quarters.

Before a crowd of 4,500 spectators at the stadium, the fast-cutting, rangy Duquesne team dropped Ford City far behind after the first quarter.

In the WPIAL junior tournament, Swissvale defeated Parnassus, 24-20, at New Kensington last night to gain the finals. In a quarter-final game Monessen defeated Bentleyville, 30-25. Monessen plays Port Vue in a semi-final match at a site to be chosen tomorrow. The winner plays Swissvale for the Junior League championship.

TRUANTS' I.Q. LOWER

BERKELEY, Cal (UP) — Why students play hookey has been solved by Dr. Lillian Bray Hill, psychologist. A survey of 130 truant boys and 130 non-truants, showed the hookey players were less intelligent.

DOG HAS LIFE ANNUITY

WABASH, Ind. (UP) — Mike, a Dobermann pinscher, is assured a comfortable existence for the rest of his life. A life annuity amounting to $240 a year provides for the dog's care under the will of his late master, Dr. E. S. Drunks, of Wabash.

Weather Forecast

Snow flurries and continued cold tonight; generally fair and slightly warmer Tuesday afternoon and Wednesday.

THE DAILY TIMES

ROCHESTER-BEAVER-MONACA

FREEDOM—BRIDGEWATER—CONWAY—VANPORT—MIDLAND

Local History

The only school building in Beaver Falls before 1873 was an old two-room structure on Seventh avenue.

ESTABLISHED APRIL 2, 1874 | BEAVER AND ROCHESTER, PA., MONDAY, MARCH 17, 1941 | BY CARRIER 15 CENTS A WEEK—

G-MEN PROBING BADEN TRAIN WRECK; FOUR KILLED, 113 INJURED IN CRASH

WRECK VIVIDLY DESCRIBED BY INJURED MAN

"Riding in the third coach, I did not notice any trouble until the car began bumping over the ties and then went over the embankment into the river," is the account of the train wreck at Baden given by Gregg D. McBride, Mulberry street, Bridgewater, the man who spread the alarm last evening.

"There were no screams until the car struck the water and baggage, seats and passengers were thrown into a jumbled heap. I was tossed to the other side of the car and found myself in water waist-deep as the coach settled."

Mr. McBride was enroute to work in Pittsburgh where he is employed as a baggage-handler in the Union Depot of the Pennsylvania Railroad.

He stated he was riding in the second from last seat when the wreck occurred. The other end of the coach was deeply submerged in the Ohio river.

Following is Mr. McBride's account of the aftermath of the wreck:

"I was the first person out of the car and the first thought I had was of No. 474, "The Buckeye Limited" due along the same track in six minutes.

"I climbed back up the bank to the tracks and went to the rear of the train where the last car was near the tracks. A flagman came to the coach and I asked him for two fusees.

GIVES ALARM

"He gave me two and I told him I was going back to stop the other train and told him to follow me. After walking a way in my drenched clothes, I noticed two houses on a small hill near the tracks.

"At the first house I asked if there was a telephone and a woman there told me no but there was one next door. I went there and explained what had happened and told the woman answering the door to call Rochester and Sewickley hospitals for all available ambulances.

"I went back to the tracks and started to walk westward (toward Baden) and flagged down No. 474 with a fusee when it come along. The train stopped about three-quarters of a mile from the scene of the wreck.

"I told the engineer and conductor of the accident and asked them to rush all possible help to the wreck.

TAKEN TO HOSPITAL

"I walked on to the Baden signal tower and told the towerman there of the wreck. Another towerman there went home, got his car and took me to Rochester hospital."

The Bridgewater man suffered a gash on the head and received severe bruises about both legs. Apparently he is suffering no ill ef-

(Continued on Page Two)

Statement On Wreck Issued By Railroad Officials Here Today

Spikes Removed From Both Sides On Outer Rail; Splicer Plates Unbolted

Emphasizing they believed the tragic train wreck at Baden Sunday evening was caused by sabotage, officials of the Pennsylvania Railroad today issued the following statement:

"That the train was wrecked deliberately was established upon inspection of the track," the statement said. "All spikes on both sides had been pulled from the outer rail, next to the river. "One end of the rail, the end facing the oncoming locomotive, was moved in 22 inches. The bolts had been removed from the splice-bars which spliced this section of rail to the adjoining rails.

"That the derailment was the result of deliberate action was further indicated by the fact that the end of the section of rail involved had been moved only 22 inches from its normal position, or the length of the bond wire, which connects the rail sections and carries the electric current operating the signals.

"The bond wire itself was not disturbed, and the railroad signal system was unaffected. The fact that the bond wire was undisturbed definitely indicates that it was intended that the train should get a clear signal and run into the re-

(Continued on Page Two)

Rochester Home Is Damaged By Fire

Damage estimated by firemen at about $600 resulted from fire at the home of Dr. and Mrs. S. H. Peirsol, 330 Adams street, Rochester, at 4:10 o'clock Saturday afternoon. The fire, reportedly caused by a defective flue, started in the top of a clothes closet next to a chimney on the second floor.

The flames burned through the top of the closet and for a short distance under the roof of the dwelling. Little damage was done by water. Furniture was removed from the room and the hardwood floor prevented the water from a booster tank used by the Rochester Volunteer Fire Department from doing any damage on the first floor of the home. Damage is covered by insurance.

Woman Overcome By Gas In Home

Miss Emma Mulheim, well-known resident of Bridgewater, was overcome by gas in the bathroom of her apartment on the second floor of the Mulheim building in Bridge street this morning and was revived by a Duquesne Light Company first-aid crew.

Miss Mulheim was found lying unconscious on the floor of the bathroom shortly before nine o'clock by Miss Nora Baker, Fallston, owner of the wallpaper store on the first floor. The aged woman apparently had been overcome while endeavoring to light a small gas stove.

Miss Baker summoned Officer King Gallagher of the Bridgewater police and physicians and members of the light company crew worked until 10:30 before Miss Mulheim was finally revived. Physicians later indicated that Miss Mulheim had suffered a stroke while in the act of lighting the gas stove.

Big Housing Project Planned In District

Federal and local officials moved today to speed action on plans for gigantic defense housing project involving the construction of some 10,000 homes for industrial workers in the Pittsburgh district. The project would cost $30,000,000.

Armed with detailed figures on defense housing needs, B. Frank Bennett, regional defense housing co-ordinator, will confer with Federal officials in Washington today, returning to Pittsburgh on Wednesday to complete plans for the housing program.

A four-day survey of Pittsburgh and other industrial towns indicated a need of between 15,000 and 18,000 houses for defense workers.

Death Coach In River After Tragic Wreck

TIMES Photos by Russell D. Porter

Overturned on its side in several feet of water, the first passenger coach of the Cleveland-Pittsburgh passenger train wrecked Sunday evening at Baden is shown above in the Ohio river.

Policemen, firemen, railroad employes and other rescue workers are standing on and around the wrecked coach, from which the bodies of all the dead except the engineer were taken.

Snapped during the raging snow-storm, the upper side of the coach is covered with snow, oil from a broken river pipe-line and river mud.

Call Extended To Pittsburgher By Rochester Church

Grace Lutheran Church Congregation Votes Unanimously To Call Minister

The congregation of Grace Lutheran church, Rochester, at a special congregational meeting Sunday morning, voted unanimously to extend a call to Rev. Elmer A. Ortner, now pastor of Christ Lutheran church, East End, Pittsburgh, to become pastor of Grace church.

At the invitation of the Church Council, Rev. Ortner occupied the pulpit of the Rochester church Sunday, March 9, morning and evening. The Church Council at a special meeting Wednesday evening, March 12, voted unanimously to recommend Rev. Ortner to the congregation for election as pastor at the congressional meeting held Sunday. Rev. Ortner also was recommended by the Synodical President, Rev. H. Reed Shepfer, Edgewood, former pastor of Grace church, and by Rev. O. W. Carlson, Butler, president of the West Conference of the Pittsburgh Synod.

Attorney George A. Baldwin, Sr., vice president of the Church Council, presided at the congregational meeting, which followed immediately at the close of the church service. George H. Davis, secretary

(Continued on Page Two)

Fire Causes Damage At Home In Monaca

Fire at the Robert Werner homestead, 816 Washington avenue, Monaca, occupied by Mrs. Clara Hoffman and son, Werner, at 9:50 o'clock Saturday evening, caused damage estimated by firemen at about $1,200. Monaca Volunteer Fire Department prevented a greater loss.

The fire started in the cellar and reportedly was caused by a short circuit electric wire. The flames burned a hole about six by eight feet through the floor to the dining room, where the heavy floor rug checked the fire. However, the heat was so intense that the woodwork and furnishings throughout the home were badly blistered.

The firemen played water from two lines of hose on the flames, which were confined to the living room and cellar. No damage resulted on the second floor.

Lost and Found

EERIE SCENE AS WORKMEN CLEARED DEBRIS OF WRECK

Snow, driven by a high wind, swirled along the railroad tracks and over the nearby river. From across the broad Ohio, the belching fire of a Bessemer converter and the flame from a waste gas exhaust at the Aliquippa Works of the Jones and Laughlin Steel Corporation cast an eerie glow.

Flickering torches, bobbing lanterns and winking flashlights partially illuminated the Pennsylvania right-of-way at Baden, where the five cars, the locomotive and tender of the wrecked Cleveland - Pittsburgh passenger train lay scattered along the river bank and in the cold black water of the silent Ohio.

Here and there along the railroad were wood fires lighted by railroad workers and spectators to ward off the sub-freezing temperature.

Policemen were everywhere—county detectives, state troopers from Beaver, New Castle and Perrysville, officers from all nearby towns and railroad police. Firemen, wearing slickers and safety helmets, quietly searched through the overturned coaches for bodies.

OFFICIALS ON SCENE

Standing around a roaring fire and partially sheltered by a canvas tarpaulin erected as a windbreak, railroad officials directed train operations over emergency telephone lines. Others supervised the work of wrecking crews and work gangs.

Steam hissed from the two wrecking cranes—one from Conway Yard and one from Scully Yard. Occasionally a wreck crew foreman shouted an order to the craneman or other workers hooking cables on an overturned car or removing the torn-up rails and crossties.

Wrecking crews and labor gangs alike worked swiftly and surely in the glare of sputtering torches, pausing only long enough to step back to allow stretcher bearers to pass carrying blanket-covered figures. His weather - beaten face standing out in bold relief in the light from a torch, one laborer quickly touched his cap and made the sign of the cross as a body was carried past him.

Occasionally a police whistle shrilled to warn the workmen and curious spectators as a train approached, its headlight knifing through the blizzard.

OIL LINE BROKEN

Over everything hung the stench of crude oil which had spread over the river and around the wrecked coaches after a Southern Pipeline

(Continued on Page Three)

HIGHLIGHTS OF WORST TRAIN WRECK IN COUNTY'S HISTORY

The heroism of one passenger on the ill-fated Cleveland-Pittsburgh train was revealed today. Frank Bisnak, Pittsburgh, received a fractured leg in the wreck but managed to make his way to the river bank from the partially submerged coach in which he was riding. He dived back into the icy waters to bring an unidentified girl ashore and then dived back to bring out his five-year-old son "Jimmy." The latter suffered a fracture of the skull in the wreck.

Mrs. Elizabeth McDonald, 42, Altoona, mother of the nine-month-old baby, Donald Raymond McDonald, who was killed in the accident, is in a critical condition, and has been placed in an oygen tent at Rochester hospital. She continually called for her baby and later told nurses she was sure he was dead as she had seen him thrown out of the window, but was unable to reach him. However, her condition would not permit her being told of her little son's death. The child was dead on admission to the hospital. He had been in the water and it is believed that he had [illegible] as he had [illegible] cars. An aunt from Niles, O., early this morning identified the body. It was at first believed to have been the child of another woman at the hospital.

William W. Wallace, 350 Iroquois place, Beaver, one of the victims, is superintendent of the Treadwell Engineering Company, Midland. He was able to make his way from the wrecked train to the highway, where he was picked up by a young couple in a car and driven to his home. He was treated by a physician for severe bruises about his head and body. Mr. Wallace was en route to New York.

A number of youths went to Rochester hospital last night to learn what they could of the wreck and remained to aid in the treatment of the victims, Miss Diana Milligan, superintendent of nurses, stated today. Miss Milligan reported a number of neighborhood youths filled hot-water bottles, carried mattresses and did other odd jobs to aid the hospital staff.

Rev. Father Agatho Briegal of St. Cecilia's Roman Catholic church was in Rochester hospital during the night ready to lend any spiritual

(Continued on Page Two)

List Of Train Wreck Dead, Injured

Folowing is a list, subject to corrections, of the four known dead and 113 injured in the Baden train wreck. Seventy-two were still in hospitals and at the Penn-Beaver Hotel, Rochester, at noon today and 41 others had been treated at hospitals and were sent home.

The dead:

Albert Rhinehart Wiegal, 57, 2357 Shunk street, Alliance, O., engineer; crushed; removed to Batcheler Funeral Home, Rochester, pending arrival of relatives.

Harry C. Kennedy, 35, 4404 Highridge street, Pittsburgh, train clerk, body and head crushed; removed to Batcheler Funeral Home, Rochester, pending arrival of relatives at noon today.

Donald Raymond McDonald, nine-months-old son of Mrs. Elizabeth McDonald, 321 First avenue, Lakemont, Altoona; body removed to Hartzel Funeral Home, Rochester.

An unidentified woman, believed to be an Italian, 38-40 years of age; five feet or five feet, two inches in height; 125-135 pounds; black hair; wearing a wedding ring and engagement ring; clad in a blue polka-dot dress which buttoned down front with dark blue buttons.

Injured at Rochester hospital—

Jacob Adler, 54, 300 McKee Place, Oakland, Pittsburgh; head and leg injuries; condition serious.

Frank Bisnak, 32, 906 Fifty-sixth street, Pittsburgh; head and leg injuries; and son, James Bisnak, 906 Fifty-sixth street, Pittsburgh, possible fracture of skull; condition serious, but slightly improved today.

John L. Hoffman, 48, 1230 E. 101st Street, Cleveland, O.; severe hip fracture; condition serious.

Mrs. Elizabeth McDonald, 42, 321 First avenue, Lakemont, Altoona; lacerated face and arm, suffering from exposure; condition poor.

Mrs. Philomena Sylvester, 38, 1612 Spring Way, Pittsburgh; possible fracture of leg.

Mrs. Hilda Rambo, 44, 422 Taylor avenue, Pittsburgh; compound fracture of left leg and simple fracture of right leg; condition poor.

Gregg D. McBride, 1212 Mulberry street, Bridgewater; head lacerations and bruises about legs; treated at hospital and removed to home.

Wasyl Shabatura, 57, 364 Becks Run road, Carrick; both legs badly injured; condition poor.

Mrs. Mary Lipella, 50, 2304 Penn avenue, Pittsburgh; chest injuries.

Mrs. Thomas Henry, 54, 940 Or-

(Continued on Page Two)

Rochester Man Injured When Hit by Automobile

Emmett Reader, Rochester, was injured when struck by a car reportedly driven by Ray Stobert, Vanport, at 11:30 o'clock Saturday night in lower Brighton avenue, Rochester and was taken to Rochester hospital.

RAIL REMOVED, SPIKES PULLED, RAILROAD SAYS

Federal Bureau of Investigation agents today began an investigation of the tragic Pennsylvania Railroad train wreck Sunday evening at Baden in which at least four persons are known dead, and 113 injured, several seriously.

Railroad officials charged that the crash was "definitely" due to sabotage.

The Federal Bureau of Investigation at Washington today said that it has assigned agents to investigate the wreck of a Pennsylvania Railroad passenger train at Baden, Pa.

A spokesman said that the FBI will make a preliminary investigation to determine whether sabotage was the cause of the wreck.

The Interstate Commerce Commission assigned four inspectors to the case. Director of Safety Shirley N. Mills said H. E. Nason, E. C. Horning, W. R. Preese and Gordon Morris will conduct that agency's inquiry.

Railroad officials charged that after the wreck they found a 39-foot section of the rail on the river side of the track—undamaged and not twisted like other sections of the rail—moved 22 inches to the left towards the other rail.

In addition, they said, spikes had been pulled from both sides of several "double-shoulder" tie plates and "splice bars" had been removed from the ends of the dislodged rail, on which the signal wire had been left intact.

At the edge of the river, where railroad officials believe they were thrown in an attempt to sink them in the nearby Ohio river, were found a claw-bar and the splice-plates from one end of the rail. The splice plates from the other end were found on the steep embankment several feet below the roadbed, half-buried in mud and snow.

Bolts which allegedly were removed from the splice plates had not been found this morning, it was said.

Speeding through the night in a driving blizzard, the train, No. 316 enroute from Cleveland to Pittsburgh, left the rails at the mouth of Logan hollow, near Logan Stop at Baden, about 9:05 o'clock.

Tearing up rails and ties for 200 yards, the locomotive and tender turned over on their sides at the edge of the 50-foot river bank, the baggage car plunged over and came to rest upright in the river, the first passenger coach rolled over and stopped on its side in the water, the second passenger coach stopped at the edge of the river, the third passenger coach came to rest on its side in the water and the fourth coach—a sleeping car—hung precariously over the river bank.

All of the dead except the engineer were removed from the first passenger coach. The body of Donald Raymond McDonald, nine-months-old, Altoona, was the first taken out.

Buried under five feet of coal, the body of A. R. Wiegal, 57, Alliance, O., veteran engineer, was removed from the overturned locomotive at 10:45 o'clock.

The body of the unidentified woman, believed to be Mrs. Rose Jagielski, Pittsburgh, was taken from the coach at 10:55 o'clock, while the coach still lay in the water.

The body of Harry C. Kennedy, Pittsburgh, railroad clerk, was removed at 2:20 o'clock this morning, after a wrecking crane had pulled the coach partially up on the bank out of the river. Lights in the coach, powered by batteries, were still burning when the body was taken out.

Immediately after the wreck a general call was sent out for all available doctors and ambulances in the Valley. While they were speeding through the storm to the scene, Train No. 474, enroute from Erie to Pittsburgh and running six minutes behind the wrecked train, was halted and most of the injured were placed aboard it and taken to Pittsburgh, where ambulances, doctors and nurses were waiting when it arrived.

The Cleveland-Pittsburgh train had stopped at New Castle and Rochester and was scheduled to stop at Sewickley. It was due at Rochester at 8:56 o'clock and at Baden at 9:02 o'clock. The train left Cleveland at 6:15 o'clock and was due in Pittsburgh at 9:30 o'clock.

At the spot where the wreck occurred, the four tracks of the railroad are straight and level on the roadbed fifty feet above the river. No. 1 track, on which the train was running, is only a few feet from the edge of the river bank.

The Pennsylvania Public Utility Commission today sent Guy R. Johnson, head of its accident section, to the scene of the wreck to make an investigation. Commission Chairman John Siggins, Jr., ordered Johnson to make a thorough probe.

Railroad officials said that someone familiar with the block signal system had loosened the rails without breaking the electric signal circuit, and that the wreckers apparently had the crowded, 12-car [illegible] Limited as their target. The limited, a [illegible], had passed the scene 15 minutes ahead of the wrecked train.

(Continued on Page Two)

Flu Bars Viking Tilt; Faculty To Play

.. A Night In The Alleys ..

★ ★ ★ ★

Pretty Good Form

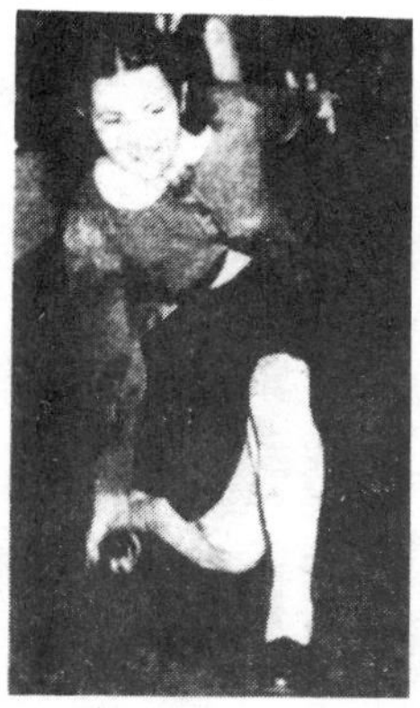

LILLIAN SHAFFALO

★ ★ ★ ★

—PHOTOS BY TONY CRISI

★ ★ ★ ★

Checking Up On Kapolka—

Johnny Kapolka, knight of the mortar and pestal who mixed medications in a local drug store until his transfer to Uniontown last week, crayons the strikes and spares during the P. M. Company employes' night at the bowling alleys.

First row, from left, Virginia Joeph, Annie Mae Davis, Frances Matajasic, Helen Powers, Kapolka, and Hen Schultheis.

Second row, Dorothy Miller, Virginia Drake, Madge Sicklesmith, Justine Dobish, Jim Laing, Lillian Shaffalo, Sharp Bailey, Roberta Hill.

Bowling has grown more popular his year with Aliquippa indoor sports enthusiasts both as a social and athletic pastime, managers of ocal alleys report.

Shown here are some of the bowlers in action. Miss Shaffalo is among the best of the femme pintopplers, but then she springs from a pin-wise family, her brother Bill ranking among the county's best.

Bustin' To Bust 'Em

JUSTINE DOBISH

The Ballet Pose

HELEN SCHULTHEIS

Determination

HELEN POWERS

Aliquippa Sports Gazette

TUESDAY, JANUARY 14, 1941 ★ ★ ★ PAGE FIVE

Team Fails To Appear So Clippers Go Idle; Play St. Ann's Next

The West Aliquippa Clippers were forced to remain idle for a few more evenings when Ambridge failed to appear for their scheduled match last night at the Franklin Junior High school.

The Clips are slated to make their next appearance Thursday evening at St. Joseph's Lyceum with the St. Ann's basketeers of Homestead as their opponent.

Oros' Goal Cinches Triumph For Jednotas

J. Oros' field goal in the last minute of play turned the victory tide in favor of the Jednotas quint of West Aliquippa, who beat the Warriors, 29-27, yesterday at St. Joseph's Lyceum floor. The losers threatened to overtake the Jednotas in the final period after trailing throughout the contest.

Herkys Drop Jr. Choir

The Herky's of Ambridge overpowered the St. Joseph's Choir quint of West Aliquippa, 39-27, last night at St. Joseph's Lyceum floor with Garibo and Harzynka leading the victors and Voynik and Oros pacing the losers.

Want Ads Have Special Appeal!

High School Basketball

GAMES TODAY

Non-League

Beaver Falls at Shady Side Academy

Farrell at New Brighton

Ellwood City at Duquesne

Section 10

Hopewell at Neville

Section 11

Mars at Beaver

Rochester at Midland

Evans City at Monaca

Freedom at Zelienople

Junior High

Ambridge at Midland

Aliquippa at Freedom

TOMORROW

(Postponed)

Non-League

Hopewell Twp. at St. Veronica

FRIDAY

Midland at Freedom

Rochester at Evans City

Monaca at Beaver

Zelienople at Mars

(Section III)

New Brighton at Aliquippa

Ellwood at Ambridge

New Castle at Beaver Falls

WARC BASKETBALL LEAGUE STANDINGS

JUNIOR LEAGUE

Team	WON	LOST	PCT.
Tigers	8	0	1.000
Redwings	5	2	.714
Brewery Aces	2	5	.286
Washington Aces	0	8	.000

No games today.

Tomorrow

Redwings vs. Tigers, 6 p. m.

P.C.'ERS MEET MONACA GRADS IN PRELIMINARY

Oilers Host Jr. Quips, Township Cancels Week's Tilts

Because even a "Yeah, team," whispered by the smaller-lunged feminine fan can scatter influenza bacteria, Hopewell high school officials today decided to avoid any possibility of spreading the disease which caused closing of township schools and called off tonight's scheduled Section 10, WPIAL encounter at Neville township high.

But Aliquippa high school's faculty cagers and the borough's semipro P. C. basketeers will go on with their scheduled games against the combined faculties of Harmony and Darlington townships and the Monaca Alumni.

The P. C.'ers, beaten once in eight starts, will play Monaca in the preliminary to the faculty tilt starting at 7:15 p. m. Both games are for the benefit of the Quippian, high school year book.

Aliquippa's Junior high quint, showing a victory and a defeat so far in Junior WPIAL competition, goes to Freedom while Ambridge battles at Midland in another Junior loop fray.

With the 35 per cent of the student body flu aching, Hopewell officials cancelled the week's athletic program of basketball games with Neville, St. Veronica and Robinson high schools.

In Section 11 (Class B) contests, Monaca plays host to Evans City, both teams undefeated in two starts. Rochester goes to Midland, Mars plays at Beaver and Zelienople hosts Freedom.

FRANKLIN INTRAMURAL BASKETBALL

Buzzards 26, Silver Streaks 19

Steelers 2, Trisigs, 0 (Forft)

Harriers 2, Hollywood 0 (Forft)

Five Stars 20, Redskins 19.

TIGERS ANNEX WARC 1ST HALF COURT HONORS

The Tigers carried off first half honors in the W. A. R. C. Junior basketball league by administering a 50-26, setback to the Washington Aces, last evening at the West Aliquippa Recreational Center.

With only one game to play, the champions hold a two and one-half game lead over their nearest opponent, the Redwings.

The jubilant victors took the offensive from the word go and salted away the bacon before the third period was very old. They then proceeded to coast in to an easy win while allowing their outclassed adversary to outscore them in the final stanza.

John Maly and John Rovnak, ace shot-makers of the victors, again sparked their club's attack, chalking up 14 and 12 points respectively, with Manager George Glomb of the Aces accounting for 8 of his five's tallies.

Tigers			
J. Rovnack, f	6	0	12
J. Maly, f	7	0	14
M. Petrick, c	3	1	7
M. Ondovchik, g	5	0	10
M. Modrak, g	3	1	7
Totals	24	2	50
Washington Aces			
F. Ciccarelli, f	3	0	6
N. Perza, f	3	0	6
G. Glomb, c	4	0	8
A. Dzugan, g	0	0	0
J. Martin, g	3	0	6
R. Kosanovich, g	0	0	0
Totals	13	0	26

Dodson Is Oakland Open Golf Champion

OAKLAND, Cal. (INS) — The proud record of Leonard Dodson, the Ozark's contribution to professional golfing, who never lost a playoff match, went untarnished today as the Springfield, Mo., player pocketed first prize money of $1,200 in the $5,000 Oakland Open Championship.

Dodson's 71 in a drenching rain at Sequoyah country club proved three strokes better than the score posted by little Ben Hogan of White Plains, N. Y. who took a 74 and five strokes better than E. J. "Dutch" Harrison's 76.

MACK RE-ELECTED

PHILADELPHIA. — (INS) — For the fifth consecutive year, Connie Mack was re-elected president-manager of the Philadelphia Athletics at the annual stockholders meeting, it was announced today.

Weather Forecast

Cloudy tonight and Thursday, with light showers tonight and Thursday morning; slightly cooler Thursday.

THE DAILY TIMES

ROCHESTER - BEAVER - MONACA

FREEDOM—BRIDGEWATER—CONWAY—VANPORT—MIDLAND

Local History

The Beaver County Institute was founded in New Brighton in 1887 "to promote science, literature and natural history."

ESTABLISHED APRIL 2, 1874 | BEAVER AND ROCHESTER, PA., WEDNESDAY, APRIL 23, 1941 | BY CARRIER 15 CENTS A WEEK—3 CENTS PER COPY

COUNTY TO WELCOME CURTISS-WRIGHT

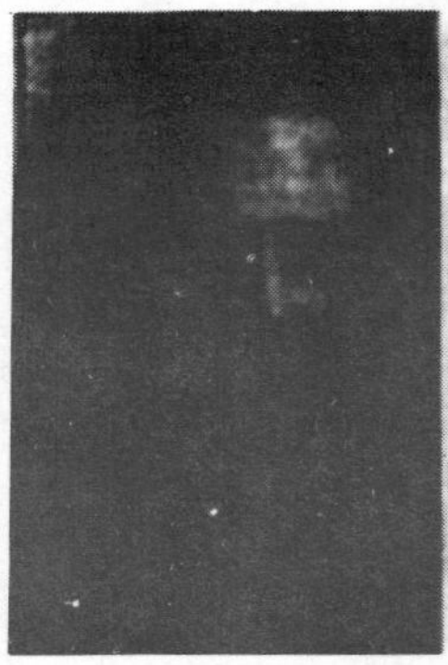

ROBERT L. EARLE
Vice President Curtiss-Wright

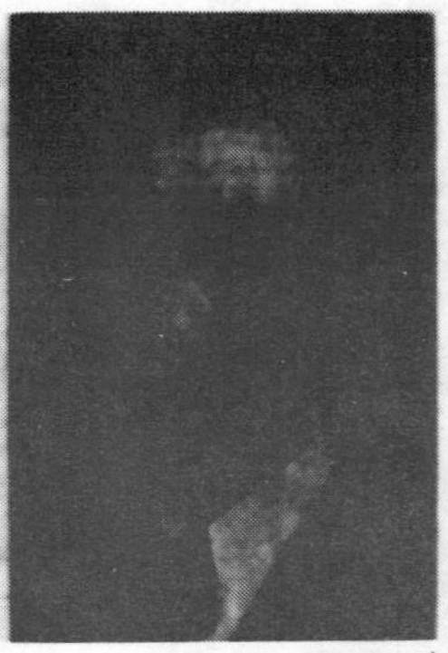

J. H. McKEE
Will Head New Plant

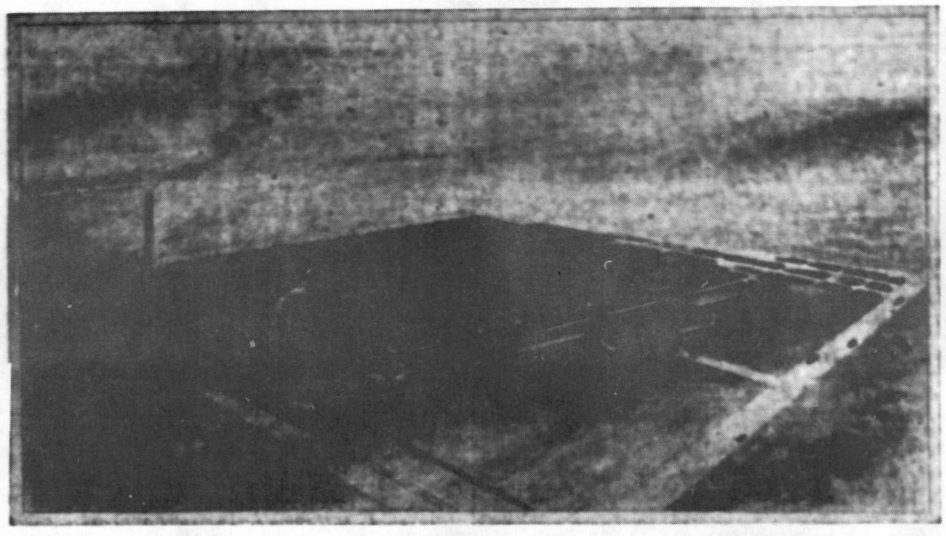

Pictured above is an architect's sketch of the new $5,221,000 Curtiss-Wright Corporation propeller plant to be erected in Borough Township, for which ground will be formally broken Thursday afternoon at the plant site near the Tuscarawas road, adjoining Beaver.

The plant will have approximately 415,000 square feet of floor space and will employ between 3,500 and 4,000 men.

In the accompanying photos are Robert L. Earle, general manager of the Curtiss-Wright Corporation, Propeller Division, Caldwell, N. J., and a director and vice-president of the corporation; J. H. McKee, manager of the company's Neville Island plant, who will be general manager of the new plant; Frank R. Phillips, president of the Duquesne Light Co. and the Philadelphia Company, and Karl Knapp, all of whom will speak at the testimonial banquet for Curtiss-Wright officials to be served Thursday evening in the Beaver United Presbyterian church.

FRANK R. PHILLIPS
Pres. Duquesne Lght Company

KARL M. KNAPP
Will Be Toastmaster

GROUND-BREAKING, BANQUET WILL BE HELD TOMORROW

All Beaver County will unite on Thursday to welcome the Curtiss-Wright Corporation to the Valley as ground is formally broken for the new $5,221,000 propeller plant to be erected by the company near the Tuscarawas road in Borough Township, adjoining Beaver.

The ground-breaking ceremony will mark the start of actual construction on the first large industrial plant ever established in the Beaver-Vanport area, and the first new plant to be built in Beaver County under the National Defense program.

The plant is expected to be placed in operation early next Fall and will employ between 3,500 and 4,000 persons.

Ever since the date for the actual start of work was fixed, committees have been working with officials of the Curtiss-Wright Corporation to arrange all details of the program that will cover the day's events.

It was not until Tuesday night that hope was finally abandoned to obtain the presence of Lowell Thomas, radio news commentator, who could not change his arrangements and be in Beaver for his broadcast. Mr. Thomas has promised, however, to participate in the dedication ceremonies.

A large number of Army and Navy men will fly from Washington tomorrow in government planes, but the time of their arrival had not been determined at noon today. Several private cars, bearing notable guests, will reach Pittsburgh tomorrow morning and the Curtiss-Wright Corporation will entertain at a luncheon at the Duquesne Club before the trip to Beaver. All reservations have been made for the banquet, to be held at six o'clock, insuring a capacity crowd of 400.

PARKING ARRANGED

Special details of the Pennsylvania Motor Police will escort the visitors from Pittsburgh to Beaver. Motor traffic will be blocked at Fourth and Buffalo streets, Beaver, to all except official cars at three o'clock tomorrow. A special parking space has been arranged for these machines.

Public parking will be available in nearby recreation park and adjacent streets. Special police will handle the parking.

Following the ground-breaking exercises there will be an aerial circus, with a daring parachute jump to the new plant site by Mal Henry of the Conway airport. The demonstration and air show will bring together planes from several states.

BUSINESS LEADERS COMING

Nearly all of the transportation, utility and manufacturing interests of the Pittsburgh district will be represented at the ceremonies.

The Pennsylvania Railroad will be represented by D. K. Chase, general superintendent; F. R. Rex, superintendent, Easter Division; R. H. Miller, general freight agent; E. W. Saville, division freight agent; E. J. Isarel, Jr., industrial agent, and J. B. Slemmons, industrial representative.

The Pittsburgh and Lake Erie Railroad will be represented by F. T. Ketterer, superintendent; O. S. Braden, assistant to the general

(Continued on Page Fifteen)

Beaver Home Scene Of Minor Fire Today

The Beaver Fire Department was called shortly before four o'clock this morning to extinguish a fire in the Bartholomew home, Beaver street, Beaver. A fire in a fireplace is believed to have spread to the floor and was burning beneath the tile of the fireplace, firemen reported. Damage was reported slight.

The department was called at five o'clock Tuesday afternoon to Center Way, where a brush fire was threatening a house, but the fire was out when firemen arrived.

Alternative Means Of Taxation Being Considered Today

More Luxury Taxes Suggested; Secrecy Surrounds Plan Under Consideration

By the United Press

WASHINGTON, April 23 — The House ways and means committee, faced with treasury proposals for drastic income taxes on the little taxpayer, today studied "alternative" suggestions for more luxury taxes.

The committee still was bound to official secrecy about the plan that reportedly would increase income taxes in the lower brackets from 300 to 600 per cent through a graduated surtax to start at 11 per cent on the first dollar of taxable income.

The secrecy will be lifted tomorrow, however, when Secretary of the Treasury Henry Morgenthau, Jr., will testify at the first public hearing on the new tax program.

Several members of the ways

(Continued on Page Ten)

Freedom Education Board Sets Budget

Freedom Board of Education adopted the 1941-42 budget, totaling $79,958, at a special meeting in the high school building Tuesday evening. The total of the budget exceeds the past year's amount by about $700.

Approval was given the Supply Committee on orders for janitor and school supplies, the majority of bids being given to the lowest bidders, except in cases where the quality was in question.

All members of the board were present. The president, Dr. John H. Boal, presided.

Legislature Seeking Halt In Relief Job Cuts In State May 6

Bill Providing For More Relief Funds Goes To Senate For Approval

By the United Press

HARRISBURG, April 23. — The Legislature seriously considered today urgent bi-partisan requests for efforts to prevent "wholesale dismissal" of WPA workers in Pennsylvania as Democratic tax abatement and road subsidy measures passed finally and exchanged House positions.

Resolutions by Reps. Robert J. Cordier, R., Lackawanna, and James J. McLane and Joseph C. Gallagher, Luzerne Democrats, urged both houses to memorialize Congress immediately to halt the relief job cuts after Col. Philip Mathews, State WPA Administrator, said 25,000 workers must be dropped by May 6.

At the same time, the administration's deficiency appropriation bills providing an additional $6,300,000 for relief until end of May were placed in position for final passage in the Senate next Monday. Given House approval, the bills were speeded through the upper cham-

(Continued on Page Ten)

Beaver Falls Housing Awards To Be Made

Awarding of contracts for two Beaver Falls Defense Housing projects will be made Saturday, April 26, according to Beaver County Housing Authority officials. These projects include the Harmony dwellings of 50 units, to be located near Tenth street, and the Morado dwellings of 142 units, in College Hill.

Bids will be received on the Aliquippa Defense Housing project Saturday, May 3, with contracts to be awarded Monday, May 5.

Beaver Stores Will Close For Ceremony

Beaver merchants and businessmen have agreed to close their places of business at three o'clock Thursday afternoon to permit participation in the ground-breaking ceremony to be held at four o'clock, marking the inauguration of construction of the propeller plant to be erected in Borough Township by the Curtiss - Wright Corporation. The announcement was made today by J. T. Anderson, president of the Beaver Businessman's Association.

GROUND-BREAKING PROCLAMATION ISSUED BY BURGESS OF BEAVER

Burgess D. A. Moore of Beaver has issued the following proclamation in connection with the ground-breaking exercises to be held Thursday to mark the start of operations on the new $5,221,000 plant of the Curtiss - Wright Corporation in adjacent Borough Township:

"Whereas, the Citizens' Welcoming Committee of Beaver and Vanport has arranged an elaborate program to indicate to the officials of the Curtiss-Wright Corporation a spirit of genuine co-operation in order that this great defense industry may be built and placed in operation as rapidly as possible and

"Whereas Beaver is to be honored Thursday by the presence of a large number of representatives of the National and State governments, including Gov. Arthur H. James of the Commonwealth of Pennsylvania, and

"Whereas the town of Beaver appears in the best of Nature's garb at this glorious spring season, citizens of our town are asked to contribute to this occasion by showing a spirit of welcome and hospitality to representatives of the Propeller Division of the Curtiss - Wright Corporation, their guests and visiting dignitaries.

"All citizens are urged to display the American flag at their homes and places of business throughout the day and merchants and other business houses are requested to close their establishments during the period from three until five o'clock, to permit the full participation of everyone in the ground breaking ceremonies. Citizens of Beaver are requested to aid in the parking of cars of visitors by not using their own machines during this period."

—D. A. Moore, Burgess, Borough of Beaver.

NEW PLANT TO BE PLACED IN OPERATION NEXT SEPTEMBER

Under present plans the new $5,221,000 plant to be erected in Borough Township by the Propeller Division of the Curtiss-Wright Corporation will be placed in operation next September, according to company officials.

With Gov. Arthur H. James and other high officials of the state and Federal governments, industrial leaders and other prominent persons in attendance, ground for the new plant will be formally broken Thursday afternoon near the Tuscarawas road, adjoining Beaver.

The Hughes-Foulkrod Company of Pittsburgh and Philadelphia has been awarded the general contract for construction of the plant, while the fabrication of steel for the structure already is well underway at the plant of the American Bridge Company in Ambridge.

The boiler contract went to the Combustion Engineering Company

(Continued on Page Ten)

WELCOME CURTISS-WRIGHT

Beaver County will join tomorrow in extending a warm, friendly, and whole-hearted welcome to the Curtiss-Wright Corporation. The occasion will be the ground-breaking for the new $5,221,000 propeller plant to be erected by the company in Borough Township, adjoining Beaver.

THE TIMES joins with all the people of the county in welcoming the company and its personnel, with the sincere wish that the plant may meet with all possible success, and that its employes enjoy life and success to the full here in the Beaver Valley.

The plant is not a Borough Township industry only; nor is it a Beaver industry only. It is a welcome addition to the growing industrial life of the entire county. Not only Borough Township and Beaver, but the entire Valley and county will benefit from the big plant, which is expected to employ between 3,000 and 4,000 persons.

Present employes of the company will locate in all sections of the Valley, and new employes will come from all communities in the district. The company's huge payroll will affect the whole Valley as it increases purchasing power, stimulates trade, and encourages building of new homes, business buildings and improvements.

For a hundred years and more Beaver Valley has been known far and wide as an outstanding industrial region. A century ago a great variety of small industries—boatyards, tanneries, and numerous other small factories—were in operation here.

As the demand for increased production in volume and variety steadily mounted, these small industrial plants were replaced by ever-larger factories which produced an innumerable variety of products in great volume.

So, with Beaver County's fine industrial and labor record, with the strategic location of the county in relation to railroads and the Ohio and Beaver rivers, with its proximity to the vast Pittsburgh industrial region, and its many other natural advantages, it is easy to believe that officials of the Curtiss-Wright Corporation have made a very wise choice in selecting the site for the new propeller plant.

Beaver County people are justly proud of our beautiful and modern homes, our fine stores, our many industrial plants, our streets and parks, our churches and schools, our rolling hills and fertile valleys, our farms and woodlands, our rivers and streams.

To all of these, we welcome the Curtiss-Wright Corporation, its officials, and its employes. And again we say:

May the company meet with every success, and its personnel enjoy life and success to the full here in our busy, bustling, friendly and beautiful Beaver Valley.

Duquesne Light Co. President To Speak At Beaver Banquet

Philadelphia Company Head, Other Officials to Attend Curtiss-Wright Affair

President Frank R. Phillips of the Philadelphia Company and subsidiary companies, including the Duquesne Light Company, which will supply all electrical power for the new Borough Township plant of the Curtiss-Wright Corporation, Propeller Division, will be one of the speakers at the ground-breaking banquet in Beaver, Thursday evening.

Mr. Phillips has long been interested in obtaining new industries for the Beaver Valley and members of his staff have rendered every assistance toward the construction of new plants in this district.

The Duquesne Light Company has started the erection of a new generating station, to cost approximately eight million dollars, to be named in honor of Mr. Phillips, at the Beaver-Allegheny county line adjacent to South Heights.

VETERAN UTILITY MAN

Since 1909 Mr. Phillips has been engaged in the utility business in Pittsburgh and is one of the best-known men in this field in the United States. He has served as President of the Philadelphia Com-

(Continued on Page Ten)

New Draft Quotas Announced Today

Quotas for the seven draft boards of Beaver County for the May 12-20 contingent have been released in Harrisburg.

The local quotas are: Draft Board No. 1, eleven; No. 2, eight; No. 3, eight; No. 4, nine; No. 5, nine; No. 6, ten, and No. 7, four. Pennsylvania is to supply 4,062 men in the draft call for May 12-20.

Program For Ground-Breaking

Following is the official program for the ground-breaking ceremony Thursday for the new Curtiss-Wright Corporation propeller plant to be erected in Borough Township, adjoining Beaver:

- 12:30—Luncheon at Pittsburgh honoring officials of the Army, Navy and Air Corps and Gov. Arthur H. James, given by officials of the Curtiss-Wright Corporation.
- 1:00—Flights of Pennsylvania-Central Air Lines rerouted to pass directly over Beaver.
- 1:30—Special motor caravan leaves Pittsburgh for Beaver with escort of Pennsylvania Motor Police.
- 2:00—Arrival of planes from various airports at Conway and Patterson Heights and start of demonstrations of Beaver and Vanport.
- 3:00—Beaver schools, business places and Court House close. Beaver high school band will leave high school building. Start of one-hour salute to Curtiss-Wright.
- 3:30—Concert on grounds by band; aerial demonstration.
- 3:45—Arrival of motor caravan from Pittsburgh.
- 4:00—Salvo of 12 bombs will mark start of ground-breaking ceremonies.
- 4:30—Salvo of 18 bombs; visiting officials and guests taken for motor tour through Beaver Valley.
- 4:45—Parachute jumping and continuation of airplane demonstration.
- 6:00—Banquet—Guild Hall, United Presbyterian church.

REVIVAL OF COOKING TO TAKE PLACE AT TIMES FREE SCHOOL

"The Revival of Cooking."

That was the subject of a leading editorial carried recently in the New York "Herald-Tribune." THE TIMES is in hearty agreement with the reminder in the opening editorial paragraph that:

"In the course of the last few years there has been a tremendous upsurge of interest in this country in the art and science of cookery."

THE TIMES confidence in that interest is finding practical expression in the modern, eagerly-awaited Cooking School, which will open its

(Continued on Page Fourteen)

ALLIED DEFENSE COLLAPSES TODAY

By the United Press

ATHENS—King George II, Greek Crown Prince, and Government flee to Crete; King says fight will go on, charges capitulation of Army of Epirus unauthorized; fate of British expeditionary force uncertain.

LONDON—End of Greek campaign believed near; Australian criticism reported over sending of BEF; Germans may be concentrating for attack on Southern Egypt; Plymouth blitzed again; reveal British raid on Bardia Saturday.

BERLIN—Germans move on Athens; Greek Arms of Epirus and Macedonia quits, conquest of Greece expected to be completed shortly; nearly 160,000 tons of shipping reported sunk in Greek harbors and waters, thousands of British troops claimed drowned.

ROME—Greek Army of Epirus and Macedonia, reported to number close to 300,000, surrendered to Italian 11th Army; British attempt to break out of Tobruk fails.

STOCKHOLM—Germans reported sending motorized troops to Northern Norway, either to repel British attack or for use in Finland against Russia.

ALGECIRAS—British strengthen Gibraltar in preparation for possible siege.

TOKYO—Press suggests adjustment of relations with United States and settlement of China "affair"

GOVERNMENT FLEES

Only a thinning British and Greek rear guard stood between Adolf Hitler's war machine and Athens today as King George II and the Greek government fled to Crete to carry on the war from that island fastness.

It seemed only a miracle could delay Germany more than a few hours in completing her conquest of the 14th nation in Europe to succumb to Nazi arms. There was no hope either in London or Athens that such a miracle would occur.

The war bulletins indicated that Thermopylae Pass — the mountain gap 85 miles north of Athens where Leonidas and 300 men fought to the death against the Persian Xerxes—had been breeched.

The Greek army of the west, trapped between German and Italian forces as it retreated out of Albania, had capitulated.

King George, the Greek Crown Prince and government had fled to Crete. The end of the war in Greece, obviously, was near.

ALLIES OUTNUMBERED

For 18 days the Greeks and an elite British expeditionary corps had stood off the pounding of the Wehrmacht. Outnumbered in manpower by odds of anything from five to ten to one and in machines by a far greater margin, the Allies had fought as stubborn a battle as was within their capability.

Collapse of the southern Serbian army, enabling the Nazis to slice through the Vardar Valley and twist down through Bitolj Pass, turned the Allied campaign into one long rear-guard action.

Today the Germans had cut through the last barrier, that of Thermopylae and there was nothing but a broad flat highway and rear guard detachments who were prepared to sell their lives as dearly as possible between the Nazi spearhead and Athens.

Today two questions were uppermost in London. How many British

(Continued on Page Ten)

Commissioners Plan Surfacing Of Rural Roads This Summer

State to Be Asked to Approve Black-topping Projects in Six Townships

Improvement of approximately five miles of county and township roads during the current year is being planned by Beaver County Commissioners, it was revealed today.

Cost of the work, which will consist of black-topping road projects that already have been completed except for bituminous surface course, is estimated to cost $28,503.

Commissioners explained, however, that the proposed projects are subject to approval of the State Highway Department. Applications for approval of the Highway Department under the County Aid law are being prepared for submission to the department.

The roads on which the county proposes to place black top surface material are located in six different townships and total 26,803 feet.

ROADS ON LIST

The various roads listed in the applications are:

North Sewickley township, road

(Continued on Page Ten)

Real Estate Board Formed In Valley

Twenty-five real estate brokers of Beaver County, at a dinner meeting Tuesday evening in the Penn-Beaver Hotel, Rochester, organized the Beaver County Board of Realtors and applied for a charter that will associate the newly-formed organization with the National Board of Realtors.

Officers elected are: President, Chester A. Lewis, Beaver Falls; secretary, Ben H. Ross, New Brighton; treasurer, Robert F. Garvin, Beaver.

Speakers were Harry [illegible], Reading, president of the Pennsylvania Board of Realtors, and [illegible] C. Fisher, Jr., Harrisburg, secretary of that board.

Boosters To Sponsor Boxing Show Here

CELTICS HUMBLE RIVAL REDS, 16-2

Board Will 'Cut' USO Branch In On Receipts

Show Marks Revival Of Borough Boxing For First Time In Years; Card Not Complete

The Boosters Club Planning Board voted last night at a meeting in the Board of Trade office to sponsor an outdoor boxing show at the high school stadium, contributing part of the gate to the United Service Organizations—a nation-wide group providing recreation for U. S. army troops.

The show will mark a revival of boxing in Aliquippa after an absence of several years as well as in Beaver Valley where the sport has declined in recent months. The board did not decide whether to sponsor a professional or amateur card.

The show will serve a patriotic cause, one member of the planning board said. In contributing to the U. S. O., the Boosters' club not only will be helping in the national defense program but will be complying with its purpose of providing recreation, he said.

He added that the U. S. O. is designed to provide recreational facilities at army camps and that Aliquippa draftees would benefit from any local contribution.

The county U. S. O. is headed by Judge Frank E. Reader. A local committee is being organized.

The club's boxing committee will investigate the possibilities of both professional and amateur bouts.

Club officials announced that the school board had granted the Boosters' request to rent the stadium for the patriotic benefit show.

The club also voted to contribute 10 per cent of the gate to the U. S. O.

Dr. J. F. Campbell of the Boosters' playground and street showers committee, reported that installation of the showers in West Aliquippa has been delayed again because of difficulty in obtaining proper devices for connecting the showers to hydrants.

The company from which the devices will be purchased required detailed specifications of the hydrants before the equipment could be prepared for local use, he said.

Dr. Campbell said he expected a report soon on the Woodlawn Water company's answer to the club's request to use hydrants in other parts of the borough for the showers. The borough owns only the hydrants in West Aliquippa.

Rudy Tatalovich of the swimming committee, reported that junior life saving classes had been started at the Plan 12 swimming pool under the direction of George Krivonak and that Senior Life saving classes open to men, women and children would be started around Aug. 1.

Miss Leotta Caldwell, chairman of women's activities, said that Mrs. Louise Carmalt would co-operate in providing swimming instruction for women and girls.

The board authorized a committee to consult the Woodlawn Land company in order to learn if the company-owned Ravine park could be obtained for development by the borough as a community park.

It was reported that the American Legion had donated a flag for the Boosters' leased Fireman's field. The board voted to write a letter of gratitude to the Legion.

The board will meet next Friday night at the board of trade office.

PANTHERS WHIP BLOCKS; CARDS BOW TO AMERCS

The Black Panthers and Americans chalked up triumphs in the West Aliquippa Mushball league yesterday at the expense of the 100 Block and the Golden Eagles. Final scores showed the Panthers winning 9-to-3 and the Amerks topping the Birds, 6-to-4.

The 100 Blockers hopped off to a three run margin in the opening frame and threatened to upset the undefeated Jungle Cats, as Twirler "Dutch" Schultz blanked the loop-leaders until the fifth. However, they could not stand prosperity and blew the chance, when they bungled in the field as the Panthers were cutting loose with their heavy artillery.

"Ibe" Pinkosky limited the losers to two hits, both by Tony Corsi, while Danny McLister with a single, a double, and a triple sparked at the plate.

In a game, that ended up being played under protest, the Amerks broke a 4-4 deadlock with a two run push in the eighth to spring a surprise on the opening half champions.

It is doubtable, though, that the protest will be upheld, as it is an argument against an umpire's decision on a base-runner. The summary:

Panthers	AB.	R.	H.	PO.	E.
B. Ross, ss	3	1	0	1	0
A. Palombo, cf	4	1	2	2	0
D. McLister, 1b	5	1	3	8	0
L. Ross, lf	5	0	1	3	0
T. DiNardo, c	5	1	3	5	0
M. Vince, lf	5	1	1	2	1
R. Recht, rf	3	1	1	2	0
A. Vargo, 3b	3	0	1	2	0
P. Matich, 2b	3	1	0	2	0
I. Pinkosky, p	3	2	2	0	0
Totals	39	9	14	27	1

100 Block	AB.	R.	H.	PO.	E.
R. Walters, 2b	2	1	0	1	1
E. Opsatnik, rs	4	1	0	1	0
W. Shaffalo, c	4	0	0	6	0
M. Zernich, cf	2	1	0	2	0
R. Zapar, 1b	3	0	0	9	1
T. Corsi, lf	3	0	2	2	1
D. Schultz, p	3	0	0	0	0
F. DiAntonio, 3b	2	0	0	2	1
A. Dzvonar, ss	3	0	0	3	1
A. Pinkosky, rf	3	0	0	1	1
Totals	29	3	2	27	6

100 Block	300	000	000—3
Black Panthers	000	023	04*—9

Home run — D. McLister. Three-base hit—T. Corsi. Two-base hit—D. McLister. Base on balls: Off—I. Pinkosky 7; Off—D. Schultz 8. Struck Out By — I. Pinkosky 2; By — D. Schultz 5. Winning pitcher—I. Pinkosky. Losing pitcher — D. Schultz. Umpire—J. Krnyevich.

Americans	AB.	R.	H.	PO.	A.	E.
J. Dzurko, c	4	0	2	3	0	0
R. Ciccone, p-3b	3	3	1	2	3	2
S. Meli, lf	2	1	0	1	1	0
A. Degovine, ss	2	0	0	1	0	0
G. Gaydos, 1b	2	0	0	7	1	0
N. Ciccone, 2b	3	0	0	3	0	0
A. Timko, 3b-p	2	0	0	2	1	1
J. Durkin, rss	2	0	0	1	0	0
P. Ciccone, cf	2	1	0	2	0	0
T. Rosati, rf	1	0	0	1	0	1
E. Klacik, rf	2	1	1	1	0	0
Totals	25	6	4	24	6	4

Eagles	AB.	R.	H.	PO.	A.	E.
R. Neish, ss	2	1	0	1	1	0
M. Neish, rf	3	1	1	2	1	0
J. Mihok, 1b	2	1	0	5	0	0
F. Cercone, 2b	2	1	2	6	2	0
E. Pager, cf	3	0	2	1	0	0
P. Sylvestri, 3b	3	0	0	3	2	0
G. Baljak, lf	3	0	1	3	0	0
A. Serjack, rss	3	0	1	0	0	0
F. Dascanio, c	3	0	0	6	0	0
A. DiAntonio, p	2	0	0	0	0	0
E. Delisio, p	1	0	0	0	0	0
Totals	27	4	7	27	6	0

Golden Eagles	000	102	010—4
Americans	000	040	02*—6

Two-base Hits — M. Neish, E. Pager. Base on Balls: Off—Ciccone 7, Off Timho 4, Off DiAntonio 5, Off Delisio 2. Struck Out By—Ciccone 2, By Timko 2, By DiAntonio 3, By Delisio 4. Winning pitcher — A. Timko. Losing pitcher—E. Delisio. Umpires—Donina, Seamen.

Rooms in Demand—Advertise Yours!

NEVER BETTER - - By Jack Sords

RED RUFFING, 37-YEAR-OLD NEW YORK YANKEE PITCHER STILL AT HIS PEAK IN EFFECTIVENESS
SORDS
MUST HAVE BEEN THE WRONG PITCH!
HE JUST MISSED A NO-HIT SHUTOUT AGAINST THE WHITE SOX RECENTLY, GIVING UP HIS FIRST HIT IN THE EIGHTH INNING

Homers Cinch Redskin 5-2 Win Over Dinovas

Homers by J. Hodanovich and Larry Zagar clinched a 5-2 over the Ambridge Dinovas for the West Aliquippa Redskins last night on the River avenue field.

Big Redskin inning was the fifth when Hodanovich round-tripped to right center field. Not to be outdone, Zagar followed the example with another circuit clout in the same spot. Steve Chalfa was called out and Mike Minnich worked Bucci for a pass.

Mike Dzugan singled to left, sending Minnich to third. On the throw-in Dzugan took second. Matzie fumbled Nick Markovich's ground ball, Minnich scoring and Dzugan taking third on the error. Markovich was trapped between first and second and Dzugan raced in from third.

The summary:

Redskins	AB	R	H	PO	A	E
N. Markovich, ss	1	1	0	1	1	0
B. Ludwico, cf	4	0	0	0	0	0
D. Casoli, r-ss	4	0	1	3	0	0
S. Hodovanich, 3	3	0	1	1	0	1
C. Leonard, lf	3	0	1	1	0	0
J. Hodovanich, 2	3	1	1	1	2	0
L. Zagar, rf	3	1	2	4	1	0
S. Chalfa, 1b	3	0	0	5	0	0
M. Minnich, c	2	1	0	11	0	0
M. Dzugan, p	3	1	1	0	0	0
Totals	29	5	7	27	4	1

Dinovas	AB	R	H	PO	A	E
R. Rosenberger, 2	4	0	0	4	2	0
Dinino, rf	3	1	1	1	0	0
Niesnak, r-ss	4	0	2	1	0	0
Simons, 3d	3	0	0	1	1	0
Knafelic, 1st	4	0	0	7	0	0
Chincilla, c	3	0	0	7	1	0
Mitzie, ss	3	0	0	0	3	1
Minkel, cf	3	1	1	0	0	0
Uhernik, lf	2	0	0	2	0	0
Bucci, p	3	0	1	1	0	0
Totals	32	2	5	24	7	1

Dinovas	000	000	011—2
Redskins	100	040	00x—5

Runs batted in, Bucci, Knafelic, S. Hodovanich, J. Hodovanich, L. Zagar. Two base hits, C. Leonard. Home runs, J. Hodovanich, L. Zagar. Stolen bases, Niesnak, B. Ludwico, S. Hodovanich, L. Zagar.

Double plays, L. Zagar, S. Chalfa. Left on bases, Dinovas 8, Redskins 4. Bases on balls, M. Dzugan, 5, Bucci 3. Strike outs, M. Dzugan 10, Bucci 4. Hits off, Bucci 7, for 5 runs in 9 innings; M. Dzugan, 5 for 2 runs in 9.

Winning pitcher, M. Dzugan; losing pitcher, Bucci. Umpires J. Leheny, A. Clay. Scorer, J. Bradovich.

Walsh, PGA President, Opposes Tourney Bets

CHICAGO— (INS)—Tom Walsh, president of the Professional Golfers Association of America, today prepared to take a poll of the PGA's executive committee on a proposal that the association take a public stand against betting on tournaments it sponsors.

Walsh said the poll would be taken by mail, probably beginning today. He added:

"The PGA never has favored betting on its tournaments, and this will be merely a formal statement of its position. In fact, there never has been any extensive betting of which I have been aware, but there have been incidents which might grow into something serious, and that is what we are trying to avoid."

WEST ALIQUIPPA MUSHBALL LEAGUE

Yesterday's Results

Black Panthers 9, 100 Block 3.
Americans 6, Golden Eagles 4.

Second Half Standings

Teams	Won	Lost	Pct.
Black Panthers	3	0	1.000
Redwings	1	1	.500
Americans	1	1	.500
Golden Eagles	1	2	.333
100 Block	1	2	.333
Logstown	0	1	.000

Games Today

Redwings vs. Logstown, 6:30 p. m.
Golden Eagles vs. 100 Block, 10:30 a. m.

Games Tomorrow

Americans vs. Redwings, 6:30 p. m.

MAJOR LEAGUE LEADERS

Home Runs

National—Ott, Giants, 18; Nicholson, Cubs, 18; Camilli, Dodgers, 16.

American—Keller, Yankees, 24; J. DiMaggio, Yanks, 22; Johnson, Athletics, 18; Williams, Redsox, 18; York, Tigers, 18.

Runs Batted In

National—Nicholson, Cubs, 70; Slaughter, Cards, 63; Camilli, Dodgers, 62.

American—J. DiMaggio, Yanks, 84; Keller, Yanks, 83; York Tigers, 75.

CELTS LAM OVER 15 RUNS FIRST THREE INNINGS

Pitcher Bar Stars For Winners; Frank Hits 4

A 15-run Celtic attack in the first three innings last night at Fireman's Field cooked the Reds' goose.

And the Celtics got sweet revenge for three previous Red defeats in borough baseball competition by pasting their hilltop rivals 16 to 2.

Four times Mike Pollack's Celts crossed the gum in the first. They counted five in the second and slashed over six more in the third.

Red batsmen went to work in the fourth for two lone runs when Sutlick singled to center field and J. Jones lammed one out past the mound for a single. Both came home when T. Suder punched a single into deep right center field. Glad struck out to retire the side.

Pitcher Paul Bar was stingy with hits, giving the Reds four scattered blows. Not an enemy batman reached first base until the run-producing fourth when Sutlick broke the ice.

The Celtics chased Pitcher George Duplaga early in the second. Mike Diaddigo, sent in to the rescue, pitched to only five batters. Brother Tommy Diaddigo replaced Mike and yielded seven runs on seven hits. He gave way to Johnny Jones in the fifth. Darkness halted the tilt in the sixth.

Sparking the Celt attack, Charles Frank hit four-for-four, batting in three teammates and scoring three himself.

The Boro loop will be idle tonight to permit the Celtics to play Midland of the Beaver Valley league here at 6:30 p. m. Play will be resumed Sunday afternoon when the Reds tack the league-leading Kleins at 2:30 p. m. The summary:

Celtics	AB.	R.	H.	PO.	A.	E.
Rusinko, cf	3	1	0	0	0	0
Cycholl, ss	3	4	1	1	3	0
C. Frank, 2b	4	3	4	3	3	0
Kulcyk, lf	4	2	2	0	0	0
Moskola, 1b	2	1	0	8	0	0
Riggins, rf	3	2	2	0	0	0
Faber, 3b	4	1	0	0	0	0
A. Frank, c	4	1	2	6	0	0
Bar, p	3	1	0	0	0	0
Totals	30	16	11	18	6	0

Reds	AB.	R.	H.	PO.	A.	E.
G. Suder, 2b	3	0	1	1	0	1
Vuich, 1b	3	0	0	4	0	0
Sutlick, lf	3	1	1	2	0	0
J. Jones, cf-p	3	1	1	1	2	0
T. Suder, ss	2	0	1	0	0	2
Miskulin, rf	0	0	0	2	0	0
Glad, rf	2	0	0	0	0	0
Fallagan, 3b	0	0	0	0	0	1
Palsa, 3b	2	0	0	0	0	0
Bucilli, c	0	0	0	0	0	0
J. Gnup, c	2	0	0	5	0	0
Duplaga, p	0	0	0	0	0	0
M. Diaddigo, p	0	0	0	0	0	0
T. Diaddigo, p-rf	2	0	0	0	1	0
Totals	22	2	4	15	3	4

Reds	0 0 0	2 0 0—2
Celtics	4 5 6	1 0 *—16

Runs batted in—T. Suder (2), Riggins (3), Faber, C. Frank (3), Kulcyk (2), A. Frank (2), Moskola, Bar. Two-base hits—Kulcyk. Three-base hits—C. Frank. Left on bases—Celtics, 5; Reds, 1. Bases on balls—Bar 0, Duplaga 4, M. Diaddigo 1, T. Diaddigo 0, Jones 0. Strike-outs—Bar 6, Duplaga 0, M. Diaddigo 0, T. Diaddigo 4, Jones 0. Hits off—Duplaga 2 hits 4 runs in 1 inning; J. Jones 0 hits 0 runs in 1 inning; M. Diaddigo 2 hits 5 runs in 1-3 inning; T. Diaddigo 7 hits 7 runs in 3 innings. Hit by pitcher, by—T. Diaddigo (Moskola). Winning pitcher—Bar. Losing pitcher—Duplaga. Umpires—Kaletz and Alexander.

BORO BASEBALL LEAGUE

Second Half Standings

Teams	Won	Lost	Pct.
Kleins	4	1	.800
Celtics	2	2	.500
Grays	2	3	.400
Reds	1	3	.250

Games To Be Played

Sunday: Reds at Kleins.
Monday: Reds at Grays.
Tuesday: Celtics at Kleins.

Results This Week

Kleins 7, Grays 6.
Celtics 16, Reds 2.

Aliquippa Sports Gazette

Baseball Standings

NATIONAL LEAGUE

Yesterday's Results

Pittsburgh 3, Philadelphia 2.
Chicago 5, Boston 4.
*St. Louis 3, New York 2.
*10 innings.
Only games scheduled.

Standings

	Won	Lost	Pct.
St. Louis	59	31	.656
Brooklyn	58	31	.652
Cincinnati	47	40	.540
Pittsburgh	44	40	.524
New York	44	40	.524
Chicago	40	49	.449
Boston	31	52	.373
Philadelphia	21	65	.244

Games Today—Pitching

Brooklyn at Pittsburgh (2)—Wyatt (13-7) and Davis (6-3) vs. Sewell (9-9) and Lanning (4-6).

Boston at St. Louis (Night)—Tobin (6-5) vs. Gumbert (6-5).

New York at Chicago — Lohrman (5-7) vs. Olsen (7-3).

Philadelphia at Cincinnati—Hughes (5-9) vs. Vander Meer (8-9).

AMERICAN LEAGUE

Yesterday's Results

New York 4, Cleveland 1.
Boston 11, Chicago 1.
Philadelphia 9, St. Louis 7.
Washington 6, Detroit 5.

Standings of the Clubs

	Won	Lost	Pct.
New York	62	28	.689
Cleveland	53	39	.576
Boston	47	43	.522
Chicago	45	46	.496
Philadelphia	42	47	.477
Detroit	43	50	.462
Washington	34	54	.391
St. Louis	34	54	.386

Games Today—Pitchers

Chicago at New York—Smith (9-10) vs. Chandler (6-4).

Cleveland at Boston—Harder (5-4) vs. Grove (6-4).

St. Louis at Washington — Auker (7-11) vs. Kennedy (2-10).

Detroit at Philadelphia—Benton (6-2) vs. Marchildon (6-7).

BASEBALL'S BIG SIX

	G	AB	R	H	Pct.
Williams, Redsox	79	257	78	102	.397
DiMaggio, Yanks	92	365	87	137	.375
Travis, Senators	84	338	58	126	.373
Reiser, Dodgers	77	298	66	101	.339
Mize, Cardinals	71	270	39	89	.330
Cooney, Braves	73	273	31	89	.326

MOORES TAKE 2 TENNIS MATCHES

Playing a match postponed from July 15, the Aliquippa Moores took two double matches away from the Coraopolis Reserves last night in the Ohio Valley Twilight Tennis League.

Bernard Bailey and Sam McNutrie teamed up to trounce Coraopolis' Bob Berkey and Bill Hartsough 6-0 and 6-2.

William Anderson and Charles Bohn found the going harder against Tom Fauntleroy and Frank Warrington, taking the match 6-4 and 6-5.

The victories boost the Moores' win column to eight compared with only two losses.

RUPPERT NEVER SOLD YANKS

NEW YORK — (INS)—A supplementary accounting filed in New York county surrogate's court by executors of the estate of the late Colonel Jacob Ruppert disclosed today that the New York Yankees baseball club has not been sold. Nearly all the Yankee stock is held by the estate.

Ninth Annual Hershey Golf Tourney Aug. 28

HERSHEY, PA. — (INS) — The ninth annual Hershey $5,000 open golf tournament will be played on August 28, 29, 30, 31 on the championship course of the Hershey Country club.

There are tense moments in the Hershey opens. Take the third Hershey open of 1935, when Ted Luther and Felix Serafin tied the 72-hole tournament with 290. That demanded a playoff the next morning.

In the Hershey open of 1936 on the final Sunday afternoon, more than a thousand people crowded around the 18th green to see the finish of the tournament.

Take Advantage of Bargain Days!

The Aliquippa Gazetteer

—DEAN C. MILLER—

CENSORSHIP

Francis (Nippy) Bates, who fishes a great deal in Aliquippa and quite frequently in Canada, has a new hobby . . . taking motion pictures.

The film he snapped on his last northern fishing excursion was something to see, colorful and as fast-moving as Nippy's chatter. But Bates made one mistake.

Instead of carrying the film back with him from Canada he sent it by mail. Censors in Toronto screened the pictures, started using scissors and sent Bates a polite little letter saying "we're sorry."

They didn't hack too much, he says, just a couple shots of a new power plant under construction and a bridge just sprung up. Potential information for "the enemy" was the reason advanced.

As a fisherman Bates was a howling success. But, and even he admits it under pressure, Wife Jean caught more. His excuse, just like a man, is, "You kept me too busy taking them off the line for me to fish."

* * * *

CONFIDENTIAL ASIDES

What well-known numbers "pick-up" agent just bought a new Packard! A big one at that. Must be doing OK by himself to afford a jalopy that big plus a motor boat . . . And while we're on the subject of gambling, what's this we hear about slot machines—jokingly called one-armed bandits—popping up in the rest rooms and backrooms of certain confectionery and other stores?

* * * *

RAMBLING 'ROUND THE BOROUGH

Druggist W. C. Young, we're told, is vacationing in Mexico. Cecil is another motion picture fan as the many who viewed his last year's film can vouch . . . Even barnyard chickens are following the effects of national defense. Washington officials are urging poultrymen to send to collection headquarters discarded aluminum leg bands . . . Many have tried and many have failed: We're talking about the lads who have tried to date enigmatic Kay Dufala, Board of Trade stenographer.

PLATTER PATTER

by—miller

(Ed. Note—We feel especially fortunate today in offering readers of this column a name known anywhere in the musical world. We give you Eugene Ormandy, conductor of the Philadelphia orchestra and RCA Victor recording star.)

By EUGENE ORMANDY
Conductor, The Philadelphia Orchestra

* * *

So many letters of inquiry are addressed to me on the subject of how the Philadelphia orchestra prepares to make phonograph records that I welcome the opportunity of reaching as many persons as possible through this column.

The first thing which must be determined after we have decided on the composition to be recorded is the timing. I use a stop watch while preparing a score at home to find the best possible place or places to end each record so it will have as logical a conclusion as can be found within the actual time limit of the recordings themselves.

Unfortunately, the composer of the symphony, who has perhaps been dead for fifty or a hundred years, was not thinking in terms of phonograph record sides, and it falls upon the conductor to make the best of the situation. By studying the score with these timing problems in mind, it is usually possible to find a not too annoying break which might occur at the end of three and a half minutes. It may also be possible to balance that with the next record, which may play as long as four and a half minutes. In this way I finally space the entire score into eight time divisions that do not destroy the all-important line of the music itself. Of course, the individual movements within the symphony offer the best stopping places whenever it is possible to utilize them.

Then we come to the actual recording which takes place in the Academy of Music, the famous old hall where the Philadelphia Orchestra plays all of its home concerts.

Since the advent of electrical recording we have been able to stress the naturalness of orchestral balance. We do not change the seating arrangements of a single player in the orchestra from the customary set-up which is used for the Orchestra's regular concerts. We strive to reproduce as accurately as possible the effect which the orchestra would have for a listener sitting in the hall. Many years of experimentation have taught the engineers where to place their microphones. Even so, the process of experimentation continued, keeping step with the extraordinary technical advances which have revolutionized the science of recording in less than twenty years.

Now about the music which we select for recording. I try to maintain some sort of balance between new and unrecorded works and older masterpieces which may already have been recorded. The music of American composers is rightfully assuming an ever increasing importance in the newer lists of recorded compositions. How much will be recorded depends to a large extent upon the reception which such music receives at the hand of the record-buying public.

It is interesting and slightly amusing to recall some of the problems which faced musicians in the old days of acoustical recording. I remember well, as concertmeister of an orchestra, having to use a Stroh violin. A Stroh violin is something you will never meet in the concert hall. It is a skeleton of the regular violin, enabling the player to hold it up with his chin and to get to the various positions. It has horns on it, one leading into the large horn which was connected with the recording machine, and the smaller one leading towards the player's ear so he could hear what he was playing. It was especially designed to project the violin's' tone in one direction so that its full intensity could be concentrated into the big horn which was used in place of the present day microphone. Aside from the player's inability to hear much of what he was playing, he was forced to almost climb into the horn for sole passages and even turn his back upon the conductor in doing so. With the invention of the microphone and the development of electrical recording, most of these contrivances were happily done away with.

Practice Economy—Read the ADS

Radio

FRIDAY, AUGUST 8

WCAE

5:00—Home of the Brave.
5:15—Portia Faces Life.
5:30—We, The Abbotts.
5:45—Jack Armstrong.
6:00—Star Gazer.
6:30—Chet Smith, Sports.
6:45—Musical Spotlight.
7:00—Fred Waring.
7:15—News.
7:30—Lone Ranger.
8:00—Lucille Manners
8:30—Information Please.
9:00—Waltz Time.
9:30—Uncle Walter's Dog House.
10:00—Wings of Destiny.
10:30—"Listen, America."
11:00—News.
11:15—Ray Herbeck's Orchestra.
11:30—Everett Hoagland Orchestra.
12:00—News; Guy Lombardo's Orch.
12:30—News; Johnny Long's Orchestra.
12:45—Art Kassell's Orchestra.
1:15—Johnny Davis' Orchestra.
1:15—Ernie Heckscher's Orchestra.
1:30—Jimmy Joys' Orchestra.

KDKA

6:00—News; Temp.
6:15—Shall We Waltz.
6:30—Sports; Serenade.
6:45—Lowell Thomas.
7:00—Bridge to Yesterday.
7:15—Radio Magic.
7:30—Hunting and Fishing Radio League.
7:45—Men of Melody.
8:00—News.
8:15—Pat Haley's Party.
8:30—Death Valley.
9:00—Vox Pop.
9:30—Happy Birthday.
9:55—Nickel Men.
10:00—Romance and Rhythm.
10:30—First Piano Quartet.
10:45—Dramas by Olmstead.
11:00—News; Let's Be Friends.
11:15—News Roundup.
11:30—Music You Want.
12:00—News.
12:15—Goodman's Orchestra.
12:30—Will Bradley's Orchestra.

WJAS

5:00—Mary Marlin.
5:15—Columbia Concert Orchestra.
5:30—The O'Neills.
5:45—Wings Over Jordan.
6:00—E. C. Hill.
6:10—Sports.
6:15—News.
6:30—Paul Sullivan.
6:45—Dinner Music.
7:00—Amos 'n' Andy.
7:15—Lanny Ross.
7:30—American Cruise.
8:00—Claudie and David.
8:30—Proudly We Hail.
8:55—Elmer Davis.
9:00—Great Plays.
9:30—Hollywood Premier.
10:00—Penthouse Party.
10:30—Symphonettes.
10:45—Evening Serenade.
11:00—News.
11:15—Tommy Tucker Orchestra.
11:30—Sonny Dunham Orchestra.
12:00—CBS News.
12:05—Powell's Orchestra.

KQV

5:00—Melody Parade.
5:30—Diminutive Classics.
5:45—Homespun Harmonies.
6:00—Modernaires.
6:10—News.
6:15—Modernaires.
6:30—Bob Prince, Sports.
6:45—Dinner Interlude.
7:00—Fulton Lewis, Jr.
7:15—Mark Lane's Orchestra.
7:30—Radio Mart.
7:45—Vocalettes.
8:00—Double or Nothing.
8:30—Castles in the Air.
9:00—Christian Science.
9:15—Civic Forum.
9:30—Show of the Night.
9:45—Organ Moods.
9:55—News.
10:00—R. G. Swing.
10:15—Korn Kobblers.
10:30—Symphonic Gems.
10:45—Dance Favorites.
11:00—News.
11:15—George Wells Music.
11:30—Music for Reading.

WWSW

3:15—Popular Potpourri.
3:45—Warm Up Time.
4:00—Pirate Game.
6:15—Entertainment Time; News.
6:15—Entertainment Time.
6:30—Building for Defense.
6:45—Club Hollywood.
7:15—Walt Schuman Music.
7:30—B. C. Sports.
7:45—D'Artega Orchestra.
8:00—Parade of Melody.
8:30—Pied Piper, Jr.
9:00—Pop Concert.
10:30—News—Leon Walters; Scores.
10:45—Stardusters.
11:00—Dance Parade.
12:00—1500 Club.

EARLY SATURDAY PROGRAMS

WCAE

7:00—Morning Express.
7:30—Morris H. Siegel.
8:00—Morning News.
8:15—Pick of Picnics.
8:30—Bandstand.
8:45—Nancy Dixon.
9:00—Good Things To Eat.
9:15—Tuneful Tidbits.
9:30—Want To Build?
9:45—Jungle Jim.
10:00—Balladeers.
10:15—Musical Tonic.
10:30—America the Free.
11:00—Lincoln Highway.
11:30—Vaudeville Theater.
12:00—News.
12:15—Front Page Drama.
12:30—Call To Youth.
12:45—Matinee in Rhythm.

WJAS

7:30—Breakfast Serenade.
7:45—News.
8:00—Cheerie Melodies.
8:15—Rev. James R. Cox.
8:45—Musical Revue.
9:00—Press News.
9:15—Melodic Moments.
9:30—Old Dirt Dobber.
10:00—Burl Ives.
10:30—Gold If You Find It.
11:00—News.
11:05—Life of Riley.
11:30—Voice of Broadway.
11:45—Hillbilly Champions.
12:00—Country Journal.
12:30—News.
12:45—Musicale.
1:00—Let's Pretend.

KDKA

6:00—Farm Program.
6:45—News.
7:00—Musical Interlude.
7:15—Musical Clock.
8:00—News.
8:15—Musical Clock.
8:45—From A to Z.
8:55—Janet Ross.
9:00—Orchestras on Parade.
9:15—Musical Interlude.
9:30—Slim Bryant.
10:00—Andrini Continentales.
10:15—Cadets Quartet.
10:30—News.
10:45—Billy Leech.
11:00—The Band Played On.
11:30—Our Barn.
11:45—Children's Program.
12:00—News.

.. Society ... Clubs ... Women's Activities ..

Merle V. Dudley, Society Editor—Phone Aliquippa 934

American Girls' Club Of Center Township

In the photograph above are ten of the 18 members of the American Girls club of Center Twp., with their sponsor, Mrs. Dorothy Sapp, seated in the center of the group. They are wearing uniforms in red, white and blue.

Front row (left to right) are Betty Leonard, Leola Irwin, Joan Huff and Lois Roscoe. Second row (l. to r.) Katherine Patton, Mrs. Sapp and Elsie Solkovy. Back row (l. to r.) Dolores Farland, Lorain Sutton, Vivian Sutton and Betty Sutton.

The girls are organized for social purposes and meet the first and third Friday evenings in the Riddle residence, Center Twp. Miss Sutton is chairman of the entertainment committee, which will meet today to plan a play to be given by the club.

Virginia Joseph Guest Of Honor At Dinner Here

Mrs. Dan Kovac entertained at dinner Sunday in honor of Miss Virginia Joseph. Decorations in yellow and green and a birthday cake were featured at the table.

Among the guests were Mrs. Edward Joseph, Mamie Casoli, Daisy Yackish, Mitzie and Tillie Novah, and Mrs. Paul Dukavich.

After dinner the party attended a theater in Pittsburgh.

Miss Joseph and her father, A. Joseph, were feted at a family dinner in the evening.

Girl Scout Troop Will Stage Over Night Hike Today

Girl Scouts of Mrs. Margaret Raffle's Troop will go to the Boy Scout Camp, Kane Road, for a weiner roast and over night hike, starting at 6 p. m. today.

Each Scout is requested to bring her own food and blankets. The troop will leave from Mrs. J. B. Diewald's residence, McMinn St.

Shippingport Items Of Interest Listed

Margaret Morrow, Pittsburgh, is spending her vacation with her parents, Mr. and Mrs. William Morrow, Shippingport.

The Rev. and Mrs. Floyd Wycoff and children, Beaver Falls, visited at the home of his sister, Mrs. Floyd Rogers, at Shippingport Sunday.

Mrs. Calla Johnson and grandson, Leslie McLaughlin, and Mrs. Marie Overberk, Aliquippa, visited with Mrs. Meada Johnson.

Mr. and Mrs. Baldwin Riddle, Aliquippa, were guests of Mr. and Mrs. Carl Gardner, Shippingport.

William Snodgrass has been ill for a week at his Shippingport home.

Charles McFadden, employed at Pittsburgh, spent the week-end with his family in Shippingport.

Jack Blair and Mrs. Hazel Storey, New Brighton, visited at the home of the latter's mother, Mrs. S. E. Gamble.

Bobbie Rambo, Midland, is visiting his grandparents, Mr. and Mrs. Harry Rambo.

Mr. and Mrs. Leslie Jones, Washington, visited her father at Shippingport Sunday.

Chester McFadden left Sunday night for Washington, Pa., where he is employed.

Smith Christy, Bellevue, visited his brother, Clarence Christy.

Mrs. S. G. Noble has returned to her home after a two weeks' visit with her daughter in New York City.

Mr. and Mrs. Frank Anderson, Aliquippa, visited at Shippingport.

Thomas McNeely, Pittsburgh, is visiting Mrs. Florence Cook.

Bill Highburger and Louis Cook were Pittsburgh visitors.

Mr. and Mrs. Leslie Williams, Ohioview, visited at the McCloud residence in Shippingport.

Millicent Mamula Honored At Party

Millicent Mamula, 162 Superior Ave., was feted at a birthday party at her home Sunday.

Mrs. Ann Zarnich and Mrs Dorothy Vucenich were the hostess' aides when refreshments were served. The table was decorated with an arrangement of flowers and a pink and white cake.

Guests included Ann Zarnich, Theodore Vucenich, Olga and Anne Milanovich, Yvonne Kozlina, Nick Milanovich, Ann Muselin, Theodore Maravich, Mike Marovich, Marion Hope Jurech and Millicent Opacich.

Today's Calendar

American Girls club executive board meeting at the Center Twp. club rooms.

Fellowship club of the First Methodist church will hold an outing at the Watson residence near Five Points, starting at 6 p. m.

Friendly Eight club will meet at the home of Mrs. Mark Ferris, 149 Spring St.

Mrs. Toner Bathurst, McLean St., will entertain the Donors' club.

Mrs. Frank Manges, Beech St., will be hostess at a meeting of the O. U. R. club.

Women of the Moose will meet at the Moose Temple, starting at 8 p. m.

UNDERGOES OPERATION

Janet Mullen, 129 Seventh St., Aliquippa, underwent a tonsilectomy at Beaver Valley General hospital this morning.

W. W. Class Of U. P. Church Fetes Member

Mrs. Robert Johnston [illegible] was honored at a handkerchief shower at the United Presbyterian church last evening. The affair was given by members of the W. W. class of the Sunday school.

Refreshments were served by Mrs. W. H. Shaffer, Mrs. D. J. Davis and Mrs. Ralph Redick. Prizes for games were won by Mrs. J. H. Stewart and Mrs. Homer Harshberger.

Five members of the class wearing old fashioned gowns impersonated famous operatic stars of the past in singing old fashioned songs. They were Mrs. Earl Cook, who accompanied at the piano, Mrs. John Anderson, Mrs. Richard Nelson, Mrs. Earl E. Davis and Mrs. Dorothy Smith.

Mrs. Jennett Orr closed the evening's activities with a prayer.

W.B.A. Guards Party At Brown Residence

Mrs. John Dobbin, Mrs. Ben Mosely and Mrs. Charles Metzler were awarded prizes at the W. B. A. Guards card party at the home of Mrs. H. M. Brown, River Ave., last night.

Mrs. Edith Smith, Walnut St., will be hostess at a card party next Monday, starting at 8:30 p. m.

Five Hundred Club Entertained At Hill Residence

Miss Sally Hill, 510 Grand Ave., entertained members of her 500 club last evening. Prizes went to Mrs. Beatrice Kuhl and Miss Annabelle Stewart. Guest prize was awarded Miss Marie Short and draw prize to Mrs. Charles Stamm.

Miss Marcella Haggerty, 1744 Garfield Ave., will entertain Sept. 29.

FELLOWSHIP CLUB HERE CHANGES MEETING PLANS

The outing scheduled by the Fellowship club of the First Methodist church at the Watson residence near Five Points has been changed. The affair will be held in the church social rooms starting at 6:30 p. m., today. For reservations call R. M. Williams, Aliquippa 2204-W.

LOCAL YOUNG MAN GETS TRANSFER TO ICELAND

Howard D. Smith, son of Mr. and Mrs. Andrew Smith, 1714 Main St., who had been stationed at Langley Field, Va., has been transferred to Iceland with Company A of the 21st Engineers and Aviators.

WOMAN CRITICALLY ILL

Mrs. C. Oscar Evans, Sheffield Terrace, is critically ill in the West Penn hospital, Pittsburgh.

Congratulations

ANN BISH, 2117 McMinn St., is celebrating her 17th birthday.

Local Topics

Mr. and Mrs. James Campbell and daughter, Ardelle, Wade St., spent the week-end in Crafton.

Mr. and Mrs. Fred Webberking, Sunset Hills, and her sister, Miss [illegible] Falls, Canada.

Mrs. Robert Irwin, Kansas City, Mo., is a guest of her nephew, James Bagshaw, Wade St.

Mrs. Zella Jones, Mr. and Mrs. Grover Bates, Mr. and Mrs. Herman Carlyle and Mr. and Mrs. Roy Howells, Aliquippa, were week-end guests at the cottage of Mr. and Mrs. Milo Prosser at Geneva-on-the Lake.

Mr. and Mrs. Martin Lytle, West Wade St., returned home yesterday after a vacation with friends from from Donora and Tarentum, at Conneaut Lake.

Lucille Kiefer, daughter of Mr. and Mrs. James Kiefer, Irwin St., has returned from a vacation at the home of her grandmother at Punxsutawney, Pa.

Mr. and Mrs. J. W. McElheny and daughter, Lucille, Brodhead Road, are vacationing at Geneva-on-the-Lake.

Mr. and Mrs. Edward Staley and daughter, Cherry St., have returned from a fishing trip in Canada.

Mrs. Jeannett Orr, Cherry St., visited at the home of Mrs. Olive Ingraham, Monaca, Sunday.

Mr. and Mrs. George Gourley and children, Irwin St., returned yesterday from a vacation trip to Niagara Falls and Erie, stopping at the Olean, N. Y., home of relatives.

Paul Henderson and Jack Villa, Aliquippa residents, spent the week-end at Geneva-on-the-Lake.

Joan and Billy Gourley, Irwin St., spent last week at the home of relatives in Big Run, Pa.

Mrs. Elizabeth Williams, Kiel St., has returned home after a visit at the home of her daughter, Mrs. David Francis, New Castle.

Miss Lillian Thomas, Orchard St., and Mrs. Marsue McChesney, Brodhead road, are vacationing in New York and Baltimore.

Mrs. George Parry, Youngstown, has concluded a visit with Mr. and Mrs. Henry Brownscombe, Franklin Ave.

Miss Mary Reese, Ellwood Ind., is the guest of Mr. and Mrs. Griff Jones, Irwin St.

Mrs. Ann Fleming and daughter, Phyllis Ann, Long Beach, Cal., are guests of Mr. and Mrs. Charles E. Coulson, Boundary St.

Miss Winnifred Weisenmiller, Spring St., is vacationing in Ohio.

Mrs. William Ritter and daughter, Jean, Chicago, have returned home after a visit with Mrs. Annie Brown and H. M. Brown, River Ave.

In Center Twp.

By MRS. MILDRED DYKE
Gazette Correspondent

LILY POND BLOOMING

The lily pond on Brodhead road, below Union cemetery, has four shades of lilies in boom and is attracting much attention.

"BIG TENT" GOES UP

The "big tent" for the Center Township Firemen's street fair has been raised. The fair will be held this Thursday, Friday and Saturday.

CLUB ENJOYS PICNIC

The American Girls' club of Center township picnicked Saturday. Mothers of members were guests. Mrs. Dorothy Sapp was hostess, assisted by Mrs. J. C. Riddle, her mother.

Miss Mildred Rebich and friends from the township were guests at the Oak Ridge Riding Academy on Brodhead road Sunday.

Wilbur Knight, Aliquippa visited his parents in Center Twp., recently.

Congratulations to Walter Davis Huff, Jr., who will celebrate his 16th birthday Aug. 28.

Mr. and Mrs. Arthur Ellis and daughter, Dorothy, Jack Ellis and Miss Gertrude Ellis visited in Center Twp. Sunday.

Gary Martin and Glenn Irwin have returned to their homes in Center Twp., after visiting in Baltimore, Md.

Billy Anderson is celebrating his birthday today.

Mrs. Ethel Ewing, who had been away for her health, has returned to her Center Twp. home.

Mr. and Mrs. L. F. Bimm, Harrisburg, were week-end guest at the H. G. Martin home, Center Twp.

W. Weigel, Youngstown, visited his sister, Mrs. Harmer Hill, Brodhead road, over the week-end.

Time Is Short If You Desire That Chinchilla Coat

LOS ANGELES. (INS)—Only two chinchilla coats — $30,000 worth—will be made in the United States this year because of scarcity of the little animals whose pelts are worth their weight in gold.

Willard H. George of Los Angeles, who grades and appraises the Chinchilla output of the United States, made this prediction today. He said that if things go right with the little animals probably four chinchilla coats will be made next year.

Of the 15,000 chinchillas in the United States, only 300 skins were tanned during the year to make the two coats, which probably will retail for $15,000.

Most of the chinchilla population, George said, is being protected for breeding purposes. At one time chinchillas were as plentiful as rabbits in South American countries but because they were so easy to trap and because their fur was in such demand the breed became all but extinct.

Experts are attempting to breed them in captivity until the time will come when "someday white-collar workers will be able to buy chinchilla for their wives," George declared.

Dines With FDR

Harlan F. Stone

Chief Justice Harlan F. Stone is pictured as he left the White House after a luncheon date with President Roosevelt. The visit was Stone's first since his elevation to leadership of the Supreme Court.

State's Now Richer Than Any Nazi Prize In Hitler's Bundle

STATE COLLEGE, Pa.—If the Commonwealth of Pennsylvania were in Europe, it would be the richest prize of the continent and the cause of endless struggles among warring powers.

This is the observation of Dean Edward Steidle, of the School of Mineral Industries at the Pennsylvania State College.

Calling attention to the recent British military expedition to Spitsbergen, Dean Steidle pointed out that the exports of coal from the Arctic island previously amounted to about 600,000 tons yearly, the same amount that can be produced from Pennsylvania mines in one day.

Since the first Automobile Show, the wages generated by the use of motor vehicles have amounted to more than 85 billion dollars, or five times all the monetary gold now held in the United States.

From a few mechanics and bench hands who puttered away in barns making a handful of cars at the turn of the century, present-day automobile manufacturing makes possible, directly and indirectly, an annual employment of 6,500,000 people.

Anything You Want—Want Ads!

With rapid improvements in cars in recent years, the automobile industry has become the nation's No. 1 customer for steel, malleable iron, nickel, lead, mohair and other commodities. The motor plants spend about $1,000,000 an hour for raw materials and fabricated parts when production is good.

South Heights News

Members of the H. H. H. club met at the home of Mrs. Pete Menosky, Crawford St. Mrs. Menosky served her club a chicken dinner and used roses and gladioli as her floral decorations. After dinner the members played cards and prizes were won by Mrs. George Wright, Mrs. Dave Milliken and Mrs. John Depta. The next meeting will be Oct. 15 at Mrs. Milliken's home on Buchanan Heights.

Mr. and Mrs. Clarence Okuly, Jordan St., returned home after a three week motor trip in the West. They visited with Mr. Okuly's brother-in-law and sister, Mr. and Mrs. George Smith, of Los Angeles, Cal. Their last stop was at the home of Mrs. Okuly's aunt, Mrs. Grace Millett, Columbus, O.

Mr. and Mrs. Avery Hartman and children, Jackie and Virginia, with Mrs. Clifford Stine, of Penn Way, spent Wednesday evening as guests of the former's uncle and aunt, Mr. and Mrs. Roth, and Mr. and Mrs. Smith, of Pittsburgh.

Albert, son of Mr. and Mrs. Warren Sarvey, of Wireton, is quarantined with scarlet fever. He is the second member of the family ill with the disease.

Congratulations to Mr. and Mrs. Charles Wright, McCoy Heights, who celebrated their 11th wedding anniversary yesterday.

Mr. and Mrs. Harry Davis, Los Angeles, were recent guests of Mr. and Mrs. Sam Thompson, Jordan St.

Mrs. Floyd Swanson, of Los Angeles, who had been visiting with her mother, Mrs. Lulu Barnes, of Whitwell, Tenn., has arrived at the home of her sister, Mrs. Maude Laney, of Curtiss St., and will visit a few days before returning home.

Mrs. Louis Whitefield and children, of Ambridge, returned home after spending three weeks with her brother and sister in the absence of their parents, Mr. and Mrs. Clarence Okuly, Jordan St.

The Weather Forecast
Cloudy, with occasional rain tonight; warmer tonight; Saturday cloudy, with occasional rain, and warmer

THE DAILY TIMES

ROCHESTER-BEAVER-MONACA
FREEDOM—BRIDGEWATER—CONWAY—VANPORT—MIDLAND

Beaver County History
Plans were made October 17, 1917, for a parade in Midland to boost the sale of Liberty Bonds.

ESTABLISHED APRIL 2, 1874 | BEAVER AND ROCHESTER, PA. FRIDAY, OCTOBER 17, 1941 | BY CARRIER 15 CENTS A WEEK

U. S. WARSHIP TORPEDOED

ARMY MAN HEADS JAPANESE CABINET

By the United Press

LONDON: Moscow becomes fortress city awaiting Nazi assault; Diplomats and many Government Officials move east, probably to Kazan; no indication German drive has been halted although may be progressing more slowly; RAF attacks Duisberg, Ruhr area, Dunkirk and Calais; expect new Cabinet will bring showdown in Japan; Bangkok broadcast warns of Thailand crisis.

BERLIN: High Command reticent on Moscow drive; Nazi spokesmen claim Moscow flanked north and south, only accessible from east; Luftwaffe bombs Moscow, Leningrad, ships fleeing Odessa.

ROME: British bomb Naples, killing 12, wounding 37, starting fires.

TOKYO: Emperor Hirohito commissions War Minister Hideki Tojo to form new Cabinet; seeks Navy support for Tojo who is regarded as Moderate Nationalist.

SHANGHAI: Diplomats regard Tojo as likely to go slow in involving Japan in war which he is said to believe may last 30 years; not regarded as close to Germany but Nazi pressure for Axis rapproachment expected.

MOSCOW POUNDED

Emperor Hirohito called on an army man today to form Japan's crisis cabinet as Nazi legions pounded against home guard battalions mustered to reinforce the tiring defenders of Moscow.

The Germans were slashing without pause against the Soviet capital. North and south of Moscow, Nazi flanking columns drove forward and it was believed that access to the city now was possible only from the east. One Russian report said the Nazi advance had been slowed but there was no claim that the Germans had been halted.

Japan's cabinet crisis reflected the intensity of the combat for Moscow.

Hirohito picked War Minister Hideki Tojo, war minister under Premier Prince Fumimaro Konoye, to attempt to form a government to succeed Konoye. It was expected that Tojo would succeed although he asked for a brief interval in which to consult political figures.

DETAILS LACKING

Regarding Moscow there was an actual dearth of specific information. The German high command cast no light on the situation, saying only that operations are proceeding according to plan with the Luftwaffe making heavy attacks on Leningrad, Moscow and ships evacuating Soviet troops from Odessa. Six of these ships totalling 30,000 tons were sunk, it was claimed, and eight of them damaged.

Nazi spokesmen offered little more information beyond the suggestion that Nazi flanking arms from Kalinin to the north and Kaluga to the south now probably had reached the Moscow parallel or gone beyond it, making access to the capital possible only from the east.

London admitted that the Germans appear to be going forward slowly on Moscow. The Soviet metropolis was virtually an armed camp. Diplomats and many government departments had evacuated east, probably to Kazan, on the Volga some 450 miles away.

There was no direct word from Moscow. Moscow radio stations were heard broadcasting the usual communiques and dispatches from the big newspapers Izvestia and Pravda but there had been no direct communication from the United Press staff correspondents in the Soviet capital for 24 hours.

BRITISH LEAVE CAPITAL

The big Nazi offensive was in its 16th day. The only official Russian word in the daily communique, heard on the Moscow radio station, which merely said that fighting was

(Continued on Page Eight)

U. S. Relieved At New Appointments To Japs' Cabinet

Selection Of Other Cabinet Members Anxiously Awaited In Washington, London

By the United Press

WASHINGTON, Oct. 17—First reaction today to selection of Gen. Hideki Tojo to form a new Japanese cabinet was "relief," but diplomats cautioned against jumping to conclusions before the make-up of the cabinet was learned.

Tojo was regarded here as among the more conservative of the aggressive Nationalist group in Japan, and observers believed that a less favorable choice, in the eyes of the United States, could have been made.

There was only guarded unofficial comment on Tojo's selection, all sources contending that speculation on future Japanese policy must await selection of the other cabinet officers — especially the Foreign Minister.

Officials have made no secret of their concern over the fall of Prince Konoye's cabinet yesterday and are aware that the make-up of its successor may change the future course of Japanese-American relations.

U. S. LEADERS CONFER

The outcome of the recent "peace" talks between the United States and Japan probably depend upon whether the Japanese war party or the moderates win ascendancy in the new cabinet. They would collapse immediately if a majority of the new ministers are of the aggressive faction, dedicated to full collaboration with Germany.

President Roosevelt conferred for several hours yesterday with Secretary of State Cordell Hull and other high diplomatic, army and navy officials on the Japanese crisis and continued reverses for Russia. He will keep in touch with Hull by

(Continued on Page Eight)

Bid For Housing Project Approved

Approval has been received by the Beaver County Housing Authority on the $722,600 construction bid for the West Mayfield defense housing project. The bid, submitted originally as $755,700 by Joseph O. Burgwin Construction Company, Pittsburgh, was reduced by negotiations.

The project will include 170 units and will be located on 37 acres of land above the B. and W. Tube Company's plant. It is estimated the project will be completed within about 135 days.

Speed Trap Operated In Rochester Twp.

Fifteen motorists of the county will receive summons to appear for hearings before Rochester township justices within the next fifteen days for violation of the speed limit of 35 miles per hour, as a result of a "speed trap" operated by Rochester township police Thursday night from 10 to 12 o'clock.

Township Police Chief Ralph B. Batto said all of the fifteen motorists were driving over 45 miles per hour.

Women's Committee For Judge Reader Plans Meet Monday

The Women's Committee of the "Beaver County Committee to help re-elect Judge Frank E. Reader," composed of Marguerite Shaw, Beaver, vice-chairman of the Republican County Committee; Brownen James, Aliquippa, president of the Beaver County Council of Republican Women; Ida Geer Weller, New Brighton, president of the Nancy Hanks Republican Women's Club, have called a meeting of the women of these several groups for working out plans for action, in the assembly room at the Court House, Monday, October 20, at 7:30 o'clock.

The interest and co-operation of Republican women from the entire county is desired by the sponsors, and all willing to work for the party will be welcome.

Laughing Lady

Boylin Photo

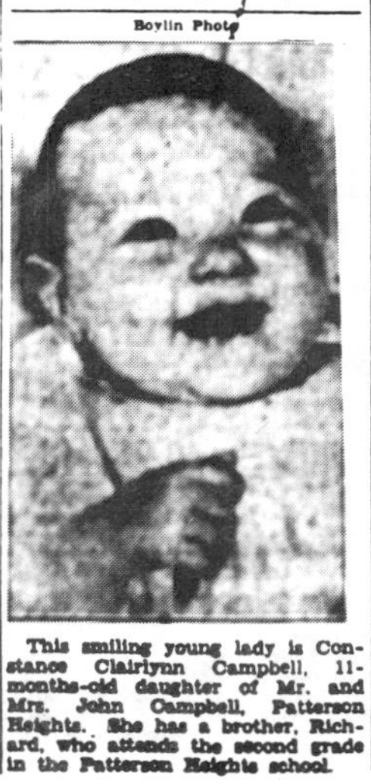

This smiling young lady is Constance Clairlynn Campbell, 11-months-old daughter of Mr. and Mrs. John Campbell, Patterson Heights. She has a brother, Richard, who attends the second grade in the Patterson Heights school.

Youth Admits Killing Man To Steal Automobile

A 16-year-old youth admitted today at Portland, Me., that he shot and killed a man to obtain his auto, repudiating his contention that he had been defending the honor of two adolescent girls.

Confronted by the conflicting stories of his cousin, Leona Ellen Cunningham, 14, and Ida A. Price, 15, sob-wracked Herbert H. Cox, Jr., told County Attorney Albert Knudsen: "I shot the man to take his car and keep going."

Victim was Grainger G. Browning, 38, of Mount Olive, N. C., who in recent months had been living at an Alexandria, Va., trailer camp. His body was discovered yesterday hidden in bushes some six miles south of Conowingo, Md.

The boy and girls, held pending arrival of Sheriff Walter E. Bennington of Hartford county, Md., with murder warrants, were to be returned later today to Bel Air, Md., for arraignment.

According to Knudsen, the three met Browning in an Alexandria

(Continued on Page Eight)

Forty-Five Draftees Named By Board No. 1 For Induction Oct. 27

Large Contingent Will Leave In Ten Days For New Cumberland, Pa.

The following 45 men have been selected for induction into the army by Local Board No. 1, Baden. They are to report to the office of the board on the second floor of the borough building, Baden, at 6:45 a. m., October 27, whereupon they shall be sent to the Army Reception Center at New Cumberland, Pa.

The men are:

Joseph Palsa, Jr., Aliquippa; William Eugene Hartswick, Baden; Kenneth Earl Price, near Ellwood City; Michael William Savie, Ambridge; Chester Raymond Shaffer, Frisco; Wilbert Samuel Paar, Baden; Jacob George Becker, near Conway; Milo Shimrak, Conway; Ralph Nickalos Reda, Ellwood City; Daniel Kowal, Jr., Harmony Twp.

Peter Allen Miskow, near Beaver Falls; William Ernest Ivey, near Valencia; Edward Tellish, near Aliquippa; Frank James Rogoz, near Freedom; Michael Paul Karpa, Monaca; William Krokonko, near Freedom; Harold LeRoy Shaffer, near Ellwood City; Russell Lemoyne Matthews,

(Continued on Page Eight)

Youth Killed, Two Wounded At Prison

WHITE HILL, Oct. 17.—An attempted break from the new White Hill Industrial School brought death from gunfire Thursday to one youthful inmate and wounds to two others.

A fourth youth was unharmed by the guards' gunfire but suffered badly lacerated hands in scaling the barbed wire fence in the third break in four months at the school, located in Cumberland county, across the Susquehanna river from Harrisburg.

Major Henry C. Hill, superintendent of the school, said the boys ignored the warning shouts and whistles of guards, who saw them scaling the fence.

Paul Selfridge, 20, of Butler, died in the institution hospital shortly after the break from a wound in the chest.

Baptist Convention Of State Is Ended

By the United Press

PHILADELPHIA, Oct. 17 — The Pennsylvania Baptist convention today was on record in opposition to "the establishing of diplomatic relations with any ecclesiastical body" as reaffirmation of its historic code of separation of church and state.

Delegates, at closing sessions of their two-day annual conclave yesterday, forwarded to President Roosevelt a resolution which also condemned "the extension of special courtesies by our government to any ecclesiastical official as such, and the employment of any of the branches of our national defense in connection with religious services that are to honor any ecclesiastical leader."

The Rev. Dr. H. E. Slade of Philadelphia was elected president and the First Baptist church of Altoona was selected as the site of the next convention, October 14 and 15, 1942.

Upper Ohio Valley Ass'n. Protests To Congress On Canal

President Of Body Sends Letters To Congressmen, Senator On Waterway

The Upper Ohio Valley Association, representing business and industrial interests of Western Pennsylvania, Ohio and West Virginia, today filed its protest with Congressmen and Senators of this area in opposition to the construction of the proposed dead-end canal from Rochester to Struthers, O., via the Beaver and Mahoning rivers.

In a letter sent to members of the Rivers and Harbors Committee of the House, the Commerce Committee of the Senate and to individual Congressmen of the tri-state district, L. F. Rains, president of the Association, stated that his group is unalterably opposed to the waterway project.

His letter stated: "As president of the Upper Ohio Valley Association, representing many of the leading business and industrial interests of Western Pennsylvania, Ohio and West Virginia, I am writing to express our opposition to the proposed construction of a dead-end canal to Struthers, Ohio, through canalization of the Beaver and Mahoning rivers.

HUGE COST CITED

"Building of this waterway, which could benefit only a few interests in the Youngstown district, would cost $86,411,000—or $2,270,000 per mile for the 35 miles of construction.

"We believe that the expenditure of such a sum is entirely unjustified, particularly at a time when the efforts of industry and the nation are being strained to the ut-

(Continued on Page Eight)

District Lutheran Men Hold Annual Rally In Rochester

Speaking, Music And Election Feature Dinner-Meeting In Grace Church

The annual Fall rally of the Beaver and Ohio Valley Lutheran Men's Association was held Thursday evening at Grace Lutheran church, Rochester, Rev. Elmer A. Ortner pastor.

About 150 men attended the banquet and rally. The banquet was served by women of the host church in the social hall. Attorney George A. Baldwin, Sr., Rochester, served as toastmaster.

The invocation was offered by Rev. Hans O. F. Simoleit, pástor of St. Paul's Lutheran church, Rochester. Group singing and special selections by the Rochester Male Chorus, under the direction of A. D. Kommel, with Paul Albright as accompanist, were enjoyed.

ERIE MAN SPEAKS

Following the dinner the rally and business session was held in the church auditorium. Rev. Fortunato Scarpitti, pastor of the Italian Mission work in Erie, was the principal speaker.

The speaker unfolded an interesting story of the home mission enterprise of the Pittsburgh Synod of the United Lutheran Church in America in the Italian settlement in Erie, of which he has been in charge the past 22 years. Rev. Scarpitti organized the first Italian Lutheran church in Erie and has been instrumental in founding other Lutheran mission centers among the Italians in Western Pennsylvania and Ohio.

A. D. Albright, Rochester, conducted the devotions and introduced the speaker. A special feature of the service was selections by the chorus.

OFFICERS ELECTED

Arthur S. Dambaugh, Ellwood City, president of the Lutheran Men's Association, presided during the business session. The election

(Continued on Page Eight)

Beaver Man Builds Real Autos For Son

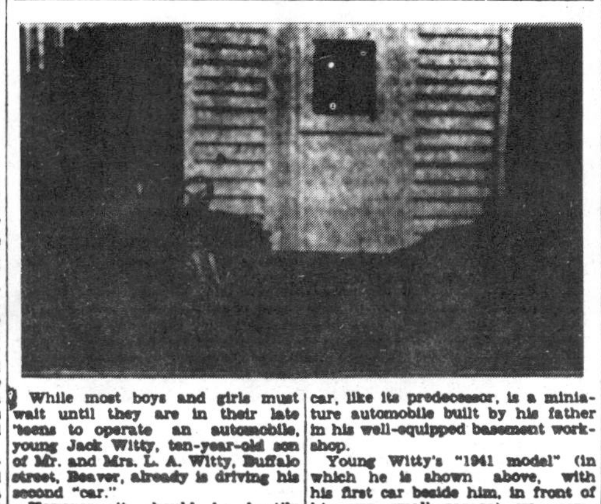

While most boys and girls must wait until they are in their late 'teens to operate an automobile, young Jack Witty, ten-year-old son of Mr. and Mrs. L. A. Witty, Buffalo street, Beaver, already is driving his second "car."

However, it should be hastily added that the Beaver boy's latest car, like its predecessor, is a miniature automobile built by his father in his well-equipped basement workshop.

Young Witty's "1941 model" (in which he is shown above, with his first car beside him, in front of his own small garage) was com-

(Continued on Page Eight)

STRIKE THREATENS AT BIG AIRPLANE FACTORY IN WEST

Company Demands That Federal Government Pay Cost Of Wage Increases

Settlement Believed Near In Cleveland Steel Strike; AFL Convention Ends

By the United Press

Strike action affecting $750,000,000 worth of airplane orders threatened today at the huge Consolidated Aircraft plant at San Diego, Cal., unless the federal government offers to bear the cost of wage increases agreed upon by the company and an AFL union.

Other labor developments included prospect of early settlement of the Midland Steel Products Company strike at Cleveland which has idled 15,400 workers and the final action of the American Federation of Labor convention driving 125,000 welders and brewery workers from the AFL.

Apparent company-union peace at the giant aircraft plant, employing 27,000 men, was shattered by angry protests from AFL machinists against a company statement that negotiated wage increases would not be forthcoming unless the federal government bore the cost.

The proposed wage increases — granting a 75 cents hourly minimum for skilled workers and a 13 cents hourly increase in lower paid brackets—ended an earlier strike threat at the plant.

TO INVOKE CLAUSE

Company spokesmen said the government was expected to pay for the increases, estimated at $82,000,000, under a clause in airplane contracts provided compensation to manufacturers for increased production costs. The war department was believed to be studying the case to determine if the wage boost should be paid by the government.

In the 17-day strike of 1,400 United Automobile Workers at the Midland Steel Products Company, details of a wage gain compromise tentatively accepted by the union and company for ending the walkout were expected to be worked out in conferences today.

From the Cleveland dispute, Conciliator James F. Dewey will go to Ecorse, Mich., to attempt settlement of a strike of 400 CIO steel workers delaying production of high tensile steel and other defense orders at the Great Lakes Steel Corporation. The walk-out, denounced as unauthorized by the parent union and leaving some 7,600 employes unaffected, was staged to protest new wage schedules negotiated by the union and company.

RAIL WORKERS ASK RAISE

In its final convention action, the AFL suspended the charter of 42,000 brewery workers until they agree to give jurisdiction over 3,000 drivers to the teamsters union and denied a separate union to welders, now divided among eight unions. Spokesmen for the welders said an independent organization embracing 75,000 to 90,000 members of their craft would be formed.

The American train dispatchers passed a resolution at Chicago yesterday demanding a 20 per cent wage increase for 3,500 members.

The new demand came as a presidential fact-finding commission finished hearing evidence from the railroads in the wage controversy involving demands by 1,800,000 employes for 30 to 41 per cent wage increases.

"SLOWDOWN" TO END

The board will hear a separate wage case involving Railway Express Company employes and rebuttal arguments from the carriers and the

(Continued on Page Eight)

British Veterans To Attend Service

The annual memorial service of Edith Cavell Post, British Empire War Veterans Association, will be held at the Providence Baptist church, near Elwood City, Sunday, October 19 at 8 p. m. All Post, Auxiliary and Junior Band members are to meet at the Post rooms, 919 Third avenue, New Brighton, not later than 6:15 p. m.

Report Given On State Pay Boosts

HARRISBURG, Oct. 17.—Governor James' office reported today 41,322 promotions and salary increases have been granted state employes since the beginning of his administration in January, 1939.

The increases and promotions included 1,971 in the department of public assistance last October 1, with 1,867 prior to that time; a total of 2,604 employes under the liquor control board and 2,058 on October 1 to salaried employes in all other departments under the governor, with 5,613 prior to October 1.

U. S. Merchant Ships Ordered From Pacific

No Casualties On Destroyer

By the United Press

SAN FRANCISCO, Oct. 17—Headquarters of the Twelfth Naval District said today that orders have been issued to all American merchant ships in Asiatic waters to put into "friendly ports" immediately. The district's public relations office said the orders went out by radio.

Shipping circles took the orders to confirm that the international situation in the Pacific was rapidly approaching a climax.

It was reported one U. S. flag merchantman, the Maritime Commission freighter Perida, already had turned back to Shanghai.

SHIP ATTACKED IN ATLANTIC

WASHINGTON, Oct. 17—The USS. Kearney, one of the United States' newest destroyers, was damaged by a torpedo today in the first successful attack on an American naval ship in the Atlantic since the European war started.

The attack, according to the Navy Department's brief announcement, occurred 350 miles southwest of Iceland. The preliminary Navy dispatches indicated that there were no casualties among the crew.

At the time of the attack, the Kearny was on patrol duty, carrying out its assignment in the North Atlantic patrol which is under President Roosevelt's orders to shoot Axis submarines, war planes or surface raiders on sight in American defensive waters.

The sea lanes to Iceland are considered American defensive waters.

The Navy did not identify the attacker, but officials believed that it undoubtedly was a German submarine.

On September 4 a German submarine attacked the USS Greer with torpedoes in the same general area, but missed.

Despite damage, the Navy said, the Kearney was able to proceed under her own power. It was not indicated whether she would seek the shelter of a harbor in Iceland or Greenland, or would cross the North Atlantic to a base in this country.

The Kearney is a 1,600-ton vessel under command of Lieut.-Comm. A. L. Danis. She was completed in 1940 and is armed with standard five-inch guns and torpedo tubes customary for a destroyer of her class.

IN "DEFENSE WATERS"

WASHINGTON, Oct. 17 — President Roosevelt said today that the USS Kearney was clearly within the American defensive zone when torpedoed this morning.

Mr. Roosevelt said the Navy is operating under its regular orders as far as retaliation against the assailant is concerned. That statement seemed to imply that since the attack occurred within the defensive zone, that other American naval

(Continued on Page Eight)

House Votes Today On Bill Permitting Arming Merchantmen

Vote Not Seen As Test Of Roosevelt's Foreign Policy, Leaders Say

By the United Press

WASHINGTON, Oct. 17 — The House was scheduled to vote today on the administration's armed ship bill. Passage was virtually assured.

Leaders of both sides said that the vote will not be a major test of President Roosevelt's foreign policy, contending that that will come when the House is asked to send those armed ships into war zones now proscribed by the Neutrality Act.

Administration leaders predicted a 100 to 150 vote majority for passage of the armed ship bill and their claims were not disputed. Noninterventionists were not expected to try to attach restrictive amendments to the one-paragraph resolution that would permit the President to put guns aboard American merchant ships.

The House met an hour earlier than usual to dispose of one remaining hour of general debate. There were nine hours of oratory yesterday.

SENATE FIGHT LOOMS

Those opposed to the bill planned only one major fight, seeking to recommit the bill to committee for further consideration.

House Speaker Sam Rayburn predicted the 100 to 150 vote majority for passage, but leaders admitted privately that the armed ship issue

(Continued on Page Eight)

Adam W. Miller, 68, Died This Morning

Adam W. Miller, 68, Darlington road, Beaver Falls, former well-known resident of Beaver, died at seven o'clock this morning in Rochester hospital.

Friends are to be received at the Lutton funeral home, Beaver Falls, where private services are to be held at 2:30 o'clock Sunday afternoon. Rev. George D. Massey, pastor of the Beaver Falls Christian church, is to officiate. Interment will be in Beaver Falls cemetery.

Surviving are the widow, Mrs. Mary M. Miller; one son, Robert Miller, at home; three daughters, Frances Miller, at home; Mrs. Gilbert Trumpeter, Monaca, and Mrs. George Marshall, Rochester; three grandchildren; one brother, Joseph Miller, Ripley, W. Va., and two sisters, Mrs. Thomas Compston and Mrs. George Lee, Ravenswood, W. Va.

Midland Solons Hold Discussion On Fire

Discussion of the recent fire which caused $65,000 damage marked the monthly meeting of Midland Council held Thursday evening in the council chambers of the borough building.

Fire Chief Edward J. [illegible] recommended the procurement of additional fire equipment.

Council approved the recent trip of borough officials to Philadelphia where they sought approval of the new sewerage system for the Midland housing project from William J. Finley, regional director of the Federal Works Agency, Defense Public Works Division.

Three Men Sought Here In New Castle Robbery

Police in all Beaver county communities and State Motor Police from the Beaver barracks searched Thursday for three men reported to be fleeing in this direction after stealing eleven dollars from a service station in New Castle.

The men, all colored, were riding in a 1941 Buick coupe bearing Ohio license plates, the alarm sent out by New Castle police reported. Several roads were watched, but no trace of the men was found [illegible]. They were last seen in [illegible] toward Beaver Falls.

The Weather Forecast
Cloudy and continued cold, with occasional snow flurries; cloudy and warmer Tuesday.

THE DAILY TIMES

ROCHESTER-BEAVER-MONACA

FREEDOM—BRIDGEWATER—CONWAY—VANPORT—MIDLAND

Beaver County History
Word of a huge counter-attack by the Allies in Flanders was received in the county November 10, 1917.

ESTABLISHED APRIL 2, 1874 | BEAVER AND ROCHESTER, PA., MONDAY, NOVEMBER 10, 1941 | BY CARRIER 15 CENTS A WEEK—

TRAFFIC ACCIDENTS CLAIM TWO LIVES HERE

★ ★ ★ ★ ★ ★ ★ ★ ★ ★ ★ ★ ★ ★ ★ ★ ★ ★ ★ ★

MONACA READY FOR ARMISTICE DAY

O. H. LOCKE
Ways and Means

H. D. BAILEY
Veterans of Foreign Wars

MRS. O. H. LOCKE
Entertainment

MRS. RALPH D. HOUSER
Window Display

ROBERT E. McCREARY
Speakers

RALPH D. HOUSER
Athletics

FRANK T. DINDINGER
Memorial

FRANK H. ZINKE
Badges and Novelties

Pictured above are eight committee chairmen for the annual Beaver County Armistice Day celebration to be held Tuesday in Monaca. Photos of others will be found elsewhere in the paper. (Pictures of all of the numerous committee chairmen were not available).

TWELVE KILLED IN OHIO TRAIN WRECK

By the United Press

DUNKIRK, O., Nov. 10— Work crews clambered over a mass of twisted wreckage today, seeking additional victims in the derailment of a fast Pennsylvania passenger train in which at least 12 persons were killed when the flyer left the tracks while roaring through this central Ohio town at a speed of 70 miles an hour.

Coroner J. A. Mooney of Hardin county, said that 12 bodies had been removed and that he believed "there are more inside the cars." At least 42 persons were injured, four of them perhaps seriously.

The fast Chicago-New York train "the Pennsylvanian" jumped the tracks almost directly in front of the small village depot as it sped through the night. The derailment occurred at 10:22 p. m.

The locomotive flopped on its side and skidded for about 100 feet. The first coach was cut cleanly in two and piled up ahead of the locomotive. Part of the train smashed into and demolished a nearby signal tower. Several cars were "telescoped" into one another and the others were left in crazy zig zag positions along the right of way.

The train had eight coaches in all. A lounge car, a diner, and a combination baggage and smoking car also were smashed. The Pullmans, although derailed, were comparatively little damaged.

CAUSE REPORTED

At Chicago H. E. Newcomet, vice president of the road, announced that a preliminary investigation indicated a cylinder head, blown from a freight train on an adjoining track, derailed the limited before there was time to flag it.

Railroad officials at the scene of the wreck announced that an inves-

(Continued on Page Eight)

Legion Commander

Photo by Graule Studios

John B. Prather, (above) widely-known Monaca attorney, is commander of Monacatootha Post, American Legion, and secretary of the committee in charge of the annual county-wide Armistice Day program to be held at Monaca on Tuesday. As post commander, Attorney Prather has been active in arranging plans for the celebration.

NOTICE—I. O. O. F.

Members of S. M. Kane Lodge No. 786, I. O. O. F., are requested to meet in the Odd Fellows Hall, Rochester, at 8 o'clock this evening to conduct ritualistic services for our late brother, Stanton Durr.

GEORGE SCHROEDER,
Noble Grand
11 10

ARMISTICE DAY

No Armistice Day since 1918 has seemed so much an anticlimax as this, the twenty-third anniversary of the peace. For months on end, the themes to which the day is dedicated by custom, the thoughts it naturally evokes, have been our daily concern and our main preoccupation.

Set aside originally to mark the triumphant end of the effort to safeguard democracy through the world and to outlaw war as an instrument of international policy, the day has now become one of sad reckoning of how far short of fruition these dreams have fallen.

Democracy, since it first arose from the ruins of older governmental forms, has never seemed in so precarious a state. And far from being relegated to the past, war, or thoughts of war, now possess the earth.

The World War and the peace growing from it left a situation which finds a greater proportion of man's ingenuity and energy and wealth put to preparation for annihilation of one another than nations have ever lavished before.

And yet, while democracy could scarcely find itself

(Continued on Page Six)

TWO KILLED, TEN INJURED IN LOCAL WEEK-END MISHAPS

Bridgewater Child Fatally Injured In Car-Truck Crash Saturday

Traffic Mishaps Leading Cause Of Injury Cases Reported Here

Two persons were killed and ten others were injured in accidents over the week-end. The two fatalities and eight of the injury cases resulted from traffic mishaps. One of the injury cases resulted from a mill accident while the tenth was the result of a football game.

CAR, TRUCK CRASH

Five persons were injured, one fatally, when the automobile in which they were riding collided with a truck at the intersection of the new Darlington road and the cut-off road to Fallston.

The automobile, operated by Charles William Parsons, Sr., Sharon road, Bridgewater, at six o'clock Saturday evening pulled from the side road into the path of a truck driven by Charles J. Fellenstein, Cleveland, according to State Motor Police.

Parsons suffered a crushed chest and possible internal injuries. His son, Charles, Jr., 12, received lacerations of the left thigh and head and cheek injuries. A daughter, Joan, nine-years old, suffered a fractured skull. Mrs. Elizabeth Leach, 54, Sixth avenue and Sixth street, Beaver Falls, suffered lacerations of the face and chest in-

(Continued on Page Eight)

Beaver County Armistice Celebration

Tuesday, November 11
Monaca

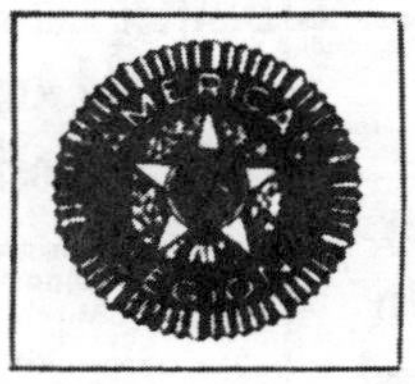

ROUTE OF PARADE

ASSEMBLE 9:45 A. M. in Indiana avenue, between Sixth and Ninth streets. Parade moves promptly at 10 east in Indiana avenue to Sixteenth street, south on Sixteenth street to Pennsylvania avenue, west on Pennsylvania avenue to Sixteenth street and disbands.

10:55 A. M. Parade Halts, 21 Bomb Salute.

11 A. M. "Taps".

11:05 A. M. Parade Resumes.

12 Noon. Program at High School Auditorium.

1 P. M. Gold Star Mothers' Dinner, Lyceum Hall.

2 P. M. Awarding of Prizes; Exhibition by winning Drum Corps and Bands at High School Athletic Field.

2:30 P. M. Football—Monaca High vs. St. Joseph High of Oil City.

2:30 P. M. Card Party and Bingo for Women.

(Continued on Page Eight)

HANDSOME AWARDS TO BE PRESENTED AT MONACA PARADE

Trophies, Cash Offered For Winners In Armistice Day Celebration Tuesday

Prizes To Be Given Veterans' Posts, Auxiliary Units, Bands And Scouts

Joseph M. Clerc, Ambridge, county Armistice Day committee chairman, announces the following awards for the parade at Monaca on Tuesday:

Most Legionnaires in line, trophy; most members of Legion Auxiliary in line, trophy; most members in line, Junior Auxiliary, $5; most members in line, Sons of Legion, $5; best outside drum and bugle corps, $15; best senior Legion drum and bugle corps, $20; high school band, first $25, second $10; best Boy Scout troop, $5; best Girl Scout troop, $5; best Cub pack, $2.50; best firemen's unit, trophy; most members in line, Veterans of Foreign Wars, trophy; most members in line, VFW Auxiliary, trophy; most service men in line, not including Legion or VFW, $15; best float, trophy.

SAYS U. S. NAVY IN WAR

LONDON, Nov. 10—Prime Minister Winston Churchill declared today that a large part of the American navy was in action against the Axis, that the Royal Air Force had achieved at least equality with the Luftwaffe and that Great Britain would come to the aid of the United States "within the hour" in event of war with Japan.

HUGE CROWD TO ATTEND PARADE

Monaca residents prepared today to welcome thousands of tri-state district folk who are expected to swarm into the town early Tuesday for the annual Beaver County Armistice Day celebration. A monster parade, a program of speaking, luncheons for junior marching units and Gold Star Mothers and Fathers, a band concert, football game and parties for visiting American Legion Auxiliary women will feature the all-day program.

Tonight, past commanders' of county Legion posts will have their annual banquet in Monaca, while the annual parade and "wreck" of Beaver County Voiture, 40 and 8 humorous organization of the Legion, will be held in the South Side town.

The annual memorial service for the dead of all wars was held Sunday by Monacatootha Post, American Legion.

Flags and bunting floated from poles, business houses and homes in Monaca today and all preparations had been completed for the gala celebration. Monaca was last host at the Armistice Day program in 1932.

Sponsored by the Beaver County Committee of the American Legion and Monacatootha Post, the event will be featured by a monster parade in which hundreds of men, women and children, together with floats, fire trucks, American Legion posts and Auxiliaries, Junior American Legion Auxiliaries, Sons of Veterans Squadrons, Boy Scouts, Girl Scouts, Veterans of Foreign Wars posts and Auxiliary units, British war veterans, high school bands, civic and

(Continued on Page Eight)

General Chairman

County Commissioner E. H. Markey, (above) widely-known Monaca war veteran, is general chairman of the committee in charge of the county Armistice Day celebration to be held Tuesday. Mr. Markey was first commander of the host post.

He served overseas with Company E, 319 Infantry, and following

(Continued on Page Eight)

ARMISTICE DAY COMMITTEES

General Chairman .... E. H. Markey
Secretary .... John B. Prather
Treasurer .... Mont D. Youtes
Executive Committee .... Chairmen of All Committees

ENTERTAINMENT
Mrs. O. H. Locke, Chairman
Mrs. William H. Kunzler
Mrs. Hattie Timmons
Mrs. E. H. Markey
Mrs. Alice Moorehouse
Mrs. Harry M. Houser
Mrs. Carl Mattauch
Mrs. H. S. Fogg
Mrs. John Keefe

PUBLICITY
Mrs. Mae L. Gaertner, Chairman
Ernest F. Konvolinka
Mrs. Hattie Timmons
Mrs. Franklin J. Hood
Mrs. Charles J. Renner
Mrs. Elmer E. Johnson

PARADE
John J. Hanlon, Chairman
Mrs. Walter Miller
William Irons
Horace D. Bailey
George E. Dietrich
Frank H. Zinke
Franklin J. Hood

MENU
Ralph G. Clarke, Chairman
Mrs. Charles J. Renner
Mrs. David W. Sinclair
Mrs. John Webber, Sr.
Mrs. Paul E. Shroads
Mrs. H. S. Fogg
Mrs. W. C. Bonett
Mrs. Ben F. Crawford
Michael K. Frenko
Charles W. Dalzell
Miss Vdena Majalik

WINDOW DISPLAY
Mrs. Ralph D. Houser, Chairman
Mrs. Walter Miller
Mrs. Allen I. Henry
Mrs. Caroline Beringer
Mrs. Erma Lawson
Mrs. Helen O'Keefe
Mrs. Howard R. Koehler, Sr.
Mrs. Bertha Bussang
Mrs. Robert F. Cain
Mrs. Richard Histner
Mrs. Ruth Vogt

(Continued on Page Eight)

BEAVER VALLEY PRINTERS HONOR FIVE 40-YEAR UNION MEMBERS

(See other photograph on Page 6)

Photo by Graule Studios

Members of the Beaver Valley Typographical Union, No. 250, their wives and friends, honored five of their 40-year union members at a banquet and dance Saturday evening in the American Legion home at Rochester. The five honor members (pictured above) are: Standing left to right—Frank L. Anderson, James W. Carson, James G. Alexander; seated, left to right—William G. Newlon, and John Clark. Four of the five, all but Mr. Carson, have been employes of THE TIMES.

The meeting was opened with a very fine course turkey dinner. The invocation was by the Rev. Ross Hunt, pastor of the Monaca Methodist church, a former printer, af-

(Continued on Page Six)

NEWS OF THE UPPER VALLEY

New Brighton News

Green Laurel To Be Used In Christmas Street Decorations

Revised Plans Made By Yule Committee Following Ban On Electric Lights

A new plan for decorating local streets for the Yule season was worked out Wednesday evening at the meeting of the Christmas Committee of the Association of Brighton Citizens. Green laurel is to replace the lights used in former years due to the ban on electric lights this year. Strands of laurel are to be used in the various business districts and more will be used at the corners of streets entering the town, with a green wreath on the center of each string.

The Bethany Bible Class of the Presbyterian church is to hold a covered dinner at 6:15 o'clock Monday evening in the social rooms of the church.

The meeting of the Berean Bible Class of the Methodist church originally scheduled for Thursday evening is to be held tonight. Important business is to be transacted at the meeting, in the home of Mrs. Warren Enke, Mercer road. Plans for the coming year are also to be discussed.

Mrs. Ed Frishkorn, Fifth street, is reported confined to her home by illness.

Members of the New Brighton Board of Education are to meet at eight o'clock Tuesday evening in the local high school.

The Mary Myler Welfare League is to meet at eight o'clock this evening in the home of Mrs. Mildred Warren Hampe, Marion Hill.

Robert Walker, son of Mr. and Mrs. George R. Walker, Penn avenue, who enlisted recently in Pittsburgh as yeoman, third class, U. S. Navy Reserves, left Wednesday evening for duty at Newport, R. I.

Oranges have been grown in Florida for more than 200 years.

Beaver Falls News

Dr. John Coleman Gave Address At Woman's Club Meet

Geneva College Professor Spoke At Meeting Of Local Junior Woman's Club

Dr. John Coleman, Geneva College, was the guest speaker at the meeting of the Beaver Falls Junior Woman's Club held recently in the Council Community House. His subject was "After the War, What?" Virginia Irwin was chairman of the committee in charge of the program. Refreshments were served by the hostesses, Helen Elmes and Miriam Latto. A Thanksgiving motif was used in decorations.

Mr. and Mrs. John K. Krivak, Seventeenth street, were honored recently in their home by their children, Mr. and Mrs. Robert Krivak, Beaver Falls, and Mr. and Mrs. Arthur Hall, New Brighton. The affair was held in observance of the silver anniversary of Mr. and Mrs. Krivak.

The monthly meeting of the Thoburn Society of the Methodist church was held recently at the home of Misses Helen and Myrtle Purviance, Eleventh street. Lunch was served by the hostesses. Plans for a covered-dish dinner Tuesday, December 2, was discussed at the business session.

Mrs. J. F. Kinsel, Patterson Heights, has been visiting her daughter, Mrs. R. B. Sweney, Cincinnati, O.

Mr. and Mrs. R. L. Porter, Edgewood Park road, near Beaver Falls, are the parents of a daughter, Ruth Ann, born last Friday in Jamison Memorial hospital, New Castle.

A pantomime social is to be held at eight o'clock Saturday evening in Moose hall by the newly-organized Beaver Valley Society for the Deaf. Music by an orchestra, a floor show and dancing are also to be enjoyed. The local group, newest addition among the deaf of the state, is fast building toward a successful future under the direction of W. Upton T. Rosenmund.

Medical Society Meets In Beaver

Dr. George B. Rush, Aliquippa, was in charge of the program at the monthly meeting of the Beaver County Medical Society, Thursday afternoon in the assembly room of the court house. The subject was "Acute Exanthemata."

Dr. Rush, Dr. J. D. Stevenson, Beaver, and Dr. W. C. Merriman, Beaver Falls, spoke on the subject. Dr. P. F. Martsolf, New Brighton, president, presided. About thirty-five members attended.

The next meeting will be held Thursday, December 11, at the Beaver Valley Country Club. Afficers for the ensuing year will be elected and the program will include case reports by Dr. T. S. Boyd, Midland; Dr. D. R. Patrick, Monaca; Dr. H. A. Black, Aliquippa, and Dr. V. I. Markson, Beaver Falls.

The difference between high and low tides amounts to as much as 50 feet, as measured in the Nova Scotia basin of Minas.

Rural Churches

CONCORD PRESBYTERIAN — 2, Sunday school; 3 worship service, "Wrestling Not Against Flesh and Blood." Rev. J. R. Mohr.

NEW SEWICKLEY TWP. HOUSE OF MERCY — 10 a. m., Sunday school. Rev. E. Victor Roland.

THE HOSPITALS

Rochester hospital: Total patients —84. A son was born Thursday to Mr. and Mrs. Jack Bradley, Aliquippa. Admitted—Carl Aschman, Aliquippa; Harry E. Roan, South Heights, and Gail Michael, Industry. Discharged—Mrs. Andrew Bunish and daughter, Vanport; Mrs. John Ristich, Aliquippa; Floyd Shrum, Rochester; Lester Deane, Mt. Lebanon; James Hill, New Castle; Charles Parsons, Jr., Bridgewater; Robert Bloom, Beaver, and Mrs. William Dugan, Freedom.

Beaver Valley hospital: Discharged—Mrs. Harry Dickson and son, Monaca, and Amelia Shutey, Bridgewater.

AMUSEMENTS

ORIENTAL THEATRE

Reuniting Bob Hope, Paulette Goddard and Director Elliott Nugent, the trio responsible for that smash laugh hit of a few seasons ago, "The Cat and the Canary," the new laugh special, "Nothing But The Truth," opens today at the Oriental Theatre.

For comedy, Bob Hope is just about the hottest thing on the screen right now and movie fans don't seem to get enough of him, despite the fact that he's been making numerous appearances. The important — and the wondrous — thing, is that Hope can keep on making pictures, and keep on topping previous side-splitting performances. To see beautiful, saucy Paulette Goddard teamed with him is an extra treat for us film fans.

In "Nothing But The Truth" Hope come to us fresh from his hilarious adventures as a rookie in "Caught in the Draft." The lusty laughs over Hope's gags and antics as an infantryman, parachute jumper and tank driver still haven't died down yet. Now here he is again, this time in a story that is noted for its laugh-loaded situations.

Taken from the famous stage comedy, "Nothing But The Truth" concerns a bet of $10,000 made by a certain veracious young man that he can tell the truth for twenty-four consecutive hours. That's the basic idea of the plot, and it just seems to be fairly bursting with opportunities for screamingly funny situations. With Hope in the role of that certain veracious young man who has to out-Washington Washington to win that $10,000 bet against Edward Arnold, Glenn Anders and Leif Erickson, the comedy should be uproarious.

MAJESTIC THEATRE

Starring Gladys George, Barton MacLane, the Dead End Kids and The Little Tough Guys, "Hit the Road" opens tonight at the Majestic Theatre. The picture is probably one of the most powerful screen offerings yet to display the talents of the well-known Dead Enders.

The Dead End Kids in "Hit the Road" are Billy Halop, Huntz Hall, Gabriel Dell and Bernard Punsley.

The significant story deals with the fate of four boys, sons of gangsters slain in a mass underworld killing. Imbued with the thought of revenge against their fathers' murderers, the boys live for the day when they will be released from reform school.

They are paroled and placed in the custody of a former underworld character, once head of their fathers' gang, now an ex-convict endeavoring to go straight.

Barton MacLane is seen in this role which will be remembered as one of the actor's strongest characterizations.

Gladys George is particularly effective in scenes dealing with the difficult reformation of the boys.

Highlighting national defense activities and the ever-present threat of sabotage on the high seas, Universal's timely 12-chapter serial, "Sea Raiders," starts tonight when the first episode, "The Raider Strikes," will be shown.

Starred in the film are the Dead End Kids, including Billy Halop, Huntz Hall, Gabriel Dell and Bernard Punsley; and The Little Tough Guys who portray a gang of tough waterfront boys. John McGuire has the role of a boat builder who constructs a new type of torpedo boat for the U. S. Navy.

BEAVER THEATRE

A highly colorful and dramatic event in motion picture history takes place to-night at the Beaver Theatre with the screening of "Foreign Correspondent." "Foreign Correspondent" must be put down as the thrill spectacle of the year, a motion picture which unreels gripping drama, breath-taking excitement, red-blooded romance and high-pitched intrigue.

"Foreign Correspondent" is played brilliantly by a top-notch cast headed by Joel McCrea, Laraine Day, George Sanders, Robert Benchley, Albert Basserman and Herbert Marshall. Its story, which unwinds on the screen with amazing speed and tempo, keeping the audience on tenterhooks, concerns a crime reporter on a New York daily who is dispatched to Europe to dig up facts. The reporter, played masterfully by Joel McCrea, digs up more than he bargains for, cracking open an international intrigue that has never before been matched on the screen for thrills and excitement.

A double screen bill opens Saturday featuring Kay Harris as "Tillie The Toiler," also Sidney Toler as "Charley Chan In Rio."

GRANADA THEATRE

When Bob Hope makes a bet of $10,000 that he can tell the truth for twenty-four hours, you can bet considerably more than the price of admission to the Granada Theatre, that what will follow will be high-speed, gag-glorious comedy.

Hope makes the wager in the new Paramount farce comedy, "Nothing But The Truth," co-starring Paulette Goddard, and featuring a comedy cast packed solid with favorite names, including Edward Arnold, Leif Erickson, Helen Vinson, Catherine Doucet, Glenn Anders, Grant Mitchell, Rose Hobart and Willie Best. An added recommendation is the fact that the new laugh opus was directed by Elliott Nugent, comedy-wise director of one of the two previous Hope-Goddard adventures into the laugh sphere, "The Cat and the Canary."

Right now Hope is just about tops in film comedy, following sock-successes in such comedies as "Road to Singapore," "Road to Zanzibar" and "Caught in the Draft." His film following has been increasing by leaps and bounds with each new picture, until now his eminence as a comedian is almost undisputed. As for Paulette Goddard, that young lady has been shuttling back and forth between comedy and drama.

RIALTO THEATRE

"How to Ride a Horse," a unique laugh-provoking Technicolor animation, is one of the most popular episodes in Walt Disney's feature-length production, "The Reluctant Dragon," featured this evening and tomorrow at the Rialto in Beaver Falls. Goofy, famous Disney character, plays the main role in the horse subject, while Mickey and Minnie, Donald and Clara, Pluto and many other Disney favorites are seen in the film.

"The Reluctant Dragon" is laid within the Disney studio itself, with Robert Benchley playing himself, a shy, bewildered "average man" tossed by a set of circumstances into the middle of the highly amusing and confusing workings of the colorful Disney plant. Audiences, through Benchley's eyes, will see, as a background to the comedian's adventures, the steps in making animated pictures, from the first funny story sketches to the finished film, along with new deluxe Technicolor comedies projected on the screen.

Included on the program is the hilarious Laurel and Hardy comedy, "Great Guns." Masters of slapstick, the slow burn and the delayed take, they take over the army in such a way as to make the Navy glad they weren't chosen. Tough sergeant Edmund MacDonald makes things miserable for them, and though they fall for lovely Sheila Ryan . . . handsome Dick Nelson already has that situation well in hand. But the pay-off is the usual climax . . . unusual even for Laurel and Hardy . . . and the funniest in many a moon.

"The Reluctant Dragon" and "Great Guns," now at the Rialto, is a sure "blues-chaser"!

Wife Preservers

If your fur coat gets wet, brush it, then hang up in the air away from heat. Don't wear it again until it is thoroughly dry.

THAT'S NO LADY—That's Bob Hope, just trying on a snappy little frilly number (heh, heh) for size, and getting the ha-ha from Paulette Goddard. This is just a sample of the things that go on (and off) in "Nothing But The Truth," new comedy opening today at the Oriental Theatre.

BIG KNOB GRANGERS TO ELECT OFFICERS

Motion pictures were shown by Frank Swick at the meeting of Big Knob Grange in the Grange hall near Unionville. At the next meeting of the Grangers, November 20, officers will be elected for the ensuing year. The meeting has been changed from the regular date.

NEW AIRMEN ARRIVE

By the United Press

A BRITISH PORT, Nov. 14. — Hundreds of additional Canadian fliers and soldier arrived in Britain last night. Officials described the group as the largest sent from Canada under the commonwealth air training program. It also included Australians, New Zealanders and Britons trained in Canada.

Maximum mercury reading on record in Puerto Rico was 90 degrees Fahrenheit.

Dry field bean production in the U. S. increased 66.2 percent from 1909 to 1934.

Midland News

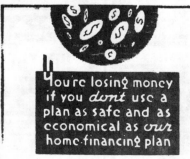

Officers Named At Recent Meeting Of Men's Brotherhood

James McClaskey Elected President Of Methodist Church Organization

Election of officers marked the recent meeting of the Men's Brotherhood of the Methodist church held in the social rooms of the church. The officers are: James McClaskey, president; Roy Grissinger, vice-president; Leroy Turner, treasurer, and Wade Stevens secretary. An oyster supper was enjoyed after the business session. The committee in charge included Robert Wirth, Merrill Campbell and Mr. Stevens.

Mr. and Mrs. Frank Delvaux and sons, Fred and Frank, Charleroi, visited over the week-end with Mrs. Delvaux' parents, Mr. and Mrs. George Wick, Penn avenue.

Mr. and Mrs. James Scholl and children, Neil and Barbara, Ohio avenue, and Carl Erickson, Penn avenue, visited recently with Mrs. Scholl's brother and sister-in-law, Mr. and Mrs. Richard E. Lawson Donora.

Mr. and Mrs. John Mueller, Midland, have returned home after a brief visit with the latter's parents, Mr. and Mrs. J. P. McGovern, Youngstown, O.

Mrs. W. H. Fulmer, Ohio avenue, left Monday to visit her parents, Mr. and Mrs. George W. Mains, McKeesport.

Mrs. Jack Laswell, Mendota, Ill., is visiting this week at the home of her parents, Mr. and Mrs. Frank Chaffin, Penn avenue.

Baden News

Mrs. F. C. Coulter Entertained Club

Mrs. F. C. Coulter, Dettmar avenue, entertained her contract bridge club recently in her home. Favors were claimed by Mrs. Jerome Hessler and Mrs. C. L. McMillen.

Members of the O. L. N. club met recently at the home of Mrs. Clarence Marr, Athalia avenue. Awards were made to Mrs. Helen Shiveley, Mrs. Jesse Romigh and Mrs. Hampton Marr.

John Scobie, Phillips street, has been visiting several days with friends in Erie.

Trails Peruvian Loot

Victor Rubio

Victor Rubio, above, has arrived in New York from Peru as a special investigator seeking trace of a pair of 4,500-year-old bracelets, allegedly stolen from the Peruvian exhibit at the New York World's fair two years ago. These bracelets were found in the ruins of a civilization that preceded the Incas.

Rochester Woman Is Feted On Birthday

Miss Elizabeth McCoy, Rochester, retired principal of Rochester high school, was honored at a birthday dinner in the home of Dr. Grace Cornelius, Ambridge, Monday evening, an annual event.

The guests, members of the A. B. C. club, included Rochester high school teachers who taught under Mrs. McCoy in Rochester. An attractive arrangement of fruit formed the centerpieces for the table. Miss Mayme J. Campbell, Rochester, a sister of the honor guest, was a special guest.

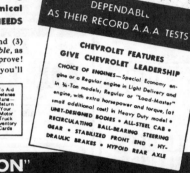

Rochester News

Officers Chosen By Lutheran Sunday School Group Here

All Officers Retained By St. Paul's Sunday School Association For Year

Officers for the ensuing year were elected and plans for the Christmas entertainment by the Sunday school were made at a meeting of the Sunday School Association of St. Paul's German Lutheran church Monday evening in the home of the superintendent, Charles Teapole, Sr., Jackson street. The entertainment will be given on Christmas night in the church auditorium. All officers were re-elected: Superintendent, Charles Teapole, Sr.; assistant superintendent, Clarence J. Conrad, Sr.; secretary, Miss Jean Evans; treasurer, Mrs. Charles E. Ruth. Devotions were conducted by Mr. Teapole. The meeting was concluded with a special hour during which Mrs. Teapole served refreshments.

Mrs. Carl Stormfels will entertain the Dorcas Bible class of Grace Lutheran church at the monthly meeting Thursday evening at her home in Case street. Miss Luella Shafer is teacher of the class.

Mrs. George O. Curry is improving at her home in Ohio avenue, where she has been confined to bed since last Friday by illness.

The weekly session of the Leadership Training School will be held this evening at 7:30 o'clock in the Sunday school room of Grace Lutheran church. Lutheran churches of the Valley are conducting the school.

Chapters from the Gospel of St. John will be discussed at the weekly prayer service this evening at eight o'clock in the First Baptist church by the pastor, Rev. Samuel Wade Stewart.

Circle No. 5 of the Ladies' Aid society of Grace Lutheran church will meet in the home of Mrs. Hilda Brenner, Ohio avenue, Thursday noon for the annual covered-dish dinner and bazaar.

Joyce Bittner is confined to her home in Center street by illness.

Rev. Rodney F. Cobb, rector of Trinity Episcopal church, is spending a few days with his mother, Mrs. B. M. Cobb in Davenport, Ia. He will return to Trinity rectory early Friday morning.

The Clabida Bible class of the Methodist church will meet Thursday evening in the home of Mrs. C. C. Jarrett, Pennsylvania avenue.

Joan and Richard Eckhardt, children of Mr. and Mrs. Paul Eckhardt, are confined to their home on Sunflower road by illness.

The senior choir of the Second Baptist church will meet for rehearsal Thursday evening at 7:30 o'clock in the church.

The Catechetical classes of Grace Lutheran church will met Thursday afternoon, the Junior class at 4:15 and the Senior class at 5:15 o'clock, in the church.

Mrs. J. C. Heim, Virginia avenue, is recovering from a fractured wrist received in a fall in her home.

Myrna and John Damon, children of Mr. and Mrs. Melvin Damon, are improving at their home in East Madison street where they have been confined by illness.

A group of local people will attend the annual "Donation and Reception Day" activities Thursday, November 20, from 2 to 8 p. m. at the Passavant hospital, Pittsburgh.

Thomas Richards, injured in a motor accident near Cumberland, Md., on October 19, was removed to his home in Jefferson street from the Allegheny Valley hospital, Cumberland, Md., where he had been confined since the accident. He is slowly recovering in his home, where he is confined to bed. Mrs. Richards, also injured in the same accident, spent the first week following the accident in the same hospital. She is recovering at her home and is able to be out.

Mrs. H. W. Boulton, Cleveland, arrived here Tuesday evening to spend several days with her parents, Mr. and Mrs. Fred Smith, Pennsylvania avenue. Mrs. and Mrs. Smith also will have as weekend guests, Mr. and Mrs. A. C. Floyd, Hoddonfield, N. J.

Misses Elverne, Bess and Mary Esther McCoy, Ohio avenue, Louise Heppel, Connecticut avenue, Priscilla Smith, Community Springs, and Jean Harris, New York avenue, all students at Muskingum College, New Concord, O., will arrive home this evening to spend the Ohio Thanksgiving vacation in their respective homes. Ohio is observing Thursday, November 20 as Thanksgiving Day.

J. F. Pflug is recovering at his home in Pinney street from injuries received when struck by an automobile at Brighton avenue and Adams street, on November 6 and is able to be about the home on crutches.

Mrs. R. C. Shay and son, George Clinton, Madison, N. J., arrived here today to spend a few days in the home of Mrs. Shay's brother-in-law and sister, Mr. and Mrs. L. C. Wagner, and her brother, John C. Irvin, East Reno street. George Shay is a sophomore at the Stephen Engineering College, New York City.

At the weekly prayer service this evening at 7:30 o'clock in the Presbyterian church, the pastor, Rev. A. E. Driggers, will have as his theme, "Sixth Chapter of Hebrews."

A meeting of Rochester Girl Scout Troop No. 1 will be held in the American Legion home this evening at 7:30 o'clock.

The Navy sent 2,500 books to its men in Iceland and are adding 1,500 more; fiction and non-fiction.

Company B News

WITH THE "BLUE" ARMY IN THE FIELD, Nov. 19.—The attacking "Blue" Army continued to advance on the north wing of the Carolina "battle front" today, although Lt. Gen. Hugh A. Drum's headquarters acknowledged a counter-blow by enemy tanks on the South flank.

("Red" Army dispatches said the "Blues" had launched an all-out offensive. The "Reds" said they were flanked strongly on north and south, and were experiencing a somewhat slower general retreat in the center, under the weight of superior "Blue" numbers.)

Late Monday, "Red" armored forces occupied the southern part of Cheraw, S. C., capturing the "Blue" 30th division headquarters, together with its chief of staff, Lt. Col. Paul R. Younts, according to late reports at Drum's headquarters. Headquarters said, however, that "Red" gains were "limited to some advance in the south."

Drum continued to advance on the northern front, swinging southwest in a semi-flanking movement against the "Rolling Fourth," lightning fast mobile experimental division that is expected to play a large part in the "Red" defense. A communique issued early today said the advancing "blues" had captured the headquarters of the "Rolling Fourth." No details were given, however.

The communique said the "Blues" were continuing their attacks on the whole front, but stressed the advance on the North.

Paper towels produced in American factories last year weighed 129,105 tons, according to the Census.

Steel from the USS Washington, scrapped in 1922, was used in building the stands of Thompson Stadium at the Naval Academy.

The Weather Forecast
Western Pennsylvania: Clear and colder tonight; fair and warmer Tuesday.

THE DAILY TIMES
ROCHESTER-BEAVER-MONACA
FREEDOM—BRIDGEWATER—CONWAY—VANPORT—MIDLAND

Beaver County History
The Camp Sherman football team played the Geneva College team November 24, 1917, at Beaver Falls.

ESTABLISHED APRIL 2, 1874 | BEAVER AND ROCHESTER, PA. MONDAY, NOVEMBER 24, 1941 | BY CARRIER 15 CENTS A WEEK—3 CENTS PER COPY

TANK BATTLE RAGES IN LIBYAN DESERT

Five Hurt When Train Hits Auto

MOTORIST DRIVES CAR ON RAILROAD TRACK BY MISTAKE

Two Midland Men, Three Gallitzin Residents Hurt At Beaver Falls

Freight Train Drags Machine Two Blocks After Crash Early Sunday

Five men were injured, one seriously, early Sunday morning when the automobile in which they were riding was struck by a Baltimore and Ohio Railroad train at Third street and Sixth avenue, Beaver Falls, and dragged two blocks before the train could be stopped.

Joseph J. Pavlock, 21, Gallitzin, Cambria County, driver of the car, told Beaver Falls police he was driving south on Sixth avenue and passed the Tenth street bridge, thinking Sixth avenue continued further toward New Brighton.

When he saw the railroad tracks he thought they were street car rails and proceeded onto them just as the east bound freight tram approached, Pavlock stated.

He admitted he saw the light and heard the whistle of the train and attempted to turn, but the front of the locomotive struck the rear left of the automobile and dragged it to the Pennsylvania railroad bridge before the train could be stopped.

ALL IN HOSPITAL

Pavlock escaped with slight lacerations of the head, but four friends riding with him were more seriously injured. James Foreso, 25, 460 Ohio avenue, Midland, suffered from internal injuries, a probable fracture of the skull and shock. His condition is regarded as critical today.

John Foreso, 29, Gallitzin, a brother of James, received injuries to the chest, head and face; Teno Travino, 31, Midland avenue, Midland, suffered lacerations of the face and head, and George Knapp, 21, Gallitzin, suffered a fracture of the left leg. All suffered from shock.

The injured were removed to Providence hospital where they are confined today.

RAILROADER HURT

James Bailey, 27, East Liverpool, O., is in Rochester hospital today suffering from an injury to his left foot reportedly received while at work Saturday evening for the Pennsylvania Railroad. Bailey was reportedly coupling a "yoke" when it slipped and fell on his foot.

ELLWOOD MEN HURT

McKEESPORT, Nov. 24. — The automobiles of Alexander Ursu, 26, of Ellwood City, and Harry A. Dunstan, 25, McKeesport, came together at an intersection.

The drivers were exchanging information when Ralph Luca, 22, of Ellwood City, a passenger in Ursu's car, started to argue with Dunstan. Dunstan suggested they all go to a police station.

En route, Ursu's car struck a railroad shifting engine. Richard Cogan, 25, Ellwood City, also a passenger in the car, was seriously hurt, and Ursu and Luca also were injured.

As a result, Ursu was held for the grand jury on a charge of drunken driving, following a magistrate's hearing. Cogan was in the hospital and Luca forfeited $10 on a disorderly conduct charge.

Freedom Resident Claimed By Death

Wesley E. Piersol, 65, well-known citizen of Freedom, died Sunday morning at 5:50 o'clock in his home, 1196 Fourth avenue, following a four-day illness from a heart ailment.

Funeral services will be held Tuesday afternoon at 2:30 o'clock in the Methodist church, Freedom. Burial will be in Sylvania Hills.

Mr. Piersol was born in Watkins, O., and the past 41 years had been a resident of Freedom. He was a retired Pennsylvania Railroad locomotive engineer, in which occupation he had been employed 42 years. He was a member of the Methodist church, Rochester Lodge, Free and Accepted Masons, and the New Castle Consistory.

Surviving are: the widow, Mrs. Linna L. Piersol; three sons, George W. Piersol, Freedom; Dr. Merle Fay Piersol, Tiffin, O., and Mark L. Piersol, Beaver; two daughters, Mrs Claire Brink, of near Freedom, and Mrs. Willis Kelly, Freedom; two brothers, Joseph T. Piersol, Freedom, and Orville Pierson, Birmingham, Ala., and two sisters, Mrs. George Stoney, Erie, and Mrs. William Smith, Ostrander, O., and eight grandchildren.

Lost and Found

LOST: Strayed or stolen, a black and tan dog (slightly lame). Finder kindly return to "Pete" Daumiller, 989 Sixth avenue, Freedom. 11|24-26

The Army Tests the 'Tank Destroyer'

Under the critical eyes of Army ordnance officials, the "tank destroyer" is demonstrated at Arlington, Va. Designed by William Bigley of Hoboken, N. J., the destroyer is built to carry a 75 mm. cannon across country at 75 miles an hour. It is basically a metal-tread tank, powered by an airplane engine.

Checks Are Mailed For Delinquent Tax Collections Here

Boroughs, School Districts To Receive Funds Collected By County Treasurer

Handsome checks will be received by several of Beaver County's municipal governments and school districts covering delinquent tax collections made in the office of County Treasurer William V. Kennedy during October.

The collections were largely made by taxpayers who have their filed taxes on the installment payment plan. The total amount collected in October to be remitted was $126,415.33.

Among the amounts certified today by County Controller, Ralph C. Bennett for remittance to the local government treasurers are the following:

Aliquippa Borough, $3,658.10; Aliquippa School, $6,796.90; Ambridge Borough, $3,663.28; Ambridge School, $8,706.54; Baden Borough, $946.64; Baden School, $1,906.11; Beaver Borough, $2,413.84; Beaver School, $2,733.19; City of Beaver Falls, $8,040.17; Beaver Falls School, $11,638.52; Conway Borough, $850.73; Conway School, $1,425.29; Freedom Borough, $943.87; Freedom School, $1,492.81; Midland Borough, $1,184.55; Midland School, $1,587.59; Monaca Borough, $3,355.42; Monaca School, $6,193.94; New Brighton Borough $2,168.06; New Brighton School, $4,059.94; Rochester Borough, $3,630.19; Rochester School, $4,958.48; Rochester Twp., $3,244.97; Rochester Twp. School, $5,868.02.

Dentist Wounded In Mystery Shooting

By the United Press

PITTSBURGH, Nov. 24— A 40-year-old Bridgeville dentist was in Mercy Hospital today with wounds suffered when he was struck by a shotgun blast fired from a parked automobile in the Hill District last night.

Physicians removed more than 75 pellets from the neck, chest, abdomen and upper thighs of the victim, Dr. C. B. Carman. He was struck by the full force of the blast as he walked past the automobile on the darkened street.

The dentist could give no explanation for the shooting, and said he thought he was mistaken for someone else.

Two shots were fired from the automobile, a dark green sedan containing two men. The first struck a window in a house directly opposite, while the second, fired a moment later, struck Dr. Carman.

Center Twp. Home Is Damaged By Fire

Fire at the McKelvey home in Center Township Sunday evening caused twelve families in the vicinity to be without electric light for about an hour.

The home, located near the Elkhorn Run road, was reported burned to the ground.

Falls Man Files Suit Against Railroad Co.

Joseph Bushless, Beaver Falls, today filed a suit against the Pennsylvania Railroad Company, claiming damages totaling $916.61. Bushless alleges that on October 4, 1940 his truck was struck by a railroad car at a crossing on Fifteenth street, Beaver Falls. The car, he avers, was not attached to a locomotive at the time.

Ousting Of Major Upheld By Court

By the United Press

PHILADELPHIA, Nov. 24—A Beaver County common pleas court action holding that Mayor Glenn W. Major, Beaver Falls, could not be legally appointed as a member of a Municipal Authority was affirmed today by the State Supreme Court.

Justice James B. Drew's opinion upheld the ouster of Major from the Beaver Falls Municipal Authority, pointing out that a councilman in a third class city cannot sit on a Municipal Authority.

The action against Major was brought by "quo warranto" proceedings in the name of District Attorney Robert E. McCreary.

Mrs. Anna Tezber Dies At Beaver

Mrs. Anna Tezber, 86, died at 1:35 o'clock Sunday afternoon in the home of her daughter, Mrs. Alexander Gulla, 371 Fourth street, Beaver, with whom she had made her home the past 16 years.

Friends are to be received at the Gulla home where services are to be held at 2:30 o'clock Wednesday afternoon. Rev. Peter Gulla, a grandson, pastor of the Gospel Mission in Beaver Falls, is to officiate. Interment will be in Sylvania Hills.

Surviving are the daughter, six other grandchildren and a brother, Michael Morrick, New York City.

Beaver Falls Firemen Answered Two Alarms

Beaver Falls firemen answered two alarms today in 65 minutes but no serious damage resulted in either case.

They were called at 11:06 o'clock to the home of Mrs. Helen Wagner, 718 Third avenue, Beaver Falls, where the explosion of coal gas in the furnace had blown out a piece of the chimney pipe, but caused no other damage.

At 12:10 o'clock this afternoon the department was summoned to Fifteenth street and Seventh avenue where the automobile of Joe Bushless, Beaver Falls had caught fire. The fire was in the carburetor and no damage resulted.

FLASHES:

By the United Press

RAF MAKES RAIDS

LONDON, Nov. 24—The Royal Air Force carried out attacks upon German naval facilities at Lorient and Brest and the docks at Dunkirk during the night, the Air Ministry reported today.

PROBE PROPAGANDA

WASHINGTON, Nov. 24. — The special grand jury on foreign propaganda in the United States begins its 10th week of deliberations today. Special prosecutor William P. Maloney, as assistant to the attorney general, declined to reveal the names of witnesses to be summoned this week.

MURDER TRIAL OPENS

FARMINGTON, Me., Nov. 24. — Fred G. Wheeler, 48, cattle dealer, goes on trial today for the death of blonde Florence Buzzell, 20, a business college student, whose love diary listed 122 boy friends. If convicted of murder, he would face life imprisonment. He is married and father of three daughters.

BOMBING IN PARIS

NEW YORK, Nov. 24 — Private advices to the United Press today said that a bomb which exploded in Paris destroyed a German bookshop in the St. Mihiel district.

Anti-Communistic Meeting Convenes In German Capital

Representatives Of Eight Nations Gather In Berlin To Sign Pact Today

By the United Press

BERLIN, Nov. 24.—Authorized sources said today that the anti-comintern pact of 1936 would be extended for another five years tomorrow when representatives of Germany and ten or more of her salellite states meet at the chancellory.

Eight foreign ministers attended a "state ceremony" at noon, when a five-year extension of the anti-comintern pact, signed originally by Germany, Italy and Japan, will be signed.

They said that the French Vichy government will not be represented nor will Sweden nor Switzerland.

The extension agreement will be signed by the foreign ministers of Germany, Italy, Spain and Hungary, and the ambassadors of Japan and Manchukuo. All these nations signed the first anti-comintern pact, which expires tomorrow.

HITLER MAY ATTEND

Spokesmen refuse dto say whether Adolf Hitler would attend, but it was assumed he would. Nor would they say whether other non-signatory countries would adhere to the pact.

Although no specific announcement was made regarding other participants, it was believed that the conference would combine the signers of the tri-partite Axis agreement, the anti-comintern pact and Germany's other allies against Russia.

Germany, Japan, Italy, Spain, Hungary, Manchukuo, Slovakia, Bulgaria, Croatia, Finland and Rumania were expected to send delegations.

Shief of State Marshal Henri Philippe Petain and vice-Premier Jean Francois Darlan are to meet Reich Marshal Hermann Wilhelm Goehing at Fontainebleau, near Paris, on Wednesday.

'Women's Land Army' To Be Organized

WASHINGTON, Nov. 24 — Mrs. Franklin D. Roosevelt, assistant director of the Office of Civilian Defense disclosed today that the OCD is planning to organize a "women's land army" to help harvest next year's crop.

The need for "farmerettes", she said, is due to the lack of farm labor caused by the migration of young people from farms to industrial work.

U. S. CONSULATE BOMBED

By the United Press

WASHINGTON, Nov. 24. — The State Department announced today that the United States Consulate at Saigon, French Indo-China, was wrecked by a bomb last night.

BOARD PREPARES TO ARBITRATE IN MINERS' DISPUTE

Three-Man Group To Study Union Shop Demand For "Captive" Coal Mines

Final Decision In Controversy To Be Up To Federal Official

By the United Press

WASHINGTON, Nov. 24. — A three-man arbitration board prepared to meet today or tomorrow to consider United Mine Workers' demands for a union shop in "captive" mines amidst increasing belief among observers that the board's decision would be satisfactory to John L. Lewis.

Since the government has no official representative on the arbitration board a decision to grant the union shop would not place the government in the position of forcing union membership on any worker—action that President Roosevelt has said it would never take.

There was another school of thought, however, which believed that pressure of public opinion and the threat of drastic anti-strike legislation forced UMWA President Lewis to call off his strike and accept arbitration. Those observers considered Lewis' decision a victory for President Roosevelt.

Those who predicted that the arbitration decision would be acceptable to Lewis believed that if the recommendation is not for a union shop it would propose a similar provision which would protect the Union's present membership, but not force non-union members to join the UMWA.

BINDING DECISION

The week-old strike of 53,000 captive miners and the sympathy strike of an estimated 150,000 commercial miners ended Saturday after Lewis accepted President Roosevelt's proposal that the dispute be submitted to an arbitration board. The miners and the Steel Companies are bound to accept the board's decision.

Despite the return of miners to the pits, Congress went ahead with

(Continued on Page Two)

One Dead, 68 Hurt In Railroad Wreck

By the United Press

CORINTH, Miss., Nov. 24 — A broken rail wrecked the express train, "The Seminole," killing one person and injuring 68, authorities said today.

En route from Jacksonville, Fla., to Chicago, the Illinois Central Railroad's Express, was derailed one mile south of here at 5:02 p. m. yesterday while moving at 20 miles an hour. Three Pullmans, four chair cars, and the diner rolled down a 25-foot embankment. The diner was set on fire by its range and burned.

Mrs. Dovie Robertson, 69, of Selmer, Tenn., a passenger, was killed. Three of the injured, all passengers, were in critical condition. Six others were seriously hurt, including members of the train crew.

State Relief Rolls Show New Decrease

By the United Press

HARRISBURG, Nov. 24 — Pennsylvania's general assistance rolls continued their decline during the week ended November 15, Public Assistance Secretary Howard L. Russell reported today, reaching the lowest level since 1933.

The unemployment relief load stood at 74,378 cases comprising 136,826 persons, or a drop of 65 per cent from the level a year ago.

A net decrease of 1,070 cases brought the number of employables down to 29,000, as compared to last week's 30,000.

In addition to general relief rolls, 102,000 cases received old-age aid, 57,000 aid to dependent children, and 14,000 blind pensions.

THANKSGIVING DINNERS TO BE SERVED BY INSTITUTIONS HERE

Thanksgiving Day will be observed with the traditional turkey dinner in the three local hospitals, the Beaver County Children's Home and the Beaver County Home for the Aged, New Brighton, the Beaver County Sanatorium and the Beaver County Home, South Side, and the Passavant Memorial Homes, Rochester, it was revealed today with the announcement of the menus at the various institutions. A special dinner also is planned at the Beaver County jail.

ROCHESTER HOSPITAL

At Rochester hospital, more than 100 pounds of turkey will be needed to serve the patients and staff, it was reported today by Miss Diana Milligan, superintendent of the hospital. This is an increase over the amount usually needed at the hospital, she reported

BEAVER VALLEY HOSPITAL

The menu at Beaver Valley hospital includes fruit punch cocktail, potato chips, roast turkey and dressing, giblet gravy, mashed potatoes, peas, jello salad and saltines, cranberry sauce, date pudding, celery and olives and brick ice cream.

PROVIDENCE HOME FOR AGED

Roast turkey and dressing "with all the trimmin'," will also be the order of the day at Providence hospital and the Beaver County Home for the Aged, New Brighton.

CHILDREN'S HOME

At the Beaver County Children's Home, New Brighton, dinner will consist of turkey and dressing, mashed potatoes and gravy, green beans, candied sweet potatoes,

(Continued on Page Two)

Democrats Seek Full Recount Of Midland Ballots

Votes cast in Midland's four precincts at the November 4 election for all borough officers will be recounted by a special recount board named by the court as a result of petitions filed with Judge Henry H. Wilson Saturday evening.

Shortly before the court house offices closed at noon Saturday, Republican leaders filed petitions to open the ballot boxes of the Third and Fourth precincts of Midland and recount the votes cast for burgess.

About eight o'clock Saturday evening Midland Democrats filed petitions with Judge Wilson asking recounts in all four precincts, not only of the votes for burgess, but also for council, auditor, tax collector, and school director.

On the basis of the original returns made by Midland election boards, the only Democratic candidate to win a borough office was Thomas J. Dublin, candidate for burgess against W. I. McInerney, Republican incumbent. Dublin, who it was said had not campaigned for the office, defeated McInerney by 13 votes. The Republican petitions to recount the third and fourth precinct votes for burgess was in the interest of McInerney, but the Democrats' petitions cover the entire borough election.

BEAVER FALLS RECOUNT

The Midland recount, however, probably will not be started until the special board has completed recounting Beaver Falls ballots. Beaver Falls Democrats have asked for recounts of the votes for mayor and school director in the First, Second, Third, Fourth and Sixth wards, while Republicans have petitioned for recounts of the votes for council in the First, Second, Third, Fourth and Sixth wards, and the Second precinct of the Seventh ward. The

(Continued on Page Two)

House Opens Debate On Price Control Legislation Today

Battle Expected On Proposal To "Freeze" Wages, Rents And Prices

By the United Press

WASHINGTON, Nov. 24 — The House begins debate today on a price control bill that would provide selective controls on individual prices but exempt wages from regulation.

A final vote is expected by the end of the week. But the real battle probably will begin Wednesday when Rep. Albert Gore, D., Tenn., offers his substitute bill to "freeze" all wages, rents and prices. His bill embodies the principles of "overall" price control advocated by Bernard M. Baruch, chairman of the 1918 war industries board.

Gore, predicting support from both Republicans and Democrats, said House Democrats were "split wide open" on the issue. He said Chairman Carl Vinson, D., Ga., of the House naval affairs committee, would speak for his bill.

The House banking committee today adopted an amendment which would restore to the price-control bill the controversial licensing system to force business compliance with price-control regulations.

REPUBLICANS TO MEET

If Gore's plan should be endorsed by a substantial body of Democrats, the fate of price control legislation would lie in the hands of the Republicans. House Republicans have scheduled a party caucus for Wednesday.

The administration will make a last-minute attempt to strengthen the bill it must support on the House floor at a special, secret session of the banking committee this morning.

The committee drastically revised the original administration bill, exempting farm prices from controls until they had reached their 1919 to 1929 levels, and striking from the bill provisions setting up a system of business licensing to enforce price edicts and empowering the government to buy and sell commodities to stabilize prices.

Committee Chairman Henry B. Steagall, D., Ala., has prepared two amendments restoring in part the business licensing provisions and the power to buy and sell. These probably will be presented as committee amendments when the House nears a vote on the bill.

FARM BLOC STRONG

Administration leaders have privately conceded that farm bloc strength in the House is too strong to eliminate the farm price exemptions, even though government farm experts have predicted it would permit average food prices to rise

(Continued on Page Two)

NOTICE—F. & A. M.

The members of Rochester Lodge No. 229, F. & A. M., are requested to meet at Masonic Temple, Rochester, Tuesday afternoon, November 25th, at two o'clock for the purpose of attending the funeral of our late Brother, Wesley E. Piersol.

By order of the
Worshipful Master,
J. HAROLD THOMPSON.
J. J. Zimmerman, Secretary. 11|24.

GERMANS DRIVE NEARER MOSCOW

By the United Press

CAIRO British and Germans locked in giant tank battle south of Tobruk as Axis resistance in Libya stiffens; Gambut taken by British forces; navy believed to have sunk Italian cruiser and destroyer in breaking up Axis reinforcements by sea.

ROME—Axis claims British suffering heavy casualties in Libya, including loss of 50 tanks and destruction of 4th armored brigade; British general captured.

BERLIN—Germans claim capture of Solnechnogorsk, 31 miles northwest of Moscow, as Luftwaffe deals furious blows at Soviet capital.

KUIBYSHEV—Red army withdraws on four vital sectors defending Moscow but maintains new lines against "supreme" Nazi offensive against capital. Russian counter-attacks launched on four fronts.

MOSCOW IN DANGER

The fate of Moscow and of the British offensive in North Africa appeared to be at stake today in big mechanized battles on the frozen eastern front and in the Libyan desert.

Dispatches from Cairo reported that fighting in Libya was spreading over a vast 500 square miles battlefield as the British seized Gambut, Bardia, Sidi Azeis and Fort Capuzzo from the Axis defenders but ran into increasingly severe resistance by German tanks in the region of Tobruk and Sidi Rezegh.

Fighting is "very hard and very confused," the British said, but with American tanks and airplanes showing that "they pack a wallop" the trend continues in favor of the attacking Allied forces.

About 15,000 Axis prisoners were reported captured, more than 260 tanks were knocked out and 76 enemy planes were downed by the RAF, according to preliminary reports, while the British Navy said that an Italian cruiser and a destroyer were believed sunk, and other vessels hit by torpedo and aerial attacks in the Mediterranean.

The Germans apparently were encountering such dangers in attempting to reinforce the Libyan units by sea that they had resorted to extensive use of aid transports, including gliders.

FIFTH FRONT FORMING

The battle of Libya continued on four main fronts, while Italian dispatches indicated that a fifth front was forming far to the west of Tobruk where it was said a British column from Giarabub oasis had reached a line south of Derna.

Neither Rome nor Berlin gave any specific positions in regard to the fighting, but both said that Axis counter-attacks were continuing. The Italians reported that the British had been pushed back in the Tobruk sector with heavy losses, including destruction of 50 tanks, that the British 4th armored brigade had been destroyed and a general taken prisoner west of Solum.

On the eastern front, the Red

(Continued on Page Two)

Miners Return To Work Today After Week-Long Strike

Huge Amount Lost In Wages; Steel Production Suffers From Walk-Out

By the United Press

PITTSBURGH, Nov. 24.—Coal miners returned to work today, ending a week-long strike which had threatened steel production.

Members of the United Mine Workers (CIO) approved with only minor criticism the action of president John L. Lewis in submitting the union shop demand to arbitration.

More than 53,000 miners in the captive mines owned by the steel companies, had struck for a union shop, and were joined by approximately 150,000 workers in commercial mines who walked out in sympathy.

The miners' return forestalled wide-spread shut-downs of steel mills because of coal shortages. Several plants had curtailed operations. The Carnegie-Illinois Steel Corporation, hardest hit, shut down 11 blast furnaces and estimated that it would be mid-week before it returned to full operation. By that time, officials said, 30,000 tons of steel will have been lost.

COSTLY WALK-OUT

In addition to the 11 blast furnaces banked in the Pittsburgh and Chicago areas, the corporation suspended operations in the 80-inch hot strip mill of its Irvin works here, reduced production by 30 per cent at the Clairton By-Products Coke Plant and banked 12 open hearths at the Clairton steel mill.

Neutral statisticians familiar with the industry estimated that commercial miners who struck lost a total of $2,747,000 in wages and the captive miners, $1,510,000. In addition, the commercial miners, under the terms of their contract, face an aggregate union fine of $500,000 for calling an unauthorized strike. The fine is levied on the basis of $1 a man per day. Whether the fine will be imposed is problematical.

These sources said production losses in the Pittsburgh area would amount to 14,000 tons of steel in-

(Continued on Page Two)

Three Children Burn To Death In Home

NORTHFIELD, O., Nov. 24 — Three small children were burned to death Sunday when a gasoline stove exploded and destroyed the home of their parents.

Daniel Huntington, his wife and five children were asleep on the second floor of their home when they were warned of the fire. Huntington dropped his wife from a window and then rescued his two youngest sons, James, 6 months, and Donald, 1 year.

Two Men Executed At Rockview Today

By the United Press

BELLEFONTE, Nov. 24 — Their parallel lives converging on the death house, a McKeesport negro and a Bucks county carpenter went calmly to their deaths today in a double execution by Pennsylvania's electric chair at Rockview Penitentiary.

Willie Jones Fox, 27-year-old negro, walked unaided to the execution chamber he had tried unsuccessfully to avoid for almost a year, to pay for the holdup-murder of Frank Acherson, 60, McKeesport packing house foreman, June 1, 1940.

Harold Frisbie, 33, of Fountainville, Pa., followed a few minutes later for the slaying of Edward Lee, wealthy Sullivan county lumber man during a holdup, October 17, 1940. Frisbie, too, had exhausted all efforts to escape the chair.

The similar lives the two had lived 200 miles apart continued in parallel in their final hours. Neither Fox nor Frisbie made special requests, neither received visitors.

Beaver Draft Board Selects Seven Men

Beaver County Draft Board No. 4, at Beaver, announced today a list of seven men to be inducted at New Cumberland, December 3. They are: Henry C. Podbielski, near Beaver Falls; William L. Fenell, Darlington; Ralph B. Webster, Beaver Falls; William C. Myers, Jr., Wilbert D. May, Robert S. Hall, all near Beaver, and Harry B. Cater, near Beaver Falls.

Cater holds the highest number—1542.

Sign Illuminated By Flare Gives Warning Of Local Speed Trap

Freedom police operated a speed trap in the west end of town, but failed to apprehend the usual number of motorists exceeding the speed limit.

During the six hours the trap was in effect, only about a score of drivers were apprehended traveling over 40 miles per hour, well over the speed limit for the section in which the trap was in effect, according to Police Chief Steve [illegible].

Investigation revealed some "Good Samaritan" had placed a large sign at the east end of town bearing the warning: "Caution, Speed Trap", and had left a flare with it to illuminate his warning.

Warnings were also telephoned among the district trucking terminals and as far east as Harrisburg to inform truckers of the trap.

25 SHOPPING DAYS 'til Christmas
SHOP EARLY

Young Republicans Of County Ready For Dinner-Dance

Large Crowd Expected To Attend Fourth Annual Affair Friday Evening

With many prominent state and district political leaders expected to attend, the fourth annual banquet and dance of the Young Republicans of Beaver County will be held Friday evening, December 6, at 6:30 o'clock, in the General Brodhead Hotel, Beaver Falls.

Over 200 men and women from all sections of Pennsylvania have made reservations for the affair and even more are expected to attend.

Following is the program as announced today by the committee:

Invocation, Rev. James M. Barnett, Monaca; introduction of toastmaster, Harold J. Howarth, Beaver Falls, chairman of the banquet committee; toastmaster, George H. Marvin, Ohioview, chairman of the Beaver County Young Republicans; remarks, Attorney Frank E. Reed, chairman of the Beaver County Republican Committee; remarks, Mrs. George L. Shaw, Beaver, vice-chairman of the county committee; remarks, Judge Frank E. Reader; address, Frank C. Hilton, chairman of the Young Republicans of Pennsylvania; introduction of guests; address, William S. Livengood, state Secretary of Internal Affairs; benediction, Rev. Fr. C. P. Koscisz, Beaver Falls.

Dancing, cabaret style, will follow immediately after the dinner.

Several other state Young Republican leaders, in addition to Hilton, will attend the banquet, along with at least one other state cabinet member and various other state officials.

Boy, 14, Indicted In Killing Of Aged Woman

MEDIA, Dec. 4—John Leeds, 14-year-old Germantown boy, was indicted by a Delaware county grand jury on a charge of murder in the fatal beating of Mrs. Elizabeth Watson, 83. He will go on trial January 12.

The youth is accused of beating Mrs. Watson and her sister, Miss Belle Geary, 80, near their Media home September 24, the day he escaped from Glen Mills School, a reformatory. Mrs. Watson died three days after the attack. The boy was apprehended in Columbus, O.

New Brighton News

Officers Elected By Brighton Club Here At Recent Meeting

James Mills Elected Director At Meeting Of Local Musical Organization

Officers were elected Tuesday evening at the meeting of the Brighton Club Band. The officers elected are: Director, James Mills; assistant director, Vic Mathis; president, J. R. Hoskins; vice - president, A. Cooper; treasurer, James Duff; secretary, R. Franke; manager, E. L. Steele; assistant manager, Vic Mathis, and trustees, R. Hilberg, W. Powell and J. Burch. Rehearsal was held after the business meeting.

Members of the New Brighton WCTU are to hold a Christmas party in conjunction with their monthly meeting at 2:30 o'clock Friday afternoon in the home of Mrs. E. Joe Vandervort, Eleventh avenue. Miss Cora Burry is to speak on her recent trip to Mexico.

The meeting of Miss Cora Burry's Class of the First Methodist church, originally scheduled for this evening, has been postponed until Friday, December 12.

Members of the Ladies' Bible class of the First Baptist church are to meet at eight o'clock this evening at the home of Mrs. G. E. Kaufman, Second street.

The Philathea Class of the Fifth Avenue Methodist church is to hold a Christmas dinner at 6:30 o'clock this evening in the social rooms of the church. A "grab-bag" is to be the feature.

The Helping Hand Circle is to meet Friday evening at the home of Mrs. Ethel Gephart, Penn avenue.

Street Lights Out In Upper Valley Section

One circuit of street lights in the lower end of Beaver Falls, Patterson Heights and Patterson Township was out for two and one-half hours Wednesday evening after trouble on the wire had caused a transformer to burn out at the Beaver Falls sub-station of the Duquesne Light Company.

The necessary clearance of the source of trouble was made more difficult for the repair crew as the dence fog enveloping the county hampered operations.

Rochester Woman Host To Members Of Club

Mrs. Edwin Shank, Rochester, entertained the Lucky Star club at her home Tuesday evening. A brief business session preceded the cards. Awards in "500" were won by Mrs. Garfield Adams, Mrs. Edward Hunter and Mrs. Louis Polce.

The hostess, in serving refreshments, was assisted by Mrs. Hinsman of Rochester,. Special guests were: Mrs. Robert Shank, Mrs. Pearl Selsridge and Mrs. Louis Heeter, Rochester.

TO ISSUE BONDS

HARRISBURG, Dec. 4. — The State Authority has agreed to issue $750,000 worth of bonds to construct the new executive mansion, Gov. Arthur H. James said today. That sum will cover cost of land and construction.

CLASSIFIED ADVERTISING

This classified advertising department is for the convenience of the public. To insure publication the same day orders should be received by 10 a. m. Orders not received in time will be published the following day. All copy received subject to being edited or rejected by us. When sending advertisements by mail care should be used to write plainly giving complete instructions so that we may give efficient service in the preparation and publication of the advertisements. When possible, payment should accompany the order. This will be expected with orders from strangers. Cash with order, one cent a word for each publication, no advertisement published for less than 25 cents for each publication. Six consecutive publications for price of four. Extra charge will be made for use of large type. Classified advertisements not accompanied by cash will be charged at two cents per word with a minimum of 50 cents for each publication. This is absolutely necessary on account of the clerical work involved. Fifty per cent discount will be allowed on charge classified advertisements if paid for before expiration date. Usual cash rates will apply to advertisers having other running open accounts with us. The above is a local schedule applying only within Beaver County.

Beaver 1800 Rocheste- 3300

Wanted

WANTED: Paper to remove by steam, no dirt or muss, Fred Hamilton, Vanport. Phone Beaver 2155-W. 12|1-6 inc

Help Wanted—Female

WANTED: Salesgirl. Must live in Beaver or vicinity. Reply giving complete details about self, including salary expected. Address replies P. O. Box 438, Beaver Falls. 12|3-5 inc

WANTED: Middle-aged woman to do housework and be companion to aged woman in suburban home. Phone Roch. 2326-W, evenings. 12|3-9 inc

WANTED: Girl for general housework, no laundry work. Call Beaver 2019 or apply 358 Beaver St., Beaver. 12|3-9 inc

WANTED: At once, girl for light housework; apartment of 4 rooms, evenings free. Apply 488 Sharon Road, Beaver. 12|3-4

WANTED: All your clothes to clean and press. Miller's Cleaning Shoppe, next to City Building. Beaver. Phone Beaver 2235-J. 11|29-12|12 inc

Help Wanted—Male

WANTED: Experienced meat cutter. Write Box A-90 c/o THE DAILY TIMES, Rochester, stating experience. 12|3-9 inc

WANTED: Man to work on farm. Phone Beaver 1864 or apply at 940 Third street, Beaver. 12|3-9 inc

CREDIT MAN
Large financial institution wishes to add several young men to its local staff. Must be between the ages of 24 and 28. Must present good appearance, have pleasing personality, ability to contact people. Must be high school graduate, college training helpful. Straight salary basis plus car allowance. Fine opportunity for permanent connection and advancement. Please call in person between 9 and 5 and ask for Mr. Armagost, Personal Finance Company, 723 12th St., Beaver Falls. 12|1-6 inc

WANTED: Let us clean and press your suit or topcoat, at Beaver's only dry cleaning plant. Miller's Cleaning. Phone Beaver 2235-J. 11|28-12|11 inc

Wanted—Salesmen

GOOD OPENING in Conway, Baden, Monaca and North Rochester. Full time route selling Rawleigh Household Products. Start immediately. Must have car. Get more particulars. Rawleigh's, Dept. PNL-29-208K, Chester, Pa., or see G. E. Kaufman, 1345 Second St., New Brighton, Pa. 11|28-12|4-11-18

Wanted—To Rent

WANTED: To rent in Beaver or lower valley town, a six or seven room house. Must have at least three bedrooms. Rent not over $50 a month. Call Beaver 1094-R. 12|2-8 inc

WANTED: To rent three unfurnished rooms, Rochester preferred, rent must be reasonable for possession in two weeks. Phone Roch. 3213-W. 12|1-6 inc

Wanted—To Buy

WANTED: To buy wardrobe, wooden preferred; single bed, radiant gas stove, in good condition and reasonable price. Phone Rochester 733-J. 12|4-10 inc

For Sale

FOR SALE: Macey sectional book case (5 sections) price $15, good condition. Also "Easy" electric washer, price $10. Inquire 501 Second St., Beaver. 12|3-4

FOR SALE: Motorola automobile radio, practically new heater equipped for defrosters, one 6.00x16 white side wall tire, one set rear fender skirts, one set of chromium wheel rings. Call Beaver 1329-M or inquire 371 Fourth St., Beaver. 12|3-9 inc

FOR SALE: Repossessed Philco auto radio, complete with aerial, cost $37.50, can be had for balance. Call at 723 Twelfth street, Beaver Falls. 12|3-9 inc

THE PERFECT GIFT—
A CALORIC FURNACE FOR THE HOME
Call Us At Once — We Will Install Before Xmas
G. W. WALTON HDWE. CO.
BEAVER
12|1-6 inc.

FOR SALE Save 60 per cent or more buy new recapped tires. Large variety to choose from. Used tires cheap. Come to White. 451 Deer Lane, Rochester 12|1-6 inc

For Sale

FOR SALE: Lady's brand new camel hair coat, size 16. Will sell reasonable. Call Beaver 1563-W or inquire 863 Corporation street, Beaver. 12|4-10 inc

FOR SALE: Used furnace with new firepot, 22-inch size; Furbrick firepot lining, Blue Ribbon soot destroyer. G. W. Walton Hdwe. Co., Beaver. 12|4-10 inc

FOR SALE: Gas heating furnace for house; in good condition; will sell very reasonable. Inquire 264 Fourth street, Beaver. 12|4-10 inc

FOR SALE: Child's roll top oak desk, like new, also pair men's skates. Inquire 817 Riverside Drive, Bridgewater. 12|4-10 inc

FOR SALE: Grande enamel top gas range, excellent condition, good baker, reasonable. Inquire 365 New York avenue, Rochester. 12|3-9 inc

Call your orders, name engraved Christmas cards. Beautiful artistic designs 50 for $1. Call for free demonstration. Phone Roch. 3935. 12|3-4

FRASER'S POTTERY SHOP, SUNFLOWER ROAD — Select your Christmas Gifts. We have a nice selection of dinnerware, 32-53-95 piece sets; 32-piece sets, pastel shades, $1.98 and up; mixing bowls, casseroles, cookie jars, also full line of vases and whatnots. Many other useful gifts. Shop early—a small deposit will hold merchandise until Christmas. 12|3-9 inc

FOR SALE: All wool mackinaw with parka; brown leather jacket, reversible; pair girl's figure ice skates, white shoes, size 6. Phone Beaver 2019. 12|3-9 inc

FOR SALE: Persian lamb coat, size 14, good condition, will sell reasonable. Inquire 187 Shields St., Rochester. Phone Roch. 2110. 12|2-8 inc

FOR SALE: Good piano, very reasonable. Also gentlemen's suits, large size. Phone Beaver 1664-R or inquire 888 Fourth St., Beaver. 12|2-8 inc

FOR SALE: Golden Oak buffet, pair quilting frames, two hot plates, gas heating stove. 383 Vermont Ave., Rochester. Phone 493-J. 12|2-8 inc

FOR SALE: Two circulating oil heaters (small type), also drum of kerosene oil. Inquire 518 Oregon avenue, Rochester, or phone Roch. 1434-W. 12|2-8 inc

FOR SALE: Just arrived, large stock of late model sweepers, including Streamline Hoovers and Electroluxs; many others as low as $15; washer and sweeper repairing a specialty. Harper's Sweeper Shop, 386 Brighton Ave., Rochester. Phone 9099. 12|1-6 inc

Magazine subscriptions, either new or renewal. Special prices for gift subscriptions until Christmas. All publishers' prices met. Phone Roch. 3373-R. Esther A. Shoop. 12|1-6 inc

FOR SALE: One New Process kitchen stove. Call Beaver 925. 12|1-6 inc

BIG WALLPAPER SALE: ½ off Thousands rolls. Save, buy now before prices go up. Real bargains, engraved papers. We deliver. HELMICK'S, 390 Brighton Ave., Rochester. 11|12-12|10 inc

FOR SALE: Duo-Therm circulating oil heater. Will heat five rooms. One month old. Moving. Will sell for $100. Cost new $135. Phone Rochester 252-R. 11|28-12|4 inc

AT LOHRY'S
Sweet CIDER every day. Several varieties of good cooking and eating apples — Winesap, Senator, Rome Beauty, Baldwin, Red and Gold Delicious. Also APPLES for Apple Butter. Call Beaver 1433-W. 11|3*

STORM WINDOWS
Redwood, Combination Glass and Screen, completely installed. Free Estimate. Hamilton Glove & Awning Co., phone Beaver 74. 9|16*

For Sale—Dogs

FOR SALE: Scottish Terrier puppies. Registered in American Kennel Club. Will make splendid Christmas gifts. 767 Sixth street, Beaver. Phone Beaver 1442. 12|1-6 inc

For Sale—Lots

FOR SALE: Level lots 80x395 feet, ¾ mile from Propeller plant, 35 feet to concrete road. Gas, electric, phone and bus service. Fine location. George Dobbs, Tuscarawas Road, Beaver. 12|4-10 inc

FOR SALE: In Monaca, lot on Virginia avenue, size 35x100, at bargain price. Easy terms. People's Building and Loan Association, Beaver Falls. 12|2-8 inc

LARGE LEVEL LOTS on good road, near Monaca, $150 each, $15 down payment, $5.00 per month. Inquire H. F. Morgan, Sylvan Crest. Phone Roch. 756-M. 12|2*

For Sale—Acreage

FOR SALE: Twenty-five acres land with large barn 40x60, level, good location, terms. E. Jay Hineman, Beaver R. D., Ohioview. 12|3-4

2½ ACRES — TERMS — $400
170 feet on hard road, 600 feet deep, good land, high elevation, back of Beaver. E. M. Standley, Realtor. Phone Beaver 957. 11|28-12|4 inc

For Sale—Real Estate

Investment Property—Business Block in Freedom, two store rooms, house - apartment over store. An excellent paying proposition as an investment. Sacrifice. Must be sold to settle estate. Call Rochester 559-J. C. E. Snead 12|3-9 inc

For Sale—Used Cars

FOR SALE: Special Deluxe 1941 5-passenger Plymouth; radio, heater, low mileage, private owner. See Mr. Hall, Penn-Beaver Hotel, Rochester. 12|4-5

FOR SALE: Two-door Ford, A-1 condition, 5 good tires and heater, cheap. Phone Roch. 1656-R. 12|3-5 inc

FOR SALE: 1933-34 Ford coach, in good condition with excellent motor, $50. Sim Holmes, 506 Fourth St. Phone Beaver 1294-J. 12|2-8 inc

1940 Pontiac Six 4-dr. Sedan
1936 Pontiac Six Coupe
1937 Dodge 4-dr.
1936 Dodge Coupe
1938 DeSoto 4-dr.
1937 DeSoto Coupe
1936 Ford Tudor
1936 Ford Conv. Coupe
1939 Studebaker Champion 2-dr.

NEW DE SOTOS AND PLYMOUTHS IN STOCK
STUMP BROS.
Ohio and Reno Sts., Rochester
Phone 1615
12/1-6 inc.

AT LOW BANK RATES
Finance your next automobile, a New Home, Repairs to your present home, through The Freedom National Bank, Freedom, Pa. 12|1-31 inc

GOOD USED CARS

1939 Dodge sedan, radio, heater	$695
1937 Chevrolet sedan	$350
1938 Plymouth coupe	$400
1937 Ford Tudor	$275
1937 DeSoto coupe	$350
1937 Dodge sedan	$385
1936 Packard sedan	$295
1936 Plymouth 2-door	$250
1935 Plymouth sedan	$225
1935 Plymouth 2-door	$200
1935 Plymouth coupe	$145
1935 Chevrolet 2-door	$185

Christy Motor Co.
469 Market St., Beaver
Phone 1456
11/29 - 12/5 inc.

FOR SALE: 1936 Chrysler 8, two new tires, heater; sell for $115 cash. Inquire C. W. Mason, Noss Plan, Rochester. Phone Roch. 3117-J. 11|29-12|5 inc

YOU OWE YOURSELF A LOOK AT
A. R. C. H. SNYDER'S
CONWAY, PA.
USED CARS
BEFORE YOU BUY
Low Finance Rates.
Large Stock To Choose From.
Lifetime Service Policy.
10/22*

For Sale—Used Trucks

FOR SALE: G. M. C. U-plate dump truck $350; two welding torches and gauges at Eighth St. Garage, Freedom. Phone Rochester 1908-M after 3 p. m. 11|28-12|4 inc

For Sale—Coal

CLINTON 4" lump coal $4.75; 2" lump $4.50; 2x4 egg. $4.25, by the truck load. Call Beaver 386-J. E. M. Sayre. 12|2-15 inc

FOR CLEAN COAL, call Kenneth White at Alexander Service Station, Rochester. Phone Rochester 9021. 11|29-12|5 inc

CHAMPION or local coal, priced from $4.25 up. For prompt delivery call Thos. Summers, Beaver 872. 11|3-15 inc*

BE WISE
Fill your coal bin with PORT Coal Now
Call Beaver 2564
KIERNAN-COURTNEY COAL CO.
9/12*

Business Opportunities

Your opportunity to buy a home with a small business to help pay for home — 5-rooms with storeroom attached and equipped for business. Good location. Phone Roch. 458. 12|4-6 inc

FOR SALE: Meat and grocery store in good industrial town, all new fixtures, splendid location. Write "Grocery" c/o DAILY TIMES, Rochester. 12|2-15 inc

For Sale—Livestock

FOR SALE: Three pigs, weight 150 to 200 pounds, nice for sausage. Phone Rochester 6138-R-2. 12|4-6 inc

SELL with WANT-ADS

For Sale—Houses

FOR SALE: Brick house located on Sunflower road — gas, water, electric, bath, hot water heat and garage. Large frontage. Price $4000. Terms 25% down, balance monthly payments. For information call Roch. 283 (evenings); Roch. 787-J (daytime). 12|4

FOR SALE: WEST VIEW—Beautiful bungalow-type frame house, seven rooms; bath, furnace, laundry trays, hardwood floors, large living room, mantel, built-in bookcases, double lot nicely shrubbed. $600 will handle; balance like rent. Ben H. Boss, 815 Third Ave., New Brighton. 12|4-10 inc

FOR SALE: Five-room house in Rochester; gas, water and electric. Price $600 cash. Inquire after 4:30 p. m. at 125 Atlas Ave., Rochester. 12|4-10 inc

FOR SALE: 4-room house, one acre ground, necessary outbuildings. Located Brighton Twp., 4 miles from Beaver. Inquire 1221 Third St., Beaver. 12|2-8 inc

FOR SALE: Six-room house, corner lot, located 477 Connecticut avenue and Webster street, Rochester. Inquire Lucille Houlette, 410 Connecticut Ave., Rochester. 11|29-12|5 inc

FOR SALE: Six-room house, bath, 1 acre ground, 2-stall garage, gas, electric, well and cistern water, electric pump; price very reasonable. 2 miles from Monaca, 1 mile from Union Cemetery gate on blacktop road. Sidney Huffmyer. 11|29-12|5 inc

4-ROOM HOUSE, CENTER ST., ROCHESTER
Price $1,000, down payment $300, balance the same as rent. House has slate roof, cistern water, gas and water. E. M. Standley, Realtor. Phone Beaver 957. 11|28-12|4 inc

FOR SALE: In Freedom, 6-room house, completely reconditioned, ready for immediate occupancy. Like new inside and out. Small down payment, balance like rent, including taxes. Call Roch. 1546. 11|12*

For Rent—Rooms

FOR RENT: Two furnished rooms for light housekeeping, sink in kitchen, private entrance. Inquire 416 14th St., Monaca. Phone Rochester 574-R. 12|4-10 inc

FOR RENT: One large front furnished room, all conveniences; one block from P. & L. E. depot. Phone Beaver 1234-R, or inquire 294 East Second street. 12|3-9 inc

FOR RENT: Two cheerful furnished rooms for light housekeeping, nicely papered, modern conveniences, electric refrigerator; on bus line, adults only. 487 Adams street, Rochester. 12|2-8 inc

FOR RENT: Large double sleeping room, modern conveniences. Inquire 144 College avenue, Beaver or phone Beaver 1399-R. 12|2-8 inc

FOR RENT: One sleeping room for two gentlemen, with board. Inquire 468 Washington St., Rochester or phone Rochester 1113-R. 12|1-6 inc

FOR RENT: Two 2-room furnished apartments, all conveniences, in Freedom. Inquire 577 Fourth Ave., Freedom. 11|28-12|1 inc

FOR RENT: One modern furnished sleeping room, centrally located in Monaca. Inquire 911 Washington avenue. 12|1-6 inc

For Rent—Houses

FOR RENT: Three-room house on Brodhead Road, gas and electric. Reference required. Call Rochester 6125-R-4. 12|4-5

FOR RENT: In Monaca, 8-room dwelling, bath, furnace, garage; suitable for two families. Inquire O. H. Locke, 1231 Pennsylvania Ave., Monaca. Phone Roch. 2394. 12|4-5

FOR RENT: Property at 230 Beaver street, Beaver. All modern conveniences. Reference required. Available January 1st. Phone or write Wm. H. Garver, Brodhead Hotel, Beaver Falls. 12|3-9 inc

FOR RENT: East Liverpool, Ohio, best location, 6-room modern house, clean, adults. Immediate possession. 509 Maryland Ave., East End. Phone Jack Mason, E. L. 4167-J. 11|29-12|5 inc

Modern 8-room house with three baths, gas heat, in good location in Beaver, $85 month. Shown by appointment. Eugene R. Hurst Agency. Beaver 1043-J. 11|28-12|4 inc

For Rent—Apartments

FOR RENT: Two-room unfurnished apartment. Inquire 440 College Ave., Beaver or phone 1239-R. 12|3-4

FOR RENT: Two furnished apartments. Private entrance and baths. Phone Beaver 2306-J. 12|1-6 inc

Miscellaneous

Patterson Township Firemen Penny Carnival every Friday night. New system 35c per card. No award less than $3.00. Door award. Play starts at 8:30 o'clock. 11|5*

For Dependable Maytag service, call Beaver County Maytag Store, New Brighton—3484. We have some good bargains in used ironing and washing machines. 10|29*

Carnival every Thursday Night 8:30 sharp. Cards 50c or 3 for $1.00. Special games and special double awards. Protected parking. Pulaski Township, Marion Hill Firemen. 11|5*

INDOOR CARNIVAL
New Legion Home
Adams St., Rochester
TUES. & FRI. NITES
8:30 P. M. (Eastern Standard Time)
23 Games 50c—Prizes $1, $2, $3, $5 in Merchandise

Miscellaneous

FOR FLOOR SANDING call E. J. Cochran, Rochester 6108-J-2. Hardwood floors layed, sanded and finished. Old floors finished like new. 11|1*

Repairs—Service

FACTORY-TO-YOU
Re-Upholstering
Dress up your home for the holidays. Our experts will rebuild or recover your furniture to make it look like new. Our work is guaranteed ... prices reasonable. All work accepted now will be returned in time for Christmas.
KANE CHAIR MFG. CO.
Old Opera House. Rochester, Pa. Phone Roch. 2610-J
12/2-8 inc.

TO PROPERTY OWNERS: Clogged sewers opened without digging with Ideal Electric Sewer opener. Phone Roch. 931-W or Roch. 1578-W. Mayhue Brothers. 11|4-E.O.W.*

Having trouble with your washer? Call Hudson's Appliance Shop. We service all makes. All work guaranteed. Prices reasonable. Phone Roch. 306. 9|9*

Amusements

The Cozy Nook—bar, dancing, grill. Couples' entrance on Fifth street. Tonti Hotel, Midland, Pa. 11|29-12|12 inc

Legal Advertisements

IN THE ORPHANS' COURT OF BEAVER COUNTY, PENNSYLVANIA.

In the matter of the FIRST AND FINAL ACCOUNT OF RALPH E. CHAMBERS, EXECUTOR of the ESTATE OF LUELLA McKEE, deceased. No. 11 September Term, 1941.

NOTICE OF HEARING AND DISTRIBUTION

All parties in interest are hereby notified that on the 26th day of November, 1941, the above Court made an order fixing Saturday, the 3rd day of January, 1942, at 9:00 o'clock A. M. Eastern Standard Time, at the Court House, Beaver, Pennsylvania, as the time and place for hearing on said Account and for distribution of the balance shown thereby to and among those legally entitled thereto.

HAZEL G. KENNY, Clerk.
Moorhead, Marshall & Sawyer, Attorneys for Accountant, Beaver Trust Bldg., Beaver, Pa.
12|4-11-18

EXECUTRIX NOTICE

Estate [illegible] Konvolinka, deceased, late of the Borough of Monaca, Beaver County, Pennsylvania. Letters Testamentary upon the above estate having been granted to the undersigned, notice is hereby given to those indebted thereto to make immediate payment, and to those having claims or demands to present them for settlement.

WILHELMINA KONVOLINKA, Executrix, 1114 Pennsylvania Ave., Monaca, Penna.
Eckert & Sohn, Attorneys.
11|6-13-20-26-12|4-11

EXECUTRIX NOTICE

Estate of ROSE CALDERONE, deceased, late of the Borough of Rochester, Beaver County, Pennsylvania. Letters Testamentary upon the above estate having been granted to the undersigned, notice is hereby given to those indebted thereto to make immediate payment, and to those having claims or demands to present them for settlement.

VIRGINIA HAMILL, Executrix, 117 East Park St., Rochester, Penna.
Eckert & Sohn, Attorneys, Beaver, Pa.
11|6-13-20-26-12|4-11

EXECUTRIX NOTICE

Estate of JAMES M. MATEER, deceased, late of Center Township, Beaver County, Pa., letters Testamentary upon the above estate having been granted to the undersigned, notice is hereby given to those indebted thereto to make immediate payment, and to those having claims or demands to present them for settlement.

ELIZABETH P. MATEER, Executrix, Monaca Pa., R. F. D. No. 1, Box 108-A.
Lawrence M. Sebring, Attorney.
11|20-26-12|4-11-18-24

ADMINISTRATRIX NOTICE

Estate of William P. Brown, deceased, late of Clermont, Lake County, Florida. Ancillary Letters of Administration upon the above estate having been granted to the undersigned, notice is hereby given to those indebted thereto to make immediate payment, and to those having claims or demands to present them for settlement.

HELEN M. BRAY, Ancillary Administratrix, 982 Second St., Beaver, Pa.
Eckert & Sohn, Attorneys.
11|6-13-20-26-12|4-11

Legal Papers
Notarized efficiently.
Hours 8 to 4.
Maude F. McBrier
DAILY TIMES Office
570 - 3rd St., Beaver

NOTARY PUBLIC

Read THE TIMES Classified Ads

PRIVATE BUCK .·. By Clyde Lewis

RIFLE RANGE
CAMP WOLTERS
SUGGESTED BY PVT. STEVE KOLITA 58 BAT. CO. B. FORT WOLTERS, TEX.
CLYDE LEWIS
12-4

"You haven't hit the target all morning, Private Buck. I'd suggest you fix your bayonet and CHARGE it!"

THE OLD HOME TOWN By STANLEY

I JUST PICKED UP TWO NEW MEMBERS FOR YOUR ORGANIZATION, FOLKS!!
IF YOU'RE FOR IT WE'RE AGIN IT SOCIETY
IT TOOK GRANDPAPPY GALE WINDPENNY JUST TWO MINUTES TO BREAK UP A SECRET MEETING OF ONE OF THOSE CRACK POT ORGANIZATIONS
STANLEY
12-4

Green Blames Lewis In Labor Dispute

CINCINNATI, Dec. 4 — Blaming John L. Lewis, CIO mine chieftain, for anti-labor sentiment and pending anti-strike legislation, William Green, president of the American Federation of Labor, declared today he "would leave the country before I would make myself responsible for such disservice to the American worker."

Green addressed the AFL-affiliated United Automobile Workers at that union's first national convention since its disaffection from the CIO.

Referring to Lewis' stand in the "captive mines" dispute, Green said, "Before the coal strike, Congress showed no disposition to enact the score or more anti-labor bills before it."

He denounced bitterly all forms of anti-strike legislation.

"There is none mild enough," he shouted at one point, "to meet with my approval."

Al Smith, Jr., May Be Disbarred Soon

NEW YORK, Dec. 4—A special grand jury today handed up a presentment to justices of the appellate division of the state supreme court calling for the disbarment of Alfred E. Smith, Jr., son of the former governor of New York, on 11 specific charges of malpractice.

The presentment said:

"From the evidence, the grand jury are of opinion that Alfred E. Smith, Jr., has committed acts of professional misconduct, fraud, deceit, crime and misdemeanor, and conduct prejudicial to the administration of justice which render him unfit to remain an attorney and counsellor-at-law in the state of New York."

The presentment charged that Smith accepted money in 11 separate instances.

Self-sealing fuel tanks for airplanes have been in use for some time. Now comes word of the development of a process to manufacture self-sealing hose, thus making a completely protected, bullet-sealing fuel system.

The USS Solace, new Navy hospital ship, distills 40,000 gallons of drinking water daily from sea salt water.

CHAMPION COAL
6 in. lump and furnace
Lowest prices — Prompt delivery
PURE, CRYSTAL CLEAR ICE
SAM CUTRONA
Phone 123 or 294 Rochester

MOVING
TRANSFER and PIANO MOVING GENERAL HAULING
S. E. WALTON
BEAVER
Phone Beaver 164
560 Corporation Street

Bridgewater News

Club Members Will Meet Friday Night

The semi-monthly meeting of the J. G. club will be held Friday evening in the home of Mrs. Alecta Pickens, New Brighton.

Members of the Dorcas Circle of the Methodist church enjoyed their Christmas party Tuesday evening in the parsonage. A covered-dish dinner was served at 6:30 o'clock. At the conclusion of a short business session, a social time was enjoyed with a "grab-bag" as a feature.

"Bill" Weyand and "Jim" Bayes, Market street, Lester Holt and David Shroads, Brighton Township and Hobart Shroads, near Rochester, returned home Wednesday morning after a several days hunting trip in McKeane county. Hobart Shroades bagged an eight-point buck.

David Love, Detroit, has returned home after a several days visit with Mr. and Mrs. H. S. Thomas and son, Harvey, Riverside Drive, and other Valley relatives.

Mrs. C. M. Lindsay, son Francis and nephews, David and Danny Lindsay, Washingtonville, visited over the week-end with Mr. and Mrs. Alfred Gallagher, Beaver, and local relatives.

Hartzel's Sell Quality Furniture.

Especially designed equipment permits sponge fishermen to work at depths of 150 feet, according to the Department of Commerce.

ROYAL TYPEWRITERS
With the Magic Margin
Exclusive Agents for Beaver County.
Service—Supplies—All Makes Repaired
C. F. BROWN
218 Federal Title & Trust Bldg., Beaver Falls

This Year Give a Practical Gift!
Corona, Underwood and Royal portable typewriters make ideal gifts for students or for the home.

All makes of standard office typewriters and supplies
W. P. POLLOCK CO.
Beaver Trust Bldg. Phone Beaver 1011

SMART! HOME OWNERS
Have your bin filled with Shane Bros. coal now, so you'll be snug when cold weather comes.

ORDER COAL NOW

SHANE BROS. TELEPHONE ROCH. 1444

The first lighthouse in the United States after the founding of the republic was built at Cape Henry, Virginia, in 1792.

The Department of Commerce says that 4,500,000 motor trucks move over the nation's highways.

Quick LOANS $25 to $300
SIMPLIFIED METHOD
On Your Own Signature
NO credit inquiries of friends, relatives or employer
NO red tape or delays
LIBERAL TERMS
Plenty of Time to Repay
Phone and tell us how much you want, then come in and get your money
Guardian FINANCIAL CORP.
1400 Seventh Avenue
Phone 968 Beaver Falls

SEARS 20 YEAR GUARANTEED
Indestructo Furnace
- Written 20 Yr. Guarantee
- Automatic Humidifier
- Indestructo Metal Castings

18-Inch $69.95

PHONE OR WRITE TODAY FREE ESTIMATING SERVICE
Complete Estimates Given on All Types of Heating Plants
SEARS, ROEBUCK AND CO.
Phone [illegible] Ambridge, Pa.

OUR QUALITY

COAL

Makes Warm Friends
Campbell Bros.
Phone BEAVER 2230

INSELBRIC
The smart trend in home modernization. Looks like brick, wears a lifetime. Saves fuel and outside repair and painting. Free Estimates Given. Phone Roch. 3252.

WEDDING INVITATIONS AND ANNOUNCEMENTS, INFORMALS AND CARDS
GLADYS A. GIBBONS
489 College Ave., Beaver

The Weather Forecast
Light snow or rain, with rising temperature tonight; snow flurries and colder Tuesday.

THE DAILY TIMES

ROCHESTER-BEAVER-MONACA
FREEDOM—BRIDGEWATER—CONWAY—VANPORT—MIDLAND

Beaver County History
Word was received ... of a huge explosion which wrecked the city of Halifax, Nova Scotia.

ESTABLISHED APRIL 2, 1874 | BEAVER AND ROCHESTER, PA., MONDAY, DECEMBER 8, 1941 | BY CARRIER 15 CENTS A WEEK—

BOMBS KILL, INJURE 3,000 IN HAWAII

★ ★

U.S. MAKES WAR ON JAPAN

American Losses Heavy In Attack By Japs' Planes

BULLETIN

WASHINGTON, Dec. 8—Casualties on the Hawaiian Island of Oahu in Sunday's Japanese air attacks will amount to about three thousand, including about 1,500 fatalities, the White House announced today.

(The maximum casualties for any one 24-hour period in London during the heavy raids were about 1,200—450 killed and 750 injured. That would indicate that the Japanese attack on Pearl Harbor was exceptionally intense or else the bombs landed on barracks or some other place where many persons were concentrated.)

The White House confirmed the loss in Pearl Harbor of "one old battleship" and a destroyer which was blown up.

Several other American ships were damaged and a large number of Army and Navy planes on Hawaiian fields were put out of commission.

The United States and Great Britain today fought off surprise attacks by Japanese air, naval and land forces that overwhelmed Thailand's defenses and menaced almost every strategic war sector in the Pacific.

Losses in men and machines were reported heavy on both sides in the first phase of fighting that spread the war to every quarter of the globe and brought hints that the Axis might soon be lined up solidly beside the Japanese. Two or three American battleships and an aircraft tender were reported knocked out.

The Japanese imperial forces, said to have suffered severe losses of airplanes and several warships, were in action on these fronts:

A major naval battle was reported west of Hawaii, with the American fleet attempting to destroy enemy warships and airplanes that blasted Pearl Harbor naval base and Honolulu.

BATTLE IN MALAYA

A fierce land battle was in progress on the northeast coast of the Malaya states where British defense forces attacked Japanese troops landed on the beaches despite severe air bombing and machinegun fire.

About 30,000 Japanese troops in 60 vessels, escorted by warships, were believed to have landed on the Malaya coast.

Japanese invasion forces bombed and shelled Bangkok, crashed into Thailand by land and sea, and were reported in a British broadcast to have forced that government to capitulate. The occupation of Thailand would open the way for Japanese drives on Burma and the Burma road supply route to China and would set up a base for a drive southward against Singapore.

Waves of Japanese bombers battered northern, central and southern areas of the Philippine Islands, reportedly causing several hundred casualties.

The great British naval base at Singapore was attacked from the air, with 60 persons reported killed and 133 injured.

LANDING REPULSED

A Japanese landing in North (British) Borneo was reported repulsed with heavy casualties, according to London dispatches, but the same source heard that the American island of Guam had been attacked from all sides and that aerial bombardment had started several big fires.

The American island of Wake, a base for trans-Pacific air routes, was reported by a British source to have been captured, while a Japanese naval squadron of one cruiser, four destroyers and other ships were sighted off the Cocos Islands in the Indian Ocean.

Australia and the Dutch East Indies joined in the war on Japan, but there were increasing hints from Berlin that the conflict would become an outright Axis battle against the Allied powers. A Nazi spokesman said that an important statement might be forthcoming later and the Berlin press hinted that Germany would aid Japan. There was still no word of the position of the Soviet Union.

On the China coast, the Japanese attacked Hong Kong by air and by land and occupied the International Settlement at Shanghai after sinking the British gunboat Peteral and seizing the American gunboat Wake. American Marines at Peiping and Tientsin were disarmed and interned.

JAPS LAUNCH BLITZ

The Emperor of Japan, "seated on the throne of a line unbroken for ages eternal," declared war on the United States and Great Britain on the grounds that the Allied powers had threatened the existence of the Japanese empire and

(Continued on Page Two)

Japs Bomb Five Points Today In The Philippines

By the United Press

MANILA, Dec. 8.—Japanese airplanes bombed five widely separated points in the Philippines today.

Naval authorities said they had no confirmation of reports that the Japanese had effected troop landings in the Philippines, including reports of the dropping of parachute troops in Japanese-peoples areas.

The Japanese planes attacked Baguio, "winter capital" of the Philippines on Luzon Island 125 miles north of Manila; Davao, chief Japanese-colonized center, on Mindanao to the south; Tarlac, 70 miles north of Manila, Clark field, the great army air base, and Aparri, chief port of northern Luzon.

Maj. Le Grande Miller, aide to Lieut. Gen. Douglas MacArthur commander in chief of American forces in the Far East, announced the bombings of Baguio, Davao and Tarlac. He said 24 Japanese planes bombed Davao at 6:30 A. M. and Japanese planes attacked Baguio half an hour later. No casualties were reported. There were no details of the Tarlac bombing.

SHIPS REPORTED DAMAGED

Navy officers denied reports that an aircraft carrier had been damaged.

(There were other reports that

(Continued on Page Two)

American Gunboat Taken By Japanese; British Craft Sunk

Crew Of U. S. Warship Overwhelmed, Taken Prisoner At Shanghai Today

By the United Press

SHANGHAI, Dec. 8.—The British gunboat Peterel sank in the Whangpoo River off the Shanghai waterfront under blasting Japanese fire today and the United States communications ship, Wake, its crew overwhelmed as it lay in anchor, was captured.

Lieut. Commdr. John Polkinhorn, 63, British naval reservist and a former Tientsin river pilot who commanded the Peterel, was believed, with most of his crew, to have gone down with his ship.

The Peterel opened fire, under odds it knew were hopeless, when the Japanese ordered it to surrender.

The Wake had no chance to fire. The Japanese, in a sudden attack as they took over the water front of the International Settlement off which the two tiny gunboats were anchored, boarded it and forced its surrender.

JAPS OPEN FIRE

Japanese gunboats had opened direct fire on the Peterel, which had

(Continued on Page Two)

Government Imposes Rigid Censorship

By the United Press

WASHINGTON, Dec. 8 — The government today censored publication of military information in this country and all cable and radio messages originating in the United States and her outlying possessions.

The Army, Navy, Federal Communications Commission, Treasury and Postoffice Department suppressed information that might be of value to the enemy.

The Navy and FCC said the control over cable and radio communications is censorship. The Army called the limitation on publication of military information "restriction" rather than "censorship."

Secret service agents were ordered to take press credentials from Japanese newspaper correspondents immediately after it was learned here that Pearl Harbor had been bombed.

The War Department enforced the 1917 Espionage Act which prohibits publication of secret military information.

Four Children Die In Fire Near Butler

BUTLER, Dec. 8.—Four girls, all below six years of age, were burned to death Sunday morning when fire swept through their farm home at Isle, small Butler county community near here.

Coroner J. Charles Dengler identified the children as Lillian Marie, 6, Edna Jacqueline, 4, and Madeline, 2, all daughters of Mr. and Mrs. Wayne C. Perring, and Dorothy Marie Perrine, one, daughter of Mrs. Catherine Perrine. The mother of the three victims was critically burned in attempting to save her daughters after throwing her youngest child to safety from a second-floor window.

WHERE UNITED STATES, BRITAIN BATTLE JAPANESE

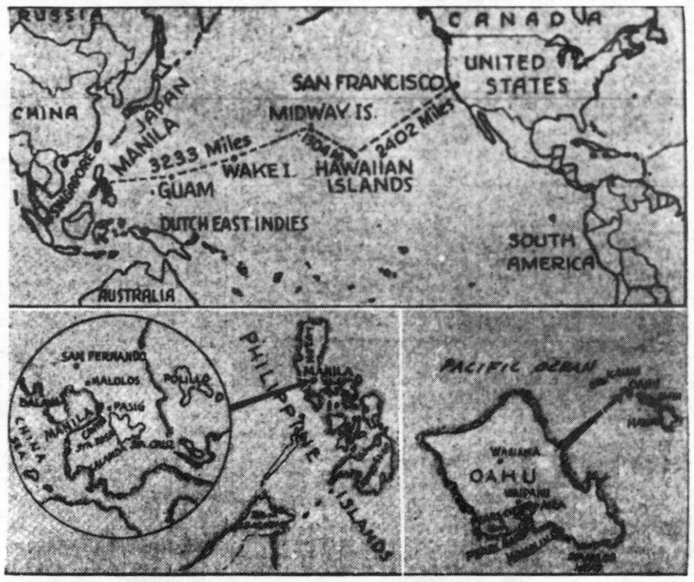
RUSSIA
CANADA
UNITED STATES
SAN FRANCISCO
CHINA
JAPAN
MIDWAY IS.
MANILA
3233 Miles
2402 Miles
WAKE I.
GUAM
HAWAIIAN ISLANDS
DUTCH EAST INDIES
SOUTH AMERICA
AUSTRALIA
SAN FERNANDO
MALOLOS
MANILA
PASIG
PACIFIC OCEAN
OAHU

Areas in which fighting has occurred between forces of the United States and Great Britain and those of Japan are shown on the maps above. Map at top shows strategic points of the entire Pacific area. Map at lower left shows Philippine Islands and area around Manila and the U. S. Naval base at Cavite. Map at lower right shows Hawaiian Islands and close-up of the island of Oahu, attacked by Japanese bombers.

More war pictures on page 6.

U. S.- JAPANESE FLEETS BATTLE

By the United Press

HONOLULU, Dec. 8—United States and Japanese fleets were believed fighting in mid-Pacific today after a Japanese aerial bombing attack on the Hawaiian Islands opened war between the two great Pacific powers.

The American fleet steamed out of the Pearl Harbor naval base shortly after Japanese planes, attacking without a declaration of war or any warning whatever, had bombed the great Pearl Harbor base, Honolulu City, and scattered army and navy bases on Oahu Island.

Naval gun flashes were seen from the coast, and the roar of the guns was heard soon after the fleet had steamed out to seek the Japanese aircraft carriers from which, it was believed, the planes had taken off and their escorting warships.

It was feared that navy, army and civilian casualties were heavy in the bolt-from-the-blue aerial attack.

Many Japanese planes were reported shot down but not before they had wrought severe damage on objectives centered on Oahu Island.

PEARL HARBOR TARGET

It was estimated that there were between 50 and 150 planes in the attacking fleet, including four-motored bombers, dive bombers and torpedo carriers.

They arrived over the islands at 7:55 a. m. (1:25 p. m. EST) yesterday, and machine-gunned an American civilian pilot who was taking

(Continued on Page Two)

Japanese Believed In Possession Of Southern Thailand

British Say Japanese Fighting To Hold Northeast Malaya Foothold

By the United Press

SINGAPORE, Dec. 8—Maj. Gen. A. E. Percival, British commander-in-chief for Malaya, reported today that the Japanese are believed to be in possession of southern Thailand and are fighting to retain their foothold on the beaches of northeast Malaya.

Percival reported to the legislative council that "confused fighting" is going on at Kota Bahru where Japanese troops still hold their positions between the beaches and the Kota Bahru airdrome which is held by British forces.

He reported that the Japanese aimed their attack at five main points in Malaya—Selatar, Tengah, Kelamtan, Sungei and Patani—all

(Continued on Page Two)

DISTRICT DEFENSE PLANTS ARE CLOSELY GUARDED BY OFFICERS

Western Pennsylvania defense plants producing $200,000,000 worth of armaments, together with vital public utilities, were placed on a complete war footing today as Government agencies ordered 24-hour armed guards at key points to protect them from sabotage.

Army, Navy and FBI officers individually warned more than 300 defense plants to increase police guards and take special anti-sabotage measures following Japan's declaration of war against the United States.

At the same time about 1,200 smaller defense plants heeded broadcast warning to be on the "alert."

Plant entrances and vulnerable points within factories were placed under double guard and floodlights were used on the grounds at many mills for the first time. Employe identification systems were tightened.

G-MEN ON DUTY

The Pittsburgh office of the Federal Bureau of Investigation ordered all its agents on duty for factory protection and anti-espionage work.

Pittsburgh officials here called 250 additional police to duty today and Allegheny county detectives were sent to industrial areas.

Reservoirs, power plants and pumping stations also were placed under heavy guard. Arterial bridges were watched closely and floodlights were being installed on more important spans.

Transportation systems also were taking emergency measures. Pennsylvania-Central and Transcontinental & Western Airlines revealed that special guards had been posted at all their stations for the past month and were now strengthened and put on day and night duty. District railroads reported precautionary measures were being taken at all bridges and tunnels and vulnerable spots along the right-of-way.

Relatives Worried Over Local Youths In Foreign Lands

Many Stationed In Army In Hawaii, Philippines, Panama, Puerto Rica

Many Beaver County families are expressing some concern today over relatives enrolled in the armed forces of the United States and stationed in possessions outside the continental limits of this country, in Hawaii, the Philippines, Panama Canal Zone and in Puerto Rica.

Investigation revealed there are 30 Beaver County youths in the army in Hawaii and one civilian living there. Sixteen other local lads are in the Panama Canal Zone; two in the Philippines and two in Puerto Rica.

IN HAWAII

Those in Hawaii include: Second Lieutenant Homer Jones, Rochester; Pvt. Clarence Ross Gradey, Rochester, 31st Comb. Squadron; Pvt. Leo. S. Parrish, Monaca, Co. A, 2d Battalion, ERTC, recently transferred from Fort Belvoir, Va.; Pvt. Raymond P. Rupple, Beaver, Battery D, 55th Coast Artillery; Pvt. Nicholas Kunder, Rochester; Pvt. Earnest R. Davis, Rochester; Pvt. David A. Wassum, Freedom; Pvt. Fred E. Swartz, Freedom, Signal Sorps; Pvt. Daniel Krokonko, infantry, Freedom; Harry L. Hamill, Coast Artillery, Freedom; Pvt. Walter Olash, infantry, Monaca; Nicholas Didich, Jr., infantry, Monaca; Joseph Blasche, infantry, Monaca; Joseph Lecker, Air Corps, New Brighton; George E. Grim, Signal Corps, New Brighton.

Wilfred Ledford, infantry, Aliquippa; William L. Peck, Ambridge, infantry; Fred K. Cassidy, Ambridge, infantry; Hubert C. McLaughlin, Coast Artillery, Industry; John N. Shellito, Industry, Field Artillery; Eugene E. Farmer, infantry, Beaver; Grover E. Kistler, Beaver, medical department.

Robert E. McClure, Beaver, Coast Artillery; Gail G. Montgomery, Beaver, Field artillery; Fred Gordon, infantry; Olin L. Mott, Beaver Falls, infantry; Mike Zabeck, Beaver, infantry; George McCarter, Darlington, infantry; James L. Huddox, Beaver Falls, infantry; Michael Kotuby, Beaver Falls, infantry, and Steve Kasper, Koppel, infantry.

IN PHILIPPINES, PANAMA

Local soldiers in the Philippines are Paul L. Luwarchik and Steve

(Continued on Page Two)

Fleet Battles As Congress Declares War

By the United Press

WASHINGTON, Dec. 8—While the American and Japanese fleets reportedly battled in the Pacific, Congress today proclaimed existence of a state of war between the United States and the Japanese Empire, 33 minutes after the dramatic moment when President Roosevelt stood before a joint session to pledge that we will triumph—"so help us, God."

Democracy was proving its right to a place in the sun with a split-second shift from peace to all-out war.

The Senate acted first, adopting the resolution by a unanimous roll call vote of 82 to 0, within 21 minutes after the President had concluded his address to a joint session of both houses.

The House voted immediately thereafter, 388 to 1 for the resolution.

CHARGES JAPS WITH DECEIT

President Roosevelt in his personal appearance summoned the nation to all-out war to "win through to absolute victory" over the Japanese Empire.

Mr. Roosevelt charged the Japanese with deceit and an "unprovoked and dastardly attack" yesterday on our Philippine and Hawaiian Island possessions. He asked Congress to recognize that since that moment a "state of war has existed between the United States and the Japanese Empire."

He promised, in his seven-minute, 500-word address that we never would forget the treacherous manner of the onslaught and that before we are through Japan will be powerless to offend so again.

GIVEN BIG OVATION

"Yesterday, December 7, 1941—a date which will live in infamy—the United States of America was suddenly and deliberately attacked by the naval and air forces of the Empire of Japan," he said.

The President, preceded by the escorting Senate-House committee, went into the House chamber supported by his son James, who wore his uniform of a Marine captain. He was greeted by a thundering ovation after he was presented to the assemblage by Speaker Sam Rayburn.

The ovation swelled in volume as the President reached the speaker's stand and a rebel yell went up from the Democratic side. The chamber was jammed to its four corners. Members of Congress and spectators listened gravely and quietly as the President began his speech at 12:33 P. M.

It was so quiet then that the snap of camera plates could be heard as they were changed by photographers in the galleries.

WILDLY CHEERED

But, there was wild cheering when the President reached the point in his brief state paper asking for a declaration that a state of war exists. The Senate was assembled with the House and among all those hundreds of men chosen by the American people to represent them as their government there seemed to be almost no dissent from the proposition that it must be war.

We were at peace, the President told the Congress and the millions of persons throughout the world who heard our answer to the Axis attack. We were at peace and even negotiating with Japan's chosen representatives to maintain it when the blow fell, the President declared.

"It will be recorded," he continued, that the distance of Hawaii from Japan makes it obvious that the attack was deliberately planned many days and even weeks ago. During the intervening time, the Japanese government has deliberately tried to deceive the United States by false statements and expressions of hope for continued peace."

State Ready For Emergency Action

HARRISBURG, Dec. 8—Governor James said today that Pennsylvania is ready for whatever call may be made on her in the present international situation. The chief executive contacted Colonel Lynn G. Adams to have all state police held in readiness for any eventualities.

He also instructed Adjutant General Robert M. Vail to have the Pennsylvania Reserve Defense Corps in readiness for a possible call to action.

A State Council of Defense meeting scheduled for Wednesday was moved up to 2 p. m. today by the governor. Dr. A. C. Marts, executive director of the defense council, said the group would "listen to what the President had to say, see what Congress does and act accordingly."

Roosevelt Surprised By Japanese Attack

By the United Press

WASHINGTON, Dec. 8. — News that Japan was at war with the United States descended upon President Roosevelt with the same startling suddenness that it did upon the American public.

Early Sunday afternoon Mr. Roosevelt received an urgent telephone message from Hawaii. Japanese airplanes had bombed Pearl Harbor. American men had been killed and wounded. American property had been damaged.

One of the president's first acts was to call his No. 1 liaison man, Secretary Stephen T. Early who immediately telephoned the major press associations. At 2:22 p. m., the United Press flashed the news that Japan and the United States were in a state of war.

14
SHOPPING DAYS to Christmas
SHOP EARLY

The Weather Forecast
Western Pennsylvania: Cloudy and slightly colder tonight; light snow and colder Wednesday.

THE DAILY TIMES

ROCHESTER-BEAVER-MONACA
FREEDOM—BRIDGEWATER—CONWAY—VANPORT—MIDLAND

Beaver County History
Many lives were reported lost December 9, 1917, in the sinking of the U. S. ship Jacob Jones.

ESTABLISHED APRIL 2, 1874 | BEAVER AND ROCHESTER, PA., TUESDAY, DECEMBER 9, 1941 | BY CARRIER 15 CENTS A WEEK—

Defense Corps Guards County Bridges

★ ★ ★ ★ ★ ★ ★ ★ ★ ★ ★ ★ ★ ★ ★ ★ ★ ★ ★ ★

JAPANESE PLANES OFF WEST COAST

JAPS STAGE LAND, AIR RAIDS TODAY ON PHILIPPINES

Residents Of Manila Take To Hills As Enemy Planes Bomb Area

Reports Of U. S. Casualties In Mid - Pacific, Philippines Made Today

By the United Press

MANILA, Dec. 9—Japanese struck at the Philippines by land and air today, and 200,000 residents of Manila went to the hills for safety.

Enemy planes bombed the Manila area by moonlight early today and flames leaped up on the southern side of the city after an air raid alarm at 3 a. m. There were two earlier alarms, but no planes appeared.

Reliable sources said Japanese troops had landed on the small island of Lubang, only 80 miles from the city. Reports said Japanese had landed only a small force, and it was assumed preparations were being made by American forces to attack.

An announcement said one person was killed and 12 wounded in the raid at Nichols Field, an army air base near Manila. In addition, headquarters of the U. S. Asiatic fleet said Ensign Robert George Tills had been killed by a Japanese air raid on Davao, island of Mindanao.

OTHER CASUALTIES

(Royal Arch Gunnison, Mutual Broadcasting System correspondent, reported from Manila that Ensign R. E. White, of the U. S. Navy, was killed in action at Guam. He also said three Marines were in a serious condition as a result of the attack at Davao. Gunnison said a Japanese aircraft carrier from which 200 planes had been operating had been sunk, but the Navy refused to confirm or deny the report).

The Columbia Broadcasting System correspondent in Manila said the city had not suffered heavily from bombing, but that damage elsewhere in the Philippines had been heavy.)

About 400,000 persons may be evacuated from Manila. President Manuel Quezon is directing their removal to safety.

RADIOS BOMBED

The BBC, heard by CBS, reported that the Japanese also bombed two short wave transmitting stations. BBC said the Japanese planes continued their attack for 10 minutes in face of heavy anti-aircraft fire.

(NBC reported that two persons were wounded by a bomb which struck near Fort McKinley.

(BBC reported that a Japanese had been arrested as he was cutting telephone lines.

United States naval authorities confirmed that America's mid-Pacific Guam Island had been attacked but had no details.

Hong Kong Awaits Japanese Attack

By the United Press

HONG KONG, Dec. 9. — British Imperial and Japanese patrols are maintaining activity along roads in the mainland part of Hong Kong colony, it was said officially today, as the garrison awaits a full scale Japanese attack.

Chief patrol activity centered in the neighborhood of Taipo and along the Castle peak road.

(This indicated that the Imperial Garrison, including Canadian troops, some distance within the limits of the mainland part of Hong Kong.

(Taipo, on the Canton railroad, is about seven miles inside the border and Castle peak is on the southwest mainland corner, indicating that Japanese troops might have effected a landing from the Pearl River.)

Defense Council To Open Monaca Office

A central office of the Monaca Local Defense Council will be opened Thursday, December 11, at 1 p. m., in the Monaca municipal building. The office will be open through Friday from 1 to 5 p. m., and all day on Saturday.

Members of the Women's Defense Unit will be on hand to receive applications for workers in the local Council of Defense. The office will be located in the room on the second floor of the municipal building used by the Centennial Committee.

Has Big Job

SHERIFF O'LOUGHLIN

Armed Guards On Duty At County Highway Bridges

Blue-gray uniformed members of the Pennsylvania Reserve Defense Corps were standing guard today on the principal highway bridges in Beaver County following their unexpected state-wide mobilization Monday evening.

Company B, First Battalion, met as usual last night in the armory at New Castle for what started to be a practice assembly but turned into actual mobilization at 9:30 o'clock, according to Major Frank A. Weber, Beaver Falls, commanding officer of three companies of the battalion.

Major Weber is in command of

(Continued on Page Six)

Horbelt Trial For Manslaughter Is In Hands Of Jury Today

New Jersey Man Claims Shooting Of Mrs. Viola Moffett Accidental

The trial of Edward J. Horbelt, 35, Maplewood, N. J., for involuntary manslaughter in connection with the fatal shooting of Mrs. Viola Moffett and for violations of the firearms act, was placed in the hands of the jury at 11:30 o'clock today, by Judge Henry H. Wilson.

Horbelt, testifying in his own defense, declared the shooting of Mrs. Moffett in a bedroom over a Beaver dairy store last September 29, was accidental.

He told the court and the jury that Mrs. Moffett and Mrs. Margaret Shewak, New Brighton, and O. R. Wallace, Rochester, were in

(Continued on Page Six)

WAR BULLETINS

By the United Press

BULLETIN 1:50 P. M.

"All Clear" sounds at New York City.

FLEET PROBE DEMANDED

WASHINGTON, Dec. 9 — Sen. Charles W. Tobey, Rep., N. H., said today it was "reported on the Senate floor that a large part of the Pacific fleet has been wiped out" and demanded that the American people be informed of the true situation.

TWO JAPANESE HELD

HUNTINGTON, W. Va., Dec. 9—Two Japanese arrested here yesterday by state troopers and FBI agents as "potentially dangerous" were held today for removal to Cincinnati, where they will be given a hearing by immigration officials.

TAX COLLECTOR ON TRIAL

UNIONTOWN, Dec. 9 — After a one-day delay, John W. Jose, South Union Twp. tax collector, was called to trial here today on charges of embezzling approximately $15,000 in tax money.

GUARD SHOOTS WOMAN

SAN FRANCISCO, Dec. 9—Mrs. Marie Sayre, 27, of San Francisco, was shot and seriously wounded by a California home guard on patrol duty at the San Francisco-Oakland Bay bridge during last night's blackout. Her husband, Don Sayre, said he did not hear Private A. Rownd's challenge for him to stop his car.

ARENA WHERE UNITED STATES, GREAT BRITAIN LOCK WITH JAPAN

AIR & NAVAL BASES
U.S.
BRITISH
DUTCH
JAPANESE
HEAVY OUTLINE SHOWS TERRITORY CONTROLLED BY JAPANESE.
U. S. S. R. (SIBERIA)
MONGOLIA
TIBET
CHINA
JAPAN
ALASKA
CANADA
U.S.
DUTCH HARBOR
SITKA
SAN FRANCISCO
SAN DIEGO
YOKOHAMA
HONG KONG
PHILIPPINE ISLANDS
GUAM
YAP
MIDWAY I. (U.S.)
WAKE I. (U.S.)
PEARL HARBOR
HAWAIIAN IS.
6245 MI. TO PANAMA CANAL
PACIFIC
OCEAN
INDIAN OCEAN
DUTCH EAST INDIES
JAVA
BORNEO
RANGOON
AUSTRALIA
BRISBANE
SYDNEY
PERTH
KING GEORGE SOUND
TASMANIA
SAMOA
PITCAIRN I.
AUCKLAND
NEW ZEALAND
KERGUELEN

Central Press Map

In complete detail, the map above shows the vast arena in which the ABCD powers now are locked in a death struggle with Japan for supremacy in the Pacific ocean and the Far East. From the hills of China's interior eastward to the area between Hawaii and the American mainland, fighting now rages between land forces, battle fleets and swarms of airplanes. Principal bases of the powers and the distances between them are indicated on the self-explanatory map above.

German And Italian Aliens Rounded Up By Federal Agents

Nearly 400 Taken Into Custody, Along With 900 Japanese Nationals

By the United Press

WASHINGTON, Dec. 9—Federal Bureau of Investigation agents seized nearly 400 German and Italian aliens in nation-wide raids last night, an authoritative source said early today.

Those seized were considered dangerous to the "peace and security" of the United States. There were said to be "more than 300" Germans and about 40 Italians in the group.

The raids were staged under a proclamation secretly promulgated by President Roosevelt, it was understood. He acted under the same section of the U. S. code which permitted seizure of about 900 Japanese nationals within 12 hours of Japan's declaration of war.

Instead of declaring that invasion or predatory incursion was being perpetrated against this nation, as was the case in the proclamation permitting the Japanese seizures, the government declared that an "invasion or predatory incursion" was "threatened".

TO PREVENT PERSECUTION

Meanwhile, the Justice Depart-

(Continued on Page Six)

Lindbergh Appeals For Unity In U. S.

CHICAGO, Dec. 8.—Charles A. Lindbergh, leading isolationist spokesman, said today that now that war has come "We must meet it as united Americans" regardless of any past attitude toward Government policy.

"We must now turn every effort to building the greatest and most efficient army, navy and air force in the world. When American soldiers go to war, it must be with the best equipment that modern skill can design and that modern industry can build," Lindbergh said.

SEVERE FIGHTING REPORTED IN NORTHERN MALAYA TODAY

SINGAPORE, Straits Settlements, Dec. 9—Japan has succeeded in landing additional troops in Northern Malaya and savage fighting continued throughout last night for the important Kota Bharu airdrome, a communique of the Malaya command said today.

It was indicated that the Japanese had succeeded in landing additional troops also in the Patani and Singora areas on the east coast of Thailand, up the coast from the Malaya border.

There were three air raid alarms between dawn and 9 a. m. today in the Singapore area after one alarm during the night but no bombing planes appeared, and it was believed that Japanese reconnaissance planes might have caused the alarms.

There was also an alarm at Kuala Lampur on the west coast.

Japanese planes were believed to be laying mines off the west coast between Malaya and Netherlands Sumatra, dispatches from local officials said.

AWAIT CASUALTIES

A casualty clearing bureau was established in Singapore today in anticipation of the arrival of wounded from the northern Malaya front and the outbreak of fighting in the Singapore zone.

A communique admitted that the Japanese had put "considerable numbers" ashore and that Japanese

(Continued on Page Six)

U. S. Air Fields Placed 'On Alert'

By the United Press

WASHINGTON, Dec. 9—The War Department today ordered all Army air fields placed "on the alert" as a precautionary measure against possible enemy attacks.

Officials said the order was a general precaution and was not based on any information that enemy bombers were approaching New York City or elsewhere.

The "alert" was ordered by Maj. Gen. Harry H. Arnoldl, chief of the U. S. Army air forces. At the same time, officials said that no personnel was being evacuated from Mitchell Field, N. Y., or elsewhere.

There had been rumors that enemy planes were within two hours of New York and that Mitchell Field was being evacuated by non-essential personnel.

Midland Recount Makes No Changes

Recounting of the votes for borough offices in Midland's four precincts was completed today and made no changes in the originally-announced election results.

Thomas J. Dublin, the only Democrat to win a borough post, gained two votes on Willlaim A. McIrnerney, Republican and present burgess. Dublin's total by the recount was 1,072, as compared with 1068, his total by the original count by election boards. McInerney who had 1,065, 13 less than Dublin, by the original count, had 1,067 after the recount.

Only very minor changes were made in the total votes for other candidates.

Four Killed Today In Freight Wreck

By the United Press

POTTSTOWN, Dec. 9.—Two heavily-laden freight trains collided at nearby Frick's Lock today, killing four trainmen and derailing 16 cars to completely block the Pennsylvania Railroad's important industrial Schuylkill division.

Both trains were moving toward Philadelphia when one crashed into the rear of the other, railroad officials said. The engine of the rear train overturned, killing three occupants and ripping up several hundred feet of the main single track.

Congress Ready For War With Nazis And Italy If Necessary

Action Looms If Axis Partners Join Japan In War With U. S.

By the United Press

WASHINGTON, Dec. 9. — Congressional leaders were ready today to acknowledge war with Germany and Italy if those Axis powers join their Japanese partner in hostilities against the United States.

Speaker Sam Rayburn told the United Press another war resolution would be adopted immediately if either Italy or Germany move against this country.

President Roosevelt, still apparently uncertain of the intentions of Rome or Berlin, addresses the nation at 10 p. m., tonight in his new and virtually all-powerful role of "war president." He will give an amplified report of fighting in the Pacific where Japan has dealt our naval and air arms a punishing blow.

There is a scattering of sharp and bitter congressional protest against

(Continued on Page Six)

More Local Youths In Danger Zones

Relatives today eagerly awaited word from two Monaca brothers who are with the U. S. Army in Hawaii. Sergt. Leonard Hutchinson and his brother, Private Milford Hutchinson, have been with the Field Artillery at Schofield Barracks. They enlisted together 2¼ years ago and have been together since that time. Their enlistment period would have expired in six months.

Staff Sergt. Paul K. Wylie, Beavar, is a member of Battery F, Coast Artillery, at Fort Shafter, Hawaii.

Private First Class Kenneth L. Crawford, Rochester, is another local youth serving with the U. S. Army in foreign lands. He is stationed in the Panama Canal Zone with the 14th Infantry.

BLACKOUTS, AIR RAID ALARMS IN CALIFORNIA AREA

BULLETIN

NEW YORK, Dec. 9—Mitchell Field reported today that all military planes at east coast points had been ordered into the air. Families of soldiers were evacuated from the post.

SAN FRANCISCO, Dec. 9—A night of blackouts and air raid alarms ordered by military authorities brought the war close to the west coast today.

Army authorities asserted enemy aircraft was operating off California's shores, and before dawn two blackouts had been ordered for the San Francisco Bay region while the Pacific Northwest and San Diego remained in darkness nightlong.

Considerable confusion surrounded the alert signals which many persons assumed to be practice alarms and which even the police twice mistakenly announced were test warnings.

The first was ordered when planes were detected about 100 miles off San Francisco. Brig. Gen. William Ryan, commanding the Fourth Interceptor Command, was convinced they were enemy craft.

He said the Navy was attempting to "locate and give battle" to the invaders.

The second warning presumably was caused by U. S. Navy patrol bombers that failed to identify themselves.

The initial "enemy" force was believed to number 60 planes, which ventured to the entrance to the Golden Gate. The planes were flying too high to be caught by searchlights. They soon disappeared to sea.

RADIO STATIONS SILENT

The report was relayed up and down the coast. Radio stations were ordered off the air lest their signals afford direction posts. Blackouts were imposed at Army posts, Navy bases, defense plants and numerous cities.

Los Angeles radio stations that had been restricted to broadcasting identification calls each half hour, were ordered off the air completely "until further notice."

In San Francisco the city pulled the switches on street and bridge lights, including the big span across the Golden Gate, and Mayor Angelo Rossi's staff hastily began a telephone campaign to get commercial signs and residential lights turned off. Ferry sirens screamed the air raid warning.

For 65 minutes the alarm, originally broadcast by the police radio system, was in effect before the police anounced an all clear. At no time, police said, was there panic here. Motorists, stopped by police on street corners and ordered to dim their lights, drove to nearby hills to watch for the reported enemy raiders. Police and volunteers went from door to-door warning residents to pull their shades.

WIDE AREA DARK

Portland, most of the Pacific Northwest, San Diego, and all the province of British Columbia were blacked out. Los Angeles was not.

"Planes were originally detected at a point about 100 miles off-shore,

(Continued on Page Six)

Action Is Reported All Along 6,000-Mile Pacific Front Today

No New Major Development Reported Today In Pacific Ocean

On the Pacific war front there was action over a 6,000-mile front but no major new developments.

The situation:

HAWAII: Apparently quiet. No reports of renewed Japanese activity; no new word on operations of the U. S. battle fleet.

PHILIPPINES: Japanese inflict small casualties in moonlight air raids directed chiefly at Nichols Field and Ft. McKinley, in Manila area; Japanese landing reported—but not confirmed—on Lubang Island, 80 miles from Manila.

GUAM: U. S. Army communique admits sinking of 840-ton minesweeper Penguin and a handful of casualties in Japanese attack on Guam; no confirmation that Japanese now hold Guam.

JAPS SEIZE SHIPS

Japanese claims: Offensive started against Burma Road; 200 "enemy" ships seized in Pacific including 10,509-ton liner President Harrison; Japanese troops enter Bangkok; Midway Island attacked, 1,300 miles west of Hawaii; claim destruction of 300 American planes at Hawaii and Philippines.

SINGAPORE: More Japanese troops land on Malaya coast but British forces are successfully resisting; London claims number of Japanese landings is so small operation is only "mop up."

HONG KONG: British and Japanese patrols deploy for action;

(Continued on Page Six)

Rochester School Funds Transferred

An adjourned meeting of the Rochester Board of Education was held Monday evening in the high school building to transact business heldover from the annual organization meeting the previous Monday. George H. Davis presided as president for the seventh consecutive year.

Authorization was made for the transfer of $22,600 from the general fund to the sinking fund to meet bonds coming due between December first and July first.

The Athletic Committee presented a preliminary report on the football season. Following the payment of outstanding bills, a detailed report will be presented at the next meeting, together with recommendations for changes in the 1942 football schedule.

Completion of work on the athletic field was announced. Top soil, turf builder and seed have been placed on the field and additional work is planned next spring.

Following the meeting, members of the Board and Superintendent Robert Barner were guests of George H. Davis at social hour spent in his home.

BOSTON ALARMED

By the United Press

BOSTON, Dec. 9.—All police were ordered on duty today, manufacturers were notified to prepare for air raids and hospitals were told to prepare for possible casualties after enemy planes were reported off the Atlantic coast

President To Speak On Radio Tonight

By the United Press

WASHINGTON, Dec. 9 — White House Secretary Stephen T. Early announced that President Roosevelt will make a nation-wide broadcast at 10 p. m. tonight to give "a more complete documentation" of the Japanese attack on Hawaii, the Philipines and other areas.

Early said the broadcast, over all networks, will be for half an hour.

He said the speech will contain information on hostilities in greater detail than "has as yet been possible."

The Weather Forecast
Western Pennsylvania: Generally fair and continued cold tonight; light snow and warmer Friday.

THE DAILY TIMES

ROCHESTER-BEAVER-MONACA
FREEDOM—BRIDGEWATER—CONWAY—VANPORT—MIDLAND

Beaver County History
Plans were made in Beaver Dec. 11, 1917, to aid in raising a $3,000,000 war fund for Knights of Columbus.

ESTABLISHED APRIL 2, 1874 | BEAVER AND ROCHESTER, PA., THURSDAY, DECEMBER 11, 1941 | BY CARRIER 15 CENTS A WEEK—3 CENTS PER COPY

Japanese Attacks Repelled By Philippine Forces

★ ★

WAR DECLARED ON AXIS

ANSWER TO WAR DECLARATIONS ON UNITED STATES BY GERMANY AND ITALY EARLIER TODAY

U. S. PLANES SINK JAPS' BATTLESHIP

By the United Press

Secretary of War Henry L. Stimson today confirmed the sinking of the 29,000-ton Japanese battleship Haruna off the northern coast of Luzon yesterday by U. S. Army bombers. Stimson told a press conference that the office of naval intelligence confirmed the sinking.

Stimson said there was a "heavy loss" of planes in Hawaii as a result of Sunday's surprise raid, but said that it "can and is being made good at the present moment."

Germany and Italy formally joined Japan in war against the United States today and Adolf Hitler shouted that the Axis would "always strike the first blow."

American diplomats in Berlin and Rome were handed their passports as the formal declarations of war were announced—completing the line-up of major powers in a World War that has now carried hostilities to every quarter of the globe on a scale never before known in history.

Hitler and Fascist Premier Benito Mussolini completed the mobilization of total Axis strength against the Allied powers in speeches at Berlin and Rome declaring that Europe is "impregnable" and that "we shall wage war to conquer."

But before the House of Commons in London Prime Minister Winston Churchill, anticipating the declarations, replied for the Allies with a statement that this is a life or death fight and "we will go forward to victory—not over Japan alone but over the Axis and all of its works."

And on the blood-smeared beaches of the Philippines and Malaya, in the air over Singapore and Manila and on the vast Pacific Ocean front American and British fighting men were speaking for themselves with the blazing weapons of war.

JAP LOSSES HEAVY

In the Philippines province of Luzon, where strong Japanese expeditionary forces crashed through a hail of American bombs to land on the coast, an official war communique said that the invaders were being mopped up near Lingayen and—in the historic words of the Marine Corps—the situation is in hand.

Japanese losses in a number of attacks on northern Luzon were described as heavy and off the coast the 29,000-ton Jap battleship was blazing fiercely as a result of hits by United States bombers. Over Manila, the skies were clear again as American interceptor planes drove back new Japanese bomber squadrons and the wreckage of 15 enemy craft was scattered across the low hills behind the capital.

On the eastern coast of Malaya, British imperials aided by British and Dutch fighting planes fought back against a Japanese invasion headed toward the great naval base of Singapore and reported that, after losing Kota Bharu airdrome near the Thailand border, they had prevented any farther advances. The Japanese still were hammering at the Kuantan area, 200 miles north of Singapore, however, in an effort to gain a foothold there.

Two thousand survivors of some 3,000 men on the great British dreadnaughts Prince of Wales and Repulse reached safety and told how the two warships fought for three hours against attacks by 60 "suicide" Japanese bombers, shooting down at least seven of the enemy craft before they went down with guns still firing.

BRITISH HOLD OUT

Behind the barricade at Hong Kong, besieged by Japanese warships, hammered by Japanese airplanes and assaulted from land by Japanese infantry, the British forces

(Continued on Page Six)

U. S. Admiral Killed

Phonephoto

Rear Admiral Isaac Campbell Kidd, 57 (above) commander of a battleship division of the U. S. Pacific fleet, was reported killed in action during the surprise Japanese attack on Pearl Harbor, Honolulu. Admiral Kidd was the first casualty to be identified by the navy department after the attack. His home is Cleveland, Ohio.

FRENCHMEN EXECUTED

VICHY, Dec. 11—German authorities at Brest, occupied France, have executed 11 Frenchmen for illegal possession of arms.

GERMANY BOMBED

LONDON, Dec. 11—The Air Ministry said today that British planes attacked northwest Germany yesterday. A communique said RAF bombers effectively attacked a tanker at the mouth of the River Ems, a railway junction near Wilhelmshaven and raided two airdromes in Holland.

Air Raid Warning System On Alert

HARRISBURG, Dec. 11 — The State Council of Defense today placed the air raid warning districts of 19 Eastern and Central Pennsylvania counties "on the alert" until further notice as a precautionary war measure.

Dr. A. C. Marts, executive director, and Ralph E. Flinn chief air raid warden, sent the following message to each air raid warning district:

"We are instructed by Mitchell Field via the third civilian defense region headquarters to immediately alert your chief air raid warden and instruct him to have someone on duty at the 'black warning box' 24 hours a day until further notice."

PUC HEARINGS ON BUS SERVICE AT PLANT CONTINUE

Better Transportation Facilities Sought For New Curtiss-Wright Plant

Committee Of Workers Supports Application Of Local Motor Coach Company

Hearings on the Public Utility Commission investigation into transportation facilities for workers at the Curtiss-Wright Propeller Corp. plant at Borough Township continued today at Pittsburgh with testimony of a CIO union committee.

The five-man committee represented 1,700 workers at the plant, many of whom travel long distances to and from work daily.

A committee spokesman said a delegation of 25 Steel Workers Organizing Committee (CIO) members originally was scheduled to appear in support of complaints that present facilities are "inadequate," but that many workers refused to leave their jobs in the interest of national defense.

Hearings on the complaints, coupled with an application of the Beaver Valley Motor Coach Company, to provide temporary "emergency" service to carry workers from the Pittsburgh area, opened yesterday.

PROPOSE THREE TRIPS

Asking permission to provide three round-trips daily, connecting with plant shift schedules, the bus company presented testimony of W. C. Lehew, Curtiss-Wright personnel manager.

Lehew testified that all of the workers at the plant were of skilled

(Continued on Page Six)

Trade Board Studies Traffic Congestion

Traffic improvement to relieve congestion on the Rochester-Monaca bridge between 4 and 6 p. m. was discussed at the weekly luncheon meeting of the Rochester Board of Trade, Wednesday noon in the Penn-Beaver Hotel.

The board also recommended elimination of the sharp right turn off Brighton avenue to Rhode Island avenue, around the soldier's monument in the public park. Ben F. Ellis, vice president, presided.

Rochester Women To Have Defense Meet

Sponsored by a group of Rochester housewives, a home defense meeting will be held Friday evening at 7 o'clock in the Rochester Veterans of Foreign Wars Home.

Charles Evans and two other Red Cross first-aid instructors will be present to assist in organizing a first-aid class. Burgess F. A. Pearson and Fenton H. Farley, principal of Rochester high school, will speak.

The meeting is open to all men and women and efforts will be made to launch an intensive civilian defense program in the town.

FORMER COUNTY MAN RESCUED IN SINKING OF BRITISH SHIP

The first eye-witness account of the sinking of the British capital ships, Prince of Wales and Repulse, was received by the Columbia Broadcasting System today from its Singapore correspondent, Cecil Brown, formerly of New Brighton. Brown was aboard the Repulse.

Brown was the CBS correspondent in Rome until he was banned from the air this spring by the Italian government. Leaving Rome he went to the Near East and then to Cairo. He went to Singapore two months ago.

On Monday he sent CBS's New York office this terse message: "Outtowning four days. Swell story." His account of the disaster was the first heard from him since.

SAW WALES GO DOWN

His account follows:

"I was aboard the battle cruiser Repulse when she was sent to the bottom under the fiercest Japanese attack in the South China Sea far off the Malaya coast. As I was swimming in thick oil water I also saw the Prince of Wales go to the bottom a half mile away in the greatest British naval loss of this war. Like hundreds of others I jumped 20 feet into the water when the Repulse was already on its side and swam as fast as possible to avoid the suction and the expected explosion.

"The Japanese pressed the attack home with all the daring of the British at Taranto. I saw six Japanese bomber planes shot down in a burst of flames five hundred yards distant.

"At least 700 have been saved on the Repulse. Perhaps the same number were saved on the Prince of Wales.

"Admiral Sir Tom Phillips, commander-in-chief of the Far Eastern fleet and Captain Leach of the Prince of Wales were last seen sliding into the water from the bridge of the Wales.

COMMANDER SAVED

"Captain William Tennant of the Repulse was saved.

"When it was obvious that the Repulse was sinking and numerous dead were lying beside the guns, I was standing on the flag deck with the only other reporter to witness this great blow to British naval strength. He is O'Dowd Gallagher of

(Continued on Page Six)

WHERE SHIPS SANK, JAPS INVADE

KUNMING
CANTON
AMOY
HONG KONG
PACIFIC OCEAN
BURMA
HANOI
HAIPHONG
HAINAN
VIGAN
APARRI
RANGOON
THAI-LAND
BANGKOK
FR. INDO CHINA
SAIGON
MANILA
PHILIPPINES
DAVAO
CHINA SEA
KUANTAN
BORNEO
SINGAPORE
NETHERLANDS INDIES

This map shows where the battle cruiser Repulse and the battleship Prince of Wales were sunk by the Japanese off Malaya, arrow left; the Philippine area where the Japanese made landings, arrow right, and reported Japanese air attacks on the vital Burma Road, Chinese supply line. One landing was said to have occurred at Aparri at the northern tip of Luzon island and another at Vigan, 75 miles south. In the first official government communique, the war department announced the defeat of a "hostile attack" against the west coast of Luzon.

New Order Of OPM May Affect Big Power Plant Here

Order Issued In Washington Being Studied By Officials Of Light Company

Whether an OPM order issued in Washington late yesterday will affect the Duquesne Light Company's huge new Wireton power plant, on the Ohio river at South Heights, will not be known until after a study of the order which may require several days, a company spokesman said.

Expansion projects which were at least 40 per cent complete December 5 will not be affected, OPM said, according to the Associated Press, and may be finished if the utility has supplies on hand or is granted priority assistance to obtain them. Otherwise the OPM prohibited public utilities from undertaking any substantial expansion of property or equipment without Government approval.

NEARLY COMPLETE

Under construction since last spring, the Wireton plant, also known as the Phillips plant, is part of a $16,000,000 expansion program undertaken by the company and now substantially completed except for the Wireton project and installation of a third unit at the Reed power station, Brunot's Island, which unit is reported about 99 per cent ready.

A giant electrical turbine generat-

(Continued on Page Six)

Sale Of Tires Is Suspended Today

WASHINGTON, Dec. 11 — The Government today banned sale of any new automobile tires to the public until December 22 to stop "a consumers' buying wave."

The order, effective today, was issued by Donald M. Nelson, priorities director, on the recommendation of the OPM's civilian supply division.

"The prohibition means," the announcement explained, "that no new automobile, truck, bus or motorcycle, farm implements or other type of tire or tube may be sold by anyone—including tire stores both wholesale and retail; filling stations, automobile dealers or any others—except on preference rating orders of A-3 or higher.

"The restriction, however, does not apply to the sale of used tires and tubes, retreaded tires or to the sale of tires and tubes furnished with new or used automotive vehicles."

County Plant Is To Be Expanded

Republic Steel Corporation contemplates construction of an addition to its Union Drawn Steel division at Beaver Falls, it was revealed today. The new addition will require 530 tons of structural steel.

Closing Witnesses To Testify Today In Palmer's Trial

Ellwood City Police, Others Testify At Trial Of Bank Robber

By the United Press

PITTSBURGH, Dec. 11—Closing witnesses were summoned today by the government in the trial of Kenneth Palmer, Detroit, only one of three men to survive a hail of police bullets as they sped away from the $2,000 hold up of a Harrisville bank.

A Federal jury, which is trying Palmer on charges of violating the Federal firearms act and bank robbery, yesterday heard police authorities and witnesses describe the gun battles in which Palmer was severely wounded and his two companions killed.

Ellwood City Chief of Police Ernest Hartman told how he stopped the get-away machine on a city street and exchanged fire with the men only to have them escape.

Later, he said, he found them three miles from the city on a narrow road to Beaver Falls. One—Earl Everets, Smithfield—was dead from a bullet fired from his own

(Continued on Page Six)

West Virginia Body Opposed To Canal

The West Virginia Chamber of Commerce is on record in opposition to the proposal for construction of the $70,000,000 Beaver-Mahoning Canal, the Upper Ohio Valley Association announced today.

The West Virginia Chamber claimed in a resolution that the proposed canal from Rochester to Struthers, O., would "ruinously" affect many West Virginia industries.

Two Hurt In Local Traffic Accidents

Fred Kcszur, 47, Beaver Falls, was admitted to Providence hospital at 8:30 o'clock Wednesday evening suffering from a shoulder injury received in a traffic accident in Ninth avenue, between Ninth and Tenth street, Beaver Falls. Koszur was riding in a car with Bart Verick, Beaver Falls, when a passing automobile crowded Verick's car to the side of the street and it struck a parked auto owned by Carl Grossglass, Beaver Falls according to Beaver Falls police.

George F. Hartman, 44, Beaver Falls, was arraigned before Justice Orrin Swick, North Sewickley Township, Wednesday evening after he had driven through a stop sign and struck a milk truck operated by Clarence G. Billian, 23, Fombell, in Franklin Township, according to State Police. Mrs. Georgia Hartman, wife of Hartman, suffered a minor laceration of the forehead. Hartman was released after paying the fine and costs.

WEST COAST SEEKS TO CONTINUE WORK DURING AIR ALARMS

Four Plane Plants Closed During Three-Hour Air Raid Alarm

Shipyards Also Affected; Practice Blackouts Are To Be Eliminated

By the United Press

LOS ANGELES, Dec. 11—Southern California's defense industries, including aircraft plants building $1,000,000,000 worth of warplanes, sought today to bolster defense precautions to prevent costly shutdowns during air raid alarms.

Four aircraft plants were closed last night, their production of vital planes and parts halted because of a three-hour air raid alarm during which the army said an enemy plane was overhead.

Consolidated Aircraft, building $750,000,000 worth of heavy bombers, Ryan Aeronautical and Solar Aircraft, building training planes, and Rohr Aircraft, manufacturer of equipment, were told by the army to order their 17,000 night shift workers home because their plants could not be completely blacked out.

SHIPYARDS HAMPERED

Shipyards, where most of the

(Continued on Page Six)

VFW Offers Home To Any Defense Group

Junction City Post, Veterans of Foreign Wars, Rochester, at meeting in the home Wednesday evening voted unanimously to permit use of the post home to any committee or group for national defense work, or to aid in any way possible in this work. The post also resolved to buy defense bonds.

County Commander H. D. Bailey, Monaca, announced the Military Order of "Cooties", is planning for a dance at Junction Park pavalion, February 19, the entire proceeds of which will be used for purchasing Defense Bonds. The annual Christmas party and "treat" for the children has been set for Sunday morning, December 21, from 9 to 12 o'clock, according to C. C. Bailey, chairman, to be assisted by his post committee. Lawrence Nugent, senior vice-commander, presided.

Two More Police Hired At Monaca

Monaca Council at a short regular session Wednesday night decided to augment the borough police force by the addition of two more patrolmen, temporarily, to better protect borough property because of war conditions. The extra police will go on duty at once.

The report of Burgess Elmer E. Hicks and the Police Department for November showed six arrests and fines amounting to $15. Charles W. Lay, president, presided.

Congress Acts Swiftly Today

By the United Press

WASHINGTON, Dec. 11—The United States today went to war against Germany and Italy, making it an all-out battle against the Axis, including Japan.

President Roosevelt sent to Congress his second war message within seventy hours and the legislators snapped through resolutions recognizing the existence of hostilities with Germany and Italy.

Notification of German and Italian declarations of war against the United States reached the State Department at 9:25 and 9:50 a. m., respectively, today.

Congress received Mr. Roosevelt's message at 12:24 p. m. and adopted appropriate war resolutions by 1:04 p. m. The Senate vote was 90 to 0.

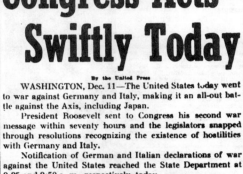

"The long known and the long expected has thus taken place," the President told Congress in his message, read separately by clerks in each house.

"The forces endeavoring to enslave the entire world are now moving toward this hemisphere."

First move in the Atlantic may be a race, for seizure of neutral islands which Germany or Italy could use as bases for aerial attacks against the richest and most populous seaboard in the world—the Atlantic coast of the United States.

Among the islands which lie far out as stepping stones for bomber attacks on North, South or Central America are the Canaries, which belong to Spain, and the Azores and Cape Verde island, which are Portuguese.

And, within our own hemisphere are islands belonging to Vichy, France, notably Martinique in the West Indies, where the French gold hoard is cached. The aircraft carrier Bearn and a French cruiser also lie there and on the flying field are many American planes which were en route to France when that country fell in June, 1940.

FIRE IN ALIQUIPPA

The Aliquippa Fire Department was called this morning to the home of Lawrence Augustino, where an overheated furnace had set fire to floor joists, the first floor and a partition. Damage was estimated at $125 by firemen.

"NOTHING NEW" IN MANILA

MANILA, 11:30 A. M., Dec. 11—A war communique today said that there were "no new developments" in connection with the Japanese landing forces in northern Luzon province.

In Danger Zone

Ralston M. Shannon, (above) radio operator on the destroyer, "Dorsey", with headquarters at Pearl Harbor, has not been heard from since the bombing at Honolulu. He is the son of Mr. and Mrs. W. C. Shannon of the Tuscarawas road. His last letter was mailed from Honolulu on December 4, stating that he was again returning to sea duty.

CASUALTY LIST RECEIVED

WASHINGTON, Dec. 11—Chairman David I. Walsh, D., Mass., of the Senate naval affairs committee said today that the Hawaiian casualty list was received by the Navy this morning but will not be made public for two or three days so that next of kin can be notified first.

BEAVER YOUTH NAMED PRINCIPAL FOR NAVAL ACADEMY APPOINTMENT

Congressman Louis E. Graham today announced the following appointments to the United States Naval and Military Academies based on the results of the competitive, qualifying examinations conducted by the Civil Service Commission on October 4:

Naval Academy—Beaver County—Principal, Reed Campbell, Beaver; first alternate, Peter Compagnoni, Ambridge; second alternate, Edward Supe, Ambridge; third alternate, Leonard Shevchik, Ambridge. Campbell, son of Mr. and Mrs. Charles G. Campbell, graduated from Beaver high school last Spring and is now a freshman at Muskingum College, New Concord, O.

Butler County—Principal, Jason W. Eury, Butler; first alternate, Tom Wigton, Butler; second alternate, George P. Young, Jr., Butler; third alternate, James V. Loucks, Butler.

Lawrence County — Principal, Howard L. Weigle, near New Castle; first alternate, John Scott Drake, Jr. West Pittsburgh; second alternate, William McClelland, New Castle; third alternate, Herbert S. Kraus, Ellwood City.

Military Academy — Principal, A. Leroy Shoaff, New Castle; first alternate, Harvey S. Boyd, Butler; second alternate, Gale Oberndorfer, New Brighton.

REED CAMPBELL

Thomas A. Chantler, Beaver, Passes Away

Thomas Albert Chantler, 33, widely-known resident of 1620 Second street, Beaver, died at 9:55 o'clock Wednesday evening in Rochester hospital following a three-week illness which started from an attack of bronchitis. He had been admitted to the hospital at 7:45 o'clock.

Mr. Chantler was the son of the late Mr. and Mrs. William G. Chantler, Beaver. Mr. Chantler was a graduate of Beaver High school, Class of 1926, and starred there in athletics. He was employed 13 years by the Jones and Laughlin Steel Corporation but had been elected secretary of the Dollar Building and Loan Corporation, Beaver, last September 1. Mr. Chantler was also a member of the Beaver Presbyterian church.

Surviving are the widow, Mrs. Martha Baker Chantler, and one sister, Mrs. Frank E. Lennox, Tuscarawas road, near Beaver. Friends are to be received at the Anderson funeral home, Beaver, where services are to be held at 2:30 o'clock Saturday afternoon.

The Weather Forecast
Western Pennsylvania: Fair tonight; somewhat colder.

THE DAILY TIMES

ROCHESTER-BEAVER-MONACA
FREEDOM—BRIDGEWATER—CONWAY—VANPORT—MIDLAND

Beaver County History
Due to bad weather, the K. of C. war fund drive in Beaver County was extended December 18, 1917.

ESTABLISHED APRIL 2, 1874 — BEAVER AND ROCHESTER, PA., THURSDAY, DECEMBER 18, 1941 — BY CARRIER 15 CENTS A WEEK—3 CENTS PER COPY

JAPANESE POUNDED IN PHILIPPINES

County Sailor Dies In Air Mishap

BADEN YOUTH IS KILLED IN NAVY AIRPLANE CRASH

Five Others Also Lose Lives In Accident At Elizabeth City, N. C.

Navy Patrol Plane Crashed, Burned In Take Off, Reports State

Another Beaver County youth was killed Wednesday when a United States Navy patrol plane crashed during a take-off at Elizabeth City, N. J., the second from the county to be killed within a week in an accident involving a plane from a branch of the armed services.

Francis J. A. Suttelle, 26, State street, Baden, was one of the six men killed yesterday in the crash. Private Vincent P. Papa, Rochester, United States Air Corps, was killed last Thursday in a plane crash near Puerto Rica.

Suttelle, a radio operator in the Navy, the pilot and co-pilot and three other men in the crew were all killed when the plane crashed on the take off and burned. Reports from the scene of the mishap said the plane was a Lockheed bomber.

FORMER BALL PLAYER

The local youth had enlisted in the Navy last January and had been stationed at Norfolk, Va., after he had completed his training in radio operation.

He was well-known in the county having played baseball in the County League for Baden three or four years.

Surviving are the father and three brothers, Jack Suttelle, Baden, Dan Suttelle, United States Navy, and Clay Suttelle, United States Army.

Son Of Former Local Woman Killed In War

John C. Watson, Jr., 27, San Francisco, Cal., a son of a retired United States Army captain, was killed in action in the Manila district, according to word received in Monaca Wednesday evening. Mrs. Maude Kuhn, Washington avenue, and Mrs. E. B. Winkle, his aunts, were informed.

Watson, eldest son of Captain and Mrs. John C. Watson, visited in Monaca last Spring while on a leave of absence. His mother formerly of Monaca, is the former Lillian Simpson.

In addition to the parents, he leaves a brother, stationed at an Army camp near San Francisco, and one sister, Mrs. Maude Alice Mitchell, San Francisco, Cal.

Labor Board Studies Precedent Of 1918

By the United Press

WASHINGTON, Dec. 19—President Roosevelt's labor industry conference, called to plan for uninterrupted arms production, today studied the procedure followed by the 1918 World War Labor Board.

Conferees said no agreement has been reached by the 12 industry and 12 labor representatives, but, it was learned, they have pledged "unstinted cooperation" toward meeting Mr. Roosevelt's request for an agreement not later than tomorrow night.

Mr. Roosevelt, asserting that "we haven't won the war by a long shot," told the conferees that "we can't have (work) stoppages . . . we have got to do perfectly unheard of things."

Both labor and management representatives appeared anxious to have all disputes considered as quickly as possible and in the localities where they occur. The first step would be conciliation, then mediation and finally arbitration.

Practice Blackouts Looming For State

By the United Press

HARRISBURG, Dec. 18—The state defense council said today practice blackouts may be held throughout the commonwealth, but officials must first get approval of the council and the U. S. army's first interceptor command at Mitchell Field, L. I.

Those instructions were sent to 590 county and local defense councils. The Third Regional Defense Headquarters explained state councils must pass on advisability of practice blackouts so that civilian and military aviation will not be confused by unheralded extinguishing of lights.

Practice alerts, however, may be held without first consulting the interceptor command, the council said.

Dr. Arnaud C. Marts, defense council director, announced he rejected a chance to assume directorship of civilian defense for the entire Third Army Corps area comprising six states because present duties require all his time.

Senate Asked To Lower Draft Age For Larger Army

By the United Press

WASHINGTON, Dec. 18 — The Senate was asked to approve today a bill making 19 to 44 years, inclusive, the age span of military service liability.

The House, which approved the legislation yesterday without record vote, refused to draft men younger than 21, and similar opposition to lowering the age appeared developing in the Senate.

Sen. Sheridan Downey, D., Calif., announced he would move to recommit the bill to the Senate military affairs committee, believing the measure had been approved too hastily. He said the nation had been "so neglectful" that training of more than 1,000,000 men in the next 12 months would be impossible.

Most Senators, however, withheld judgment pending the opportunity to study the printed record of secret hearings at which Army officials gave their reasons for wanting the age limits extended. Lack of the printed record yesterday was what caused Sens. Robert A. Taft, R., O., and Arthur H. Vandenberg, R., Mich., to request postponement of the final vote at least until today.

PLAN HUGE ARMY

The hearings revealed that the Army is thinking in terms of more than 4,000,000 men in service.

Referring to the House report refusing to lower the draft age from 21 to 19 years on the ground that 4,000,000 men would be available to the Army without it, Brig. Gen. Wade H. Haislip, assistant chief of staff for personnel, testified before the Senate military affairs committee:

"Four million men isn't an army today. The Germans have over 8,000,000 men under arms today, and to limit the War Department in a war where we don't know where it is going to reach, whether it is going to touch every part of the country, to say 'You can only have an army of 4,000,000 men,' I think is dangerous."

He added that "our air force will be 1,000,000 men before we are through."

RESTRICTIONS OPPOSED

A letter from Secretary of War Henry L. Stimson urged that no restrictions be placed on priorities in calling men, and that the War Department not be pinned down as to the ultimate size of the army

(Continued on Page Eight)

Firemen's Relief Group Of County Elects Officers

Annual Banquet Scheduled January 21; County Treasurer Gives Defense Talk

At the meeting of the Beaver County Firemen's Relief Association Wednesday night at Monaca, officers for the ensuing year were elected.

Harold Howarth, Beaver Falls, was elected president, succeeding Enlow Groom, Fallston, who could not succeed himself. Milton Crider, Freedom, was elected first vice-president. Roy Guy, New Brighton, was elected second vice-president. Warren Miller, Rochester, who had no opposition for financial secretary, will begin his fourth term in that capacity. Charles Casner, Patterson Township, who also had no opposition for treasurer, will also enter upon his fourth term.

The death benefits of the association were raised to $60 instead of $50.

Frank Bucholz reported elaborate

(Continued on Page Eight)

Monaca Youngster

Photo by Graule Studios

Donna Jean Beckman (above) is the four-months-old daughter of Mr. and Mrs. Fred Beckman, 728 Indiana avenue, Monaca. Her mother is the former Lois Bond of Beaver Falls.

Figures In Pacific High Command Shake-Up

The United States army and navy announce a sweeping shakeup of the Pacific high command on the land, on the sea and in the air as a result of the Pearl Harbor disaster. Rear Admiral Chester V. Nimitz (top left) is given command of the Pacific fleet, relieving Admiral Husband E. Kimmel (lower left). Lieut. Gen. Delos C. Emmons (top center) takes over the duties of Lieut. Gen. Walter C. Short (center bottom) who headed the army's Hawaiian department. Brig. Gen. C. L. Tinker (right top) will relieve Major Gen. Frederick L. Martin (bottom right) as commander of the air forces.

CHANGES MADE IN U. S. ARMY NAVY COMMANDERS IN HAWAII

By the United Press

WASHINGTON, Dec. 18—A major shift in American strategy in waging the war in the Pacific, with heavy stress upon aerial attack, was believed today to be involved in the drastic wartime shakeup of army and naval forces.

The shakeup, apparently carried out under orders of President Roosevelt, placed a new triumvirate of strategists in command in the Hawaiian - Pacific battlefront on land, sea and in the air and answered Congressional and public clamor stirred by Japan's "infamous" attack on Pearl Harbor 11 days ago.

A fighting general of the air, who is an exponent of the heavy bomber as a major striking force, became commander of Hawaii's land and air defenses, replacing an infantry general of the same rank.

The naval change places a full admiral, who was a pioneer submarine commander and expert, in charge of all naval vessels in the Pacific.

The shakeup came in the midst of a secret Presidential inquiry into the Japanese surprise attack which plunged the United States into war and which Secretary of the Navy Frank Knox said had caught the American defenders "not on the alert." The joint Army-Navy inquiry board, which will seek to fix the blame—if there is any—for the Hawaiian forces being caught off

(Continued on Page Eight)

Reports Heard By Hospital Board At Monthly Meeting

Purchase Of New Equipment, Repairs Authorized At Rochester Institution

Routine business, finances and reports were considered by members of the Board of Trustees of the Rochester General hospital at their monthly meeting Wednesday evening. The Board authorized the Superintendent, Miss Diana Milligan, to purchase some new equipment to be used in various departments of the hospital. The House committee was authorized to make repairs where needed in several places. Another report revealed that the hospital has recently acquired two pieces of Beaver property at Sheriff's sale to protect judgments held by the hospital. The report of Miss Milligan revealed details of work done in the hospital during the last month.

Red Cross Issues Call For Nurses

WASHINGTON, Dec. 18 — The American Red Cross issued a call for 50,000 graduate nurses to build up its reserve strength to meet the emergency requirements of the armed forces and the civilian population.

Nurses for the armed forces are recruited by the Red Cross, and a reserve of 74,000 registered trained nurses is needed to place the nation's program on a full wartime basis. It now has 24,000 in the reserve.

Ten Youths Killed When Bus Ignites After Overturning

NYA Enrollees Lose Lives In Tragic Crash Near Marshall, Illinois

By the United Press

MARSHALL, Ill., Dec. 18 — The bodies of 10 NYA enrollees were recovered early today from the flaming wreckage of a bus which overturned near West Union, 10 miles south of here.

Coroner H. E. Swinford reported that the bus apparently had skidded on a wet highway and slipped off the road about 11 o'clock last night. He said the bus driver, Ferris Williams, Casey, and at least two other youths were seriously injured.

The bus was en route from an NYA school at Oblong, 25 miles south of here, to deliver the boys to their homes at Marshall and Casey.

FIVE OTHERS HURT

It was reported that five youths escaped without injuries serious enough to require hospitalization.

Swinford said he reached the scene of the crash about 1:45 a. m., while the bus still was smouldering despite efforts of Robinson firemen to extinguish the blaze. Bodies of the victims were removed and brought to Marshall, where authorities were trying to round up uninjured youths and to contact NYA

(Continued on Page Eight)

CONTROLLED SALES OF TIRES TO BEGIN IN U. S. ON JAN. 4

By the United Press

WASHINGTON, Dec. 18 — The ordinary man who uses his car principally to drive to work, to scout around Saturday nights and for Sunday driving may not be able to buy a new tire for the duration of the war, or until Far Eastern shipping lanes are reopened.

That news—perhaps more than any other—today brings the impact of the world wide war directly to the home front. War needs for all materials — especially rubber—will be placed uncompromisingly ahead of less-essential civilian demands.

Price Control Administrator Leon Henderson, who also is director of the OPM's civilian supply division, revealed that state and local machinery is being set up to ration automobile tires beginning January 4 only to persons and agencies classed as essential to industrial efficiency and civilian health.

The same machinery, he said, may be used to carry out rationing programs for other scarce commodities.

MUST CUT CONSUMPTION

Henderson disclosed that civilian consumption of crude rubber must be reduced to at least 10,000 tons a month. Current consumption has been at the rate of nearly 47,000 tons a month.

Under the severe overall rubber rationing program, producers would be required to eliminate production of golf and tennis balls, bathing suits, stationers goods such as rubber bands, toy balloons and hundreds of other items. Rubber supplies would be guaranteed for the production of fire hose, hot water bottles, syringes, protective clothing, jar rings, surgeons' gloves, friction tape and essential mechanical goods.

Defense officials estimated that the United States probably will produce only 30,000 tons of synthetic

(Continued on Page Eight)

YOUTH NARROWLY ESCAPES DEATH BY ELECTROCUTION

Resident Of Wellsville Struck By High Voltage Wires At Vanport

Misfortune Turns To Good Fortune As Youth Gets Job On Housing Project

Misfortune may have been good fortune in disguise for Vincent (Jimmie) Amato, 17, Wellsville, Ohio, who had a miraculous escape from electrocution this morning when he was caught by falling power lines, carried down by a tree, at the Vanport housing project.

Despite the fact that he laid on three sputtering wires, carrying 4,000 volts of electricity, until pulled to safety by Harvey Cox, 352 New York avenue, Rochester, Amato was able to leave Rochester hospital within an hour after the accident—and this afternoon expected to start to work as a laborer on the housing job.

All customers of the Duquesne Light Company in Beaver, Bridgewater, Vanport and adjacent districts were without electric current for 13 minutes following the accident, the current being shut off by a breaker operation at 10:26 o'clock. The power remained off until the lines were cleared. Hundreds of telephone calls were received at the operating headquarters in Bridgewater from alarmed residents.

RESCUER DARES DEATH

Duquesne light first-aid men rushed to Vanport and were amazed to find the Wellsville boy little the worse for his experience aside from brush burns over his left eye. He was examined at the hospital and discharged.

Amato and Domenick Gullace, 18, Center street, Wellsville, hitch-hiked to Vanport this morning to apply for a job and were looking for the employment office when a 53-foot poplar tree, being removed, got away from a crew of workmen and fell over the power lines.

Cox was working in a ditch nearby and himself narrowly escaped the falling wires. He saw the Amato youth lying on the smoking wires and despite his own danger and with heavy gloves as his only protection, grasped the belt of the boy's jacket and pulled him to safety. Amato regained consciousness in a few moments.

Plane With Army Officers Missing

By the United Press

WASHINGTON, Dec. 18—Secretary of War Henry L. Stimson announced today that Major General Herbert A. Dargue, commanding general of the First Army Air Force, Mitchell Field, N. Y., and a group of high ranking army officers have been missing since December 12 on a transcontinental flight.

The plane, according to Stimson, was last reported at 7:55 p. m. last Friday as about two miles south of Palmdale, Calif., and a search has been instituted.

Thermos Bottle Taken From Bridge Guard Hut

Major Leslie Watson of the Salvation Army Corps Rochester, reported today that a thermos bottle belonging to the corps had been taken between 8 a. m. and 4 p. m. Wednesday from the small shelter hut for guards on the Cleveland and Pittsburgh bridge of the Pennsylvania Railroad at Rochester.

Thermos bottles filled with coffee are left late every night by Major Watson for the guards on duty at the several bridges in the Rochester district. Major Watson hopes the person who took the bottle will return it.

Veteran Worker

On the day after Christmas, Charles F. Bierer, (above) 325 Maine avenue, Rochester, will complete 25 years of service with the Bell Telephone Company. Starting in 1916 as a lineman, he has become an all round central office man, telephone installer and repairman.

Married and the father of six children, Mr. Bierer is a member of the 100,000 Mile Club, a group of 771 Bell workers who have driven company cars more than 10 years without an accident.

TIMOR OCCUPIED BY ALLIED ARMY

By the United Press

LONDON—Dutch and Australian troops carry out protective occupation of Portuguese Timor off eastern Netherlands East Indies; Japanese occupation of Portuguese Macao adjacent to Hong Kong rumored.

CAIRO—Axis forces in eastern Cyrenaica in full retreat; resistance broken after five-day tank battle near Mekili south of Derna.

SINGAPORE—British seek to halt heavy Japanese drive through flooded western Malayan rice fields toward positions flanking Britain's secondary naval base at Penang; Empire forces fall back on 50-mile North Borneo front; Hong Kong rejects Japanese ultimatum, rakes Japanese positions with artillery fire.

MANILA—American forces pound Japanese patrols in Vigan and Aparri sectors; new air raid alarm in Manila.

BATAVIA—Dutch bombers blast Japanese warships and transports off North Borneo; set Japanese cruiser afire.

TOKYO—Official radio claims troops advancing in Philippines; Japanese bombers attack Kunming, Burma road terminus.

MOSCOW—Red army reported "pursuing" Germans on main fronts.

HELSINKI—Communique admits general Russian offensive.

The Allies took the initiative in the East Indies today by seizing the island of Timor to prevent establishment of a dangerous Axis air and submarine base north of Australia.

Seizure of the island, owned by the Dutch and the Portuguese, brought Portugal directly within the war orbit but so far had led to no definite repercussions other than a protest by Lisbon authorities. Dutch and Australian troops took over the little island after assuring Portugal that the action was only temporary and precautionary.

On other fronts:

PHILIPPINES—American defense forces defeated and chased a Japanese patrol south of Vigan on the west coast and smashed an enemy motorized advance from Aparri on the north, killing about 40 and losing one dead. The Manila area again was attacked by enemy planes. Tokyo broadcasts claimed that three Japanese columns were advancing on Luzon island from Vigan, Aparri and Legaspi.

PENANG THREATENED

The Japanese also claimed to have destroyed American barracks in the Legaspi sector and sunk three U. S. submarines.

MALAYA—Japanese forces, using one-man tanks and infiltrating through the flooded rice fields, advanced to a point opposite the British naval base on the Island of Penang, on the east coast of Malaya. British forces withdrew and reorganized while reinforcements arrived from the south for a counter-drive believed already under way. The threat to Penang was described in London as serious. On the west coast of Malaya the Japanese were driven back in fighting in the Kelantan sector, where they suffered heavy losses.

BORNEO—British and Dutch land forces held strong positions after withdrawing from the Miri oil sector on the north coast, where all oil facilities were destroyed. The Allies held the Borneo airdromes, which the Japanese apparently sought to seize for attacks on Singapore and the Philippines.

HONG KONG—British defenders rejected a second Japanese ultimatum and replied strongly to Japanese artillery and air bombing. Chungking reported that a Chinese drive on the mainland to relieve Singapore was progressing and th

(Continued on Page Eight)

Will Head Drive

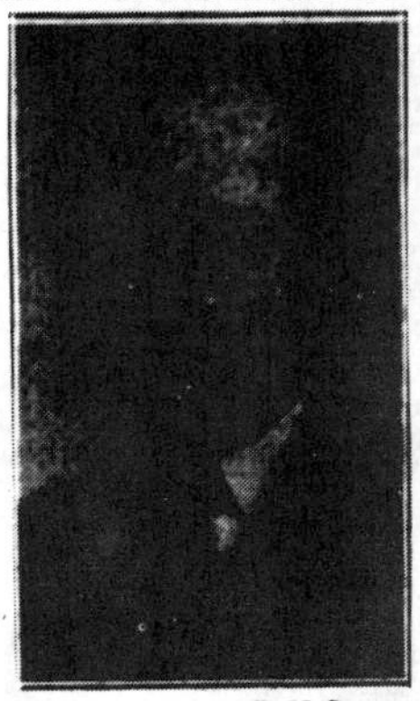

Dist. Atty. Robert E. McCreary

He has accepted the County Chairmanship of the Beaver County Red Cross drive to raise a $75,000 war relief fund.

Directors Elected By Rochester Board Of Trade Members

Organization Opposes Assessment Of Damages on County If Canal Is Built

When the Rochester Board of Trade met Wednesday noon in its weekly luncheon at the Penn-Beaver hotel, announcement was made of the results for the election of directors for the ensuing two years.

Those elected are: Ben F. Ellis, Attorney George A. Baldwin, Sr., Paul J. Huth, William J. Toner, H. Earl Kirk, Robert C. Stout and Armin K. Barner. The directors will meet soon and organize.

NEUTRAL ON CANAL

The organization went on record as neither opposing or supporting the construction of the proposed canal from the Ohio river to Youngstown, O., but opposed the assessment of damages that may be caused by the construction in Beaver County to the county. The action was taken in reply to a communication of the Ohio River Improvement Association at Cincinnati, O.

The next meeting will be held December 31. James W. Doncaster, president, presided. W. A. Hartzel received congratulations on his 82nd birthday, observed recently.

Small Steamer Hits Mine In Manila Bay

By the United Press

MANILA, P. I., Dec. 18—Approximately 200 persons were killed when the inter-island steamer Corregidor struck a mine and sank in Manila Bay yesterday, a witness estimated today.

The disaster was described as the worst Philippine maritime tragedy in recent years. The vessel, formerly engaged in trans-channel service between England and France, carried 326 passengers and crew members.

Among the missing were the wife and two children of Assemblyman Dominador Tan, who visited the United States last year to obtain President Roosevelt's signature on Philippine constitutional amendments. Tan was reported saved, but several other assemblymen were believed lost.

Aliquippa Borough Offices Entered

Who ransacked the Aliquippa City Building, and why. What were they after? What, if anything, did they get?

These questions were baffling Aliquippa police today as they sought an answer. Offices of the Central Relief agency, a local relief set-up, the health office, and various other departments were visited during the night. In the same building are housed the police and fire departments, the office of the Burgess, etc.

A member of the police department said today that "no report has been made to us" regarding the matter.

5
SHOPPING DAYS
Christmas
SHOP EARLY

Rochester News

Sauerkraut Dinner Features Meeting Of Church Group

Gleaners Class Of Evangelical Church Hosts To Husbands At Affair

A sauerkraut dinner featured the December meeting of the Gleaners Bible class of Zion Evangelical church Tuesday evening in the church social room. Husbands of the members were special guests. Covers were laid for thirty. The pastor, Rev. Thomas O. Fuss, voiced the invocation. A brief business session was conducted by the president, Mrs. D. R. Woods, and hostesses for the year 1942 were named. Games featured the social period. The next meeting will be held Tuesday, January 27. Mrs. Fuss, wife of the pastor, is teacher of the class.

Mrs. Robert D. Fleming observed her eighty-first birthday Tuesday at her home in Monroe street. Members of the family gathered in the homestead in the evening and spent several happy hours together. Mrs. Fleming received gifts, and also numerous greeting cards bearing congratulatory messages and best wishes from relatives and friends. Lunch was served. Among those present from out of the county were Mr. and Mrs. Fleming's son-in-law and daughter, Mr. and Mrs. George O. Sewall, and children, George, Jr., and Elmira Jane Sewall, Newton Falls, O., formerly of Rochester.

Second Lieutenant Paul H. Baldwin, of the U. S. A. Signal Corps stationed at Fort Monmouth, near Red Bank, N. J., left Wednesday to report for duty after spending a seven-day furlough with his parents, Attorney and Mrs. George A. Baldwin, and family, Connecticut avenue.

Miss Peggy Watson has returned to New York City, where she is a private pupil of Evan Evans, of the Juilliard School of Music, after spending the Christmas holidays with her parents, Major and Mrs. Leslie Watson, of the local Salvation Army Corps. While in the Valley, Miss Watson was contralto soloist at a midnight service Christmas eve in St. Stephen's Episcopal church, Sewickley.

The Christmas display of the Rochester Volunteer Fire Department in the municipal building is attracting hundreds of visitors from all parts of the county. The display is open to the public during the day and in the evening and is one of the finest in this section of the country.

Miss Beatrice Gardner is confined to bed by illness at her home in East Washington street.

The monthly meeting of the Dorcas Circle of Zion Evangelical church will be held Friday evening at 8 o'clock in the church social room. The choir will meet in the church for rehearsal the same evening at 7:30 o'clock.

George Day, son of Mr. and Mrs. George E. Day, is improving at his home in Delaware avenue, where he has been confined to bed since Christmas suffering from influenza.

Miss Mary Steinacker, a student nurse at Sewickley Valley hospital, is spending today and Friday with her parents, Mr. and Mrs. George A. Steinacker, Ohio avenue.

James McBurney, Denver, Col., will leave Friday morning for his home after a two-week visit with Mr. and Mrs. Max Kroen and family, Webster street.

Mr. and Mrs. Carl Sommer, Sr., Vermont avenue, spent the Christmas holidays with their son-in-law and daughter, Mr. and Mrs. Anthony Herman, and family, Struthers, O.

Mrs. Mary Irons, who has been ill the past three weeks of bronchitis and pleurisy at her home, 435 Brown street, was reported somewhat improved.

Many people from all parts of the county have viewed the Christmas display in the home of Street Commissioner and Mrs. Roy E. Powell, 522 Hull street. The display is one of the finest in the county and is open to the public.

Mr. and Mrs. Harry H. Cable, Alexandria, Va., formerly of Rochester, returned home today after spending a week with Mrs. Cable's parents, Mr. and Mrs. A. N. Gutermuth, and her brother-in-law and sister, Mr. and Mrs. Walter M. Dunham, and family, Delaware avenue.

Mrs. Jennie Canal entertained the Lucky Star club Tuesday evening at her home in North Rochester. Three tables of "500" were in play and favors were awarded to Mrs. Brady Jacobs, Mrs. M. Evans and Mrs. Ruby Plevell, who was honor guest. The hostess was assisted in serving refreshments by Mrs. Louis Polce.

Burma Road Abuses Reported Reduced

WASHINGTON, Jan 1. — Abuses interfering with delivery of American supplies to China over the Burma Road have been reduced to a minimum, official circles reported today coincident with a renewed request by China for an inter-allied commission to operate and control the road.

Reports of graft and corruption in connection with the supplies that move over the Burma Road have been investigated by United States Officials and in many cases the reforms they recommended have been put into effect.

Government official recognize that it would be impossible completely to separate Burma Road traffic from the multiple taxes and commissions which have existed for generations and which provide the only source of income for many poverty-stricken Chinese.

Government officials likewise concede that they do not expect Chinese chauffeurs, mechanics and workmen to operate with the same efficiency of Americans.

RADIO PROGRAMS

6:00 p. m.
WWSW, News.
WCAE, Song at Six.
WJAS, Paul Sullivan.
KQV, Modernaires; News.
KDKA, News; Pat Haley.

6:15 p. m.
WWSW, Golden Gate Quartette.
WCAE, Evening News.
WJAS, Beckley Smith, News.
KQV, Modernaires.
KDKA, Shall We Waltz.

6:30 p. m.
WWSW, Starlit Hour.
WCAE, Bob Chester Orch.
WJAS, Bob Hannon, Songs.
KQV, Bob Prince; Sports.
KDKA, Friendly Four.

6:45 p. m.
WWSW, Club Hollywood.
WJAS, Dinner Music.
KQV, Dinner Music.
KDKA, Lowell Thomas, News.

7:00 p. m.
WCAE, Fulton Lewis, Jr.
WJAS, Amos 'n' Andy.
KQV, Easy Aces.
KDKA, Fred Waring.

7:15 p. m.
WWSW, The Mandolettes.
WCAE, Here's Morgan.
WJAS, Lanny Ross.
KQV, Mr. Keen.
KDKA, News of the World.

7:30 p. m.
WWSW, Sports Slants.
WCAE, Confidentially Yours.
WJAS, Mickey Ross Orch.
KQV, Baron Elliott.
KDKA, Cugat Rhumba Revue.

7:45 p. m.
WWSW, Restyled Rhythms.
WCAE, Inside of Sports.
KQV, Lum and Abner.

8:00 p. m.
WWSW, Stand. String Ensemble.
WCAE, Morton Gould Orch.
WJAS, Death Valley Days.
KQV, March of Time.
KDKA, Coffee Time.

8:15 p. m.
WWSW, Sundown Serenaders.

8:30 p. m.
WWSW, Music of Maestros.
WCAE, For Your Information.
WJAS, Duffy's Tavern.
KQV, Service With a Smile.
KDKA, Aldrich Family.

8:45 p. m.
WCAE, Uncle Sam Calling.
WJAS, Tavern; E. Davis.

9:00 p. m.
WWSW, Parade of Melody.
WCAE, Gus Steck Orch.
WJAS, Bowes Amateur Hour.
KQV, Town Meeting.
KDKA, Music Hall.

9:15 p. m.
WCAE, A. Gunnison, News.

9:30 p. m.
WCAE, American Preferred.

10:00 p. m.
WWSW, Grotto Orch.
WCAE, R. Gram Swing.
WJAS, Glenn Miller's Orch.
KQV, Opera Guild.
KDKA, Rudy Vallee.

10:15 p. m.
WWSW, Dorothy and Squires.
WCAE, Spotlight Bands.
WJAS, The First Line.
KQV, First Piano Quartet.

10:30 p. m.
WWSW, News.
WCAE, True to Life.
KQV, Album of Memories.
KDKA, Frank Fay.

10:45 p. m.
WWSW, Art Farrar Orch.
WCAE, Under Western Skies.
WJAS, Evening Serenade.
KQV, C. Cavallero's Orch.

11:00 p. m.
WWSW, Interlude at Eleven.
WCAE, N. Twigger, News.
WJAS, K. Hildebrand; News.
KQV, News.
KDKA, News; Let's Be Friends.

11:15 p. m.
WWSW, Gardens Sports Parade.
WCAE, Hal McIntire Orch.
WJAS, Sports News; Orch.
KQV, Songs We Love.
KDKA, Music You Want.

11:30 p. m.
WWSW, Masterworks of Music.
WCAE, Baron Elliott Orch.
WJAS, Vaughn Monroe Orch.
KQV, Music for Reading.

11:45 p. m.
KDKA, News.

Conway News

Volunteers Sought For Defense Council

Volunteers are being sought for the Conway Defense Council, according to Paul Copeland, Eleventh street, who is in charge of enrolling those desiring to serve.

Mr. and Mrs. Walter Hudspeth and three children, Sharon, visited this week with Mr. and Mrs. Grover Spicher, Second avenue, and other local friends. The Hudspeths formerly lived in Conway.

Rev. and Mrs. Charles D. Beatty and infant daughter, Freedom, spent the Christmas holidays with Mrs. Beatty's parents in Baltimore, Md. Rev. Beatty is pastor of the Conway and Freedom Methodist churches.

Liars' Club Makes Its Annual Award To Man Who Told "Fish Story"

By the United Press

BURLINGTON, Wis., Jan. 1. — The Burlington Liars Club went "hook, line and sinker" for a fish story today and awarded its annual world's championship for a tale about catching fish with a barber pole.

R. C. Cross of Wausau, Wis., won the title and the diamond-studded 10-cent lyre symbolic of International preeminence in prevarication. Cross told of catching fish by pouring hair tonic in a stream. The fisherman needs only to set a barber pole and the Police Gazette on the bank and shout, "next," he said. The fish jump out of the water.

The revolutionary techique was developed, Cross said, in the land of Unadilla, where fish grew beards after a native accidentally spilled hair tonic in their habitat.

E. C. Hulett, the club's president, said Cross, story was picked from among 6,259 entries and that the war hadn't interfered with the output of lies.

Each person's quota of peanuts is ten pounds a year, because 1940 Census reports showed that 1,155,316,299 pounds are grown annually in the United States.

Demand Renewed For Separate Air Force

By the United Press

WASHINGTON, Jan. 1. — Japanese use of air power in the attack on the Philippines today renewed congressional demands for creation of a separate air force. Some influential members warned, however, against disturbing the existing setup in wartime.

Regardless of their views on the wisdom of a new organizational arrangement for military aviation, legislators generally favored army acceptance of Charles A. Lindbergh's tender of his services for war duty.

Sen. Pat McCarran, D., Nev., author of a pending bill to create an aviation department and to raise military aviation to rank coordinate with the Army and Navy, advocated that Lindbergh be given back his commission as Colonel and "a prominent place in the councils of our national military forces."

"His training, experience, and knowledge in the whole field of aviation justifies this," he said. "Whatever views he may have held about our getting into war, he had millions of his countrymen with him. But those same millions together with Mr. Lindbergh, now are unified against the enemy."

W. & J. Will Offer Navy Officer Courses

WASHINGTON, Pa., Jan. 1 — Preparations were underway today at Washington and Jefferson College to install courses which will qualify students as officers in the U. S. Navy, according to President Ralph C. Hutchinson. Students will be given a months sea training upon graduation and then transferred to a government training station for final courses leading to commissions.

THE DAILY TIMES
Established April 2, 1874

THE BEAVER ARGUS
Established November 1803
Consolidated July 1, 1930

BEAVER OFFICE
Third Street

ROCHESTER OFFICE
20? Brighton Ave., at Jackson St.

Published each evening except Sunday by THE DAILY TIMES COMPANY, INC. Entered at the Beaver postoffice as second class matter. E. I. Freeland, owner and general manager. Jack Malone, managing editor. Bill Anderson, sports editor. Gladys Gibbons, society editor. William T. Dentzer, M. F. McBrier, advertising manager. Corporation officers, E. L. Freeland, President; Edward J. Hahn, secretary-treasurer; William I. Dentzer, vice-president.

Member Pennsylvania Publisher's Association and National Editorial Association. Served by the United Press Association and Central Press, Inc.

TELEPHONES

Beaver 1800
Rochester 2500

SUBSCRIPTION RATES

By mail $5.00 per year to all subscribers in Beaver County, $6.00 per year to all points outside Beaver County, 50c per month, 25c per week, 2 weeks 30c. By carrier 18c week. 3c per copy at news stands. All communications should be addressed to THE DAILY TIMES, Rochester or Beaver, Pa. No attention paid to unsigned communications.

Let it be impressed upon your minds, let it be instilled into your children that the liberty of the press is the Palladium of all civic, political and religious rights of all freemen.—Junius.

Let the people know the truth and the country is safe.—Abraham Lincoln.

Lest We Forget

Congress shall make no law respecting an establishment of religion, or prohibiting the free exercise thereof; or abridging the freedom of speech or of the press.

—U. S. Constitution

ONLY ONE YARDSTICK

The American people will soon realize, if they do not already, that an all-out national war effort, 1942 style, is considerably more than just a phrase.

The key to the situation is supplied in the words of Brig. Gen. Lewis B. Hershey, national selective service director. General Hershey says that the size of the United States Army can be measured by only one yardstick—it must be big enough to win the war.

No one knows at the moment just how big the Army—and, of course, the Navy and Marine Corps—will have to be to accomplish that purpose, but there is little doubt that to assure victory over experienced and determined foes the armed forces of the United States will have to grow to a point heretofore regarded as imaginary.

Millions of men will be in uniform before the war is won. Millions are already available through selective service and millions more will be on call after all men 20 through 44 register on February 16. Not all these men will be fit for combat duty, but it is reasonable to expect that many of them will be used for duties behind the lines to free other men who are qualified to fight.

And the industrial army must grow, too. Staggering amounts of munitions must be produced for the use of the increased armed forces. For the time being, students, men with families and men needed in the production of food and weapons will be deferred from military service. But General Hershey makes it clear that as apprentices become skilled workers and as women can be substituted in industry and agriculture, more men will be called to the colors.

This is a national fight. It can be won only by a national effort greater than anything the world has yet seen.

DRAFT REGISTRATION

Acting under authority of the recently revised Selective Service Act, the President has set February 16 for the registration of all men born on or after February 17, 1897, and on or before December 31, 1921. This comprises the 20-44 age group of approximately 9,000,000 men. It leaves the remainder of the 18-64 group for later registration. Those who registered in 1940 and 1941 are not required to register again.

The registration is represented as preliminary to further drafts of men for the armed services. Whether it means that volunteer enlistments will soon be stopped has not been disclosed, but if the selective service principle is to be carried out as intended, with the government judging the best use that can be made of the abilities of every man, the volunteer plan will soon be abandoned.

The new draft forms will call for much information about the training and experiences of registrants. This is the first step in what may become a draft of defense labor. When the draft extension act was passed, much was said about conscription of the country's man power. Many members of Congress declared that the country must prepare itself to correct the injustice involved in requiring some men to join the armed forces and allowing others whose ability is useful in defense industries to work or loaf, as [illegible] dictates.

Judging by the program laid out by the President, this authority may be invoked before long. Individual liberty will disappear more and more as the war progresses. Only if victory can be won speedily can restoration of the people's traditional liberties be looked for.

ON THE HOME FRONT

Secretary of the Interior Harold L. Ickes reappears in the news with the announcement that he does not think gasoline rationing will be necessary, intimating that he thinks lack of tires will cut down consumption of gasoline. The Secretary ordered a speed limit of forty miles an hour in all national parks, and while he emphasized that he was not advising states what to do, he thought it would be a good idea to enforce a similar speed limit in state parks to conserve gasoline.

Whisky distillers have been ordered by the OPM to cut production of potable spirits by 60 per cent, to conserve sugar and to make facilities available for the production of industrial alcohol needed by the war effort.

United States tax stamps on automobiles will go on sale January 26 in post offices and Federal internal revenue offices throughout the nation. Under a new law, one of these stamps must be affixed to every automobile. Cars parked in garages for lack of tires are not exempt. The tax is $5 a year per car, but the stamps which must be affixed by February 1 will cost $2.09 and will be good until July 1, the beginning of the government's new fiscal year.

The OPM told a meeting of the newly-formed dairy industries committee that it favors every-other-day delivery as this would conserve 40 to 50 per cent of the rubber now used in truck tires, save large quantities of gasoline and prolong the life of delivery vehicles.

Dairies, stores and other retail businesses can not buy tires under the rationing plan. Wholesalers and manufacturers delivering goods to retail outlets can buy them.

EFFECT OF A RUMOR

There is an undercover rumor abroad in the United States, which breaks out occasionally in spots here and there, to the effect that the Federal government contemplates the commandeering of individual deposits in banks.

This rumor is wholly without foundation, but it is being given sufficient credence by the ignorant to cause hoarding of currency, which is as foolish as the commandeered deposit story.

There was an increase of $500,000,000 in the last month in total money circulation. In the last year this circulation figure has grown by 2,300,000,000 and now stands at the unprecedented figure of $11,000,000,000. This is almost three times the amount of money which the country required to do business during its last period of prosperity.

Hoarding is not going to help anybody in this situation. The bank deposit story probably grew from talk of withdrawing a portion of pay from wage-earners' envelopes, investing the money in government securities and returning the sum with interest after the war. This plan, even if it should be finally adopted, has nothing to do with bank deposits and hoarded money would have no effect upon it.

The hoarder is taking money out of circulation that might otherwise be usefully employed and he is not helping himself in any manner.

THE JAP MIND

There is a strong probability that before the United States is finished with Japan expanded in sight into the mental processes of its peculiar people may come to Americans. Almost a century of contact with the Japs has not been revealing. Intellectually they appear to have added little to the world's store of wisdom.

Recently a student in New York compiled a number of Japanese folk sayings. Some that he presented were familiar, but others were not.

If power of epigram is shown sharply in the Japanese brain it is in the comment on liquor: "First the man takes the drink; then the drink takes the drink; then the drink takes the man."

Much of epigrammatic offering by Japan is acid and packs a sneer and in that respect may disclose a national attitude of mind. One old saying is: "Who can speak well can lie well." Another: "He who steals gold is put in prison; he who steals land is made a king."

Many of the proverbs are quite commonplace. One runs: "A journey of a thousand miles begins with one step." Another says: "Cold tea and cold rice may be endured, but not cold looks and words." Another reads: "He who hunts two horses leaves one and loses the other."

And there is one Japanese proverb that the foolhardy Nipponese are to re-learn shortly, to wit: "It is difficult to be strong and not rash."

All Males In Family Serve In Armed Forces

By the United Press

HARRISBURG, Jan. 12—All males in the family of Ray E. Taylor, Republican minority member of the State House of Representatives and Commander of a local American Legion Post, will be on duty in the armed forces today.

Taylor, who was a chief petty officer in the navy during the last war, was ordered to return to service today. His son J. Harvey Taylor has been on duty with the 28th Division since February. Ray E. Taylor, Jr., another son, left for air corps duty. Their brother, J. Frank Taylor, entrains today for Newport, R. I., to attend the naval training school.

"COUNTY SEAT"

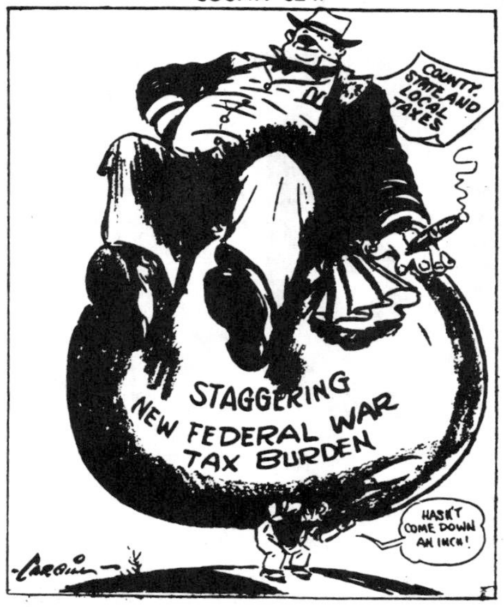
COUNTY, STATE AND LOCAL TAXES
STAGGERING NEW FEDERAL WAR TAX BURDEN
HASN'T COME DOWN AN INCH!

Books for Buddies

WE WANT BOOKS
VICTORY BOOK CAMPAIGN

Ten million books will be sought for men of the United States armed forces and Merchant Marine through this poster, designed by the Nationally known illustrator, C. B. Falls. Sponsors of the Victory Book Campaign are the American Red Cross, American Library Association and the United Service Organizations.

State's Industries Play Important Part In National Defense

More Than One-Fourth Of Pennsylvania Industries Making Defense Materials

HARRISBURG, Jan. 12—Pennsylvania's coal mines, steel mills, knitting mills, shipyards and farms play a great role in the nation's all-out effort for victory over the Axis forces.

At present, more than one-fourth of the state's industries are engaged in defense production, and with the greater demands of war are expected to carry a large burden of national production in the future, according to the state commerce department.

Shipping is a large industry of the state as shown by the fact that the port of Erie and Philadelphia together handle a greater volume of water-borne commerce than all New England ports. The Port of Philadelphia in 1940 handled 27,178,534 tons of merchandise, second only to the Port of New York.

Shipyards in Pennsylvania now have under construction $750,000,000 worth of ships for the United States Navy and Merchant Marine. Yards along the Delaware River hold contracts for more than 200 vessels whose total cost will be $1,500,000,000.

Pennsylvania employs more factory workers than in all the 19 states between the Mississippi River and the Sierra Nevada Mountains, with annual payrolls amounting to $220,000,000 more than these combined states, a department survey discloses.

Steel furnaces of this state have a capacity three times those of Japan and produce 30 per cent of all the steel melted and manufactured in the United States. Pennsylvania's iron works produce nearly one-third of America's pig iron, while its coke ovens produce 30 per cent of our nation's coke and by-products.

One-third of the nation's coal supply is mined in Pennsylvania.

The knitting mills of Pennsylvania will help clothe our soldiers and sailors. The mills, which in peacetime dominate the nation in their production of hosiery and underwear, will be called upon to produce a major part of the output of knitted textiles needed by the government.

In the value of farm products, the state ranks 11th in the union, but frequently is the first state in the country in the cash value of its potato crop.

DO YOU REMEMBER.

THIRTY YEARS AGO

FRIDAY, Jan. 12, 1912—Officers elected recently by the Ladies' Aid Society of the Rochester Methodist Episcopal church include: President, Mrs. James A. Warrick; vice-president, Mrs. James Ambrose; secretary, Mrs. Lee Jackson; assistant secretary, Miss Tillie McIlvain; financial secretary, Mrs. Henry Gordon, and treasurer, Mrs. Lyon.

TWENTY YEARS AGO

THURSDAY, Jan. 12, 1922—Election of officers and appointment of standing committees marked the meeting of Walter S. Roth Post, American Legion, held Tuesday evening in the municipal building. Raymond Stedman was named post commander.

TEN YEARS AGO

TUESDAY, Jan. 12, 1932—Reports of the various committees for the past year were presented and officers for the ensuing year were elected Sunday at the annual congregational meeting of St. Paul's German Lutheran church, Rochester, held in the church.

Sugar Conservation Order Made By OPM Will Be Modified

Ceiling Prices To Be Increased 20 Cents Per Hundred Pounds Under Plan

By the United Press

WASHINGTON, Jan. 12—Modification of the OPM sugar conservation order will provide additional supplies for retailers who have been limiting their customers to specific purchases because of depleted stocks, defense officials said today.

The OPM announced that the order, which froze sugar deliveries this year to 1940 monthly levels, will be revised by February 1 to allow deliveries at 1941 rates, which were much higher. That revision also will provide additional sugar supplies for businesses set up since 1940 or which have increased their business.

Ceiling prices for refined cane and beet sugar will be increased by 20 cents per 100 pounds, it was announced. The advance in price will compensate refiners for a recent government-approved price increase of 24 cents a hundred pounds for raw cane sugar.

That price increase, Price Administrator Leon Henderson said, probably will be passed along to the consumer when present stocks are depleted. Supplies acquired at the lower price by retailers, he added, should not be sold at higher prices.

Because of a heavy run on retail sugar stocks following start of the war, defense officials said that hoarding has created a temporary sugar shortage this month. Imports of sugar from Cuba, it was said, probably will be adequate to forestall a permanent shortage.

They warned, however, that sugar stocks may have to be rationed to civilians by a card system if hoarding persists.

To replenish civilian sugar supplies, OPM officials indicated, stocks in the hands of bottling, candy companies and other large industrial users may be requisitioned if they are above a 60-day supply.

COLLIES WATCH DOGS

VAN NUYS, Cal. (UP)—As a new protection against airplane sabotage, German shepherd dogs are being trained at the Van Nuys airplane factory as night guardians. They are taught to tackle anyone who seeks to board a plane.

The heart of the teak tree is the most valuable part of the tree. It is a native of South Asia and the Malayan islands, grows from 100 to 150 feet high, with a circumference of 20 to 25 feet at 100 years of age.

AMUSEMENTS

ORIENTAL THEATRE

That amazing young man of the screen, Mickey Rooney, came to town yesterday at the Oriental Theatre and literally "went to town" in the most entertaining performance of his career in the new musical, "Babes on Broadway."

Co-starred with Judy Garland, and aided by a large suporting cast featuring Fay Bainter and such youthful song-and-dance artists as Virginia Weidler, Ray McDonald and Richard Quine, the latter two graduates of the New York musical comedy stage, Rooney and his gang deliver an evening of entertainment worth anybody's time and money.

"Babes on Broadway" is built for entertainment from start to finish. Dealing with the scores of youngsters who yearly invade Broadway to fight for their "break" on the stage, it covers a wide panorama of theatrical life both front and backstage, with its tragedy and humor adroitly balanced by the musical interludes.

These cover a wide latitude of dances and song numbers ranging from such old-timers as George M. Cohan's "Yankee Doodle Dandy" to such brand-new numbers as "How About You" and "Hoe Down."

There is so much entertainment packed into "Babes on Broadway" that it is hard to single out any one specially, but a definite highlight of the procedings are the imitations done by Rooney and Miss Garland.

MAJESTIC THEATRE

A South American setting, strange, mysterious and fascinating, provides the background for the exciting film, "Law of the Tropics," starring Constance Bennett and Jeffrey Lynn, which opens at the Majestic Theatre tonight.

The cast turns in fine performances with lovely Constance Bennett showing versatility in a difficult role, and Jeffrey Lynn whose roles have mostly been on the light romantic side, does very well in a strongly dramatic portrayal.

A young planter (played by Jeffrey Lynn) on one of South America's largest rubber plantations leaves to meet a girl who is coming down from the United States to marry him. He receives a wire from her, saying that it's all off and that she is married to someone else. Drowning his troubles in a tropical cafe, he meets a singer, played by Constance Bennett, who he asks to marry him and assume the name of the girl he intended to wed originally. Being anxious to keep on the move because the police are on her trail for a past crime, she consents.

The added feature, "The Stork Pays Off," stars "Slapsie" Maxie Rosenbloom with Rochelle Hudson and Victor Jory.

GRANADA THEATRE

Noah Webster described "skylark" as a term meaning "to frolic boisterously; to indulge in antics; to run or skip about in a sportive or playful manner . . ." which doesn't nearly begin to do justice to the "Skylark" Claudette Colbert, Ray Milland and Brian Aherne indulged in last night at the opening of their new picture at the Granada Theatre.

Setting a new comedy pace aboard a fast-moving "marry-go-round," Claudette thumbs her nose at a marriage of five years which has made her and her home just a prop and a background to impress her husband's business clients. Ray Milland, the husband, is nonplussed at the fact that his wife considers love more important than his business career. Brian Aherne, the "other man," takes one look at Claudette and from then on realizes how empty his bachelor life has been. Binnie Barnes, the straying wife of Milland's biggest client, has no intention of letting Claudette steal Aherne, her part time boy friend. And caught in the dizzy domestic whirlpool are Walter Abel and Mona Barrie, a happily married couple who try to straighten everything and everybody out.

That's the set-up of Paramount's "Skylark" which worked itself up into a frenzied climax that had last night's audience roaring with laughter.

BEAVER THEATRE

Headed by a cast of comedy luminaries including Jimmy Gleason, William Tracy, Noah Meery, Jr., and Elyse Knox, "Tanks a Million," the laugh-filled story of Uncle Sam's draft army, opens tonight at the Beaver Theatre.

The story of "Tanks a Million" concerns Dodo Doubleday, played by William Tracy, who has a photographic memory and whose genius for memorizing data gets him in and out of a series of rollicking episodes. By mistake he broadcasts in the name of the Colonel, played by Jimmy Gleason, and lands in the guard house. How he manages to win the day and the girl brings the story to a fun-filled conclusion.

"Buy Me That Town" with Lloyd Nolan and Constance Moore in the leading roles, is an added feature. Nolan plays a big-time gangster, who actually buys a bankrupt town and sets about remodeling it as a hideaway haven for income tax evaders, phony stock brokers and others "on the lam" who can pay him $1,000 a week for sanctuary in the town jail. The crooks live the life of Reilly in the jail renovated to resemble a luxury club, while Nolan's beetle-browned pals hold down jobs as chief of police, fire chief and town treasurer.

How another mobster tries to "muscle in" and how the town belle, played by Miss Moore, turns the gangsters into respectable citizens is the story of "Buy Me That Town."

Heads New U. S. War Production Board

PRODU

President Roosevelt has placed American war production under the supreme authority of Donald Marr Nelson (right) who will head a war production board on which Vice President Henry Wallace (left) now Chairman of the Economic Defense Board, will serve as a member. Nelson, until his new appointment, was Executive Director of the Supply Priorities and Allocations Board. Placing war production under one authority incisively answers the criticism which was mounting in Congress over the de-centralized offices, say political observers.

Air Raid Alarm Sounds In Hawaii

HONOLULU, T. H., Jan. 15—The Pearl Harbor naval base sprang to instant readiness for battle Wednesday when air raid alarms shrieked throughout Oahu Island on the approach of "unidentified aircraft." No raiders appeared, however, and it was assumed the airplanes either were friendly or were driven off.

United States fighting planes zoomed to the sky, battle stations were manned, and citizens of Honolulu scurried to air raid shelters built since Japan's sneak air attack on December 7, which set off the Pacific war and gave America its war cry, "Remember Pearl Harbor."

The alarms sounded shortly before noon and the all clear came at noon sharp. No official announcement was made on the reason for the alarm but it was learned "unidentified aircraft" had been sighted.

World War Pension Bill Passed Up

WASHINGTON, Jan. 15—House approved proposals to pay veterans of the last World war and their widows and dependents an estimated $10,000,000,000 in pensions in the years to come failed to obtain either approval or disapproval of a Senate finance sub-committee.

The sub-committee, headed by Senator Clark, Democrat, Missouri, referred the two bills to the full committee without recommendation.

One bill would grant $40 a month pensions to World War veterans when they reached the age of 65.

The other would pay dependent widows of veterans $20 a month.

Red Cross News

ROCHESTER CLASS

Much interest is being shown in the first-aid course being conducted in the American Legion Home, Rochester, in connection with the local Civilian Defense program. The course is being sponsored by the American Red Cross with Walter S. Roth Post, American Legion, cooperating.

About fifty women and men enrolled at a meeting Wednesday evening of last week and that number was doubled by the enrollment of as many more at the meeting last night, which was the last opportunity to enroll for the complete course.

Meetings will be held every Wednesday evening at 7:30 o'clock in the Legion Home. Mrs. Alice Beckert and Eugene Geist, both of Rochester, are the local Red Cross instructors.

War News In Brief

By the United Press

LONDON, Jan. 15—Russian troops still are landing at Feodosiya, eastern Crimean port, the German radio acknowledged in a broadcast telling of Nazi air attacks on that place. "The Luftwaffe bombed continuously large Russian shipping concentrations, disembarking troops, and war materials of all kinds," the broadcast said.

CHUNGKING, Jan. 15— Further successes in North Hunan Province, a flare-up of fighting around Canton and Chinese attacks in South Honan and North Hupeh Provinces were announced in Chinese communiques this morning.

MOSCOW, Jan. 15—The Russians announced today the recapture of Medyn, 30 miles west of the Moscow-Bryansk railway in a continuing advance toward Vyazma.

WASHINGTON, Jan. 15 — The Navy Department announced today that the entrance to Delaware Bay had been mined. Inbound vessels were warned to obtain permission and direction for entering from the naval vessel stationed southward of the Overfalls lightship, or in bad weather, from the harbor control post.

OTTAWA, Jan. 15—The Government announced today that all enemy aliens would be removed from the defense areas of British Columbia, where there are some 25,000 Japanese. The only exception will be those holding police permits to remain.

Bridgewater News

First Meeting Held By First-Aid Class For Local Women

Twenty-Three Enroll In Red Cross Class Being Formed In Community

The first meeting of the Woman's First-Aid class was held Wednesday morning in the school auditorium. Twenty-three members enrolled, but the enrollment will be held open until next Wednesday, when instructions will begin. It was planned to meet Wednesday and Thursday mornings of each week, classes to begin promptly at 9:30 o'clock and close at 11:30. This will be done until the required twenty-hour course is completed. All those enrolling must attend every session and be ready to start not later than 9:30.

Members of the Presbyterian church choir were entertained at the conclusion of choir rehearsal Wednesday evening by Rev. J. W. St. Clair and Sutherland Campbell. A social time was enjoyed in the social rooms, after which lunch was served.

Mr. and Mrs. Oakley Harkins, Market street, are the parents of a daughter, born Saturday morning at their home.

Secret Marriage Recently Revealed

Photo by Graule Studios

Pictured above are Mr. and Mrs. Ralph L. Weaton, Monaca, whose secret wedding was revealed in the home of Mrs. Weaton's mother last Friday evening. Mrs. Weaton is the former Miss Elojean Mateer, Brodhead road, and Mr. Weaton is a son of Mr. and Mrs. George F. Weaton, Potter Township. They are residing in Monaca.

SOCIETY

Betrothal Of Beaver Teacher, Betty Munson, To Thomas J. Davidson Of Beaver Falls Told

Mr. and Mrs. C. A. Munson of Beaver, announce the engagement of their younger daughter, Betty Jane, to Thomas J. Davidson, son of Mr. and Mrs. C. R. Davidson, Beaver Falls. No date has been chosen for the nuptial event.

The bride-elect is a graduate of Beaver high school and Wilson College, Chambersburg, and is a teacher in Beaver high school. Mr. Davidson was graduated from Beaver Falls high school and Geneva College. He is employed by the Curtiss-Wright Corporation, Beaver.

BETTY MUNSON

Marriage Of Local Couple Last October Is Announced Here

Miss Margaret Pander, John Draganza Wed in St. Louis, Mo.

Announcement is made of the marriage of Miss Margaret Pander, daughter of Mr. and Mrs. James Pander, Rochester to John Draganza, son of Michael Draganza, East Rochester. The wedding was an event of October 25, 1941, at St. Louis, Mo.

Mrs. Draganza will make her home with her parents while her husband is serving in the United States Army, at present stationed at Ft. Leonard Wood, Mo. Mrs. Draganza returned a few days ago to her home in Rochester.

Recent Bride

Photo by Graule Studios

Mrs. James Tooch, (above) a bride of this month, is the former Mary Bedich of Fallston. She became a bride at a pretty wedding in St. Joseph's Roman Catholic church, New Brighton. The young couple is residing with the bridegroom's parents in Marion Hill, New Brighton.

VALLEY EVENTS OF FORMER YEARS

THIRTY YEARS AGO

MONDAY, Jan. 15, 1912—Plans are being completed for a dance Monday evening, January 29, by the Young Men's Progressive League of St. John's Roman Catholic church. The affair is to be held in the Lyceum hall, Fifteenth street.

TWENTY YEARS AGO

SUNDAY, Jan. 15, 1922—The Josephine White Missionary Society of the Beaver United Presbyterian church met Friday evening at the home of Mrs. L. E. Todd, Third street, Beaver. Several interesting papers were presented and lunch was served.

TEN YEARS AGO

FRIDAY, Jan. 15, 1932—Members of the Freedom Women's Christian Temperance Union met recently in the home of Mrs. Reed S. Shirey, Freedom, and heard the presentation of a number of interesting papers. Refreshments were served by the hostess at the conclusion of the evening.

Law Hampering Plane Production In West

SAN DIEGO, Cal., Jan. 15—Major Edgar N. Gott, Consolidated Aircraft Corporation executive, said today that President Roosevelt's order for 185,000 airplanes in the next two years could not be filled unless California's restrictions on the employment of women were relaxed.

Present state laws restrict employment of women between the hours of 11 p. m. and 6 a. m. and in emergency shifts exceeding eight hours.

MENNONITE SENTENCED

PHILADELPHIA, Jan. 15—Harry Zimmerman Kilmer, 22-year-old Lancaster county Mennonite, was sentenced to a year and a day in Federal prison after he refused to report to a civilian work camp for conscientious objectors in Fulton county.

MALTA HEAVILY RAIDED

VALETTA, Malta, Jan. 15—Axis planes have raided this British, Mediterranean outpost 90 times since January 1, but officials said today that casualties were few and damage slight. Raids were almost continuous Monday night and Tuesday.

RADIO PROGRAMS

6:00 p. m.
WWSW, News.
WCAE, Song at Six.
WJAS, Paul Sullivan.
KQV, News.
KDKA, News; Pat Haley.

6:15 p. m.
WWSW, Golden Gate Quartette.
WCAE, Evening News.
WJAS, Beckley Smith, News.
KQV, Modernaires.
KDKA, Shall We Waltz.

6:30 p. m.
WWSW, Starlit Hour.
WCAE, Saxomaniacs.
WJAS, Dinner Music.
KQV, Bob Prince—Sports
KDKA, Friendly Hour.

6:45 p. m.
WWSW, Club Hollywood.
WCAE, Song Sampler.
KQV, Dinner Music.
KDKA, Lowell Thomas, News.

7:00 p. m.
WCAE, Fulton Lewis, Jr.
WJAS, Amos 'n' Andy.
KQV, Easy Aces.
KDKA, Fred Waring.

7:15 p. m.
WWSW, The Mandolettes.
WCAE, Rio Conference.
WJAS, Lanny Ross.
KQV, Mr. Keen.
KDKA, News of the World.

7:30 p. m.
WWSW, Sports Slants.
WCAE, Confidentially Yours.
WJAS, Mickey Ross Orch.
KQV, Baron Elliott.
KDKA, Al Pearce.

7:45 p. m.
WWSW, Charlie Spivak Orch.
WCAE, Inside of Sports.
KQV, Lum and Abner.

8:00 p. m.
WWSW, Stand. String Ensemble.
WCAE, Max Adkin's Orch.
WJAS, Death Valley Days.
KQV, March of Time.
KDKA, Coffee Time.

8:15 p. m.
WWSW, Sundown Serenaders.

8:30 p. m.
WWSW, YWCA—In Defense.
WCAE, For Your Information.
WJAS, Duffy's Tavern.
KQV, Service with a Smile.
KDKA, Aldrich Family.

8:45 p. m.
WWSW, Walter Remsen.
WCAE, Uncle Sam Calling.
WJAS, Tavern; E. Davis.

9:00 p. m.
WWSW, Parade of Melody.
WCAE, Legion Convention.
WJAS, Major Bowes.
KQV, Amer. Town Meeting.
KDKA, Musical Hall.

9:30 p. m.
WWSW, Concert Gems.
WCAE, Sinfonietta.

9:45 p. m.
WWSW, Mayor's Civic Forum.

10:00 p. m.
WWSW, Lennie Martin Orch.
WCAE, Gram Swing, News.
WJAS, Glenn Miller's Orch.
KQV, Metropolitan Opera.
KDKA, Rudy Vallee.

10:15 p. m.
WWSW, Dorothy, Her Esquires.
WCAE, Spotlight Bands.
WJAS, The First Time.
KQV, First Piano Quartet.

10:30 p. m.
WWSW, News.
WJAS, Defense Reporter.
KQV, Album of Memories.
KDKA, Frank Fay.

10:45 p. m.
WWSW, Colonial Orch.
WCAE, Bette Smiley.
WJAS, Fay Wray.
KQV, Joe Sudy Orch.

11:00 p. m.
WWSW, Interlude at Eleven.
WCAE, E. Twigger, News.
WJAS, K. Hildebrand, News.
KQV, News.
KDKA, News; Music.

11:15 p. m.
WWSW, Gardens Sports Parade.
WCAE, Frankie Master Orch.
WJAS, Alvino Rey's Orch.
KQV, Songs We Love.
KDKA, Music You Want.

11:30 p. m.
WWSW, Masterworks of Music.
WCAE, Baron Elliott's Orch.
WJAS, Guy Lombardo's Orch.
KQV, Music for Reading.

11:45 p. m.
KDKA, News.

12:00 Midnight
WWSW, 1500 Club (til 6 a. m.)
WCAE, Alvino Rey Orch.
WJAS, News; Orchestra.
KQV, News; Music.
KDKA, Music; Tomlinson.

12:15 a. m.
WJAS, Shep Field's Orch.
KQV, Music for Reading.
KDKA, Peaceful Valley.

12:30 a. m.
WCAE, Del Courtney Orch.
KQV, Dance Music.
KDKA, Freddie Ebener's Orch.

12:45 a. m.
KQV, Music; News.

FOUR DIE IN FIRE

DETROIT, Jan. 15 — A young mother and her three small children perished Wednesday in a fire which destroyed their Dearborn township cottage, built by the husband and father, who was at work.

Seven new coal mines have been opened recently in unoccupied China and others have been modernized, according to the Department of Commerce.

Living costs are moving ahead at a rapid rate and reflect the earlier advance in primary markets, the Department of Commerce says.

Micro-photography is being used to expedite mail between Great Britain and British armed forces in the Middle East, according to the Department of Commerce.

Rochester Twp. Brother And Sister Wed At Double Ceremony In West Virginia

The Methodist church parsonage at New Cumberland, W. Va., was the scene of a double wedding ceremony Saturday morning, January 10, at 11:30 o'clock, when Miss Linora Barkley, Rochester Township, became the bride of Franklin H. White, New Brighton, and Miss Ruth Inman, New Brighton, became the bride of William H. Barkley, Rochester Township, brother of Mrs. White.

The nuptial lines were read by Rev. Wayne W. Moore. For her wedding Mrs. White wore a powder blue silk crepe dress with brown accessories and Mrs. Barkley wore teal blue crepe with brown accessories.

The newlyweds spent several days visiting points of interest in West Virginia. Mr. and Mrs. White are residing at 341 Pennsylvania avenue, Rochester, and Mr. and Mrs. Barkley are living at Mr. Barkley's home in the Noss Plan.

Mr. White is employed at the Pittsburgh Tool Steel and Wire Company mill in Monaca, and Mr. Barkley is employed by the Mid-West Abrasive Company.

Beaver News

Church Census Is Planned By Local Ministerial Group

Pastors Plan Survey At Meeting Held Wednesday In Lutheran Church

The Beaver Ministers' Association held its January meeting in the Lutheran church Wednesday morning, with Rev. H. J. Schmid, president, in charge. The pastors voted favorably on a proposal to conduct a church census in Beaver in the near future, in view of the recent influx of new people to the borough, and a layman in one of the churches will be sought to lead the work.

The regular meeting of the Department of Literature of the Beaver Woman's Club will be held Friday afternoon, January 16, at two o'clock, in the Presbyterian church, with the chairman, Mrs. W. W. Rinehart, presiding.

Lynn B. Oppelt has returned to his post at Camp Shelby, Miss., after spending a week here with his parents, Mr. and Mrs. F. R. Oppelt, Market street.

The Busy Bee Class of Holy Trinity Lutheran church held its first meeting of the year recently at the home of the teacher, Mrs. T. E. Allebach, East end avenue. Officers were elected for the ensuing year. They are: President, Reba Gillespie; vice-president, Sara Belle Segmiller; secretary, Patricia Schmid; treasurer, Phyllis Hawthorne; sunshine secretary, Rose Romigh, and publicity chairman, Billie Gene Bickerstaff. Plans were made for future activities and lunch was served by the hostess. The next meeting is to be held at the home of Reba and Ethel Gillespie, Dutch Ridge road.

AIR CORPS AGE REDUCED

PITTSBURGH, Jan. 15 — The Army Recruiting station here announced today reduction of the age limit for Army Air Corps cadets to 18 years. Cadet pilots, navigators and bombardiers now will be accepted at ages from 18 through 26.

PROBE DEMANDED

WASHINGTON, Jan. 15—Sen. Allen J. Ellender, D., La., today demanded a "thorough investigation" of charges of nepotism and waste in the construction of the Louisiana ordnance plant, Minden, La.

Separate Air Force Hearings Deferred

WASHINGTON, Jan. 15 — The Senate Military Committee has announced indefinite postponement of hearings on proposals to create a separate air force.

With nearly a full attendance, an announcement said, the committee voted unanimously to reconsider its earlier decision to hold hearings.

"This," the statement said, "for the reason that since our country is now at war it is not now appropriate to bring up this controversial question.

"Unified command in our army making an harmonious whole is, in the judgment of the committee, what the completely unified people of our country are entitled to in the successful conduct of the war."

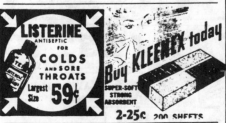

The Weather Forecast

WESTERN PENNSYLVANIA: Continued cold tonight, with light snow late tonight in west portion

THE DAILY TIMES

ROCHESTER · BEAVER · MONACA

FREEDOM—BRIDGEWATER—CONWAY—VANPORT—MIDLAND

Beaver County History

ESTABLISHED APRIL 2, 1874 — BEAVER AND ROCHESTER, PA., THURSDAY, FEBRUARY 12, 1942 — BY CARRIER 18 CENTS A WEEK—3 CENTS PER COPY

British Continue To Fight In Singapore

★ ★ ★ ★

COUNTY TAX REMAINS AT TEN MILLS

CONFERENCE HELD BY SCHOOL BOARDS TO STUDY PROGRAM

School Directors In Beaver Area To Continue Present Plan Of Schooling

Beaver Pupils To Present Patriotic Pageant During May

To discuss educational problems in the various districts, a conference was held Wednesday evening by the Beaver, Bridgewater, Borough Township, Brighton Township and county school boards.

The State Department of Public Instruction was represented by Dr Ray Robinson and Dr. Karl Morneweck. The U. S. Office of Education and the Defense Housing Authority were represented by Dr. Donald Davis.

The first decision was whether the area was going to develop a "six-six" program of education or retain the present "eight - four" plan. After all factors were taken into consideration, with the financial problem bearing the greatest emphasis, it was unanimously decided by the township boards that they preferred to continue their responsibility in caring for the first eight grades, with their pupils going to Beaver high school for the upper four years.

This decision means that the preliminary plans for the development of a Junior high school in Beaver are withdrawn and that the Beaver board is under no obligation whatever for additional building facilities as it is within the Beaver board's power to accept or reject non-resident pupils.

PICNIC SITE NAMED

During the meeting of the Beaver board preceding the conference the bids for general school and janitorial school supplies were opened and awarded.

The Activities Committee reported that the pupils from the fourth grade up had overwhelmingly selected Idora Park at Youngstown, O., for their annual school picnic and the officers of the school were authorized to sign the contracts.

The Finance Committee presented the bills payable and drew attention to the preparation of the coming budget which will necessitate considerable study since the costs of operating a school program have increased tremendously and the fact that considerable long term indebtedness will be falling due this coming year.

Plans for a spring festival were presented. A committee of ten teachers and principals met last week to discuss the feasibility of consolidating some of the spring activities on account of the irregularity of the times. A consolidation was deemed advisable for the following reasons: To conserve parents' energy since so many are engaged in defense activities, to minimize expenses on activities of a non-patriotic nature, to conserve the energy of the teachers who are assisting in defense activities, to present one mammoth activity with a patriotic theme which would include or substitute for all spring activities.

TO STAGE PAGEANT

About May 8 or 15 a pageant with a musical background will be staged in the stadium which is intended to consolidate the following activities:

Spring music festival, gym exhibition (Junior and Senior high school boys and girls), general school exhibition, May Day.

Many pupils from the fourth through twelfth grades will be used in this program. The committee is open for suggestions and ideas. The committee includes: Lincoln Building—Mr. Schaffer and Mrs. Hartley; Ft. McIntosh building — Mr. Linn, Mrs. Campbell, Miss Anderson, and Miss Schewe; High school building — Miss McKinley, Mrs. Detzel, Mr. Economos, Mr. Brammer.

County Schools To Receive Payments

Three local school districts are among those scheduled to receive checks from the state, according to an announcement made by State Treasurer G. Harold Wagner.

Monaca is to receive $338.30 for training N.Y.A. youths, Midland is to get $799.60 for vocational education for defense and Beaver Falls is to receive $5,475.49 for vocational education for defense. The checks are to be placed in the mails Friday.

Lost and Found

LOST: In Rochester A. & P. store, miniature gold football with initials W.E.W. Raised "R" on front. Highly valued. Liberal reward. Return Rochester Senior High School Office. 2 12

WAR!
U.S.A.
THEN!
NOW!
LINCOLN
LIFE · LIBERTY · PURSUIT · OF · HAPPINESS
HE STARTED US—ON THE RIGHT ROAD, LET US KEEP GOING---"THAT THE GOVERNMENT, OF THE PEOPLE, BY THE PEOPLE, AND FOR THE PEOPLE, SHALL NOT PERISH FROM THE EARTH."

Officers Named At Meeting Of County Agricultural Group

B. A. Caven Re-elected President Of Agricultural Extension Association

At the annual meeting of the Beaver County Extension Association held at Center Grange hall yesterday, B. A. Caven of North Sewickley Township was re-elected president.

Other officers re-elected are: Elmer L. Goehring, Marion Township, vice president, east side; Earl Nichol, Green Township, vice president, south side; and T. N. Gillespie, North Sewickley Township, secretary-treasurer. E. E. Duncan, Brighton Township, succeeds J. W. Denny, Chippewa Township as vice-president of the west side.

Project reports were given by E. E. Duncan, Brighton Township, Mrs. C. E. Buckley, Brighton Township; Scott Baker, Brighton Township; Mary Throckmorton, Chippewa Township; William Thompson, Green Township, and John Elder, Chippewa Township.

TWO TALKS GIVEN

The highlight of the morning session was the address given by Miss Eleanor Winters, nutrition specialist, Pennsylvania State College, on the subject "What to Eat and Why." The principal address of the day was given by Earl L. Moffitt, Farm Management Specialist, State College.

Annual reports of work within

(Continued on Page Ten)

A. M. F. STITELER DIES IN ROCHESTER HOSPITAL TODAY

In the death of Allen M. F. Stiteler, aged 60 years, at the Rochester hospital at 8:10 o'clock this morning, Beaver county lost one of her outstanding citizens and business men.

Taken By Death

A. M. F. STITELER

He had been critically ill for several weeks. Several times he had rallied and appeared to be on the road to recovery. Last evening he suffered a collapse, and the end came early today.

Funeral services will be conducted in his home in Brighton township Saturday afternoon at 2:30 o'clock. Burial will be in Beaver cemetery.

Mr. Stiteler came from Philadelphia to Beaver as a young man more than thirty years ago to represent the Pew interests here. He was, for many years, actively engaged in the management of the Beaver Valley Railroad, a connecting road between the Pennsylvania and the New York Central systems here. While more recently engaged in other business enterprises, chiefly the Beaver Falls Planning Mill company, Mr. Stiteler continued to represent the Pew interests here until his death. He was an active Building and Loan man, and a director of the First National Bank of Beaver Falls.

He was a World War veteran, a member of the American Legion, for many years active in the Beaver Post, and a former commander. He served in a wide area abroad during the World War more than twenty years ago. While in France, he had charge of large transportation outfits engaged in moving troops and supplies by rail through-

(Continued on Page Ten)

Freedom Teachers Granted Pay Boost By School Board

Ten Per Cent Pay Increase Voted By Directors; No School Monday

The Freedom Board of Education, in monthly session Wednesday evening, voted to give the teachers a ten per cent increase in salary beginning March 1, for the balance of the fiscal year. This action was taken in view of the emergency and increased living conditions.

The board also voted to assist the Local Draft Board with the registration next Monday and in order that the teachers will be free to help, there will be no school on that date.

The report of the supplies and equipment committee, Frank Holsinger chairman, dealing with supplies and equipment for the next school year, was approved. It was voted to install a new drinking fountain in the First Ward school building.

SUBSTITUTE NAMED

Mrs. Katherine E. Zahn, who represented the Board at the State

(Continued on Page Ten)

Men To Be Accepted For Defense Corps

Capt. Lester W. McClelland, commander of Company B, Pennsylvania Reserve Defense Corps, will be at the New Brighton armory this evening at 8 o'clock to accept men 18 to 50 years of age for enlistment in the newly-formed local platoon of the company.

Battle Rages On Singapore

By the United Press

British guns still pounded the Japanese today in defense of Singapore.

Enemy invasion forces were reported by Axis radio broadcasts to be pressing a "general offensive" on the strategic islands at the tip of the Malayan peninsula, but it was acknowledged that the battle which Tokyo claimed to have won on Wednesday was not yet over.

London reported that battered British troops carried out four desperate counter-attacks against the Japanese—only one of which was successful. A spokesman said tonight that "the situation at Singapore is very grave."

A British military commentator said at 10 a. m. (EWT) today that communications with Singapore still appeared to be functioning.

Heavy artillery in the British fortress of Changi at the northeast corner of the island still was in action, the Tokyo radio admitted, and fighting was in progress along a line that indicated the defenders held a large part of the eastern section of Singapore island.

Radio Tokyo said that the main Japanese army entered the city of Singapore this morning and that furious aerial bombardment had blasted or set fire to at least 25 ships in the harbor.

A number of British troops—the Axis estimated them anywhere from 25,000 to 75,000—were reported cut off as a result of the Japanese advance across the island, and London sources acknowledged that lack of warships and merchant vessels made it highly unlikely that any large force could be evacuated from Singapore even with unusual luck.

MANY EVACUATED

The Singapore radio had not been heard since 5 a. m., when it said that fighting still was in progress and that ships still were evacuating women and children from the harbor. A huge cloud of smoke hung over the harbor area and other parts of the island as a result of the application of the "scorched earth" policy, the Calcutta reports said, but other dispatches indicated that much equipment had not been destroyed.

No official word from Singapore had been received by London military authorities since Wednesday noon, but the Axis broadcasts made it certain that the defenders still were fighting on various parts of the island.

Changi fortress apparently was the main center of resistance as it was under heavy attack by Japanese airplanes which were attempting to silence the long-range British guns that were still hammering at Japanese lines on the Johore coast.

CHURCHILL UNDER FIRE

But there also appeared to be serious political repercussions in London where a parliamentary revolt against the conduct of the war

(Continued on Page Ten)

Lights For Water Works, Reservoirs Approved At Monaca

Council Members May Have Special Meeting To Approve Budget For 1942

The proposed budget for 1942 was not adopted by Monaca Council at a meeting Wednesday night because of the 15-day period for its public inspection not having expired. A special meeting of council may be called in the near future for final adoption of the budget.

Council decided to have floodlights installed at the municipal water works and at the reservoirs.

The use of the fire department quarters in the municipal building by the American Flint Glass Workers Local Union for payment of dues was discontinued as a safety measure during the duration of the war.

BURGESS' SALARY DISCUSSED

The payment of a salary to the burgess in accordance with an act of the Legislature, in place of him receiving the costs for hearings, was discussed and the matter was referred to the Police committee for further consideration.

The purchase of a light truck for the Water Department was discussed and the Water committee was instructed to obtain prices and other data and report at the next meeting of council.

The fence being built around the new reservoir is nearing completion, it was reported. Council appropriated $25 to the Monaca Local Council of Defense for incidentals. George E. Dietrich, president, presided.

Special Meet Held By Board Of Health

The Beaver Board of Health held a special meeting Wednesday evening in the borough building and discussed the misunderstanding in quarantine laws for measles, whooping cough, chicken-pox, German measles and mumps.

Many persons have not been notifying the board of health of such cases or when the children who had been ill are returning to school. Despite the belief of some persons, the periods of quarantine have not been changed, the board stated.

Any child suffering from one of the five most common children's diseases must be quarantined the full period, but others in the house need not be quarantined, according to the board.

Unless the parents cooperate and see that the health officer is notified, enforcement of the law will be necessary, the board decided.

Nation At War Pays Homage To Lincoln

By the United Press

WASHINGTON, Feb. 12—A war-conscious nation paid tribute today to a man whose name is irrevocably linked with war—Abraham Lincoln.

This is the 133rd anniversary of Lincoln's birth. In cities and towns throughout the nation patriotic organizations will sponsor gatherings paying homage to him.

In Washington a representative of President Roosevelt will appear at the white marble Lincoln memorial to place the president's wreath alongside the many others there. Last year the president made a trip to the memorial himself.

An army band, color-bearers and an armed guard of soldiers, sailors and marines were on the program at the memorial ceremonies. More than a score of patriotic organizations were prepared to participate.

Lincoln was born in Hardin county, now Larue county, Ky., February 12, 1809. He was shot April 14, 1865, and died the next day.

Big Crowd Attends Annual Dinner Of Lead Firm Employes

St. Joseph Lead Company President Speaks At Tenth Safety Dinner-Dance

Employes of the St. Joseph Lead Company and their wives and friends—more than 600 strong—attended the tenth annual safety dinner and dance Wednesday evening in the General Brodhead Hotel, Beaver Falls.

Featuring the affair were the annual presentation of awards to employes, an address by President Clinton H. Crane, New York City, and an excellent program of professional entertainment.

"Democracy—life, liberty and the pursuit of happiness — was bought with blood, sweat and tears and is worth fighting for." Mr. Crane declared in his address.

For the duration of the war we must temporarily give up some of our liberties and follow our leaders," he said. Stating that the nation must be closely united as one large family against a common enemy, Mr. Crane stated that "when the enemy is outside the family there can be no squabbles inside the family."

OVERTAKING ENEMIES

The United States was unprepared for the war and started slowly and clumsily, but is fast overtaking its enemies, he said. The present war has proven, Mr. Crane aid, that a navy without a powerful air force is helpless.

Commending the workers for their loyalty and industry, the com-

(Continued on Page Ten)

BUDGETS ADOPTED BY COMMISSIONERS TOTAL $1,628,043

Eight-Mill Tax Levied For County And One Mill For Sanatorium

Institution District Tax Levy Is Reduced From Three Mills To One Mill

Beaver County Commissioners Art W. Coombs, J. S. Edwards and E. H. Markey have set the Beaver County tax levy for 1942 at ten mills, the same as for many years, and adopted County and Institution District budgets for this year totaling $1,628,043.01.

While the total county levy of ten mills is the same as last year, the commissioners have reduced the Institution District levy from three mills to one mill, and increased the general county levy from seven mills to nine. One mill of the nine-mill county levy is allocated for the County Tuberculosis Hospital. Last year the levy for the Sanitorium was one-half mill.

The county budget for 1942 lists estimated receipts of $1,474,027.35 and appropriations totaling $1,428,368.01, leaving an unappropriated balance of $45,659.34.

The estimated receipts include a cash balance of $63,852.35 on hand at the beginning of the current fiscal year; tax receipts—estimated on the basis of an 83 per cent collection of the duplicate and including anticipated income from taxes of prior years and from the four-mill personal property tax—of $909,000 and receipts of $162,000 from miscellaneous sources.

TO BUILD HIGHWAY

By far the largest single appropriation for the year is for debt service. The budget appropriates

(Continued on Page Ten)

Defense Council To Meet At Conway

Final arrangements have been completed for the meeting of the Conway Civilian Defense Council at 7:30 o'clock this evening in the auditorium of the Conway school.

Rev. Dr. W. W. McKinney, Ambridge, is to deliver the principal address and George Roark, New Brighton, executive secretary of the Beaver County Civilian Council of Defense, and William J. Toner, Beaver, manager of the Rochester exchange of the Bell Telephone Company, will also speak.

A program of patriotic songs and a novelty number will be presented by students of the First, Second and Third grades of the Conway school. The first-aid team of the Conway Fire Department is to present a demonstration in conjunction with the meeting.

William S. Veder Dies At Beaver

William S. Veder, 79, 509 Sharon road, Beaver, died at 10:45 o'clock Wednesday evening in Beaver Valley hospital. He was admitted to the hospital on Monday, February 9, his birthday anniversary.

Friends are to be received at the Anderson funeral home, Beaver, where services are to be held at 2:30 o'clock Sunday afternoon. Interment will be in Grandview cemetery, Beaver Falls.

Mr. Veder was born in Rochester and had resided in the county all his life. He had lived in Fallston the past few years but had moved to Beaver last September. He was a retired bricklayer.

Surviving are the widow, Mrs. Jennie Veder; one son, Glenn Veder; one brother, Henry Veder, Pittsburgh; three grandchildren and several nephews.

Nine Killed In Bomber Crashes

By the United Press

SEATTLE, Wash., Feb. 12 — A twin-motored army bomber from McChord Field crashed near Tolt, north of here, today. Sheriff's officers said four men were killed.

Military and civil authorities found wreckage scattered over a wide area of swamp land.

Two bodies were found 100 feet from the main wreckage. Part of the fuselage was submerged in the swamp, hampering investigation.

Witnesses said they heard the plane's motors apparently running perfectly, then the crash.

WINDSOR LOCKS, Conn., Feb. 12 —A statement issued by Col. Clyde V. Finter, commander of Bradley Field, today disclosed the names of five army flyers who were killed yesterday afternoon when their multi-motored bomber crashed at nearby Granby.

2c **The Aliquippa News** 2c

VOL. 2. No. 6 ALIQUIPPA, PA., FEBRUARY 27, 1942 PRICE: TWO CENTS

142 MORE DRAFTED HERE

Teachers, Police, Merchants Called for March Induction

One-hundred-forty-two Aliquippa men, the most since the war began, will leave homes and businesses early next month for the Army.

Borough draft officials revealed the names of the men, ranging from school teachers to laborers but withheld date of their departure on grounds that the information might be valuable to "the enemy."

The men passed rigid Army physical examinations in Pittsburgh Feb. 19, the day 86 borough boys left for New Cumberland amid the cheers of more than 1000 spectators who "saw them off" at the P. & L. E. station here.

Approximately 77 of the group examined in Pittsburgh that day failed the physical tests and were placed in deferred classifications. Principal reason for rejections, it was understood, was the prevalence of tuberculosis and venereal diseases.

Waiting Period Eliminated

Less than a week ago Selective Service officials announced that

diseases would be accepted and "cured while in the service" and that severe cases would be given temporary (1-B) deferments .

Tubercular cases, as in World War No. 1, will be deferred, perhaps indefinitely.

Draft officials in Washington also announced this week that the normal waiting period of 10 days between the time a prospective selectee is examined by army physicians and the time he is inducted has been eliminated to speed-up expansion of the Army.

Hereafter, it was disclosed, registrants will report for induction after they have passed the "screening" (blood test) examination by local draft boards. When they report in compliance with orders they will be examined by Army doctors and, if accepted, inducted immediately.

Officials explained, however, that "in cases where the immediate induction would cause undue hardship to the registrant he will be given an immediate furlough to adjust his civilian affairs."

Names of selectees leaving in this next group appear in an adjoining column.

They Go Next Month

Harry W. Brungard
Earl Blanton, Jr.
Herbert A. Ayoob
Paul T. Slater
Howard W. Kemp
Nick De Francesco
Donald Eugene Swarts
Gilbert P. Grabnegger
Benedict C. Espey
Alexander Kosanovich
Robert G. McIlvain, Jr.
John Thomas
John E. Sebes
Theodore F. Voyvodich
Fred T. Ferris
Daniel F. McDonald
William L. Galupi
Francis J. Dowling
Ralph P. Romanna
Mike Yesko
Whittiel A. Booker
Clayton M. McMutrie
Albert S. Mihok
James P. Anthony
John M. Evanstanko
Albert J. Vincenzini
Andrew B. Oros
Frank Krotec
Joseph J. Madren
Smillie A. Nixon
George Brewer
Melvin Cannon
Joseph Girata
Joseph T. Trella
Leonard B. Morris
Daniel Britza
Robert G. Churney
Fred Blankenhorn
Michael Delenko
Stephen Dufala
Melvin W. Acklin
Albert P. Staman
Carmen De Francesco
Michael Dzugan
William J. Paczak
Charles Powell
Romaine A. Williams
Luther M. Thornton
David Betters
Aaron Garrett
Harold O. Dean
Richard Dorsett
Wilson A. Cook
Charles R. Carter
Theodore Illuminati
John Chismar
Jay A. Neish
Paul F. Hojdila
Ralph Reich, Jr.
Edward Poola
John A. Owens
Eli M. Rebich
Paul Opsatnik
John Kimak
James R. Moore
Arthur McCall
Joseph J. Ayoob
Joe J. Basco
John C. Kaluza
George Pinkosky
George D. Walker
John Gratson
Henry J. Delisio
George J. Gardlik
Joseph Kovacic
Frank V. Ceanfaglione
John Allen
Mario Vincenzini
David C. Allen
George Veligdan
Eugene Semenchuk
Steve W. Kost
Quirino Di Sante
Panfilo Filippi
Joseph M. Puskarich
Matt J. Shetek
Albert E. Oliker

(Continued on Page Two)

Two Die Here

Mike Fokas, 66, 256 Station St., died yesterday of complications after an illness of three years; born in Greece, a resident of Aliquippa for 14 years and a former borough employe; survived by two daughters, Sophia Buclou, Aliquippa, and Jennie Xilas, Athens, O., and two grandchildren; services not arranged.

John Badura, 58, Jones and Laughlin Steel Corp. worker, was found dead of a heart attack Wednesday at 255 Calhoun St., where he roomed. Burial today at 9 a. m. from Darroch Funeral home; High mass of requiem at St. Titus Church; interment at Mt. Olivet cemetery.

Passenger Cars Going Out; Sugar Rationers Lack Plan

Dr. J. F. Campbell, chairman of the Aliquippa Rationing Board, said today that recent government letters indicated that passenger cars would be forced off the road soon to conserve rubber for war industries and transportation.

"Restrictions on issuing permits for tires and recapping are so strong today," he said, "that since Feb. 19 you can't get recapped tires back from the dealers without a certificate from the board.

Meanwhile, rationing officials were uncertain about how or when sugar rationing cards would be issued.

Schools Superintendent L. M. Wilson said he "thought" rationing would go into effect early next month and that elementary school buildings would be kept open four nights for registration of families, but none here could say what procedure would be instituted for rationing sugar.

Capmbell said that the March quota of tires and tubes for this district—Hopewell and Independence townships, South Heights and Aliquippa—was:

Passenger tires, 14; passenger tubes, 12; commercial truck tires, 26; commercial truck tubes, 29; and 11 recapping jobs (Class A rating).

Fair Rent Judges Balk at Linmar

Aliquippa's Fair Rent Committee was on record today as being "without authority" to lower rents or utility charges on 250 homes the U. S. government built, owns and rents to defense worers on Linmar Plan.

After hearing complaints from ten tenants of the U. S. H. A. project, not yet completed, the committee announced through Member Charles Lucas:

"This committee is of the opinion that a fair rent date of July 1, 1941 having been established and no rentals having been fixed by the landlord, the United States Government, on or before July 1, 1941, this committee is therefore without authority to render a decision on the merits of this case."

Principal protests were over rates charged for electricity, water and gas. Tenant John Konowal said he "thought 60 cents per month for water, especially when it comes from a master meter" was too much to pay. He intimated the project was making a profit on its utility charges.

One tenant said he paid a $6.70 gas bill for 30 days and $2.41 for 16 days of electricity. He said he thought the tenants were being charged for utilities used in 132 vacant "upper level" homes at the project. Project manager J. Perry Kennedy denied this, saying that contractors were responsible for that charge.

Kennedy's explanation for high utility rates on the project, divided among tenants according to the size of their homes, was that "the tenants are playing with the thermostat control button and as soon as they quit using them as toys the rate will seek a lower level."

Girls Prepare to Fill Men's Jobs Here

Girls stepped in today to fill the gap in Aliquippa's war effort weakened by large draft calls which have been taking Jones & Laughlin workers to Army camps.

Schools Superintendent L. M. Wilson said "quite a few" girls had enrolled in the free Penn State Defense courses which started last night at the high schools. Girls enrolled principally in metallurgical inspection, preliminary accounting and elementary radio courses, he said.

Twenty-two different courses are offered in the Penn State study and classes will be formed as "the need arises," officials said.

Boro Represented in Valley Planning

Aliquippa was represented today on the Citizens' Planning Committee of Beaver County, headed by Prof. E. D. Davidson, county schools superintendent.

Named as officers of the committee were Albert Smith, Hopewell township, and Mary Louise Hornstein, Aliquippa.

Alien Registration to End Tomorrow

Registration of Aliquippa's "enemy" aliens ends tomorrow.

Postal employes in charge of the registration of Japanese, Italian and German aliens at headquarters in borough council chambers said that approximately 500 aliens had registered by yesterday.

John Miller to Join Naval Air Corps

John L. Miller, Jr., son of Dr. and Mrs. J. L. Miller of West Aliquippa until this week kept as a secret from his parents his volunteering for the naval air corps.

Still one year shy of a degree in his pre-medical course at Westminster College, the councilman's son has been studying ground work preparatory to flying in classes conducted by the Civil Aeronautics Association.

He was not expected to go to Pensacola, Fla., for active duty for several months.

Four Boro Children Ill of Pneumonia

Officials of the Aliquippa Board of Health announced today that four borough youngsters were stricken with pneumonia.

They are: Gloria, year-old daughter of Mr. and Mrs. Oscar Varpness, 211 Baker St.; Arthur, 9, son of Mr. and Mrs. Flavino Di-Donato, 140 Riverview Ave.; John, 3, son of James Rickert, 132 Riverview Ave.; and Charles, year-old son of Mr. and Mrs. Charles David, 312 Station St.

Six residents were quarantined with pneumonia and one with German measles.

Son for Cebalos

Mr. and Mrs. Martin Cebalo, 716 Tyler St., Sheffield Terrace, were proud parents today of an eight-pound, nine-ounce son, born 2 a. m. Monday at Providence hospital, Beaver Falls.

Mrs. Cebalo is the former Olga Batz and worked at the Keyser Real Estate and Insurance office, Franklin avenue. The son has been named, Martin, Jr.

BADEN NEWS

Mrs. C. E. Vignere, Byersdale, accompanied by her mother and her daughter, Miss Betty Vignere, are enjoying a two-week vacation in Florida.

Mrs. R. W. Warner, Rotteck street, is undergoing observation in Rochester hospital.

Miss Betty Suprock, Schiller street, is confined to her home by illness.

The deathwatch beetle, once believed to foretell the death of the listener, is really signaling its mate. It does this by tapping on the timbers in old houses with its hammerlike head.

MRS. W. L. MELLON DIES

By the United Press

PITTSBURGH, March 20—Funeral services will be held Saturday afternoon for Mrs. William Larimer Mellon, wife of the chairman of the Gulf Oil Corporation. Mrs. Mellon became ill several weeks ago and died Wednesday aboard the yacht, Old River, at Miami, Fla.

IRISH PLOT CHARGED

BELFAST, March 20—A special court today disclosed an Irish Republican Army plot to determine the number and disposition of American and other armed forces in Northern Ireland. It was believed the plot may have been Nazi inspired.

The average citizen of the United States is said to eat 70 oranges a year.

Monaca High Cage And Grid Team Honored At Banquet

Indian Passers Get WPIAL Class B Basketball Trophy

District Attorney R. E. McCreary Is Principal Speaker; Gridders Presented Letters, Emblems Awarded Cagers

Monaca high school athletes, members of the 1941 football squad, and the boys who brought the W. P. I. A. L. Class B basketball championship to the Southside community for the second time in four years, were feted at the annual banquet at the Beaver Valley Sportsmen's club Thursday evening.

Presentation of the Western Pennsylvania Interscholastic Athletic League's trophy, emblematic of the Class B championship, was one of the highlights of the program. The trophy is in plaque form with a six-inch figure of a basketball player on an ebony pedestal, and flanked on one side by a metal tablet on which is inscribed the names of the squad members, team managers, Coach Stanley J. Berkman, and Faculty Manager Don Measel, and on the other side by a tablet which carries the team's complete record for the season.

E. G. Groleau, high school principal, presided at the after-dinner program. He congratulated the members of the football team on the excellent record compiled last Fall under Coach Louis Blistan and Assistant Coach Berkman. He said he was proud of the fact that he is the high school principal in Western Pennsylvania who can boast that his basketball team won the Class B championship twice.

Mr. Groleau introduced several guests, including Carl Brody, Rev. Ross Hunt, Charles Renner, John Thomas, Harold A. Fox of the school board; Superintendent of Schools Philip H. Petrie; W. W. Anderson and Ernest Konvolinka.

The speaking program was short, featured by a brief talk by District Attorney Robert E. McCreary who declared that winning of the WPIAL Class B basketball championship was an honor to the entire county as well as for Monaca.

Faculty Manager Measel presented letters to the following members of last Fall's football team: Joe Antoline, Tony Battaglia, Ed. Bobrowski, Earl Brummitt, John Dietrich, Eugene Knopp, Willard LeGoullon, William Milne, Tom Namadden, Ed. Ofcharka, Marshall Olshanski, Dan Sabella, Joe Turbish, Joe Trella, John Vogt, Stan Wywrot, Joe Yuran, Matt Zupsic, and Theodore Stanik, senior football manager.

Members of the championship basketball team were awarded emblems suitable for attaching to sweaters, in place of letters. The emblems carried the words, "Class B Champs, 1942, Monaca," in red letters on a blue background. Basketball players receiving these emblems were: Joe Trella, David Sinclair, Tony Scassa, Bob Pickrell, William Holle, Ed. Ofcharka, Steve Ogrizek, Al. Vlasic, Eugene Knopp, Jack Kinkead, Jim Hill, senior manager Calvin Swink.

Letters were awarded to two senior cheer leaders, Betty J. Figley and Helen Schuller.

Coach Stanley Berkman was indisposed and unable to be present when his championship cage team was honored.

Each member of the Red and Blue floor team and Coach Berkman also received a gold basketball watch charm inscribed with "Class B Champs, 1942," and his name. John Schmidt, Monaca, presented the charms on behalf of Monaca merchants and fans who contributed to the fund to purchase them.

Halfback Joe Antoline, on behalf of the football squad, presented Football Coach Louis Blistan with a gift in appreciation of his work with the team last Fall.

The program closed with a motion picture, "Highlights of the College Football Season."

About seventy - five persons attended the banquet. The dinner was served by the Auxiliary to the Beaver Valley Sportsmen's Club.

SPORT SLANTS

By BILL ANDERSON

The Pittsburgh Pirates spend a good part of the training season in Pullman cars. By the time the bold Buccos get back to Forbes Field for their home opener with St. Louis on April 17, they will have traveled nearly 7,000 miles on the rattlers alone, not counting side jaunts by bus and taxi.

Manager Frank Frisch of the Corsairs has made a lot of changes in the club since he succeeded Pie Traynor at the helm in 1940. The squad taken to training camp this spring included only three regulars and four pitchers from Traynor's last team in 1939. The regulars were Outfielder Bob Elliott, Second Baseman Frankie Gustine and Third Baseman Lee Handley. Handley, who has been sent home to Peoria, Ill. to wait until his ailing right arm mends, may not be on hand when the Bucs return home. The four pitchers held over since 1939 include Rip Sewell, Ken Heintzelman, Bob Klinger and Bill Clemensen.

In rounding-up the Pirate crew, Manager Frisch and President Bill Benswanger roamed far and wide. No less than 17 different states were represented in the original training squad with California contributing six, North Carolina four, Illinois three, West Virginia, Indiana, Michigan, Missouri, Maryland, Florida and Massachusetts two each, Ohio, New Jersey, Georgia, Texas, Oregon, and Washington one each—not a single player from the home state. William Richard Cox, the young infielder procured from Harrisburg last fall, is a resident of Newport, Pa., but he went to the army before the training trip was started. The army also got Pitcher John Copple, a native Pennsylvanian.

The ancestral background of the Pittsburgh players is just as varied as their home states. Their ancestors came from 16 countries. Five of the Buccos are the only representatives of their nationalities in the National League. The only Basque in the senior loop is Infielder Pete Coscarart; Maurice Van Robays the only Belgian; Nick Strincevich the only Serb; Eddie Fernandes the only Portuguese, and Aldon Wilkie the only Canadian in the National League.

Ancestral derivations of other Pirate players include: Stu Martin and Bill Baker, English; Loyd Deitz, Ken Heintzelman, Bob Klinger, and Ken Jungles, German; Frank Gustine, Joe Sullivan, John Barett, Alf Anderson and Don Kerr, Irish; Vince DiMaggio, Italian; Hank Gornicki and John Wyrostek, Polish; Rip Sewell, Scotch; Al Lopez, Spanish; Max Butcher, Dutch-German; Babe Phelps and Eddie Stewart, English-German; Lee Handley and Jimmy Wasdel, English-Irish; Luke Hamlin, English-Scotch; Elbie Fletcher and John Lanning, Irish-Scotch.

Mention of Honus Wagner's having been a nationally prominent independent or professional basketball star at the peak of his athletic career, as well as the greatest baseball player of all time, recalls to sports veterans the fact that the famous Pirate coach turned down what was probably a record theatrical offer for an individual athletic act. The late John P. Harris, then one of the leading showmen of the country and manager of Pittsburgh's vaudeville theater, the Grand Opera House, offered Wagner $1,500 for a week of two-a-day at his showhouse, just to toss around a basketball, etc., in an athletic act lasting about ten minutes. Engagements at other theaters around the country at the same salary also were in prospect. Harris figured that Wagner's nationwide renown would make him a great boxoffice attraction. But Honus turned it down. He said he wasn't an actor.

COUNTY PAROCHIAL GRADE SCHOOL CHAMPS

Pictured above are members of the Presentation Parochial school basketball team, Midland, champions of the Beaver Valley Parochial School Basketball League, who defeated an All-Star team Thursday evening by a 33 to 17 count in a benefit game.

Members of the squad pictured above are: Seated, left to right—Toncic, Balint, Migliore, Conelly, Roach and student manager Curto; Standing—Coach Sammy Rosatone, Miccucci, Relic, Wasko, C. Kennedy, W. Kennedy and Manager Rev. Fr. Paul Leger.

Fame Team Leads Close Race For Team Honors In Beaver Women's Dux League

Lancers Now Trail Leaders By Three Games; Frances Gagliordony Posts High Individual Scores This Week

In Tuesday evening's matches in the Beaver Women's Bowling League, Frances Gagliordony, of Wises team, carried off both high one and three game honors for the week with scores of 182 and 482.

The high team scores for the week included a single game of 669 by Wises, and Anderson's three game total of 1901.

The Fame entry boasts a three game lead over Lancers for first place in the race for team laurels. Fame won three games from Morrows, while the second place Lancers slipped a bit by dropping one out of three games to Wises.

In other matches Anderson and Smiths won all three games from Bennetts and Isalys, respectively, while Bakery copped two from LaBelle. The Daily Times-Akins match was postponed.

Individual high scores for each team were: Andersons — Dorothy Weaver, 169 and 475; Bennetts — Catherine Morris 122 and 341; Fame — Grace Lehman 170 and Florence Vaughn 378; LaBelle — Marion Bechtel 137 and 351; Isalys —Ann Shemone 143 and 373; Morrows—Lois Nelson 134 and Virginia Barstow 331; Bakery—Leone Townsend 147 and 336; Lancers—Aurelia Hoffner 156 and 441; Smiths—Lillian Shaffalo 159 and 412.

TEAM SCORES

Andersons	681	583	637—1901
Bennetts	417	451	464—1332
Fame	629	593	640—1862
Morrows	501	473	465—1439
Smiths	622	566	538—1726
Isalys	510	565	534—1609
Lancers	612	664	597—1873
Wises	592	636	669—1897
Bakery	593	497	514—1604
LaBelle	446	495	544—1485

TEAM STANDING

	Won	Lost
Fame	72	15
Lancers	69	18
Andersons	58	29
Wises	57	30
Smiths	55	32
Daily Times	52	32
Bakery	42	45
Isalys	38	49
Bennetts	30	57
Akins	21	63
LaBelle	21	66
Morrow	4	83

Presentation Cage Team Tops All-Stars In Benefit Contest

Parochial League Champs Trounce All-Stars 33 To 17 In Game At Midland Gym

Swamping their opponents under a barrage of points in the first half, the Presentation school cagers of Midland, champions of the Beaver Valley Parochial School Basketball League, topped an All-Star aggregation Thursday evening on the Midland floor by a score of 33 to 17 in a benefit game.

The All-Stars, composed of the cream of the crop of the other seven league teams, were handcuffed by the classy Presentation outfit through the first two periods when they managed to score only eight points while the league champions were pouring 24 counters through the hoop.

The winners substituted freely in the last half and each team counted nine points in the final two periods. Migliore of the winners outscored the All-Stars single-handed as he dropped in eight field goals and a brace of fouls for a total of eighteen points.

Gouldsberry was high for the losers with two goals and five conversions from the charity shot line for a total of nine points.

In the first preliminary game the Eighth Grade girls' team of the Presentation school topped the Seventh Grade team to take the intramural championship of the school. The final score was 2 to 0, Mary Ross accounting for the only score.

In the boys' preliminary game, the St. Titus cagers of Aliquippa, runners-up in the league, scored a 23 to 19 victory over a second All-Star team.

The lineups:

PRESENTATION

	G.	F.	Pts.
Balint, f	0	1	1
Migliore, f	8	2	18
Relic, c	0	0	0
W. Kennedy, g	3	2	8
C. Kennedy, g	3	0	6
Totals	14	5	33

Substitutions: Wasko, Toncic, Miccucci, Roach, Connelly, Sieni, Flora, Farman, Pressuti, Roman, Lozzi.

ALL-STARS

	G.	F.	Pts.
Gouldsberry, f	2	5	9
Tovey, f	0	0	0
Oras, c	1	0	2
J. Shaughnessy, g	0	0	0
M. Shaughnessy, g	0	0	0
Banko, f	1	0	2
E. Shields, f	1	0	2
Crowd, g	0	2	2
Totals	5	7	17

Substitutions: Ferra, Barroud.

Like Washington, D. C., Raleigh, North Carolina's capital city, was laid out originally for a capital.

Elliott Paces Bucs To 12 To 9 Victory

By the United Press

LOS ANGELES, March 27— Mr. Big of the heavy-hitting Pittsburgh Pirates today was Third Baseman Bob Elliott who smashed out his second home run within a week on the exhibition circuit. Elliott rapped out number 2, a 400-footer, yesterday as the Bucs dispatched Sacramento, 12-9, with both collecting 12 hits. It was the Pirates' 10th victory in 11 starts—a record they hoped to extend against the Whitesox at Long Beach this afternoon.

British demands for bacon have forced the Canadian Government to limit the consumption of pork products to those which do not qualify for the British market, reports the Department of Commerce.

Going to Tigers?

Joe Medwick

According to reports in the southland, Joe Medwick, the Brooklyn Dodgers' outfielder, may go to the Detroit Tigers in a trade for Buck Newsome, the big Tiger pitcher who is a holdout. Medwick has lost his left field job with the Dodgers, Augie Galan, ex-Chicago Cub infielder, taking over.

IN PLAYOFF—Bryan Hextall of Rangers, left, and Syl Apps of Maple Leafs, seen during Stanley Cup playoff game in New York.

District Track And Field Meet Shifted To May 9 At Geneva

Annual Championship Meet Is Moved Ahead One Week; Covies Start Practice

Geneva College authorities announced today that the annual District Intercollegiate track and field championships, originally scheduled for Saturday, May 16, have been moved forward one week, and will be staged at Reeves Stadium, Beaver Falls, on Saturday, May 9.

The shift in dates was made to accomodate several schools which are closing the semester earlier than usual because of the war-time speed-up schedule.

The Covenanters' dual meet with Westminster, previously carded for May 9, will be held on May 16.

Coach Slim Ransom has already started track and field practice sessions and has a good-sized squad working out daily.

Prospects for a successful season were brighter today when it was announced that Andy Matter, classy hurdler who was scheduled to be inducted into the army on April 4, has been granted a stay of induction until June to permit him to finish his Junior year of college. Thus he will be available for the entire track season.

Geneva will have tennis and golf teams this spring but indications are that the schedule will be shortened because some other district schools have abandoned these sports. Duquesne, for instance, has dropped both tennis and golf.

Following is the revised Geneva track and field schedule:

April 25—Grove City, away.
May 2, Carnegie Tech, home.
May 5—Wash.-Jeff., away.
May 9—District intercollegiates, Reeves Stadium.
May 16—Westminster, home.

LOUIS PREDICTS THIRD ROUND KNOCKOUT OVER BIG ABE SIMON

By JACK CUDDY
United Press Staff Correspondent

NEW YORK, March 27—Within three rounds, Madison Square Garden is expected to reverberate to the thunder of a falling giant tonight as Champion Joe Louis again unleashes the most destructive fists in heavyweight history on the gargantuan jaw of huge Abe Simon.

Private Louis, fighting for the first time since he joined the army and making a second historic free defense of the ring's most valuable crown, says he will try to knock out in three sessions the mauling monster who lasted 13 frames against him at Detroit last March.

Brown-skinned Joe, never a man to make rash promises, set the time limit on Simon's activities in an attempt to bear out the three-round prediction made by old Jack Blackburn, his trainer and pal, who is recovering from pneumonia in a Chicago hospital and who will be absent from Joe's corner for the first time since Louis turned professional.

In this record-shattering 21st defense of his title, Louis is fighting without pay to benefit army emergency relief, which receives all profits of the bout in addition to Joe's 47½ per cent purse and 2½ per cent of Simon's 15 per cent check. Promoter Mike Jacobs expects a crowd of more than 16,000 and a gate of more than $125,000. In which case, army relief's total will exceed $50,000.

In Bomber Joe's last fight as a civilian, January 9, he tossed leather free for the Navy Relief Society, attracting a gate of $189,700 for his first-round knockout of big Buddy Baer. Tickets then were topped at $30, but tonight the pasteboards range only up to $25.

Because Louis is a soldier and the bout is for army relief, a large contingent of army officials and soldiers will witness the bout. Robert P. Patterson, undersecretary of war, is scheduled to address the fans from the ring. His address and the fight will be broadcast over the Mutual network and short-waved to soldiers in both hemispheres.

Kentucky, Stanford Play For NCAA Title

By the United Press

KANSAS CITY, Mo., March 28—The two greatest college basketball aggregations in the United States in 1942—Dartmouth and Stanford—square off here Saturday night for the brightest of cage glories—the National Collegiate championship of America.

Betting odds varied as the report circulated that hawk-eyed Don Burness, co-captain of the Stanford quintet, has recovered sufficiently from an ankle injury to allow him to take his place in the lineup. If the high-scoring Stanford ace plays, the bookmakers indicated, the Californians probably will rate a two or three-point edge. If not, they said, the two teams may go to the post on a five-to-four "take your choice" basis.

Dartmouth earned the right to participate in the national finals by defeating Kentucky in the eastern playoffs at New Orleans last Saturday. Stanford went into the finals by virtue of a win over Colorado in the western playoffs here at the same time.

In pre-tournament play, Stanford won 24 out of 28 games, proceeding then to lick Rice Institute, 53 to 47, and Colorado University, 46 to 38, in the finals of the western tournament here last weekend.

Dartmouth lost three engagements out of twenty-two in games previous to the eastern playoffs in which they downed Penn State in the preliminary Friday night, 44 to 38, and followed through with a winning stroke to fell Kentucky in the climaxer, 47 to 28, capturing the eastern crown.

The Weather Forecast
WESTERN PENNSYLVANIA: Rain tonight; slowly rising temperature.

THE DAILY TIMES

ROCHESTER-BEAVER-MONACA
FREEDOM—BRIDGEWATER—CONWAY—VANPORT—MIDLAND

Beaver County History
Plans for a celebration to be held soon to dedicate a huge borough service flag were being made April 9, 1918, in Rochester.

ESTABLISHED APRIL 2, 1874 | BEAVER AND ROCHESTER, PA., THURSDAY, APRIL 9, 1942 | BY CARRIER 18 CENTS A WEEK—3 CENTS PER COPY

One Killed, Three Hurt In Conway Yard Mishap

★ ★

U. S. FORCES GIVE UP IN BATAAN

LAWMAKERS ARE TO QUIT SPECIAL SESSION FRIDAY

Differences In Major Legislation Expected To Be Adjusted By House, Senate

Committees To Iron Out Difficulties In Bills To Permit Adjournment

By the United Press

HARRISBURG, April 9.—Barring printing delays, the special wartime session will adjourn finally "on the nose" at 4 p. m. tomorrow, House Majority Floor Leader Leo A. Achterman said today, confident "difficulties" will be adjusted on major legislation to:

1. Provide approximately $9,000,000 in annual unemployment compensation benefit increases to Pennsylvania's qualified jobless.

2. Broaden sabotage prevention regulations and set penalties for intentionally defective workmanship at $10,000 or 10 years imprisonment.

3. Allow local governments to appropriate funds for civilian defense, with authorization to borrow, but not levy additional takes, for that purpose.

4. Enable the highways Department to issue special permits, on the present fee basis, allowing trucks to haul war materials in excess of present weight and length restrictions.

TO NAME COMMITTEES

Conference committees will be appointed in the Democratic-dominated House and Republican-controlled Senate to iron out differences on those issues. An impasse was reached on the unemployment compensation and anti-sabotage measures as result of House amendments to Senate bills.

The House made the saboteur measure conform to the federal wartime law of 1918, deleting many sections opposed by organized labor. Major provisions of the jobless benefit bill, including an $8-$18 weekly benefit range, were untouched, but argument ensued on changes supposedly threatening the fund's reserve.

The House placed in position for final passage the "big truck" bill after inserting amendments of Rep. Homer S. Brown, D., Allegheny, requiring defense material truck haulers to pay a $5 special permit fee and 2 cents per ton mile for the excess load, as at present.

Deleted from the Senate measure was a section allowing truckers to haul any kind of material without payment of any fee. Brown pointed out that permits for overweight

(Continued on Page Six)

New Teacher Named In Beaver Schools

Miss Mary Robinson of Mercer, has replaced Mrs. Lyle Kimple, Beaver kindergarten teacher, as substitute for the remainder of the school year.

Miss Robinson was graduated from the Pasadena, Calif., high school and the Orton School for Girls in Los Angeles, after which she attended the National College for Education for four years. This college is in connection with Northwestern University. She has also done graduate study at Columbia University. Since completing her college work she has taught three years in kindergarten in Saginaw, Mich., and an additional two years in the Kent School for Girls at the Walton Unit School at Olivet, Mich. She is making her home with Rev. and Mrs. Charles Wolf.

Mrs. Kimple, formerly Dorothy Rodger, prior to her resignation as kindergarten teacher had been employed by the Beaver School District the past thirteen years, most of which has been spent in the kindergarten. She formerly taught the second grade.

Four Local Boys Join Up With U. S. Army

Four local youths enlisted in the U. S. Army Wednesday at the recruiting office in Pittsburgh. They are: James R. Jeffries, New Brighton; Eugene K. Gahles, Beaver Falls; John R. Dudash and Michael V. Trone, Aliquippa.

Marion Hill Man Killed Today In Railroad Accident

One man was killed and three others were injured when a four-car "cut" collided with a freight train in the Conway Yards of the Pennsylvania railroad at three o'clock this morning, derailing the engine of the train and buckling several cars in the cut.

The four cars running down the "hump" and loaded with coal crashed into the thirteen-car train being shifted across the yards. Henry Jerome (Hank) Brown, 24, Marion Hill, a brakeman riding between the first and second cars on the cut was crushed when the two cars were buckled by the impact. He was killed instantly.

The cut struck the tender of the switching engine and overturned it and derailed the locomotive. Engineman Carl J. Sandahl, 49, Alliance, O., suffered injuries to the face and neck and a fracture of the leg and severe shock, when struck by falling coal.

Richard E. Beebout, 25, 77 Fourth avenue, Freedom, received a possible sprained shoulder and Thomas Leo Fairley, 22, Pittsburgh, brakemen, suffered an eye injury.

TRIO IN HOSPITAL

Brown's body was removed to the Hartzel funeral home, Rochester, and the three injured men were taken to Rochester hospital.

Brown had been employed by the

(Continued on Page Six)

Monaca People To Have Parade For Draftees Saturday

Numerous Organizations To Participate In "Send-Off" For Men Going To Army

Selective Service Board No 5, Monaca, has completed plans for a "send-off" for the large group of selectees who are leaving Monaca Saturday morning to join the armed forces. All Monaca will turn out to demonstrate its appreciation for the sacrifice the boys are making for their country and a parade will feature.

Draft Board officials, Council, Police, the Board of Education, Monacatootha Post and color guards, the Monaca High School Band of 65 pieces and town folk will parade.

Forming at the Junior high school, at Washington avenue, the parade will move down Washington avenue to Eighth street, to Pennsylvania avenue, and thence to the Pittsburgh and Lake Erie station.

SELECTEES CHOSEN

The selectees include:

William Johnathan Jacober, Monaca; Harrison Trueman Rowley, Georgetown; John Vendell Didich, Monaca; Alfred John Nevish, Midland; Dwight Francis Glancy, Monaca; Ben Sochor, Monaca; Joseph Harvilla, Ambridge; Michael W. Milnarcik, Jr., Monaca; Harold Nelson Bowersock, Hookstown; Edward Jackson Deem, Industry; Pete Tessler, Midland; Nick Vranes, Midland; Albert Joseph Rieth, Bridgewater; Oliver James Smith, Beaver; Mitchell Vukelich, Midland; Pete Tucker, Midland; George Konzeleski, Georgetown; Guy Edward Horm, Midland; Frank Joseph Kovac, Monaca; Mike Frank Fresty, Midland; Ross Arwell Renc, Smiths Ferry; Albert Adamek, Monaca; George Vignovich, Midland; Joseph Zenich, Midland.

Joseph Alfred Alexander, Mon-

(Continued on Page Six)

Local Boys to Compete In Forensic Contest

Five Rochester High school students will be the only Beaver county competitors in the district Forensic and Music contest to be held Saturday at California State Teachers' College.

Harry Carcaise is to compete in the clarinet solo contest and the boys' quartet, composed of Vernon McDade, Gail Boyde, Clarence Conrad and Leslie Marietta, will enter the vocal competition. Marietta is also slated to compete in the baritone solo contest.

The Ambridge high school debate team, representative of Beaver county schools, defeated Centerville, Washington county representative last week and earned the right to compete in a triangular meet on Monday, April 13, at the University of Pittsburgh.

The Ambridge debaters will meet debate teams from Redstone Township, winner of the Fayette-Greene county contests, and Latrobe, winner of the Allegheny-Westmoreland county contest. The winner of this contest will move into the state finals.

These Made Heroic Stand Against Japanese In Bataan

SUBIC
OLONGAPO
DINALUPIHAN
ORANI
BALANGA
MORONG
ABUCAY
SAMAL
PILAR
BAGAC
LIMAY
CABCABEN
CORREGIDOR
FT. HUGHES
FT. DRUM
Manila Bay
MANILA
South China Sea

Three-inch anti-aircraft guns on Corregidor

Maj. Gen. Jonathan Wainwright

A 12-inch disappearing gun on Corregidor

Chaplains Assigned At Monthly Meeting Of Rochester Pastors

Ministers Named To Serve At Rochester Hospital, County Sanatorium

Assignment of chaplains to serve at Rochester hospital and ministers to conduct services at the Beaver County Sanatorium was made by Rev. Rodney F. Cobb, secretary of the Rochester Ministerial Association at the monthly meeting of the association Wednesday afternoon in the Presbyterian church.

Chaplains at Rochester hospital are: Weeks beginning April 12, Rev. C. E. Read, Monaca; April 19, Rev. A. E. Driggers, Rochester; April 26, Rev. E. Victor Roland, Freedom; May 3, Rev. Hans O. F. Simoleit, Rochester; May 10, Major Leslie Watson, Rochester; May 17, Rev. Rodney F. Cobb, Rochester; May 24, Rev. Thurman McCracken, Rochester; May 31, Rev. Elmer A. Ortner, Rochester; June 7, Rev. Thomas O. Fuss, Rochester; June 14, Rev. D. C. McCoy, Rochester; June 21, Rev. Dr. W. M. Baumgartner, Rochester; June 28, Rev. J. W. St. Clair, Bridgewater.

SANATORIUM CHAPLAINS

Ministers to conduct services at Beaver County Sanatorium: April 9, Rev. D. C. McCoy; April 23, Rev. Dr. W. M. Baumgartner; May 7, Rev. St. Clair; May 21, Rev. R. H. Ling, Bridgewater; June 4, Major Leslie Watson; June 18, Rev. Ortner.

Rev. John C. Steele, pastor of the Presbyterian church, Vanport, was appointed to represent the ministers on the Beaver County Planning Board.

At the next meeting on May 13,

(Continued on Page Six)

Los Angeles Area Has Raid Blackout

LOS ANGELES, April 9. -- A blackout was ordered in Southern California Wednesday night by military authorities, presumably because of the suspected presence of unidentified planes in the region.

Radio stations were ordered off the air at 8:33 p. m. (PST) by the Federal Communications Commission at the request of the Fourth Interceptor Command as the entire region was placed on the "yellow" alert.

Less than 15 minutes later, at 8:45 p. m. the area was ordered on the "blue" alert, the second warning stage and the last step before a blackout is ordered.

Seven persons died of heart attack during the blackout, receiving hospitals said. Two died in the street, four at home and one in an ambulance.

NAVAL-AIR BATTLE IN BAY OF BENGAL MENACES INDIA

Far to the east a grim naval-air showdown—with the fate of Ceylon if not India at stake—appeared to be underway in the Bay of Bengal between British warships and Japanese naval and air forces. The British admiralty admitted the loss of the heavy cruisers Cornwall and Dorsetshire, sunk by Japanese planes off the coast of India.

The fall of Bataan—and the opening of the siege of rock-girt Corregidor which may become the Alamo of Manila Bay—probably will release large numbers of Japanese troops and planes for action of the India Burma front and at the northern approaches to Australia.

However, the Japanese must still knock out Corregidor and its battleship guns as well as nearby Forts Drum, Hughes and Frank either by aerial assault or landings.

The Bengal Bay naval fight was the first definite word on previous Axis radio reports of a British naval squadron led by the 31,100-ton battleship Malaya steaming into the Indian Ocean to challenge the Japanese fleet.

American flying fortresses have attacked the Japanese warships at Port Blair in the Andaman Island base of the Japanese and presumably were aiding the British warships.

AXIS CLAIMS GAINS

The Japanese, according to radio bulletins, claimed not only the sinking of the two British cruisers but 44 merchant ships in the Bay of Bengal. The German radio added a claim—unsupported elsewhere — that a Japanese expeditionary force supported by cruisers and destroyers had landed on the Bay of Bengal coast.

The German radio said that "major Japanese forces" also were ashore north of the Burmese port

(Continued on Page Six)

Ban Imposed On All Construction Work Not Needed For War

Non-Essential Homes, Roads And Commercial Buildings Affected By Order

WASHINGTON, April 9. — The war production board today prohibited new construction of nonessential residences, roads and commercial buildings, and indicated that projects already underway might be halted if the materials going into them could be used more effectively in the war program.

The order is effective today. Specifically it bans any residential construction other than maintenance and repair work if the cost is $500 or more, unless specific Gov-

(Continued on Page Six)

Prominent Resident Of Freedom Hurt In Fall

Mrs. Katherine Rockenstein, 64, wife of Burgess John H. Rockenstein, 612 Fourth avenue, Freedom, suffered a fracture of her left ankle early Wednesday afternoon when she fell while attending a lodge meeting in the Freedom municipal building. She was removed to Rochester hospital.

BEAVER FALLS SCHOOL BOARD REFUSES TWO RESIGNATIONS

More than one hundred citizens attended the special meeting of the Beaver Falls Board of Education held Wednesday evening to act on the resignation of J. B. Jamison, president of the board, and the letter from J. Roy Jackson, superintendent of schools, stating he would not seek re-election, both as a result of petty politics in the school board.

The large attendance forced the school directors to move their usual meeting room into a double room.

Citizens expressed themselves as opposed to the "secret meeting" method reportedly used by a part of the board to discuss the ousting of Jackson this year. They spoke for two and one-half hours and the meeting was not closed until after midnight.

MET LAST SATURDAY

Several members of the board reportedly met last Saturday evening unofficially and discussed a possible successor for Jackson. Word of the reported meeting got around and Jamison submitted his resignation, asking that action be taken on it no later than Wednesday.

Meanwhile, Jackson wrote a letter to the board stating he would not seek re-election to another four-year term this Spring.

The Board voted last night not to accept Jamison's resignation and Jackson's letter was withdrawn after a number of highly-incensed citizens expressed themselves on the subject of his leaving at the meeting.

Agreement On Water Rate Is Approved At Monaca Council Meet

Rate For Supplying Water to Housing Project Is Approved By Solons

Monaca Council at a regular meeting Wednesday night passed a resolution authorizing the president, George E. Dietrich, to sign a water rate agreement with the Beaver County Housing Authority to supply water from the municipal water plant for the 100-unit housing project now under construction in the borough.

Laying of additional sewer and water lines in the Fourth and Fifth Wards was discussed and Borough Secretary Guy Grater was instructed to get bids on the price of material necessary for this work.

Secretary Grater also was instructed to write a letter to E. L. Schmidt, state highway engineer, requesting that Pennsylvania avenue, from Ninth to Twenty-first streets, be repaired with asphalt.

TO BUY POLICE GUNS

Secretary Grater was instructed to get prices on two high-power rifles, one sub-machine gun and

(Continued on Page Six)

Further Cut In Gasoline Ordered

WASHINGTON, April 9. — The War Production Board today cut gasoline deliveries to filling stations and other bulk consumers in the East and West coast curtailment areas from the present 80 per cent to 66 per cent of the average amounts they received in December, January and February.

The order is effective April 16.

The curtailment areas include the 17 eastern seaboard states, the District of Columbia and the Pacific northwest states of Washington and Oregon. The order provides that seasonal variations may be adjusted in computing the delivery figure on which the 66 per cent volume is computed.

Pay Increase Asked By Monaca Teachers

At a special meeting of the Monaca Board of Education, Wednesday evening, a committee representing the Monaca school teachers met with the board to seek an increase in salary.

A joint meeting of the board and Monaca Borough Council will be held Wednesday evening, April 16, when efforts will be made on a more equalized tax assessment in the borough. Charles J. Renner, president, presided.

Four Forts In Manila Bay Still Fighting

By the United Press

WASHINGTON, April 9—Yanks and Filipinos on Bataan went down fighting today under an incessant pounding from land, sea and air by vastly superior Japanese forces.

A special war department communique announced that the situation "indicates the probability that the defenses on Bataan have been overcome."

It said Lieut. Gen. Jonathan M. Wainwright's men were in a state of "complete physical exhaustion."

Resistance virtually has ended on Bataan, it was believed certain from the tenor of the communique and informed quarters held little hope that the broken defenders could be gotten by boat to Corregidor fortress, which lies off the southern tip of Bataan. The Japanese were overrunning the peninsula too rapidly to permit that.

The closing days of the battle of Bataan were complicated by the large number of noncombatants crowded behind the lines in the narrow confines of the peninsula, it was learned. Caring for and feeding these people was a drain on the fighting forces and may have hastened collapse of the defense.

Outnumbered from the start, low on supplies, lacking air support, and wearied beyond human endurance by days of fighting against fresh enemy troops — the defenders fulfilled to the end their promise and their purpose. That was to make the Japanese pay and pay, in men, in equipment, and in time, for every inch of ground gained.

In that they succeeded. The battle for the Bataan peninsula, a 13-mile wide stretch of jungle and mountains, will be remembered always as a national epic of valor.

The nation through President Roosevelt and Gen. Douglas MacArthur have pledged that Bataan and all the rest of the Philippines will be re-won when American striking forces in the Southwest Pacific are ready.

TO FIGHT ON

The fateful message from Wainwright was announced by the War Department shortly after 5 a. m. Wainwright was on Corregidor fortress, which lies two miles out from Bataan in Manila Bay. There the battle for control of the bay will be carried on. But there was no indication whether Wainwright would be able to evacuate many of his Bataan forces to the fortress.

The War Department's special communique said:

"A message from General Wainwright at Fort Mills just received at

(Continued on Page Six)

Forts In Manila Bay Last U. S. Footholds In Philippine Isles

Four Rock-Bound Fortresses Only American Possessions Left In Islands

WASHINGTON, April 9. — Collapse of Lieut. Gen. Jonathan M. Wainwright's defenses on Bataan Peninsula means that the last major American footholds in the Philippines will be four small rock-bound islands in Manila Bay.

The largest of these islands is Corregidor, an almost solid piece of rock about five miles long and three miles wide. The Spaniards first fortified it, and American forces have turned it into a bristling arsenal with 12-inch guns which command the entrance to Manila Bay.

Fort Mills is the main fortification on Corregidor, and its anti-aircraft gun crews have established a reputation for accuracy by shooting down more than 30 of the hordes of Japanese Bombers which have attacked it. Big galleries and tunnels have been dug out of the rock for storerooms and shelters for the Corregidor garrison. How many

(Continued on Page Six)

Would Serve Again

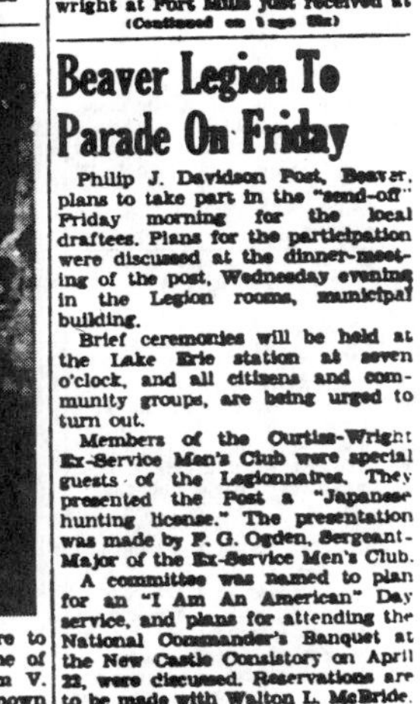

Impelled by a patriotic desire to serve his country again in time of war, County Treasurer William V. Kennedy, (above) widely-known veteran of World War I, is seeking to "join up" with the army once more for the duration. Mr. Kennedy, former county sheriff, saw intensive action in France as a member of the Machine Gun Company of the 10th Regiment. He was wounded September 27, 1918, and was discharged as a sergeant February 14, 1919. Later he received a commission as a captain in the Officers' Reserve Corps. Since the war, Mr. Kennedy has been active in American Legion and civic affairs in the county and since the outbreak of the present war has taken a leading part in civilian defense work.

Beaver Legion To Parade On Friday

Philip J. Davidson Post, Beaver, plans to take part in the "send-off" Friday morning for the local draftees. Plans for the participation were discussed at the dinner-meeting of the post, Wednesday evening in the Legion rooms, municipal building.

Brief ceremonies will be held at the Lake Erie station at seven o'clock, and all citizens and community groups, are being urged to turn out.

Members of the Curtiss-Wright Ex-Service Men's Club were special guests of the Legionnaires. They presented the Post a "Japanese hunting license." The presentation was made by F. G. Ogden, Sergeant-Major of the Ex-Service Men's Club.

A committee was named to plan for an "I Am An American" Day service, and plans for attending the National Commander's Banquet at the New Castle Consistory on April 22, were discussed. Reservations are to be made with Walton L. McBride, post commander.

"Andy" Stiveson, Pittsburgh, showed colored motion pictures of an extensive fishing trip through Tweedsmuir Park, British Columbia.

Woman Is Burned When Dress Catches Fire

Mrs. Ida Crowley, 77, 346 Brighton avenue, Rochester, was admitted to Rochester hospital Wednesday evening suffering from burns about the body, right arm and left hand. Mrs. Crowley was reported burned when her dress was ignited by a small gas stove while she was drying clothes in her home.

CARDINALS PICKED TO WIN NATIONAL LEAGUE PENNANT

CARDS, REDS, DODGERS, GIANTS MAY FINISH IN THAT ORDER

United Press Scribe Thinks Glorious Bums Have Had Their Day; Bucs Will Fight For Fourth Place

By GEORGE KIRKSEY
United Press Staff Correspondent

NEW YORK, April 10—The glorious bums of Brooklyn have had their day. They'll have to come down off their National League throne this season and make way for the St. Louis Cardinals—a frisky, swashbuckling gang imbued with "they can't lick us" spirit.

The Cards still think they had the best ball club last season when they trailed the Dodgers 2½ games despite a season-long injury jinx which deprived them of their full strength for all of but five days of the season. St. Louis has a better ball club this season. It has speed, pitching, balance and strong reserve strength.

If the Cardinals have any weakness, it's lack of long distance punch. But that they may not need. To make up for the loss of Mize and Padgett, the Cards have added speed and consistency to their attack. They have six potential .300 hitters in their batting order. The Cards never won a pennant with Mize playing first, and insiders think that they'll be better off without him. The Cards will open up with two rookies in the regular lineup—Stan Musial in left field and Ray Sanders at first. If either fails, Johnny Hopp, who hit 303 last year, will take over.

The tipoff on the strength of the Cards is the fact that they may be able to keep a man as fast and able as Hopp on the bench. The Cards' infield is high class regardless of who plays first. Crespi and Marion with a year's experience under their belts, may be the league's best keystone combination.

But the Cards' main strength lies in their pitching. It is not only good but it's deep. Cooper, Warneke, White, Lanier, Pollet, Gumbert, Lohrman, Shoun and Krist represent one of the best all-round pitching staffs in baseball. With five lefties on their staff, the Cards have the best southpaw group. Righthander Mort Cooper, who had to take time out for an arm operation last season, is the man to watch. He looks like a sure 20-game winner.

Brooklyn may not be able to save second place. The Reds, who slumped from world's champs in 1940 to third last season, are likely to hit the comeback trail and finish second. Cincinnati's pitching still must be rated baseball's best. Walters, Derringer, Vander Meer, Riddle, Thompson, Moore and the surprise veteran-rookie Starr, will put the Reds up close.

The Dodgers will be far from pushovers but already their good luck charm seems to have deserted them. Dolf Camilli and Billy Herman have just been treated at Johns Hopkins hospital for ailing backs. Pete Reiser, National League batting champion, has been reclassified 1-A Even partial loss of any one of these key men would hurt the Dodgers plenty.

Brooklyn, while it still has tremendous hitting power, can't match either Cincinnati or St. Louis in pitching. Four of the Dodger pitchers are old men, as pitchers go. Fitzsimmons is 41, Johnny Allen 36, Curt Davis 35, and Larry French 34. Any or all of them might go at the same time.

The Giants, who have looked horrible this Spring, aren't as bad as the records indicate. In fact Mel Ott, feeling his way in his new job, has built the framework of a fairly good club. It may surprise, especially if Fiddler Bill McGee pitches up to expectations and Hank Leiber and Johnny Mize hit well, and battle Pittsburgh for fourth place.

The Pirates, with plenty of power, are nevertheless in the question mark class. They have no standout pitcher and the left side of the infield—with Pete Coscarart at short and the converted outfielder Bob Elliott at third is definitely a problem.

There seems little hope for the Cubs getting out of sixth place. Neither their pitching or attack looks any better. The Boston Braves still have too many old men to be more than an occasional annoyance. The Phillies will finish last again—a sure thing.

Forecast Of Finish Of National League Race

By the United Press

NEW YORK, April 10.—How George Kirksey, United Press baseball writer, forecasts the finish of the 1942 National League pennant race compared with the 1941 finish:

1942 Prediction	1941 Finish
1. St. Louis	1. Brooklyn
2. Cincinnati	2. St. Louis
3. Brooklyn	3. Cincinnati
4. New York	4. Pittsburgh
5. Pittsburgh	5. New York
6. Chicago	6. Chicago
7. Boston	7. Boston
8. Philadelphia	8. Philadelphia

Injury To Hand Forces Yarosz To Cancel Bout

An injury to his right hand, received in his bout with Curley Denton of Cincinnati at Louisville, Ky., Monday night, has forced Tommy Yarosz Monaca middleweight boxer, to cancel a scheduled fight at Rochester, N. Y., tonight.

Yarosz was matched with Rocky Luciano of Williamsport, for a six-round bout tonight, but had to cancel the engagement because of a badly-stoved thumb. He suffered the injury in the third round of his ten-round bout with Denton. The Monaca boy won the decision over Denton, a highly rated fighter in the mid-west, despite being handicapped by the sore hand during the last seven heats. He might have stopped Denton if he had not been hurt.

Irish Bobby Berger, Akron, who, like Yarosz, is managed by Ray Foutts of East Liverpoool, is to meet Jimmy Mandell on the card in Rochester tonight.

Yarosz is scheduled for a return bout with Johnny Lawer, Cleveland scrapper, at Cleveland, on April 17, but may have to cancel that appearance too, unless his hand mends rapidly. The bout is billed as one of the preliminaries to the Bob Pastor-Jimmy Bivins fight.

Melio Bettina Boxes Beckwith Tonight

By the United Press

CHICAGO, April 10—Melio Bettina, former world's light heavyweight champion who is gunning for recognition as the No. 1 challenger for the heavyweight crown, risks two long winning streaks tonight when he faces Booker Beckwith, youthful Gary, Ind. negro.

Bettina has never been beaten by a heavyweight and holds 27 consecutive victories in the division. The other mark he puts on the block is that of not having lost to a negro fighter in his nine years of professional campaigning.

ZALE ENLISTS IN NAVY

GREAT LAKES, Ill., April 10 — Middleweight Titleholder Tony Zale, 28, fourth world's champion boxer to enlist in the nation's armed forces, was ordered by the navy today to report for active duty as a boxing instructor April 27.

Club Fighters To Mark Garden Show

PITTSBURGH, April 10—Two of the best club fighters in the East will perform for the first time before local fans Monday night at The Gardens when Maxie Berger, the Canadian welterweight champion, meets Fritzie Zivic in the ten-round headliner and Wickey Harkins of New York faces Carmen Notch of East Liberty in the semi-final scheduled to go eight rounds.

Both Berger and Harkins come from the same school of wade-in and throw-a-lot-of-leather fighters, who please the fans. They are the type that try to knock out the other fellow or be knocked out in the attempt, although surprisingly enough each boy has only been kayoed once.

Berger's buzz-saw style is combined with a hefty punch and he may give Zivic plenty of trouble. The former welterweight champion, who has scored consecutive knockouts over Izzy Jannazzo and Wild Bill McDowell in his latest starts, will be out to add Berger to his list, which will enhance his brightening chances of meeting Red Cochrane for the championship sometime here before June.

THE POCKETBOOK of KNOWLEDGE BY TOPPS

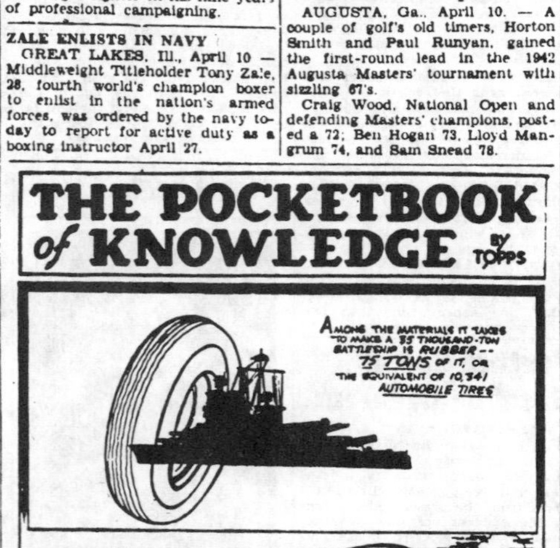
AMONG THE MATERIALS IT TAKES TO MAKE A 35 THOUSAND-TON BATTLESHIP IS RUBBER-- 75 TONS OF IT, OR THE EQUIVALENT OF 10,341 AUTOMOBILE TIRES
FOR HEALTH
FOR SAFETY
$6,000,000
ONE LARGE COMPANY SPENT 6 MILLION DOLLARS
ALASKA

PLAY BALL!
Sam Chapman
Morrie Arnovich
Hank Greenberg
More night baseball games
1942
Bob Feller

"PLAY BALL!" That old familiar cry, heard each year by more than 60,000,000 sports fans in the United States, rings out again with the spotlight on the major league races getting underway April 14. War, the world over, has affected the way of life of all and caused the cancellation of many big sporting events. Baseball, America's national game, has felt the effect of the conflict but, as in the past, it has survived as a necessary medium of wartime recreation and relaxation. The 1942 season will be marked by an increase in night games, suggested by President Roosevelt himself; two all-star major league games, and probably many other games between service teams and the major league clubs. Many of the stars of the past are absent from the national scene, called or having volunteered for service. More than 60 men from major league rosters are in the service, including such established stars as Bob Feller of the Indians, Hank Greenberg of the Tigers, Sam Chapman of the Athletics, Cecil Travis of the Senators, Carvell Rowell of the Braves and Morris Arnovich, ex-Phil star. New managers include Lou Boudreau, boy pilot of the Indians; Mel Ott, replacing Bill Terry at the helm of the Giants, and Hans Lobert, new mentor of the Phils. Defending champions are the New York Yanks in the American league and the Brooklyn Dodgers in the National circuit. Favorite in the American again is the Yanks with the Cardinals, Dodgers and Reds one-two-three choices in the National loop.

Freedom High To Open 1942 Football Season On Sept. 4th

Red And White Eleven To Play Ten Games; Open With Beaver Falls Tigers

Faculty Manager J. Richard Fruth of Freedom high school has completed the Red and White's 1942 football card, listing ten games. The Bulldogs, as usual, open with a tough assignment. They meet the Beaver Falls gridders, on Friday night, September 4, at Reeves Stadium, Beaver Falls, three days before Labor Day.

One week later, September 11, the Red and White eleven ill meet Rochester on the Junction City field, and their first home game will be with Leetsdale on September 18.

Other opponents include Millvale, Zelienople, Hopewell township, Beaver and Sharpsburg away from home and Monaca at home. The Freedom eleven will play four night games, at Beaver Falls, Rochester, Millvale and Beaver.

The schedule:
- *Sept. 4—Freedom at Beaver Falls.
- *Sept. 11—Freedom at Rochester.
- Sept. 18—Leetsdale at Freedom.
- *Sept. 25—Freedom at Millvale.
- Oct. 2—Freedom at Zelienople.
- Oct. 9—Freedom at Shenango.
- Oct. 16—Freedom at Hopewell Twp.
- Oct. 24—Monaca at Freedom.
- *Oct. 30—Freedom at Beaver.
- Nov. 13—Freedom at Sharpsburg.

*Night Games.

Runyan And Smith Lead Masters Open

AUGUSTA, Ga., April 10. — A couple of golf's old timers, Horton Smith and Paul Runyan, gained the first-round lead in the 1942 Augusta Masters' tournament with sizzling 67's.

Craig Wood, National Open and defending Masters' champions, posted a 72; Ben Hogan 73, Lloyd Mangrum 74, and Sam Snead 78.

Bucs Demonstrating Powerful Punch And Good Pitching As League Opener Nears

Current Pirate Club Best Conditioned In Several Years; Better Defense Expected With Coscarart And Fletcher On Left Side Of Infield

By the United Press

ENID, Okla., April 10—Showing more fire and dash than in years, the Pittsburgh Pirates are heading north for the opening of the National League season with the best conditioned and strongest looking club in several years.

Demonstrating a powerful punch combined with good pitching, the Pirates have kicked the Athletics, White Sox and Cubs around in exhibition games to run up 15 victories against five defeats. Not in a long time has a Pittsburgh team been in as fine condition as the 1942 club. In recent years one of the big draw-backs of the Pirates has been their failure to get away from the barrier fast.

In building the Pirates, Manager Frankie Frisch had several delicate problems to solve. Loss of Rookie Bill Cox, who had expected to play shortstop, and complications resulting from Lee Handley's ailing arm didn't help his problem any. The Pirates finished last in fielding a yer ago and one of Frisch's big jobs was to improve the defense.

Frisch had to rebuild the whole left side of the Pittsburgh infield. Pete Coscarart, one of the four obtained from the Dodgers in the Arky Vaughan deal, has been converted from a second baseman into a shortstop and Bob Elliott, who played right field last year, has been installed at third base. Coscarart's work has been sensationall. Teaming up with Frank Gustine at second, the Keystone pair have averaged more than one double play a game. In addition Coscarart's hitting has been a big surprise. He's batting .325 and has clouted three homers, one with the bases filled.

Manager Jimmy Dykes of the White Sox, himself an old third baseman, who's seen Elliott at third base in seven games, has placed the stamp of approval on him. Elliott, five pounds heavier than last year, has shown an improvement in his hitting over a year ago. Afield he has a strong arm and handles ground balls naturally.

Elbie Fletcher will be at first again and Stu Martin and Alf Anderson will handle the infield utility jobs. Handley has gone home with his sore arm and may be out all year.

The Pirates' outfield will lineup with Maurice Van Robays in left, Vince DiMaggio in center, and Rookie Johnny Barrett, who hit .313 for Hollywood, in right. John Wyrostek, a left-handed hitter who batted .316 for New Orleans last year, gave Van Robays a good run for the left field job but didn't quite make it. He'll stick along with Jimmy Wasdell from the Dodgers and Eddie Stewart as reserve outfielders.

The Pittsburgh catching staff of Al Lopez, Babe Phelps, the ex-Dodger, and Bill Baker is considered by many as the league's top staff.

The Pirates lack a standout mound star but the hurling corps has balance and Frisch may get considerable mileage out of it, particularly if the defense is improved as hoped. The "big five" figure to be Max Butcher, Rip Sewell, John Lanning, Ken Heintzelman and Lloyd Dietz, ho came fast late last season. Luke Hamlin, another of the Brooklyn castoffs, Aldon Wilkie, Joe Sullivan and Nick Strincevich are in the second line along with Bob Klinger, the No. 1 relief man. Han Gornicki, bought from the Cardinals, and Ken Jungles, ex-Clevelander, also are fighting for mound jobs.

Pittsburgh seems to have an abundance of power with almost anybody in the lineup capable of driving the ball out of the park. The big question, however, seems to be the Pirates' left side of the infield. If Coscarart and Elliott hold up the Pirates could make considerable trouble.

Semi-Pro Group Changes Rules

By the United Press

ST. LOUIS, April 10—The National Semi-Pro Baseball Congress announced changes in its rules that will allow every sandlot team to participate in its tournaments.

Commissioner George H. Sisler said there will be no age restrictions on any of the estimated 65,000 teams which will begin play on May 3. Only organized professional clubs or those classified as barnstorming teams will not be allowed to take part in league, district or state tournaments under sanction of the Congress.

Sisler said state champions, after qualifying for the national semi-pro championship tournament at Wichita, Kans., Aug. 14 to 26, will be permitted five changes in their roster. Any players substituted, however, must come from the State the team represents.

Charley Burley Stops Cleo McNeal In Fifth

MINNEAPOLIS, April 10—Charley Burley, 150, of Pittsburgh knocked out Cleo McNeal, 146, of Akron, O., in the fifth round of a scheduled eight-round bout last night.

Burley had McNeal down twice in the second round for nine counts. He floored him again in the fourth for another count of nine, the bell saving him. Two left hooks followed by a smashing right to the chin scored the knockout in the next round.

Veteran Bookie Picks Yanks And Cardinals

By the United Press

NEW YORK, April 10 — Jack Doyle, the bespectacled Broadway odds-maker who will give you a price on anything from turtle races to President Roosevelt's 1944 re-election, established the New York Yankees and the St. Louis Cards today as favorites in the major league pennant races.

The little Irishman, who figures odds on everything but horse races, believes the whole opening line may be upset by the war effort and that despite the war there will be considerable wagering.

Pirates Send Kerr To Toronto Club

By the United Press

HUTCHINSON, Kan., April 10—The Pittsburgh Pirate pitching staff was reduced to 12 today with the optioning of Don Kerr to Toronto. Release of the 24-year-old Baltimore hurler left only two more deductions to be made from the mound corps to reach the 10-limit Manager Frankie Frisch plans to carry this year. The Pirate-Athletic final series was stymied for the third straight day yesterday because of the weather and they will try to resume here today.

New Steffen System To Aid Tech Sports

By the United Press

PITTSBURGH, April 10—Barring unforeseen developments due to the war, Carnegie Tech hopes one day to resume its position as a power in intercollegiate football, according to Dr. Robert E. Doherty, president of the school.

At his annual dinner for sports writers yesterday, Dr. Doherty said that a new Steffen fund system has been worked out by Chester C. Williamson, chairman, and a committee of 15, under which it is hoped to gradually build up the team during the next four years.

Gay, Colorful Musical, "Song Of The Islands" Now At The Rialto In Beaver Falls

Betty Grable steps out in her own streamlined version of the hula aided by Harry Owens and His Royal Hawaiian Orchestra in "Song of the Islands," the Technicolor musical which opened this afternoon at the Rialto in Beaver Falls. Vic Mature and Jack Oakie are co-starred with Betty in the film.

SPORT SLANTS

By BILL ANDERSON

The traditional inter-class track and field meet will be revived at Geneva College next Wednesday and Thursday afternoons starting at 3:15 P. M., with field events on Wednesday and track events Thursday. Considerable interest is being shown in the affair and all four classes are trying to organize full teams. The class winning the meeting will be well-rewarded according to Carl Hughes, Geneva athletic publicity director. A few days ago Hughes unearthed an old trophy cup from a closet in the athletic office and it will be presented to the winning class. The cup is dated 1910, and from data engraved on it was donated by a Beaver Falls jeweler to be awarded each year to the class winning the annual track and field meet. How many years it has been hidden away no one seems to know.

The Ambridge high school cage team and an Alumni team composed chiefly of college players staged a thrilling contest this week when their game featured a benefit program at the Ambridge high gym. The Collegians, paced by Eddie Ziolkowski of Pitt, defeated the high school boys, 39 to 37, after two extra periods. Rallying in the last half, the high school team tied the score at 33-33. In the first period each side scored two points but in the second overtime the Collegians counted four points to two for Coach Rubenstein's pupils and emerged the victor. On the Alumni team in addition to Ziolkowski was Tony Kubec, and Bobby Palmer of Geneva; Hank Holets of Carnegie Tech, and Papasodero and Dubensky.

The name of Col. E. R. Bradley and his Idle Hour Farms are synonymous with thoroughbred horses and the Kentucky Derby, which is to be run at Churchill Downs for the 68th time on May 2. The Colonel has sent 26 of his famous "B"-named horses to the post in 17 different Kentucky derbies starting with 1921, and has seen the victory wreath placed on four of them—Behave Yourself in 1921, Bubbling Over in 1926; Burgoo King in 1932 and Brokers Tip in 1933. This year his entry will be Bless Me and the colt is said to have more than an outside chance of winning.

Usually more than one hundred colts and fillies are nominated for the Kentucky Derby, but seldom more than a ten go to the post. Only 678 different horses have run in all the derbies to date. It costs $25 to nominate a colt, and $500 more to start him. The owner of the winning horse receive $53,000, second place wins $8,000; third place $3,000; and fourth place, $1,000. There are also substantial prizes for the trainers, jockeys and breeders. The total purse is composed of the stakes, plus $75,000 contributed by the track management.

Briefs: The Blackhawk Public golf course, now an 18-hole layout and one of the finest in this district, will be officially opened to the public this coming week-end... Paul Frable, capable greenskeeper, has the course in fine shape and local niblick swingers, it is said, are in for a pleasant surprise..... Adam Wolicki, former Ambridge sports writer, is now in the Army and is stationed at Fort Francis E. Warner, near Cheyenne, Wyo.

Lou Boudreau wants no lofty goals to face his Cleveland Indians, so he's in complete concordance with the sports writer's poll that selected his club as a candidate for fourth place. He said that that was the spot he had picked for them. However, he's not saying that is where they'll finish.

Babe Ruth Better

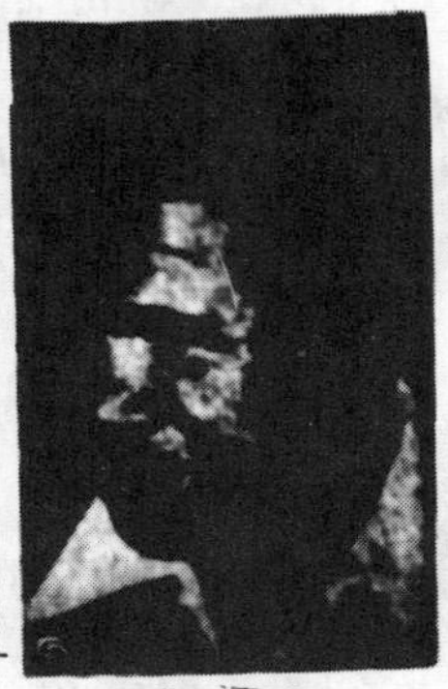

Babe Ruth

George Herman Ruth, baseball's mighty Babe, is reported in better condition in Hollywood hospital, Hollywood, Cal., where he has been working in a movie on the life of Ruth's late teammate, Lou Gehrig.

Pittsburgh Club's Rookie Outfielder

JOHN J. BARRETT, outfielder—Born December 18, 1917, in Lowell, Mass. Now a resident of Lawrence, Mass. Hits and throws left-handed. Height, 5 feet 10¼ inches. Weight, 170 pounds. Purchased by Pittsburgh from Hollywood in the Pacific Coast League. Played football and baseball at Lowell high school prior to his graduation in 1935. Went in for semi-pro ball in 1936, and in 1937 made his professional start with Mansfield in the Ohio State League, where he not only batted for the fancy average of .378 but startled the circuit by stealing the amazing total of 51 bases, causing the fans to wonder if he should not be called Jackrabbit instead of Jack Barrett. Established in the Red Sox chain, Barrett appeared on the rosters of the Haselton, Scranton and Louisville clubs in 1938 and 1939, and in 1940 was all set for a big league chance with the Boston Americans. However, the Red Sox managed to get Dominic DiMaggio from San Francisco, and this left no room on the outfield squad for Barrett. So Johnny was turned over to San Francisco to fill the vacancy there, and so well did he do the job that he led the league in triples with 22, an indication of his rare speed in view of the fact that his batting average was only .267, and again assaulted the base-stealing records of late year by rolling up a total of 40 thefts. His hitting was very timely, too. Transferred to the Hollywood club last year, Johnny was the talk of the Pacific Coast League. During the first part of the campaign he went along at only an ordinary pace, and on July 17 he was hitting a mere .267. Then Barrett suddenly found himself, and from that stage to the finish he was a sensation. In his 74 games after July 17, he batted .357, and the big jump enabled him to finish with an average of .313 for the year. Johnny scored 75 runs, his 162 hits included 27 doubles, 14 triples and 4 homers, he knocked in 66 runs, drew 57 walks, struck out 49 times, and kept up his base-stealing reputation by purloining 24. His fielding average was .965. As evidence of his own sincerity and ambition, two essential qualities in the making of a real ball player, Barrett requested that he be permitted to go to the El Centro camp with the first Pirate squad this spring in order to get himself in the best condition possible.

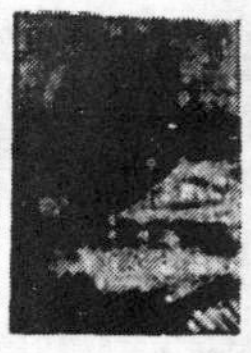

A pledge canvasser will call on you soon. Give your government full support by agreeing to purchase U. S. Savings Bonds and Stamps regularly.

Only necessities belong in your budget now. And the biggest necessity of all is the regular purchase of U. S. Savings Stamps and Bonds.

Everyone should sign the Bond Pledge Card. If you are already buying to your fullest ability through Payroll Savings, say so on the Pledge Card, but sign it.

The Weather Forecast

WESTERN PENNSYLVANIA Continued warm tonight.

THE DAILY TIMES

ROCHESTER-BEAVER-MONACA

FREEDOM—BRIDGEWATER—CONWAY—VANPORT—MIDLAND

ESTABLISHED APRIL 2, 1874 | BEAVER AND ROCHESTER, PA., THURSDAY, APRIL 16, 1942 | BY CARRIER 18 CENTS A WEEK— 3 CENTS PER COPY

Beaver County History

Plans were being made on April 16, 1918, for a ceremony to be held to mark the dedication of a service flag for Monaca borough.

FREEDOM TEACHERS GIVEN INCREASE IN PAY

★ ★ ★ ★ ★ ★ ★ ★ ★ ★ ★ ★ ★ ★ ★ ★ ★ ★ ★ ★

ALLIED FLIERS CONTINUE BIG RAIDS

AMERICAN PLANES BOMB PHILIPPINES

By the United Press

GENERAL MacARTHUR'S HEADQUARTERS, Australia, April 16—Brig. Gen. Ralph Royce said today that about 110 tons of bombs were dropped on the Philippines in the "two-day picnic" attack of 13 American bombers and added, "I'll bet those damned Japs still don't know what hit them."

More than 35 passengers returned to Australia on the American bombers, including the crew of 10 men of one flying fortress which was lost on the expedition.

Royce, the leader of the mission which challenged Japan's hold on the Philippines, said that during the two-days assault he communicated with Lieut. Gen. Jonathan M. Wainwright, commander of the besieged garrison at Corregidor fortress in Manila Bay, several times.

The American airmen who staged the 4,000-mile round trip attack were the heroes of Australia today, but they were impatient to get back into action for another crack at the Japs.

Seated serenely in his hotel here, Royce told how the three flying fortresses and 10 North American B-25 bombers under his command smashed at four key enemy objectives in the Philippines.

At Manila they attacked Nichols airfield, struck at the port of Batangas in southern Luzon, Cebu and Davao at from 2,000 to 5,000 feet under ferocious enemy fire.

JAP SHIPS SUNK

Fighting off fighter plane attacks, they sank four transports, probably sank a fifth, damaged three large vessels and probably several smaller ones, destroyed five enemy planes and damaged many. Hangars, airdrome runways, warehouses and Japanese troop concentrations were bombed.

The whole plan of attack was drawn by Gen. Douglas MacArthur—a mission of vengeance for Bataan and of hope and cheer for the defenders of Corregidor, Royce said.

Around Corregidor in Manila Bay, he added, the bombers hunted for Japanese cruisers and destroyers, but found none.

Royce, who piloted one of the bombers for five hours en route to the secret base of operations in the Philippines, said that the number of evacuees flown back to Australia from the Philippines were chosen by Wainwright.

"We made one of our attacks on Davao synchronized with an attack by the American forces in Mindanao Island, and we dropped many bombs

(Continued on Page Six)

Firemen Of County Hold Monthly Meet In New Brighton

Relief Association Invited To Participate In Parade At Rochester June 14

The Beaver County Firemen's Relief Association held its monthly meeting Wednesday night at the New Brighton Fire Department's rooms.

The county firemen have been invited to participate in a big parade to be held by the Rochester Elks, June 14. Members of the Aliquippa Fire Department announced there would be a meeting of the Western Pennsylvania Firemen's Association Board of Control at Aliquippa in July.

The Aliquippa firemen were awarded the annual convention for 1942, in August, but owing to the war there will be a general business session held only Friday and Saturday, August 14 and 15.

Carl Taylor, of the Defense committee, reported that before any defense material could be obtained a bond would have to be procured by the person in charge of the equipment.

Chief Charles Cooper, Beaver Falls, reported there would be a bigger "Fire Prevention Week" this year and that a parade would be held if possible.

HEAR TWO SPEAKERS

Principal Alf M. Asper, of Freedom high school, spoke on the topic "The Life of a Volunteer Fireman." He also spoke on "Priorities."

Thomas Hopkins, Pittsburgh, an authority on the two per cent foreign fire insurance, gave a general review of the funds. He stated that Pennsylvania is the only state in the nation which has a complete program for the distribution of these funds.

A program was received from Captain Joseph Fay, of the Pittsburgh Fire Department, showing how to protect children if and when an air raid should occur, whether in school or at home, and the kind of shelters and air drills. Walter Anderson, veteran member of the Freedom Fire Department, was reported still in a serious condition at the Veterans' Hospital, Aspinwall.

The meeting was attended by 100 firemen and several new members were received. The New Galilee Fire Department was awarded the May meeting. Lunch was served by the New Brighton firemen. Harold Howarth, Beaver Falls, president, presided.

Trade Board Calls Off Boat Excursion

The Rochester Board of Trade held its monthly luncheon meeting Wednesday noon at the Penn-Beaver Hotel with President William J. Toner, presiding.

A communication from the Ohio Valley Improvement Association, Cincinnati, was read but no action was taken. The letter referred to H. R. 6886 sponsored by Congressman Snyder, of Pennsylvania, which would create a board authorized to determine an equitable toll on inland rivers.

O. E. Kunsman, Chairman of the boat ride and picnic Committee reported it would be impossible to secure the steamer Washington this year.

Action was taken to observe Memorial Day, May 30, and Independence Day, July 4, by closing their places of business. Merchants, in order to serve their customers, will remain open the previous day until 9 p. m. The Board also voted to donate $10 to the Rochester United Memorial Association to help defray expense in the observance of that day.

Draft Board No. 3 Ready For "R" Day

Draft Board No. 3, Rochester, has completed plans for the fourth national "R" day registration to be held Monday, April 27, according to announcement made today by Charles W. McDonald, board secretary.

Men under the jurisdiction of the board are to register at the Rochester post office, the New Brighton post office or the Fourth Ward borough building at New Brighton, Mr. McDonald said. Registration hours will be from 7 a. m. to 9 p. m.

Thirty-Year Man

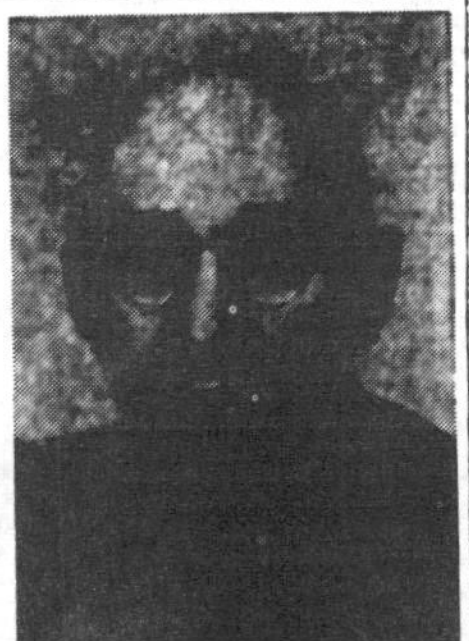

George M. Nippert, (above) 1207 Fifth street, New Brighton, today completes thirty years of service with the Bell Telephone Company. He is a commercial representative, assigned to the Rochester central office. A member of the Telephone Pioneers of America, Mr. Nippert also is affiliated with a number of Masonic organizations as well as the Eagles, the Moose and the United States Commercial Travelers.

Lost and Found

LOST: Brown Shephard - Chow dog (female), in Rochester, Wednesday. Answers to name "Porky." Phone Rochester 886-M. Reward. 4-16-18 inc.

Beaver High May Queen and Her Court

CHRISTINE WILSON

NANCY KINCAID

PHYLLIS McBRIDE

DELLA JEAN McPHERSON

That Beaver high school students prefer blondes was again emphasized yesterday afternoon when they chose for this year's "May Queen," lovely Della Jean McPherson. Her pretty maid of honor, Christine Wilson, is dark-haired in contrast.

Among the five attendants selected for the Queen's attendants, are both blondes and brunettes. In the retinue are: Mary Jane McClarey, Kate Marshall, Nancy Kincaid, Phyllis McBride and Alice Gregory.

The entire student body voted yesterday on the seven nominees, presented by the Senior girls. This election is always one of the highlights on the school calendar and is entered into with much enthusiasm.

The May Day exercises this year will be a part of a huge Patriotic May Festival in which more than 800 school students, including those from both the elementary grades and high school, will participate, to be presented on Friday evening, May 15.

Primarily the festivities will include musical features, physical education demonstrations, etc. A number of the teachers are assisting with the pageant.

KATHERINE MARSHALL

ALICE GREGORY

MARY JANE McCLAREY

Conference On Race Relations Scheduled Saturday Afternoon

Numerous Speakers To Participate In Meeting At Beaver Court House

Beaver county citizens interested in promoting a greater interracial unity in the local war effort have been invited to participate in a Race Relations conference Saturday afternoon in the court house assembly room.

Dr. Robert Weaver, chief of negro employment and training for the war production board, and Dr. Laurence Foster, University of Pennsylvania professor and executive director of the state temporary commission on conditions of the urban colored population, will be featured speakers at the conference, co-sponsored by the Andrew Tanner Welfare Association and the newly-organized race relations commission of Beaver county.

The program will be marked by a series of short speeches and by individual panel discussions of "Civilian Defense," "Housing," and "Employment and Training", followed by a summary of the conference by Dr. Foster and the main address by Dr. Weaver.

Other speakers include William H. Miller and S. Edward Yancy, president and executive secretary, respectively, of the Andrew Tanner group; Rev. G. C. Thomas, Rochester, chairman of the race relations commission; Clemons M. Roark, sub-regional coordinator for the National Housing Agency; Homer Brown, Pittsburgh, member of the Pennsylvania legislature; Ralph C. Bennett, county controller; Sam H. Boyles, business representative of the Beaver Valley Building Trades Council; Earl Hodge, staff representative of the Steel Workers Organizing Committee; Mrs. Charles Craighead, member of the board of directors of the Andrew Tanner Welfare Association; and Arthur Mart-

(Continued on Page Six)

OCD Reorganized By Roosevelt

WASHINGTON, Apr. 16—President Roosevelt today reorganized the Office of Civilian Defense in a manner that will give the army and navy an active voice in the operation of the Civilian Defense program.

Under the new set-up, James M. Landis continues as OCD director. But, Mr. Roosevelt created within the OCD a "Civilian Defense Board consisting of the director, who shall serve as chairman; the Secretary of War, the Attorney General, the Secretary of Navy, the director of the Office of Defense, Health and Welfare services, and such other members as the President may designate."

New Terrorism Is Reported In France

VICHY, France, April 16—A fresh wave of terrorism broke out in Nazi-held France as Pierre Laval prepared to assume full power over the Vichy government with a cabinet of his own choosing.

Production Records Broken By Crucible Steel Last Quarter

President Reports Increase In Net Profit For First Quarter Of Year

The Crucible Steel Company of America broke all previous production records in the first quarter of this year, F. B. Hufnagle, president and board chairman, said at the annual meeting today in reporting consolidated net profit for the period at $1,951,111 against $1,489,851 a year earlier.

Earnings for the first three months this year equaled $3.46 a common share when provisions for preferred dividends were made, compared with $2.42 a share in the initial three months last year.

Asserting that for several months the company's actual output has exceeded the hitherto estimated capacity, Hufnagle said that this was accomplished despite priority and allocation orders which involve frequent schedule revisions.

He expressed confidence that still

(Continued on Page Six)

AUXILIARY POLICE TRAINING IN COUNTY DISCUSSED AT MEETING

A clear picture of the duties of auxiliary police instructors was presented last night by County Law Enforcement Chairman C. J. O'Loughlin, and County Instruction Chief W. S. Bazard, at a joint meeting of local law enforcement chairmen and instructors.

The meeting, held in the assembly room of the court house, was attended by representatives of 16 of the 22 local councils of defense. They heard Sheriff O'Loughlin warn that "the regular police and their auxiliaries have the most important job in the protective organization of the civilian defense program and their training for this work should be thorough and of the highest order."

TO START SCHOOLS

In a talk outlining the instruction procedures, Mr. Bazard declared that one of the first jobs of the instructors was to become thoroughly familiar with the materials issued by the state council for training purposes and then to supplement their teaching in the light of their practical experience as protectors of the public.

Instruction manuals and other materials relative to auxiliary police work were distributed and the instructors were urged to start training schools immediately.

SALARY INCREASE GRANTED TEACHERS BY FREEDOM BOARD

Tentative School Budget Totaling $88,299 Adopted At Meeting Of Directors

Date Set For Annual School Picnic; Commencement Speaker Is Announced

A general increase in salaries for teachers in the Freedom schools was voted at the postponed meeting of the Freedom Board of Education, Wednesday evening. This action was taken due to the increased cost of living conditions.

A budget, amounting to $88,299, was tentatively adopted and is to be on file in the offices of the supervising principal in the high school ten days for inspection. This is an increase of approximately $8,000 over last year's budget, taking into consideration the increase in the cost of supplies, etc. The tax levy will be set at the next regular meeting of the Board.

Provided transportation will be available, the annual school picnic will be held on Tuesday, May 26, at West View Park, Pittsburgh.

Dr. Weir C. Ketler, president of Grove City, has been procured as speaker for the annual Commencement on Thursday evening, May 28. The Baccalaureate service will be on Sunday, May 24.

The Board agreed to cooperate with the request of Governor Arthur H. James in closing the schools on Monday, April 27, so that the teachers might assist with the registration of men for service, also to arrange the school schedule in order that the teachers might also assist in the rationing of sugar during the first week in May.

Provision was made for the high school band to again participate in the Memorial Day parade on May 30. Various reports, including that of the treasurer, were given. Dr. John H. Boal, president, presided and all members were in attendance.

Plumbing Equipment Stocks Are "Frozen"

WASHINGTON, April 16 — The War Production Board today froze all stocks of new plumbing and heating equipment, but excluded retail sales of $5 or less, or any sale made on a military priority rating.

Acting to prevent dissipation of equipment needed in defense housing and military construction, WPB prohibited the sale or delivery after 12:01 a. m., of any fixtures, fittings, pipe furnaces, oil burners, coal stokers and a wide range of other equipment for non-essential purposes.

In an earlier order vitally affecting the plumbing and heating industry, the board prohibited production of oil burners, and coal stokers for residential use after May 31.

Contracts Awarded For School Addition

The Cook-Anderson Company, Beaver, has been awarded the contract for the general construction work on the new addition to be made to the Pulaski Township school building on a bid of $25,862 it was announced today by the Federal Works Agency which is handling the government grant to defray the cost of the addition.

Contracts awarded on other phases of the work are: Plumbing, H. W. Butler Company, Beaver Falls, $3,850; electrical work, Prothero Electric Company, Beaver, $1,990, and heating, Columbia Heating and Ventilating Company, $4,890, the agency announced.

The school addition is to be constructed as a wartime Public Works project. Contracts call for the completion of the work in 135 calendar days or in ample time for the opening of school in September. The addition is to provide school facilities for the families of workers engaged in war production here. The total Federal grant for the work is approximately $46,990.

SURPRISE "ALERT" HELD

WASHINGTON, Pa., April 16.—Air raid authorities agreed today that the Washington County protection system was in need of a little "toning up" following the county's first surprise air raid "alert" in which 21 communities participated.

MAN, WIFE DIE

WAYNESBURG, April 16. — Double funeral services will be held for Mr. and Mrs. William Roupe of Deep Valley, Greene County. The couple died yesterday within eight hours of each other. Mrs. Roupe, 77, succumbed first and the husband died eight hours later.

BOMBS RAINED ON WESTERN EUROPE

By the United Press

LONDON—RAF, with American and Canadian pilots, resumes non-stop offensive against Axis in west; urgency of British talks with Gen George C. Marshall, American Chief of Staff, may postpone Prime Minister Churchill's parliamentary review of war situation.

RUSSIA—Red Army captures dozens of enemy strong points in pressing effort to break up Hitler's offensive plans; first great battle of spring believed raging on Bryansk front but Kuibyshev says Bryansk itself not yet reached.

FRANCE—Pierre Laval forms new Cabinet expected to aid Axis war effort; Hitler reportedly shifts Marshal Von Brundstedt from Russian Front to take charge of occupied France, guarding rear against Allied invasion attempt.

BURMA—Six Japanese columns, with 100,000 reinforcements, threaten encirclement of Allied positions in Central Burma by new flank attack from Thailand.

AUSTRALIA—Americans report dropping 110 tons of bombs on Japanese in Philippines; Allies renew attacks on Koepang.

Allied aerial squadrons, including American pilots, pressed a non-stop offensive against the Axis western front today and the Red army reported that it had captured dozens of strong points in heavy fighting in the east.

The hammering at both ends of the Axis in Europe continued on a big scale following successful American air blows against enemy bases in the Philippines where 110 tons of bombs were dropped and a new raid on the Japanese base of Koepang on Timor Islands, north of Australia.

Only in Burma did today's dispatches tell of serious reverses for the United Nations forces, which were under attack on the Central Burma front by six Japanese columns which apparently had received about 100,000 reinforcements and were threatening to encircle the British and Chinese positions.

The aerial offensive against Hitler in Western Europe entered its fifth day of intensive fighting with every indication that the British air force—probably with the aid of American squadrons later—intended to keep on hammering enemy targets every hour.

AMERICANS IN RAID

Big British bombers, with Americans and Canadians at the controls of some, ranged over the German industrial cities of the Ruhr during the hours of darkness and big formations of Spitfires and Hurricane fighter-bomber planes resumed the attack on the European coast as soon as daylight permitted.

Factories, railroads, docks, shipping and any other targets that could be found were attacked by the planes, which frequently have been forced to fight off strong enemy fighter squadrons. The air ministry, reporting four British craft missing, said that a German torpedo boat was one of the targets damaged by a diving Spitfire's cannon.

The British aerial attacks were designed primarily to break up the enemy rear lines and thus weaken Hitler's preparations for a summer offensive in Southern Russia, but they also were regarded as a token of the Allies determination to reply ruthlessly to any attempt by the new Vichy French government under Pierre Laval to give further military aid to the Axis.

LAVAL ACTION AWAITED

Laval, forming a new cabinet as soon as he returned to Vichy after conferring with Fascist leaders in Paris, was believed to have been ordered by Hitler to protect the French coast against invasion during the showdown fighting in Russia this summer. To aid in this task, it was reported in London that Hitler had withdrawn Marshal Karl R. G. Von Rundstedt from the Rus-

(Continued on Page Six)

Joint Meeting Of Borough Officials Held On Southside

Monaca Assessors, Councilmen, School Directors Discuss Drop In Assessments

A joint meeting was held Wednesday by the assessors, members of the Borough Council and Board of School Directors at Monaca. The purpose of the meeting was to talk over the shrinkage of assessments in Monaca during the past six or eight years.

It is evident that there has been a decrease in assessed valuation of real property as the present assessment totals $3,185,582, while in 1934 it was $3,655,369, or a drop of $469,787. During this same period there has been, from a conservative estimate, at least $100,000 assessment in additional and new construction.

The decrease on old assessments, plus the increase in new construction which has been assessed, make a grand total of $569,787 during this time.

One mill tax levied on this amount means a loss in actual revenue to the borough and school district of $569.79, it was said. Based on the total present levy of 31 mills school and 15 borough, it means a decrease in revenue of $26,210 annually.

TAX INCREASE LOOMS

There is only one alternative for any governing body if standards are to be maintained—raise the millage to meet the decrease, it was pointed out. In the past the shortage in revenue has been partially offset through borrowing and curtailment of operation. Now, both of these recourses have been exhausted and the inevitable is at hand—"raise the millage"—the conferees said.

It was not the purpose of the joint meeting to find fault or condemn any one or group, but to seek some way to reach a fair and equal assessment between all wards so that any millage increase would be fair and equal tax on all property alike.

It is hoped by the conferees that this may come about in an amicable way and thus allow all property owners to share alike in helping to maintain the borough and schools and receive the benefits in the same way.

New Casualty List Is Announced Today

By the United Press

WASHINGTON, April 16. — The War Department today announced the names of 57 soldiers, who were kill in action or died of wounds in the East Indies and Australia. It was the first casualty list issued on Army action in the far East.

The list included 30 officers and 27 enlisted men. The majority were killed in the Dutch East Indies, although a few lost their lives "in or near Northern Australia." Most of the dead were members of the army air forces. The list did not include any casualties in the Philippines.

"The list is incomplete, and the War Department will make public the names of additional soldiers who meet death in this area whenever verified reports are received and checked," the Department said.

Previously the Department had announced the names of 226 men and officers killed as a result of the Japanese attack on Hawaii, Dec. 7. Today's list brings the total announced army dead to 283.

Four County Youths Enlist In Army, Navy

Four county youths enlisted Wednesday in the armed forces at Pittsburgh recruiting offices. Leonard Moss, Rochester, and James Tselepis, Aliquippa, joined the Navy while Delbert M. Greathouse, Ambridge, and Theodore W. Rygalsky, Ambridge, enlisted in the Army.

Corregidor's Guns Blast Japanese

WASHINGTON, April 16—The big guns of Corregidor fortress in Manila Bay blasted Japanese troop and truck concentrations on Bataan yesterday, blowing up ammunition dumps and inflicting "numerous" casualties on the enemy, the War Department said today.

In its first communique from the besieged fortress in two days, the War Department said that Lieut. Gen. Jonathan M. Wainwright's gunners had hurled a roaring challenge to the Japanese just one week after the fall of Bataan.

NOTICE—I.O.O.F. NO. 786

All members of S. M. Kane Lodge No. 786, I. O. O. F., Rochester, are requested to meet at the lodge rooms tonight, Thursday, April 16th, at 7:30 to attend the ritualistic service for our late brother Henry Fremont Steel.

It is also requested of all brothers who have cars to drive same.

Signed—

GEORGE H. SCHROEDER, Noble Grand

Lester W. Smith, Secretary

4896

The Weather Forecast

WESTERN PENNSYLVANIA Moderately cold tonight.

THE DAILY TIMES

ROCHESTER-BEAVER-MONACA

FREEDOM—BRIDGEWATER—CONWAY—VANPORT—MIDLAND

ESTABLISHED APRIL 2, 1874 | BEAVER AND ROCHESTER, PA., SATURDAY, APRIL 18, 1942 | BY CARRIER 18 CENTS A WEEK—3 CENTS PER COPY

Beaver County History

Farmers of Beaver County were being urged on April 18, 1918 to relinquish all holdings of wheat to aid in feeding people of Allied nations

Japanese Capture Cebu City In Philippines

★ ★

U. S. PLANES BOMB JAPANESE CITIES

SECOND LARGEST PHILIPPINE CITY CAPTURED BY JAPS

War Department Reports Cebu Apparently In Hands Of Invading Forces

Guns Of Manila Bay Forts Continue To Hammer At Japanese Positions

By the United Press

WASHINGTON, April 18—Cebu, the second largest city of the Philippine Islands, apparently has fallen to the Japanese, the War Department reported today.

But the big guns of American island forts in Manila Bay continued to disrupt enemy forces on Bataan.

A communique said aerial bombardment and shelling of Corregidor from enemy artillery continued throughout yesterday, "though with somewhat decreased intensity," and "little damage was done."

Artillery on Corregidor and other island forts returned the fire, and "silenced several enemy batteries and blasted roads and bridges in Bataan, disrupting communications."

CITY SAID BURNING

Reports from Cebu Island, where 12,000 Japanese troops landed a week ago, indicated that Cebu city is in enemy hands. The city was reported to be burning, although fierce fighting is still continuing in that general area.

Some 8,000 Japanese troops, who landed on the island of Panay, near Cebu, are meeting stiff opposition from our troops.

The communique made no mention of the reported bombing of Japanese cities by American planes.

Yesterday's communique did not mention any action on the island of Mindanao, in the southern Philippines, where American-Filipino patrols have been harassing supply columns and storehouses by hit-and-run raids.

Marimba Playing By Woman Is Restricted By Philadelphia Judge

By the United Press

PHILADELPHIA, April 18.—Mrs. Barbara Ernst, whose marimba playing upset the neighborhood, today was limited to one-hour periods for her music, but a judge had shredded her repertoire to bits.

Neighbors of Mrs. Ernst yesterday asked Judge Harold L. Ervin to issue an injunction against her playing such numbers as "When Irish Eyes Are Smiling," and "Jingle Bells." An unnamed naval officer asked that "Anchors Aweight" be stricken from the daily recitals.

Mrs. Ernst, the neighbors admitted, had a nice touch with the hammers, but the volume from the marimba was too great. She had selected, they said, a piece for each person in the neighborhood, and played it as they walked by.

Judge Ervin told Mrs. Ernst to confine her serenades to the hours between 9 A. M. and 10 P. M. on weekdays, and 1 P. M. to 10 P.M. on Sundays, and not to play more than one hour at a time, nor more than three hours in any one day.

Frank Floccari Dies In Veterans Hospital

Frank Floccari, 49, 419 Adams street, Rochester, veteran of World War I, died at 10 o'clock Friday night in the Veterans Administration Facility, Aspinwall.

He was born in Italy and was a cabinet maker by occupation. He served in the war as a private in the 162nd Infantry and was a member of St. Cecilia Roman Catholic church Sons of Italy Lodge and Walter S Roth Post, American Legion, Rochester.

Surviving are one son, Frank, Jr., and two daughters, Angeline and Marie Floccari, all at home; three sisters and his mother-in-law, Mrs Angelina Morelli.

The body was removed to the family home, where friends will be received. Funeral services will be held Tuesday morning at 9 o'clock in St. Cecilia church. Burial will be in St. Cecilia cemetery, with military honors.

Lost and Found

LOST: Gentleman's yellow gold ruby ring, Wednesday night, corner Walnut and Second streets, Beaver. Reward. Phone Beaver 781-R or return 1411 Second street.

4 18-24 inc

LOST: White gold Elgin wrist watch, probably between Beaver Cash Market and Bank St., Beaver. Finder please call Beaver 1383-W or return to 740 Bank street.

4|18-20

IN NEWS AS LAVAL FORMS PRO-AXIS VICHY CABINET

ADMIRAL DARLAN
Land, Sea, Air Chief

MARSHAL PETAIN
Chief of State

PIERRE LAVAL
Chief of Government

GENERAL BRIDOUX
Minister of War

Assuming control of Unoccupied France with the new title of "Chief of the Government," Pierre Laval, ardent pro-Nazi, has organized a pro-Axis cabinet which was believed to include General Bridoux, as war minister and Pierre Cathala as finance minister. Laval's cabinet succeeds that of Admiral Jean Francois Darlan who now assumes the new post of chief of French land, sea and air forces. Though retaining the rank of "Chief of State," aging Marshal Henri Petain is reduced to the status of the figure-head presidents of pre-armistice France. Laval, in addition to his office as chief of the government, has also assumed the portfolios of foreign affairs, interior and propaganda.

PIERRE CATHALA
Minister of Finance

Relief Payments In County Show Slight Decline This Week

Payments Total $1,941, State Treasurer Reports; Total Payments Are $41,832

Direct relief payments made to needy Beaver Countains during the week ended today show a decrease of $77 from those of the previous week, according to State Treasurer G. Harold Wagner.

Payments for the week totaled $1,941 which was $10,744 lower than those of the comparable week of last year. Current payments required 1,485 fewer checks than those of a year ago.

Payments by the Bureau of Assistance Disbursements in the State Treasury Department follows: Current week—$1,941, made with 470 checks; previous week—$2,018, made with 486 checks; comparable week 1941—$12,685, made with 1955 checks.

TOTAL PAYMENTS $41,832

At the same time, Treasurer Wagner announced total payments of $41,832 for all types of categorical assistance—that is, Old Age Assistance, Aid to Dependent Children,

(Continued on Page Eight)

County Fire Chiefs To Meet Sunday Evening

Reports on activities pertaining to the auxiliary firemen's work in the Civilian Defense program are to be submitted Sunday evening at the monthly meeting of the Beaver County Fire Chiefs' Association in the White Township fire station.

Geneva Speaker

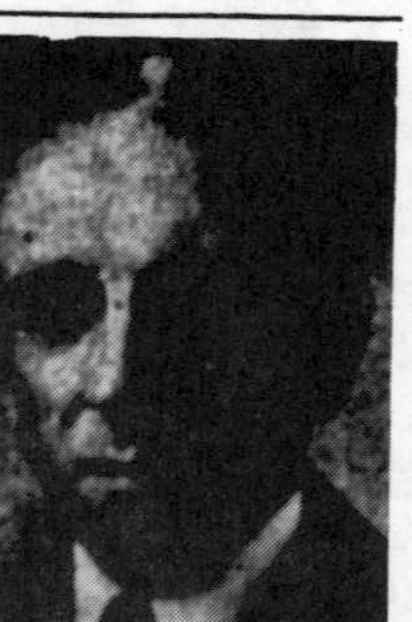

Dr. John G. Bowman

The principal address at the annual Commencement of Geneva College on May 19 will be given by Dr. John G. Bowman, Chancellor of the University of Pittsburgh.

Rochester Boy Enters Hospital For Tenth Operation In 4 Years

Oliver Buck, Jr., 14, son of Mr. and Mrs. Oliver Buck, Rochester, entered St. Francis hospital, Pittsburgh, on Thursday for the tenth operation he has undergone in the past four years.

The boy will undergo an operation Monday on his left hand as the result of a compound fracture of the arm suffered when he fell four years ago.

His younger sister, Nancy Lee, who left a few days ago to visit her uncle and aunt, Mr. and Mrs. John Glew, Aliquippa, is ill from pneumonia.

House Committee To Start Next Week On Writing Revenue Bill

New Bill May Include Sales Tax And Modified Corporation Levies

By the United Press

WASHINGTON, April 18.—The House ways and means committee begins next week to write the 1942 war revenue bill—slated to total at least $7,600,000,000, possibly including a general sales tax and modified corporation levies.

The committee completed nearly seven weeks of public hearings on the tax program late yesterday. It plans to study the thousands of pages of testimony from administration officials and special interests during executive sessions that are to start next Wednesday and last from six weeks to two months.

Later the committee is expected to take up President Roosevelt's recommendation for increasing social security payroll taxes by another $2,000,000,000.

There also is a possibility that when the revenue bill reaches the

(Continued on Page Eight)

Civil Service Law For Police Upheld

By the United Press

PITTSBURGH, April 18 — The state law establishing civil service protection for police officers in boroughs and first-class townships was declared constitutional today, according to an opinion by Common Pleas Judge John J. Kennedy.

The opinion was handed down on a petition by council members and Burgess John H. Bragdon of Bellevue, asking a declaratory judgment on the Civil Service Act of last June 5. The Bellevue Fraternal Order of Police lodge and three civil service commission members were named defendants in the action.

The petition charged the act was class legislation and therefore unconstitutional because it does not apply to municipalities having less than three policemen.

Annual Legion Essay Contest Outlined At Committee Meeting

Monthly Meeting Of County Legion Committee Held Friday In Midland

The annual Legion essay contest for high school seniors was outlined Friday evening at the monthly meeting of the Beaver County American Legion Committee in the Midland borough building.

District Attorney Robert E. McCreary, Monaca, outlined plans for the contest, details of which are to be sent to all high schools in the near future. The contest winner is to receive a four-year scholarship at the Unversity of Pittsburgh.

C. C. Sweesey, New Castle, outlined plans for the National Commander's banquet to be held Wednesday evening in the Consistory

(Continued on Page Eight)

Beaver Presbytery To Meet Next Tuesday

The annual Spring meeting of the Beaver Presbytery is to be held at nine o'clock Tuesday morning, April 21, in the New Brighton Presbyterian church.

NEW PASTOR OF FREEDOM CHURCH RECENTLY RETURNED FROM INDIA

Rev. Harold E. Buell, former missionary-teacher recently returned from Lucknow, India, has been appointed by Bishop James H. Straughn of the Pittsburgh Conference, Methodist church, to serve as pastor of the Freedom and Conway Methodist churches. His appointment becomes effective this month in the Freedom church and May 1 in the Conway church. Rev. Buell has occupied the pulpit of the Freedom church the past two Sundays He is moving today from Pittsburgh and will occupy the church parsonage in Parkway.

He succeeds Rev. Charles D. Beatty as pastor of the two churches Rev. Beatty is now serving as a chaplain in the United States Navy and, according to the last word received by former parishioners here, he is at Norfolk, Va., and his wife and little daughter, Carolin Virginia, are with him there.

Rev. Buell, 26, got out of India and the Far East just three days ahead of the Jap bombings and took a southernly route on a Dutch cargo vessel home. In the Antarctic seas, little traveled by merchant marine, or navy boats, his ship zigzagged to America, taking nine weeks.

He was almost half-way home when the Nipponese started dropping bombs in Pearl Harbor, and other Pacific areas. From then on, his voyage on a small, 10-000-ton Dutch cargo vessel became a nightmare of anxiety—sleepless nights,

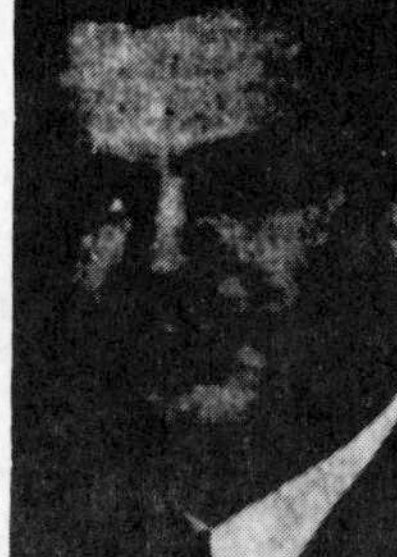

REV. H. E. BUELL

watchful days spent in constant fear of attack.

A graduate of Pitt, Boston Uni-

(Continued on Page Eight)

U. S. AND FRENCH RELATIONS NEAR BREAKING POINT

American Policy Toward Laval Government Maintained On Hour-To-Hour Basis

Diplomatic Relations To Be Continued For Time Being Despite Strain

By the United Press

WASHINGTON, April 18 — The American policy toward the new government of France was developing today on an hour-to-hour basis to offer quick counter-strokes to any threat against the United Nations which might spring from Pierre Laval's pro-German activities.

The United States already has expressed its sharp disapproval of Laval by recalling Ambassador William D. Leahy and informing the French Ambassador here in strong terms that it was "notorious" that German authorities had influenced a recent communication from Vichy.

Leahy's recall—coming as collaborationist Laval took over reins of the French government from aged Marshal Henri Philippe Petain—brought relations between the two traditionally friendly nations to the worst impasse in 150 years—but not to a complete rupture.

The United States will continue to maintain diplomatic relations for the time being, because of considerations of the gravest political and military importance. But it will not lend the dignity of an ambassador's presence in Vichy.

U. S. ON GUARD

If Laval swings France or the French fleet into any open alignment with the Axis, the American diplomatic mission in France will be recalled immediately.

In the meantime the United Press, through its observers at various points in France and French possessions, will be on guard against any overt or hidden hostility. Places of particular strategic importance are French North Africa and the French possessions in the Western Hemisphere.

One of the primary objectives in maintaining relations with Vichy after the fall of France in 1940 has been to sustain and encourage the French people against the collaborationists and the Axis dictators who are attempting the subjugation of the whole French population.

A severance of those relations now, it was felt, would have a dispiriting effect upon the French people who are giving evidence of repugnance for all Laval represents. Any action by this government which would weaken the will of the French people to resist, or discourage their aspirations for liberation, would also weaken the cause of the United Nations.

LAVAL VS. DARLAN

If Germany is attempting to force a break between Vichy and the United States because of the advantages of isolating the French people from contact with their potential liberators, the Nazis may cause Laval to recall Gaston Henry-Haye, French Ambassador here since the late summer of 1940.

The new line-up in France may

(Continued on Page Eight)

Promoted To Captain

Lieutenant William G. Franz, (above), son of Mr. and Mrs. W. Elmer Franz, Fourth avenue, Freedom, has been promoted to Captain in the United States Army, according to word received here by his parents. Captain Franz is in the chemical warfare service at Edgewood Arsenal, Md. He has been in service since last October.

Dr. R. B. Dawson, 74, Prominent Physician, Died Friday Evening

Well-Known Rural Physician Succumbed In East Liverpool City Hospital

Dr. R. B. Dawson, 74, is dead at his home at Fairview, Ohio township. He died in the City hospital, East Liverpool, at 8:45 last night, of complications, following a ten days illness.

Funeral services are to be held in the home Monday at two o'clock. Friends will be received in the home beginning this evening. Interment will be in Sylvania Hills Memorial Park.

Dr. Dawson, a general practitioner, had practiced at Fairview for forty-seven years. He knew well the country physicians experiences in the horse and buggy days. He was a member of the pioneer Dawson family, widely known for more than a century in the eastern part of the county. He was a graduate of Western Reserve Medical College at Cleveland.

Survivors include a son, Robert D. Dawson, of Fairview; two grandchildren, and a sister, Mrs. Flora Taylor, of East Rochester, Ohio.

He was a member of the Reformed Presbyterian church, at Fairview, and of the Beaver County Medical Society. For nearly half a century he was widely known as one of the most active country physicians in Western Pennsylvania.

Striking Students To Return To School

By the United Press

PITTSBURGH, April 18—Brentwood school students who went on strike in protest to the dismissal of O. H. English, formerly of Ambridge, as supervising principal planned today to return to classes on Monday following an appeal from English to end their walkout.

The high school and grade school students voted last night to go back to school on Monday and Tuesday, but warned they would resume their strike Wednesday unless the school board decides on favorable action at a meeting next Tuesday night.

English, whose dismissal last Tuesday by a four-to-three vote of the school board prompted the strike, appealed from his hospital bed in Elmira, N. Y., where he underwent an appendicitis operation, that the walkout be called off.

A meeting has been scheduled in the high school auditorium for next Tuesday night when the four board members who voted for English's removal will be asked to explain their vote. The three dissenting members resigned in protest.

TO CALL COUGHLIN

WASHINGTON, April 18—Father Charles E. Coughlin, founder of the magazine "Social Justice," which was banned from the mails as "seditious" and "non-mailable", probably will be called to testify before a Federal grand jury here, it was learned today. Attorney General Francis Biddle disclosed yesterday that the grand jury will begin an investigation of the publication next week.

TOYKO, YOKOHAMA AND KOBE RAIDED; BIG FIRES STARTED

By the United Press

JAPAN—American bombers attack Tokyo, Kobe, Yokohama and Nagoya in surprise blows at Japanese war centers; first raid on enemy homeland starts fires in flimsy, crowded industrial and shipping areas Nine planes reported shot down.

AUSTRALIA—Allied bombers again attack Japanese invasion base at Koepang; MacArthur, with new instructions, creating supreme staff for United Nations

BURMA—U S. flying fortresses batter Japanese reinforcements at Rangoon; enemy offensive continues without important change in Central Burma.

GERMANY—British bombers in daring low-level attack bomb vital German submarine engine factory at Augsburg, only 110 miles from Hitler's mountain retreat; new attacks on Hamburg, St. Nazaire, Lorient and other bases on Nazi-held European coast.

RUSSIA—Red army reports break through and capture of number of towns on Karelian (Finnish) front; Russian pincers pressed deeper into Smolensk front possibly menacing city of Smolensk.

American bomber squadrons carried the war to Japan with surprise raids on Tokyo and three other great enemy war centers today in the boldest of many United Nations aerial blows from France to the tropical Islands of the Southwest Pacific.

The glow of fires—greatest fear of Japanese in crowded, flimsy cities—spread in the wake of high explosives crashing down on Tokyo (7,000,000 population), Yokohama (650,000 population), Kobe (800,000 population) and the vast naval-industrial city of Nagoya (990,000 population).

News of the attack came only from Radio Tokyo immediately after the five-hour aerial attack which was launched from many directions and which the Japanese said resulted in destruction of nine attacking planes, possibly from aircraft carriers but perhaps flown from distant bases in China. The Japanese obviously didn't know where the attackers were based.

RANGOON ATTACKED

But the sensational aerial onslaught was only part of a world-wide picture of growing Allied aerial armadas in action.

At New Delhi, it was disclosed that United States flying fortresses under Brig. Gen. Lewis H. Brereton

(Continued on Page Eight)

Seventy-Six Tires Stolen From Conway Garage Last Night

Loss Of 46 New Tires And 30 Used Ones Is Estimated At $2,000

Seventy-six automobile tires valued at about $2,000 were stolen from the Snyder Garage, Conway, last night, by thieves who smashed a rear window and jimmied a door to gain entrance to the sales room where the tires were stored.

The robbery was discovered by A R. C. H. (Red) Snyder, proprietor at seven o'clock this morning when he opened the garage. He reported immediately to Police Chief Frank D. Whelen of Conway, who called state police.

The thieves, police say, hauled the tires away in a truck after carrying them out a rear door. The tires were nearly all of the popular 6:00 and 6:50 sizes and included 46 new tires and 30 used tires.

SOME IGNORED

Some odd makes and retreads were ignored by the robbers. Serial numbers of the new tires were not available, it was said.

State Police said this was the biggest theft of tires that has occured in Beaver county since rationing made bootlegging of tires a dangerous but profitable racket.

Production Of United Nations Exceeds Axis

By the United Press

NEW YORK, April 18.—Donald M. Nelson, chairman of the War Production Board, said last night that the combined war production of the United States, Britain and Russia now exceeds that of the Axis.

"It is safe to predict" that by the end of this year, the Allies will have overcome the reserve that Japan began building in 1930, and that Germany began laying up in 1933. From then on, the Allies will have their enemies "at an increasing disadvantage."

Nelson spoke at the annual dinner of the American Society of Newspaper Editors.

He said there still was no room for over-optimism; it was not enough to top Axis production, all must work harder and harder until the enemy's "enormous" reserve, plus the booty he has seized from his victims, is overcome.

He said the American standard of living must be substantially lower for the duration, because materials for civilian consumption would not be left from production.

Bids For Bridge Go Down Instead Of Up

Beaver County Commissioners are losing ground in their effort to dispose of the old Sharon bridge over the Beaver river at Junction Park as scrap iron.

Several weeks ago an advertisement brought only two bids from scrap dealers, and they were rejected as being too low. One dealer offered about $1,100 for the structure and remove it.

The commissioners decided to re-advertise the bridge, but only one proposal was on hand the morning at the time set for opening bids. The lone bid was by Charles Zubik, Pittsburgh, who offered a mere $606. The commissioners took no action regarding the bid today.

Containing at least 150 tons of heavy scrap, the bridge would be worth probably $3,000 laid down in the mill yard at the price fixed by Federal regulations, but the shortage of labor and the cost of removing the steel and transporting it to the mill has kept the bids down, it is believed. One bidder, in response to the first advertisement, wanted a substantial sum plus the steel for removing the bridge.

Welfare Group To Have Program Here

The education committee of the Andrew Tanner Welfare Association of Beaver County will sponsor a program Sunday, April 19, in the Beaver County Court House, at 2:30 p. m., as a climax to the Race Relations Conference held at the Court House today.

The theme will center around the findings of the Race Relations Conference, together with the work the Andrew Tanner Welfare Association is doing among the Negroes of the county, and patriotic unity.

The chairman of the education committee, Charles Peyton, Beaver Falls, will preside. The guest speakers will be J. K. Lott, assistant executive director, Pennsylvania State Temporary Commission on Conditions of the Urban Colored Population," who will give a summary of the conference; Rev. S. S. Booker, secretary, West Federal Street, Y. M. C. A., Youngstown, O., and Francis Farmer, Rochester.

Vocal selections will be given by Mrs. Virginia Sweet, Miss Helen James and William Hicks.

MacARTHUR IN COMMAND

GEN. MacARTHUR'S HEADQUARTERS, Australia, April 18—All United Nations now are in complete agreement on Gen. Douglas MacArthur's Southwest Pacific command and it can be anticipated that formal organization of his area will be effected in the immediate future, it was announced today.

LEND-LEASE AID GROWS

WASHINGTON, April 18. — The White House disclosed today that lend-lease aid amounted to more than $3,000,000,000 by the end of March and that war supplies sent to Russia last month were 2 1-2 times as great as those sent in February.

Three Local Hearings Before Liquor Board

The Liquor Control Board held hearings today at Pittsburgh on three citations against three Beaver County licensees.

Angelina Cutrona, proprietor of the Frank Cutrona Company, Rochester beer distributor, was charged with selling beer on credit and falsification of records; the Order of Sons of Italy, Rochester, was charged with purchasing beer on credit, selling to non-members, keeping improper records; Gus Markis, proprietor of the Dairy Lunch, Aliquippa, was charged with maintaining a gambling device.

An auditor o fthe board testified that in 82 instances, from January 10, 1941, to February 10, 1942, checks paying for beer delivered to the Sons of Italy were deposited by the Cutrona company from four to 19 days after delivery of the beer.

The lodge was charged with paying with checks dated later than delivery of the beer. Ben Colamarino, treasurer of the House committee, and Sam Cutrona, chairman of the lodge's House committee, explained that the checks were dated after delivery of the beer because they had to sign the checks and were not always available to do so.

Mrs. Mamie Martino, daughter of Mrs. Cutrona and manager of the distributing concern, denied that she extended credit to the lodge. She said she did not think she violated the law. "I got the checks as soon as I could," she testified.

Simon Donatell, club steward, testified that he did not recall selling drinks to two liquor board agents. He explained, however, the date the agents said they visited the clubroom was Columbus Day and a celebration was in progress.

In the Markis hearings, State Motor Policeman Herman Perstine testified that he played a nickel slot machine in the restaurant last February 6 and was paid off in cash when he "hit" for five games. He said he arrested Markis who pleaded no defense last March 21 and was fined $100 and costs in the county court.

Legion Drum Corps To March In Parade

At the weekly meeting of Walter S. Roth Post, American Legion, Rochester, Monday evening, it was decided that the post drum and bugle corps participate in the "Navy Week" parade in Ambridge, Sunday evening, May 17, at 7 o'clock.

Further plans also were made for participation in the Memorial Day celebration, May 30, and the Elks' Flag Day celebration, June 14, in Rochester. Albert Howe, commander, presided.

Tommy Yarosz Wins Bout At Louisville

Tommy Yarosz, Monaca middleweight boxer, outpointed Gene Luker of Cincinnati in a ten-round bout at Louisville, Ky., last night.

The bout was co-featured with fight in which Mike Raffa, of Fort Knox, scored a second round knockout over Joe Marinelli of Dayton. Yarosz weighed 158 and Luker 162.

Registration Opens

(Continued from Page One)

totaling $8,986,126 were collected on 224,653,173 gallons.

A breakdown of motor vehicle registration figures for 1941 showed 1,252,172 passenger automobile and 8,285 motorcycle owners in the ration area. Beyond the line of demarcation in the exempted region were 777,748 auto and 5,140 motorcycle operators. Busses, trucks and other commercial vehicles clearly identifiable will not need cards.

The majority of the registrants were expected to get "A" cards, good for 21 gallons of gasoline during the 47-day period from May 15 to July 1, when a permanent rationing system will be set up. Card "B-1" will be good for 33 gallons, "B-2" for 45, and "B-3" for 57. The "X" cards —for unlimited purchases—will go to doctors, government officials and others in essential services.

MILLIONS TO REGISTER

WASHINGTON, May 12—Approximately 8,500,000 motorists in 17 eastern states begin registering today for the gasoline rationing program which starts Friday.

Registration, which will determine how much gasoline a week a motorist will be permitted to buy, continues tomorrow and Thursday. Beginning Friday a ration card as well as money will be necessary on the eastern seaboard to buy gasoline for passenger cars.

Meanwhile, transportation officials are studying all possibilities for increasing the amount of oil moved into the shortage area. The Office of Defense Transportation is considering the use of the Atlantic intracoastal waterway. Today a Senate commerce subcommittee begins an investigation of all inland waterways for the transportation of oil and other commodities.

An ODT official said the chief difficulty in obtaining gasoline over the Atlantic coastal waterway was to find oil-carrying barges. Some transportation experts have suggested that wooden barges could be built.

The Long and The

(Continued from page one)

members. Dancing will be from 9 to 12 o'clock.

Capt. Conrad has announced that the Curtiss - Wright Corporation, through its local plant management, will present the Corps with its national colors at a ceremony to be held either on Memorial Day, or on Flag Day, June 14th. Capt. Conrad is the organizer of the Corps.

At the last regular drill the Corps members elected First Sergeant Harry Hollenbaugh to be its First Lieutenant; Sergt. Harold Price has been promoted to First Sergeant; Corp. Joseph Steuger to Technical Sergeant, Privates Paul Steuger and Gerry Laughlin to Corporals.

Some Members Of Beaver Valley Military Training Corps

Front row, kneeling, left to right—Capt. Charles L. Conrad, Tech. Sergt. Joseph Steuger, Corp. Gerry Laughlin, Joseph Kohlman, Fred Koble, Jr., Robert Weber, William Wilson; rear row, standing—First Lieut. Paul E. Hollenbaugh, Corp. Paul Steuger, John Boris, Jack Martin, Gerald R. Shannon, Robert France, Paul Lambert, First Sergt. Earl Price.

WAR BULLETINS

By the United Press

CHINESE MAKE RAIDS

CHUNGKING, May 12—Chinese guerrilla forces have killed 310 more Japanese in a series of raids over a wide area, the official Central News Agency reported today.

REDS CHECK ADVANCE

LONDON, May 12—Axis armies attempting to start an offensive through the Crimea toward the Caucasian oil fields appeared today to have been smashed back at most points with severe losses by what the Berlin radio called "numerically superior" Red army forces.

JAP PLANES DESTROYED

AN ADVANCED ALLIED BASE, Southwest Pacific, May 12—Forty-one Japanese planes have been destroyed and 200 Japanese fliers have been killed since the Japanese began raiding this northwestern Australia area, it was estimated today. Destroyed planes include 21 bombers and 13 fighters shot down by American interceptor planes.

BLACKOUT ORDERED

SAN DIEGO, Cal., May 12— A five-minute blackout was ordered in San Diego last night because of the presence of an unidentified plane, which later was identified as friendly. The western defense command announced that radio stations were silenced at 11:10 p. m.

PASSENGER SHIP SUNK

VICHY, France, May 12—Paris newspapers reported today that the small passenger ship Albatross, returning to the French mainland from Oleron Island off La Rochelle, struck a mine and sank with its 30 passengers and crewmen.

BRITISH REVEAL LOSSES

LONDON, May 12.—British Empire forces throughout the war have suffered the loss of 183,500 men, an official statement disclosed today. The losses included: Killed—48,973; wounded 46,363; taken prisoner, 58,458; missing, 29,756.

PRISONERS RECAPTURED

LONDON, May 12.—Seven of 10 Italian war prisoners, aviators and seamen, who escaped from a middle England prison camp, have been recaptured, it was announced today.

ALLIES CLAIM BIG TOLL

LONDON, May 12. — Allied air forces, taking an ever-increasing toll of Axis aerial strength, have destroyed or damaged 1,363 enemy planes during the past 10 days, a compilation of United Nations communiques disclosed today.

Germans Launch

(Continued from page one)

mechanized invasion column from the border of Yunnan Province above Mandalay and Lashio, forcing a 50-mile enemy retreat from the west bank of the Salween river to the Yunnan town of Mangshih.

The Japanese still held a foothold on Chinese territory with heavy fighting reported in the Chefang and Mangshih sectors more than 25 miles inside the Yunnan-Burmese border.

About 5,000 Japanese troops were in Yunnan Province along the Burma Road and 15,000 others were along the Salween Valley in northern and Central Burma. The Chinese were attempting to cut off the entire Japanese column along the Salween by attacking Lashio and also to trap an enemy force which moved northwest from Lashio to Myitkyina, 195 miles northward.

The Japanese, meanwhile, sought to encircle the Chinese forces between Mandalay and Myitkyina and, according to a Chinese spokesman in Chungking, the outcome of the battle of Burma seemed to depend upon the outcome of these Chinese and Japanese encirclement operations.

MORE JAP SHIPS SUNK

The toll of Japanese ships sunk or damaged in the battle of the Coral Sea and Allied "mopping up" attacks rose to 24 today when Gen. Douglas MacArthur announced that U. S. bombers had sunk or damaged two more enemy transports and a tanker at Japanese invasion islands off northeast Australia.

The two transports, undoubtedly loaded with troops, were bombed off Kessa in the Solomon Islands. The tanker was hit during a bombing of a Japanese seaplane base at Deboyne Island in the Louisiades on the southeastern tip of New Guinea.

There were indications that a strong Japanese fleet might be lurking off northeastern Australia ready to resume the battle which began on May 4, inasmuch as Japan is attaching great importance to the naval-air struggle.

The Tokyo radio revealed that Japan's foremost Admiral, Isoroqu Yamamoto, onetime naval attache in Washington and a leading exponent of naval air power, led the Japanese forces in the battle. He is commander in chief of Japan's combined fleets.

VIOLENCE IN PARIS

New outbreaks of anti-Nazi sabotage and violence in Nazi-held Paris piled up new troubles for Pierre Laval and his Vichy government and for Gestapo Chief Reinhard Heydrich who was sent to Paris in an effort to stamp out the troubles.

Six Paris hotels and restaurants requisitioned by the Germans were bombed, following a dynamiting of the Bourges radio station in Paris. It is the strongest Nazi-operated transmitter of the Nazi-held capital.

After the bombings, which included the Ambassador Hotel on the Boulevard Haussman in the heart of the City, the Germans isolated entire areas and suspended subway service in an effort to trap those responsible.

A German freight train was derailed near Parthenay by a mine.

The new outbreaks undoubtedly will result in more Frenchmen dying before German firing squads, which are estimated to have killed between 100 and 200 Frenchmen in the past week or 10 days.

SOCIETY

Rochester C. D. Of A. Names Officers, Plans For 25th Anniversary Dinner

Officers were elected and plans were made for the 25th anniversary of Court St. Rita, Catholic Daughters of America, at the monthly meeting held in the Knights of Columbus Home, Rochester, Monday evening. Mrs. Charles J. Renner, Monaca, was elected Grand Regent.

MRS. C. J. RENNER

Other officers are: Vice-regent, Mrs. Mary Boyle; prophet, Miss Grace Heyman; monitor, Mrs. Jean Dugan; sentinel, Mrs. Anna Vinceguerra; treasurer, Mrs. Sadie Smith; financial secretary, Mrs. Marie Grandey; historian, Mrs. Clara Straile; lecturer, Mrs. Merse F. Kuhn; organist, Miss Francis Heyman. Trustees—Mrs. Mayme Bruehl, Mrs. Margaret A. Joyce, Mrs. Margaret Goedeker, Mrs. Mary Malloy.

The anniversary dinner will be held the evening of May 25, in Beaver. Reservations are being received by Mrs. Dugan, Mrs. Kuhn and Mrs. Malloy. Cards followed with six tables of "500" in play. Awards were presented Miss Marie Devine, Mrs. Christine Genevie, Mrs. Mary Wright, and the door award to Mrs. Dugan.

Mrs. Kuhn was chairman of the committee and her aides were Mrs. Smith, Miss Heyman and Mrs. Bruehl.

In the absence of the retiring regent, Mrs. S. R. Stuehling, Monaca, Mrs. Mary Boyle, vice regent, presided.

County Gold Star Mothers And Fathers Honored At Dinner By Purple Heart Group

Seated at tables in the social auditorium of the New Brighton Presbyterian church, Monday evening, sixteen Beaver County Gold Star mothers and fathers were honor guests at the annual Mother's Day dinner sponsored by the Ladies' Auxiliary to Beaver County Chapter, Military Order of the Purple Heart.

As the guests assembled at the table, Mrs. Mildred E. Carey, Rochester, past president, softly played appropriate music. Decorations at the table in the traditional colors of both groups—purple and gold—were effectively carried out.

A huge bowl of flowers centered the festive board. The invocation was voiced by Mrs. Ferd Buquo, Ellwood City, chaplain of the Gold Star Mothers organizations. The Auxiliary presented each guest a gift.

Mrs. Kenneth C. Sands, Rochester, led in the pledge of allegiance to the flag and later in the singing of the "Star Spangled Banner." Mrs. Dora Beitsch Carothers, Beaver Falls, sang, accompanied by Mrs. E. E. Woods, Beaver Falls. Mrs. Carothers later led in group singing. Several humorous readings were given by Miss Lois Reda and Miss June Glover, Beaver Falls.

Greetings were extended the honor guests by Adrian W. McGee, Beaver Falls, commander of the Beaver County Chapter of the Purple Heart, followed by brief remarks by Kenneth C. Sands, Rochester, vice-commander, and Past Commander Albert Thumm, Beaver Falls. Mrs. Ella Hennon, vice-president of the Gold Star Mothers, extended greetings for the mothers. Mrs. Ada Bevington, a Gold Star mother of Beaver, also spoke. Mrs. Harry Brewer, New Brighton, a member, was absent because of illness. Ferd Buquo, Ellwood City, spoke for the Gold Star fathers.

The event marked a dual celebration for Mrs. Alice Engle, Girard, O., formerly of New Brighton, one of the Gold Star Mothers, who celebrated her 80th birthday Monday, and Mrs. W. J. Veal, one of the older Gold Star mothers, who celebrated her birthday on Sunday.

The committee in charge of the arrangements included Mrs. Adrian W. McGee, Mrs. Dan Baker, Sr., Mrs. Robert Shaw and Mrs. Wilbur Brewer.

Hospital News

Rochester hospital: Total patients—99. A daughter was born this morning to Mr. and Mrs. Carlton Chaffee, near Beaver. Admitted—Hazel Nannah, Freedom; Mrs. Harry Steinacker, Rochester; Edgar McDowell, Wellsville, O.; Franklin Smith, Alliance, O.; Mrs. Frank Carter, Conway, and J. J. Aldridge and Theresa Palumbo, Beaver. Discharged — Norman Moxley, Frank Felkey and Rade Ejalajac, Midland; Wilmer Emerick, Rochester, and Mrs. Carmine DiPietro and Walter Yarbrough, Aliquippa.

Beaver Valley hospital: Admitted—Harry Williams, near Rochester; John A. Hays, near Beaver, and Hazel Eisenbrown, near Freedom.

FOURTEEN SEAMEN KILLED

MIAMI, Fla., May 12.—Fourteen seamen died in the flaming wreckage of a medium-sized Dutch merchant ship kindled into a "fiery torch" by two torpedoes from two Axis submarines, survivors said today.

HOLLANDERS EXECUTED

LONDON, May 12.—German occupation authorities executed 24 more Hollanders on charges of leading a secret anti-Nazi organization, bringing the total executed to 95, the Aneta news agency said today.

Plans For Combating

(Continued from Page One)

of the State Council of Cooperative Organizations, and Horst.

The meeting of the farm-milk organization chiefs representing approximately 125,000 Commonwealth farmers, like the New York City session, will be devoted chiefly to methods of thwarting Lewis' drive to sign up 3,000,000 dairy farmers in District 50 of the United Mine Workers of America.

MONOPOLY CITED

Horst emphasized that all groups mentioned "are united against" the Lewis drive. The state's dairy farmers were urged last week by C. L. Dickinson, secretary of the Free Farmers, Inc., formed by farmer foes of Lewis' move in Northeastern Pennsylvania, New York and New Jersey, to join in their fight.

"If Lewis can gather together under his leadership all the farmers of one kind in connection with a great labor organization, we could have the greatest monopoly the country has ever seen," Dickinson claimed.

Dairy farmer organization officials were believed spurred by findings of a nationwide poll which purportedly showed farmers are the least sympathetic to the labor union movement.

Meantime, the UMW's District 50 regional directors pushed organization work and denounced attacks against the Lewis move as "tirades from the milk trusts and not the dairy farmers." A drive to organize Western Pennsylvania dairy farmers will be started Thursday at a meeting of the United Farmers of America.

Budget Adopted

(Continued from Page One)

girls' dressing room in the high school building.

TO ADMINISTER TOXOID

Dr. Edward Davis, school physician, will administer diphtheria toxoid on Wednesday to more than 190 school children who have received parental permission.

Wellsville, O., high school will be added to the 1942 football schedule, rounding out a ten-game schedule. The game will be played Friday night, November 13, at Rochester. If a two-year contract is effected, the 1943 game will be played at Wellsville.

The report of Superintendent Robert Barner was heard and current bills were approved and ordered paid.

Scrap Metal Collection Totaled 9,275 Pounds

The amount of scrap metal collected in Monaca Friday and Saturday, May 8 and 9, was 9,275 pounds, it was reported today by Borough Secretary Guy Grater. The metal was sold to a junk dealer and the proceeds go to the Monaca Civilian Defense Council to be used for defense purposes.

Ernie Pelaia Wins Bout In Chicago

Ernie Pelaia, Monaca, boxer, punched out a split decision over Bill Parsons, a hard-hitting colored boy, at Marigold Gardens, Chicago, last night.

Parsons, who subbed for Jimmy Pierce of Milwaukee, proved a tough opponent, Pelaia advised his manager, Walter Miller of Beaver Falls, in a telegram today.

Pelaia probably will remain in Chicago this week, and expects to box in the same ring next Monday night.

ORDER POSTPONED

WASHINGTON, May 12. — The Office of Defense Transportation today postponed until June 1 its order restricting to one a day local deliveries by newspapers, dairies, laundries and other establishments. The order had been scheduled to become effective May fifteenth.

CHURCH GROUP TO MEET

The monthly meeting of the Hodge Band of the Beaver Presbyterian church will be held in the church parlors on Wednesday afternoon at 2:30 o'clock.

FIVE MINERS KILLED

FORT SMITH, Ark., May 12—State Mine Inspector J. W. Fitzjarrel said today that coal dust or gas probably caused an explosion which killed five miners and injured two others near here late yesterday.

DEATHS and FUNERALS

Mrs. Laura Hahnoddle

Mrs. Laura B. Hahnoddle, 69, Ohio Township, near Darlington, died at one o'clock Monday afternoon in the home of Russell Davidson, Ohio Township, after an illness of two weeks. Funeral services are to be held at 2:30 o'clock Wednesday afternoon in the Anderson funeral home, Beaver. Interment will be in Beaver Falls cemetery. Mrs. Hahnoddle was a member of Salem Presbyterian church and a past member of Rebekah Lodge, Beaver Falls. Surviving are one brother, Earl Riddle, Detroit; three sisters, Mrs. Annie Bonnett, Petersburg, O., Mrs. Dilly Pollyblank, West Pittsburgh, and Mrs. Ada Morrow, New Brighton; four nephews, S. L. Morrow, New Brighton, George Duncan, Enon, Herbert Bonnett, Detroit, and Keith Riddle, Beaver Falls, and three nieces, Grace Houston and Mildred Brownlee, Enon, and Mrs. John Frazier, Beaver.

PLATT FUNERAL

Funeral services for Forest J. Platt, 311 Ohio avenue, Rochester, who died last Friday in Magee hospital, Pittsburgh, were held Sunday afternoon in the home of his aunt, Mrs. Alice Orgill, 4377 Stanton avenue, Pittsburgh. The services were conducted by Rev. Thomas O. Fuss, pastor of Zion Evangelical church, Rochester, of which Mr. Platt was a member. He also was a member of the Board of Trustees and a teacher in the Sunday school. A number of the church members attended the funeral. Mrs. D. R. Woods, John H. Buckenheimer and Leslie Marietta of the church choir sang. Burial was in the Presbyterian cemetery, Bakerstown.

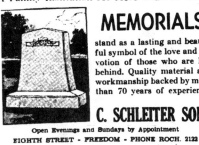

School Exhibit On Display In Beaver

The Industrial Arts Department of the Beaver high school has placed an interesting display in the window of the J. T. Anderson store, Third street. This exhibit gives a cross-sectional view of the offerings and type of work of this department.

According to present arrangements, a boy can take three years of work in either shop or mechanical drawing. The shop program consists of wood work, ornamental iron, art metal and a little machine lathe work. The mechanical drawing starts with very simple working drawings done in pencil to tracing, and blue print making.

Included in this exhibit are several of the airplane models which are being made for the Bureau of Aeronautics. Fifty such models are under construction by various boys in the high school.

The display includes: Drawings, blueprints and tracings, hack saws, center punches, hammers turned on lathe, hammers made with files, pliers, metal matazine basket, flower pot holders, several different kinds of end tables, radio tables, footstools, book cases, model airplanes, coffee tables, lamps and ash stands.

This work is all under the direction and supervision of Donald Higbee, a graduate of California State Teachers College and is in his third year of teaching in Beaver high school.

House May Decide

(Continued from Page One)

was prepared to offer an amendment. He will propose that the revised pay schedule be effective for the duration of the war only, on the grounds that the Army and Navy pay schedules already are too complicated and should be overhauled completely when the war has ended.

Comdr. H. G. Hopwood, testifying before the naval affairs committee yesterday, estimated that the proposed pay increases would cost the Navy $203,000,000 in 1942.

WAR DEPT. COST HIGHER

No accurate estimate of the cost to the War Department, with its rapidly expanding forces, was available, but the military affairs committee said in its report that, based upon the strength as of last January 1, the cost would be approximately $285,000,000.

The only officers who would be granted increases in their base pay are second lieutenants in the Army and ensigns in the Navy. Each of those groups would be increased from $1,500 to $1,800 a year. Most officers would receive increased allowances for rations and rent.

The military affairs committee planned to open hearings today on a bill providing family allowances for the dependents of enlisted men. Federal Security Administrator Paul V. McNutt will testify.

The average work week for employes in manufacturing industries in this country is now 41.5 hours.

The Weather Forecast

WESTERN PENNSYLVANIA: Scattered showers and thunder storms, with mild temperature, tonight. Grass pollen count, 266.

THE DAILY TIMES

ROCHESTER-BEAVER-MONACA

FREEDOM—BRIDGEWATER—CONWAY—VANPORT—MIDLAND

Beaver County History

A large German ammunition dump north of Commercy, France, was destroyed by American Artillery, it was announced here on June 1, 1918.

ESTABLISHED APRIL 2, 1874 | BEAVER AND ROCHESTER, PA., MONDAY, JUNE, 1, 1942 | BY CARRIER 18 CENTS A WEEK—

AMERICAN PILOTS TO BOMB GERMANY

SCENES AS BEAVER COUNTY OBSERVED MEMORIAL DAY

—TIMES Photos by Bill Heyman.

Pictured at the left above are scenes from the Rochester Memorial Day parade, the top view showing the Rochester High school band with pretty Phyllis McNees, drum-majorette to the right. The center picture shows the color guard of the Rochester Cub Packs, and the two lower pictures show children of the Rochester schools who also participated in the parade, with each youngster bearing a small American flag.

Photo at right shows section of Beaver parade. Heading the delegation of employes from the Pennsylvania plant of the Curtiss-Wright Corporation, Propeller Division, who took part in the Beaver Memorial Day parade was an honor guard composed of guards Harry Kier (left), Frank McAllister (carrying flag), and William Spiers. Immediately behind them are nurses from the First Aid room and guard delegation led by Captain Philip Pastine. Small insert at lower right shows Chapel in Beaver cemetery, with Doris Irons, Beaver high school graduate this year, giving Lincoln's Gettysburg address. The insert photo at the cemetery chapel was made by Charles Schendel, a Beaver high school boy.

COLOGNE WRECKED BY BIG RAF RAID

By the United Press

United States bomber and fighting squadrons soon will join the aerial offensive against Germany, increasing threefold the fury of the RAF's great week-end assault that wrecked industrial Cologne under the impact of 6,720,000 pounds of bombs.

The Cologne attack by a fleet of 1,500 British planes, biggest in the history of aerial warfare, was revealed by the chief of the U. S. Army Air Corps, Lieut. Gen. Henry H. Arnold, and British officials to have been merely a forctaste of what is in store for Germany.

Soon a great armada of 5,000 Allied planes — United States and British—will be flying against the Reich, it was stated.

While planes staged a carnival of "victory rolls" in the sky over London, Gen. Arnold ended secrecy around the consultations which he and other U. S. war leaders have been holding in London and announced that a balance force of American bombers and fighters soon will join the attacks on Germany.

The Germans retaliated last night with an attack on ancient Canterbury, cradle of British Christianity, with a force of about 25 planes, choosing "Kultur targets" and causing heavy destruction that left homes and ancient edifices in ruins.

A heavily-censored dispatch from Canterbury indicated that the city's famous cathedral, dating back 772 years, had been wrecked and perhaps destroyed and that parts of the town were a mass of flames. Schools and hotels in the nonmilitary city also were wrecked.

PLANE LOSSES LOW

The Germans boasted that thousands of bombs had been hurled upon Canterbury in the vengeance attack and they admitted heavy damage to Cologne where it was claimed that 78 of the British raiding planes had been shot down. The British admitted the loss of 44 planes.

The loss of 44 planes was not great, however, considering the size of the armada and the damage done—seven-eighths of one of Germany's greatest cities and great Rhine port and railroad center left in blazing, broken ruins.

The British had anticipated that they might lose six per sent, or 90 planes, of their attacking force but their losses were less than three per cent whereas the Germans, on the May 10, 1941, crescendo of the blitz against London lost 6.6 per cent of a fleet of 500 planes. Other attacks during the battle of Britain cost the Germans up to 10 percent of their planes.

The Cologne attack by 1,500 bombers and fighters launched from 60 British airdromes lasted

(Continued on Page Ten)

Youngster Killed, Eight Injured In Week-End Mishaps

Lone Fatality And Six Of Injured Hurt In Automobile Accidents

One dead and eight injured was the accident toll for Beaver County for the holiday week-end. The one fatality and six of the injury cases were caused by traffic mishaps; one man lost part of a finger in a meat grinder and a woman was hurt in a fall.

Evelyn Smith, colored, four-year-old daughter of Mr. and Mrs. Percy Smith, 1933 Penn avenue extension, New Brighton, was fatally injured Friday evening when struck by an automobile at Third avenue and Twentieth street, New Brighton, according to New Brighton police.

The child reportedly ran into the path of an automobile operated by R. A. Ashcroft, near Hookstown, and the driver swerved his car to avoid striking the child and side-swiped another auto and hit the youngster, police stated today.

The girl received a fracture of the skull and a fractured shoulder and was removed to a physician's office and then to Beaver Valley hospital. She lived but a short time after the accident.

Funeral services were held this afternoon in the family home and interment was in Union cemetery, Monaca. Surviving are the parents, six sisters and four brothers, Ernestine, Alma, Etheline, Vongray, Doris Jean, Larry, Roger, Percy, Jr., and Elmer, at home, and Mrs. Gladys Scott, Canton, O.

FIVE MEN HURT

Five Pittsburghers were injured early Sunday morning in a traffic mishap while enroute to work at the Curtiss-Wright propeller plant at Beaver. The car in which they were riding swerved off the highway near the Mount Gallitzin Academy, Baden, and crashed into a utility pole.

William Moore, 21, and Richard Bryan, 21, received injuries to their backs while Albert James Duff, 19, the driver of the car, and two other passengers, Hale Korb, 26, and William Parker, 28, escaped with miscellaneous lacerations and bruises.

Duff told State Motor Police he had fallen asleep while driving. Moore and Bryan are confined to Rochester hospital today but the other three were treated and discharged.

STRUCK BY AUTO

Charles Ammon, 33, near Beaver was admitted to Rochester hospital at 12:40 o'clock Sunday morning suffering from a fracture of the leg reportedly received when struck by an automobile operated by George Ade, East Liverpool.

STOREKEEPER HURT

Joseph Hogan, near Rochester, lost the tip of the middle finger on his right hand late Friday evening when the member became caught in a meat grinder at his store in Rochester. He was treated by a physician and returned to his home. The tip of the finger was severed almost to the first joint.

INJURED IN FALL

Mrs. Hattie Kester, Marion Hill, is in Beaver Valley hospital today suffering from a fracture of the hip reportedly received late Saturday afternoon in a fall in a Beaver Falls theatre.

Two Lose Lives In Railroad Wreck

By the United Press

WASHINGTON, Pa., June 1.—Two crew members were killed and a third was critically injured late yesterday when a Pittsburgh-bound freight train left the Baltimore and Ohio Railroad tracks on a curve east of Taylortown, and plunged over a 15-foot embankment into a corn field.

The dead were Fireman Chester H. Frazier, of Glenwood, who died before rescuers could extricate him from the cab; and Engineer G. H. Van Buren, of Hazelwood, who died early today in Washington Hospital.

Brakeman George Walden, 27, of Alabama City, Ala., suffered severe burns and lacerations and was reported in critical condition in Washington Hospital.

The three crew members were buried in tons of earth scooped up by the locomotive as it plunged over the hillside. Frazier died as he struggled to shut off the escaping steam in the locomotive cab. The other two were buried in the loose dirt and John Dague and neighbors ignored the steam and used their bare hands to remove Van Buren and Walden.

A total of 16 freight cars were derailed and scrap steel and oil were strewn over the roadbed. Unofficial estimates placed the damage at $100,000.

Further Plans Are Made For Flag Day Parade In Rochester

Monster Celebration Planned By Elks Lodges Of 26th District June 14

Further arrangements for the county-wide observance of Flag Day, Sunday, June 14, in Rochester by Elks lodges of the 26th District, were made when representatives of all organizations planning to participate met in the Rochester Elks' Home, with Charles S. Edwards, general chairman, presiding.

The District comprises Beaver, Butler and Lawrence counties. Elks lodges of Rochester, Beaver Falls, Ellwood City, Ambridge, Aliquippa and Coraopolis are sponsoring the holiday observance, which is expected to be the greatest celebration of Flag Day ever held in the 26th District.

The program will begin with a big parade at 2:30 p. m. It is expected 19 bands and drum corps will furnish music.

FLAG DISPLAY ASKED

Negotiations are under way to bring some U. S. Army mechanized forces to Rochester to participate in the parade. The committee asks that all citizens display the American Flag at their homes and business places and anyone not having a flag can get one at the Rochester Elks' Home at cost.

Judge W. H. Dietrich, Allegheny county, will be the principal speaker. The program will be completed at the next meeting, Friday, June 12, at which all organizations will be represented to receive final instructions.

A radio station will pbroadcast the ceremonies at the Rochester High School athletic field, where the public may gather for the event.

The committee is asking for 100 per cent cooperation of borough councils, police and other organizations and citizens of the county in the celebration of Flag Day, next Sunday.

PARADES, SPEAKING FEATURE MEMORIAL DAY OBSERVANCE

With no more Civil War veterans surviving here to take part in the exercises as in former years, Beaver County residents observed Memorial Day on Saturday with fine parades and excellent programs of speaking.

American Legion and Veterans of Foreign Wars posts and their auxiliary units, along with community memorial associations, were in charge of the observance in the various Valley towns.

Except in the Ambridge-Aliquippa district, rain which fell in the early afternoon failed to mar the local programs, which were concluded before the downpour.

Although war industries worked as usual, most business houses, banks, offices and the court house were closed for the holiday. Swimming pools opened for the season, baseball games and golf matches were played and numerous family dinners and picnics were held in the county.

Impressive Service Is Held In Junction City

Memorial Day was observed in traditional manner in Rochester Saturday morning, when hundreds of people congregated along the streets and in the central park to witness the parade and hear the fine program arranged by the Rochester United Memorial Association. The parade included representations from many of the local organizations, with two musical units—the Rochester high school band and Walter S. Roth Post drum and bugle corps.

The main speaker at the park ceremonies was Bernard Regner, of the Pittsburgh Chamber of Commerce, who for 19 years was a correspondent for a Chicago newspaper in Paris.

He said, "If we want to win this war, and we are going to win it, we must work, maintain discipline and, in addition to patriotic faith, we must have religious faith. France did not work and lacked faith in the cause and was defeated. Germany worked and has patriotic faith in

(Continued on Page Ten)

Ambridge Man Dies Suddenly At Work

Stricken ill while at work in the printing shop of the Ambridge Citizen Printing and Publishing Company, Ambridge, this morning, John Goerman, Economy Township, died at 8:20 o'clock from a heart attack shortly after he was removed to a nearby physician's office for treatment.

Mr. Goerman, son of the late Henry Lee and Sarah Schwalm Goerman, was well-known in valley printing circles. The body was removed to the O'Donnell funeral home, Ambridge, where services are to be held Thursday.

Barrymore Funeral To Be Held Tuesday

HOLLYWOOD, June 1.—John Barrymore's body lay in state today to be viewed by intimate friends who will attend private funeral services tomorrow at Calvary cemetery.

Barrymore's family asked that there be no public view of the body and invited only friends and relatives to the funeral services.

Pallbearers will be John Decker, the artist; Gene Fowler, the novelist, producer E. J. Mannix, actor W. C. Fields, C. J. Brider and Stanley Campbell.

Honorary pallbearbers will include Edward Sheldon, Charles MacArthur, Ben Hecht, Roland Young, Thomas Mitchell, Alan Mowbray, Arthur Hopkins, George M. Cohan, Herbert Bayward Swope and Bramwell Fletcher.

County Students Get Pitt Degrees

When the University of Pittsburgh held its second commencement excises under the accelerated program this afternoon, 535 students in graduate and professional schools received degrees.

Previously, on April 26, 648 seniors in undergraduate schools received degrees. Thus a total of 1,183 degrees have been awarded this spring.

Among the degree candidates were.- Beaver — William Reed Rowse, B. S. in Pharmacy; Ambridge—Vincent Elden Rice, Master in Letters; Virginia Rosemary Skapik, Master in Letters, Harold S. Irons, Doctor of Education; Aliquippa—John Joseph Nolan, Doctor of Medicine.

County Grand Jury Begins Session At Court House Today

John W. Hunter Of Rochester Is Named Foreman; Talesmen Summoned

With John W. Hunter, Rochester, named as foreman, the June grand jury of Beaver County convened at the courthouse this morning to begin consideration of approximately 55 cases in which District Attorney Robert E. McCreary will seek indictments.

Actual deliberations of the Grand Jury were delayed about an hour while Sheriff Charles J. O'Loughlin summoned five talesman to take the places of several persons who were excused. Only eleven of the original list of 24 persons drawn for duty were on hand when the roll was called at ten o'clock.

Bernard Walker, Tarrs, Pa. pleaded guilty to driving while intoxicated. Walker was paroled for three years on payment of the costs and a fine of $25 to the court.

ALIQUIPPAN SENTENCED

Ernest Berry, colored, Aliquippa, pleaded guilty to felonious assault and battery charges preferred by his estranged wife, Geraldine. He was sentenced to pay the costs and serve six months in jail. Police said Berry cut his wife with a razor.

In addition to the foreman, members of the grand jury are: J. F. Anderson, Ohio Twp.; W. C. Kinsley, Beaver Falls; Agnes King, New Brighton; Fred P. Noss, New Brighton; J. A. Richard, Beaver Falls; Paul E. Rosenbaum, Freedom; Emma M. Ripper, New Brighton; Lester E. Terry, South Heights; Frederick Webster, New Brighton; George Wise, North Sewickley Twp. and the following talesmen; George Hunter, Sr., Beaver; Theo H. Eckel, Bridgewater; Mrs. Joseph R. Edwards, Beaver. Mrs. Mildred Gratty, Rochester Twp., and Sidney Huffmyer, Center Twp.

Rochester Service Station Is Looted

Police are investigating a robbery that occurred Sunday night at the Schaughency Service Station, Pleasant street and Rhode Island avenue, Rochester.

Thieves gained entrance to the station by forcing open a rear window. They obtained $13 in change, a cigaret machine, battery, two home radios, one automobile radio and a spotlight.

The robbery was discovered when the station was opened this morning.

Decrease Reported In Holiday Deaths

Gasoline rationing in Eastern states and conservation of tires appeared today to have contributed to a sharp reduction of the nation's Memorial Day week-end traffic toll.

A United Press survey showed at least 73 persons were killed in Traffic accidents, 50 were drowned and 39 were killed in miscellaneous mishaps.

The Memorial Day week-end last year, however, extended over three days. Gasoline rationing curtailed driving in 17 eastern states; motorists hesitated to use their irreplaceable tires, and an increased number of workers in armament factories remained at their jobs for holiday work.

Two New State Motor Patrolmen In Beaver

Two new State Motor patrolmen, Pvts. Motily and Barger, reported at the Beaver barracks today from Butler to replace Edward Buehler and George Mazza. Buehler and Mazza are to go to Butler the latter part of the month when several patrolmen now on vacation return to duty, according to Corporal Paul Rittelmann, commanding officer at the local barracks.

Heads Woman's Club

Mrs. H. D. Washburn, (above) well-known county seat resident, has assumed her duties as the new president of the Beaver Woman's Club, succeeding Mrs. C. A. Mengel. Story on Page 10.)

Awards Presented To Brighton Twp. 8th Grade Pupils

Boys And Girls Entertained By Township P.-T.A.; Cash Prizes, Medals Presented

The eighth grade students of the Brighton Township schools were guests of the Brighton Township Parent-Teacher Association. Twenty-four of the group of thirty from the six schools were entertained at a "movie-party" at the Beaver theatre, where they saw the picture, "Dumbo", followed by a lunch at the Court House restaurant, Beaver.

Mrs. Arthur B. Clark, president of the organization, presented the three honor awards, in silver dollars, to the following students: First, $5, to LaVerne Blair, son of Mr. and Mrs. LaVerne Blair, student in the Stokes school; second, $3, to Austin Grove, son of Mr. and Mrs. Charles Grove, a student in the Barclay school, and third, $1, to Joanna Reisinger, daughter of Mr. and Mrs. Daniel M. Reisinger, a student in the Stokes school.

Medals were awarded to LaVerne Blair and Joanna Reisinger, chosen the outstanding boy and girl, by Attorney and Mrs. Sam B. Wilson, representing the Philip J. Davidson American Legion Post and Auxiliary, Beaver.

Mrs. Clark also presented the diplomas to the graduates and to each one she gave, as a gift from the PTA, an autograph book.

Rochester Man Dies Enroute To Hospital

William R. Johnston, 61, of 435 Harmony avenue, Rochester, died suddenly at 4:45 o'clock Friday afternoon while en route to Rochester hospital.

The body was removed to the Hartzel funeral home, Rochester, where friends were received and where funeral services were held at 10:30 o'clock this morning, conducted by Rev. Waldron, Episcopal minister of Bellevue. Burial was in Sylvania Hills Memorial Park.

He was born in Little Valley, N. Y. He had been a resident of Rochester the last four years and was proprietor of the Valley Roller Garden, Rochester. Surviving are: the widow, Mrs. Emma M. Johnston; one son, Joseph W. Johnston, Bellevue, and one brother, C. L. Johnston, McKees Rocks.

ELABORATE PARADE PLANNED AT BEAVER ON INDEPENDENCE DAY

Preliminary plans for the huge Beaver County defense mobilization parade to be held in Beaver on July Fourth were made Sunday at a meeting of the parade chairman, Major Frank A. Weber, Pennsylvania Reserve Defense Corps, of Beaver Falls, with members of his committee at the Court House assembly room.

About a dozen men representing several Beaver Valley communities were present, and heartily endorsed the general parade plans outlined by Chairman Weber.

Arrangements were made for another meeting next Sunday afternoon at the court house in conjunction with the semi-monthly meeting of the executive committee of the County Defense Council.

In outlining tentative plans for the parade and program Major Weber declared every effort would be made to make the affair the biggest and most elaborate of its kind ever staged in the Beaver Valley.

PLAN TOWN UNITS

The parade plan adopted was to have each town in the county represented as a separate unit, with the chairman of each local defense council responsible for getting the various organizations—defense, civic, fraternal, industrial, religious and educational — represented. Having the various organizations of each town parade as a unit, it is believed, will create competition.

It is tentatively planned to form the parade in River Road, and parade in Third street, to East End avenue, with the reviewing stand located in McIntosh Square, opposite the Court House.

Major Weber's plan to decorate McIntosh Square as a memorial to

(Continued on Page Ten)

Live Alligator Found By Rochester Woman

Many Beaver Countians agreed it "rained cats and dogs" Saturday afternoon and early Sunday but Mrs. John Liebentritt, Jr., 410 Jackson street, Rochester, was wondering if the weather man went one better in her ease.

She found a live baby alligator in her yard Sunday. Rochester police were called to dispose of the animal and expressed the belief the "critter" had been sent here from the South as a novelty and had escaped from its owner.

Regular meeting S. M. Kane Lodge No. 786 Tuesday night, June 2 at 7:30 P. M., I. O. O. F. Hall, Rochester. Members of Third Degree team requested to be present. Surprise-lunch by committee. 6/1.

County Young GOP To Meet Tuesday Night

With the Beaver Falls Young Republican Club as host, the mothly meeting of the Beaver County Young Republican Board of Control will be held Tuesday evening, June 2, at 8 o'clock in the Beaver Falls Polish Falcon hall, 218 Eleventh street.

The meeting is open to members of all county Young GOP clubs and dancing, entertainment and lunch will follow the business session.

Plans will be discussed for the intensive participation of the Young Republicans in the General Election campaign next Fall.

Beaver Nurse Enlists For Military Service

The first nurse from Beaver to enter the service of her country is Miss Helen Anderson, daughter of Mr. and Mrs. George A. Anderson, Second street. She has been assigned to Langley Field, Va., and will leave Jun 10. Miss Anderson, a graduate of Sewickley Valley hospital, has been commissioned a second lieutenant.

Quarantine Imposed At Hospital Today

McKEESPORT, June 1. — The McKeesport hospital today placed 59 patients, including 34 children, under quarantine as authorities sought to check an epidemic of pneumococcic meningitis, which has claimed the lives of five babies in the hospital in ten days.

Included among those under quarantine were 25 mothers and 26 babies in the Palmer Memorial Home, the maternity section of the hospital. Nurses and other hospital personnel also were confined to their quarters. Children under 14 years were barred from visiting the hospital.

Twenty-four children died in the hospital last month, many as a result of meningitis and infectious diarrhea.

The Aliquippa News

329 Franklin Avenue, Aliquippa, Pa.
Telephone 187

Published by the Aliquippa Unit of the Newspaper Guild of Pittsburgh, American Newspaper Guild

LOCAL RETAIL DISPLAY RATES
OPEN NON-CONTRACT

General, Political and Transient..........60c per Inch
Local Display..........50c per Inch
(Retailers who have been in business at least one year, or who have a year's lease on their store building.)
Full Page..........40c per Inch
30 Inches to Full Page..........45c per Inch

ALL NON-CONTRACT ADVERTISING CASH WITH ORDER.

Contract Rates on Application

Delanko-Casoli Betrothal Announced

Announcement was made today of the engagement of Miss Mary J. Delanko, daughter of Mr. and Mrs. Nicholas Delanko, of 316 Fourth avenue, Aliquippa, to Fred Ralph Casoli, son of Mr. and Mrs. Anthony Casoli, of 252 Station street.

Casoli, an aviation cadet stationed at Maxwell Field, Ala., was home on leave and brought the engagement ring with him.

He is a graduate of Edinboro State Teachers' College, where he was a stellar athlete, a member of the varsity basketball team. He is a graduate of Aliquippa high school, and was a member of the Ambridge high school faculty before he joined the air corps.

Miss Delanko, also a graduate of Aliquippa high school, attended a Beaver Falls business school, and is now doing secretarial work for the H. H. Robertson Co., in Ambridge.

No date has been set for the wedding, but it will be sometime this fall.

Couple Honeymoons After Military Wedding

A West Aliquippa girl and her soldier husband were honeymooning today after a military wedding Tuesday morning in St. Joseph R. C. church, West Aliquippa.

Pvt. Alden Bonchitti, son of Mr. and Mrs. Samuel Bonchitti, Broadhead Rd., and Miss Justina Rossi, daughter of Mrs. Angeline Rossi, Main Ave., exchanged wedding vows that day in front of the Rev. Joseph Altany.

The bride wore a finger-tip veil and all white nylon chiffon gown with train. An attendant, Miss Roslyn Bonchitti, sister of the bridegroom, was attired in a white gown. Joseph Cukrovany was attendant for the bridegroom.

Both the bride and Miss Bonchitti carried white Colonial bouquets.

A reception at the bride's home followed the wedding. On return from the honeymoon, Bonchitti will go to Ft. Monroe, Va. The bride will live at the Bonchitti home.

KEEP 'EM FLYING—BUY WAR VICTORY STAMPS & BONDS!

Mrs. Schaller and Mrs. Nolan Entertain

Mrs. Robert Schaller and Mrs. John J. Nolan were hosts Tuesday at a dessert bridge at Mrs. Schaller's home, 708 Hall St., where two visitors to Aliquippa were guests of honor.

They were Mrs. Carroll Uolan of Indiana and Mrs. Fred Blatt, of Houston, Tex.

Eight tables of bridge were in play. The decorations were yellow and white.

Prize winners at bridge were Mrs. William Pyle, Mrs. R. J. McGinley, Mrs. J. B. Scott and Mrs. C. W. Smith.

Grand-daughters Visit

Twin granddaughters, the Misses Peggy Jean and Ruth Ann Perrine, of Farrel, Pa., today were visiting Mr. and Mrs. Ivor L. Jones, 161 Hopewell Ave.

Zaremba Visits

Corporal Wallace Zaremba, former director of the Boosters' community baseball league, has been visiting in Aliquippa.

He obtained a seven-day leave from his army post at Fort Eustis, Va.

Miss Padgett To Marry B. Ball

Miss Pauline Padgett, only daughter of Mr. and Mrs. A. E. Padgett, 1109 Irwin St., will become the bride tomorrow in a quiet ceremony at the United Presbyterian church of Horace Ball, son of Mr. B. Ball, Atlanta, Ga.

The couple will honeymoon in Chicago and points west and on their return will reside at the Padgett home.

15th Anniversary

Mr. and Mrs. Christy Paglieri, Allegheny Ave., West Aliquippa, observed their 15th wedding anniversary Tuesday.

Miss Marks Returns

Miss Elinor Marks, Allegheny Ave., returned this week after a week's visit with her uncle, Morris Klein, of Pittsburgh.

— CLASSIFIED ADS —

FOR SALE—6 good properties on Broadhead Rd., with 3 acres and more.
Brick building on 501 Washington St., Plan 11. $1000 down.
5-room new house, Sheffield, $4700.
8-room house, corner lot, $5000. $800 down. Two 5-room bungalows $3300 each. 9-room house, with extra lot, $6000. 3 good farms for sale. Chas. Tatalovich, 145 Hopewell Ave. Phone 9449.

FOR SALE—2-story dwelling, Beaver Road, Ambridge, $5900.00. $600.00 down.
Double dwelling, 1100 block Beaver Road, Ambridge, $6000.00. $700.00 down.
6-Room brick dwelling, Larimer Ave., $6600.00. $700.00 down.
7-Room brick dwelling, Larimer Ave., $6500.00. $700.00 down.
7-Room brick dwelling, Larimer Ave., $4750.00.
6-Room frame dwelling, corner lot, Main St., $5500.00.
2-story frame dwelling, Sheffield, $4750.00.
Insurance. Notary Public
Walter S. Cameron, Broker
Phone 11. 375 Franklin Ave.

FOR SALE—75 acres of farm land, on good road, in Independence Twp. Call Gringo 14-4.

FOR RENT — Three unfurnished rooms, 1608 Polk St. Phone 2246-W.

FOR RENT—Furnished room. 549 Highland Ave. Phone 276-J.

WANTED — Experienced girl for grocery store. Apply 1724 Main St. Inquire 378 Franklin Ave.

WANTED—Experienced girl for general housework and laundry. Call 2044-M after 7 p. m.

WANTED TO BUY — 6 or 7-room home on Highland Ave. Full details in first letter. Write Box M, The Aliquippa News.

FOR SALE—Roper range. Inquire 686 Franklin Ave.

INSELBRIC — Will give your home the modern beauty of real brick. No matter what the present condition of your house may be INSELBRIC will make it the showplace of the neighborhood. HOME IMPROVEMENT CO., 1002 Merchant St., Ambridge, Pa.

FOR SALE—1941 Dodge 4-door Town Sedan, fluid drive; radio and heater; excellent tires; 2-tone paint job. Low mileage. Terms: $375 cash, balance in terms. Call Aliq. 752 between 9 a. m. and 4 p. m.

FOR RENT—Four unfurnished rooms, furnace heat. 1419 Green St.; also For Sale—7-room brick bungalow, same address.

LOST OR STOLEN — Red leather purse containing cards and money. Finder may keep money. Please return cards. Return 329 Franklin Ave., or to address on cards.

FOR RENT — Three-room apartment. Inquire 378 Franklin Ave.

FOR SALE — Two lots on Sheffield Terrace. Inquire 2338 Sheffield Ave.; call 567-R.

FOR RENT — Three unfurnished rooms, sink in kitchen. Adults only. Inquire 1719 Irwin St.

FOR RENT — One nicely furnished room, suitable for one or two gentlemen. Inquire 119 Orchard St.

WANTED—Housekeeper, middle-aged lady, willing to work in country home. Phone Gringo, 14, ring 4.

FOR SALE—All kinds of Baby Chicks, U. S. approved and Pullorum tested. Jimmie's Fish and Poultry Market, 222 Franklin Ave.

WANTED—Experienced girl for general housework and laundry. Must like small children. References. Call 2044-M after 7 p. m.

FOR RENT — Two-room apartment. Furnished or unfurnished. Modern conveniences. YOUNG'S 5c & 10c STORE, 360 Franklin Ave.

FOR RENT — 2 unfurnished rooms. Inquire 1727 Davidson.

FOR RENT—One furnished room, 101 Grand Ave., Sheffield Terrace; call 9404.

Cetlin And Wilson To Entertain Kiddies

The children at the Beaver County Children's Home in New Brighton will be entertained as special guests of the Cetlin and Wilson Shows at a matinee on Saturday. The entertainment will include a featured performance of the trained elephants and other animals in the circus ring on the midway.

Members of the Central Labor Council will furnish transportation for the children to and from the show grounds.

The Saturday matinee also offers a special advantage to all other children who wish to attend, as all shows and rides will be reduced to five cents for the afternoon.

Barbara STANWYCK
Joel McCREA
in
The GREAT MAN'S Lady
with
BRIAN DONLEVY

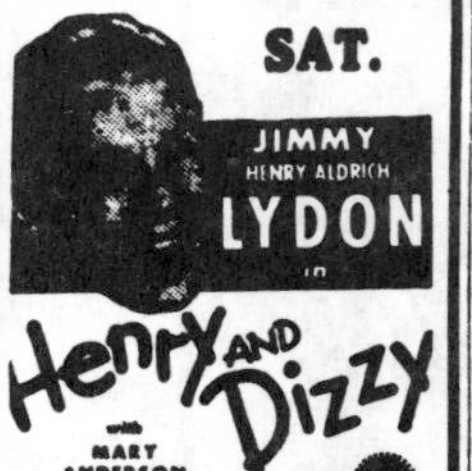
JIMMY
HENRY ALDRICH
LYDON
in
Henry AND Dizzy
with
MARY ANDERSON
CHARLES SMITH

Straight from a whole year at advanced prices!
NOW
POPULAR
PRICES!

HOWL!
MALE ANIMAL

"Chicko" Struts His Stuff For Laffs!

"Chicko," three year old chimpanzee is the only living monkey that can ride a two-wheel bike without the aid of his trainer. "Chicko" is featured in the Monkey Show on the mile-long gladway of the Cetlin and Wilson Shows now playing at Junction Park.

Amusements

ORIENTAL THEATRE

"Mrs. Miniver," Jan Struther's best-selling novel, dealing with the high courage of the English middle classes under air raids and war terrors, is brought to the screen as a living, breathing reality by Greer Garson, Walter Pidgeon and a perfectly chosen cast in the picture now showing at the Oriental Theatre for a solid week's run.

The story deals with Mrs. Miniver and her husband, Clem, played by Miss Garson and Pidgeon. Their son, at Oxford, joins the R. A. F. and becomes engaged to the granddaughter of a noblewoman of the village in which they live. How they do their best to carry on life as usual: their bravery under raid alarms; how the older men aided at the rescue at Dunkirk; figure in moving human interest episodes mingled with comedy. The destruction of the village by bombers is climaxed by the villagers, in their wrecked church, inspired by their vicar, resolving to "carry on" with the same cool courage and with an abiding faith.

Miss Garson's role is touchingly human, and Pidgeon typifies the valor of the British under fire. The love angle is in the hands of pretty Teresa Wright and Richard Ney, and Dame May Whitty is dominant as the noblewoman to whom the trials of war bring a new conception of democracy. Typically English characters are enacted by Reginald Owen, Henry Travers and Christopher Severn. Henry Wilcoxon has an inspiring speech as the vicar.

MAJESTIC THEATRE

A thrilling and highly absorbing story is told in "Black Dragon," the drama which opens tonight at the Majestic. Dealing as it does with the all-out war against the Japanese, the picture is as timely as tomorrow's newspaper, and is interesting to an unusual degree.

Bela Lugosi is the star, and his sinister personality is ideally suited to his role. He is the central figure in an amazing series of events, which picture in a convincing manner a possible situation directly affecting the welfare of the United States. As far as we know, it hasn't happened yet, but Americans are fast becoming persuaded that there is no limit to the possibilities of the present era.

The cast is uniformly excellent. John Barclay plays the principal feminine role, and other important parts are in the hands of George Pembroke, Clayton Moore, Max Hoffman, Jr., Irving Mitchell, Robert Frazer, Edward Peil, Sr., and Kenneth Harlan.

The added feature, "Stardust On The Sage," stars Gene Autry.

RIALTO THEATRE

"Mrs. Miniver," now playing at the Rialto in Beaver Falls, starring Greer Garson and Watler Pidgeon, is one of the greatest films ever made. When you've said that and advised everybody to see it without fail, you've said about all there is to say about it. For when a photoplay is as brilliantly directed, acted and written, so full of tender humor, exalted courage and humanity as "Mrs. Miniver" is, it speaks for itself more eloquently than any words of praise from a reviewer.

To divulge this masterpiece would destroy some of the excitement, emotion, exaltation you will experience when you see it. Put it down though as the first really great film to come out of World War II, as a film that will be remembered in years to come for its dramatic impact, its emotional appeal, the way it recaptures the faith and courage of a people fighting a people's war.

"Mrs. Miniver" is the only picture to play Radio City Music Hall over six weeks and it has been held-over in all key citites.

Yes, masterpiece is the only word for "Mrs. Miniver."

BEAVER THEATRE

"Sergeant York," which has been brought back by popular demand, received heaps of favorable comment from newspaper critics and local audiences alike. All agree that this is the type of film biography which makes excellent screen fare. The picture ends tonight at the Beaver Theatre.

The dramatic story of the man who captured 132 German prisoners during the World War, stars Gary Cooper who was given an "Oscar" for his performance, and Joan Leslie. Other prominent players are Walter Brennan, George Tobias and Stanley Ridges.

One of the most charming comedies of the season, "The Male Animal," which opens tomorrow, is a sparkling film that brings together three grand performers — Henry Fonda, Olivia de Havilland and Joan Leslie. It has a delightful story that will take you out of the realm of worry and trouble, with comedy that is both riotous and plausible.

GRANADA THEATRE

Catchy song numbers, plenty of laughs, and a generous share of thrills and shudders, make Paramount's "Sweater Girl," the mystery musical film that opened last night at the Granada Theatre, something to see, hear and get excited about.

With Eddie Bracken, June Preisser and Betty Jane Rhodes in the top singing and acting spots, "Sweater Girl" is a swiftly-paced picture and altogether one of the most amusing musical movies to come this way in quite some time. Frank Loesser and Jule Styne wrote the songs, William Clemens was the director, and Sol Siegel, who has given us many a delightful film, was the producer. The hit tunes include "I Don't Want to Walk Without You," sung by Betty Jane Rhodes; "What Gives Out Now," a hilariously funny comic number by the Bracken - Preisser team; "Sweater Girl," sung by Eddie Bracken, and "I Said No," a nicely naughty number by Betty Jane.

The plot hinges around a college musical show and the murder of the student song writer. By the time the mystery has been solved everyone with the exception of the detective, has been suspected. The murder theme, however, doesn't prevent a goodly flow of gags and a plentiful supply of good clean fun.

GREER GARSON
WALTER PIDGEON
Mrs. Miniver
with
Teresa Wright · Dame May Whitty

DAVIS
IN THIS OUR LIFE
Olivia DeHavilland · Geo. Brent · Dennis Morgan

CUTE CO-EDS and CAMPUS CUT-UPS!
MURDER ON THE LOOSE!
Sweater Girl
EDDIE BRACKEN
JUNE PREISSER
BETTY JANE RHODES
It's full of swing, songs, dance, romance!

STOLEN RANGE FINDER
CAPTAIN MIDNIGHT
A COLUMBIA CHAPTER PLAY

—Bomb the Japs with Junk!—

"THE WORLD ON PARADE"
SHOWS
Everything New But the Name
1942 TOUR
BIG NEW FREE CIRCUS ACTS
ELEPHANTS
DOGS - PONIES

ADMISSIONS:	Day	After 6 p. m.
General Admission—Adults	40c	Free
Automobile Parking, All Week	25c	25c
Grand Stand	40c	25c

YOU MUST SEE THE PICTURE EVERYBODY IS PUTTING ON THEIR 10-BEST LIST OF ALL-TIME!
Exciting...tender...real..."Mrs. Miniver" is a picture to make your heart beat faster...your eyes shine brighter...and set your pulse to racing! BIG...in its immortal telling of little things...DRAMATIC...in its human angle on world-sweeping events..."Mrs. Miniver" adds up to the most vivid story of love and life, courage and daring you've ever seen.
GREER GARSON · WALTER PIDGEON
Directed by WILLIAM WYLER · Produced by SIDNEY FRANKLIN
MRS. MINIVER
WITH
TERESA WRIGHT · DAME MAY WHITTY · REGINALD OWEN
HENRY TRAVERS · RICHARD NEY · HENRY WILCOXON
NO ADVANCE IN PRICES!
TIME OF SHOWS — 1:45, 4:20, 7:00, 9:40 P. M.
10-BEST ILLUSTRATORS PORTRAY "MRS. MINIVER"
Ten of the country's leading magazine illustrators were invited to see "Mrs. Miniver" and create a symbolic illustration which visualizes their conception of its most stirring scenes. The drawing reproduced here is the work of DEAN CORNWELL

Beaver Valley Country Club Golf Tournament Begins

QUALIFYING ROUND OF ANNUAL TOURNAMENT PLAYED SAT.

George M. Hunter, Jr. Claims Medalist Prize Saturday, Marsh Posts Low Score; P. J. Davidson Is Defending Champ

Elimination matches in the Beaver Valley Country Club's annual golf tournament will get underway today. First round pairings were announced yesterday at conclusion of the 18-hole qualifying round in which about 65 men competed. Four flights of 16 men each were arranged.

Among the 16 men who qualified for championship flight, Bill Marsh had the low gross score of 72, but he did not play his qualifying round on Saturday, which was the official qualifying day. The club's golf committee offers a prize for the low score played on the official qualifying day, but allows members ten day period in which to qualify. Marsh posted his 72 earlier in the week, while George M. Hunter, Jr., Beaver, shot a 74 in the official qualifying test Saturday, and won the club prize. Hunter has withdrawn from the tourney.

W. H. Wise, Jr., turned in a card of 76 and Ralph Connolly was next with a 77. P. J. Davidson, the defending champion, Lynn Pettler, and Frank E. Reed, tied with 78s.

Following are the 16 golfers who will compete in the first or championship division of the annual tournament, together with their qualifying scores and first round pairings:

Upper Bracket

P. J. Davidson, 78, vs. Bill Martin, 79.

Lynn Pettler, 78, vs. R. B. McKee, 81.

W. H. Wise, Jr., 76, vs. W. J. Thomas, 80.

J. Walter Lehman, 79, vs. Newell Hamilton, 82.

Lower Bracket

Bill Marsh 72, vs. H. C. Weidner, Jr., 79.

Frank E. Read, 78, vs. Dr. G. C. Camp, 81.

Ralph Connolly, 77, vs. Sam Smith, 81.

Dr. M. F. Pettler, 79, vs. T. E. Poe, Jr., 83.

First round matches in all of the four divisions of the championship tournament must be played off on or before next Sunday. Second round matches will begin on Monday, August 17.

Sunday the Beaver Valley Country Club held medal play, full handicap tournament, for benefit of the Red Cross, with 46 members participating, and tomorrow a women's tournament for the same worthy cause will be held.

In the first division of the Red Cross tournament yesterday M. J. Thomas and George M. Hunter, Jr., tied for the honors with net 68s. Thomas had a gross score of 80 and a handicap of 12 while Hunter posted a gross 71, and had a handicap of 3.

Charles Bourne Jr., was the leader in the second division with a 97-26—71.

Fourth Ward Beats Monaca Sportsmen

Behind five-hit pitching by Bill Fritzius, the Rochester Fourth Warders defeated the Monaca Sportsmen, 14 to 1, at Rochester. Fritzius fanned ten batters.

The Fourth Warders collected 12 hits of B. Davis and H. Bailey, Sportsmen pitchers. Rowe, R. McElhaney and Fritzius were the leaders with three hits apiece. D. McElhaney and Fritzius clouted home runs. The scores:

Fourth Warders	AB.	R.	H.	P.	A.	E.
Rowe, ss.	4	3	3	0	2	0
R. McElhaney, 2b.	3	4	3	2	0	0
Goehring, c.	3	1	0	10	2	0
D. McElhaney, 3b.	4	3	2	1	0	1
Radcliffe, 1b.	2	2	1	6	0	0
Whitten, cf.	3	0	0	0	0	0
Fritzius, p.	4	1	3	0	3	0
DiFrancisco, lf.	3	0	0	0	0	1
Eakin, rf.	3	0	0	2	0	0
Total	29	14	12	21	7	2

Monaca Sp'tsmen.	AB.	R.	H.	P.	A.	E.
B. Davis, p-3b.	3	0	1	2	1	0
E. Davis, 2b.	3	0	1	2	0	1
Weekley, cf.	3	0	0	1	0	0
F. Bailey, c.	3	0	0	8	2	0
Harrison, 1b.	3	0	1	3	0	0
Pollak, 3b-ss.	3	0	0	1	2	1
H. Bailey, ss-p.	2	0	0	1	1	0
Sinclair, lf.	1	0	0	0	0	0
Trombulak, rf.	3	1	2	0	0	0
Bailey, rf.	2	0	0	0	0	0
Total	26	7	5	18	6	2

Monaca .... 0 0 1 0 0 0 0— 1
Fourth Ward .... 2 0 5 3 0 4 —14

Two-base hits—R. McElhaney, B. Davis.

Home Runs — D. McElhaney, Fritzius.

Hit by pitcher—Goehring.

Stolen bases—Rowe 2, R. McElhaney, E. Davis, Trombulak, Harrison.

Struck out—By Fritzius 10, Davis eight.

Umpire—Bingle.

WIVES FEAR WORST

PORTLAND, Ore. (UP)—They're sending shirts to Congress now! Figuring that Congress may soon amend the Federal income tax law to the worst for the "white collar class," five Portland housewives anticipated their husbands' "losing their shirts" and so promptly mailed the shirts in advance to the Oregon delegation in Congress.

Pirates Drop Both Ends Of Twin Bill To Cards, 4-3, 2-1

Double Loss Snaps Bucs' Five Game Winning Streak; Musial Paces Hitters

The five-game winning streak of the Pittsburgh Pirates came to an end Sunday afternoon when the St. Louis Cardinals took both ends of a double-header 4 to 3 and 2 to 1 at Forbes Field.

The Cards lost little time in scoring in the opening game as they pushed across three runs in the first.

The pirates tied up the count in the sixth but the Cards were not to be denied and counted again in the eighth to take the game. Sewell and Lanning hurled for the Pirates and allowed an even dozen hits while their mates were collecting seven from the slants of Beazley and Dickson.

In the nightcap the Cards counted single tallies in the first and second innings and the Pirates scored in the last half of the second but both teams were unable to push across another run before the game was called at the end of the eighth inning due to the Sunday law.

White and Krist held the Pirates to six hits while Klinger and Dietz returned the compliment as they handled the slab duties against the winners.

Musial, Cardinal left fielder, paced the batters with four hits for the afternoon while Slaughter and Moore of the Cards and Wasdell of the Pirates each had three hits.

The second game score:

St. Louis	AB.	R.	H.	P.	A.	E.
Kurowski, 3b.	4	0	0	0	2	0
Walker, cf.	4	1	1	2	0	0
Slaughter, rf.	4	0	1	3	0	0
Musial, lf.	2	0	2	6	0	0
Sanders, 1b.	4	0	0	6	0	0
O'Dea, c.	4	1	0	4	0	0
Marion, ss.	2	0	1	2	1	0
Crespi, 2b.	2	0	1	1	3	0
White, p.	1	0	0	0	2	0
Krist, p.	2	0	0	0	0	0
Totals	29	2	6	24	8	0

Pittsburgh	AB.	R.	H.	P.	A.	E.
Coscarart, ss-2b.	4	0	0	0	2	0
Wasdell, rf.	2	0	2	2	0	0
Van Robays, lf.	4	0	1	0	0	1
Elliott, 3b.	4	0	1	0	2	0
Fletcher, 1b.	4	1	0	9	2	0
DiMaggio, cf.	3	0	2	2	0	0
Gustine, 2b.	1	0	0	4	3	1
Phelps, c.	1	0	0	2	0	0
Lopez, c.	2	0	0	4	0	0
*Barrett	1	0	0	0	0	0
Geary, ss.	0	0	0	0	0	0
Klinger, p.	2	0	0	1	3	0
**Stewart	1	0	0	0	0	0
Dietz, p.	0	0	0	0	0	0
Total	29	1	6	24	12	2

*Batted for Lopez in Sixth.
**Batted for Klinger in seventh.

St. Louis .... 110 000 00—2
Pittsburgh .... 010 000 00—1

Two-base hits—Walker, Musial, Wasdell. Three-base hit—Marion. Runs batted in—By Musial, Crespi, Gustine. Stolen base — DiMaggio. Double play — White to Crespi to Sanders. First base on balls—off White 1; off Krist 3; off Klinger 2. Sacrifice hits — Marion, Musial. Struck out—By Krist 3; by Klinger 3. Winning pitcher—Krist. Losing pitcher—Klinger. Umpires—Goetz, Conlan and Reardon.

Joe Morbito To Teach In Youngstown School

EAST LIVERPOOL, O., Aug. 10—Joseph Morbito, who recently resigned after seven years as high school football coach here, accepted a contract to teach mechanical drawing at the Youngstown Rayen high school.

A former Carnegie Tech grid star, Morbito said he will not be a member of the Rayen coaching staff, but he may accept an outside coaching offer in addition to his teaching duties.

He has resigned, effective August 22, his vacation position in the drafting department at the Pittsburgh Crucible Steel Company, Midland, preparatory to assumption of his teaching post September 8. He and his family will move to Youngstown.

Notch To Fight Vines Tonight

By United Press

PITTSBURGH, Aug. 10. — The twice-postponed 10-round bout featuring Carman Notch, Pittsburgh welterweight, against Vinnie Vines, of New York, will be staged at Hickey Park tonight with a supporting card of two six-rounders and one eight.

SIT-SLIDE—Clyde McCullough of the Cubs slides into second on the seat of his pants but is forced out by Billy Herman of the Dodgers.

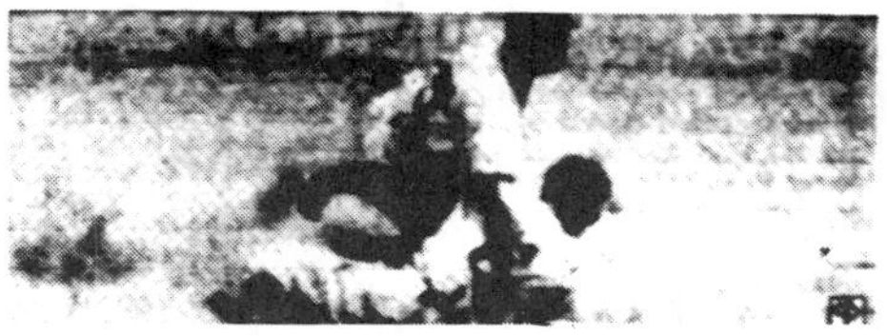

TANGLE—Both Second Baseman Mickey Witek of the Reds and Lonnie Frey of the Giants hit the dust as Witek is forced at second.

Baseball Summary

NATIONAL LEAGUE

Results Sunday

St. Louis 4, Pittsburgh 3.
†St. Louis 2, Pittsburgh 1.
*New York 3, Philadelphia 2.
New York 2, Philadelphia 0.
‡Chicago 10, Cincinnati 8.
§Cincinnati 2, Chicago 1.
Brooklyn at Boston (2), postponed.
*Ten innings. †Eight innings, Sunday law. ‡Eighteen innings. §Five innings, darkness.

TEAM STANDING

	W.	L.	Pct.
Brooklyn	74	33	.692
St. Louis	65	40	.619
Cincinnati	57	50	.533
New York	58	51	.532
Pittsburgh	48	55	.466
Chicago	50	61	.450
Boston	45	65	.409
Philadelphia	31	73	.298

Games Today

St. Louis at Pittsburgh.
Philadelphia at Brooklyn (twilight).
Others not scheduled.

Games Tuesday

Cincinnati at Pittsburgh.
St. Louis at Chicago.
New York at Boston.
Others not scheduled.

AMERICAN LEAGUE

Results Sunday

Detroit 9, St. Louis 3.
Detroit 3, St. Louis 1.
Chicago 11, Cleveland 1.
Chicago 3, Cleveland 2.
Philadelphia at New York (2), postponed.
Boston at Washington, postponed.

TEAM STANDING

	W.	L.	Pct
New York	71	35	.670
Boston	59	47	.557
Cleveland	60	49	.550
St. Louis	56	56	.500
Detroit	53	60	.469
Chicago	48	55	.466
Washington	43	61	.413
Philadelphia	43	70	.381

Games Today

Boston at Washington, (2—Twilight and night).
Philadelphia at New York (2).
Cleveland at Chicago (night).
Others not scheduled.

Games Tuesday

Chicago at St. Louis.
Detroit at Cleveland.
Washington at Philadelphia.
Boston at New York.

BEAVER COUNTY LEAGUE

TEAM STANDING

	W.	L.
Conway	12	2
Curtiss-Wright	10	3
West Mayfield	8	4
Aliquippa	7	4
Beaver	6	8
New Galilee	4	8
Rochester	4	10
Beaver Falls	1	13

Games Today—Umpires

Conway at Curtiss-Wright (Anderson and Stewart).
New Galilee at Beaver Falls (Goehring and Smith).
West Mayfield at Rochester (Montani and Triance).
Beaver at Aliquippa (Popik and Starr).

Games Tuesday—Umpires

West Mayfield at Curtiss-Wright (Montani and Triance).

INDUSTRIAL SOFTBALL LEAGUE

TEAM STANDING

	W.	L.
J. & L.	7	0
Colonial Steel	4	2
Townsends	4	3
Mack-Hemphill	3	3
Tool Steel Wire	1	6
Hydril	0	5

Games Today

Mack-Hemphill vs. Hydril at P. B. I. field.
Tool Steel Wire vs. Colonial Steel at Colona.

PENN STATE ASSN.

First Game

Butler .... 400 000— 4- 5-5
Oil City ...... 012 135—12-12-0

(Called at end of 6th inning. Second game postponed.)

Holmes, Gustafson and Warren; Chir, Fain and Leone.

Washington and Johnstown, postponed.

Robinson To Meet Cowboy Ruben Shank

By United Press

NEW YORK, Aug. 10—Ray (Sugar) Robinson, undefeated Harlem welterweight, has been matched for a 10-round bout with Cowboy Ruben Shank of Denver at Madison Square Garden, August 21.

SECOND IN LICENSES

COLUMBUS, O. (UP) — Ohio ranked second in the number of fishing licenses sold in 1941, the State Conservation Division has revealed. Michigan came first with 773,228 licenses issued and Ohio's total was 714,342.

GLAMOROUS
GLORIA

When the nation's sport fans turn their attention to Neenah, Wis., for the National Women's Swimming and Diving championships to be held there Aug 14-16, what interested party could help but concentrate his attention on glorious Gloria Callen, above, the New York gal who holds 34 American backstroke titles and one of the outstanding competitors in the meet. Miss Callen is a member of the New York Women's Swimming association. She recently set a new record in winning the Canadian senior women's 100-yard backstroke championship.

Fiddler Bill McGee Of Giants Credits His Return To Old Time Form To Built-Up Shoe

McGee Aids Giants In Taking Two From Phils; Cardinals Cut One Game From Lead Of Dodgers; White Sox Drop Indians Back To Third Place In Sweeping Double-Bill

By United Press

NEW YORK, Aug. 10—Bill McGee, the "pitchless wonder" of the National League, provided the New York Giants with an exasperating problem for nearly two years, but today Manager Mel Ott seems to have "the fiddler" on the road back.

McGee, who became famous as a "fiddler" with the St. Louis Cardinals, became as celebrated for his inability to win with the Giants. His fast ball, which had made him a 16-game winner and one of the top men on the Cards' pitching staff two years ago, left him—and apparently his confidence went along.

McGee himself credits his current rejuvenation to a built-up shoe which has brought his vertebrae back into line.

"That chronic weakness of the spine," said McGee, "has bothered me on and off for a long time. When that vertebrae shift happens it causes the bones in my body to shift and makes my left leg about an inch and a half shorter than my right. Naturally, that makes it painful to throw and, of course, leaves me without any confidence in my pitching delivery. I think this new shoe has turned the trick, though."

And apparently it has, because the Giants took the Phils twice, 3-2 and 2-0, yesterday to move within one percentage point of third place. Ott's squeeze bunt with the bases loaded and one out in the 10th inning won the first game. But it was McGee's work in the night-cap that was more significant.

Pitcher Hiram Bithorn was both a winner and a loser as the Cubs divided with the Reds. Bithorn Pitched the last 6 1-3 innings in an 18-inning first game as the Cubs won a 10-8 decision in the Major's longest game of the year. He was credited with the victory in this contest, but lost the nightcap, 2-1, when the game was called by darknes after 4½ innings.

The Cardinals cut the idle Dodgers National League lead to eight games by winning two from Pittsburgh, 4-3 and 2-1.

The White Sox knocked the Indians back into third place in the American League by winning both ends of a doubleheader, 11-1 and 3-2. The double win stretched the Sox' win string to eight straight. Ted Lyons extended his own winning streak to seven in a row by winning his 10th victory with a four-hit job in the first game.

Detroit hung up two over the Browns, 9-3 and 2-1. A six-run explosion in the fourth enabled the Tigers to end a five-game losing streak in the opener as the Browns made five errors.

Stone Quarry, J-L Game Tonight On Green Garden Field

The site of the big softball game scheduled this evening between the Jones and Laughlin team, unbeaten leader of the County Industrial League, and the Stone Quarry team, champs of the Aliquippa Softball League, has been changed, it was announced today.

Originally scheduled to be played on the Stone Quarry field, Colona Heights, the game has been transferred to the J. and L. field at the Green Garden golf course, and will be played tonight starting at 6:30 o'clock.

The change was necessary, it was stated, because an Industrial League game between Colonial Steel and Pittsburgh Tool Steel Wire is scheduled for the Stone Quarry field.

The Stone Quarry outfit will meet the Midland softball team Tuesday evening.

Aliquippian Named S. Huntingdon Coach

Officials of South Huntingdon Township High school near Greensburg, Pa., today announced the selection of Elmer Gross, of Aliquippa, Pa., as football and basketball coach. Gross, a sports star at Slippery Rock State Teachers College until 1941, will replace William T. Overand, who is now in the army.

Hawaiian Swimmers Set World Records

NEW LONDON, Conn., Aug. 10—Two Hawaiian buddies, Big Billy Smith, Jr., and pint-sized Keo Nakama shook hands as they lined up for the 880-yard free style race yesterday, wished each other a world's record, and then both proceeded to accomplish the trick as the three-day National AAU men's swimming championships closed.

The 17-year-old Smith of Maui, Hawaii, and Nakama, now an Ohio State sophomore, fought it out stroke for stroke until the home stretch when the former spurted and won by inches.

The broad-shouldered Smith, winning his third crown of the meet, hit the finish in 9 minutes and 54.6 seconds. Nakama, the 1941 champion, was a fraction of a second slower. The victor looped 13 seconds off the listed international standard recorded seven years ago by Ralph Flanagan of Miami, Fla.

Send THE TIMES to your boy in the Army or Navy. "It's like a letter from home every day."

Bladesmen To Meet Conway; Pirates Play W. Mayfield

Grays To Oppose Aliquippa Nine Tonight; New Galilee Visits Beaver Falls

With the Conway and Curtiss-Wright teams as leading contenders Beaver County Baseball League teams continue their second half campaign this evening. Four games are scheduled.

Most interst is being exhibited in the Conway-Curtiss-Wright contest at Beaver's Gypsy Glen field. Conway is about one and one-half games ahead of the Bladesmen, who must win tonight's game if they wish to remain in the running.

The Beaver Grays travel to Aliquippa, Rochester's Pirates will tangle with West Mayfield on the Junction City diamond, and Beaver Falls will be host to New Galilee.

Send THE TIMES to your boy in the Army or Navy. "It's like a letter from home every day."

SPORT SLANTS

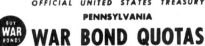

By BILL ANDERSON

The Allie Stolz-Chalky Wright fight in New York last Thursday evening provided a contradiction of the oft-expressed belief that boxing fans, for the most part, are a bit on the blood-thirsty side, enjoying the sport most when the claret runs red and someone is rocked to sleep with a lightly-padded fist. Stolz, the 23-year-old youngster, got a bigger hand from the 12,000 spectators for not knocking out the aging colored scrapper when he could easily have done so, than he would have had he pounded Wright to the canvas. Inasmuch as a big-money fight with Sammy Angott, lightweight champion, hung in the balance, Stolz could not have been blamed for ending the fight in the tenth round, but he voluntarily chose instead to carry the venerable Negro along and allow him to finish the bout on his feet. It is also refreshing that the fans approved.

BRIEFS: Hank Greenberg, one of the first major league baseball stars to be called into Army service, has been commissioned a lieutenant after completing an officers' training course at Miami . . . Bloomsburg State Teachers College is the latest to drop football for the duration . . . One reason the Cardinals are trailing so far behind the Dodgers is that Carl Hubbell, Giant veteran, has pitched three of his six victories against them . . . Bob McNamara, former Freedom high coach, who will take over the coaching duties at Sewickley in the Fall, has been getting in shape by working in the Bethlehem Steel plant in Leetsdale. McNamara resides at the Springer Apartments, in Leetsdale.

CUB POW WOW IS PLANNED FOR AUG. 22 AT GYPSY GLEN PARK

The Fort McIntosh District, Boy Scouts of America, announce a Cub Pow Wow to be held August 22, 1942 at the Gypsy Glen Park in Beaver. All Cub Packs in the Fort McIntosh District are invited to attend this affair which will begin at 3:30 in the afternoon with Estimation and Guessing Hunt and end up at 8:30 after a Campfire. Supper will be in the form of a basket picnic, each family bringing their own food. Gas burners have been reserved for those who wish to heat their food.

Games will be in charge of Mr. D. I. Hutchison of Rochester; physical arragnements, Mssrs. Charles Cole and J. P. Jones of Beaver; campfire program, R. Judd Irwin of New Brighton, Don Cook, Sr. of Rochester and Rev. Hutchison of New Brighton. Other members of the Ft. McIntosh District Camping and Activities Committee from Midland, E. E. Glaser and Arron Lloyd along with Mr. James Machen of Beaver Falls are expected to assist with the program.

Mr. Amos K. Meader, Field Scout Executive and Cubbing Director of the Allegheny Council, Boy Scouts of America, will be on hand to announce other Cubbing Activities of the Allegheny Council.

Gordon Is New American Loop Batting Leader

By United Press

NEW YORK, Aug. 10 — Second-baseman Joe Gordon of the New York Yankees regained the American League hitting lead last week, batting his average seven points to oust Ted Williams of the Boston Red Sox.

Gordon, who led the league for three consecutive weeks earlier in the season, had an average of .343. Williams fell from .350 to .341. The figures are based on games played through Thursday.

FOUR-LEGGED CHICKEN

ATHENS, O. (UP)—Attracting visitors to the farm of Mr. and Mrs. Ted Janthorey is a four-legged chicken. The chick is four weeks old and as lively as the others of the same hatch.

Tennis Champion

Louise Brough of Beverly Hills, Cal., is pictured above in action at the Eastern Grass Court Tennis Championships at the Westchester Country Club, Rye, N. Y. She swept through the eliminations and Saturday defeated Defending Champion Pauline Betz, Los Angeles, 6-3, 7-5, in the finals to capture the title.

An average of 3,600 persons per program attended 15 midget auto races at Akron this year.

OFFICIAL UNITED STATES TREASURY
PENNSYLVANIA
WAR BOND QUOTAS
FOR AUGUST

WASHINGTON, D. C., Aug. 10.—Henry Morgenthau, Jr., Secretary of the Treasury, today announced the August War Bond Quotas for the 3,070 counties in the nation totalling $815,000,000.

The August quota for the State of Pennsylvania is $63,-250,000.

In arriving at the county quotas for August the Treasury Department took into consideration major factors affecting incomes which in turn cause significant variations in sales during the twelve-month period.

Hereafter actual Bond sales in the various states will be compared with quotas on a cumulative basis. The amount by which sales fall short of or exceed quotas in any month will be added to or subtracted from quotas for future months.

Quotas by counties are:

Adams, $144,100; Allegheny, $11,-135,200; Armstrong, $239,200.

Beaver, $704,700; Bedford, $51,000; Berks, $1,364,800; Blair, $483,300; Bradford, $243,100; Bucks, $437,400; Butler, $386,600.

Cambria, $745,600; Cameron, $26,-800; Carbon, $228,500; Centre, $175,-600; Chester, $620,800; Clarion, $102,-000; Clearfield, $225,000; Clinton, $100,200; Columbia, $347,900; Crawford, $338,800; Cumberland, $302,600.

Dauphin, $1,185,500; Delaware, $1,-659,000.

Elk, $146,800; Erie, $1,245,000.

Fayette, $573,100; Forest, $9,500; Franklin, $352,800; Fulton, $21,100.

Greene, $89,800.

Huntingdon, $87,900.

Indiana, $155,700.

Jefferson, $145,700; Juniata, $35,-200.

Lackawanna, $1,080,000; Lancaster, $1,145,800; Lawrence, $453,900; Lebanon, $414,600; Lehigh, $885,500; Luzerne, $1,875,000; Lycoming, $397,200.

McKean, $274,000; Mercer, $713,-500; Mifflin, $140,100; Monroe, $100,-500; Montgomery, $1,607,800; Montour, $61,500.

Northampton, $1,563,000; Northumberland, $547,200.

Perry, $74,100; Philadelphia, $22,-350,600; Pike, $18,600; Potter, $43,-900.

Schuylkill, $903,300; Snyder, $44,-900; Somerset, $222,500; Sullivan, $19,500; Susquehanna, $66,600.

Tioga, $103,000.

Union, $49,200.

Venango, $255,200.

Warren, $162,400; Washington, $870,900; Wayne, $89,800; Westmoreland, $1,257,700; Wyoming, $44,400.

York, $1,303,500.

U. S. Treasury Department

Vacationers returning from Canada must have photographic films censored.

Send THE TIMES to your boy in the Army or Navy. "It's like a letter from home every day."

Center Township 4-H Club Officers And Leaders

TIMES Photo by Bill Heyman

Pictured above are officers of Center Township 4-H Cook-If-You-Can club and the club sponsors. They are: President, Irene Johnston; vice-president, Joanna Embree; secretary, Jean Milne; song leader, Patricia Patterson; game leader, Dorothy Boak; reporter, Mary Louise Callaghan. Mrs. Ralph W. Hartenbach and Mrs. Gorman Johnston, the club leaders; Miss Marian Rapp, Beaver County Home Economics representative, and Miss Johnston, president, are seated in the front row.

CONWAY NEWS

Ladies Bible Class Plans Picnic Supper

Members of the Ladies' Bible class of the Methodist church are to hold a picnic supper Thursday evening in the church social rooms.

Mrs. Dana Par. Second avenue, has been ill at her home.

George Micheletti, Jr., Second avenue, has returned home after a one-week vacation trip.

Miss Vandecasty, Pittsburgh, has been visiting her uncle and aunt Mr. and Mrs. Ian Work, here.

Rochester News

Meetings Scheduled At Zion Evangelical Church This Evening

Prayer Services To Be Held This Evening; Missionary Society Meets Thursday

Rev. Thomas O. Fuss, pastor of Zion Evangelical church, will have charge of the adult prayer service in the church this evening at 7:30 o'clock. The Young People's prayer service at the same hour will be under the leadership of Miss Dorothy Fields. Thursday evening at 8 o'clock the Woman's Missionary Society will hold its monthly meeting in the home of Mrs. H. M. Myers, Lincoln street.

Mr. and Mrs. Dan Donatell and daughter, Joyce Ann, Deer Lane, returned Tuesday from Richmond, Ind., where they were guests several days of relatives. They accompanied Valley relatives.

Walter C. Gordon, pharmacist mate in the Naval hospital, Philadelphia, visited the week end in the home of his parents, Mr. and Mrs. Walter A. Gordon, Jefferson street. Mrs. Gordon, who is ill, has been removed to the home of Mr. Gordon's mother, Mrs. W. T. Gordon, Jackson street.

Dr. A. M. Klingelhofer, Burbank, Cal., is visiting his parents, Mr. and Mrs. Louis Klingelhofer, and family, Jefferson street.

Technical Sergeant Lester Berkihiser, stationed at an army camp near Washington, and Private George E. Berkihiser, Ft. Eustis, Va., left Tuesday for camp after spending a few days in the home of their parents, Mr. and Mrs. C. P. Berkihiser, Kossuth street.

Mr. and Mrs. Emile Traubel, Jersey City, N. J., left for home Sunday after spending a week at the home of Mr. and Mrs. E. A. Blackburn, Adams street, and Mr. and Mrs. F. W. Niehaus, Reno street. Mr. and Mrs. Blackburn accompanied them as far as Johnstown. Mrs. Traubel is a sister of the two local women.

Frank Creese, Vermont avenue, spent several days with his son, Corporal Glenn Creese, at Camp Kilmore, N. J. Father and son visited in New York City Saturday and spent Sunday together at Camp Kilmore.

Miss Virginia Kaste, Beaver, spent the week end with Miss Betty Hood, Clay street, who is spending her vacation with her sister, Mrs. Clifford Aultman at North Girard. Miss Anna Margaret Hood, who has also been vacationing at the Aultman cottage, entertained Miss Gay Stroup, Mecklem avenue, over the week end and returned home with her.

Rev. Richard Kennedy, Butler, was the guest speaker in the United Presbyterian church Sunday morning.

Mrs. Zelda Frazier has returned from a two-week vacation from Barnett's shoe store, Rochester. One week was spent at Chautauqua, N. Y.

Mrs. James H. Ewing, Beaver, formerly of Rochester, left Tuesday to spend two weeks in Mt. Washington, Cincinnati, O. She was accompanied there by her son-in-law, daughter and grandson, Mr. and Mrs. G. C. Stewart and son, Jimmy, and Mr. and Mrs. H. S. Cover, Cincinnati, O. Jimmy Stewart has been staying with his grandmother the past month.

The mid-week prayer service of the Baptist church will be held this evening in the church and Rev. W. A. Binkley, pastor, will present the second of a series of studies on "The Church and the World."

Mrs. Harry Berger and Mrs. Walter Hight, Pittsburgh, were guests of Mr. and Mrs. Harry Clayton, Connecticut avenue, Sunday.

Pfc. Willard H. Kidd spent a week end furlough with his parents, Mr. and Mrs. Earl W. Kidd, Jefferson street. He is stationed with the machine record unit of the Army in Providence, R. I., having recently completed a two-month course at the school of International Business Machines, Boston.

Mrs. Louise C. Southwick, Pennsylvania avenue, returned home Saturday after spending two weeks with her nieces in Wheeling, W. Va.

Mr. and Mrs. Wilbur Roush, daughter, Aloha Jean, and son, Wilbur, Webster street, spent the past week end at the Woodward Hotel, Woodward, near Altoona, returning home Monday. They were accompanied by Mrs. Roush's brother-in-law and sister, Mr. and Mrs. R. E. Davis, Beaver.

There will be no meeting of the surgical dressing group in Rochester Thursday due to the lack of materials.

Harold C. Kornman, son of Mr. and Mrs. George T. Kornman, Jane street, is to leave Friday for the Aviation Cadet Replacement Center at Santa Ana, Calif.

Miss Rhea Andreas, assistant librarian at the Rochester Public Library, has returned from a one-week vacation spent with relatives in Midland.

BEAVER NEWS

Rebekah Lodge Of Beaver Plans For Covered-Dish Event

Birthday Anniversaries Of Members In July, August, September To Be Observed

A meeting of Lady Bonnar Rebekah Lodge, will be held Thursday evening, August 20, in the lodge hall, Third street. The meeting will be preceded by a covered-dish dinner at 6:30 o'clock, celebrating the birthday aniversaries of members during July, August and September. Degree practice will also be held.

Mr. and Mrs. Albert Renner of Philadelphia visited Sunday with Mr. Renner's sister, Mrs. Hilda M. Dickenson, and family, Fifth street. Mr. Renner is a former Monaca resident.

Mr. and Mrs. R. E. Davis, Corporation street, and Mrs. Davis' brother-in-law and sister, Mr. and Mrs. Wilbur Roush, daughter, Aloha Jean, and son, Wilbur, Rochester, spent the past week-end at the Woodward Hotel at Woodward, near Altoona. They returned Monday.

Mrs. Homer H. Hogsett and son, Melvin, Park street, are spending several days in Pittsburgh at the home of Mr. and Mrs. J. W. Federkeil.

Mr. and Mrs. Henry Steel and daughter, Ann, Third street, spent last week-end at Lake Erie.

Members of the Susannah Wesley Guild of the Methodist church will meet to sew Thursday from ten to three o'clock at the home of Mrs. Lewis H. Urling, Windyghoul Estates. Those desiring transportation to the Urling home are to contact Mrs. John M. Horter.

Miss Marjorie Warrick, daughter of Mrs. Elsie J. Warrick of Turnpike street, is improving satisfactorily following an appendectomy in the Beaver Valley hospital, New Brighton, Monday morning.

Miss Phyllis Ethlyn Neely, Beaver street, underwent a tonsilectomy in Providence hospital, Beaver Falls, on Tuesday morning, and is improving satisfactorily. Miss Neely, employed by the Pennsylvania State Highway Department, with offices at East Rochester, is on her vacation.

Mr. and Mrs. D. J. McCoy and daughter, Nancy Joan, Dutch Ridge road, are returning today from Tionesta, where they have been visiting the past week with Mr. McCoy's parents, Mr. and Mrs. I. N. McCoy. After a week, they expect to return to Tionesta for another visit of several days.

Mr. and Mrs. O. S. Braden, Beaver street, have concluded a vacation of three weeks spent at Madison-on-the-Lake, O.

Mr. and Mrs. J. W. Crary of Fourth street have returned home from Linwood Park, Vermilion, O., where they enjoyed a one-week vacation. Mr. and Mrs. Edwin P. Parrott, Wilson avenue, spent the week-end there with the Crarys.

ECONOMY HINT

To make your meat balls grow in size and so go farther combine them with chopped spinach.

Waunita Hot Springs and Ouray, Colorado, each have two medicinal springs.

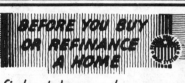

The Weather Forecast

WESTERN PENNSYLVANIA: Somewhat warmer, with scattered showers. Pollen count, 173.

THE DAILY TIMES

ROCHESTER-BEAVER-MONACA

FREEDOM—BRIDGEWATER—CONWAY—VANPORT—MIDLAND

Beaver County History

Seven more towns were wrested from German troops by the Allies. It was reported in Beaver County on August 22, 1918.

ESTABLISHED APRIL 2, 1874 | BEAVER AND ROCHESTER, PA., SATURDAY, AUGUST 22, 1942 | BY CARRIER 18 CENTS A WEEK

MARINES SMASH JAPANESE IN PACIFIC

STATE LEGION CONVENTION IS CLOSED TODAY

Legionnaires Elect Commander, Vote On Resolutions; Decide to Move Headquarters to Harrisburg; Parade Today

By United Press

PITTSBURGH, Aug. 22 — Delegates to the State American Legion convention moved toward adjournment today in a strenuous business session to elect a department commander and act on resolutions that were tabled by a decision to remove state headquarters from Philadelphia to Harrisburg.

To an already jammed agenda, the 1,000 delegates added consideration of important policy legislation which included: whether or not veterans of the present war should be eligible for Legion membership; a decrease in occupational deferments and abandonment of conscientious objectcs' camps and provisions for Legionnaires to get "necessary gas and tires" to man aircraft spotting posts.

Candidates for Pennsylvania Commander, succeeding I. G. Gordon Forster, of Philadelphia, were Daniel C. Hartbauer, Pittsburgh; John G. Love, Bellefonte, and Richard H. Klein, Sunbury.

TO MOVE HEADQUARTERS

The convention was thrown almost a half-day behind schedule when the Internal Organization committee late yesterday presented to the convention floor two plans for moving Legion offices to the state capitol. One plan was passed by the narrow margin of 519 to 495 after delegates overwhelmingly defeated another that would have required the forfeit of the department's $50,000 in war bonds to finance the move.

The successful resolution was presented by the Brook-Doll Post No. 33, Bellefone, providing for sale of stocks and bonds held by the department treasury to finance the removal. A similar resolution adopted last year at Altoona never was acted upon for lack of financial ways and means.

Proceding on schedule, the Women's Auxiliary convention closed today following presentation of committee reports and installation of officers. Newly-chosen officers are: Mrs. Archie W. Miller, of New Cumberland, president, and Mrs. G. W. Dressler, Pittsburgh, re-elected secretary-treasurer, and Mrs. Mabel Stark, West Pittston, re-elected chaplain.

The Legion, Auxiliary and the two branches of the 40 and 8 Society participated in the 24th annual grand parade this afternoon with 30,000 veterans and their wives marching through the downtown section.

War Revenue Bill Headed For Revision

WASHINGTON, Aug. 22. — The $6,200,000,000 house-approved war revenue bill today appeared headed toward major revision along lines recommended by administration economists who believe taxes should absorb most individual income not used for bare essentials.

Chairman Walter F. George, D., Ga., of the Senate Finance Committee, which begins shaping the legislation on Monday, jolted a press conference yesterday with the flat statement that he is convinced heavier taxes on income are necessary "if we are serious about paying for the war and checking inflation".

Emphasizing that the time to "harvest" dollars is here, he called for a system of savings to be superimposed on present taxes and those contained in the House bill which would dig more deeply into the pockets of individual taxpayers.

FOKINE DIES

NEW YORK, Aug. 22 — Michel Fokine, 62, famous ballet master who created the "dying swan" dance for the late Anna Pavlova, died early today of pneumonia.

Four Beaver Brothers Serving Uncle Sam

J. CRAWFORD KENNEDY

Graule Photo

JOHN E. KENNEDY

Graule Photo

RICHARD R. KENNEDY

PAUL E. KENNEDY

Mr. and Mrs. C. H. Kennedy, well-known Beaver residents, spend much of their "spare" time these days writing letters to their four sons, now serving in the armed forces of their country. Mrs. Kennedy says "three or four letters every day keep one busy".

J. Crawford Kennedy, oldest of the four boys, entered the service on June 24, 1941. He took his basic training at Camp Wheeler, Ga., and was soon promoted to Corporal. For several months, he was detailed to train new inductees in the first rudiments of military training. Later, he applied for officers' training and was immediately accepted and sent to Fort Benning, Ga., to an officers' training school. He received his commission as a second lieutenant last July 4 and was sent to take command of the 81-mm. mortar gun platoon in the 383rd Infantry at Camp Adair, Oregon, where he is now stationed.

Richard R. (Dick) Kennedy, better known as "Kelly" to his many Beaver friends, entered the service on March 18, this year. He was at once appointed to the Quartermaster Corps, with basic training headquarters at Fort Warren, Cheyenne, Wyo. After an intensive training program, he was one of ten "hand picked" men out of a group of several hundred to make up a headquarters company for foreign service. It is the duty of the headquarters company to establish new Quartermaster posts, break in a staff of operatives and then move on to the next new base. He left for overseas in late June and is now stationed "somewhere" in Great Britain.

Paul E. Kennedy, the third son, enlisted in the Aviation Cadets in March of this year and was sent to Maxwell Field, Ala., for his basic training. After a series of rigid examinations in mathematics and other intensive studies, he passed all with high marks and was classified as a pilot. Upon completion of this course, he will be transferred to another field where his training in flying maneuvers will be pursued to qualify him for his "wings" and a commission as a second lieutenant in the Air Forces.

John E. (Jack) Kennedy, fourth to

(Continued On Page Eight)

Minister Convicted By Jury In Trial On Spying Charge

Philadelphia Pastor Awaits Sentence; Three Others Sent To Prison

By United Press

HARTFORD, Conn., Aug. 22.—Convicted by a Federal jury of betraying American military secrets to the Axis powers, Rev. Kurt Emil Bruno Molzahn, 47, pastor of Old Zion Lutheran church, Philadelphia, and former German cavalry officer, was in jail today, awaiting sentence—which the government demanded be the maximum penalty of 20 years.

His conviction paved the way for the sentencing of three others involved in the conspiracy.

Gerhard Wilhelm Kunze, American born leader of the German-American Bund, drew a sentence of

(Continued On Page Eight)

Freedom Infant

Pictured above is brown-haired, brown-eyed Marla Rae Neuber, daughter of Mr. and Mrs. Raymond R. Neuber, Rochester. Mrs. Neuber is the former Dorothy Sweeney, Freedom. The baby is one of five generations of which the great-great-grandmother is Mrs. L. H. Evans, Washington. Her daughter, the great-grandmother of Marla, is Mrs. Warren E. Kilgore, Freedom.

Two-Foot Alligator Found By Boys In Beaver Falls Friday

Three youngsters playing in West Second street, Beaver Falls, early Friday afternoon wondered for a few minutes if their eyes were deceiving them when they saw an alligator near the tracks of the Pennsylvania railroad.

One of the youngsters, George Russ, 13, near Rochester, stepped on the animal back of the head while his brother, John 15, and the third boy, Thomas Stauffer, 13, 228 Ninth avenue, Beaver Falls, aided him in holding the two-foot long "critter."

Stauffer went home, procured a sack and the three boys placed the alligator in it without mishap. Stymied as to what to do with their prize, they called Beaver Falls police and turned the sack and its contents over to an officer.

Later the alligator was turned over to John Jersey, Virginia avenue, Rochester, to add to his collection of animals.

Local Engineer Is Awarded Contract For War Project

Michael Baker, Jr., To Supervise Troop Ferrying And Glider Bases Construction

Michael Baker, Jr., civil engineer and surveyor of Rochester, was called to Washington today to receive his newest assignment. Accompanying him was Francis G. Neilan, assistant field engineer, who will be in charge of the operations.

Mr. Baker will supply architectural design and supervise construction, as well as the complete survey and engineering service for two troop ferry command bases and glider training bases, costing $3,000,000, lo-

(Continued On Page Eight)

Local Draft Board To Send 92 Men For Army Examination Tuesday

Preparations are being made by Draft Board No. 3, Rochester, to send 92 men to Pittsburgh for their final army physical examination on Tuesday, August 25.

Accompanied by the national colors, members of the draft board and others, the men will march from the draft board office to the Pennsylvania Railroad station to board the 8:06 a. m. train.

Sixteen Aviation Cadets From County Go To California

Ten Other County Youths Enlisted Friday In Armed Forces At Pittsburgh

Ten Beaver County youths enlisted in the armed forces Friday at Pittsburgh recruiting offices as sixteen others from the county were sent to the west coast as aviation cadets for basic flying training.

The enlistees are: Army Air Forces — Wilbert H. Householder, New Brighton; Coast Guard — Emil A. Alam, Aliquippa, and Gene S. Smiley, Freedom; Navy—George A. Babish, Frank and John Kochanowski, Aliquippa, and Warren H. McConnell, Beaver; and Marine Corps —Joseph F. Thomas, Monaca, and James L. Martin, Beaver Falls.

The aviation cadets, sent to Santa Ana, Calif., by the Aviation Cadet Board, are: Ivon J. Broz and Andrew A. Mihok, West Aliquippa; David M. Carl, Robert Allen Doty, Jack Clark Hixenbaugh and Benjahin T. Kline, Aliquippa; Elwood V. R. Cromwell and Robert C. Mennell, Beaver Falls; Martin M. Cypher, Smiths Ferry; Michael Danylo, Koppel; Harold Chester Kornman and Paul R. Patterson, Rochester; Ira Mansfield Heckathorne, Jr., New Brighton; Kenneth S. Leasure and James W. Reese, Beaver, and Andrew J. Parkinson, Bridgewater.

COST OF RELIEF IN COUNTY SHOWED DECREASE IN JULY

Direct relief payments made to needy Beaver countians during the week ended today show an increase of $7 over those of the previous week, according to State Treasurer G. Harold Wagner.

Payments for the week totaled $1,428, which was $1,950 lower than those of the comparable week of last year. Current payments required 450 fewer checks than those of a year ago.

Payments by the Bureau of Assistance Disbursements in the State Treasury Department follow:

Current week—$1,428, made with 349 checks; previous week—$1,421, made with 348 checks; comparable week 1941—$3,378, made with 799 checks.

TOTAL COSTS DROP

At the same time, Treasurer Wagner announced total payments of $37,031 for all types of categorical assistances—that is, Old Age Assistance, Aid to Dependent Children, and Pensions for the Blind — paid Beaver countians during July. Following is a comparison of payments made last month and during June:

These payments were:

July—Old Age Assistance, $19,026, made with 862 checks; aid to dependent children, $12,276, made with 365 checks; pensions for the blind, $5,728, made with 191 checks.

June—Old Age Assistance, $19,276, made with 873 checks; aid to dependent children, $12,889, made with 382 checks; pensions for the blind, $5,758, made with 192 checks.

WAR EFFORT HAMPERED BY MANY STRIKES

Labor Leaders, Company And Government Officials Striving To Settle Walkouts, Aluminum Workers To Vote On Strike

Labor leaders, company and government officials sought today to stave off or settle "grievance" walkouts that threatened war production in basic industries in the east, middle west and on the Pacific coast and Canada.

In Los Angeles, 3,000 United Automobile Workers (CIO) voted to resume work today after a one day walkout at the large Vernon, Cal., plant of the Aluminum Company of America. William B. Taylor, UAW west coast director, urged a return to work and read a telegram from the War Labor Board which said "this is an inopportune time to strike against the government."

The walkout, unauthorized by the union, had been called in protest against dismissal of 30 workers. The shutdown of the aluminum plant threatened closing of the Vultee Aircraft, Inc., and airplane parts plants. The workers had been denied a $1-a-day wage boost by the WLB.

At Pittsburgh, President N. A. Zonarich of Aluminum Workers of America (CIO) announced he would appeal directly to President Roosevelt to help avert a strike of 32,000 CIO workers in seven vital Alcoa plants. The workers have a wage grievance and called for a strike poll of its members on Aug. 27. They also were denied a $1-a-day wage increase by the WLB.

PLANT PICKETED

At Louisville, Ky., a group of CIO aluminum workers picketed the 11 plants of the Reynolds Metals Company in what they termed a "lockout" despite a refusal by the NLRB to call a bargaining election. Operations at the plant continued with the help of AFL workers, who, the NLRB said, were in the majority. They also had been denied.

The WLB has not said what it would do, if the aluminum union strikes, but the two previous cases of WLB defiance brought quick action from Mr. Roosevelt.

He ordered the Navy to seize the General Cable Corporation's Bayonne, N. J., plant when a union struck for a 10-cent-an-hour wage increase the WLB had denied and made it plain that this action was not against the management. Subsequently, he ordered the Army to seize the Wood Machine Company in South Boston, Mass., when the management would not accept a

(Continued On Page Eight)

Objectors To War Must Go To Court

By United Press

PHILADELPHIA, Aug. 22 — The U. S. Circuit Court of Appeals ruled late yesterday that conscientious objectors must be inducted into the army and then petition for writs of habeas corpus if they wish to have their classifications by local draft boards changed.

The ruling was made in the case of Leland W. Drumheller, 26, of Boyertown, who is serving a two-year sentence for failure to report for induction into a work camp. Drumheller, who said he was an ordained minister of the Jehovah's Witnesses' sect, was classified as an objector by his draft board.

He sought to have the court restrain the board from inducting him and to set aside his classification.

Enlists In Marines

Graule Photo

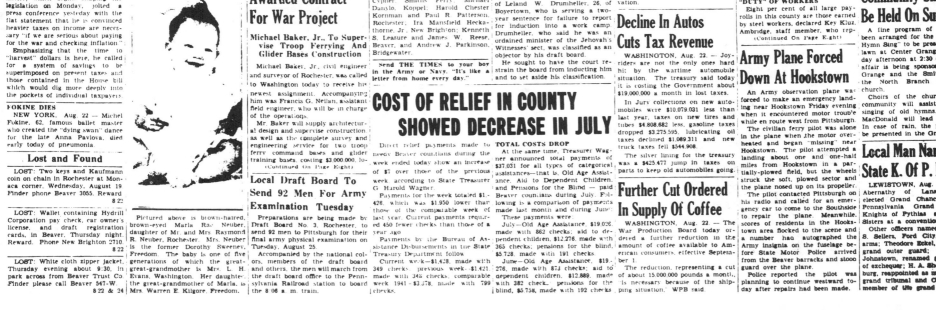

Robert Howard McCandless, (above) oldest son of Mr. and Mrs. C. Guy McCandless of Forest Homes, near Rochester, has enlisted in the United States Marines. He was graduated from Freedom high school in the class of 1940 and had been employed as a shell inspector by the National Supply Company, Ambridge. The McCandlesses, before moving to Rochester, lived in Freedom.

Four Persons Hurt In Local Accidents Friday And Today

Three Injured In Traffic Accidents And Another Hurt In Fall

An Ellwood City man received slight lacerations of the wrist when the automible in which he was riding collided with a truck shortly after midnight this morning near Ellwood City.

Both the truck and the car rolled over after the collision but the truck driver and other occupants of the car were not hurt, according to State Motor Police investigating the accident.

The injured man, Jack Glogosky, Ellwood City, and three other occupants of the car were arrested on a charge of disorderly conduct and lodged over night in the county jail at Beaver, police stated today.

HURT IN AUTO ACCIDENT

Willis Knatz, 1011 Bernadine street, Ambridge, was admitted to Rochester hospital this afternoon for treatment of lacerations of the leg reportedly received in an automobile accident on the Fallston road.

FALLS ON BOTTLE

Harold Douglass, 17, near Beaver Falls, was treated at Providence hospital this morning for lacerations of the hand reportedly received when he fell on a broken milk bottle while working for the Hart Dairy Company.

HURT IN TRAFFIC

Leonard Schillinger, Oil City, was treated at Rochester hospital early this morning for minor injuries reportedly received in a traffic accident on the Sunflower road, near Rochester.

FALLS ON STREET

Mike Vukovich, 30 Sheffield avenue, Aliquippa, was admitted to Beaver Valley hospital Friday evening after having fallen on a street in Aliquippa. Examination failed to reveal any injuries but he was confined to the hospital for observation.

Decline In Autos Cuts Tax Revenue

WASHINGTON, Aug. 22. — Joy-riders are not the only ones hard hit by the wartime automobile situation. The treasury said today it is costing the Government about $19,000,000 a month in lost taxes.

In Jury collections on new automobiles were $10,079,031 less than last year, taxes on new tires and tubes $4,808,682 less, gasoline taxes dropped $3,275,595, lubricating oil taxes declined $1,089,311 and new truck taxes fell $544,908.

The silver lining for the treasury was a $425,477 jump in taxes on parts to keep old automobiles going.

Further Cut Ordered In Supply Of Coffee

WASHINGTON, Aug. 22. — The War Production Board today ordered a further reduction in the amount of coffee available to American consumers, effective September 1.

The reduction, representing a cut of about 15,000,000 pounds a month, "is necessary because of the shipping situation," WPB said.

NEW SUCCESSES SCORED BY U. S

By United Press

LONDON—Predict daylight flying fortress attacks on Berlin; RAF and U. S. planes sweep English Channel; new reports of unrest from occupied Europe.

BERLIN—Nazis claim capture of Krymskaya and Kurchanskaya, close to Russian naval base of Novorossisk.

PEARL HARBOR—American Marines killed 842 Japanese, take 30 prisoners in Southeast Pacific battles.

GENERAL MacARTHUR'S HEADQUARTERS—Allied bombers attack Timor.

MOSCOW—Germans press hard on approaches of Stalingrad despite Soviet counter-attacks.

American forces in the southwest Pacific today fought to widen the successes already won in their initial offensive operation against the Japanese.

U. S. Marines in the Solomons—backed up by high-flying bombers of Gen. Douglas MacArthur's command—made it plain to the Japanese that they are engaged in a fight to the death.

Official American communiques revealed that in three bloody encounters with the Japanese the marines had taken only 30 prisoners while 842 Japanese were slain in combat. Against these heavy enemy losses the only stated marine casualties were 34 men killed and 85 wounded.

The actions were fought both in the Solomons where the Marines steadily mopped up the areas under their control and fought off Japanese counterattacks and on Makin Island of the Gilbert group.

DESTRUCTIVE RAID

The Gilbert action was revealed to have been a raid of destruction. Marines fought their way onto the island, destroyed Japanese installations, crippled the small Japanese garrison and then withdrew, their mission accomplished.

Second in command in the Gilbert battle, it was revealed, was President Roosevelt's son, Maj. James Roosevelt. He was unscathed in the action.

In the Solomons fighting was continuous and bloody. When a Japanese landing party of 700 troops attempted to dislodge the Americans from one position, it was destroyed with 670 killed and 30 prisoners. In another Solomon battle 92 Japanese were slain.

Long range bombers from Australia were in action to harass Japanese bases from which rein-

(Continued On Page Eight)

County CIO Leaders Pledge Aid In USO Drive For $50,000

Plans For Campaign Mapped By Local Presidents At Meeting In Beaver

President of the various locals of the United Steel Workers will immediately meet with the management of the various industrial plants with which C. I. O. contracts are held, as the first step in a plan for the complete cooperation of some 37,000 steel workers in Beaver County in support of the local campaign to raise $50,000 here for the United Service Organization.

This decision was reached at an enthusiastic meeting of the official C. I. O. group in the assembly room at the court house last night.

Manuel Wood, Baden, International Representative, with headquarters in Ambridge, was named as chairman for the U. S. W. in the county U. S. O. drive. Mr. Wood declared that through plant management and labor, working hand in hand, the campaign to provide funds in support of the morale of the United States soldiers and sailors will be realized.

SEEK $1 PER MAN

Every effort will be made to obtain a contribution of at least one dollar from each member of the C. I. O. organization, the chairman declaring that the fact must be taken into consideration that heavy demands have already been made upon this group in the various war activities.

Charles Yoho, president of the county C. I. O. Council, presided and declared that there was no question as to the endorsement of organized labor in the campaign.

The educational sound movie, "The Private Letters of Private Dobbs," was shown and was followed by an interesting talk by Mrs. R. Henry Carothers, Beaver Falls, mother of the first county soldier to enlist after the Pearl Harbor attack, who gave a detailed description of her personal observation of U. S. O. clubs and activities in the communities where there are large numbers of soldiers in training.

District Attorney Robert E. McCreary, campaign chairman, expressed to the executive group of the U. S. W. his appreciation of the splendid work of this organization that made it possible to raise over $100,000, for the Red Cross War Relief instead of the quota of $75,000, and said that the same spirit of United effort would result in the U. S. O. quota being exceeded in this county.

"DUTY" OF WORKERS

Eight per cent of all large payrolls in this county are those earned by steel workers, declared Key Kluz, Ambridge, staff member, who rep-

(Continued On Page Eight)

Army Plane Forced Down At Hookstown

An Army observation plane was forced to make an emergency landing near Hookstown Friday evening when it encountered motor trouble while en route west from Pittsburgh.

The civilian ferry pilot was alone in the plane when the motor overheated and began "missing" near Hookstown. The pilot attempted a landing about one and one-half miles from Hookstown in a partially-plowed field, but the wheels struck the soft, plowed sector and the plane nosed up on its propeller.

The pilot contacted Pittsburgh on his radio and called for an emergency car to come to the Southside to repair the plane. Meanwhile, scores of residents in the Hookstown area flocked to the scene and a number had autographed the Army insignia on the fuselage before State Motor Police arrived from the Beaver barracks and stood guard over the plane.

Police reported the pilot was planning to continue westward today after repairs had been made.

Source Of Blackout 'Leaks' Discovered

HARRISBURG, Aug. 22.—Dr. A. C. Martz, director of the State Defense Council, revealed today that he has "discovered the sources" of information "leaks" on the starting time of the Tuesday night Pennsylvania-New Jersey blackout.

Declaring that "the guilty persons have been reprimanded," Marts said "measures which we hope will be effective have been taken to prevent further leaks."

He would not enlarge further on the situation, which marred perfection of the 25-minute drill. Philadelphia, where the leaks apparently were most widespread, has scheduled a "completely surprise" blackout for some future date.

Community Sing To Be Held On Sunday

A fine program of music has been arranged for the "Community Hymn Sing" to be presented on the lawn at Center Grange hall, Sunday afternoon at 2:30 o'clock. The affair is being sponsored by the Grange and the Smith Circle of the North Branch Presbyterian church.

Choirs of the churches in the community will assist with the singing of old hymns. George F. MacDonald will lead the singing. In case of rain, the program will be presented in the Grange hall.

Local Man Named To State K. Of P. Post

LEWISTOWN, Aug. 22. — W. P. Abernathy of Lansdowne, was elected Grand Chancellor of the Pennsylvania Grand Lodge of Knights of Pythias and Pythian Sisters at a convention yesterday.

Other officers named included J. S. Sellers, Ford City, master-at-arms; Theodore Eckel, Bridgewater, grand outer guard; Henry Fox, Johnstown, renamed grand master of exchequer; H. A. Sheaff, Canonsburg, reappointed as member of the grand tribunal and Chester Nagel member of the grand tribunal.

SQUAD OF 47 GREETS NEW GRID COACH AT BEAVER HIGH

CANDIDATES FOR 1942 BOBCAT TEAM INCLUDES 11 LETTERMEN

Coaches Harold Leffler and Max Martin Plan Two-a-Day Sessions for Maroon Squad Until School Starts Sept. 9

Beaver High school's 1942 football squad, about 47 strong, is hard at work under direction of Head Coach Harold C. Leffler and Assistant Coach Max Martin in preparation for the opening game with Midland on Thursday night, September 10, at Midland. Drills were started Tuesday and will continue twice daily until the Beaver schools open for the Fall term on September 9.

Coaches Leffler and Martin, who succeeded John Economos and Sam Milanovich this year, found eleven lettermen on hand when the squad reported this week, including nine linesmen and two backs.

The returning lettermen include: Don Carlon, center; Jack Deeley, Roger Netherland and Lawrence Deemer, guards; Dick Hume, Bob Pinkerton and Milt Patterson, tackles; Clarence Black and Tom Holt, ends; Don Parsons and Dick Scherrbaum, backs.

Carlon, Deeley, Hume, Netherland, Parsons and Pinkerton are seniors this year, Black, Deemer and Holt are juniors, while Patterson and Scherrbaum are sophomores.

Other candidates who gained some experience last season but did not earn letters are: Tom Cochran, Cleo Davis, and Bob Patterson, seniors; Frank Cascio, Bill Douds, Duard Fisher, Harry McKelvey, Frank Moravec and Frank Morris, juniors, and Dominic Cascio, sophomore. Tom Fitzgerald, center, a junior, has not reported for practice but is expected out later.

Squad members who are trying out for the first time include: Fil Mecklem, and Vernon Keener, seniors; Gordon Lees, Jack Good, Bob Holt, John Cool, Ted Gooch, Eugene Kirk, Jack Wright, Jack Gibson, Bob Boyd, Kramer Bradshaw, Charles Wallace, Raymond Tabay and J. Boeh, juniors; George McCormick, Joe Houk, Harold Firestone, Bob Mellon, Charles Schendel, Paul Courtney, Jack Martin, Eugene Morgan, J. W. Coates and Jim Black, sophomores.

Five backs and two linesmen were lost from the 1941 Beaver high team, including Bill Emmerich, Gilbert Flocker, Bud Grove, Gail Perault and Dick Bundy, backs, and Tom G[illegible]ford, tackle and end, and Bob Gridley, guard.

Practice sessions of the Beaver gridders yesterday consisted chiefly of conditioning exercises, but rougher stuff is ahead. Yesterday student managers were busy putting the finishing touches on a huge new charging machine.

Coach Leffler, who comes to Beaver after 12 years as assistant coach at Martins Ferry, O. high school, plans to hold morning and afternoon drills until school opens on Wednesday, September 9. The opening game with Midland is on Thursday, September 10, which gives the Bobcat mentors more than two weeks to whip a team into shape.

There appears to be enough experienced linesmen on hand, but Leffler and Martin will have to develop backfield men to replace last year's quartet of regulars who included Bill Emmerich, Gail Perault, Gilbert Flocker and Bud Grove.

However, the Bobcat squad includes several boys who showed promise last year of developing into fine backfield players, Bill Douds, Frank Morris, Don Parsons, Dick Scherrbaum, Frank Cascio. There are also several promising candidates among the members of last year's junior high team who have joined the varsity squad.

In addition to the game with Midland, the Bobcat eleven will play Avalon, Leetsdale, Monaca, Zelienople, Avonworth, New Brighton, Freedom and Rochester. The first home game is with Avalon on Thursday night, September 17. Portable lights will be used. The final game with Rochester is booked for November 6, at the Junction City field.

Segura Favored In Amateur Tourney

By United Press

NEW YORK, Aug. 27—The 61st national amateur tennis championships open at Forest Hills today with a bounding South American favored to become the first foreign winner of the men's title in eight years and a husky California girl an odds-on favorite to capture women's honors.

Francisco (Pancho) Segura, the undersized Ecuadorean with the two-fisted attack, was rated at even money to take the men's singles title and Louise Brough of Beverly Hills, Calif., was favored for the new women's championship.

Victory for Segura would make him the first invader to carry off the crown since Fred Perry, the Belting Briton, turned back Wilmer Allison in 1934 for a repeat triumph.

ARMSTRONG WINS

OAKLAND, Cal., Aug. 27—Henry Armstrong won another fight in his comeback drive last night with a technical knockout over Rodolfo Ramierz, Mexico City, in the eighth round of the scheduled 10-round main event.

Aliquippa Team Quits League Title Series

The Aliquippa Y.N.R.C. club has pulled out of the Beaver County Baseball League championship series with Conway, it was reported last night after League President Don Bailey refused a protest on the game played Tuesday night at Aliquippa and won by Conway, 2 to 1.

Unless plans are changed later today there will be no game at Conway tonight, as scheduled, and Manager Eddie Gratty's club will win the League title for the second straight year.

Conway won the first game of the series Monday night, by a score of 7 to 1, and captured the second contest, 2 to 1, although Lefty Cepull held Gratty's outfit to two hits over nine innings.

According to reports it was in the ninth inning of the second game that the controversy arose, when the umpires refused to call a balk against Pitcher Frank Birner of Conway. President Bailey said it was purely a matter of the umpires' judgment, but when he refused to act on the protest last night the Steeler management announced their team would not appear at Conway tonight for the third game of the series.

Umpires, Bladesmen Enjoy Ball Game

The Beaver County League umpires didn't defeat Curtiss-Wright in their exhibition game at Beaver last night, but all hands had a good time.

The final score was reported as 6-0 in favor of the Bladesmen.

Graham (Grimmy) Smith pitched for the Umpires and Popik did the catching. Other arbiters on hand were Starr, Triance, Stewart and Goehring.

Manager Ray Davis of the Rochester Pirates showed the Umpires how to call balls and strikes, and League President Don Bailey umpired on the bases.

West Virginia Will Use Freshmen Gridders

By United Press

MORGANTOWN, W. Va., Aug. 27—West Virginia University has discontinued the freshman rule in athletics for the duration of the war, Athletic Director Roy Hawley announced yesterday.

The one year residence (freshman) rule was abandoned by the athletic board because the school lost a number of athletes who enlisted or were drafted into the armed services.

The black drum, a fish inhabiting southern waters, has stone crushing machinery in the back of its mouth. It preys upon oysters and various kinds of marine animals.

IT'S PAPA CROSETTI OFF DIAMOND

When he's off the baseball diamond, Frankie Crosetti, New York Yankee infielder, fills very well the role of a proud papa. He's pictured above with his 10-month-old daughter, Ellen, as they got a breath of fresh air in a New York park.

BEAVER HIGH SCHOOL FOOTBALL SQUAD FOR 1942

TIMES Photo by Bill Heyman

Shown in the above photo is the Beaver high school football squad which is in training under Coaches Harold C. Leffler and Max Martin in preparation for the 1942 gridiron season. The Bobcats will hold two drills daily until the start of the school term on September 9, and open the season against Midland on September 10.

Dodgers Cinch To Take Flag, Experts Say, Despite Recent Sprint Of St. Louis Cards

Brooklyn Now Only 4¼ Games Ahead As Cards Win Third Straight From Pace-Setters; Giants Snap Five-Game Losing Streak; Red Sox Now Trailing Yanks By 7½ Games

By United Press

NEW YORK, Aug. 27—On the face of it, the National League flag race looks tough for the Brooklyn Dodgers but take it from the historians, the Flatbushers cannot lose.

It is a mere matter of mixing psychology with facts supplied by the game's historians. So well has the course of baseball been charted that it is almost indisputable that a team beaten in a hard-fought campaign almost never bounces back to win the follow season.

Two years ago, the Tigers edged past the Indians and went into the big money and the Cleveland club has never recovered. The same thing happened in 1938 when the Pirates blew up and three years before when the Cubs stormed through a 21-game winning streak to nip the Cards at the post. The Pirates have never been a contender since and St. Louis is still trying to come back.

Psychologists explain that the shock of final defeat after months of strain and effort is too much for a team to withstand. That's what happened to the Cards last year and regardless of what has happened in St. Louis so far during this Cardinal - Dodger series and what may happen in the final game today, the Red Birds haven't ever been the club that gave Brooklyn such a spirited brawl in '41. Then, they had youth, speed, spirit and drive and although they lost in '41, they were figured a cinch to follow up this year. But Brooklyn has been in front almost all the way and that's the way it's going to finish, according to the form charts.

The Cardinals trimmed the Dodgers' National League edge to 4¼ games, scoring their third straight victory, 2-1, in 10 innings at Sportsmen's Park yesterday.

The Cards staged another garrison finish, breaking a 1-all tie in the 10th when Second Baseman Jimmy Brown charged from third and bowled over Catcher Mickey Owen with the winning run.

The Giants cracked a string of five straight defeats with a 15-hit attack on three pitchers and whipped the Reds, 11-2.

Doubles by Danny Litwhiler and Nick Etten in the 11th gave the Phils a 3-2 victory over the Cubs in the first game of a doubleheader but Les Fleming brought the Bruins an even break by holding the Phils to five hits for a 3-0 win in the nightcap.

Excellent relief pitching by Joe Haynes and timely round-trippers by Myril Hoag and Wally Moses helped the White Sox defeat the Yankees, 5-3.

Bill Butland, recently made over into a starting pitcher, won his fourth victory in a row as the Red Sox defeated the Indians, 4-1. A single by Tony Lupin with the bases loaded and another one-bagger by Joe Cronin with the bases packed, sent home two more in the eighth. It was the Sox' ninth consecutive win and cut the Yankees' lead to 7½ games.

The Tigers took both ends of a double-header from the Athletics, winning the first game, 1-0 for Virgil Trucks, and the nightcap, 4-2, behind the five-hit pitching of Hal White.

Baseball Summary

NATIONAL LEAGUE

Results Wednesday

New York 11, Cincinnati 2.
*Philadelphia 3, Chicago 2.
Chicago 3, Philadelphia 0.
·St. Louis 2, Brooklyn 1.
Only games scheduled.
*11 innings. ·10 innings.

TEAM STANDING

	W.	L.	Pct.
Brooklyn	84	38	.689
St. Louis	80	43	.650
New York	66	58	.532
Cincinnati	60	62	.492
Pittsburgh	56	63	.471
Chicago	59	70	.457
Boston	50	75	.400
Philadelphia	36	82	.305

Games Today

Boston at Pittsburgh.
Brooklyn at St. Louis.
New York at Cincinnati.
Others not scheduled.

Games Friday

New York at Pittsburgh.
Boston at Cincinnati (night).
Philadelphia at St. Louis.
Brooklyn at Chicago.

AMERICAN LEAGUE

Results Wednesday

Chicago 5, New York 3.
Boston 4, Cleveland 1.
Detroit 1, Philadelphia 0.
Detroit 4, Philadelphia 2.
Only games scheduled.

TEAM STANDING

	W.	L.	Pct
New York	82	43	.656
Boston	75	51	.595
St. Louis	66	59	.528
Cleveland	64	61	.512
Detroit	63	64	.496
Chicago	54	65	.454
Washington	48	73	.397
Philadelphia	48	84	.264

Games Today

Cleveland at Boston.
Others not scheduled.

Games Friday

Chicago at Boston.
Detroit at Washington.
Cleveland at New York.
Others not scheduled.

PENN STATE ASSN.

Johnstown	109 300 100	14-17-2
Washington	034 200 030	12-14-5

Brenning, Akers (3) and Jackson; Babbey, Robinson (3), Schoendinest (4), Graham (6) and Alsnauer.

Oil City	103 100 130	9-12-5
Butler	130 404 51x	18-15-3

Gustafson, Shapiro (6) and Corley; Faine, Rapach (8) and Leone.

Reindeer herds continue to increase in the Canadian Arctic, and the recent fawning season indicates an estimated 1,000 fawns added to the main herd, according to E. G. Poole, game and fish representative at Winnipeg. The year's fawn crop will be likely to boost the reindeer population of the Northwest Territories to about 10,000 animals, says Poole.

BLADESMEN LEAVE TOMORROW FOR GAME WITH JERSEY TEAM

The Curtiss - Wright baseball team, runner-up in the second half in the Beaver County League, will seek to gain the championship of the Propeller Division of the Curtiss-Wright Corporation in a series with the team representing the two New Jersey plants of the company, starting next Saturday afternoon at Patterson, N. J.

The Keystone Bladesmen will leave Rochester about 9:45 o'clock Friday evening on a sleeper train and will arrive in Newark, N. J., Saturday morning. They will visit the Caldwell, N. J., plant Saturday morning and Saturday afternoon at 4:30 o'clock, will meet the New Jersey plant team at Patterson.

The second game of the series will be played at Gypsy Glen Field, Beaver, starting at 4:30 o'clock, on Saturday, September 5, when the New Jersey team will visit the Beaver plant. If a third game is necessary it will be played immediately after the second contest.

Following the game next Saturday at Patterson, the local Bladesmen will go to New York to have dinner with members of the New Jersey team, and will remain there overnight, and return home Sunday night. Most of the players making the trip are utilizing their week-end vacation periods.

Those who are slated to make the trip are: Manager Frank Madva, center field; Earl Meyers, third base; Frank Mason, shortstop; Paul Watson, left field; Mike Babin, second base; Stan Navage, first base; Paul Rosenlieb, right field; Ed. Sandusky, catcher; Ira Curtiss and Lefty Boren, pitchers; Ross Gibbs, outfielder; Harold Smith first base, and Tom Murray, catcher.

SPORT SLANTS

By BILL ANDERSON

A crowd estimated at 400 persons turned out Monday night to witness the opening game of the County League championship series between the Conway and Aliquippa clubs at Conway. An even larger attendance had been anticipated for the game scheduled at Aliquippa last Sunday, called-off because of rain.

Monday night's boxing show at Hickey Park, in which three local fighters scored victories, attracted a goodly number of Valley mitt fans. The show was a good one, every bout being interesting. Trouble was experienced with the ring lights. Part of the lights went out when the first bout was in progress and only four of the nine burned during the remainder of the show.

The Beaver Falls Police Department is planning its annual amateur boxing show for the evening of October 19. John Loscianno, of Ellwood City, will be the matchmaker and arrange the bouts, and Milt Weiner is handling the promotional details. Ted Corcoran, a member of the Beaver Falls police force, it is said, will make his fistic debut.

Ambridge high school has placed adult season tickets for the Bridgers' six home games, all night attractions, on sale. Student session tickets will go on sale when school opens September 1. . . The Ellwood City and Wampum Rod and Gun clubs will hold their third annual field day on October 8. . . There will be at least a 20 per cent decrease in the number of colleges playing football this Fall . . Baseball Commissioner Landis has arranged for the world series to be broadcast so all games can be heard by all men in the U. S. services overseas.

Bill Daddio, former Pitt star, has given up his job as physical director at a Meadville plant, to return for a second season of pro football with the Chicago Cardinals.

BOUT POSTPONED

CHICAGO, Aug. 27—Ray (Sugar) Robinson, New York, and Tony Motisi, Chicago, meet tonight in a welterweight boxing match in Comiskey Park. Scheduled for last night, the fight was postponed because of weather.

PITCHING FOR U. S. - - By Jack Sord

'TAINT ANYTHING TO WHAT I'LL DO TO THE JAPS!
TED LYONS,
41-YEAR-OLD VETERAN PITCHER OF THE CHICAGO WHITE SOX, READY FOR HIS CALL TO THE ARMY
IN 20 YEARS WITH THE WHITE SOX HE HAS PITCHED

K. Of C. Tournament Set For Sunday At Blackhawk Course

The golf party scheduled for last Sunday by the county Knights of Columbus was postponed due to the bad weather until Sunday afternoon, August 30. Teeing-off time has been set for 2 o'clock and the Blackhawk course will be the scene of action.

Arrangements have been made to serve a grilled dinner at the K. of C. Council Rooms at Rochester following the golfing. The approximate time for the dinner will be 6:30. It has been decided to hold the dinner party Sunday evening regardless of the weather, so in case of rain again, the entire day will not be spoiled. The evening event is open to members and their friends, regardless of whether they play golf or not.

No additional charges are being made for the tournament as only the regular green-fees are collected and the contestants have a chance to enter the blind-bogey contest by setting their own handicap score, this method giving all golfers, regardless of their ability, the same opportunity for the awards.

If any persons so far not having been contacted by the committee for these activities desire to phone for reservations they may do so by getting in touch with any of the following: M A. Marino, John Slyman or F. N. Joyce.

Jack La Motta To Test Jimmy Edgar Friday Evening

By United Press

NEW YORK, Aug. 27. — Jimmy Edgar of Detroit, the "Little Brown Bomber," gets his all-important test at Madison Square Garden Friday night when he proves to the boxing world that he is either (1) a second edition of Joe Louis, or (2) just another ham-and-egger.

Edgar is compared with heavyweight champion Joe Louis in his every move because he comes from Detroit, the champion's home town, because he is managed by John Roxborough—one of Louis' co-managers—because he apparently is one of the hardest hitting welterweights ever to toss leather. And because he admittedly apes jolting Joe's shuffling style.

Edgar caused a mild quake in the boxing fraternity on July 31, when he knocked out Vern Patterson in the second round at the Garden, after exhibiting one of the grandest displays of straight punching New Yorkers have noted in a comparative novice in years.

Because of that kayo, 21-year-old Edgar is being thrown into the ring Friday night with Jack La Motta, a tough middleweight who will out-weigh welterweight Edgar seven or eight pounds. And La Motta is favored to win at 7-5 because La Motta is a rough, tough operator who never has been knocked out and who has lost only four decisions in two years.

If the little brown bomber gets past La Motta in their 10-rounder Friday night, he will be in position to demand a big-money shot with any of the country's top-flight welters—such as Ray Robinson, Fritzie Zivic—or even champion Red Cochran of the Navy.

Young Edgar fights like Louis largely because Corporal Joe spent nearly two months teaching him what to do with his fists. That was at the Louis farm near Detroit, where there's always a welcome sign out.

Tri-State PGA Tourney Opens At Sunnehanna

By United Press

JOHNSTOWN, Aug. 27—The annual championship tournament of the Tri-State chapter, Professional Golfers' Association opened today at the Sunnehanna Country Club, with Perry DelVecchio of Greensburg in the role of defending champion. Between 25 and 30 professionals teed off in the 18-hole qualifying round.

FREEDOM NEWS

Miss Rosey Bell Is Hostess To Cheer Leaders At Her Home

Freedom High School Girls Making Plans For Ensuing Year; To Visit Pittsburgh

Miss Rosey Bell, captain of the cheer leaders of Freedom high school, entertained the other cheer leaders, including Misses Mila Morton, Dolly Sparato and Anna Linta, at her home in East Fifth avenue, Wednesday evening. Misses "Evie" Heslip and Jane McCauley were guests. The girls discussed plans for the ensuing year and for electing another cheer leader. Friday, they expect to go to Pittsburgh to purchase some equipment and uniforms. At the close of the evening, the hostess, assisted by her mother, Mrs. Joseph Bell, served lunch.

Joseph Hattinger of Buffalo, N. Y., visited Tuesday and Wednesday in the home of his brother and sister-in-law, Mr. and Mrs. Leonard J. Hattinger, and family, West Fifth avenue. Miss Irene Barry of Pittsburgh arrived Wednesday to visit a week with the Hattingers.

Walter M. Otto, Sixth avenue, is expected to return Friday evening from Geneva - on - the - Lake, O., where he is vacationing a week with a group of young men from Carnegie Tech, Pittsburgh.

Mr. and Mrs. Elmer H. Otto, Conway-Wallrose road, formerly of Freedom, have named their daughter, born Monday morning in Sewickley Valley hospital, Ellen Lucille. She weighed six pounds and fourteen ounces.

Mrs. Gilbert Chapman and daughter, Joy, of East Liverpool, O., have concluded a visit of ten days with Mr. and Mrs. Robert Rich, and son, "Bobby," West Fourth avenue. Mrs. Chapman is an aunt of Mrs. Rich.

Mr. and Mrs. William Witts, Crows Run, have received word that their son, Corporal William Witts, Jr., has arrived in England.

At the Freedom National Bank during Wednesday's first daylight air raid test, it took exactly 2½ minutes to put away cash and lock up the vault, it was reported today.

The grunion is a peculiar fish which comes up on the southern California beaches to spawn in July and August. In a heavy run an in-washing wave may litter the sands with the fish, where anglers can catch them with their hands.

French is the mother tongue to five million North Americans, three million of them in the province of Quebec.

Invited to U. S.

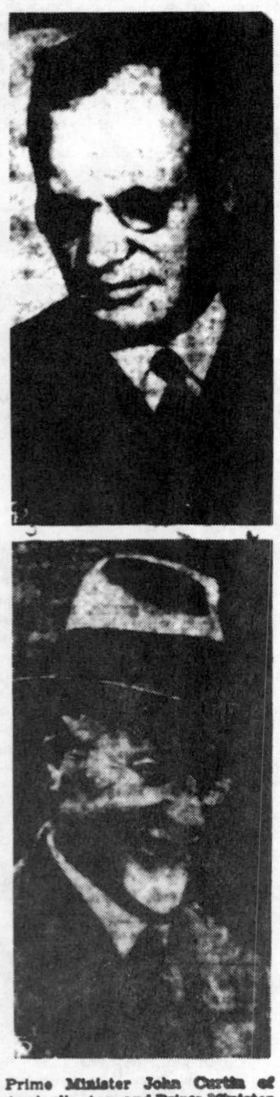

Prime Minister John Curtin of Australia, top, and Prime Minister Jan Smuts of the Union of South Africa, bottom, have been invited by President Roosevelt to visit the United States. The purpose of the invitation was not disclosed. Prime Minister Peter Fraser of New Zealand is now in the United States.

Amusements

ORIENTAL THEATRE

Clark Gable and Lana Turner, the titanic twosome who made screen history in "Honky Tonk," are reunited in one of the year's important pictures, "Somewhere I'll Find You," currently showing at the Oriental Theatre today for the last time.

A musical show idea teeming with originality and packing more solid entertainment per foot than the movie public has been offered in a long time, is due tomorrow when the long-awaited Irving Berlin's "Holiday Inn" bows into town with Bing Crosby, Fred Astaire, Marjorie Reynolds, Virginia Dale and Walter Abel.

The idea was to make a picture revolving around our national holidays. This they have done in "Holiday Inn," setting these holidays to music and wrapping around them a fascinating love story.

Crosby, as a night club singer, breaks away from his partners, Fred Astaire and Virginia Dale, because he's tired of grinding away at singing and dancing in these clubs. He's just plain lazy. So he retires to a Connecticut farm, but working it single-handed leaves no time at all even to look at a calendar, let alone do any celebrating. He conceives the idea of turning the farm into an inn to be open only on holidays when guests will be fed and entertained with a floor show. There being only 15 important holidays during a year, Bing figures he can rest the other 350.

"Holiday Inn" sparkles with eleven great new Berlin tunes you've already been hearing, and two favorite old ones. The picture is said to represent the best efforts of Bing Crosby and Fred Astaire to date, which should make it an entertainment "must" for anybody and everybody.

MAJESTIC THEATRE

Four pairs of eyes saw the crime; but four pairs of lips told different stories, while a man's life hung in the balance—proving that, when it's murder, seeing isn't always believing! But previewers who have seen 20th Century-Fox latest baffler, "Thru Different Eyes," coming to the Majestic Theatre Friday insist that it's one of the most unusual mystery thrillers of the year.

Tantalizingly unfolded in the flashback manner, the story concerns the tribulations of a county district attorney beset by an unfathomable killing and a meddlesome wife.

As far as the state is concerned, the case was closed with the conviction of the fiance of the D. A.'s own niece. That's where the missus steps in. She is very close to her niece and, since her intuition tells her the guilty one is still at large, she takes matters into her own hands.

"Boss Of Hangtown Mesa," starring Johnny Mack Brown, is the added attraction for Friday and Saturday.

Chester Morris and Harriet Hilliard are co-starred in "Canal Zone," the feature attraction at the Majestic tonight. "Billy The Kid's Smoking Guns," starring Buster Crabbe, is also included on tonight's billing.

Send THE TIMES to your boy in the Army or Navy. "It's like a letter from home every day."

On Miami Honeymoon

Walking along a palm-tree-studded lawn in Miami are Lieut. and Mrs. Edgar L. Hinton. She is the former Marguerite Roach, daughter of Major Hal Roach, Hollywood motion picture producer. The couple was married in San Antonio, Texas, eight days before Roach was married for the second time. Roach's new bride is Lucille Prin, of Los Angeles. *(Central Press)*

HOLIDAY INN

"HOLIDAY INN" ENTERTAINERS STEP OUT between shows. Bing Crosby and a few of the lovelies from Irving Berlin's smash hit musical, "Holiday Inn," which opens tomorrow at the Oriental Theatre. Bing shares starring honors with none other than Fred Astaire in this jamboree of songs, dances, romance and hilarity. The girls in this case are Marjorie Reynolds and Virginia Dale.

BEAVER THEATRE

Joan Crawford returning to the type of romantic comedy characterization which led to her original success, joyfully returns to the Beaver Theatre in "They All Kissed the Bride," a tender and warmly human love story with Melvyn Douglas delightfully co-starred. The stellar cast includes Roland Young, Billie Burke and Allen Jenkins.

"They All Kissed the Bride" presents Miss Crawford as a million dollar doll who toys with love, until she discovers she's playing with fire; Douglas is seen as the gentleman who believes there's nothing wrong with a woman that a man's lips won't cure.

One of the most delightfully entertaining movies of this or any other season, the new Irene Dunne comedy, "Lady in a Jam," opens tomorrow for an hour-and-a-half's laugh relaxation.

The film will have you chuckling in the opening scenes, laughing in the middle and howling at the end. It's solid and perfect entertainment.

GRANADA THEATRE

It isn't often that an Irving Berlin musical hits the screen, but there's one coming along soon! It's the song-filled, laugh-filled Paramount musical, dancing picture, "Holiday Inn," starring Bing Crosby and Fred Astaire, with Marjorie Reynolds, Virginia Dale and Walter Abel, opening today at the Granada Theatre.

For his latest film Mr. Berlin has written more new songs than have ever been composed for any one picture before. Eleven brand new hits, among them "White Christmas" and "Be Careful, It's My Heart," is something of a record even for America's foremost words-and-music man. As if eleven new Berlin songs weren't enough to set "Holiday Inn" head and shoulder above any other musical ever made, there are two old Berlin favorites thrown in for good measure—"Lazy," and "Easter Parade."

In the story, Crosby turns his farmhouse into an inn which is open only on holidays. Shows appropriate to the holidays, with music to match, are put on by Bing and Marjorie Reynolds.

Having more dances in this film than he's ever had before, Astaire divides them between Marjorie Reynolds and Virginia Dale, both of whom, from all accounts are terpsichoreally terrific. And Bing, of course, sings those Berlin melodies as only Bing can.

Send THE TIMES to your boy in the Army or Navy. "It's like a letter from home every day."

RIALTO THEATRE

A command for Love from movie fans the world over, brought Lana Turner and Clark Gable together again in the new romantic drama "Somewhere I'll Find You," featured this evening through Friday at the Rialto in Beaver Falls.

"Somewhere I'll Find You," an up-to-the-minute yarn written by Marguerite Roberts and Walter Reisch for the screen and based on a Cosmopolitan Magazine story by Charles Hoffman, sparkles with brittle dialogue, and excites with today's fast-moving action.

Clarke Gable is thoroughly at home in a newspaper reporter characterization while Lana Turner adds another vivid portrayal to her list of exciting roles, as a fiery girl reporter. As Gable's brother and reporter teammate is Robert Sterling in his biggest role to date.

"Somewhere I'll Find You," a fast-moving, full of action, modern adventure film is one you can't afford to miss.

Outstanding short subjects are included on the program.

Extra! Extra! Ann Rutherford, Lynn Bari, Carole Landis, Virginia Gilmore and Mary Beth Hughes are the "Orchestra Wives" or sweethearts in the musical triumph opening Saturday at the Rialto! Glenn Miller and his band who made history with their rendition of "Chattanooga Choo Choo" in "Sun Valley Serenade" are again featured in "Orchestra Wives".

Read THE TIMES Classified Ads

Restoring the Neck's Beauty

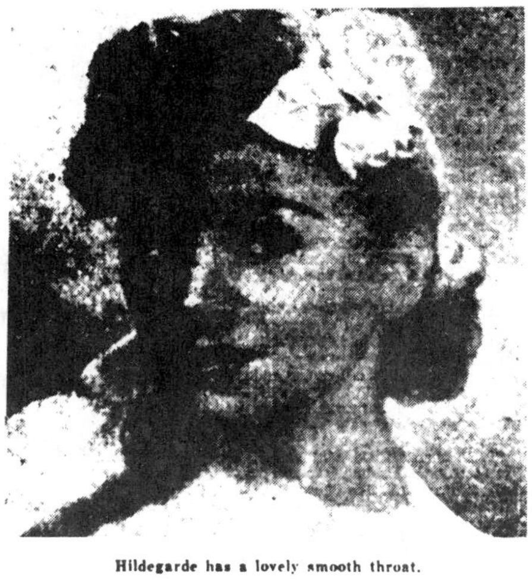

Hildegarde has a lovely smooth throat.

By HELEN FOLLETT

WHEN THE neck tuckers out and folds itself into plaits, a woman suspects that she is getting along. Hair can be made attractive no matter how thin it may be. Complexions can be brightened with counterfeit blushes and the flattering lipstick. If eyebrows are pale, mascara serves as first aid. But what can be done with a neck that has gone to seed? Hang a necklace around it and it looks just that much more forlorn and crestfallen.

When the face is happily lapping up cold cream or being refreshed with tonics and astringents the poor neck doesn't get even the leavings. It is often forgotten.

Take out an insurance against fiddle strings. Don't wait until the cross lines appear. Apply as much cream as you can force into the flesh. Start on the neck; then you won't forget and overlook its needs. Slap and pat. Smooth up and down with flattened fingers. In the morning dash on cold water.

Practice carrying the head splendidly, always on the level, never thrown forward. The forward pose relaxes muscles and tissues.

A plump, short neck gets wider and fatter if the head droops forward. The thin neck gets thinner under the same condition because fibers have no work to do.

The cure for neck troubles is found in a spirited body pose and such exercises as will assist the functions of glands, tissues, muscles and blood streams.

Stand erect, hands on hips. Tilt the head back slowly, forcing the under lip up over the upper one, pulling up the flesh of the chin until chin and neck are smooth and firm. Send the head back as far as it will go, then turn it slowly from side to side. There will be a pull on muscles way down on the chest and the shoulders. This pulling will make them strong and will stimulate circulation.

Read THE TIMES Classified Ads

CLASSIFIED ADVERTISING

This classified advertising department is for the convenience of the public. To insure publication the same day orders should be received by 10 a. m. Orders not received in time will be published the following day. All copy received subject to being edited or rejected by us. When sending advertisements by mail care should be used to write plainly giving complete instructions so that we may give efficient service in the preparation and publication of the advertisements. When possible, payment should accompany the order. This will be expected with orders from strangers. Cash with order, one cent a word for each publication. No advertisement published for less than 25 cents for each publication. Six consecutive publications for price of four. Extra charge will be made for use of large type. Classified advertisements not accompanied by cash will be charged at two cents per word with a minimum of 50 cents for each publication. This is absolutely necessary on account of the clerical work involved. Fifty per cent discount will be allowed on charge classified advertisements if paid for before expiration date. Usual cash rates will apply to advertisers having other running open accounts with us. The above is a local schedule applying only within Beaver County

Office Telephones
Beaver 1800 Rocheste- 3300

Wanted

WANTED: To apply insulated stone or brick style siding for home owners who really can appreciate a bargain. We have the best selection of shingles, the best price and the best applicators. F. H. A. loans can be arranged as low as $5 month, first payment starting 45 days after job is completed. Call Beaver 1601-W. 9|2-8 inc.

WANTED: For clients in Rochester, Sunflower, Tuscarawas and Brodhead road district, 5 and 6 room bungalow type homes — second floor available not necessarily finished, from $3,000 to $5,800. George C. Gremer, Real Estate & Insurance, office 236 Adams St., residence 315 Virginia Ave., Rohester. 9 2.

AT LOW BANK RATES
Finance repairs to your present home, a new home, or your next automobile through The Freedom National Bank, Freedom, Pa. 9|1-30 inc.

WANTED: Moving and hauling. Equipped for moving refrigerators. Inquire at Grocery Store, 832 Case St., East Rochester. Phone Roch. 9141. 9|1-14 inc.

BEAVER AIR RAID WARDENS' scrap collection every Thursday p. m. Iron, copper, brass, aluminum, rags, rubber and paper wanted. Call Hayes at Beaver 1629. 9 1-2

Help Wanted—Male

WANTED: Collector and investigator. Apply at Price's Clothing Store, 1000 Seventh avenue, Beaver Falls. 9 2-8 inc.

LARGE national organization needs men of clear record, in Beaver County or other Western Penna. cities. Will make insurance and credit investigations through personal contact with public. No selling or collecting. Permanent salaried position plus carfare. Good chances for advancement. Give age, education, employment record, present income and military status. Replies strictly confidential. Address P. O. Lock Box 1286, Pittsburgh, Pa. 9 1-3 inc.

WANTED: Life insurance man. For Rochester, Monaca debit. Good salary and commission. Car not necessary. Good future for the right man. Write Rochester P. O. No. 27. 9 1-3 inc.

WANTED: Reliable store boy for ladies dress shop. Phone Beaver Falls 2752. 9|1-3 inc.

WANTED: Men to work on track. Apply Pennsylvania Railroad Freight Station, Rochester. 8|31-9|2 inc

WANTED: High school or college graduate with some knowledge of chemistry for production control work in local chemical laboratory. Give age, draft status, experience and salary expected. Write Box X-10 c/o DAILY TIMES, Beaver. 8|28-9|3 inc

WANTED: Let us clean and press your suit or topcoat at Beaver's only dry cleaning plant. Miller's Cleaning Shoppe, next to city building, Beaver. Phone 2235-J. 9 8*

Help Wanted—Female

We pay you $25 for selling fifty $1.00 boxes. 50 beautiful assorted name imprinted Christmas cards sell $1.00—your profit 50c. Free samples. Cheerful Card Co. 28A0 White Plains, N. Y. 9 2

WANTED: Young lady to take charge of small child in afternoons. Call Beaver 2667-J between 9 A. M. and 12 noon. 9 2-4 inc.

WANTED: Girl for full time housework. Phone Beaver 2573 or apply 337 3rd Street, Beaver. 9 2-8 inc.

WANTED: Waitress. Apply Dan's Dairy Bar, 916 Pennsylvania Ave., Monaca, between 9 a. m. and 5 p. m. 9 2-8 inc

WANTED: Seamstress by Weiss Cleaners, 159 Brighton Ave., Rochester. 9 2

WANTED: Two experienced waitresses. Apply Center Restaurant, 103 Brighton Ave., Rochester. 9 1-2

WANTED: Girl or woman for general housework or mother's helper. Apply 1093 Bank street, Beaver. 9|1-7 inc.

WANTED: Middle-aged woman, light housework, 4 days a week, no washing, no cooking, stay nights, permanent, no children; room and board. Write "Box R-10" c/o DAILY TIMES, Beaver. 8 31-9,5 inc

WANTED: Experienced cleaning woman several days a week. Phone Beaver 2028. 8 31-9 5 inc

Help Wanted—Female

WANTED: Dishwasher. Phone Beaver 1101-R. 9|2-4 inc

WANTED: Girl for general housework, go home nights. Phone Rochester 20. 9|2-4 inc

WANTED: Experienced girl for general housework. Phone Beaver 1562-R between 7 and 9 p. m. 8|29-9|4 inc.

WANTED: Woman, capable of managing ladies' dress shop. Write P. O. Box 284, Rochester, Pa., giving references and experience. 8|29-9|4 inc.

WANTED: A girl for light housework between the ages of 18 and 25. Inquire at 369 Beaver St., third floor. 8|27-9|2 inc

LADIES—Let us renew your garments, coats, suits, dresses, etc., drapes. Miller's Cleaning Shoppe, next to city building, Beaver Phone 2235-J. 9 8*

Male and Female Help

WANTED: Caretaker for Council Community House, Beaver Falls. Phone Beaver Falls 1346-J. 9|1-7 inc.

Wanted—To Buy

Cash for your late model used car if it has good tires. Henry Birnesser Motor Sales, Baden. Phone Baden 5861—after 6 p. m. Baden 4501. 9|2-8 inc

WANTED: To buy a second typewriter. Call Beaver 179-R. 9 2.

WANTED: To buy live worthless horses for mink feed. Write Clyde Liptak, R. D. 2, Aliquippa. 8|31-9|5 inc

Wanted—To Rent

WANTED: To rent two unfurnished rooms, suitable for light housekeeping in Rochester. Young married couple. Phone Roch. 2791. 9|1-3 inc.

WANTED: In Rochester by reliable couple unfurnished apartment. Private bath. Phone Rochester 2206. 8|31-9|5 inc

WANTED: To rent furnished apartment or house in Beaver Valley. Must have two bedrooms. Call Beaver Falls 1303-J or write P. O. Box 258, Beaver Falls, Pa. 8|31-9|5 inc

For Sale

FOR SALE: 15½ foot Mullins boat, inboard motor. Call New Brighton 9926. 9 2-8 inc

FOR SALE: Piano, in good condition; 43" high. Inquire 1298 Penna. Ave., Monaca. 9 2.

FOR SALE: Daybed inner-spring mattress; good condition. Reasonable. Phone Rochester 3409. 9 2

FOR SALE: White oak 6-piece breakfast set including table, 4 chairs and buffet. Call Beaver 1217. 9 2-8 inc

FOR SALE: Acorn white enamel, left hand oven gas range, in good condition. Price reasonable. Call Beaver 386-W before 10 A. M. 9 2-3

FOR SALE: Coal cook stove; in good condition, a good baker. Will sell very reasonable. Inquire at Clover Farm Store, Vanport. 9|1-2

FOR SALE: Boys' bicycle, fully equipped, excellent condition; $27.00. Inquire 3rd floor, 499 3rd St., Beaver, Pa. 9|1-2.

FOR SALE: Home-grown Bartlett pears, prune plums, apples, grapes, pickles, tomatoes and potatoes, also pure honey. Fraser's Market, on Sunflower Road. 8 28-9 3 inc

FOR SALE: Top soil $2.00 a truck load, loaded in your trucks. The world's finest, Brown's at Unionville. Phone N. B. 3778-R-12. 8 31-9 5 inc

FOR SALE: Grapes, Pears, Damson Plums. H. B. Koehler, Allendale. Route 68. 8 31-9 5 inc

AT LOHRY'S

FOR SALE: SWEET CIDER, ice cold, beginning Tuesday, Sept. 1st. Also good cooking and eating APPLES well sprayed. Follow Tuscarawas Road 3 miles, make a left hand turn at our sign, on a new improved road, follow one mile. Call Beaver 1433-W. 8|29*

LAWN SEED
for Fall Planting
At
G. W. Walton Hdwe. Co.
BEAVER
8 27-9 2 inc.

FOR SALE: One 1½ h. p. Stover gasoline engine; one 3x3½ Curtiss Air Compressor, no tank. Separate machines. Phone Baden 4715. D. A. Stewart, R. D. Baden. 8 27-9 2 inc

THIS WEEK ONLY! SPECIAL GROUP OF 47 NEW FALL "NAN CARSON" 2-PIECE DRESSES, REGULAR $4.95-$5.95-$6.95 VALUES, YOUR CHOICE, $1.00 OFF. FRICK'S, NEXT TO FORT McINTOSH BANK, BEAVER. 8 31-9 5 inc

BIG WALLPAPER SALE: ½ off. Just received big factory shipment thousands of rolls new papers, on sale at factory dealer prices, 8c to $2.00. Wm. Helmick, 390 Brighton Ave., Rochester. (The Big Store). 8 29-9 4 inc

FOR SALE: 8-piece dining room suite. Good condition, $35. Inquire 717 Maplewood Ave., Ambridge. Ambridge 1118-J. 8 31-9 5 inc

For Sale

AT WALTON HDWE.
HUMPHREY RADIANTFIRES AND CIRCULATING GAS HEATERS
9|2-8 inc.

Rexair sweeper like new, new and used Premier, Hoovers. Parts and repairs for all makes. Wringer Rolls, Washer Rebuilding. Harpers, 386 Brighton Ave., Roch. Phone 9099. 9|1-7 inc.

FOR SALE: The only grocery and confectionery in East Rochester; brick building, fixtures, equipment and merchandise, doing good business. Inquire 832 Case St., before 8 p. m. 9|1-7 inc.

FOR SALE: Blackstone automatic washing machine, like new; one porch glider, also nearly new, and lawn mower. Phone either Rochester 610 or 3679-J. 9|1-7 inc.

FOR SALE: Beauty Shop equipment, chrome furniture; reasonable. Phone Beaver 2306-J. 8|29-9|4 inc.

FOR SALE: Automatic carpet loom, like new. Inquire Alois J. Adamek, Sr., 1340 Atlantic Ave., Monaca. 8|29-9|4 inc.

FOR SALE: Good cooking and eating apples, Sickle pears and Blue Concord grapes at Emerick's farm, Sunflower-Knob road. 8|28-9|3 inc

FOR SALE: Apples for apple butter, Blue Damson plums, prune plums, eating grapes, also little pigs, (O.I.C.) Matt Slavik Fruit Stand, Sunflower Road, Route 68. 8|28-9|3 inc

We buy, sell and repair all makes of washers. Beaver County Maytag Store, 9th St. & 10th Ave., New Brighton. Phone 2484. John W. Young, Proprietor. 6|1*

RAINCOATS FOR MEN, all sizes. Miller's Cleaning Shoppe, next to city building, Beaver, Phone 2235-J. 9 5*

For Sale—Houses

VANCLYFF HOMES in Vanport. Small, modern Dwigs. FHA approved and financed. Open for inspection daily including Saturday and Sunday P. M. BOVARD-ANDERSON COMPANY, Exclusive Agts. 9|2-8 inc

FOR SALE: 2536 Colonial street, Monaca—5-room and bath frame dwelling, gas, electric, city water, price $2500. Cash required $250, monthly payments $22.37. Immediate possession. Inquire O. H. Locke, 1231 Pennsylvania avenue, Monaca. Phone Rochester 2394. 9|2-8 inc

FOR SALE: Six room house, large lot, available immediately, priced to sell. Inquire at 700 5th St., Beaver, Pa. Phone 1222-W. 9|1-7 inc.

FOR SALE: In East Rochester, 8-room brick blockhouse, also 12-room frame house, modern conveniences. Inquire at store, 832 Case St., Rochester. 9|1-7 inc.

FOR SALE: 6-room modern house, 2½ acres ground. Located Conway-Wallrose road. Call Baden 6761. 8|31-9|5 inc

FOR SALE: House, 8 rooms and finished attic, 2 large rooms; new hot air furnace; basement, 4 large rooms, brick walls; cistern water piped throughout house; excellent location, large lot. See interior for unusual value. Would duplex to advantage. Any reasonable terms accepted. Owner within; 138 College avenue, Beaver. 8 27-9 2 inc

FOR SALE: Nine-room house, consisting of two apartments. Electric, gas, well. Bathroom shared. Corner lot. Close downtown Rochester. Call Roch. 1997-R evenings Owner entering service. 8|28-9|3 inc

FOR SALE: 4-room frame house, Sunflower road; gas, water, electric. Large lot. Inquire L. Liberty, top of Unionville Hill, Sunflower road. 8 27-9 2 inc

For Sale—Farms

BRIGHTON TOWNSHIP
Farm of 48 acres with six room house, barn and other out-buildings. House has electricity and running water. $3500. Terms or will consider town property in trade.
1¾ Acres on improved road with house foundation started and enough blocks to complete. Drilled well with casing. $600.
JAMES S. STROUSS
458 3 St. Phone 815 Beaver 9|1-7 inc

For Sale—Livestock

FOR SALE: Bay mare, weight 1300, good for farm work; also two Shepherd and Collie female pups, $2.00 each. Phone Roch. 6122-J-1. 9 2-8 inc

FOR SALE: Guernsey cow, has been fresh two weeks. Call Beaver 515-J. 9 2-8 inc.

FOR SALE: One saddle horse with military saddle, and one springer spaniel dog. Phone Rochester 3661-J. 9|1-2

For Sale—Flowers

Gladioli, dahlias, cut fresh as ordered—hospital and cemetery bouquets, funeral pieces or dozen. Reasonable. Helm's Gladahlia Gardens Brodhead Road, 3 miles from Monaca. Phone Roch. 6132-R-3. 8 29-9 4 inc.

For Sale—Used Cars

NO PRIORITY NEEDED!
'41 PLYMOUTH Dlx. Cpe. Radio. Spot Light. Excellent.
'41 PONTIAC 6 Dlx. Club Cpe. Radio. Heater.
'41 HUDSON 6 Dlx. 4-Door. Driven little. "A-1".
'40 BUICK Special (Smallest) 4-Door. Radio. Heater.
'40 WILLYS Station Wagon.
'39 BUICK Special. 4-Door.
—Also many 38's, 37's, 36's, including several good '36 Chevrolets.
TRADES and TERMS!
WAGNER AUTO SALES
Near Rochester End, Monaca Bridge. Open evenings for War Workers.
9 2-3

FOR SALE: 1941 Nash 2-door, 5-passenger coupe, 12,000 miles. Owner going to army. Call Beaver 1995. 9|2-4 inc.

1941 Oldsmobile 6 Club Coupe, Hydromatic trans. 1941 Pontiac 6 Club Sedan. Cars fully equipped, fine condition, priced to sell without trade-in. Ralph D. Ewing, Oldsmobile Garage, Beaver, Pa. Used Car Lot. 9|2-4 inc.

FOR SALE: 1939 Plymouth Deluxe sedan. A-1 condition 5 good tires, radio, heater and seat covers. Call Beaver 1948-W. 9|2-8 inc.

FOR SALE: 1940 DeSoto, fine condition, 7-passenger, excellent tires, low mileage. Mrs. Juergens, Conway-Wallrose Road. 9 2

FOR SALE: Ford Fordor Deluxe sedan, good tires, heater, a real value, $125. Inquire Batto Bros. 329 Maine avenue, Rochester. 9 2-8 inc

FOR SALE: 1939 Buick sedan, excellent condition; low mileage; 6 good tires. Call Beaver 2773. 9 2-8 inc

FOR SALE: 1937 La Fayette sedan. Heater. Good condition. Reasonable. Phone Rochester 2597 any evening. 9 2.

FOR SALE: 1936 Cheve dump truck, one and one-half ton, U-plate, A-1 condition, tires like new, $350. Inquire 1215 Washington Ave., Monaca. Phone Rochester 615-J-1. 9 2-8 inc.

FOR SALE: 1939 Hudson 6 sedan $250.00; 1938 Chevrolet coach $250.00; 1938 Plymouth sedan $200.00; 1937 Chrysler Imperial sedan $225.00; 1937 Chrysler 6 sedan $135.00; 1936 Terraplane sedan $50.00. Will trade for motorcycle or pickup truck. Inquire Eugene Cox. 388 Lloyd street, Rochester. Phone 4099-R. 9|1-7 inc.

FOR SALE: 1937 Ford Dump Truck, good tires. Inquire 270 East End Ave., Beaver after 6:00 P. M. 9|1-7 inc.

FOR SALE: 1937 Chrysler Royal Sedan. Good condition. Extra tires. $325. 1729 Corporation St Phone Beaver 2785-W. 9|1-7 inc

NOTICE TO THE PUBLIC—Highest cash price paid for used cars—1930 to 1941. All makes, regardless of condition. Quick service. White Used Car Lot, corner Deer Lane and Penna. Ave., Rochester. Phone 3236. Open evenings. 8|31-9|5 inc

FOR SALE: 1941 Nash 600 2-door sedan, good tires. No trade-ins. Call Ohio View 28201. 8|31-9|5 inc

FOR SALE: Haywood-Wakefield reed baby carriage. Phone Roch. 3859-W. 8|28-9|3 inc

FOR SALE: 1939 Plymouth Deluxe coupe, good tires and heater, $325 cash (leaving for Army). Inquire 1751 Seventh Avenue, Freedom. Phone Rochester 1609-J. 8|28-9|3 inc

Business Opportunities

FOR SALE: Meat and grocery business on Patterson Heights, doing fine business, good reason for selling. Inquire 2346 (rear) 7th Ave. Phone Beaver Falls, Phone 2573-R. 9 2-8 inc

FOR SALE: Business opportunity—the only restaurant in Potter Township and only about ½ mile from new Synthetic Rubber Plant. Clientele well established, building will qualify for application for liquor license. For details call Rochester 458. 9|1-3 inc.

FOR SALE: Established grocery, meat and confectionery business. Excellent opportunity at reasonable price. Living rooms connected. Inquire 250 Virginia Ave., Rochester. 8|31-9|5 inc

For Sale—Coal

Clinton Coal by truck load. 4" lump $5; 2" lump $4.75; 2x4 egg $4.50. Ohioview Coal: ¾ lump $4.50. Call Beaver 386-J. E. M. Sayre. 8|31-10|3 inc

For Sale—Dogs

FOR SALE: Male black Cocker Spaniel pup. Pedigreed, $25. Must phone no later than Thursday night. Rochester 282-W. 9 2-3

For Rent—Houses

FOR RENT: Three room house, unfurnished, one block rear of Fire Dept. Inquire George Davis, corner Irwin and Vine streets, Vanport. 9|2-8 inc.

FOR RENT: House boat, 5 rooms and bath. Phone Roch. 1917-W. 8|31-9|5 inc

FOR RENT: 8-room house, completely furnished in desirable neighborhood in Monaca. Phone Rochester 54 or 393. 8 31-9 2 inc

LEGAL ADVERTISEMENTS

NOTICE

Notice is hereby given that the following report of the Auditors of the School District of the Borough of Beaver, Pennsylvania, was filed in the Court of Common Pleas of Beaver County, Pa., at Number 238, September Term, 1942, on September 1, 1942, and that the same will be confirmed absolutely unless an appeal is taken therefrom within thirty (30) days after the filing thereof.

EDWIN M. WALLOVER,
Prothonotary.

AUDITORS' STATEMENT

Beaver School District, Beaver, Pa.
Year Ending July 6, 1942
Assessed valuation $4,253,475.00 Mills levied—17.

GENERAL FUND

RECEIPTS		DISBURSEMENTS	
Balance July 5, 1941	$ 3,006.50	General Control	$ 8,330.05
Taxes	81,695.50	Instruction	71,663.44
State appropriation	17,285.26	Auxiliary Agencies	776.52
Tuition—non-residents	18,814.70	Operation of plant	11,487.75
Short term loans	10,000.00	Maintenance of plant	2,573.34
Interest	753.36	Fixed charges	3,199.16
Rents	1,120.55	Debt Service	20,919.81
Other receipts	460.45	Capital Outlay	7,947.70
Total	$133,136.41	Total	$126,897.27

SINKING FUND

RECEIPTS		DISBURSEMENTS	
Balance July 4, 1941	$ 11,757.26	Bonds retired	$ 10,000.00
From General Fund	1,107.34	Interest on bonds	950.00
Interest	57.97	Refund to General Fund	217.74
Total	$ 12,922.57	Total	$ 11,167.74

BALANCE SHEET

ASSETS		LIABILITIES	
School Buildings and sites	$410,610.46	Bonded Indebtedness	$ 64,000.00
Text books and equipment	59,448.29	Temporary Loans	10,000.00
Taxes receivable	27,401.57	Accounts payable	4,188.49
Academy Trust Fund	17,660.00		
Unexpired insurance	2,500.00	Total	$ 78,188.49
Rents and tuition receivable	560.65		
Sinking Fund balance	1,754.83		
General Fund balance	6,239.14		
Total	$526,174.94		

(Detailed statements filed in Prothonotary's Office and in office of School Superintendent.)

WALTER CHURM,
D. M. CARVER,
Auditors.

Beaver, Pa., August 10, 1942. 9 2-9-16

For Rent—Rooms

FOR RENT: Two cheerful furnished light housekeeping rooms. All conveniences. Electric refrigeration. On bus line. Adults only. 487 Adams street, Rochester. 9 2

FOR RENT: Near Curtiss-Wright, furnished sleeping room for one or two gentlemen. Phone Beaver 1420-J. 9|2-8 inc

FOR RENT. Furnished sleeping room in new home for one or two young ladies. Board if desired. Call Beaver 1472-R or inquire 1425 Corporation St., Beaver. 9 2

FOR RENT: Four unfurnished rooms with bath, on third floor; redecorated; $40.00 per month. Also one furnished sleeping room and kitchenette, $25.00 per month. Utilities paid. Phone Beaver 1126-W. 9 2

FOR RENT: One private room in a separate building suitable for two gentlemen; modern conveniences. Do own cooking if desired. Phone Beaver 1553-M after 9:00 p. m. 9|2-8 inc

FOR RENT: Furnished room, suitable for one or two gentlemen. Bath, electricity, use of telephone, furnace heat. Inquire 434 Dravo Ave., Beaver. 9|2-4 inc.

FOR RENT: Furnished room for one or two gentlemen. 1140 Third street, Beaver. 9|2-8 inc

FOR RENT: One sleeping room suitable for one or two gentlemen. Rochester 875 or inquire 198 Brighton Ave., Rochester. 8 29-9 4 inc.

FOR RENT: Large furnished room 12x22 for housekeeping, couple only. One mile from Monaca. Bus line. At Union Cemetery. Rochester 811. 9|1-7 inc.

FOR RENT: Two nicely furnished rooms for light housekeeping, all modern conveniences, centrally located. Inquire 471 Kossuth street, Rochester. 9|1-7 inc.

FOR RENT: Two furnished rooms for light housekeeping. Inquire 711 Market street, Bridgewater. 9|1-7 inc.

FOR RENT: 3 furnished rooms and bath. Use of telephone. Inquire 416 Fourteenth St., Monaca. 9|1-7 inc.

FOR RENT: Two unfurnished rooms for light housekeeping. Inquire 250 Eleventh St., Conway. 9|1-3 inc.

FOR RENT: Two nicely furnished rooms on bus line in Monaca. All utilities. Adults only. 802 Pennsylvania avenue, Monaca. 8 31-9 5 inc

FOR RENT: Large front sleeping room in home of two adults, suitable for one or two men. Use of phone. 179 Clay street, Rochester. Phone Roch. 3069-W. 8 31-9,5 inc

FOR RENT: Two furnished rooms for light housekeeping. All conveniences. Adults only. Inquire 577 Fourth Avenue, Freedom. 8|31-9|5 inc

FOR RENT: Sleeping room for one or two men. New home, modern conveniences including shower bath. 377 Sixth St., Beaver (off Beaver street). Phone Beaver 3459-M. 8|31-9|5 inc

FOR RENT: 2 large unfurnished rooms, kitchen and bedroom, modern conveniences. Paul Komare, Industry. Phone Ohioview 28428. 8|28-9|3 inc

FOR RENT: Two large nicely furnished rooms for light housekeeping, middle-aged employed couple (adults only) preferred, semi-private bath, entrance. 1007 Indiana Ave., Monaca. Roch. 733-J, until 7:30 p. m. 8|29-9|3 inc

FOR RENT: Furnished sleeping rooms, single and double. Inquire 490 Lincoln Ave., Beaver. 8|26-9|3 inc

Read THE TIMES Classified Ads

Miscellaneous

Carnival every Thursday Night 8:30 sharp. Cards 50c or 3 for $1.00. Special games and special double awards. Protected parking. Pulaski Township, Marion Hill Firemen. 8 3*

Patterson Township Firemen Penny Carnival every Friday night. New system 35c per card. No award less than $3.00. Door award. Play starts at 8:30 o'clock 7|6*

Having trouble with your washer? Call Hudson's Appliance Shop. We service all makes. All work guaranteed. Prices reasonable. Phone Roch. 306. 9|9*

INDOOR CARNIVAL
New Legion Home
Adams St., Rochester
TUES. & FRI. NITES
8 P. M.
33 games 50c—Prizes $2, $3, $5, $10
In Merchandise

Lost and Found

LOST: In vicinity of Tamaqui Village, Thursday morning, Collie 6 months old (brown with white face, 4 white paws). Child's companion. Answers to "Paddy." Phone Beaver 2693-R. Reward. 8 31-9 5 inc

LOST: In lower valley, a pair of rimmed glasses. Reward if returned to F. G. Baker, Jefferson street, Vanport. 8|28-9|3 inc

Repairs—Service

TO PROPERTY OWNERS: Clogged sewers opened without digging or disturbing lawns. Ideal Electric Sewer opener. Phone Roch. 931-W or Roch. 1578-W. Mayhue Brothers. 11,4-E.O.W.*

FACTORY-TO-YOU
Re-Upholstering
Let our upholsterers put new life into your old living room suite, and give it the same bright freshness of new furniture. Everything stripped to the bare frame — Frames are repaired, tightened and polished—Interiors rebuilt and refilled—Cushions are completely new. Do it now while we still have a big selection of fabrics.
BUY U. S. WAR BONDS
KANE CHAIR MFG. CO.
Old Opera House. Rochester, Pa. Phone Roch. 2810-J
8|26*

Money to Loan

MONEY TO LOAN: On first mortgage, to refinance, buy, build, repair or modernize, on our Easy Payment Loan Plan. Quick, convenient. First Federal Savings Loan Assn., 713 Eleventh street, Beaver Falls, Pa. 8 1*

Professional Service

CHIROPRACTIC and Sulphur Vapor Baths Treatments for your Rheumatism, Arthritis, Lumbago and general run down condition. DR. MAUDE E. BLEAKNEY Beaver 9052 for appointment. 8 29-9 4 inc.

REAL ESTATE FOR SALE

$2500. 2 story frame 5 room dwelling, lot 30x62, Reno St. $600 down payment.

$3100. 2 story concrete block 6 room dwelling, lot 40x113, Connecticut Ave. 15% down payment

$6000. 2 story brick 6 room dwelling, lot 50x100, Irvin Ave. $1000 down payment.

For appointment see
The
James W. Doncaster Agency, Inc.
177 Brighton Ave., Rochester, Pa.
Phone 283
9 1-2

ADMINISTRATOR'S NOTICE

Estate of ELIZABETH A. LAWSON, deceased, late of the Borough of Monaca, Beaver County, Pennsylvania, letters of Administration d.b.n. upon the above estate having been granted to the undersigned, notice is hereby given to those indebted thereto to make immediate payment, and to those having claims or demands to present them for settlement.

BEAVER COUNTY TRUST COMPANY,
Administrator, d.b.n.,
New Brighton, Pa.
Eckert & Sohn, Attorneys,
331 Commerce Street,
Beaver, Penna.
8 12-19-26-9 2-9-16

EXECUTOR'S NOTICE

Estate of JOSEPH EBERLE, deceased, late of the Borough of Aliquippa, Beaver County, Penna., letters Testamentary upon the above estate having been granted to the undersigned, notice is hereby given to those indebted thereto to make immediate payment, and to those having claims or demands to present them for settlement.

WOODLAWN TRUST CO.,
Executor,
392 Franklin Avenue,
Aliquippa, Penna.
Eckert & Sohn, Attorneys,
515 Franklin Avenue,
Aliquippa, Penna.
8 5-12-19-26-9 2-9

EXECUTOR'S NOTICE

ESTATE of Frederick Swingle deceased, late of the Borough of Beaver, Beaver County, letters Testamentary upon the above estate having been granted to the undersigned, notice is hereby given to those indebted thereto to make immediate payment, and to those having claims or demands to present them for settlement.

Beaver Trust Company,
Executor,
Beaver, Penna.
Reed & Ewing,
Attorneys.
7 29-8 5-12-19-26-9 2

Household & Office Furniture
MARINO
Furniture Exchange
We buy scrap iron and junk for defense 9 2-29 inc.

CASH
for
SCHOOL
EXPENSES

Loans to buy school books and equipment, and other necessities. Money advanced to parents for grade school, high school or college educational expenses. Borrow up to $300. Repay monthly. Come in or phone.

FURNITURE & AUTO LOANS
$25 to $300
The Old Reliable Company
35 Years in Beaver Falls
UNION LOAN CO.
ROOMS 2 & 4 2nd FLOOR
BENSON BUILDING
CORNER 12th ST. & 7th AVE. PH. 2-4-4
BEAVER FALLS

Read THE TIMES Classified Ads

Send THE TIMES to your boy in the Army or Navy. "It's like a letter from home every day."

THEY'RE GOOD BUYS!
SEE THEM TODAY!
1936 G. M. C. Pick-up
1934 Ford Dump Truck
1938 Chevrolet Sedan
1938 Plymouth Sedan
1937 Plymouth Sedan
1936 Chevrolet Coupe
Collect Scrap and Destroy The Jap!
BAKER
CHEVROLET CO.
444 Third St. Beaver
Phone 1661

DO YOU NEED MONEY
to pay taxes, insurance premiums, auto repairs, Doctor and hospital bills, vacation expense or to consolidate all those small accounts? If so, see us for the money; have just one place to pay; make us your only creditor, you will not find a more considerate and friendly one.
We invite you to compare our rates with those of any other company in the Beaver Valley.
"WHY PAY MORE?"
Rochester Thrift and Loan Corporation
218 Brighton Ave.
Rochester - Phone 2100

NEED MONEY?
TO BUY COAL . . .
TO PAY DOCTOR or HOSPITAL BILLS
OR ANY OTHER PRESSING NEED?
Loans granted on furniture to husband and wife.
On automobiles or personal signature.
No endorsers or embarrassing investigations.
Fast, confidential, convenient service.
ALEX BENTLEY, MGR.
A.B.C.Credit Inc
"A Unit of the Well-Known ABC Plan"
814 Seventh Ave. Phone 81
Beaver Falls, Pa.

REPAIR NOW!
We Specialize In -
- Brick Veneering
- Brick Work
- Concrete Work
- Fire Places
- Chimney Work
- Carpenter Work

Repair and modernize now while materials are still available. Fine workmanship — Satisfaction guaranteed.
A. DOMENICO
392 Maryland Ave., Rochester
Phone 3211-R

Keep 'Em Writing
Have your typewriter serviced by a service man that is a TYPIST and really knows how a typewriter should work.
Service and supplies for all makes of office machines
C. F. BROWN
Royal Typewriters—Adding Machines — Supplies
218 Federal Title & Trust Bldg.
Beaver Falls 2079

CHAMPION COAL
6 in. lump and furnace
Lowest prices — Prompt delivery
PURE CRYSTAL CLEAR ICE
SAM CUTRONA
Phone 128 or 836 Rochester

WEDDING INVITATIONS AND ANNOUNCEMENTS, INFORMALS AND CARDS
GLADYS A. GIBBONS
[illegible] College Ave., Beaver

BURGAWAY AHEAD—Burgaway comes across the wire in front of [illegible] to capture this race at Aqueduct track near New York.

SPORTS NEWS-TRIBUNE

OUT OF THE BUSHES to split a pennant purse have come [illegible] back, Cullenbine, Hassett, Hemsley and Turner of the Yanks.

Rochester Opens Tonight At Home With Freedom

Photo and Engraving by News-Tribune.

Defeated only once last season, the Rochester Rams tonight herald the opening of what they hope will be another successful season. Flashy new jerseys will appear on the Junction City boys when they take on Freedom's Bulldogs at 8:15 o'clock on the Rochester field. Coaches Ernie Meyer and Earl Ewing have chosen the above performers as likely starters, left to right, as follows: Dave McElhaney, John Friend, John Silipigni, Charles Rowe, Andy Mignanelli, Phil Sciaretta, and Bill Krouse; backfield—Bill Fritzius, halfback; Lester Ratcliffe, quarterback; Charles DeFrancesca, fullback; Eddie Prospero, halfback, and Phil Colella, halfback.

Rep. Weiss New Pro Grid Referee

WASHINGTON, Sept. 10.—(A.P.) — Representative Samuel Weiss, Democrat, Pennsylvania, thinks the National Football league is in for its biggest year, and as Referee Weiss he hopes to have a large hand in its success.

The congressman, who has refereed high school and college games for 18 years, is starting his first year as a pro and believes he and his fellow officials have an added responsibility during the war.

"War workers nowadays are accustomed to speed," he said, "and the football officials must see to it that the games are speeded up, also. People just aren't in the mood to watch a lot of wrangling and disputes out on the field this year, and it's up to the officials to see that the games are conducted as snappy as possible."

Pro football, he feels, will furnish workers in such war-boom cities as Washington, Pittsburgh and Detroit with their chief entertainment this fall.

Weiss, expressing sharp disagreement with Lieutenant Commander Gene Tunney's recent statement that "you can't learn to fight by playing football," declared there was nothing like the action of pro football to put a player in condition, both physically and psychologically, for duty in the armed forces. He cited a letter recently received from Edgar Jones, the former Richmond university speed merchant who performed last season with the Pittsburgh Steelers.

"Jones, who now is in the army, told me if it hadn't been for that year with the Steelers, he would have been a gone gosling when he got into the service," the congressman said. "He says that one year gave him a tremendous jump on his fellow soldiers in the matter of physical condition, and the experience he gained in studying methods of attack really has been advantageous."

In his college years at Duquesne Weiss ran the 100-yard dash in ten seconds and was named quarterback of the second all-time Duquesne team. The first-team signal caller graduated in 1894.

Who would the congressman say is the greatest player he has ever seen?

"That's easy. Cliff Battles. That guy couldn't do anything wrong."

SOUTHWORTH, EDWARDS IN NET SEMI-FINALS

Jack Southworth and H. Edwards advanced to the singles semi-finals as they won quarter-final matches in the annual Allegheny county tennis tournament at the Pittsburgh golf club yesterday.

National Amateur Tennis To Continue

From the looks of things in general, the national amateur tennis championships will be carried on for the duration. That's the prediction of Holcombe Ward, president of the U. S. Lawn Tennis Association.

Quoting from his statement, "I don't think it will be difficult to continue the championships, unless something really disastrous happens. Tennis is not like other sports, demanding older players. We have literally thousands of youngsters, many as young as 15, who can carry on the competition."

Ward stresses that the best players on hand will be made use of to be trained and made ready to recapture the Davis Cup.

Yesterday's Stars

Howie Pollet, Cardinals — Stopped Giants with four-hit hurling.

Lon Warneke, Cubs — Kept Dodgers smothered on eight hits.

Danny Litwhiler, Phils—Tripled in 11th inning for winning run against Pirates.

Ted Lyons, White Sox, and Bruce Campbell, Senators — Former pitched seven-hit ball to win first game and latter singled with bases loaded in eighth inning to decide second session.

Dennis Galehouse, Browns — Pitched three-hit shutout against Yankees.

League Leaders

(By the Associated Press)

NATIONAL LEAGUE

Batting — Lombardi, Boston, .333.

Runs—Ott, New York, 105.

Runs Batted In — Mize, New York, 96.

Hits — Slaughter, St. Louis, 170.

Doubles — Medwick, Brooklyn, 36.

Triples — Slaughter, St. Louis, 17.

Home Runs — Ott, New York, 27.

Stolen Bases — Reiser, Brooklyn, 15.

Pitching — Krist, St. Louis, 12-3.

AMERICAN LEAGUE

Batting — Williams, Boston, .350.

Runs—Williams, Boston, 125.

Runs Batted In — Williams, Boston, 127.

Hits—Pesky, Boston, 190.

Doubles — Clift, St. Louis, 39.

Triples—Heath, Cleveland, and DiMaggio, New York, 13.

Home Runs — Williams, Boston, 31.

Stolen Bases — Case, Washington, 38.

Pitching — Borowy, New York, 14-3.

EAGLES OBTAIN JEFFERSON

The Philadelphia Eagles recently obtained Billy Jefferson, a 210-pound, six-foot-two speed lad who played his college football at Mississippi State, from the Chicago Cardinals.

MacPhail, Army Bound, Doubts Bums Will Win

BROOKLYN, Sept. 11—(AP)— Larry MacPhail, the magnetic mastermind of the Brooklyn Dodgers, says he doubts his ball club can win the National League pennant, so it may be just as well that he is in Washington today while the St. Louis Cardinals set siege to Ebbetts Field.

The president of the Brooklyn club went to the capital last night to complete arrangements for his entry into the army — probably with a commission in the Field Artillery in which he was a captain during the first World War. But before he left he witnessed the 10-2 debacle which his Dodgers dropped to the Chicago Cubs and it apparently made him happier that he was marching off to war.

Anyway he was laughing as he declared to newspapermen, "I doubt if my club can win it" and recalled the warning he had given his players three weeks ago that they would have to hustle harder to stay on top.

PACKERS SIGN CROFT

GREEN BAY, Wis. — (AP) — Milburn (Tiny) Croft, former Ripon (Wis.) College tackle, was obtained by the Green Bay Packers from the Washington Redskins yesterday. A 285-pounder, Croft is the biggest man in the National Football League. He stands 6 foot 3.

Probable Lineups For Stadium Game

BEAVER FALLS		MONACA
78—Earley	L.E.	Ciccozzi—86
70—Jackson	L.T.	Bobroski—75
79—Campese	L.G.	Namaden—77
65—Anderson	C.	Milne—87
61—Tkacik	R.G.	M. Zupsic—72
67—Carbone	R.T.	Vogt—83
77—Thellman	R.E.	Dietrich—79
74—Cleary	Q.	Knopp—81
62—Massey	R.H.	Olshanski—76
66—Bricker	L.H.	Yuran—82
71—Tate	F.	Battaglia—73

TIGER SUBS—Purri 76, C. James 75, Lesinski 63, LaRocca 78, Omogrosso 81, Brown 72, Thomas 80, Barnett 25, Podbielski 49, Brizzi 30, Scario 79, J. James 24, Reed 23, Hornacek 40, Balzer 47, Dreher 66, Barsottini 26, Gaugler 44, McGee 52, Marsico 37, Pietro 60, Zarnecki 31

INDIAN SUBS—LeGoullen 90, Brummitt 91, Milne 87, Bell 88, Deveney 93, Renzo 84, James 80, T. Taormina 61, Laughner 57, Kramer 69, Busang 71, Ballish 89, Stakic 68, Hlebo 85, Zupsic 70, Redjaneck 92, P. Taormina 60, Donovan 62, Fedeles 56, J. Palumbo 66, Joe Palumbo 65, Baxa 64.

OFFICIALS

Oatey Shanks — Joe Rider — C. P. Deemer

Tiger-Monaca Game Heads Night Card

4 Other Valley Tilts Tonight; Brighton at Sharpsville Saturday

By ERNIE KONVOLINKA

Scholastic football has moved strictly into high gear among Beaver Valley teams in this, the second week of war-time gridiron experiences.

Five games tonight and one tomorrow afternoon will complete the eight-tilt county card which started last night and continues this afternoon when Hopewell plays at Zelienople.

Tiger-Monaca Game

Topmost among the nocturnal struggles tonight is the Beaver Falls-Monaca High game at Reeves stadium at 8:15 o'clock. Rochester baptizes its season at home with Freedom, Donora goes to Ambridge; Sewickley to Aliquippa and Union township to Ellwood.

A single Saturday afternoon attraction of interest to the valley is the New Brighton opener at Sharpsville at 2:30 p. m.

Coach Alex Ufema will field the same team of Tigers whose claws last week wounded Freedom 55-0. Coach Lou Blistan, however, has to shift his Monacans, sending Jay Yuran from center to the backfield on offense due to the leg injury of Fullback Joe Turbish, who can barely hobble after the Indian defeat at Ambridge last week. Milne takes over for Yuran at center.

Lynn Cleary, at quarterback; Paul Massey and Loyal Bricker, halfbacks, and Earl Tate, fullback, will comprise the starting Tiger backfield, with Fullback [illegible] Omogrosso, who scored 28 points against Freedom, ready for quick entry. The Indians will start Knopp at quarterback, Olshanski and Yuran at halfbacks, and Battaglia, fullback.

Rochester-Freedom

Coaches Ernie Meyer and Earl Ewing at Rochester expect Freedom to put up a different kind of battle than the Bulldogs did in losing 55-0 to Beaver Falls.

Six lettermen are included in the Ram starting array and Meyer hastens to remind that most of the squad is "green." The veterans are Friend and Sciaretta, tackles; Silipigni, a guard; Krause, an end; and Phil Colella, standout halfback, and Prospero, who saw action at half last season. Other backfield posts will be filled by Fullback DiFrancesca, a reserve last season; Bill Fritzius, senior, out for his first year, who vies with Prospero for a starting bid, and Quarterback Radcliffe. Rowe, a center, and Mignanelli, guard, are both senior recruits, and McElhaney, an end, is a newcomer. Sixteen Rochester lettermen graduated last spring.

Freedom's coach, Michael Josephs, probably will use Ripper and Corklic, ends; Genova and Asper, tackles; Cornelius and Holman, guards, and Arbutina, center; Miller, quarterback; Sabolic and DePaolis, halfbacks, and Genevie, fullback.

Brighton-Sharpsville

Coach George Roark, with a flock of inexperienced players, will inject Nemecek and Farrow at ends; Reina and Summa, at tackles; Haddox and Ayers, guards; Gillespie, center; and Albert Peluso, Schwartzel, Pappa-rodis and Wurzel in the backfield at Sharpsville. Of these only Gillespie, Nemecek and Summa are

Continued On Page Twenty.

Beaver Off To Good Start By Defeating Midland High, 12-0

Scherrbaum, Parsons Spark Second Straight Win Over Leopards

Coach Harold Leffler, new mentor of Beaver High school, sent his gridders off to a fast 1942 start last evening when the Bobcats outbattled the Midland Leopards, 12-0, under the portable lights at the Midland field.

The victors spent most of the time in Midland territory and chalked up nine first downs to two for the losing side in scoring a second win in two years after 18 seasons without a triumph over the Midlanders.

The first score came early in the second chapter on a march from the Beaver 32 though the Bobcats were halted momentarily on the two-foot line. Starting all over again when a Midland punt traveled out only 27 yards, Don Parsons, Bill Douds and Dick Scherrbaum drove to the six, where Parsons punctured left end for the initial touchdown. C. Black, moving back from his end post, missed the conversion.

Late in the third quarter, the scrappy Beaver backfield set the stage for the second six-pointer that came two plays after the start of the fourth canto.

The sustained march began from the Beaver 34 where Midland's hard-plugging fullback, Bob Onuska, aimed a punt out of bounds. Sparked by the running of Scherrbaum and McKelvey, and two passes caught by Don Parsons, the 'Cats' gathered three first downs in a hurry, with Scherrbaum crossing from seven yards out. Black again missed via placement but the County seaters had a 12-0 margin which held.

Midland started the second half with a bang when Halfback Cherene grabbed a 25-yard pass from Onuska to the Beaver 34 but the movement died there. Late in the contest, when Leffler entered 10 subs at once, the Leopards came closest when Steve Germusa, a halfback, carried a short pass to the 25 yard stripe where the threat ended.

Beaver's Deeley and Netherland matched in line play the glistening work of Scherrbaum and Parsons in the backfield. Onuska, whose educated punting toe kept Midland out of many another hole, carried the Leopard burden.

	Beaver—12	Midland—0
LE	Deely	De Marzio
LT	Pinkerson	D'Ieri
LG	Deemer	Bastile
C	Carbon	Bires
RG	Netherland	Bomestar
RT	Hume	Hunter
RE	C. Black	Tepovich
QB	M. Patterson	W. Germusa
LH	Scherrbaum	Cherene
RH	Parsons	S. Germusa
FB	Douds	Onuska

Scoring by periods:

Beaver	0	6	0	6	—12

Touchdowns: Parsons, Scherrbaum. Referee, Grahame; umpire, Harr; head linesman, H. L. Mann.

Beaver Subs: McKelvey, Coates, Holt, Fisher, Morris, Keenen, McCormick, Cochran.

Midland Subs: Daniels, Diciccio, Katich, Kukich, Migliore, Muller.

Boxing Notes

NEW YORK — Fritzie Zivic, 147¼, of Pittsburgh, outpointed Freddie (Red) Cochrane, 146, Elizabeth, N. J. (10). Willie Pep, 130, Hartford, Conn., stopped Frank Franconeri, 125, Bayonne, N. J. (1).

FALL RIVER, Mass. — Billy Buckley, 130, Fall River, stopped Eddie de Angelis, 128, Boston (5).

ROCHESTER, N. Y. — Harvey Dubs, 144½, Toronto, outpointed Tommy Hogan, 142½, New York (10).

ELIZABETH, N. J. — Ike Williams, 135, Trenton, N. J., outpointed Charlie Davis, 130, New York (8).

The Weather Forecast
WESTERN PENNSYLVANIA: Continued warm today and tonight, with scattered showers tonight. Pollen count, 534.

"The Paper That Goes Home"

THE DAILY TIMES

ROCHESTER-BEAVER-MONACA
FREEDOM—BRIDGEWATER—CONWAY—VANPORT—MIDLAND

Beaver County History
The rumor that the Kaiser was about to abdicate as head of the German government was heard here on September 17, 1918.

ESTABLISHED APRIL 2, 1874 | BEAVER AND ROCHESTER, PA., THURSDAY, SEPTEMBER 17, 1942 | BY CARRIER 18 CENTS A WEEK—3 CENTS PER COPY

STREET FIGHTING RAGES IN STALINGRAD

LINEMAN DIES AFTER MISHAP AT WORK HERE

Injuries Fatal To Mike Pavlinich, Bridgewater Utility Worker, Following Accident In Hopewell Township On Wednesday

Mike Pavlinich, 48, first class lineman employed by the Duquesne Light company and a resident of 1408 Mulberry street, Bridgewater, died at Rochester Hospital at 12:50 o'clock this morning from the effect of head injuries and shock sustained while at work in Hopewell Township at 4:15 o'clock yesterday afternoon.

According to George W. Tissue, operations superintendent in the Western Division, Pavlinich was a member of a crew working in the Green Garden road district and was near the top of a pole at the intersection of Hopewell avenue and Hall street. He apparently came in contact with a primary wire and suffered electric shock, falling a distance of 30 feet to the ground.

Fellow-workmen immediately began administering artificial respiration and Pavlinich partially revived but did not fully regain consciousness. He was removed in an ambulance to the hospital and Mr. Tissue stated today that his condition was not thought to have been serious.

VETERAN LINEMAN

Mr. Pavlinich was a member of a well-known Bridgewater family and early next year would have completed 25 years of service with the utility company, having been a first class lineman for nearly 20 years of that period. He was respected and admired by other employes and well regarded in his home community.

A son, Sergeant George Michael Pavlinich, is attached to the Engineers Utility Detachment, United States Army, in Iceland and only a few days ago wrote his parents that he was looking forward to returning to "the good old U.S.A." A daughter, Clara Ann Pavlinich, last week entered the nurses' training school at St. Elizabeth's Hospital, Youngstown, Ohio, hoping to become an army nurse. Both are graduates of Beaver High school.

In addition to the wife and two children, Mr. Pavlinich is survived by the mother, Mrs. Mary Pavlinich, Bridgewater; and the following sisters: Mrs. Frank Brozich, Mrs. Frank Moravec, Mrs. John Schutey and Mrs. Lawrence Longher, Bridgewater.

The body will be removed to the family home early this evening. No arrangements have as yet been made for the funeral services, as efforts are being made to contact the son through the American Red Cross, in the hope that arrangements can be made for him to fly to the United States immediately.

Mr. Pavlinich was a member of SS. Cyril and Methodius Roman Catholic church, New Brighton.

Two Persons Hurt In Local Mishaps

William H. Jackson, 65, 816 Fifth avenue, New Brighton, was admitted to Beaver Valley hospital Wednesday afternoon suffering from a laceration of the head. He was injured when struck by a shovel on a passing truck at Ninth street and Fifth avenue, while crossing the street, according to New Brighton police.

William Hodgkinson, 12-year-old son of Mrs. Mabel Hodgkinson, 902 Penn avenue, New Brighton, was admitted to Beaver Valley hospital Wednesday evening suffering from a possible fracture of the wrist received in a fall from a tree near his home.

Local Woman To Be Honored At Dinner

A testimonial dinner is to be held at 6:30 o'clock Friday evening by the Beaver Valley Sabbath School Association, honoring Mrs. David Anderson, New Brighton, who has been secretary of the Association the past fifteen years and was children's superintendent two years prior to that.

The dinner is to be held in the social rooms of the Fifth Avenue Methodist church, New Brighton.

With Government

Pictured above is Eugene C. Myers, Rochester, who recently was appointed a junior engineering draftsman in the Department of Commerce and U. S. Coast and Geodetic Survey, Washington. He is the son of Mr. and Mrs. Chester W. Myers, Rochester.

Rochester To Have Community Flag For Those In Service

When the Rochester Board of Trade met Wednesday noon at the Penn-Beaver Hotel an order for the "Service Flag" was placed.

In the field will be a single star with numerals to indicate the number of men and women from the community now in the armed services. The numerals will be changed from time to time as enlistments increase. The flag will be placed in the vicinity of the public park.

The board also is contacting borough council again about the marking of the various streets with their names as a convenience to the public. It is believed the work can be done inexpensively by stenciling the names in paint at the curb line.

Also, donating of the cannon in the public park to the scrap drive for the war effort was discussed.

Many To Attend Draft Conference

Reservations for the draft deferment dinner-meeting to be held Thursday evening, September 24, at the General Brodhead Hotel, Beaver Falls, now total 185, according to Charles W. McDonald, secretary of Local Draft Board No. 3, Rochester, which is sponsoring the affair.

Any interested industrial executive, business man or other employer may attend the dinner, Mr. McDonald said, but all reservations must be received by him not later than Tuesday, September 22.

Major R. W. Dodds, occupational adviser of the State Selective Service System, will be the principal speaker and will explain latest developments in regulations regarding draft deferments because of occupation.

Likes Trains

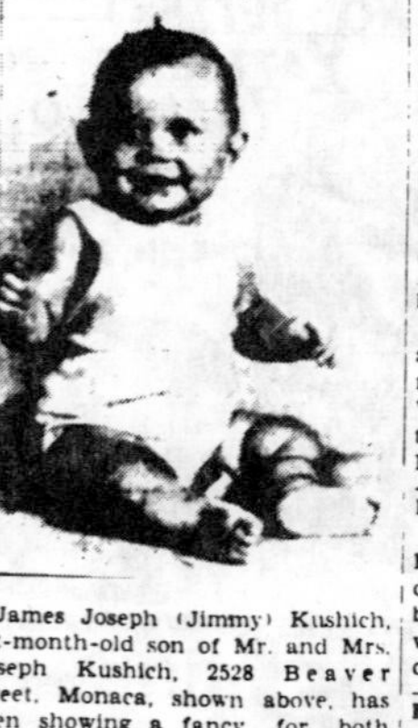

James Joseph (Jimmy) Kushich, six-month-old son of Mr. and Mrs. Joseph Kushich, 2528 Beaver street, Monaca, shown above, has been showing a fancy for both trains and animals. Jimmy has brown eyes and brown hair.

DECISION ON MANPOWER IS URGED TODAY

Lack Of Definite Manpower Policy Said Endangering War Effort; Division Between Armed Forces, Industry Necessary

By United Press

WASHINGTON, Sept. 17—Wendell Lund, director of the WPB's Labor Production Division, said today that lack of definite manpower policy endangers the war effort and makes it impossible to determine the largest and most efficient possible army that can be serviced by the United States.

So long as voluntary enlistments are permitted, no positive policy on the division of manpower between industry and the armed forces can be made effectively by the Selective Service System, he said in a statement prepared for presentation to the special House Defense Migration Committee.

"As yet no machinery or principles have been established by which we can determine the largest and most efficient possible army which can be fully serviced by those who are left outside the armed forces," he said. "Our government agencies are preparing themselves to make that decision. But until it is made, twin dangers face the nation's war effort.

DANGERS CITED

"On the one hand, workers may be taken out of jobs into the army in such a way as to cripple the production the armed forces need for their maximum efficiency. On the other hand, there is danger that the armed forces may be denied the men they need to operate the war machine."

Lund testified two days after Maj. Gen. Lewis B. Hershey, director of Selective Service, told the committee that an army of between 10,000,000 and 13,000,000 men would require the drafting of married men with children. War Manpower Commission Chairman Paul V. McNutt told the committee yesterday a National Service Act appeared inevitable. It would compel men and women to serve on the home front where needed and vest control of all manpower in a single authority.

Lund's statement came as congressional sources reported that a contest already is developing among three government agencies over which of them would administer a national service act if it is enacted. The agencies were said to be the War Manpower Commission, the Selective Service System and the War Production Board.

Aliquippan Indicted On Extortion Count

Nick Godich, 52, Aliquippa mill worker, today was indicted by the Federal grand jury at Pittsburgh on a charge of sending a threatening letter through the mails.

He is accused of sending a letter to Nick and Barbara Spehar, 1808 Tyler street, Aliquippa, demanding $1,000 be placed at a spot near Glenwillard. Threats of bodily harm were made unless the demand was met, authorities claimed.

FLASHES:

By United Press

DAVIS TO TESTIFY

WASHINGTON, Sept. 17—Director Elmer Davis of the Office of War Information makes his first appearance as a witness before a Senate committee today. He will be the first witness of the Interstate Commerce sub-committee's investigation of James C. Petrillo, head of the American Federation of Musicians.

POSTMASTER RENOMINATED

WASHINGTON, Sept. 17—Nomination of postmasters for re-appointment, sent to the Senate by the White House today for confirmation, included Postmaster James P. Bryan, Beaver.

LABOR BODY TO MEET

HARRISBURGH, Sept. 17 — The Pennsylvania Labor Federation will decide its position in the state gubernatorial election and discuss war labor problems at an executive committee meeting September 22.

BLAST INJURES 16

NEW HAVEN, Conn., Sept. 17—An explosion in a unit of the Winchester Repeating Arms Division of the Western Cartridge Company late last night injured 16 persons, two of them critically.

JAPS LOST THESE IN NEW GUINEA

Here are some of the trophies taken from the Japanese by United Nations forces operating in New Guinea. An American and an Australian soldier are seen examining the arms and other Nipponese war material.

Plans Being Made By County Firemen For Annual Rites

Announcement of the annual county memorial service for deceased firemen—to be held Sunday afternoon, October 11, in Midland high school auditorium—was made by the Midland Volunteer Fire Department, the Beaver County Firemen's Relief Association, and Beaver County Fire Chiefs' Association at the meeting of the Beaver County Firemen's Relief Association, Wednesday night in Chippewa township.

Fire Chief E. J. Barrett, Midland, announced that an impressive service will be held to honor the deceased members of the various fire departments and Ladies' Auxiliaries whose death lists are higher this year than in previous years.

Further plans for the memorial service will be made at the monthly meeting of the Chiefs' Association, Sunday evening, September 20, in the Center Township fire house.

HEAR TALK ON DEFENSE

The meeting of the Relief Association was attended by 250 firemen. The principal speaker was George Roark, secretary of the County Defense Council, who gave an interesting talk on the part in the war program to be played by the firemen. He also pointed out the duties of all firemen, auxiliary firemen, air raid wardens, and fire watchers and the education of school children during air raid drills.

Fire Chief Cooper of Beaver Falls announced there would not be any county parade in connection with Fire Prevention Week this year, but posters and fire prevention programs would be carried out by each town or city.

Fire Chief Rittelman of Am-

(Continued On Page Six)

Three County Men Wounded In Action

Official announcement was made today in Washington by the Navy Department of three county men wounded in action.

The list includes Corp. Carl W. McCracken, Marine Corps, son of Mrs. Bertha McCracken, 1111 Third avenue, Freedom, formerly of Rochester; John Joseph Miazgowicz, storekeeper in the Navy, son of Michael Miazgowicz, 208 Third avenue, Aliquippa; and Corp. Kenneth L. Canonge, Marine Corps, son of Mrs. Maude Canonge, 511 Merchant street, Ambridge.

Annual Campaign For Funds Planned By Valley Y.M.C.A.

The Finance Committee of the Beaver Valley Y.M.C.A. announces that plans are under way for the annual campaign for memberships and subscriptions to support the "Y" for the current budget year. Dan Evans, trust officer at the Beaver County Trust Company, is chairman for this year's drive.

Dates for the campaign have been set for October 15 to 22, opening on a Thursday night and closing one week later. A meeting will be held at the "Y" Friday night at 8 o'clock, at which Mr. Evans will begin building the drive organization.

The Y.M.C.A. has been a force for good in the communities of the Beaver Valley for fifty-three years. Its four-fold program — embracing religious, health, recreational, and morale building activities—is especially appropriate in these days when the stress and strain of war conditions touch almost every individual.

As in the past several years, no financial solicitation will be made in Beaver Falls, since the Y.M.C.A. receives its support in that town from the Community Chest, but will be confined to New Brighton and the lower valley towns. However, memberships during the drive will be available at a reduced rate to anyone.

Farm Machinery To Be Rationed In State

By United Press

HARRISBURG, Sept. 17— James E. Walker, chairman of the U. S. Agriculture Department's state war board, today disclosed that "frozen" farm machinery will be rationed in Pennsylvania by county committees comprising two farmers and the county AAA chairman.

Walker characterized the federal agriculture department's order temporarily freezing all farm machinery in the hands of dealers as "necessary to insure fair distribution of available equipment and its placement where it will do the most good in wartime farming production."

Sheriff O'Loughlin In Hospital For Operation

Charles J. O'Loughlin, Beaver County Sheriff and Burgess of Aliquippa, underwent an operation at Rochester Hospital today for a kidney ailment. Following the operation his condition was reported as good.

SCRAP SALVAGE CAMPAIGN IS PUSHED HERE TO AID IN WAR

The drive for vital scrap materials needed for America's war industries which began last Monday in Rochester is being continued.

About 30 tons of scrap metals and other materials have been collected since the drive was started, C. D. McDonald, chairman of the Rochester Salvage Committee, announced today.

Citizens are urged to conduct an intensive search around their homes and garages for scrap, whether in large or small quantities, and if possible, take it to the official salvage depot opposite the high school, or place it in a container on the curb in front of the home and trucks will pick it up.

Persons having scrap to contribute can leave word with Mr. McDonald or at the municipal building and trucks will be sent to collect it.

DRIVE ON AT MONACA

The salvage drive for scrap metals and other materials needed for America's war effort being conducted this week in Monaca is meeting with much success. Friday, September 18, will be the last day collections will be made.

Citizens are urged to gather every bit of scrap about their premises, place it on the curb line at their homes, notify Borough Secretary Guy Grater, chairman of the Salvage Committee, at the municipal building and trucks will collect it.

JAPS BLASTED BY YANKS IN PACIFIC AREAS

American Forces Slow Enemy Drive In Solomons; Ships, Planes, Shore Facilities And Troops Hammered In Aleutians

By United Press

WASHINGTON, Sept. 17—American forces have delivered new setbacks to the Japanese at both ends of the far-flung Pacific battle line, slowing the enemy drive to recapture the Solomon Islands and inflicting shattering blows on ships, planes, shore facilities and men in the Aleutian Islands.

Eight enemy ships were blasted by American planes at Kiska Island in the Aleutians, two of them being sunk.

From Guadalcanal came the cheering news that navy and marine corps dive bombers have damaged two Japanese cruisers while marine land forces not only are holding their positions on that main American base in the Solomons but have diminished the initial ferocity of the Japanese counter - attacks which started last Saturday.

These reports on developments in the Pacific war theater were issued last night in two naval communiques.

ALEUTIANS HIT HARD

The communique on two attacks on the enemy in the Aleutians was the first mention of that fog-shrouded area since August 22. But it told of a large-scale attack by fighter - escorted American army heavy bombers to Kiska which must have left much of that main enemy base in the island chain off Alaska destroyed.

In addition to the enemy ships sunk and damaged, 500 troops were killed or wounded, six planes were destroyed and fire was set to storehouses and supply dumps ashore.

Not a single American plane was lost during the attack as a result of enemy action, the navy reported. Admiral Chester W. Nimitz reported in Pearl Harbor, however, that two pilots of P-38 fighters were killed when their planes collided.

MORE JAPS BOMBED

Meanwhile, army flying fortresses and navy and marine corps dive bombers and torpedo planes ranged over the Northwestern Solomons, carrying the fight to the enemy. They intercepted a force of Japanese cruisers and destroyers off Choiseul Island, about 200 miles from Guadalcanal. Two of the cruisers were hit, raising to at least 22 the number of Japanese ships sunk or damaged since the marines launched the Solomons offensive August 7.

The flying fortresses, for the second time in two days, struck at Rekata Bay on Santa Isabel Island, about 140 miles northwest of Guadalcanal. Shore installations were bombed and set afire.

Nine More Youths Join Armed Forces

Nine more Beaver Countians have enlisted in the armed forces at Pittsburgh recruiting stations, six joining the Navy while the Army, Ordnance Enlisted Reserve and the Marine Corps each claimed one.

The enlistees:

Navy—Robert C. Bell, Beaver Falls; Michael M. Bires, Jr., Joseph T. Brehany and Albert L. Turner, Aliquippa, and Paul A. Cooney and Vincent J. Kamicker, West Aliquippa.

Army—Herbert K. Daman, Beaver Falls.

Ordnance Enlisted Reserve—John P. Budris, Ambridge.

Marines—Norman Lorencz, New Brighton.

Report Is Filed By Grand Jury

The Beaver County Grand Jury, following an inspection tour of county institutions yesterday, filed a brief report at the office of the clerk of courts recommending small pay increases for nurses at the County Home Hospital.

The report follows:

To Court of Quarter Sessions, Beaver County Court House, Beaver, Pa.

"We the Grand Jury of the September 1942 sessions do hereby recommend an increase of $5 per month to the nurses at the County Home Hospital.

—C. J. Ingraham, foreman; H. E. Reed, Secretary."

RAF MAKES BIG RAID ON RUHR

Today's War Summary

MOSCOW—Germans battle way into Stalingrad from foothold gained in city's northern outskirts.

LONDON—RAF deals smashing blow to German war industry with major-scale raid on Ruhr; Soviet agitation for second front increases.

CHUNGKING—Reports of Japanese troop movements and Tokyo conferences strengthen belief new Japanese military blow is pending.

GEN. MacARTHUR'S HDQTS. — Japanese increase pressure on mountain trails leading to Port Moresby, Allied base in New Guinea.

The Royal Air Force reported today that its Bomber Command had struck another deadly blow at the German war industries of the Ruhr in a great night attack that apparently fell only little short of the crushing 1,000-plane mark.

The RAF blow fell as Russian troops battled in the streets and bomb-blasted buildings of Stalingrad to hold off one of the greatest Nazi attacks of the war. Repercussions of the Stalingrad battle were felt sharply in London where Soviet agitation for an immediate second land front in the west rose higher.

The Air Ministry described the RAF night attack as having been carried out by a "very strong" force of planes, and estimates of the raiding squadron ranged upwards of 700. The RAF lost 39 planes in the night's operation, the heaviest loss sustained in a single night since the 1,000 plane attack on Bremen.

RUSSIANS RETREAT

Reports from the eastern front indicated the Germans were fighting their way forward in Stalingrad, driving into the city and slowly forcing the Russians back. Moscow dispatches described the German attack as one of the most vicious of the war and said the Nazis had a foothold in the northwestern outskirts of the city, nine to 12 miles from the center of the city.

An estimated 450,000 German and Rumanian troops were smashing ahead in the northwestern sector and it was believed the total Nazi force engaged in the Stalingrad operation was about 1,000,000 men.

Chungking reported that Emperor Hirohito had conferred with the cabinet of Premier Hideki Tojo, an unusual event which was thought might be linked with some momentous decision or impending event, such as a possible attack on Siberia. The meeting coincided with the appointment of Masayuki Tani as Japanese Foreign Minister. At the same time the Chinese reported that two Japanese divisions had been spotted at Shanghai, apparently bound for some unknown destination.

The tempo of action in the southwest Pacific was rising, particularly in New Guinea where Gen. Douglas MacArthur reported heavy Japanese pressure on the trail leading down the Owen Stanley mountains toward Port Moresby.

PORT MORESBY MENACED

The Japanese were said to be in the vicinity of Ioribaiwa, about 32

(Continued On Page Six)

In Army Radio Corps

Corporal Homer L. Alford, son of Mr. and Mrs. H. L. Alford, Fifth avenue, Freedom, is with the army radio corps "somewhere" in Australia.

Lieut. Walter Coss Is Home On Leave From Fighting Front

Captain Walter (Bud) Coss, 1109 Third avenue, New Brighton, is spending a brief leave of absence from his duties in the United States Army Air Forces—in which he has won considerable fame—with his parents, Dr. and Mrs. W. L. Coss, New Brighton.

The local aviator arrived home Wednesday, but is forbidden by regulations to state from where he came or his method of transportation.

Reports from the Southwest Pacific, though, have informed local friends of the New Brighton pilot of his exploits in the current war against Japan.

Coss was stationed on the Island of Luzon in the Philippines when the Japs struck on December 7. While on patrol during the early battles for the American stronghold in the Pacific, Coss encountered a cluster of Japanese Navy Zero fighters over the northern tip of Luzon.

ESCAPES DEATH

A burst of machine gun fire struck the cooling system of his plane and he was forced to bail out. Coss did a delayed jump, waiting until he was near the ground before pulling his ripcord. His delay allowed him only one swing of the canopy before he landed in water.

One Jap plane had followed him down and sprayed his floating parachute with bullets. Fearful that his yellow life jacket would be a good target, the local pilot discarded it and dove deep underwater when the Zero came back to the spot.

Each time the Jap dove, Coss went back underwater and, when the plane finally left, discovered his swimming jacket was riddled by bullets.

He swam ashore and found he was near Aparri, a considerable distance from his home field. Walking with one Filipino ahead of him and another behind, Coss returned to duty after an eight-day walk through the jungles.

GIVEN PROMOTION

As the Japanese forces overran Luzon, American airmen were removed to Java, where Coss was notified on February 19 of his promotion to the rank of captain.

Friends in this vicinity knew of his promotion before he did as the result of a newspaper story from Batavia on February 18. Coss was at the opposite end of the island at

(Continued On Page Six)

Six Men Killed In Army Plane Crash

BIRMINGHAM, Ala., Sept. 17.—Six men were killed Wednesday in the crash of an army bomber on Double Oak Mountain, some 20 miles southeast of here.

The ship struck a mountain peak 400 yards from the Birmingham-Childersburg highway, after apparently turning sharply to avoid another peak.

First news of the accident came in a call to the state highway patrol from an unidentified motorist who witnessed the crash as he drove along the highway.

J. And L. Executive Invited To Join OPA

By United Press

PITTSBURGH, Sept. 17—A veteran employe of Jones and Laughlin Steel Corp. has been invited to join an industrial committee of the Office of Price Administration, it was revealed today. A. W. Herron, Jr., manager of warehouse sales for the company, was asked to join the steel warehouse and jobbers advisory committee of the OPA. He has been with J. & L. 22 years and was made warehouse manager four years ago.

Many County Boys, Girls Enrolled At Penn State College

A record freshman class totaling more than 2,100 students has been enrolled at the Pennsylvania State College for the fall semester, according to William S. Hoffman, registrar.

These figures indicate an increase of 500 first-year students over the 1,600 freshmen enrolled last fall. There are approximately 150 more freshman co-eds this year than last. The increase swells the freshman women enrollment to an all-time high of about 600.

Beaver county first-year students are:

Aliquippa—John V. Battles, lower division; Lois E. Cohen, lower division; John R. Connelly, civil engineering; Dale A. Eberle, chemistry; Howard S. Gilliland, lower division; Herbert D. Maneloveg, chemical engineering; John W. Morgan, lower division; Robert B. Sankey, chemical engineering; James K. Schell, dairy husbandry; Joe Smisko, chemical engineering.

Ambridge—John Athens, chemical engineering; Robert E. Bires, lower division; Elsie F. Blanarik. lower division; Raymond E. Boyle, metallurgy; Peter Compagnoni, civil engineering; Anthony J. Krol, pre-medical; Leonard J. Shevchik, chemistry; Stephen J. Skapik, electrical engineering; Charles J. Weber, Jr., pre-medical.

Baden — Charles M. Cook, Jr., chemical engineering; William R. Cummings, mechanical engineering.

Beaver—Patrick J. Cody, agriculture; William M. Gordon, poultry husbandry; Robert R. Gridley, industrial engineering; Jean M. Grimm, lower division; Lewis H. Urling, pre-medical.

Beaver Falls—Donald L. Gaudio, lower division.

Conway—William F. Bena, metallurgy.

Freedom—William A. Peirsol, electrical engineering.

Hookstown—Richard M. Laughlin, mechanical engineering; Ada L. Mansfield, lower division.

Midland—James E. Brown, mechanical engineering; Olen C. Gibson, mechanical engineering.

Monaca — Marian H. Batchelor, lower division.

New Brighton—Richard N. Golden, civil engineering; John J. Helbling, horticulture; David A. Lonkert, electrical engineering; Martha J. Tritschler, lower division.

Rochester—Shirley M. Camp, lower division; Edward E. Dawson, Jr., architectural engineering; Edward J. Holler, chemical engineering; Robert H. Robinson, pre-medical; Sarah J. Schmidt, medical technology.

Bridgewater—Samuel C. Holland, chemical engineering.

New Sheffield

Bunco Club Members Are Entertained

The monthly meeting of the Bunco Club was held at the home of Mrs. Guy Hineman, Maple avenue. Prizes were captured by Mrs. Jenny Sission, Mrs. Ralph Davis, Jr., Mrs. Roy Hineman and Mrs. Joe Gully. Mrs. Ralph Davis, Sr., Fairmont, was a guest of the club.

Mr. and Mrs. John Rupnick and family have moved into their newly-built home in Maple avenue.

Mrs. Ralph Davis, Sr., Fairmont, W. Va., visited recently at the home of Mr. and Mrs. Ralph Davis, Jr., Maple avenue.

Charles Janes, Brodhead road, is a patient in Sewickley Valley hospital where he underwent an appendicitis operation.

Joe Belich, West Wade street, and Mafalda DiNardo, Maple avenue, announced their engagement at a farewell and birthday party held recently.

By November, 1931, British Empire purchases in the United States since the outbreak of the war had mounted to over $5,000,000,000—more than 10 times the value of goods exported under Lend-Lease to that date.

National Grange Objects To Tax On Transportation

At hearings before the finance committee of the United States Senate, the National Grange registered objections to the imposition of the proposed 5 per cent tax on the transportation of property throughout the country.

In the opinion of the Grange, such tax would be objectionable for several reasons:—First, because it would be inflationary; second, because the tax would be pyramided, compelling the ultimate consumer to pay more than the government would receive; and third, because such an impost would be discriminatory, resting more heavily on those sections of the country that are farthest removed from market than it would on other sections within easy reach of their markets.

The Grange takes the position that the distance a man lives from market is not a just measure of the tax he should pay to support our war effort, but that war taxes should bear equally on all parts of the country.

The Grange declares that if this tax proposal is to be enacted, notwithstanding all its objectionable features, it would be more fair and equitable to impose a flat rate, regardless of the distance a shipment might travel. A rate of 1½ cents per hundredweight or 30 cents a ton on livestock and agricutlural products, says the Grange, would produce approximately the same revenue as a 5 per cent tax.

Draft Boards Urged To Fight Disease

HARRISBURG, Sept. 18.—Dr. Edgar S. Everhart, chief of the State Veneral Disease Division and medical head of the State Selective Service system, today called on local draft boards to give "active coperation" in rehabilitating 3,000 draft registrants infected with syphilis.

Everhart said many syphilitics rejected for service by the army in Pennsylvania had started ourses of treatment under the program conducted by the State Health Department and Selective Service system. "But," he added, "we have no way of knowing how many of the men continued receiving treatment after once starting them."

Emphasizing he had no desire to have local board members "take on the additional duties of health officers," Everhart declared the local boards "could do much toward making this program a real success." He pointed out that "the program has potentialities of being a tremendous benefit to the general public welfare as well as to the army."

BADEN NEWS

Mrs. Helen Vignere has returned to her home in Providence, R. I., after visiting several weeks with her mother, Mrs. Frank McCale, Market street, and her sister, Mrs. Roland Henderson, Rochester.

Frank W. McCale, Market street, has been confined to his home several weeks by a severe attack of bronchitis.

Mrs. Richard Smith has been confined to Sewickley Valley hospital where she underwent a major operation.

San Francisco's world-famous Golden Gate park contains 17 miles of improved driveways, two museums, a zoo, an aquarium, a stadium, a music pavilion, tennis courts, croquet grounds, bowling greens and lakes

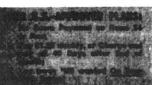

The Weather Forecast

WESTERN PENNSYLVANIA: Rain and continued cold tonight; rain and snow near Lake Erie. Pollen count, 73.

"The Paper That Goes Home"

THE DAILY TIMES

ROCHESTER-BEAVER-MONACA

FREEDOM—BRIDGEWATER—CONWAY—VANPORT—MIDLAND

Beaver County History

A new drive was started by Allied troops in the Champagne district of France on Sept. 26, 1918, it was reported in the county.

ESTABLISHED APRIL 2, 1874 | BEAVER AND ROCHESTER, PA., SATURDAY, SEPTEMBER 26, 1942 | BY CARRIER 18 CENTS A WEEK—5 CENTS PER COPY

RUSSIAN COUNTER-DRIVE SLOWS NAZIS

VALLEY SINGERS TO BROADCAST COAST-TO-COAST SUNDAY AFTERNOON

This is the Beaver Curtiss-Wright Chorus which will be heard from coast to coast Sunday on the Mutual Broadcasting System from the Beaver High School stadium, where a pre-broadcast program will open at 2 p. m. Members of the chorus are (left to right):

First row—Evelyn Chambers, Laura McConnell, Mary Alice Bayes, Wanda Calder, Ruth Reich, Kathleen Reutter, Louise Grine, Ruth Clark, Mary Campbell, Eleanor Kirtland, Ethlyn Neely, Dorothy McDonald, Marion Symons, Florence Ogden.

Second row—Virginia Kaste, Betty McKee, Jean Lynch, John Pontis, Dick Dodds, John Bralkowski, Tom Davidson, George Douglass, Lloyd Stevenson, Jr., Leila McDonald, Betty Davidson, Jane Smith, Ruth Ewing.

Third row—A. K. Johnson, Bill Wetzel, Edwin Ewing, C. A. Stratthaus, M. J. McCarthy, Wayne Patterson, Frank Gallio, William Bailey, Sam McCallum, Jim Mace (director), Jim McCormick, John Fink, Frank Horne, Joseph Hildman, Harry Hinds, Harry Douthett, Jr., Robert Wine.

Following is the pre-broadcast program:

"America", audience, chorus and orchestra; "Beaver At Work", W. B. Avery, industrial relations, Curtiss-Wright Corporation, Propeller Division; selection from "Orchestra Wives"; "Education and the War," G. A. McCormick, superintendent of Beaver schools; "Gopak", chorus; "The Army Air Corps", Curtiss-Wright Orchestra; "Aviation", Colonel Howard H. Couch, Army Air Forces; "Johnson Rag", Curtiss-Wright Orchestra; "The Community and Industry," Oscar W. Nelson, Beaver plant manager; orchestra.

GERMAN DRIVE IS REPORTED SLOWING DOWN

Reds Believed To Have Severed Nazi Rail Supply Line; Japs Blasted By Allied Artillery In Pacific; R A F Planes Make Sweeps

By United Press

MOSCOW—Nazi drive on Stalingrad lags as Soviet counter-attack gains momentum; Red forces believed to have cut rail line supplying Germans.

VICHY— Laval discovers alleged plot to remove his power, ousts French cabinet secretary for relations with Germany.

GEN. MacARTHUR'S HDQTRS. —Allied artillery blasts Japanese columns attempting to reach Port Moresby as Allied aircraft continues bombing of Japanese bases.

LONDON — RAF attacks enemy shipping along European coast, interrupts Quisling party meeting at Oslo with bombs.

BERLIN — German radio claims American troops swarming along African coast for attack on Dakar.

OFFENSE CHECKED

The massive Nazi drive on Stalingrad today appeared to be spending its force with the momentum of the attack lagging in the face of the Red army's last ditch defense.

Soviet reports indicated that Marshal Semyon Timoshenko's defense plans had thwarted, for the time being, Adolf Hitler's attempt to capture the Volga river key and that the Nazis may be forced to start a new offensive if they hope to capture the city this Autumn.

Military experts in London believed that the Red army would still have sufficient strength to wage a winter war against the Germans and pin down a major portion of the Nazi armies in Russia during the cold months. These experts believed that the heavy losses suffered by both the Germans and Russians have not yet been so severe as to impair the major fighting strength of either side.

The Soviet counter-attack northwest of Stalingrad was developing steadily, reports from Moscow said, and appeared to be pinching the big German forces assembled on the Stalingrad battleground.

DRIVE FOR HILLS

The Russians fought off several Nazi counter-attacks northwest of the city and were driving in with a flanking maneuver designed to force the Nazis to pull out the

(Continued On Page Eight)

Rochester To Have Big Army Rally On Wednesday, Sept. 30

A United States Army rally, sponsored by the Air Forces, Signal Corps, Ordnance Department, and WAAC, will be held Wednesday, September 30, at 12 o'clock noon on the steps of the Rochester post office.

The speakers will be: Major Harmar D. Denny, Pittsburgh, Air Forces; Lieutenant Patrick L. Mohardt, Monmouth, N. J., Signal Corps; Lieutenant W. G. Kirk, Pittsburgh, Ordnance, and Mrs. Dorothy Kolbum, Pittsburgh, WAAC.

Entertainment will include music by the Pittsburgh WPA Band of sixteen pieces, directed by Mr. Barolette. Ten sound trucks will parade through the streets.

Sam M. McCune, Rochester, will master of ceremonies.

The purpose of the rally is to secure specialists in the line of machinists, aircraft and radio mechanics, welders, aircraft radio operators, metal workers and other craftsmen. Representatives of the different army groups will interview men for the various occupations.

Women To Receive Same Pay As Men

By United Press

WASHINGTON Sept. 26 Wage discrimination against war workers because of sex appeared to be out the window today following adoption by the War Labor Board of a policy granting "equal pay for equal work" for women in armament industries.

The policy was set forth in a unanimous decision, written by Dr. George W. Taylor, the Board's vice-chairman, who said any other condition was "not conducive to maximum production."

The decision, handed down in a dispute involving 7,600 employes of the Brown & Sharpe Manufacturing Co., Providence, R. I., was regarded by labor officials as of equal importance to the "Little Steel" ruling fixing wage increases at 15 per cent above January, 1941 levels.

Manpower Draft Is Proposed In Bill

WASHINGTON, Sept. 26 — A manpower draft of all men between 18 and 65 years of age was proposed today in legislation introduced by Sen. Warren R. Austin, R., Vt., who said it provides an opportunity for men in that age group to serve their country "by fighting or working."

The bill would apply to all men over the 45-year maximum draft age and to all below that age who have been deferred from military service.

Railroad Workers Make Demands For Increase In Wages

By United Press

CHICAGO, Sept. 26 — The nation's major railroads receive demands from their "non-operating" employes today, reopening the wage issue on which the carriers and unions were deadlocked for five months last year.

The demands were sent by the 14 non-operating unions, who asked a minimum wage of 70 cents an hour, a wage increase of 20 cents an hour and a closed shop for 950,000 employes. Similar demands were submitted by the Hotel and Restaurant Employes Alliance and Bartenders International League.

The closed shop issue was introduced in negotiations for the first time, a union spokesman said, "to prevent chiselers from profiting by improved working and wage conditions negotiated by the unions."

A management spokesman said the National Railway Labor Act explicitly forbade closed shop contracts.

BIG PAYROLL BOOST

Although the "Big Five" operating brotherhoods, representing 350,000 employes, usually act in concert with the non-operating unions, they have given no indication whether they intend to open negotiations.

Management representatives declined to comment on the demands, but it was estimated that the requested wage increase would boost payrolls more than $200,000,000.

An agreement reached last December after five months of negotiations, ultimately settled by a Presidential fact-finding board, gave the non-operating employes an increase averaging nine cents an hour and raising their average wage to 73.5 cents an hour. At the same time the operating employes were given an increase of 7.5 per cent.

The agreement expires December 31. The fact-finding board last year recommended that the rail-

(Continued On Page Eight)

Serving Overseas

Now serving with the U. S. Army in England is Pvt. Marshall C. Killian, son of Mr. and Mrs. M. C. Killian, Tuscarawas road, near Beaver. He graduated from New Brighton high school in 1940 and attended Geneva College. At the time of his induction into the army he was employed by the St. Joseph Lead Company.

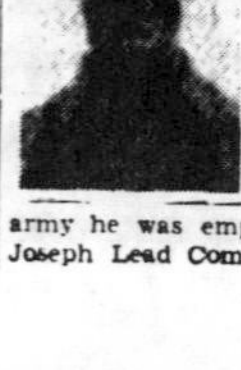

INTERESTING PROGRAM IS ARRANGED FOR CURTISS-WRIGHT RADIO PROGRAM SUNDAY

The voices of twenty-seven Beaver Valley residents will be heard from coast to coast Sunday as the Beaver Curtiss-Wright Chorus, broadcasts over a 135-station hook-up of the Mutual Broadcasting System. The broadcast will be the closing feature of a 90-minute program beginning at 2 p. m. in the Beaver High school stadium, where the chorus will make its first formal appearance.

The program preceding the broadcast will feature addresses by Colonel H. H. Couch, chief of the Propeller Laboratory in the Air Forces Research and Development Center, Wright Field, Dayton, Ohio; George A. McCormick, superintendent of Beaver Schools, and Oscar W. Nelson, manager of the Curtiss-Wright Corporation, Propeller Division, plant in Beaver.

In the event of rain, the entire program, including the broadcast, will be held in Beaver High school auditorium.

A number of officials from nearby communities are expected to attend the program, which will pay tribute in song and drama to the manner in which communities like Beaver are meeting their wartime responsibilities.

Dramatic roles in the script will be taken by members of the recently-organized dramatic society at the propeller plant. They are George Douglass, Jane Smith and "Lil" Dempsey, all of Beaver and Eleanor Bloom, Aliquippa.

TO EXHIBIT BLADES

Extensive preparations have been made to handle traffic and visitors in the vicinity of the broadcast scene. The local police force, under the supervision of Chief Lisle Kimple, will be augmented by eight uniformed guards of the Curtiss-Wright plant. Uniformed girl employes from the plant will act as ushers.

A special feature of the program will be an exhibit of propeller

(Continued On Page Eight)

Aliquippa Sailor Is Reported Dead

James P. Campbell, son of James F. Campbell, 1210 McMinn street, Aliquippa, was reported as dead among the 2,355 seamen listed as dead and missing by the U. S. Navy today in the first American merchant marine casualty list.

The casualties included 434 known dead and 1,921 missing.

The report covered the period from Sept. 27, 1941, when the merchant vessel, I. C. White, was torpedoed and sunk in the South Atlantic, to August 1, 1942. Pennsylvania listed 29 dead and 152 missing.

The list included only those casualties resulting directly from enemy action while sailing under the American flag. Names of personnel on United States merchant vessels which are overdue and presumed lost are considered casualties of enemy action.

FLASHES:

By United Press

FIREMEN KILLED

PITTSBURGH, Sept. 26 — Tripping over a hose in the attic of a home where hew as fighting a fire, Fireman Henry C. Schaefer, 46, was killed last night when he fell to the second floor.

THREE ESCAPE FIRE

PITTSBURGH, Sept. 26 — Firemen early today battled a two-alarm blaze for four hours after they rescued a young mother and her infant son, and a hysterical girl leaped to safety from the third floor of a burning home.

STRIKERS RETURN

CLEVELAND, Sept. 26 — Some of 400 men involved in a three-day wildcat strike in the smelter division of the Aluminum Company of America plant were back at work today, and officials of the Mine, Mill and Smelter Workers' Union (CIO) were trying to get the rest back.

OFFICERS GRADUATE

CARLISLE, Pa., Sept. 26 — The medical field service school today graduated 241 new officers for administrative duties as 2nd lieutenants in the medical corps, releasing more army physicians and dentists for strictly professional assignments.

LABOR TO GET VOICE

WASHINGTON, Sept. 26 — War Production Director Donald M. Nelson today was expected to complete streamlining of his agency soon by giving labor an increased voice in its policies and operations and by junking its priority system in favor of allocations.

COAL ORDERS RESTRICTED

HARRISBURG, Sept. 26—Anthracite users through the hard coal marketing states will be asked by the government to keep their fuel orders down to about a 40 or 60-day supply until after November 1, the United Press learned today.

SCRAP DRIVE GRATIFYING

HARRISBURG, Sept. 26—Incomplete reports from 53 counties revealed today that Pennsylvania's scrap harvest drive yielded more than a third of its estimated 75,000-ton goal in the first ten days of the campaign.

Beaver Speaker

Col. H. H. Couch, (above) Chief of the Propeller Laboratory in the Air Forces Research and Development Center, Wright Field, Dayton, O., will speak Sunday afternoon in the Beaver high school stadium at ceremonies attending the first formal appearance of the Beaver Curtiss-Wright Chorus.

Rationing Of Dairy Products Predicted Within Two Months

By United Press

HARRISBURG, Sept. 26—Chairman John M. McKee of the Milk Control Commission, although declining to predict outcome of recent hearings in Erie and Scranton to consider increases in milk prices paid to dairy farmers, said today the Office of Price Administration now has "factual data" on which to act.

Although Federal ceilings froze wholesale and retail milk prices, the Commission scheduled hearings on demands by producers that increased costs of labor, feed, supplies and equipment justify a better return.

Any Commission order coming out of the hearings raising prices would have to have OPA approval before taking effect.

Meantime, the Federal Agriculture Department predicted rationing of dairy products within two months—thus bearing out McKee's prediction 60 days ago that farmers would be unable to supply the demand for milk unless dairying was made as

(Continued On Page Eight)

New Compromise Is Offered In Battle Over Farm Parity

By United Press

WASHINGTON, Sept. 26 — Sen. Walter F. George, D., Ga., today offered a new compromise in the bitter tussle between administration and farm bloc forces over legislation granting President Roosevelt broad powers to combat inflation.

He recommended further revision of an administration amendment—requiring the President to consider farm labor costs in fixing farm price ceilings — to include a date from which higher labor costs would be figured.

The farm bloc has demanded revision of the present formula for computing parity prices for agriculture to include all labor costs. The proposal, embodied in an amendment by Sen. Elmer Thomas, D., Okla., has been opposed flatly by the President.

George said the administration amendment, as now drawn, applies "only to future increases" in labor costs and should be revised to permit price ceiling adjustments to compensate for rises in labor and other costs since September 1, 1939, or, possibly, from January 1, 1940.

BARKLEY OBJECTS

Senate Democratic Leader Alben W. Barkley of Kentucky, however, objected and challenged George's contention that future increases alone would be affected under the original compromise.

Barkley, who yesterday adjourned the Senate until Monday after five days of debate, reiterated his confidence that the administration would win through. He felt a showdown vote would come on Monday or Tuesday.

Administration leaders have asserted that the anti-inflation bill, if it contains the Thomas amendment, will be vetoed by the President who then would establish farm price control by executive order.

George contended that the revision he proposed would accomplish all that the farm bloc de-

(Continued On Page Eight)

Beaver Merchants To Meet Tuesday Night

The Beaver Merchants and Professional Men's association has announced a dinner meeting of the organization at the Beaver Presbyterian church, Tuesday evening, September 29, at 6:30 o'clock.

Guests will include Beaver High Coach Harold C. Leffler and Assistant Coaches Max Martin and James Scarfpin.

CORRECTION!

Anacin 50 for 59c, not 100 for 59c as quoted in error in Jordan's Friday advertisement. 9 26

Gasoline Rationing Program Expected To Start In November

WASHINGTON, Sept. 26. — The Office of Price Administration today rushed preparations to ration gasoline to the nation's 27,000,000 civilian motorists as ordered by Rubber Czar William S. Jeffers to keep the country's economic life from breaking down.

Jeffers did not specify a date for starting the program, but the unofficial guess was either Nov. 1 or Nov. 15.

His order to OPA was coupled with an appeal to motorists to curtail gasoline consumption until the new restraints become effective, and to observe a 35-mile-an-hour speed limit. And he implied that more drastic curbs will be necessary if motorists fail to cooperate voluntarily.

The rationing, on a coupon basis, will follow the program which has been in operation since last July in 17 East Coast states and the District of Columbia. It restricts non-

(Continued On Page Eight)

She's Army Nurse

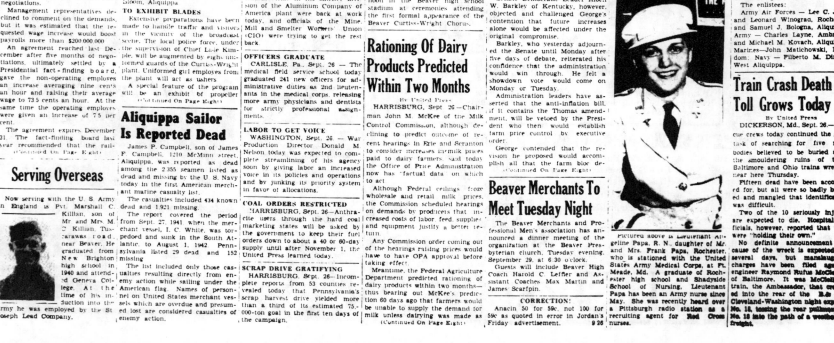

Pictured above is Lieutenant Angeline Papa, R. N., daughter of Mr. and Mrs. Frank Papa, Rochester, who is stationed with the United States Army Medical Corps, at Ft. Meade, Md. A graduate of Rochester high school and Shadyside School of Nursing, Lieutenant Papa has been an Army nurse since May. She was recently heard over a Pittsburgh radio station as a recruiting agent for Red Cross nurses.

Seven Boys Enlist; 75 Selectees Pass

Seven more Beaver Countians have enlisted in the armed forces at Pittsburgh recruiting offices and seventy-five selectees from Local Board No. 6, Ambridge, passed their final physical examinations Friday at Pittsburgh.

The enlistees:

Army Air Forces — Lee C. Joyce and Leonard Winograd, Rochester, and Samuel J. Bologna, Aliquippa; Army — Charles Layne, Ambridge, and Michael M. Kovach, Aliquippa; Marines—John Matichowski, Freedom; Navy — Filberto M. Dinello, West Aliquippa.

Train Crash Death Toll Grows Today

By United Press

DICKERSON, Md., Sept. 26.—Rescue crews today continued the grim task of searching for five more bodies believed to be buried amid the smouldering ruins of three Baltimore and Ohio trains wrecked near here Thursday.

Fifteen dead have been accounted for, but all were so badly burned and mangled that identification was difficult.

Two of the 10 seriously injured are expected to die. Hospital officials, however, reported that they were "holding their own."

No definite announcement on cause of the wreck is expected for several days, but manslaughter charges have been filed against engineer Raymond Rufus McClellan of Baltimore. It was McClellan's train, the Ambassador, that crashed into the rear of the B.& O.'s Cleveland-Washington night express No. 18, tossing the rear pullman on No. 18 into the path of a westbound freight.

SIX BEAVER COUNTY MEN ACCEPTED FOR SERVICE WITH MARINES

ALBERT REVESKE

LOUIS A. PAGANI

ROBERT McGEE

CHESTER B. KOAH

C. LLOYD DIEHL

FRANK LUPO

Headquarters of the United States Marine Corps Recruiting in the Pittsburgh area has announced that six Beaver County men have recently been accepted for service with the fighting "Leathernecks" and have been assigned to Parris Island, S. C., for basic training. The men are Albert Reveske, 1503 Fourth avenue, Beaver Falls; Louis A. Pagani, Morris street, Darlington; Robert McGee, 2511 Eighth avenue, Beaver Falls; Chester B. Koah, 1215 Third avenue, Beaver Falls; C. Lloyd Diehl, 324 Morado Dwellings, Beaver Falls and Frank Lupo, 828 Fourth avenue, Beaver Falls. They were sworn into the service by Major A. E. Simon, officer in charge of the Pittsburgh headquarters.

SERVING WITH U. S. ARMED FORCES

PVT. JAMES LOREY

Private James E. Lorey, 1801 Eighth avenue, has returned to Fort Bragg, North Carolina, after spending a seven-day furlough at his home. He entered the armed forces on June 23.

PVT. ROBERT E. JACKSON

Private Robert E. Jackson of College Hill has been stationed with the armed forces "somewhere in Australia" since last February.

RICHARD F. FULTON

Richard F. Fulton, son of Mr. and Mrs. N. A. Fulton, of Beaver Falls, is with the Army Air Corps at Gowen Field, Idaho.

ROBERT L. SHIPLEY

Robert Lee Shipley, son of Mr. and Mrs. O. L. Shipley of R. D. 1, Beaver Falls, has joined the enlisted reserve of the United States Army Air Forces and in the near future will be called to active duty as an Aviation Cadet.

CORP OHNSMAN

Corporal Elliott Ohnsman, son of Mr. and Mrs. Clyde Ohnsman of the Oakdale Road, Chippewa Township, is stationed with an engineers' division at Fort George Meade, Md. The local youth has been in the service for two months.

PVT. WM. SHAFER

Private William Shafer, son of Mr. and Mrs. Norman G. Shafer of Eighth avenue, New Brighton, who enlisted in the Army Air Forces last January has recently been transferred to a Texas air field. He is a mechanic.

SGT. GEO. SHAFER

Sgt. George Shafer, who enlisted in the Army Air Corps some two years ago, is located at Boling Field, Washington, D. C. He is the son of Mr. and Mrs. Norman G. Shafer, of Eighth avenue, New Brighton.

Attired in Latest Desert Garb

Mesquites can be a nuisance anywhere, including the Western desert, so these British tank men have outfitted themselves with the latest mosquito-net headgear. They are shown writing letters home while waiting for the order to go into action. Their tank is in the background.

GARRY C. MYERS Ph. D. DR. CLENDENING

WOMEN'S PAGE

HELEN FOLLETT FASHION NOTES

Best Type of Dressing as First Aid for Minor Injuries

By LOGAN CLENDENING, M. D.

SOMEONE has been asked or inspired to compose a new First Aid Manual and has written in to inquire what disinfectants they are to recommend and why. My feeling is to answer both, "Don't." Don't write another manual on First Aid, and don't put anything on disinfectants in the one you don't write.

Dr. Clendening will answer questions of general interest only, and then only through his column.

I'll admit I'm a little cynical about civilian first aiders, having seen several of them in action. In the article I wrote on the subject a week or two ago, it will be remembered I dwelt on some other "don'ts." When a person falls down unconscious on the sidewalk, don't try to move him or rub him, and don't try to be too efficient. Just make him comfortable and let him rest. The doctor is on the way anyhow.

Dressing a Minor Injury

We are considering now, of course, a minor injury—an open wound not serious enough to call the doctor. Every step but one in the dressing of such a wound, simple as it appears, is subject to some discussion. One undebatably good procedure is to put on a piece of sterile gauze and strap it down with adhesive plaster.

The only safe and dependable means of removing foreign particles from a wound is by picking them out with a sterile forceps.

Disinfectants are measured by a standard known as the phenol coefficient, and are classified as bacteriostatic (which means they prevent the growth of germs), and bacteriocidal (which means they kill the germs). The mercury disinfectants are very good bacteriostatic agents, but not very good bacteriocidal. That would be all right and make them useful for skin wounds except that the skin, sweat, wound and blood secretions contain sulfides and other reducing agents which have more or less neutralizing effect on mercurials.

Bacteriocidal Agents

Tincture of iodine is a good bacteriocidal agent and a good skin disinfectant, but somewhat destructive, although this is not important in a small abrasion. Except for tincture of iodine there is no use using alcohol solutions of disinfectants. They sting and the aqueous solutions are just as effective. A crust forms quickly which seals the open spot off, and healing takes place under the crust.

The conclusion drawn by a large hospital staff after considerable study should be fairly easy to remember: "Fresh lacerations of a minor nature which do not require treatment by a physician usually do well if they are merely covered with a sterile unmedicated gauze pad, held in place with adhesive with gentle pressure."

QUESTIONS AND ANSWERS

W. B., Chico, California: Does extraction of teeth cause deafness to any degree? Will a properly fitting plate help deafness to any degree whe the deafness is due to extraction?

Answer: Sometimes. When all the teeth in the lower jaw are removed, the jaw bone presses against the Eustachian tube opening into the middle ear, causing partial deafness. It can be remedied by a good plate.

EDITOR'S NOTE: Dr. Clendening has seven pamphlets which can be obtained by readers. Each pamphlet sells for 10 cents. For any one pamphlet desired, send 10 cents in coin, and a self-addressed envelope stamped with a three-cent stamp, to Dr. Logan Clendening, in care of this paper. The pamphlets are: "Three Weeks' Reducing Diet", "Indigestion and Constipation", "Reducing and Gaining", "Infant Feeding", "Instructions for the Treatment of Diabetes", "Feminine Hygiene" and "The Care of the Hair and Skin".

Marian Martin Patterns

9210

A TWO-WAY DIRNDL

Youngest, most beguiling of the new-season frocks is Pattern 9210 by Marian Martin! It's in the favorite dirndl style, and makes either a contrasting blouse and skirt or a one-piece dress. Ruffling is crisp.

Pattern 9210 may be ordered only in junior miss sizes 11, 13, 15, 17. Size 13, blouse, requires 1½ yards, 39 inch fabric; skirt, 2⅛ yards 35 inch velveteen.

Send SIXTEEN CENTS in coins for this Marian Martin pattern. Write plainly SIZE, NAME, ADDRESS and STYLE NUMBER.

Save for Victory—with our helpful new Fall and Winter Pattern Book! It's the best guide to home sewing, with smart, easy-to-sew, thrifty designs for work, play, school. Pattern Book is ten cents.

Send your order to News-Tribune Pattern Department, 232 West Eighteenth street, New York, N. Y.

BARCLAY ON BRIDGE

By Shepard Barclay

"The Authority on Authorities"

HOW MANY ARE SURE?

VULNERABILITY is a mighty factor in considering whether to pass or to overcall a bid at your right. Many an opponent, who seldom even considers doubling your overcall if you are not vulnerable, is ready to think about cracking down on you when you are vulnerable. At such a time, you must weigh carefully your prospects in case you find your partner with a virtually blank hand, and the other side giving you the old whipsaw with practically all of the outstanding strength.

	1.	2.
♠	8 5	8 5
♥	A K 6 4 2	Q J 10 9 8 3
♦	A 7 5	K Q J
♣	6 3 2	3 2

Those two hands illustrate emphatically the main difference between a sound opening bid and a sound overcall. No. 1 would be a good original bid, in any system, with its top trick content and a promising suit, whereas No. 2 would not be, due to lack of defensive trick strength.

But, to overcall a hostile 1-Spade at your right with No. 1 would be unthinkable to an advanced player, whereas a 2-Heart overcall on No. 2 would be viewed by most of them as thoroughly sound and well worth trying. Why?

First of all is the negative reason. If you are doubled with No. 1, you may take only four tricks and be down four, at a cost of 1100 points. With No. 2 you are almost certain to take six tricks and be down only two at the outside, for a maximum loss of 500. And, to set you that badly, the opponents would probably have to give up a slam.

Second is the positive reason. There is a quite fair chance for a game with No. 2 if your partner has nearly an opening bid, with a fortuitous fit. With No. 1 his chance of holding enough to produce a game is lower. Also with No. 2 you require little help from him to make 2-Hearts, whereas with No. 1 you need quite a bit.

In a nutshell, total playing tricks rather than high ones, are most important when making an overcall.

• • •

Tomorrow's Problem

	North	
	♠ A Q ♥ K Q J 4 ♦ A J 10 9 8 2 ♣ 10	
West ♠ J 10 5 ♥ 7 ♦ 6 5 3 ♣ Q J 9 6 5 3	N W E S	**East** ♠ K 8 7 4 3 2 ♦ 10 8 2 ♦ K 7 ♣ A 8
	♠ 9 6 ♥ A 9 6 5 3 ♦ Q 4 ♣ K 7 4 2	

(Dealer: East. Neither side vulnerable.)

If East's diamond K wins the first trick, and he returns the suit in hope of a ruff by West, how should South try for all the rest of the tricks at hearts?

Distributed by King Features Syndicate, Inc.

Grandma's Beauty Secret

By HELEN FOLLETT

Listen to this. Here are the words of a woman of 60 who looks 10 years younger. Her children and grandchildren adore her. She is tolerant, gracious, poised and contented. She says:

"No woman can have charm or beauty who has not inner poise, who isn't getting along happily with herself. One should find oneself a good companion. That is not possible if one broods, harbors grudges or goes around with a chip on the shoulder.

"I refuse to let life kick me around, even in these troubled days. By being tranquil, I am keeping myself strong, not wasting energy. I've taken care of my health, had respect for the laws of hygene. I have a grand time. Every day I find simple pleasures, one way or another, to keep myself cheerful.

"I've got my own teeth in my head, my own hair on my scalp, because I learned long ago to take proper care of them. I haven't developed a meal bag figure because I have restricted appetite and taken daily exercises. I still do my daily dozen before breakfast.

"The mistake many women make is in not realizing that mental health is necessary for physical health."

The foregoing sermonette should be taken to heart by the woman who fusses over little things.

Take life as it comes. Enjoy blessings, bear ills bravely. It is the only way to live happily in mind and spirit.

Ambergris, a costly ingredient of the rarest perfumes, is an abnormal growth in the body of a whale.

What You Buy With WAR BONDS

Tracer bullets, generally used in night combat, enable the gun operator to note the accuracy of fire, since course of the bullet may be followed to the target. This is important in air combat, especially.

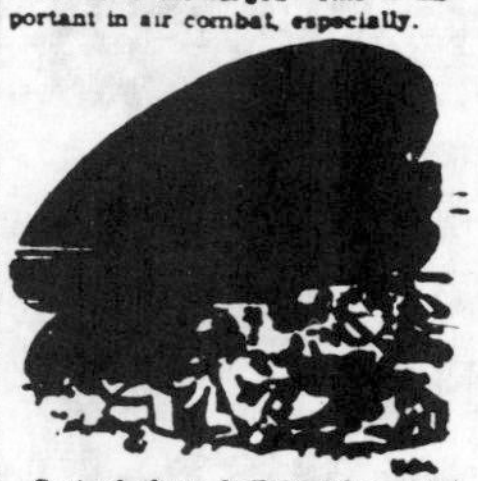

Cost of these bullets, of course, varies with the caliber, but 1,000 rounds of 50-caliber machine gun tracer bullets cost in the neighborhood of $250. Your purchase of War Bonds and War Stamps will help pay for the millions of rounds of ammunition needed for tracer bullet-fire. Invest AT LEAST TEN PERCENT of income in War Bonds every payday. Buy them from your bank, postoffice, radio station, and other outlets. U. S. Treasury Department

Cat Says Birds Are Rude

"I didn't do a thing." Tells Shadowland Folk They Fly Away When She Comes

By MAX TRELL

Chirpy Sparrow, Rob and Roberta Robin, the Wrens and the Thrushes were all agreed that something must be done.

Knarf and Hanid, the shadows with the turned-about names, met the birds on Sparrow's Lookout, near the chimney of the house. Rob Robin explained the trouble. "It's the cat," he said. "We never do her any harm at all. Yet she is always trying to pounce on us. Why only yesterday—"

At that moment all the birds uttered shrill cries and flew off as fast as they could.

Knarf and Hanid looked toward the chimney at that moment. They were surprised to see a furry head and a pair of green eyes just to one side of it.

"I didn't do a thing," the cat said when they went up to her. She stroked her whiskers. "Those birds are just rude. They fly away the moment I come near. It isn't right."

"You shouldn't come near them," Hanid said.

Mrs. Cat Learns a Lesson

"But I like them. I like them almost as much as I do the mice. I don't think they are being polite. But I'll go right on liking them."

The two shadows decided that the cat must be taught a lesson. They had a long talk with Chirpy Sparrow. Then they hit on a plan. A few minutes later they went to the cat again. "Do you like birds?"

"Of course. There isn't a single one I wouldn't like to meet. But as I told you before, they don't like to meet me. They always fly away when they see me coming."

"Well, we've just spoken to the birds and there's one of them who would like to meet you very much. He's waiting for you now on the fence at the edge of the cornfield."

"How wonderful! I'll go there at once. I never like to keep a bird waiting who's waiting for me!"

She Hurried Away

With that the cat hurried off to the fence at the edge of, the cornfield. Knarf and Hanid and Chirpy Snarrow and the rest of the birds waited to see what would happen.

The cat reached the fence and who do you suppose was waiting for her?

It was Yoho the Black Crow. She wasn' afraid of cats at all. She flew right at her. Mrs. Cat ran so fast that her back legs were ahead of her front legs and her tail had trouble keeping up with the rest of her.

"'Fraid cat! Go hide in a hat!" the birds mocked her.

Mrs. Cat didn't go out looking for birds for quite a while after that. "I like mice much better than birds," she told the next-door- neighbor's cat that night. "They haven't got beaks and they haven't got wings. I certainly wouldn't care for them if they had. Let's climb on a fence and singa song. It might make me feel better."

And that's what they did.

Child Should Not Oppose Parent's Second Marriage

By MARIAN MAYS MARTIN

Mary Doe had been a widow five long years and was heartily sick of living alone. She was not young and her chances of remarriage were anything but bright, even though she was an attractive woman with a little money in the bank, a nice little home in the country and a car with five good tires. Along came, not Prince Charming, but the father of a couple of boys and a girl in the throes of discovering romance. Mr. Opportunity, he might be called. He also was tired of living alone, his wife having died, his boys having been called into the service and his girl having gone back to college. So, Mr. Opportunity took careful account of what the lady could bring to the bargain, and Mary Doe, taking inventory of all Mr. Opportunity could contribute to her advantage, said, "Yes, thank you," when he suggested that they marry and run the chance of living happily ever after.

Their marriage was a great and pleasant surprise to everyone but their respective families; his sons were understanding, if amused; his daughter was neither. She resented the idea of anyone taking her mother's place and was much too young and inexperienced to understand that when one remarries it isn't the place of the departed husband or wife that is being filled, it is simply that one chapter in one's life is finished and another begun.

Needed Each Other

It isn't an easy task to mother another woman's children, but, in this case, they were grown and gone from the home, so Mary Doe decided to do her best to make Mr. Opportunity happy and to contribute what she could to the happiness of his children.

Having had a previous matrimonial experience, she was capable of figuring out that she was not usurping anyone's place, but making one for herself. She respected her husband's first marriage and his memories, as she expected him to respect hers. She admitted, to herself at least, that she did not love Mr. Opportunity as she had loved her first husband, and she also admitted that it was altogether likely that she was not loved by Mr. Opportunity as much as his first wife, which was quite all right with her.

"I need him and he needs me," she said, "and that seems to me sufficient reason for our marriage."

"But it didn't justify it to the daughter, who, like all young girls, saw no excuse other than love for marriage. It is, of course, the ideal incentive; no young person can be expected to understand the awful aching loneliness that comes especially to one who has known the satisfaction and happiness of true companionship.

Life Goes On

It seems absurd to deny oneself companionship of one person because that of another has been taken away. Life must go on and it is perfectly natural to hope to get as much out of it as one can. Sensible folks know that life is a series of compromises, that no life is exactly as one would wish it, that the picture is never perfect.

A father who has brought his children up to love and revere their mother's memory must, I suppose, be prepared for them to feel a resentment over his remarriage, but he should try to make his children see his new wife, not in the light of a usurper, but someone who enters after the first act, or chapter, and who is creating her own place, not filling or attempting to fill that of another.

This man is entitled to a life of his own, and so is this woman. The children are entitled to theirs. It is quite unlikely that the girl will be willing to sacrifice her happiness to remain with her father; she is expecting too much when she expects her father to deny himself what comfort he can get because of her selfish prejudice and jealousy.

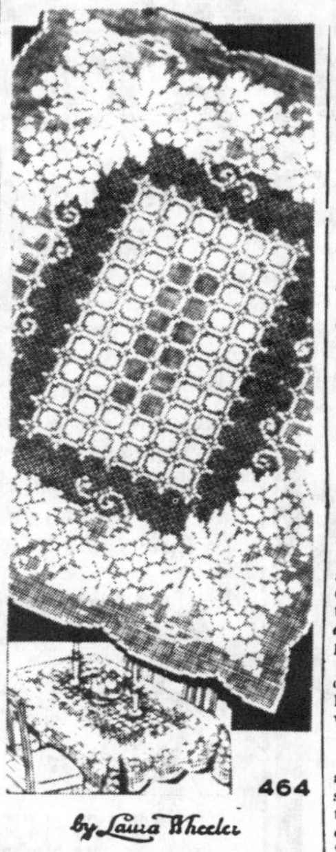

464

by Laura Wheeler

CLOTH EASILY YOURS

Imagine how pretty your finest China will look on this rich grape design cloth; Get started crocheting it now! It's 72x90 inches in string—smaller in finer cotton. Pattern 464 contains charts and directions for cloth and scarf each in 3 sizes; illustration of it and stitches; materials required.

Send ELEVEN CENTS in coins for this pattern to News-Tribune Needlecraft Dept., 82 Eighth avenue, New York, N. Y. Write plainly PATTERN NUMBER, your NAME and ADDRESS.

Help Build Courage In Young People

By Garry Cleveland Myers, Ph. D.

Because of children's anguish over school failures some report cards avoid the term, "Failure," and many principals and teachers avoid the use of this word in speaking to the child or his parents. While this procedure does save some children from needless sorrow, the facts cannot long be hidden.

A few school systems, of ocurse, promote practically all children, aiming to have the teacher receiving the unprepared children, do only the kind of work at which they can succeed. This is a big step forward if the teacher does set the lagging child to do only what he can do well and takes him and his parents into her confidence. Unfortunately relatively few teachers have advanced so far in their thinking and practice.

Whatever the procedure, the child and his parents eventually know when he has not advanced with his class.

Unintelligent

The human, though unintelligent thing most parents, even some teachers, are inclined to do then is to shame and scold the child for his lagging or failure. Some children are brutally compared at home with a more fortunate brother, sister, cousin or playmate; scolded, even beaten when their failing grades come home.

One wonders why any intelligent parent would be so foolish and cruel. They should know that the child, even though he seems to be indifferent toward the failure, is already humiliated and discouraged. They should know that shaming, scolding or other punishment won't inspire the child to want to work harder at his lessons. It will on the other hand make him less ready to do his best.

Correct Procedure

The wise and thoughtful parents will observe the facts, and express neither anger nor condemnation. These parents will sit down together to consider what is the best thing to do for the child from now on. They will confer, courteously, with the teacher, principal, or school psychologist, or iwth all three, trying to learn all they can about the child, why he afiled, what his specific learning difficulties are and what can be done to help him learn. In some instances the parents will consult a psychologist (probably at a nearby college or university), having had the youngster's vision, hearing and general physical conditions first checked.

Success Gives Courage

Whoever tries to help this child now or later at learning should set him to learn in reading, arithmetic, spelling or any other subject, only what he can succeed at, no matter at what grade level this work will have to be. He must succeed in order to gain courage and interest to try harder, and enjoy still more success.

It may be necessary to require the child to be home at desirable periods and o sit down at his lessons at a definite, regular (but not too long) time. Beyond these requirements force will hinder more than help his learning progress.

Solving Parent Problems

Q. Have you a special bulletin on fears in the child?

A. Yes; to be had in the usual way, by writing me in care of this paper, enclosing a self-addressed envelope with a three-cent stamp on it.

MODEST MAIDENS

Trademark Registered U. S. Patent Office

MASH HIT
40TH WEEK

"My boy friend asked for my picture to tack up in his barracks."

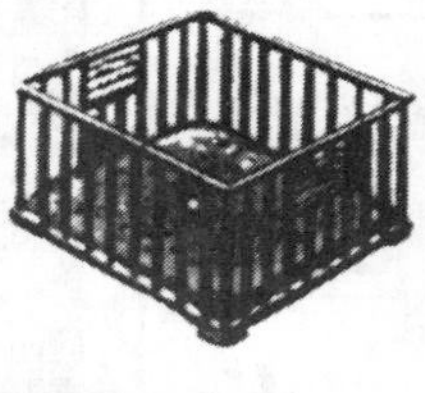

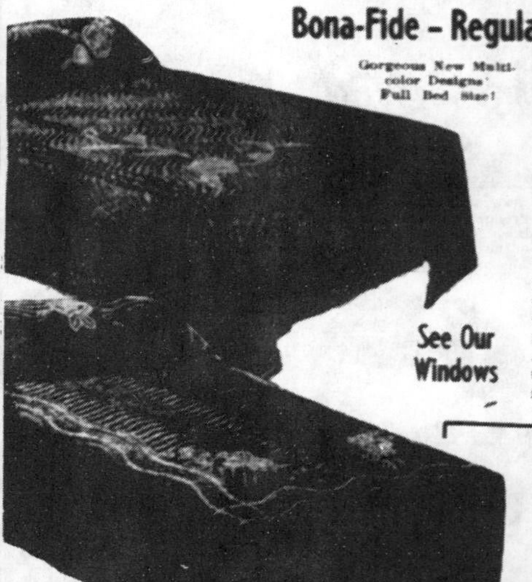

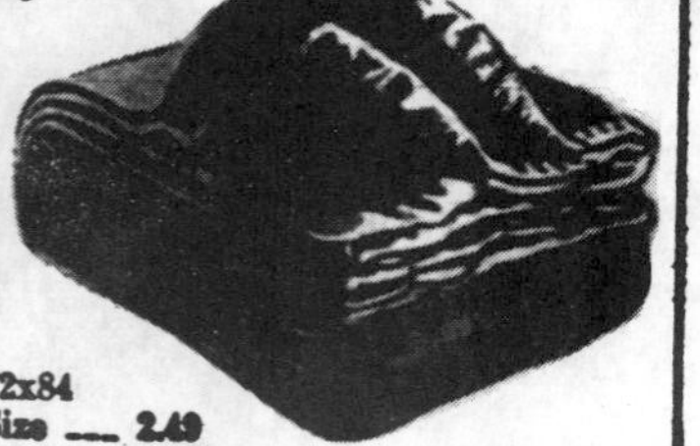

LOWER VALLEY NEWS

MONACA

CURFEW ENFORCED

Police Chief Dan Liston said today that borough council's recent adoption of the curfew at 10 o'clock carries with it the responsibility of police picking up persons under 17 years of age who are out after that time. Youngsters will be brought to the municipal building, according to Liston, and their parents notified to come after them. The curfew is one blast of the siren at the municipal building.

TRI-HI-Y TAG DAY

Members of both the Junior and Senior Tri-Hi-Y clubs will conduct a "Tag Day" tomorrow for the Monaca public library, it was decided at a meeting of the Senior group on Wednesday evening. Plans are also under way to sponsor a "Salvage Dance" on October 30 at the high school when the admission will be a piece of scrap metal. At this week's meeting Miss Marjorie Dindinger presented a book report on the publication titled, "The Raft."

Brotherhood Sunday will be observed Sunday in St. Peter's Lutheran church at 9:30 o'clock and in the Redeemer Lutheran church at 10:45 o'clock. "Faithful Men" is to be the topic in both churches.

Tax Collector Isobel Ramsey, of Jackson avenue, is spending the week in Washington, D. C., Baltimore, Md., and other points.

Rev. Dr. E. Conn Pires, pastor of the Beaver Presbyterian church, will speak at both services Sunday in the Monaca Presbyterian church.

The Brotherhood of Redeemer Lutheran church will meet on Tuesday evening at 8:00 o'clock in the parsonage with Rev. C. E. Read, pastor.

Doris Sickles, daughter of George Sickles, Atlantic avenue, a junior in the local high school, is reported improving at her home following a two weeks' illness of grip. She is still confined to bed, however.

Jack McCarthy, of Atlantic avenue, recently passed all examinations to become an air cadet and is awaiting a call to service.

Apprentice Petty Officer Ferman Massey, son of Councilman and Mrs. William Massey, of Ninth street, will leave Sunday night for Chicago, Ill., reporting to the Great Lakes Naval Training base after spending eight days here. He is expected to attend navy radio school upon his return.

Mrs. Mary McCarthy, Atlantic avenue, is able to be out following an operation several weeks ago in Rochester hospital. Her daughter, Rosemary McCarthy, employed in the St. Joseph's Lead company office, is enjoying a vacation of two weeks.

Mrs. John R. Skinner, of Atlantic avenue, is confined to her home with the grip.

Mr. and Mrs. Albert Siee, of Meadville, have returned home after visiting their cousins, Mr. and Mrs. Daniel J. Vogt and family, Virginia avenue.

The Junior Missionary Society of the Redeemer Lutheran church will meet Thursday evening, October 22, at the home of Mrs. George Dagen, Ninth street.

high school band will be held this evening and Saturday.

Homer Grimm, Webster street, is confined to his home by illness.

Mrs. Thomas R. Amrheim, Mr. and Mrs. Frank Lutz, Miss Eleanor Zeck and Mrs. Paul Hoffman and children, West View, Pittsburgh, spent Wednesday with Mr. and Mrs. Joseph Gomory and family, and Mrs. Mary Ann Gomory, Deer lane.

The Lions' club met Thursday evening at the Penn-Beaver hotel when David C. Locke, Monaca, was the speaker. His subject was "History of the Races of Warring Nations."

Charles Rosen, son of Mr. and Mrs. Jack Rosen, Vermont avenue, is confined to his home by illness.

Employees of the Outdoor Advertising company and families were guests of E. A. McKee, president and manager of the company at a dinner Wednesday evening in the Penn-Beaver hotel. Covers were laid for twenty. Following the dinner the group was entertained at the Oriental theatre.

The resignation of Wade Hoffman as janitor of the Adams street school building was accepted at a meeting of the board of education on Wednesday evening. The resignation was tendered because of ill health, and is effective today. The position will be filled temporarily by Phillip Gordon, retired janitor.

BEAVER

SALES CLASS PROJECT

The salesmanship class of Beaver High school has resumed its downtown store decoration project started last year under the direction of the instructor, R. G. Smith. Decorating committees in this week's project are Effie Moldovan, chairman, Clifford Schnuth, Irene Romigh and Lube Plodinac; and Mary Bankovich, chairman, William Hetrick, Sara Jane Baker and Helen Posgaj. Mr. Smith and members of the class will appreciate constructive comment on criticism which may be written and left at the store where the class has completed its project. It is the plan to decorate a different store window each week.

Mrs. Carl Oliver and infant son, Richard Stephen, of Beaver Falls, formerly of Beaver, have been removed to their home from the Beaver Valley General hospital.

Mr. and Mrs. F. A. Ray and son, Billy, of Baltimore, Md., have returned home after visiting for a few days with the former's parents, Mr. and Mrs. E. H. Ray, of Lincoln avenue.

Ms. Don Struthers, Second street entertained her bridge club at her home Wednesday evening when favors were claimed by Mrs. Don Morris and Mrs. Paul Jones.

Sorme 15 members of the Beaver Quota club plan to attend the third district meeting and birthday party of the Butler Quota club in the Nixon hotel, tomorrow afternoon and evening.

Miss Helen Jeffers, of Canal street, was feted last evening on the occasion of her sixteenth birthday at a party in her home. Some 20 guests, students of the local high school, attended.

Cop. Charles D. Stone, Camp Pickett, Va., medical corps, is visiting at his home in Fourth street and with Mrs. Stone, Aliquippa, while on a furlough of two weeks.

Eight members of the Youth Fellowship group of the United Presbyterian church this week enjoyed a wiener roast and social gathering at the Gypsy Glen Recreational park.

Mr. and Ms. R. W. Wander, of the Hyllmede Farms, has as their guests, Mr. and Mrs. Samuel Whitlock, Bedford, O.

Mr. and Mrs. Earl Reed, of the Dutch Ridge road, parents of a baby daughter, born Monday at their home, have named the 8½ pound arrival, Lillian Pearl.

Mrs. Harry Duncan, of Second street, much improved following three weeks' of treatment at the Bashline-Rossman hospital, Grove City, has been removed to her home.

Richard Fuerst, son of Mr. and Mrs. Earl Fuerst, Tamaqua Dive, who enlisted recently as an aviation machinist's mate, left this week for naval training.

The Junior class of High school will sponsor a Victory dance this evening in the school gym when the purchase of a war stamp will serve as admission.

Mr. and Mrs. James Harton, of Lynn street, Vanport, have returned from Volant where they visited relatives for three months.

Pvt. John Farley, son of Mrs. Ernestine Farley, Sixth street, who is attending clerical school at Camp Wheeler, Ga., is expected to graduate November 10.

Sgt. Frederick Krohe, son of Mrs. Ella Beaner, Dutch Ridge road, is here from Fort Bragg, N. C., for a five-day furlough.

Mrs. Eve Swearingen, Dravo avenue, has returned home from Harrisburg and Philadelphia after visiting relatives.

Full coordination of the muscles of the eyes is not believed to be attained in children until their fifth year.

ROCHESTER

GLEANERS MEET

The Gleaners' Bible class of St. Paul's Lutheran church met at the home of Mrs. Oscar Medeke, Jefferson street, Wednesday evening, with the devotions and business meeting in charge of Mrs. Louis Hartman, president. Plans were made for fall activities. A social time was enjoyed and in guessing game contests favors went to Mrs. Floyd Simms and Mrs. Albert Sulser. Lunch was served by the hostess, assisted by Katherine Kebhardt and Derothy Kehna. The November meeting will be held at the home of Mrs. Susan Spearhaus, Adams street.

Jeanne Anderson, Pinney street, confined to her home suffering with laryngitis.

Mrs. Harry Dagen, Jackson street, has returned home after visiting friends in Steubenville, O.

A daughter was born to Mr. and Mrs. A. E. Brown, Monaca, Thursday evening in the Providence hospital. Mrs. Brown is the former Mary C. Erlwein, Rochester.

Mrs. Charles McCourt, New York avenue, who was removed to the Rochester General hospital Sunday for treatment, is reported improving nicely.

The F. R. E. S. H. club met Wednesday evening at the home of Miss Margaret Bloom, Clay street. A social hour followed at which dancing and games were enjoyed. Lunch was served by the hostess, assisted by her mother, Mrs. Fingol Bloom.

Tag day for the benefit of the

SERVING WITH U. S. ARMED FORCES

PVT. MINNETTI

Private Lee Minnetti, son of Mrs. Rose Minnetti, 914 Eleventh street, rear, New Brighton, with the U. S. Army for the past twenty months, is stationed at Leesville, La.

PVT. SPALDING

Private Elmer Spalding, son of Adam Spaulding of the Patterson hotel, has been in the U. S. Army since last January. He is stationed with a quartermasters' motor supply and evacuation unit in New York. Shown with him in the picture above is his father.

PVT. HARKINS

Private Regis Harkins, son of Mr. and Mrs. M. Harkins of Jackson street, New Brighton, is stationed at Robin's Field, Ga.

PVT. MAJCHER

Private Mike Majcher, left in the picture, son of Mr. and Mrs. Mike Majcher of West Mayfield is stationed at Camp Wheeler, Ga. He entered the service August 7th. With him are several of his camp buddies.

PVT. EVERETT

Private DeWayne L. Everett, who is serving in an anti aircraft division at Washington, D. C., is the son of Mr. and Mrs. C. W. Everett of 1624 Sixth avenue, Beaver Falls.

U S NAVY

ELI MUSSI

Eli (Billie) Mussi, son of Mr. and Mrs. Joseph Mussi of Homewood enlisted with the U. S. Navy last April 27th and is on duty with the Naval Air Forces at Lakehurst, N. J. He likes his job with Uncle Sam and would like to hear from his valley friends.

WILLIAM H. CLARK

Nineteen-year-old William Harold Clark, son of Mrs. Nellie Clark of 1105 Darlington Road, Beaver Falls, has been placed in the Army Air Forces' enlisted reserve and in the near future will be called up for training as an aviation cadet.

He graduated from Beaver Falls High School in June 1941 and has been employed by the Babcock & Wilcox Tube Company. Clark was one of the Orange and Black cheerleaders in his senior year.

PVT. JOHN GUZZETTI

Private John Guzzetti of New Galilee is stationed with the Army Air Forces at Santa Monica, Calif.

RAYMOND ALTSMAN

Raymond L. Altsman, 1022 Twenty-fourth street, has been accepted in the enlisted reserve of the Army Air Forces and after eight months of training will become a flying officer and receive his wings.

The son of Mrs. Julia Altsman, he graduated from Beaver Falls High School and was employed by the Babcock & Wilcox Tube Company before his enlistment.

PVT. WALTER BETHE

Private Walter Bethe, son of Mr. and Mrs. Fred Betke of 1611 Sixth avenue, Beaver Falls, is stationed with the armed forces in England. The local youth entered the service January 27.

GOOD EVENING
Luxuries are the things that make people go without necessities.

The News-Tribune

News Established May 22, 1874 · Combined March 1, 1923 · Tribune Established August 25, 1884

THE WEATHER
Western Pennsylvania—Warmer today and tonight, rain tonight.

Member Associated Press
American Newspaper Publishers Association

BEAVER FALLS—NEW BRIGHTON, PA. THURSDAY, NOVEMBER 5, 1942 Three Cents

AXIS SUFFERS WORST DEFEAT OF WAR· ROMMEL DESERT ARMY IN FULL FLIGHT

Today In Washington

History Is Repeating Itself In the Recent Election, Possibly In 1944

By DAVID LAWRENCE

WASHINGTON, Nov. 5—Twenty-four years ago this week—November, 1918—the American people woke up to read about a Republican landslide that captured both houses of congress in the midst of war, and everybody wondered what had happened but couldn't quite explain it. It took two years more before the explantion came in the 1920 Presidetnial landslide. History has repeated itself.

This year, as in 1918, a large group of protesting voters—a minority in itself—swung away from the party in power and joined with the straight-ticket Republicans to bring about a majority in numerous districts and in many states.

Wartime restrictions caused the upheaval in 1918, and it is primarily responsible today. Along with this are the shifting minorities registering a protest "against things." Thus a sizeable group of folks who want victory, but don't think the administration is operating efficiently, voted Republican on Tuesday. Still another dissatisfied group thinks the administration is using war powers to put over a social revolution and voted Republican to tell Washington that there's a limit to that sort of high-handed tactics. A third group consists of foreign-born as well as some second generation Americans whose loyalty to America is unquestioned but who still [illegible] America should have kept out of the war either by appeasing Germany or Japan or Japan or both. The fourth group, the straight-ticket voters, merely believed that America is better off with a Republican than a Democratic congress.

It doesn't take a big percentage of the electorate in each district to swing a congressional election. Sometimes a shift of less than 5 per cent among the voters, as compared with a previous election, can turn the election. It will be recalled that although will be recalled, that although Willkie's electorate vote was small in 1940 the margin of victory for Roosevelt in nearly every state showed a substantial reduction as compared to 1936. A tide began to run two years ago against the New Deal, and it is still running strong.

It is most unfortunate that the

Continued On Page Three.

MacKenzie's War Analysis

Hitler's Grip On North Africa Is Starting To Slip

By DEWITT MACKENZIE

LONDON, Nov. 5.—The Allied triumph in Egypt gives strong hope that we are witnessing the beginning of the not far distant end to Hitler's hold on North Africa.

The Nazi all-highest also is having visions of disaster for Berlin claims a "remarkable concentration" of British warships and transports at Gibraltar.

The Vichy government is reported to be holding conferences about North Africa and from Rear Admiral Luetzow of the German naval staff we get this:

"Casablanca, on French Morocco's west coast, is a danger spot far overshadowing Dakar.

"Africa swarms with United States agents whose gaze turns to Casablanca."

Is Hitler conjuring up bugbears to torture his sleep? He will know in due course and so shall we. Meantime, it is a most comfortable feeling to see him worry.

We must temper our natural optimism with caution because there is hard and bitter work to be done before the Axis armies are annihilated. That is the task before us—the destruction of the fighting machine in all [illegible] Africa.

Once before we had our dreams when Wavell drove defeated enemy columns far to the westward across the desert.

But the Axis still was strong then and the Allies weak. Indeed, just at the crucial moment, Wavell had to rush troops off to the defense of Greece, thereby depriving him of a chance to follow up his victory.

Now, however, the Hitlerites

Continued On Page Three.

GOP Ends New Deal Control Over Congress

Retains Bare Majority But Not Enough For Working Control

FACES FUSION PERIL

WASHINGTON, Nov. 5—(AP) For practical legislative purposes, the New Deal lost control of congress in Tuesday's elections although the Democratic party maintained a bare majority, with 218 house seats and a larger margin in the senate with 56 members.

While late returns in a few closely contested races held the possibility of slight increases in these majorities, there remained little doubt that Republicans and anti-New Deal Democrats could control legislation in either body any time they chose to unite.

GOP HOLDS 208

This was especially true in the house, where the 208 seats already clinched by the Republicans gave them their largest representation since the last days of the Hoover administration in 1931. The bloc of Democratic members who often vote against New Deal proposals there is such that a coalition could effect a substantial working majority on any controversial legislation.

In the senate, the Democrats elected 15, to combine with 41 holdovers for a total of 56, seven above the 49 necessary for control. They appeared likely to make their total 57 since Senator James E. Murray, Democrat, was leading his Republican opponent, Wellington D. Rankin, in Montana.

8-VOTE MARGIN

This possible eight-vote margin for the Democrats, however, would leave the out-and-out New Dealers in the minority any time five of a dozen or more majority party members who have been critical of administration policies elected to go along with a solid Republican lineup on some issue.

The effect of this realignment was expected to result in sharpening congress' control attitude toward conduct of the war, its possible rejection of any more social reform legislation for the duration, and the strengthening of demands for stricter legislative control of the operations of such agencies as the Office of Price Administration.

President Roosevelt might well meet the changed situation by acting more frequently in an executive capacity, instead of setting in motion the relatively slower and less certain legislative machinery.

George M. Cohan Takes Last Call

NEW YORK, Nov. 5 (AP) George M. Cohan, greatest song and dance man of them all, died at 5 a. m. today.

His death came just as he would have had it, for the only people around Times Square were either actors on their way home or policemen and air raid wardens on their patrols. Those were the people he knew best.

Cohan, seriously ill for a year, died peacefully in his Fifth avenue home, close beside the Central Park path where he used to take long walks every day. He was 64 years old, but even a month ago he seemed to be recovering from his illness and was actively planning to return to the stage and to service as air raid warden.

Because of this liking for long walks in Central Park Cohan liked people, the kind who ask you for a dime for a cup of coffee, and he liked pigeons, the kind which swooped down on the park walk for a peanut. So in 1933 he produced a play called "Pigeons and People" which fictionized that philosophy. In his real life he carried it on, for there were many actors and actresses who remained on his payroll long after they had ceased appearing in his shows.

With him when he died were his wife, Mrs. Agnes Cohan, his daughters, Mrs. George Ronkin, and Helen and Georgette Cohan, and his first friend, Gene Buck.

STRUCK BY CAR

Daniel Kraft, three-year-old son of Mr. and Mrs John Kraft of Eighteenth street and Twentieth avenue, suffered a fractured right leg and bruises about the face and head about 4 o'clock yesterday afternoon when hit by an automobile near his home.

At Providence hospital, where the child was admitted for treatment attaches said the machine was operated by H. H. McCabe, Willets Road, Glenshaw. Daniel was later removed to his home.

FAMED ARMY AIR LEADER ON LOOKOUT FOR JAPS

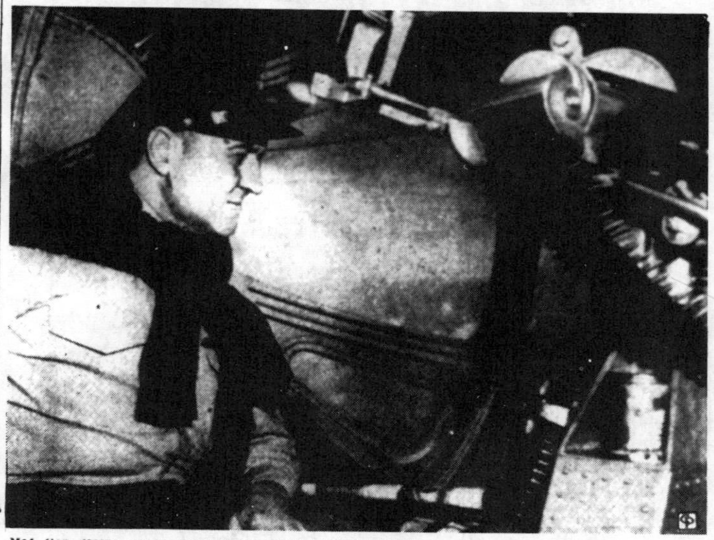

Maj. Gen. Ralph Royce, who led the famous flight of bombers over the Philippines from Australia recently, is pictured here on the lookout for any sign of the enemy as he flies between Australia and New Guinea.

Martin Turns Immediately To Planning War-Time Program

Governor-Elect Confers With James and Other State Executives

HARRISBURG, Nov. 5—(AP)—Governor-elect Edward Martin tackled the job of planning his war-time leadership of the arsenal state today after a hurried trip here from his Washington, Pa., home for conferences with Governor James and other governmental executives.

The tall, lean, 63-year-old world war hero, refreshed after only a few hours sleep, resumed his work early and had little to say immediately beyond the statement:

"I'll be busy. We've got to get things moving because of the war effort. It takes time, you know."

"The Democrats will help me, too," he added, referring to the Republican legislative majority assured him by the GOP's sweep in Tuesday's general election.

Observers pointed out that the Republican victories were insufficient to provide the two-thirds Senate majority necessary for the confirmation of executive appointments.

The same lack of Republican power has confronted James for two years. His appointments of Commissioner Lynn G. Adams of the State Motor Police and Chairman John M. McKee of the Milk Control Commission have lacked confirmation, but never have been rejected because Republicans, controlling committees, have kept the appointments from coming to a

Continued On Page Three.

Monaca To Start "Skip-Stop" Plan

The inauguration of "skip-stop" bus service in Monaca next Monday was announced today by Harry Feely, Jr., Monaca administrator for the Beaver county war transportation committee.

A total of nine stops will be eliminated under the conservation system designed by the Office of Defense Transportation to save vital gasoline, tires, oil and manpower.

"I am sure every patriotic citizen will be glad to sacrifice convenience and walk a few steps more in order to help win the war," asserted Burgess John H. Bell who, with other borough officials, assisted the Beaver county war transportation committee in making out the new schedule of stops.

Monaca is the second Beaver county community to be affected by the wartime measure. "Skip-stop" service was begun in Midland last Monday with the discontinuance of ten stops for the duration.

On the west-bound run through Monaca, beginning next Monday, busses will no longer stop at the U. S. Sanitary plant, Fifteenth street, and Twelfth street.

On the east-bound route busses will skip the stops at Washington avenue, Twelfth and Fifteenth streets, the U. S. Sanitary plant, Monaca Lumber and Twenty-first street.

American Troops Landed In Cairo

CAIRO, Nov. 5.—(AP)—The arrival of 7,000 American troops and a large unit of nurses in the land of the Pharaohs on Hallowe'en night was disclosed for publication last night.

The troops formed the largest body of American soldiers ever sent to the Middle East in one transport and they made the long voyage from New York without the loss of a single man.

They included a variety of technically trained specialists, ground crewmen for United States Air Force units, machinists, engineers and members of the Quartermaster Corps, the Medical Corps, the Signal Corps and ordnance, hospital and postal men."

Control Centers Of County Criticized

Colonel William E. Pierce, Third Corps Area, O. C. D., made a tour of the county's civilian defense control centers yesterday and declared he was disappointed generally in the setup.

The county control center is too small, Colonel Pierce said, and the same is true of most of the other control centers in other communities of the county.

The inspector said "The Japs and Nazis have not had time yet to get around to bombing us, but that time will come,—then maybe civilian defense organizations will make adequate plans to protect the population."

Freedom Nimrod Shot In Hunting Accident

Joseph Martino, 46, of Tenth street and Seventh avenue, Freedom, suffering gunshot wounds in the back, yesterday became the first Beaver Valley casualty of the small game hunting season.

Shot accidentally by V. A. Hazenstab, 1040 Seventh avenue, Freedom, Martino was rushed to Rochester hospital at 4:15 o'clock yesterday afternoon. His condition today is reported as "good."

State's New "First Lady" To Leave Running Pennsylvania To Husband

WASHINGTON, Pa., Nov. 5.—(A. P.)—Mrs. Charity Martin, a motherly little woman five-foot-two and with eyes of blue, is going to leave the business of running Pennsylvania strictly to her governor-elect husband, Edward Martin.

"It's my husband's place to do that," the state's first-lady-to-be said at her home here last night.

"I don't believe in women interfering in things of that kind unless they're in a political office, like Miss O'Hara (secretary of the commonwealth)."

Explaining she's "no speechmaker," Mrs. Martin pointed out that her role in the campaign was "going to meetings, talking to people and shaking hands."

Although Adjutant General Martin has been in politics since 1905 and served as state auditor general, state treasurer and state Republican chairman, Mrs. Martin said she had never aspired to be Pennsylvania's "first lady."

"I have been in the governor's mansion at Harrisburg a great many times, but I never expected to live there," she said.

Like her husband, Mrs. Martin took Tuesday's election results calmly:

"I feel just the same. I suppose you become accustomed to it."

Receiving the congratulations of home town folk until 4:00 a. m. and answering the door yesterday to get several hundred telegrams from well-wishers left her somewhat tired but very congenial and informal.

"I haven't had time to get my hair fixed or my nose powdered—I've been answering the 'phone all the livelong day," she apologized.

Reds Break Up Nazi Drives

Germans Revert Vainly To General Offensive In Stalingrad

MOSCOW, Nov. 5—(AP)—The Russians have broken up all the latest Nazi efforts to expand the invasion salient in northern Stalingrad and, in some places, have forced the Germans to abandon several basic points, dispatches said today.

While bitter attacks and counter-attacks developed about the ruined Volga river city, Red Army troops were credited with local gains northwest of Stalingrad, on the Black Sea front and in the Mozdok sector of the Central Caucasus.

A successful Soviet holding action was indicated before the Caucasian slopes and passes southeast of Nalchik.

Izvestia said the battle of Stalingrad was characterized by a growing maneuverability of Red Army units.

Observers stressed the heaviness of the German attacks, however, and at least one point they threw in a new division. There were many hand-to-hand clashes. The latest German loss reported was 1,000 slain yesterday.

The Nazi air force bombed the city's defenses steadily in support of the ground operations. There

Continued On Page Eleven.

James Going Back To Luzerne County

HARRISBURG, Nov. 5 (AP) —Governor James said today he definitely was going back home to Luzerne county and practice law when his term ends in January.

"I probably will take a vacation—I've never taken a real one in my life—and then go home," he declared. "I hope I can do better practicing law the first year than I did after leaving college. I only made $198 that year."

Asked if he'd like to return to the governor's office four years hence, James replied.

"Any man who tries to look four years ahead these days is certainly an optimist."

Allies Plunge Thru Jungle For New Gains

Widen Attempted Japanese Vise On Island Airfield

ARMAMENTS TAKEN

WASHINGTON, Nov. 4.—(A. P.)—Persistent battering of the Japanese by land and air gave American and Allied fighters fresh ground gains today in besieged Guadalcanal and New Guinea.

Further widening an attempted Japanese vise that threatened to close on the American-held airfield in Guadalcanal, United States marines and soldiers forced back the enemy's western flank, capturing about 20 machine guns and two small field artillery pieces in the process.

In New Guinea, westward of the Solomon islands, Allied troops under General Douglas MacArthur's Australian command overcame "strong enemy resistance" and plunged on through the jungles toward the Japanese coastal base at Buna.

GUADALCANAL GAINS

The navy reported the continued American advances in Guadalcanal last night. Supported by army and navy planes that strafed and bombed the Nipponese troops and positions, the United States forces inched forward along beaches and through the dense underbrush Monday (South Pacific time) to relieve the pressure on the important airbase.

At the other end of the newly installed enemy vise, east of Henderson airport, recently landed Japanese troops presumably were manipulating for a thrust at the springboard of the American aerial assault on the foe's ships, troops and installations.

MacArthur's headquarters reported today (Australian time) that the Nipponese New Guinea invasion which in late September had penetrated as far as 32 miles from the Allies' Port Moresby base, now had been pushed back several miles beyond Kokoda, midway point across the island's 120-mile waist.

While the ground advance continued, Allied planes sought to blast away obstacles on the way to the Japanese Buna base. The air assault which strafed the beaches and landing areas at Buna, itself, also fanned out to subsidiary Nipponese bases of Lae and Salamaua up the coast.

The attacks, executed to hinder any Japanese efforts to bolster Buna by sea, set many fires and probably destroyed an enemy munitions dump, the raiders reported. Medium bombers also announced "heavy damage" inflicted on Dilli and the Japanese-occupied villages of Maobisse and Alley in Portuguese Timor.

Dinner Given For Selectees

Parade Tomorrow Evening To Mark Send-Off Of Local Contingent

Beaver Falls selectees who leave tomorrow night for Fort George Meade, Md., were honored last night at a sumptuous dinner in First Methodist church, but only about half of those who comprise the contingent were in attendance and committee members hinted that if the men themselves aren't interested in the affairs the affairs may be discontinued.

The soldiers who attended enjoyed a full-course turkey dinner with all the trimmings. During the repast, an orchestra directed by Charles Conti contributed music. Afterwards, the Rev. George M. Chester of St. Mary's Episcopal church and the Rev. C. S. Applegath, new pastor of the host church, spoke briefly.

The send-off committee presented each man with a sewing kit and the Salvation Army gave each new service man a package containing stationery, candy, etc. Protestant men each received a New Testament and Catholic men a prayer book.

Tomorrow night the group will depart at 7:26 o'clock from the Pennsylvania station and will march to the depot from City Hall, led by members of the high school band. Townspeople are urged to join in the parade and to be at the station to bid the men Godspeed.

Parking of automobiles on Eleventh street from Seventh avenue west to Eleventh avenue

(Continued on page eleven)

COMMISSIONER DIES

E. H. "DEWEY" MARKEY

County Commissioner Ewing Hicks Markey succumbed last evening to a heart attack which struck him last Friday evening. The former county treasurer and American Legion leader is being mourned by a host of friends throughout the county.

Death Claims E. H. Markey

County Commissioner, Prominent Democratic Leader Dies At Monaca

County Commissioner Ewing Hicks Markey died in his home, 810 Pennsylvania avenue, Monaca, at 6:40 o'clock last evening following a heart attack suffered last Friday evening.

A life-long resident of the county, Mr. Markey was active in the political, civic and fraternal life of the community in which he lived and in recent years was one of the dominant forces in the Democratic party, and in the affairs of the American Legion.

He was employed for years by the Jones & Laughlin Steel corporation at Aliquippa and resigned to become a candidate for county treasurer in 1935. He was elected to that office and served four years. In 1939 he ran for county commissioner and was elected with the highest vote ever given a Democratic candidate for that office.

Mr. Markey had not been in good health for some time but declined to take an extended rest. He was a highly-strung, hard-working official and continued active in all community affairs up to the time he was fatally stricken.

He had a host of friends, having had the faculty of keeping friends regardless of the outcome of any

Continued On Page Eleven.

Army Heavily Favored In Local Enlistments

District men joining the service heavily favored the Army in yesterday's recruiting, ten being recruited in this branch as compared to one each in the Navy and Marines. They were:

Army: John H. Nicely, Darlington; Frank Fazio, New Brighton; Rudolph Pinotich, Ambridge; Harold D. Scott, Aliquippa; Jack E. Frishkorn, New Brighton; Robert L. Burzese, Baden; Arthur D. Morrifield, Jr., East Rochester; Robert C. Brown, Jr., Beaver; Frank Meronski, Ambridge, and Dominic A. Farsoni, Ellwood City.

Navy: John H. Tucker, New Brighton.

Marines: Dave J. Florentine, New Brighton.

British Close In Pursuit Of Fleeing Foe

Rommel Army Racing West In An Effort To Escape Destruction

FRONT CRUMBLED

Axis Loses Thousands In Captured, Killed, Wounded, Isolated

BULLETIN

LONDON, Nov. 5.—(AP)—An official British source said today that Marshal Rommel's army "is busted" and predicted that its fate would be finally sealed soon.

The United States and British air force, the British army and navy are engaged in what amounts to a mopping-up process, this informant, who must remain anonymous, declared.

CAIRO, Nov. 5—(AP)—Weakened by the loss of thousands of men captured, killed, wounded or isolated in their desert strong points, a once-proud Axis army was in full flight today across Western Egypt in a frantic hunt for position to avert destruction.

Only a rearward moving screen of anti-tank guns and tanks shielded the bulk of Marshal Rommel's African corps from the pressing advance of a United Nations army—the Eighth British—while a comparatively impotent air force sought to parry the combined blows of American and British Imperial airmen.

While 9,000 prisoners (by count already 24 hours old) streamed dejectedly to the British rear, the Allied air forces kept hitting at the foe, and the main coastal line of retreat was described as a veritable graveyard of smoking, twisted tanks, armored cars and trucks.

HAS NO RESERVES

It was believed that Rommel had no large reserves behind him either in Western Egypt or Libya.

ONLY BEGINNING

LONDON, Nov. 5—(AP)—The defeat of Marshal Rommel's armies in Egypt will be followed by other Allied offensives which will give relief to the embattled Russians, Sir Stafford Cripps, lord privy seal, told an audience of war workers today.

"This is not the only diversion we can or shall make to help our Russian allies," Sir Stafford, former ambassador to Moscow, declared. "As our strength and that of our American allies builds up other offensives wil be started in other areas."

He said the Eighth Army was "destroying German and Italian land and air forces which might otherwise be joining in the attack on the Soviet armies."

Most military observers among the British held that his full force had been marshaled on the now crumbled El Alamein line where Rommel had pushed nearly to Alexandria and the Nile.

The sudden collapse of the Axis defenses was announced last night in a British communique after 12 days of furious fighting in which the Allies were said to have taken a tremendous toll of Rommel's men and equipment.

Today's communique told of a

Continued On Page Three.

Bulletins

NEW YORK, Nov. 5—(AP)—William Coffman, general manager of the Shrine's annual East-West All-Star Football Game, announced today he had received authorization from Lieut. Gen. John L. Dewitt, commanding the western defense command, to proceed with plans for holding the contest next New Years Day at Kezar Stadium, San Francisco.

LONDON, Nov. 5—(AP)—The Air Ministry said today that the RAF had been on offensive operations over Europe 11 nights and 21 days during October. Bombers were over Germany seven nights and one day and over Northern Italy three nights and one day.

Throughout most of the month weather conditions were unfavorable for raids over Germany, but advantage was taken of cloud conditions to press home daylight attacks, the Ministry said.

WASHINGTON, Nov. 5—(AP)—The Army disclosed plans today for adding five new infantry divisions in the next two months, while Secretary of War Stimson spoke out against what he called the "pre-war mentality" of those who insist on requiring a full year's training for younger draftees.

The activation of five additional infantry divisions in November and December would bring the strength of the Army to some four score divisions and well past 4,500,000 men.

LONDON, Nov. 5—(AP)—Fighting French parachute soldiers have dropped far behind the Axis' desert lines and knocked out almost 100 planes on enemy airfields, Reuters reported today in a dispatch from Beirut, Lebanon.

It said the parachutists were picked men from a corps of highly trained specialists who had made forays at Barka, near Bengasi, and Martuba, 60 miles northwest of Tobruk.

JEFF ERTZ DIES IN PLANE CRASH

WEATHER
Light snow today and tonight with little change in temperature but with a tendency towards rising.

ALIQUIPPA
NEWS-GAZETTE

Aliquippa needs airplane spotters. Volunteer today.

SERVING A GROWING INDUSTRIAL COMMUNITY OF 50,000 — ESTABLISHED 1922

VOL. 21—NO. 39 — ALIQUIPPA, PA., THURSDAY, JANUARY 7, 1943 — 4 CENTS

THIRD FRONT COMING-FDR

Lewis Pledges J. & L. To Break More Output Records

Boulevard Open; Engineers To Confer In Boro

Schmidt Says Road Safe If Cliff Frozen; To Discuss Permanent Solution Next Week

The State highway department opened Constitution boulevard for motor traffic today for the first time since the bus disaster in which 22 of 25 passengers were crushed to death by a 2000 ton avalanche of cliff rock.

F. L. Schmidt, enigeneer at the highway department's Pittsburgh office, said:

"The boulevard is safe while the cliffside is frozen. There are a couple of places we want to scale off yet. It wasn't entirely safe until it was frozen. Otherwise we would not have opened it."

Schmidt said he and a representative of Lamont Hughes' highway office in Harrisburg would confer here next week, either Monday or Wednesday, with Board of Trade, mill, and county officials to discuss what should and can be done to prevent a recurrence of the disastrous rock slide.

Asked how future slides might be prevented, Schmidt said:

"To guarantee that there will be no recurrence, you would have to take that cliff away. It will always be a source of danger.

"Anything can be done if you have enough money," he added.

Schmidt said that "probably a slide will never occur on a split second like that," referring to timing of the recent bus disaster.

"The place the slide occurred was not the worst looking. People might scoff at fate, but one second sooner or later and the bus would not have been hit."

Schmidt pointed out that the highways department encountered slides on numerous roads in western Pennsylvania.

"One slide on the Lincoln highway covered four lanes of

(Continued on Page Three)

traffic, but no one was hurt, and there is four times as much traffic on the Lincoln highway as on the boulevard. The slide in Aliquippa was just one of those things."

While declaring that a disastrous slide such as that of two weeks ago might never occur again, he agreed that the danger would always be present.

He stressed the singularity of conditions that caused the recent avalanche, pointing out that the slide was caused by a quick atmospheric change from freezing to a quick thaw.

"It was as quick a change as you can get," he said.

"The weather changed from near zero temperature to warm. Any hillside would loosen under those circumstances," Schmidt said.

The slide was caused by the flow of rain into fissures in the cliff rock. With freezing, the water expanded, exerting what Schmidt called "a push."

With the sudden thaw, the ice melted, the water seeped out, and larger fissures were left unsupported and came down.

Asked if moving of the Ambridge bridge to span the Ohio from Franklin ave., or construction of a ramp cliff high along the present boulevard would solve the problem, Schmidt said he could not suggest a solution until after he and associate engineers completed their survey of the terrain next week.

He said his office was swamped with letters demanding opening of the highway.

One coal firm, servicing the mill, had asked to travel the road at its own risk and even offered to sign papers releasing the state of a responsibility.

WICKARD PLANS LOCAL BOARDS FOR FOOD JOB

Committees to Solve Shortages

WASHINGTON.—(INS) — In his first recognition of the series of critical local food shortages that have been reported throughout the nation, Food Administrator Claude Wickard today set about establishing food industry committees to solve food problems.

The committees, Wickard said, will be responsible for providing food wherever a shortage occurs and for striking at the roots of the problem by correcting the specific causes of local shortages.

Each committee will be set up within 10 days, he pledged.

With the armed forces and lend-lease taking more and more of America's food and with the people at home in the midst of a war prosperity, local shortages of meats, dairy products and other commodities have sprung up in many communities, agriculture experts admitted.

The situation has been especially serious in war-swollen cities where distribution systems were taxed by populations beyond normal, it was reported. Dètroit, Boston, Washington, D. C., and several West coast cities, where war work or government is now the main industry, have felt serious shortages of some products, especially beef, butter, milk and eggs.

There were several reports of horse-meat being offered for sale because no beef was available.

Wickard's plan calls for using the technical skill and experience of food manufacturers, distributors and processors.

Grocers as well as meat packers, vegetable processors and super-market managers, will be represented on each local committee, although the committees will be headed by a food distribution administration expert.

Wickard's assistant, FDA Head Roy F. Hendrickson, outlined the steps the committee system will take to solve food problems:

1. Each local committee will establish publicly-announced complaint centers, verify each complaint brought in by the public within one day, and "take immediate steps to relieve the shortage through voluntary co-operation locally, calling upon manufacturers or distributors to expedite food movement to the point of shortage."

2. If this fails to fill the shortage, state committees should be called in to locate the needed food within the state.

3. Should this move also fail, the regional FDA chiefs or FSA headquarters in Washington should be called into action to scour the country for the requirements.

Wilson Returns From Hawaii On Sick Leave

Lieutenant Kendall Wilson, son of Mrs. Harry Hetrick, 1318 Irwin St., was home today on a 21-day sick leave after Army service which found him in Hawaii when the Japs landed their sneak punch.

Lt. Wilson, only 19, served in Hawaii for three years and returned from there to United States to attend Officers' Training School at Ft. Benning, Ga. He volunteered for officer's service with the U. S. paratroopers.

BOROUGH YOUTH KILLED FLYING AT ARMY SCHOOL

Would Have Won Wings Next Month

An Aliquippa student Army pilot who would have received his silver wings next month today was dead — victim of an airplane crash.

He was Jeffrey C. Ertz, Jr., 21, son of Mr. and Mrs. Jeffrey Ertz, Sr., 1625 McMinn St.

His parents received word at 4:30 a. m. today of the crash of an Army plane at Gunner Field, Ala. where he had been training.

A graduate of Aliquippa High school's 1939 class and a prominent borough athlete, the deceased enlisted in the Army Air Force Feb. 15, 1942.

He was president of the High School [illegible] the cross country team, second baseman for the Aliquippa Bucs and Hollywood Aces, a member of the Aliquippa Methodist church and secretary of the church's Epworth League.

Survivors include the parents and a brother, James.

Funeral services have been tentatively set for Sunday. Friends will be received at the C. E. Douds Funeral home.

Don't Ask How, But Two Parked Autos Collide

It sounds impossible and even the police couldn't explain it but two parked cars collided last night and $7 damage resulted.

According to police, Angelo Ricci's coupe was parked near his home at 112 Economy St.

Another parked car belonging to Henry Rittiger, 185 Hopewell Ave., allegedly bumped it.

How? Well, that was a subject of heated discussion, not only by the car owners but also police who listened to their complaints.

Closest solution to the scientific impasse was that Rittiger had jacked up his car, the jack slipping and lurching his car into the Ricci coupe.

Anyway, Rittiger paid $7 damage, protesting all the time that damage was "old damage," not caused by the crash.

Car Crashes

Slippery roads caused a $1200 accident at 5:15 a. m. today when a truck driven by Bill Pochy, Cleveland, O., crashed into a gas station near Darlington.

Pochy, traveling north on Route 51 lost control of the truck and it ran amuck, crashing into the building which housed a gas station and a family's home.

No one was injured, State Motor Police reported this morning, but total damage to the truck and building was estimated at $1200.

Indications Against Tax Cut

HARRISBURG — (INS)—Evidence began piling up today indicating that there would be no substantial reduction of taxes by the legislature after it reconvenes Jan. 18 to receive the administartion program of Governor-Elect Edward Martin.

Despite outgoing Gov. Arthur H. James' estimate that taxes could be slashed more than $50,000,000, Martin has refused to comment on the governor's statement.

STATE GETS COUNTY SALVAGE QUOTA

HARRISBURG.—(INS)—The Advisory Salvage Committee of the State Council of Defense today assigned a quota of 156 tons of tin can salvage during January to Beaver county.

Long Time No See

Photographed for the first time as a group, the [illegible] New Republicans elected to Congress are seen on the Capitol steps just before the opening of the 78th Session. They have been gone in those numbers since the advent of the New Deal a decade ago. G.O.P. Leader Joseph Martin pledged the Republicans to the war effort.

Trade Board Asks Street Improvement; Advocates Change In Tax Set-Up Here

Members of the Board of Trade last night recommended a revaluation of property for tax assessments, overhauling of the tax system and demanded road and sidewalk improvements in Aliquippa.

The board also announced that highway department representatives would confer here next week with industrial, civic and governmental leaders on a means of preventing future rock slides on Constitution boulevard.

The board voted to extend to the management and employes of the Jones and Laughlin Steel Corporation congratulations and praise for winning the Army Navy "E" production award.

The street improvements sought by the board were:—

1 A sidewalk, "ash, concrete or marble," from the Stone Arch to the Brodhead Road to safeguard the lives of children going to school and others walking the road.

2 Roughening of the surface of sidewalks to prevent danger of slipping

3 Filling of holes in borough streets which endanger tires needed in the war effort as well as other automobile parts such as springs and axles.

4—Ashes at crosswalks so that autos can stop quickly to avoid skidding in event of quick stops for traffic lights.

5—Inspection of defective rain spouts on downtown buildings.

6 -Use of the street sweeper to keep borough streets clean.

7—Enforcement of the ordinance requiring property owners to clear sidewalks of ice and snow.

Trade Board President Winton Hoffman named W. C. Young, M. A. Staman, J. Harvey Moore and Morris Gastfriend members of a nominating committee to choose candidates for election of trustees, president, vice-president and treasurer

The nominations were to be submitted the first meeting in Wednesday. The election will be the third Wednesday of February.

MARDSEN RECOVERS

Charles Marsden, borough mortician, was reported in a "good" condition today at the Beaver Valley general hospital, New Brighton.

He underwent a mastoid operation yesterday.

15,000 DEFY UMW IN STRIKE

WILKES-BARRE, Pa. (INS) —The Revolt of an estimated 15,000 anthracite miners over the payment of increased dues assumed more serious proportions today as an appeal by John L. Lewis and other mine union officials that they return to work was flatly rejected. Meanwhile, production dropped as the need for winter fuel increased.

Lewis, president of the United Mine Workers of America, joined with other union officials in requesting the miners to halt their strikes with submit their grievances through regular channels. Five unions in the Wilkes-Barre area formally voted to reject the proposal and strikers predicted that others would follow suit."

The miners are protesting the increase in union dues voted last October by the United Mine Workers union at its international convention in Cincinnati. The dues, which were increased from $1 to $1.50 a month, are deducted from the miners' pay envelopes by the coal companies in accordance with the provisions of the union-operators contract.

WAGNER KILLED AS PLANE SPINS OUT OF CONTROL

EGLIN FIELD, Fla. (INS) Lieut. Col. Boyd D. "Buzz" Wagner, 26, one of America's first air heroes of this war who disappeared on a routine flight Nov. 30, met his death when his plane got out of control and plunged into the ground from a steep spin, evidence of the wreckage indicated today.

Discovery of the air hero's crushed body in the wreckage of his plane near Freeport, Fla., 25 miles from Eglin Field, was announced by Brig. Gen. Gardner Grandison, commanding officer of the air base

The body of Col. Wagner, who was credited with shooting down from 15 to 50 Japanese warplanes, was found crushed in the wreckage of his P-40 pursuit plane in which he disappeared while on a flight between Eglin Field and Maxwell Field, Ala., according to the general's statement.

"The plane was wrecked and partially buried, indicating that it had plunged into the ground out of control and probably from a steep spin," Gen. Grandison said.

Police Ready To Nab Pleasure Drivers

Police Chief Trevor Jenkins announced that effective noon today borough officers would keep a sharp lookout for violators of the new "no pleasure driving" ban by Washington rationing officials.

But, like other Western Pennsylvania police officers who lacked clarification of the Office of Price Administration's shut down on pleasure driving, Jenkins awaited instruction on just what constituted pleasure driving before attempting to enforce the curtailment order

Pittsburgh Superintendent of Police Harvey Scott declared that the police there "will do our best," but added that he believed it would be a tremendously difficult task to single out motorists who are driving "for fun."

Walter R. Cartwright, district manager of the OPA with authority in 16 western counties, said he has requested the co-operation of all municipal officers in western Pennsylvania communities in enforcing the ban

"Enforcement officers were asked to check the use of automobiles parked near amusement places or those possibly being driven at the time for pleasure and make reports to local rationing boards," Cartwright said.

He added that the owner's name, license number, and the type of ration sticker should be reported in cases of violation.

President Appeals For Worldwide Freedom From Want, Asks Congress' Aid

Roosevelt Asks Congress Not to Make Issue of "Freedom from Want" But Says "Country Knows Where I Stand On" The Post War Aim

WASHINGTON.—(INS)—President Roosevelt, in a fighting speech before the 78th Congress, today pledged to the American people that the Axis and Fascist enemies in Europe and Japan will be bombed and smashed in their own countries.

"The Nazis and the Fascists have asked for it—and they are going to get it," the President declared in a spirited and stirring address before Congress on the state of the Union.

The President declared that while he could not for military reasons disclose where the United Nations would strike next in Europe, "we are going to strike—and strike hard."

[illegible] growing American might, "will become evident to the Japanese people themselves when we strike at their own home islands, and bomb them constantly from the air."

For the United States forces, the President said that the period of defensive action in the Pacific is passing and "now our aim is to force the Japanese to fight.

"The period of defensive attrition in the Pacific is passing," the President said. "Now our aim is to force the Japanese to fight. Last year, we stopped them. This year, we intend to advance."

ARMY GROWS

In his message the Chief Executive disclosed that there are now one and one-half million United States soldiers, sailors, marines and flyers in service in foreign areas throughout the world. During 1942, he related, the American armed forces grew in size from 2,000,000 to 7,000,000 men and officers.

Turning his attention to the domestic front, Mr. Roosevelt told Congress and the nation through the radio networks that "our forward progress in this war has depended upon our progress on the production front."

After recounting the battle and the production progress of 1942, the first year of war, the President turned his attention to planning for the post war years.

HIGH ON LIST

High on the list of war aims, the President placed the third of the four freedoms—freedom from want.

After the war, the President declared that the people of the United States "expect the opportunity to work, to run their farms, their stores, to earn decent wages. . . .

"They do not want a post-war America which suffers from undernourishment or slums—or the dole. They want no get-rich-quick era or bogus prosperity, which will end for them in selling apples on a street corner, as happened after the bursting of the boom in 1929."

Emphasizing his disagreement with some of his advisers, Mr. Roosevelt declared that this was the "time to speak of a better America after the war . . .

"If the security of the individual citizen, or the family, should become a subject of national debate, the country knows where I stand.

"I say this now to this 78th Congress, because it is wholly possible that freedom from want—the right of employment and the right of assurance against life's hazards—will loom very large as a task of America during the coming two years.

"I trust it will not be regarded as an issue—but rather as a task for all of us to study sympathetically, to work out with a constant regard for the attain[illegible] objective."

3000 WITNESS ARMY-NAVY 'E' AWARD AT MILL

Management, Labor Lauded for Work In War Program

The management-labor team at the Aliquippa Plant of the Jones and Laughlin Steel Corporation won its "letter" yesterday.

More than 3000 assorted steel workers stuffed the bunting-decked tin mill store house annex and half the store house behind it yesterday afternoon to hear J. and L. President H. E. Lewis, promise to smash more war production records.

Lieutenant Colonel John S. Swauger executive officer of the Pittsburgh Ordnance district, presented the Army-Navy "E" (for excellent) pennant for war production to Harry Saxer, general superintendent of the Aliquippa works, and Robert Pursley of the welded tube department, representing workers.

"Only the untiring, unselfish teamwork, with both labor and management putting their shoulders to the wheel, could have won it (the award), and did win it," Colonel Swauger said.

"The production line becomes the first line of defense, the first front, the point where victory must begin," he declared

"In presenting to the men and women of this plant the Army-

(Continued on Page Three)

HEART ATTACK FATAL TO WOMAN

Mrs. Carmela Ciccone, 69, died suddenly at 4:30 a. m. today of a heart attack at her home, 328 Main Ave.

She is survived by her daughter, Mrs. Chris Ciccone and six grandchildren

Funeral arrangements have not been completed

Patuc Joins Marines, 3 Others Enlist

Steve A. Patuc, 1512 Liberty Ave., left yesterday for duty with the U. S. Marines, Recruiting Sergeant Michael Wynn of Aliquippa announced today

Three other borough boys who enlisted last month are Emil Bochak, 204 Oak St., leaving Jan. 22, Thomas E. Matsko, 401 Allegheny Ave., West Aliquippa, leaves Jan. 19, and James W. Doyle, 1722 Davidson St., leaves Jan. 21.

CELTICS WIN 1st HALF FLAG

Tigers Aim to Knock Quips Out Of First Place Slot In Sec. 3

Falls Win Against Duquesne Hi Compared With Quips' Loss Show They May Just Do That Very Thing

Our Quips have a big argument on their hands tonight.

Coach Nick Ufema and his Beaver Falls Tigers come to the Aliquippa high school gym tonight and they don't seem to think that Coach Nate Lippe's boys should be roosting with such select company as Ambridge at the top of the Section 3 Western Pennsylvania Intercollegiate Athletic Association.

It is their problem, then, to make Nate and his boys see eye to eye with them, and the only way the Tigers will be able to do this is to paste a licking on the Aliquippa team tonight. Perhaps the Quips will have a little rebuttal in the argument.

Strictly off the season's records, Beaver Falls should come off with a victory. Ufemas' team took seven of their eight pre-WPIAL games and have split even in two league games. Ellwood City gave their title hopes a rude jolt in the league opener with a 40 to 33 defeat. However, Ufema's team came back Friday night to administer a convincing walloping to a New Castle squad, 45 to 20.

Against this same New Castle team, the Quips could only squeeze through by the narrowest of margins in the last 30 seconds of the game, 30 to 28. In the only other two games in which both teams met a common foe, the Tigers own a clear cut advantage as far as comparative records.

Both squads met and defeated Monaca by similar scores, the Quips winning 27 to 21 and the Beaver Falls five by 30 to 23. In the Duquesne games, however, a different story unfolds. Tonight's invaders were able to brush the Duquesne team 36 to 30, while the Quips were falling unwilling victims to the same squad 31 to 19.

Thus, the average seem to point to the fact that Lippe's string of four straight victories is about to end. But the Aliquippa boys have been showing steady improvement after a rather shaky season's start, and they could tuck their third straight league triumph in their vest pocket if they play the kind of ball they exhibited in the first half of the New Brighton game last Friday night.

"We looked good in the first half of the New Brighton game, Coach Lippe said, "but we seemed to lose our head and poise in the third quarter and reverted back to earlier season form."

The Quip coach said that the team was improving and that he hoped they could hold their heads for the full game tonight.

Ufema has a wealth of material from which to pick his starting lineup. In fact, two lettermen from last year's team are gathering the sharp splinters that come from the Tiger bench, having been replaced by two reserves, Podbielski, a forward, and Jack Hair, a 6 ft., 2 in. center.

Other starters for the Ufema men find Ours teaming with Podbileski at the other forward and Anderson and Peete at the guard posts. Lippe's starting lineup will be the same that has opened the last few games.

The starting lineups:

Pos.	Aliquippa	Beaver Falls
F.	Suder	Ours
F.	Zernich	Podbielski
C.	Chizmar	Hair
G.	Glad	Anderson
G.	Odlevak	Peete

Brush with Death

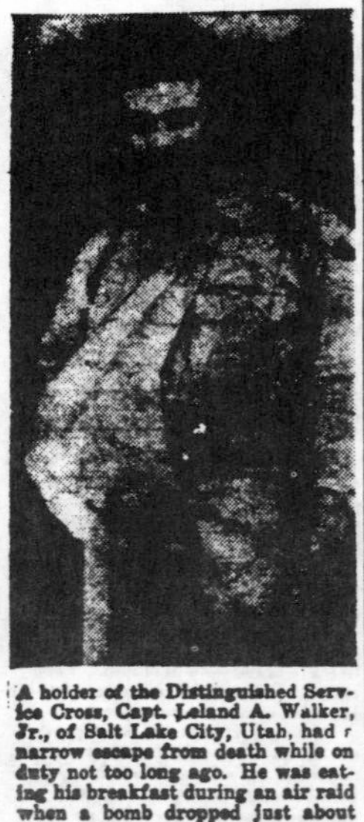

A holder of the Distinguished Service Cross, Capt. Leland A. Walker, Jr., of Salt Lake City, Utah, had a narrow escape from death while on duty not too long ago. He was eating his breakfast during an air raid when a bomb dropped just about fifty feet from him. Fortunately, it was a dud. (Central Press)

JV's Will Win Tonite 'Or Else'--Milanovich

Quip Coach Hints Shakeup If Juniors Don't Perk Up

Quote Coach Fred Milanovich—"My starting Junior Quip five better make a good showing tonight against Monaca or else—"

Coach Milanovich was referring to the five boys who have started in all of the Jayvee losses this year and the shake-up the squad is going to receive if play doesn't improve.

"I'm going to give these boys another chance tonight," Milanovich said. "Then if there isn't some great improvement shown, you can look for a good, big shake-up among the first five."

The Quip Juniors travel to Monaca tonight to take on George Dietrich's junior five. The argument in the Monaca gym won't revolve around any championship or even a second place position. Rather it will be a fight to see whether Monaca or Aliquippa is going to be the first to break into the victory column this year.

Monaca has taken it on the chin from Beaver Falls, Ellwood City, and Ambridge this year, while the charges of Coach Milanovich have "came, saw, and gone down to defeat" before Freedom, Ellwood City, and Beaver Falls.

Coach Dietrich said that he would probably start Guinto and Kazar at the forwards for the Monaca team, with Stauffer at center and Karak and McFadden filling the guard slots.

Milanovich's "Last Chance" five will be made up of Prisuta and Smisko at the forwards, Barkovich at center, and Wright and Haney at the guards.

If the Quip Jayvees are to see the daylight of victory this year, tonight is as good as any to do it. The threatened shake-up may put a little more verve and bounce into Milanovich's youngsters and bring them their first triumph of the year.

Callura Tops Wilson For "Feather" Crown

PROVIDENCE, R. I.—In a wild and wooly batle that combined as much wrestling as boxing a la Marquis de Queensbury, Jackie Callura of Hamilton, Ont. shoved and kicked his way to the NBA's world featherweight title last night by gaining a 15-round unanimous decision over Pittsburgh's Jackie Wilson.

Thomas Jefferson tasted waffles in Holland and had a waffle iron sent to him from Europe. He is generally credited with introducing the waffle to the United States.

Guatemala estimates its 1941-coffee crop at over 85,000,000 pounds.

TALK OF CHANGE IN STRATEGY OF ALLIES BREWING

WASHINGTON — (INS) — Reports were current in Washington today that important developments in connection with Allied strategy are impending as a result of discussions which have taken place between the United States and Great Britain.

These discussions are believed to have touched upon the question of determining the next major move in Allied strategy.

They are also believed to have considered methods of combatting the Nazi submarine menace.

In connection with future grand strategy, the view prevails in some Allied diplomatic quarters in Washington that the United Nations should consider the question of concentrating their forces in an all-out attack on Japan before Germany is completely knocked out of the war.

This suggestion for a possible change in Allied grand strategy is underrstood to have been prompted by the fear that when Germany has finally been defeated, the peoples of the Allied countries in Europe, including the British and Russians, may be so war weary that there will be little enthusiasm for a continuation of the war in the Pacific.

In such an event, the danger is seen that there might be popular support for a compromise peace with Japan, or that America might be left holding the bag in the Far East.

Those who are advocating consideration of this question do not believe the time has arrived for any immediate change in the present strategy of concentrating on the defeat of Germany as the first major objective of the United Nations.

They believe the United Nations should continue concentrating on Germany until Hitler's military might has been crippled beyond repair.

When Germany's power to launch major offensive campaigns in this war has been defintely crushed, and the German armies are pushed back to their own soil, then it is felt the United Nations should consider turning their main attention to Japan.

VIKINGS VISIT AT ROCHESTER HIGH TONIGHT

Seek Elusive First Win In Two Years Of Hopewell Play

Hopewell High school travels to Rochester tonight still in quest of the "Holy Grail," or in words of the layman, still in quest of their first basektball victory.

"Hope springs eternal in the human breast," is an oft-quoted phrase, and Coach Leland Shachern and his young squad have done their best to prove its truth in the last two years.

Purely on the record that Rochester and Hopewell have compiled for the year, it looks as if Hopewell will still be "questing" after tonight's encounter. Rochester has nine games under its season belt and have been returned winners four times. In league games, however, they are the "cocks of the walk" with two victories against no reverses.

Hopewell's record? Well, they have only played two games and both have ended in reverse as far as their backers are concerned. One of the Viking defeats came at the hands of Midland, 88 to 17, a team that Rochester took into camp with comparative ease. Thus, if you are hoping for a Hopewell victory in tonight's engagement, just ignore the records.

Bill Peacock, coach of the league leaders, said that he would probably start Fritzius and Pandak at the forwards, Supak at the center post, and Krouse and Di-Francesce at the guards.

Shachern's lineup will probably be the same as that which started the two previous games. This will find Metro and S. Mervis at the forwards, Shannon jumping center, and Milich and Dobal humping it along at the guard posts.

Probable starting lineups:

Pos.	Hopewell	Rochester
F.	Metro	Fritzius
F.	S. Mervis	Pandak
C.	Shannon	Supak
G.	Milich	Krouse
G.	Dobal	DiFrancesce

He Was Lucky

Coast Guardsman James D. Fox holds his fingers through a blanket that was ripped by a Jap shell that struck his bunk on Guadalcanal a minute or two after he had left it. On one occasion the tent occupied by Fox had 72 holes in it after a Jap artillery attack. This is a U. S. Coast Guard photo. (Central Press)

RUSSIAN WAR MACHINE ROLLS ON ACROSS CAUCASUS

KURSK
VORONEZH
RUSSIA
Scale of Miles
0 50 100 150
Volga River
Ural River
Don River
STALINGRAD
KHARKOV
ASTRAKHAN
ROSTOV
SALSK
DIVNOE
TIKHORETSK
Sea of Azov
Caspian Sea
MINERALNYE VODY
KIZLYAR
GROZNY
Black Sea
BAKU

German attempts to halt the Russian drives forward have failed as the Soviet armies continue their advances on all fronts. On the southern front, Moscow reports new gains in the direction of Rostov. Shaded areas on the Central Press map above indicate territory recaptured by the Red Army on this front since its winter offensive got under way. Note the pocketed German forces before Stalingrad

Aliquippa News-Gazette SPORTS

STILL AT IT - - - By Jack Sords

ED "STRANGLER" LEWIS, VETERAN OF THOUSANDS OF WRESTLING MATCHES AND FIVE TIMES WORLD CHAMPION STILL ACTIVE AT GRAPPLING
LEWIS WON HIS FIRST TITLE BACK IN 1921, THROWING JOE STECHER
HE BECAME POPULAR AS "THE STRANGLER" WITH HIS CRUSHING HEAD-LOCK
SORDS

Cauliflower, domestic cabbage, and kohl-rabi, all are descendants of wild cabbage. They are modifications of the flowers, leaves and stems, respectively.

Grade School Cage Loop Opens Card

The Laughlin-New Sheffield grade school team is going to have to find some scoring threats in order to compete in the newly organized Grade School league.

Against Washington Junior High school in the opening game of the league last night, the kids from Laughlin went through the first half without finding the net for either a field-goal or a free toss.

The third quarter started and still no score. Things looked bad for the "scoreless wonders," so bad, in fact, that it looked like a basketball "blackout" with Laughlin-New Sheffield lost in the dark.

Then in a fast and furious scramble for the ball, Mancini of Washington fouled Grabski. Grabski, visibly tense with a chance to put his team into the scoring column after nearly three quarters of play, stepped to the foul line, sighted, and tossed. The ball hit the rim, sagged a moment and then dropped through, giving Grabski high point honors for his team with one marker. That was the end of the scoring for the boys from Laughlin-New Sheffield.

The Washington Junior five, while putting up their iron-clad defense, found time enough to hoop 13 field goals and a charity toss for 27 points. Their showing last night stamp the Washington boys as definite threats to captur ethe flag in the newly organized grade school league.

The box score:

Washington Jr. High School—27

	FG	FT	PF	TP
Klopovich, f	2	1	0	5
Reszytelo, f	0	0	0	0
Passeri, f	1	0	1	2
Matthews, f	0	0	0	0
Dinardo, c	3	0	0	6
Petronio, c	0	0	0	0
Mancini, g	2	0	1	4
Shepel, g	1	0	0	2
Decolo, g	2	0	0	4
Jinnini, g	0	0	0	0
Ross, g	0	0	1	0
Ilov, g	1	0	0	2
Rostato, g	1	0	0	2
Totals	13	1	3	27

Laughlin-New Sheffield—1

	FG	FT	PF	TP
Davies, f	0	0	0	0
Grabski, f	0	1	0	1
Robison, f	0	0	0	0
Brown, c	0	0	1	0
Thomas, g	0	0	1	0
Williams, g	0	0	0	0
Gartley, g	0	0	0	0
Murphy, g	0	0	0	0
Brown, g	0	0	0	0
Totals	0	1	2	1

Score by quarters:

Washington Jr. Hi.	12	21	23	27
Laughlin-N. Sheffield	0	0	1	1

Referee, Lloyd Cable.
Umpire, George Senchek.
Timekeeper, Dan Nelson.

CHAMPS RALLY IN LAST HALF TO CINCH BORO LOOP BUNTING

The first-half bunting of the Boosters' basketball league is all salted down today and stored in the vest pockets of the Celtics.

Fred Ferry, Vincich, Moskola and the other Celts had plenty of anxious moments last night, but they finally proved themselves the champs with a scintillating last half rally to dump the Sons of Italy into the also-ran class 43 to 35. In the other game, the Quippans pushed the hapless Mihaliks deeper into the league cellar and raised themselves to within a game of the second-place Sons.

For the first three quarters of the Celt-Son game last night, it looked as if the S of I. five would prolong the first half race a little longer. The game started off with a bang and the Sons had an 11 to 8 lead at the end of the first period. Holding Ferry well in check throughout the first half, the Sons kept up a blistering pace but couldn't stay in front. The score at the half was knotted 22 to 22.

The game slowed to a walk in the third period which ended 28 to 28.

Then in true championship style, the Celts started to pour it on when the pressure was there.

Ferry and his mates finall broke through the Sons defense and before the game ended they had run up a 43 to 35 lead on the fighting second-places.

With the first half championship settled, the remaining two nights of play will be a mere formality, at least as far as the Celtics are concerned. There is still a fight going on for the second place spot between the Sons of Italy and the Quippan five.

Ferry, after being held down the first half of last night's game, finally sifted through the Sons for six field goals and a free tors for 13 points and high honors for the night. Hodovonich was high for the Sons with 5 buckets and two free throws for good for 12 points.

The Boxscore:

CELTICS

	FG	FT	FTM	F	TP
Ferry, f	6	1	2	0	13
Moskola, f	3	0	1	4	6
C. Frank, f	0	0	0	0	0
Radovinski, f	0	0	0	0	0
Vincich, c	1	0	1	1	2
Faber, c	2	1	0	3	5
Gnup, g	2	3	1	1	7
Rusinko, g	1	1	1	0	3
Joseph, g	3	1	1	2	7
Dzurko, g	0	0	0	0	0
Totals	18	7	7	11	43

SONS OF ITALY

	FG	FT	FTM	F	TP
Casoli, c	1	0	0	2	2
Fuderich, f	4	0	2	2	8
Voltich, f	1	0	0	2	2
Miskulin, f	1	0	0	0	2
Ferezon, c	3	2	2	3	8
Ludwico, g	0	0	1	2	0
Hodovonich, g	5	2	1	1	12
Buccilli, g	0	1	1	1	1
Shafflo, g	0	0	0	0	0
Totals	15	5	7	13	35

Score by Quarters—

Celtics	8	22	28	43
S of I	11	22	28	35

Sec. 3 Results

New Brighton 43 Ellwood City 35

Sec. 3 Standings

	W.	L.
Aliquippa	2	0
Ambridge	2	0
Beaver Falls	1	1
Ellwood City	1	2
New Brighton	1	2
New Castle	0	2

GAMES TONIGHT

WPIAL—Class A

Section 3—Beaver Falls at Aliquippa, Ambridge at New Castle, New Brighton at Ellwood City.

Class B

Section 11—Midland at Beaver, Monaca at Freedom, Hopewell at Rochester.

CLASSIFIED ADS

NEWS-GAZETTE PHONE 934

RATE — One insertion, 4c a word. 2 to 5 insertions, 3c a word. t.f. after 5th insertion, 2c a word.

Rates for Classified Display—Apply.

CARD OF THANKS

We wish to express our sincere thanks and appreciation to our many friends, neighbors and relatives for their many acts of kindness extended to us during our recent bereavement, the death of our beloved wife and mother, Millie Babish. We especially wish to thank the Rev. Edward G. Zauner, of St. Titus R. C. church, the choir boys, those who donated flowers, and cars and all who in any way tended to lessen our sorrow.

Steve Babish and Family.

PERSONAL

JOE'S BARBER SHOP on Plan 12, now operating 5:30 to 9 p. m. Thursdays, Fridays, Saturdays, due to shortage of manpower and JOE giving all extra time on Defense Industry.

LOST AND FOUND

LOST—One sugar rationing book by Kiriako Nicola. Return to the Rationing Board.

LOST—Sugar rationing books. Mike, Susie, Anna, Dorothy and Mike Elko. Return to Rationing Board.

LOST—Sugar rationing books. No. 383125 and 383116. Williams. 136 Beech St.

LOST—One sugar rationing book. No. 388478. Return to Rationing Board.

LOST—One sugar rationing book, by Matt Prigorac. Return to the Rationing Board.

LOST—Card case containing "A" and "B" Gasoline Rationing coupons. Harold Lamb. Return to News-Gazette.

LOST—Black wallet containing driver's license, belongs to Edward Zima. Call 1059.

LOST — Male Biegel Hound. Brown, black and white with mark on one ear. Answers to name, "Don." License No. 8716. Reward. Phone 2046, or return to 1929 Irwin St.

AUTOMOTIVE

FOR SALE

'31 Model A Ford Coach, 2 new tires, new battery—$50.
'33 Chrysler 4-door Sedan—$40.
'36 Chevrolet Coupe—$100.
BILL'S AUTO WRECKING CO.
104 Waugaman St. Phone 1411

FOR SALE — LaSalle de Luxe, 1937 Sedan. Radio, heater. Bargain. Must sell. 1126 Third Ave., Beaver Falls.

EMPLOYMENT

8 Female Help Wanted

WANTED — Girl or woman for light housework and take care of child. 1596 Main St.

WANTED — Girl for general housework. Call 836-R.

WANTED — Girl or woman for general housework. Excellent references necessary. Good wages. Apply 658 Merchant St., Ambridge. Phone Amb. 368.

WANTED—Young lady to work in Drug Store. Experienced preferred. Apply in person. Woodlawn Drug Store, 246 Franklin Ave.

WANTED
An experienced shoe saleslady. Steady position. Excellent wages. Good references required. Write Box D, Aliquippa News-Gazette.

WANTED—A TALL, EXPERIENCED SALESLADY TO WORK IN LADY'S READY TO WEAR STORE. CAPABLE OF MANAGING AND BUYING. GOOD WAGES. STEADY POSITION. WRITE BOX F, ALIQUIPPA NEWS-GAZETTE.

WANTED
A young lady to work as cashier in Lady's Ready to Wear Store. Steady position. Must be reliable. Good references required. Write Box B, Aliquippa News-Gazette.

WANTED—Colored woman for housework. 716 Franklin Ave.

WANTED—Girl or woman to do housework part time. 1204 Franklin Ave. Call 213-W.

9 Male Help Wanted

WANTED — Stock boy. Sol's Store. 363 Franklin Ave.

MERCHANDISE

16 Miscellaneous for Sale

FOR SALE—Heatrola, Lounge, Occasional Chairs, Lamps, Dishes, etc. Rear 3rd floor, 322 Franklin Ave.

FOR SALE—An occasional table and table lamp. Very reasonable. 308 Main St., West Aliquippa. Call 360.

26 Musical - Radio

"THE HOUR OF CHARM," by Phil Spitalny. Price, $2.68.—ALIQUIPPA RADIO SALES, 154 Kiehl St. Phone 1988.

30 Wanted to Buy

WANTED TO BUY—If you have old electric iron you do not want, state the price you want for it. Write P. O. Box 457.

WE PAY CASH
For used Refrigerators, Radios, Washers, Sweepers. Buy anything electrical.
DeSALLE ELECTRICAL APPLIANCE CO.
303 Sheffield Ave. Phone 2397

WANTED—Highest prices paid for used furniture, washing machines, stoves, etc. FIELD'S USED FURNITURE OUTLET, 845 Merchant St., Ambridge, Pa. Phone 1169.

ROOMS FOR RENT

FOR RENT — Nicely furnished room, suitable for 1 or 2 gentlemen. One block from Wye. Inquire 268 Franklin Ave., 2nd floor front.

FOR RENT — Two unfurnished rooms. Sink and stove in kitchen. 115 Oliver St.

FOR RENT — Two unfurnished rooms. 109 Third Ave. Plan 11.

FOR RENT — Two unfurnished rooms in Plan 6. 302 Kiehl St.

FOR RENT—Three unfurnished rooms. 303 Seventh Ave.

FOR RENT—Six-room unfurnished apartment. 1828 Main St. Apply next door.

54 Wanted Room and Board

WANTED—3, 4 or 5 room apartment. Phone 1414-R.

HOUSES FOR SALE

FOR SALE—Six room house with electric and cistern. Two acres. Route 18. Mechanicsburg. Write E. D. Littell, R. F. D. No. 1, Hookstown, Pa.

FOR SALE—6 room house with extra lot. 1221 Main St. Phone 967.

REAL ESTATE

FOR SALE — 1¼ acres land. Brodhead Road, Center Twp. A restricted home plan. Call 1362-M.

WANTED TO BUY—Have customers for five and six room houses. Medium prices preferred. List for sales, with us now. Robert Simpson, 411 Franklin Ave. Phone 2281.

SITUATIONS WANTED

WANTED — Would like steady job as driver. Age 24. Call 1646-R.

The News-Tribune
BEAVER FALLS — NEW BRIGHTON, PA. MONDAY, MARCH 15, 1943

ING-RICH TO GET ARMY AND NAVY "E" AWARD TOMORROW

★ ★ ★ ★ ★ ★ ★ ★ ★ ★ ★ ★ ★ ★ ★ ★ ★ ★ ★ ★

To Present Army-Navy "E" Pins

LT. COMMANDER H. H. McCLINTIC, JR., USNR

Commander McClintic, Naval Advisor to the War Production Board in this district, will present the Army-Navy "E" pins to Ingram-Richardson employes tomorrow afternoon. A native of Pittsburgh, Commander McClintic served in the first World War as a Lieutenant in the U. S. Field Artillery. Following his graduation from Massachusetts Institute of Technology in 1919, he was employed by McClintic-Marshall Construction Company until 1934 when he became executive vice president and director of Pittsburgh Piping Equipment. In 1937 he was appointed president of the Ferguson & Edmundson Company, from which office he resigned to enter the armed services. Commander McClintic is the son of Howard H. McClintic, who was for many years head of McClintic-Marshall Construction Company.

Congratulations

Again Beaver Valley's chest swells with pride as the employés and management of another of its manufacturing plants wins the coveted Army and Navy award for excellence in production.

This time the Ingram-Richardson plant is added to the growing list of factories all over the Nation whose management and employes have gone all out for production and whose contribution to the war effort has been so outstanding and commendable as to merit and deserve this special recognition.

The management and employes of Ingram-Richardson can be justly proud of the honor bestowed upon them, and upon their record of achievement that brings the honor. A vast conversion program transformed the local industry almost over-night. After years of making American homes more pleasant, comfortable and convenient, today's products go toward protecting those very homes. In the operation of this plant is embodied the drastic change that has taken place throughout the Nation—a change from peacetime pursuits to all-out war production, and a change entered wholeheartedly into by management and employes alike. That is the American spirit.

Therefore, congratulations to everyone connected with Ingram-Richardson. Everyone of you has had a part in setting this commendable production record. The symbolic pennant can proudly fly o'er your plant, an important unit in our arsenal of democracy, and individuol "E" pins can gleam from the lapel of each proud executive and proud worker, equally important on the Nation's production line.

Beaver Falls and all of Beaver County joins a grateful Nation in applauding you and your commendable contribution toward Victory. The cooperative spirit of your industry, wherein its various units, formerly competitors, combined to make possible the mighty wartime conversion program, demonstrates to all the world, and most emphatically to the Axis — the Spirit that is America!

ERNEST RICHARDSON
President, Treasurer

E. E. REAGLE
Vice President in Charge of War Products

J. H. E. McMILLAN
Vice President in Charge of Sales

BERT F. CAROTHERS
Factory Superintendent

Ingram-Richardson Record Of Production Is Featured By Numerous First Achievements

Plant Wins "E" Soon After Conversion To Wartime Manufacture

AN AMAZING FEAT

Award of the Army-Navy "E" for excellence on the production front to the Ingram-Richardson Manufacturing company, within a few months after the company began the manufacture of war materials without any experience in that endeavor at all, is only one of the many amazing accomplishments of Ing-Rich which has marked forty-two years of manufacturing in Beaver Falls.

The history of the company is full of "firsts." Known all over the globe for its enameled signs Ing-Rich was not only one of the first companies in the world to make such products, but were really pioneers in the manufacture of table tops, plain and decorated, exteriors and interiors of refrigerators, laundry covers, sink drainboards, enameled gas ranges and heaters.

It all started 'way back in England when the late Louis Ingram, for many years head of the local company, learned his trade as a glass sign worker in his uncle's factory at six pence (twelve cents) a week.

Mr. Ingram and his partner, Ernest Richardson, were born in England and met here when they accepted positions with the Enameled Iron company of Beaver Falls in 1892. The company was started by P. W. and S. W. Smith who brought their manufacturing idea here from Netherland, England.

Mr. Richardson was factory superintendent and Mr. Ingram the company's general manager. The plant was on the site of the Rohrkaste property near the foot of Steffin Hill. One of the Smith brothers was killed in a railroad accident near the factory and his brother soon sold the business to William M. Gillespie of Pittsburgh.

STARTED IN 1901

In May, 1901, Messrs Ingram and Richardson started their own porcelain enameling business. Others who embarked with them upon this venture were Dr. J. S. Louthan, Witt A. Eckles, a druggist here, the late Frederick Davidson, the late J. Rankin Martin and E. L. Hutchinson.

A year later they purchased the plant where they formerly worked and merged it with their own.

About that time they became associated with M. N. Hurd, who had been connected with various phases of the iron enameling business in Ohio and West Virginia and in 1915 when the company built a factory in Frankfort, Ind., Mr. Hurd was made general manager of the western plant.

In 1924 they started a plant in Bayonne, N. J., and operated it for eight years but finally disposed of it, continuing operations here and at Frankfort.

It is a far cry from the group of frail little buildings which housed the company's manufacturing business back in 1901 to the present modern plant. Mr. Richardson shows a picture of the original "factory" and says "a lot of water has gone over the dam since then."

START NEW LINES

But the partners were not content to stand still. They started manufacturing enameled iron signs and specialties. One of the first of these was "The Farmers National Bank." As new products appeared upon the market of the rapidly growing industrial country of their adoption they set about to discover whether or not they might not adapt their business to the trade, making new articles more appealing to the eye by coating them with porcelain enamel.

Gas ranges were becoming all the rage and Mr. Richardson still has the first porcelain enameled range ever made by the company in the kitchen of his home. The idea soon caught on and the black, unattractive kitchen stove was soon being replaced by shiny white porcelain ranges which brightened up gloomy kitchens delighted the hearts of housewives from Maine to California.

READY TO SERVE

Mr. Richardson in commenting upon the recent change in their manufacturing—changing the factory over completely to turning out war materials said:

"Well, we've tried a lot of things around here. We were the first to make enameled table tops. We made them plain and they sold. We fixed them up a bit with decorations here and there and they sold too. We figured if enameled steel looked good on a cook range it would improve the appearance of an ice box. It did and we made enameled exteriors and interiors for refrigerators.

"We tried to keep up with the trend of the times but we never expected to be in the manufacture of war goods. When the war situation became really serious we were not equipped to handle war contracts, but we soon recognized that we might be able to convert and our own business was just about finished. There was a shortage of metals vital to our industry. So we secured the services of Mr. Reagle to aid in the change over from peace time to war time manufacturing.

"We did convert in as short a time as possible and are now turning out material the war effort needs as rapidly as it is possible to do so. We expect to exceed our present output in the future and are planning accordingly. We are very happy that the Army and Navy have seen fit to recognize our efforts in this new endeavor and we feel sure that every Ing-Rich employe will redouble his efforts if that will bring peace any quicker."

Army-Navy Group To Attend Rites

The following Army and Navy personnel are scheduled to be present at tomorrow's joint Army-Navy War production award to the Ingram-Richardson Manufacturing Company.

Army—F. B. Bell, district chief, Pittsburgh Ordnance District; Major Harold G. Garvis, chief, Tank branch, Pittsburgh Ordnance district; Major Walter E. Landgraf, Production Service branch, Pittsburgh Odrnance district; Captain W. H. Marsh, officer in charge, Ellwood City sub-office, Aetna Standard Engineering Co., Ellwood City; Captain W. S. Rial, Jr., Public Information officer, Pittsburgh Ordnance district, and Lt. T. A. Strommen, Production Service branch, Pittsburgh Ordnance district.

NAVY—Commander C. E. Egeler, officer in charge, Office of Inspector of Naval Material, Munhall; Lt Commander H. H. McClintic, Jr., USNR, Naval Advisor to War Production Board, Pittsburgh; George S. Miley, Navy department, Babcock & Wilcox Co., Beaver Falls; and L. M. Meneice, Navy department, Babcock & Wilcox Co., Beaver Falls.

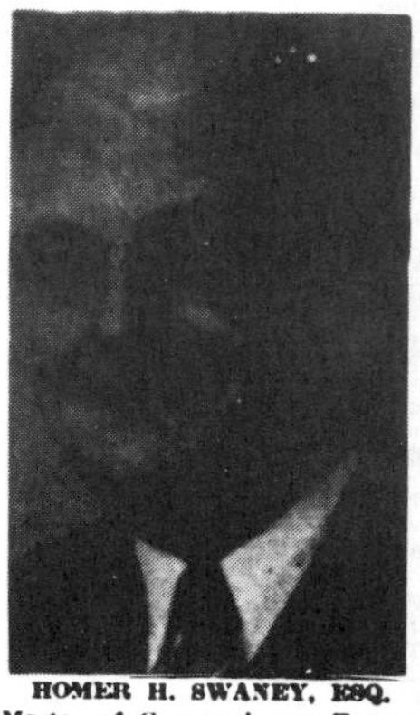

HOMER H. SWANEY, ESQ.
Master of Ceremonies at Tomorrow's Program

WILLIAM TRESS
Secretary and Assistant Treasurer

CHARLES H. FREDERICK
Chief Designer

To Award Army-Navy "E" Pennant

MAJOR HAROLD G. GARVIS

Major Garvis, Chief of the Tank and Motor Transport Branch, Pittsburgh Ordnance District, will make the awards of the Army-Navy "E" pennant tomorrow afternoon to employes of Ingram-Richardson Manufacturing Co. Major Garvis had a practical background in industry before entering into active army service. He holds a degree in mechanical engineering from the University of Pittsburgh. Following his studies he entered the employ of Westinghouse Electric & Manufacturing Company where he served in various supervisory capacities. Major Garvis was commissioned in the Infantry Reserve in 1929 and transferred to the Ordnance Department in 1938. In 1940 he was granted a leave of absence from Westinghouse when ordered to active duty with the Pittsburgh Ordnance District. He was stationed as Army Inspector of Ordnance, Aetna-Standard Engineering Company in charge of Ellwood City Area until 1941, when he was placed in charge of Artillery, Tank, Small Arms Inspection in the Pittsburgh office. In August, 1942, he was made chief of the Tank and Motor Transport Branch.

PRESENTATION PROGRAM

Star Spangled Banner — Mrs. Dorothy Jones Miller
Soloist,
Accompanied by Beaver Falls High School Band

Opening Remarks — Homer H. Swaney, Esq.
Master of Ceremony

Presentation Address — Major Harold G. Garvis
Chief of Tank Division,
Pittsburgh Ordnance District

Acceptance — Mr. Ernest Richardson
President Ingram-Richardson
Manufacturing Company

Raising Army and Navy "E" Flag
Employes' Color Guard
All World War 1 Veterans
Frank Rachuba
William Schuler
Earl Thatcher
Edward Kraft
Charles Jones
William Stanyard

Music—"Caissons Go Rolling Along"
Beaver Falls High School Band
Adolph Pletincks, Director

Token Presentation Army and Navy "E" Pins
Lieut. Commander H. H. McClintic
Advisor to War Production Board
Pittsburgh Branch

Acceptance of Pins — Hugh Murphy
Pres. Local 112 U. S. W. A.
Harry McClane
Representing Male Employes,
with a 37-year record of employment
Miss Bess L. Demorest
Representing Women Employes,
with a 32-year record of employment

Closing Song—"America" Mrs. Dorothy Jones Miller
Soloist,
Accompanied by Beaver Falls High School Band

Three Ing-Rich Employes Selected To Receive Token Award Of "E" Pins

Three Ingram-Richardson employes have been chosen to receive token award of the Army-Navy "E" pins at tomorrow's ceremony. They are Hugh Murphy, Harry McClane and Miss Bess L. Demorest.

When the Army-Navy "E" is awarded, all employes of the honored company are presented with "E" insignia to show that they are doing their part in the production of war materials. As it would be practically impossible to give out pins to all during the broadcast, the above trio has been selected to appear on the program for the token presentation. Following the broadcast, all Ingram-Richardson employes will then be presented with their own individual pins.

The pin is a colorful, red, blue and silver insignia with the Army-Navy "E" in the center.

An employe of the Ingram-Richardson Manufacturing Company for eight years, Mr. Murphy is president of Local 1112, United Steel Workers of America. He is in the Inspection Department. Born in Motherwell, Scotland, Hugh Murphy came to America when he was 16 years old. He became an American citizen in 1940.

HUGH MURPHY

MISS BESS L. DEMOREST

HARRY McCLANE

Miss Demorest will be awarded an "E" pin tomorrow as a representative of the female employes of Ingram-Richardson. She has seen 32 years of service with the company, and is head of the Order Department. Miss Demorest is very active in church and civic activities of the district.

Scheduled to be awarded an "E" pin tomorrow, Mr. McClane is one of Ingram-Richardson's oldest employes, having been with the company for 37 years. Prior to the company's conversion to war production, he mixed colors for Ingram-Richardson advertising signs and colored table tops. He is the guiding light behind the Ing-Rich employes' sports activities, and is responsible for the prominent position Ing-Rich teams occupy in Beaver county industrial sports circles.

The Weather Forecast
WESTERN PENNSYLVANIA: Occasional rain; not much change in temperature.

"The Paper That Goes Home"

THE DAILY TIMES

ROCHESTER-BEAVER-MONACA
FREEDOM—BRIDGEWATER—CONWAY—VANPORT—MIDLAND

Beaver County History
Conclusive proof was available that Germany had caused the war, it was reported here on March 13, 1919.

4 Cents

ESTABLISHED APRIL 2, 1874 | BEAVER AND ROCHESTER, PA., SATURDAY, MARCH 13, 1943 | BY CARRIER 24 CENTS A WEEK

ESSEN HEAVILY BOMBED BY RAF PLANES

COAL MINERS THREATEN TO STAGE STRIKE

Danger Of Walk-Out By Bituminous Miners Grows After Northern And Southern Operators Refuse Wage Demands; Contract Expires March 31

By United Press

NEW YORK, March 13.—Threats of a strike by 585,000 soft coal miners that would tie up bituminous production developed today after both northern and southern operators refused demands by the United Mine Workers (CIO) for wage increases and minimum wage levels.

The threats were made by several district presidents of the union at conferences of union and operator representatives attempting to negotiate a new contract. The present agreement expires March 31.

James Mark, president of District 2, charged the mine workers were "hiding behind the skirts of the War Labor Board," and warned that "no matter what the Labor Board says or does, if the men don't get a contract by April 1, they won't go into the mines."

"We are out to get a substantial increase," he added, "and we are going to get it no matter what the consequences."

LEWIS SILENT

John P. Bussarelo, president of District 5, said the miners want $2 a day more "and we won't take less," while John Seddon, spokesman for the same district, warned of "drastic and unpredictable" consequences if the demands are not met.

John L. Lewis, president of the UMW, would not comment on the situation.

The northern operators first refused the union's demands for a wage increase of $2 a day with a minimum of $8 a day for all miners, readjustments in working conditions and inclusion of 50,000 minor bosses in the agreement.

The southern operators turned down the demands yesterday, offering counter-proposals for a 40-hour week, instead of the present 35 hours, with payment of overtime after 40 hours. But the union refused these and also voted down an operators' proposal that the present agreement continue until three months after the war ends.

The conference was adjourned yesterday until Monday.

Brothers In Service

Fred John

Richard

Three sons of Mr. and Mrs. Fred J. Knott, Sr., 404 Fourth street, Beaver, are serving in the armed forces, two of them outside the United States.

They are: Seaman 2nd Class Fred J. Knott, Jr., in the Navy; Pvt. Richard T. Knott, U. S. Marines, and Corp. John M. Knott, Army Air Forces.

Fred apparently met his brother, "Dick," in the South Pacific theatre of war and presumably at Guadalcanal several months ago, as he wrote home that Dick "was looking well." John, the oldest, 21, is an instructor at Sioux Falls, S. D., and has been in the service since January 10, 1942. He formerly played basketball, football and baseball at Beaver high school.

"Dick", 18, was the first to enlist, leaving on December 15, 1941, eight days after Pearl Harbor. He also played football and basketball at Beaver high. Fred enlisted on January 10, the same day as John, and is a former football and basketball star at Beaver high school where he graduated in 1941. He will be 20 years old on March 29.

Relief Payments In County Declined During Last Month

State Treasurer G. Harold Wagner announced total payments of $35,080 for all types of categorical assistance — Old age assistance, aid to dependent children and pensions for the blind—paid Beaver Countians during February.

Following is a comparison of payments made last month and during January:

February—Old age assistance, $19,547; aid to dependent children, $9,781; pensions for the blind, $5,751.

January—Old age assistance, $19,946; aid to dependent children, $10,409; pensions for the blind, $5,721.

Anti-Black Market Steps Taken By OPA

By United Press

PHILADELPHIA, March 13—Farmers, butchers and meat packers in Philadelphia and other Pennsylvania areas will operate under a federal permit system beginning April 1, James E. Walker, chairman of the Pennsylvania War Board of the U. S. Department of Agriculture, announced today.

The system, designed to stamp out black market practices and assure equal meat distribution, will be administered by local ration boards in Philadelphia, Reading, Allentown, Harrisburg, Pittsburgh and Erie.

All who buy livestock, including farmers and small butchers who slaughter their own stock, will require permits, Walker said. In addition, all slaughterers operating under federal inspection must reserve a percentage of their production for war uses.

EDEN IN U. S. FOR PARLEYS ON WAR AIMS

British Foreign Secretary Flies Atlantic In Bomber For Series Of Conferences; Plans Visits To Other Sections Of Country During Stay

By United Press

WASHINGTON, March 13—Complete agreement of views between the American and British governments on post-war problems is the objective of the conversations begun here today by British Foreign Secretary Anthony Eden.

It was learned from a highly authoritative source that while the consultations will not involve binding commitments between the two governments, it is hoped that a complete understanding will develop which ultimately will embrace all of the United Nations.

The handsome 45-year-old Eden, who arrived yesterday after flying the Atlantic in an American bomber, was scheduled for a visit with President Roosevelt today after a press conference at the British Embassy.

Secretary of State Cordell Hull, who has been resting in Florida, will return over the week end. Undersecretary Sumner Welles, a key figure in American post-war planning, also will be prominent in the discussions.

TO PLAN ALLIED PARLEY

The talks of President Roosevelt and the other high ranking American officials with Eden and members of his party will be preliminary to general discussions to which all the United Nations will be asked to send representatives.

Eden's presence in Washington, anticipated for weeks by insiders here and postponed until now because of the illness of Prime Minister Winston Churchill, was announced by the White House last night.

The announcement stated that Eden came here at the invitation of this government and said he was here "to undertake a general exchange of views with the United States government on all aspects of the war situation, and to discuss the most effective method preparing for meetings between the governments of all United Nations to consider questions arising out of the war."

The Eden discussions undoubtedly will cover various post-war European settlements. And consideration of post-war Europe unquestionably makes Russia an important subject.

Relations of both Great Britain and the United States with the Soviet Union have not been improved by developments of the last year, despite the urgency given to Allied help to the Red Army in its magnificent performance against the Nazi invaders.

RELATIONS TROUBLED

British refusal to undertake a second front in Europe last year and the unfortunate remarks in Moscow this week by U. S. Ambassador William H. Standley are highlights of the troubled relations between London and Washington on the one hand, and Moscow on the other.

Both the United States and Britain wish to smooth over the present agitated state of relations with the Soviet, and the Eden talks are counted on to accomplish much in that direction.

The Russians get along well with Eden and it is believed here that, despite occasional flurries in American-Soviet affairs, Moscow has trust and confidence in American policies.

Other topics on the Eden agenda are European post - war security. (Continued On Page Eight)

HITLER'S DISABILITY REPORTED, LEADERS CHANGE

COMPLETE BREAKDOWN, nervous and physical, of Adolf Hitler is reported, sending him into near retirement at his Berchtesgaden retreat, above, high in the Bavarian Alps. Der Fuehrer is pictured, left, during earlier days at his favorite rest spot, and, center above, looking haggard and worn as he appeared in most recent picture to reach the United States. Military strategy is said to have passed into the hands of Gen. Fritz von Mannstein, while Herman Goering, upper left, and Paul Joseph Goebbels, upper right, may be vying for political leadership—as Hitler's Nazi "heirs." *(International)*

Motorists Must Aid In Ride Sharing To Get Extra Gasoline

By United Press

WASHINGTON, March 13.—Motorists today faced loss of supplemental "B" and "C" gasoline rationing books issued for occupational uses if they refuse to participate in ride-sharing clubs.

Price Administrator Prentiss M. Brown has ordered local rationing boards to insist that applicants for supplemental ration books belong to full ride-sharing clubs when the books become renewable, beginning March 22.

If arrangements to carry three other persons to and from work regularly have not been made, the applicant will have to produce evidence that alternative means of transportation are not available, and that he is sharing his car with as many people as possible.

Brown said that ride-sharing must be made a universal practice if passenger car mileage is to be reduced to the 5,000 mile-a-year average recommended by the Baruch Rubber investigating committee.

UP TO BOARDS

An OPA spokesman said today that supplemental rations may be either denied completely or drastically curtailed to motorists who refuse deliberately to cooperate. He said many reasons of inconvenience hitherto given for inability of motorists to participate in the clubs probably would not hold as much weight with the boards as in the past.

The "B" and "A" books provide 378 miles of driving a month in the (Continued On Page Eight)

Vegetable Prices To Be Equalized

By United Press

PITTSBURGH, March 13—Establishment of equalized price ceilings for fresh vegetables in all major cities is expected to end within a week a shortage of certain vegetables in the Pittsburgh area.

Office of Price Administration representatives here said they expect "momentarily" receipt of notice of the price equalization. Because the ceiling price on peas and beans has been higher in mid-West cities than in Pittsburgh, shippers have diverted their produce to those points.

American Materials Of War Sent To French Patriots

By United Press

LONDON, March 13—American arms, including even field artillery, have reached thousands of French patriots engaged in sabotage and terrorist raids against the Axis in eastern France, Swiss dispatches said today.

More than 1,500 men in Savoi Province under the organized command of a Gen. Cartier now are armed with American machine-guns, rifles and revolvers and some have 75 millimeter guns and shells, a Zurich report said.

Gen. Cartier was not otherwise identified, but French army registers list two generals of that surname, Gen. Georges Cartier and Gen. Francois Cartier. The dispatch gave no hint as to how the American weapons reached the patriots.

French frontier dispatches said the Savoi Province frontier army altogether numbered more than 50,000 men, all well equipped and under the command of officers demobilized from the French army after the Nazi occupation of south (Continued On Page Eight)

Home Gardens Are Urged By Governor

HARRISBURG, March 13.—Gov. Edward Martin wants Pennsylvanians to plant and harvest Victory gardens and to can the surplus foods.

Noting the important part food will play in winning the war, Martin called on owners of suitable land to volunteer its use and for schools to encourage and guide students with Victory gardens.

Martin expressed confidence that the state's goal of 1,400,000 gardens—double last year's total—will be reached.

Agriculture Secretary Miles Horst advised Victory gardeners to forego planting of potatoes in their backyard plots "since experience shows that the returns do not warrant the use of seed and the effort." He pointed out that "potato growing requires highly specilized care."

ARRIVES IN AFRICA

Word has been received by Mrs. Donald Y. Shaffer of New Brighton, of the safe arrival of her husband, Lieutenant Colonel Shaffer, in North Africa. Mrs. Shaffer is the former Katharine Hughes of Beaver.

Fayette Probe To Be Resumed Monday

By United Press

UNIONTOWN, March 13. — The Fayette county grand jury which has been conducting a two-fold investigation of fiscal affairs and rackets in this county, is expected to resume its work Monday to complete its findings in the latter phase of inquiry.

The jury already has returned indictments against five county officials and a former state senator in connection with payment of a $10,000 attorney's fee in settlement of the county's indebtedness to the state. The jurors were off duty this week due to absence of Deputy Attorney General James I. Marsh, head of the investigation.

Court observers believe that the grand jury may report on Tuesday or Wednesday its recommendations resulting from the inquiry into pinball and slotmachine operations.

Couple Overcome By Monoxide Gas In Parked Auto

Sitting in an automobile parked in front of the girl's home with the motor running almost proved fatal to a local couple Friday evening as both were overcome by carbon monoxide fumes.

The couple, Dorothy Sterling, 16, Eighteenth avenue, New Brighton, and Paul Bolland, 22, near New Brighton, had been riding and parked at the Sterling home for a few minutes before entering the house.

Dorothy's mother, Mrs. John Sterling, became alarmed as they (Continued On Page Eight)

J. P. Morgan Dies In Florida Today

JOHN PIERPONT MORGAN

By United Press

BOCA GRANDE, Fla., March 13.—John Pierpont Morgan, called "the younger" though 75 years old, international financier, head of a famous financial dynasty, and one of the world's wealthiest men, died at 3:15 A. M. today.

The president of J. P. Morgan and Company, Inc., a name prominent in the financing of empires through the life-times of two John Pierpont Morgans and creator of such industrial giants as United States Steel Corporation, succumb- (Continued On Page Eight)

RAID BELIEVED BIGGEST OF WAR

Today's War Summary

By United Press

LONDON—Royal Air Force delivers one of war's heaviest blows against Essen, home of Krupp Arms Works.

ALLIED HEADQUARTERS IN NORTH AFRICA—Gen. Dwight D. Eisenhower, in order of the day, calls for "destruction" of Axis armies; big push appears imminent.

MOSCOW — Germans smash closer to Kharkov; Red army told to defend city "to last drop of blood."

LONDON, March 13—The Royal Air Force drove home a pulverizing blow to the heart of the Nazi war-making machine today with an attack by hundreds of planes on Essen—the Pittsburgh of Germany—where hundreds of acres of industrial plants already lay wrecked and shattered.

Early reports on last night's crushing raid indicated that it may well have been the heaviest of the war which, of course, would be the heaviest in history.

Although there was no indication that the total of RAF planes participating in the attack exceeded the 1,000-plane figures set last spring, there was every indication that the Lancasters and Stirlings carried a greater tonnage of high explosives than had rocked the land of the Nazis heretofore.

It also was indicated that the Allied air offensive had by no means reached its crescendo. Instead, the air attacks of the USAAF and the RAF were regarded as finally having started upward to the point where astronomical bomb tonnages will have softened the Reich until invasion forces can crack its hollow shell.

EISENHOWER CONFIDENT

The tempo of Allied preparation for the ground assault in Tunisia had reached the point where Gen. Dwight D. Eisenhower, Allied North African commander-in-chief, could predict that the Axis armies would be pushed back "into the sea and to destruction." Eisenhower warned that the Germans and Italians would make "further and separate efforts" to break the Allied ring, however.

The RAF's admitted losses in the attack on Essen were 23 planes, more than one-third again as many as the Nazis claimed in their initial reports. But informed sources insisted that the raid was economical from a percentage standpoint, indicating the large number of planes and crews involved.

Such attacks as last night's are certain to have direct effects on Nazi military power on all fronts. It was estimated that more than 450 acres of Essen were devastated by the attack only a week ago. It was reasonable to suppose that even greater devastation was wrought last night.

The frequency of the air attacks has not given the Nazis time to clear up the damage and rehabilitate factories and machinery. This certainly will be reflected in smaller and slower production of guns, cannon, tanks and planes.

REDS HARD PRESSED

That these trip hammer blows to German industry are sorely needed is indicated by developments on the eastern front where the Red army obviously is engaged in its most (Continued On Page Eight)

Six Persons Hurt In Local Traffic And Work Mishaps

Richard Dawson, 34, near Monaca, was admitted to Rochester hospital early this morning suffering from a head injury received while at work for the Koppers Company at Kobuta. His condition was regarded as serious late this morning.

SECOND WORKMAN HURT

Angelo C. Mooney, 34, New Castle, was admitted to Rochester hospital Friday afternoon suffering from fractures of the ribs received while at work for the Koppers Company at Kobuta.

STRUCK BY TIRE RIM

Charles Pyle, 38, McKees Rocks, was admitted to Rochester hospital early Friday evening suffering from severe lacerations of the face received when a tire rim was blown off a truck while he was checking the air pressure at a Bridgewater service station.

THREE HURT IN CRASH

Three employes of the local Curtiss-Wright plant were injured in an automobile accident Friday in Duss avenue, Ambridge, and were removed to Sewickley hospital. The automobile was operated by Andrew Kaintz, McKees Rocks, a foreman at the plant, when it collided with a parked car, according to Ambridge police.

Those injured are James Humenny, who received lacerations of the head and a knee injury; William Wagner, a possible fracture of the nose, and John Arena, bruises and minor lacerations. All three are from McKees Rocks. Kaintz was uninjured and Arena was only treated at the hospital, where the other two were admitted.

TWO DIE IN PLANE

GLENDALE, Calif., March 13.—Staff Sgt. Merle F. Robinson, Louisburg, O., was one of two army fliers killed yesterday when the plane he was piloting crashed near here, army officers announced today. Two others were injured seriously.

Thousands Join CD Forces In State

By United Press

HARRISBURG, Mar. 13.—Over 71,000 Pennsylvanians volunteered for civilian defense duty during February to record the biggest enrollment gain since last October, it was announced today.

The State Defense Council said a gain of 20,000 in the Citizens' Defense Corps brought the number of air raid wardens and other protective volunteers to 592,000—more than double the figure of a year ago.

Reports from 29 counties showed an increase of 51,000 in the non-protective activities. Block leaders and other miscellaneous service volunteers in the reported counties now total 202,165.

Women comprise most of the non - protective volunteers and about 13 per cent of the citizens' defense corps.

Five Men Killed In New York Hotel Fire

LITTLE FALLS, N. Y., March 13—Five men were killed early today when fire swept through the third floor of the Murray Hotel.

They were trapped in their beds and firemen found their bodies after the fire had been extinguished.

The Murray Hotel is a three-story frame structure and the fire originated on the third floor. Persons on the lower floors escaped without difficulty. Only two persons escaped from the third floor.

WARNING TO BUSINESSMEN

Inquiry has been made at the District Attorney's office by businessmen and cleric of Beaver County concerning solicitations being made by strangers for advertising space in a magazine called the AMERICAN SLAV. These strangers represent to the businessmen that they have great influence with the ten groups of American people of Slavic origin and that the man who advertises in this magazine will get all of the business of these ten groups.

The brains of the combination appears to be Ante Marko Doshen, alias Dochen Kovatchevich, an ex-staff officer of the Russian Imperial Army, and the professional solicitors who do the actual canvassing are usually Arthur and Philip Fisher.

We have in our possession a writing sent out by John H. Pankuch, a former editor of the magazine, to the effect that the paid circulation of this magazine is less than five hundred for all of United States, and less than one hundred in Beaver County.

We are informed that they do not have the endorsement of the Slavic Societies of Beaver County, and that they make no effort to induce the Slavic people here to deal exclusively with the advertisers, except through a printed request in a magazine which has no circulation.

We feel it our duty to warn businessmen of this situation in order that they might not be victimized by slickers. The many good people of Beaver County of Slavic origin have a right to be properly represented.

—R. E. McCREARY, District Attorney.

Two Youths Held In Theft Of Auto

Two youths held by Beaver Falls police for stealing and wrecking an automobile Thursday morning in Beaver Falls were to be arraigned today before Alderman George B. Johnston on charges of larceny of a motor vehicle.

The youths, Joseph Baumgartner, near Ellwood City, and Robert M. Tennant, New Castle, reportedly stole an automobile owned by Mrs. Grace Sterling, College avenue, Beaver Falls, damaged the rear of it a few blocks away in a collision with a truck and abandoned it, according to police.

Bankers Prepare For Bond Drive

In preparation for the Victory Bond Sale, beginning April 12, Beaver County bankers, executive bank officers, regional and district chairmen, held a three-hour organization meeting in the Court House last night. T. C. Swarts, of the Woodlawn Trust Co. was leader of the group of 150 present.

Details of the organization setup were explained. Announcement was made that when the organization is completed, 3,000 workers will go into all parts of the county to sell approximately eight million dollars in United States bonds to help finance our national war program. The national goal is 13 billion dollars. Up to last night's meeting no definite goal had been set for Beaver county.

Next week regional chairmen will hold meetings and complete the selling organization in all parts of the county. Every financial institution in the county was represented at last nights meeting. Area and district chairmen made reports on progress of organization in their respective districts.

WAACS HAVE OBSTACLE COURSE

LIKE THE SOLDIERS, members of the Women's Army Auxiliary Corps must be in top physical condition. To help them get that way and stay that way, an obstacle course has been laid out at Fort Oglethorpe, Georgia. WAACS are pictured above running over one of the more intricate hazards. *(International)*

Tight Situation In Steel Supplies Not Yet Alleviated

The widely heralded reduction in new war plant construction and machine tool output will not relieve the tight situation in steel supplies to any great extent, for the slack will be absorbed speedily by the need to keep the total war program up to schedule.

At most, the steel industry expects only a slight and very temporary easing of the pressure in perhaps a few departments, while in other major products the industry's flexibility and its capacity to break records probably will be tested to the limit. The use of United States materials and men so far in the war may prove to be only a fraction of the total need for complete victory.

Whether the announced review of new construction will succeed in cutting off more than "paper" plants is doubted by some officials at Washington, who point to the needed expansion in aluminum and magnesium, 100 octane gasoline, synthetic rubber, steel, and in vessel construction will prevent any substantial reduction. The review of projects may only result in taking some of the "water" out of construction requirements.

Third quarter lend-lease steel shipments are expected to show a sharp rise. It is beliezed a large portion of this tonnage will be semi-finished material for England and light railroad rails for Russia. Domestic orders for rails and other supplies have picked up recently, according to some sellers.

Because of the need for repairs on steel making equipment, ingot production for the nation dropped one point this week to 98.5 per cent of rated capacity. The only gains in output for the week have occurred in the Birmingham district which is up half a point to 102.5 per cent and the Eastern area which has jumped seven points to 96 per cent. Pittsburgh operations are down one point to 101 per cent as is Philadelphia at 95 per cent.

Chicago production has sagged half a point to 96.5 per cent, the district's lowest level since the middle of 1941. Youngstown steelmaking has fallen off half a point to 95 per cent while Cleveland has decreased three points to 99 per cent. The operating rate at Cincinnati has declined two points to 105 per cent and St. Louis production is off one point to 101.5 per cent. Wheeling and Detroit are unchanged at 89 and 104.5 per cent respectively.

Stock Of Potatoes Discovered In New York Barber Shop

NEW YORK, May 21 (UP)—Numerous city officials including Mayor F. H. LaGuardia, the OPA and even the selective service became interested today in the discovery of 16,000 pounds of potatoes in a barber shop.

The potatoes, which have become a rarity in New York, were impounded and police were questioning Benjamin Caplan, 40, Philadelphia, whom they said was the owner.

LaGuardia personally took charge of the case shortly after they were brought in by truck from upstate New York, and the trucker, Anthony Zubinsky, Plattsburgh, also was held.

Caplan said he bought the potatoes from a Chateaugay, N. Y. farmer. The city building department followed with the charge that the barber shop floor, with the potatoes on it, was carrying seven times its safe limit.

The New York market departments said the bags did not have labels giving the net weight and the producer. The fire department said they found a fire hazard in the barber shop—several five-gallon cans of kerosene.

The OPA was investigating for possible black market evidence. Finally selective service officials inquired into Caplan's draft status.

Pleasure Driving Restrictions Same As Previous Ban

WASHINGTON, May 21 (UP)—The new restrictions on pleasure driving are similar to those applied last winter. Gasoline may be used only for trips connected with the motorist's occupation or with family or personal necessity.

Family or personal necessity driving includes (but is not limited to): Essential shopping, getting medical attention, attending religious services, attending funerals, attending meetings of groups or organizations essential to the occupation or profession of the person using the vehicle; meeting an emergency involving a threat to life, health or property, or for instruction or training in meeting or preparing to meet such emergencies.

Non-essential trips specifically prohibited by the ban include (but are not limited to): Driving to places of amusement, recreation or entertainment (such as theaters, amusement parks, concerts, dances, golf courses, skating-rinks, bowling alleys or night clubs; sporting events (such as races or games); social club meetings; sight-seeing, touring and vacation travel; making social calls.

Members of the armed forces on leave or furlough are exempt from the ban to visit relatives and make other social calls.

Butcher Believes OPA Is Competitor

PITTSBURGH, May 21 (UP)—District OPA Price Executive E. G. Albright swears it's true. A housewife protested when her butcher asked 39 cents a pound for hamburger. "That's too much," she said. "I saw in the paper that the OPA price is 32 cents a pound." Evidently thinking the OPA was a new competitor down the block, the butcher retorted: "Well, why don't you go down there and buy it?" Albright said the butcher shortly will learn that the OPA ceiling price for small retailers really is 32 cents—and that the OPA is not a butcher shop.

Grapefruit canning started in Florida in 1921.

BIG AVIATION BACKLOG

LOS ANGELES, Cal.—(UP)—At a meeting here of the executives of the Eastern aircraft factories with the heads of those on the Pacific coast, it was established that between them they have an aviation backlog of nearly $17,000,000,000. Plans were formulated to speed up its liquidation.

California's first legislature which met in San Jose in 1894, became known as the "Legislature of a Thousand Drinks" for its adjournment celebration.

Freedom Seniors To Present Play, Skit Next Week

The seniors of Freedom high school will present their class play next Thursday afternoon and Friday evening in the high school auditorium. The three-act comedy-drama, "An American Is Born," by Richard Paulding, presents America and all it stands for, in terms of the present day.

The part of "Eliot James," a New York factory owner, is being taken by John Kronstain; and that of his wife, "Ina," by Mary Lou Mengel. Their pretty daughters "Madge" and "Patty" are Betty Whitehouse and Louise Wood. Edward Sabolic is taking the part of "Bernard Balch," Madge's boy friend. "Dottie Newcomb," Patty's girl friend, is Jean Guy; and Lorida Ciani will be seen in the parts of "Miss Furness," Mr. James' secretary, and "Mrs. Cruikshank," a colored lady. "Timmy Cruikshank," a cockney boy evacuated from London, who provides much of the comedy in the play, is being portrayed by Sam Mandarino.

The remaining members of the cast are newcomers on the high school stage: "Sigmund Hale," a stranger in town about whom is an air of mystery, is being played by Faye Piersol. "Pauline," the Polish hired girl, is Mary Roknick; and "Major Benson," of the War Department is John Genova.

The play is directed by Miss Elisabeth Bates. Mrs. Edna Foster is class sponsor. Other members of the staff are: Stage—R. O. Robertson, John Bonaparte, Joe Bosco, Joe DePaolis, Ben Genevie; Prompters are Lorida Ciano, Mary Roknick; properties, Jean Guy; tickets, Henrietta Skerkowski; advertising, Louise Wood; make-up, Elaine Simmons.

Preliminary to the play, a victory skit, "Democracy on the Air," by Helen Ramsey, will be performed by another group of seniors. The skit is a street broadcast in which passers-by express their views of the American freedoms.

The cast: "Man on the Street," a radio announcer, Richard Johnson; "Jim," his assistant, Joe DePaolis; "Denny," a street urchin, Tom Zinkham (6th grade); "Miss Lurena Day," a school teacher, Margaret Samchuck; "Jacob Johnson," a laborer, Bob Smith; "Polly Platinum," a debutante, Martha Concelman; "Otto Redd," an agitator, Bagdon Corklic; "Mrs. Moffett," an old lady, Ruth Franz.

The high school orchestra, under the direction of Domenico Caputo, will present several numbers before the play.

The combined total of government and private expenditures contemplated for 1943 to expand and improve iron and steel plants facilities is nearly $650,000,000.

BEAVER FALLS

Marriage Of Local Soldier In Indiana Is Announced Here

Announcement is made of the marriage of Betty Lake, daughter of Mr. and Mrs. Robert Lake, Manhattan, Kan., to Sgt. Herman Kidd, son of Mrs. Marie Chapman, near Beaver Falls. The marriage was performed February 6 in Columbus, Ind. Sgt. Kidd enlisted in the Army in July, 1940, and is now stationed at Camp Leonard Wood, Mo. He and his bride have an apartment near the camp.

Dr. and Mrs. J. Howard Swick, Eighth avenue, who have been visiting in Lakeland, Fla., are en route home. They are to stop over at Washington, D. C., and are to arrive here Saturday.

Corp. A. M. Lutheran, stationed with the Marine Air Corps at San Diego, has been spending a week's furlough with his parents, Mr. and Mrs. Joseph Lutheran, Second avenue.

Mrs. Joseph Woolslayer, Seventh avenue, has left for a visit with her son, Edward Woolslayer, Akron, O.

Miss Elizabeth Reagle, a junior at Ohio Wesleyan University, has been elected to the presidency of the university's Women's Athletic Association. She is the daughter of Mr. and Mrs. E. E. Reagle, Fourth avenue, Patterson Heights. She is affiliated with the Chi Omega sorority.

The ten-month-old son of Mr. and Mrs. Cameron Rylott, Morado Dwellings, who has been ill with pneumonia, is improving.

In Great Britain women are engaged in practically every kind of transportation work except shipping.

ROCHESTER

Lutheran Class To Meet Tuesday In Home Of Member

The Samaritan class of St. Paul's Lutheran church will meet Tuesday evening at 8 o'clock in the home of Mrs. Henry Gissel, Virginia avenue.

Second Class Seaman Richard Say is spending a nine-day leave from the Great Lakes Naval Training Station, Ill., with his wife, formerly Evalynne Vaughn, and parents, Mr. and Mrs. John Say, Sunflower road.

Pfc. Charles Bogolea has been transferred from the Marine Air Base at Kearny Mesa, San Diego, to Santa Ana, Calif. He is the son of Mr. and Mrs. Nicholas Bogolea, East Rochester.

Pvt. Louis W. Gardner, Jr., has returned to Camp Lejeune, New River, N. C., after spending a three-day leave with his parents, Mr. and Mrs. Louis W. Gardner, Atlas avenue.

Charles Grisetti, recently promoted to private first class with the Marines, has been transferred from New River, N. C., to Philadelphia where he is attending a telephone school. He is the son of Mr. and Mrs. Angelo Grisetti, Jerferson street.

Mrs. Charles Groth, Jefferson street, is confined to bed by illness.

Mr. and Mrs. William Corliss and Miss Maryellen Hollander, Denton Plan, and Mrs. Dan J. Vogt, Monaca, attended Wednesday the graduation exercises of Mrs. Corliss' nephew, John Paul Goff, from the University of Pittsburgh Medical School. The son of John P. Goff, Coraopolis, formerly of New Brighton, Dr. Goff was also commissioned a first lieutenant in the army. He will serve a period of internship at St. Francis hospital before entering active service.

Mrs. Catherine Miller and son "Billy," whose home in Beaver Falls was destroyed by fire early Wednesday morning, will reside permanently with Mrs. Miller's mother, Mrs. Matilda Schilling, Virginia avenue. Billy is at present confined to the hospital suffering from injuries received while escaping the fire.

Mrs. E. E. Stroupe, Mecklem avenue, and Mrs. C. P. Berkihiser, Kossuth street, spent Wednesday in Alliance, O., visiting relatives.

The condition of George W. Cameron, who is seriously ill in the Lincoln Hotel, is reported no better.

Wilbur Y. McNees and son, Wilbur Y. McNees, Jr., Ohio avenue, are spending a few days in Cleveland.

Winifred Lodge, Daughters of Rebekah, will meet in the I. O. O. F. hall this evening. Installation of officers will feature.

Roland Haney, Kentucky avenue, who left Wednesday evening for army service, was tendered a farewell dinner in the home of his mother, Mrs. Clara L. Haney, Tuesday evening. Mrs. Haney was assisted in serving by her sister, Vera Grant, and Mrs. Kenneth Haney. William Wiedner, East Liverpool, has been a guest for a few days in the home of Mrs. Haney, an aunt.

Mr. and Mrs. Warren Ball, Lincoln avenue, have received word of a son born March 23 at Steelton to Sgt. and Mrs. Warren Ball, Jr. Sgt. Ball is serving in the Army in North Africa.

Warnings Issued On Infectious Eye Disease Epidemic

By United Press

CHICAGO, April 2.—The American Medical Association warned today that an infectious eye disease which has swept the nation's shipyards may become more extensive in scope and listed procedures to combat its spread.

The disease, which has assumed epidemic proportions in west coast shipyards, causes an acute inflammation of the eyelids and usually lasts from 14 to 18 days, the American Medical Journal said in a special warning bulletin.

The presence of the disease, known medically as epidemic keratoconjunctivitis, is first manifested by an irritation of the eyelid similar to that caused by a foreign body, the bulletin said. One eye uually is affected first and in most cases the second becomes infected within five to eight days.

The Journal said no specific treatment had been discovered to cure the disease but advised that during the acute state the eyes be kept clean by irrigation to avoid infecting others.

SPRING FASHIONS INSPIRED BY SILHOUETTE, YARDAGE ECONOMY

walk and carry

FOR GRACIOUS MOMENTS: Soft, easy lines from the feminine, ruffled lace collar to the slimming skirt feature this Eisenberg Original.

SAVING MANPOWER, GAS, TIRES: the Business Girl "walks and carries." Her functional covert suit will last many a season.

SAVE WEAR: this smartly styled suit is fashioned of a durable Crown rayon blend fabric.

SAVE "CHANGING": have a wear everywhere spun rayon, border printed dress designed by Simplicity, simple to make.

Dutch Treat

Joan Durain designs a light blue linen weave jumper with red, yellow and green crossstitch braid trim worn over a white broadcloth blouse. Matching jacket and Dutch cap.

A Model is Murdered ~ BABS LEE

CHAPTER THIRTY-THREE

It was noon before Argus awoke the following day. He felt strangely light-headed from loss of blood and shock. He got up and called Butch.

"You got a visitor," his valet told him. "I told him you couldn't see nobody—you was too sick. But he won't leave."

"He says his name is Carstairs. He's a white-haired guy with a big bay winder."

"I wondered when he'd arrive," said Argus. "Tell him I'll be in as soon as I'm dressed. Then come back here and help me."

"Sure, boss."

Cartairs, Sr., was smoking a cigar and nervously pacing up and down the living room when Argus entered.

"What can I do for you?" the detective asked.

Carstairs whirled. "So, there you are," he said in his deep voice. "I want that check back you stole from my son's pocket."

Argus smiled.

"I'm prepared to pay you if that's what you want," Carstairs boomed. "How about it? How much do you want?" The older man puffed furiously on his cigar and glared at Argus through narrowed blue eyes.

"Sit down," the detective invited.

"I'd prefer to stand," Carstairs snapped.

"As you wish, but I hope you won't get tired. You and I have a few things to discuss."

"I can't see that we have anything to discuss."

"Why don't you tell me about this check — how Syria Verne's name happened to be endorsed on the back — and — why the police found a silk robe belonging to you in her apartment?"

Carstairs got red in the face. He blew out his cheeks like a porpoise.

"I—I was framed!" he roared.

"That's what they all say," drawled Argus. "I should have thought you could make up a better story, but for the sake of argument, who framed you?"

"Why that girl—she—told me some cock-and-bull story about my son and herself and I was fool enough to believe her. I made out that check to get rid of her. As for the robe—maybe my son borrowed it—how should I know?"

"Do you realize what you're inferring?" Argus asked.

"Well you know how it is, Mr. Steele. Young men are young men. They're impulsive, and do foolish things. My son—well, he's always been headstrong," Carstairs blustered.

"If what you've just told me is true and you bought Syria off, why should you be so concerned about getting that check back? Certainly not to protect your son's reputation."

"You're an insulting young whippersnapper, just as I've been led to believe."

"In court parlance that would be considered an ad hominem argument—an appeal to personal prejudice, and it would be ruled out. Come now, isn't it your reputation you want to preserve?"

"I'll admit I happen to be interested in politics right now and I don't want any unfavorable publicity concerning my son."

"You should've thought of that earlier," Argus snapped. "Why were you telephoning Syria Verne from the Whitsun Club?"

"She was trying to stir up trouble between my son and his wife."

"Where did you go when you left the Whitsun Club Monday night at 11:30?"

"Home."

"Then it took you two hours and a half to go from Fifth avenue and 52nd street to 645 East 56th?" Argus pressed.

"Well, maybe I stopped off and had a drink. I don't remember. Furthermore, what right have you to question me? I'm not on trial."

"How long have you known Dancer Martinelli?"

"I never heard of him, outside of newspaper stories. Now listen, young man—"

"You're in a bad spot, Carstairs. You live in the same building as Syria Verne. Your robe is found in her apartment. You make out a check for five thousand dollars which has been endorsed by her. You phone her from your club the night she was murdered. Then you barge in here and try to buy me off. I have a good mind to turn you over to the police." Argus got up and started toward the phone.

"Maybe I have been hasty," said Carstairs wiping his brow with his handkerchief. "Let's talk things over."

"Well, let's—and get it over with. I haven't had breakfast yet. How long were you—er, financing Syria Verne?"

Argus thought for a moment that Carstairs would burst a blood vessel. "How dare you suggest such a thing?" he spluttered.

"I didn't suggest it. I just asked for information," asserted Argus, smilingf.

"Well, you implied it by asking how long I'd been financing her."

"All right, then, had you been financing her?"

"Certainly not. I only met her a month ago." Carstairs looked away. "Then I used her only in a business capacity for my advertising. My son suggested it."

"How did your son happen to get hold of that check?"

"He must've found it among my papers."

"And you had nothing in common with Miss Verne—that is apart from your son and your business?"

"I've told you," Carstairs was exasperated. "But that's all part of a young man sowing his wild oats. He's married now."

"I've also learned you had a heated quarrel with your son last week. Why? Was it about the check?"

"We had a row over an entirely different matter."

"You came home Monday afternoon around four o'clock. Did you go out again?"

"No, not until I went to the club at seven. But what are you getting at? What right have you to question my actions?"

"Mr. Carstairs, I don't mind telling you that both you and your son are on a spot. In fact, both of you need a nice alibi."

"What about that check, do I get it back? All this nonsense—"

"All in due time. But about Martinelli—"

"Confound Martinelli!" rasped Carstairs, turning purple again. "I don't know the man."

"Then what were you doing in his car on Monday night at 11:30?"

"That's a lie! I've never seen

(Continued on Page Five)

The Weather Forecast

WESTERN PENNSYLVANIA: Snow flurries; warmer today. Tree pollen count — 102.

"The Paper That Goes Home"

THE DAILY TIMES

1874 — and WESTERN ARGUS — 1803

ROCHESTER - BEAVER - MONACA - FREEDOM - BRIDGEWATER - CONWAY - VANPORT - MIDLAND

Beaver County History

Germany's war indemnity was set at sixty billion dollars, it was reported in the county on April 14, 1919.

4 Cents

Established April 2, 1874 | Beaver and Rochester, Pa., Wednesday, April 14, 1943 | By Carrier 24 Cents A Week

BIG ALLIED AIR FLEETS BLAST AXIS

SCHOOL BOARD AT BEAVER TO LEVY NEW TAX

Tax Of $3 To Be Imposed Under New Budgetary Program Of School Board; Former $5 Tax Discontinued In 1937; Property Tax Levy To Be Cut One Mill

Although the tax levy will be reduced one mill, a per capita tax of $3 - $2 less than the $5 tax which was discontinued in 1937—will be imposed again under the tentative budget adopted at the monthly meeting of the Beaver school board Tuesday evening.

The budget totals $126,140, based on a 16-mill tax levy.

The school directors feel that the ever-increasing number of non-property owners should help finance the educational program more directly, since ceilings have been placed upon rents. Also, the 1939 law now makes possible the easier collection of the per capita tax. The tentative budget is available for inspection in the office of the superintendent of schools during the next thirty days and will be presented for final adoption on Tuesday, May 11.

ACTIVITIES LISTED

The Activities Committee presented the basketball report which was approved. The list of activities for the remainder of the school term was presented as follows:

April 14, Wednesday, 3 p. m. and 8 p. m., air raid warning demonstration; April 16, Friday, 8 p. m., Music Festival; April 29, Thursday, 11 a. m., Miss Fulheim (Woman's Club Speaker); April 29 and 30, 7 to 10 p. m., Fine and Practical Arts exhibition in gymnasium and auditorium; May 7, Friday, Junior-Senior Prom; May 17 to 21, Senior exams; May 21, Friday, 6:30 p. m., May Day at Stadium; May 23, Sunday, Baccalaureate service; May 28, Friday, Senior play; June 1, Tuesday, Commencement; June 3, Thursday, last day of school — Senior dance.

The Baccalaureate and Commencement dates were altered slightly in order to cooperate with the local Memorial Day Association for arrangement of speakers. The last day of school for the seniors is Friday, May 21. Baccalaureate will be Sunday, May 23, rather than May 30. Dr. E. C. Pires, pastor of the local Presbyterian church, has been extended an invitation to preach the baccalaureate sermon to the graduating class. He will be assisted by the other ministers.

REPORTS HEARD

The Education Committee reported on the status of the teachers in relation to military service and the report is encouraging, although the intervening months between the close of school and September may alter cases. However teaching is now being considered an essential occupation.

The Buildings and Grounds Committee reported on the recent visitation to all buildings and complimented the caretakers on the

(Continued On Page Ten)

County Legion To Meet On Thursday

Breaking an established custom of the last twenty years, the Beaver County Committee of the American Legion will hold the balance of its meetings this year in the Rochester Legion home, the third Thursday of each month.

Ever since its formation, the committee has rotated its meetings in the various post homes throughout the county. This year, due to limited transportation facilities, it was decided to hold the meetings in Rochester, as it is easily accessible to all posts by bus.

Many of the posts are starting plans for Memorial Day observances. This year the Legion will pay tribute to men of the present conflict who have died in the service, as well as those of past wars.

Following the action taken in Allegheny County last week, County Commander P. A. Tarter warned relatives of boys in the service to beware of fake solicitors who try to secure money by playing on the patriotism and feelings of parents of boys in the service. Parents who are in doubt as to what they should do when approached by these solicitors should contact their local Legion post.

Midland Post will be the host to the committee at Rochester Thursday night.

Beaver Doctor

Dr. Ellsworth Henderson, (above) son of Mr. and Mrs. Frank A. Henderson, Beaver, recently graduated from the School of Medicine, University of Pittsburgh, and is now interning at Mercy hospital, Pittsburgh. He graduated from Beaver high school in 1934 and graduated from Geneva College, where he took a pre-medical course, in 1938.

No Compromise Seen On Filibuster In State Upper House

BULLETIN

HARRISBURG, April 14.—State Senate Republicans today defeated the purpose of what they termed a Democratic filibuster by passing a bill to reapportion the Pennsylvania Congressional districts. After debating more than an hour on merits of the bill, following an unsuccessful attempt by Sen. Joseph M. Barr, Dem., Allegheny, to amend it, the Senate adopted the measure by a 28 to 12 vote, all Democrats except Sen. John J. Haluska, Cambria, dissenting.

HARRISBURG, April 14 — Still locked in the grip of a time-consuming Democratic filibuster with no compromise in sight, the Senate met at 7 a. m. today to pass finally the Republican Congressional reapportionment bill—root of the controversy.

Sleepy-eyed and agitated over the tiresome process of listening to bills read at length—the minority's method of protesting the reapportionment measure—the Senators came back for another ordeal after two attempts to end it collapsed.

In an effort to break down the Democrats' stand, the Republican leadership will try to hold the House and Senate in session two extra days, Friday and Saturday, it was reported.

The House reconvened at 11:30 a. m. after rejection of a Democratic proposal calling for creation of a joint 10-member committee to seek a solution to the filibuster. Rep. Homer S. Brown D., Allegheny, asked for immediate consideration of a resolution setting up the committee, but Rep. Samuel W. Salus, R., Philadelphia, objected that the Democrats "got themselves in this mess and we shouldn't help them out."

REQUEST REFUSED

Earlier, Sen. Joseph M. Barr, D., Allegheny, leading the fight against the GOP's redistricting bill, refused Republican Floor Leader Weldon B. Heyburn's request to give a number of new bills initial approval without having them read, insisting all bills be read at length.

The measure, designed to replace the "makeshift" 1942 Congressional reapportionment plan, would drop one member from Philadelphia's bloc of seven, increase Allegheny's districts from four to five, and revamp a number of other western bailiwicks. Democrats charge it is a "vicious gerrymander" which will force loss of eight party Congressmen at the 1944 elections.

Hopes for a compromise rested with Gov. Edward Martin, with whom a special six-member Demo-

(Continued On Page Ten)

Beaver Army Flier Wins Air Medal

Capt. William R. Harris, Dravo avenue, Beaver, Army Air Forces, was among 41 Pennsylvanians who have been awarded Air Medals, the War Department announced today. Five oak leaf clusters were also awarded.

Captain Harris previously was awarded the Purple Heart Medal as the result of having been wounded on a bombing raid over Europe.

Jaspan Bill Back Before Committee

By United Press

HARRISBURG, April 14 — The Jaspan parole board ripper was back in the Senate judiciary general committee today — apparently for good—as a study was started on the compromise measure of Rep. Adrian H. Jones, R., Luzerne.

Jones' proposal, backed by the administration, reduces the board's membership from five to three and abolishes civil service protection for its employes.

MANAGER IS NAMED FOR BEAVER POOL

Harold Leffler, High School Coach, Elected By Council To Supervise Borough Pool; Prices Fixed For Season Tickets; New Police Sergeant Elected; Victory Garden Ordinance Asked

Harold C. Leffler, Beaver high school athletic coach, was named manager of the Beaver municipal swimming pool for the coming season by the park committee at the monthly meeting of Beaver Council Tuesday evening.

Leffler, who has had several years experience as pool manager and playground supervisor, will succeed Lyle Mayne, who was in charge of the pool the last two summers. Mayne advised council a month ago that he had accepted a call as pastor of a church in New England and would not return to Beaver this summer.

The price of season tickets for the swimming pool were fixed as follows:

For children under high school age, $2.50, plus tax; for high school students from Freshmen to Seniors, inclusive, $3, plus tax; and for adults over high school age, $5.50, plus tax.

NEW POLICE SERGEANT

Council accepted the resignation of Ralph Logan, as sergeant in the police department, and promoted Ira Hays from patrolman to sergeant. Logan will remain on the police force as a patrolman.

Theodore Wallace, chairman of the Victory Garden Committee, appeared before council and at his suggestion council adopted an ordinance designed to protect gardens from thieves. The ordinance provides a heavy fine for any persons convicted of damaging gardens. Council also promised to have several acres of the land east of the borough water works plowed as soon as possible and Mr. Wallace stated he had already received requests from 56 persons for garden plots.

The borough officers were authorized to negotiate a temporary loan not to exceed $2,000 if needed, to meet expenses until 1943 taxes become payable. The secretary's report showed a balance of $4,145.13 in the general fund and it was said that a loan might not be necessary.

TO IMPROVE STREET

Tax Collector Russell Porter reported collections totaling $619.63 during the last month. The collector reported that 97.3 percent of the 1942 real estate tax duplicate had been collected, and 78.6 per

(Continued On Page Ten)

GOP Drafts Petition On Tax Legislation

By United Press

WASHINGTON, April 14.—House Republican leaders and Republican members of the Ways and Means committee today began drafting a petition to bring pay-as-you-go tax legislation to the House floor.

House Republican Leader Joseph W. Martin, Jr., of Massachusetts, who called the meeting, declined to say which pay-as-you-go plan would be the subject of the petition, but it was expected to be the bill by Rep. Aime J. Forand, D., R. I., which would put income tax payers on a current basis by forgiving 75 per cent of the 1942 liability.

Rep. Robert Ramspeck, D., Ga., Democratic whip and a compromise advocate, said he understood the Republicans planned to petition Forand's bill to the floor, and then offer the Ruml plan as a substitute.

Quick House action seemed impossible, however, because apparently House rules would preclude floor action on the Forand bill before the second week in May. In spite of that, Martin notified Republicans that all plans for an Easter recess to start this week end were off.

Canadian Army Is Ready For Strike

By United Press

ARVIDA, Que., April 14 — Three thousand Canadian soldiers stood ready for emergency duty in event a strike threat by AFL union workers at the big Aluminum Company of Canada plant materializes.

The Aluminum Workers of America, an international AFL affiliated union, threatened to walkout unless their demands for a wage increase of 10 cents an hour, a week's vacation and time and a half after 48 hours are met. The plant, engaged in war production orders, employs approximately 11,000.

It was the second time in less than two years that soldiers were sent to the plant. In 1941, the Catholic Union won its bargaining agreement after a strike in which troops were called to restore order.

MUSSOLINI'S ITALIAN NAVY DWINDLES DAY BY DAY

AXIS SHIPS in the Mediterranean are having a rough time of it at the hands of American Flying Fortresses and other Allied aircraft which are trying to prevent an evacuation from Tunisia of Field Marshal Erwin Rommel's forces. Allied surface vessels also are playing a role. The Italian submarine Asteria is pictured, top, surfacing after being depth-charged by a British destroyer. With their craft down for the last time, crew members swim to the destroyer, below. *(International Soundphotos)*

BEAVER SCHOOL PUPILS TO GIVE CONCERT ON FRIDAY

The Music Department of the Beaver schools will give its Spring Music Festival in the high school auditorium Friday evening, April 16, at eight o'clock. This program will be the sixth annual Music Festival to be given by students of the school, the first having been in 1938.

This year the program will feature the school's symphony orchestra and chorus. There will also be numbers by small instrumental groups and soloists. Another group that is expected to appeal to the younger set is the swing orchestra.

The program will be varied, including both classical and popular music and should appeal to everyone. Parents and friends of the pupils may attend. The program follows:

Symphony Orchestra — "Star Spangled Banner," "Gypsy Trail Overture," "Sleeping Beauty Waltz," "Pavanne," "Smoke Gets In Your Eyes."

Chorus -- "Come Away Sweet Love," "Four Slovak Carols," "Going A Maying," "Who Is Silvia," "Deep Purple," "The American's Creed."

Flute ensemble (Jane Williams, Lois Burton, Jane Ellen McCormick, Helen Whitelaw)—"Valse Stac-

(Continued On Page Ten)

Immediate Physical Exams For All Draft Registrants Urged

WASHINGTON, April 14. — Sen. Burton K. Wheeler, D., Mont., today proposed abolition of Selective Service's state quota system and immediate physical examination of all draft registrants "so that we'll all known exactly where we stand."

Wheeler said he would seek those and other changes in the draft system when the House-approved Kilday bill, designed to put fathers at the bottom of the draft list, comes up in the Senate.

Here are Wheeler's explanations of the "loopholes" in the Kilday

(Continued On Page Ten)

County Man To Be Deputy Adjutant General

Frank A. (Bridgie) Weber, (above) widely-known Beaver Falls Legionnaire, will be appointed by Gov. Edward Martin as deputy adjutant general in charge of veterans' affairs, THE TIMES learned today from a reliable source in Harrisburg.

Mr. Weber, a veteran of the first World War and a personal friend of Governor Martin, will take office April 26, it was reported. For several years he has been personnel director of the Babcock and Wilcox Tube Company, Beaver Falls,

(Continued On Page Ten)

State Control Of Church Scored At Presbytery Meet

In the only formal address given before Beaver Valley Presbytery at its spring meeting in Beaver Falls on Tuesday, Dr. Clarence J. Williamson, professor of Church History in Pittsburgh-Xenia Seminary, offered bitter complaint against the trend toward a state-controlled church in America. He said that in defending democracy we are drifting toward some of the wrongs of totalitarian government, and not least of these is a hampering of the church's freedom to train its own leadership.

He spoke in particular about a new Navy arrangement to take candidates for the Protestant ministry just out of high school, give them free college education, and then free seminary training. "The result will be," said Dr. Williamson, "that we shall develop a military clergy and also a civil clergy, and since the military clergy will be financially subsidized by the state, the unsubsidized home front may go without pastors!"

Dr. Williamson frankly reported that this would be unfair to the United Presbyterian denomination since it already had gone far beyond its quota in the supply of chaplains to the armed forces; and it would also mean that traditional separation of church and state was on the way out everywhere.

TO REPAIR "SHRINE"

The Presbytery meeting was an all-day gathering, held in the United Presbyterian church. It was presided over by the new Moderator, Rev. Daniel C. McCoy, Rochester, who was introduced by Rev. Hugh G. Snodgrass, Conway, retiring Moderator.

Note was taken of a need for repairs at Service church on the South Side. This is probably the greatest historical shrine in the United Presbyterian denomination,

(Continued On Page Ten)

Mrs. M. M. Reeder Dies At Freedom

Mrs. Amanda L. Reeder 62, 1415 Fifth avenue, Freedom, died in the family home this morning at two o'clock following a long illness. The body was removed to the Hartzel Funeral Home, Rochester, and later taken to her home where funeral services will be conducted Friday afternoon at 2.30 o'clock. Burial will be in Oak Grove cemetery.

Mrs. Reeder, the wife of Murray M. Reeder, was born in Freedom, and spent most of her life there. She was a member of a well known family and was widely known in the community. She was a member of the Freedom Presbyterian church.

Surviving, in addition to the husband are two daughters, Mrs. J. A. Mann, Rochester, and Mrs. William L. Huck, at home; two sisters, Miss Ada L. Jackson and Mrs. Pearl Andrews, Freedom; four grandchildren and three great - grandchildren. Paul H. Rosensteel, a grandson, Army Air Forces, Jefferson Barracks, Mo., made his home with the Reeders.

ITALY, GERMANY HEAVILY BOMBED

Today's War Summary

By United Press

AFRICA—Allied armies reach prepared Axis positions west of Enfidaville about 50 miles south of Tunis, clean out heights northeast of Kairouan and advance on northern flank as airmen destroy 145 Axis planes.

EUROPE—British bombers resume offensive against continent, bombing Spezia naval base in Italy and targets in northwest Germany with a loss of three planes as Allied forces from Africa pound Sicilian bases.

RUSSIA—Red Army repulses German attacks below Leningrad and southeast of Kharkov and strikes across river on Smolensk front to capture fortified positions.

AUSTRALIA—General MacArthur warns that Japanese control sea lanes in western Pacific and Allied airmen must carry burden of stopping any reinforced Japanese onslaught, freely predicted in many quarters.

The crushing weight of an American-British-Russian air offensive pressed against Axis Europe from all sides today, with the heaviest blows raining on Italy as the Tunisian campaign across the Mediterranean narrows moved toward a climax.

Allied planes were striking from Britain, from northwest Africa, from the Middle East and from Russia in a concentric assault on Germany and Italy and their occupied territory.

Home - based British bombers smashed in strong force at the Italian base of Spezia. Flying Fortresses swarmed up from northwest Africa to pound Sicilian air bases. Raiders from the Middle East hit Palermo and Messina, the key Axis strong points in Sicily.

Allied armies advanced in all the key sectors of Tunisia, drawing the noose on the German and Italian troops pocketed in the Bizerte and Tunis area, where the crucial battle shaped up rapidly.

REDS BOMB KOENIGSBURG

The Red air force, joining the air offensive against Germany for the first time in months, raided the East Prussian capital of Koenigsberg Monday night for the second time in three nights.

The British Eighth and First Armies were moving up to Marshal Erwin Rommel's mountain line some 50 miles south of Tunis, where he showed signs of making his first stand since he was thrown out of Wadi Akarit, far down the coast.

French troops completed the occupation of a strategic range of heights east and northeast of Kairouan and pushed on to join in the grand assault of the Allies against the Tunis-Bizerte fortress area.

The left wing of Lieut. Gen. K. A. N. Anderson's First Army chipped deeper into the hills above the Medjez-El-Bab sector, overcoming stiff Axis opposition.

Allied headquarters reported the destruction of at least 145 Axis planes in trip-hammer blows synchronized with the land operations and softening up the front and rear lines of the enemy

SICILY FIELD ATTACKED

Maj. Gen. James H. Doolittle's

(Continued On Page Ten)

County Purchases One-Fifth Of Bond Quota In Two Days

Beaver County apparently took the quota assigned to it by the Treasury Department seriously, for the actual bond purchases on Monday and Tuesday, the first two days of the current campaign amount to almost twenty per cent of the county's quota for the three-week drive.

Actual bond sales for the two days amounted to $1,118,932.25, it was disclosed at noon today by T. C. Swarts, Aliquippa, chairman of the Beaver County Victory Fund Executive Committee.

These sales were reported to Swarts by banks, building and loan associations and postoffices. It is believed the actual sales are much higher, Swarts stated today but warned against "over-confidence" in the campaign.

The county's quota is $5,871,000, to be met or topped before May 1 when the campaign is scheduled to close.

The drive to sell $381,000,000 in bonds in the Second area, comprising 23 Pennsylvania and West Virginia counties, was well underway today as 31,747 subscriptions pledged $25,757,087 in the first 48 hours of the drive. Clarence Stanley, Pittsburgh, chairman for the Second area, expressed satisfaction over initial results.

John W. McTaggert Dies In Hospital

John W. McTaggert, 74, well-known Vanport resident, died at 5:20 o'clock this morning in Rochester hospital.

Mr. McTaggert operated a truck farm for many years in Vanport on the present site of the Van-Buren Homes. He was a clerk thirty years for C. C. Denny, Vanport, and was a member of the Bridgewater Presbyterian church.

Surviving are the widow, Mrs. Josephine McTaggert; two sons, James C. McTaggert, Beaver, and John G. McTaggert, Potter Township, and two daughters, Mrs. Lawrence Hurst, Vanport, and Mrs. D. R. Craig, Washington, D. C.

The body was removed to the Anderson funeral home, Beaver, and later to the family home. Funeral services are to be held at 2:30 o'clock Friday afternoon in the home and interment will be in Beaver cemetery.

Six Attacks Made On Japs At Kiska

WASHINGTON, April 14—U. S. Army medium bombers, supported by Army and Navy fighters, have made six more attacks on Japanese-held Kiska in the Aleutians, the Navy disclosed today. A communique said that hits were scored on the runways, gun emplacements and the main camp area.

In the South Pacific, U. S. airmen struck two more blows at Munda on New Georgia Island. Fires were started by hits scored on an ammunition dump and in the camp area.

Rochester Sailor

Jack Messenger

First Class Seaman J. W. (Jack) Messenger, son of Mr. and Mrs. Harry Messenger, Rochester, is stationed with the Navy at Norfolk, Va. His engagement to Miss Dorothy Turney, Rochester, was recently announced.

Thief Makes Small Haul In Beaver Home

In a visit early last evening to the home of Mr. and Mrs. Lawrence D. Sheets, Second and Market streets, Beaver, a thief got little and missed much. Getting between five and six dollars from Mrs. Sheets' purse, the thief overlooked a large sum in bills folded in another compartment of the large purse.

Mrs. Sheets, suffering from a cold, had retired to her room early. Mr. Sheets and daughter Betty Ann, were out. The house was dark. Shortly after nine o'clock, Mrs. Sheets was aroused by a noise on the first floor. She called, thinking her daughter had come in. As she started down stairs, the back door slammed.

Remembering that she had failed to bank her money yesterday afternoon, Mrs. Sheets found, on examining her purse, that the change compartment had been emptied, but the thief had overlooked the larger sum in the secret bill fold.

Beaver Girl Joins Marines Auxiliary

Miss Annabelle Gulla, daughter of Mr. and Mrs. Alexander Gulla, Fourth street, Beaver, has been sworn into the Women's Auxiliary to the U. S. Marine Corps at Pittsburgh and is awaiting orders to report to Grover College, New York City, for training.

Miss Gulla is a graduate of Beaver high school, 1939, and has been employed in a clerical capacity at the local Curtiss-Wright plant. She is the second member of her family to enter the armed forces, as a brother, Pfc. Ted Gulla, is serving in the Army at Fort Mason, Calif.

THE DAILY TIMES
Established April 2, 1874

WESTERN ARGUS
Established November 1803
Consolidated July 1, 1930

BEAVER OFFICE
Third Street

ROCHESTER OFFICE
202 Brighton Ave., at Jackson St.

Published each evening except Sunday by THE DAILY TIMES COMPANY, INC. Entered at the Beaver postoffice as second class matter. E. L. Freeland, owner and general manager. Jack Malone, managing editor. Bill Anderson, Sports editor. Gladys Gibbons, society editor. William T. Dentzer, M. F. McBrier, advertising managers. Corporation officers, E. L. Freeland, President; Edward J. Harn, secretary-Treasurer; William T. Dentzer, vice-president.

Member Pennsylvania Publisher's Association and National Editorial Association. Served by the United Press Association and Central Press, Inc.

TELEPHONES
Beaver 1500
Rochester ... 3500

SUBSCRIPTION RATES
By mail $5.00 per year to all subscribers in Beaver County. $6.00 per year to all points outside Beaver County; 50c per month; 20c per week. By carrier 24c a week; 4c per copy at news stands. All communications should be addressed to THE DAILY TIMES, Rochester or Beaver, Pa. No attention paid to unsigned communications.

Let it be impressed upon your minds, let it be instilled into your children that the liberty of the press is the Palladium of all civic, political and religious rights of all freemen—Junius.

"Let the people know the truth and the country is safe." —Abraham Lincoln.

LEST WE FORGET
Congress shall make no law respecting an establishment of religion, or prohibiting the free exercise thereof; or abridging the freedom of speech or of the press.
—U. S. Constitution

The Great Game Of Politics

By Frank R. Kent

THE RIGHT ANSWER

Washington, April 15.

THE RECENT proposals of the CIO to the War Shipping Administration and their rejection on Friday by the WSA through Admiral Emory S. Land and his chief aide, Mr. Lewis W. Douglas, constitute a chapter of the country's wartime history which ought to be read by every American citizen. Nothing more revealing has happened here for a long time.

—o—

WHAT the CIO urged was, first, that all control over the many phases of ship operations, including the movement of cargo, be centralized in the WSA; second, that the administration and formation of policy concerning all these activities be vested in "tri-party bodies," one covering the entire WSA operation, one in each of its many departments and one in each of the many ports, foreign and domestic, touched by American shipping—each tri-party body to consist of representatives of labor, of management and of Government.

—o—

TO APPRECIATE their revolutionary character and what they would mean to the war effort is necessary, first, to understand the immediate effect of these proposals and, second, to understand from whom they come. The first effect would be to take away from the army and navy all control over the many vessels they now own. It would take out of their hands the operation of vast terminal facilities and warehouses in United States ports and foreign harbors. It would destroy the great and successful system of distributing cargo, of loading cargo and protecting cargo. It would wipe out of existence the army and navy organizations built up in the many years of operation of their fleets and which conduct extensive operations in all parts of the world.

—o—

IN BRIEF, what the CIO proposed was to wrest from the army and navy traditional control of their great fleets and substitute a system composed of a multitude of "tri-party bodies," dominated by labor and the Government. One has only to consider the cumbersome nature of such a setup and the enormous confusion which would follow to understand what would happen. In effect, it is a proposal for losing the war. In the end, it would give the CIO maritime unions control over all shipping. It would enable them to bottle up the country. It certainly would place the future of the war in the hands of the labor union leaders, raising them to a position of extraordinary power.

—o—

SO MUCH for the effect of the proposals—now as to their source. They were sponsored before the Truman Senate committee and the WSA by a group of CIO Maritime Union leaders, chief of whom was Mr. Harry Bridges. Mr. Bridges is the notorious Pacific Coast labor leader who, after years of litigation, was finally indicted as an undesirable alien, a member of the Communist party and declared not entitled to remain in this country. Held guilty by the court, he was ordered deported and has appealed the case. Yet here he is in Washington making to a Senate committee and the great War Shipping Administration proposals which literally would cripple our armed services in the midst of the greatest war in history.

—o—

IT IS also interesting to note that the Bridges communication was concurred in by Mr. Phillip Murray, head of the CIO. Mr. Murray is on intimate terms with the President and a frequent White House visitor. It is a rare day on which in some form or other Mr. Murray's press agents do not parade his patriotism or he does not laud the magnificent way in which organized labor is supporting the war effort. This, however, has not prevented him from using the war to extend the power of his union in every possible way. It did not prevent him from supporting last year the strike position of his enemy, Mr. John L. Lewis. It did not prevent him from scuttling the President's National Labor Mediation Board, of which he was a member. And it does not now prevent him from indorsing the radical and ruinous scheme advanced by the Communistic Mr. Bridges and his friends, who are quite the most dangerous as well as the smartest labor leaders we have. The truth is that this "tri-party body" idea which Mr. Bridges and his partners tried to force on the WSA is the CIO objective for industry generally. But this is the first time the demands have been made in writing—and put on the record.

—o—

THE "LABOR, management, government" combination has a fair sound, but it is wholly false. In reality it means labor control, as practical political considerations inevitably force government cooperation with labor as against management. Certainly, that has been the record in this Administration and that assuredly would have followed in our vast and vital shipping activities had the Bridges proposals gone through. Few things more disastrous to the national interests at this time can be conceived and it is greatly to the credit of the WSA that it made no effort to conciliate or compromise. In its reply, transmitted to the Truman committee, the WSA literally shot the proposal full of holes. It said "No" in a clear, strong voice. There are Government agencies which would not have done so and the clarity and force of the WSA decision were fine. However, its full benefit will be lost if the people as a whole fail to understand what these CIO radicals are really up to. Considering his position the effrontery of Mr. Bridges in making these proposals is exceeded only by their shocking character.

EDITORIAL COMMENT

"REGULATORY" ARMY NEEDS TRAINING:—If it were not tragic it would be humorous to see how all at once the powers-that-be in Washington have awakened to the fact that farming is an essential industry.

Those who are writing the regulations for farmers should have more practical knowledge of the sources of food supplies than is furnished by Washington restaurants.

Leading dairy organizations have long pointed out what was going to happen to our milk, cheese and butter supply. Maybe if a few of the white-collar boys in Washington had had to shovel manure and milk cows for three months as training for their regulatory jobs, there would be more dairy products today.

THE GULF GROWS WIDER:—The question of whether our country will be able to survive the cost of the war without financial collapse, looms larger daily. In ordinary times a two or three-hundred-billion-dollar debt would have been considered insurmountable. But when a nation has its back to the wall, it can often accomplish the impossible. We now have our backs to the wall financially. It remains to be seen whether the people value personal comfort more than they value personal liberty and the integrity of the nation.

Inflation and eventual bankruptcy can be avoided if the people have the determination to follow through on measures designed to curtail excess purchasing power and the accumulation of an unmanageable public debt. In the main, these measures are rigid price controls and rationing, cuts in non-essential government spending, taxation, and bond sales to the people. Except for rationing, we have adopted none of these measures fully as yet.

Too many people and public officials cling to peacetime illusions. They are even so foolish as to plan greater comforts in the future, assuming that they can skip the gulf of sacrifice that lies between. The gulf grows wider as they talk.

CLEARING DECKS: — The government is deploying its forces and clearing its decks for the long, hard pull. Chairman Nelson of WPB has simplified his organization structure and clearly defined lines of authority among Vice-Chairmen. The President has "drafted" Chester Davis as "food czar." WMC has created a new nine-man Labor-Management Policy Committee for greater efficiency and better representation among the three major economic groups—Industry, Labor, and Agriculture.

The WPB realignment will give Mr. Nelson more time to look after broad policy matters and work out major plans. The magnitude of the new program was made known when Mr. Nelson told the Senate Military Affairs Committee that the United States will carry 80 per cent of the United Nations production burden.

WPB changes came at a time when the agency faces a tremendous task of rescheduling of war orders to meet shifting strategic needs. This means some disruption for war material manufacturers, quick negotiation of new contracts, conversion to new types of production, and, in many instances, resumption of some civilian production on a limited scale.

It also means a vast increase in smaller prime contracts and in subcontracting as well as changing emphasis on such vital issues as manpower. Stressing this point, Secretary of the Navy Knox asked this question: "Isn't it true that the speed of production of all implements of war has exceeded expectations because manufacturers, when they got into production, found that they could produce far more rapidly than the original estimates?"

Modern Methods Of Treatment Saving Many War Casualties

By United Press

WASHINGTON, April 15—Sulfa drugs, blood plasma and facilities for rapid transport of wounded are major factors in reducing the percentage of fatalities among the casualties of this war.

This was the consensus among army medical men at the army medical center and Walter Reed General Hospital under command of Brig. Gen. Shelley U. Marietta, when they showed reporters some of the new equipment and technique used in caring for war wounded. Reports on the visit were released today.

Sulfa drugs are greatly reducing infection, and plasma is saving many who would otherwise die from shock, burns and loss of blood.

Airplanes are bringing casualties back from the front to hospitals where there are adequate facilities to care for complicated cases. One patient with a complicated abdominal wound was brought here from Egypt in 72 hours. Others have been flown from India, Cairo, Europe, Africa, Alaska, and the Far East.

The war is producing numbers of mental cases, it was said. Most are not insane, but psychoneurotics—persons who cannot stand the strain.

SALLY'S SALLIES

GUESS EVER'THING'S OKE NOW—THAT CLATTERING SOUND HAS STOPPED
4-15
Copr. 1943, King Features Syndicate, Inc., World rights reserved.

Amusements

ORIENTAL THEATRE

A breathtaking example of filmdom at its highest, "The Moon Is Down," the picturization of John Steinbeck's great novel which opened yesterday at the Oriental theatre, is a truly great motion picture.

Vivid, intensely moving and masterfully filmed, is this story of the Nazi invasion of a peaceful Norwegian town. The bitter destiny of the defeated overwhelms the people as the sudden appearance of the German troops takes them completely unaware. But freedom is a precious heritage and therein lies the story that a people's hopes, strength and spirit—everything that freedom stands for—even under the heel of the conqueror, will never be crushed.

The entire picture is a rare cinematic masterpiece. Not only has it captured the mood of the book, but the brilliance of the individual scenes has seldom, if ever been surpassed. There remains in your reviewer's mind, for instance the trial of a Norwegian patriot by a Nazi Colonel, convincingly played by Sir Cedric Hardwicke. Mayor Orden, whose screen counterpart is Henry Travers, sympathizes with the native who has killed a Nazi soldier, but is powerless to help him. As the doomed man goes to his death the mayor says:

"Go knowing that these men will never again have any rest, no rest at all, until they are gone from Norway, or dead."

BEAVER THEATRE

Ronald Colman and Greer Garson teamed for the first time, provide haunting romance and a dramatic story in "Random Harvest," screen presentation of James Hilton's best-selling novel, now showing at the Beaver theatre.

Closely following the book, except that the story is told in chronological order instead of in "flashbacks," it deals with a wealthy Englishman who loses all memory of his past during the first World War. Befriended by a young actress, he starts life anew and wins note as a writer. They marry. Then, in an accident, his memory of the past comes back, but memory of the space after the war vanishes. He assumes his old identity and becomes a powerful figure in industry. The wife, realizing that she now is a stranger to him, becomes his secretary, never mentioning their marriage, and essays the task of winning back his memory and love. How this is accomplished provides a haunting romantic climax.

GRANADA THEATRE

The laughs are on Henry Aldrich again and to judge by the audience at the Granada theatre where Paramount presented that fellow's newest comedy, "Henry Aldrich Gets Glamour" last night, the laughs seemed to come from way down whence only the best laughs hail.

In this latest and funniest in the Aldrich Family series Henry is once again utterly bewildered by the many amazing things that happen to him. Of course, they are always things beyond his control, but somehow, with the confused assistance of Dizzy, he manages to come through slightly the worse for wear — but he does come through.

The cast of "Henry Aldrich Gets Glamour" includes Jimmy Lydon, Charles Smith, John Litel, Olive Blakeney, Diana Lynn, Frances Gifford and Vaughan Glaser, the latter once more the inimitable Professor Bradley.

RIALTO THEATRE

The "unquenchable flame" of Norway's resistence to its Nazi conquerors is the theme of the stirring picture "The Moon Is Down," taken from the outstanding novel by John Steinbeck, which is currently featured at the Rialto in Beaver Falls through Friday.

Producer Nunnally Johnson, who wrote the screen play, went to great effort to film a realistic story and one of the most heartening pictures of the war. The film, as did the book, brings home to Americans the fact that a great and courageous people are keeping up the fight against oppression ... and, they are on our side.

In this memorable picture, which strikes a new note in the list of films concerning the present conflict, Sir Cedric Hardwicke plays the part of ruthless Nazi Col. Lanser; Henry Travers, is seen as the peaceful but heroic Mayor of the invaded village; Lee J. Cobb, as Dr. Winter, confidant of the mayor; Dorris Bowden, as wistful Molly Morden, widowed by a Nazi firing squad and Margaret Wycherly as the confused but trusting wife of the Mayor.

Added to the program are a group of outstanding short subjects including a presentation by the popular series This Is America entitled "Boom Town D. C."; an amusing cartoon, "Dumb Hounded"; adventures of a cameraman, "Climbing the Peaks" and the latest in News.

Opening Saturday, Samuel Goldwyn's outstanding production, Gary Cooper in "The Pride of The Yankees" (The life of Lou Gehrig). The stellar cast includes Teresa Wright, Babe Ruth and Walter Brennan with Ray Noble and his Orchestra. It's the story of a great public hero ... loved by everyone!

MAJESTIC THEATRE

Fun, music and mystery are the entertainment factors emphasized in the lavish recommendation which heralds the opening of "Behind the 8-Ball," coming Friday to the Majestic theatre. The talent roster includes the Ritz Brothers, Carol Bruce, Dick Foran and Grace McDonald.

In addition to these outstanding performers, Johnny Downs, William Demarest and Sonny Dunham and his Orchestra are said to occupy conspicuous spots in the picture's cleverly concocted story.

Dancing and music figure prominently in the film's action which deals with the staging of a summer theatre musical show despite the mysterious murdering of the production's guest stars. Miss Bruce and Foran appear as the producers of the show and the Ritz Brothers are seen as themselves, ribald entertainers who unwittingly substitute for the departed guest stars.

True to tradition, the show must go on and the manner in which it does is declared to be unusually comical.

The added feature for Friday and Saturday, "Texas To Bataan," stars The Range Busters.

THE WAY OF RIGHTEOUSNESS

DAILY LENTEN DEVOTIONS

Sponsored by the
Rochester Ministerial Association

By Rev. William A. Binkley, Pastor of the First Baptist Church

Romans 14:7—"For none of us liveth to himself, and no man dieth to himself."

In these days our faces turn toward Calvary. We are constrained to contemplate the miracle of the triumph of Jesus. An old question is raised anew, "What have we to do with Him?" Paul gives Christianity's classic answer: "For none of us liveth to himself, and no man dieth to himself. For whether we live, we live unto the Lord; and whether we die, we die unto the Lord; whether we live therefore, or die, we are the Lord's" (Romans 14: 7, 8).

What have we to do with Him? We live for Him! We die for Him! We belong to Him! No smallest fragment of our life is unrelated to Him. Death is swallowed up in victory—His victory. It is Christ always and everywhere. In the words attributed to St. Patrick:

"Christ with me, Christ before me, Christ behind me,
Christ in me, Christ beneath me, Christ above me,
Christ on my right, Christ on my left,
Christ when I lie down, Christ when I sit down, Christ when I arise,
Christ in the heart of every man who thinks of me,
Christ in the mouth of every one who speaks of me,
Christ in every ear that hears me, Christ in every eye that sees me."

Turn us, O Lord, from self to Thee. Reign Thou Supreme in our hearts now and evermore. Amen.

PRIVATE BUCK .·. By Clyde Lewis

GUARD HOUSE
FORT DEVENS
CLYDE LEWIS
4-15

"After this, don't try to tip the Major when he gives you a two-day pass!"

Help Wanted—Male

WANTED: Man to do carpenter work on interior of house. Phone Roch. 3393-J. 4/16-22 inc

WANTED: Truck driver. Apply Rubino Produce, near Curtiss-Wright, Beaver. 4|16-22 inc

WANTED: Man to work on truck, one with driver's license preferred. Harry E. Goll, 940 Third St., Beaver. Phone 1864. 4|16-22 inc

MAN FOR STOREKEEPER
Apply in person
Pittsburgh Bridge & Iron Works
North Rochester
4|15-16

WANTED: Man to prune apple trees. Will pay 80c per hour or let job by contract. Call Rochester 3090. 4|15-17 inc.

WANTED: Four men. Our wartime job is to render essential heating service. We need men to call on homes and take the orders. Good pay. Finest kind of preparation for learning the heating business. Tremendous post war opportunity. Do not apply if already engaged in defense work. The Holland Furnace Company, 347 Merchant St., Ambridge. 4|13-16 inc.

WANTED!
COACH OPERATORS
Apply at
Junction Park Office
Beaver Valley Motor Coach Company
3|30-tf

Men Wanted For Defense Plant
Apply Crucible Steel Co. of America, Employment Office, Seventh St., Midland, Pa.
Week-days 8:30 a. m. to 5:00 p. m.; Saturdays—8:30 a. m. to 12 noon. Open Monday, Wednesday and Friday evenings 6 to 9 P. M.
Applications from those now employed in War Industries will not be considered.
11|16 *

Help Wanted—Female

WANTED: Bookkeeper, to handle accounts and take telephone orders. Apply Rubino Produce, near Curtiss-Wright, Beaver. 4|16-22 inc

WANTED: Experienced woman to do cooking and general housework. No washing. Good wages. Phine Beaver 1346 or call at 494 Bank St., Beaver. 4|16-17

WANTED: Girl to take care of two children for mother who is employed. State wages expected in letter to P. O. Box 35, West Bridgewater, Pa. 4|16-22 inc.

WANTED: Experienced woman driver between 25 and 40, for well-established coffee route, salary $25, plus commission. Phone Beaver 1054-J., ask for Mrs. Ferguson. 4|16-19 inc

WANTED: Saleslady and seamstress for steady work. Apply Union Clothing Co., Brighton Ave., Rochester. 4|14-20 inc.

WANTED: Girl or woman. Family of two adults. Saturday afternoons and Sundays off. Stay at night optional—room with bath. Call Beaver 1061-R. 4|16-17

WANTED: Middle-aged housekeeper for working couple, housecleaning finished; good wages, modern home. Saturday afternoons and Sundays off. Call after 6:30 P. M., Beaver 1693-W. 4|14-20 inc.

WANTED: Two waitresses for day light work. Good wages. Apply Tip Top Restaurant, 157 Brighton Ave., Rochester. 4|14-20 inc.

WANTED: Waitress. Only experienced need apply. Beaver Lunch, 518 Third street, Beaver. 4|13-19 inc.

WANTED: White or colored girl for general housework (stay nights optional). Apply Mrs. T. W. McCreary, 130 Virginia Avenue, Monaca. Rochester 2529. 4|13-19 inc.

LADIES: Let us renew your garments, coats, suits, dresses, etc., drapes. Miller's Cleaning Shoppe, next to city building, Beaver. Phone 2235-J. 4|9*

WANTED: Middle-aged white woman to look after aged lady and do housework. Stay nights. Call Beaver 1383-M. 4|12-17 inc

WANTED: Experienced maid for general housework. Phone Mrs S. H. Peirsol, Rochester 212 4|12-17 inc

WANTED: Girl to do ironing, steady employment. Apply at 142 Madison street, Rochester Phone Rochester 1130. 4|12-17 inc

WANTED: Woman to care for 2 small children of employed couple. Good salary. Room if desired. Call Beaver 3266-W. 4|12-17 inc.

Help Wanted—Female

WANTED: Waitress and dishwasher. Inquire Excellent Restaurant, 153 Brighton Ave., Rochester. 4|14-20 inc.

WANTED: Housekeeper for family of five. Stay nights. Call Rochester 422-R. 4|13-19 inc.

WANTED: Middle-aged woman as housekeeper, to take complete charge. Permanent home. Call Beaver 2727-W. 4|13-19 inc.

Wanted

WANTED: To plow ground for gardens, large or small plots, tractor or team, price reasonable. Call Rochester 6133-J-1. 4|16-22 inc

Mother with child (aged 3) desires room and board in private home in Freedom, Rochester or Beaver. Phone Beaver 3108-M. 4|13-19 inc.

WANTED: All kinds of sewing and remodeling in private home by experienced seamstress. All work guaranteed. Inquire 405 Wahl St., Monaca. Phone Rochester 3048-J. 4|5-17 inc.

MOVING: INCLUDING PIANOS AND REFRIGERATORS. ROCHESTER 3389. "TOSH." 4|10-16 inc

HAULING: Ashes or anything. Also top soil delivered anywhere. Phone Rochester 2370-W. 3|30-4|26 inc.

WANTED: Let us clean and press your suit or topcoat at Beaver's only dry cleaning plant. Miller's Cleaning Shoppe, next to city building, Beaver. Phone 2235-J. 4|9*

FACTORY-TO-YOU
Re-Upholstering
Have your living room suite recovered or repaired by our factory expert method. Our quality workmanship is known everywhere.
KANE CHAIR MFG. CO.
Old Opera House. Rochester, Pa. Phone Roch. 3810-J
11|18*

Wanted—To Rent

WANTED: To rent, by May 1st, 4 or 5-room furnished apartment or house. Three adults. Best of references. Phone Beaver 1254-M. 4|16-22 inc

WANTED: To rent modern first floor private apartment or furnished house by couple. Phone Rochester 4248. 4|15-21 inc.

WANTED: To rent garage in vicinity of College Avenue, Beaver. Phone Beaver 2164-W between 1 and 3 p. m. 4|15-17 inc.

WANTED TO RENT OR BUY: 5 or 6 room house, preferably just outside of Beaver. Small down payment with monthly terms. Write Box "3" care DAILY TIMES, Rochester. 4|14-20 inc.

WANTED: To rent a two or three room apartment, furnished or unfurnished, preferably in Monaca. Phone Rochester 3387-J. 4|14-20 inc.

WANTED: To rent 2-room furnished apartment with bath, by couple with 2 children. Rent for 7-month period—monthly rental no object. Write "A 21" care DAILY TIMES, Beaver. 4|14-20 inc.

WANTED TO RENT: Two rooms with twin beds in private home for four gentlemen, either upper or lower Valley. Write Box 44, c/o DAILY TIMES, Rochester. 4|12-17 inc

Wanted—To Buy

WANTED: Kitchen cabinets, china cabinets, kitchen cupboards, breakfast sets, table top gas ranges, bed room suites, dressers, chiffoniers, chifforobes, wardrobes, chests, book cases, child's cribs, radios, high chairs, sewing machines, electric sweepers, washers, Frigidaires, coal cook stoves, coal heaters, three-burner gas kitchenette stoves, hot plates, electric motors, kitchen sinks, lavatories, bath tubs, comodes, tools, glassware, antiques. Keck Furniture Exchange, Monaca. Phone Rochester 3426-J. 3|19-24-29-4|2*

WANTED: To buy a used electric sewing machine, in good condition, price must be reasonable. Phone Beaver 2533. 4|16-22 inc

WANTED: To buy pressure cooker in good condition. Phone Rochester 3746-J. 4|16-17

WANTED: To buy electric refrigerator in good condition and reasonable. Phone New Brighton 965-R. 4|15-16

WANTED TO BUY: Used washer, must be in reasonable condition. Will pay cash. Call Rochester 3926-R. 4|14-20 inc.

WANTED: To buy outboard motor 9 to 12 hp. Inquire Elvidge Service Station, Monaca, or phone Rochester 607. 4|14-20 inc.

WANTED USED CARS
Late Models—'39- 0-'41
CHRISTY MOTOR CO.
469 Market St. Beaver
4|13-19 inc.

WANTED: To buy used trumpet or cornet, good condition, reasonable. Phone Rochester 3742-M. 4|13-19 inc.

WANTED: To buy a work horse, 1600 to 1700 pounds. Will pay cash. Joe Milkov, Tuscarawas Road, Beaver. 4|10-16 inc

WANTED: Wire clothes hangers; must be clean, not bent, tied in bundles. Will pay 1c each. Bring to Miller's Cleaning Shoppe, next to City Bldg., Beaver. 4|9*

Wanted—Salesmen

Salesmen for retail bread routes. Work five days week. Salary and commission. Apply in person. Home Science Bakery, 260 East End Ave., Beaver. 4|15-21 inc

Wanted—Situations

Boy, 17, with permit, wants work after school and Saturday. New Brighton 4611-M. 4|15-21 inc

For Sale

FOR SALE: 3-pc. walnut bedroom suite, $35; 6-pc. walnut bedroom suite, $55; 3-pc. living room suite, $10; 3-pc. living room suite, $25; heavy maple dinette set, $38.50; mahogany buffet, $12; small oak buffet, $9; walnut china cabinet and buffet, $18; sewing machine, $8; oil range, $10; new utility cupboards, $11; mattresses, $8.95; unfinished chairs, $1.50 each; 9x12 Congoleum rugs including Gold Seal, $6.75 to $7.75; yd. goods. 40c sq. yd.; inlaid, $1 sq. yd; grocer computing scale, $10; cash register, $5; typewriter, $8; new 10 ft. stepladders, $4.95. Keck's Furniture Exchange, Monaca, phone Roch. 3426-J, open evenings. 4|16

FOR SALE AT ONCE: Fry's cut glass, stem ware, oven ware, etc. One Orthophonic radio, one antique walnut dresser with marble top, one steel cot, one electric clock, two gas heating stoves, antique glassware and dishes. Martin Koehler, Virginia Ave. Ext., Rochester, across from Triangle Service Station. 4|15-17 inc

Trade your old washer on a rebuilt one. Just several left. Wringer rolls and gears. Harper's, 386 Brighton Ave., Rochester. Phone 9099. 4|16-17

FOR SALE: Air heat furnace. Will sell cheap. Phone Rochester 3257. 4|16-17

FOR SALE: Hamilton-Beach food mixer, radio, bed, dressers, tables, chairs, sectional book-case, books, desks, cabinets, pedestals, 9x13 rug, child's sled, wagon and blackboard; dishes, jars, crocks, I.E.S. lamp, garden implements and seed, tools, ladder, tubs, tub stand with hand wringer, gas stove, Aladdin oil lamp. Paul Shoop, ½ mile from Freedom on Harvey Run Road. 4|15-21 inc

WALLPAPER: Just received a large shipment of 10c wallpapers, suitable for every room. Also beautiful selection of Asam, Imperial and Peerless. George C. Gremer, Wallpaper - Gifts, 236 Adams street, Rochester. 4|12-17 inc.

FOR SALE: Lady's 2-piece navy blue wool suit, size 38, in good condition. Price reasonable. Call Beaver 589-M. 4|15-16

FOR SALE: Ladies' black seal coat, size 16, price $6. Inquire 1320 Atlantic Ave., Monaca, or phone Rochester 2097. 4|15-17 inc

FOR SALE: 1 brass bed, dresser, library table, 6-ft. porch swing, 2 opaline table tops with bases, kitchen cabinet, 3 kitchen chairs, 4-inch pipe vise, 8x10 ft. rug, 1 leather rocker. 369 New York Ave., Rochester, or call Roch. 58-J after 7 P. M. 4|15-21 inc.

FOR SALE: Girl's 24-inch bicycle, fully equipped; perfect condition. Used only a short time. Inquire 1118 Fifth Street, Beaver. 4|15-16

FOR SALE: One single metal bed, one dresser, music cabinet and rocking chair. Phone Beaver 3470. 4|15-16

FOR SALE: Quick Meal gas range, practically new, price $20.00. Inquire 823 Third avenue, Freedom. Phone Rochester 9115. 4|14-20 inc.

Hoover Premier and other popular sweeper parts & repairs. Rebuilding of all makes a specialty. We buy old sweepers. Harper's, 386 Brighton Ave., Rochester. Phone 9099. 4|14-20 inc.

FOR SALE: Daybed, round oak dining table, Steinite cabinet radio, gilt framed full-length mirror, double bed, curtain stretchers, radiant gas stove, single bed complete. Phone Rochester 6129-R-21. 4|14-20 inc.

FOR SALE: Enough rough lumber to build small 4-room house. 12 windows, 2 doors. 320 Maine Ave., West Aliquippa. 4|14-20 inc.

FOR SALE: Geese eggs for hatching. Also sweet corn seed and field corn seed. Also Burpee's dahlia roots. Matt Slavic, Sunflower Road, New Brighton, Route 68. 4|10-16 inc

FOR SALE: 4-piece maple bedroom suite and rug, one Zenith portable radio, one Mossberg 22 rifle and case. Phone Rochester 921-M. 4|12-17 inc

Home-grown Russet seed potatoes, No. 1 and No. 2; also a few Maine certified Russet seed potatoes. Bring containers. Fraser's Market, Sunflower Road. 4|12-17 inc

If you want the latest hit records, in
VICTOR, COLUMBIA, DECCA, and CAPITOL
Visit our record department. Also a full line of the finest Albums
GORDON'S CUT RATE
906 Penna. Ave., Monaca, Penna.
4|12-17 inc.

FOR SALE: Must sacrifice new maple bedroom suite (twin beds). Any reasonable offer considered. Inquire 1595 Corporation street, Beaver, after 1 p. m. 4|10-16 inc

SIMON'S Wallpaper and Paint Store. Great reductions on all wallpaper, paints and floor coverings. Shop and save. 919 7th Ave., Beaver Falls, Pa. 3|1-5|31 inc.

For Sale

BIG WALLPAPER SALE—½ off thousands rolls. We specialize in wallpaper. Come where you get factory dealer prices. Quality at low cost. 5c to $2.00 roll. We carry the largest stock in Valley. New designs. Wm. Helmick, 390 Brighton Ave., Rochester. (The Big Store). 4|16-29 inc

FOR SALE: 12 cu. ft. Frigidaire, A-1 shape. Phone Beaver 9000. 4|16-17

FOR SALE: Large level lots, 60 ft. frontage on Sylvan Crest, Monaca, $175 up, $15 down payment, $5 per month. Inquire H. F. Morgan or phone Rochester 756-M. 4|12*

112 RATS killed with box Schuttes Rat Killer — Money back guarantee. Harmless to all animals, poultry and humans. Purchased at all Hardware and Feed Stores. 3|25-4|21 inc.

FOR SALE: 3-piece living room suite with tailored slip covers Can be seen evenings, 7 to 9, 224 Jefferson street, Rochester. 4|10-16 inc

For Sale—Houses

FOR SALE
SUBURBAN BUNGALOW
5 rooms and bath on first floor, 1 room on second floor, furnace, city and cistern water, storm doors and windows, Venetian blinds. 2-car garage, double lot, well shrubbed. Near school.
BOVARD-ANDERSON COMPANY
Rental Insurance
Real Estate
617 Third Street Beaver 1121
4|10-14-16

FOR SALE: 6-room brick and shingle house, living room type, bath, furnace, garage, about ¾ acre, less than one mile from Rochester, $4,700; 13-room brick, near Brighton Ave., suitable for rooms or duplex; good six-room house in Baden, bath, new furnace, garage, chicken house, lot 50x120, $4,750. WANTED: Small farm with 6-room house within 5 or 6 miles from Rochester. George C. Gremer, Real Estate & Insurance, 236 Adams St., Rochester. 4|16-22 inc

Six room frame house in Beaver, has bath, furnace, large level lot and garden space. Price $3800. Possession in 30 days. A. Stammelbach, Realtor, 413 Third St., Beaver. 4|16

Owner must leave town. See this unusual value: Well-built home, 7 rooms, finished attic, brick basement. Excellent location. Interior recently redecorated. New furnace, thermostat control, with cool air for summer. Large garden plot. Cistern piped through house. A real sacrifice. 138 College Ave., Beaver. 4|16

FOR SALE: 6-room frame house. All modern conveniences and ½-acre ground, 4 miles from rubber plant. 1549 Marshall Road, Monaca. John Evankovach. 4|15-21 inc.

FOR SALE: Six room brick house, State street, Vanport. Price $2500. Phone Beaver 1053-J. 4|15-21 inc.

DUPLEX
With three rooms & bath on first and second floors. One available May 1st. Level lot with double garage. Wide paved street facing park. Income of $80 per month. $6500.
JAMES S. STROUSS
458 3 St., Phone 815 Beaver
4|14-20 inc.

FOR SALE: 8-room house, centrally located in Rochester. Large level lot, garage. Phone 402-R, Roch. 4|13-19 inc.

FOR SALE: In good location down town, Rochester, 7-room frame house with large porch on first floor. Sleeping porch on second floor. All conveniences. Easily duplexed. Large level lot, cistern, three garages. Phone Rochester 96. 4|12-17 inc

FOR SALE: 7 room house, hot air furnace, garage, 7 lots. Inquire at 1855 Fifth avenue, Freedom, Pa. 3|20-4|23 inc.

Frame duplex, upstairs rental carries property. Modern equipped throughout, two baths. Fine location College Hill. Must settle estate. Can easily convert into four apartments. Real bargain. Write Box "T-33" c/o DAILY TIMES, Beaver. 4|12-17 inc

FOR SALE: Six-room frame house, bath, modern kitchen, all conveniences. Nice lot, garage. Located Marion Hill, New Brighton. $5200. Immediate possession. Phone New Brighton 4375-W. 4|12-17 inc

HOMES FOR SALE
Beautiful Suburban Home. 2 miles from Monaca. Five large rooms and bath. Unfinished 2nd floor. Built 1942. 2½ acres of land. $6800.00. For appointment, call or see
WM. J. MILLER
907 Penna Avenue, Monaca, Pa.
Phone Rochester 1610
4|12-17 inc.

FOR SALE: 7-room house, good condition, near high school — $5,000; 7-room house, bath, furnace, large lot, 2-car garage, centrally located — $2,500; 6-room house, bath, furnace, garage, corner lot — $3,000; 6-room house, bath, furnace, garage, corner lot — $2,850; 6-room house, bath, furnace, garage, near College and Third St., Beaver — $3,500. Terms all ¼ down. George C. Gremer, Real Estate and Insurance, 236 Adams St., Rochester. 4|12-17 inc.

For Sale—Real Estate

Investment Property, mercantile and apartment bldgs, well rented. Will show a 25% investment — terms. Bovard-Anderson Company, Beaver 1121. 4|15-17 inc.

For Sale—Coal

BUY COAL Now and Save. Call Beaver 386-J. Clinton Coal by Truck Load. 4|14-20 inc.

For Sale—Used Cars

FOR SALE: 1942 Pontiac "8" Two-Door Sedan; driven only 10,000 miles, fully equipped. Car like new. Price $975.00. Phone Beaver 1062-J. 4|15-21 inc.

CHEAP TRANSPORTATION: 1939 Harley Davidson 74 motorcycle and side car, motor overhauled, $400. 1934 Dodge Pick-up truck, 1936 Chevrolet Pick-up, 1937 Chrysler Eight sedan, Three 1937 Chevrolet Coaches. Also new 22 Springfield repeating rifle and cartridges. Inquire Eugene Cox, New York avenue, near Fry Glass Bridge, Rochester. Phone 3994-W. 4|14-20 inc.

GOOD USED CARS
1941 Pontiac 2-dr. radio, heater
1940 Pontiac 2-dr.
1941 Chevrolet 5-pass. coupe. radio, heater
1941 Nash "600" sedan, radio, air conditioned.
1940 Dodge sedan, radio, heater
1941 Chevrolet 3-pass. coupe
1937 Chevrolet sedan
1936 Chevrolet sedan
1936 Plymouth sedan
1936 Dodge sedan
Christy Motor Co.
469 Market street, Beaver
Phone 1456
4|13-19 inc.

ONLY A FEW NEW PONTIACS LEFT
Our Used Cars will all be gone shortly, according to last week's sales. Act now if you want a good car for the duration.
A. R. C. H. SNYDER
CONWAY
4|13 *

For Sale—Farms

FOR SALE: Small farm, with 21 acres, two houses, close to town. Orchard. Spring water, electricity. Inquire 823 Third avenue, Freedom, or phone Rochester 9115. 4|14-20 inc.

FOR SALE: 100-A. farm, seven room house, large barn, ½ mi. from hard road, near Unionville on route 68. H. H. Teets, Rochester, Pa. Telephone 468-J-1 Zelienople R. D. 1. 4|13-19 inc.

FOR SALE: Farm of 32 acres, 2½ miles from Monaca, 5 miles from Aliquippa, on hard road. Call E. J. Cochran, Rochester 6161-J-2. 4|13-5|17 inc.

For Sale—Lots

FOR SALE: One 2-grave lot in Sylvania Hills Memorial Park near Chimes Tower. Inquire 713 Penna. Ave., Monaca. Tues.-Fri. *

LOTS: Rochester Township, fine garden polts — $150. and up. Terms. Bovard-Anderson Company, Beaver 1121. 4|15-21 inc.

FOR SALE: Lot 37½'x100 in Denton Plan, Rochester. Reasonable. Phone Rochester 618-W. 4|12-17 inc

For Sale—Poultry

FOR SALE: 2 pair Golden pheasants, 12 light brown bantams, 4 cockerels and 8 pullets, reasonable. Inquire Samuel Hahn, 520 Bryan Ave., Rochester. 4|14-20 inc.

For Sale—Dogs

FOR SALE: Red Spaniel pup (male) good breed, one-year-old; will sell for $25 War Bond. Inquire 950 Fourteenth St., Monaca. Phone Rochester 3247-R. 4|15-21 inc

For Rent—Rooms

FOR RENT: Attractive double sleeping room, gentlemen preferred, on bus line. Inquire 1036 Allaire Ave., Colona Heights, Monaca. 4|16-17

FOR RENT: Sleeping room for two gentlemen (twin beds) handy bus line, no other roomers. Phone Rochester 2188. 4|16

FOR RENT: Two furnished light housekeeping rooms with twin beds. Modern conveniences. Inquire 437 Ninth St., Monaca, or phone Rochester 375-R. 4|16-22 inc

FOR RENT: 3-room furnished apartment with private bath and entrance. Adults only. 415 Eighth St., Monaca. 4|16-22 inc

FOR RENT: Two-room furnished apartment; also one large light-housekeeping room and sleeping room. Clyde House Hotel, 1328 Fifth Ave., New Brighton. Phone 3042 or 9888. 4|16-22 inc

FOR RENT: Sleeping room, 416 Ninth St., Monaca. 4|15-21 inc.

FOR RENT: Large front sleeping room for 2 gentlemen. Near Curtiss-Wright plant. 434 Dravo Ave., Beaver. Phone Beaver 1161-W. 4|15 *

For Rent—Apartments

FOR RENT: May 1st, desirable unfurnished 4-room apartment. Convenient location in Beaver. Third floor. Adults only. Call Beaver 2074. 4|16-22 inc

OHIOVIEW
Two & Three Rm. Apts. with private bath. Inc. heat & water. $32-$40. Adults only.
JAMES S. STROUSS
458 3 St., Phone 815 Beaver
4|14-20 inc.

FOR RENT: Three room unfurnished apartment; all utilities furnished. Phone Beaver 2592-R. 4|13-19 inc.

Miscellaneous

WEEK END SPECIAL — Limited amount fancy Delicious and Stayman apples, subject to prior sale. Also wanted, farm hand, steady or intermittent periods; tools, wood or metal working, farm equipment, livestock and implements. State price and description in letter to George H. McGinness, Construction Assembly & Repair Service, Darlington, Pa. 4|10-16 inc

LEGAL ADVERTISEMENTS

LEGAL NOTICE

The Board of School Directors of the School District of the Borough of Aliquippa requests sealed proposals as follows for the school year 1943-1944.

1. Incandescent Lamps, Fluorescent Tubes and Starters
2. Printed Forms
3. Medical Supplies
4. Science Supplies
5. Shop Supplies

Complete information and bid forms may be secured from A. D. Dungan, Assistant Superintendent, Aliquippa High School, Aliquippa, Pennsylvania.

All proposals must be enclosed in an envelope, sealed and plainly marked "Proposal" and delivered to Louis A. Smith, Secretary, General Office, Aliquippa High School, Aliquippa, Pennsylvania, before 4:00 P. M. Eastern War Time, April 19, 1943.

BY ORDER OF THE BOARD
G. Rees Carroll, President.
ATTEST:
Louis A. Smith, Secretary.
4|2-9-16

ADMINISTRATOR'S NOTICE

Estate of JAMES C. BOYD, deceased, late of Hanover Township, Beaver County, Pennsylvania, letters of Administration upon the above estate having been granted to the undersigned, notice is hereby given to those indebted thereto to make immediate payment, and to those having claims or demands to present them for settlement.

HARVEY C. BOYD,
Administrator,
R. D. No. 1, Hookstown, Pa.
Reed and Ewing, Esqs.,
Attorneys,
Beaver, Penna.
3|26-4|2-9-16-23-30

BOROUGH OF ALIQUIPPA OFFICIAL

Sealed proposals will be received by the Borough of Aliquippa for furnishing and delivering approximately 35,000 gallons of gasoline and approximately 1,000 gallons of oil; also greases for the Borough motor equipment.

All proposals must be in the hands of the Borough Secretary on or before 5:00 P. M. Eastern War Time, Monday, May 3rd, 1943. The right is reserved to reject any or all bids.

JOHN J. TODORA,
President of Council.
E. W. Devitt, Secretary.
4|9-16-23

BOROUGH OF ALIQUIPPA OFFICIAL

Sealed proposals for furnishing F.O.B. cars, Aliquippa, Pennsylvania, approximately 500 tons of crushed slag or crushed limestone in sizes as specified on date of order. All proposals are to be in the hands of the Borough Secretary on or before 5:00 P. M. Eastern War Time, Monday, May 3rd, 1943. The right is reserved to reject any or all proposals.

JOHN J. TODORA,
President of Council.
E. W. Devitt, Secretary.
4|9-16-23

Miscellaneous

Patterson Township Firemen Penny Carnival Every Friday Night. New System—Cards 50c, or 3 for $1.00. No award less than $3.00. Door Award. Play starts 8:30. 3|2*

Carnival every Thursday Night 8:30 sharp. Cards 50c or 3 for $1.00. Special games and special double awards. Protected parking. Pulaski Township, Marion Hill Firemen. 10|5*

INDOOR CARNIVAL
New Legion Home
Adams St., Rochester
TUES. & FRI. NITES
8:30 P. M.
33 games 50c—Prizes $2, $3, $5, $10 In Merchandise

Repairs—Service

TYPEWRITERS cleaned, repaired, sold and rented. All kinds in any condition bought for cash. David H. Miser, 252 East End Ave., Beaver. Phone Beaver 1426-M. 4|15-21 inc

TO PROPERTY OWNERS: Clogged sewers opened without digging with Ideal Electric Sewer opener. Phone Roch. 931-W or Roch. 1578-W. Hayhue Brothers. 11|4-E.O.W.*

GENUINE HOOVER SWEEPER Service and Parts. Sahli Motor Company. Phone Beaver Falls 1440. 4|7-20 inc

If your MAYTAG washer or ironer needs attention, call The Maytag Store, New Brighton 2484. John W. Young, proprietor. 1|2*

CLASSIFIED ADVERTISING

This classified advertising department is for the convenience of the public. To insure publication the same day orders should be received by 10 a. m. Orders not received in time will be published the following day. All copy received subject to being edited or rejected by us. When sending advertisements by mail care should be used to write plainly giving complete instructions so that we may give efficient service in the preparation and publication of the advertisements. When possible, payment should accompany the order. This will be expected with orders from strangers. Cash with order, one cent a word for each publication. No advertisement published for less than 25 cents for each publication. Six consecutive publications for price of four. Extra charge will be made for use of large type. Classified advertisements not accompanied by cash will be charged at two cents per word with a minimum of 50 cents for each publication. This is absolutely necessary on account of the clerical work involved. Fifty per cent discount will be allowed on charge classified advertisements if paid for before expiration date. Usual cash rates will apply to advertisers having other running open accounts with us. The above is a local schedule applying within Beaver County.

Office Telephones
Beaver 1800 Rochester 3300

IN THE COURT OF COMMON PLEAS OF BEAVER COUNTY, PENNSYLVANIA.

MARY COMO vs. PASQUALE COMO. No. 141 June Term, 1942.

NOTICE
OF MASTER'S HEARING

To Pasquale Como, Respondent:

You are hereby notified that the undersigned has been appointed to take testimony in the above case and report the same, together with his recommendations thereon, to the Court; that he will meet for the purposes of his appointment at Court Room No. 3, Court House, Beaver, Pa., on Saturday, May 1, 1943, at 11:00 o'clock A. M. Eastern War Time, at which time and place you may appear and be heard if you so desire

GEORGE A BALDWIN,
Master.
4|9 & 16

ADMINISTRATOR'S CTA NOTICE

Estate of Carrie Schwartz, deceased, late of Rochester Borough, Beaver County, Pennsylvania, letters of Administration upon the above estate having been granted to the undersigned, notice is hereby given to those indebted thereto to make immediate payment, and to those having claims or demands to present them for settlement.

REBECCA SCHWARTZ,
Administrator, c.t.a.
435 Pinney Street,
Rochester, Penna.
Moorhead, Marshall & Sawyer,
Attorneys,
Beaver Trust Bldg.,
Beaver, Penna.
3|12-19-26-4|2-9-16

BIDS — GARBAGE COLLECTION

The Borough of Freedom Borough Council will receive bids during the next ten days, for the collection of garbage. The Borough reserves the right to reject any or all bids.

G. L. WERNER,
President of Council.
4|14-16-19

What You Buy With
WAR BONDS
Safety From Infection

If you thought your investment in Government Bonds would save the life of your own boy or your neighbor's boy you would buy every dollar's worth you could, wouldn't you. As a matter of fact your War Bonds have already saved the lives of thousands of our soldiers.

Every soldier and every marine gets a package of Sulfanilamide in his first aid kit. And this tiny package is a vital item, for it has literally saved thousands upon thousands of lives on the battle fields. The packet of sulfa pills costs 16 cents; in powder form the cost is 3¼ cents. "They give their lives—You lend your money." *U. S. Treasury Department*

Call Beaver 2564 For
PORT COAL
Fill Your Bin Now!
COURTNEY COAL CO.

ROYAL TRAINED FACTORY SERVICE for ALL OFFICE MACHINES
C. F. BROWN
Royal Typewriters—Adding Machines — Supplies
818 Federal Title & Trust Bldg.
Beaver Falls 3379

WEDDING INVITATIONS AND ANNOUNCEMENTS
INFORMALS AND CARDS
GLADYS A. GIBBONS
429 College Ave., Beaver

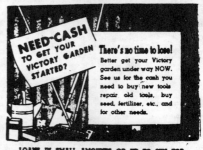

NEED CASH
TO GET YOUR
VICTORY GARDEN
STARTED?

There's no time to lose! Better get your Victory garden under way NOW. See us for the cash you need to buy new tools, repair old tools, buy seed, fertilizer, etc., and for other needs.

LOANS IN SMALL AMOUNTS OR UP TO $300 FOR ALL WORTHY PURPOSES. COME IN OR PHONE!

UNION LOAN CO.
The Old Reliable Company—35 Years in Beaver Falls
Rooms 2 & 4, 2nd Floor Benson Building
Cor. 12th St., 7th Av. Phone 2-4-4 Beaver Falls

AN ESSENTIAL WAR INDUSTRY NEEDS HELP TO "KEEP 'EM ROLLING"
FREIGHT BRAKEMEN
YARD CLERKS
TELEGRAPH OPERATORS
The Pittsburgh and Lake Erie Railroad Co.
APPLY:—
The Pittsburgh and Lake Erie Railroad Company, General Yard Master, College Station, Beaver Falls, Pa., or West Aliquippa, Pa.
(Applications from those now employed in war industries will not be considered.)

You Get
CASH plus
with a Loan from *us*
You get the cash you need, plus these advantages at 'Personal':
LOANS, $10 to $250 or more, are made promptly and without co-signers.
SPECIAL service for employed women, single or married.
BETWEEN-PAY-DAY LOANS. $30 for 2 wks. costs less than 33¢.
1-VISIT LOANS. Apply by phone. Pick up the cash by appointment.
If you need cash for any worthy purpose, come in, write or phone us today.
Personal FINANCE CO.
723 12th St. Beaver Falls
Phone 3540

LOANS
to pay taxes, insurance premiums, auto repairs, doctor and hospital bills, or to consolidate all those small accounts and furnish cash for Spring home improvements.
Rochester Thrift & Loan CORPORATION
218 Brighton Ave., Rochester
Phone 2100

CHAMPION COAL
6 in. lump and furnace
Lowest prices — Prompt delivery
PURE, CRYSTAL CLEAR 30B
SAM CUTRONA
Phone 128 or 384 Rochester

MOVING
TRANSFER and PIANO MOVING
GENERAL HAULING
MRS. S. E. WALTON
OWNER - MANAGER
BEAVER
Phone Beaver 164
500 Corporation Street

LEGAL PAPERS
NOTARIZED EFFICIENTLY
Maude F. McBrier
DAILY TIMES Office
570 - 3rd St., Beaver

Read THE TIMES Classified Ads

WEATHER
Warmer today and tonight; light rain in west portion tonight and in east tonight.

The Aliquippa Times

ALIQUIPPA, PA., FRIDAY, APRIL 23, 1943

Four Cents

Details of "The Mishalin Case," bared on sports page of today's Times. Turn to Page 6.

4 Bandits Confess; Face Court Action

Churches Mark Easter With Special Services

Ingenuity Reward

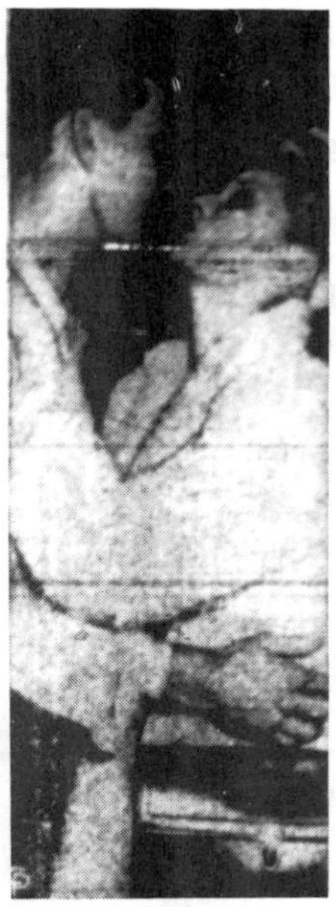

WHEN JOHN BRITTAIN contributed suggestions at the Downey, Cal., plant of Consolidated Vultee Aircraft corporation that have saved 12,000 man-hours in building planes since Pearl Harbor, he jokingly suggested that his reward be a kiss from Film Star Rita Hayworth. Rita, hearing of it, thought it might be a suitable reward at that, so she did, as pictured above. *(International)*

RATION BOARD GRANTS TIRES, TUBES TO MANY

The Aliquippa Ration Board today had granted requisitions to 31 persons and seven business houses for 105 tires, 20 tubes, seven recaps and one pair of boots.

The following business firms were awarded tires:

Jones & Laughlin Steel Corporation, nine; P. M. Moore, four truck tires and four tubes; Wilson Furniture, four truck tires; John Ondilla, three truck tires and four truck tubes; Emerson Parrish, two truck tires and two truck tubes; Nick Machuga, one truck tire and tube, and the Borough of Aliquippa, seven recaps.

Passengers awarded tubes and tires are:

Allen M. Brooks, two grade 1 tires; Joseph F. Bontempo, three grade 1 tires; William Marquard, three grade 1 tires; Michael Torbic, two grade 1 tires; Eleanor Van Bloom, four grade 2 tires; John Holobinko, two grade 2 tires; Robert Mervis, four grade 2 tires.

Charles R. Shumaker, two grade 2 tires; Mark Hilliker, two grade 2 tires; Lee McCoy, two grade 2 tires; Albert Burkhardt, three grade 3 tires; William Haubner, two grade 3 tires; Neal Maples, four grade 2 tires; J. Raymond Eberle, five grade 3 tires and five new tubes; John Dulay, two grade 3 tires; Steve Yanchik, four grade 3 tires; Nicholas Welles, two grade 3 tires; Joe Palsa, four grade 3 tires; Philip S. Stewart, three grade 3 tires and one new tube; A. L. Nairn, five grade 3 tires; Jennie Giammanco, five grade 3 tires; John Lowe, one new tube.

Edward Schlack, two grade 3 tires; Cecel L. Lynn, four grade 3 tires and two new tubes; Aloysius M. Pierce, two grade 3 tires; J. H. Harmon, two grade 3 tires; Raymond F. Thomas, one grade 3 tire. Mike Corsi was awarded a pair of boots.

Business Activity Declines In Region

Business activity in the Pittsburgh district declined last week to the lowest level since mid-January, the University of Pittsburgh bureau of business research said today.

The bureau reported that the decline affected nearly all lines of activity and the weekly index of activity dropped to 116.0 of the 1923-25 average, a decrease of 1.6 points from the previous week.

SMITH PROMOTED

An announcement from Randolph Field, Texas, today said that Robert L. Smith, of Aliquippa, was promoted and commissioned a second lieutenant.

ANNUAL EASTER SERVICES SET AT LOCAL CHURCHES

Masses, Communion, Cantatas & Music To Be Highlights

Highlighted by cantatas, Communion, Solemn High Mases and special music, Easter services will be held at all Aliquippa churches Sunday to culminate the celebration of Holy Week.

Today, Good Friday, was being appropriately marked at several of the edifices, with the Community service at the First Methodist church and masses in other churches as the outstanding observances.

As Aliquippa awaited Easter 1943, merchants reported the usual rush of the season and they expected another large turnout of patrons tomorrow.

An Easter cantata titled "The Easter Triumph," will be presented at the First Baptist church here Sunday at 11 a. m. under the direction of Wilmer Weight, choir director. The annual Easter message will be delivered by the Rev. E. C. Poole, pastor, at 8 p. m., with baptism also to feature. Other services at the church Sunday school at 9:45 a. m. and a Young People's meeting at [illegible] p. m.

The Rev. E. W. Byers, retired, will deliver the Easter sermon Sunday morning at Woodlawn Presbyterian church. Tonight there will be Communion services and a reception for new members, with the Rev. J. W. St. Clair presiding.

(Continued on Page Five)

COUNCIL CALLS BOND MEETING

Borough Secretary E. W. Devitt announced that Aliquippa council will convene in a special meeting at 8 p. m. today.

The councilmen will consider the purchase of War Bonds. Money from available sinking funds will be used for the purchase, he indicated.

Motions To Quash Indictments Seen

UNIONTOWN, Pa., April 21.—(UP)—Individual petitions on motions to quash indictments against a former state senator and five Fayette county officials probably will be placed before President Judge H. S. Dumbauld tomorrow morning.

The petitions were presented yesterday after the judge had requested that the quash motions be separated in a petition apart from the reasons cited for removal of himself as judge in the pending cases which go on trial May 10.

BICYCLE STOLEN HERE

A bicycle owned by Robert Boring, 135 Temple street, was reported stolen sometime last night. The license number of his bicycle was 769.

Police are checking on all bicycles that are traveling at night without lights.

Pastor, Tried As Spy By Japs, To Speak At VFW Banquet Here

The former head of a Shanghai China, university who was captured by the Japs and tried as a spy will speak in Aliquippa next Thursday evening.

He is Dr. Francis Cox, now pastor of the Church of The Redeemer in Pittsburgh.

He will deliver the principal address at the annual banquet of Louis Waugaman post of the V.F.W., an event scheduled to begin at 6:30 p. m. Thursday at the B.P.O.E. clubrooms.

Dr. Cox was among the group of Americans released in the exchange of prisoners by the Japs and the U. S.

Russell W. Cochran will be installed as new post commander. He succeeds John J. Serdensky.

63 German Planes Destroyed By U. S.

LONDON, April 23—(UP)—American heavy bombers destroyed 63 Germas planes in their unescorted raid on Bremen last Saturday, the Eighth United States air force announced today.

U. S. MERCHANT VESSEL SUNK

WASHINGTON, April 23. —(UP)—A medium-sized United States merchant vessel was torpedoed and sunk by an enemy submarine in the south Altantic early in March, the Navy announced today. Survivors have been landed at Miami.

Youthful Vandals Rounded Up Here

Answering numerous complaints of Temple and Oliver street residents of youngsters breaking street lights, destroying property and not listening to curfew rules, Officers Tom Diaddigo and Andrew Palochak last night rounded up a mob of boys raging from eight to 15 years of age.

The boys had been disturbing residents of Plan 12 for some time and were running over garage roofs and otherwise causing commotion.

They were taken before Chief of Police Trevor Jenkins, who advised their parents to be more considerate to the properties of others and to abide by the 9 o'clock curfew.

Rationing Board Lists New Hours

New office hours for the Aliquippa Rationing board were announced today by Dr. J. F. Campbell, chairman.

The office will open at 8:30 a. m. and close to the public at 3:30 p. m., but the office force will work until 5:45 p. m.

On Tuesday and Fridays the office will be open from 6:30 to 9 p. m. The office will be open on Saturday afternoon unless regulations are changed Dr. Campbell said.

VISIT IN ALIQUIPPA

Srgt. Technician Robert H. Reinel, with his parents, Mr. and Mrs. Frank Nichol of Carlisle, Pa., are visiting here with his aunt, Mrs. J. H. Robb 2018 Main St. He is on furlough from Camp White, Oregon.

Miss Beulah Robb Holden, with the Signal Corps at Harrisburg, accompanied Srgt. Reinel to Aliquippa to visit her mother, Mrs. Elizabeth Holden.

Lieut. St. Clair, Aliquippa, Directs WAAC Recruiting

Lieut. Myrtle L. St. Clair, daughter of Mr. and Mrs. H. C. St. Clair, Moreland St., here is officer in charge of recruiting for the WAAC at Harrisburg, having graduated from Officers Training school at Des Moines, Ia., recently, it was learned today.

Mrs. St. Clair, who was present at her daughter's graduation and "pinned on" Lt. St. Clair's bars, was accompanied to Des Moines by Mrs Theodore Yoho, Shaw St.

Another daughter of the St. Clair's, Mrs. Glenn St. Clair Leonard, is stationed at the WAAC training center, Camp Edwards, Boston Mass. Mrs. Leonard, an auxiliary in the WAACs, is on duty as a driver for officers at the camp. She operates a nine-passenger station wagon.

Lt. Myrtle, who was an instructor at the University of Miami in Florida, and her sister, Mrs. Leonard both rendered one year's service there as plane spotters prior to entry in the WAACS.

MAN, 68, DROPS DEAD IN DEPOT

Stricken with an acute heart attack, Mile Gvoich, 68, of Woodlawn Park here, dropped dead this morning at the P.&L.E. railroad station.

The man was pronounced dead by a physician summoned to the depot.

His body was removed to the C. E. Douds' Funeral home to be prepared for burial.

WAR HONOR ROLL COMMITTEE WILL CONVENE MONDAY

Aliquippa's War Honor Roll committee will meet at the U.S.O. assembly room on Franklin Ave., next Monday commencing at 8 p. m., Chairman Cliff J. Smith said today.

More than $2,000 has been donated to the fund to defray expenses of erecting the Honor Roll, he revealed. Additional contributions came in after publication of the first list of donors earlier this week.

Officials are still awaiting word from the Post Office department at Washington, D. C., concerning approval or rejection of the site selected for the Honor Roll. The local post office lawn has been picked as the site.

Germans Over 10 Disallowed Milk

LONDON, April 23—(UP)—Germans over 10 years of age are allowed no milk under the rigid rationing, but adults receive from 140 to 175 ounces of potatoes and from 12½ to 33 ounces of meat per week.

The information was contained in a written answer by Dingle Foot, parliamentary secretary to the ministry of economic warfare, to questions submitted to parliament.

Court Hands Down Opinion In Shafer Bus Lines Appeal

PHILADELPHIA, April 23.—(UP)—The Pennsylvania Supreme court handed down the following decisions yesterday:

By Justice Patterson:

Moore V. Meyer & Power Co., appt. C. P. Butler. Judgment reversed and judgment entered for appellant on the whole record.

Kennuir V. City of Pittsburgh, appt. C. P. Allegheny. Judgment affirmed.

By Justice Stearne:

In re petition of W. A. Shafer T/A etc. as Shafer Coach Lines, Appt. C. P. Allegheny. Order of the July term of court below affirmed. Order of the court at No. 2682 July term is reversed and the record is remitted to the Pennsylvania Labor Relations Board for further proceedings consistent with this opinion. Costs in both appeals to be equally divided between appellant and appellee.

11 O'Clock Curfew For Teen-Age Girls Set In Pittsburgh

PITTSBURGH, April 23.—(UP)—As part of a drive against vice conditions, the City of Pittsburgh next week will put into effect an 11 p. m. curfew prohibiting unescorted teen age girls from appearing on downtown streets.

YANKEES SEIZE LARGE ISLAND FROM JAPANESE

Strategic Range Of Hills Captured By British Troops

The War In Brief

By UNITED PRESS

Africa: British First Army advances in new offensive to capture range of hills southwest of Tunis, Eighth Army beats off counter-attacks and holds gains, and Allied air forces shoot down 38 enemy planes including 20 big German transports.

Europe: Russian planes bomb East Prussia and Royal Air Force mines enemy waters, losing two planes with bad weather limiting operations.

Russia: Red Army beats off repeated German attacks in northwest Caucasus thwarts attempt to cross Donets southeast of Kharkov, and penetrates Nazi positions northeast of Smolensk.

Australia: New type of Japanese plane reported in action north of Australia coincident with sharp increase in air activity over New Guinea coast. Allied planes bomb Japanese bases.

WASHINGTON April 23.—(UP)—The Navy revealed today that the U. S. has occupied the largest of the Ellice Islands in the south Pacific which had been seized by the Japanese early in the war.

The Ellice group is within easy striking distance of the Japanese occupied Gilbert Islands and is close to the Allied supply lines to the South Pacific.

Disclosure of the occupation was made in a Navy communique reporting that enemy bombers attacked U. S. positions on Funafuti in the Ellice group on Thursday.

When the island was occupied was not revealed by the Navy.

The communique said merely that light casualties and minor damage were suffered in the attack.

BY UNITED PRESS

British troops have captured a strategic range of hills in a new offensive southwest of Tunis and Allied air forces have destroyed an entire fleet of 20 giant German transport planes off the Tunisian coast, Gen. Dwight D. Eisenhower's headquarters announced today.

Steadily mountaing Allied pressure on the shrinking Axis bridgehead in northeast Tunisia won new ground, and the resumption of the American and British air offensive accounted for 38 enemy planes altogether with a loss of only five.

The British Eighth Army beat off stubborn counter-attacks along the Enfidaville mountain line south south of Tunis, inflicting heavy losses on the Afrika Korps, and clung firmly to all its hard-won gains in the rugged hills.

Lieut. Gen. K. A. N. Anderson's first army struck eastward in force yesterday along a nine-mile front in the Bou Arada sector at the center of the Tunisian battle Arc. An Allied communique said

(Continued on Page Two)

1942 Plates Good Only One More Week

HARRISBURG, April 23.—(UP)—Pennsylvania motorists today had only one week more to drive their automobiles with 1942 registration plates.

Revenue Secretary David W. Harris reminded motorists that the 1943 tab must be attached to license plates after midnight, April 30.

Automobile owners were granted a one-month extension of the deadline last month when the Welfare department reported its prison labor would not be able to complete the required number of tags by March 31.

The Jap claim that U. S. fliers had bombed non-military objectives and machine-gunned civilians was branded an outrageous lie by Capt. Ted Lawson (left) and Capt. Harold F. Watson. They took part in the Tokyo raid and, along with the rest of the nation, were stunned to learn some of their comrades had been executed by the Japs. They are pictured in Washington where they expressed a desire to bomb the Nipponese Capital again. (International soundphoto)

'Little Bo Peep': Harry Mallis Has Lost 1,800 Sheep

WORLAND, Wyo., April 23.—(UP)—Like Little Bo Peep, Harry Mallis lost his sheep—1,800 of them.

Not content to leave them alone and trust them to come home, Mallis appealed to the [illegible] planes in a search for the flock [illegible] was this way. He was [illegible] the flock last Friday in the mountainous Big Bend country, and while watching the sheep jump over rocks, he became sleepy and dozed off.

When he awoke, the sheep were gone.

"I started out to look for them," he said, "but I got lost, too."

Finally, he found his way back to civilization and appealed to officers at the Casper air base.

The Army said it would have to get permission from Washington.

Execution Of U. S. Fliers Justified, Berlin Radio Says

BY UNITED PRESS

The Berlin radio broadcast today a splurge of Nazi press comments attempting to justify the execution of captured American fliers by the Japanese.

"If the U. S. airmen are instructed by their superiors to go out for murder, they cannot expect to receive another treatment than that becoming murderers," one comment said.

Most of the press reports as recorded by the United Press in New York tried to say that the fliers had been told to deliberately attack civilians. They even said that leaders toured the U. S. describing this activity.

The Newspaper Voelkischer Beobachter purported to give the German people a long series of statements by British and United States leaders advocating raids on civilians.

'Captive' Miners Strike At Six Fayette County Plants

PITTSBURGH, April 21—(UP)—A spreading strike of coal miners today shut down or curtailed operations at six district "captive" mines producing approximately 10,000 tons of coal daily for war manufacturing steel mills.

Approximately 3,000 miners were idle at five mines of Republic Steel Corp., and at one mine of Weirton Steel Co.

The strike spread this morning to the Brownsville Junction mine of Republic Steel, employing approximately 800, when 30 men left their jobs. The walkout threatened continued production by 296 coke ovens at the mine.

The strike at the Republic mines apparently constituted a protest by the workers against a proposed contract covering small strip mines. The workers were said to be opposed to a caluse requiring submission of the agreement to the War Labor Board for approval. The Weirton's Isabella mine, near Uniontown, employing 900 men, was on strike reportedly over the concern of the transfer of three workers from one part of the mine to another.

FARMERS WILL GET 'WORK OR FIGHT' ORDER

PITTSBURGH, April 21.—(UP)—Orders to "farm or fight" will go out in Allegheny county next week to former farmers in [illegible] and those in the 38-44 age group who are not now employed in an essential activity, Charles P. Shenot, chairman of the Allegheny County War board, announced today.

The letters will direct the affected men to go into dairy farming within 30 days or face induction into the Army despite physical disabilities or age. Shenot said a survey by his board has disclosed a severe shortage of dairy farmers in Allegheny county, and similar conditions exist in surrounding counties.

Coal Operators To Appear Before NWLB

NEW YORK, April 21.—(UP)—Northern Appalachian soft coal operator announced today they would appear before the National War Labor board at Washington tomorrow, despite the anticipated refusal of the United Mine Workers to join them at the government hearing.

John L. Lewis, UMW president, holding a caucus with his union associates, was not immediately available for a statement when Charles O'Neill operators' spokesman, announced his intention to answer the summons of the WLB. O'Neill said his broup would leave for Washington late today and appear before the board at 10 a. m. tomorrow as the WLB had requested, in an effort to end the deadlocked soft coal contract negotiations.

HELD FOR ROBBERY

COLUMBUS, Ga., April 23.—(UP)—Wilbur Land, who said he was a labor organiser from Toledo, O., was held in jail here today under bond on a charge of robbery by snatching. He was arrested a week ago.

NEWCASTLE MAN FOURTH MEMBER OF BANDIT GANG

Remand Quartet To Beaver County Jail After Arraignment

Four self-confessed bandits, arrested this week after a series of crimes in the Beaver valley, today awaited court action at Beaver following their arraignment before Justice Ivor L. Jones here yesterday afternoon.

Fingerprinted and photographed at the borough police station prior to being arraigned, the quartet held in jail without bond includes:

James Nemeth, Rochester, formerly of West Aliquippa; James Zangara, New Castle; Robert Corless, Rochester, and Jack Beltz, Freedom.

Zangara was taken into custody by police later in the week, while the others were nabbed Sunday following the armed robbery of the Slovak club in West Aliquippa.

Some of the group is expected to appear before Beaver county court tomorrow for sentence. They waived hearing to court.

The quartet is charged with burglary, larceny and carrying firearms, police said.

The bandits admitted taking 100 bottles of whisky, 25 cartons of cigarets and six [illegible] of cigars from the Berger [illegible] Main St., Plan 12, officers disclosed.

They also pleaded guilty to holding up the West Side club, where they escaped with $230 in cash and five cartons of cigarets.

The bandits menaced [illegible]chek, bartender, with a gun and forced him and a club member to walk to a lavatory, where the pair were locked up.

Insurance Policy With Every Uniform, Goal Of Sen. Walsh

WASHINGTON, April 23.—(UP)—An insurance policy with every uniform is the goal of Chairman David I. Walsh, D., Mass., of the Senate Naval Affairs committee, who would make it mandatory for every servicemen to carry at $10,000 insurance policy.

Walsh introduced a bill in the Senate yesterday providing "that all persons now in active service of the land and naval forces, and all persons who hereafter enter upon such service, shall be considered as having (automatically) applied for government insurance up to the maximum amount allowed—that is, $10,000."

If the bill becomes law it would make the United States government the greatest insurance company in the world. With the United States having 11,000,000 men and women in the armed forces by the end of the year, each holding a $10,000 policy, the government would have $110,000,000,000 worth of insurance in force. The largest American life insurance company, the Metropolitan, has $28,000,000,000 worth of insurance in force.

Evidence brought out in a hearing of subcommittee of the Senate Finance committee last month revealed that 15 per cent of the naval personnel and 25 per cent of the army personnel do not have national service life insurance. A large number of those in the service have only a few thousand dollars worth of insurance.

REMEMBERS CHARITY

NEW YORK, April 23.—(UP)—The will of Louis Dudley, Beaumont, founder of the May Department store chain provides for a trust fund leaving from $12,000,000 to $15,000,000 to charitable and educational institutions, an accounting filed in Supreme court yesterday disclosed.

BOOS GIRL ILL

Carol, daughter of Mr. and Mrs Carl Boos, 1809 Davison St., is a patient at Rochester General hospital.

The Weather Forecast
WESTERN PENNSYLVANIA: Continued cold today and tonight. Frost in the north portion tonight. Tree pollen count—220.

"The Paper That Goes Home"

THE DAILY TIMES

1874 — and WESTERN ARGUS — 1803
ROCHESTER - BEAVER - MONACA - FREEDOM - BRIDGEWATER - CONWAY - VANPORT - MIDLAND

Beaver County History
German peace envoys were preparing to accept the treaty offered, it was reported here on May 14, 1919.

4 Cents

Established April 2, 1874 | Beaver and Rochester, Pa., Friday, May 14, 1943 | By Carrier 24 Cents A Week

ATTU INVADED BY AMERICAN TROOPS; EUROPE ROCKED BY ALLIED BOMBERS

COUNTY MAN, GIRL FOUND DEAD IN AUTO

Murder, Suicide Seen In Death Of Tobacco Shop Proprietor And Avalon Girl On Lonely Road In Allegheny County; Man Leaves Letter To Wife, Two Sons

An Ambridge man and a 22-year-old Avalon girl were found dead Thursday afternoon in the former's automobile parked along a lonely road in Sewickley Township, apparently the result of murder and suicide.

The man, Patrick J. Napolitan, 40, Melrose avenue, had been shot through the left temple and the girl, Elinor M. Knauff, daughter of Mr. and Mrs. J. Arthur Knauff, Chestnut street, had gunshot wounds in the chest, stomach and abdomen.

Allegheny County detectives expressed the belief Napolitan had shot the girl and then killed himself. The death weapon, a .32-calibre revolver identified as the property of Napolitan, was found on the automobile seat close to Napolitan's left hand.

The bodies were discovered by Clarence W. Profator, Sewickley Township constable, who was driving a school bus. He saw the Napolitan car parked along the Hitzel hill road and pulled up along side. From the higher seat in the bus, Profator could see the bodies inside the automobile.

LEFT LETTER TO WIFE

Constable Profator immediately notified the detectives and returned to the scene. The time of death was estimated at noon yesterday and the bodies were found three hours later.

In Napolitan's coat was found a letter to his wife, Leota, 37, telling of his inability to break his friendship with Elinor. The letter was dated May 12, Wednesday, and was signed, "Your Damn Fool Husband.

Napolitan had first met Miss Knauff three months ago when she went to work in a paint store across the street from his Ambridge Smoke Shop, Merchant street. Mrs. Napolitan told police that she had heard her husband was "going around" with Elinor and offered him a divorce, but both he and the girl refused and promised to quit seeing each other.

REPORTED MISSING

Mrs. Napolitan had reported her husband to the Ambridge police as missing at four o'clock yesterday afternoon and called them again at 4:50 o'clock, according to Police Chief Andrew Bires.

Five minutes after her second call, Ambridge police were notified Napolitan's body had been found across the county line.

Meanwhile, the Knauffs had

(Continued On Page Eight)

County Sodalities To Crown May Queen

Plans are being completed for the annual "Beaver County Sodality Day," to be held in St. Veronica's Roman Catholic church, Ambridge, Sunday, May 16, at 7:30 o'clock. Miss Florence Gigler, (above) prefect of the Sodality of St. Veronica's church, has been selected May Queen by the Beaver County Union of Sodalities. She will place a floral crown upon the statue of the Blessed Virgin Mary.

Miss Mary V. Anthony, Rochester, president of the Beaver County Union, and Miss Elsie Hallas, Ambridge, corresponding secretary, will be the attendants to the Queen.

Miss Theresa Wilson, prefect of St. Cecilia's Sodality; Miss Angeline Tooch, prefect of St. Anthony's Sodality, and Miss Cecelia Burek, prefect of St. John's Sodality, will be members of the queen's court. Members of the county sodalities will form a living Rosary.

Churchill Speaks To Britons Today

WASHINGTON, May 14.—Prime Minister Winston Churchill speaks to the British people by radio today. His speech was scheduled for 3 P. M., and was to be broadcast in this country and Great Britain.

Churchill's remarks were to be directed to the people of his own country on the occasion of the anniversary of the British Home Guards, but he also was expected to use the opportunity to explain in a general way the purpose of his visit here.

While the Roosevelt-Churchill conferences continue at the White House their staff chiefs are conferring elsewhere in the capital.

Churchill also has been conferring with Secretary of State Hull and other American leaders, and with British and Australian officials in Washington.

Canadian Prime Minister W. L MacKenzie King will join the conferences for a brief period next week and it was believed possible that Madame Chiang Kai-Shek wife of the Chinese Generalissimo, would see Churchill here.

One of the high spots of Churchill's visit will come next Wednesday when he speaks before a joint session of congress. He made a similar congressional appearance shortly before he concluded his visit to this country, in January, 1942.

School Tax Millage Is Set For Conway

The Conway Board of Education met Thursday evening and adopted a tentative budget for the 1943-44 school year. The board set the tax rate at 30 mills with a five dollar per capita tax.

Dr. E. M. Nesbitt, pastor of the Beaver United Presbyterian church, is to be the principal speaker at the commencement exercises, it was announced.

Monaca Ready To Give Blood To Armed Forces

Monaca is ready for the Mobile Blood Donors' unit Monday morning. Notices were in the mail today to pledged donors telling them the hours and place to report beginning Monday morning.

Telephone — Rochester 3574 —has been installed in the library in the city building. Headquarters there will be manned day and night until the job is finished. Persons seeking to register, or desiring information, are asked to call that number, or go there in person.

Coffee Rationing Increase Is Urged

PITTSBURGH, May 14—(UP)—With a 30-day supply of coffee claimed to be on grocers" shelves and imports steadily increasing, the Tri- State section of the National Coffee Association urged the OPA to increase rations from one pound per person every five weeks to one pound every four weeks.

In all, 50 Tri-State coffee roasters besieged the OPA with telegrams, urging modification of the rationing laws, not only for civilian home consumption but also for restaurants and institutions. The action was voted at a regional meeting of the association here where delegates said curtailment of the beverage has the industry genuinely worried.

Two Men Hurt In Truck Accident

Robert Campbell, 52, Charles street, Monaca Heights, and Wilkie Salter, 42, Connecticut avenue, Rochester, were admitted to Rochester hospital this morning suffering from injuries received in a truck accident along the Brodhead road. Campbell suffered a head injury and Salter had an injury to one shoulder.

FINAL VOTE NEARS TODAY ON TAX PLAN

Battle Looms Over Ruml Plan In Senate Amid Charges Against Administration And Manufacturers' Association; Democrats Offer Substitute Proposals As Delaying Measure

WASHINGTON, May 14.—(UP)—The Senate neared a final vote on pay-as-you-go tax legislation today amid alleged administration delaying tactics and a National Association of Manufacturer's pressure campaign against the Ruml plan.

The NAM was accused of "deluging" Senators with anti-Ruml plan telegrams lest complete forgiveness of a year's income taxes result in pressure for higher corporation taxes.

The administration, according to cloakroom reports, was trying to delay the final vote long enough for leaders to corral support for a compromise on the Ruml plan—the 75 per cent forgiveness bill of finance committee chairman Walter F. George, D., Ga.

Delaying strategy also was seen in the sudden introduction late yesterday of several subtsitutes by Democratic opponents of the Ruml plan. The last on ewas offered by Sen. Allen J. Ellender, D., La., who would forgive no taxes but collect the 1942 levy on a five-year installment plan, reaching complete pay-as-you-go on June 15, 1948.

MORE VOTES SOUGHT

There were reports that Ellender had administration support, not that Ruml opponents had any hope of getting his plan approved but to give the time to get more votes for the George bill.

The charge against the NAM was made by Sen. Homer Ferguson, R. Mich., Ruml plan advocate. He said his office was deluged with telegrams supporting the George proposal and that upon investigation of their source he found that the NAM had instructed its members "to exert every possible effort to induce each senator" to vote for the George amendment.

The third day of debate opens with Ellender's "installment plan" pending and a limit of 15 minutes per senator on discussion of it.

VARIED PROPOSALS

As the showdown aproaches, the senate has these proposals before it:

1. The 100 per cent forgiveness, or Ruml, plan.
2. George's 75 per cent forgiveness plan.
3. Ellender's no forgiveness bill
4. An amendment by Sen. W. Lee O'Daniel, D., Tex., to ignore pay-as-you-go completely but to inaugurate withholding taxes at the source on July 1 anyway.
5. An amendment by Sen. Tom Connally, D., Tex., to make 1942 income taxes subject to the lower 1941 rates and higher 1941 exemptions, giving those liable to taxation three years to pay what they owe at the lower rate. That would put taxpayers on pay-as-you-go March 15, 1946.
6. The original House-approved bill wiping out 1942 tax liability for all taxpayers in the first surtax bracket and putting them on pay-as-you-go immediately. Higher brackets never would become current unless they paid two years' taxes in one.

Each proposal would retain the Ruml bill's plan of starting 20 per cent withholding taxes on all wages and salaries over $624 for a single man and $1,248 for a married man (with an additional allowance of $312 for each dependent in either case) on July 1. Each of them, with the exception of O'Daniel's amendment and the House-approved bill, would put the individual taxpayer on a pay-as-you-go basis eventually.

Dr. M. M. Pearce Named To Post

Dr. M. M. Peace, president of Geneva College, was slated for election to the state committee of the Young Men's Christian Association at the 74th state convention today in Harrisburg. Plans were to be discussed to increase the wartime effectiveness of the youth movement.

R. C. STOUT ASKS RELEASE AS CHAIRMAN OF RED CROSS

ROBERT C. STOUT

Completing five and one-half years of devoted service, Robert C. Stout, of Beaver, has told the Board of Directors of the Beaver County Chapter, American Red Cross, that he desires to be relieved of the chairmanship at the end of his present term on June 30. His statement came at the end of the monthly board meeting last night.

After giving a lengthy review of the Chapter's work and growth in recent years, he said:

"I have no right to anticipate a reelection by the board, nor am I taking that for granted. But I feel that it is my duty to make my desires clear at this time, 30 days before the annual election, so that your board may not come face to face with an emergency at the time of the annual meeting."

Continuing, Mr. Stout stated:

"My desire to be relieved entirely of the chairmanship is partly because of the condition of my own personal health, the tremendous demands which the chairmanship of this board makes on my time, the fact that my own personal business has suffered much because I am away from it too much, and that the work has grown too heavy to be carried on by me without injustice to myself, my business, my health and my family. I shall gladly continue to take an active interest in the work and welfare of the Chapter in any other way, and will support the Chapter to the best of my ability."

He thanked the board members,

(Continued On Page Eight)

Valley Students To Graduate From Geneva On Tuesday

Of the 47 students graduating from Geneva College in the May division next Tuesday morning, the following are from the Beaver Valley:

Miss Margaret L. Urling, Roy S. Grissinger, Arthur K. Najarian, and Harrison N. Richardson, all of Beaver; Misses Virginia M. Napoli, Florence M. Lawson and Jack A. Meredith, all of Rochester; Miss Elizabeth Fauser, Monaca; Paul C. Headland, Baden; John G. Hallisey, Aliquippa; Miss Lenora Gimmatteo, Robert C. Palmer, and Arthur Ostrowski, all of Ambridge; Miss Anna Hopta, Leetsdale, William C. Martin, Freedom; Miss Elsa DeBona, William G. Gillespie and Robert J. Hamilton, all of New Brighton.

Mrs. Irene Hohenthaner Elm, Mrs. Jean Hemphill and the Misses K. Kathryn Coleman, Virginia M. Kroen, M. Isabelle Murphy, Allison Tweed, Willard E. Brown, Willard E. Hemphill, Richard T. Metheny, James A. Moore, and Paul C. Stole, all of Beaver Falls.

Prizes will be announced and honors, high honors and highest honors awarded the graduates of high standing and who have pursued a rather extensive course of reading outside of that required in the pursuit of their regular studies.

Adolph Pletincks, Beaver Falls high school, who is taking the place at the college of Prof. Robert Boyle of the Department of Music since his call to the service, will be in charge of the music by the college ensemble.

President McLeod M. Pearce will deliver the address to the graduates and present their diplomas at the close of the commencement address by Dr. John H. Bowman, Pittsburgh.

Navy Commissions Two County Men

George F. Wheaton, Jr., near Monaca, and Frederick A. Kelsall, Ambridge, have been commissioned lieutenants, junior grade, in the U. S. Naval Reserve, according to the Pittsburgh office of Naval Officer Procurement

New Industry To Be Established In Monaca Next Week

Monaca is to have a new industry, according to announcement made today by Ralph Shattuck of the American Soil Builder Company, manufacturers of soil builders and conditioners.

Starting next week, the company will begin production in the United States Sanitary Manufacturing Company plant, closed since last June.

Under present plans, first production will be carried on by the skeleton maintenance crew retained by the Sanitary company at the plant, and additional employes will be hired later as production is increased.

The Monaca plant is well-equipped to manufacture the Soil Builder Company's products, Mr. Shattuck said, as a large battery of heat treating furnaces is available for processing the coal which is the principal ingredient of the soil builder.

INVENTOR TO COME HERE

Containing coal, limstone and salt, the soil builders are covered by four patents owned by Charles Peter, Salt Lake City, who has spent ten years in testing and experimenting with soils all over the county and on many types of vegetation. Mr. Peter expects to arrive in Monaca early next week to supervise initial production and instruct the Sanitary company employes.

A license for manufacturing and selling rights under the Peter patents is held by Mr. Shattuck, identified with the coal industry in Ohio, and James Marr, an importer and manufacturer in New York City. Under their contract they have the manufacturing and selling rights in 36 states east of the Rocky Mountains and in Cuba and Puerto Rico. Offices of the company are in the Commonwealth Annex Building, Pittsburgh.

While a plant has been in operation in the Rocky Mountain area several years and the business there has shown rapid growth, the Monaca plant is the first to be es-

(Continued On Page Two)

LEWIS IN NEW YORK

NEW YORK, May 14—John L. Lewis, United Mine Workers' president, has returned to his New York office after conferences in Washington, his secretary said today.

Beaver Army Pilot Wounded In Mid-East

Mr. and Mrs. Ernest W. Fogel, Sr., 464 Fourth street, Beaver, received word last night from the War Department at Washington that their son, First Lieut. Ernest W. Fogel, Jr., Army Air Forces pilot, (above) was wounded in action May 4 in the Middle East area.

The telegram from the Adjutant-General read: "Deeply regret to inform you that your son, First Lieutenant Ernest W. Fogel, was wounded in action May 4, in the Middle East area. Report further states making normal improvement. Reports of condition expected every fifteen days. You will be advised as reports are received."

Lieutenant Fogel widely known in Beaver Valley, arrived overseas March 1 and has seen considerable action. He was pilot of a B-24 bomber.

He trained as an aviation cadet at Maxwell Field, Ala., completed his training at Columbus, Miss., and on July 26, 1942, was graduated and received his "wings," and his commission as lieutenant. Later he was stationed at a bomber field in Utah.

Nazi-Incited Revolt Sweeping Holland; Many Die In Clashes

LONDON, May 14 (UP)—A Nazi-incited revolt was reported sweeping Holland today, resulting in street clashes in which 70 patriots died, while at the other end of the Axis defense line Premier Benito Mussolini prepared the Italian people for an Allied invasion.

Twenty patriots were machine gunned to death during riots in Amsterdam as shootings, sabotage and mass strikes spread everywhere, a Dutch refugee government spokesman said.

The Germans spread leaflets calling for the uprising to speed the "hour of liberation" in an effort to find the leaders of Dutch resistance, it was believed. The spokesman said a liberation army of 75,000 was in hiding in the Neherlands to

(Continued On Page Eight)

Navy Nurse At Midland Home

Lieut. Helen Walker, U. S. Navy nurse, stationed at Pearl Harbor for more than a year, arrived last night at her home in Midland after a quick voyage. She flew to Pittsburgh from San Francisco.

ROCHESTER SOLDIER DESCRIBES BLOODY FIGHTING WHICH RAGED ON GUADALCANAL

By BILL HEYMAN

Friends and relatives of Corp. Eugene E. Farmer, U. S. Army, Reno street extension, near Rochester, formerly of Beaver, are hearing of the bloody fight for Guadalcanal first-hand as Farmer is home after three and one-half months spent on that South Pacific island.

The local youth is spending a 30-day sick leave with his mother, Mrs. W. A. Farmer, and his grandparents, Mr. and Mrs. John Boyce Farmer, after contracting malaria fever on Guadalcanal and being shipped back to the States to recuperate.

For his service in Guadalcanal and in Hawaii, Corporal Farmer wears the American Defense ribbon with Pearl Harbor star, the Southwest Pacific Campaign bar and the Asiatic-Pacific ribbon with a star for a major battle.

In addition to these, he has three gold "V's" on his left forearm, each denoting six months of overseas duty in the current war. On his left arm at the shoulder is a sky-blue diamond with five white stars and a red numeral "1" on which tiny, white letters spell "Guadalcanal".

Guadalcanal is not the only place he saw action, for Farmer was at Schofield barracks, Hawaii, when the Japs pulled their sneak attack on December 7, 1941.

The local youth enlisted in the Army on July 3, 1941, after completing his sophomore year at Beaver high school and spent three weeks at New Rochelle, N. Y., before being sent to Hawaii. He remained at Hawaii from August 17, 1941, until October, 1942, when he embarked for the South Pacific and Guadalcanal.

Although the Marines had made the first landings on the Jap-held island, Farmer's regiment was among the first Army men to be sent to reinforce the Leathernecks.

Farmer remained at Guadalcanal until last January 15, when he was evacuated to an American base elsewhere in the Southwest Pacific and returned to this country on April 4 and to Rochester on May fifth.

Upon the completion of his furlough, he is to report to the Lawson Army hospital at Atlanta, Ga. for further orders

Farmer enlisted with Earl Rader, Fifth street, Beaver, and the two remained together until they en-

(Continued On Page Four)

Big Offensive Drive Opened

BULLETIN

WASHINGTON, May 14—U. S. forces landed on Attu Island in the Aleutian group on Tuesday and are now fighting the Japanese there for possession of the westernmost island of the chain. The Navy Department said details of the operation will be released when the situation is clarified.

The Navy also announced that U. S. fliers have shot down 16 Zeros and probably destroyed two more in a furious air battle in the Solomons. Five U. S. planes were lost, but two of the pilots were saved. The battle took place near the Russell Islands, just northwest of Guadalcanal, on May 13 (Island Time).

Allied Planes Bombard Axis On European Fronts

Nazi Europe rocked today under an Allied pre-invasion aerial bombardment the like of which the world has never seen.

The long awaited big push of the American and British air forces against Adolf Hitler's continental fortress was on.

A ceaseless, trip-hammer pounding shook the fortress and ripped into the enemy war base, softening it up for the land assault which many quarters believed was near.

The Royal Air Force, the United State Army Air Force and the Red Air Force shuttled over Europe in unbroken relays, smashing from all sides and unprecedented strength at Germany, Italy, occupied territory and island outposts.

MANY POINTS HIT

Berlin, the Ruhr, Czechoslovakia, Northwest Germany, Warsaw, Naples, France, Sicily, Sardinia—all of them and widely scattered intermediate targets had quaked and blazed under the full scale Allied offensive gathering momentum like a downhill snowball.

The attack reopened the question of how long a beleaguered target—even as big and strong as continental Europe—could withstand such a scourging from the air. None would say, but the Allied command evidently was bent on finding out.

By night British bombers "in very great strength" swarmed over Berlin, the Ruhr, and Czechoslovakia far to the east in a triple-pronged drive following its record assault on Duisburg 24 hours earlier.

By day American heavy bombers, following up a record-breaking attack on Nazi bases in North France, struck mightily at the North German coastal district, according to the Berlin radio with substantiating evidence that a "great force" of Allied planes roared over the coast of England on the shuttle route to Europe.

BERLIN BLASTED

The RAF bombed Berlin and struck simultaneously last night at Germany's great industrial citadels in the central Ruhr and Czechoslovakia. Thirty-four planes in all were lost, the same number lost the previous night during the heaviest raid of the war on the inland port and industrial center of Duisburg.

American crews made the heav-

(Continued On Page Eight)

Price Ceiling Set On Soaps By OPA

WASHINGTON, May 14 (UP)—The Office of Price Administration today established specific dollars-and-cents maximum prices for soap, effective May 24.

The ceilings, which will reduce prices in some stores, were described by OPA as the "ideal form of price control." The maximum prices start at the manufacturing plant where prices are set by the case. Wholesale and retail ceilings also are established under the order.

An OPA spokesman said the ceilings are nation-wide and will prevent any form of chiseling. For the time being, the only retail stores affected by the order will be gorcery stores. These stores make the major part of the retail soap sales.

Did Japs Shoot Down Woman Flier?

Widely circulated radio speculation today indicated a widespread belief that Paps shot down Amelia Earhart, famous woman flier, who disappeaerd three years ago while flying over the Pacific ocean.

Japanese Report Battle Raging On Aleutian Island

Strong American units have landed on Attu Island, westernmost of the Aleutians, and a violent fight for the Japanese base is in progress, a Tokyo broadcast said today.

The brief Tokyo report said the landing took place May 12. The assertion was not immediately verified by Allied sources.

DNB, German news agency, broadcast the Tokyo imperial headquarters announcement shortly after it had been picked up in the United States by the Federal Communications Commission and reported by the British Broadcasting Corporation.

The announcement followed by seven days the disclosure in Washington of the occupation of Amchitka, 244 miles east of Attu and only 72 miles from the other Japanese Aleutians base at Kiska. The capture of Amchitka was accomplished January 12.

WOULD THREATEN JAP ISLES

Amchitka itself is within theoretical operating range of Tokyo with the new type bombers reportedly being built by the United States and Attu is even closer. Attu is 2,005 airline miles from Tokyo.

Occupation of Attu would put the northern Japanese islands — the Kurile group—in direct danger of American air assault by present bombers such as the Liberator.

The reported action against Attu came amid widespread predictions of an impending drive against Japan at all points in the Pacific, including the Aleutians.

The latest air attack on Kiska was reported yesterday. A Washington communique said Mitchells bombed the airplane runway and main camp area on the barren island Tuesday in the 221st attack since March 1. The enemy is believed to have a submarine base on Kiska.

Legion Medals Are Awarded At Freedom

Dolores Bilotto, only daughter of Mr. and Mrs. Joseph Bilotto, Third avenue, Freedom, has been chosen the outstanding girl, and Joseph Borro, Jr., younger son of Mr. and Mrs. Joseph Borro, Unionville road, near Freedom, the outstanding boy in the eighth grade of the Freedom public schools.

They were selected by their fellow-students from a list of students eligible for this honor compiled by their teachers, and, before the student body and guests in the high school auditorium, were presented medals.

June Metzger, a high school freshman, representing both the Freedom American Legion and Auxiliary, who annually present medals to the outstanding boy and girl in the Eighth grade, made the presentation speech. Miss Metzger's father, Fred G. Metzger is commander of the Legion and her mother, who died several months ago, was Americanism chairman of the Auxiliary, and officially would have been the representative from the Auxiliary to present the awards.

Miss Metzger, in her brief talk, stressed the five points which were considered in the selection of the two students—honor, courage, leadership, scholarship and service.

British Veterans To Have Memorial

All members of the Edith Cavell Post, British Empire War Veterans Association, are to meet at New Brighton high school, Sunday evening, May 16, at 7:30 to take part in the memorial service.

WEATHER DELAYS START OF COUNTY LEAGUE SEASON

PIRATES TO PLAY TONIGHT GRAYS, C-W MEET WEDNESDAY

Rain yesterday afternoon resulting in wet playing fields delayed the opening of the Beaver County Baseball League season last night, but the lid will be lifted this evening if there is no further interference by bad weather.

The Rochester Pirates and Beaver Falls clubs have made arrangements to play their initial game at Beaver Falls this evening if the weather permits and the Curtiss-Wright and Beaver teams plan to play their opener at Gypsy Glen Field, Beaver, on Wednesday evening at 6:30 o'clock.

The four clubs of the county circuit were all set for their initial battles last night but by mid-afternoon it became apparent that the games would have to be postponed.

Manager Tony Fubio of the Falls club has announced that Jimmy Boren, left hand pitcher who performed for the Beaver Falls Browns in the Penn State League two or three years ago, will start on the mound tonight against the Junction City nine.

Friday night the County League schedule sends Rochester into action against Curtiss-Wright on the Beaver Field while Beaver Grays invade Beaver Falls.

The diamond at Rochester has not been put into shape for playing, but if possible the work will be done this week, so the Pirates can make their first home appearance the early part of next week.

Baseball Summary

NATIONAL LEAGUE

Results Monday

Cincinnati 3, New York 1.
Philadelphia 8, Chicago 4.
Brooklyn 1, St. Louis 0.
Only games scheduled.

TEAM STANDING

	W.	L.	Pct.
Brooklyn	17	7	.696
Boston	11	8	.579
St. Louis	11	9	.550
Cincinnati	11	12	.478
Philadelphia	10	11	.476
Pittsburgh	9	10	.474
New York	10	13	.435
Chicago	7	16	.304

GAMES TODAY

Pittsburgh at Boston.
Cincinnati at New York.
St. Louis at Brooklyn.
Chicago at Philadelphia (night).

Games Wednesday

Pittsburgh at Boston (2).
Cincinnati at New York.
St. Louis at Brooklyn.
Chicago at Philadelphia.

AMERICAN LEAGUE

Results Monday

All games postponed, weather.

TEAM STANDING

	W.	L.	Pct.
New York	14	8	.636
Cleveland	13	9	.591
Washington	14	11	.560
St. Louis	9	9	.500
Detroit	10	11	.476
Philadelphia	11	14	.440
Chicago	8	11	.421
Boston	8	14	.364

GAMES TODAY

New York at Detroit.
Boston at Cleveland (night).
Washington at St. Louis.
Philadelphia at Chicago.

Games Wednesday

New York at Detroit.
Boston at Cleveland.
Washington at St. Louis.
Philadelphia at Chicago.

BEAVER COUNTY LEAGUE

Results Monday

Beaver - Curtiss-Wright, postponed.
Rochester - Beaver Falls, postponed.

Game Tonight

Rochester at Beaver Falls.

Games Wednesday

Beaver at Curtiss-Wright.

Games Thursday

Rochester at Curtiss-Wright.
Beaver at Beaver Falls.

Hagg Should Spur Track Interest

NEW YORK, May 18 (UP)—The impending visit of Sweden's Gunder Hagg for a series of races with America's crack runners will do much for the salvation of track and field, officials admitted following the IC4A championships.

Although the draft-stricken collegiate ranks still are turning in creditable performances, the sport needs the post - graduate "name" competitors to attract respectable crowds.

This point was proved when the IC4A, oldest track meet in the country and limited to collegians, drew a bare 1,500 fans to Triborough Stadium. It was expected that even without the rest of the graduated headliners, Hagg and galloping little Greg Rice would pack the stands with 25,000 persons when they meet in the same stadium June 20 in the national AAU chapmionships.

Draft Depleting Jockeys

BALTIMORE, Md., — (UP) — Along with all other sports, racing is beginning to feel the manpower drain, particularly among jockeys. Henri Mora, Patsy Grant and Al Boscon received their draft notices at Pimlico.

BIG NOISE FROM ST. LOUIS JUST WHISPER IN BROOKLYN

NEW YORK, May 18 (UP)—The big noise from St. Louis was just a whisper in Brooklyn today as the Bums looked down their ancient noses at the World Champion Cardinals, now reposing in third place in the National League, and prepared to do battle for the second straight day in defense of their three-and-a-half game lead.

Durocher's Doddering Dandies played like nine frisky kids yesterday in putting the skids under the Cardinals by a 1-0 count that dropped them a half-game below the second place Boston Braves.

Rube Melton scattered five hits among the Redbirds in winning his first game as a Dodger and extended his heroics to the plate by driving in the game's only run. Howie Pollet, Cardinal southpaw, faced a long line of right-handed hitters tailored specially for the occasion by Durocher and gave up seven hits in losing his first game.

The Cincinnati Reds came out best in the percentage point scramble down around the bottom of the first division by giving the New York Giants the 3-1 treatment.

When the statisticians had cleared their figures away, the Reds had moved from sixth to fourth, Philadelphia's Phillies were two points away in fifth place—after spending the previous day in seventh—and the Pittsburgh Pirates were in sixth place, two points south of Philadelphia.

Ray Starr, Cincinnati right-hander, kept pulling the string on the Giants with a maddening slow ball which they bounced around for eight ineffectual hits. Starr, moreover, singled two runs home in the second with the bags loaded and was followed to the plate by Lonnie Frey, who punched home the Reds' final marker.

Harry Feldman, Ace Adams and Bobby Coombs gave up a total of nine hits, which might have been a trifle more respectable if the Giants hadn't let 13 runners die on base.

The Philadelphia Phillies spotted the Chicago Cubs three runs in the first inning and then came back in the last half of the same inning with a five-run outburst that sent Claude Passeau and Eddie Hanyzewski fleeing. Les Fleming, Dick Barrett and Ray Prim also appeared for Chicago and allowed a total of 12 hits in company with their predecessors. The final score: Philadelphia 8, Chicago 4.

Johnny Podgajny gave up eight hits over the full nine innings for the Phillies and Danny Litwhiler, Philadelphia outfielder, hit his fourth homer of the season in the second inning.

Pittsburgh and Boston were idle in the National League. All scheduled games in the American League were postponed.

Yesterday's star — Rube Melton, Brooklyn pitcher who gave the Dodgers an important edge in their series with the Cardinals with a superb five-hit performance.

THE OLD HOME TOWN Registered U. S. Patent Office By STANLEY

HEY! MAW!--WAIT-ONE OF YOU GIRLS GOT MY PANTS ON BY MISTAKE!!
BUS STOP
THE EARLY MORNING SHIFT

Propeller Plant Softball Loop To Open Season Today

Twelve of the twenty-two teams in the Softball League at the Beaver Plant of the Curtiss-Wright Corporation, Propeller Division, were to get into action today at the Beaver municipal recreation center to officially open the 1943 softball season.

The first game was scheduled to take place at 8:15 a. m., with the Expeditors meeting the Welders. Games are to be played at 8:15 and 9:00 a. m. and 2:00, 4:30, 6:00 and 7:15 p. m.

Play in the league will be divided into three sections to facilitate scheduling among the three shifts of the plant.

Immediately after the close of the season in the early part of July, the three section champs will meet in a play-off tournament for the plant championship.

Meanwhile, six teams have been entered in the girls' softball league now being organized. The girls are scheduled to open their league on June 4.

The following is a complete list of the men's teams and their managers, participating in the men's softball league: Expeditors, O. McKenzie; Welders, R. Englert; Hornets, W. Schiller; Cubs, E. Snyder; Pirates, J. Burby; Yanks, F. Mooney; Bombardiers, W. Turek; Cards; J. Deyber; Blue Devils, C. Kinkopf; Phils, R. Pampe; Senators, T. Wylie.

Millers, E. Wagoner; Hawks, E. Gombosh; Braves, S. Hixon; Dodgers, S. Fortunato; Indians, H. Krumpleman; Spitfires, R. Sheets; Minute Men, S. Helliar; Dwellers, S. Sulkin; Reds, R. Erb; Bears, T Murray; Hot Spots, J. Lednak.

SPORT SLANTS

By BILL ANDERSON

There will be a new set-up in the Geneva College athletic office when the next term begins in September. A. C. Edgecombe, graduate manager of athletics for 19 years, has been given a leave of absence for the duration and has begun his duties as administrator of the Beaver County Housing Authority, and Carl Hughes, student sports publicity director and Edgecombe's right hand bower for the last two years, was graduated at the commencement exercises today. Hughes plans to spend the next few weeks at his home in South Fork. He expects to be inducted into the Army in June.

Don Bailey tried to get the Beaver County League to elect someone else to head the loop this summer, but the club managers had no one immediately available, so Bailey remains at the helm. Bailey said he would like to be free of the responsibility of directing the county league in order to have more time for umpiring in the junior loop. He has an idea for writing a baseball book and wants a chance to develop it.

Meetings of the county league and the junior association are to be held next Sunday evening at 8:30 o'clock to discuss any problems which may come up during the first week of the county league season, and to complete the organization of the Junior Association. There is still time for any junior clubs in the lower valley to join the circuit.

Alvin (Mote) Bergman, of Leetsdale, former Ambridge barber, who always celebrates his birthday by walking a mile for each year of his age, completed 56 miles at the Leetsdale high school field last Thursday afternoon. He finished the trek in 10 hours and 55 minutes and then went to work at the National Supply Company plant where he is employed. Bergman thinks walking is the greatest and most beneficial of all sports, and plans to try a 100-mile marathon next September.

Leo Nobile, former All-County guard at Ambridge high, is home from Penn State awaiting a call to Army service about May 26. Nobile was a regular on the Nittany Lion eleven last football season after starring on the great 1941 Penn State freshman team. Ray Ulinski, Ambridge, quarterback on the 1941 Lion yearling team, has been in the Army for several months. He's an M. P. and located in Alabama.

Jake (One-Man-Riot) Lamotta of the Bronx looms as a threat to Fritzie Zivic's record of 24 straight victories in Pittsburgh rings, when they meet at Forbes Field next Monday night. Fritzie says he can beat LaMotta, but the "One-Man-Riot" has been established the favorite. Zivic hasn't lost a decision before a Pittsburgh audience since Charley Burley beat him in June, 1938. In the meantime, he has scored 24 consecutive wins in Smoky City bouts, but in most of them he was the pre-fight favorite.

BROWNS LOSE STEPHENS

ST. LOUIS, May 18 — The St. Louis Browns faced the problem today of fielding an adequate replacement for Vern Stephens, sharp-hitting young shortstop, who will be out of action for at least six weeks because of a fractured knee-cap. X-rays disclosed yesterday that Stephens had injured his knee sliding into second base in a game with the New York Yankees.

Send THE TIMES to your boy in the Army or Navy. "It's like a letter from home every day."

GLAD TO (CATCHER'S) MITT YA

OUTFIELDER BABE BARNA of the New York Giants knocks both ball and glove from the hands of Catcher Hernandez of the Cubs as he scores on a line drive to center field. *(International)*

Rabid Mexican Baseball Fans Often Show Displeasure By Setting Fire To Stands

By EDWARD L. THOMAS
United Press Staff Correspondent

MEXICO CITY, May 18.—(UP)—Mexico today claimed the most rabid baseball fans in the world and offered as solid proof the fact that disgusted rooters often set the bleachers afire when their favorite team blows a game.

When it comes to howling at an umpire, giving the imported Bronx Cheer to a butter-fingered player or going all-out with a physical display of displeasure, your Mexican fan takes a back seat to no one —not even a Brooklynite.

Normally there are six ball parks in which the Mexican major league teams perform. But sometimes there are only five and a half plants —half of one having gone up in flames—after a group of fans shouting the Spanish equivalent of "you bums" and struck the match.

The situation resulting from this enthusiasm is critical, however, for Mexico's ball parks are far too few to care adequately for the ever-increasing baseball public.

The six-team major circuit netted private owners a cool 500,000 pesos (about $100,000) after all expenses were paid last year. The largest park has a capacity of 14,000, but 18,000 squeezed through the turnstiles for the most recent North-South all-star game.

Mexico's major league was founded by Alejandro Aguilar Reyes and Ernesto Carmona in 1925. They had watched baseball operations in the United States and decided Mexico should have her own major league. It has been going strong since its founding, increasing in popularity and quality.

Aguilar Reyes was high commissioner of the league until last year when he resigned to devote full time to his job as publisher-editor of Mexico's only sports daily, "La Aficion."

The six teams in the major league are Mexico City, Vera Cruz, Monterrey, Torreon, Puebla and Tampico. They play a 90-game season — a round-robin schedule that parallels that in the United States.

Last season's pennant race was the closest in years. Torreon won the flag in the last game. Four teams remained tied for third place, only a few games behind the leaders.

Mexicans apparently do not care for night baseball. They prefer having the warm sun on their backs.

Baseball terms retain their flavor while being uttered in Spanish. Many of them have retained their English spelling, such as home run, pitcher, catcher and hits. You can find those words on any sports page, for the Spanish language does not embrace any that could fittingly take their place.

Jackie Wilson Wins Over Petro By TKO

WASHINGTON, May 18—Jackie Wilson of Pittsburgh, former NBA featherweight champion, scored a 10-round technical knockout over Danny Petro, Washington, before 5,000 spectators here last night.

Petro, who had won 13 of the 14 bouts in his professional career, started last and hurt Wilson with a series of hard lefts in the first two rounds. After that, however, the ringwise Wilson found the range and peppered his young opponent with stinging rights to the body and occasional hard lefts.

Al Tribuani Wins Over Bummy Davis

PHILADELPHIA, May 18—Al Tribuani, Wilmington, Del., welterweight, survived a ninth round count of nine to win a referee's decision over Al (Bummy) Davis, of Brooklyn before 9,000 fans at the Arena last night. The fight, straight from Pier 6, had the crowd on its feet from start to finish.

Kept Laudry Job

PHILADELPHIA — (UP) — Bob Montgomery, leading lightweight contender, was a laundry worker in 1937 when he decided to become a fighter. For his first nine fights as an amateur, he paid his handlers out of his laundry earnings. Seeing his development, they then agreed to work for nothing until he was ready to turn professional.

Avonworth Player Wins Golf Honors

PITTSBURGH, May 18.—(UP)—Paul Lawry, No. 2 player on the Avonworth high school team, captured the WPIAL individual golf championship yesterday, scoring an eight over par 79 at the Longue Vue Club. Tommy Smith, of Greensburg, and Leonard Zigo, of Har-Brack, tied for the runner-up post with 82 each. In a run-off, one-hole match, Smith, who had a 42-40, defeated Zigo, for second position.

Nick Noval, Penn Township, carded an 83 stroke total for fourth place, while Cliff Andres, top player on the Munhall team, could do no better than fifteen with a 44-40—84.

Each Has Own Name

NEW YORK. — (UP) — Count Fleet, Mrs. John D. Hertz's Kentucky Derby and Preakness winner, is known around the barns by several names. His groom calls him "Old Zeke"; the stable foreman refers to him as "The Champ"; newspapermen call him "The Flee," and to the public at large he is "The Count."

Hutchinson Crack Shot

NORFOLK, Va.—(UP)—Freddie Hutchinson, the former Detroit Tiger pitcher, is one of the best rifle and pistol shots at the Norfolk Naval Station. He's an instructor on the rifle range.

ACROSS THE TRACK—It's wet going in Big Ten meet but Dallas Dupre of Ohio State, star of meet, extreme right, whips a big field in century.

EASY ENOUGH—Devil Diver, Greentree stable entry, wins the Metropolitan Handicap at Belmont Park easy enough. Marriage, second.

Catholic League Winners Honored At Annual Banquet

One hundred and eighteen members of the Beaver Valley Catholic Bowling League gathered in St. Cecelia's school gymnasium to pay tribute to the winners of their respective divisions and partake of a delicious banquet served by the Christian Mothers of that parish.

St. Marys of Beaver Falls for the fourth straight year was the winner in the men's division, defeating St. Cyril of New Brighton. On the winning team were: Tom Caruso, Ernie Derose, Tully Alberti, Elmer Morelli, Augie Gatto, Roy Featherstone, Tony Menzina, John Luraghi, while on the losing outfit were Tony Czortorski, George Zivitz, Father John Sima, Walter Czortorski, Frank Pavkovick, Joseph Pavkovick and Pete Palijash.

Individual awards were won by Ralpk Wick, Al Nitsche, Tony Czortorski, Alex Roman, Leo Doyle, Tony Fiorucci, Ernie Derose and Tully Alberti.

Winner of the second half in the ladies division, St. Cecelia of Rochester emerged the victor in the roll-off with St. Cyril of New Brighton. Mary Murphy, Mary Anthony, Frances Farina, Ann Shemone, McCusker and Schumney composed the Championship team. St. Cyril's roster included Margaret Zivitz, Helen Pakovick, Dora Kasparik, Betty Smieska, Pauline Budiscak, Ann Flanick, Rose Namecek and Ann Pakovick.

Flo Monce led the individuals, followed by Mary Murphy, Betty Smieska, Ruth Hoodnick, Ann Shemone, Betty Darrow, Frances Farina, Hilda Curti and Rosa Tatko. Although handicapped by transportation and the war the League turned in its biggest season.

CHALKY WRIGHT WINS

BALTIMORE, May 18 — Chalky Wright, former featherweight champion, scored a technical knockout over Frankie Carto, Philadelphia, in the eighth round of a scheduled 10-round fight here last night.

Left-Handed Catchers

NEW YORK, — (UP) — Mickey Owen, first-string catcher for the Brooklyn Dodgers, confirms a general baseball theory that there is no reason why left-handed catchers can't make the grade in major league company. Apparently, says Owen, it is simply tradition working against the few southpaw receivers in existence.

Send THE TIMES to your boy in the Army or Navy. "It's like a letter from home every day."

Tournaments To Be Held In 48 States

WICHITA, Kan. — Forty-eight state championship baseball tournaments, each featuring brackets from 4 to 32 teams, will be staged under the sanction of the National Semi-Pro Baseball Congress this summer, President Ray Dumont announced here today.

The events will be open to any sandlot or semi-pro team, which includes those from the service, industrial or "town" ranks.

Under the nation-wide plan, each visiting team entering a state tournament will share in a mileage allowance, prorated from gross receipts. Leading teams will receive cash prizes. The champion will be awarded the official state championship trophy by the national organization and credited for competition, if it desires, in the annual National tournament in Wichita, August 13 to 25, with an estimated $25,000 in cash prizes to teams, including a $5,000 guarantee to the winner.

WALKER STOPS BROWN

CHICAGO, May 18—Buddy Walker, Columbus, O., heavyweight, ended Clarence Brown's string of four straight knockout victories last night by scoring a technical knockout over the Chicago fighter in the fourth round of a scheduled 10-round bout.

Coast Guardsmen Asked To Help In Drive On Rabbits

PHILADELPHIA, May 18.—(UP)—The U. S. Coast Guard motto, "semper paratus," literally interpreted means always prepared, but the Coast Guard probably never looked ahead to victory gardens—and rabbits.

The West Oak Lane Lions Club has appealed to the guard to help them in their nightly battle against marauding cotton tails who converge on 800 victory gardens at 19th street, and Cheltenham avenue. A nightly patrol is kept and, so far as nature will permit, the tender young lettuce shoots are being conooyed safely through infancy, adolescency and into the adult, or salad, stage.

The gardens are on the P. A. B. Wedener Estate, where the Coast Guard trains dogs, and members of the Lions Club and their friends, amateur gardeners all, decided not to plant corn, because of the corn borer; potatoes, because of potato bugs, nor tomatoes, because of scald and black rot.

Lettuce was decided upon because it is almost insect-free and quite nutritious. That's what the rabbits thought.

TODAY'S RADIO PROGRAM

6:00 p. m.
WWSW, Bill Cullen, news.
WCAE, Baron Elliott Orch.
WJAS, Frazier Hunt.
KQV, Dinner Music.
KDKA, News; Music.
WKBN, News.

6:15 p. m.
WWSW, Entertainment Time.
WCAE, Evening News.
WJAS, Beckley Smith, news.
KQV, Sports with Evans.
KDKA, Designs for Listening
WKBN, Don Gardner; You Won't Believe It.

6:30 p. m.
WWSW, Memory Songs.
WCAE, Fgn. News Roundup.
WJAS, Edwin C. Hill.
KQV, News.
KDKA, Songs for Service Men.
WKBN, John B. Kennedy.

6:45 p. m.
WWSW, Entertainment Time.
WCAE, Uncle Sam Program.
WJAS, Bob Prince, sports.
KQV, Modernaires.
KDKA, Lowell Thomas, news.
WKBN, The World Today; Joseph C. Harsch.

7:00 p. m.
WWSW, Baron Elliott Orch.
WCAE, Fulton Lewis, Jr.
WJAS, I Love a Mystery.
KQV, Victor Borge; Music.
KDKA, Fred Waring.
WKBN, I Love a Mystery.

7:15 p. m.
WCAE, Walter Durante.
WJAS, Harry James Orch.
KQV, Men, Mach. & Victory.
KDKA, News of the World.
WKBN, Harry James Orchestra.

7:30 p. m.
WWSW, Sports.
WCAE, Confidentially Yours.
WJAS, Melody Hour.
KQV, Pop Stuff.
KDKA, Tap Time.
WKBN, American Melody Hour.

7:45 p. m.
WWSW, Don Allen
WCAE, Treasury Star Parade.

8:00 p. m.
WWSW, Ben Selvin.
WCAE, Cisco Kid
WJAS, Lights Out.
KQV, Earl Godwin, news.
KDKA, Johnny Presents
WKBN, Lights Out.

8:15 p. m.
WWSW, Lawless Twenties
KQV, Lum and Abner.

8:30 p. m.
WWSW, Evening Serenade
WCAE, Pass in Review.
WJAS, Al Jolson
KQV, Duffy's
KDKA, Horace Heidt.
WKBN, Al Jolson; News

8:45 p. m.
WWSW, Ted Fiorito
WJAS, Jolson; News

9:00 p. m.
WWSW, Golden Hour.
WCAE, Gabriel Heatter.
WJAS, Burns and Allen
KQV, Famous Jury Trials.
KDKA, Battle of Sexes
WKBN, Burns and Allen.

9:15 p. m.
WCAE, Date with WAACs.

9:30 p. m.
WCAE, Return of Nick Carter.
WJAS, Suspense
KQV, Spot Light Bands.
KDKA, Fibber McGee & Molly.
WKBN, George Wald Orchestra.

9:45 p. m.
KQV, Bands; Organ.

10:00 p. m.
WWSW, Mayor's Civic Forum.
WCAE, John B. Hughes.
WJAS, Jazz Laboratory.
KQV, Raymond G. Swing.
KDKA, Bob Hope.
WKBN, Jazz Laboratory.

10:15 p. m.
WWSW, Uncle Sam Speaks.
WCAE, Ramon Ramos.
KQV, Gracie Fields.

10:30 p. m.
WWSW, Bill Cullen, news.
WCAE, U. S. Marine Pgm.
WJAS, John B. Kennedy.
KQV, This Nation at War.
KDKA, Red Skelton.
WKBN, Soldiers of the Press.

10:45 p. m.
WWSW, Scores; Music.
WCAE, Baron Elliott Orch.
WJAS, Mary Small.
WKBN, Mary Small, Songs.

11:00 p. m.
WWSW, Music for Your Mood.
WCAE, Norman Twigger.
WJAS, Ken Hildebrand.
KQV, News.
KDKA, News.
WKBN, News; Quincy Howe

11:15 p. m.
WCAE, George Duffy Orch.
WJAS, News; Pgh. Prepares
KQV, Treasury Star Parade.
KDKA, Eleven-Fifteen Local.
WKBN, Baseball Scores; Gordon MacRae, Songs.

11:30 p. m.
WWSW, Masterworks of Music.
WCAE, Sinfonietta.
WJAS, Greater Pgh. Prepares.
KQV, Music for Reading.
KDKA, "Uncle Sam".
WKBN, Invitation to Music.

11:45 p. m.
WJAS, Invitation to Music.
KQV, Music; News.
KDKA, Jack Swift, news.

12:00 Midnight
WWSW, 1500 Club (till 6 a. m.)
WCAE, Lawrence Welk Orch.
WJAS, News; James Orch.
KQV, Music for Reading.
KDKA, Hawaiian Echoes.
WKBN, Signature

12:15 a. m.
WCAE, Buddy Franklin.
WJAS, Harry James Orch.
KDKA, Frank Andrini Orch.

12:30 a. m.
WCAE, News; Barrie Orch.
KDKA, Roy Shields & Company.

12:45 a. m.
WCAE, Gracie Barrie Orch.

Swank School For Girls Now Hospital For U. S. Soldiers

WASHINGTON, May 18.—(UP)—Irene Castle, the dancer, or Martha Knudsen, daughter of the former General Motors president, wouldn't recognize their old alma mater today.

It isn't the swanky girls finishing school they knew as National Park Seminary. It's now Forest Glen Annex of Walter Reed Hospital—a place where soldiers are sent to recuperate from wounds or illness they may have suffered in Tunisia, or the Solomons, or the Aleutians, or wherever else American fighting men are in action.

Even as a hospital, though, the place retains many of its unusual features.

Convalescent officers live in luxurious sorority houses.

Soldiers wearing maroon-colored hospital uniforms pace the heavily carpeted halls.

Gold-framed mirrors still hang on the walls, and some soldiers like to stop in front of them and preen themselves.

The Army took over the school last September on the theory that sick and wounded soldiers, when no longer bed-fast, would get well quicker in an unhospital-like atmosphere.

OCD Intensifies Fat Salvage Drive

HARRISBURG, May 18.—(UP)—The State Defense Council today asked each Pennsylvania housewife to save at least one tablespoon of waste kitchen fats every day in a drive to boost state collections to 1,500,000 pounds per month.

Salvage chairman Warren R. Roberts explained that the waste fats should be placed in a wide-mouthed tin container and kept in a cool place. Butchers will pay 4 cents a pound for the fats, converted into nitro-glycerin, a powerful explosive.

Inquest Planned In Traffic Death

A coroner's inquest into the death of Carl B. Elbell, 55, 1140 Third street, Beaver, and Big Run, Pa., who was fatally injured when struck by an automobile in Third street, Beaver, on April 30 and died three days later, is to be held at seven o'clock Wednesday evening in the Beaver municipal building. Robert F. Smith, near Beaver Falls, driver of the automobile, posted $1,000 bond following the accident to insure his appearance at the inquest.

Unemployed Here Get $647 Fund

Checks totaling $647 were distributed to the unemployed during the week of May 14 by the Rochester office of Unemployment Compensation, it was announced today in Harrisburg by State Treasurer G. Harold Wagner. The state total was $87,392.55.

Brighton Township

Girls' 4-H Club To Meet On Wednesday

The Sewing-for-Victory 4-H club will meet Wednesday evening at seven o'clock in the home of Miss Patsy Whitehill, Dutch Ridge road, for the fortnightly session.

Amusements

(Continued From Page Four)

an American flyer attached to the Chinese Army. Preston is ordered to fly the travellers, including a French officer, an aged Chinese lady, a clergyman, a Russian Countess, and the nurse, across the border into India. From this point on the film moves from one thrill to another with speed enough to give any audience the jitters. There's an air battle with Zero fighters, a crash in the steaming jungles and some exciting moments when the fugitives are caught by Jap troops.

Adding a mystery flavor to an already spine-tingling picture, one of the airplane passengers is a spy.

"Taxi, Mister," the added feature, stars William Bendix and Grace Bradley.

HOME–FASHIONS–SEWING–HEALTH HINTS

After 35, Keep Eye on Scales

Leslie Brooks recommends badminton to keep weight down.

By HELEN FOLLETT

UP TO THE age of 35 it is all right for a woman to carry a few extra pounds. From that birthday onward she must keep a weather eye on the bathroom scales; if they show an increase she must get busy. It won't do to let fat cells become established. The longer they reside on the premises the tougher they are. And they have a way of multiplying that is discouraging to the one who is inclined to add to her measurements.

The safe reducing diet does not mean that all fat producing foods must be eliminated—sweets, starches and fats—because they are necessary to create energy, but it does mean that these elements should be greatly reduced. One egg daily is the rule, two or three servings of fruit, raw or cooked without sugar, one very small serving of potato, one of meat and at least two vegetables besides potatoes. Green salads are especially necessary. Buttermilk and unsweetened lemonade are ideal beverages.

Training the Appetite

The trouble with the heavyweight is that her appetite demands groceries that build adipose tissue. If war conditions cut down her allowance of fats and sweets, she fills up on bread and pastries. Her first effort should be to train her appetite to enjoy foods that will keep her healthy, make her slender.

Long hours of sleep and little exercise are factors that make for too abundant curves. Activity is the law of life. To keep muscles strong we must be alert, on the move. When muscles go slack, they attract fat cells.

Ten minutes of calisthenics every morning and a brisk walk every day will not only make a woman look better, but feel better. The woman who runs a carpet sweeper or vacuum cleaner over the rugs every day is getting an exercise that is likely to slither down the hips. The chair sitter is bound to acquire spread amidships.

Physical Examinaton One Step In Diagnosis

By LOGAN CLENDENING, M.D.

I AM WRITING this in a series of articles on diagnosis in order to try to give you a sympathetic understanding of your doctor. In order to treat you successfully, he must make a successful diagnosis. Recently I emphasized that the first step in diagnosis which the modern physician uses, and the most important, is to obtain a history—the patient's account of the illness in the patient's own words. This week I wish to discuss the second step in diagnosis, which is the physical examination.

> Dr. Clendening will answer questions of general interest only, and then only through his column.

The physical examination consists in endeavoring to accumulate data about the patient's appearance and the signs he displays which are evident to the physician's trained senses—sight, feeling and hearing.

It may seem to some of my readers that I am neglecting methods of diagnosis by machines. We live in a machine age and it is notorious that people in telling you about their doctor will tell you how he took the blood pressure with a machine and how he had an x-ray made and how he examined the heart with an electrocardiogram and how he examined the blood and used a microscope.

Importance of History

These things are all very fine, but they do not take the place of the history and the physical examination. According to the best authorities the history of the patient's illness, as told by the patient, is of 50 per cent importance in the final diagnosis, the physical examination, 25 per cent, and all the mechanical, microscopical and instrumental methods are worth about 25 per cent in the final summary of the average diagnosis.

Let me illustrate by taking a common condition, jaundice or yellow jaundice. The patient can see this and to that extent it is a symptom, so the patient tells you when it started and other things about it. You can see it and to that extent it is a sign, and part of the physical examination. Your seeing the fact that the patient is jaundiced confirms the patient's statement.

Now you begin to analyze it and you find that the patient says it came on without pain. In making a physical examination of the abdomen over the gallbladder, you find that there is no tenderness and you cannot feel any lump which would indicate the gallbladder or an enlargement of the liver. The patient says that attacks of jaundice have occurred a number of times in the last few years.

Blood Examinations

You can make some blood examinations, which would give a mechanical interpretation of the jaundice. The icteric index would tell you mathematically just how deep it is, and what is called the Vandenbergh test would tell another fact and an x-ray of the gallbladder would show whether the jaundice could be due to gallstones.

But as a matter of fact, you do not need this mechanical help because you can analyze the situation from your physical examination.

The fact that there is no pain and no tenderness and no palpable gallbladder indicates that there are no gallstones or gallbladder disease. The fact that you cannot feel the liver rules out cirrhosis. The fact that the patient is subject to recurrent attacks would indicate that the jaundice was due to blood destruction rather than to stoppage of the bile.

QUESTIONS AND ANSWERS

A. C. C.:—Are exercises of the muscles of the eye, as recommended by some people, good for astigmatism?

Answer: No. The only muscles of the eye that you can exercise are not attached to any portion of the eye which controls accomodation. You might as well open and shut the hood of your radiator 20 times a day in order to get your engine to quit missing.

C. N.:—I have been using saccharine tablets in my coffee and tea in place of sugar and was told it is hard on the heart. Could you please tell me if this is so?

Answer: Irresponsible and gossipy people are always saying something about saccharine to make those who take it uncomfortable. An extensive investigation, carried out over a period of years, showed that people can take saccharine indefinitely without any harm whatever.

Casserole Makes Meat Go Far

By BETSY NEWMAN

MAKING THE meat ration do for entertaining guests is really a problem, especially when the family consists of one or two. However, by giving thought, it can be done. You may have to have two or three meatless dinners thereafter, but after all, who cares? We have cheese, eggs, nuts, fish, etc., to take the place of the protein we miss in meat. And we don't have to go on week after week with no meat, as many persons are doing in other countries. Here's a casserole dish that will show you one way to make a small amount of meat go a long way.

Today's Menu

Casserole of Spaghetti, Tomatoes and Meat Balls
Asparagus or Green Peas
Carrot Sticks, Lettuce, Radishes, Onions
Hot Rolls
Strawberry Shortcake
Coffee

Casserole of Spaghetti, Tomatoes and Meat Balls

1 pkg. spaghetti or macaroni	2½ c. canned tomatoes
1 lb. chopped meat	1 medium sized onion
4 tbsps. bacon fat	¼ c. chopped green pepper
⅛ tsp. pepper	1 tsp. salt

Cook spaghetti or macaroni in boiling, salted water until tender, drain, rinse and pour into 2-quart casserole. Melt fat in frying pan. Brown meat which has been formed into small balls, add chopped onion and green pepper and cook for 1 minute; add tomatoes and seasonings and taste to see if it is seasoned. Mix with spaghetti and pour all, well mixed, into casserole. Cover top with bread crumbs or corn flakes, crumbled, and bake ½ hour. You can sprinkle grated cheese on top if you wish or slice cheese on top and brown. Serves 6.

SALLY'S SALLIES

Registered U. S. Patent Office.

I THINK HENRY BECOMES MORE LIKE HIS FATHER EVERY DAY
REALLY? AND CAN'T YOU DO ANYTHING ABOUT IT?
6-8

Serve Greens With Rice

By BETSY NEWMAN

IF YOU cannot get your family to eat their spinach or other greens plain, you might try serving them with rice.

Today's Menu

Lamb Chops Greens with Rice
Carrot, Radish, Green Onion, Lettuce Salad
Lemon Milk Sherbet Iced Tea

Greens with Rice

2 tbsps. fat	1 clove garlic, peeled
1 medium-sized onion, sliced	1 c. cooked rice
2 c. chopped, cooked greens	Salt, pepper

Melt fat in heavy frying pan, add onion and garlic, and cook over medium heat for 3 minutes. Remove garlic, stir in greens and rice, heat and season to taste with salt and pepper. Serves 6.

Lemon Milk Sherbet

1 tsp. plain gelatin	Salt
1 qt. milk	Juice of 3 lemons
1 c. sugar	

Soak gelatin in ½ cup milk for about 5 minutes; dissolve over hot water and add to remainder of milk. Mix lemon juice and sugar, add slowly to milk mixture, and freeze. For a richer sherbet use half cream and half milk. Serves 8.

New Dance Dress

Black crepe with lace inserts.

By VERA WINSTON

SHORT SKIRTED gala after-dark frocks are certainly long in public favor, since women enjoy their comfort and men admire them. This one, in black crepe has cap sleeves and an interesting neckline. It fastens in back with tiny covered buttons and is molded to the figure without any defining of the waistline. Diagonal inserts of black lace terminate in bows at one side.

There's Always Mañana

by LOIS EBY and JOHN C. FLEMING

WRITTEN FOR AND RELEASED BY CENTRAL PRESS ASSOCIATION

SYNOPSIS

Notified that her brother,
MELVIN MARSDEN, is missing in action,
JEAN MARSDEN, who has risen to the top as a fashion model, quits her job to become secretary to
STEVE LANDIS, director of a new rubber plant in Mexico. Jean has an abrupt introduction to carefree, handsome
CURLEY, employed by
MR. AND MRS. PARKINSON, owners of the Rancho Casolina.

* * *

YESTERDAY: Jean suddenly realizes that she misses Curley, who is away on a trip with Mr. Parkinson.

CHAPTER ELEVEN

AN ORANGE rim of sun still was spilling its bright color down the mountain side to the west when Jean whirled the station wagon into the courtyard. Mrs. Parkinson put down her book and smiled from her deck chair in the patio. "Welcome home, dear," she called. "Did you have a busy day?"

"And how!" Jean called as she jumped from the car and started toward her hostess. "If business keeps pouring in this way I'll have to be a one-woman swing shift!"

"How about a swim before dinner?" Mrs. Parkinson suggested. "And then we'll have our dinner in our robes, by the edge of the pool."

"You have a positive genius for thinking of just the right thing at the right time!" Jean smiled.

The two women, arm in arm, went in to change for their swim. Jean was ready first, and came out to sink into a deeply cushioned bamboo chair to wait for Mrs. Parkinson. As her wide blue eyes looked away to the mountains, that were shaded now from almost an orchid of color to deep purple, she found herself wondering what a certain dark-eyed young man was doing in Mexico City? Whether he had given her a thought since he left Rancho Casolina? The slamming of the screen door and the slap of Mrs. Parkinson's huaraches on the flagstones brought her back. Flinging her crimson bathing cape on the chair, Jean crossed to the high-dive platform. On the top platform she was poised a moment, a perfectly molded figure in a white suit, her arms and legs the color of Mocha. She sprang lightly from the board and cut a perfect arc to the green pool below. When she came to the surface, Mrs. Parkinson called to her, "As perfect a swan dive as I ever saw! Looked professional to me. Sure you're not holding out on some of your talents?"

". . . I did do a bit of amateur diving for the Ocean Spray Athletic Club a few years ago."

Jean laughed. "I never was a professional, but I did do a bit of amateur diving for the Ocean Spray Athletic club a few summers ago."

"I used to do a good deal of swimming myself when I was younger," Mrs. Parkinson said. "In fact, Mr. Parkinson and I judged several meets at the Grande hotel one winter while we were staying on the French Riviera."

"It's great sport, I think," Jean said. "And there's nothing better for the figure."

Just then Mrs. Parkinson turned down the flagstone walk. Her eyes met the figure of Rosita, walking with her head down and small fires blazing from the depths of her dark eyes. "Hello, child," she called. "Where have you been all day? I haven't had a glimpse of you since early morning."

"I have been riding in the hills," Rosita said with a sharp tone to her voice. She smiled a faint, quick smile at Mrs. Parkinson as if in apology for her curt reply, and then through narrowing eyes glowered at the poised figure of Jean on the high-dive platform.

"We're having dinner out here by the pool, Rosita," Mrs. Parkinson said gently, ignoring the girl's bad humor.

"Thank you, no, senora. I will eat in the kitchen with Elena!" Rosita snapped loudly. "Elena, she is a veree nice girl!"

Jean dived again and again, and finally, when she saw Jose coming with a small table with dinner service for two, she climbed from the pool, tossed her rubber cap to the ground, and threw her cape around her shoulders.

"I feel completely refreshed," she said as she watched Mrs. Parkinson ladle out steaming creamed turkey from a silver chaffing dish. "And that smells delicious."

"Elena is a splendid cook," Mrs. Parkinson smiled. "I hope your factory won't lure her away from me with the high wages I understand they are paying."

"If she makes application for work I shall be completely selfish and tell the personnel manager she has fits or something." Jean laughed.

Halfway through the meal Jean glanced up from her plate suddenly with a puzzled look on her face. "Why is it that Rosita hates me so?"

Mrs. Parkinson laid her fork aside before she answered. "I'm afraid she has, in that frighteningly fertile imagination of hers, conceived the notion that she is Curley's sweetheart. And you are a rival."

"For Curley?" Jean's laugh was nervously self-conscious. "Why, the poor child—but how utterly fantastic!"

There was an awkward moment of silence and then Mrs. Parkinson put the subject aside lightly as she reached out and patted Jean on the hand. "It's nothing to worry about, dear; it will all pass quickly, but you know Latin blood—it boils easily, and cools the same way."

They had just finished eating when they heard the crunch of automobile tires on the driveway and looked to see Steve come racing across the patio, a yellow envelope in his hand. Jean's heart stood still. She thought of the last telegram she had opened so gaily—"Melvin Marsden—missing—"

Steve gave her a worried glance as he handed it to her. "After what you said about your brother, I thought maybe . . . well, I thought this might be urgent, so I brought it right out."

Jean's hands were shaking so she could hardly break the seal. Steve watching the tenseness of her white face as she started to read, saw it slowly relax. He drew a breath of relief at her light tinkling, amused laugh.

"Well! I guess it isn't bad news," he said, mopping his forehead.

Jean read the message again before she looked up with a smile. "The idiot!" she murmured, folding the paper. "It's just a crazy message from—Curley! Nothing really, of any importance."

She saw Steve's face tighten with irritation and for an instant she was afraid of what he might say. But abruptly he grinned, with forced good nature. "I should be taking my good time to come dashing out here delivering messages from Dan Cupid."

"Thank you so much anyway," Jean cried. "The road to heaven also is paved with good intentions, you know. I think there's been a mistake in the name on this, however. From all I hear, it should have been addressed to Rosita."

Mrs. Parkinson smiled at Steve. "Won't you have a scotch and soda after your mad dash, Mr. Landis?" He thanked her politely, but refused. He had a mountain of work on his desk that was paging him—he could hear it even out here.

As Jean turned back from waving goodby, she saw Rosita on the balcony. From her baleful glare, it was apparent she had seen and heard about the telegram.

Jean and Mrs. Parkinson sat on the patio rather late that night talking. Finally, Mrs. Parkinson suggested they go to bed. Jean slipped into pale green pajamas and stood by the open window a long time. She looked off to the west and saw the dark mountains sleeping under a cloudless sky. Suddenly something silver flashed past her face to sink itself with a dull thud into the heavy bedroom door. Jean could see it glinting across the room in the thin moonlight. She crossed and saw a delicately wrought silver machete still quivering. A note was attached. She drew the knife quickly from the door and read the message printed in childish scrawl, "You let Senor Curley alone or else . . ." It was not signed. It didn't have to be.

(To Be Continued)

YOU CAN SEW THESE YOURSELF

COOL YOUNG BASQUE

9031

Marian Martin

Make this fetching young basque frock as a change from sports or work clothes. Marian Martin Pattern 9031 has a pretty neckline, with contrast of yoke, cuffs and skirt band. The skirt band may be omitted, and cap sleevelets are optional.

Pattern 9031 may be ordered only in misses' sizes 12, 14, 16, 18 and 20. Size 16 takes 3 yards 35-inch fabric, 1 yard contrast, and 8½ yards lace edging.

Send SIXTEEN CENTS in coins for this Marian Martin pattern. Write plainly SIZE, NAME, ADDRESS, STYLE NUMBER.

The Marian Martin Summer Pattern Book is full of styles to make sewing easy. Send TEN CENTS more for this book.

Send your order to THE DAILY TIMES, Pattern Department, Beaver, Pa.

COUPON

Name ....
Town ....
Street No. ....
Pattern Size ....
Pattern Number ....

Simplification of cotton fabrics will add approximately 230 million yards of cotton textiles annually through increased loom capacity.

Artists are feeling the pinch of war metals savings through an order halting production of metal easels and metal picture frames.

Home Helps for Scholars

By GARRY CLEVELAND MYERS, Ph.D.

WHEN A CHILD fails or lags at school, we parents usually place the blame on him or his teacher or both, rarely on ourselves. In these days when very low or failing grades come home, many parents charge the child with not having tried or worked hard enough. Many parents beat him or abuse him in some other way.

In the last analysis, as measured over the years, perhaps the parent should take the blame, even though he had always tried conscientiously to do the very best by the child.

Anyway, before any reader lets himself scold or punish his child who brings home a low or failing report card, he should sit down calmly, preferably with the other parent, and do some careful, serious thinking.

If you have a child who has failed, or barely passed this last school term, let me entreat you to put no trust in venting your emotions on him. Instead, please consider that your problem now is to find a way to help this child do better at school from now on. First you want him not to dwell on his failure remorsefully but to look hopefully ahead to a way to greater school success. You will want to have assurance from a medical expert that your child is physically well, that he has not been handicapped by poor sight or hearing.

Seek Out Experts

Then you will try to find out from his teacher and other learning experts just where his difficulties have been and specific ways to help him overcome them. If any teacher merely tells you the child is lazy and indifferent, insist on more definite reasons. What is back of these? Has he reading difficulty, for example? In case he reads poorly, he can hardly be expected to work very hard at reading or on subjects which consist chiefly of reading. If he is a miserable speller or poor at arithmetic, he won't normally work enthusiastically at these subjects.

My "Home Helps for Poor Spellers," "Home Helps for Poor Readers, I and II," may be had by sending a self-addressed envelope with a three-cent stamp.

Your older child might have neglected to do his home work at a regular time and place. He might not have been home at night to do it. Your problem is to see to it that your child shall cultivate day-by-day homework responsibility. In hundreds of other ways you may have been responsible, through your emotional expression, especially when he works at lessons, for his success or failure. Besides, no matter how smart their parents are, some children are just naturally slow learners.

Solving Parent Problems

Q. Do insane parents, other adults and youths who are sent to a mental hospital, really ever return cured?

A. Yes; the majority of those sent there in time return permanently cured.

Q. Do you think it safe for the mother to leave a sleeping child alone in the house long enough to go shopping?

A. I do not. The greatest danger is that he might awaken in her absence and grow seriously frightened at being left alone.

Shadows Learn About Clouds

—Mr. Punch Describes One He Found in Tree—

By MAX TRELL

KNARF AND Hanid, the shadows with the turned-about names, were in the playroom with their very good friend Mr. Punch. Suddenly Knarf, who had been looking out of the window at a cloud floating by overhead, said:

"Mr. Punch, why do clouds float? What makes them stay up in the air?"

"Well," answered Mr. Punch, "if they didn't stay up in the air, they wouldn't float. And if they didn't float, they wouldn't be clouds. I think that answers your question."

With that he stretched out in a chair, shut his eyes and started to take a nap. But the shadows weren't satisfied with Mr. Punch's answer. They still didn't know what made clouds stay up in the air, or why they floated about. They kept shaking Mr. Punch until finally he opened his eyes again.

"Clouds are very curious," he went on. "They don't always float. I remember once when a little cloud floated right through the house where I was living."

A Strange Event

The shadows were very eager to hear about this strange event and begged Mr. Punch to tell them all about it.

"It happened one summer's day," he said, "quite early in the morning. "I had just awakened. I hurried to the window to look out and see what kind of a day it was—and there, in the birch tree standing in the garden, was a cloud."

"In the birch tree!" Knarf and Hanid exclaimed in astonishment.

Mr. Punch nodded. "It had got itself caught in the branches. Yes, there it was, poor thing, unable to float off, or rain down, or do any of the things that clouds do. So I decided to set it free again. I went up to the tree and shook it. Dear me!" Mr. Punch sighed.

"Clouds are very curious," Mr. Punch said.

"What happened? Didn't you set it free, Mr. Punch?"

Set Cloud Free

"Indeed I did! The next instant I found myself in a thick white mist. The cloud had tumbled down, right on top of me! I groped my way back into the house. Alas—I had left the door open and it had come in too. The only thing I could do was to get back into bed and pull the covers over my head. That's what I finally did.

"And when I woke up again—I mean, when I looked out from under the covers again, the cloud was gone. It wasn't out in the garden either. It had just gone. But this will surprise you!—everything in the house, the spoons, the mirrors—everything looked silvery. And the leaves of the birch were silvery too. And that," concluded Mr. Punch as he got ready to continue his nap, "was because of the cloud. It had a silver lining, you see . . . a silver . . . lining."

Today's VICTORY GARDEN-GRAPH

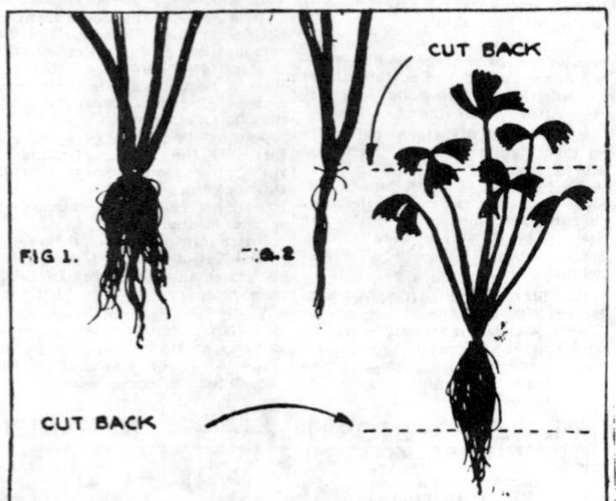
CUT BACK
FIG 1.
CUT BACK
6-7

So You Want to Grow Your Own Celery in Victory Garden?

By DEAN HALLIDAY

Released by Central Press Association

MANY VICTORY gardeners wonder if they can grow their own celery. It can be done and successfully if the gardener is willing to take extra pains with his plants.

Delicious celery can be grown successfully in the average Victory garden providing it has rich soil and lots of moisture as well as careful handling for the purpose of blanching.

It is advisable, however, for the average Victory gardener to buy celery plants ready to be set out in the garden. Celery seed germinates slowly and the young plants should be transplanted at least twice before setting out. The transplantings retard growth but help to develop a bushy root system, as illustrated in Figure 1 of the accompanying Garden-Graph, instead of the long tap root shown in Figure 2.

When planting celery plants prune the roots leaving only two or three inches long, and, as illustrated, also cut back the tops of the plants about one-third to check excessive evaporation while the roots are becoming established.

Be careful not to let the roots dry out and set the plants a little deeper than they formerly stood. During transplanting and later when cultivating take care not to get any soil between the stalks or into the heart of the plant.

Comic *The News-Tribune* Page

BRICK BRADFORD By William Ritt and Clarence Gray

COME, BRICK, WHY DO YOU NOT RESUME YOUR REST ?
I'M NOT TIRED, I—
OH, BUT YOU ARE, SEE ?

FELIX THE CAT ENFORCED BATH

NOPE! TOO COLD!
I WOULDN'T GO IN BATHING FOR A MILLION!
HORNETS!

NANCY THE NEW ORDER By Ernie Bushmiller

FLOY FLOY HAS INVITED ME FOR LUNCH AT A REAL CHINESE RESTAURANT
OH, BOY! THIS OUGHT TO BE A WONDERFUL TREAT
TWO ORDERS OF HAM AND EGGS!
ERNIE BUSHMILLER

HAP HOPPER, Washington Correspondent WASTED EFFORT Edited By Drew Pearson

LOLITA
FIND

TOOTS AND CASPER PAINFUL PAYING By Jimmie Murphy

GOODNESS! HERE COME SOME MORE BILL COLLECTORS! WHAT ARE WE GOING TO DO?
KEEP ON RINGING THEY CAN'T BE OUT ALL THE TIME!
I'M GOING TO WAIT HERE TILL THEY DO ANSWER!
I'M GETTING CALLOUSES ON MY KNUCKLES!
OH DEAR! THAT CONSTANT KNOCKING IS GIVING ME A HEADACHE!
IT'S NOTHING COMPARED TO THE HEADACHE I'VE GOT SOPHIE!
JIMMY MURPHY

TIM TYLER—FLYING LUCK GIRL MEETS BOYS By Lyman Young

TIM WAITS TENSELY, AS HURRYING FOOTSTEPS DRAW CLOSER AND CLOSER
...A MOMENT LATER...
ALL CLEAR, SPUD! COME ON BACK! I'VE CAUGHT OUR FOLLOWER—
G-GALLOPING GRAVY! IT'S—
TRIXIE KEENE!!

SALLY'S SALLIES

DON'T STIR A FOOT FROM YOUR POST, BUT KEEP WALKING UP AND DOWN AND SEE WHAT YOU CAN HEAR

BACK HOME AGAIN By Ed Dodd

JOE'S JOINT
POST OFFICE
THAT HELPLESS FEELING

SCORCHY SMITH DUD Trademark Registered U. S. Patent Office

TOO LATE, TOOT! AWAY FROM THAT COCKPIT, OR I'LL FIRE!
WHAT'S HE...? HE'S REACHING FOR THE MACHINE-GUN BUTTON! CAN'T LET THAT...!
CLICK!

DIXIE DUGAN EARLY AMERICANS By McEvoy and Striebel

DIXIE ASKS PA'S PERMISSION TO CONDUCT HER SUMMER OUTDOOR SCHEDULE ON THEIR PROPERTY
PLAYIN' PIONEER?? AW—THAT'S A GRAND IDEE, DIXIE! IT'LL BUILD CHARACTER! GO RIGHT AHEAD
THANKS, PA
IT'LL ALSO BUILD THEIR LITTLE BODIES AND BROADEN THEIR MINDS
PULLIN' WEEDS! SPRAYIN' MY TOMATO PLANTS! LOOSENIN' TH' GROUND AROUND MY CORN! DIGGIN' MY POTATOES! THERE ARE TH' TOOLS!
I THINK YOU MISUNDERSTAND, PA—
—THEY'RE GOING TO BE EARLY AMERICANS SO THEY CAN'T HAVE ANYTHING TO DO WITH A MODERN VICTORY GARDEN
OH, THEY CAN'T, EH?

JOE PALOOKA BIG TALK By Ham Fisher

DID WE
WHY UH GEE YOU GUYS SURE DONE A GREAT JOB WHILE WE WERE AWAY.
C'MON, WHAT DECORATION DID JA GET?
WHAT DID YA STOP ME FER WHY DON'T WE SHOW OUR DECORATIONS
OH, I DON'T KNOW. I GUESS I'M KINDA FUNNY.
NICE GUY THAT JOE.
LEMMY'S OKAY TOO. JUST A KID.

JOE JINKS MEET THE MASTER

PETE HUMUS CONNECTED A BEAUTIFUL RIGHT TO COWBOY CROWLEY'S JAW! THE COWBOY IS TAKING THE COUNT AGAIN!
1-2-3-
CROWLEY IS UP AT THE COUNT OF "8"! THE COWBOY IS FIGHTING A LOSING BATTLE AS HUMUS STEPS IN FOR THE KILL. PETE LANDS A HARD RIGHT, AT THE BELL
SOK
CLANG
PETE, YOU'RE TERRIFIC! YOU'RE TH' NEXT CHAMP!
NUTTIN' CAN STOP ME NOW, BOSS!
HELLO, MESSMORE!
(GULP!) P-PRESTO—! W-WHAT ARE YOU D-DOING HERE?

LITTLE MARY MIXUP DANGER By R. M. Brinkerhoff

KEEP UNDER COVER—I'LL LISTEN AT THE WINDOW SOME MORE—
SOMEONE'S COMING! A STRANGER!
WHAT IS—A FELLOW LIKE THAT DOING HERE IN SHANTY TOWN?
PETER IN HERE. QUICK!

BRONCHO BILL AT LONG ODDS By Harry F. O'Neill

TO SAVE A MAN FROM LYNCHING BILL FOUND THE WOUNDED BONETA SHERIFF, IDENTIFIED HIMSELF AND TOLD THE STORY OF WOULD-BE LYNCHERS — THE OFFICER GAVE HIM MORE ARMS AND THE NAMES OF SOME DECENT CITIZENS
THANKS! WITH THEIR HELP I CAN FETCH THE MAN TO YOUR JAIL
MEANWHILE, BILL'S PRISONER, DICK PORTER, ALSO FALSELY ACCUSED OF MURDER, WAS DEFENDING ANOTHER WHO WOULD BE HANGED WITHOUT TRIAL
HERE THEY COME!
HURRY WITH THAT BATTERIN' RAM— WE'LL BUST DOWN THE DOOR—

TARZAN CORNERED By Edgar Rice Burroughs

THORWALD WAS THUNDERSTRUCK BY THIS SUDDEN ENCOUNTER. HE VOICED A CRY OF ASTONISHMENT.
A MOMENT LATER, HITLER HIMSELF APPEARED ON A LEDGE ABOVE WITH TWO NAZI OFFICERS.
"TARZAN—TARZAN HAS RETURNED," THORWALD SHOUTED. "KILL HIM!"
INSTANTLY TWO PISTOLS LEAPED FROM THE HOLSTERS OF THE NAZI OFFICERS.

THE OLD HOME TOWN By Stanley

SARAH SAYS SHE'S TAKING NO CHANCES ON OUR LOSING THE WAR WHILE MRS OSWALD TWITTS STATION WAGON IS IN THE SHOP WITH A BUSTED FENDER SO SHE'S RUNNING ERRANDS FOR THE WOMEN'S WAR WORK CENTER
AUNT SARAH PEABODY ON THE HOME FRONT

ROOM AND BOARD By Gene Ahern

BROTHER PINKY HAS JUST RETURNED FROM BRAZIL, WHERE HE HAD QUITE AN EXTENSIVE COFFEE PLANTATION! AH KMF— SO YOU SEE, UNCLE BERT, WE PUFFLES CAN BE SUCCESSFUL!
WEREN'T YOU THE ONE THE PUFFLE FAMILY SPOKE ABOUT IN A HUSH? ... RUNNING A ROULETTE WHEEL, A RACE TRACK TOUT—AND OTHER THINGS!
UNCLE BERT,—OH YES, I PLACE YOU NOW!—USED TO BE SAID YOU WERE A STAGE-DOOR JOHN QUITE A BLADE IN YOUR DAY! SAY! DID THAT MARRIAGE EVER COME OFF WITH THE ORIENTAL DANCER?
GOING BACK IN THE PUFFLE ALBUM

The Weather Forecast

WESTERN PENNSYLVANIA: Continued warm tonight; thunder showers this evening. Grass pollen count—608.

"The Paper That Goes Home"

THE DAILY TIMES

1874 — and WESTERN ARGUS — 1803

ROCHESTER - BEAVER - MONACA - FREEDOM - BRIDGEWATER - CONWAY - VANPORT - MIDLAND

Beaver County History

An early German acceptance of Allied peace terms was expected, according to word received here on June 22, 1919

4 Cents

Established April 2, 1874 | Beaver and Rochester, Pa., Tuesday, June 22, 1943 | By Carrier 24 Cents A Week

CONTINUED U. S. CONTROL OF MINES SEEN

TROOPS QUELL RACE RIOTING IN DETROIT

Twenty-Five Persons Killed, 700 Injured In Sporadic Battles Between Whites And Negroes; Order Reported Restored Early Today

DETROIT, June 22.—(UP)—Federal troops in full battle regalia—armored equipment and powerful guns—restored order in Detroit today after the nation's worst civil disturbance since the first world war.

They moved into the city shortly before midnight under direct orders from President Roosevelt to quell rioting bands of negro and white mobsters whose 24-hour reign of terror resulted in the death of 25 persons, injury to nearly 700 others and wanton destruction of property.

The Presidential orders, issued at the request of Gov. Harry F. Kelly, whose declaration of a state of emergency was ignored by the rioters, commanded all persons engaged in "unlawful and insurrectionary proceedings" to disperse and return to their homes at once.

Almost simultaneously Secretary of War Henry L. Stimson announced at Washington that he had directed Maj.-Gen. Henry S. Aurand, commanding the Sixth Service command at Chicago, to use troops to suppress the disturbances.

STREETS CLEARED

But even before the orders of Mr. Roosevelt and Stimson were made public 1,100 federal troops swung up Woodward avenue—Detroit's main thoroughfare—and into debris-littered "Paradise Valley"—the city's shabby negro quarters.

With fixed bayonets the soldiers marched slowly behind armored cars whose machine guns were trained upon second story windows from which there had been sniping earlier in the evening. Within a few minutes streets were cleared and peace was restord. Hoewever, the streets still bore evidence of the rioting — overturned and demolished cars and trucks, looted shops, broken glass and bloody remnants of clothing scattered almost everywhere.

Brig.-Gen. William E. Guthner, in charge of federal troops here, said 1,200 additional soldiers were being held in reserve at Fort Wayne and Silfridge Field, Mich. Detroit's 3,500 weary city police also were to be joined today by 1,500 state troopers from as far north as the upper Peninsula of Michigan and by Michigan guardsmen mobilized by the Governor.

STARTED SUNDAY

The death toll reached 25 — 22 negroes and three whites—at 4:25 a. m. today with at least 15 of the victims reportedly slain by police. Dr. Austin Z. Howard, chief surgeon at Receiving Hospital, which alone treated more than 500 of the injured, described the rioting as

(Continued On Page Ten)

MARTIAL LAW DECLARED AS DETROIT RACE RIOTS SPREAD IN CITY

MARTIAL LAW HAS BEEN DECLARED in certain sections of Detroit as race riots spread through the city, bringing death to at least 25 persons and injuries to 700 more. A Negro is pictured, left, as he was cornered by police during the fighting. A mob of white persons is pictured, top right, as they waited for Negroes to alight from street cars or appear on the streets. Smashed and burned automobiles litter a street in the Negro district, lower right.

Eighty-Six County Men Are Inducted Into Armed Forces

Eighty-six Beaver County men from Local Draft Board No. 1, Baden, and Board No. 2, Beaver Falls, passed their physical examinations Monday in Pittsburgh and were inducted into the armed forces.

Those inducted are:

Raymond F. Cook, Chester A. Elak, Charles T. Goosby, John T. Jackson, Jr., Robert Neal, Beaver Falls; Charles W. Klein, New Brighton; Phillis G. Whipple, Freedom; Charles J. Krepps, Conway; James C. Oppelt, Ambridge; Walter Kolakowski, Ambridge; Frederick J. Hacker, Jr., New Brighton; Norman A. Welling, Baden; Vincent O. McDonough, Freedom; George F. Groeller, Ambridge; Billy Why, Beaver Falls.

Paul C. Stolz, Beaver Falls; Ernest V. Bilotto, Freedom; Theodore N. Hilnes, Frank J. Gasper, Paul J. Muto, Albert D. Nusser, Beaver Falls; Emerson J. Mooney, Howard B. Emery, New Brighton; John Sherba, Jr., Ambridge; Fred L. Blankenbicker, Henry M. Brzozowski, Joseph F. Sicchitano, Robert W. Gayhart, Jr., Louis R. James, Jr., Victor F. Fabiani, Rich-

(Continued On Page Ten)

Man Hit By Auto Dies In Hospital

Kostanty Hoynesky, Ambridge, died this morning in Beaver Valley hospital from injuries received when struck by an automobile at eleven o'clock Sunday evening at Duss avenue and Eighth street, Ambridge. The driver was Erland S. Rote, Sewickley, according to Deputy Coroner Mrs. H. C. McCarter. The body was removed to the O'Donnell funeral home, Ambridge.

FIRST EARLY-MORNING TEST BLACKOUT IS FAILURE HERE

Beaver Valley would have been an easy target for enemy bombers had the practice blackout held early this morning been a real air raid instead of a practice called by the Third Army Command in Baltimore.

The fan-out system for alerting civilian defense groups broke down at the very source and as a result street lights were never extinguished in many places and in all communities the Civilian Defense Corps was late getting mobilized.

George W. Roark, executive secretary of the County Defense Council, reported today that the mix-up resulted from failure of the personnel manning the black box to realize that the "yellow" warning, which came through about 4:13 a. m., was the signal for a practice blackout, and not, as they thought, merely a test of the telephone lines and other signal equipment.

Roark explained that the Third Army Service Command tests the special telephone line frequently at any hour of the day or night, but this morning was the first time a practice blackout had been ordered by that method.

FAN-OUT DELAYED

The phraseology used by the Army operator to test the lines is very similiar to that used to signal a blackout or air raid, and the men manning the "black box" did not realize their mistake until sometime after receiving the first blue signal about 4:30 a. m. The "yellow" alert had been received about 4:13 a. m.

Then, an effort was made to fan-out the alerts on yellow, blue, red, and blue in succession as rapidly as possible, but considerable confusion resulted and there were numerous break downs caused by the failure or inability of other key persons to complete their calls. Telephone lines were jammed for a half hour or more.

Roark said today the mistake

(Continued on Page Ten)

Two Boys Blamed In Trolley Crash

PITTSBURGH, June 22.—(UP)—Two boys who allegedly tampered with the air tank which controls the brakes on one of the cars were blamed by detectives for a rear-end collision of two trolleys early today, resulting in injury to 35 passengers. None of the 35 was injured seriously but 21 of them were treated at hospitals. It was the third wreck involving trolleys in eight days.

The accident happened at Murray and Flemington avenues, Squirrel Hill, as the two Homestead cars were inbound.

J. Raymond Metzger, 35, of Pittsburgh, operator of the first car, a streamliner, told officers he stopped to discharge a passenger, and was just starting to go when the second trolley, an old style car, crashed into the rear.

Operator of the second trolley, William Chuba, 30, Canonsburg, said his brakes would not function when he tried to stop as he saw the car in front.

A youth, John Cole, passenger on Chuba's car, told detectives that while the car was stopped at an earlier intersection, he saw two boys who had been loitering on the corner, apparently let the air out of the tank which controls the brakes.

Driver Acquitted Of Failure To Stop

Richard Harlen Davis, near Darlington, was acquitted of failure to stop and render assistance at the scene of an accident by a jury late Monday afternoon following a trial before Judge Henry H. Wilson. The jury directed that the county pay the costs. Davis denied, as charged in the indictment, that his car had struck Frank Barejcza, of West Mayfield, on Oct. 28, 1942.

Valley Presbytery Approves Pastoral Call, Supply Pastors

Formation of plans to install a new pastor at the Steffin Hill church and approval of several stated supply pastors marked the morning session of the summer meeting of the Beaver Valley Presbytery held today in the New Brighton United Presbyterian church.

Rev. D. C. McCoy, Rochester, moderator, and Dr. Thomas P. Graham, Ambridge, clerk, were in charge of the session.

The opening sermon was delivered by Henry L. Millison, a member of the Second United Presbyterian church, New Castle, who has just completed his second year at Pittsburgh Xenia Theological Seminary. He was licensed by the

(Continued On Page Ten)

Beaver Woman Died In Home Monday

Mrs. Alice Tresa McClintock, widow of Edward McClintock, died at six o'clock Monday evening in her home, 493 East End avenue, Beaver.

Mrs. McClintock was a member of SS. Peter and Paul Roman Catholic church, Beaver; Rochester Court, Catholic Daughters of America; the Ladies Catholic Benevolent Association and the Tabernacle Society of the church. Surviving are one son, Officer Candidate Paul Dolan McClintock, Fort Benning; Ga.; one daughter, Margaret Dolan McClintock, at home; one brother, Martin J. Dolan, Pittsburgh, and one sister, Mrs. Anna Diskin, Los Vergas, Nev.

The body was removed to the Anderson funeral home, Beaver, and later to the family home where friends are being received.

URGE END OF STRIKE

PHILADELPHIA, June 22.—The United Labor committee, at a meeting last night, adopted a resolution urging the striking coal miners to return to the mines and to permit government agencies to negotiate a satisfactory contract.

Brighton Workers In Scout Campaign Top Other Towns

New Brighton workers in the annual Beaver County Boy Scout financial campaign for $10,500, holding their initial meeting Monday evening in the Beaver Valley Y. M. C. A., reported $880 already contributed in the drive. That figure is the highest yet reported at any town meeting in the Fort McIntosh Boy Scout District, topping Rochester by six dollars.

Judge Frank E. Reader, co-chairman of the campaign, and Prothonotary E. M. Wallover, vice chairman of the Fort McIntosh District Committee, were the principal speakers, stressing the need for all-out support of county Boy Scouts and Cubs. F. E. Garvin, Fort McIntosh sectional chairman, also spoke briefly, urging full support of the campaign.

NEXT REPORT FRIDAY

Charles M. Arnold, town chairman, presided and introduced the campaign workers. John Merriman, New Brighton Neighborhood Commissioner, discussed Scouting activities. Charles G. Robertson, Beaver, Boy Scout field executive in the Fort McIntosh District, and secretary to Judge Reader in the campaign, gave instructions to the workers.

W. W. Wilson, member of the Merchants and Employes Division in the New Brighton solicitation, asked the invocation. Rev. G.

(Continued On Page Ten)

McCreary Not To Be Candidate For Election In Fall

District Attorney Robert E. McCreary, Monaca, will not be a candidate for re-election at the coming county primaries. First information as to the decision of the official now completing his eighth year as prosecuting attorney, was contained in the following statement issued today by Mr. McCreary:

"My greatest desire at this time is to see a Republican victory in Beaver County next November, a very necessary step if this county

(Continued On Page Ten)

MENACE TO STEEL OUTPUT GROWING

BULLETIN

PITTSBURGH, June 22—The coal strike will force United States Steel Corporation to bank more than half of the 37 blast furnaces in the Pittsburgh operating district by Thursday, with a resultant loss of thousands of tons of steel for the war effort, it was announced today. A spokesman for the company disclosed that lack of coke due to the coal walk-out will result in a shut-down of six blast furnaces by tomorrow and a total of 19 by Thursday.

WASHINGTON, June 22 (UP)—Solid Fuels Administrator Harold L. Ickes and United Mine Workers President John L. Lewis confer again today, presumably to lay the groundwork for discussion of government operation of struck coal mines for the duration of the war.

Virtually all bituminous and anthracite miners stayed home from work for the second day. Their strike already has affected war production, officials of the Carnegie-Illinois Steel Corporation in Pittsburgh announcing that some of their blast furnaces would be shut down today because of lack of coal.

Ickes and Lewis began their talks yesterday after the UMW rejected the War Labor Board's proposed contract between miners and operators, but said the miners would work for the government.

Neither Ickes nor Lewis would hint about the details of their talks, but a spokesman for Ickes revealed that officials of the Solid Fuels Administration already had discussed "permanent" operation of the mines just in case it should prove necessary. The mines were seized by the government, presumably on a temporary basis, after the strike of May 1.

It was believed that Ickes was given a go-ahead by President Roosevelt or War Mobilization Director James B. Byrnes before he proceeded. When Ickes intervened in the dispute before, the WLB blocked him with President Roosevelt's support so Lewis could not succeed in by-passing the Board.

WLB STILL IN COMMAND

Even after yesterday's conference, one of Ickes' aides reiterated that the WLB still retained jurisdiction over the wage dispute.

Earlier, Wayne L. Morse, WLB public member and compliance officer, said that not only Lewis but "all the agencies of government were bound by the Board's directive "subject to such action as the President may wish to take."

(Continued On Page Ten)

Fleets Of Allied Bombers Blast At Germany And Italy

War Summary

By United Press

EUROPE — Allied air offensive mounts to new pitch with American bombing raids on German Ruhr and Belgium after Royal Air Force makes one of the biggest raids of the war on Krefeld at western edge of Ruhr.

MEDITERRANEAN — American and British bombers blast Naples day and night and smash at widely scattered targets in Italy and island outposts.

RUSSIA—Red Air Force pounds German bases behind eastern front; Soviet proclamation on second anniversary of war with Germany calls for second front this year, says defeat of Nazis without it is impossible.

SOUTHWEST PACIFIC— Allies shoot down 14 to 23 planes from Japanese fleet of 36 in dogfight over New Guinea base of Lae, running two-day bag to 47.

NAZI CITY RAIDED

American heavy bombers in strong force raided targets in the Ruhr and Belgium today after powerful Allied air armadas had carried out one of the biggest raids of the war on the German production center of Krefeld and blasted the Italian port of Naples day and night.

The two-pronged aerial offensive from Britain and Africa against both ends of the European Axis was mounting toward unprecedented scope and intensity.

The trip-hammer blows at key Axis war centers by United States and British bombing fleets in action around the clock were accompanied by subsidiary thrusts into widespread territory occupied by the Nazis and against the ramparts of Southern Europe.

Today's double blast by the Eighth U. S. Air Force followed a crushing attack on Krefeld by the RAF, the plastering of Naples Sunday night and yesterday by Anglo-American aerial teams, and a broadside hail of blows against oth-

(Continued On Page Ten)

Horse Runs Into Auto; Five Hurt

Five men were injured this morning when the automobile in which they were enroute to work at Kobuta was struck by a stampeding horse and crashed into a ditch near St. Joseph Park.

Five or six horses, believed to be owned by a farmer by the name of Pollis, near Aliquippa, had stampeded and one of the animals struck the workers' car as they galloped across the highway, Aliquippa police report.

The three injured—Brick Dudley, Elmira street; Lonnie Mitchell, 316 Sixth avenue, and Hayward Walker, 426 Monaca road, all of Aliquippa—were removed to the Aliquippa police station where they were treated by a physician. All received lacerations and bruises about the face and body. Two other occupants of the car escaped with bruises, according to police.

The horse which struck the car received a long, deep cut across the chest, according to the story told Aliquippa police.

Rochester K. Of C. Elects Officers

Election of officers marked the semi-monthly meeting of Father James Reid Council, Knights of Columbus, held Monday evening in the council home.

John R. Murtha, deputy grand knight, was elected grand knight succeeding Attorney J. Frank Kelker, Jr. Other officers elected are Deputy grand knight, Joseph V. Mazzocca; chancellor, . F. Kelker, Sr., re-elected recorder, William D. Heyman; treasurer, Leo Scracnek, re-elected; warden, Michael Marino; advocate, Thomas D Stablow; inside guard, Michael Marino; outside guard, Amgelo Stablow; trustee, Frank Guda; delegates to 1944 state convention, John R. Murtha and J. Frank Kiker, Jr., and alternate, Charles T. Welsh and William D. Heyman.

Permission was granted for the use of the home grounds for a Cub Pack "pow-wow" in July. A program of horseshoes, ping-pong and other games was enjoyed following the business session.

Lost and Found

LOST: Between new road in Colona and Hill Top Bus line, Virginia avenue, Rochester, one $50.00 bill, Monday. Reward. Call Rochester 1711. 6 22-28 inc.

LOST: 2 ration books, No 1 With name Anna Marie Scruci and No. 2 with name Francis Gilbert Scruci, Virginia Ave Extension, Rochester 6 22-24 inc.

LOST: In New Sewickley Twp., female wire haired Fox Terrier 'Black and tan markings. Answers to name "Crickie" Liberal reward for any information Phone Rochester 6148-J-1 6 22-28 inc.

LOST: No 1 Ration Book in Rochester or Monaca between June 1st and 5th, 1943 Raymond S. Doak, R. D. No. 1 Monaca, Pa. 6 22-24 inc.

Red Cross Setup Here Is Revised, Stout Accepts Chairmanship Again

BOB STOUT

JOSEPH J. SPRATT

Reorganization and redistribution of the war time work of the Beaver County Chapter, American Red Cross, resulted last night in the reelection of Robert C. Stout, Beaver to the chairmanship of the Chapter for another year. He has accepted the post under the new setup.

One month ago he had declined to accept reelection. He gave a long list of reasons. Among them were that he had already served five and one-half years as head of the Chapter; that the war-time work of the Chapter had expanded tremendously, and that the condition of his health would not permit him to continue to carry the load; that so much of his time and effort had

(Continued On Page Ten)

KOBUTA COMMUNITY AT KOPPERS PLANT ON SOUTHSIDE CALLED "HOME" BY OVER 1,500

By BILL HEYMAN

Life-long residents of Beaver County, familiar though they may have been with the Potter Township area, show considerable surprise when they visit the location of the butadiene and styrene plant being erected for the Defense Plant Corporation by the Koppers United Company.

The plant itself extends over 200 acres, and there is probably not a more interesting or higher specialized sector than Kobuta Village, the trailer camp, and Camp Beaver, the barracks area at the plant.

Together the two communities separated only by a wire fence, form a small city of over 1,500 persons, almost entirely new arrivals in the county.

A visit to the two communities, better known to local residents by the common term "Kobuta", reveals the conditions under which men working at the plant and their wives and families are living due to the unavailability of sufficient permanent housing facilities in Beaver county.

While the trailer camp is for the workers with families, the barracks area is for bachelors or men who came here to work without bringing their families. They are housed in Nissen huts, similar to those used by American troops in Iceland and other overseas posts.

Kobuta also has a modern cafeteria capable of seating 500 persons. The building is well-lighted, being glassed on three sides, while the kitchen, storerooms and three up-to-date refrigerator rooms are located on the fourth side.

Many mornings the cafeteria serves breakfast to 1,200 or 1,300 persons, while two thousand meals for one day is considered only average. The record for one day is 6,837 meals, according to Patrick Murphy, cafeteria manager, a jovial Irishman who is extremely proud of his layout.

Murphy will, on the slightest provocation, show a visitor his well-stocked larder, his spotless kitchen with its bakery, the commissary where sandwiches to take out are available and his pet refrigerator rooms.

He reports warm weather is a little hard on the soft-drink supply. No alcoholic beverages are sold on the area, and the sale of 1,000 cases of soda pop is not a bit out of line. Two canteens located in the plant proper aid in this distribution.

The trailer camp, now Kobuta Village, was started last December and the first occupant moved in on February 15 of this year. Complete occupancy was achieved on March 15 and there are now waiting lists for both the government-owned trailers and parking space for private trailers.

In the village at present are 250 government-owned units, 30 privately-owned units and 21 utility units. Ninety of the government trailers are of the expandable type

(Continued On Page Three)

FREEDOM ARMY NURSE FORGOT TO SALUTE CLARK GABLE IN ENGLAND

LIEUT. ALDA M. BEECHER

"Captain Clark Gable is at the same post where I am now stationed and the first time I saw him I was so excited I forgot to salute," wrote Second Lieutenant Alda Mauk Beecher, pretty U. S. Army nurse, from England to her parents, Mr. and Mrs. Roy A. Mauk, Rochester, formerly of Freedom.

Lieutenant Beecher wrote that she has talked to the famous screen idol and said that he is very much the same in real life as in the movies.

"We are given bicycles here and do most of our traveling by bike," Lieutenant Beecher said. She has just recently arrived in England. Before leaving for overseas duty, she was located at Fort Belvoir, Va. Previously, she had been stationed at Fort Eustis, Va., for six months training.

Her husband, Captain Jess S. Beecher, U. S. Army, was stationed on the West Coast the last time the Mauks heard from him. The Beechers were married last July at the army post at Fort Eustis, culminating a romance which began at the fort only a few months before.

Pfc. Thomas N. (Bucky) Mauk, son of the Mauks, with the U. S. Marines, is on a small island in the South Pacific, according to word received by his family. He had been stationed at the Hawaiian Islands and was at Honolulu.

Amusements

ORIENTAL THEATRE

Parading a lineup of extraordinary youthful talent, the novel comedy musical, "Mister Big," ends tonight at the Oriental Theatre. Donald O'Connor, one of Hollywood's most remarkable juvenile performers, is starred. Headlined with him are Gloria Jean and Peggy Ryan.

Jive versus the classics, is the theme of "Mister Big" and the idea is said to have been developed for the screen in entertaining style. Locale of the bright story is a School of the Theatre, where a gang of jive-minded kids mingle boogie-woogie with highbrow compositions.

Other popular players in the cast are Robert Paige, Elyse Knox, Samuel S. Hinds and Bobby Scheerer.

Singing and dancing are featured throughout the picture with unusual specialties contributed by The Ben Carter Choir and Ray Eberle with Eddie Miller's Bob Cats.

Paramount's "Aerial Gunner," the exciting action film story of the Air Corps gunners, opening tomorrow, shows the important role the aerial gunners play in flying warfare.

In an action packed scene, Zeros attack a lone bomber, meeting the blazing guns of our Air Corps sharpshooters, who blast them out of the sky.

Chester Morris and Richard Arlen head the cast of the thrilling film, in which Jimmy Lydon, Dick Powell and Lita Ward are featured

MAJESTIC THEATRE

"Good Morning, Judge," announced as one of the season's most zestful action comedies, comes Wednesday to the Majestic Theatre. The film co-starring Dennis O'Keefe and Louise Allbritton, is said to deal comically with the gay complications and altercations pertaining to a $100,000 plagiarism suit. Mary Beth Hughes, J. Carrol Naish, Louise Beavers and Samuel S. Hinds are featured in the supporting cast.

O'Keefe appears as the head of a large music publishing house against which the lawsuit is filed. Miss Allbritton is seen as the talented young woman attorney who represents two irate song-writers. Miss Hughes portrays the blonde vocalist romantically inclined toward the publisher. She also figures in the frenzied legal proceedings and in a knockdown-dragout cafe battle which brings the story to its hilarious courtroom finale.

"Night Plane from Chungking," starring Robert Preston and Ellen Drew, is the added feature for Wednesday and Thursday.

BEAVER THEATRE

With the war headlines getting us down daily, and tired war workers in urgent need of relaxation, it is pleasant to be able to recommend a film that offers temporary escape at least from all our problems. It is "Lady of Burlesque, ending tonight at the Beaver Theatre and is as gay and tuneful and mirth-provoking as the doctor ordered.

The famous strip tease artist, Gypsy Rose Lee, authored the story, "G-String Murders," from which this brittle, streamlined story running from the zaniest farce to tense, suspense-filled drama, was adapted. And who, better than Gypsy, could describe so perfectly the exciting, colorful life behind the scenes as well as in front of the footlights in a Broadway burlesque theatre.

Barbara Stanwyck plays the starring role, that of Dixie Daisy, a small town burlesque performer who suddenly gets her big chance at The Old Opera House, a famous burlesque theatre on Broadway.

A double screen bill opens tomorrow, presenting Laurel and Hardy in "Jitterbugs," also "Calaboose" with Jimmy Rogers and Noah Beery, Jr.

SALLY'S SALLIES

GENTLEMEN PREFER BLONDES, ANYWAY
WELL, YOU OUGHT TO KNOW, DEAR, YOU'VE BEEN BOTH

RIALTO THEATRE

Pat O'Brien and Randolph Scott are the official stars of "Bombardier," RKO Radio's thrill-paced saga of the Air Force now playing at the Rialto. But in simple justice it must be recorded that there are a couple of other stars in the gripping film that in their way are as important as the human one—the famous Norden bombsight and the Flying Fortresses.

How that closely-guarded instrument which, in Bombardier's language, "drops 'em in a barrel from 20,000 feet," was developed, and how this country came to have the priceless weapon, and men trained to use it, when war flared across Pearl Harbor, is here told for the first time. And it is told in a brilliant and authentic fashion which makes the picture deftly entertaining as well as revealing.

The big fortresses, too, have a vital role in the film, which is said to be a nod to the professional career of Colonel "Paddy" Ryan, whose foresight and persistence brought about adoption of the Norden device, and who created the schools where Bombardier cadets are taught the secret of its intricate mechanism.

Absorbingly interesting details of the training and the rigorous routine the cadets go through are woven into the plot to lend realism. A romance with pretty Anne Shirley as the heroine is also featured.

Deluxe shorts complete this outstanding program.

GRANADA THEATRE

Murder, espionage and romance are the explosive ingredients of the new film, "Background to Danger," now playing at the Granada.

Starring George Raft and Sydney Greenstreet the picture's strong supporting cast is headed by Peter Lorre, accomplished player of spine-tingling roles, Brenda Marshall and Osa Massen, pretty Danish actress. Locale of this exciting story is Turkey, a focal point of international intrigue and counter-espionage.

Slacks And Oxfords For Women Workers At Propeller Plant

Female employes in the Curtiss-Wright Corporation plant in Borough Township are now required to wear slacks and sensible oxfords with low heels, preferably safety shoes.

A reminder to that effect was issued to all Beaver bladeswomen through a safety bulletin bearing the signatures of Plant Manager Oscar W. Nelson and Safety Supervisor Sam McNaugher.

"All women employes, who work on the shop floor, are required to wear slacks," a bulletin said.

"This is a condition of employment. Women in enclosed offices are exempt."

Another bulletin posted at the same time advised: "All women who work on the shop floor are required to wear a sensible oxford with low heels, preferably safety shoes. Shoes with high spike heels, bedroom slippers, and open toe or heel shoes, are prohibited anywhere in the plant. This is a condition of employment."

Seeks Divorce

SUPERIOR COURT in Los Angeles is hearing the divorce suit filed by Film Actress Jean Parker, above, against her husband, H. Dawson Sanders, a radio announcer. She charged "grievous mental suffering." (International)

British Glider Troops Have Tea Before Invasion

ADVANCED BRITISH AIRBASE North Africa, July 11.—(Delayed)—(UP) — The British glider-borne troops who with parachutists helped pave the way for the invasion of Sicily had their cup of tea just before they landed on the Italian island.

These men without nerves thought that was a joke. They're in there fighting now and haven't had time to report how that last cup went. But the fliers who pulled the gliders over said the troops had wisecracks on their lips just before they filed into their craft in Africa.

The cup of tea was due to be handed out as they pulled in toward the landing spot and while their pilots awaited word to unhook the steel cables linking the gliders to the towing planes.

The first groups surprised the Italians. The later ones came down through searchlights and anti-aircraft fire that spurted near their shadowy craft as they glided toward the earth.

PRIVATE BUCK .·. By Clyde Lewis

FORT SILL

"Today is Buck's birthday, so he fired a 21-gun salute for himself!"

SCOTT'S SCRAP BOOK By R. J. SCOTT

W. G. GEORGE - VET ENGLISH TRACK STAR HELD 12 CHAMPIONSHIP TITLES AT ONE TIME - HIS TIME OF 4 MINUTES 12 3/4 SECONDS FOR THE MILE STOOD FOR 35 YEARS
PAGODA-SHAPED ANT HILLS ARE BUILT BY WHITE ANTS OF THE BELGIAN CONGO
SCRAPS
ANYWAY, I'M STILL IN TH' RIVER
HOW WIDE IS THE AMAZON RIVER WHERE IT ENTERS THE SEA?
150 MILES FROM HEADLAND TO HEADLAND
PANPIPES ARE PLAYED UPON THE ARRIVAL AND DEPARTURE OF COURIERS, IN BOLIVIA

THE OLD HOME TOWN By STANLEY

I AINT ACCUSIN' NOBODY- BUT SINCE A HALF-A-HAM WALKED OUT OF THE ICE BOX YESTERDAY MORNIN'- I'M STAYING RIGHT HERE UNTIL I SEE YOU TWO BABIES ARE SAFELY ON THAT BUS!
GR-R-R
THE EARLY MORNING SHIFT TAKES OFF FROM MRS SULPHURO BRIMSTONE'S BOARDING HOUSE UNDER A CLOUD
STANLEY
7-13

There's Always Mañana

by LOIS EBY and JOHN C. FLEMING

WRITTEN FOR AND RELEASED BY CENTRAL PRESS ASSOCIATION

CHAPTER THIRTY-NINE

THE NEXT day the "national police" of both Mexico and the States had arrived. Four quiet, sharp-eyed men in civilian clothes, they had trickled through Jean's office into Steve's to hold short, tense conferences, and then disappeared again on their mysterious errands around the countryside. She was not asked to take notes at these conferences, and Steve gave her no inkling of what was transpiring in them.

She had no desire to discuss them. Her curiosity was dead. She was conscious only of a dull, apprehensive terror as she watched the federal agents of two countries co-operating in a smooth, confident routine of closing in on their quarry.

Steve understood the daze through which she was carrying on her work. He was patient with her when he saw her mind go blank in the midst of a dictated sentence, stopping to repeat it casually, slowly for her. He could feel the grinding torture she was enduring each time Manzanares burst in with fresh reports. Out of sheer sympathy, he was beginning to feel a definite relief when Manzanares or one of the FBI men admitted, "No working evidence on the gang around here."

But he could not always shield her. There was the morning of the second day when he had pantomimed through the glass partition for her to bring into the conference the report she was typing. She had brought it, looking pale and remote in her apple-green suit, a small carbon smudge on her high brow where he had seen her press her hand to her aching head.

At sight of her, Manzanares, in the circle of FBI men around Steve, came momentarily from his absorption in the work.

"Did you know," he demanded, "of the fine work the Senorita Marsden has accomplished for us?"

The FBI men didn't. They regarded the embarrassed Jean with friendly admiration as Manzanares launched forth into a glowing and detailed description of her spying activities at the Rancho Casolina.

"And it was the senorita herself," he finished triumphantly, "who saw with her own beautiful eyes the limping man talking to the one undoubtedly Jeffries in the hallway of the hacienda."

At the last words, Jean's eyes focused sharply on Manzanares. "They have found the limping man, then?" she whispered.

Manzanares nodded joyfully. "But, yes, senorita! Only this morning he was recovered by the police in Mexico City. He is one of the gang of Jeffries, and with him was discovered explosives sufficient to destroy another defense factory."

"Oh!"

Steve leaped to the rescue, alarmed at the closed, dull hopelessness settling over her face. "I wonder if you'd mind typing this report immediately, Jean?" he said casually.

Jean nodded gratefully and fled.

One of the FBI men chuckled. "I'll give you the job, Landis, of selecting my next secretary. I like your taste."

"Would it not perhaps be a wise thing," suggested one of the Mexican detectives, "to allow her to pay another visit to the rancho? Our activities have been most discreet. She could still return there in the guise of friendship and, who knows, be successful once more."

"No!"

The men looked up surprised at Steve's violence.

"You're crazy if you men think your presence has gone unnoticed in the village," he said irritably, "or that any members of the gang in this vicinity aren't nervous as cats about it. Jean is not going near that rancho. In fact, I'm concerned over her safety now, even in the hotel."

The FBI men dropped the subject immediately. Steve felt in their tactfulness a sympathetic realization of his feeling for her. It embarassed him, but didn't change his determination to protect her from any further participation in this sordid business in which her heart had so treacherously involved her.

When they had gone, Steve sat on at his desk, his work before him for once going unnoticed. He WAS concerned about Jean. In the next few days, if the FBI men accomplished what they seemed confident they would, her part in the round-up would certainly be known by the criminals involved—if not actually broadcast by the garrulous Manzanares. And vengeance often was swift in this country. A stool-pigeon of the law was hated with virulent ruthlessness, as Manzanares himself had often told him in his rambling tales of capture. Reluctantly he reached a decision and rang Jean's buzzer.

Through the glass partition she sent him a quick smile and held up a hand in the pantomime they had worked out, meaning, "With, or without notebook?"

"Without," he signaled, and watched her approach his office door with the graceful, erect swinging walk he loved.

"Sit down." He pulled one of the conference chairs to the side of his desk for her. "I want to talk to you."

Her blue eyes fixed on his face in a swift stab of frightened questioning. "They've—found their evidence?"

"No," he reassured her. "This has nothing to do with the sabotage gang. I want to talk about you."

"Oh!" She dropped into the chair relieved, making a pretense of humorous defiance. "What's the matter with me?"

Steve's eyes searched her face gravely. "You're tired. You've been on a long straining pull for two months now, helping me get this factory into running order. I think you've earned a short vacation—some place far away. The shorter you make it, of course," he added humorously, "the better I'll like it personally. But I want you to take several weeks at least."

She smiled back wanly. "You're a pretty swell guy, Steve Landis," she told him softly. "You're giving me a chance to get away until this sabotage thing is over. To get hold of myself."

He shrugged. "Put it any way you like. It's the right thing. You've gone through more than a couple of women ought to stand. If you get back into the city for a while — see the old sights — old friends, you'll find the world will be a different place."

She sighed. "Maybe you're right." Suddenly she leaned forward to lay a crumpled telegram on his desk.

"It came this morning," she said unsteadily. "At first I put it in the wastebasket. That's why it's crumpled. But later I fished it out. I'm in pretty much of a dither, I guess. I—I can't seem to reason very well. Do you think I ought to consider it?"

Steve read the lengthy telegram through with sinking heart. The thing he had most feared had come. The wire was from her New York agent. A Hollywood motion picture producer had been interested in her picture and background in the national magazine. He was offering her the leading role in his next defense story. Would she leave for Hollywood immediately or would the agent be forced to come out there and carry her?

Steve handed the telegram back to her. "I think," he said with forced cheerfulness, "that it's the thing for you to do. Absolutely."

(To Be Continued)

Cost Of Living In June Showed Drop

WASHINGTON, July 28 (UP)—Secretary of Labor Frances Perkins today reported that the drop in fresh vegetable and butter prices cut the Bureau of Labor Statistics' cost-of-living index by 0.2 per cent in the month ending June 15.

It was the first month since a year before Pearl Harbor that the index has dropped.

"This small decrease," Miss Perkins said, "compares with increases of 0.8 per cent for the month ending May 15, 1.1 per cent in the month ending April 15, and 1.5 for the month ending March 15."

Despite the small drop in June, the cost-of-living index now stands at 124.8 per cent of the 1935-39 average—23.8 per cent above January, 1941, base date of the Little Steel formula which permits wage increases of 15 per cent, and 7.6 per cent above May, 1942, when the Office of Price Administration started retail price control.

Miss Perkins' report revealed that food prices still were the major factor in the cost-of-living index, clothing, rent, fuel, electricity, ice, housefurnishings and other items having remained relatively stable since May, 1942.

Food prices, which make up over 40 per cent of the index, now are 45 per cent above January, 1941 and over 16 per cent above May, 1942. They declined 0.8 per cent during the month ending June 15.

Beef cattle are moving to the markets in record numbers. Perhaps soon the beef shortage will go the way of the potato, sugar and coffee scarcity.

BEAVER FALLS

Local Girl Weds Ohio Man Here At Quiet Ceremony

Miss M. Beatrice McCann, daughter of the late Mr. and Mrs. Floyd L. McCann, Middlebourne, W. Va., and Richard C. M. Carr, son of Mrs. Malinda Carr and the late David Carr, Newark, O., were married at a simple ceremony in the bride's home in College Hill. Dr. John C. Lorimer, pastor of the First United Presbyterian church, officiated. Miss McCann chose a street-length dress of white silk pique with white accessories for her wedding costume. Talisman roses formed her corsage and a pair of silver pins belonging to her mother were her "something old." A buffet lunch served by Misses Ruth and Mary McCann, sisters of the bride, assisted by Mrs. Estelle Mennell, New Brighton, followed the ceremony. The couple is at home at 2824 Fifth avenue, College Hill.

At a party in their home, given by Mrs. Frank Frumen and daughter, Ann, Beaver Falls, announcement was made of the wedding date of Miss Victoria Frumen to Harry F. Reid, son of Mrs. Arbelin Reid, Columbus, O. The date, September 15, was revealed on small scrolls concealed in corsages of fuchsia and baby breath. Prizes were awarded Mrs. Purdy McKean and Miss Elsie Gross. A surprise feature was the arrival of Cpl. Harry Frumen, en route from Seattle, Wash., to Marietta, Ga.

The meeting of the W.S.C.S. this evening at 7:30 o'clock in the College Hill Methodist church is to be marked by a canning demonstration.

Miss Linnie Long, College Hill, is attending a board meeting of the State Woman's Christian Temperance Union in Harrisburg this week. Before returning she will visit relatives in Altoona.

The annual children's picnic given by the Salvation Army will be held Wednesday, August 4, in Ing-Rich park. All refreshments will be provided. Tickets are being issued at the Salvation Army office from 9 to 12 o'clock every morning.

A wiener roast will be held by the American Legion Auxiliary Thursday evening at the home of Mrs. R. S. Horner, Fifteenth avenue.

Post-War Aviation, Merchant Marine Planning Is Urged

WASHINGTON, July 28.—(UP)—Sen. Henry Cabot Lodge, Jr., R., Mass., today proposed that the United States begin planning for a post-war aviation and Merchant Marine policy which would provide job opportunities for some 3,000,000 aviation war veterans and more than 200,000 wartime merchant seamen.

"These men, having lived for the war years on the air field and aboard Merchant ships, have a right to use their training in peacetime aviation and the Merchant Marine if they want to," Lodge said in an interview. "Our post-war policy should be built around such job opportunities."

He said that our policy should include nothing that would threaten either our post-war Commercial Aviation or our Merchant Marine, or that would make it less attractive or impossible.

Lodge believes Congress itself should have a hand in dictating the aviation policy when peace comes. Similarly, he added, the United States now is back on the seas and care should be exercised in the disposition of the huge merchant fleet that will exist when the war ends.

With such policies in mind, Lodge said, he will talk with as many enlisted men as possible during the globe-girdling air tour of war theaters on which he and four other Senators are bout to embark.

MARINE GETS THRILL

PHILADELPHIA, July 28.—(UP)—Marine private Edward Perkins, of Reading, Pa., escorting his mother through the Philadelphia ordnance district exhibit, stopped suddenly and pointed to a Japanese anti-tank gun. "Hey, Mom!" he exclaimed. "I captured that one myself at Guadalcanal."

FLASH STRIKE ENDS

PITTSBURGH, July 28.—(UP)—Ending a flash strike over dismissal of a rebellious workman, welders and cranemen at the Blaw-Knox Company plant returned to work today and company and union officials were to meet this afternoon to consider the case of the discharged worker. The strike, which started last night, made 650 workers idle.

California averages 35 meat animals per square mile of area.

MONACA NEWS

Local Boy Scouts Spending Week At Camp Umbstaetter

Local Boy Scouts who are spending a week at Camp Umbstaetter, near Fair Oaks, include Joseph Gallagher, George Godfrey, Jack Paley, James Weigle, Edward Fox, Charles Brockmiller, Harry Glass and Billy Manderson.

Miss Adeline Johnson, Indiana avenue, and her niece, Miss Ann Skoog, Pittsburgh, are vacationing in Gainsville, Fla.

George W. Barber, Atlantic avenue, Labor Supply officer in the county, will leave Thursday for Bedford to attend a conference Friday of the International Association of Public Employment Service.

Eugene Spisak, son of Mr. and Mrs. Michael Spisak, has left for Spangler to visit his grandmother, Mrs. Susan Dunchak.

Mrs. Helen O'Keefe, her daughter, Mary, Pennsylvania avenue, and Miss Eva Heyman, Rochester, visited over Sunday with Mrs. Marie McCann, New Castle.

Mrs. Thomas Thornburg, Indiana avenue, was called to Clinton by the illness of her father, William Herschberger, who suffered a stroke of paralysis a few days ago.

Miss Mary Lou Millen, Stockdale, has returned home after visiting the past two weeks with her uncle and aunt, Mr. and Mrs. John Cronin, Washington avenue. Her cousin, Frances Cronin, accompanied her home for a visit.

Miss Wilma Jean Jutte, Eckert Road, returned home Tuesday after visiting ten days with her grandparents, Mr. and Mrs. John Kebart, Aliquippa.

Mrs. Emma Werner, Washington avenue, who suffered an injury to her right hand several days ago, is improving.

The daughter born Friday in Rochester hospital to Mr. and Mrs. Earl McKnight, Stephen Phillips Homes, has been named Barbara Jean. Cathie, another daughter of the McKnights, is visiting several weeks with her aunt in Pittsburgh.

Mrs. Joseph Gill and family are spending a one-week vacation at Geneva-on-the-Lake, O.

Pfc. Henry Reigel, Ft. Monroe, Va., is spending a several day furlough with Mrs. Reigel, in the home of her parents, Mr. and Mrs. Fred Featherstone, Atlantic avenue.

Mr. and Mrs. Frank J. Hradesky, Stephen Phillips Homes, have returned after visiting several days with friends in Uniontown.

Mr. and Mrs. Claude Gerould and granddaughter, Rosanne Feeny, Newark, O., have returned home after visiting a few days with Mr. Gerould's son-in-law and daughter, Mr. and Mrs. Howard D. Johnston, and family, Fourth street.

Mrs. Louise Dixon, Fourth street, and her niece, Miss Anna Ciccozzi, Pacific avenue, have left for Fresno, Cal., to join Mrs. Dixon's husband, Cpl. Clark Dixon.

Air Raid Wardens, members of the Red Cross and other Civilian Defense units are to meet at the Community Hall of Stephen Phillips Homes Wednesday evening at 8 o'clock.

Sgt. Orazio Ciccozzi, son of Mr. and Mrs. Dominic Ciccozzi, Pacific avenue, serving in the Army Air Forces at Salt Lake City, Utah, has been transferred to Miami Beach, Fla., according to word received by his parents.

Miss Freda Featherstone, Atlantic avenue, returned home Tuesday evening from Geneva-on-the-Lake, O., where she had been a guest of Mr. and Mrs. John C. McCreary and family, Atlantic avenue, who are vacationing there. Miss Kitty Lou French, Atlantic avenue, is spending the week with the McCrearys.

Mr. and Mrs. Frank Morell, Stephen Phillips Homes, have returned after vacationing a week at Conneaut Lake.

A son was born Sunday to Mr. and Mrs. Thomas Shaffer, Stephen Phillips Homes. This is the first child born at the Homes.

Mrs. Andrew Semivan and children, Richard and Dolores, returned Monday to their home in Youngstown after visiting ten days with Mrs. Semivan's parents, Mr. and Mrs. William Macirynski, Nimick avenue.

W. L. Gallagher, Elm street, is ill in his home.

Raymond Gallagher, U.S.N., is spending a few days with his parents, Mr. and Mrs. John Gallagher, Elm street. He also is visiting Mrs. Gallagher in the home of her father in Beaver Falls.

Over 100 File For State Judgeships

HARRISBURG, July 28.—(UP)—The State Elections Bureau announced today that 101 candidates filed petitions before yesterday's deadline to seek nominations in the Sept. 14 primary for the 49 judicial posts to be filled in the Nov. 2 elections.

Neither candidate for the Superior Court Judgeship, only statewide office to be filled, will be opposed in the primary. Both Judge Claude T. Reno, Allentown Republican, who was appointed to that post last December, and Curtis Bok, Philadelphia, Democratic Common Pleas Judge, are backed by their state organizations.

A new cement joins metals more firmly together than riveting or welding, it is claimed.

Classified Advertising

CLASSIFIED ADVERTISING

This classified advertising department is for the convenience of the public. To insure publication the same day orders should be received by 10 a. m. Orders not received in time will be published the following day. All copy received subject to being edited or rejected by us. When sending advertisements by mail care should be used to write plainly giving complete instructions so that we may give efficient service in the preparation and publication of the advertisements. When possible, payment should accompany the order. This will be expected with orders from strangers. Cash with order, one cent a word for each publication. No advertisement published for less than 25 cents for each publication. Six consecutive publications for price of four. Extra charge will be made for use of large type. Classified advertisements not accompanied by cash will be charged at two cents per word with a minimum of 50 cents for each publication. This is absolutely necessary on account of the clerical work involved. Fifty per cent discount will be allowed on charge classified advertisements if paid for before expiration date. Usual cash rates will apply to advertisers having other running open accounts with us. The above is a local schedule applying within Beaver County.

Office Telephones
Beaver 1800 Rochester 3300

Rooms and Board

ROOM AND BOARD — Home-cooked meals. 245 Commerce St., Beaver. Phone Beaver 2667-R. 8|13-19 inc

Miscellaneous

CARNIVAL every Thursday 8:30 sharp. Special awards up to $10. Door awards. Cards 50c or 3 for $1.00. Benefit of Marion Hill Firemen. 8-17*

Lost and Found

LOST: On Colona Heights, a Blue Tick and Beagle hound, female. No collar or license. Answers to name "Tillie." White with black spots. Phone Roch. 4117-J. 8|14-20 inc

LOST: Food Ration Book No. 2. Oscar Stone, 517 Connecticut avenue, Rochester. 8|14-17 inc

LOST: Saturday night between Rochester and Beaver Falls, gent's billfold, money, license card, B gas ration books. Floyd Caplinger. Return DAILY TIMES Office, Rochester. Reward. 8|16-18 inc

Repairs—Service

Typewriters, cleaned, repaired, rented and bought. Make arrangements now to have your machine gone over, as parts are hard to get, and no work can be done for a week. David H. Miser, 252 East End Ave. Phone Beaver 1426-M. 8|17-23 inc.

TO PROPERTY OWNERS: Clogged sewers opened without digging with Ideal Electric Sewer opener. Phone Roch 931-W or Roch. 1578-W Mayhue Brothers. 11|4-E.O.W.*

GENUINE HOOVER SWEEPER Guaranteed Service and Parts. Sahli's, phone Rochester 792. 8|6-9|2 inc.

If your MAYTAG washer or ironer needs attention, call The Maytag Store, New Brignton 2484. John W. Young, proprietor. 1|2*

WANTED: Plumbing repair work. Phone Rochester 3106-W-2. 8|15-21 inc

Beauty Culture

BLANCHE'S BEAUTY SHOPPE: Closed for week or 10 days—on vacation. 8|17

Legal Notices

NOTICE

Notice is hereby given that the following accounts have been filed in the Court of Common Pleas of Beaver County, Pa., and that the same will be allowed by said Court on Monday, September 6th, 1943, unless cause be then shown against their confirmation:—

FIRST and FINAL ACCOUNT of BEAVER TRUST COMPANY, Beaver, Pa., Guardian of Estate of CHARLES TORRENCE, weak-minded person.

FIRST and FINAL ACCOUNT of BEAVER COUNTY TRUST COMPANY, New Brighton, Pa., Guardian of MAGGIE M. FULLERTON, a weak-minded person.

FIRST and FINAL ACCOUNT of MIKE N. MARTIN, Guardian of ADELINA ROSSORELLI, a weak-minded person.

FIRST and FINAL ACCOUNT of BEAVER TRUST COMPANY, Beaver, Pa., Guardian of Estate of MARIE HOLIK, a weak-minded person.

FIRST and FINAL ACCOUNT of BEAVER TRUST COMPANY Guardian of Estate of OTTO ABEL, a weak-minded person.

EDWIN M. WALLOVER,
Prothonotary.
Aug. 2, 1943.
8|3-10-17-24

EXECUTORS' NOTICE

Estate of FLORENCE V. THOMPSON, deceased, late of Borough of Beaver, Beaver County, Pennsylvania, letters Testamentary upon the above estate having been granted to the undersigned, notice is hereby given to those indebted thereto to make immediate payment, and to those having claims or demands to present them for settlement.

FRANKLIN B. THOMPSON,
LAUREN THOMPSON,
Executors,
Beaver, Pa.
8|10-17-24-31-9|7-14

NOTICE OF DISTRIBUTION IN THE ORPHANS' COURT OF BEAVER COUNTY

In the matter of ROY W. SHAFFER and ALBERT W. SHAFFER, Executors of the Estate of Emma C. Shaffer, late of the Borough of New Brighton, County of Beaver and State of Pennsylvania. No. 6 June Term, 1943.

Notice is hereby given that the court has fixed Monday, September 20, 1943 at 9 o'clock A. M., in open court, as the time and place for distribution of the balance shown by the account in the above entitled estate to and among those legally entitled thereto, at which time and place any and all persons interested therein may appear and be heard if they so desire.

Signed,
ROY W. SHAFFER,
ALBERT W. SHAFFER,
Executors of the Estate of Emma C. Shaffer.
A. G. HELBLING,
Attorney.
8|17-24-31

MIDLAND HIGH GRIDDERS GET SET FOR TRAINING SEASON

FORTY CANDIDATES REPORT AT MEETING MONDAY NIGHT

About 40 candidates for the 1943 Midland high school varsity football team reported at the high school last night for a pre-training season meeting called by Head Coach William Walters. The Leopards will begin their drills on August 25 at Crucible field.

Coach Walters counted nine lettermen from last year's squad among the 40 candidates, and eight other boys who gained some experience in the 1942 campaign. The remainder of the group was made up of inexperienced boys. A few more candidates are expected to report before the opening game with Beaver high on September 9th.

The nine lettermen returning this year are: Bob Bires and Steve Germusa, backs; Tony DiMarzio, Bob Kadelak, Bob Katich, Willie Love, Angelo Migliore, Vincent D'Itri, and Howard Coughlin. Two other boys who played last season are now serving in the armed forces, Nick Relic who was drafted and assigned to the Navy and Russell Simmons who enlisted in the Navy.

Midland schools will open for the Fall semester on September 8, and the next night the Leopard eleven will open its football season against Beaver's Bobcats at Beaver. The following week the Midland club will meet Rochester at the Rams' field. Other opponents are Monaca, Aliquippa, New Brighton, East Liverpool, Beaver Falls and Ambridge in the order named. The season ends on October 30.

Candidates for the Midland team will be given physical examinations at the high school on Saturday, August 21, from 9:30 a. m. to noon and on Monday, August 23, from 2:30 to 4:30 p. m. Uniforms and equipment will be issued on Tuesday, August 24, between the hours of 10 a. m. and 6 p. m.

Coach Walters plans to hold two practice sessions each week day except Saturday and holidays. Morning drills will start at 10 o'clock and afternoon drills at 2:30. On Saturdays and on Labor Day only morning practices will be held.

The Midland coach will be assisted again this year by Jack Grewell, and Ben Kaye, junior high coach, will assist during the pre-school training period. Midland is planning to revive junior high football this Fall, after a lapse of one year.

SPORT SLANTS

By BILL ANDERSON

Many young American soldiers and sailors will testify that the world isn't as large as they had been led to believe. For instance, Walter A. Gordon, Jr., son of Mr. and Mrs. Walter A. Gordon, Sr., Jefferson street, Rochester, a pharmacist mate in the Navy, serving somewhere in the African theater, recently had the pleasure of meeting Al Schacht, former big league catcher, and in late years known as the "Clown Prince of Baseball." Schacht, his partner Nick Altrock and several others are entertaining service men in North Africa. The surprising feature of the meeting to Gordon was that Schacht, when he learned the young sailor was from Western Pennsylvania asked: "Do you know Alex Pearson." And Gordon replied, "Sure, he's my home town burgess." Finding he and the famous athlete and entertainer had a common acquaintance lent special significance to Gordon's introduction to Schacht. Burgess Pearson, it is well known here, was a professional ball player for many years and has known Schacht for a long time. Schacht has visited Beaver Valley at least twice. The first time was during the early 1920's when the late Howard Shanks of Monaca, then an infielder for the Senators, brought a team of professional all-stars to Rochester for a post-season exhibition game with a Rochester team of which Burgess Pearson was the manager. Schacht played for Shanks' outfit. A few years ago the clown of baseball put on his act at Beaver Falls during a Penn State League game. ....

Midland high school's coach, Bill Walters, held a pre-practice meeting of candidates for the Leopard varsity grid team last night, and candidates for Ellwood City Senior and junior high school squads have been notified to visit the high school Wednesday afternoon for their physical examinations. It won't be long now until the air will be filled with inflated pigskins.

Coach Harold C. Leffler of Beaver, and Lee Schachern of Beaver Falls, very likely will hold a scrimmage or two between their respective teams during the week both will be in training at the camp at Epworth Woods. The Tigers and the Bobcats are to be in camp at Epworth Woods at the same time, starting Wednesday of next week, and a couple of scrimmage sessions between the two squads would no doubt be beneficial. Neither coach need worry about revealing any secrets to the other for the schools are not scheduled to meet this Fall.

The Los Angeles baseball club, which is making a walkaway of the Pacific Coast League championship race, boasts one of the youngest if not the youngest player in organized baseball this year. He is Billy Sarni, 15 years old, who, it is said, does a fine job of catching. Clarence Rowland, president of the Angels, once manager of the Chicago White Sox, says Sarni is a cinch to be in the majors next season. In his first 12 games with the Angels he batted .321, hitting a homer his first time at bat. In those 12 games he threw out 11 runners trying to steal.

The State of Ohio is to have its first open deer hunting season in recent years this coming Fall, starting on December 6. Nearby Columbiana County is one of the 10 counties in which it will be legal to shoot either does or bucks and in three others the season will be open for bucks only.

Plans for an Industrial Tenpin Bowling League are being made by the Manufacturers Division of the Ellwood City Chamber of Commerce. Seven plants have applied for berths in the loop. Play will begin about September 16.

Center Line Rule Will Help Defending Team In Ice Hockey

TORONTO, Aug. 17.—(UP)—Better individual stick work and old fashioned hockey playing will result this season from passage of a new rule by officials of the National Hockey League and the Canadian Amateur Hockey Association at their meeting here.

The new rule calls for adoption of a center line behind which the defending team can make forward passes without penalty.

The change, advocated for some time, is designed to permit defending teams to break away from power plays more easily, thus cutting the use of the lunging attack by making it too hazardous for the offensive players.

Use of the power play, which permits several of the attacking players to go down ice and accept a long pass from a team mate, has increased to such an extent in recent years that the rule makers believed it a serious threat to the life of Canada's national game.

Under the revised ruling, attackers will fear to venture at great length down the ice because of the possibility of being trapped out of position in case the puck is stolen by an opposing player. Thus, the stick work and brilliant offensive play of the individual in getting the puck into the scoring zone will be brought forth.

Baseball Summary

NATIONAL LEAGUE

RESULTS MONDAY

Pittsburgh 5, Boston 1.
Cincinnati 5, New York 2.
Brooklyn 7, St. Louis 3.
Philadelphia 4, Chicago 3.

TEAM STANDING

	W.	L.	Pct.
St. Louis	69	36	.657
Cincinnati	59	49	.546
Pittsburgh	58	50	.537
Brooklyn	56	53	.514
Boston	48	55	.466
Philadelphia	51	60	.459
Chicago	49	58	.458
New York	39	69	.364

GAMES TODAY

Pittsburgh at Boston.
Cincinnati at New York.
St. Louis at Brooklyn.
Chicago at Philadelphia.

GAMES WEDNESDAY

Pittsburgh at New York.
Cincinnati at Boston.
Chicago at Brooklyn.
St. Louis at Philadelphia.

AMERICAN LEAGUE

RESULTS MONDAY

Washington 6, Cleveland 3.
New York 7, Chicago 0.
Boston 9, St. Louis 0.
Only games scheduled.

TEAM STANDING

	W.	L.	Pct.
New York	66	40	.623
Washington	59	52	.532
Cleveland	55	50	.524
Detroit	54	50	.519
Chicago	55	52	.514
Boston	53	55	.491
St. Louis	45	60	.429
Philadelphia	40	68	.370

GAMES TODAY

New York at Chicago.
Boston at St. Louis.
Philadelphia at Detroit.
Others not scheduled.

GAMES WEDNESDAY

Washington at Chicago.
Philadelphia at St. Louis.
New York at Cleveland.
Boston at Detroit.

BEAVER VALLEY ASSOCIATION

RESULTS MONDAY

Merchants 10, Shamrocks 3.
Beaver Falls - East Rochester, postponed.

TEAM STANDING

	Won	Lost
Truckers	10	1
E. Rochester	4	5
Beaver Falls	4	5
Merchants	4	7
Shamrocks	3	8

GAMES TONIGHT

Beaver Falls at Merchants.
Shamrocks at E. Rochester.

STANFORD DROPS FOOTBALL

PALO ALTO, Cal., Aug 17 Stanford University has cancelled its 1943 football schedule because of lack of manpower. Graduate Manager Al Masters said Coach Marchmont Schwartz and staff would remain and handle the army's physical fitness program for the approximately 2,500 cadets now enrolled at the university.

Finalists In Curtiss-Wright Softball Tourney

Winners of the recent Beaver Softball tournament, the Braves, are shown with five faithful rooters. Back, (l. to r.) Kent Halsted, B. Inman, F. Anderson, J. Thompson, C. Ober, and J. Mance. Middle: Russ Book, manager; E. Cox, captain; B. Anderson, J. Pfeiffer, and M. Rebrrovich. Front, Helen Roseler, Marge Mc Clure, Jean Barto, Dora Demarchi, and Thelma Serafine.

GENEVA COLLEGE ABANDONS FOOTBALL FOR 1943 SEASON

Geneva College football became a casualty of the war today when Dr. M. M. Pearce, president, announced that due to scarcity of players the athletic board had decided to drop the gridiron sport for the 1943 season.

The decision to abandon football and cancel all scheduled games for 1943 was reached after it became definite last week that the Army was not going to relax its ban against Army student trainees participating in intercollegiate athletics.

Geneva officials explained that almost the entire 1942 football squad is missing from the campus. Only a few players were lost by graduation but calls to the armed forces have taken nearly all the under grads.

The Covenanter schedule for this Fall had originally included nine games, but three' schools, Grove City, Westminster and Youngstown, had previously abandoned the sport. Geneva officials have notified the others, West Virginia U., Waynesburg, Bethany, Lock Haven, Washington and Jefferson, and Carnegie Tech of the decision to drop the sport this year.

This will be the first season in about 50 years that the Covenanter school has not fielded a football team. The first team was organized early in the 1890's and each year since, even throughout World War I, the gold and white was represented on the barred field.

Calendar makers passed from 1 B. C. to 1 A. D., disregarding the Zero year, so that there are only 1,942 years since 1 B. C. rather than 1,943.

TODAY'S RADIO PROGRAM

6:00 p. m.
WWSW, Scores; Bill Cullen.
WCAE, Sing a Song at Six.
WJAS, Mickey Ross Orch.
KQV, Terry and Pirates.
KDKA, War Needs Wires.
WKBN, Alan Freed-News.

6:15 p. m.
WWSW, Entertainment Time.
WCAE, Evening News.
WJAS, Beckley Smith, News.
KQV, Sports With Evans.
KDKA, Designs for Listening.
WKBN, Don Gardner-Sports.

6:30 p. m.
WWSW, Song Souvenirs V. N.
WCAE, Foreign News.
WJAS, Edwin C. Hill.
KQV, News.
KDKA, Songs for Service Men.
WKBN, Jeri Sullavan-Songs.

6:45 p. m.
WWSW, Entertainment Time.
WCAE, Dinner Music.
WJAS, Bob Prince, Sports.
KQV, Modernaires.
KDKA, Lowell Thomas, News.
WKBN, The World Today; Jos. C. Harsch-News.

7:00 p. m.
WWSW, News.
WCAE, Fulton Lewis, Jr.
WJAS, I Love a Mystery.
KQV, Rine's Orch; News.
KDKA, Fred Waring.
WKBN, I Love a Mystery.

7:15 p. m.
WWSW, Entertainment Time.
WCAE, Wohl's Sophisticants.
WJAS, Harry James Orch.
KQV, Men, Mach., Victory.
KDKA, News of the World.
WKBN, Harry James Orchestra.

7:30 p. m.
WWSW, Joe Tucker, Sports.
WCAE, Confidentially Yours.
WJAS, Amer. Melody Hour.
KQV, Pop Stuff.
KDKA, Tap Time.
WKBN, American Melody Hour.

7:45 p. m.
WWSW, Don Allen.
WCAE, Date With WACs.

8:00 p. m.
WWSW, News; Edna Peterson.
WCAE, Amer. Forum of Air.
WJAS, Lights Out.
KQV, Watch the World.
KDKA, Johnny Presents.
WKBN, Lights Out.

8:15 p. m.
WWSW, Lawless Twenties.
KQV, Lum and Abner.

8:30 p. m.
WWSW, Dance a While.
WJAS, Judy Canova Show.
KQV, Noah Webster Says.
KDKA, Horace Heidt.
WKBN, Judy Canova Show; Alan Freed-News.

8:45 p. m.
WJAS, Judy Canova News.

9:00 p. m.
WWSW, News.
WCAE, Gabriel Heatter.
WJAS, Robert J. Alderdice.
KQV, Famous Jury Trials.
KDKA, Battle of Sexes.
WKBN, The Colonel.

9:15 p. m.
WWSW, Golden Hour.
WCAE, Mutual Music.
WJAS, Treas. Song Parade.

9:30 p. m.
WWSW, Time to Dance.
WCAE, Cisco Kid.
WJAS, Report to the Nation.
KQV, Spotlight Bands.
KDKA, Passing Parade.
WKBN, Report to the Nation.

9:45 p. m.
KQV, Bands; Organ.

10:00 p. m.
WWSW, News; Dance Music.
WCAE, John B. Hughes.
WJAS, Passport for Adams.
KQV, Raymond Gram Swing.
KDKA, Music Shop.
WKBN, Passport for Adams.

10:15 p. m.
WWSW, Audrey Lynn-Organist.
WCAE, Songs, Sunny Skylar.
KQV, Lulu and Johnny.

10:30 p. m.
WWSW, Bill Cullen, News.
WCAE, Brad Hunt Orch.
WJAS, Congress Speaks.
KQV, This Nation at War.
KDKA, Beat the Band.
WKBN, Bob Astor Orchestra.

10:45 p. m.
WWSW, Scores; Maples Orch.
WCAE, Treasury Star Parade.
WJAS, Ted Husing, Sports.

11:00 p. m.
WWSW, Music for Mood.
WCAE, News Parade.
WJAS, Ken Hildebrand.
KQV, News.
KDKA, News.
WKBN, News; Bill Henry.

11:15 p. m.
WCAE, Geo. Hamilton Orch.
WJAS, Joseph Harsch, News.
KQV, Treas. Star Parade.
KDKA, Eleven-Fifteen Local.
WKBN, Baseball Scores; Joan Brooks-Songs.

11:30 p. m.
WWSW, Masterworks of Music.
WCAE, Sinfonietta.
WJAS, Raymond Scott Orch.
KQV, Music for Reading.
KDKA, Hawaiian Echoes.
WKBN, Raymond Scott Orchestra.

11:45 p. m.
KQV, Music; News.
KDKA, Jack Swift, News.

12:00 Midnight
WWSW, 1500 Club (till 6 a. m.)
WCAE, Geo. Hamilton Orch.
WJAS, News; Sherwood Orch.
KQV, Music for Reading.
KDKA, Roy Shield & Co.
WKBN, Signature.

12:15 a. m.
WJAS, Sherwood Orch.

12:30 a. m.
WCAE, Horace Heidt Orch.

Baseball Experts Hail Comeback Of Schoolboy Rowe

NEW YORK, Aug. 17 (UP) — Baseball experts today were hailing the pitching of Schoolboy Rowe as one of the greatest comebacks ever seen in the National League.

The long righthander, who was leading the league in a number of hurling departments 10 years ago, was given up for lost by the Brooklyn Dodgers last season and was released to the Montreal farm club. Winning only two games and losing one, Rowe was sold by Montreal to the Philadelphia Phillies in March of this year.

But last night, Rowe hurled his 11th victory, one of the top records in the league, to defeat the Chicago Cubs, 4-3, with a five hit performance. The victory put money in Rowe's pocket as his contract called for a bonus of $1,000 if he won more than 10 games and an additional $100 for every victory thereafter.

Newcomer Howard Schultz, obtained Sunday by Dodger President Branch Rickey from the St. Paul Saints of the American Association, brought new joy to Brooklyn hearts as the Dodgers nipped the league leading St. Louis Cardinals, 7-3.

Schultz, six foot six and one-half inch first baseman, made a spectacular debut with an excellent fielding job and two hits, one a double, in four appearances at the plate.

Johnny Gee pitched the Pittsburgh Pirates to a 5-1 victory over the Boston Braves. Vince DiMaggio broke a 1-1 tie to start the Bucs on the victory path when he tallied on Catcher Clyde Kluttz's error.

Hank Borowy dealt out four hits in miserly fashion, enabling the New York Yankees to defeat the Chicago White Sox, 7-0, under Chicago lights.

The Cincinnati Reds made it three straight with a 5-2 victory over the hapless New York Giants.

Bill Lefebvre, acquired last week from Minneapolis in the American Association, pitched the Washington Senators right into second place in the junior circuit with a 6-3 victory over the Cleveland Indians.

In the only other American League game scheduled, the Boston Red Sox defeated the St. Louis Browns, 9-0.

Louis Will Start Tour On Aug. 30

WASHINGTON, Aug. 17.—Sergeant Joe Louis will start an exhibition trek on August 30, that eventually will carry him overseas for a display of the fistic skill that won him the heavyweight boxing crown.

The War Department, disclosed that the champ will tour army camps in this country for 100 days and then go abroad for workouts before combat troops.

At first, it had been decided to start the tour on Wednesday, but a postponement resulted when Louis told army officers at Fort Meade, Md., today that he would like to take the extra time to get back into shape for boxing.

Father-Daughter Wins Golf Tourney

GREENSBURG, Pa., Aug. 17. — For the first time since the event was started, a father-daughter combination won the annual father-and-son-or-daughter golf tournament at the Greensburg Country Club yesterday.

W. F. Euwer and his daughter, Jean Euwer, of Jeannette, took top honors with a net of 67.

Runners-up with a net of 68 were Dr. H. J. Thomas and his son, James, of Greensburg, defending champions.

Batting Changes Lifted Musial To Top Of Averages

By JACK CUDDY
United Press Staff Correspondent

NEW YORK, Aug. 17 (UP)—Two little batting changes early in July lifted Stan Musial from "goot hitter" to top man in the major leagues.

The Cardinals slender, brown-haired right fielder explained these significant alterations between games of a doubleheader with the Dodgers at Ebbets Field.

Musial, just in from the "sun garden," was drenched but happy as he plumped down on a dressing room bench and pulled off his gray blouse and sopping undershirt. His two homers and a single had driven in five runs as the champions downed Brooklyn, 11-2, in the opener.

Perspiring mates smacked him on the back as they herded past, with noisy spikes, to their lockers. He's "aces" with them because of his prowess and sunny disposition. Success hasn't spoiled this 22-year-old Donora (Pa.) dynamiter — this stream-lined six-footer with the aquiline nose and laughing brown eyes.

Stan laughed off the home run congratulations and said, "Homers are alright. I'll certainly never refuse them; but I like triples better. Triples are almost as effective as homers, and they give you a chance to run. I like to run." He leads the majors in three-baggers, with 15.

The Polish pellet pounder tops both leagues with a batting average of .354, registered on 153 hits, including 30 doubles.

In late June, Musial was hitting about .325. At least four National League rivals were above him. This was a robust figure—an improvement over his .315 of last year, his first season with the Cards. But Stan wasn't satisfied. He thought he could do better.

"So I made two changes about July first," he explained. "I changed to a bat that was a half-ounce lighter, to get more speed into my swing. I started using a 34½ ounce bat instead of a 35. Then I shifted my grip about two inches, from a half-choke clear to the end of the bat handle. This increased the power of my drive.

"I figure that these changes—along with a bit more confidence this season helped my batting a lot."

Doubtless some of Stan's confidence stems from his relish for the right field post. Since he throws as well as bats left-handed, it is much easier for him to make the long heaves from the sun field than from the left field, where he played last season, in the World Series and early this season. Quick turns often necessary in pegging from the left field, aggravated an old shoulder injury—suffered while pitching in the minors. He has had no shoulder trouble since shifting to the right garden.

What pitcher gives Musial the most trouble?

Stan said, "Kirby Higbe is toughest for me. He throws those fast knuckle balls, and I can't seem to do much with them."

Musial's remarks were prophetic. Higbe pitched the nightcap for the Dodgers, and the majors' leading batsman went hitless. Higbe emphasized his mastery over Musial by making him hit into a double play, with the bases loaded, in the seventh inning.

Terranova Is New Feather Champion

NEW ORLEANS, Aug. 17 (UP)—Phil Terranova of New York reigned as National Boxing Association featherweight champion today following his eight-round knockout of Jackie Callura, Hamilton, Ont., in a scheduled 15-round bout at Pelican Stadium last night.

As nine thousand fans watched, the 23-year-old Bronx Italian pounded Callura into the canvas with hard, sharp jabs from both hands. He set the champion on the floor early in the round for a nine count and then loosed an uppercut after less than a minute of the second to bring the bout to a close.

Beaver Gridders To Meet Tonight

Beaver high school principal Charles S. Linn announced today that all candidates for the Maroon and Gray football squad are to meet in the high school at seven o'clock this evening for a check-up on the progress of the Booster Club's campaign to raise funds to send the gridders to camp at Epworth Woods next week. About 40 boys are expected to go to camp for the week of pre-school drills.

Plane Bought By School Does Job

SOMEWHERE IN NEW GUINEA Aug. 17. — (Delayed)—(UP)—Progress report to the students at Endicott, N. Y., Union High School:

The Airacobra which you bought with war bonds led a force in a dog-fight against the Japanese over New Guinea today and the enemy got a sound thrashing, losing 11 medium bombers and three fighters in less than a minute.

It was your plane's baptism of fire and the pleased pilot, Capt. Grant Dudishire of Williamsburg, Ia., trained her guns on three enemy bombers and a fighter and got all of them. The Endicott Special—it still bears that name—came through unscratched.

At the height of the Shaker settlements there were about 6,000 in the United States. According to a recent estimate there are only about 200 remaining.

Forty million pounds of lead foil have been saved by substituting paper wrappings on cigarets, smoking and chewing tobacco.

Today's Victory Garden-Graph

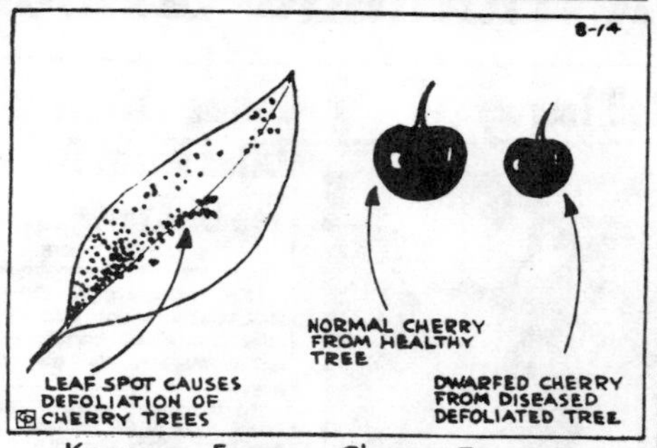
8-14
NORMAL CHERRY FROM HEALTHY TREE
LEAF SPOT CAUSES DEFOLIATION OF CHERRY TREES
DWARFED CHERRY FROM DISEASED DEFOLIATED TREE

Keep an Eye on Cherry Trees in Victory Garden

By DEAN HALLIDAY

Released by Central Press Association

IF YOU have one or two sweet and sour cherry trees in your home orchard and the leaves have turned yellow and fallen early, especially those on the sour cherry trees, you can suspect a disease known as yellow leaf or cherry leaf spot.

The three outstanding diseases on cherries are brown-rot, yellow leaf and black-knot.

The brown-rot attacks the fruit after it has begun to ripen. The fruit decays and is covered with a gray mold. When the affected fruit drops to the ground and is not gathered up and destroyed, the fungus causing the disease remains alive until spring, when it produces a large number of spores which float upward and finally infect the new crop. The blossoms may be blighted, the fruit rotted and the leaves affected. The fungus spreads rapidly in wet weather during the summer.

The yellow leaf of cherry causes defoliation, after the leaves have become spotted, as illustrated in the accompanying Garden-Graph. This loss of foliage not only weakens the tree so that it may winter-kill, but it also reduces the number of fruit buds for the following year. The yellowed, fallen leaves should be cleaned up from the ground and burned, otherwise the fungus which causes the disease will survive the winter in the old leaves and spores in the spring will infect the new foliage.

Black-knot is a fungus disease which occurs on cherry trees which have been neglected for some time, and affects only the woody parts.

Lime-sulphur or Bordeaux sprays are recommended for cherry diseases but should be used carefully else the foliage will be burned and fruit dwarfed, as illustrated.

BARCLAY ON BRIDGE

By Shepard Barclay

"The Authority on Authorities"

CAN STAND REPETITION

THERE IS one admonition for average players which can stand any amount of repetition. It is that usually a trump suit is dangerous if the opponents hold as many as six cards in it. Less than half of the time these will be divided evenly, with three held by each defender. More often, some one of them will have four and the other two. This means that the declarer must be prepared to compete most of the time against a four-card trump holding by one defender. Such being the case, it is frequently better to try for a fit in some other suit, or for No Trumps in preference to a suit in which your side holds only seven cards.

North:
♠ A Q 10 4 2
♥ A 6 4
♦ 5 2
♣ Q 10 6

West:
♠ 6 5
♥ Q 9 8 7
♦ 6 4 3
♣ A J 8 7

East:
♠ J 9 8 3
♥ 5 3 2
♦ Q 9 8
♣ 9 5 2

South:
♠ K 7
♥ K J 10
♦ A K J 10 7
♣ K 4 3

(Dealer: North. North-South vulnerable.)

North	East	South	West
1 ♠	Pass	3 ♦	Pass
3 ♠	Pass	4 NT	Pass
5 ♥	Pass	6 ♠	

No matter how this hand gets played, North hasn't a chance in the world to make his contract. The club A is a sure winner, and so is the spade J, if the hand is played in spades. That contract was reached by a fair number of the pairs in a social duplicate, and all of these were, of course, set.

At some of the tables, South, instead of using a conventional slam call of 4-No Trumps, after hearing North's spade rebid, 3-Spades, called 4-Diamonds. The main purpose of this was to see if North would bid spades a third time. If so, he would be proclaiming possession of a six-card suit, in which event South's doubleton would have been adequate support.

But North in those cases bid 4-No Trumps, whereupon South immediately slammed the hand at 6-No Trumps. After East led a heart or club, this contract had a good chance to make as, after three rounds of spades got tried and the suit failed to break, the diamond finesse still remained as a chance for the contract, and of course it worked.

The real point of this, however, is that in No Trumps the declarer had two tries for his contract, whereas in spades he had only one, with the odds against that one chance.

* * *

Tomorrow's Problem

North:
♠ 7 5 3 2
♥ 6 4 3
♦ A K Q
♣ 10 9 7

West:
♠ A K Q J 9
♥ 9 8 7 5
♦ 6 4
♣ A Q

East:
♠ 10 8 6
♥ 2
♦ 8 7 2
♣ 8 6 5 4 3 2

South:
♠ 4
♥ A K Q J 10
♦ J 10 9 5 3
♣ K J

(Dealer: South. East-West vulnerable.)

What is the soundest way for South to play this hand at 4-Hearts, after ruffing the second spade lead?

Distributed by King Features Syndicate, Inc.

THE POCKETBOOK of KNOWLEDGE by TOPPS
SAVING EXPENSIVE BULLETS AND GUNPOWDER WHEN TRAINING SOLDIERS TO USE MACHINE GUNS, UNCLE SAM NOW EMPLOYS INDUSTRY'S NEWLY DEVELOPED PLASTIC PELLETS WHICH COST ONLY ONE CENT INSTEAD OF 30 CENTS FOR REGULAR BULLETS
A NEW ELECTRONIC SEWING MACHINE USES NEITHER NEEDLE NOR THREAD....... IT "RADIATES" A SOLID SEAM ON THERMOPLASTIC COATED FABRICS
OOF!
NEW ELECTRICAL FISH "NETS" KEEP FISH FROM SWIMMING FROM RESTRICTED AREAS IN A STREAM OR LAKE, YET DOESN'T KILL THEM
NEW COMBAT GLOVE FOR AVIATORS REALLY IS THREE GLOVES IN ONE...
IN ARMENIA, JAM IS PREPARED IN JAM "ROBES": THE JAM IS SPREAD ON CLOTH, DRIED, AND ROLLED UP AND STORED FOR FUTURE USE.

PRIVATE BUCK

QUARTERMASTER'S DEP'T.
8-25
Copr. 1943, King Features Syndicate, Inc., World rights reserved

"He says his uniform takes less material than the average, so could he have the difference in cash?"

THE OLD HOME TOWN Registered U. S. Patent Office By STANLEY
WASHINGS TOOK IN
YOU WORM! - IF I HAD MY WAY YOU'D STAY IN HOT WATER FOR THE DURATION---- KEEP RUBBING IF YOU DON'T WANT TO CARRY A GUN!
HE'S BEEN IN HOT WATER MOST OF HIS LIFE!
SEE ED FINALLY HAS GOTTEN INTO ESSENTIAL WORK!!
AN ARMY OFFICIAL IS CHECKING UP THE LOCAL MAN POWER SUPPLY -
STANLEY 8-25

SALLY'S SALLIES

Registered U. S. Patent Office.

IF YOU HAD YOUR LIFE OVER AGAIN, WHAT WOULD YOU DO WRONG?
8-25
Copr. 1943, King Features Syndicate, Inc., World rights reserved

SCOTT'S SCRAP BOOK By R. J. SCOTT
NATURE DID NOT INTEND HUMAN BEINGS TO SWIM - OUR TRUNK IS NOT ADAPTED FOR THE PURPOSE AND THE RATE OF PROGRESS IS OUT OF ALL PROPORTION TO THE ENERGY EXPENDED
SCRAPS
WHAT TREE IS MOST SUSCEPTIBLE TO LIGHTNING?
A TALL OAK
SOME WOMEN OF THAILAND WEAR A CANOPY HEAD-DRESS - A SORT OF RUG, RIGGED ON A FRAME AND EXTENDING BEYOND THE FOREHEAD
THERE ARE AS MANY ATOMS IN A TUMBLER OF WATER AS THERE ARE TUMBLERS OF WATER IN AN OCEAN
8-25

Wife Preservers

If a small amount of mold is present on canned or preserved food, it may be removed from the surface and the remainder of the food may be safely eaten. If a heavy growth is present, however, discard the food.

BLONDIE

Listen to "Blondie" on the air every Monday night at (7:30 P. M. EWT)

By Chic Young

NOPE, YOU CAN'T HAVE A DIME -- YOU'VE GOT TO LEARN TO HAVE MORE RESPECT FOR MONEY
I GUESS I'M JUST A FAILURE AS A SON
OH, NO, ALEXANDER I DIDN'T MEAN THAT!
IT'S NOT YOUR FAULT, DAD! YOU'VE BEEN A WONDERFUL FATHER! I'M JUST NO GOOD
I'M SORRY IF I MADE YOU FEEL THAT WAY, SON -- HERE'S YOUR DIME
GEE, IT WORKED SWELL, ALVIN! WHERE DID YOU LEARN THAT TRICK?
G'WAN, I'VE BEEN USING IT FOR YEARS
8-25

RIGHT AROUND HOME

By Dudley Fisher

I'M GOING LIGHT THIS NOON, ROSIE, 'CAUSE TONIGHT WE'RE HAVING STEAK!
THAT'S CABBAGE! ELLA'S SISTER DROPPED IN ON HER AND I LOANED HER OUR STEAK!
THIS IS FUN! I LIKE TO GO OUT FOR DINNER!
THREE DOUBLE HAMBURGERS!
YOU SHOULD HAVE SAID THAT AT NOON! I'VE GOT NOTHING LEFT BUT CABBAGE.
8-25

MUGGS AND SKEETER

By Wally Bishop

SAY, GRAMPS, I WONDER IF YOU COULD GIVE ME A HAND WITH SOMETHIN'?
WHAT IS IT, SKEETER?
VACATION IS NEARLY OVER, SO I'M GETTIN' READY FOR THE OPENING DAY OF SCHOOL.
THAT'S FINE, SKEETER. I'LL BE GLAD TO GIVE YOU A HAND WITH YOUR NEW LESSONS!!
THAT ISN'T WHAT I HAD IN MIND, GRAMPS, ALL I WANT FROM YOU IS A LETTER TO MY TEACHER...
FOR WHAT PURPOSE, SKEETER?
...JUST ASKIN' HER TO EXCUSE ME, IN CASE I HAPPEN TO GET SICK OR SOMETHIN' THAT DAY!
8-25

BRICK BRADFORD—On the Throne of Titania

By William Ritt and Clarence Gray

BRICK ENTERS THE PEDESTAL OF — THE TITANIC CAVERN IDOL —
HERE'S HOPING I DON'T FALL THROUGH ANY MORE TRAPDOORS!
SAY! THIS IS NOT A ROOM! IT'S A LONG, NARROW TUNNEL!
I'M GOING TO FIND OUT WHERE THIS LEADS TO — EVEN IF I NEVER GET BACK!
8-25

ETTA KETT

By Paul Robinson

WAIT HERE, I'LL GET CAPTAIN FAIRCHILD TO IDENTIFY YOU!
JEEPERS!
AT EASE! HE'LL FIX IT UP, SO YOU'LL GET INTO THE BALL!
OH, -- BUT YOU'LL HAVE TO HELP ME
THAT WAS ONLY A TRICK OF MINE -- I'M NOT CAPTAIN FAIRCHILD'S FIANCÉE! IN FACT, I'VE NEVER EVEN SEEN HIM!
JUST LEAVE EVERYTHING TO ME!
GEE, YOU'RE SUPER! SH-H!
8 25

BIG SISTER

By Les Forgrave

NOW I DON'T WONDER AT MRS. BETTS' FRAIL HEALTH. THE FOOD SHE LIVES ON! NO EGGS, NO BUTTER.
NOT MUCH ELSE BUT TEA AND CRACKERS, AND A BIT OF DRIED FRUIT. IT'S A MARVEL SHE'S ALIVE AT ALL!
SOME FRESH VEGETABLES WOULD DO HER WORLDS OF GOOD. WHILE SHE GETS HER NAP I'LL SLIP DOWN TO OUR GARDEN!
8-25

DONALD DUCK

By Walt Disney

FOR WORKING SO HARD WASHING MY WINDOWS, I'M ASKING YOU TO SUPPER!
BOY THAT'S A RELIEF! I'M ALL-IN!
HOW ABOUT SOME CHOPS? AND NEW POTATOES? AND A GREEN SALAD? AND ASPARAGUS?
FINE!
DELICIOUS!
SWELL!
GREAT!
AND HOT ROLLS? AND APPLE PIE A LA MODE?
WONDERFUL!
SERVE SELF STORE NO 2
8 25

JUST KIDS

By Ad Carter

HERE COMES THAT LITTLE MONKEY AGAIN - WHAT NOW?
MARJORY - DO YOU THINK YOU ARE PLAYING FAIR WITH ME? YOU LET ME GO IN MY OWN GARDEN - BUT I CAN'T DO ANY WEEDING - AND I BOUGHT SHORTS FOR THAT PURPOSE
THEY ARE VERY PRETTY SHORTS - TOO
THIS IS A PROBLEM - I'LL THINK OVER
I'VE GOT HER
SIR - COULD YOU GIVE YOUR SHORTS A WORK-OUT - MOWING THE LAWN?
8-25

The Weather Forecast
WESTERN PENNSYLVANIA: Continued cool with scattered showers this afternoon and evening.

"The Paper That Goes Home"

THE DAILY TIMES

1874 — and WESTERN ARGUS — 1803

ROCHESTER - BEAVER - MONACA - FREEDOM - BRIDGEWATER - CONWAY - VANPORT - MIDLAND

Beaver County History
General Pershing was given a huge welcome home in New York on September 8, 1919, it was reported here.

4 Cents

Established April 2, 1874 | Beaver and Rochester, Pa., Wednesday, September 8, 1943 | By Carrier 24 Cents A Week

Blood Bank Returns To County Next Month

★ ★ ★ ★ ★ ★ ★ ★ ★ ★ ★ ★ ★ ★ ★ ★ ★ ★

ITALY GIVES UP!

STALINO TAKEN BY RUSSIANS

KEY CITY IN DONETS BASIN IS RECAPTURED

Fall Of Stalino To Advancing Russian Army Gives Reds Railway Hub In Important Donets Sector

MOSCOW, Sept. 8 (UP) — The Red army has captured Stalino, industrial capital and railway hub of the Donets basin.

(Berlin announced by radio that the Germans had evacuated Stalino "according to plan in the course of elastic disengaging operations after the complete destruction of war important installations" — the Nazi verbiage for losing the city.)

The report that Stalino again was in Russian hands put the seal on Russian claims that the complete reconquest of the mineral-wealthy Donets basin was assured and that the Germans were being swept westward at a growing pace.

The capture of Stalino, with a pre-war population of nearly 500,000 and control point of the dense network of railroads sparking the Donets industries, rivaled the taking of Kharkov as a major victory in the summer campaign of the Red army.

NAZIS FACE TRAP

It served to collapse the core of Nazi resistance in the thin and dangerously extended salient at the flank of which the advancing Russians were threatening to slice down to the Sea of Azov and trap tens of thousands of invasion troops.

The Germans took Stalino on October 21, 1941, in their invasion sweep eastward through the Ukraine and had held it ever since. Military quarters said that after losing this city the Nazis would have little reason for trying to hold on in the Donets basin.

The battle for the complete liberation of the eastern Ukraine appeared to have reached its final phase, even as Soviet forces to the northwest all but severed rail communications between the Axis central and southern fronts.

During the last 24 hours the Russians had taken more than 300 other places, advancing up to 12½ miles on a 700-mile front. The Soviets captured Chesnokovka, six miles northwest of Bakhmach, yesterday and cut the Gomel-Bakh-

Continued on Page Ten

Lost and Found

LOST: Monday evening, on Union Cemetery Road near Chapel Cemetery, 2 black and white spotted pigs, 8 weeks old. Reward. Call Rochester 6129-R-3. 9 8-14 inc.

LOST: Large red woven grass pocketbook Wednesday morning on Dutch Ridge Road or in Beaver containing War Bonds, cash, driver's license, keys, etc. Mrs. John J. Young, Dutch Ridge Road, Beaver. Liberal reward. Phone Beaver 320. 9 8-9-10

LOST: Sailor's black Morrocan wallet containing necessary papers, sum of money and identification, Tuesday evening in Freedom. Reward. Phone Zelienople -M. 9 8-14 inc.

LOST: Orange and cream Persian male cat, vicinity Houdeshells, Vanport. Phone Beaver Falls 2712-R, or return to Houdeshells. Reward. 9 8-10 inc.

FOUND: A wagon. Owner may have same by identifying property and paying for this adv. Phone Rochester 310 or inquire 395 Adams street, Rochester. 9 8-9

LOST: Two No. 1 and Two No. 2 Ration Books, also Savings Account Bank Book, in Beaver, Wednesday morning. Susan Spurlock Wilkins, Leonard Wilkins, Atlanta, Georgia. Call Beaver 1584-J. 168 Dravo Ave., Beaver. 9 8-10 inc.

KILLED 38 JAPS, GETS MEDAL

ONLY ENLISTED MARINE to receive the Congressional Medal of Honor so far in this war is Platoon Sergt. John Basilone, 26, pictured above during a New York press conference that flustered him more than did the Japs. He personally killed 38 enemy soldiers last October during a battle for Henderson field on Guadalcanal. *(International)*

TRAIN WRECK DEATH TOLL NOW 78; OTHERS MAY DIE

PHILADELPHIA, Sept. 8 (UP)—Workmen cleared the last of the Congressional Limited wreckage from the Pennsylvania Railroad's main line right-of-way in Philadelphia today as physicians battled to keep the wreck's death toll of 78 from rising.

At least six other persons were listed as critical among the 115 injured in the nation's greatest railroad tragedy since 1918, when a crash at Nashville, Tenn., killed 115.

Full operation over the four-track stretch near Frankford Junction was resumed—but at speeds reduced far under the limit of 45 miles per hour.

Work crews labored by floodlight until early today to remove the wreckage. Six cars of the Limited upset when a burned-out journal box dropped an axle on the first coach.

MANY UNIDENTIFIED

Meanwhile, friends and relatives filed through the city morgue attempting to identify many of the crushed and mangled victims. Twenty-one were still unidentified, most of them women, whose loss of handbags made even paper identification impossible.

Twelve bodies were removed from around the base of the signal tower girder which was struck by the first of the wrecked cars—an old-type day coach. The car twisted to its side and was sliced in half just over the windows as it hurtled into the upright girder.

Six governmental agencies, headed by 20 FBI agents, continued separate investigations, and the Interstate Commerce Commission and the Pennsylvania Public Service Commission scheduled a joint hearing for today to hear the results of an examination of the journal box which the railroad said caused the crash.

The meeting will be behind closed doors at the office of J. L. Cramwell, superintendent of the railroad's Philadelphia Terminal Division. The journal box was exam-

Continued on Page Ten

Colonel To Speak At Luncheon Here

Lt. Col. William E. Pierce, liaison officer for Pennsylvania, Third Civilian Defense Region, will be the principal speaker at the management luncheon to be held under auspices of the Beaver County Civilian Defense Council at the Penn-Beaver Hotel at 12:15 o'clock tomorrow, it was announced today.

The luncheon is planned as a preliminary to the Plant Protection Conference for Beaver County to be held Wednesday and Thursday, September 15 and 16, in the Court House Assembly Room. It is anticipated that all industrial plants in the county will be represented at the luncheon, George W. Roark, executive secretary of the county Civilian Defense Council, said today.

Ballot Contract Is Awarded Today

The Beaver County Commissioners today awarded a contract to the Beaver Falls Printing Company for printing the ballots to be used at the general election on November 2, for $856.25. Only two bids were submitted, with the contract going to the low bidder.

Only one bid was received by the commissioners today in answer to an advertisement for coal to heat the county buildings during the coming winter. The commissioners postponed awarding a contract until later.

Red Cross Blood Bank To Return Here In October

Twenty thousand, two hundred and fifty persons will be asked to register for the second visit of the American Red Cross Mobile Blood Bank Unit to Beaver County between the period of October 11 and January 29. Official confirmation of these dates was received Tuesday by R. C. Stout, chairman of the Beaver County Red Cross Chapter.

In making the announcement of the visit of the unit, Mr. Stout also revealed that William J. Toner, Beaver, well known Bell Telephone Company executive, had been named county chairman of the blood donor campaign.

Sufficient time has elapsed since the first visit of the mobile unit last spring to permit all persons who then were donors, to again contribute to the blood bank. During the earlier campaign the demand of the United States armed forces for blood plasma was 70,000 pints per week. This demand is now 100,000 pints per week, with still further need for plasma—ranking first in the saving of lives of wounded—expected as military action is expanded.

Many individuals who registered as donors during the first campaign here and who were not able to contribute for various reasons, have been anxiously awaiting the return of the Red Cross unit. Calls are being received daily at Chapter headquarters from persons wanting to aid in this movement of mercy.

Extent to which the blood plasma is used is shown in a recent statement that 92 pints were required to save the life of a single soldier, terribly wounded in Sicily.

NEED 1,500 WEEKLY

Based on the requirement of 1,500 donors being signed up for each of the thirteen and one-half weeks the unit will be in Beaver County, a total of 20,250 registrants will be required, according to Mr. Stout, who has called attention to the fact that the county has been extremely fortunate in obtaining the mobile unit at this particular time.

Anticipated severe winter weather conditions were taken into consideration in arranging the schedule of the unit by Red Cross executives, who have booked the more distant points from Pittsburgh for the fall season, with the last six weeks, extending to the end of January, being assigned to Aliquippa and Ambridge.

DATES LISTED

Definite location of the unit in the eight larger communities of the county during the period of the campaign and the hours to be observed are as follows:

Beaver Falls: October 11, 12, 13, 14,—1:30 to 5:30 p. m.; 15 and 16—10:30 a. m. to 2:30 p. m.; Oct. 18,

Continued on Page Two

Argentina Denied Lend-Lease Military Supplies By U. S.

WASHINGTON, Sept. 8 (UP)—Argentina today faced the post-war prospect of having to relinquish her domination of South America to Brazil and to continue her self-imposed isolation from other Western Hemisphere nations.

That implication was contained in a letter to Argentina's Foreign Minister, Segundo Storni, in which Secretary of State Cordell Hull bluntly rejected Argentina's appeal for airplanes and other munitions on grounds that she has refused to contribute her share to the defense of the hemisphere, has failed to live up to her inter-American commitments, and has in many ways given aid and comfort to the enemies of the United Nations.

The correspondence between Hull and Storni was released by the State Department last night. Hull's reply to Stornis' appeal that his country's neutrality was misunderstood was the most severe rebuke delivered to a Latin American government in many years.

BRAZIL'S MIGHT GROWING

It was in marked contrast to the warm Independence Day message

Continued on Page Ten

Transient Is Found Dead In Old Quarry

A 24-hour search for a homeless transient ended Tuesday afternoon when the missing man, William Carden, 70, was found dead at the foot of a 65-foot quarry wall near Homewood.

Carden had stopped Sunday at the Mike Haney farm near Homewood as he had been in the habit of doing. No one had seen him after Sunday evening and a search was made for him Monday.

Tuesday afternoon the search ended when the body was found in the abandoned quarry. Carden had apparently wondered too near the edge, according to Dr. John M. Jackson, deputy coroner, and had plunged to the bottom of the quarry.

Fighter Planes Raid Over Europe Again

LONDON, Sept. 8 (UP)—Marauder medium bombers of the Eighth U. S. Air Force attacked German air fields in the Lille area of Northern France today, carrying the Allied offensive against the Continent into its seventh straight day.

British fighters flew over the Dover Strait today toward Europe on the seventh straight day of Allied raiding on the continent after night attacks on enemy airfields in France and Belgium and shipping in the channel.

A Berlin broadcast said two British "nuisance raiders" were over Reich territory last night and one of them, a Mosquito bomber, was shot down by anti-aircraft fire at the German-Dutch frontier.

Mosquitoes, on intruder operations, hit at railroad targets along with the airfields, the air ministry reported, and naval aircraft sank a German E-boat in the channel without loss.

ALLIES SWEEP THROUGH JAP LAE DEFENSES

Airborne Allied Reinforcements And Steady Bombing Crack Japanese Outer Defenses And Tighten Siege Lines Around Lae

ALLIED HEADQUARTERS, Southwest Pacific, Sept. 8.—(UP)—Allied troops, aided by airborne reinforcements and a steady bombing campaign, have swept through Japanese outer defenses at Lae to tighten the siege lines around the New Guinea coastal base, it was announced today. A force of Australians who crushed an enemy outguard at Singaua Plantation advanced five miles and was approaching the mouth of the Busu river, barely four miles east of Lae.

Liberators, Flying Fortresses and Mitchells dropped explosives that kept enemy defenses staggered in the perimeter around Lae while other planes brought in troops to hastily cleared Nadzab airfield, captured Sunday by American and Australian paratroops.

(Tokyo radio said 1,000 American parachutists landed on the left bank of the Markham river, 20 miles northwest of Lae Monday and that soldiers from the Lae garrison "nearly wiped out the enemy ground troops as well as the majority of the parachute unit.")

BOMBERS POUND JAPS

The ground forces that had gone ashore northeast of Lae never gave the Japanese a chance to get set in Singaula Plantation, roughly nine miles from Lae, smashing their light units and moving ahead. Behind them, the Allied beachhead established last Saturday was broadened.

Heavy bombers attacked enemy defenses at Jacobsen's Plantation, west of Lae, with 80 tons of explosives, setting fires visible 30 miles, Monday while Mitchells hit the Malahang Plantation, just across Busu River toward Lae, with 65 tons of bombs and 75,000 rounds of shell fire.

The bombers were unopposed but later in the day Allied fighters supporting the ground action met and defeated 30 enemy planes, including 20 medium bombers and 10 fighters. At least seven and probably 13 of the enemy aircraft were destroyed. One Allied plane was lost.

Exact location of the troops moving toward Lae from Nadzab Airstrip, 20 miles west of Lae, was not announced but they had turned the port into an Allied landing ground within 24 hours after brushing aside surprised enemy forces and were believed pushing ahead rapidly.

JAPS TRAPPED

At Salamaua, about 25 miles southeast of Lae on the New Guinea coast, American and Australian troops carried out patrol actions. Twenty thousand Japanese troops were trapped and probably doomed in Lae and Salamaua.

In minor air actions north of New Guinea, Allied planes sank six barges and damaged five enemy supply vessels. Other planes raided

Continued on Page Ten

QUOTA CLUB GARDEN FAIR TO BE HELD AT BEAVER SATURDAY

The Quota Club's "Victory Garden Fair", an event of Saturday, is expected to attract many Beaver Valley folk. It will be held in the Beaver high school gymnasium from two until ten o'clock. It is open to the public and anyone may exhibit in the "fair".

There are various classes, including fruits, vegetables, canned goods, jellies and jams in the competitive group, and flowers, paintings, painted articles, antiques, handicraft, "home management" and children's exhibit in the non-competitive group.

Ross M. Gridley, Beaver County farm agent, will judge the fresh articles and Miss Elizabeth McKinley, Home Economics Director of Beaver high school, will judge the canned goods. Gladys Boyd is chairman and Jean Rowse is co-chairman of the affair.

Special prizes will be awarded, including a "door prize" and "entry prize."

A feature attraction will be a group of "shadow-boxes" to be displayed by the Beaver Garden Club.

The rules governing the "fair" follows:

COMPETITIVE GROUP

Division 1—Fruit:

Class 1. Apples—5 speciments to a plate—any variety.

Class 2. Peaches—5 specimens—any variety.

Class 3. Pears—3 specimens—any variety.

Class 4. Plums—5 specimens—

Continued on Page Ten

Fighting Is Ended Today By Armistice

Today's War Summary

By United Press

ITALY—Italy surrenders unconditionally to Allies; British Eighth Army extends Italian bridgehead at least 13 miles, capturing Bova Marina on the south coast and advancing five miles northward from Palmi; Allies now control 200 square miles of Southern Italy.

RUSSIA—Red Army reported to have captured Stalino, rail-industrial center of Donets Basin; Russian cut Gomel-Bakhmach railroad to disrupt German nort-south movements.

SOUTHWEST PACIFIC—Air-borne reinforcements bolster Allied troops advancing on Lae, New Guinea from both sides.

WESTERN EUROPE—British fighters attack continent.

ALLIED HEADQUARTERS, North Africa, Sept. 8 (UP)—Italy surrendered today—unconditionally.

Gen. Dwight D. Eisenhower announced the capitulation of the Italian armed forces five days after the British Eighth Army had invaded Italy.

The Allied commander-in-chief in the Mediterranean area, in announcing the collapse of Italian resistance, said Italy had been granted a military armistice.

The break at the weak end of the European Axis climaxed a brief invasion campaign against the "toe" of Italy, where the resistance encountered by the British Eighth Army was described as no more than a "token" defense.

Gen. Sir Bernard L. Montgomery's troops had been advancing cautiously up the tip of the Italian peninsula, retarded by little more than Axis demolitions and the rugged terrain.

Eisenhower himself announced the Italian surrender over the Allied headquarters radio.

"As commander-in-chief, I have granted a military armistice, approved by the British, American and Soviet governments," Eisenhower said.

"The Italian government has surrendered unconditionally!"

The surrender was effective "this instant" and hostilities terminated at once.

The Italians made an approach with a view to an armistice some weeks ago, Eisenhower said. A meeting was arranged and took place in neutral terirtory.

It was explained to the Italians that they must surrender unconditionally. Further meetings took place in Sicily.

The armistice was signed on September 3 at headquarters there.

The representatives agreed that a simultaneous announcement of the armistice would be made by both sides.

A proclamation by Marshal Pietro Badoglio, Premier of the Italian government, was read over the Allied radio. In it he said the government recognized the impossibility of continuing, and with the object of preventing further harm to the Italian nation, had requested an armistice, which had been granted.

Under the armistice, the Italians not only agreed to all the terms laid down by Eisenhower, but pledged to use force against Germany if the Nazis try to prevent them from carrying out the terms of the agreement.

The Germans were estimated to have several divisions in Italy, and were expected to try to increase them.

ADVANCE CONTINUED

The British Eighth Army had advanced another 13 miles around the toe of the Italian boot, it was announced today, and was pouring arms and stores into its bridgehead at a rate that presaged an early extension of the offensive within Italy.

(A German communique broadcast by Radio Berlin asserted that Allied forces have landed in the Gulf of Eufemia on the northwestern coast of the Italian foot, presumably about 25 miles northeast of the main British forces.)

(Radio Algiers quoted an Allied spokesman as saying that the bridgehead had been extended 18 miles.)

The Allied South Coast column captured Bova Marina in an eight-mile advance from Melito, while other forces on the rocky north or northwest coast drove five miles beyond Palmi to within one mile of Gioia Taura, terminus of a cross-peninsula road.

BOMBERS ACTIVE

Allied medium and fighter bombers gave the enemy a taste of his own medicine with around-the-clock raids on the Calabrian peninsula that cut the coastal railway near a bridge at Sapri behind the retreating Axis troops, damaging the railway bridges at Trebisacce on the Gulf of Taranto and wrecked motor vehicles on two roads in the Lauria-Lagonegro area.

American Flying Fortresses hit at the network of air fields [illegible]

Continued on Page Ten

BEST WISHES

To Coach Carl Aschman And The Fighting QUIPS

for VICTORY in '43

LINEUPS FOR TONIGHT'S GAME

Aliquippa HIGH SCHOOL

Pos.	Player	No.
LE	Walters	39
LT	Mancini, 32 or Thomas	51
LG	Drevna	29
C	Kosanovich	36
RG	Gratson	28
RT	Georgakis	52
RE	Stoken	42
QB	Smallwood, 30; Branchetti	24
LH	Nan	31
RH	Sylvester, 23 or Zanath	46
FB	Young	22

ALIQUIPPA SUBS

Cleary	38	Swan	50
Gilbert	37	Jones	21
Pettis	44	De Fonso	49
Bonomi	33	Lampone	48
Prisuta	35	Potozny	34
Vagercik	45		
Diocquidio	40		
Genario	41		
Leviser	27		
Currie	26		
Mihalcin	53		
Morris	43		
Cerrelli	47		

Petronio, Talepsis, Cable, Twaddle, Barnes, Gula, Kolenda, Huell, Girata, Ayoob, Battles, Tormey, Bradford, Unis, Marshall, Manojlovich, Moskos, Passedellis, Hock, Hook, Colonna.

Freedom HIGH SCHOOL

Pos.	Player	No.
LE	Trompetta	75
LT	Farls	79
LG	Kronk	76
C	DePoalis	80
RG	Ripper	77
RT	Ruckert	81
RE	Fox	74
QB	Meehan	72
LH	H. Martin	70
RH	Petcovic	71
FB	Shingler	73

FREEDOM SUBS

Fztezepanic	28	McIntosh	11
Liberato	78	E. Martin	23
Swager	14	Smith	27
Tianetti	24	Masoni	15
Erzen	18	McCracken	26
Johnson	19	Whitehouse	25
Lathan	13	Vargo	21
Polbert	30		

Kickoff at 8:30 p. m.

P. M. Moore
Plodinec's
Woodlawn Trust Co.
Pete Cost Auto Service
Automotive Service Garage
Henderson & Son
Velonis Furniture Co.

Eger's Jewelry Store
Culp's Shop
Wilson Furniture
Sol's Stores
White Poultry Market
City Cab Co
Staman's

Apollo Soda Water Works
Oliker Bros.
Keifer's Dairy
Woodlawn Hotel
Wyke's Auto Parts
Villa's Inn
Jacobson's

W. C. Young Drug Co.
Klein's Jewelry Store
Todd Motor Sales
Drinkmore Dairy Co.
Ruffner & Moore
Hoffman Drug Co.
Detroit Auto Body & Radiator Works

WEATHER
Warmer today and somewhat warmer tonight.

The Evening Times

"Serving the Ohio Valley Industrial Area"

Quips unimpressive in 20 to 7 win over Butler. Read story on sports page today.

VOL. I—No. 113 — ALIQUIPPA, PA., MONDAY, SEPTEMBER 27, 1943 — FOUR CENTS

71 ALIQUIPPANS INDUCTED

★ ★ ★

German Fortress Hit Hard

REDS BOOST BONDS

THIRD WAR LOAN DRIVE is given a boost by Josef Stalin, who sent a special message to the U. S. asking Americans to buy U. S. War Bonds. Maj. Gen. A. I. Belyaev, chief of the Soviet purchasing commission, is shown reading the message at capital's "Back the Attack" show. *(International)*

Union Launches Drive Here To Enroll Members

7,500 Now Signed, Several Thousand More Non-Members

Aliquippa Local No. 1211 of the United Steelworkers of America (CIO) today announced it is launching a drive to enroll several thousand employes of the J. & L. Steel Corp. here as members of the union.

With approximately 7,500 men and women now belonging to the U. S. of A. local, the union said it will be "the first line of defense in the fight against post-war reaction, wage cuts and unemployment."

Officials emphasized the part the women employes should play in the union, pointing out they now get men's wages and "we expect them to do their part toward the protection of those gains."

Solicitation of new members will be continued at the entrance to the J. & L. Works for an indefinite period of time, it was revealed.

Men and women who have been in the service of Uncle Sam or those off work because of illness or injury will not be required to pay the $3 initiation fee.

Pamphlets explaining formation of the union and how it works were being distributed at the plant.

Jack Atkinson is president of Local 1211; Mike Katcher, financial secretary; James Downing, vice president; Kenneth Parsons, treasurer, and Regis Brennan, recording secretary. The union's organizing committee is composed of Louis Fontana, general chairman; James Cipolla, vice chairman, and John Konowal. The organizing committee is comprised of nine zones covering the various departments at the local plant.

WAC Recruiter Will Be Here Wednesdays

Lieut. Agnes Coutts, of the Beaver Falls recruiting station, will be at the Aliquippa post office every Wednesday between the hours of 10 a. m. and 12:30 p. m. for the purpose of interviewing those who are interested in enlisting in the Women's Army Corps. On Wednesday afternoon of each week she will be at the Laney Motor Sales Co., Merchant St., Ambridge.

MRS. YOUNG HOME

Mrs. Leaman Young, 1818 Grant St., returned home from Rochester hospital over the week-end.

Nazi Fortress Pounded Heavily By Allied Armies

Fifth, Eighth Armies Move On; Emden Hit By U. S. Fortresses

By UNITED PRESS.

Germany's European fortress was under heavy attack today from American and British Armies in southern Italy, from Russian forces that were getting dangerously near the old Polish frontier, from Yankee bombers, and from Jugoslav patriots carrying on guerrilla warfare in northeastern Italy.

Both the American Fifth and the British Eighth Armies made substantial gains as they straightened their front in Italy along a line running eastward from the Salerno sector. The Fifth Army seized Calabritto, 25 miles northeast of Salerno, and Cassano after an 11-mile advance, and the Eighth pushed across the Ofanto river and captured Cerignola on the Foggia plain.

As British pressure increased on the eastern side of the Italian peninsula, the Germans abandoned 13 important airdromes in the Foggia area. When the Allied air fleets begin using these bases, they will have an excellent springboard for attacks on northern Italy, the Balkans and Greater Germany.

The heaviest fighting in Italy was in progress in the rugged mountains guarding the approaches to Naples. Here, the Germans had thrown in reinforcements for a stern delaying stand.

Reynolds Packard, United Press war correspondent who flew over Naples in an Allied reconnaissance plane, said that the city appeared to have been evacuated.

The Soviet Army threw its main weight against Kiev, capital of the Ukraine and Russia's third largest city. One Red force was attacking the city frontally from its eastern suburbs while flanking columns were sweeping across the Dnieper river to the north and south. One unconfirmed report stated the Germans were evacuating Kiev.

Russian troops were believed to have crossed the Dnieper at several points on a 300-mile front between Kiev and Dniepropetrovsk. To the north of Kiev, Soviet forces were advancing into White Russia along a 250-mile front and moving swiftly toward the Polish border.

British military analysts believed that the Russian offensive had achieved such success that the Allies might be forced to hasten plans for an invasion of western Europe.

It was pointed out that the Allies either must open a second front or face the possibility of the Russians defeating the Nazis sin-

(Continued on Page Three)

Pvt. Robert Risher Assigned To Lehigh

Pvt. Robert Risher son of Dr. and Mrs. Robert R. Risher of 406 Franklin Ave. has been assigned to Lehigh university at Bethlehem Pa. as a member of the Army's Specialized Training unit. He will begin his study of basic ngineering Oct. 11.

The training will be given in three 12-week terms. When the new term starts more than 1,300 soldiers will be stationed at Lehigh under this AST program.

Storekeeper R. Thomas Graduates At Sampson

Second Class Storekeeper Roy C. Thomas, son of Mrs. W. J. Thomas, Aliquippa, and husband of Mrs. Anna Mae Thomas, Coraopolis, R. D., has been graduated from the Storekeeper's school at the U. S. Naval Training station, Sampson, N. Y.

MRS. F.D.R. BACK FROM TOUR

Mrs. Franklin D. Roosevelt steps down, above, at La Guardia field, New York, from the Liberator plane that carried her on a 23,000-mile tour of United Nations bases in the Pacific war zone. Shown are, left to right, M/Srgt. Norman Long, engineer of plane; Mrs. Roosevelt; Maj. George E. Durno, press relations officer who accompanied her, and M/Srgt. Richard Funk, steward. (International Soundphoto)

J-L Works Gets 'M' Award Today

Ceremony Scheduled At Pittsburgh Plant

The coveted Maritime "M" award will be conferred upon the Pittsburgh Works of the Jones & Laughlin Steel corporation by Charles E. Walsh, Director of Procurement of the United States Maritime Commission, at a ceremony in the strip-sheet mill today at 4:30 p. m.

In advising J. & L. that its Pittsburgh Works had been awarded the highest honors of the Commission, Rear Admiral H. L. Vickery, chairman of the Board of Awards, said in part:

"I take pleasure in advising you that the Board, in recognition of outstanding production achievement has awarded the Pittsburgh Works the Martime "M" Pennant, the Victory Eagle Flag, and Maritime Merit Badges for all employees of that Works."

A wide variety of steel products is being made by J. & L. for use in the construction of the famous Liberty Ships and the new speedy Victory Ships, including steel hull plates which are being made on the strip-sheet mill that was quickly and ingeniously converted from producing light sheets for auto bodies to the heavier hull plates.

Davies' Infant Dies At Rochester Hospital

Judith Ann Davies, two-day-old daughter of Elias and Margaret Komar Davies, 2200 Davidson St., died at 7:30 a. m. yesterday in Rochester hospital.

Blessing services will be held at 3 p. m. today at the Douds Funeral Home with the Rev. Fr. Edward G. Zauner officiating. Burial will be in Mt. Olivet cemetery.

Center Twp. Firemen Will Stage Bazaar

The Center Twp. Volunteer Firemen and the Ladies' Auxiliary to the Firemen have planned to hold their annual bazaar and card party Sept. 30, Oct. 1 and Oct. 2, at the Center Township Firemen's hall, beginning at 7:30 p. m.

Entertainment, "something for everyone," is under the direction of Jack Combs and Mrs. Harold Heller.

PATIENT IN HOSPITAL

Albert Evans, Monaca Heights, who formerly lived here, an employe of the South mills electrical shop of the Jones and Laughlin Steel Corp., is a patient at the Beaver County Sanitarium.

Former CCC C[illegible] Is Up For Sale

Sealed Bids To Be Received This Week

Sealed bids will be received until Monday, Oct. 4, for the purchase of 32 one-story frame buildings comprising a former CCC camp in Beaver county.

The exteriors of the buildings are covered with tar paper while the interiors are lined with fiber board.

The entire group of buildings must be sold as one unit and the bids may be mailed to war department real estate representatives at the Raccoon recreational demonstration area, R. D. 1, Hookstown, Pa.

Housing Authority's Main Offices Moved

The central offices of the Beaver County Housing Authority was moved Saturday to the permanent location on the site of the county's largest war housing project, Van Buren Homes, 400 units, State St., Vanport.

Temporary offices were located in the Tamaqui Village Administration and community building about a year and a half ago. The new building, a one story brick structure, contains private office rooms, two general office rooms, reception rooms, stock room, furnace room and foyer.

Offices to be housed will be the administration, management, accounting, activities, tenant selection and maintenance.

Christen Bomber In Honor Of Girl Here

In a letter received here Saturday from Tech. Srgt. Osman Zubchevich, of Chicago, Ill., stationed with the U. S. Air Force in Sicily, he informed Miss Daisy Dragovich, 105 Sheffield Ave., here, that his new $150,000 plane had been christened "The Daisy" in her honor.

Miss Dragovich is employed in the metallurgical department of the Jones and Laughlin Steel Corp.

DISTRICT FOLK ILL

Mrs. Pete Belsky, 235 Superior Ave., and Merle Rhines, R. D. 2, Aliquippa, were discharged from Beaver Valley hospital yesterday. A daughter was born today to Mr. and Mrs. Charles Sycyn, Walnut St., Baden, and Miss Kay Hessert, 1311 Ridge Rd., Ambridge, was was admitted to the hospital yesterday. Mrs. John Spear, 237 Anthony Wayne Village, Baden, was discharged yesterday.

Six Injured In Area Accidents Over Week-End

Ambridge Man Hurt Badly; Auto Mishaps Injure Several Here

Six persons were injured, one critically, in industrial and vehicular accidents in the district over the week-end.

The most seriously hurt was James Ostrowski, 30, of 276 13th St., Ambridge, who is fighting for his life at Sewickley Valley hospital.

An employe of the A. M. Byers Co., he was hurt Friday night when a pin broke, causing equipment to fall and hit him on the head.

Jimmie Burns, 1827 McMinn St., received a gash above the left eye and suffered painful brush burns when struck by an automobile driven by Frank Simonich, Jr., of 2611 Mill St., yesterday. Three stitches were required to close the gash. Simonich paid the medical fees.

Raymond W. Troup, while backing his automobile out on Harding Ave. after the football game at the local stadium [illegible] foot of Ann Kovalenko, 10, 317 Second Ave. Miss Kovalenko was treated by a physician.

Albert Winowich, R. D. 2, Aliquippa, was motoring on Brodhead road when a rear tire went flat, causing him to lose control of the vehicle and collide with a parked automobile, besides damaging a service pump belonging to the Foushee Service station. Damage to Winowich's car was estimated at $100, while damage to the parked vehicle, owned by Barnett Feldman, 716 Franklin Ave., was placed at $75. Damage to the service pump was not estimated.

Katherine DeJovin, 5, 333½ Main St., suffered a two-inch cut on the left hand when she fell while at play near her home. Eight clips were required to close the wound.

A schoolboy football game accounted for injuries to Edward Jujan, 12, 620 Neal St., Saturday. The boy was taken to the office of a physician after he received a deep laceration of the lip during the game with other lads.

Mrs. Hazel Hill, New Brighton, is a patient in Rochester hospital suffering head injuries received when she fell through the floor of a building at Kobuta.

11 Arrested In Pool Room Raid

Proprietor Held To Court At Hearing

State Motor police and county detectives raided a pool room at Beaver Falls Saturday night and arrested 11 men on gambling charges.

The proprietor, named Chiodo, was held for court under $500 bond, charged with maintaining a gambling house. The ten others were released after posting $5 forfeits.

Pvts. Robert O. Bechdel and Michael Motily of the Motor police and County Detectives M. J. Kane and L. H. Pinkerton conducted the raid.

McMillin Candidate For Navy Commission

As a candidate for a commission in the U. S. Navy, Bruce B. McMillin, son of Dr. and Mrs. H. C. McMillin of 381 Franklin Ave. here, is among 500 apprentice seamen in training at Middlebury college in Vermont under the Navy V-12 program.

This group received special commendation from Secretary of the Navy Frank Knox during his recent review of the Middlebury regiment. McMillin attended Yale university before going to Middlebury.

'Quota Week' In Third War Bond Drive Announced

Upturn In Purchase Of E Bonds Urged By Chairman T. C. Swarts

This is "Quota Week" in the Third War Loan Drive, County Chairman T. C. Swarts announced today in disclosing Beaver county's sales of Series E Bonds have been less than 10 per cent of the $1,580,900 quota fixed by the Treasury department.

"Special attention has been directed to sales of E Bonds during this campaign," he said, "because such sales represent more directly the support from individuals on the home front."

The county chairman urged persons to buy an extra bond this week to "back the attack."

He said the nation has only responded 60 per cent to its quota of buying E Bonds while the figure in the entire state is only 20 per cent of the quota fixed by the Treasury.

A total of $7,209,543, repres[illegible] been sold in Beaver county to date. The quota is $9,181,600.

Aliquippa, with 7,230 subscriptions amounting to $2,081,755 continued to lead the county, followed by Beaver Falls, with $1,364, 851 subscribed, and New Brighton, with $1,009,794.

Brush Fire Put Out By Borough Firemen

Mischievous children playing on the hillside overlooking the upper end of Superior Ave. ignited the surrounding brush shortly after noon today. Firemen and volunteers battled the blaze unsuccessfully with an Indian pump but when the wind-swept blaze threatened nearby residences, the firemen resorted to the booster pump and the conflagration was extinguished.

Corp J. B. Forrester Now In North Africa

Recently promoted from private first class, Corp. James B. Forrester, serving with the U. S. Air Force, has written his mother here that he has "arrived safely somewhere in the North African War area."

Formerly stationed at Greenville, S. C., he was married last summer to Miss Carlene Delancy, who is living at Pittsburgh with her father.

Court Refuses To Quash Charges Against Judge

PITTSBURGH, Sept. 27 (U.P.) — The State Supreme court today refused to quash a writ of mandamus against President Judge J. Hilary Keenan of Westmoreland county, who had been charged with neglect of duty, but accepted proof that Keenan had complied with an order to dispose of a backlog of cases on his docket.

At the same time, however, the high court ruled that upon payment of costs in the case by Judge Keenan, the writ of mandamus may be returned to the court marked "satisfied."

UNDERGOES TONSILECTOMY

Louise, daughter of Mr. and Mrs. Robert Conrady, 1711 McMinn St., is recovering at her home after undergoing a tonsilectomy at Mercy hospital Friday.

RETURN FROM OHIO VISIT

Mrs. A. D. Davenport, McMinn St., and Mrs. E. W. Beyer, Milton St., have returned from a short stay with friends at Martins Ferry, O.

RETURN HOME

Mrs. Vincent Horvath and infant daughter, 236 Beaver Ave., West Aliquippa, returned home from Rochester hospital over the week-end.

TROUBLES OVER

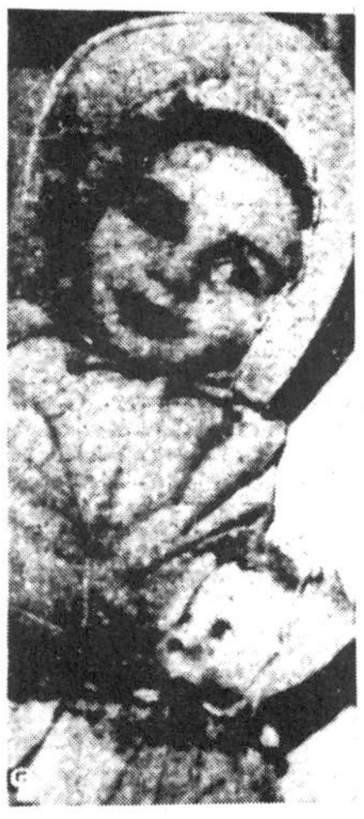

"PENICILLIN BABY," two-year-old Patricia Malone, is pictured as she was about to leave Lutheran hospital, New York, to go home after the successful fight to save her life. She had been given only a few hours to live when the New York Journal-American obtained a supply of penicillin, a new drug, and saved her life. (International)

John A. Gancarz, J-L Foreman, Dies

In Hospital Several Days; Rites Tomorrow

John Anthony Gancarz, 58, 27 High St., Temple Heights, died at 12:50 p. m. Friday in Beaver Valley hospital, where he had been a patient since last Tuesday. Death was due to complications.

Born in Poland, he had been a resident here for the last 32 years and was employed as gauger foreman at the Wire mill of the Jones & Laughlin Steel Corp., here.

Besides his widow, Mrs. Jennie Gancarz, he leaves one daughter, Mrs. Stella Radwanski, Ambridge; his mother, Mrs. Gancarz, Temple Heights; two brothers, Joseph, Aliquippa, and Frank, Cleveland.

Two sisters, Mrs. Mary Tattar, Ambridge, and the other living in Europe, also survive.

He was a member of St. Titus R. C. church, Alisuippa, and St. Stanislaus lodge No. 354, Ambridge.

Funeral services will be tomorrow with High Mass of Requiem from St. Titus church at 9:30 a. m. Burial will be in Mt. Olivet cemetery.

Office Of Civilian Defense Open 2 Nights

Mrs. Eugene Young today announced she will be at the Civilian Defense office in the municipal building two nights weekly. from 7 to 10 p. m. each Monday and Thursday, to help members of the Civilian Defense Corps fill out their questionnaires.

Other hours she will be there will be Monday, 9 to 12 noon; Tuesday, Wednesday and Friday, 9 a. m. to 4 p. m.; Thursday, 9 to 12, and Saturday, 9 a. m. to 12:30 p. m.

George L. Kiefer, executive director of Civilian Defense, today announced:

"I heartily endorse Mrs. Young's action in this matter and she is to be congratulated on her splendid spirit of Americanism."

Station Street Boy Is Bitten By Canine

Sam Treamtafello, 140 Station St., was bitten on the left leg by a dog belonging to a Farber family, residing on Franklin Ave., yesterday. The youth was treated by a physician and sent home.

HOME FROM HOSPITAL

Mrs. Bruno Ulatoski and son, 1606 Main St., are home from Rochester hospital.

Selectees Will Entrain In Three Weeks For Service

Three Accepted As Aviation Cadets; 126 In All Undergo Exams

One hundred, twenty-six selectees from the Aliquippa Draft Board reported to the Pittsburgh induction station for final physical examination Friday and of that number 71 were inducted but will not leave for service with the armed forces until three weeks hence. The inductees are:

Paul F. Bliss, Lindsay Whitaker, Mike Sudak, Jr., Gather H. Brooks, Norman R. Wilkins, William E. Glover, John J. Ruby, Eldon T. Abee, George Mandich, Charles W. Smith, Jr.

Spyros Mukanos, Sam Boldasair, John R. Shorsher, Charles A. Wagner, Mike Maruhnich, James N. Vallese, Mike P. Dzugan, John Siktar, Raymond S. Pawlowski, Robert Mingo.

John A. Seech, Walton Werme, Jack Feigar, Charles Phillips, David Chambers, David [illegible] igan, Benny W. Glenn, Edward F. Winterbauer.

Lawrence A. Beer, Jr., Joseph S. Golixer, Patsy J. DiVecchio, James J. Ertz, Richard Rock, Alonzo Moore, John R. Zaluski, Walter J. Quantz, Jr., John Walke, Anthony Haluka.

Cleophas Johnson, William A. Tilly, Albert J. Silla, William F. Roberts, James J. Jackson, Andrew Blocker, Jr., Robert E. Stevens, Daniel Schram, Jr., Nick Radovich, Walter Montini.

Andy Bible, James Hallisey, Richard Myers, Joseph Miller, Eugene Montini, John Nordberg, Michael Barron, Emlyn Charles, Peter Crisi, Mike Sudar.

Nicholas Hayden, Reed Salvati, William Marquard, Eugene Biletto, Donald Follet, Robert Symons, Jr., and William Martin.

Three local registrants were accepted as aviation cadets. They are: Paul A. Hamilton, Leon F. Block and William E. Davies. Arnold W. Cable was accepted as a engineer.

LATE FLASHES

By UNITED PRESS

PITTSFIELD Mass. — John F. Noxon Jr., 48, prominent attorney and Harvard graduate was charged today with electrocuting his six-month-old son.

The baby one of two sons of Mr. and Mrs. Noxon, died Tuesday in the Noxon home. Police recorded the death as accidental when Medical-Examiner Albert C. England's preliminary report said it had resulted from electrocution. But following an autopsy, police lodged a first degree murder charge against Noxon, who is the son of a former Berkshire county district-attorney.

LONDON. — The British Press association's diplomatic expert said today that Premier Josef Stalin, President Roosevelt and Prime Minister Winston Churchill were "confidently expected" to meet before Christmas.

CHARLOTTESVILLE, Va., Sept. 27.—(U.P.)—Military authorities today investigated the derailment of a west-bound Chesapeake and Ohio passenger train carrying German war prisoners.

The engineer and fireman, C. R. Dillar and Jake Pritchett, both of Charlottesville, were killed. The brakeman and 10 military personnel were injured.

None of the prisoners was killed and none escaped, the Third Service Command at Baltimore said. It reported that only two prisoners were injured seriously enough to require hospitalization. The two were taken to a nearby hospital under guard.

Beaver And Monaca Elevens Meet Under Lights Tonight

FREEDOM SET FOR VISIT OF ZELIENOPLE TEAM TOMORROW

The week end football program in the Valley opens this evening at Beaver's Gypsy Glen Field where the Bobcats will meet Coach Lou Blistan's Monaca Indians in their annual grid battle. Freedom's Bulldogs tackle Zelienople Friday afternoon at Freedom. Three other contests are scheduled Friday night and two Saturday afternoon.

While the Maroon and Gray probably will be without three players who were regulars at the start of the season, Milt Patterson, Lawrence Deemer and Bob Rhinelander, all nursing injured hands, the Bobcats see tonight's game as a chance to get back on the victory train and get even, to some extent, for trouncings administered by the Indians over the last four years.

Local football followers are anticipating a close game tonight. The Red and Blue eleven, although beaten 19 to 0 by Midland last week, showed considerable improvement in the ground gaining department, and it may be that Coach Blistan's boys are just recovering from the early season poundings by Class AA Ambridge, Beaver Falls and New Brighton teams.

LEFFLER REVISES BACKFIELD

Coach H. C. Leffler of Beaver has been grooming a revised backfield combination this week, which probably will be in the lineup at the kickoff. Jack Good and Dick Scherrbaum remain at the quarterback and left halfback posts, respectively, but indications are that Courtney will be at righthalf in place of Joe Taormina and Firestone at fullback, instead of Buckenheimer.

On the line the Bobcat lineup will likely include Staub and either Willoughby or Gibson, ends; R. Hawkins and either D. Hawkins or Holt, tackles; Fisher and either Cascio or Black, guards, and either Fitzgerald or McCormick, center.

Several assignments on the Monaca starting lineup will not be decided until game time. Coach Blistan announced that J. Hill and James will be the ends, Rubino, center, Ridjanek and either Slaughter or Danny Taormina, guards. Any two of four tackles may be starters, Bell, Sproull, Brummitt and Coombs. In the backfield it will be either Busang or Laughner, quarterback; Korak and either Renzo or Barkhurst, halfbacks, and A. Taormina, fullback.

The Indians will wear blue jerseys for tonight's game and the Beavers will be in red outfits.

BULLDOGS READY

On paper at least Zelienople's veteran eleven would appear to have an edge over Freedom's eleven but the Bulldogs are paying no attention to past performances and are primed for a determined battle with the Purple and Gold. The game, on Freedom's East End Field, is scheduled to get underway at 2:30 o'clock tomorrow afternoon.

While the Bulldogs have dropped their three games to date, to Aliquippa, Shenango and Millvale, the Zelienople gridders have won two and lost two. They lost to Ellwood City and Beaver, but defeated Hopewell and Shenango, a team that edged the Bulldogs, 13 to 0.

Coach Dick Fruth expects to start about the same team that was effective against Millevale in the second half of last week's game. Trombetta and Bill Meehan are the ends. Pectovic and either Faris or Liberato will be the tackles, with Ripper and Kronk, guards and C. DePaolis, center. The backfield probably will be Tolbert at quarterback, Bud Martin and Dick Smith, halfbacks, and Shingler, fullback.

Clyde Clements, Zelienople coach, hasn't announced a starting lineup for tomorrow's game, but the usual combination employed in previous contests, has Sweeney and Altemus or Wilson, ends; Lampard and Bartley, tackles; Yohn and Wardle, guards, and Jeffries center; Burkett is the regular quarterback, Young and R. Weigle, the halfbacks and Captain Goehring, fullback. Merle Young, Weigle and Goehring are all capable ball carriers, but Young is the speedboy of the outfit.

RAMS PREP FOR CRIMSON

The Rochester - New Brighton clash at Rochester tops Friday night's grid program. These two old rivals are getting set for a hard battle. Interest among the fans is high and another overflow crowd is certain to jam the Junction City field.

In other games Friday night the Beaver Falls Tigers will meet Ambridge on the Bridgers field and the Ellwood City's eleven will invade Butler.

On Saturday afternoon Aliquippa will appear at Midland to battle the Leopards and Hopewell township's Vikings will tangle with Shenango Township on the Lawrence County team's gridiron.

.PITCHING ARM NEEDED HERE.

PITCHER BERNARD C. KUCYNSKI, who starred at the University of Pennsylvania before hurling for the Philadelphia Athletics earlier this season, finds a new use for his throwing arm at Parris Island, S. C., Marine base where he is a private. Kucynski takes a lesson in hand grenade throwing. (International)

Probable Lineups Beaver-Monaca Game

No.	BEAVER	Pos.	MONACA	No.
30	Staub	LE	J. Hill	23
24	R. Hawkins	LT	Sproull or	33
			Bell	41
22	Fisher	LG	Slaughter or	37
			D. Taormina	31
13	Fitzgerald or	C	Rubino	35
11	McCormick			
26	Cascio or	RG	Ridjanek	42
34	Black			
32	D. Hawkins or	RT	Brummitt or	40
14	Holt		Coombs	21
15	Willoughby or	RE	James	39
18	Gibson			
16	Good	G	Laughner or	28
			Busang	38
19	Scherrbaum	LH	Korak	24
29	Courtney	RH	Renzo or	29
			Barkhurst	30
21	Firestone	F	A. Taormina	22

SUBSTITUTES

BEAVER—Buckenheimer 25, Moravec 23, Albright 28, Cameron 20, Taormina 10, Deemer 31, Patterson 27, Rhinelander 12.

MONACA—P. Hill 20, Thornburg 25, Grosshans 27, Loughead 32, McPadden 19, P. Taormina 36, Donovan 34, Krosky 18.

OFFICIALS: Richard Phillips, Paul Hoskins, A. P. Wildman. KICKOFF—8:00 p. m.

Ladies Church Dux Loop Opens Season

The Ladies' Church Bowling League of New Brighton has been reorganised with eleven teams enrolled and the first matches were rolled this week. Fifth Avenue Methodist 1, Presbyterian 2 and United Presbyterian 1, started off with three-game victories.

Helen Druschel, of First Methodist 1, had the high single game of the opening week, 162, and Jane McDanel's 399 was the best three-game score. Following are the high individual scores for each team:

Lutheran 1—Mrs. D. F. Harvey, 132 and 321; Lutheran 2—Julia Ragula, 132 and 373; Fifth Ave. Meth. 1—Peg Dickey 150, Jane McDanel 150 and 399; Fifth Ave. Meth. 2—Winifred Wilderoder 130 and Helen Beatty 363; First Meth. 1—Helen Druschel 162 and 331; First Meth. 2—Mable Kester 142 and 397; Presbyterian1—Mary Lou Fritz, 118 and 327; Presbyterian 2—Mildred Reutter 152 and 377; Presbyterian 3—Mary Catherine Moersch 106, Sara Bingham 106, Betty Hasely 244; nited Presby. 1—Vesta Conray 139 and 334.

TEAM STANDING

	Won	Lost
Fifth Ave. Meth. 1	3	0
Presbyterian 2	3	0
United Presbyterian 1	3	0
First Meth. 2	2	1
Lutheran 2	2	1
Lutheran 1	1	2
First Meth. 1	1	2
Fifth Ave. Meth. 2	0	3
Presbyterian 1	0	3
Presbyterian 3	0	3
United Presbyterian 2	Idle	

Durocher's Status Is Left In Doubt

PITTSBURGH, Sept. 30 (UP) — The 1944 status of Manager Leo Durocher of the Brooklyn Dodgers was left in doubt today by one of President Branch Rickey's typical maneuvers.

Rickey announced late yesterday that Durocher will be given his unconditional release as player-manager when the club concludes its season against Cincinnati Sunday but that Leo would have an equal opportunity, along with other aspirants, to negotiate for the job as bench manager of the Dodgers next year.

Rickey said Durocher also would be free to negotiate for some other job in baseball, in radio or in Hollywood. The reference to radio and Hollywood may have been directed at the several radio appearances Leo has made in the past few months and the fact that he has many friends among film stars.

CADET CAPTAIN
By Jack Sords
CASIMIR MYSLINSKI
CAPTAIN AND CENTER OF THE ARMY

Pirates Purchase Columbus Hurler

PITTSBURGH, Sept. 30.—(UP)— The Pittsburgh Pirates have completed the deal for the purchase of Pitcher Elwin (Preacher) Roe from Columbus of the American Association, releasing outright Pitcher Johnny Podgajny and outfielder Johnny Wyrostek to the Red Birds.

The Bucs agreed to give Columbus two players in addition to a cash consideration for Roe.

Five Pirates On Nation's Team To Tour Pacific

Five members of the Pittsburgh Pirates, including Manager Frank Frisch, have been selected on the National League All-Star team that will tour the Southwest Pacific battle area this Fall to play for American service men.

In addition to Frisch, who was honored by being chosen manager of the National League team, the following Pirates were selected: Rip Sewell, pitcher; Fletcher and Elliott, infielders, and DiMaggio, outfielder.

Joe Cronin of the Boston Red Sox, will be manager of the American League team. The tour will begin soon after the world series.

The players selected are:

National League: Pitchers—Sewell, Pirates; Vander Meer, Reds; Javery, Braves; Gerheauser, Phils; Bithorn, Cubs; Walters, Reds; Catchers—Cooper, Cardinals; Mueller, Reds; Infielders—Klein, Cardinals; Fletcher, Pirates; Miller, Reds; Elliott, Pirates; Bartell, Giants; Outfielders — DiMaggio, Pirates; Musial Cardinals; Galan and Walker, Dodgers, and Medwick, Giants; Manager—Frankie Frisch, Pirates.

American League: Pitchers—Chandler, Yankees; Leonard, Senators; Hughson, Red Sox; Trout, Tigers Grove, Whitesox; Reynolds, Indians; Catchers—Dickey, Yankees; Hemsley, Yankees; Early, Senators; Infielders — York, Tigers; Doerr, Red Sox; Gordon and Johnson, Yankees; Appling, Whitesox; Outfielders—Keller, Yankees; Fox, Red Sox; Case and Spence, Senators; Manager—Joe Cronin, Red Sox.

Alliance Riders Top Darlington

The Alliance, O., polo team defeated the Darlington riders by a 7 to 6 margin Wednesday evening on the latter's field. Play was very fast throughout the game and was decided in the last 18 seconds when Votah converting a number three foul for the winning tally.

Darlington defeated the Alliance team last week 8-5 and a playoff is scheduled for Wednesday evening, October 6.

The lineups:

Darlington	Pos.	Alliance
Braden	1	Johnson
G. Camp	2	Murphy
Boren	3	Fernangle
Drake	4	Votah

Spares: Darlington — McMillen, Moore; Alliance—T. Wilson, Reese.

Scoring—Braden 3, Camp 2, Drake 1, Johnson 2, Votah 2, Murphy 1, Fernangle 1, Wilson 1.

Score by chukkers:

Alliance	1	1	2	1	1	1—7
Darlington	2	2	1	0	1	0—6

Senators Clinch Second Place; Bucs Beaten By Dodgers

NEW YORK, Sept. 30.—(UP) — Baseball men agreed today that the prize for most improvement in a ball club this season should by all means go to the Washington Senators and their first-year manager, Ossie Bleuge.

The Nats clinched second place in the Junior Circuit last night by winning both ends of a doubleheader from the Cleveland Indians, 6-2 and 7-4.

The Chicago White Sox and the New York Yankees traded shutouts. Bespectacled Bill Dietrich hurled the Sox to a 3-0 triumph in the opener and Charley Wensloff pitched the Yankee victory, 4-0.

The Philadelphia Athletics won their first Wednesday ball game of the season in the first of two games with the Detroit Tigers. Jess Flores pitched the "A's" to an 8-2 decision. Paul (Dizzy) Trout received credit for his 19th decision in the nightcap as his mates hammered out a 9-1 Tiger triumph. Rudy York clouted his 34th homer in the second game.

The St. Louis Browns clinched sixth place with a 4-3 triumph in a 13-inning first game and battled to a nine inning, 3-3 draw with the Boston Red Sox in second.

In the National League the Brooklyn Dodgers regained third place with a 19-hit 14-7 victory over the Pittsburgh Pirates. Trailing 4-1 in the sixth, the Dodgers went to work on starter Max Butcher and three other pitchers to score nine runs in the eighth inning and walkaway with the game.

The St. Louis Cardinals made it 19 decisions out of 22-games with the Boston Braves when Alpha Brazle southpawed his way to a 3-2 victory.

The New York Giants and the Chicago Cubs battled to a 14-inning 3-3 tie.

Johnny Vander Meer pitched his second consecutive four hit shutout when the Cincinnati Reds defeated the Philadelphia Phillies, 3-0.

Wildcats Win Over Buckeys, 19 To 8

The Bickerstaff Wildcats took a 19-5 decision from the West Park Buckeyes Wednesday afternoon on the West Washington Street Field, Rochester.

Bill Bickerstaff paced the scoring with 12 points. Glenn Ross and Jim Shaffer were next with 6 points each. Dietz ran off tackle for the extra point for the Cats. The Buckeyes also scored a safety.

OPERATION SUCCESSFUL

CHICAGO, Sept. 30.—(UP)—The Chicago White Sox announced that an operation on Thornton Lee's pitching arm was "wholly successful." Several bone chips were removed from his elbow and a shoulder growth was treated by Dr. Daniel Leventhal. Lee is convalescing in a hospital.

Big League Leaders

By UNITED PRESS

LEADING BATTERS

AMERICAN LEAGUE

Player, Club	AB.	H.	Pct.
Appling, Chicago	573	187	.326
Wakefield, Detroit	624	195	.313
Hodgin, Chicago	396	124	.313
Cramer, Detroit	606	182	.301
Case, Washington	605	176	.291
NATIONAL LEAGUE			
Musial, St. Louis	610	218	.357
Herman, Brooklyn	571	190	.333
W. Cooper, St. Louis	445	141	.317
Witek, New York	608	192	.316
Elliott, Pittsburgh	575	182	.316

Football Calendar

HIGH SCHOOL

TONIGHT

*Monaca at Beaver, 8 p. m.

FRIDAY

*New Brighton at Rochester, 8 p. m.

*Beaver Falls at Ambridge, 8:15 p. m.

*Ellwood City at Butler.

Zelienople at Freedom, 2:30 p. m.

SATURDAY

Aliquippa at Midland, 3:00 p. m.

Hopewell at Shenango.

*Night games.

COLLEGE

SATURDAY

Pitt at Great Lakes.

Carnegie Tech at University of Rochester.

Penn State at North Carolina.

Georgia Tech at Notre Dame.

MAURIELLO WINS

SYRACUSE, N. Y., Sept. 30 (UP) —Tami Mauriello, New York heavyweight, registered an eighth-round technical knockout over Gunnar Barlund, Finnish veteran, last night in the main event of Jack Kearns' service athletic equipment show.

THE OLD HOME TOWN
By STANLEY
I JUST REMEMBER, IT WAS THE NON-EXPLOSIVE CLEANING FLUID I WAS SUPPOSED TO GET!
ORDER YOUR COAL HERE
TOBACCO DEPT
GROCERIES
DRUGS
AUTO SUPPLIES
HARDWARE DEPT
SCHOOL SUPPLIES
LET IT BE A LESSON TO YOU, CHUM!

SPORT SLANTS

By BILL ANDERSON

The writer keenly enjoyed a letter from Alex J. Scassa, formerly of Monaca and promoter of some fine amateur boxing shows at Rochester several years ago. Scassa has been living near Russellville, Alabama, and working in a war plant there the last two years or more. Picking cotton can hardly be classed as sport, but Alex's account of his experience on a big cotton plantation, we think, will prove entertaining to both our readers.

Following are several paragraphs from Scassa's letter describing the art of picking cotton a la Scassa:

"The cotton plantations were short of cotton pickers, so a bunch of us war workers decided toput in a few extra licks for the war effort and try our hands at cotton picking.

"Cotton picking time begins at daybreak, and at 6 a. m. I was up and on the field raring to go.

"As other cotton pickers arrived I was amazed at the heavy clothing they wore. I asked a Negro why all the heavy clothes. He said, 'To keep de heat out boss, to keep de heat out.' They all wore big straw hats to protect them from the sun. I laughed at the way they were dressed, but it wasn't long until I found out how wrong I was.

"At the weighing wagon they gave me a nine-foot sack that resembled a folder tent, which I slung across my shoulder. It dragged several feet on the ground. With the sack went these instructions. 'Stay in one row. You can pick one row or two, one on each side, or you can pick "snatch", two pickers working one row together.

'I employed a 'snatch system' of my own. That is, I roved wild and snatched where the cotton seemed the most abundant. But the boss soon put a stop to that. "I thought I was doing pretty good, separating the dry leaves from each ball, when a veteran Negro picker, called out and said: "Boss, if you is doing that for a living you is apt to go hungry. At the rate you're going you won't fill that sack in three weeks!

"Cotton picking is really an art. These experienced pickers work in a semi-squat position as they nimbly and lightly run their fingers over the stalks, just as a pianist runs his fingers over the keyboards.

"The rate of pay is $1.50 a hundred pounds. The average picker can pick 200 pounds a day. I have heard that the real experts will pick around 600 pounds.

"All it really takes to be a cotton picker is willingness, rhythm and an exceptionally strong back. I'm afraid I do not possess any of these qualities and that my days of cotton picking are over.

"After about six hours of this, hot weary and hungry, I decided to throw in the towel. It was more than 100 degrees in the shade, and where I was, there was no shade.

"Tired and weary I trudged to the weighing wagon. The boss weighed my cotton, and when he said 50-pounds, I almost keeled over. I thought sure I had picked at least a ton.

"My labors brought me the sum of 75 cents, which I donated to charity. That is, I applied it on a bottle of liniment which saved a man's life."

Red Birds, Chiefs Open Series Friday

COLUMBUS, O., Sept. 30.—(UP) —The Columbus Red Birds of the American Association and the Syracuse Chiefs of the International League, winners of the Governor's Cup playoffs of their respective circuits, prepared today for the Little World Series.

The Red Birds won the right to represent the American Association last night with a 2-0 victory over the Indianapolis Indians.

The Little World Series opens Friday night at Syracuse in a best of seven playoff.

TODAY'S RADIO PROGRAM

6 p. m.
WWSW, Bill Cullen, News.
WCAE, Babe Rhodes Orch.
WJAS, Major Eliot.
KQV, Terry and the Pirates.
KDKA, News; War Needs Wires.
WKBN, News; Window Shopper.

6:15 p. m.
WWSW, Rosey Rowswell.
WCAE, Evening News.
WJAS, Beckley Smith, News.
KQV, Sports with Evans.
KDKA, Design for Listening.
WKBN, Don Gardner, Sports.

6:30 p. m.
WWSW, Song Souvenirs.
WCAE, News Everywhere.
WJAS, Chats About Dogs.
KQV, News.
KDKA, Songs for Service Men.
WJAS, Major Geo. F. Elliott.

6:45 p. m.
WWSW, Entertainment Time.
WCAE, Dinner Music.
WJA, Bob Prince, Sports.
KQV, Modernaires.
KDKA, Lowell Thomas, News.
WKBN, The World Today; Joseph C. Harsch.

7 p. m.
WWSW, News.
WCAE, Fulton Lewis, Jr.
WJAS, I Love a Mystery.
KQV, Wings To Victory.
KDKA, Fred Waring.
WKBN, Bill Seth, News.

7:15 p. m.
WWSW, Entertainment Time.
WCAE, Wohl's Sophisticates.
WJAS, Harry James Orch.
KDKA, News of the World.
WKBN, Harry James Orch.

7:30 p. m.
WWSW, Joe Tucker, Sports.
WCAE, Bulldog Drummond.
WJAS, Easy Aces.
KQV, Fighting Coast Guard.
KDKA, Life with Fred Brady.
WKBN, W. O. R. Johnson and Fred Heim.

7:45 p. m.
WWSW, Two Queens.
WJAS, Mr. Keen.
WKBN, Emil Cote, Auto Drama.

8 p. m.
WWSW, News; Captain Floro.
WCAE, This Is Our Enemy.
WJAS, The Roma Show.
KQV, Watch the World Go By.
KDKA, Baby Snooks.
WKBN, Roma Comedy Show.

8:15 p. m.
WWSW, Four Vagabonds.
KQV, Lum and Abner.

8:30 p. m.
WWSW, Time To Dance.
WCAE, Adventure.
WJAS, Death Valley Days.
KQV, Town Meeting.
KDKA, Aldrich Family.
WKBN, Death Valley Days; Alan Freed, News.

8:45 p. m.
WJAS, Bill Henry, News.

9 p. m.
WWSW, News; Roller Derby.
WCAE, Gabriel Heatter.
WJAS, Major Bowes.
KDKA, Music Hall.
WKBN, Major Bowes.

9:15 p. m.
WWSW, Golden Hour.
WCAE, Fight Night

9:30 p. m.
WCAE, U Tell Em Club.
WJAS, Dinah Shore Program.
KQV, Spotlight Bands.
KDKA, J. Davis & J. Haley.
WKBN, Dinah Shore Show.

9:45 p. m.
KQV, Treasury Program.

10 p. m.
WWSW, News; Organ Interlude.
WCAE, Raymond Clapper.
WJAS, The First Line.
KQV, Raymond G. Swing.
KDKA, Moore-Durante Program.
WKBN, The First Line.

10:15 p. m.
WWSW, Oklahoma.
WCAE, M. Spitalny Orch.
KQV, Miniature Minstrels.

10:30 p. m.
WWSW, Bill Cullen, News.
WCAE, Camp Wheeler.
WJAS, Suspense.
KQV, Gertrude Lawrence.
KDKA, March of Time.
WKBN, Suspense.

10:45 p. m.
WWSW, Scores; Music.

11 p. m.
WWSW, Homer Ochsenhirt.
WCAE, News Parade.
WJAS, Ken Hildebrand, News.
KQV, News.
KDKA, News.
WKBN, I Love a Mystery.

11:15 p. m.
WWSW, Gardens Sports Parade
WCAE, Treasury Star Parade.
WJAS, Joan Brooks.
KQV, Treasury Star Parade.
KDKA, Eleven-Fifteen Local.
WKBN, Touchdown Tips.

11:30 p. m.
WWSW, Masterworks of Music.
WCAE, Johnny Messner Orch.
WJAS, Flashgun Casey.
KQV, Music for Reading.
KDKA, Treasury Star Parade.
WKBN, Flashgun Casey.

11:45 p. m.
WCAE, Lionel Hampton Orch.
KQV, Music; News.
KDKA, News, Jack Swift.

12 Midnight
WWSW, 1500 Club (till 6 a. m.)
WCAE, George Duffy Orch.
WJAS, News; Open House.
KQV, Music for Reading.
KDKA, The Music You Want.
WKBN, News.

12:15 a. m.
WJAS, Open House.
WKBN, Open House.

12:30 a. m.
WCAE, Al Donahue Orch.
KDKA, The Groover Boys.
WKBN, Johnny Long Orch.

Baseball Summary

NATIONAL LEAGUE

RESULTS WEDNESDAY

Brooklyn 14, Pittsburgh 7.
St. Louis 3, Boston 2.
*Chicago 3, New York 3.
Cincinnati 3, Philadelphia 0.
*14 innings, called; darkness.

TEAM STANDING

	W.	L.	Pct.
St. Louis	101	49	.673
Cincinnati	85	65	.567
Brooklyn	79	70	.530
Pittsburgh	80	72	.526
Chicago	71	77	.480
Boston	66	82	.446
Philadelphia	62	90	.408
New York	55	94	.369

GAMES TODAY

New York at St. Louis (night).
Boston at Chicago.
Brooklyn at Cincinnati.
Others not scheduled.

GAMES FRIDAY

New York at St. Louis.
Brooklyn at Cincinnati.
Boston at Chicago.
Others not scheduled.

AMERICAN LEAGUE

RESULTS WEDNESDAY

Chicago 3, New York 0.
New York 4, Chicago 0.
Philadelphia 8, Detroit 2.
Detroit 9, Philadelphia 1.
*St. Louis 4, Boston 3.
**St. Louis 3, Boston 3.
Washington 6, Cleveland 2.
Washington 7, Cleveland 4.
*13 innings. ** 9 innings, called, darkness.

TEAM STANDING

	W.	L.	Pct.
New York	95	55	.633
Washington	84	67	.556
Cleveland	79	71	.527
Chicago	79	72	.523
Detroit	75	76	.497
St. Louis	71	77	.480
Boston	68	71	.456
Philadelphia	49	101	.327

GAMES TODAY

Chicago at New York.
St. Louis at Boston (2).
Detroit at Philadelphia.
Cleveland at Washington (night).

GAMES FRIDAY

St. Louis at New York.
Cleveland at Philadelphia.
Others not scheduled.

BITHORN AWAITS CALL

CHICAGO, Sept. 30. — (UP) — Hiram Bithorn, Chicago Cubs Puerto Rican pitcher, is awaiting orders from his San Juan draft board to report for a physical examination. Bithorn, current ace of the Cub moundsmen, received a tentative 1-A classification during the team's recent eastern trip.

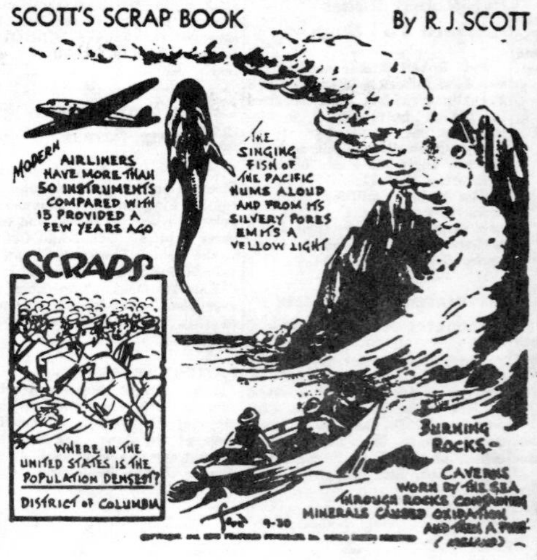

SCOTT'S SCRAP BOOK
By R. J. SCOTT
MODERN AIRLINERS HAVE MORE THAN 50 INSTRUMENTS COMPARED WITH 15 PROVIDED A FEW YEARS AGO
THE SINGING FISH OF THE PACIFIC HUMS ALOUD AND FROM ITS SILVERY PORES EMITS A YELLOW LIGHT
SCRAPS
WHERE IN THE UNITED STATES IS THE POPULATION DENSEST?
DISTRICT OF COLUMBIA
BURNING ROCKS

Fayette Officials Facing New Trial

UNIONTOWN, Sept. 30 (UP) — Anthony Cavalcante, Fayette county attorney and former State Senator, and four Fayette county officials will go on trial next Monday on charges of conspiracy to cheat and defraud Fayette county taxpayers in connection with payment of a $10,-000 fee to Cavalcante for compromising the county's indebtedness to the state.

Besides the attorney, the other defendants in the case—the seventh trial resulting from an inquiry into the county's fiscal affairs by a grand jury last March—are County Commissioners John W. Rankin, Arthur Higinbotham, and Michael Karolcik, and County Controller Albert Montgomery.

Among the commonwealth witnesses at the trial next week will be two deputy state attorneys general, Ralph B. Umsted and C. P. Kiely, who testified last week at the trial of the three commissioners on charges of altering the Fayette county minutes to show authorization of a fee for Cavalcante. The commissioners were convicted in that case.

Women are said to make better spies than men. Intelligence officers of state departments say men are apt to tell all they know when under the influence of liquor.

NEWS-TRIBUNE

NEW BRIGHTON

HISTORY IN TABLOID

[illegible]

Mrs. Amy [illegible] er of [illegible] rix and wife of [illegible] former [illegible] of New Brighton [illegible] of McKeesport [illegible] Saturday at McKeesport hospital after a long illness. She was 70 years of age.

Mrs. Richey, who lived at 3003 Jenny Lind street, McKeesport, was born in New Brighton, the daughter of the late C. F. and Adelaide R. Winter, and moved to McKeesport 47 years ago. She was a past president of the Burt Foster Post Auxiliary of the American Legion and a member of the Central Presbyterian church, McKeesport.

In addition to her husband and Miss Richey, she leaves two other daughters, Mrs. G. P. Gamble of McKeesport, and Mrs. T. W. Smith Jr., of Akron, O., and a son, Lieutenant Joseph W. Richey of the United States Army, and a brother, A. T. Winter, of Beaver Falls.

Friends are being received at the Hunter - Edmondson - Striffler funeral home, 600 Market street, McKeesport, where funeral services will be held at 2 P.M. tomorrow. Interment will be in Versailles cemetery.

Shivering Police Make Urgent Plea For Heat

"We're freezin' to death!" came the chattering plea from the temporary police station in the borough building annex this morning.

Holding forth at a desk in the corner of the firemen's recreation and meeting room, the valiant minions of the law had but one reply for requests for routine reports—"We who are about to freeze to death, salute you! Please can you do something? We have no heat nor nothin'!"

It develops that heat from the borough building furnace "just doesn't get around to that corner" of the annex until the "shank" of the morning, and a plan is being studied to keep a night fire going until police find permanent headquarters.

W. C. T. U. Enjoys Talks On Citizenship Phases

"Legislation and Citizenship" proved an interesting topic for discussion at the end-of-the-week meeting of the New Brighton W.C.T.U. The meeting was held at the home of Mrs. E. Joe Vandervort. Mrs. Nellie Phillips led the program.

Mrs. Vandervort very ably spoke on "Get Out the Vote," and "The Crusade Spirit," was the topic of a talk by Mrs. Phillips. Mrs. Elizabeth Kennedy led the devotions in a talk on past Sabbath school lessons.

After a brief business session presided over by Mrs. H. P. Miller, a short social period was enjoyed. Mrs. Vandervort served cookies and tea. Mrs. John Caughey presided at the tea table.

STUDY VIOLATIONS

Circumstances surrounding a number of minor violations during the recent night air-raid test will be aired tomorrow evening by the decisions board of the local OCD. The board will meet in the local control room at 7:30 o'clock.

A meeting of the control center personnel will be held at 8 o'clock.

READIN' AND RIDIN' AND 'RITHMETIC'

THIS IS A WHOLE LOT TOUGHER PROBLEM THAN I THOUGHT
RATIONING
NEW GASOLINE REDUCTIONS B-C
PUBLIC
(UNSOLVED PROBLEM) IF A HAS 10 RED POINTS AND BUTTER IS 16, HOW IN HECK DO YOU GET ANY BUTTER?
BRGILL
KING FEATURES SYNDICATE, Inc.

HAWKINS HOME PARTY

A record attendance marked the party for members of the Hawkins Home Circle held Friday evening at the home of Mrs. Kenneth Burgess, Mercer road. Patriotic colors were used throughout the appointments and decorations.

Mrs. Edwina Burgess, Mrs. Hazel Guy, Mrs. Elsa Guy and Mrs. Mabel Boggs received the awards in the games. Lunch was served by the hostess, assisted by her mother, Mrs. Linnie Cole, and her sister, Mrs. Walter Anderson.

New Brighton Briefs

Joseph Anderson, U. S. Navy, has returned to his post after a furlough spent with his parents, Mr. and Mrs. James Anderson, Mercer road.

Choir rehearsal at the First Methodist church will be held Wednesday evening at 7:30 o'clock.

Mr. and Mrs. John Dewhirst, Marion Hill, entertained a group of relatives and friends on Saturday evening at their home, in honor of the first birthday anniversary of their daughter, Patricia Jean.

Mrs. William Barger, Mercer road, is reported confined to her home by illness.

Pvt. William Mittner, U. S. Marines, is spending a furlough at his home here.

Miss Sarah Mitchell, Sharon, is visiting with her cousins, Mr. and Mrs. B. E. Arnold, Crescent Heights.

Patty McClane, daughter of Mr. and Mrs. Patrick V. McClane, North Mercer avenue, is reported ill at her home.

The Beaver Presbyterial will meet tomorrow in the Rochester Presbyterian church. The morning session will open at 9:45 o'clock.

Mr. and Mrs. Glenn Funkhouser and family, Mercer avenue, visited over the weekend with relatives at Elyria, O.

Mr. and Mrs. Ralph Ferrell, Bellevue, have concluded a visit with relatives here and in Beaver Falls.

Robert Shaffer, who has been stationed at Fordham University, New York, is enjoying a furlough with his wife and his parents, Mr. and Mrs. R. T. Shaffer.

Rev. and Mrs. M. M. Boose, of the Four-Mile U. P. church, are the parents of a daughter born Saturday night in the Beaver Valley General hospital. The baby has been named Sylvia Joyce.

Mrs. Paul Sheets, Marion Hill, who has been ill, is reported much improved and able to be about her home.

Attendance yesterday at the Christian and Missionary Alliance Sunday school was reported as 201. The church board will meet this evening at the church, and the teachers and officers of the Sunday school will meet tomorrow evening.

Miss Mary Ewing of Cabot, Butler county, a former resident and teacher in the New Brighton schools, visited over the weekend with relatives and friends here.

Mr. and Mrs. William McWhitter and baby, Pittsburgh, have returned home after a visit of several days with Mr. and Mrs. John Dewhirst, Marion Hill.

The Fallston surgical dressing class will meet Wednesday from 9:30 until 3 o'clock at the borough building.

Mr. and Mrs. Lester Sheets and family have concluded a visit with relatives at Independence, W. Va.

Charles Smith, janitor at the Marion Hill school, is reported ill at his home.

Mrs. Alice Bolland of this place is in Ellwood City at the home of her son, John W. Bolland and is spending a great deal of time with her daughter, Mrs. Bernice Denhart, a patient in the Ellwood Hospital. Mrs. Denhart's condition is much improved and she will be able to receive company in a few days.

Mr. and Mrs. Jack P. Headland have named their son born on September 27th at the Beaver Valley General hospital, Jack Roger. Mrs. Headland is the former Marjorie Strayer, daughter of Mr. and Mrs. A. C. Strayer of Beaver, formerly of this place.

Attendance yesterday at the First Presbyterian Sunday school was reported as 199. Classes reporting perfect attendance were those of Mrs. R. M. Kenah and Miss Nellie Couch.

Rally day attendance at Trinity Lutheran Sunday school yesterday was 242. Four classes report attendance of 100 percent—those of Arthur Martsolf, Mrs. Elsie Lowery, Lulu Zimmerman and Alice Hartman.

Group No. 2 of the Women's Society for Christian Service of the First Methodist church will meet tomorrow evening with Mrs. Paul Stanley. A good attendance is asked.

Items of Interest From Fifty-Five Years Ago

(From the Beaver Valley News of October 4, 1888)

Attendance at the third day of the county fair was one of the largest ever known and was roughly estimated at from 5,000 to 6,000. The number of family tickets which have been sold is over 2,300. The inpouring began as early as 8:00 o'clock in the morning and it was continuous until after 2:00 o'clock. After people have made the tour of the various halls and the grounds in general [illegible] ready to [illegible] to the [illegible] they [illegible] hour and [illegible] the clanging of the [illegible] bell, which calls the races. This was the case yesterday and the sea of faces which lined the track for several hundred yards on either side of the judges' stand and the grand stand was an interesting spectacle to behold. The trotting race had but three entries which were Pat McLaughlin's bay gelding, S. E. Gallagher; a Pittsburgh bay mare called Gypsy owned by Harry Rea, and a bay gelding called Lynn W. owned by Lynn Bros. of Youngstown. It was a pretty little race but was won easily by the latter horse. During the later afternoon Lynn W.'s owner agreed to let him trot a mile for an exhibition, to beat the best trotting time ever made on the Beaver track. This was done by Mohawk Gift, owned by a gentleman named Adams living beyond Youngstown three years ago under similar circumstances and his time was 2:30¼. Lynn W. did it yesterday in 2:26¾ by several watches.

Nellie, the six-year-old daughter of Mr. and Mrs. John Nolan of near the Tumbler works, Rochester, had quite an accident on Saturday afternoon which came near resulting fatally. She was standing on the railing of the porch getting some morning glory seeds when she accidentally slipped and fell to the ground, a distance of 14 feet, alighting on her head. She was unconscious when picked up and remained so for several hours. Dr. Hillman was called in, who found that her collar bone was shattered.

The Sourbeck hotel has been sold to Mager F. Scott of the St. Charles hotel, Pittsburgh, and he will take possession about the 15th of the present month.

H. Noss has secured J. J. Sheets of Ashland, O., an experienced photographer, to take charge of his gallery. Mr. Noss is getting new backgrounds and otherwise improving his gallery.

T. J. Powell of Franklin township was in town on Thursday, walking with the aid of a cane. He has been quite sick since last June, unable to do any work. At that time he was kicked in the left knee by a cow, which resulted in a stove that kept him in the house for weeks.

Thursday evening as William Powell attempted to alight from a Lake Erie train at the New Brighton station, he was attacked by three men, two of whom grasped him by the arms. The other one held him down by the neck, and in this position took a pocketbook containing $500 from his hip pocket. Mr. Powell made considerable outcry and went back on the train in an effort to discover the perpetrators, but all efforts proved unavailing.

Our townsman, Albert Marquis, Sr. with Marcus T. C. Rose of New Castle, former members of Company H. 9th Pennsylvania Reserves, were eye witnesses to the assassination of President Lincoln at Ford's theatre on April 14, 1865. The above mentioned gentlemen were seated in the parquette circle at the time the infamous deed was committed and their account of the tragic affair and the incidents immediately following, are very interesting and realistic.

Hospital News

The Beaver Valley General hospital today reported the birth yesterday of a daughter to Mr. and Mrs. Milton Boos, R. D. 1, Beaver. Admissions included: Mrs. Thomas Gilkey, R. D. 2, Beaver Falls; Mrs. Anthony Fadool, Aliquippa; William Garmen, 933 Sixth avenue; Arthur Teets, R. D. 1, Rochester; Mary Beatty, 797 Third avenue, Freedom; Clarence Davis, R. D. 2, Beaver Falls; Mrs. Roy Dripps, 1505 Eighth avenue, Beaver Falls; Daniel Lasco, Baden; Mrs. Paul Barord, Patterson Heights, and Matthew Cisowski, N.S. Pittsburgh.

Discharges were: Mrs. Ford Shane, Beloit, Ohio; Mrs. Angelo Trombetto and son, 1326 Second avenue, Conway; Mrs. James Sullivan and daughter, 1319 Riverside drive, West Bridgewater; Mrs. Elmer Mallick, 522 Eighteenth avenue, Beaver Falls; Emerson and John Barr, 1341 Sixth street; Virgil Conkle, Aliquippa; Mrs. Charles Ferry, Aliquippa; Mrs. Frank Huddy and son, 120 Shields street, Rochester; Kay Hessert, Ambridge; Betty Kistner, 724 Tenth avenue; Elva Maylone, Vanport; Barbara Ann Trgovac, 912 Thirteenth street, and Fred Herman, N.S. Pittsburgh.

Mr. and Mrs. Frank McClain, 3806 Third avenue, are the parents of a baby girl born at Providence hospital yesterday morning. Mr. and Mrs. Joseph Vekasy, 1525 Third avenue are also the parents of a baby girl born Sunday morning at the hospital.

Admissions over the week-end included Mrs. Rose Marcus, 1504 Seventh avenue, medical; Frank Louis Persetti, 406 Third avenue, New Brighton, surgical; Mrs. A. R. Patterson, 509½ Bell avenue, Ellwood City, surgical, and [illegible] DeGiandu, Morado, tonsils.

The hospital discharged [illegible] Podlaski, 717 [illegible] street; Mrs. [illegible] R. D. 2; [illegible] Twenty-second street; [illegible] avenue; Mrs. [illegible] Mrs. Catherine Beighley, 401 Thirty-fifth street, and Mrs. Thomas Welsh, 1506 Sixteenth

[illegible] interest.

Peter [illegible], Aessica, a Pennsylvania [illegible] employe, suffered a [illegible] Saturday and was admitted to Rochester General hospital.

A son was born Sunday to Mr. and Mrs. Harold [illegible], Freedom; a son to Mr. and Mrs. Arthur Michler, Beaver, Sunday; and a daughter Sunday to Mr. and Mrs. Allen Ruckert, Freedom, the hospital reported.

Admissions include Joseph Bersoni, Aliquippa; William Ness, Freedom; Mrs. Sebastian Suffaletti, Midland, and Dorothy Padomnia, Freedom.

Those discharged were Mrs. Walter Foley and daughter, Monaca; Andrew Harvie, near Monaca; Levie Starr, Mt. Airy, N. C., Lawrence Cozad, Rochester; Mrs. Dominec Verrico, Rochester; Mrs. William Warden and son, Rochester; Mrs. Elias Davies, Aliquippa; Mrs. Paul Gibson and daughter, near Coraopolis; Mrs. Earl Herbine and daughter, Baden; Frank Koper, Ambridge; Charlotte Belick, Aliquippa; Mrs. Charles Emler and daughter, Monaca; and Mrs. Gus Servatius, Beaver. A total of 100 patients was reported.

Today In Washington

(Continued From Page One)

10. Germany's new submarine tactics and resumption of attacks on Allied convoys.

Now nobody questions the right of the Prime Minister to make any announcement he wishes or when he wishes but it is difficult to understand why when these items of news arise spontaneously they are not given to the press in the customary form. Reasons for holding up certain news for days at a time are, of course, recognised but it would be difficult to believe that all the news items released in the Prime Minister's speech just happened to "break" on the same day.

The danger in Mr. Churchill's action is that the press, which is constantly being accused of being overoptimistic or of emphasizing minor items of military progress, will because of these unique accumulations of news for use in public addresses be less able to serve the public the way it can and should in wartime. Something appears to be vitally wrong in London and it is no secret that officials of our own Office of War Information are dismayed and discouraged by the manner in which American and British reporters are prevented from writing the big news because it is being saved up for use in the Prime Minister's speeches. This is not a happy commentary on the freedom to report. For there is no problem here of complying with the rules of censorship but simply a question of misuse of that power by a high official of government.

News Of Local People From The Service Camps

Technical Sergeant Steve J. Boller, of the parachute school at Fort Benning, Georgia, has been promoted to master sergeant. He is the son of Mrs. Catherine Boller, 1030 Twenty-fourth street, and went to the parachute school February 16, 1942 from headquarters of an infantry training battalion at Camp Croft, South Carolina. He qualified as a parachutist March 21, 1942.

Robert Park of Manhasset, N. Y., flight surgeon at the Station hospital of the Independence, Kan., army air field, has been advised by the war department of his promotion from first lieutenant to captain in the medical corps.

Captain Park, the son of Robert Park of Beaver Falls, holds a B. S. from Geneva college, and won his M. D. from the Syracuse university college of medicine, Syracuse, N. Y. He was engaged in private practice and the practice of industrial medicine and surgery in Brooklyn, N. Y., before receiving his commission as first lieutenant in the medical corps August 6, 1942.

He attended the army air forces school of aviation medicine at Randolph field, Texas, attaining an A. M. E. rating. He came to the air base from duty at Randolph field, reporting March 12 of this year.

[illegible] in a New York apartment. Now he lives in a tent. (International)

"STRICTLY PRIVATE"

Trademark Registered U. S. Patent Office

U. S. ARMY
SOMEWHERE IN ENGLAND
DEAR MOM:—
A GUY OUGHTA LEARN TO THINK BEFORE HE ACTS. ESPECIALLY IN A ARMY.. TODAY THEY ASK FOR VOLUNTEERS FOR GLIDER PRACTICE & I SAID YES WITHOUT GIVING IT ANY CONSIDERATION.
YOUR SON
P.S. I GUESS I HAD MY MIND ON TORCH SINGER..
AP Features

Seek Printer Of Bogus Gas Coupons

PHILADELPHIA—(AP)—Federal agents spread a dragnet today for the operator of a Philadelphia printing plant, following a raid in which counterfeit gasoline ration coupons worth more than 10,000,000 gallons were seized.

A tip from a gasoline dealer, approached as a possible customer, and subsequent defective work led U. S. marshals and Office of Price Administration agents to the two-room headquarters of the Hill Printing Service yesterday.

There, Myron M. Coffey, chief OPA investigator said, they found stacks of counterfeit coupons of all types, along with plates and dies and two presses, one nearly new. Coffey estimated that the plant could have turned out coupons worth 100,000,000 gallons of gasoline in its four months of existence.

A warrant charging illegal manufacture, possession and transfer of federal ration currency was sworn out for Dennis A. Hill, 39, identified by Coffey as the owner of the plant. No one was on the premises when they were raided.

The man who attempted to sell the coupons to the gasoline dealer was followed to a telephone booth in which stamps worth 37,000 gallons were found after he left. The trail led to another suspect, and a search of his home uncovered counterfeits worth 500,000 gallons, along with the cards of eight printing concerns.

DAILY CROSSWORD

ACROSS
1. Soft palates
5. Act of selling
9. Red cedar
10. Type of daisy
12. Opposed to vacuums
13. Discolored
14. Relative
15. Furnish
16. To set again
18. Lyric poem of lament
19. Climbing plant
21. Peaks
24. Float
28. Exclamation
29. June bug
30. Mail
32. The Milky Way
35. Run away and marry
37. Snake
40. Kind of duck
44. Across
45. Covered with small figures
46. Species of goat antelope
48. Chasm
49. Because
50. Medieval helmet
51. Punt
52. Carry on the [illegible]

DOWN
1. [illegible]
2. [illegible]
3. [illegible]
4. Prescription term
5. The sun
6. One of feathers of underwing
7. Morning reception
8. Ogling
9. Box scientifically
11. Whirlpool
17. A titmouse
18. Half an em
20. Similar
21. Mass of yarn on spindle
22. Greek letter
23. Goddess of dawn
25. Girl's name
26. Crafty animal
27. Attempt
31. Bank of turf
32. Depart
33. Simian
34. Convenience
36. Music note
37. Gear teeth
38. Egglike
39. Capital of Switzerland
41. Layer of skin (anat.)
42. Glowing coal
43. Pause
47. Guided
48. Cry of a crow

Saturday's Answer

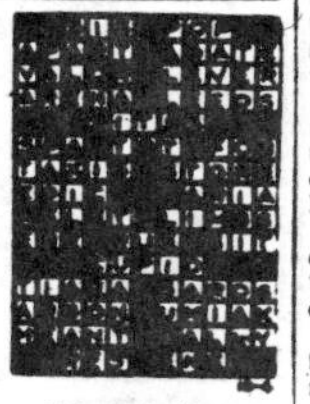

10-4

SVA SEEN SOSENTAKA FTULFMFGA
[illegible]

LAFF-A-DAY

"Junior's named his tank after me!"

MONACA NEWS

Mrs. Miriam Stevens returned Tuesday to Harrisburg, where she is employed by the Workmen's Compensation Board, after visiting since Friday with her parents, Mr. and Mrs. E. B. Steiner, Indiana avenue.

George Evans, Sr., has returned to his home in Atlantic avenue after visiting several days with his son, George Evans, Jr., Washington, and with another son, Curtis Evans, pharmacist's mate second class, who recently graduated from Dental school at Bainbridge, Md.

Mr. and Mrs. Norman Harrison, Marshall road, have returned from New York where they spent several days visiting their sons, Pvt. John Harrison, stationed in Farmingdale, N. Y., and Norman, Jr., bugler second class, stationed at Long Beach. They were accompanied by John's wife.

Pvt. Stephen Ogrizek, with the U. S. Marines, has returned to Allentown, where he is attending school, after visiting several days with his parents, Mr. and Mrs. Stephen Ogrizek, Pennsylvania avenue.

Charles Calhoon, who recently completed his "boot" training at Great Lakes, Ill., returned there today after visiting a week with his wife at her home in Pennsylvania avenue and with his parents, Mr. and Mrs. Ralph Calhoon, Colona Heights.

Aviation Cadet Melvin O. Larson returned Monday to Wilkes-Barre, where he is attending Bucknell Junior college, after visiting over the week end with his parents, Mr. and Mrs. Oscar Larson, Pennsylvania avenue.

Mrs. Mary McClenahan is seriously ill at her home in Virginia avenue.

Mrs. Howard Knopp, Jr., and sons, Jimmy and Tommy, Sixth street, will leave the first of the week for Los Angeles, where they will make their home. Mr. Knopp has been employed there several months.

Pvt. Samuel Taormina will return Thursday to Camp McCaw, N. C., after visiting his parents, Mr. and Mrs. Samuel Taormina, Pennsylvania avenue. Another son of the Taorminas, Pvt. Joseph Taormina, is also visiting here and will return Saturday to Camp McCoy, Wis.

Miss Elsa Hild, Indiana avenue, Miss Lillian Theil, Marshall road, and Miss Janet Hlebo, Virginia avenue, visited over the week end in Cleveland and attended the Navy - Notre Dame football game.

Mrs. Howard Glass is confined to her home in Linden street by illness.

Sgt. Patsy Pictrandea, who has been visiting ten days with Mr. and Mrs. Anthony Taormina, Indiana avenue, returned Tuesday to his base in New Mexico.

Mrs. Chester Karlberg is recoverng at her home in Elm street following an operation on her jaw, performed Monday at Rochester hospital.

The first observance of Thanksgiving Day at Plymouth began on Thursday, Nov. 3, 1621, and closed with a state dinner on Saturday.

Potter Twp. Votes Solidly Republican

Potter Township residents voted solidly Republican in the general election on Tuesday, GOP nominees for both county and local offices winning by wide margins.

In the only local contest, Ruth Larson, Rep., defeated Martha Phillis, Dem., in the contest for school director for a four-year term.

Following are the returns:

Treasurer—Smith, Dem., 11; O'Loughlin, Rep., 74.

District Attorney — Caputo, Dem., 13; Coghlan, Rep., 74.

Register—Grater, Dem., 17; Holland, Rep., 69.

Recorder—Nagel, Dem., 12; Murray, Rep., 73.

Commissioner (three elected) —Pearson, Dem., 19; Gilkey, Dem., 15; Coombs, Rep., 72; Edwards, Rep., 67.

Sheriff — Schulte, Dem., 11; McKenny, Rep., 75.

Clerk of Courts—Kenny, Dem., 15; Mowry, Rep., 73.

Controller — Patterson, Dem., 13; Bennett, Rep., 74.

Prothonotary — Courtney, Dem., 12; Wallover, Rep., 74.

Coroner—Werner, Dem., 13; Davis, Rep., 74.

Surveyor — Baker, Dem.-Rep., 86.

Assessor — Mahlon Douds, Rep., 81.

School Director (two elected for six years)—Virginia Douds, Rep., 75; Fred Thomas, Rep., 77.

School Director (four years)—Martha Phillis, Dem., 12; Ruth Larson, Rep., 71.

School Director (two years)—Martha Phillis, Rep., 71.

Constable—Frank Robert Adams, Rep., 79.

Auditor—Eugene R. H. Doutt, Rep., 78.

Justice of Peace—Ira E. Sullivan, Rep., 76.

Supervisor (six years) — Charles Lotz, Rep., 75.

Supervisor (four years)—Carl A. Larson, Rep., 75.

Tax Collector—Alfred Hohage, Rep., 75.

Judge of Election—James L. Johnston, Rep., 77.

Inspector of Election—Martha Hohage, Rep., 73.

Daugherty Township Favors Republicans

All Republican candidates for county offices were winners in the voting in Daugherty Township.

Results were:

Treasurer — Smith, Dem., 72; O'Loughlin, Rep., 197.

District Attorney — Caputo, Dem., 54; Coghlan, Rep., 220.

Register — Grater, Dem., 58; Holland, Rep., 215.

Recorder — Nagel, Dem., 74; Murray, Rep., 197.

Commissioner (three elected) — Pearson, Dem., 83; Gilkey, Dem., 106; Coombs, Rep., 160; Edwards, Rep., 185.

Sheriff—Schulte, Dem., 38; McKenny, Rep., 236.

Clerk of Courts—Kenny, Dem., 69; Mowry, Rep., 207.

Controller — Patterson, Dem., 75; Bennett, Rep., 194.

Prothonotary—Courtney, Dem. 72; Wallover, Rep., 194.

Coroner — Werner, Dem., 58; Davis, Rep., 206.

Surveyor — Baker, Dem.-Rep., 268.

BRIDGEWATER

Methodist Circle To Meet Thursday

The monthly meeting of the Thoburn Circle of the Methodist church will be held Thursday evening in the parsonage. Donations for the Deaconess Home at Pittsburgh will be collected at that time.

Mrs. John Shephard continues to improve at her home in Sharon Road after a several days illness.

Mr. and Mrs. Norman Montgomery moved Tuesday from Market street to New Castle. Mr. Montgomery will leave in several days for service with the SeaBees.

Word has been received by Mrs. D. M. Baker, Jr., that her husband, who recently left for service in the army, is stationed at Greensboro, N. C.

Pvt. Matt Pupich, Fort Glenn, N. C., is spending a several days furlough with his parents, Mr. and Mrs. Matt Pupich, and family, Sharon road.

Donald Winters, Bridge street, left Tuesday for service in the SeaBees.

WINNERS IN CONTEST FOR COUNTY GOVERNMENT OFFICES

RALPH C. BENNETT

S. CLIFFORD HOLLAND

DANIEL C. BAKER

THOMAS D. GILKEY

WILLIAM COGHLAN

JOSEPH S. EDWARDS

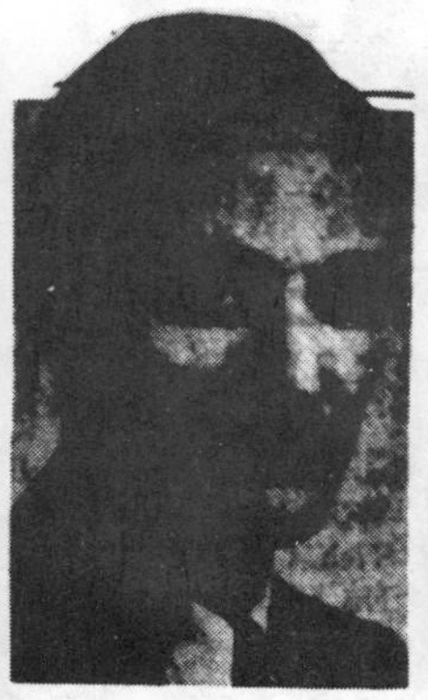

EDWIN M. WALLOVER

ART W. COOMBS

Pictured above are eight of the newly-elected county officials, seven Republicans and one Democrat, County Commissioner Thomas D. Gilkey. Art W. Coombs, Center Township, chairman of the county commissioners, and Joseph S. Edwards, Rochester, were re-elected as commissioners. Mr. Gilkey is completing the unexpired term of the late E. H. Markey, Monaca. County Controller Ralph C. Bennett, New Brighton, was re-elected to serve his third term. Register and Recorder S. Clifford Holland, Bridgewater, was elected to the new post of register of wills. Edwin M. Wallover, Midland, was re-elected to serve his second term as prothonotary. William Coghlan, Beaver, who has served two terms as assistant district attorney, was elected district attorney to succeed Robert E. McCreary, Monaca, who was not a candidate for re-election and served as Republican campaign manager. Daniel C. Baker, nominated on both the Republican and Democratic tickets, was re-elected as county surveyor.

SOCIETY NEWS

Beaver Quotarians Hear Of Juvenile Delinquency At Meet

Speaking on 'Juvenile Delinquency" before members of the Beaver Quota club at the fortnightly dinner-meeting Tuesday evening in the Penn-Beaver hotel, Rochester, Attorney Paul H. Baldwin, Rochester, county juvenile probation officer, placed the blame upon parents and adults in most cases, and conditions caused by war for the great increase in juvenile delinquency at the present time.

Delinquency is prevalent in homes where both the father and mother are working, also in "broken homes", he pointed out. The attraction of young girls for the "man in uniform" has created a difficult sex problem and is the main reason for the greater increase of delinquency among girls than boys, he stated. Although there are delinquents coming from good homes, the speaker said they are usually not "repeaters". Most delinquent children do not attend Sunday school or church, and there are very few Boy Scouts or Girls Scouts among delinquents, Mr. Baldwin mentioned.

He advocated a "Big Brother-Big Sister" system, which if properly worked out as a community project, backed by churches or civic groups, might greatly help to solve the probation problem. In this system, individuals would "sponsor" a delinquent boy or girl, at the suggestion of the probation officers.

Elma Graham, co-chairman of the program committee, introduced Attorney Baldwin. Gladys Boyd, ways and means chairman, announced that the club's annual card party is to be held at the hotel Friday evening, November 19, at eight o'clock. This will take the place of the next meeting.

Mrs. Irene Ohye, Beaver, a Quotarian, who the past two years has been engaged in the Valley as social worker for the Lutheran Inner Mission Society, spoke a few words of farewell to the clubmembers. She will leave about November 19 to assume her new duties as a social worker at a children's institution near Harrisburg.

On the dinner-table was a huge bowl of gourds, nuts, etc., forming a colorful centerpiece.

Rochester Class Has Monthly Meet

The Fay Shanor Bible class of the Rochester Methodist church was entertained Monday evening at the home of Mrs. Percy Boren. A guessing contest was directed by Mrs. Louise Musgrave and Miss Shanor led devotions. Lunch was served by the hostess, assisted by Mrs. Jesse Zahn, Mrs. Ann Zahn and Mrs. David Shanor. Mrs. Shanor will be hostess to the group in December.

Raccoon Township Couple Married

Miss Margaret C. Gleason, daughter of Mrs. Violet Gleason, Raccoon Township, and the late Earl Gleason, and Pvt. Peter A. Johnston, son of Mrs. Viola Johnston, Raccoon Township, and the late Grant Johnston, were united in marriage in the office of J. L. Aultman, Brodhead road, at noon Monday.

Mrs. Johnston, who attended Glenwillard high school, will reside for the duration with Pvt. Johnston's mother. Private Johnston attended Aliquippa high school.

Banquet Planned For Band, Orchestra

Plans for the annual banquet for members of the band and orchestra of Rochester high school were discussed at the monthly meeting of the Band and Orchestra Parents' Association Monday evening.

Mrs. Floyd Goehring was appointed to fill the vacancy in the office of secretary, caused by the resignation of Mrs. Fingol Bloom. Mrs. Ira Wallace was appointed publicity chairman.

District Governor Visits Rotarians

R. Donald Yauch, Uniontown, 176th district governor, made his official visit to the Rochester Rotary club at its weekly dinner-meeting Tuesday evening in the Penn-Beaver hotel.

Fifty-one members and two guests, R. A. McElhinney, Owosso, Mich., and Frank M. Potts, Midland, were present.

Newspapers Lead In War Bond Publicity

WASHINGTON, Nov. 3. — Newspapers contributed $21,000,000 of the more than $36,000,000 worth of advertising and publicity donated during the third war loan, the treasury reported today.

The treasury said war bond advertising in newspapers aggregated 129,549,946 lines valued at $8,639,540, while 61,226,060 lines of publicity was valued at $12,207,555.

Radio's contribution was estimated at $12,000,000; outdoor advertising, $1,600,000; magazines, $1,380,000; national advertisers in various media, $1,799,467.

Springfield, Mass., was sacked by the Indians on Oct. 5, 1675.

Pulaski Residents Elect Republicans

In Pulaski Township, there were two contests for local offices and Alex Pearson was the lone Democratic nominee for county office to win over his Republican opponents.

Thomas Roser and Floyd Klitz, Rep., won the two school board posts over Eunice Edwards and Harry Klitz, Dem., while Paul T. Goehring, Rep., defeated R. O. Weber, Dem., for the single supervisor post.

Following are the results of the voting:

Treasurer — Smith, Dem., 82; O'Loughlin, Rep., 96.

District Attorney — Caputo, Dem., 63; Coghlan, Rep., 112.

Register — Grater, Dem., 60; Holland, Rep., 115.

Recorder — Nagel, Dem., 79; Murray, Rep., 94.

Commissioner (three elected) — Pearson, Dem., 92; Gilkey, Dem., 83; Coombs, Rep., 78; Edwards, Rep., 94.

Sheriff—Schulte, Dem., 53; McKenny, Rep., 122.

Clerk of Courts—Kenny, Dem., 78; Mowry, Rep., 101.

Controller -- Patterson, Dem., 66; Bennett, Rep., 113.

Prothonotary—Courtney, Dem. 81; Wallover, Rep., 95.

Coroner -- Werner, Dem., 68; Davis, Rep., 109.

Surveyor — Baker, Dem.-Rep. 177.

Assessor—Raymond E. Miller, Rep., 132.

School Director (two elected for six years)—Eunice Edwards, Dem., 76; Harry Klitz, Dem., 74; Thomas Roser, Rep., 108; Floyd Klitz, Rep., 93.

Constable—Edwin S. Mason, Dem.-Rep., 173.

Auditor — John Karr, Dem., 104.

Justice of Peace (two elected) —Harry C. Wallis, Rep., 108; Oscar Gordon, Rep., 99.

Supervisor—R. O. Weber, Dem., 78; Paul T. Goehring, Rep., 102.

Tax Collector—Matilda Brewer, Rep., 128.

Judge of Election—Mary Davis, Rep., 124.

Inspector of Election—Nellie Knauff, Dem., 85; Bertha Hartman, Rep., 91.

GOP Candidates Win In Shippingport

In the balloting at Shippingport on Tuesday, Republican candidates for both county and municipal offices were victorious over their Democratic opponents.

In the voting for school director, Sarah Christy, Dem.-Rep., and Hattie Hayward, Rep., defeated J. A. McLane, Dem. In the race for three council vacancies, Homer Allison, Dem.-Rep., Carl Calhoon and George Bates, Rep., were winners over Carl Gardner and Richard Barnhart, Dem.

The returns:

Treasurer — Smith, Dem., 19; O'Luoghlin, Rep. 43.

District, Attorney — Caputo, Dem., 12; Coghlan, Rep., 48.

Register — Grater, Dem., 20; Holland, Rep., 37.

Recorder — Nagel, Dem., 20; Murray, Rep., 36.

Commissioner (three elected) — Pearson, Dem., 13; Gilkey, Dem., 16; Coombs, Rep., 48; Edwards, Rep., 42.

Sheriff—Schulte, Dem., 20; McKenny, Rep., 41.

Clerk of Courts—Kenny, Dem., 25; Mowry, Rep., 34.

Controller — Patterson, Dem., 18; Bennett, Rep., 38.

Prothonotary—Courtney, Dem. 15; Wallover, Rep. 46.

Coroner — Werner, Dem., 12; Davis, Rep., 45.

Surveyor — Baker, Dem.-Rep., 59.

Assessor— Velma Rambo, 27 (write-ins).

School Director (two elected for six years)—J. A. McLane, Dem., 20; Sarah Christy, Dem.-Rep., 51; Hattie Hayward, Rep., 54.

Auditor — Smith Hayward, Dem., 27; Ethel Allison, Rep., 36.

Council (three elected)—Homer Allison, Dem.-Rep., 46; Carl Gardner, Dem., 25; Richard Barnhardt, Dem., 20; Carl Calhoon, Rep., 42; George Bates, Rep., 29.

Tax Collector— Cathryn Calhoon, Rep., 58.

Judge of Election—Ruth Marker, 20 (write-ins).

Inspector of Election— Ethel Allison, Rep., 46.

ROSE MAGESTRO BRIDE OF PVT. FRED PRICE

Ceremony Is Performed At Parsonage In S. Carolina

Mr. and Mrs. Michael Magestro entertained 15 members of their family at a dinner at their home, 47 Miller road, Saturday evening when announcement was made of the marriage of their daughter, Rose, to Pvt. Fred Price, son of Mrs. Nora Price, 208 Highland Ave.

The wedding was an event of New Year's Day at the parsonage of the First Methodist church at Bennettsville, S. C., with the Rev. John F. Kinney officiating.

Mrs. Price wore a corsage of white gardenias with her poudre blue wool ensemble, with black accessories and was attended by Miss Ruby Cunningham of 176 Franklin Ave., who wore a corsage of Talisman roses with her beige and brown two-piece suit.

Cpl. M. J. McCorkley, of Ft. Bragg, N. C., was best man.

Following the ceremony a wedding dinner was served the bridal party at a Bennettsville hotel.

Mrs. Price, an employe of the Woodlawn Laundry, returned here last week but will rejoin her husband in the south sometime next month.

Pvt. Price, a former employe of the electrical department of the Jones and Laughlin Steel Corp., has been in the service more than a year and is stationed at Fort Bragg with the U. S. Field Artillery.

Local Topics

Mrs. A. E. Sisson, 114 Carrol St., has returned from Latonia, Ky., where she attended the funeral of her brother, E. J. Bingham, who died there last week.

Clifford, Jr., son of Mr. and Mrs. Clifford Schofield, of Wireton, is recovering in Sewickley hospital after a serious illness.

Miss Sara Harper, of South Heights, who has been seriously ill at her home, is reported today as much improved.

Mrs. S. C. McCallister, South Heights, has returned from a short visit with relatives at Emsworth.

Mrs. Donald Nelson, student at the Indiana State Teachers college, has returned to her studies after spending the week-end with her parents, Mr. and Mrs. Howard Erwin of South Heights.

Mrs. A. Rulenz and Mrs. Roy McCellum, of Baltimore, Md., have returned home after spending the past week at the home of Mr. and Mrs. C. A. Stine of South Heights.

Miss Jean Ditter, a student nurse at McKeesport hospital, spent the week-end at South Heights with her parents, Mr. and Mrs. George Ditter.

Charles and Henry, sons of Mr. and Mrs. Joseph Neugebauer, Jr., Bon Meade, are able to be out again after a two weeks' illness with measles.

Mrs. Martha Feber Brown and son, Roy, of South Heights, have recovered from a recent attack of flu.

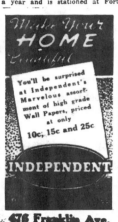

ALIQUIPPANS IN SERVICE

Ralph Cochran Leaves For Air Corps Service

Ralph Edward Cochran, son of Mr. and Mrs. W. G. Cochran, 532 Highland Ave., who graduated Wednesday from Aliquippa High school, left Sunday night for Fort Meade, Md., where he will be sent today to Miami, Fla., for classification as an air cadet with the U. S. Air Force.

Enlisting last summer in the Air Forces' Reserve Corps, he received his notice to enter training immediately after his graduation.

His brother, William Richard Cochran, is stationed with the U. S. Air Corps at Peru, Ind.

Aviation Student Sam Rebich At Lynchburg

Aviation Student Samuel Rebich, of 111 Locust St., Aliquippa, has reported to the 14th College Training detachment at Lynchburg college in Virginia to undergo Aircrew Training preparatory to receiving specialized training as a pilot, bombardier or navigator.

During his stay there, he will receive academic training in mathematics, physics, English, history and geography. In addition, he will receive over 100 hours of military training and 120 hours of physical training. Then, during his last month there, will receive 10 hours of actual flight instruction in a light airplane.

After leaving there he will undergo specialized training as a pilot, bombardier or navigator and then approximately nine months later, if he has successfully completed his training courses, he will receive the coveted silver wings and either a Commission as a 2nd lieutenant or a warrant as a flight officer.

SOLDIER TRANSFERRED

Having been transferred from Los Angeles, Cal., S/Sgt. Michael Basalyga, son of Mr. and Mrs. John Basalyga of South Heights, is enroute to Louisiana for a new assignment with the U. S. Air Force.

SEAMAN TRANSFERRED

Walter Tranter, of Wireton, who completed his 'boot' training with the U. S. Navy at Sampson, N. Y., has been transferred recently to Dearborn, Mich.

PFC WRIGHT TRANSFERRED

Pfc. Carl Wright, son of Mr. and Mrs. George Wright of South Heights, has been transferred from Kearns, Utah, to his new assignment with the U. S. Air Force at El Paso, Texas.

SON FOR MOARRIS'

A son was born yesterday at Rochester hospital to Mr. and Mrs. Joe Morris, 2003 McLean St.

Joseph R. Hennessy Promoted To Corporal

CPL. JOSEPH R. HENNESSY

While confined to the base hospital at Camp Stewart, Ga., with an attack of influenza, Pfc. Joseph R. Hennessy, son of Mr. and Mrs. J. V. Hennessy, 600 Reed St., was advised that he had been promoted to the rank of corporal.

A range setter in the U. S. Anti-aircraft Division, he left for the armed service upon his graduation from High school here last May and recently was appointed as an instructor in air-craft identification.

Pfc. E. Svetichan Serving Overseas

PFC. ELIAS SVETICHAN

Pfc. Elias Svetichan, son of Nick Svetichan, 14 Cedar Ave., New Sheffield, is serving overseas with the U. S. Marines.

A former employe of the seamless tube department of the Jones and Laughlin Steel Corp., he enlisted in the U. S. Marine Corps Oct. 1, 1942, receiving his "boot" training at Parris Island, S. C., and upon completing further training at Portsmouth, Va., he was assigned to the U.S.S. Birmingham and ordered into active service in the Atlantic.

Returning to the United States after participating in the invasion of Sicily, he spent a six-day furlough at home last August. He was transferred at the conclusion of his furlough to the West Coast and has been in combat service in the "Southwest Pacific" since that time.

E. Grimshaw Is Officer Of Sorority

Miss Eugenia Grimshaw, daughter of Mr. and Mrs. E. V. Grimshaw, of 101 Wayne St., here, has been elected corresponding secretary of Alpha Xi Delta national social sorority at Bethany college, Bethany, W. Va.

Miss Grimshaw is a sophomore at Bethany and is a graduate of the 1942 class of Aliquippa High school, where she was a member of the Girl Reserves, the Library club and the Forum club.

At Bethany Miss Grimshaw is active in the Y. W. C. A. and the Women's Athletic Association.

REMARRY TO HAVE LICENSE

KANSAS CITY, Kan.—(U.P.)—A Kansas City, Mo., couple, married for 33 years, was remarried here recently so they could replace their marriage license which was lost in a fire 15 years ago. The two, who gave their names as Edward Stacy, 61, and Minnie E. Bicknell, 60, said a marriage license was requested in so many cases and they thought it would be easier to be remarried than to check back in the license records for a duplicate.

WOMAN GETS QUICK AID

KANSAS CITY, Mo. (U.P.)—The stage was all set for an accident when Mrs. Louise P. Bartlett slipped and broke her right ankle recently. She fell in front of a doctor's home. The physician saw the accident and went out to offer his help. A private ambulance was passing by, so the driver stopped to assist. A police car was parked half a block away. The police officer was summoned, and he aided the doctor in applying the splint. The ambulance then took the patient to a hospital.

ASKS DIVORCE FOR SPANKING

SALEM, Mass. (U.P.) — Because her husband took her over his knee and spanked her with a hair brush when she returned home at midnight after visiting an aunt, Mrs. Muriel A. Roland, 26, of Boston, has petitioned for divorce in probate court.

OFFICIALLY Roger W. Heald, 22, above, of Nashua, N. H., may be an Army aviation cadet, but he certainly is no rookie flyer. When he leaves Albion, Mich., college to start cadet training, his log will show 2,310 flying hours. A former flying instructor, he turned down a commission because he would have had to remain a flight instructor. (International)

Ration Reminders

Meats, butter, fats: brown stamps R, S, T and U now valid; all expire Jan. 29.

Canned, frozen and dried foods: Green stamps D, E, F in ration book No. 4 are effective through Jan. 20. G, H and J stamps valid through Feb. 20.

Sugar: stamp 30 in ration book No. 4 is good through March 31.

Shoes: coupon 18 of Book No. 1 and coupon 1 on the "airplane" sheet in book No. 3 are valid for an indefinite period.

Fuel oil: period 2 coupons, effective through Feb. 7; and period 3 coupons valid through March 13, are good for 10 gallons per unit.

STARTS 62ND DIARY

KEENE, N. H.—(U.P.) The height of regularity and persistence has been achieved by George G. E. Congdon, who is starting his 62nd consecutive diary despite the fact he is in his 75th year.

Junior Italian Council To Mark 4th Anniversary

When the Junior Italian Council met Sunday night in the Service Canteen here, plans were completed for the spring membership drive and the anniversary party marking the fourth birthday of the organization, to be held in February.

Miss Betty Ceravolo was named general chairman of the affair, with Orlando Piroli as co-chairman.

Miss Frances Fricano, president, conducted the meeting and the general committee served refreshments and was in charge of a social hour that followed.

Junior Woman's Club Board Plans Meeting

The Executive Board of the Junior Woman's club will meet tomorrow at 8 p. m. at the home of the club's president, Miss F. Jane Hanna, 408 Highland Ave., with Mrs. Harold Vest and Mrs. John Wykes as hostesses.

TOWN OWES NO ONE

WENHAM, Mass. (U.P.)—As a fitting part of the celebration of the 300th anniversary of its incorporation, the town of Wenham announces a surplus of $64,000 in its treasury, with all bills paid and no indebtedness on its books.

Laughlin P.T.A. Will Convene In School Tomorrow

The Laughlin Parents and Teachers Association will meet tomorrow in the Laughlin school auditorium at 2:30 p. m.

Following the business session and program, tea will be served by Mrs. George Marshall and her committee.

Fidelis Class To Meet Here On January 28

A meeting of the Fidelis class of the First Baptist church scheduled for Friday evening, Jan. 21, has been postponed until Friday, Jan. 28, when they will convene at 8 p. m. at the home of Mrs. Roy Gilmore, 313 Kiehl St.

Read the Want Ads Every Day

U. S. Fighter Group Has "Funeral" For Returning Veteran

AMERICAN FIGHTER BASE, Italy, Jan. 21 (UP)—The "corpse" sat up in the coffin, waved a bottle and yelled "Yippee." It was considered a very fitting remark.

That explains something of the 57th U. S. Fighter Group which this week began its fourth year as a fighting unit in a very sad state of mind.

The "corpse" was a member of the 57th who was being sent home because of a bad ear. Men of the 57th go home so rarely that they made a big occasion of it.

They got the ailing member drunk, loaded him in a coffin and the funeral procession paraded down the street. Staid British Eighth Army soldiers, thinking the funeral was real, stood at attention.

As the procession passed between two lines of soldiers, the pilot reared up, and voiced the group's feeling toward the world in general and the war in particular.

Navy Man Overseas Yearns To Return On Traffic Charge

NEW YORK, Jan. 21 (UP)—The Warrant Officer at downtown traffic court had been looking a long time for the owner of a Louisiana automobile cited for overtime parking last November.

Almost ready to give up the search, he received a letter yesterday from the owner. It read:

"My dear brother Warrant Officer: "There was a slight bit of inconvenience on the 19th of November, which made it impossible for me to be law abiding—I was shipped overseas.

"However, if you can use your legal power or influence to get me to appear in dear ole New York—even for one day—and spend it in the brig at that—brother—I'm waiting fo' yo' answer.

"Uncle Sam's Nephew, Frank Falot, C.S.P. U. S. Navy.

"P.S. The car was junked."

Save KITCHEN FATS to win the war.

The Weather Forecast
WESTERN PENNSYLVANIA: Fair with moderate temperatures today; fair and cold tonight; Sunday, fair.

"The Paper That Goes Home"

THE DAILY TIMES

1874—and WESTERN ARGUS—1803

ROCHESTER - BEAVER - MONACA - FREEDOM - BRIDGEWATER - CONWAY - VANPORT - MIDLAND

Beaver County History
British aviators made raids on Ostend and Zubrugge, Belgium, on January 22, 1915, it was reported here.

4 Cents

Established April 2, 1874 | Beaver and Rochester, Pa., Saturday, January 22, 1944 | By Carrier 24 Cents A Week

ALLIED TROOPS LAND NEAR ROME

CONTROL OF FARM WAGES IS ORDERED

War Food Administration Extends Government Control To Agricultural Workers; To Set Up Wage Boards

WASHINGTON, Jan. 22 (UP) War Food Administrator Marvin Jones today announced plans for extending government control over farm wage rates "wherever necessary" to check inflationary increases.

Farm wage rates have increased during the past year due to the labor shortage which tends to force wages upward. The WFA felt the need to apply a check to prevent production costs from getting out of hand.

Acting at the direction of Economic Stabilization Director Fred M. Vinson, Jones issued regulations to govern procedure "for establishing wages and salaries of agricultural workers."

"State agricultural wage boards will be appointed where necessary to hold public hearings and assist in the establishing of specific wage ceilings and in determining penalties for violations by either employer or employes," the announcement said.

TO NAME BOARDS

The boards will be named by Jones to function in states where he deems wage controls necessary. The boards will function for agricultural workers in a manner similar to War Labor Board control over industrial wages. They are intended to prevent rises in farm production costs out of line with the stabilization program.

Vinson ordered wages and salaries of agricultural workers earning more than $2,400 a year frozen and ruled that they cannot receive increased pay without prior approval of Jones.

Vinson also directed that no reduction be made in wages or salaries for any particular work below the highest rates paid for that work between January 1 and September 15, 1942.

Jones has been given authority over farm wages up to $5,000 a year. Those in excess of that amount come under jurisdiction of the Commissioner of Internal Revenue.

The state wage boards will have authority to fix wage ceilings for specific farm work. In any state where a board is not set up any farm employer may increase his wage rates up to $2,400 a year without government permission.

Any employer in a state where a board is established may increase wages up to the ceiling established for any particular work without authorization from the board. Appeals from board decisions may be made directly to Jones.

The order defines agricultural workers as those engaged in the production, cultivation, growing and harvesting of agricultural or horticultural commodities in greenhouses, nursery or enclosed shed or hotbed as well as on farms. In poultry raising the work is defined as agricultural whether performed on the farms or in hatcheries.

Maximum penalty for violation of the wage order is a $1,000 fine, one year imprisonment, or both. The penalty would apply equally to employer or employe found guilty by a federal court.

Man Burned To Death In Ship Collision

LEWES, Del., Jan. 22 (UP)—One man burned to death in flaming oil and 15 other crew members of a small coastwise tanker were rescued last night when their vessel collided with the 8,000-ton Liberty ship Charles Henderson, five miles off the Delaware capes.

The tanker burst into flames immediately after the vessels collided. Motorists who lined the shore said the ship's storage tanks apparently burst, releasing a large quantity of burning oil on the water. Searchlights were turned on the scene as the blazing tanker drifted within approximately three miles of the shore and Navy and Coast Guard boats went to the crews' rescue.

The tanker, its fire extinguished, was towed to port and the Liberty ship was ordered back into harbor for inspection.

The collision was the third along the Jersey-Delaware coast within two months.

FLYING FORTS AND FIGHTERS LEAVE WEIRD TRAILS

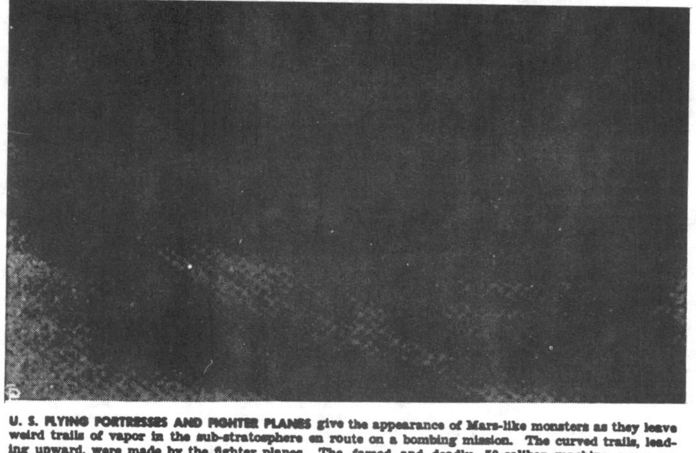

U. S. FLYING FORTRESSES AND FIGHTER PLANES give the appearance of Mars-like monsters as they leave weird trails of vapor in the sub-stratosphere en route on a bombing mission. The curved trails, leading upward, were made by the fighter planes. The famed and deadly .50-caliber machine guns are plainly visible on the Flying Fortresses. Army Signal Corps photo. *(International Soundphoto)*

John E. Bittner Dies In Monaca

John Edward Bittner, 77, well known Monaca resident, died in the home of his son, James G. Bittner, 932 Washington avenue, Friday evening at 8:30 o'clock. Friends will be received in the home, where funeral services will be conducted Monday afternoon at 2:30 o'clock. Burial will be in Sylvania Hills.

For many years Mr. Bittner conducted a restaurant in Monaca, and in later years was engaged in the same business in Ellwood City. He was a member of Monaca Council, Sons and Daughters of Liberty, and an honorary member of Watercure Lodge, Knights of Pythias, Monaca. He was born near Wheeling, W. Va.

Surviving are the son; two daughters, Mrs. Beryl Miller and Mrs. William W. Massey, Monaca; three sisters, Mrs. Louise Southwick, Rochester; Mrs. Carrie Helble and Mrs. Mathilda Thomas, New Brighton; three brothers, Fred Bittner, Cleveland; Louis Bittner, New Brighton, and Edward Bittner, Jeannette.

FLASHES:

FOOD HOARDER HELD

CLEVELAND, Jan. 22. (UP)—Adelbert Beelman, 29, a restaurant employe, was held for investigation today after police found his room packed with so much canned goods that it was difficult to turn around.

SIX DIE IN FIRE

Evansville, Ind., Jan. 22. (UP)—The death of Charles Mills, 24, Robinson, Ill., increased to six today the victims of a fire at Evans Hall, war housing project, yesterday. Four of the six victims were unidentified.

STAMP RING SMASHED

NEWARK, N. J., Jan. 22. (UP)—Police believed today they had smashed one of the leading distribution centers of a black market gasoline ration stamp ring, which operated in at least four eastern states. Eleven men were arrested in a series of raids, in which both counterfeit and valid coupons, representing more than 100,000 gallons of gasoline, were confiscated.

MAN DIES IN FIRE

WASHINGTON, Jan. 22 (UP)—One person was killed and four persons were made homeless in a fire which destroyed a Strabane home. John Kordell, 62, died in the second floor of the home where he was sleeping.

STRIKE ENDED

SEATTLE, Jan. 22. (UP)—A four-day strike of 6,000 molders and foundrymen, which tied up war production in 79 plants in Washington and Oregon, ended today when the strikers voted to return to work pending a National Labor Board review of their wage demands. The strike had affected 20,000 workers and was described as the worst in the northwest since the war began.

U-BOAT SUNK

LONDON, Jan. 22. (UP)—American and British warships, supported by RAF planes, sank one German U-boat, probably destroyed another and damaged several in standing off a major German attack on an Allied convoy in the Atlantic a few weeks ago, it was announced today.

Argentina Reports Probe Of Spy Ring Is Being Pushed

BUENOS AIRES, Jan. 22. (UP)—The Argentine government announced today that it was pressing a "complete investigation" of an alleged Axis spy ring in this country following the arrest of a member of the Argentine Consular Service by British counter-espionage officials at Trinidad.

British authorities at Trinidad disclosed late yesterday that the consular employe, Alberto Osmar Helmuth, was arrested while en route to Europe and held after it was found he was "an enemy of the United Nations." The Argentine foreign office immediately announced Helmuth's dismissal from the consular service.

Argentine government spokesmen said the country's federal police, created recently along the lines of the FBI, had been investigating Axis spy activities for some time.

(The London radio, in a broadcast recorded by CBS, quoted "an official Argentine broadcast" today asserting that Helmuth was not dismissed but "has been exonerated" of the charges against him.)

"Some arrests already have been made," one spokesman said, "but due to the bearing of the inquiry on the interests of the belligerent nations the matter has been kept secret."

The current investigation was believed the first against Axis activities conducted by the Gen. Pedro Ramires government, although several minor inquiries were carried out during the Castillo regime at the request of the American and British governments.

HANNEGAN ELECTED

WASHINGTON, Jan. 22 (UP)—The Democratic National Committee today unanimously elected Robert E. Hannegan, St. Louis, as chairman.

Three Young Men Sentenced Today

Three county youths, one a paratrooper AWOL from his station in South Carolina, were committed by the Beaver County courts today to the State industrial training school at White Hill for larceny of automobiles and burglary.

James Hussher, 20, New Brighton, the paratrooper, pleaded guilty to two charges of stealing automobiles and to a charge of burglary, and was committed to the White Hill institution by Judge Henry H. Wilson. The two younger boys, Kenneth Valentine, 17, New Galilee, and Norman Eckles, 17, Beaver Falls, were before Judge Wilson in Juvenile court and were also committed to White Hill.

Taken into custody by Beaver Falls police a few days ago, the three youths were accused of the theft of automobiles belonging to James Flusher, Beaver Falls, and Jack Richard Hilfinger of Fallston, and to robbing the Eagles Club of Beaver Falls, taking about $72 in currency and eight bottles of whiskey. Beaver Falls police said the boys also had admitted to theft of a car in East Palestine, another in New Castle and to robbery of a service station near Grove City.

Guy A. Parsons, Bridgewater, entered a plea of guilty today to robbery. He was charged with taking about $165 from Dampsey D. Dye in Beaver Falls on January 16. He was paroled for five years upon payment of the costs and restitution of the money taken from Mr. Dye.

CREMATION COSTLY

NEW YORK, Jan. 22 (UP)—Dr. Charles Fletcher, veterinarian at the Marble Hill Crematory for Pet Animals, Inc., has cremated all kinds of pets. But his most unique was "Joe," a 25-cent turtle, which a soldier in Italy sent to his girl friend here. The girl spent $15 to have the turtle cremated.

Help the boys on the firing line by saving KITCHEN FATS. They will thank you.

RED CROSS, FELLOW-WORKERS AID OHIO TP. FIRE VICTIMS

Within three hours after the total destruction by fire yesterday of the uninsured home of Mr. and Mrs. Albert L. Chevalier in Ohio township, with all of its contents, representatives of Beaver County Chapter, American Red Cross, were on the scene to help the couple and their five small children.

Meanwhile, fellow-employes of Chevalier in the Duquesne Light Company took prompt steps to furnish immediate needs of clothing and other articles, and to assure Chevalier that they would stand solidly behind him in his announced intention to rebuild the house that he had shaped with his own hands over a period of six or seven years.

Mrs. Chevalier, her cut and lacerated right hand and forearm dressed by utility first aid men, related in detail how she had stood at the bedside of her sister, Mrs. Erma Goddard, less than 200 feet away, watching her own home and worrying about her three youngest boys, ranging from one to four years, when she saw a sudden burst of flame and smoke roar from the rear of the seven-room frame structure.

She ran to her home, and, blocked by flames, was unable to enter the house through the doors. Two of the children stood with their faces pressed against the living room window, while the youngest sat on the floor. The mother shouted a warning to the youngsters to stand back. She smashed the large glass in the living room window with her bare fist and climbed in through the shattered glass to rescue her children.

The courageous mother and the three smallest youngsters were taken last evening to the home of her parents, Mr. and Mrs. Ned W. Mowen, 1505 Fourth street, Riverview, Beaver Falls. The six and eight-year-old sons, in school at the time of the tragedy, will stay with kind-hearted Ohio Township neighbors, while the father will live during the emergency at the home of his mother in New Brighton. Offers of assistance came from all sides late yesterday and today, and it was apparent that the plight of the family and the courage of the mother had attracted the deepest sympathy.

Mrs. Chevalier, whose every personal possession and those of her family were burned, including ration books, has one happiness in the tragedy, that a community prayer service was held in the farm home the night before it was destroyed.

JAPS BLASTED FROM AIR, SEA IN SO. PACIFIC

Attacks By Planes, Ships May Presage Two-Way Drive On Enemy Base At Madang

ADVANCED ALLIED HEADQUARTERS, New Guinea, Jan. 22 (UP)—Allied naval and air blasting of Japanese attempts to reinforce their New Guinea garrisons were reported today by Gen. Douglas MacArthur's communique, with the operations hinting a determined two-way drive on the strong enemy coastal base of Madang, on the northern coast.

Allied medium bombers and fighters dropped 74 tons of bombs on Japanese positions in the upper Ramu Valley, American P-T boats, speeding through the Japanese-controlled waters off Madang, sank four enemy troop-laden barges and other medium bombers and fighters sank 20 barges and damaged others at Hansa Bay 100 miles north of Madang.

The concentrated air attacks in the Ramu Valley, a headquarters spokesman said, indicated a possible Australian offensive with limited objectives as the veteran jungle fighters continued to improve their positions only 30 miles south of Madang.

The attacks by the P-T boats Thursday night carried them farther north than at any time previously and followed Allied successes in extending their control of the coast to a point 45 miles below Madang.

OTHER BASES HIT

Navy crews reported that the equipment of the 160 Japanese troops killed when the barges sank indicated they were replacements for the Madang area, rather than troops being evacuated.

Other Allied planes in night air patrol off Wewak, 200 miles above Madang, damaged a 1,000-ton enemy freighter, while at Hansa Bay, midway between those two points, medium bombers, fighter-escorted, struck at enemy supply dumps and small shipping. The target area was covered with fire.

Heavy bombers over the Dutch East Indies dropped 45 tons of bombs on the naval base at Ambon, Amboina Island, Wednesday, and shot down five enemy fighters. Two Allied planes were lost.

American bombers on Bougainville Island, in the Solomons, blasted the Kahili airfields on the southern coast and naval units again bombarded enemy shore installations at the northern tip of the island.

ATOLLS RAIDED

PEARL HARBOR, Jan. 22. (UP)—United States Army and Navy bombers raided three Atolls in the Japanese-held Marshall islands Wednesday and Thursday, damaging two enemy cargo ships.

Admiral Chester W. Nimitz' communique said that Liberators of the Seventh Army Air Force raided Wotje Wednesday, losing one plane.

A Navy search Liberator of Fleet Airwing Two, damaged two cargo transports near Maleolap, Wednesday, and Navy Venturas made a low-level attack on Imieji and Tmiet islands of the Jaluit Atoll Thursday. One of the Venturas was shot down by anti-aircraft fire.

Defense Official Blackout Violator

HONESDALE, Jan. 22 (UP)—"Turn out that light," an air raid warden yelled during a New Year's Day blackout test here. The light stayed on and today A. H. Howell, chairman of the Wayne county civilian defense council held a receipt for a $5 fine he paid as the offender. Howell, who also is county superintendent of schools, pleaded guilty before a justice of the peace and with two other violators was fined.

Slight Increase In Relief Cost Noted

State Treasurer G. Harold Wagner reported that direct relief payments made to needy residents of Beaver County during the week ended today show an increase of $4 over those of the previous week. Payments for the week totaled $635 which was $1012 lower than those of the comparable week of last year.

TRAP NAZIS

LATVIA
LITHUANIA
NORTHERN FRONT
(RUSSIA)

STRELNA CORRIDOR, where an unidentified number of German soldiers have been trapped, is indicated on this map of the northern Russian front. The corridor is southwest of Leningrad, long-besieged city now being freed by Russian offensive. *(International)*

Three Youngsters Die, Mother Hurt When Home Burns

NEW CASTLE, Jan. 22 (UP)—Three children were asphyxiated and their mother was burned seriously today when fire swept their two-story frame home here.

The dead were: Rose Ann, 9; Eileen, 8, and William Sweeney, 2, children of Mr. and Mrs. John Sweeney, of 501 Division street.

Mrs. Sweeney, who tried unsuccessfully to rescue Rose Ann, who was found lying on the kitchen floor, was burned when her night clothing caught fire. The other children were found on the second floor of the building. The three children also were burned.

The husband and father was at work when the fire started. Apparently originating in a closet, the fire spread quickly, and when firemen arrived the building was a mass of flames.

Hard Workers Are Suspended At Ford Plant By CIO Union

EDGEWATER, N. J., Jan. 22—(UP)—A dispute between the Ford Motor Company and the United Automobile Workers (CIO) over the suspension of two men reportedly because they worked faster than other employes, was to be submitted to an umpire at Detroit today.

The men were transferred to an open shop by the company after their suspension, and the action threatened to cause a walk-out of the 4,000 workers in the Ford assembly plant here.

The men, John Elvin and Neil Smith, tested 22 to 24 trucks a day, compared with an average of 10 to 12 by other workers, although they all were paid the same wages. The union local, in suspending them, said briefly that the action was taken "for conduct unbecoming union men."

Elvin, a veteran of World War I and the father of several sons in the armed forces, said he sent telegrams to President Roosevelt and Secretary of War Henry L. Stimson seeking their advice.

OPA Pegs Prices Of Fresh Vegetables

WASHINGTON, Jan. 22—The Office of Price Administration, seeking to prevent sharp increases in fresh vegetable prices during the winter and early spring, announced a schedule today for pegging the retail prices of carrots, spinach, peas, snap beans, egg plant, peppers and cucumbers.

The schedule fixes ceilings at all sales levels prior to retail and will be the basis for retail prices to be set in February.

To Save Paper—

Today's TIMES is smaller than usual. Some news and advertising features are eliminated from this issue. This may be frequently necessary until essential and mandatory war time restrictions are modified or lifted. Meanwhile, by printing small papers occasionally, the saving in paper will be sufficient to enable us to publish the customary news, features and advertising several days each week.

HARBOR 32 MILES FROM CAPITAL IS REPORTED SEIZED

TODAY'S WAR SUMMARY

ITALY — American, British, French forces establish beachheads below Rome in biggest Allied invasion since Salerno; Allied launch simultaneous advance on German lines to the south.

RUSSIA—Red armies pursue Germans through collapsed fortifications west and south of Leningrad, massacre hundreds; open another Leningrad-Moscow rail line.

WESTERN EUROPE—RAF drops more than 2,240 short tons of bombs on Magdeburg, arms center, hits Berlin in diversionary attack.

PACIFIC—Allies prepare two-pronged drive on Madang, New Guinea as bombers hammer Japanese in upper Ramu Valley; American P-T boats sink four, planes sink 20 enemy barges.

American, British and French invasion forces landed on the Italian west coast between Rome and the main German defense lines to the south today in the most powerful Allied amphibious assault since the Salerno landing last September.

The new drive for Rome came as the Allied aerial bombardment of Axis Europe was carried into its second day with a heavy RAF raid on the German war center of Madgeburg. In Russia, Soviet armies rounded up and annihilated German forces fleeing from their collapsed northwestern defenses.

Landing under cover of darkness and a heavy air and naval bombardment, Lt. Gen. Mark W. Clark's Fifth Army invasion troops led by American Ranger units and British Commandos, outflanked the two most formidable German defense lines guarding Rome and prepared for a drive on the Italian capital itself.

WIN BEACHHEADS

An official German DNB agency said the invasion forces won beachheads between the harbor town of Nettuno, 32 miles south of Rome and 55 miles northwest of the main front, and the Tiber estuary, which empties into the Tyrrhenian Sea 16 miles southwest of Rome and 30 miles north of Nettuno. The port of Anzia, a few miles west of Nattuno also may have fallen.

Allied air forces under the command of Lieut. Gen. Ira C. Eaker, former chief of the 8th Air Force in England, paved the way for the invasion thrust with two days of heavy raids that temporarily cut off Rome from rail and other communication with German reserves and supply depots to the north.

The air offensive reached its climax yesterday with the heaviest and most widespread assaults since Salerno. German airfields as far away as Marseilles, France, were attacked. In their final attacks on airfields near Rome, the bombers did not even encounter anti-aircraft fire, indicating the degree of saturation achieved by the raiders.

TROOPS POUR ASHORE

Then under the cover of darkness last night huge invasion ships packed with troops, guns and probably tanks slipped along the Italian coast and took up positions offshore while Allied warships and night bombers sent tons of explosives into the coastal sector marked for the landings.

A steady stream of Allied troops and trucks were pouring ashore with virtually no opposition from the German air force, the first American pilots to return from flights over the new beachhead reported.

The assault forces closed in

Continued on Page Eight

Beaver Marine Home From So. Pacific

Veteran of a year in the Southwest Pacific war area, Capt. George R. Wilson, U. S. Marine Corps, arrived this morning for an indefinite leave with his parents, Mr. and Mrs. Karl D. Wilson, Buffalo street, Beaver.

A member of a signal company, Captain Wilson spent six months in active combat duty. After his leave he will report to the Fleet Marine Force at San Diego, Calif. He was called to active service in February, 1941, after being commissioned a second lieutenant upon his graduation from Renssalaer Polytechnical Institute, Troy, N. Y., in 1940.

House Expected To Reject Tax Bill As Passed By Senate

WASHINGTON, Jan. 22 (UP)—The 1944 tax bill, carrying $2,275,000,000 in additional revenue as it passed the Senate late yesterday, today was headed for the House again where it will be speedily rejected and sent into conference for compromise next Monday.

Amounting to less than a quarter of the $10,500,000,000 asked by the treasury to help finance the war and prevent inflation, the present bill has been denounced as "unrealistic" by President Roosevelt.

Considerable conference debate on the measure was indicated by House ways and means committee member Harold Knutson, R., Minn., who said the House would insist on its integration of victory and regular individual income taxes—which the Senate rejected.

However, Democratic members of the committee predicted that agreement would be reached in two days. Neither quarter expected any difficulty over the renegotiation law amendments which snarled Senate debate for more than a week.

DELAY FORESEEN

Approving the Senate-incorporated December 31, 1944, termination date for renegotiation, Knutson said:

"Personally, I'm in favor of terminating renegotiation. As a matter of fact, we should have provided for termination next December 31 on the theory that if the Procurement Division hasn't acquired an understanding of production costs by this time, President Roosevelt should get some new members at work making contracts. They have had nearly three years experience. They should be able to negotiate contracts that will stand up.' '

If Knutson's belief that the House will stand pat on its integration of victory and regular income taxes proves correct, there is a bare possibility that the bill will not be enacted in time for the new schedule of excise taxes to go into effect March 1. The bill must be signed by the President 10 days before March 1 to put the higher rates into operation then. The next effective date under law would be April 1. It appears unlikely that the Senate will accede to any House demand that the income tax schedule be as completely rewritten as the House desires.

VERSIONS DIFFER

The Senate took final action on the bill late yesterday, passing it by voice vote. The $2,275,600,000 yield of the measure was $136,300,000, more than the House-approved total of $2,139,300,000.

As it left the Senate, the measure did not change present individual income tax rates but

(Continued On Page Eight)

Wanted

ESTIMATES QUOTED ON ESSENTIAL HOME REPAIRS. WORK SUBJECT TO PROCUREMENT OF MATERIALS. FOR FURTHER INFORMATON CALL CHARLES E. HANEY, LUMBER, FREEDOM. PHONE ROCH. 725. 1|27-2|2 inc.

WANTED: Curtains to wash and stretch in my own home. Phone Roch. 3003-R, or inquire 604 Case St., Rochester. 1|27-2|2 inc.

WANTED: High school girls will care for children evenings. Call Beaver 303-R. 1|27

MOVING: INCLUDING PIANOS AND REFRIGERATORS. ROCH. 3380 "TOSH." 1|22-2|4 inc

WANTED: All kinds of sewing and remodeling in private home by experienced seamstress. All work guaranteed. Inquire 405 Wahl St., Monaca. Phone Rochester 3048-J. 1|21-2|3 inc.

GENERAL HAULING: Ashes or Rubbish. Phone Rochester 2370-W. 1|15-2|11 inc.

Why pay rent when $39 a month pays for your own home in Tusca Glen? $600 down payment, plus closing costs, balance payable like rent. For further information, phone Roch. 725. 1|11*

WANTED: Plastering. Bids given on new work. Patch work a specialty. Phone Rochester 794-W. Ray Berry, 468 Webster street, Rochester. 1|4-31 inc

We do hauling of ashes and rubbish. Call Beaver 328. 1|26-2|9 inc.

WANTED: To buy wire clothes hangers, in good condition. 1c each. Bring to Miller's Cleaning Shoppe, next to City Building, Beaver. 1|9*

Help Wanted—Male

WANTED: Man to drive truck. Apply American Oil Company, West Bridgewater, Pa. 1|25-27 inc.

WANTED: Meat cutter, part or full time. Good wages. 1301 Penn avenue, Monaca. Steve's Clover Farm store. 1|25-27 inc

COACH OPERATORS WANTED!
Apply at
Junction Park Office
Beaver Valley Motor Coach Company
If now employed in Essential Industry, statement of availability is required.

Help Wanted—Female

WANTED: Kitchen help. Apply Beaver Lunch, 518 Third St., Beaver, 8 a. m. to 8 p. m. 1|27-2|2 inc

WANTED: Typist. Apply at the Employment Office of the Hydril Corporation, North Rochester. 1|27-29 inc

WANTED: Waitresses for hotel dining room. Apply Mrs. Snapp, Penn-Beaver Hotel, Rochester. 1|27-29 inc.

WANTED: Girl or woman, 21 or over, with selling experience to work in men's furnishing store. Steady employment to right party. Apply in person to Morris Rubinoff, 680 Third avenue, Freedom. 1|24-29 inc

WANTED: Young lady, 20 to 31 years, for house to house bread route. Union wages $5.00 day through training period, work 5 days week. Must be steady worker and good driver. Apply Home Science Bakery, 260 East End Ave., Beaver. 1|22-28 inc

WANTED: Kitchen helper—must be neat and clean. Apply Dietician, Rochester General Hospital. 12|30*

WANTED: Saleslady for ladies' store, permanent position. Apply in person at Edmin's, 156 Brighton avenue, Rochester. 1|26-2|1 inc.

WANTED: Stock girl, white or colored, apply in person at Edmin's, 156 Brighton avenue, Rochester. 1|26-2|1 inc

WANTED: Girl for general housework, no washing, mother employed. Phone Rochester 116-W. 1|25-31 inc.

WANTED: 2 waitresses and one dishwasher for after school. Tip Top Restaurant, 157 Brighton Ave., Rochester. 1|25-31 inc

WANTED: Cook (40 years of age or over preferred) at Beaver County Home. Call Beaver 1488-J for appointment. 1|19-2|1 inc.

You all want mesh non runs and you can get them for $1.23 and $1.45 at Ed Frick's Men's Shop, Beaver. 1|21-27 inc

Help Wanted—Male

MAN BETWEEN 38 and 45
for tractor trailer driver
Apply
Keystone Bakery
West Bridgewater
1|26-28 inc.

Pittsburgh Tube Co.
100% WAR INDUSTRY
NEEDS MEN
Work requires no particular skill or previous training and is steady. Well paid and essential to the war effort. 48 hours a week. Rotating shifts. Upgrading to higher paid jobs when qualified.
Apply at plant, Monaca, Pa., or U. S. Employment Office, 101 Brighton Ave., Rochester
If now employed in Essential Industry, statement of availability is required.
1|7 *

HELP TO MAKE STEEL
Needed By Our Army & Navy
Men 16 to 60
NO EXPERIENCE REQUIRED
APPLY
CRUCIBLE STEEL COMPANY
of America
Employment Office—Seventh Street, Midland, Pa., or to U. S. Employment Service, Rochester, Pa.
Midland Office Open 9 to 5 daily except Saturday 9 to 12.
If now employed in Essential Industry, statement of availability is required.

Male and Female Help

WANTED
MEN and WOMEN
Mechanics — Semi-Skilled — Laborers
to Produce
SLAB ZINC - ZINC OXIDE - SULPHURIC ACID
Slab Zinc for Cartridge and Shell Brass, Ship Propeller Bronze, Bomb Parts, etc. Zinc Oxide for Natural and Synthetic Rubber, Chemical Warfare, Electrical Insulation, etc. Sulphuric Acid for Munitions and Steel Manufacture.
All of these products are raw materials for the manufacture of material of offense
ST. JOSEPH LEAD COMPANY
Of Pennsylvania, Josephtown, Pa.
Telephone for appointment, Roch. 3281
If now employed in Essential Industry, statement of availability is required.
12|16 *

WANTED
EXPERIENCED MEN
To Work On Army and Navy Ordnance Materiel
Floorhands — Oilers
Machinists — Brakemen
Electricians — Cranemen
Laborers
ALSO BOYS 16 AND 17
Who Are Able To Procure Working Certificates
No Experience Required
WE CAN PLACE A FEW WOMEN
NO EXPERIENCE REQUIRED
APPLY EMPLOYMENT OFFICE
SPANG-CHALFANT
DIVISION OF THE NATIONAL SUPPLY COMPANY
DUSS AVENUE AT 23RD STREET, AMBRIDGE, PA.
If employed in essential industry statement of availability is required.
1|19 *

WANTED
MEN and WOMEN
INSPECTORS - LABORERS
MACHINE OPERATORS
Apply
Hydril Corporation
North Rochester
If now employed in Essential Industry, statement of availability is required
1|21-2|3 inc.

Read THE TIMES Classified Ads for Bargains

Help Wanted—Female

WANTED: Girl to operate pressing machine. Good pay. Steady work. Experience preferred. Apply at Sanitary Cleaners, 223 Brighton Ave., Rochester. 1|27-2|2 inc.

WANTED: Girl to work in dry cleaning plant, one willing to learn to press. Weiss Cleaners, Water street, Rochester. Phone Roch. 676. 1|26-27

WANTED — COOK
Steady daylight work, no experience necessary. Apply in person, Dan's Dairy Bar, 916 Pennsylvania avenue, Monaca. 1|25-31 inc.

Wanted—Male or Female

Counter man or woman experienced in retail meat selling, no cutting, steady position, good salary. Inquire in person Moss Cash Market, 145 Brighton Avenue, Rochester. 1|27-2|2 inc

WANTED: Night clerk for hotel. Knowledge of book keeping helpful. Apply manager, Penn-Beaver Hotel, Rochester. 1|27-29 inc

Wanted—To Buy

WANTED: To buy Panel Truck, must be in A-1 condition and priced right. Phone Rochester 2622-W. 1|27

WANTED: Clock keys. I have clocks but I need keys. Will pay 25c each. Coombs Furniture Exchange, 308 9th street, Monaca. 1|27-2|2 inc

WANTED: To buy a 2 or 3 piece living room suite, also a maple bed room suite. Must be in good condition and reasonable. Call Roch. 149. 1|27-2|2 inc

WANTED: Highest cash price paid for used cars, any make or model. Call us today or come to White, 461 Deer Lane, Rochester. Phone 1540 or 3236. 1|24-29 inc.

WANTED: To buy modern 4 or 5 room bungalow with some ground, handy to Beaver or Rochester. Needed March 1st. Write Box "M-402" c/o DAILY TIMES, Beaver, Pa. 1|24-29 inc

WANTED TO BUY: Class C or similar gasoline motor for gas model airplane. Must be in good running condition, with all necessary connections, tools, etc. Will pay good price for good equipment. See Eddie Freeland, 375 Dravo Ave., Beaver, after 4:15 p. m. Do not make telephone calls. 1|25-31 inc.

WANT TO BUY something? Tell what you want through the TIMES "wanted ads. In that way, perhaps you'll find what you want. The cost is small. Thousands of people read these small ads daily.

Wanted—To Rent

WANTED: To rent furnished apartment or house, must have 2 bedrooms. Possession March 1st. Preferably in Beaver. Call Beaver 2164-M. 1|24-29 inc.

WANTED: To rent 4 or 5 room house in Rochester, by couple without children. Phone Roch. 2303-R. 1|21-27 inc.

For Sale

FOR SALE: Reversible tweed coat, size 16; pair brown pumps, size 7-AAA, also pair size 6½-AAAA. Phone Rochester 3070. 1|27-28

FOR SALE: Grunow refrigerator in excellent condition. Call Roch. 6107-R-13. 1|27-2|2 inc

FOR SALE: Antique Chickering grand piano, $35.00. Owner leaving town — must sell. Phone Beaver 1231-J or inquire 270 Dravo avenue, Beaver. 1|27-2|2 inc

FOR SALE: Ladies ½ Carat Diamond Ring with two side diamonds. Write "D-31" c/o THE DAILY TIMES, Beaver, Pa. 1|26-2|1 inc.

EXPERT SWEEPER REPAIRING
Quick service on your Hoover, Premier, Eureka, etc. All work guaranteed. CLAUSEN'S 1039 3rd St., Beaver. Phone Beaver 2099 or 6168-J-3. 1|26-2|1 inc

FOR SALE!
BUILDINGS and USED LUMBER
Phone Roch. 39-J
12|21*

GIRLS—You'll want a pair of Rollins Bemberg sheers. They just came in and quantity is limited. Colors good at $1.01. Ed. Frick's Men's Shop, Beaver. 1|21-27 inc.

PUMPS
All Kinds Delivered From Stock. Can Also Supply Pipe and Fittings
A. H. McMINN
619 11th St., Beaver Falls, Pa. Phone B. F. 812
1|18-2|14 inc.

BIG WALLPAPER SALE: ½ off thousands rolls. Bargains. Direct Factory dealer prices. 5c to $2.00 roll. WM. HELMICK, 390 Brighton Ave., Rochester. (The Big Store). 1|14-27 inc.

For Sale

Cast Iron and Steel Furnaces In Stock
BEGLIN STOVE AND FURNACE CO.
AUTHORIZED
KALAMAZOO
DEALER
Repairs For All Makes Of Furnaces
1408 7th Ave. Beaver Falls, Pa. Phone 467
1|25-31 inc.

FOR SALE: Red Star gas range, walnut dining room table, 10 walnut dining room chairs. Inquire 1621 Corporation St., Beaver. Phone 3338. 1|27

FOR SALE: Frigidaire electric refrigerator, cheap. Inquire 376 New York avenue, Rochester. 1|27-28

FOR SALE: 1 new riding bridle, one saddle used very little, $37.50. See E. R. Brubaker, 1138 4th St., Beaver, before 6 p. m. 1|25-31 inc.

FOR SALE: One coal circulating heater, like new—heats 4 rooms. Inquire 1222 Linden street, Monaca Heights. 1|24-29 inc.

FOR SALE: Used cameras and camera supplies. Jordan's, "The Little Store On The Square," Beaver. 1|26-2|1 inc.

Bicycles— boys and girls— rebuilt, repainted. Complete line of parts, expert repairing. Highest prices paid for used bikes and parts. Dunny's Bike Shop, 235 College Ave., Beaver. 1|22-28 inc.

FOR SALE: Fresh eggs 55c dozen. Jordan's — "The Little Store On The Square," Beaver. 1|26-27

FOR SALE: Frigidaire, gas range, Apex electric washing machine and 4-piece walnut bedroom suite. Call after 7 p. m. Beaver 1553-M-2 or 488 Sharon Road, Beaver. 1|26-28 inc

FOR SALE: Cow manure $6 a ton in a yard. Stephen White, 9th St. Ext., 3 miles back of Freedom, Freedom Knob Rd. 1|26-27

FOR SALE: 4-piece maple bedroom suite, child's high chair and crib, axminster rugs. Inquire 938 14th St., Monaca. 1|25-27 inc.

FOR SALE: One bedroom suite, 5 pieces; 14 steel Venetian shades, and one door shade; one breakfast nook, black and white; one porch glider, one coffee table, green chair and ottoman; 3 piece maple sun porch set. Phone Roch. 54 or 576-R-1. 1|25-27 inc.

FOR SALE: Workmen's gloves—fuzzy palms; gauntlets, knit wrist, leather palms and brown jersey, at Miller Super Market, Monaca. Phone Roch. 1504. 1|22-28 inc.

Highest Cash Prices Paid
For Refrigerators, Washers, Sewing Machines, Stoves, Rugs, Radios and Modern Furniture
MARINO FURNITURE EXCHANGE
Rochester — Phone 984
1|11-2|7 inc.

FOR SALE: Men's 2 trouser wool suits, short, stout, 175 to 200 lbs.; man's new hat, tan, size 7¼; shirts, size 18; 2 pair boy's trousers, size 16; 1 leather jacket, size 14; 1 ladies Polo coat, size 36; man's canvas Suiter traveling bag; G-E Broil-O-Mat; Selmer brass trombone; 2 sleds; boys books, new; 2 tennis racquets; 2 army cots; 4 card table chairs; sun lamp. Phone Beaver 1653. 1|22-28 inc.

WE PAY CASH FOR USED WASHERS, SWEEPERS, RADIOS, REGARDLESS OF CONDITION. WASHER, SWEEPER REPAIRING, PARTS FOR ALL MAKES. HARPER'S, 386 BRIGHTON AVE., ROCHESTER. PHONE 9090. 1|25-31 inc.

FOR SALE: Complete living, dining, bed-room suites and other furnishings, lamps, tables, dishes. Phone Beaver 3169-M. 1|22-29 inc.

HAVE YOU something to sell? Somebody needs what you no longer have use for. Advertise it in the TIMES FOR SALE ads. Chances are you will find a ready buyer.

Read THE TIMES Classified Ads.

For Sale

FOR SALE: Now we can offer Prompt Service on Genuine Firestone Factory recaps. Have your Tires recapped now. Schaughencys, Rochester, Beaver and Beaver Falls. 1|20*

FOR SALE: Visit Coombs Furniture Exchange, 308 Ninth St., Monaca, for new and used furniture and many other "hard-to-get" articles. We buy and sell. Roch. 4369. 1|6-3|2 inc

120 New Guns to be sold to Farmers—30-06. 16 Ga. Pump and 22 Repeating Rifles, all with shells. Smith Bros. Gun Store, Unionville, Pa. 1|21-27 inc.

Accordion for sale. Young man leaving for Army. Will sell cheap. Inquire 1100 Penn Ave., New Brighton. Phone 1374. 1|22-28 inc.

For lovely legs that attract lingering admiring glances everywhere they appear, get those lovely Bembergs at Ed Frick's Men's Shop, Beaver. 1|21-27 inc

FOR SALE: Twin cylinder air compressor, quick operating, used in gas station short time. For information call Beaver 4287-W. 1|21-27 inc

For Sale—Houses

$2100
Buys this 4-room house, gas, water, electric, bath and cement cellar. Also 2-room house at rear, gas, water and electric. Income $35 per month. Located on improved street in Rochester. $500 down payment, balance like rent. For information, inquire
DANIEL B. MYERS
201 Brighton Ave., Rochester
Day phone: Rochester 767-J
Eve. Phone: Rochester 233
1|27-29 inc

FOR SALE: $6,000 six room brick house, concrete block garage. Transportation in front of house. $6,000 six room brick house, finished attic, new brick garage, level lot. Transportation in front of house. See or phone Eugene R. Hurst Agency, 588 Third St., Beaver 1043-J. 1|27-2|2 inc.

FOR SALE: 6 room house, Pennsylvania avenue, Monaca, completely furnished, including Beauty Shop with complete equipment. Phone Roch. 9038. 1|27-2|2 inc

FOR SALE: New 3-room house, gas, water, electric, furnace, one acre ground, 4 miles from Conway, on Conway-Wallrose Rd. Phone Baden 6840. 1|27-2|2 inc

979 CANAL ST., BEAVER
6 room frame house, enclosed sunporch, good furnace, modern bath with shower, garage, owner occupied. Price $5950. Possession in 30 days. E. M. Standley, Realtor, Beaver. 1|26-28 inc

IN BEAVER
6 rm. frame dwlg., 4 car garage, paved st., alley two sides. House in A1 condition, practically new furnace—$6,000.
Frame duplex, 516 - 2nd St., 3 rm. down, 4 rm. up, 2 baths, 2 kitchens. Hot-air furnace—$5500—Terms.
Large brick dwlg., paved st., large lot, 3 car brick garage, 3 baths, forced air furnace.
Brick duplex or large one family house. 302 River Road, 5 rms. & bath first; 5 rooms, bath & porch, 2nd floor.
BOVARD - ANDERSON COMPANY
A Real Estate Office For 40 Years
617 Third Street, Beaver 1121
1|25-27 inc.

FOR SALE: 6 room house and bath, all modern conveniences, excellent condition, now vacant, located corner Reno St., and Vermont avenue, Rochester. Inquire 244 Adams street, Rochester or phone Roch. 2368. 1|25-31 inc.

IN BEAVER, near bus and P. & L. E., 8 room brick, slate roof, baths on first and second floors, cistern water throughout, finished 3rd floor, brick garage. Phone Beaver 867-J or write "H 44" c/o DAILY TIMES, Beaver. 1|24-29 inc

Here is one of the Best Offers. A new 5-room house and integral garage, level lot. Good material. Good workmanship. Come and see them at 201 Wayne street, Baden or call Baden 6591. J. P. Parry. 1|21-27 inc.

FOR SALE: New home at Tusca Glen, Tuscarawas road. 6 rooms and bath, all modern. Ready for occupancy. $6000. $600 down payment, $39 per month pays principal, interest, taxes and insurances. Phone Roch. 725. 11|16*

FOR SALE: Five room modern brick house, garage in basement. Lot 75 x 150. On 1262 Eckert Road, Monaca Heights. Call Roch. 3475-J. 1|25-31 inc

FOR SALE: Frame house, 5 rooms and bath, 1 car garage, good condition, located on Pennsylvania avenue, Monaca. $4,700.00. Phone Roch. 257-R. 1|24-29 inc.

WANT TO BUY something? Tell what you want through the TIMES "wanted ads. In that way, perhaps you'll find what you want. The cost is small. Thousands of people read these small ads daily.

For Sale—Used Cars

FOR SALE: 1939 Ford Tudor sedan. Owner leaving for army. $100 down, balance monthly payments. Phone Rochester 730. 1|27-2|2 inc.

FOR SALE: 1939 Buick sedan, deluxe equipment & good tires, excellent condition. Inquire 434 Market St., Beaver, Pa. 1|27-2|2 inc

GOOD USED CARS
1942 BUICK super, 6 passenger coupe, radio, heater.
1942 PONTIAC 8 streamliner, 6 passenger coupe, radio, heater.
1942 PLYMOUTH special deluxe, 5 passenger coupe, radio, heater.
1942 PLYMOUTH special deluxe, 2 door, radio, heater.
1941 PLYMOUTH special deluxe, 2 door, radio, heater.
1941 DODGE 2 door, fluid drive, radio, heater.
1941 DODGE sedan, fluid drive, radio, heater.
1941 CHEVROLET special deluxe, 5 passenger coupe, radio, heater.
1941 CHEVROLET special deluxe sedan.
1941 CHEVROLET special deluxe, 2 door.
1940 CHEVROLET special deluxe sedan.
1940 BUICK special sedan, radio, heater.
1940 DESOTO sedan, radio, heater
1939 PLYMOUTH deluxe sedan.
1939 CHEVROLET deluxe 2 door.
1934 CHEVROLET sedan.
Christy Motor Co.
469 Market Street, Beaver
Phone 1456
1|25-31 inc.

WANTED USED CARS
Late Models—'39-'40-'41
CHRISTY MOTOR CO.
469 Market St. Beaver
1|25-31 inc.

FOR SALE: 1941 Buick Super sedan, like new. Call Roch. 225—9 a. m. to 5 p. m. 1|24-29 inc

FOR SALE: 1930 Buick, good tires (recapped), good condition. Inquire 485 New York Ave., Rochester. 1|21-27 inc

A. R. C. H. SNYDER
PAYS MORE
For Good Late Models Pontiacs and Chevrolets
CONWAY, PA.

For Sale—Livestock

FOR SALE: 2 milk goats; will kid in March. Call Beaver 6116-J-11. 1|25-31 inc.

FOR SALE: One light colored sorrel horse with gold mane and tail, 16 hands, 3 gaited, rides and drives, 7 years old. Also beautiful, chestnut sorrel stallion colt, 2½ years old and one black and white stallion pony, 46 inches tall, nine years old, a beautiful animal. Also one Western and one English saddle. Call Sim Holmes, Beaver 6154-J-11. 1|24-29 inc.

FOR SALE: Rabbits, good breeding stock, mostly Flemish Giants, also one checkered Giant petigreed buck. Call Rochester 6118-R-12. 1|21-27 inc

For Sale—Dogs

FOR SALE: "Sadie", a remarkably well bred black female Cocker Spaniel registered in American Kennel Club Book under the name of Good Cheer of Marjolear, born in April, 1940. Sire — Champion Dungarvan Trader Horn and Dan Selka Belle of Marjolear. Sadie has a fine coat and beautiful head. She is of gentle disposition, used to children and would make anyone a fine pet with also show and breeding possibilities. For further information call Beaver 1837. 1|27-29 inc.

For Sale—Poultry

FOR SALE: 12 laying White Leghorn hens. Inquire 752 Canal street, Beaver. Phone Beaver 3818-R. 1|22-28 inc.

BABY CHICKS
State blood-tested New Hampshire Reds from 100% nonreactor breeding flocks. All under state supervision. Cunningham Poultry Farm & Hatchery, Darlington Road. Phone Beaver Falls 1014. 1|10-2|5 inc

For Sale—Farms

FOR SALE: Farm of 50 acres, Hanover Township, 4 miles from Laughlin's Corner off Route 168 on Route 093. A room house, barn, good spring water, electricity and telephone at door, ½ mile to school. M. W. Nichol, Georgetown, Penna. Phone Hookstown 2355, R. D. No. 1. 1|21-27 inc.

Call Beaver 2564 For
PORT COAL
PROMPT DELIVERY
COURTNEY COAL CO.

Read THE TIMES Classified Ads.

For Sale—Coal

QUALITY COAL, also Ashes. Fred Summers, West View, Beaver. Phone Beaver 1562-R or 572. 1|21-2|3 inc.

Trade or Exchange

WANTED to trade late model gas range for late model oil stove in good condition. Phone Ohioview 38181. 1|27-29

For Rent—Apartments

FOR RENT: 3 or 4 room furnished apartment in modern home on Mercer Road, New Brighton, ½ mile from town. Employed couple preferred. Adults only. Phone N. B. 3361-J. 1|27-30 inc.

FOR RENT: Two room apartment with bath, furnished for house-keeping, first floor, private entrance. Also one housekeeping room, bath, first floor, private entrance. 332 Wayne St., Beaver. 1|27-2|2 inc

FOR RENT: Three room furnished apartment, private bath, on first floor, all utilities furnished. Inquire 1224 Poplar St., Bridgewater. Phone Beaver 1841-R or Beaver 634-R. 1|26-2|1 inc.

FOR RENT: Duplex, 4 rooms & bath, immediate poss. —$40.00. BOVARD - ANDERSON CO. Beaver 1121. 1|26-28 inc.

FOR RENT: Modern, well located, efficiency apartment. All hardwood floors, incinerator, use of laundry and private locker in basement. Reasonable rental. Inquire at Walton Hdwe. Co., Beaver, Pa. 1|26-2|1 inc

FOR RENT: 3 and 4 room apartments. For details inquire 209 Beaver Trust Bldg., Beaver or phone Beaver 1585. 1|26-2|8 inc

FOR RENT: 2 three room apartments, second floor, one four room apartment, third floor. Phone Baden 3431. 1|26-2|1 inc

FOR RENT: Furnished 3 room apartment, electric refrigerator, garage, heat supplied, $40 monthly. Immediate occupancy. 480 Beaver St. Phone Beaver 988-W. 1|25-31 inc

FOR RENT: Three room unfurnished apartment with bath, heat, light and use of laundry. Private entrance. Fine location. Call Beaver 3348. 1|25-31 inc.

FOR RENT: 3 room apartment, 499 Third St., Beaver. Suitable for couple, heat furnished. See Eugene R. Hurst Agency, 588 Third St., Beaver 1043-J. 1|24-29 inc.

IMMEDIATE POSSESSION
Four room apt. with H. W. Floors, and Tile bath, adults only, $55.
JAMES S. STROUSS
458 3rd St. Phone 815 Beaver
1|21-27 inc

FOR RENT: Three room unfurnished apartment, light and heat furnished, modern conveniences, 3 miles from Kobuta on bus line to Aliquippa. Phone Roch. 6131-J-4. 1|21-27 inc.

FOR RENT: Apartment, three rooms with bath. Utilities furnished. Phone Beaver 2592-R. 1|22-28 inc.

HAVE YOU a room for rent? Advertise it in the TIMES "for rent" section. You probably will rent it quickly. The cost is small.

ROYAL TRAINED FACTORY SERVICE for ALL OFFICE MACHINES
C. F. BROWN
Royal Typewriters—Adding Machines — Supplies
818 Federal Title & Trust Bldg., Beaver Falls 3879

CASH
FOR YOUR CAR
See us now for Top Dollar while Prices Are High. We Buy All Makes From '36s to '42s.
TODD MOTOR SALES
1725 MAIN ST., ALIQUIPPA
PHONE 2088

MONEY to Loan
To pay taxes, insurance premiums, auto repairs, doctor and hospital bills and furnish cash for your winter coal and home improvements.
Rochester Thrift & Loan CORPORATION
218 Brighton Ave., Rochester Phone 2100

AWNINGS
For spring delivery, order now, while labor and material are available.
STORM WINDOWS & STORM DOORS
Redwood combination with removable glass and screens.
WINDOW SHADES - TRUCK COVERS - VENETIAN BLINDS
All items furnished and installed complete.
For free estimate call
HAMILTON GLOVE & AWNING COMPANY
468 Buffalo St., Phone Beaver 94

UNITED STATES MARINES, using machine guns and carbines, halted and pushed back a Japanese counter-attack on their position on Cape Gloucester, New Britain island. The Nips retreated into the jungle until they had gathered what they considered enough strength to counter-attack. The Marines, however, soon had them in full retreat again. This is a U S Marine Corps photo. *(International)*

Army-Navy Tests Here Wednesday

Qualifying tests for high school and college men eligible for the Army-Navy College qualifying examinations take place next Wednesday, March 15, at Beaver Falls high school and Geneva College. Leaflets describing the tests and containing application blanks are available at the local school offices.

The test is open to young men who reach their 17th but not their 22nd birthday by next July 1, who are in the final term of their senior year of high school; recent high school or prep school graduates, or college students without certificates of graduation from high school and not now enrolled in any service program. Those who failed to qualify on previous Army-Navy college qualify tests are eligible provided they are not already in the armed forces. Candidates are required to designate a choice of service, but those designating the Navy, which includes the Marines and Coast Guard, must be between 17 and 19 years inclusive by July 1.

Obituary

MRS. GEORGE F. BLINN

Mrs. Maggie V. Blinn, wife of George F. Blinn of 711 Tenth Street, New Brighton, died at 6 o'clock Friday night in Providence hospital. She was born November 6, 1871 in Smiths Ferry, and had resided in New Brighton for many years.

Mrs. Blinn leaves her husband and two sons, Edwin C. Blinn and Earl W. Blinn, both of New Brighton, and one grandson. Surviving also are the following brothers and sisters: Perry Wilson, Frank Wilson, Miss Blanche Wilson and Mrs. Cora Hays, all of Smiths Ferry.

Friends are being received at the Loyal B. Young Funeral Home.

Funeral Notices

BLINN: Funeral services for the late Mrs. Maggie V. Blinn will be held at 2:30 o'clock Monday afternoon in the Loyal B. Young Funeral Home in charge of the Rev. Wm. H. Marburger of Trinity Lutheran church. Burial will take place in North Sewickley cemetery.

CARD OF THANKS

We acknowledge with grateful appreciation the kind expressions of sympathy extended to us during our recent bereavement in the loss of our beloved father, Andrew Jackson Tennant.

We also wish to thank all who aided us in any way, particularly the Rev. Alden Green and Rev. Henry A. Young for their very comforting words.

Family of Andrew Jackson Tennant. 3-11-1t

Helpful Hints For Victory Gardeners

Locate your garden site now. It may be a private garden on your own ground. But be sure that you select a sunny location, free from trees or shrubs.

If you are employed in one of Beaver county's industrial plants, request a plot in the factory victory garden tract. If your plant does not have gardening facilities for its employes, ask why not. Many large industries are doing it, and the program has a place in their labor plan.

See your local civilian defense chairman about a plot in the community victory garden.

Vacant lots should be plowed and prepared for people seeking ground. This would transform ugly, weedy places into gardens of food and beauty.

Juniors interested in school gardens should take the matter up with school authorities. Ask your nature science teacher for garden discussions and an outdoor school garden nature's laboratory where you can observe nature by growing vegetables and flowers. Information for introducing gardening in schools may be obtained from the National Education Association, Washington, D. C., or Paul Young, Board of Education, Cleveland, Ohio.

A kitchen garden is the best security a family can have. Ask your labor union to help you find the best social and economic security for your family.

PRUNING TIME NOW

Grape vines, fruit trees and ornamental shrubs and fruit-bearing shrubs can be pruned now. All shrubs that bloom on new wood can be pruned now, but shrubs blooming on old wood should be pruned after blooming.

The principles of pruning are: First, remove all dead and diseased wood;

Second, remove all excess growth so as to remove the struggle for existence;

Third, strive for gracefulness of effect.

Now is the time to put your garden tools in order. You will need a spade, a hoe, a rake and a good dust gun. Buy your Rotonone dust and fertilizer, and order your seed.

The soil as a rule requires from 3 to 4 pounds of commercial fertilizer for every 100 square feet. Fertilizer is toxic and should be spaded into the ground. If it is too near the surface it is apt to escape into the air.

Send your questions and problems on gardening to the News-Tribune and they will be answered in this column.

Circular 253, "Growing Vegetables for Home Use," obtainable from Ross M. Gridley, Agriculture Extension Office, Beaver, is one of the best sources of gardening information.

Yankees Bomb

(Continued From Page One)

the night.

The air ministry said three aircraft factories and a small bearing factory in central and southern France were hit in a "bomber's moon" operation in the continuing campaign to knock out Germany's aircraft production facilities. The specific objectives were not named.

The air ministry said one aircraft was lost.

It was the RAF's fourth sizable mission this week and the fifth in a new campaign in which seven airplane plants and two big railroad centers have been bombed.

These raids are capitalizing on a period of bright nights which are excellent for pinpointing targets but which are not good for the concealment required for deep penetrations of the continent.

On the night before the four-engined Lancasters hit an aircraft factory near Marseille in southern France.

American fighters again escorted the four-engined Flying Fortresses and Liberators on today's strikes.

Tot Burned To Death

PHILLIPSBURG, Pa., (AP)—Ronald Erickson, three, was burned to death yesterday after he left go his mother's dress as she was leading him and his sister, Joyce, four, from their flaming home at Glassflat near here. The mother and baby, two, whom she carried in her arms, were burned about the face and hands. Gust Erickson, the father, was at work.

LITTLE GIRL DIES

CHESTER, Pa., (AP)—Kathryn Hobbs, 4, dragged from the icy waters of a creek near here yesterday died a few minutes after she was admitted to the Chester hospital.

Mrs. Sadie Hobbs, the child's mother, said they were walking along the creek when the little girl slipped on the muddy bank and slid into the water.

ROTARY RESERVATIONS

Any member of the Beaver Falls Rotary Club anticipating inviting a guest to the organization's 25th anniversary meeting at the Brodhead Hotel next Tuesday night must so notify the hotel no later than 10 o'clock Monday morning, it was announced today.

Since accommodations for the dinner are limited to the capacity of the Colonial room, the hotel must be informed by the hour stated as to how many are to be expected for the event.

Free-For-All Primary Fight For State Superior Court Develops

HARRISBURG—(AP)—A free-for-all fight for a Pennsylvania Superior Court judgeship developed today with former Governor Arthur H. James, Republican, now a member of the court, seeking both the Republican and Democratic nominations for a full ten-year term in the $18,000 a year post.

James filed for the Democratic nomination yesterday, countering an opposition made several weeks ago when another incumbent, Judge Chester H. Rhodes, Democrat, was entered in the Republican nomination. Rhodes also is in the Democratic primary. Both have organization backing.

The former governor was appointed to the court last month by Edward Martin, who succeeded him as governor, to fill a vacancy.

James Democratic filing came during a final day rush of candidates to file for the April 25 primaries. Petitions of more than [illegible] candidates were filed before the 5 P. M. deadline swamped the State elections bureau and sent the number entered to 1,369.

James, who was sitting with the Superior Court in [illegible] when his petitions were presented, said he [illegible] comment."

The [illegible] ignoring a [illegible] challenge to [illegible] "[illegible] jurists," also have [illegible] Judge J. Frank [illegible] of Armstrong county for the second Superior Court place.

Slated with Rhodes by the [illegible] is Auditor General F. [illegible] with whom James re[illegible] [illegible] ballot the nominations will go to those two receiving the highest votes.

Outside of the Superior Court fight, no opposition appeared to the GOP organization's slate headed by U. S. Senator James J. Davis, who is seeking a third term.

The Democratic State Committee ticket however, was challenged by John F. Breslin, Carbon county, who is opposing State Treasurer G. Harold Wagner for Auditor General, and Henry Arthur Morris, Mahanoy City, who is running against Third Assistant Postmaster General Ramsey S. Black for State Treasurer. Congressman Francis J. Myers, Philadelphia, is the Democratic candidate for the Senate.

President Roosevelt was the only candidate placed in the presidential preference primary, the Democratic state committee placing his name on the ballot to give voters a chance to register "approval of his leadership." The outcome is not binding on convention delegates.

The Republicans called for an uninstructed convention delegation. Only one Republican—John E. Philpot of Philadelphia—and one Democrat—Daniel J. North of Beaver Meadows—filed for convention delegate-at-large in opposition to organization slates.

The state's entire congressional delegation is seeking re-election with the exception of Myers, who is running for the senate, and William I. Troutman, congressman-at-large, whose state-wide district was eliminated by the 1943 reapportionment act. Troutman filed for the state senate from [illegible]

Brighton Township Woman Has Notable Service Record As 4-H Club Leader

[illegible] parts of a [illegible] Mrs. [illegible] Buckley of Brighton [illegible] is one of these leaders. [illegible] years of [illegible] as a 4-H club leader for [illegible] Club work in [illegible] township was started by [illegible] in 1924. Her first club group [illegible] of eight members, many of whom are still residing in the township. The members in her first club were Misses Elizabeth and Jeanette McCain, Ruth Heimes, Stella Novakovic, Mrs. Betty Stahl, Mrs. Ruth Small, Mrs. Mary Hagie Funk, and Mrs. Eva Bryner.

After two years of 4-H Club work, two members of Mrs. Buckley's club who were sisters, were left alone by a sudden death in their family. Visiting them sometime later and noticing how well these girls kept their home and put into practice the things they learned in 4-H, Mrs. Buckley said, "Then I knew how valuable 4-H work really was, and I kept on with it ever since."

Seven of Mrs. Buckley's first club members completed seven years of club work. In 1930 the club selected the canning project. They worked hard that year and took their canned products to the State Farm Show at Harrisburg. Of the $40 awarded in prizes for 4-H canned goods in the state, Mrs. Buckley's club won $30.

They were one of the first clubs to select the room improvement project in the state. Their exhibit at the Farm Show stimulated interest in this project in many other clubs throughout the state.

SECOND GENERATION

In 1942 Mrs. Buckley had her largest club group, consisting of 26 members. Three of the members, Grace, Velva, and Betty Bryner, were daughters of Mrs. Eva Bryner, whom she had in her first 4-H Club group.

While many people don't have time for service activities, there are few people that are busier than Mrs. Buckley. Yet she has always found time for 4-H Club work. She says that the work means much to her, not only because of the help she has given the girls, but also for the many useful things she herself has learned from the various projects her girls have carried. She passes on much of this information to others. She has gained many people's confidence. Her family feel it would be interesting if she had kept a record of the various problems that people in the community have brought to her for advice. Her family call her the "Information Bureau." Even though the problems were varied, she has always been able to help in some way.

MANY OTHER ACTIVITIES

In addition to 4-H Club work, Mrs. Buckley has many other activities. She was the first woman to serve on the county agricultural extension executive committee. She was the only woman member of the committee for three years, until two other women were added to the committee. Her other activities include Eastern Star, Grange, and church work. She also has duties to her family of seven children, four of whom were active in 4-H and did outstanding work. Ruth Buckley, now Mrs. Ruth Small, completed seven years of club work; Betty Buckley, now Mrs. Betty Stahl, completed eight years of club work and won the honor of being sent to the Eastern 4-H Conference in Massachusetts; and Marion Buckley, now Mrs. Marion Shroads, completed eight years of outstanding club work. Mrs. Buckley's son, Robert, now in the armed services, also completed eight years of club work.

Mrs. Buckley is proud of all her 4-H Club girls. When there are girls in the club who cannot afford to pay their expenses for camp, etc., the club makes cookies, sometimes picks berries to raise money so that all club members are given the same opportunity.

If you talk to Mrs. Buckley about 4-H Club work, she will tell you about experiences she has seen where the 4-H club has helped girls to manage for themselves. She will also tell you that she wouldn't take a fortune for the experience of being a 4-H Club leader. She feels she has benefited as much as the club girls from it.

BEAVER FALLS SCHOOL NEWS

"The future of America depends upon the girls and boys of today."
—Theodore Roosevelt.

LATIN WEEK CELEBRATED

Latin Week was celebrated in Pennsylvania this year during the week of February 28 to March 3. This year's program consisted of each class making four large posters. These posters portrayed the value of Latin in mathematics, science, and English. Together with these were testimonials, in poster form, from local professional people showing how Latin had benefited them. Included were ministers and lawyers, a nurse, a doctor, a dentist, a pharmacist, a secretary, a druggist, a business man, and a teacher.

The school library cooperated by displaying attractive bulletin board suggestions for reading fiction and non-fiction books with a Latin background.

This Latin Week celebration was a departure from that of last year because a Latin exhibition was staged in connection with the Diamond Jubilee held in Beaver Falls, January 16-23. The usual features which mark a Latin Week program include an assembly program, an exhibition, and a guest speaker. Miss Mary Dougherty is the Latin instructor in the high school.

—Marguerite Davidson.

SENIOR HIGH ASSEMBLY

An assembly on March 8 at Beaver Falls Senior High featured movies on "How to Choose Your Occupation" and a "Pete Smith Specialty" on George Washington Carver, the famed colored scientist.

The assembly opened with the flag salute and singing of the Star Spangled Banner. Hobart Seigal then spoke a few words on the educational value of the movies to be presented. James Patterson acted as chairman. Bill Schroeder and Charles Martin were the flag bearers. This program was sponsored by the Hi-Y.

—Betty Jane Shuber.

LEAP YEAR DANCE HELD

On February 28th, in the high school cafeteria, the Rhythm Club held a Leap Year dance.

The girls observed the formality generally followed by the boys. They invited the boys, escorted them to the cafeteria, bought their corsages, "asked for the dances," and later "saw them home."

The highlight of the evening was the judging of the "corsages" the girls bought the boys. These were judged according to "beauty only."

The first prize went to Donald Coleman, who was under a most beautiful corsage of eight round cream puffs formed in a circle, and one long cream puff in the middle with green and white icing, which was presented to him by Joline Schoemer.

Second prize went to Charles Merriman whose corsage was presented to him by Norma Jean Davis. It consisted of two sprays of ivy and a little lamb, with a card behind it, signifying that little lambs eat ivy.

Third prize went to Charles Gerson and his corsage was presented to him by Elinor Hagerman. It consisted of three carrots, and an ostrich feather, a snake (artificial) and a veil from an 1890 hat.

The judges were: Lila Gibson, Neal Bricker, Thom Muir, Peggy McClain.

Mary Catherine Goll was general chairman for the dance. Committees were: Decoration: Bernice Webb, chairman, Catherine Hummel, Rosemary Spagnola, Mickey Caruso, Don Garvin and Bob McLanahan. Food: Jeanne Warren, chairman; Eleanor Searfoss, Chuck Ford, Jack Weir. Checking: Betty Fredrick, chairman, Evelyn Meine, Mary Alice Mulford, Eleanor Stanford. Reception: Sue Sahli, chairman, Wilhelmena Scheeler, Jean Brown, and Carolyn Miller.

This was the first time a dance of this kind has been held in high school, and everyone agreed it was a very unusual and enjoyable evening.

—Eleanor Shont

JUNIOR BANQUET COMMITTEE

Plans are under way for the Junior banquet to be held April 15 in the high school cafeteria.

Members of the program committee are: Joan Frantz, Elinor Hagerman, Edward Ifft, Emogene Keeler, Charles Martin, Edward Newman, Edward Perencevic, Peter Pettler, Lois Schaefer, and Shirley Whitslar.

The decorating committee is composed of: Mary Jane Ewing, chairman; Alice Biro, Mary Jane Carody, Adela Clearwater, Virginia Mary Coon, Eleanor Demeter, Carolyn Edgecomb, Jacqueline Lane, Norma Parsons, Peggy Powell, Elinor Stanford, Martha Terdik, and Bernice Webb.

—Phyllis Redmond

BOND AND STAMP SALES

Students of B. F. H. S. are still continuing in their campaign for buying a P-51 Mustang Pursuit plane with the school name on it. A model of the plane has been made and each week it will be given to the home-room having the highest total. This week the hangar for the P-51 was room 309.

Many home-rooms have won new stars in "The Flags for Freedom Contest" still in progress. Room 309 received its 12th to 32nd star, 304 its 31st star, 117 its 21st star, 207 its 18th, 312 its 17th, 218 its 11th, 311 its 6th, 215 its 5th and 6th, and 301 its 4th star.

Also, in the "Flags for Freedom Contest" four home rooms have added stripes to their flags. The sixth stripe was added in room 114, room 106 [illegible] and rooms 301 and 118 their [illegible].

No [illegible] contributed 100 per cent [illegible]. There were, however, [illegible] rooms with 100 per cent. [illegible] were 301, 214, 120, [illegible] 117, 218 and 109. The [illegible] sophomore room to [illegible] 100 per cent in the [illegible].

Room 309, [illegible] highest total, has [illegible] the sum of $1066.[illegible].

This week the school total was $1991.70. This means that to date there is $26,010.[illegible] toward the P-51 Mustang. To this week's total the Sophomores contributed $1290.30, the Juniors [illegible] and the Seniors $418.40.

—Rosemary [illegible]

Prosecutions Held Interference With Individual Rights

WEST CHESTER, Pa.—(AP)—Miles Horst, State Secretary of Agriculture, asserted today he regards federal prosecutions of a Lebanon county farmer and farm auctioneer on charges of price ceiling violations "as unwarranted interference with individual rights and destructive of our farm economy."

"If the federal government had devoted half the energy to the prevention of strikes in farm implement manufacturing plants as it has to snooping," declared Horst in a prepared address to the Delaware-Chester County Farm Bureau, "there might now be plenty of new farm implements, instead of a perilous shortage."

Paul E. Sanger, Myerstown, the auctioneer, and L. E. Bucklew, South Annville Township, were arrested last month on federal warrants at the request of the Harrisburg OPA district office, which accused them of selling two farm tractors for more than OPA ceiling prices at the auction on Bucklew's farm. The warrants are returnable to the U. S. district court at Scranton.

Asserting he recognized the need of price regulation as an anti inflationary measure in wartime, Horst charged "an effort is now being made to break down and wreck the long-established and generally popular system whereby Pennsylvania farmers rid themselves of surplus stock, equipment and implements thru the medium of the traditional Pennsylvania method of public sale when they give up farming."

Geneva News

The members of the French and English clubs attended a performance of "Ladies in Waiting," given by the Carnegie Tech drama students in the Carnegie Tech playhouse, Thursday evening. Dr. and Mrs. Pearce, Dr. and Mrs. Ketcham, Mrs. J. C. Twinem, Dr. Morrill, Miss Holtom and Miss Patton accompanied the students.

Dr. and Mrs. J. S. Martin returned this week from a three months trip to the west coast. Enroute home Dr. Martin attended Geneva Alumni club meetings in Los Angeles, Cal., Denver, Col., Sterling, Topeka and Kansas City, Kan., Morning Sun, Ia., and Chicago, Ill.

Thomas N. Anderson, general superintendent of the Armstrong Cork Co., at Keyport, N. J., visited at the college on Friday. Mr. Anderson is formerly from Enon Valley and graduated from Geneva in 1926.

The Economics club met in the home of Dr. and Mrs. Robert Haley on Monday evening. C. Brainerd Metheny addressed the club members.

Drastic Steps

(Continued From Page One)

that Ireland had been swept by waves of invasion jitters.

Several further measures appear to be open to the United States and Britain, which had backed the American request to the limit. All of them, and possibly others are believed to be under consideration here and in London. They include:

1. Closing and fully guarding the border between Eire and Northern Ireland as an emergency military measure.

2. Breaking diplomatic relations with the Dublin government. This appeared to be the most improbable step of all since it usually creates more problems than it solves.

3. Clamping down on economic collaboration with Ireland. The country is an integral part of the British economic system and dependent entirely on British and American shipping.

Japs Strike Back

(Continued From Page One)

tion against the Japanese. Allied planes plastered suspected gun positions with 50 tons of bombs.

This was not the only sign of life shown by the large but isolated enemy garrison on Bougainville. Under cover of a heavy rainstorm, patrols of Japanese jungle fighters slipped through American barbed wire and seized several machine gun pillboxes on high ground.

American artillery countered this thrust and other Japanese maneuvers by pouring 3,000 rounds into enemy positions.

NEWS OF OUR MEN and WOMEN IN UNIFORM

IN NAVAL TRAINING

JULIAN J. TUNNO

Julian J. Tunno, A/S, son of Mr. and Mrs. Alfred A. Tunno of College Hill, has resumed his studies at Northwestern University, Evanston, Ill., in the College V-12 Navy training unit after spending a week at his home.

FRED L. HAHN

Fred Leroy Hahn, son of Mr. and Mrs. F. Hahn of R. D. 3, has completed basic training at the Submarine School, New London, Conn., for duty with the Navy's growing fleet of undersea fighters. He is a graduate of Beaver Falls high school and joined the Navy last March, going to Sampson, N. Y., for recruit training.

AWARDED SILVER WINGS

LT. WM. E. FLICKNER

William E. Flickner, son of Mr. and Mrs. Edward H. Flickner of Thirty-seventh street extension, a recent graduate of the Army Air Forces bombardier school at Kirtland Field, Albuquerque, N. M., has been commissioned a second lieutenant and awarded the silver wings of the aerial bombardier, supplementing previously-won aerial gunner's insignia.

In civilian life he was employed at the Babcock & Wilcox Tube company and played semi-pro football and baseball.

AT NAVAL AIR STATION

DAVID A. EDGECOMBE

Naval Aviation Cadet David A. Edgecombe, son of Mr. and Mrs. A. C. Edgecombe of Beaver Falls, has successfully completed the 11-week course at the U. S. Navy pre-flight school, Chapel Hill, N. C. He has been promoted to primary flight training at the Naval Air Station, Glenview, Ill.

Cadet Edgecombe attended Geneva College, transferring to Carnegie Tech. He is a member of the American Society of Mechanical Engineers and during his college career was interested in golf and tennis.

GUNNERY INSTRUCTOR

PVT. JOHN [illegible]

Private John [illegible], son of Mr. and Mrs. Mike [illegible] of West Mayfield is stationed at Camp Carson, Colo. He entered the service August 12, 194[illegible], having formerly been employed by the Babcock & Wilcox Tube company.

WANTED

Your RED CROSS is at his side

TO LIFT RESTRICTIONS

HARRISBURG, Mar. 21 (UP) The Liquor Control Board prepared today to lift all restrictions on sales of brandy at its 579 state stores. This move will leave only sparkling wines on the list of beverages being rationed informally on a bottle-per-customer basis.

Monaca News

Local Auxiliary To Legion Post Will Meet On Wednesday

The American Legion Auxiliary will meet in the Legion home Wednesday evening. Hostesses are Mrs. Allen I. Henfy and Mrs. Frank Curry.

Pvt. George Adamek returned Monday to Boston after visiting several days with his mother, Mrs. Josephine Adamek, Davis Lane.

Pvt. Edward Anderson, Jr., with the Army Air Forces at Baltimore, visited over the week end with his wife, Mrs. Ada Mae Anderson, and his parents, Mr. and Mrs. Edward Anderson, Sr., Davis Lane.

Cpl. Orrie Simpson returned today to Denver after visiting ten days with his wife, Nina Kaszer Simpson, Stone Quarry road, and his mother, Mrs. Hattie Simpson, Freedom.

Mr. and Mrs. Russell McCartney and family moved Saturday from their home in Davis lane to Stephen Phillips Homes.

Mrs. Fred G. Smith, Atlantic avenue, entertained the Friday night club. Two tables of "500" were in play and prizes were awarded Mrs. Wilbur Smith, Mrs. J. Edward Harper and Mrs. George Cain. Refreshments were served by the hostess, assisted by Mrs. Edwin S. Miller.

Miss Catherine McMillan, Atlantic avenue, visited over the week end with Mrs. William J. Ross, Cleveland. Miss McMillan and Mrs. Ross were former roommates at Mercyhurst College for Girls, Erie. Miss McMillan's father, J. H. E. McMillan, is spending a few days transacting business in Olean and Brooklyn, N. Y., and Erie.

Pfc. Robert O. John, Shreveport, La., is spending a ten-day furlough with his parents, Mr. and Mrs. William C. John, Sixth street.

Pfc. Frank W. Basar is spending a fifteen-day furlough with his parents, Mr. and Mrs. George Basar, Front street. He is with the Army Air Forces at Drew Field, Tampa, Fla.

Pvt. Paul D. Smith, Parris Island, S. C., is spending a ten-day furlough with his wife and children, Judy and Jackie, Linden street. He will leave Sunday to resume his duties as an instructor on the rifle range.

Mrs. Ross E. Boren, Allaire avenue, entertained her card club in her home and awarded prizes to Mrs. Wallace Sehur, Mrs. James Whittington, Mrs. Clayton Willard and Mrs. Robert Harvie.

Mrs. John R. Guthrie, Pennsylvania avenue, has returned home from Fairmont, W. Va., where she visited a week with relatives and friends.

Mrs. Josephine McComas and her sister, Miss Caroline Witterman, Washington avenue, returned from New Orleans, La., after spending ten days with Mrs. McComas' husband.

Norman Harrison, U. S. Navy, New York, has been promoted to bugler first class. Word has been received by his parents, Mr. and Mrs. Norman Harrison, Marshall road.

Ensign and Mrs. Joseph Weigel, Johnstown, visited over the week end with Ensign Weigle's parents, Mr. and Mrs. H. B. Weigel, and family, Washington avenue.

Miss Emma Larant, Pennsylvania avenue, spent Monday with friends in Pittsburgh.

Miss Mae Patterson, Brodhead road, is improving in her home, where she is confined to bed suffering from grippe.

Charles K. Sullivan and his daughters, Beryl and Ethel, Pennsylvania avenue, were guests Monday of friends in Pittsburgh.

Beaver News

Susannah Wesley Guild Plans "Sew" And Monthly Meet

The Susannah Wesley Guild of the Methodist church will sew all day Wednesday in the home of Mrs. Floyd W. Supler, Seventh street. Thursday evening at 7:45 o'clock, the Guild will meet in the home of Mrs. J. Paul Jones, River road, for its monthly session. The assistant hostesses are Mrs. Earle D. Engle, Mrs. Roy Gillespie, Mrs. Harry W. Long, Mrs. Claude E. Lutton and Mrs. Harry S. McCleery.

Robert A. Gibson, Beaver, has graduated from the Norfolk Naval hospital at Portsmouth, Va., and has been assigned to the Naval hospital staff at Quantico, Va., according to word received here. He is an hospital apprentice second class.

Pvt. Eugene I. George has arrived in England, according to word received by his parents, Mr. and Mrs. Wade E. George, Elm street. He was stationed at Camp Campbell in Kentucky and for a month before leaving for overseas duty, he was at Fort Meade, Md.

Tech. Sgt. Chester D. Harris, son of Mr. and Mrs. Chester L. Harris, Corporation street, has returned to the United States after spending two years in South America and the jungles of Trinidad. He is now at Camp Claibourne, La., and is expected home soon.

Petty Officer First Class James Shoemaker and his wife, visited recently with his brother-in-law and sister, Mr. and Mrs. Clarence L. Wagner, Fair avenue. Shoemaker is home on leave after spending more than a year in active service on a destroyer in the Southwest Pacific and expects to return to the west coast by March 25.

Mr. and Mrs. L. Dean Berry, Fourth street, spent the week end as guests of Mr. and Mrs. Raymond A. Berkihiser, Crafton Heights. The Berkihisers are former residents of Rochester.

Mrs. Edson Rodgers, Beaver, has procured a position as assistant to Dr. Andrew W. Culley, local physician, succeeding Miss Dorothy Whitehouse, Freedom, whose resignation became effective a week ago.

Miss Helen Lehew, a student at Hood College, Frederick, Md., was one of the leading characters in the dramatic production, "Ladies in Waiting," staged Saturday at the college. Miss Lehew is the daughter of Mr. and Mrs. W. C. Lehew, Dutch Ridge road.

CONFERENCE CALLED

CHICAGO, March 21 (UP)—The National Republican Agriculture Committee today scheduled a meeting with representatives of the five major farm organizations here April 3-4, prior to drafting the party's agriculture plank for the 1944 platform.

Beaver Falls

Council Refuses To Purchase Old Post Office Here

Refusal of Beaver Falls Council to purchase the old postoffice building marked the weekly meeting of the councilmen Monday in the city building. Council voted four to one that the government be notified it was not interested in procuring the building for use as a bus terminal or any other purpose at present. This leaves the path open to private enterprise to negotiate for its purchase. Council accepted the bid of one dollar from the College Hill fire department for tearing down the old hill fire station. The firemen plan to do the work themselves and use the brick to build a training tower. City Solicitor E. Y. Calvin stated it is not necessary to pass an ordinance setting up a Beaver Falls Historical Commission as the committee in charge of the recent Diamond Jubilee celebration can do so by incorporating under the laws of the state.

Mr. and Mrs. L. L. Weir, Riverview, have received word that their son, Pfc. Garth Weir, has arrived overseas.

Lieut. Gerald Braden has returned to Goodfellow Field, San Angelo, Tex., after spending a ten-day leave with his parents, Mr. and Mrs. Harry Braden, Sixth avenue. His sister, Miss Rosemary Braden, assistant field director with the American Red Cross at Fort Meyer, Arlington, Va., has concluded a four-day visit here after completing her training course at Edgewood Arsenal, Md.

Chester Monit, seaman second class in the Navy, is spending a 14-day furlough with his wife and son in Ninth avenue after completing his "boot" training at the Great Lakes Naval Training Station, Ill.

Vaunted "Fortress Europe" Proved Roofless By Allied Bombing Fleets

By RALPH E. HEINZEN
United Press Staff Correspondent

NEW YORK, Mar. 24 (UP)—Germany's Atlantic wall and its supporting defensive barriers remain to be tested, but 13 months in German internment at Baden Baden gave ample evidence that the German fortress has no roof.

In more than 200 raids on the Reich, the war has been carried to 30,000,000 Germans in more than 70 big cities. Night after night I heard the warning sirens wail. I saw the Fortresses flying over on the first great American daylight raids of the war; I watched the bombing of Mannheim, Offenbach, Frankfort and Stuttgart. I could feel the shock of the explosions miles away.

Never once did I see the American and British bombers driven off their objectives. I saw some of them drop out of the skies in flames. I also saw German fighters crash.

The Germans know now that Germany was caught short on her aid defenses. Fuehrer Adolf Hitler believed the boast of his pompous Air Reichs Marshal Herman Goering that the Allies never would overtake the lead his Luftwaffe had established at the beginning of the war.

They know that Goering's boast that he had erected a curtain of steel — an impenetrable barrier of anti-aircraft guns—to protect the homeland was merely so much talk. Ninety per cent of the Allied bombers shot down during the past year were hit over the target by local defense batteries and nightfighters. The curtain is a myth.

All Germany and Western Europe is a network of signal alarms, according to German publications. Listening apparatus picks up the sound of invaders, often when the engines are only being warmed up on their home fields in England. Radio teletypes flash the alarm to all Germany.

When the direction of the raid becomes apparent, the system operates in zones 100 miles square. Zones in the expected path are given a five-star alarm. Those nearby get a three-star alarm to stand by for a possible change in the direction of the Allied flight.

That system enabled the Nazis to inflict fairly heavy losses as long as the Americans and British flew directly to their target. The course was plotted on the big electrical board at Berlin GHQ and fighters were sent up along the line of expected course.

But the methodical Germans were upset when the Allies began to cut zig-zag courses. If the Allies intended going to Berlin they would head for Cologne, send off a few dummy raiders to attack Cassel or Mannheim, then bolt for Leipzig. When the Germans shifted all their defenses toward Leipzig, the Allies turned left and raced for Berlin. Ten or more cities have been hit in feinting attacks while the main body of bombers reached Berlin comparatively unopposed.

Another Allied trick to fool the gunners setting anti-aircraft shell fuses down below near the coastline is to send over waves of planes at different altitudes. Each wave shifts altitude frequently.

On one occasion, the Germans, convinced that Berlin was the target, called for Leipzig to hurry over all available fire apparatus as swiftly as possible. The Leipzig firemen were hell bent for Berlin when the Allied planes shifted course and set Leipzig aflame.

What Did You Do Today, My Friend?

(Lt. Dean Shatlein, tank commander, wrote this poem on the battlefield of Africa. Wounded severely, he amputated his own foot with a jackknife, and thought he was dying when he wrote this poem, but was rescued by Americans after about 2 hours of hiding and was taken to a hospital in England, where he recovered.)

★ ★ ★ ★

What did you do today, my friend,
From morning until night?
How many times did you complain
The rationing is too tight?
When are you going to start to do
All of the things you say?
A soldier would like to know, my friend,
WHAT DID YOU DO TODAY?

We met the enemy today
And took the town by storm.
Happy reading it will make
For you tomorrow morn.
You'll read with satisfaction
The brief communique
We fought, but are you fighting?
WHAT DID YOU DO TODAY?

My gunner died in my arms today;
I feel his warm blood yet;
Your neighbor's dying boy gave out
A scream I can't forget.
On my right a tank was hit,
A flash and then a fire;
The stench of burning flesh
Still rises from the pyre.

WHAT DID YOU DO TODAY, MY FRIEND,
To help us with the task?
Did you work harder and longer for less,
Or is that too much to ask,
What right have I to ask you this,
You probably will say;
Maybe now you'll understand
YOU SEE, I DIED TODAY.

REALLY MEAN THIEF

EVANSTON, Ill., March 24 (UP)—Mrs. H. D. Mitchell, Evanston, had her own idea today of the meanest person in the world. It is the sneak thief, presumably female, who stole five pre-war, two-way stretch girdles from the clothesline in the basement of her home.

HE WAS TOO CLEAN

MIAMI, Fla., March 24 (UP) Mrs. Rita Kashins, Miami, charged in starting divorce proceedings against Benjamin Kashin of New York, that he carried his germ-dodging too far. She said he washed his hands on an average of 75 times a day.

INVASION TEST CASUALTY

ONE OF MANY real casualties in massive invasion maneuvers in England, a British soldier walks ashore from a landing barge, his trousers nearly blown off and one leg burned by an explosion. Real battle conditions were maintained throughout the tests. (International)

OPA official who says rationing may be continued after the war because people like it hasn't been shopping recently.

New Brighton

Servicemen's Boxes Packed At Recent Bible Class Meet

Boxes for forty servicemen affiliated with the Fifth Avenue Methodist church were packed at the recent meeting of the Kennedy Bible class in the church. The boxes are to be Easter gifts for the men in the service. Hostesses were Mrs. Gerald Wallace, Mrs. Craig Holland and Mrs. Kenneth Bingham.

Staff Sgt. Robert M. Corfield, 21, 701 Fifth street, has been awarded the Air Medal for meritorious achievement while participating in five bombing missions over Europe. Sgt. Corfield is stationed in England and is a waist gunner on a Flying Fortress.

Mrs. Erskine Schachern, Fourth street, is confined to her home by illness.

Sgt. William Ludwig, stationed at Fort Williams, Me., is spending a furlough with his parents, Mr. and Mrs. William A. Ludwig, Eighth avenue.

Pat McKenny, stationed at Adair, Ore., is spending a furlough with his parents, Mr. and Mrs. Ray McKenny, Sixth avenue.

Mrs. Margaret Kidd, Detroit, has concluded a visit with her son and daughter-in-law, Mr. and Mrs. F. G. Harvey, Tenth street, and other relatives here.

Corp. T. Peter Shields has returned to Barkley, Tex., after a visit with his parents, Mr. and Mrs. John Shields, Third avenue. He has a brother, Corp. J. P. Shields, serving at an air field in Tennessee.

Mr. and Mrs. J. W. Eakles, Marion Hill, have received word that their son, Corp. Harry O. Eakles, who has been confined to the hospital at Camp Gordon, Ga., several weeks by a leg injury, is improving.

Pfc. Theron Klugh will return Tuesday to Elgin Field, Fla., after visiting since Saturday with his mother, Mrs. Louis Foertsch, Concord avenue.

ONE-MAN WAR PLANT

LIMA, O.—(UP)—Lester B. Prat is a one-man war plant at the age of 67. He operates a jewelry shop equipped with a lathe, which turns out the shafts for voltage regulators which keep bombers' instruments accurate on raids over Berlin and elsewhere.

Winners In State Can Collection Contest Announced

HARRISBURG, April 18 (UP) The State Defense Council today announced the names of three boys who won a total of $150 in war bonds for spearheading collections of 9,792,633 prepared tin cans by Pennsylvania school pupils during March.

Top individual honors, marked by war bond prizes of $75, $50 and $25 respectively, went to Robert Readinger, Reinerton, who collected 22,565 cans; Fred Honeywell, Warrior Run, collector of 21,560 cans, and Roy Brindle, near Chambersburg, who brought in 17,671 cans.

For the third consecutive month the Broughton school, near Wellsboro, took first prize for the school collecting the most cans on a per-pupil basis when its 18 enrolled pupils gathered 33,737 cans.

Luzerne County led all other counties with collections of 1,95,-068 prepared cans; Berks County was second with 773,096; Allegheny was third with 708,112, and Schuylkill was fourth with 543,-598.

The council's state salvage committee announced the war bond prizes for top individual pupil collections will be continued this month.

DOBBIN TO THE RESCUE

BLYTHEVILLE, Ark.—(UP)—Gas rationing forced many stores to discontinue delivery service but the Happy Hour Super Market has solved that problem. It will resume the practice of delivery service to customers through the medium of a bright, new, horse-drawn red wagon.

Save KITCHEN FATS to win the war.

SWIMMER, 13, WINS U. S. TITLE

ONLY 13, Patricia Sinclair, New York girl rates the sports headlinies as she wins the 100-yard breaststroke in the annual A. A. U. women's swim tourney at Oakland, Cal. (International)

Iron Ore Arriving By Lake Freighter

Freshly shipped iron ore from Lake Superior mines is today moving into Pittsburgh district plants of U. S. Steel Corporation subsidiaries to replenish stock piles, worn thin by a winter of record-breaking iron and steel-making operations.

The first ore boat of the year to reach the Conneaut, Ohio, facilities of the Pittsburgh and Conneaut Dock Company, the J. J. Hill of the Pittsburgh Steamship Company, docked yesterday and within less than four hours ore from its holds was en route in railroad cars to the Pittsburgh mills.

This was 16 days earlier than the first vessel docking at Conneaut last year, the Myron C. Taylor which arrived April 29.

The chief raw material of steel, 1.78 tons of iron ore are required to make one ton of pig iron in the blast furnace, the first metallurgical step in steel-making. The other principal raw materials are coke and limestone.

MacDonald Blocked Hoover Navy Plan At Parley In 1929

WASHINGTON, Apr. 18. (UP)—State Department papers revealed today that British Prime Minister Ramsy MacDonald, at the last minute of his 1929 conference with President Herbert Hoover, eliminated from the final announcement the Hoover proposal to divide the world into two hemispheres for purposes of naval base limitation.

MacDonald became "troubled about public opinion" at home and "frightened" about possible repercussions of the naval base proposal which would have pledged the United States not to build new bases in the Far East and Great Britain not to build any in the Western Hemisphere.

He also eliminated all reference to another Hoover proposal designed to eliminate starvation of civilian populations by naval blockade as a weapon of war. Mr. Hoover wanted to grant food ships in wartime the same immunity from attack as hospital ships.

These hitherto unpublished proposals were made public by the State Department in two volumes of papers on U. S. foreign relations for 1929. Each year the department publishes papers that are 15 years old.

The Interior Department buys food for resale in Puerto Rico and the Virgin Islands from a $15,000,-000 revolving fund appropriated by Congress.

SCOTT'S SCRAP BOOK By R. J. SCOTT

THE GIANT WATER BUG WILL ATTACK A FROG
SCRAPS
AN ABANDONED 300,000-GALLON WINE BARREL WAS CONVERTED INTO A RESTAURANT, SEATING 500 PEOPLE - BAVARIA
WHAT RIVER IN ALL THE WORLD HAS THE GREATEST AMOUNT OF TONNAGE PASSING THROUGH IT?
THE DETROIT RIVER
THE AFRICAN KAFFA BUFFALO IS CONSIDERED THE DEADLIEST OF ALL WILD ANIMALS

Amusements

Oriental Theatre

When a man asks you to marry him, that's love. And when a vaudevillian asks you to be his stage partner, that's business. But when the man is a vaudevillian, asks you to marry him, and to be his stage partner as well—that's the history of Nora Bayes — one of America's best - remembered singers whose life is the basis for "Shine On Harvest Moon," now playing at the Oriental theatre. Starring Ann Sheridan as Nora Bayes, and Dennis Morgan as Jack Norworth, her husband, the film depicts the rise of the first of the torch-singers from her early days in a Milwaukee honky-tonk, to the success, which eventually befell her as one of the biggest of Ziegfeld's stars.

A rare mixture of nostalgic story and song against a background of the early 1900's, including gaslight and old time tunes — "Shine On Harvest Moon," "When It's Apple Blossom Time in Normandy," and "Take Me Out To The Ball Game" being just a few of them, "Shine On Harvest Moon," tells the tribulations which befell the young lovers before they finally "arrived."

A consistently fine cast includes Irene Manning, remembered for her outstanding performance as the singing lead in "Desert Song," Jack Carson and Marie Wilson who contribute some top-notch comedy.

Majestic Theatre

Complete with girls, tunes and zany situations, "Rosie the Riveter" opens Wednesday at the Majestic Theatre.

One of Hollywood's newer young starlets, Jane Frazee, provides the songs and contributes much to the eye-appeal of the picture which is based on the housing shortage and its effect upon four defense plant workers.

The riotous results of a "swing-shift" arrangement between two girls and two men for sharing the one available room in town, constitutes the plot of the musical. In addition to the title song, the picture features several other "hit" tunes, and several dozen beautiful girls.

Miss Frazee proves herself a capable young actress as well as a singer, and she and Frank Albertson handle the romantic roles ably while Vera Vague, who is amazingly lovely to look at, carries the comedy with the aid of top-notch comedian Frank Jenks.

"Amazing Mr. Forrest" is the added feature for Wednesday and Thursday.

Beaver Theatre

Little Margaret O'Brien, who brought a lump to the throats of millions of moviegoers in "Journey for Margaret" and "You, John Jones," is now playing in her first starring role. This time a comedy tailor-made to her talents, "Lost Angel." The film is now showing at the Beaver Theatre.

Margaret appears as a child prodigy reared scientifically by a group of professors. She is a mental marvel but has never kown the true joy and tenderness of childhood. Then James Craig, playing a breezy newspaper reporter, appears on the scene and captivates her with a promise to show her magic. Not only does he capture her imagination but her heart as well. And in return Margaret brings joy and happiness to him and girl girl1234566 ness to him and his girl, played by lovely Marsha Hunt.

"In Our Time" opens tomorrow. This remarkable love story, clouded with the hardships of current events, takes place in Poland, just at the beginning of the war.

Ida Lupino and Paul Henreid have the leading roles. Also featured are Nancy Coleman, Mary Boland, Victor Francen and Nazimova.

SAVES FOR 'OLD AGE'

DENVER, Col.—(UP) — Henry Hall, a sprucely-dressed Negro with a flowing beard and trim mustache, has a ready explanation for the thrift that has enabled him to accumulate more than $800. He is "saving the money for a rainy day or maybe old age." Hall is 104 years old.

Earlier names of the Congressional Record were the Annals of Conress, Register of Debates, and Congressional Globe.

Wife Preservers

To add a particularly good flavor to your meat gravy, add a little chopped green pepper, especially to beef or lamb

A *Model is Murdered* ~ BABS LEE

CHAPTER TWENTY-FOUR

"What are you doing here?" Argus asked Ellen.

"I have a date," she said mysteriously, "with Roger Flagg. I ran into him coming out of a jewelry store on Madison Avenue and Forty-seventh Street and he invited me to lunch."

"Where is he now?"

"Checking his hat and coat. Here he comes!"

Flagg joined them and greeted both Argus and Donna cordially. "This is fine," he smiled. "Now we can all have lunch together."

"I have another engagement," said Donna, sliding off her stool. "Thanks for the drink, Mr. Steele. Goodbye."

"Well," queried Flagg, looking squarely at Argus. "How about you?"

"Delighted," said Steele.

When they were seated, Flagg said: "I'm sorry you were put on the spot with that reporter from the *Blade* yesterday."

"Don't apologize, Roger," said Ellen. "From where I stood he seemed to be suffering no pain whatsoever."

"It was all your fault in the first place, red head," Argus demurred. "If you find you've lost a perfectly good prospective husband, don't forget you were the one wanted me to meet you in Mr. Flagg's office and come to the fashion show."

The waiter stood by attentively as Flagg consulted with Ellen and Argus and then gave the order.

"Tell me," said Flagg, when the waiter had gone. "Have the police found anything new? The papers haven't told much."

"The police have done a great deal," declared Argus. "My friend the Inspector tells me that either you, or some one in your apartment Monday night, phoned Syria Verne." Argus watched him out of the corner of his eye.

Flagg frowned. "They must be mistaken. I don't recall any phone calls having been made from my place that night. Anyway, what would that have to do with it?"

"Just a routine checkup, I guess," Argus said. "Sure that none of the fellows you were playing poker with didn't phone?"

"No," answered Flagg, puzzled. "But you can ask them if you want to. I'll give you their names and addresses before we leave here. I didn't know there was any way of checking calls on dial phones."

"Apparently the police have a way," Argus said. "Oh, and there was something else. Some one overheard you quarrelling with Syria the other day—said you mentioned something about having 'lost'."

"I don't remember," declared Flagg.

"I understand that Syria had gotten her movie contract quite independent of your organization and that she was planning not to pay you any commission."

Flagg's eyes flickered. "That's quite true," he admitted.

"I thought perhaps that was the reason you said something about having 'lost'."

"I could have," Flagg admitted. "Strange, isn't it, the significance of little things when people become involved in a murder case?"

"Speaking of movie contracts," said Ellen, "this should interest you, Argus, since I shall probably have to support you in your old age. I was offered two hundred dollars a week and a movie contract all my very own, this morning."

"Who offered it to you?"

"Your friend from Superba."

"It's not enough," objected Flagg. "I'll tell him so when I get back to the office."

"But honestly, Roger, don't you think two hundred a week is a lot for a gal that can't even act?" Ellen asked.

"And who's going to know it when they look at that lovely face of yours on the screen?" Flagg countered. "No, sir. Three hundred's the minimum you can accept." The model-agent remained adamant.

The waiter hovered about. Argus congratulated Ellen. Flagg explained why he believed he could get Ellen a better contract. Argus thought he must have told Syria the same thing, once.

"There's a pretty one," said Argus, looking across the room. A girl was sitting with a man in the far corner of the restaurant. She had fair hair, a retroussé nose and wide mouth. She was talking animatedly to her companion.

"What do you do in a case like that?" Argus asked. "Just go over and introduce yourself and say, 'Pardon me, miss, but would you like to become a famous model?' I should think it might be a temptation."

Flagg laughed. "No. Fortunately I never have to do that. If and when I am introduced to an attractive girl, I might suggest, if I think she'd be interested, that she come to my office. But usually the girls come either to me or to one of my rivals—John Robert Powers or Harry Conover."

"Lucky guys, you three!" Argus exclaimed. "You've built such fancy mousetraps. Is there any particular type of 'mice' you like especially?"

"No," said Flagg. "So long as a girl has good bone structure and a certain amount of intelligence, beauty, as such, is not so important. I can usually groom her to become a good model. You see it isn't always the beautiful girls that photograph the best."

"That's why there's so much talk about being photogenic," Ellen said.

"How did you happen to get started in this business?" Argus asked Flagg.

"Well," said Flagg, "after the war I batted around doing odd jobs all over the country. I've been a lumberjack, a wireless operator, a truck driver and—yes—at one time an actor. I played the weight lifter in a play about the circus that made a tour of the sticks one summer. Then the doctor told me I'd have to take it easy—my lungs weren't too good after that old touch of war gas. I drifted into New York and bumped into a friend of mine in the advertising business. He wanted a model for a campaign."

Flagg smiled. "He described the girl he wanted and offered twenty dollars to any one who could find her. She was a difficult type to find. But I found her. And then I started getting models for his agency and accounts. That's about it. I went on from there and opened an agency."

"Sounds like a checkered career," smiled Ellen.

Flagg glanced at his wrist watch. It was flat and gold with a tan leather strap. "It's 2:20. I've got to get back to my office. Can I drop you, Ellen—Mr. Steele?"

"Oh, swell!" said Ellen. "My job's across the street from you." She slipped into her coat.

"You two run along," waved Argus.

"Here's the list of names of the fellows with whom I played poker on Monday night," said Flagg, hurriedly scribbling them down on a piece of paper. "Oh, and I meant to ask you—did you get that letter you expected from Cynthia Lane? The one she wrote before she was killed?"

"Yes," answered Argus.

"Inspector Grange is handling that letter detail. I think it will produce fireworks."

When Ellen and Flagg had departed, Argus phoned the five men Flagg had played poker with. From each he received approximately the same reply. The models' agent had had a winning streak that had started around eleven and continued until the game broke up at 2:30. Not once during that time had Flagg left the table.

It was about 8 p.m., when Argus returned to his apartment. Butch greeted him at the door. "I thought maybe I'd cook some fried chicken and biscuits for yuh, boss," he said. "Yuh know yuh been eatin' out a lot lately. Yuh don't get the proper nourish—"

"Grand idea, Butch! Sounds swell!" He slapped him on the shoulder. "Did a package come for me?"

"Yeah. It's in the living room. It come from some air-conditioning place. I untied it and put it in de livin' room. I didn't know what you wanted done wid it."

"That's okay. We'll leave it there." The detective walked into the living room, glanced casually at the machine and sat down to read an evening paper. The front page had pictures of Syria, Cynthia Lane and a small one of himself. The caption over his read: "Sleuth Searches for Redbeard in Model Killing. He read on:

"Argus Steele, internationally known detective and mystery story writer, is searching for a man disguised with a red beard and glasses, it was learned on good authority, today. Steele heretofore has denied that he is working on the model murder mystery. Elmer Gamp, elevator boy in the apartment building atop which the late Miss Verne's penthouse was located, confirmed the story of the mysterious redbeard...."

(To be continued)

New Brighton

Speaker Announced For Memorial Day Observance Here

Lawrence D. Smith, prominent New Brighton citizen and Beaver Falls school teacher, has been procured as the speaker for Memorial Day here. Lt. L. E. Craven has again been named chief marshal of the parade. Police Chief Sam Kennedy was appointed to the city traffic committee. The committee in charge of the union church service to be held Sunday evening, May 28, has organized a tentative program. Members of the committee are: V. A. Mathis, Merran Reader, Chester K. Kennedy, Rev. F. O. Christofer, Mrs. Alice Linn, Mrs. William Mitsch and E. H. Carey.

Arriving as a surprise, Lt. Anthony P. Koricansky, son of Mr. and Mrs. Steve Koricansky, Nineteenth street, is spending a leave with his parents. He is enroute to Lincoln, Neb., where he will pilot a B-24 Liberator bomber.

A meeting of the Belle Crawford Guild of Grace Methodist church will be held this evening in the home of Esther Clarkson, Third avenue.

SHIPYARD STRIKE ENDS

CHESTER, May 5, (UP)—Full production was resumed today at the Sun Shipbuilding and Drydock Co. yards following a return-to-work vote by 300 striking piecework counters. The vote taken Wednesday assured the return of more than 6,000 piecework employes, idle for two days. The pieceworkers voted to resume if the counters returned to their jobs.

U. S.-British Oil Parley Concluded

WASHINGTON, May 5 (UP)—The joint Anglo-American Middle East Supply Council will be retained after the war and may be assigned the task of co-ordinating production and distribution of Middle East oil by both American and British interests, it was learned today.

The disclosure followed a State Department announcement that Anglo-American technical experts have ended two weeks of exploratory discussions on postwar petroleum problems and will now report their recommendations to their respective governments.

The participants revealed that both groups were agreed that fears of a world oil famine are unfounded—that known and indicated oil supplies in the world are adequate and that future plans should be built upon orderly development of those resources rather than on a prospective oil rationing program.

The conferees were said to have agreed that the control for such development should be placed in an advisory committee of experts so constituted and empowered that its recommendations would be acceptable to both governments.

The Weather Forecast
WESTERN PENNSYLVANIA: Scattered thundershowers this afternoon and tonight, becoming cooler in west portion today.

"The Paper That Goes Home"

THE DAILY TIMES

1874—and WESTERN ARGUS—1906

ROCHESTER - BEAVER - MONACA - FREEDOM - BRIDGEWATER - CONWAY - VANPORT - MIDLAND

Beaver County History
The British battleship "Goliath", was sunk May 13, 1915, local residents learned.

4 Cents

Established April 2, 1874 | Beaver and Rochester, Pa., Saturday, May 13, 1944 | By Carrier 24 Cents A Week

ALLIES HIT MAIN GERMAN DEFENSES IN ITALY

STATE DRAFT BOARDS FACE HEAVY TASK

Big Reclassification Job Confronts Local Boards As Result Of New Draft Policy; One Or Two More Induction Stations May Close

HARRISBURG, May 13 (UP) Another big reclassification job faced the state's 432 local Selective Service boards today as a result of the new national draft policy and it appeared one or two more induction stations may be closed because of the drop in Army and Navy manpower quotas.

State Selective Service headquarters said Maj. Gen. Lewis B. Hershey's latest directive, which was sent from Washington straight to local boards, was "self-explanatory" as to the reclassification of "necessary" men 26 to 29 years old and those over 30 who are merely "regularly engaged in" essential work.

Local boards will be required to review all registrants in these groups, state headquarters said, to carry out Hershey's orders that:

1. Physically fit registrants 26 through 29 are to be placed or retained in 2-A or 2-B—or reclassified from 1-A—if found by the local board "necessary to and regularly engaged in" an activity in support of the national health, safety, interest or war production.

2. Registrants 30 through 37, regardless of physical status, are to be placed or retained in 2-A or 2-B—or reclassified from 1-A—if they are merely "regularly engaged in" essential work.

JUST COMPLETED JOB

The boards have just completed a classification review of all 18-to-25-year-olds deferred for essential agriculture work or other occupation in response to Hershey's April 8 ban on induction of registrants over 25 employed in essential or war contributing activities.

Closing induction stations in addition to Greensburg, which ceased operations last month, rests with the armed forces, state headquarters said, but pointed out that Selective Service began operating in 1940 with only five centers in Philadelphia, Pittsburgh, Wilkes-Barre, Harrisburg and Altoona.

Allentown and Erie were added later followed by Greensburg. This last station was closed last month and personnel shifted to Erie. The announcement at Washington that Army-Navy calls for the rest of the year were expected to be lowered to 100,000 to 150,000 monthly will reduce the work of the Pennsylvania induction centers proportionately, it was pointed out.

Rev. Paul Freligh Gets New Charge

Rev. Paul E. Freligh, pastor of the Marion Hill Christian and Missionary Alliance church, and Mrs. Freligh, well known residents of Marion Hill, will leave May 30 for their new post in Seattle, Wash. The University Gospel Tabernacle of the Christian and Missionary Alliance church, is Rev. Freligh's new assignment.

Rev. and Mrs. Freligh, former missionaries, have spoken frequently in the Valley and are prominent throughout county religious circles.

Rochester Soldier Home From Pacific For Mothers Day

It will be a real Mothers Day Sunday for Mr. and Mrs. Joseph Nitsche, Reno street, Rochester, as they spend it with their son, Pfc. Rudolph Nitsche, who returned early this morning from eighteen months of active duty with the Quartermaster Corps in the South Pacific.

Having served a total of twenty-seven months, Private Nitsche, 41, has received an honorable discharge. While overseas he served in Australia, New Guinea and several islands. He received his early training at Camp Lee, Va. A brother, Louis J. Nitsche, fireman second class, is stationed in Gulfport, Miss.

FALL IS FATAL

PITTSBURGH, May 13 (UP)—A fall of 80 feet from a smoke stack of the LaBelle paint, Crucible Steel Company, last Thursday led to the death of Joseph Lazar, 41, yesterday in Presbyterian hospital. He suffered a fractured skull.

FREEDOM HIGH MAY QUEEN CROWNED AT CEREMONY

Freedom's "May Queen" Dorothy Borro, was crowned at colorful festivities this week in the high school auditorium. Seated upon the throne is the queen, and at her feet are little Kim McCracken, Joyce Stacel, left, and Judy Ann Borro, right. Standing, left to right, are: Jane McCauley, Nellie Keller, Peggy Black, Thelma Jean Fry, Helen Schumney, Laura West, Betty Jean Coulter and Martha Parks, the queen's attendants. — (Graule Photo)

U. S. Subs Sinking Japs Ships At Rate Of Over One Daily

WASHINGTON, May 13. (UP)—American submarines have seen sinking Japanese ships at a rate of better than one a day during the last six months, a United Press analysis showed today.

Since Nov. 1 of last year, navy announcements have added up a total of 203 enemy vessels sunk by U. S. underseas craft. This is a monthly average of more than 33 ships.

The Germans chalked up a higher daily average in the summer of 1942 when their U-boats sank Allied ships at a rate of about three a day. Nevertheless the American average is considered relatively good since our submarines do not have as many targets to shoot at as the Germans had. Furthermore, Japan's shipyard capacity is hopelessly outstripped by her merchant losses to date.

The over-all total of Japanese ships sent to the bottom by American submarines since the start of the war reached 558 with the navy's announcement yesterday that our underseas raiders had sunk 14 more of the enemy's vessels.

TWENTY U. S. SUBS LOST

In addition to the 558 ships sunk, the Navy listed 36 more as probably sunk and 115 dam-

Continued on Page Ten

Center Township To Have Graduation

The tentative date set for the Center Township Eighth Grade graduation exercises was set for Thursday, May 25, at the monthly meeting of Center Township Board of Education. Forty-seven members compose the class.

Plans also are underway for a May Day program to be presented Friday evening, May 19 in the school. May 29 marks the closing of school for the summer vacation. Richard Weigle, president, presided.

PRIEST RETURNS

SPRINGFIELD, Mass., May 13 (UP)—The Rev. Stanislaus Orlemanski, greeted with cheers on his return home from his much-criticized mission to Moscow today, announced that he will go to Washington at a later date to report to "my government" on his conferences with Premier-Marshal Josef Stalin.

ROCHESTER HOSPITAL STORK DERBY IS THREE-WAY RACE

By GLADYS GIBBONS

Hovering over Rochester hospital Friday, that long-legged bird, the Stork, somehow seemed reluctant to pay his usual visit. It was "National Hospital Day" and the hospital offered a $25 war bond to the first baby to arrive there on that day.

Day waned and the night fell, but still no sounds of a new-born babe's first cries. Two expectant mothers, in the hospital all day, were joined by another. It was nearing the hour of ten, and there was a feeling of anxiety.

Doctors were arriving, nurses were scurrying here and there, each of the three fathers-to-be was eagerly awaiting the arrival of his child, and in the corridor with the hospital superintendent, Mrs. Olive Nelson, were several members of the hospital staff and your reporter. It was a neck-to-neck race, and there was plenty of hushed excitement.

Then it happened! Movie-fashion, Nurse Twila Lundell Delp, the hospital "mother", appeared, carrying in her arms two baby boys. Hurrying to weigh and clothe the tiny creatures, she announced: "There are three of them, all boys" And there were. All had been delivered within exactly twenty minutes, the first at ten o'clock, the second at 10:14,

Continued on Page Ten

Decrease Reported In Relief Payments To County People

State Treasurer G. Harold Wagner reported that direct relief payments made to needy residents of Beaver County during the week ended today show a decrease of $6 from those of the previous week. Payments for the week totaled $565, which was $249 lower than those of the comparable week of last year.

At the same time, Wagner announced total payments of $27,808 for all types of categorical assistance—that is, Old Age Assistance, Aid to Dependent Children, and Pensions for the Blind—paid Beaver Countians during April Following is a comparison of payments made last month and during March:

April — Old Age Assistance, $17,112; Aid to Dependent Children, $5,597; Pensions for the Blind, $5,100.

March — Old Age Assistance, $28,210; Aid to Dependent Children, $5,967; Pensions for the Blind, $5,070.

WORKERS STRICKEN ILL

PHILADELPHIA, May 13 — (UP)—Eighteen employes of the West Philadelphia plant of Collins and Aikman, Inc., were detained in hospitals today for treatment of food poisoning apparently suffered in the company's cafeteria. At least 27 employes were hospitalized last night after becoming ill while at work.

Dies Not To Seek Re-Election Because Of Throat Ailment

WASHINGTON, May 13. (UP)—The sudden and unexpected decision of Rep. Martin Dies, D., Tex., to retire from Congress when his present term expires left in doubt today the future of the special committee investigating unAmerican activities over which he has presided since May, 1938.

Dies announced yesterday in Texas, after seeing a throat specialist, that an ailment of serious nature forced him to make the decision. He visited the specialist after he lost his voice during a speaking tour.

There is no doubt that the unAmerican activities, investigation will continue through the present Congress in the same tenor that has characterized it since it began. But beyond that, there is a real question as to

Continued on Page Ten

WOUNDED

Mr. and Mrs. Omar J. Davis, Fifth avenue, Freedom, have received word from their son, Lt. William J. Davis, (above) that he was wounded at Anzio Beachhead on April 27. He wrote that his right arm was injured, but tells his folk "not to worry, it is not too bad." Lieutenant Davis has been serving overseas since January. His wife, Mrs. Rachel Gage Davis, is with her parents at Merridian, Miss.

Floyd Chalfant, State Official, To Speak At Beaver

Floyd Chalfant, secretary of the State Department of Commerce, who is to be guest speaker at the annual public dinner of the Beaver County Council of Republican Women at 6:30 o'clock Tuesday, May 16, in the Methodist church, Beaver, was formerly editor of THE TIMES. He left Beaver in 1925, after having been a resident of Beaver seven years, going to Waynesboro, where he purchased the Waynesboro "Record Herald."

Mr. Chalfant became a member of Governor Martin's cabinet in January, 1943. In the Department of Commerce are vested the State Planning Board and the Pennsylvania Aeronautics Commission. Secretary Chalfant is chairman of both of these boards.

Although much of Mr. Chalfant's work has to be done in Harrisburg, he still maintains his newspaper in Waynesboro, where the Chalfants reside.

Reservations may be made with the following Council members: Miss Estella MacMillen, Court House; Mrs. Ray P. McKenny, New Brighton; Mrs. William B. Brown, Rochester; Mrs. George H. Kelley, Ambridge; Mrs. Fred S. High, Midland; Mrs. Donald L. White or Mrs. James W. Mackall, Brighton Township; Mrs. Herman T. Romigh, Freedom; Mrs. George Hemphill, Beaver Falls; Mrs. Carl Vogt, Monaca; Mrs. Isaac James or Mrs. H. M. Brown, Aliquippa, or Mrs. George L. Shaw, Beaver.

Beaver Accountant "Takes Day Off" On 87th Birthday

In the quiet dignity of his home at 340 College avenue, Beaver, Arthur S. Palfray quietly observed his 87th birthday anniversary Friday. Throughout the afternoon and evening he chatted with friends who called to congratulate and wish him well. Actually, he "took the day off" from his arduous daily work as a public accountant, except to attend to his daily business correspondence and read some of the "birthday" messages received.

He is the last surviving member of a noted New England family, has devoted himself exclusively to accounting work for more than forty years, and has been a resident of Beaver for many years. As a boy he learned much about the leather business in Boston, and as a young man he became widely known in that industry. Business connections in earlier life took him to Mexico, South America, Canada and to England.

Last March, before he had fully recovered from an attack of pneumonia, Mr. Palfray handled more than a hundred income tax accounts at his office in his home. He remarked they were not the short and easy forms either. Usually reticent about himself and his work, Mr. Palfray keeps himself well informed on local, national and world events, including progress in all phases of the war.

FOUR AERIAL FLEETS BLAST JAPS' BASES

Heavy Attacks Made On Enemy Strongpoints Over Wide Area Of Pacific; Island Captured By Chinese Forces; Allied Planes Blast Japs In China

By UNITED PRESS

The United States brought the power of four aerial forces into its concentrated campaign on the Caroline Islands today in the increasing Pacific offensive which saw American planes in new attacks on widespread Japanese bases from the Central to the Southwest Pacific.

The raids were centered on Truk, which was hit on two successive days in individual attacks by South and Central Pacific Liberators to round out the 44th and 45th assaults on the big enemy base. A total of 158 tons of bombs was dropped on the atoll's installations Wednesday and Thursday and eight enemy planes were destroyed, together with probably two others in the first attack.

OTHER BASES HIT

The combined forces also hit other Caroline bases, including the easternmost island of Kusaie; Ponape, 436 miles east of Truk; Alet Island, 200 miles west of Truk, and Murilo in the Hall Islands, 150 miles north of Truk. An enemy fighter was damaged 300 miles eat of the Palau Islands.

Two planes from Solomons bases were lost in a new raid on Rabaul, New Britain, on Wednesday, when the area was hit with 44 tons of bombs.

In the Southwest, Allied planes again struck the Wewak Hansa Bay area in British New Guinea, and the Wakde area in Dutch New Guinea. Ground troops continued to mop up the Hollandia and Aitape areas and killed an additional 69 Japanese Thursday and captured 45.

CHINESE TAKE ISLAND

In Chungking it was announced

Continued on Page Ten

Ship Blast Takes Lives Of Seventeen

BOSTON, May 13 (UP)—A naval court of inquiry began an investigation today of a series of mysterious explosions aboard a 132-foot Navy lighter carrying condemned ammunition, in which 17 sailors apparently lost their lives.

The vessel burned and sank within 35 minutes Thursday in the fog shrouded Atlantic off Boston, the Navy announced yesterday.

As the self-propelled lighter was wracked by explosions that sent pellets flying across a 14-mile area northeast of Boston, 14 officers and men leaped for their lives. One of this group died of burns at a Chelsea hospital. The others suffered only slight injuries. Navy land and sea craft were searching the area for 16 men listed as missing.

Almost two-thirds of the vessel's load of condemned ammunition from the Hingham Naval Depot had been brought up on the deck and jettisoned when the first of the mysterious detonations occurred.

Army Planes Coming To Local Airfield

C. A. P. members, cadets, and Air Forces Cadets and prospective cadets will receive their "orientation ride" May 14, 15 and 16 at the Patterson Heights airfield. Six Army liaison planes will be at the disposal of Lt. Joseph P. Russell, commanding officer of the 66th Squadron, C. A. P. Cadets may report any day they wish.

VANPORT'S OUTSTANDING PUPILS

Classmates of Juanita Mae Reed and John Waddell, Jr., (above) in the Eighth grade of the Vanport school this week chose them as the outstanding boy and girl, to receive the Beaver American Legion Post and Auxiliary awards at the annual graduation Thursday evening, May 25.

Miss Reed is the only daughter of Mr. and Mrs. Glenn G. Reed of Water avenue, Vanport. She has attended the Vanport school the past seven years, is active in school and community affairs, plays the piano, and is a Girl Scout. She is one of the brightest students.

John, son of Mr. and Mrs. John Waddell, 34-A street, [illegible] Homes, formerly of Monaca, is also one of the honor students. He is president of his class.

THREE TOWNS, FIVE HILLS ARE CAPTURED

TODAY'S WAR SUMMARY

By UNITED PRESS

ITALY—Allied armies, driving toward Rome, rout enemy from outer strongholds, capture three towns and five hills and engage main defenses of Gustav line.

AIR WAR—Big forces of Allied bombers and fighters fly against Western Germany after British night raiders dump 2,000 tons of explosives on crippled rail network behind anti-invasion wall.

RUSSIA—Red Army troops beat off new attacks on Soviet bridgehead on Lower Dnestr near Chisinau.

YUGOSLAVIA—Allied forces, supporting Yugoslav partisans offensive in Montenegro, reported to have destroyed all German strongholds near Podgorica on Albanian frontier.

PACIFIC—Four American aerial forces concentrate on campaign against Caroline islands.

Heavy fighting raged on the 25-mile front above Cassino to the Tyrrhenian Sea today as the opposing forces in Italy swayed back and forth in the first onslaught of the 1944 Allied campaign to crush Germany.

The great aerial offensive from Britain against Northwestern Europe went on uninterrupted with large forces of Allied daylight bombers again over the continent after a night during which the RAF dropped some 2,000 tons of bombs on the railway networks of France and Belgium, concentrating their heaviest attack on the junctions of Louvain and Hasselt in Belgium.

The Allied Fifth and Eighth armies in Italy drove well into the outer defenses of the German Gustav line but met with fierce resistance and had difficulty holding some of their preliminary gains. It was announced that they had taken at least three towns and five hills. London reported that in some places the Allies had advanced two to three miles but had been checked in others.

Fifth Army troops were forced to fall back to the outskirts of one town they had penetrated, while the Eighth Army at Cassino yielded a foothold it had gained at heavy cost on Hill 560 overlooking Monastery Hill, after beating off six counter-attacks.

BATTLES RAGING

The Germans were fighting from strongly prepared positions in the hills above and below Cassino and across the Rapido and Garigliano rivers. Some of the heaviest fighting was around Castelforte towards the seaward end of the line, where American troops of the Fifth Army captured four hills and the French another.

Gen. Sir Harold R. L. G. Alexander, Allied commander in Italy, warned the troops before the offensive started that the fighting would be hard and bitter and perhaps long. At the same time he reminded them that they have superior force and confidently predicted that the German armies in Italy would be destroyed.

In addition to the umbrella of

Continued on Page Ten

East Rochester Man Is Held For Buying Stolen Auto Tires

Facing a charge of buying stolen automobile tires, Charles F. Fox, 40, operator of a service station on the Rochester-Freedom boulevard, East Rochester, was in custody of the FBI and Pittsburgh city police, it was reported today by County Detective M. J. Kane.

Fox, the officers stated, was taken into custody in the course of an investigation following the arrest of the alleged leaders of a Pittsburgh stolen car ring. Phillip Lawrence, Mt. Vernon street, Pittsburgh, and John Harris, Laurel street, Pittsburgh, Detective Kane said, were arrested by Pittsburgh city detectives for stealing cars and stripping them of tires and other accessories. They named Fox, the officer said, as the purchaser of a number of tires from stolen cars. Another Pittsburgh man, Leo Brown, Kane said, is alleged to have been implicated and has been apprehended by Cleveland police.

County Detectives Kane and Howard Murray, state police, Pittsburgh detectives and FBI agents all cooperated in the investigation of the stolen car ring's activities in the Valley.

Cadet Nurses To Be Sworn Today

Members of the Providence Hospital Cadet Nurse Corps were to be formally inducted in ceremonies in the hospital at 4:30 p. m. today. The induction program will be held in connection with nation-wide ceremonies, centering about a broadcast from Washington, in which all cadet nurses in the United States will be sworn in.

Col. J. Howard Swick, U. S. Army, retired, will preside at the hospital ceremonies at which 34 girls will be inducted. A group from the Beaver Falls high school orchestra will provide instrumental music.

Grandson Of Local Folk Missing

Mr. and Mrs. Thomas Morris, Canal street, Bridgewater, received word Thursday that their grandson, Lieut. Harold Reich, is reported missing in action in the European area. Lieut. Reich is the only son of Mr. and Mrs. Fred Reich, Alexandria, Va., former Bridgewater residents. He was a pilot on an Army bomber. Mrs. Morris left Friday evening for a visit in the Reich home. Young Reich was also a nephew of Jack Morris, a well-known Valley aviator and instructor, now of Washington, D. C.

New Strike Occurs At Johnstown Plant

PITTSBURGH, May 13. (UP)—An "erroneous" report that two men who had refused to oil machinery had been discharged was blamed today in part for a strike involving 550 men at the wheel plant of the Bethlehem Steel Corp., Johnstown.

Some of the other employes involved left their jobs Wednesday in another dispute, Hough general manager, said

Committee Plans Monaca Ceremony

At a committee meeting Friday evening in the Monaca American Legion home, plans were made for the "I Am An American Day" program to be presented at 2:30 o'clock, May 21 in Monaca high school. Judge Walter Braham, New Castle, will be the speaker.

THE DAILY TIMES

1874—and WESTERN ARGUS—1803

ROCHESTER - BEAVER - MONACA - FREEDOM - BRIDGEWATER - CONWAY - VANPORT - MIDLAND

Established April 2, 1874 | Beaver and Rochester, Pa., Tuesday, May 23, 1944 | Single Copy 4 Cents — 24 Cents A Week

OFFENSIVE IS LAUNCHED BY ALLIES AT ANZIO

U. S. LOSSES LOW IN WAKDE ISLES BATTLE

Twenty Japs Killed For Every American Lost In Capture Of Islands; Airstrip Speedily Put In Use By U. S. Forces

By UNITED PRESS

American troops who wrested the Wakde Islands from the Japanese killed nearly 20 men for every American lost and began using the captured airstrip Sunday, 48 hours after it was taken, Gen. Douglas MacArthur announced today.

Meanwhile, Admiral Chester W. Nimitz maintained official silence on Japanese reports that a huge American task force had raided Marcus island, 1,150 miles southeast of Tokyo. The Japanese claimed that 32 of 132 attacking American planes were shot down.

MacArthur said 833 Japanese were killed when the Americans took over the Wakde islands and captured the airstrip, situated on Insoemoar, the larger of the two islands. Virtually no prisoners were taken.

In contrast, American losses were 41 dead, 135 wounded, two missing.

AIRSTRIP SPEEDILY USED

The speed with which American engineers repaired the 4,700-foot long Wakde airstrip, situated on Insoemoar, the larger of the two islands, was indicated by the announcement that transports bringing supplies began landings on the strip Sunday, two days after American ground forces had fought the Japanese across the strip and trapped them in a corner of the island.

The communique said that mopping up operations continued in the Wakde-Sarmi area.

American artillery and destroyers shelled enemy positions on the Dutch New Guinea mainland Saturday, with artillery fire blasting Maffin village west of the American bridgehead across the Tor river. The enemy returned the fire with mortar shells which raked the bridgehead.

BASES BOMBARDED

The destroyers joined with American fighters and bombers in blasting Japanese positions near Sarmi, 20 miles west of the Wakde islands, destroying ammunition dumps, and aiding American forces advancing westward along the coast.

Fifth Air Force bombers continued the assault on enemy positions in the western area of Dutch New Guinea, with Liberators hitting and starting fires at airdromes at Manokwari, a coastal town, and Moemi, while Mitchell mediums damaged several barges and small craft in Mawi bay to the south.

Allied air patrols along the western Dutch New Guinea coast strafed Japanese shipping, sinking one vessel and damaging others, while northwest of Manokwari another enemy coastal vessel was forced aground.

Price Regulations To Be Explained

A meeting for wholesalers and retailers who price their commodities by regulation GMPR will be held in Pittsburgh on Monday, May 29, at 10:30 a. m. in the Chamber of Commerce Building, second floor auditorium, for the purpose of explaining GMPR Amendment 61. Also, for all wholesalers and retailers of women's, girls', children's and infants' outer apparel as priced by MPR 330, Amendment 1, a new amendment pertaining to this regulation will be discussed and explained.

Should any retailer not be able to attend and desires the information, he may contact Jerry R. Herbst, District Price Specialist, for all details and information concerning this regulation.

The new 3 (a) applications must be used after June 1 and may be obtained at local War Price and Rationing boards.

Freedom Brothers, Cousin Meet Abroad

Two brothers and a cousin, all of Freedom, met in Italy on May 14, according to word received by a sister of the brothers, Miss Mary Larkin, Eighth street, Freedom. It was a happy day for Corporal David Larkin of an Anti-Aircraft division; Edward Larkin, Merchant Marine, and Sgt. Charles Carson, of a railroad battalion.

David and Charles learned that all winter they had been stationed only about a half mile apart in Italy.

Rochester High School Scholarship, Award Winners

JOHN REUTHER

BETTY HINDMAN

ANNE WALLACE

BETTY KORSAN

MARY KATHRYN SHANOR

WILLIAM BRADSHAW

GEORGE ENGLERT

Pictured here are six members of the 1944 graduating class of Rochester high school who have been awarded scholarships at various institutions of higher learning, and a seventh member who won an art award.

John Reuther, son of Mr. and Mrs. Andrew P. Reuther, Rochester, the class valedictorian, won the Pitt scholarship with a potential value of $600. He also received the "Readers Digest" Valedictorian Prize. Betty Hindman, daughter of Mr. and Mrs. James Hindman, Rochester, salutatorian, was awarded a Geneva scholarship with a potential value of $150.

Anne Wallace, daughter of Dr. and Mrs. Oren Wallace, Sunflower, won a competitive scholarship awarded by Pennsylvania College for Women, with a potential value of $660. Betty Korsan, daughter of Mr. and Mrs. P. W. Korsan, Rochester, won an honor scholarship at Westminster College, New Wilmington, valued at $200.

George Englert, son of Mr. and Mrs. George M. Englert, East Rochester, was awarded the George E. Graff Journalism Scholarship valued at $500 and the National High School Institute Scholarship to the Medill School of Journalism at Northwestern University. William Bradshaw, son of Mr. and Harris Bradshaw, Baden, was awarded a Geneva College scholarship worth $150.

Mary Kathryn Shanor, daughter of Mr. and Mrs. C. W. Shanor, Rochester, was awarded a Certificate of Merit for an oil painting hung in Carnegie Institute in the national high school art exhibit sponsored by the "Scholastic" magazine.—Graule Photos

House Committee Calls NLRB Member In Ward Inquiry

WASHINGTON, May 23 (UP) — Gerard D. Reilly, member of the National Labor Relations board, was called before the Ramspeck committee today as the House investigation of government seizure of Montgomery Ward and Company's Chicago properties moved into its second day.

An NLRB representative was asked to testify in connection with the committee's effort to make a "chronological study" of the prolonged dispute between Montgomery Ward and the government over labor policies. Reilly will also be asked to discuss immediate events leading up to the election conducted by the NLRB among the concern's Chicago employes the day the properties were returned to private ownership.

It was the company's refusal to extend its contract with a CIO union pending the NLRB election

Continued on Page Two

HEADS ALUMNI

Rev. Elmer A. Ortner, pastor of Grace Lutheran church, Rochester, has been elected president of the Alumni Association of Thiel College, Greenville. He also has been elected a member of the executive committee of the Seminary Alumni Association of Mt. Airy Theological Seminary, Philadelphia, and will serve in that capacity three years. This evening, Rev. Ortner will be the speaker at a dinner of all members of the Thiel College Alumni Association attending the Pittsburgh Synod meeting this week in Pittsburgh.

BATTLE RAGING FOR BURMA KEY POINT OF MYITKYINA

SOUTHEAST ASIA HEADQUARTERS, Kandy, Ceylon, May 23 (UP)—The bitter house-to-house battle for Myitkyina continued today for the fifth straight day and official reports acknowledged that driving rainstorms and fierce Japanese resistance had prevented the attacking Americans and Chinese from expanding their foothold inside the city.

A communique issued in Chungking said there were no substantial changes in the opposing lines inside Myitkyina yesterday, although Brig. Gen. Frank Merrill's Marauders seized new positions along the approaches to the enemy's Burma stronghold and sealed off the last loopholes in their siege lines to the north.

Allied planes dominated the battlefield throughout the day, racing in unopposed to bomb and strafe the doomed Japanese garrison, while American heavy artillery pounded their defenses relentlessly.

Simultaneously, it was disclosed that Chinese forces driving on Burma from Western China had cut the old Burma Road at Chefang, 50 miles west of the Salween river and 16 miles north of the Burma-China border on the highway to Lashio.

PLANES HIT JAPS

The communique said heavy fighting continued in the lower Mogaung Valley 43 miles northwest of Myitkyina, where Allied forces were closing in from the north and south on Kamaing.

The Chungking communique reported that U. S. 14th Air Force fighter-bombers, manned by

Continued on Page Two

Carnegie-Illinois Acquitted By Jury

PITTSBURGH, May 23. (UP) —A Federal court jury today acquitted the Carnegie-Illinois Steel Corporation on charges of falsifying tests of steel ship plates delivered to the Navy, Maritime Commission and the Treasury Department.

The jury of six men and six women delivered a sealed verdict, reached last night after 6½ hours of deliberation, to Judge Robert M. Gibson a few minutes after court opened this morning. The case went to the jury at 2:30 p. m. Monday.

At the same time, the jury, acting upon instructions of Judge Gibson, also acquitted the corporation of charges of destroying records of steel tests and analyses. The verdict ended a case which began in the Spring of 1943.

INJURED IN FALL

Mrs. John F. Dodge, Second street, Beaver, sustained a severe foot injury in a fall down a flight of stairs in her home, Monday. Last Fall, she suffered a broken wrist and other injuries in a similar fall.

Three District Men In Casualty List

Pvt. William C. Myers, Jr., Division Lane, Beaver; Pfc. Stephen Durniak, Ambridge avenue, Fair Oaks, and Pvt. Michael L. Susan, Hood street, Aliquippa, were listed as wounded in action in the Mediterranean area in the casualty lists released today by the War Department.

Rochester Sailor Burned By Acid

Mr. and Mrs. William Gauss, Center street, Rochester, received a telephone message from their son, William Edward Gauss, apprentice seaman, stationed at Great Lakes, Ill., stating that he had received severe acid burns on his right arm and hand, but that he was recovering. The accident occurred Monday afternoon when a can of acid was ov-

War History

Germany declared war on Italy on May 23, 1915, according to news dispatches received here.

Rochester Junior High Graduation To Be On Thursday

Rev. Frank Lathom, pastor of the Reformed Presbyterian church, Walton, N. Y., and brother of J. Russell Lathom, Rochester Junior high school principal, will be the speaker at the Junior high school graduation Thursday afternoon at 1:45 o'clock in the Rochester high school auditorium. The graduating class consists of 200 pupils.

Following is the program:

"Lord God Omnipotent," Girls Chorus; Devotion — Scripture reading, Lord's Prayer, J. Russell Lathom; Welcome, Patty Herold, President of Student Council; "The Shepherd Boy," Girls Chorus; Address, Rev. Lathom; trumpet trio, Frank Carevic, Jay Gabele, Henry Gardner; Legion Medal awards, Robert P. Barner, superintendent of schools; "Junior High Memories," William Dentzer; trombone duet, Joe Hutchinson, George Day; "Anticipations of High School," Harry Roth; Junior High Chorus—"The Bells of St. Mary's", "Grandfather's Clock," "Carmencita," Anthony Caputo, director; Junior High Band—"Our Director," "Anchors Aweigh," "Thunderer," directed by Mr. Caputo.

Ushers are: Mary Jane Keiser, Laureme Leonard, Dionna Cable, Peggy Grimm, Billy May, George Vonakis.

OUTSTANDING BRIDGEWATER PUPILS

Pupils in the Eighth grade of the Bridgewater school have chosen Sara Jane Douds and Gene Ferguson, above, as the outstanding members of the class. They will receive the American Legion and Legion Auxiliary awards presented annually to the boy and girl who excel in honor, courage, scholarship, leadership and service.

MIGHTY AIR ARMADA HITS REICH, FRANCE

Force Of 1,700 American Planes Blast Europe In Wake Of Bombardment During Night By 1,000 British Bombers

By UNITED PRESS

A 1,750-plane American task force lashed Germany and occupied France today after 1,000 British bombers dropped about 4,480 tons of explosives on Dortmund, Brunswick and other targets in three countries along and behind the invasion coast.

The resumed bombardment of Western Europe soared to record or near-record heights on its 5th straight day. In the first 12 hours, more than 3,000 Allied planes ranged over Germany and anti-invasion buffer areas, delivering at least 6,500 tons of bombs.

About 750 Flying Fortresses and Liberators headed the daylight parade against the continent, smashing at German airdromes and rail yards in France and targets in western Germany which were not identified immediately.

More than 1,000 U. S. Thunderbolts, Lightnings and Mustangs escorted the big bombers, which also were supported by RAF Mustangs sweeping nearby areas. It was the greatest fighter fleet ever dispatched in any theater on a single operation.

RAF LOSES 35 PLANES

The RAF opened the day with its heaviest blows in a month soon after midnight. At a cost of 35 planes its heavy bombers hammered Germany's Ruhr steel center of Dortmund and the aircraft center of Brunswick, 120 miles west of Berlin.

Other British bombers hit the French rail centers of Orleans and Le Mans southwest of Paris, and speedy Mosquitoes jabbed at the German chemical center of Ludwigshafen and an airfield in Belgium.

The extra large fighter escort apparently was dispatched over invasion-marked Western Europe to draw the reluctant Luftwaffe into battle to thin further its already diminishing numbers in advance of the impending Allied invasion.

German broadcasts reported "heavy air battles" over southeast France and Belgium, an indication that the strategy may have succeeded. The German DNB agency acknowledged that some bombers penetrated western Germany, but claimed they dropped only a few bombs.

NAZIS OVER ENGLAND

The daylight raids all followed the pre-invasion pattern of crippling enemy airdromes and communications as a prelude to the opening of a western land front. Sunny skies and the early start of today's round of attacks indicated the Allied air forces might exceed yesterday's mark of 6,000 tons of explosives

Continued on Page Two

J. And L. Workers Granted Wage Boost

Wage increases ranging from one to six cents hourly for 214 employes in the Jones and Laughlin Steel Corporation blast furnace department at Aliquippa, have been sanctioned by the War Labor Board.

The approval ends a dispute which caused a 16-hour work stoppage on May 6. The wage increases had been agreed upon by the company and the union to adjust inequities in the department, but the proposals had been twice rejected by the WLB. Although 353 men are employed in the department, only those engaged in actual operation for the five blast furnaces are affected.

Monaca Paratrooper Killed In Action

Mr. and Mrs. Telford Birge, Sharon road, Bridgewater, have received word that Mr. Birge's brother, Pvt. Waldo W. Birge, Monaca, serving as a paratrooper, had been killed in action May 1 at the Anzio beachhead. He had been wounded in the African campaign and upon recovery had been sent to Italy.

Weather Forecast

Western Pennsylvania—Scattered thundershowers today. Fair and somewhat cooler tonight. Wednesday cloudy and scattered thundershowers.

NAZIS REPORT DRIVE OPENED BY 5th ARMY

TODAY'S WAR SUMMARY

By UNITED PRESS

AIR WAR—Aerial softening of Europe for invasion gains momentum as more than 3,000 Allied planes, including 1,750 four-engined bombers, blast Germany, France and Belgium.

ITALY — Eighth Army, in battering ram advance, smashes well into whole section of surviving north end of Adolf Hitler line, Germans report heavy attack by 5th Army at Anzio beachhead.

BURMA—House to house battle sways through Myitkyina for fifth straight day as official reports acknowledge rainstorm and fierce Japanese resistance prevent Chinese-American troops from expanding toe-hold in city.

RUSSIA—Red Army reported preparing for "battles that lie ahead" as lull continues on eastern front.

PACIFIC—Admiral Chester Nimitz maintains silence on Japanese report that large American task force attacked Marcus Island.

The German DNB news agency reported today that German troops had evacuated Pico, middle hinge of the Nazi defenses on the main Italian front.

The Eighth Army in Italy, front reports said, battered its way "well into" an entire section of what remains of the otherwise broken Adolf Hitler line at the northern end of the front.

Down towards the coast the Fifth Army, held back temporarily in its frontal attack on Terracina by the arrival of German reinforcements, flanked the town by seizing a village and six peaks dominating it from the north. They also took the entrance to the 4½ mile long railroad tunnel which goes through the mountains north of Terracina to the Pontine flat lands beyond. The position is only 23 miles from the Anzio beachhead.

The Germans, who had weakened their ring around the beachhead by sending reinforcements from there to the sagging southern front, reported today that the Fifth Army had begun a heavy attack all along its perimeter. A German communique said the attack was accompanied by an intense artillery barrage and that fighting was "in full swing."

STIFF RESISTANCE

The Germans, using 17 divisions to defend the southern front and throwing in their last reserves, were putting up strong resistance in a win-or-lose effort to stop the Allied march towards Rome.

The section where the Eighth Army had broken into the northern end of their line was not specified, although it was believed to be in the Liri Valley southwest of Piedimonte. The enemy was holding out stoutly in Piedimonte, northern anchor of his line, but Polish units of the Eighth Army were reported closing in on it from three sides.

In the center, around Mt. Leu-

Continued on Page Two

Boy Drowned When He Falls Into Ohio River At Aliquippa

The Ohio river claimed its first victim of the season Monday afternoon about 5:30 o'clock when nine-year-old Edward Powell, 115 Seventh street, West Aliquippa, fell into the water near the pump house at West Aliquippa and was drowned.

The youngster was reportedly playing with several other boys in an old rowboat tied to the shore when the accident occurred.

Rescue workers, firemen and police worked forty-five minutes recovering the body from almost the exact spot where it had disappeared. The Duquesne Light Company first aid crew was also called.

The son of Mr. and Mrs. William Powell, he was one of nine children. The body was removed to the Darroch funeral home and later taken to the family home, where friends will be received. Funeral service will be held Thursday afternoon at 2 o'clock in the Methodist church. Burial will be in Woodlawn cemetery.

Local Man Injured In Dive Into Run

An expert swimmer and diver, James Cordes, Sunflower road, near Rochester, suffered a broken neck when he dived from a bridge over Brady's run, near Fallston, Monday afternoon.

Cordes and a companion, Sam Hooper, Aliquippa, had gone to the pool to swim prior to going to work at the Jones and Laughlin Steel Corporation plant, Aliquippa, where the former was employed as a boss blower on a blast furnace.

Attracted by air bubbles on the surface of the water, Cooper immediately dived to Cordes' rescue. Placing Cordes in his automobile, Hooper drove to Rochester hospital. He was later taken in a Hartzel ambulance to St. Francis hospital, Pittsburgh. Cordes is married and the father of a son and daughter. According to word received by relatives at noon today from the hospital, hope is held for his recovery.

Beaver Flier Is Missing In Action

Mrs. Dorothy Damon Reed, Beaver, has been notified by the War Department that her husband, Tech. Sgt. Clarence E. Reed, has been reported missing in action since May 7 over Germany. He was chief engineer and top turret gunner on a Flying Fortress.

Sergeant Reed was graduated from Beaver Falls high school in 1939 and before entering the service was employed by the Moltrup Steel Company, Beaver Falls. He is a son of Mr. and Mrs. G. Earl Reed, near Beaver.

Bill Jack Not To Speak In Valley

The program committee of the Beaver County Foremen's Club today announced that the public meeting scheduled in Beaver Falls high school auditorium Monday, May 29, at which famed Bill Jack, Cleveland industrialist, was to have been the speaker, has been cancelled. Due to an emergency connected with the war effort, Mr. Jack has been called elsewhere, making it impossible for him to be here.

Mr. Jack has promised the local group that if it is possible, he will appear here next Fall.

House Completes Tax Bill Action

WASHINGTON, May 23. (UP) —The House today completed Congressional action on the individual income tax simplification bill which will free approximately 30,000,000 Americans from the necessity of calculating their Federal taxes.

This measure, effective next January 1, also would simplify the returns which must be filed by the remaining 20,000,000 taxpayers and would revise withholding schedules to make amounts withheld by employers cover, as nearly as possible, all Federal income taxes due.

The bill has the Treasury's approval and is expected to be signed by President Roosevelt.

Good Evening:

Follow "Calamity Town," an absorbing mystery crime, in The Times daily. It starts today on Page 4.

The Evening Times

"Serving the Ohio Valley Industrial Area"

VOL. II—No. 31 — ALIQUIPPA, PA., WEDNESDAY, MAY 31, 1944 — FOUR CENTS

The Weather:

Considerable cloudiness but mostly sunny and warm again today and Thursday.

BAD BLAZE FOLLOWS WRECK

War Honor Roll Dedicated As Sacred Shrine

RAMBLING AROUND ALIQUIPPA

By THE STAFF

A SHRINE DEDICATED

Dedication of the War Honor Roll here last evening was marred by only one thing—a public address system that didn't carry the speakers' voices very far.

As a result, hundreds of persons left the scene before the program had been half completed. It was unfortunate that loudspeakers were not placed at several points in the big audience.

All in all, however, it was an impressive and solemn ceremony. Tears welled in the eyes of many in the crowd during the program.

After it was all over, First Lieut. John T. Dempsey and other honored guests were served dinner at the Canteen. Lieut. Dempsey refused to accept any money from the Memorial Day Committee for coming to town to speak, so he was presented a pen and pencil set.

* * *

The Plodinec Furniture Co. today donated eight cartons of cigarets to Aliquippa police for use in their vending machine.

The profits realized from sale of the smokes is spent for flowers bedecking the department's honor roll near the tax collector's office.

Yesterday, through courtesy of police, two wreaths adorned the Honor Roll at the dedication ceremony. The floral bouquets, one from the department, the other from the local lodge of the Fraternal Order of Police, were bought with finances from the vending machine.

* * *

TEACHERS SCATTER

The closing of Hopewell Township High school for the summer months disperses its teaching force from the eastern coast to the far off Pacific.

Miss Veda Yorkish, music teacher, will spend six weeks vacationing at Rye Beach, N. Y., as will Mrs. Wilma Powell, teacher of commercial subjects. Mrs. Powell will later join her husband, who is stationed with the U. S. Army at Harrisburg. Miss Yorkish will conclude the summer months in New York City.

Miss Betty Zitman, who also teaches in the commercial department will hie away to California for three months and Mrs. Lois Haspolla, English teacher, will join her husband at his parsonage at [illegible]

[illegible] and Mrs. Faye Williams, of Sheffield Terrace, physical education teacher, will enroll for summer classes at the University of Pittsburgh, when she returns from a two week's visit at Washington, D. C.

Albert [illegible], Rochester, also a math teacher, will work in a defense plant in the valley during the summer.

Mrs. Ruby Freeble, teacher of foreign languages, who lives in Leetsdale, will enroll next month at Pitt after a brief rest at home.

Miss Ellen Owens, of Cornopolis, history and language teacher, plans to study further at Indiana State Teachers college.

The high school's principal, D. D. Kretzert, who lives in New Sheffield, also will enroll for an extension course at Pitt. Fred Milanovich, the coach, can be found daily at the Plan 12 swimming pool, and the supervising principal, Mason J. Bodkin, will tour Pennsylvania, taking moving pictures of its superb scenery before enrolling at the University of Pittsburgh.

* * *

The biggest thrill of 35 years in the insurance business came the other day to S. C. Moore, veteran Aliquippa agent.

He was cited in his firm's periodical report which showed him in 179th position out of 300 leaders selected from the company's 25,000 agents in the United States for personal production during the first four months of 1944.

Moore also was named in 31st position among 50 leaders for personal production in April.

* * *

PLAN SOUTHERN VISITS

Mr. and Mrs. James Adams, Sr., and son, James, Jr., of Beaver, will leave this week to visit his family at Tampa, Fla., and her parents in Tuscaloosa, Ala. Mrs. Adams, better known here as Mrs. Jewell Adams, is a teacher in the eighth grade at Hopewell Township schools. She will enroll for summer school at the University of Pittsburgh when she returns from her Southern vacation.

Another teacher who will leave tomorrow for a vacation in the South is Mrs. Robert J. Hersberger, the former Virginia Westlake, a teacher in the New Sheffield school. She will join her husband at Camp Stewart, Ga. Second Lieut. Hersberger was recently promoted to the rank of first lieutenant.

Freedom Man Suffers Burns At Oil Works

Steve Sedyski, of Freedom, was admitted to Rochester hospital yesterday at 10:35 a.m. suffering from burns of both legs and body sustained while at work for the Freedom Oil Works. His condition this morning was given as "fairly good"

Shrine Borough's Contribution To March To Peace

Colorful Ceremony Held; Roll Praised As 'One Of Finest'

Aliquippa's $7,000 War Honor Roll, commemorating more than 4,000 of its former residents now in the armed forces, was unveiled amidst colorful surroundings last evening as thousands jammed Franklin Ave.

The realization of an 18-month dream capped a strictly local Memorial Day observance which was featured by a procession of hundreds of notables, including service, civic, religious, fraternal and government leaders.

Chief speaker at the dedicatory services was 29-year old Lt. John Dempsey, a veteran of the African and Sicilian invasions and now a convalescent at Deshon hospital in Butler.

Tracing the inception of Memorial Day back to the Civil War, Lt. Dempsey pointed out that May 30 has been accepted as the day of observance by northern states in the United States because the date coincides with France's Day of Ashes, a holiday in commemoration of Napoleon [illegible]

The speaker described briefly his experiences in actual combat. [illegible] of a troop ship to his [illegible] blown to bits by German Messerschmitts off the Sicilian coast. Luckily, he said, only a "handful" of American casualties resulted.

"This stately memorial," spoke Clifford J. Smith, Honor roll chairman, "is an indication to the people of Aliquippa of the price we must pay for freedom.

"4,000 Aliquippans," he continued, "....who were playing in lots....who knew war only from the history books....are now engaged in the deathless struggle."

"These are Aliquippa's contribution toward humanity's march to freedom. Freedom has its price in the age-long struggle of democracy and tyranny."

Smith paid glorious tribute to the first Aliquippan killed in World War II—Alex Venable, of the Marine Corps, who lost his life defending Wake Island shortly after the sneak attack on Pearl Harbor.

He added:

"This Honor Roll is symbolic of our hopes and prayers that their (Aliquippa's servicemen and women) mission cannot, shall not fail. It is symbolic of

(Continued on Page Three)

FDR Seeks More Money For OPA

WASHINGTON, May 31. (UP)—President Roosevelt today asked Congress to increase appropriations of the Office of Price Administration for the fiscal year starting July 1 to enable OPA to step up its enforcement program and to simplify price controls.

Mr. Roosevelt sent to Congress a request for $182,252,000 to finance OPA operations during the 1945 fiscal year compared with $169,500,000 provided for the agency in regular and supplemental appropriations for the current fiscal year.

A White House statement said the estimate contemplated additional regional and district enforcement manpower, and added: "Increased efforts will also be made to eliminate the counterfeiting of ration stamps and to prevent leaks of the civilian share of commodities into unauthorized channels."

Vujo Yovestic, Once Resident Here, Dies

Funeral services for the late Vujo Yovestic, former Aliquippan who died Thursday at Indiana Harbor, Ind., will be held tomorrow at 1:30 p. m. from the Pearce Funeral Home here, followed by services at 2 p. m. at St. Elijah's Serbian church. Burial will be in St. Elijah's cemetery.

A GRAND TRIBUTE TO ALIQUIPPANS IN THE SERVICE

Aliquippa's beautiful War Honor Roll, made possible by monetary contributions from many local folk and organizations, was formally unveiled and dedicated last evening as thousands watched. The above view of the shrine was snapped several days before all the names had been encased. Below is the cancelled check received by the Honor Roll committee from Treasurer James P. Walsh after the American Legion post's successful drive to get sufficient funds to complete the roll.

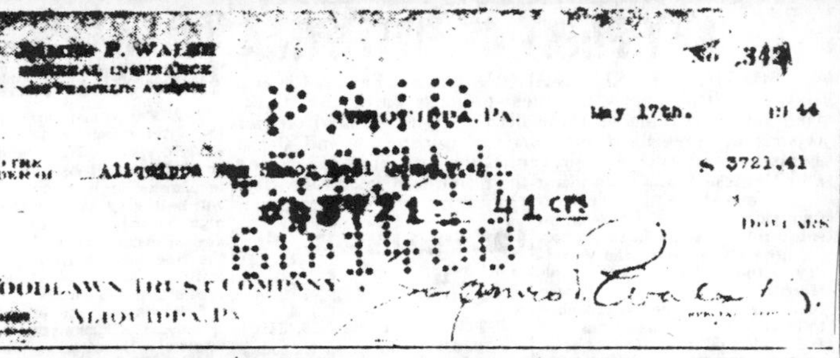

JAMES P. WALSH
GENERAL INSURANCE
FRANKLIN AVENUE
No. 342
PAID
ALIQUIPPA, PA. May 17th. 1944
PAY TO THE ORDER OF Aliquippa War Shrine [illegible] $ 3721.41
3721 41 cts DOLLARS
WOODLAWN TRUST COMPANY
ALIQUIPPA, PA

U. S. Airmen In Raid On Peiping

Former Capital Of China Is Target

By United Press

A long-distance American air raid on Pieping, former capital of China, was reported by Tokyo Radio Wednesday, which claimed one of two P-51 fighters participating in the raid was forced down and captured near Hossin in Shansi province.

The Tokyo broadcast, heard by United Press at San Francisco, said the attack took place Tuesday morning, and quoted an official communique of the north China military headquarters of the Japanese expeditionary forces.

WOMAN WINS AWARD

Mrs. Helen Lawrence, 137 Spring St., was the winner of a $50 paper doll awarded last night by the Aliquippa Service Canteen at its dance which was attended by more than 1,000 persons.

Price Meeting To Be Staged June 7

June 7 has definitely been selected as the date of Aliquippa's first open price meeting, Chief Clerk Anne Hornstein of the local OPA announced today.

The confab arranged to enlighten shoppers and merchants in the procedure of price control, will begin at 7:30 p. m. in the assembly hall of the United Steelworkers' building.

Two price coordinators from the Pittsburgh District OPA office will deliver the principal addresses.

Eger's Clock Contest Ends; 2 Winners Named

Eger's annual clock contest for Aliquippa High seniors ended Monday and two members of the June graduating class were named winners of Bulova watches. The clock was started May 15 at 4 p. m.

Recipients of the watches were Helen Pompeo, 520 Highland Ave., and Edward LeViseur, 1209 Davidson St. Judges of the contest were T. C. Swarts, Robert M. Crawford and Lytle M. Wilson.

Only Slightly Bruised . . .

Aliquippa Boy, 2, Falls 3 Stories From Porch

A two-year old Aliquippa boy was saved from serious or possibly fatal injuries yesterday by a chain protruding from a fire escape after he fell from a three-story porch at his home, 312 Station St.

The infant, Daniel Webster, landed on the sidewalk below, sustaining only slight bruises.

His fall was broken by the chain. A thorough examination by a local physician at the emergency hospital disclosed no broken bones.

He was treated for bruises on his right cheek, face and mouth. After treatment he was taken home by his mother.

Capt. Samuel Shumaker Succumbs On Cruiser

PITTSBURGH, May 31—(U.P.)—Capt. Samuel R. [illegible], Huntingdon, Pa., native, and former resident of Indiana, Pa., and Sewickley, died on board the Navy cruiser New Orleans, of which he was commanding officer, the Navy Department announced.

The announcement said the cause of death was a heart attack. He was buried at sea following his death on Friday, Navy officials said.

25,000 See LST Craft Launched

Carries Names Of Bond Subscribers

A LST fighting craft was launched before 25,000 spectators at the Dravo Shipyard yesterday representing $5,000,000 in extra war bond subscriptions from Allegheny county.

The craft, christened the LST-750 by Mrs. Clifford S. Heins, chairman of the Women's Division of the War Finance committee in the Fort Pitt area, slid sideways into the water at Neville Island to culminate ceremonies lasting one and a half hours.

Rear Admiral M. F. Draemel, commandant of the Philadelphia Navy Yard and the Fourth Naval District, Robert W. Coyne, field director of the War Finance Division, U. S. Treasury Dept., and John Green, national president of the Industrial Union of Marine and Shipbuilding Workers of America, were principal speakers at the christening. The Army-Navy "E" award with four stars was presented to the Dravo Corp. by Capt. W. R. Nichols, supervisor of shipbuilding in the Pittsburgh district.

Intense midday heat forced about 150 persons to seek shelter and first aid.

The LST-750 carried the names of every subscriber to the extra war bond drive as it hit the water. The scroll later will be presented to the commanding officer of the craft and will be carried in his quarters when the craft enters active duty.

HOME ON FURLOUGHS

Aliquippa servicemen spending leaves and furloughs include Mike Larkovich, Colo.; Stephen Mesko, Md.; John G. Mengak, Va.; Joseph [illegible]; D. J. Proino, Md.; Thomas [illegible], Cal.; George Lane, Jr., [illegible]; [illegible], Wash. D. C., and [illegible], N.C.

Stolen Auto Is Found; 1 Missing

One stolen car was recovered while another was still being sought today by Aliquippa police.

Twenty-five minutes after A. E. Oliker, local clothing merchant, had notified authorities that his 1941 Buick coupe had been stolen from the rear of his store, it was found in a ditch at Monaca Rd. and Third Ave.

Chief Trevor Jenkins and Patrolman Andrew Palochak came upon the vehicle, which was undamaged, as they were patrolling in a police car.

The other auto was stolen early today from the Jones and Laughlin parking lot near the "Wye" here.

A 1936 blue Chevrolet coupe, bearing license plates 171 U, it is the property of Ronald Smith, Economy St., South Heights, who worked the midnight to 8 a.m. shift at the local plant.

In reporting the theft, he told police he left his ignition keys in the auto before going into the mill.

HOME FROM HOSPITAL

Andrew Cabish, Jr., 146 Riverview Ave., was discharged yesterday from Rochester hospital.

$219,784 Quota Set For Aliquippa In Bond Drive

Beaver county has been set up with nine districts for the Fifth War Loan which starts June 12 and runs until July 8. Each district has been assigned a proportionate share of the quota of $10,470,000, which is the largest quota ever allotted to Beaver county.

The county organization will lend all possible aid to the various districts of the county but the success of the Fifth War Loan will depend on the active participation of all those who have worked so faithfully in the past. It is hoped that many new workers will volunteer to assist their area chairman, for Beaver county must exceed its quota in these critical pre-invasion days. It is our duty to back the attack and to sell and buy more than before.

The district quotas have been set up after very careful consideration of all the various factors concerned and are based on the percentage of increase in the county quotas.

The quotas assigned to the various districts are, Aliquippa, $2,219,784; Ambridge $2,364,919;

(Continued on Page Three)

Allies Advance To Genzano, 15 Miles Away From Rome

Pre-Invasion Air Offensive Against Europe Continues

By LOUIS F. KEEMLE
United Press War Editor

Allied forces slogged determinedly towards Rome today along the western fringe of the Alban Hills, penetrating the strongly-defended German line almost to Genzano, on the Appian Way 15 miles below the capital.

The enemy was putting up the stiffest kind of resistance and Gen. Sir Harold R. L. G. Alexander, Allied commander, noted that he is evidently determined to hold the line from Valmontone to the sea "at all cost."

The Fifth Army, however, threw its main weight towards the seaward end of the line, pounding slowly ahead on either side of the Appian Way in an effort to make a break-through to Albano, key point of the defenses on the highway 13 miles from Rome.

The pre-invasion aerial offensive against western Europe went [illegible] of Allied planes streamed across the channel in the wake of an exceptionally heavy night attack by RAF big bombers at the French coastal defenses.

The advance on Rome was closed when the Germans threw in everything they had available in a delaying action apparently designed less to save the imperilled capital than to protect the retreat of their main forces from the Liri and Sacco valley sectors at the southeastern end of the front.

The Eighth Army and the right wing of the Fifth were making steady progress in that region. Today's communique recorded the

(Continued on Page Three)

Opening Of Two Pools Delayed

West Aliquippa's Pool Opens Tomorrow

Minor repairs will cause a one-day delay in the opening of the Plan 12 and Plan 11 swimming pools but West Aliquippa's pool will open tomorrow as scheduled, Supervisor Fred Milanovich announced today.

Work at the two sites, Milanovich disclosed, is being rushed to assure their opening on Friday.

The chlorinator has been set up in the West Side pool. The bottom of the pool must be cleaned and water poured into it, jobs which should be completed today, the supervisor said.

Milanovich disclosed that he has two men under consideration for lifeguard positions at Plan 11. The posts are filled at the other two pools.

He also called upon all employes, including check boys and girls, to be present tomorrow at 10 a. m. at the Plan 11 and Plan 12 pools to aid in the cleaning up task.

Truck, Two R. R. Cars Destroyed; 5 Persons Hurt

3 Others Injured In Accidents; Fire Fought For 3 Hours

Heavy property damage and a raging fire battled for three hours by the Freedom Fire department followed the sideswiping of a heavy trailer truck and a sedan in Freedom shortly after last midnight which sent Charles Lee, 46, of Washington, N. J., to Rochester hospital with a crushed and lacerated foot.

The accident also caused minor injuries to Ralph Dauer, of New Brighton, and his father, mother and sister, all passengers in the Dauer car. They were treated at the same hospital.

The borough streets were purified with a deluge of mouth wash when the heavy trailer truck upset after striking a curb, hurling its cargo of several hundred cases of the antiseptic shipped by the Laverne Products Co., into the highway.

Gasoline in the truck ignited [illegible] the trailer. The flames spread onto nearby tracks of the Pennsylvania railroad, burning two box cars on the siding.

Leo F. Posleck, 25, of McKees Rocks, although badly shaken up, miraculously escaped serious injury when the car he was driving at 2:30 p.m. yesterday jumped the curb near Sixteenth St., Freedom, hurtling over a 50-foot embankment onto the tracks of the Pennsylvania railroad's main tracks. He allegedly was forced off the road by an approaching car.

Three aged residents of Darlington were injured yesterday afternoon in an unusual automobile accident two miles west of Beaver on the Dutch Ridge Road. Miss Mary Davis, 72, and Mrs. William McGaffic, 76, wife of the driver, were taken to Rochester hospital.

Miss Davis, who is suffering from lacerations of the scalp and shock, struck at a bee that had flown into the rear seat where she rode alone. The insect flew to the front of the car, stinging the driver, 72, on the left arm, causing him to lose control of the machine which swerved to the left side of the road and collided with a steel telephone pole.

McGaffic was treated at the hospital and taken home. His wife, whose condition today was given as "poor," is suffering lacerations and shock.

Stray Dog Shot; Believed Rabid

A stray dog, feared rabid, was shot today in Hopewell Twp. by Constable George Hill after it had bitten six other canines.

Its head was sent to Harrisburg to ascertain if a positive case of rabies exists.

Apprehension of the canine prompted Constable Hill to sound a stern warning to dog-owners that they will be prosecuted and their dogs shot if the canines are permitted to roam at large.

Patricia Ruth Kelsey On Tech's Honor Roll

Miss Patricia Ruth Kelsey, daughter of Mr. and Mrs. F. W. Kelsey, 114 Major St., here, has been named on the semester honor roll at Carnegie Institute of Technology, where she has just completed her sophomore year in the department of costume economics at Margaret Morrison.

In an announcement received from the registrar's office, honor students must have completed the semester's work with a B-plus average.

Miss Kelsey was graduated from Aliquippa High school.

PATIENT IN HOSPITAL

Elizabeth Ochaick, 1122 [illegible] St., is a patient at [illegible] hospital.

Baseball School Opens In Beaver Tomorrow

MACKEY, BREHANY TO CONDUCT TRYOUTS AT GYPSY GLEN PARK

Leo Mackey and Joe Brehany, Pittsburgh Pirates scouts, are all set to open classes at Gypsy Glen Field, Beaver, tomorrow morning, in the baseball school to be conducted by the Pittsburgh National League club Thursday, Friday and Saturday, from 11 a. m. until 4 p. m.

Mackey and Brehany, who will be assisted by Paul Jones, Beaver, will arrive early tomorrow and soon after they have checked in Gypsy Glen Field will be one of the busiest spots in the country, showing more athletic activity than has been seen around here in many a day.

First of all there will be the registration and numbering of the boys reporting for the tryouts, blouse numbers being issued to the applicants for the purpose of making identification easier while the drills are in progress and so that the two judges may be helped in listing the outstanding performers who impress them.

Then there will be a sizing up of all comers for size, speed, power and so on, and this will be followed by the real workouts and coaching and instructions in pitching, catching, fielding, hitting, throwing and baserunning. When these tests have determined the better boys in the field, the survivors will be divided into teams and a series of games will be played to give Mackey and Brehany the final dope on which they will base their decision as to what lads are qualified to go into professional ball.

The camp is open to all boys over 15 years of age who desire to take up baseball as a means of livelihood. All that the candidates have to do is to furnish their own transportation, uniforms, gloves and spiked shoes. The Pittsburgh club will provide all necessary equipment, such as bats, balls, protectors and masks, as well as free coaching.

Litwhiler Seeking Navy Commission

ST. LOUIS, June 14. — His Philadelphia draft board has deferred him but Danny Litwhiler, St. Louis Cardinal's outfield, has applied for a navy commission and expects to take his physical examination late this week.

"I'm waiting to hear from the navy any day," said Litwhiler, adding that the members of Philadelphia Board 54 "did what they think is the right thing and that's what I'm doing."

Harris, Walker Top Hickey Park Show

Johnny Walker, hard - hitting Philadelphia boy, managed by Chris Dundee, and Ossie ((Bulldog) Harris, Pittsburgh, middleweight, will headline the first boxing show to be staged at Hickey Park, next Monday night.

Walker boasts a record of 23 consecutive triumphs, 19 of them by knockouts, and will more than likely be a favorite to stop the veteran Harris.

Henry Armstrong Sees Great Future For Kieth Nuttall

By JACK CUDDY
United Press Staff Correspondent

NEW YORK, June 14. (UP)—Brown - skinned Henry Armstrong, the poetical puglist, dreams of the wonderful world of tomorrow in which he will be building his young white "miracle fighter" — Keith Nuttall—to ring championships and fabulous wealth, assisted by television.

Armstrong, former triple champion, enthused about Young Nuttall at Stillman's gym, just before he stepped into the ring for a workout with Torpedo Reed of Los Angeles, in preparation for Thursday night's dangerous brawl with Al "Bummy" Davis at Madison Square Garden.

The bull-shouldered veteran in white sweat shirt and blue trunks, who insists that he is only 31 years old, said, "I don't know how long I'll be fighting. I feel swell now; sharp as a razor, after plenty of competition. I should lick Davis all right, if I watch his left hook. I can't go on fighting forever. But I want to fight as long as I can store up a war chest with which to back Young Nuttall, the most amazing youngster I ever saw.

"This Nuttall kid is only 13—or maybe 14—now. He lives in Brigham, Utah. He weighs only about 90 pounds. He's still an amateur. But what he can do with his fists is absolutely unbelievable. I've been around fighters for a long, long time. I've looked over hundreds of experienced boxers and hundreds of youngsters; but never have I seen any human being who approached this kid Nuttall in God-given natural ability. He's positively uncanny."

Did Armstrong say that this Young Nuttall was a white boy? A reporter asked.

Yes, indeed, Hammering Henry emphasized. And for that reason Armstrong is convinced that he will become the first Negro manager ever to guide a white fighter to a title—"perhaps three titles — featherweight, lightweight and welterweight—but not at one time. The New York Boxing Commission has taken steps to prevent any fighter from holding more than one title at a time."

Armstrong, through his Los Angeles attorneys, has a "minor contract" on Young Nuttall's services until he is 21, and an option on his services thereafter.

The yungster's father, Morris A. Nuttall—a Brigham baker and former professional middleweight scrapper—asked Armstrong to become manager of his boy, after refusing an offer of $10,000 to tie up with another manager. The elder Nuttall figured Henry was the pilot he wanted for his son because of Armstrong's reputation for square-dealing and because he had been triple champion.

"When the father first wrote me, I didn't say yes or I didn't say no," explains Henry. "I figured maybe the old man was over-sold on his son—like most fathers. Anyway I looked the kid over when he was giving an exhibition with his father for soldiers at Wendover, Utah. Well—I got bug-eyed watching that kid, who is a dream fighter. To test his mind, in between rounds, I told him how to right-cross his father's left jab. He went out and nailed his old man on the chin, dropping him with a right cross. He weighed 89 pounds; his father was 166. I fell head over heels in love with that kid right there. Come victory and television, this kid will be my golden boy."

Schoolboy Is New Speed King

Charley Parker . . . Mr. Speed himself

By WALTER L. JOHNS
Central Press Sports Editor.

U. S. TRACK and field athletics, badly in need of a headliner to place it back in the top category of athletic competition for spectator attention, may have one in 17-year-old Charley Parker, the new, unoffcial "world's fastest human."

Parker, the schoolboy speed king of San Antonio, Tex., who has been undefeated in three years of competition embracing 50 races and who has run the century in 9.5 seconds, only a tenth of a second over the world record, is scheduled to hogtie the headlines the week-end of June 17 when he competes in the national A. A. U. track meet in New York.

If it hadn't been for an appendectomy, Parker would be a national figure right now.

Appendectomy Stops Him

He was scheduled to compete in the A. A. U. meet last year at this time when he was sent to the hospital a few days before the meet. In 1943 he turned in times of 9.5 for the 100 and 20.6 for the 220 and he hadn't even run against anyone who could push him to the limit.

The boy whom track observers expect will top the amazing performances of America's Olympic king of 1936, Jesse Owens, has absolutely flawless natural form, according to students of the game.

No less an authority on track than Dan Ferris, secretary-treasurer of the A. A. U., says that Parker "looks like the greatest thing that has come along in years" and confidently predicts the youth will crack both the 100 and the 220-yard marks before he's through.

This season the "Texas Tornado" has run in 14 races and set nine new records of one kind or another besides tieing two others.

Although turned down by the Navy because of color blindness, Parker still is attempting to get into the Army.

Baseball Summary

NATIONAL LEAGUE
RESULTS TUESDAY

*Pittsburgh 3, Cincinnati 2.
Boston 2, Philadelphia 1.
Philadelphia 8, Boston 7.
Brooklyn 9, New York 4.
Chicago-St. Louis, night game.
*5 innings, called; rain.

TEAM STANDING

	W.	L.	Pct.
St. Louis	33	15	.688
Pittsburgh	26	19	.578
Cincinnati	25	23	.521
New York	25	24	.510
Brooklyn	24	26	.480
Boston	23	30	.434
Philadelphia	19	27	.413
Chicago	16	27	.372

GAMES TODAY

Pgh. at Cincinnati (night).
Chicago at St. Louis.
Brooklyn at New York (night)
Boston at Philadelphia (night)

GAMES THURSDAY

Pittsburgh at Cincinnati.
Boston at Philadelphia.
Others not scheduled.

AMERICAN LEAGUE
RESULTS TUESDAY

St. Louis 5, Chicago 3.
Boston 7, Philadelphia 2.
Detroit - Cleveland, postponed, rain.
Washington 3, New York 0.

TEAM STANDING

	W.	L.	Pct.
St. Louis	29	23	.558
Boston	26	23	.531
Detroit	25	25	.500
Cleveland	25	26	.490
Chicago	22	23	.489
Washington	24	26	.480
New York	22	24	.478
Philadelphia	22	25	.468

GAMES TODAY

Detroit at Cleveland (2).
Philadelphia at Boston (2).
New York at Washington (night).
St. Louis at Chicago (night).

GAMES THURSDAY

New York at Washington (night).
Detroit at Cleveland.
Philadelphia at Boston.
Others not scheduled.

COUNTY ASSOCIATION
TEAM STANDING

	W.	L.
Beaver Falls	8	3
East Rochester	7	4
Monaca	7	5
Beaver	6	5
New Brighton	4	7
Rochester	2	10

GAMES TONIGHT

E. Rochester at Monaca.
Beaver Falls at Beaver.
Rochester at New Brighton.

MONACA BASEBALL LEAGUE
TEAM STANDING

	Won	Lost
Sportsmen	6	0
Balamuts	4	1
Pgh. Tube CIO	3	1
S. O. I.	2	3
Police Dept.	1	5
Scouts	0	6

GAMES THURSDAY

Pgh. Tube vs. Balamuts, H. S. Field.
Scouts vs. Police, Marshall Rd.
S. O. I. vs. Sportsmen, Sportsmen's Field.

A'S PURCHASE EPPS

PHILADELPHIA, June 12 —(UP)—Hal Epps, St. Louis Browns outfielder, today became the property of the Philadelphia Athletics under a straight cash transaction between the two clubs. The purchase of Epps was announced by Connie Mack, manager of the Athletics, who did not divulge the price.

PRIVATE BUCK

MARSHALL ISLANDS
"Anything to make me hungrier, Buck—His name sounds like Hashi Hash!"

Mel Ott Ignores Suggestions That He "Get Tough"

NEW YORK, June 14 (UP)—Mild Mel Ott won't play Jekyll-Hyde to spur his New York Giants to greater heights, he said today in response to suggestions that he "get tough" with his hired help.

"I am tough," he insisted. "I can be as tough as I have to be. Just ask my ball players. But I'm not going to put on a show. I'm not the fiery type, maybe, but neither is Joe McCarthy and I understand he's a pretty good manager."

Everybody has always liked the chunky little fellow who came to John McGraw as a catgher, 16 years old, in 1925, and became one of the best outfielders and power hitters in baseball.

As manager of last year's cellar inhabitants, Ott lost weight, fell off in his batting, was confined to bed with stomach disturbances.

"Nerves," he explained. "The doctor told me I'd just have to stop worrying so much, that's all. Do I worry? Sure, how can a man help it?"

Somewhere in the off-season, Ott acquired new philosophy, although he can't put his finger on it.

"I decided that a manager could be either an asset or a liability to his club," he explained. "If you strain nervously so much that you lose baseball values—jerk a pitcher too soon, or hold off too long; or hesitate to shove the infield back for a double play; or to try a 'squeeze' yourself—then the team senses it instinctively, and you're done for the day."

A manager's toughest job, Marvelous Mel said, is to take ball games "as they come, and dismiss them when the last putout is registered. Frankly, I can't do it, yet. I wish I could. But no manager ever thinks that the other team won; he conjures up scenes where his team lost."

The payoff in baseball is in common sense, plus a hunch, plus the nerve to carry through, Ott said, "and the rest is up to the boys."

A record-setter practically every time he hits a homer, walks, scores, or drives in a run, the "Little Giant" is enjoying one of his greatest seasons, but admits he has no scientific explanation either for his showing or the Giants'.

Beaver Recreation Loop Opens Season

The Beaver Recreation Baseball League had its opening at Gypsy Glen Field Monday evening when the Bridgewater Leopards defeated the Beaver United Presbyterians, 12 to 10.

Under supervision of Edward Schaffer, the four-team circuit will operate throughout the summer. On Thursday evening the Beaver Presidents will meet the Beaver Wildcats.

The Leopards leaped to an early lead and kept in front until the U. P.'s tied the count at 10-all with a four run rally in the sixth inning. Bob Schaughency's home run featured the rally.

Bridgewater came back to push across the winning tallies in the seventh. C. Rall clouted a triple and Brozich followed with a single. He scored later when Ferguson sacrificed. The hitting star of the opening game was C. Eicher of the Leopards who hit a single, double and a triple in four times at bat. The lineups:

Leopards	AB	R	H
M. Loncher, 1b	3	3	2
C. Eicher, lf	4	2	3
McBride, 2b	4	0	0
C. Rall, 3b	4	2	3
Brozich, c	4	2	1
Shutey, rf	3	1	1
St. Clair, ss	4	1	1
Ferguson, cf	4	0	0
L. Loncher, p	4	1	0
Totals	34	12	11

Beaver U. P.	AB	R	H
Howe, rf	1	1	0
Haugh, 2b	3	1	1
Staley, ss	5	0	0
Schaughency, 1b	4	2	2
Blair, cf	4	1	1
Daellenbach, lf	2	0	0
Aldridge, c	4	0	1
Davis, 3b	3	0	0
Fleming, p	3	3	0
Campbell, lf	2	2	0
Willoughby, cf	1	0	0
Totals	32	10	5

Leopards .... 208 000 2—12
Beaver U. P. .... 003 214 0—10

2-Base Hits—Eicher, Aldridge. 3-Base Hits—Eicher, Haugh, Rall. Home Run—Schaughency. First Base on Balls—Off Loncher 12, off Fleming 2. Struck Out—By Loncher 1, by Fleming 1, by Haugh 5.

PIRATES BEAT REDS, 3 TO 2, RED SOX GAIN SECOND PLACE

NEW YORK, June 14 (UP)—The Boston Red Sox, given a bare chance at an upper second division berth in pre-season reckonings, today were termed the American League's "Cinderella team" as they rested in second place, only a game and a half behind the leading St. Louis Browns.

The Red Sox, who gave such players as Ted Williams, John Pesky and Dom DiMaggio to the armed services before the start of last season, have suffered as heavily as any team in the majors from service calls and as a result, dropped from second to seventh place in the standings last year. Yet, with little talk and considerable work, Joe Cronin has put together an outfit which now rides the crest of a six-game winning streak and may threaten throughout the season.

Joe Bowman, either castoff or waived on by every club in the National League, returned Boston's latest victory, his fourth of the season, yesterday by holding the Philadelphia Athletics to seven hits while coasting to a 7-2 triumph.

The slumping New York Yankees reached a new low of seventh place at Washington as Knuckleballer Dutch Leonard shut them out on seven hits for a 3-0 triumph. The loss extended the Yankees' losing skein to seven games.

In the only other junior circuit contest played, Detroit at Cleveland having been rained out, the St. Louis Browns beat the Chicago White Sox, 5-3.

In the National League the St. Louis Cardinals, paced by Danny Litwhiler's three doubles and a single, unleashed a 16-hit attack against the Chicago Cubs to win, 8-3. Max Lanier recorded his seventh victory as the Red Birds protected their league lead.

Boston and Philadelphia split, the Braves taking the opener of two games, 2-1 behind the eight-hit pitching of Jim Tobin. The Phillies snapped their five-game losing streak in the afterpiece by outslugging the Braves to win, 8-7. Al Gerheauser lasted the route to record the triumph.

Ray Starr, making his first start as a Pittsburgh Pirate, defeated his old mates, the Cincinnati Reds, 3-2 in five innings. Three doubles and a walk broke the Bucs' string of 21 scoreless innings with three tallies in the fourth frame and gave Starr the decision before rain and hail halted the contest.

The Brooklyn Dodgers, making use of the New York Giants' favorite blow, the home run, beat their borough rivals, 9-4. Dixie Walker, Frenchy Bordagaray and Howie Schultz all hit for the circuit.

Former Grid Stars Now Military Police

ALLIED FORCE ADVANCE PRESS HEADQUARTERS, Italy, June 13. (UP) — Four former football stars are playing on the same team here—throwing blocks and tackles on Italian criminals and racketeers as members of the Military Police.

Best known member of the quartet is "Jumpin' Joe" Savoldi, one-time Notre Dame battering ram. Savoldi, who turned wrestler after his football career, is a special investigater in the black market division and likes it so well he intends to remain in police work after the war.

The others are Maj. Mike Mikulak, former Oregon and Chicago Cardinal back; Maj. Ralph Tolve, an All-Southern at Alabama, and Lt. Bob Di Natale of Boston College. Working with them is Angust McCabe, who used to do a bit of footballing for Columbia back in 1916.

They decreased the Naples traffic accident rate by 85 per cent and started a criminal investigation section that played havoc with counterfeit rings and black market gangs. Their work has been so effective that black market flour, which once sold for $1,000 a truck-load, has risen to over $3,000, which means that thefts of American supplies has been made a risky business.

"Savoldi makes every bit as good a detective as he did a football player," Mikulak said. "He had never done any police work before going to Africa in June of last year yet, he has cracked some of our toughest black market sases."

UNION CITY, N. J., June 14—Charlie (Lulu) Costantino, 133, New York, scored a decisive 10-round victory over Angel Aviles, 132, Mexico City, former Mexican featherweight champion, at Roosevelt Stadium here Tuesday night.

Collects 450 Canes Over Half Century

PITTSBURGH (U.P.)—Some people prefer collecting stamps; some shoes; not a few rare antiques, but William A. Hutchison of Tarentum has collected, within the last 48 years, odd and beautiful canes, many with highly interesting backgrounds.

In his more than 450-odd canes reposes one once owned by Horace Greeley and was a combination gun-cane used when Mr. Greeley "toured" the then wild and roaring west.

But probably the prize possession of his whole collection is the cane he bought in Mexico City in 1896, and which was responsible for his one-half century hobby. Hutchison said he bought it the day after attending a bull-fight from a peddler and found it had been made from the defunct horns of "el toros" of the previous day's battles.

Practically every country in the world is represented in his odd collection, and seven of the 450 odd canes are made from the wood near the birthplaces of Presidents James Buchanan, James Monroe, William McKinley, Abraham Lincoln, Thomas Jefferson, George Washington, and Calvin Coolidge. Not a few of the canes have Washington associations and one, our first President cut himself from a Long Island pine.

Not all of his canes represent the historical. Present-day events are signified by many of his masterpieces. He has carved a cane from a mulberry limb taken from Gen. Dwight D. Eisenhower's Denison, Tex., birthplace.

Chiggers, He Says, Go For The Blondes

LINCOLN, Neb. (U.P.)—The ubiquitous chigger, like gentlemen of two decades ago, prefer blondes, and has an unerring ability to locate same.

The pesky bugs seek and find thin-skinned victims, according to extension entymologist Don B. Whelan of the state agricultural college, and their keen sense of location leads them directly to the most likely source of food.

The majority of people fail to realize they have provided feeding ground until several hours after the unhappy event, he said, when small, red, itchy spots appear.

Whelan suggested a film of sulphur dust around the ankles, on the clothing, and at all likely points of contact to discourage the foragers' appetites. After exposure to the tiny tormentors, a dab of fly-spray on each bite will tend to kill the chiggers and soothe the itching, he said.

A warm, soapy bath was next on the entymologist's list of recommendations for scratching sufferers.

"If they have used sulphur on their skins, they'll need it," he commented, "and if they haven't, they'll need it even more."

MUSIC HATH CHARMS

OKLAHOMA CITY (U.P.)—Warden R. B. Conner of the Oklahoma penitentiary at McAlester has received authority from the state board of affairs to purchase musical instruments from the prison canteen fund for musical training of inmates of the institution.

Red Cross relief this spring to Kansas families affected by the worst floods since 1923 totaled $45,941.49, according to Harold R. Fowler, St. Louis, director of the Red Cross emergency relief office.

Six More Local Young Men Await Calls To Air Force

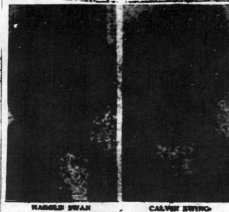

HAROLD SWAN

CALVIN EWING

MELVIN MANSUETTE

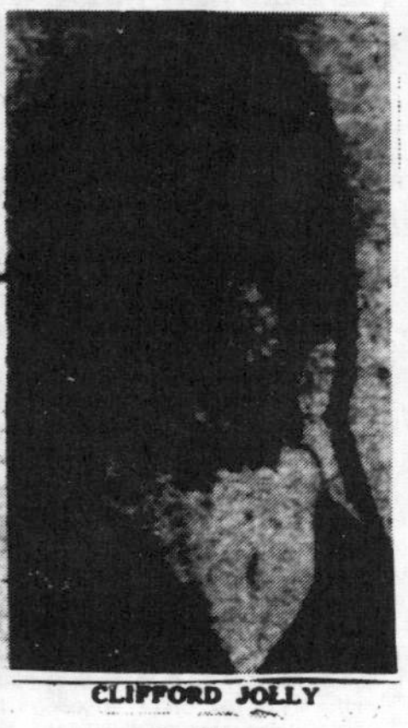

CLIFFORD JOLLY

W. K. RHODES

ANTHONY D'ALFONSO

Six more local youths have enlisted in the Army Air Force's rapidly swelling air armada for future training in air combat crews as gunners, pilots, bombardiers and navigators.

The sextette are:

Harold Leroy Swan, son of Mr. and Mrs. Robert Swan, R. D. 3, Aliquippa; Calvin Wayne Ewing, son of Mr. and Mrs. J. Calvin Ewing, R. D. 2, Aliquippa; Melvin Joseph Mansuette, son of Mr. and Mrs. Lawrence Mansuette, 134 Oakwood St.; Clifford Jack Jolly, son of Mr. and Mrs. C. J. Jolly, R. D. 3, Aliquippa; William George Rhodes, son of Mr. and Mrs. William A. Rhodes, 353 Linmar Terrace; and Anthony George D'Alfonso, son of Mr. and Mrs. Nick D'Alfonso, R. D. 2, Aliquipa.

All are students of the local High school with the exception of Jolly, and Rhodes, who are receiving their educations at Hopewell High School.

The enlistees will remain in school until they attain their 18th birthdays after which they will be called into active service.

INJURED ON - - -

(Continued from Page One)

coast the Jerry started throwing up a lot of flak at us and we started to get nervous as hell and couldn't wait to get out of those 'box cars' and get our feet on the ground so we could fight back. Finally we got the order to prepare to jump and in a few moments I found myself out in the air.

"My 'chute opened with a jolt that almost tore me in half and then I began to realize that this was the real thing, not a joy ride. For the air was filled with machine-gun slugs! Wow! It reminded me of a bunch of kids shooting Roman candles on the Fourth of July!

"All the bullets were different colors and all of them seemed to be headed for yours truly! I was thankful that we had jumped at such a low altitude when I felt myself smack the ground a few seconds later.

"I found I had landed in a little field about an acre square and, after scouting around, discovered I was the only person there. There were three sleepy looking cows, which looked up as if to say 'Hi Yank, what kept you so long?' I like to think of that little French field as Aliquippa's gift to France — one of the very first bits of their land to be liberated and handed back to them.

"When I left the field I met up with the rest of the boys and we proceeded to go to work. We knocked out a coastal gun position, quite a few pill-boxes and a great many machine gun positions during those early morning hours before the sea-borne troops began to land. But by late in the afternoon of D-Day the Jerry was beginning to make it hot for us and we were damned happy when American troops from the beach broke through to help us.

"That was a great meeting because we knew right then that the invasion would be a success.

"I remained with the outfit six days and then had to be evacuated due to injuries I received on the jump D-Day. But I'm okay now and ready for another hop on Hienie.

"The German is a tough customer and we boys respect his soldiering —but he's in for a pasting from the Yanks. He's met the better man and he knows it We may not have the experience he has, but we have guts, intelligence and a damn wonderful country to fight for.

"I wish you could have seen the tanks and guns unloading into France. It would have made you proud to see what those bonds of yours was doing. I guess every doughboy these days has a prayer of thanks in his heart for the folks at home who are doing such a great job. Keep it up and we'll kick the pants off Hitler before he can say 'Actung'.

"I sure miss the paper these days and hope it won't be too long until The Times shows up again. Until then I'll say best o'luck and jump out here.

"Ray Dye,
U. S. Paratrooper."

Thursday 500 Club Meets At Estok Home

Mrs. Mike Shandik, Wireton, entertained members of the Thursday Night 500 club last night at the home of her sister-in-law, Mrs. Michael Estok, McMinn St., here.

Prize awards for the evening went to Mrs. Michael Katchur and Mrs. Estok.

Refreshments were served by the hostess. Plans were made to meet again Thursday evening, August 17, at the home of Mrs. John Sopko, 604 Grand Ave., Sheffield Terrace.

POOR NAVIGATION

WOONSOCKET, R. I. (U.P.)—It was necessary to call a sizable crew of policemen and firemen to arrest Enest Savoie on a drunkenness charge. The suspect had become wedged between two buildings.

Information services were supplied to 2,648,929 members of the armed forces and civilians by the United Service Organizations during a single month, the most recent USO statistical report shows.

DRIVE ON FOREST FIRES

OKLAHOMA CITY (U.P.)—State and private funds in Oklahoma will be matched with $28,451 received from the Federal government to fight forest fires, according to Glen Durrell, director of state parks. An estimated 30 per cent of the state's timber lands burn out every year, the director said.

SUCCEEDS PHILIPPINES' QUEZON

SUCCEEDING President Manuel Quezon, who died after a long illness, Sergio Osmena is shown, right, being sworn in as new president of the Philippine Commonwealth. Osmena, who as vice president has been handling Philippine affairs in Washington since the Japs overran the islands, takes the oath from Supreme Court Justice Robert H. Jackson in Washington. *(International)*

SPANISH DICTATOR FRANCO KNEELS

ON THE PEAK OF THE ANGELS, a Spanish hill that was formerly known as "the red peak," Gen. Francisco Franco, El Caudillo (the leader), kneels with his wife as they attend the celebration of the enthronement of the Sacred Heart. *(International)*

Photog Killed

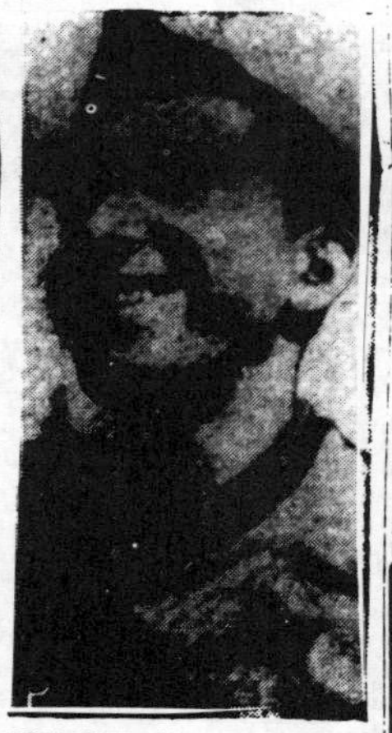

BEDE IRVIN, above, an American war pool photographer on the staff of the Associated Press, has been killed in action on the Normandy front, according to an announcement by United States Army authorities in London. Irvin was on an assignment with the U. S. Ninth Air Force when he died near St. Lo. A native of Des Moines, Ia., Irvin is survived by wife, former Kathryne Hankin, of Los Angeles. *(International)*

CRACKER PUFFS ACCOMPANY COOLING SUMMER DRINKS

Cracker Puffs that taste like popcorn are a novel acompaniment for summer drinks, go well with soups, and make appetite-provoking tidbits to serve before dinner.

The directions are simple: Soak soda crackers in cold water for 10 minutes. Lift carefully from water with perforated pancake turner and drain. Place on baking sheet far enough apart to allow for expansion. Spread a small amount of butter on each cracker. Bake in hot oven (425 degrees) for 30-40 minutes until light brown and crisp. Salt to taste.

Automobile accident statistics show that at 20 miles per hour there are 12 fatalities for each 1,000 injuries, while at 51 miles per hour and over, there are 92 fatalities—more than a seven-fold increase.

Jap Killed By Valley Marine

It took 20 days for Marine Pfc. Ray Schafer, of Little Rock, S. C., to kill his first Jap. Then he got all the action he wanted on Saipan, in the Marianas.

One night, when Schafer was waiting to be relieved from watch, two Japs suddenly appeared about 10 yards from his foxhole. Schafer let go with his fire, killing one enemy and wounding another.

A few days later, Schafer was standing watch with Corporal Bronislaw Roner, of Beaver Falls, when two Japs approached, jabbering in their native language. Thinking the enemy was about to surrender, Roner climbed out of his foxhole. Suddenly one Jap reached for a hand grenade.

Schafer fired, wounding the Jap, and then leaped out of his shelter, tackling the enemy and yelling for Roner to shoot. Roner put a bullet through the enemy's forehead. Not satisfied with one, the Marines were pretty unhappy because the second Jap got away.

Of the food packages sent by the International Red Cross committee to our wounded men who are prisoners of war, 90 per cent safely reach their destination.

$5 GOLD PIECE IN RADISH

CHICAGO (U.P.)—Jack and the beanstalk have nothing on Jack James, 12, of Oak Park, Ill., and his victory garden. When Jack went out to pull a few radishes for dinner one day he noticed a particularly juicy-looking one. He bit into it and found a five-dollar gold piece around which the radish had grown completely.

Naturalized at 10

LYNN, Mass. (U.P.)—The youngest naturalized citizen in the United States is 10-year-old Colette H. Ducette. A native of St. Raphael, Que., Colette would not have been eligible for naturalization until she reached 18 if she had not been adopted legally by Mr. and Mrs. Alfred W. Ducette.

Retired Minister "Drafted"

PITTSFIELD, Mass. (U.P.)—Though he retired from the ministry several years ago, the Rev. Oscar W. [illegible] has been "drafted" for a summer schedule which includes Sunday services in five churches.

THE DAILY TIMES

1874—and WESTERN ARGUS—1803

ROCHESTER - BEAVER - MONACA - FREEDOM - BRIDGEWATER - CONWAY - VANPORT - MIDLAND

Established April 2, 1874 | Beaver and Rochester, Pa., Monday, August 28, 1944 | Single Copy 4 Cents — 24 Cents A Week

YANKS CHOP WAY ALONG MARNE

Yanks Cut Way Up Rhone; Big Gains Reported

Dash May Prove One Of Most Important Victories Since D-Day. Open Fifth Day Of Bombing Against Badly Battered Nazis. Tanks Cut Through Defenses

ROME, Aug. 28 (UP)—American tanks and infantry have killed, wounded or captured 15,000 Germans in a fighting 40-mile dash up the Rhone Valley to Montelimar, half way between the Mediterranean and Lyon, it was announced today.

In probably the most important victory since the initial landings only two weeks ago, the Americans cut to pieces the German 19th Army in several days of battle as it attempted to withdraw north along the Rhone Valley.

Infantry, mobile artillery and hundreds of fighter-bombers and fighters joined in the slaughter of the fleeing enemy units. Bombers previously had destroyed bridges across the Rhone, preventing the Germans from escaping to the west bank.

The survivors were in full flight northward from Montelimar, 40 miles north of Avignon and 80 miles south of Lyon. Included in the decimated enemy units were elements of the 11th Panzer and 198th Infantry Divisions, possibly reinforced by elements of three other divisions.

LONDON, Aug. 28 (UP)—American heavy bombers today opened the fifth successive day of an intensified Allied aerial offensive which sent nearly 10,000 tons of explosives showering onto the Germans yesterday in their home country and in France.

SUPREME HEADQUARTERS, AEF, Aug. 28 (UP)—American tank columns knifed through weak German defenses in the valley of the Marne and drove in on the historic battleground of Chateau-Thierry today, while Nazi reports said a second thrust north of Troyes had reached the Marne at Vitry-Francois, 100 miles beyond Paris and barely ninety miles from the German border.

SUPREME HEADQUARTERS, AEF, Aug. 28 (UP) Allied forces have reached the "immediate vicinity of Romilly, 60 miles southeast of Paris, a communique announced today.

CHUNGKING, Aug. 28 (UP)—The commander of the Fourth Chinese Army, Chang Teh Neng, was executed Friday for neglect in duty which resulted in the loss of Changsha last June, the Central News Agency reported today.

MOSCOW, Aug. 28 (UP) Two powerful Soviet armies poured through the Galati Gap into Central Romania today, heading for the Ploesti oil fields and Bucharest in a momentous drive military observers believed would liberate the Balkans within a few weeks.

Mechanized Cossacks of Marshal Rodion Y. Malinovsky's 2nd Ukrainian Army paced the lightning Soviet advance, driving a spearhead through Ploesti's outer defenses and sending another racing toward the Romanian capital.

(A Berlin broadcast said "bitter battles" already were raging at Ploesti between German and Romanian troops.)

Fanning out south of Ramnicul-Sarat, where Malinovsky brought his forces to within 57 miles of Romania's rich oil fields and 72 miles of Bucharest, one column swept along the railroad to Ploesti and the other struck down the main highway to the capital. The Red Army troops, moving along the western side of the 45-mile wide gap below Focsani, were meeting only token resistance from the fleeing Germans and Romanian troops were surrendering on contact.

War History

A German air attack on Paris proved to be a failure, August 28, 1915, news flashes said.

Lost and Found

Nazis Flee Before Patton's Tanks

By UNITED PRESS

NORTHERN FRANCE—American tank columns knife through German defenses in valley of Marne and drive to historic battlefield of Chateau-Thierry while Germans report a second thrust north of Troyes had reached Vitry En Francois, barely 90 miles from German border.

SOUTHERN FRANCE—American tanks and infantry kill or capture 15,000 Germans in 40 mile drive up Rhone Valley to Montelimar, halfway between Mediterannean coast and Lyon.

RUSSIA—Two powerful Soviet armies pour through Galati Gap into Central Romania in drive that observers believe will liberate Balkans within few weeks.

AIR WAR—American heavy bombers open fifth consecutive day of intensive aerial assault which sent 10,000 tons of bombs on Germans in home country and France.

PACIFIC—Allied bombers hit 10 large Japanese bases in three-day series of attacks.

ITALY—Polish troops of British 8th Army advance seven miles beyond Metauro river and send spearheads across Arzilla river to point five miles southeast of Pesaro.

American Forces Storm Through Marne Valley Toward Germany

By LOUIS F. KEEMLE
United Press War Editor

American mobile columns stormed through the valley of the Marne east of Paris toward the German frontier against scattered enemy resistance today, while northwest of the capital Allied forces expanded beyond their Seine bridgeheads in an apparent drive to clear the robot bomb coast along the Channel.

In Southern France it was announced that American tanks and infantry had killed, wounded or captured 15,000 Germans in an advance of 40 miles up the Rhone Valley to Montelimar half way between the Mediterranean and Lyon.

On the eastern front, the 2nd and 3rd Ukrainian armies poured through the Galati Gap into central Romania, headed for the Ploesti oil fields and Bucharest and meeting only rear guard resistance from the fleeing Germans. Not only Romania but Bulgaria, Yugoslavia and possibly Hungary were slipping from the Nazi grasp in the growing collapse of the whole Balkan set-up.

The most spectacular Allied progress in France was that of Lt. Gen. George S. Patton's tank forces in the Marne Valley. Front line dispatches said the Americans in this "third battle of the Marne" were meeting sharp resistance in some places from enemy rear guards numbering up to 1,000 men but at most points only handfuls of Germans barred the way.

Over this historic battleground, where the Germans were halted in 1914 and broke in 1918 in the second battle of the Marne that preceded the end of the war, the Americans were winning almost by default. After capturing Meaux, 23 miles east of Paris, they crossed the river and were approaching Chateau-Thierry, scene of memorable fighting in the last war.

Allied headquarters said the Americans had sped on beyond captured Troyes without meeting more than token resistance, and Berlin reported they had reached Vitry, 100 miles beyond Paris and barely 30 miles from the German border.

An official announcement said General Patton's men had already captured 65,000 Germans and killed 16,000 in the eastward sweep.

A "security blackout" barred official news on the progress of the Allied forces beyond the Seine bridgeheads, but London newspapers said the battle of the robot coast had begun, and one reported the British were 25 miles north of the Seine at at undisclosed point and were headed toward Dieppe.

Public Aid Cases

ISBURG, Aug. 28. (UP)—Virtually all of Pennsylvania's 140,638 current public aid cases have resulted from "unemployability" and have been listed on relief rolls for "many years," the State Public Assistance Department reported today.

The total comprises 84,902 on old-age assistance rolls; 20,672, general assistance, 22,135 aid to dependent children, and 12,929 blind pensions.

Pershing Honored

PHILADELPHIA, Aug. 28 — (UP)—Gen. John J. Pershing, who led the American armies to victory in France in 1918, today was named recipient of the Army and Navy Union's annual medal of honor for outstanding service to the American people.

8 Fliers Killed

SMYRNA FIELD, Tenn., Aug. 28. (UP)—Eight fliers were killed in the mid-air collision of two B-24 Liberator bombers in Rutherford county Friday night, Col. Stanley M. Umstead, base commanding officer, announced. All occupants of the two planes were killed when the planes crashed. Victims of the crash included Sgt. Joseph J. Froelich, 29, crew chief, Lincoln Place, Pa.

GET EQUAL TIME

WASHINGTON, Aug. 28 (UP) All qualified political parties will be granted equal weekly time on Army shortwave radio facilities for broadcast of "political addresses" to armed forces, overseas, a War Department announcement said today.

Church Burned Mortgage at Sunday Afternoon Ceremony

By BILL BUTLER

On Sunday afternoon, Wayman Chapel A. M. E. church, New Brighton, burned their mortgage before a capacity crowd of members and well wishers from all over Beaver county.

Under the leadership of the Rev. L. J. Izzard, the pastor, a drive was launched to raise $3,500 to liquidate the indebtedness. This drive went over the top by raising $4,060 with the result the trustees were able to pay off the mortgage debt of $3,110.25 and free the church of all other indebtedness.

A program consisted of an organ voluntary by Robt. M. Brown, hymn led by Rev. M. S. Parrish, prayer by Rev. E. J. Sheffield, solo by Roy Colman, Scripture lesson by Rev. J. W. Cock and remarks by representatives of the New Brighton Ministerial Association, and Rev. George C. Thomas of the Ministers and Laymen's Alliance.

The sermon was by Rev. William McKinley Dawkins, pastor, St. James A. M. E. church, Pittsburgh, Pa.

Harry Webster, Sr., secretary of the stewards board and Miss Anna Alford, secretary of trustees board, made further remarks after which William Webster presented the mortgage to the pastor. L. A. Stanton and Mrs. Irene Webster held the mortgage while Mrs. Jennie Gardner and Robt. Brown set the flame to it. Miss Rose Alice Cephas and Master Malcourt Robert Bean, Jr., received the ashes. Mrs. William R. Webster was mistress of ceremonies.

Some of the out of town guests present were: Mr. and Mrs. Henry Howard, Mr. and Mrs. Dan Haliburton, Washington, Pa., Mr. and Mrs. Andrew Haliburton, Lexington, Ky., Mrs. Benjamin Griffin, Tampa, Fla., Mr. and Mrs. James Branch, Sewickley, Mrs. Cora J. Logan, Masury, Ohio, Mr. and Mrs. Edwin J. Izzard, Braddock, Pa., Miss Odessa Izzard and Mrs. Lucy Roy, Washington, D. C., and others.

DRIVE NEARS OLD WAR SCENES

ENGLAND
FOLKSTONE
OSTEND
DUNKERQUE
CALAIS
BOULOGNE
YPRES
BELG.
ENGLISH CHANNEL
MONS
DOUAI
ARRAS
CAMBRAI
DIEPPE
ST. QUENTIN
LE HAVRE
ROUEN
CAEN
FRANCE
MANTES
PARIS
VERSAILLES
MARNE
CHARTRES

GHOSTS OF ANOTHER WORLD WAR stalk the French areas which now lie in the path of major drives in the current Battle for France and it may well be that many a son will fight close to the grave of his father. As the drive turns northward from below Paris, the Marne River again is in the limelight and, pushing north and eastward, U. S. troops move toward World War I battlefields (indicated by circles) such as Soissons, Amiens, Ypres, St. Quentin and Cambrai. At Abbeville lies one goal which may be of vital importance in wiping out the Rocket Coast, already harrassed by the successful push to the Seine. (*International*)

MONACA PLANS GARDEN SHOW

Monaca Garden club's second annual Garden Show will be presented Thursday evening, August 31, in Monaca high school. Miss Agnes McGeary, program chairman, under whose direction the program has been arranged, is being assisted by Mrs. George C. Berry, Mrs. Fred T. Berkman, Mrs. Smith D. Hicks and Mrs. John M. Dunn.

The garden show, opening at 7 o'clock, will be followed by a style show to be presented by Center Township 4-H "Sew-if-you-Can" club girls. At 9 o'clock, an "Old-Fashioned Garden Party," under the direction of Mrs. Lucille Michael Plug, will be presented. Music will be furnished by the Monaca High School orchestra, under the direction of Russell M. Wood. There are to be awards, also a door prize.

All exhibits must be staged and ready for judging by four o'clock on August 31. The placing and staging will be under the supervision of the committee. They will be staged by class and number only. No exhibit may be entered in more than one class and all exhibits that do not conform to the specifications of the schedule will be disqualified. All flowers or vegetables entered for competition must have been grown by the exhibitor, and all canned foods, jams and jellies must have been canned by the exhibitor. Only one entry will be permitted in each class by any one exhibitor. No prizes will be given to unworthy exhibits even if there is only one entry in that class.

All entries are the property of the Garden Show committee until the close of the show. Blue ribbons will be awarded for first prize, red ribbons for second, and sweepstakes prizes for the exhibitor winning the greatest number of points.

In Division 1, Flowers will be staged in two sections, 1. specimen; 2, arrangements; in Division 2, vegetables will be judged on the following: quality and size, condition and appearance, and in Division 2, canned foods will be judged on quality—clearness of liquid, perfectness of material, and general appearance — uniformity of product, color and arrangement in jar.

Beaver Man Home After Serving In Two Wars Abroad

Lt. Col. Paul Howe (above) is home with his family in River Road, Beaver, after serving the past 2½ years in the Army. His transfer to inactive status became effective today.

He spent a year in Africa with the Second Corps under General Patton, returning to the United States last December. Since then he has been stationed at Camp Croft, S. C., and Fort McClellan, Ala.

Lieutenant Colonel Howe, also a veteran of World War I, is an honorary commander in the Army of the King of Tunisia. He was presented a medal by the King at the palace, as one of the interesting highlights of his year overseas.

GOOD WASTE PAPER is needed in our war effort. Save

Matthew Fronko To Visit Mother

Tech. Sgt. Matthew Fronko, home from England on a 21-day furlough where he participated in twenty-eight missions over German occupied countries, will visit his mother, Mrs. Susanna Fronko, and family, and other Monaca relatives. Fronko wears the Air Medal and three Oak Leaf Clusters and a Silver Star. He has been in the service for two years, and has been serving overseas the past year. Following his furlough, he will report at an army air base, Lincoln, Neb., where he will be an instructor.

Darlington Man Killed In France

Tech. Sgt. Stephen Salters, 26, son of Mrs. Mary Salters, Darlington, was killed in action in France on August 10, according to word received Saturday evening by his wife, Mrs. Caroline Stein Salters, formerly of Monaca. He left with Company B, New Brighton in February, 1941. Mrs. Salters enlisted in the WAVES in July and will leave September 6 for Hunter College, N. Y. She makes her home with her parents, Mr. and Mrs. Joseph Stein, near Beaver Falls.

Weather Forecast

WESTERN PENNSYLVANIA: Cloudy with intermitten showers today and tonight; Tuesday, fair and cooler. Pollen count, 464.

Plan To Reduce Number Of Draft Boards In State

HARRISBURG, Aug. 28 (UP) State Selective Service headquarters had plans underway today to cut expenses in Pennsylvania by consolidating as many of the 422 local draft board offices as possible since induction quotas have been reduced.

Wherever possible three or perhaps four boards will be merged to curtail personnel and save rental costs, a headquarters spokesman said, and it is probable that a number of counties will be left with only one office.

Each local board, however, will retain its previous jurisdiction and continue to operate as an individual unit, the spokesman said. Records will be kept separate and quotas will be filled only from individual districts.

Germans Renew Robot Attacks

LONDON, Aug. 28 (UP)—The Germans resumed their flying bomb attacks on London and the southern counties shortly after noon today, ending a 31-hour respite from the terror raids.

The missles which hit the affected areas today were the first since before daylight Sunday and following big stories by London newspapers speculating that the robot bombs might be on the way out.

Headlines on the stories ranged from "Battle for Flybomb Sites Has Begun" to "End of Flybomb Now in Sight."

The extent of today's attacks, however, was not disclosed.

Before the lull began, a number of bombs that penetrated a heavy cannonade caused some deaths including three in workers' homes which were hit when one weapon fell within 100 yards of where a previous one landed. Another victim was a girl, who literally disappeared when a bomb landed close after she refused to take cover.

7 District Mines Remain Closed

Seven major Western Pennsylvania mines remained closed today as a supervisory workers' dispute went before the War Labor Board in Washington, but wildcat strikes at other district pits were called off.

Back at work today were 2,200 miners at the Jones and Laughlin Steel Corporation's Vesta No. 5 at Vestaburg, Heisley Coal Company's Nanty-Glo pit in Cambria County, and the Pittsburgh Coal Company's Lindley at Houston, Washington County.

Still down are the Frances and Berry pits of the Ford Collieries Company at Curtisville and the Ernest, Yatesboro, Kent 1-2, Lucerne and Waterman of the Rochester and Pittsburgh Coal Company at Indiana.

Meanwhile, President John McAlpine and Secretary Robert Condra of the United Clerical, Technical and Supervisory Employes of the Mining Industry, an affili-

Continued on Page Two

AIR NAVIGATOR

Flight Officer Jack Hesser, (above) son of Mrs. Sarah Hesser, Deer Lane, Rochester, is stationed at the Radar School in Boca Raton, Fla. A navigator in the Air Forces, he received his wings and commission at San Marcos, Tex. A former Rochester high school grid star, he graduated in 1938 and attended Bethany and Centenary Colleges before enlisting in the Air Forces in February, 1943. He was formerly employed at the Curtiss-Wright Corporation plant, Borough Township. He received his training at Keesler Field, Miss., University of Arkansas and Laredo, Tex.

HURT IN ACTION

Pfc. Cuy R. Smith, Jr., (above) only son of Mr. and Mrs. Guy R. Smith, Deer Lane, Rochester, was seriously wounded in action in France, August 8, according to a telegram received by his parents Saturday evening from the War Department.

Serving with the infantry, the local youth has been overseas since June of this year, and in France since July. He enlisted March 11, 1943, and was called to active duty June 17, following his graduation from Rochester high school. He received his basic training at Ft. McClellan, Ala., and later trained at Ft. Benning, Ga. The last letter received from him was written August 5.

BEAVER GUNNER

Pfc. Jack R. Madder, (above) son of Mr. and Mrs. Harry C. Madder, Corporation street, Beaver, graduated from Aerial Gunnery School at Harlington, Tex., Army Air Field. In addition to a promotion in grade he received his gunner's wings.

Hunting Licenses For 1944 On Sale

Pennsylvania hunting licenses for 1944 are now on sale at the office of County Treasurer Charles J. O'Loughlin. 1943 hunting licenses expire on August 31. The license fee for residents' is the same as last year, $2.00.

Among Missing

The name of Pfc. Frank A. Tataseo, son of Mrs. Anna Tataseo, Beaver Falls, was included in a casualty list of U. S. soldiers missing in action in the European theatre of war, released by the War Department today.

COMING BACK

WASHINGTON, Aug. 28 (UP) Madame Chiang Kai-Shek, wife of the Chinese Generalissimo, is seriously ill and will come to the United States in a few weeks for urgently needed medical treatment, her brother-in-law, Chinese Finance Minister Dr. H. H. Kung, disclosed today.

DEADLINE TO REGISTER IS OCTOBER 7TH

October 7 Is Also Last Day To Change Party Or Address To Vote At Presidential Election; Several Thousand County Residents Are Not Registered

Beaver County citizens who are not now registered and eligible to vote at the presidential election this Fall, have only about six weeks in which to register, J. J. Zimmerman, chief county registrar, announced today.

Saturday, October 7, is the deadline for registrations. After that date no registrations can be made for the General election on November 7. October 7 is also the deadline for changing party affiliations and filing notices of change of address from one voting district to another.

Persons who move from one voting district to another after September 7, are not eligible to vote at the Presidential election as Pennsylvania's laws require 60 days residence in the voting district. However, persons who have moved prior to Sept. 7, may notify the registration office of change of address anytime up to and including October 7.

Electors who move or have moved to a new address within the same voting district have until ten days before the election to advise the registration office.

There are several thousand Beaver County residents, Zimmerman said today, whose names are not in the registration files. The latest count, made only a few days ago, reveals that there are 54,287 persons registered, including 34,090 Republicans, 19,775 Democrats, and 422 in the other minor political parties.

Injured In Fall, Dies In Hospital

Lester Liptak, 33, Kaye avenue, Monaca Heights, died Sunday morning at 11:20 o'clock in Rochester hospital from injuries received when he fell over a 55-foot embankment above an old abandoned stone quarry on Grove avenue, Monaca Heights, Sunday morning.

According to police, the accident is believed to have occurred about 1:45 o'clock. The body was removed from Rochester hospital to the Douds funeral home, Aliquippa.

An employe of the St. Joseph Lead Company, he is survived by the widow, Mrs. Ann Ondila Liptak; five children, Harry, Mary Ann, Richard, Stephen John and Paul, all at home; the parents, Mr. and Mrs. Steve Liptak, Aliquippa; three brothers, Clyde, Vincent and Richard Liptak, all of New Sheffield, and one sister, Miss Romaine Liptak, New Sheffield.

The body will be taken to the home of his parents, 2406 Linden avenue, Aliquippa, where friends will be received and funeral services will be held Wednesday afternoon at 2:30 o'clock. Interment will be in Union cemetery.

Four Boys Born

GAINESVILLE, Fla., Aug. 28 (UP)—Quadruplet boys, born last night to a 22-year-old farm girl, the wife of an army private, were reported in good condition today in their Hall County Memorial hospital incubators.

Their births were described by Dr. George W. Karelas as normal. The quads are the sons of Pvt. and Mrs. Charles E. Lee, Gainesville. Lee is stationed at Camp Blanding, Fla.

ROCHESTER FLIER VETERAN OF 226 MISSIONS IN CHINA AREA

A veteran of 226 missions in the China-Burma-India theatre of operations, Staff Sgt. John D. McNamee, son of Mr. and Mrs. John McNamee, Washington street, Rochester, has been awarded the Distinguished Flying Cross and the Air Medal.

A pilot of an L-5, attached to an Army liaison squadron, he has been overseas more than a year and in letters to his parents reveals many interesting incidents. He, with several of the men in his unit were asked to write of their most exciting mission and in a letter to his parents McNamee stated:

"It was hard for me to choose which was my most exciting. On two different occasions I flew out Japanese prisoners and then there was the time I cracked up my airplane right in the heart of Burma and was walking for two days with some British soldiers in Jap-occupied territory.

"One time I flew into a strip completely surrounded by Japs and evacuated three wounded soldiers. I could go on and on telling you of my exciting missions."

McNamee and his group were highly commended for their "exceptional skill and magnificent disregard for flying conditions which were continuously worse than those normally experienced in other theatres of war," according to a letter received from Brigadier Perrons, of the First Air Command, United States Army Air Forces.

A graduate of Rochester high school, he has been in the armed forces since September, 1942, and before his induction was employed at the Curtiss-Wright plant, Beaver.

The McNamees have another son, Sgt. L. F. McNamee, a classification expert with the Personnel Section of the Army Air Forces, stationed at San Francisco.

Yankees Only Two Games Out Of First Place

New York Grabs Doubleheader As Browns Lose, 4-3

Race In American Loop Now Tighter Than A Snare Drum

NEW YORK, Sept. 1 (U.P.)—Pennant fever, a chronic condition with the New York Yankees which occurs as annually as hay fever, gripped the entire squad today and the guy spreading the contagion was fiery Frankie Crosetti, the last of the old Bronx Bombers.

They're all gone but Frankie, but the sparky infielder remembers the habits he acquired with other championship teams, so he hit a ninth inning homer with two out yesterday to give the Yankees a double victory over Washington, 9 to 4 and 4 to 3, an accomplishment which reduced the lead of the St. Louis Browns to just two games.

It isn't amiss to trace the upswing of the Yankees from the late that Crosetti left a California war plant to bolster a team that appeared to be going no place. When he broke into the lineup as a regular at Philadelphia on Aug. 4, the Yankees were in third place, six games off the pace and going in reverse. Since then they have won 18 and lost 12 and Crosetti has been batting .298, 32 points above his lifetime major league average of .246.

The score was 3-all and Pitcher Alex Carrasquel was bearing down when Crosetti broke up the ball game, giving Rookie Mel Queen his third victory. The Yanks won the opener without difficulty, taking advantage of five Washington errors to score at will. Crosetti made three hits and batted in two runs in this contest, but the big offensive punch was supplied by Johnny Lindell's three run triple. Joey Kuhel hit a homer for the Nats in the first game and Nick Etten got his 15th for the Yankees in the second.

Detroit scored three unearned runs off the jittery Browns at St. Louis, to win 4 to 3 last night. Paul (Dizzy) Trout doing a two inning relief stint for Frankie Overmire gained his 23rd victory, while Willis Hudlin, up from Little Rock of the Southern Association, relieved Sig Jakucki to be tagged with the defeat. The Tigers made the winning run in the ninth when Mike (Pinkey) Higgins singled home Roger Cramer.

Yesterday's Star—Frankie Crosetti, last of the old guard Yankees, who sparked New York to a double victory over Washington with a homer, three singles and a stolen base for the day.

BASEBALL
HOW THEY STAND

National League

Yesterday's Results

No games scheduled.

Standing Of The Teams Today

	Won	Lost	Pct.
St. Louis ...	91	30	.752
PITTSBURGH	71	50	.587
Cincinnati ...	67	51	.568
New York ...	57	67	.460
Chicago	54	65	.454
Boston	50	74	.403
Philadelphia .	48	72	.400
Brooklyn ...	48	77	.384

Games Today—Pitching Selections

St. Louis at Pittsburgh (Night Ostermueller (11-4) vs. Schmidt (5-8) (8:30 o'clock).

New York at Brooklyn—Fischer (4-12) vs. Melton (7-10).

Boston at Philadelphia (2) (Twilight-Night)—Hutchings (1-2) and C. Barrett (7-14) vs. Gerheauser (7-13) and R. Barrett (9-14).

Chicago at Cincinnati—(Night)—Fleming (8-9) vs. Walters (19-6).

American League

Yesterday's Results

New York 9; Washington 4
New York 4; Washington 3
Detroit 4; St. Louis 3
Only games scheduled.

Standing Of The Teams Today

	Won	Lost	Pct.
St. Louis ...	71	56	.559
New York ...	69	58	.543
Detroit	67	58	.536
Boston	68	60	.531
Philadelphia .	62	68	.477
Cleveland ...	61	67	.477
Chicago	58	67	.464
Washington ..	53	75	.414

Games Today—Pitching Selections

Washington at New York—Lefebvre (2-3) vs. Bonham (10-6).

Detroit at St. Louis (night)—houser (21-8) vs. (13-6).

Philadelphia at Boston—Black (8-9) or Christopher (11-11) vs. Bowman (10-6).

Cleveland at Chicago—(Night)—Smith (7-10) vs. Haynes (3-4).

A 270 day food reserve for each soldier overseas and a 90-day reserve for each one in this country is maintained by the U. S. Army.

Red Peppers

BY NICK WALLACE

RACCOON NATIONAL PARK, Sept. 1—**Variety is the spice of life and battling the same foe day in and day out can get monotonous.**

Well-fed on a diet of intra-squad scrimmages, the hard-working Quips were due for a new lease on life today with the completion of arrangements to have the Baldwin Twp. squad test the Aschmanites in both morning and afternoon drills.

Encamped in the same project about a mile from Quip headquarters, the Baldwin boys this year are under the tutelage of Harold Wilkinson, former Duquesne High mentor.

Wilkinson tutored the Dukes to a widely-heralded upset victory last fall over Clairton. It was the first defeat in 26 starts for the Bears and knocked them out of the running for the WPIAL AA title.

Wilkinson moved over to Baldwin this year, taking over a post vacated by his brother, now located in Florida with the Navy. Baldwin, a thriving township near Brentwood, is only in its second year of football. It holds a Class A classification in the WPIAL.

To emphasize the importance of Aliquippa's Curbstone Coaches, it may be pertinent to point out that the Baldwin lads are paying their own way at camp. Each player dishes out $12 for the week they spend at this project.

Wilkinson has installed the T-formation and the Notre Dame shift at Baldwin. It will be interesting to see how the Quips will adapt themselves against the tricky formations.

The two teams were scheduled to stage a dummy scrimmage with no attempts being made to score touchdowns.

• • •

Coach Aschman refused to halt last evening's scrimmage session in spite of the torrential downpour. The mud-splattered gridders had no objections, however, to battling through 45 full minutes in a driving storm.

The veterans—the only term we can apply to the lads in the upper bracket since to call them varsity men is entirely erroneous—were tested both offensively and defensively by the the so-called newcomers.

It marked the first time the vets were on the defensive and the results to Aschman were just "about what were expected." Little Steve (Lindy) Tselepis was his usual rip-roaring self, representing the fifth man in the newcomer backfield. However, the stocky guard continues to have trouble with his offensive blocking.

• • •

The seasoned linemen opened up numerous holes but the backs, especially the unexperienced ones, looked bad trying to hit the gaps.

Additional plays were given the candidates in the morning and the vets surprised by assimilating them without too much refreshing. Up until yesterday, the squad had been using only fundamental plays. If they can master the newest strategems, they will be all set for a regulation ball-game, Aschman declared.

For the first time, passing and pass defense was stressed. The usual wild heaves and dropped throws were plentiful.

Edward (Headgear) Maly, 148-pound halfback hopeful, was a new arrival to camp yesterday. Without the benefit of calisthenics and preliminaries, Maly stepped into a bruising exercise in which a halfback and an end teamed together to attempt blocking an incoming tackle. Maly, at that time, was one of several tackles trying to perform the break-through.

He took plenty of punishment but showed that he relishes it. He put to shame the other tackles, who had a week's start on him and are familar with the position which is totally strange to him.

Maly, a 16-year-old junior who stands five-feet, six inches, was late in reporting because the coaching staff felt it unwise for him to aspire for a starting berth since he will be eligible only for another season.

• • •

Pat Haljisey, hard-charging halfback, was sidelined yesterday during the scrimmaging. And he was heartbroken for he wants nothing else but to be in the thick of action.

Pat, who has suffered countless bruises once scrimmaging got underway, could not run properly because of a pulled muscle in his knee. He participated in signal drills and other less strenuous phases of the workouts.

• • •

It probably doesn't make much difference but Curt Pettis, we found out the other day, is a left-footed kicker. Pettis took his turns with others who thought they could punt but he was far from a bowling standout. In fact, Coach Aschman assures us there is no chance of the speedy halfback doing the kicking this season.

There'll be many long faces when camp breaks up Monday afternoon. Coaches, players, Curbstone Coaches and school administration officials are unanimous in expressing keen satisfaction over all arrangements here. Everything points to the squad's returning next year.

OUT OF THIS PROMISING SQUAD COMES ALIQUIPPA HIGH'S 1944 FOOTBALL TEAM

Left to right, bottom row: Tony D'Alfonso, Harold Swan, Bernie Kolenda, Eddie Zanath, Dick Young, Clark Hall, Jim Battles, Lindy Tselepis, Dave Prisuta, Aldo Bononi, Tony Cerelli.

Second row: Otis Barnes, Bob Maslich, Pat Lampone, Ed Mancini, Ray Ferenan, Pete Vujicija, Buzz Leasha, Joe Petoczny, Lou Colonna, Stan Maneljovich, Paul Moshos, Mike Mihalcin, John Waters, Sidney Jones.

Back row: Pete Costanza, Bill Marshall, Bob Baldwin, Felix Mastropolli, Jack Babiak, George Skoupsis, Bob Grossi, Lloyd Cable, Jim Tormey, Jim Currie, George Walzer, George Paplamstes, Omar Christian, Tony Dercole, George Povelitis, John Suisko, Ray Kunzman, Steve Skorich, Mike Maycanich, Henry Young, Paul (Pickles) Piccirilli, Nick Klepovich, Tony Piccquidio, Pete Twaddle, George Vidonich, Steve Georgakis, Rick Fontana, Mike Yagercik, Curt Pettis.

(Photo by Times Staff Photographer)

ASPIRES FOR QUIP VARSITY BERTH

ELI (BUZZ) LEASHA

One of the early sensations at the Quips' pre-season training at Raccoon National Park has been Eli (Buzz) Leasha, 152-pound sophomore who may be the answer to Coach Carl A. Aschman's center worries. Aspiring to a regular job in his first year out for the squad, Leasha originally wanted to play a guard post. He was switched to an end and then when a shortage of snapper backs became apparent, Aschman shifted the 17-year-old youth to center. He needs loads of development offensively but in backing up the line he has been a standout.

(Photo by Times' Staff Photographer)

Dress up the everyday weiner by spreading with mustard, dipping in fine cracker crumbs and browning under the broiler.

Instead of worrying over appetizers at the last moment before a party, the calm, unruffled hostess lets guests make their own original combinations from a variety of salted crackers, cold meats, unrationed spreads, cheese, sliced radishes, cucumbers and olives.

BUY MORE WAR BONDS NOW!

Army-Navy Game May Be Shifted

Move Launched For "V" Celebration

WASHINGTON, Sept. 1—(U.P.)—Sports minded senators and representatives awaited reconsideration today of the Navy department's decision to play the annual service academy football game at Annapolis, Md., after Rep. Mike Munroney, D., Okla., appealed for it to be staged in a large city as a victory celebration, provided the German war is won before Dec. 2.

Munroney wrote Secretary of Navy James V. Forrestal and Acting Secretary of War Robert P. Patterson, suggesing the game be played in honor of service men, in a large eastern city. He said he believed that if Germany surrendered before the scheduled date of the game, Dec. 2, that the eastern transportation situation would be eased sufficiently to permit it to be played in a metropolitan center.

Forrestal announced earlier this week that the game would be played at Annapolis, and that attendance would be restricted to residents of the immediate area. Since the 1942 season, the game has been played alternately at Annapolis and West Point, N. Y.

Get In The Scrap — Save Paper!

POWELL, LOCAL PUG, WILL BATTLE CANADIAN WELTERWEIGHT CHAMP

Paul Powell, Aliquippa boxer now fighting out of Montreal, Canada will meet Dave Castilloux, Canadian lightweight and welter champion, in an exhibition bout tomorrow night.

Powell is getting loads of publicity in the Canadian city as a result of agreeing to meet the champ.

He was scheduled to fight at the Montreal Stadium this week but the card was rained out. He has another bout carded next week at Montreal.

Crucial Game Of Series Deferred

The torrential downpour of rain last evening forced postponement of the crucial game between the Celtic-Red Jrs., and the Dukes, which was slated at Franklin field.

The Celts, needing one more win to walk off with the honors, will be out to stop the Dukes, who are determined to stave off the onrushing surge of their opponents.

Should the Celts win the contest, which is scheduled for 6 p.m. today at Franklin field, and become the champs, a series between them and the Hollywood nine, Saxer league kings, will be arranged to decide the Junior champs of the community.

M.P.I.C. To Meet U.S.A. In Series

The local softball season will enter its final stages Sunday when the M.P.I. club, with an enviable record, clashes with the highly-tuted U. S. of A. softballers in the first of a five-game series to decide the mythical softball kings of the community.

The clash is scheduled for 2:30 p. m. at Fireman's field.

PIG HAS EXTRA FEET

ENID, Okla. (U.P.)—There should be no shortage of pigs' feet in the Bill Hutchinson home south of here this winter. One of Hutchinson's sows gave birth to a six-legged piglet. The many-footed animal has three left front legs.

Award Winners At Playgrounds Are Released

Logstown Moaners Capture Softball Title For Season

With the official closing of the playground season in Aliquippa yesterday, Playground Director Joe Chesnut today announced the winners of the various competitive tournaments staged at the sites.

A red and black emblem was presented each winner in their respective matches.

The Logstown Moaners copped first-place honors in the softball classic, winning 23 games and dropping four. In addition to receiving the emblem award, the team was presented a bat and ball.

The following members of the Moaners were recipients of the awards:

Ed Shaw, manager; James Bazmore, Ray Bazmore, Dom Baghetti, Arnold Thomas, Bud Shaw, Otho Thomas, Gino Pireli, Dave Prisuta, Don Tyler, Wayne Woods, "Boomie" Manojlovich, George Maravich, "Polly" Ceanfiogne and Willie Langston.

The Jones School Duchess' team won the laurels in the girls' league with 13 wins against a pair of setbacks. The following comprise the team's roster:

Lena Tarquinio, manager; Frances Russo, Dorothy Rubesin, Marie

(Continued on Page Seven)

Nine Games For Valley Elevens This Week End

Iowa, Winner Of One Game Last Season, Appears Weak Again This Year With Team Made Up Of Fresh

John Stewart
Quarter
Jim Hansen Fullback
Bob Liddy

By WALTER L. JOHNS
Central Press Sports Editor

Time changes many things.

Edward Patrick (Slip) Madigan, Notre Dame, 1920, head coach of the University of Iowa Hawkeyes, hopes that time—that which he has plenty of—will change his 1944 football squad into a Big Nine contender instead of just another doormat for the other schools.

Iowa, winner of only one game last season (over Nebraska in last game), is due for another bad season judging from the prospects of the squad at the present time.

But Madigan has plenty of time to find a winning combination for the Hawkeyes don't get under way until October 7, later than usual.

ALL CIVILIAN

Here's the way the Hawkeyes will stack up:

There will be at least eight freshmen on the first team. There are only three lettermen back, two guards and the quarterback. The squad is virtually all civilian. The line will be heavier than last season. It will average 193 pounds as against the 188-pound forward wall in '43. Punting may be done by an end. Replacements are rugged enough, but most of the boys are 17-year-old freshmen.

Iowa opened its practice season in August with 88 prospective candidates. The squad dropped to 66 and by the first week in September it was back to 77. Of this group 67 were freshmen.

The vets returning are Bob Liddy and Stan Mohrbacher, two fine guards; and John Stewart, quarter who was a part-time halfback last season. Liddy is a sound player, having put in 448 out of a possible 480 minutes last Fall. Mohrbacher, who has added 35 pounds to his frame, now weighs 220 pounds. He was a regular last Fall.

SERVICE BOYS

At the ends Madigan is working Jack Kelso, first veteran to enter the University under the GI bill of rights, and Ken Rose, a long punter from Turlock, Cal. Kelso received a medical discharge after serving over three years in the Army.

Don Winslow, freshman from Iowa City, and Bill Benksin, from Des Moines, are the probable tackles. Bob Snyder, 195-pound freshman from Sioux City, is the center.

Iowa's backfield may shape up with Stewart at quarter, Jim Hansen, 210 pounds, at full and Dick Woodard, all-state quarterback at Fort Dodge last year, and Pat Callaghan, North Platte, Neb., freshman, at the halves. Other backfield men who have looked good in practice are Nelson Smith, football letterman in 1942 at Coe College and a medical discharge from the Army Air Corps; Bill Kersten, Logan, Ia., frosh, and Irving Sword, another Coe college letterman now out of the service.

Send the DAILY TIMES to your boy in the Army or Navy. "It's like a letter from home every day."

Pirates Beat Cards 5-3 And 6-5 In Double Header, Yanks Face Athletics

NEW YORK, Sept. 13 (UP)—The New York Yankees, leading the tight American League pennant race by a scant half game—hardly enough to cheer about—lay their slender margin on the line tonight against the Philadelphia Athletics.

The Yanks, boasting 13 victories in 19 starts against the "A's" this season, were favored to swell their margin to a full game over the idle second place Detroit Tigers. But Manager Joe McCarthy, remembering how the Athletics beat the St. Louis Browns three out of four games when the latter were in first place on their last eastern road trip, was set to send his best pitcher after tonight's victory.

Hank Borowy, who has beaten the Athletics in all five of his starts against them this year, was McCarthy's choice to increase the Yankee margin in the only American League activity scheduled until Friday.

In yesterday's National League games, the Pittsburgh Pirates defeated the St. Louis Cardinals twice for their sixth and seventh wins over the league leaders in their last eight games.

The Bucs' double victory deprived the Cardinals' of their opportunity to attain mathematical certainty of clinching the flag.

Fritz Ostermueller started the chore of proving to the Cards that their 17½ game margin had been provided by the rest of the league and scattered eight hits for a 5-3 decision—his 14th of the season and his third over the circuit pace-setters. The Bucs nipped Rookie right-hander Fred Schmidt for four runs in the first two frames to make Ostermueller's task an easy one.

The Pirates came from behind in the fourth inning of the nightcap to tie the count at 2-2 when Frank Colman and Babe Dahlgren hit home runs off successive pitches by Rookie Bud Byerly. They moved in front in the same inning on an unearned run resulting from Whitey Kurowski's error and went on to win, 6-5. Three sixth inning Pittsburgh runs proved necessary, however, as the Cards knocked Buc Pitcher Preacher Roe out of the box with a three-run rally in the eighth.

Card-Pitts Beaten By Eagles, 22 To 0

PHILADELPHIA, Sept. 13. (UP) The Philadelphia Eagles of the National Football League, displaying a smooth and speedy running attack, crushed the merged Pittsburgh Steeler-Chicago Cardinal eleven 22-0 last night before 25,000 fans in an exhibition game at Shibe Park.

The Eagles scored three touchdowns in the first quater to coast to the victory.

Highlight of the game was the second tally when Jack Banta, Navy dischargee and former Southern California back, took a punt on his 19 and raced 81 yards to score.

Jack Hinkle counted the first Philadelphia points when he smashed around left end from the 15-yard line on the ninth running play of the game. Mal Bleeker, another ex-Southern California star, scored the last touchdown when he climaxed a 61-yard drive with an eight-yard smash through center.

The Eagles scored a safety in the third period when they caught Steeler-Card back Bobby Thurbon attempting to run out a punt from his end zone.

SONNENBERG DIES

WASHINGTON, Sept. 13 (UP) Wrestler Gus Sonnenberg, 44, credited with introducing the "flying tackle" to the professional mat game, died of luekemia last night at the Bethesda, Md., naval hospital. He had been hospitalized for almost eight months following service as a navy chief specialist at Great Lakes, Ill., and Brainbridge, Md.

Memphis To Meet Vols In Playoff

MEMPHIS, Tenn., Sept. 13. (UP)—Two of the masterminds of minor league baseball, Nashville Larry Gilbert and Memphis J. Thompson (Doc) Prothro, match wits here tonight when the Volunteers and Chickasaws tangle in the opening contest of a four-out-of-seven game series to determine the 1944 champions of the Southern Association.

The series will mark the sixth straight in which Gilbert has participated since joining the Vols as manager in 1939. He has led them to Shaughnessy playoff victories four times, beating Atlanta in 1939, '40 and '41 and Little Rock in 1942.

Prothro, erstwhile Phillie manager, is in his first southern play-off sinme steered the Little Rock Travelers to the pennant in 1937.

Big League Leaders

NATIONAL LEAGUE

	Ab.	R.	H.	Pct.
Walker, Bkln.	472	72	167	.354
Musial, St. L.	520	104	181	.348
Medwick, N. Y.	452	63	155	.343
Hopp, St. L...	459	98	153	.333
W. Cooper, St. Louis...	341	50	110	.323

AMERICAN LEAGUE

	Ab.	R.	H.	Pct.
Fox, Boston..	456	67	149	.327
Doerr, Boston	468	93	152	.325
Johnson, Bost.	456	100	148	.325
Stirnweiss, New York..	575	114	183	.318
Boudreau, Clev	515	83	163	.317

Home runs—Nicholson, Cubs, 32; Ott, Giants, 26.

Runs batted in — Nicholson, Cubs, 107; Sanders, Cardinals, 98; Stephens, Browns, 97.

A's PITCHER IS PRISONER

PHILADELPHIA, Sept. 13 — (UP)—Phil Marchildon, former Philadelphia Athletics' pitching star who enlisted in the Royal Canadian Air Force in 1942, has been reported a prisoner of war in Germany.

Beaver Falls Star Leads County Baseball Association In Batting

Joe Hornacek, of the championship Beaver Falls Tigers, was the individual batting champion of the Beaver Valley Association for the 1944 season according to official averages released by League President Don Bailey.

Hornacek, playing in 24 games, was at bat 82 times and collected 40 hits for an average of .488 for the season. He was followed by Dick Scherrbaum, Beaver catcher, who played in 31 games, made 47 hits in 98 times at bat for a .480 average, eight percentage points behind Hornacek.

Third place was claimed by Dick McNutt, New Brighton, who hit .438 in 11 games and by D'Alfonso, Monaca, who clouted the horsehide at a .432 clip.

These were the only players among those participating in ten or more games, who topped the .400 mark.

Scherrbaum led the league in total hits with 47 and in run scoring with 35. Following are the official batting averages including those who played in ten or more games:

BATTING AVERAGES

Player	G	AB	R	H	2B	3B	HR	SH	SB	Ave.
J. Hornacek, Beaver Falls ...	24	82	24	40	5	4	4	0	2	.488
Scherrbaum, Beaver	31	98	35	47	11	4	1	1	8	.480
McNutt, New Brighton	11	32	3	14	2	0	0	0	1	.438
D'Alfonso, Monaca	29	88	25	38	9	1	1	0	9	.432
J. Borkovic, East Rochester	28	90	22	35	11	3	1	3	12	.389
Murtha, Rochester	19	55	10	21	1	0	0	0	1	.382
D. McElhaney, E. Rochester	12	34	12	13	4	0	0	0	12	.382
C. Young, East Rochester .	25	80	15	30	9	2	0	1	5	.375
Haddox, New Brighton	25	81	21	30	7	3	2	0	8	.370
P. Shaughnessy, E. Rochester	12	36	10	13	2	1	0	0	3	.361
Perri, Monaca	11	39	7	14	2	0	0	0	7	.359
Rall, Beaver	32	84	25	30	4	2	3	0	2	.357
Wehr, East Rochester	22	73	16	26	5	1	0	2	16	.356
P. Hill, Monaca	11	31	8	11	5	0	0	0	4	.355
Firestone, Beaver	31	117	29	39	6	4	2	1	5	.333
P. Palumbo, Monaca	15	39	6	13	0	0	0	0	1	.333
Markulin, Monaca	14	18	1	6	0	0	0	2	0	.333
Richter, Beaver Falls	12	18	2	6	2	0	0	0	0	.333
Pierce, Rochester	27	80	22	26	7	3	1	0	10	.325
Peluso, New Brighton	24	71	18	23	4	0	4	0	12	.324
Omograsso, Beaver Falls ...	13	34	5	11	2	1	0	0	1	.324
Weatherly, Beaver Falls ...	17	50	10	16	1	2	0	1	9	.320
Lonnett, Beaver Falls	31	106	33	33	3	6	3	0	6	.311
J. Hill, Monaca	16	46	7	14	3	2	0	0	10	.304
Witterman, East Rochester .	16	54	15	16	1	0	0	0	12	.296
Parilla, Rochester	17	44	5	13	1	0	0	0	-	.295
Hodge, New Brighton	26	82	16	24	5	2	1	0	4	.293
Loeffler, Beaver Falls	18	58	16	17	2	1	0	3	5	.293
Kinkead, Monaca	16	48	14	14	5	0	0	0	4	.292
Courtney, Beaver	12	42	10	12	0	1	0	0	2	.286
Didio, East Rochester	14	35	5	10	0	0	0	0	5	.286
McGee, Beaver Falls	15	28	5	8	0	0	0	0	0	.286
Rihley, Beaver Falls	14	39	8	11	5	0	1	0	1	.282
Zupsic, Monaca	13	32	5	9	4	0	0	1	4	.281
T. Hornacek, Beaver Falls ..	17	50	5	14	0	0	0	0	2	.280
Somerville, Beaver	31	88	24	24	0	3	0	3	5	.273
R. Haarbauer, New Brighton	23	74	13	20	3	2	0	1	7	.270
Barnett, Beaver Falls	22	75	18	20	1	2	0	0	10	.267
Kross, New Brighton	12	34	8	9	0	1	0	0	2	.265
Shutey, Beaver	26	65	10	17	1	0	1	0	2	.262
Weiss, Beaver Falls	27	68	12	17	0	1	0	0	2	.250
Beatty, Rochester	19	56	10	14	1	1	0	0	1	.250
Stout, Beaver	31	101	15	25	6	2	1	2	3	.248
Shingler, East Rochester ..	21	57	15	14	6	0	0	1	7	.246
Chawford, Rochester	16	41	8	10	1	0	0	0	1	.244
E. Thomas, Monaca	29	91	20	22	6	1	0	1	5	.242
Radcliff, New Brighton	24	80	16	19	1	0	0	3	7	.238
Vogt, Monaca	28	69	7	16	2	0	0	0	2	.282
Lupo, Beaver Falls	16	22	3	5	0	1	0	1	2	.227
McCormick, Beaver	31	84	24	19	3	1	0	2	8	.226
Signore, East Rochester	14	36	4	8	1	0	0	0	1	.222
Jena, Monaca	32	77	13	17	1	1	0	2	8	.221
B. Thomas, Rochester	17	55	12	12	2	0	2	0	0	.218
Mike, Rochester	16	37	7	8	1	1	0	0	2	.216
Edwards, New Brighton ...	24	71	13	15	3	0	1	1	7	.211
Harley, Rochester	19	50	11	10	3	0	0	0	1	.200
Brewer, Rochester	15	31	4	6	0	0	0	0	2	.194
Spratt, New Brighton	31	97	14	18	1	1	0	2	9	.186
Lovette, New Brighton	22	59	4	11	0	0	1	0	1	.186
Irwin, New Brighton	16	44	8	8	1	0	0	1	4	.182
Swauger, Beaver	13	34	7	6	0	0	0	4	5	.176
Andrews, Beaver Falls	13	34	4	6	0	1	0	0	0	.176
Boller, Beaver Falls	15	23	6	4	0	1	1	0	3	.174
Blair, Beaver	18	41	10	7	2	1	0	0	2	.171
Dishler, Rochester	22	69	18	11	1	0	0	1	2	.159
Calder, Beaver Falls	15	38	5	6	0	1	0	1	0	.158
Macirynski, Monaca	14	32	5	5	0	0	0	0	0	.156
H. McElhaney, Rochester ..	20	66	12	10	3	0	0	0	3	.152
Fulton, Beaver Falls	22	60	12	9	0	0	0	1	0	.150
Dioguardi, East Rochester .	14	40	10	6	0	0	0	0	4	.150
Clifton, Monaca	18	40	2	6	1	0	0	1	0	.150
Trimble, East Rochester ...	17	42	7	6	1	0	0	2	3	.143
Ketterer, Rochester	20	42	6	6	1	0	0	0	2	.143
Henry, Beaver	18	40	8	5	1	0	0	0	2	.125
Casey, Beaver Falls	19	35	9	4	0	0	0	1	5	.114
Fortune, New Brighton	29	71	17	8	0	2	0	1	8	.113
Steele, Rochester	18	37	4	4	0	0	0	0	0	.108
C. Borkovic, East Rochester	13	28	8	3	1	0	0	0	5	.107
Meehan, East Rochester	12	38	2	4	0	0	0	0	1	.105
Bingle, Rochester	13	29	2	3	1	0	0	0	0	.103
Dolenak, Monaca	26	48	17	3	1	0	0	0	8	.063
Kerr, Beaver	17	19	4	1	0	0	0	1	1	.053
McClain, Monaca	12	25	2	1	0	0	0	0	0	.040

Bucknell Eleven Green But Faces 10-Game Schedule

LEWISBURG, Pa., Sept. 13 — (UP)—Bucknell University begins its 10-game football campaign next Saturday and from this historic Alma Mater of Christy Mathewson and Clark Hinkle comes the wail that the 1944 thundering herd is the most inexperienced squad to represent Bucknell since the first ball was booted on the campus back in 1881.

Head Coach Woody Ludwig, late-season successor to Johnny Sitarsky in 1943 when Sitarsky entered the Army, has a squad of 44 Naval trainees and four civilians, but from the initial group of half a hundred who reported, only ten men have college experience and 34 have only high school experience. The remainder have no organized experience whatsoever.

He has six men hold-overs from last year's Bison eleven that won six and lost four and of these, the ace back is Gene Hubda, a 175-pound Marine trainee from Perth Amboy, N. J. Hubka starred as a Temple Freshman two years ago, and for Bucknell last year.

With Hubka, allowing for sudden Naval transfers, are Ralph Grant, Ashley, Pa., a 185-pound quarterback who already has played two seasons with the Bisons; Lou Mardaga, Wilkinsburg, Pa., an end at Bucknell last year by way of Washington and Jefferson; Wayne Steele, Rockville Center, N. Y., tackle; Bob Farley, Wilkes-Barre, Pa., guard, and a 175-pound wrestling champ and Jimmy Seel, 170-pound center from Pittsburgh, Pa.

For Saturday's opener with Muhlenberg at Allentown, Ludwig plans tentatively to start Lester Heinz, Willoughby, O., and Mardaga at the ends; George Kochins, Kingston, Pa., and Steele at the tackle; Farley and Clyde Bennett, Montoursville, Pa., at the guards, with Seel at center.

The backs stand out as Grant and Hubka, aided by Al Yannelli, Philadelphia, and Ned Naffah, Pittsburgh.

Pennsylvanians are scattered plentifully through the Bison line-up.

SPORT SLANTS

By BILL ANDERSON

Congressman Sammy Weiss, Pittsburgh, who has been fighting a wordy battle in an effort to keep sports alive during the war, delivered another blast against the inconsistency of Navy officials who ordered the annual Army-Navy football classic played in the relative seclusion of Annapolis because of transportation difficulties. Weiss scores a point undoubtedly when he remarks not without some sarcasm: "The Navy cannot go to Philadelphia or New York to play the Army, but the Navy can go to Cleveland to play Notre Dame before an expected 80,000 persons. The Army cannot go to Philadelphia or New York to play the Navy, but it can go to New York to play Notre Dame before an anticipated crowd of 78,000. The drain on transportation facilities is listed as a drawback yet Navy is scheduled to go to Atlanta, Ga. This just does not make sense. The service teams are not permitted to play before crowds when they play each other but they are permitted to travel thousands of miles to play outside opposition in heavily populated centers."

And he adds: "If the strategists at home or the powers that be insist on making a dud out of the Army-Navy game, why do they not call it off entirely. Either give the game back to' the American people, where it belongs or quit giving phoney excuses."

Bernie Kolenda, first string guard, who suffered a broken collar bone in the Quips' opening game with Freedom last Friday night, is the second player Coach Carl Aschman has lost in that way this year. Jim Batchelor, a freshman, received a broken collar bone while the squad was in training at Raccoon National Park. Although only a junior, this was to be Kolenda's last year of scholastic football. He and at least four other members of the Steeler squad are enrolled in the Army Air Forces Reserve and expect to be called for active duty about December. They are Dick Young, center; Harold Swan, tackle; Tony D'Alfonso and Bill Marshall.

Baseball Summary

NATIONAL LEAGUE
RESULTS TUESDAY

Pittsburgh 5, St. Louis 3.
Pittsburgh 6, St. Louis 5.
Cincinnati - Chicago (2), postponed, wet grounds.
Philadelphia - New York (2), postponed, rain.
Boston - Brooklyn, postponed, rain.

TEAM STANDING

	W.	L.	Pct.
St. Louis	95	39	.705
Pittsburgh	79	54	.594
Cincinnati	73	57	.562
Chicago	60	70	.462
New York	61	72	.459
Boston	55	79	.410
Brooklyn	55	80	.407
Philadelphia	52	79	.397

GAMES TODAY

Pittsburgh at St. Louis (2), (Twilight and night).
Philadelphia at New York 2.
Boston at Brooklyn (2).
Cincinnati at Chicago (2).

GAMES THURSDAY

No games scheduled.

AMERICAN LEAGUE
RESULTS TUESDAY

No games scheduled.

TEAM STANDING

	W.	L.	Pct.
New York	76	61	.555
Detroit	75	61	.551
St. Louis	75	62	.547
Boston	73	64	.533
Cleveland	65	72	.474
Chicago	63	74	.460
Philadelphia	64	75	.460
Washington	58	80	.420

GAMES TODAY

New York at Philadelphia (night).
Others not scheduled.

GAMES THURSDAY

No games scheduled.

Grid Calendar

HIGH SCHOOL

Thursday

*Zelienople at Beaver, 8 p. m.

Friday

*Midland at Rochester, 8:15 p. m.
*Ambridge at Harbrack.
*Washington at Beaver Falls, 8 p. m.
Freedom at Shenango.
Evans City at Hopewell.
*Farrell at Ellwood City.
*Central Cath. at Aliquippa.

Saturday

Monaca at New Brighton, 2:30 p. m.
*Night Games.

Seven Local Schoolboy Teams Meet Outside Foes; Seven Contests Are Booked Friday Afternoon And Night

Beaver County high school football teams are prepping for a week end program that includes no less than nine games, scattered over three days and pits local elevens against outside opponents in every instance except two. The Rochester-Midland clash at Rochester Friday night and the New Brighton-Monaca fracas Saturday are the only games between Beaver county elevens on the card.

Beaver high's Bobcats open the week's show on Thursday night, meeting the Zelienople high gridders at Gypsy Glen field.

On Friday night there will be four games, besides the Rochester-Midland tilt, involving county elevens, and two others are booked in the afternoon. Beaver Falls, which topped Coraopolis, 20 to 12, in its opener last week, is scheduled to tangle with Washington high at Beaver Falls; Ambridge meets Har-Brack Union on the latter's barred field. Aliquippa will entertain the Central Catholic high team of Pittsburgh and Ellwood City will meet Farrell high at Lincoln Field, Ellwood City.

In the Friday afternoon contests Hopewell township will be host to Evans City high, and Freedom will travel to Lawrence County to renew its rivalry with Shenango township.

New Brighton and Monaca have the Saturday afternoon date to themselves for their annual engagement at New Brighton.

16TH GAME OF SERIES

The Beaver - Zelienople series has not been interrupted since 1929 at least. In the 15 games played from 1929 to 1943, both inclusive, the Bobcats have scored eight victories, Zelienople won four games and three ended in tie scores. The last Zelienople win over the Maroon was in 1939, 6 to 0. Last year Beaver won 7 to 0 in a hard-fought battle at Zelienople, and in 1942 the Bobcats triumphed, 21 to 7. In 1941 they played a 6-6 tie.

Last weekend the Bobcats opened their season by tripping Midland, 19 to 0, and Zelienople's gridders began their campaign by dropping a free-scoring contest to Coach Fred Milanovich's Hopewell township eleven, 13 to 25.

MIDLAND LOSES GERMUSA

Coach Bill Walters of Midland is preparing the Midland high eleven to meet Rochester Saturday night without Halfback Steve Germusa in the lineup. Germusa, it was reported today, has quit the Leopard squad. His older brother, Mike Germusa, was reported by the War Department recently to have been killed in action. Deeply grieved by the sad news members of his family, it was said, have asked Steve to give up football. He was one of Coach Walters' best backs and his loss will be keenly felt.

Bill Walters, son of the coach, has been shifted from a tackle spot to the backfield and probably will start at fullback against Rochester. Petties, a senior, out for football for the first time this season, is battling with Joe Dapollonia for a guard berth.

Rochester's Rampaging Rams are favored to beat the Midland eleven, but if they do the Leopards will still hold an edge in the series between th two schools which began in 1931. In the first ten years of their gridiron rivalry the Blue and White won only two games from the Leopards, in 1932 and in 1936. They tied 0-0 in 1935, and the Crucibles won all the rest. The games have been a bit one-sided since 1940, as the Rams won 25-6 in 1941, 40-13 in 1942 and 60-0 last year. In the series todate Rochester has won five games from Midland, lost seven and tied one.

FREEDOM FACES SHENANGO

Freedom's bulldogs are looking for another tough battle with Shenango high Friday afternoon. Previous games in the series have been consistantly close. From 1938 through 1940 they played three scoreless ties in a row. Freedom won 7 to 0 in 1941, lost 7 to 19 in 1942 and again last season by a 0 to 13 count.

Coach Moe Rubenstein of Ambridge is drilling his Bridgers for a hard game with the Har-Brack eleven at Har-Brack on Friday night. The Union high team was a fill-in on Ambridge's card last year and nosed out the Bridgers 7 to 6 and last week this year's Har-Brack eleven defeated New Castle, 13 to 9. It was the first home opener the Red Hurricane has lost in 22 years.

STEELERS LOSE STAR GUARD

The Aliquippa-Central Catholic game on Friday night at the Quip stadium will be the first between these two schools. The Steelers downed a fighting Freedom eleven 20 to 0 last week with Joe Potocany scoring all the points, and may encounter stubborn resistance from Central Catholic also.

Coach Carl Aschman is grooming Steve Tselepis and Dave Prisuta to share the guard post vacated by Bernie Kolenda, who suffered a broken collar bone in the Freedom encounter and was lost for the balance of the season. Kolenda suffered the injury in the second quarter while applying a block. Eddie Zanath speedy halfback, missed the Freedom game because of a wrenched knee but may be ready to go against the Pittsburgh eleven.

The Farrell-Ellwood City game at Ellwood's stadium should be one of the best of the weekend. While the Wolverines were humbling little Union Township, 44 to 0, the Farrell eleven was dropping its opening game to Erie Academy, 7 to 12.

So far Ellwood and Farrel have met four times with each winning twice. They played a home and home series in 1936 and '37 with Farrell winning in 1936, 13 to 6, and Ellwood taking the 1937 game, 25 to 12. Farrell won 7 to 0 two years ago and last season the Wolverines triumphed, 26 to 6.

BRIGHTON HOLDS EDGE

Records on Monaca-New Brighton gridiron conflicts are available as far back as 1923. They have not met every season since that date but at least 12 games have been played, with Monaca winning four, New Brighton seven and one even. Over the last four years they have split even, Monaca winning 6 to 0 in 1940 and 12 to 7 in 1942, and New Brighton taking a 14 to 0 decision in 1941 and whipping the Indians, 47 to 0 last year.

Unless a regular coach to replace Lewis M. Heeter is procured in the meantime, High School Principal E. G. Groleau and Chris Mangin will be in charge of the Indians Saturday when they collide with George Roark's big, highly-regarded New Brighton cleaters.

The Beaver Falls- Washington high battle at Reeves Stadium will be the first between the two schools.

Saturday Big Day For Local Golfers At Raccoon Course

The Field Day to be held at the Raccoon Golf Club Saturday will be a big day for the golfers of the district. Contests of all types will keep the participants busy. Events for both the top-notch golfer and those who play for exercise are on the program.

In conjunction with the "Stag Day" the Lower Valley championship will be at stake and will go to the golfer with low medal score in the 18 holes each person is to play. With the Lower Valley championship title will go a silver cup. The other prizes, about 15 in number, include golf bags, sweaters and the like, of which about 12 will go to the blind bogey contest winners, the event in which every player has an equal chance because each sets his own handicap before he starts to play.

The day's golfing starts at 8 in the morning and will run all day, with foursomes being sent out every 15 minutes until about 5 o'clock. Single and double golfers are welcome but will be made up into foursomes with others who have not formed their own foursomes. By phoning Bob Dawson, pro at the club, a starting time can be reserved to suit. Refreshments will be served throughout the day. Price of ticket includes everything, green fee, lunch and refreshments.

Bantam Champion Wins Title Bout

LOS ANGELES, Sept. 13. (UP)—Manuel Ortiz headed back to his farm in El Centro, Calif., today, the world's bantamweight championship still in his pocket after his fourth-round technical knock-out last night over spunky Luis Castillo.

It was Ortz' 11th title defense, and he disposed of the Mexican contender in 11 and one-half minutes of almost nip and tuck battling.

Referee Mushy Callahan stopped the fight in the fourth round after Ortiz cut Castillo's left eye with a couple of smashing rights. A doctor crawled into the ring, examined the eye, and ordered the bout stopped.

BOUT CANCELLED

CLEVELAND, Sept. 13 (UP)—The Jimmy Bivins-Lloyd Marshall heavyweight fight, scheduled for September 21, has been cancelled. Promoter Larry Atkins said, because Bivins re-injured a knuckle wound on his right hand while training.

St. Louis Club Wins Flag On Last Day Of Season

Brownies Defeat Yankees 5 to 2 As Tigers Lose to Senators 4-1, And Clinch Their First League Pennant

By LEO H. PETERSEN
United Press Sports Editor

ST. LOUIS, Oct. 2 (UP)—The St. Louis Browns carried he American League pennant into the World Series today or the first time in history. The Cinderella boys won it the ard way, nosing out the Detroit Tigers by a one game margin on the last day of the season.

They will go into the series pening Wednesday with their tra-city rivals, the St. Louis ardinals, underdogs, but no one ho saw them whip the New ork Yankees in four straight ames was selling them short nd with fans the country over, ey will be the sentimental vorites.

The fight that won them the rowns' first World Series gold nce the American League began perating in 1901 was magnifient. They went down to the st day to win, and, as they ad been showing all season ng, they had what it takes in e clutch. No one, including eir manager Luke Sewell, could ass them a great ball club, but ey have fight and courage.

Everyone of them was a hero all the others and outstanding these heroes was Chet Laabs, hose two home runs provided e power to down the Yankees sterday in Sportsman's Park the game that meant gold and lory. The score was 5 to 2.

It was 22 years ago that the owns made their first serious d for an American League pennt. They lost then to the ankees by one game. So it was tisfying that the Yankees were e victims this year. At Detroit, e last place Washington Senaors gave the Browns the assist ey needed by defeating the Tigs—with them the Browns were ed when the last games started 4 to 1.

When the odds are against em, the Browns are at their st. And they had one other dvantage yesterday. When they ok the field the scoreboard owed that the Senators were ading Detroit 3 to 0. But they ere jittery for the first three inngs, throwing the ball away nd practically handing the ankees two runs. It wasn't un the fourth that they showed e stuff of which champions are ade. By that time the Senators ere leading 4 to 0 with the gers at bat in the last of the nth. To the cheers of more an 37,000 fans the largest owd ever to watch the Browns ay at Sportsman's Park, Mike reevich opened with a single to ft. Up stepped Laabs, a .230 tter and part-time ball player d war plant worker. He caught ld of one of Mel Queen's hard, gh fast ones and dumped it nong the spectators in the left ld pavilion to tie the score.

After that Sig Jakucki, a five d ten cent store pitcher until e war drained major league ll clubs of many of their plays, closed the scoring door on Yankees.

With two down in the fifth, ueen once again faced Kreevh. And again Kreevich singled. aabs again stepped to the plate. nd again he put the ball into e pavilion, scoring two more ns That would have been ough, but just to make things mfortable, Vernon Stephens t a home run in the eighth off ank Borowy, the Yankees' leadg pitcher whom McCarthy had nt in to relieve Queen after aabs' second homer.

It was Jakucki's 13th victory gainst nine defeats, while for ueen it was his third defeat gainst six victories. Both clubs ot six hits.

Sewell, as happy as a school y, was too excited to think out the series—but it was dolrs to doughnuts that it would Nelson Potter pitching the first ame for him against Morton ooper, the strong man of the ardinal staff, when they square f day after tomorrow.

After First Baseman George cQuinn had snared Oscar rimes' last-out foul ball, the 37,00 fans spilled, snake-dancing, nto the field. When Jakucki ame out of the dressing room shirt sleeves after showering, he autograph fans took over.

Beaver County Grid Standings

COUNTY GAMES ONLY

	W	L	T	Pts.	Op.
Beaver	2	0	0	25	0
Aliquippa	2	0	0	65	6
Ellwood City ..	1	0	0	26	6
Beaver Falls ..	1	0	0	6	0
New Brighton .	2	0	1	60	14
Ambridge	1	1	1	46	13
Rochester	1	2	0	46	52
Monaca	1	3	0	14	79
Freedom	0	1	0	0	20
Midland	0	4	0	7	111
Hopewell	0	0	0	0	0

ALL GAMES

	W	L	T	Pts.	Op.
Beaver	4	0	0	71	13
Beaver Falls ..	4	0	0	99	24
Ellwood City ..	4	0	0	124	33
Aliquippa	4	0	0	90	26
Hopewell	3	0	0	95	13
New Brighton .	3	0	1	89	20
Ambridge	2	1	1	78	19
Rochester	2	2	0	96	52
Monaca	1	3	0	14	79
Midland	0	4	0	13	111
Freedom	0	4	0	6	67

Football Scores

COLLEGE

Notre Dame 58, Pitt 0.
Denison 40, Bethany 12.
West Virginia 32, Case 7.
Army 46, N. Carolina 0.
Bates 6, Conn. 0.
Bowling Green 19, Alma 6.
Brown 44, Tufts 0.
Columbia 21, Union 0.
Cornell 26, Bucknell 0.
Dartmouth 6, Holy Cross 6.
Harvard 13, Worcester Tech 0.
Iowa P-F 45, Ft. Sheridan 12.
NCAR P-F 21, Navy 14.
Penn 18, Duke 7.
Penn State 58, Muhlenberg 13.
Rochester 20, Colgate 13.
Villanova 14, F. & M. 6.
Yale 7, Coast Guard 3.
Baldwin Wallace 35, Oberlin 0.
Great Lakes 26, Illinois 26.
Indiana 20, Michigan 0.
Iowa State 49, Gustavus Adol. 0.
Kansas State 6, Wichita 6.
Minnesota 39, Nebraska 0.
Ohio State 54, Missouri 0.
Purdue 40, Marquette 7.
Wabash 20, Illinois Wes. 0.
Wisconsin 7, Northwestern 6.
Bainbridge 43, Camp Lee 0.
Camp Peary 20, Cherry Point 0.
Catawba 7, Va. Mil. Inst. 6.
Georgia P-F 20, S. Carolina 14.
Georgia Tech 51, Clemson 0.
Mississippi 26, Florida 6.
Miss. State 42, Jackson Base 0.
N. Car. State 13, Virginia 0.
Tennessee 26, Kentucky 13.
Wm. & Mary 46, Ft. Munroe 0.
Colorado Coll. 25, New Mexico 7.
Norman Navy 28, Oklahoma 14.
So. Methodist 49, N. Tex. Agri. 0.
Texas 20, Southwestern 0.
Tex. Chris. 34, S. Plains AAF 0.
California 6, UCLA 0.
2nd Air Force 33, Colorado 6.
S. California 18, Pacific 6.
Utah 24, Idaho Navy 0.
Washington 65, Whitman 6.

SCHOLASTIC

Altoona 7, Westinghouse 0.
Aspinwall 20, Oakmont 0.
Blairsville 31, N. Bethlehem 0.
Claysburg 13, Roaring Spring 7.
Donora 45, Latrobe 6.
East Deer 31, West Deer 0.
Farrell 26, Sharpsville 6.
Franklin Boro 13, South Fork 0.
Glassport 33, Rankin 0.
Greenville 18, Titusville 0.
Jeannette 33, Penn Twp. 0.
Johnstown 39, German Twp. 13.
Kiski 19, Derry 12.
New Brighton 19, Rochester 0.
Newton Falls 12, Brookfield 0.
Norwin 13, Wilkinsburg 6.
Patton 33, Nanty Glo 6.
Pitcairn 53, E. McKeesport 0.
Springdale 20, Leechburg 0.
Sewickley Twp. 12, Im. Conc. 0.
Stowe 13, Carnegie 0.
Swissvale 18, Ford City 13.
Turtle Creek 20, Penn 0.
Verona 6, South Fayette 6.
Williamsburg 0, Bigler 0.
Wilmerding 19, T.afford 7.
Windber 42, Portage 0.
Youngwood 19, Derry Twp. 0.

SUNDAY

PRO EXHIBITION

Pittsburgh 17, New York 16.
Chicago Bears 28, Washington 0.
Cleveland 7, Philadelphia 7.

NATIONAL LEAGUE

Green Bay 27, Detroit 6.

AMERICAN LEAGUE

Hollywood R. 49, Los Angeles 7.
San Francisco 35, Seattle Bo. 21.

HIGH SCHOOL

St. George 18, St. Luke 0.

SERVICE GAMES

Ft. Bennig 3rd 26, Maxwell Fld. 0.
Gulfport Air 30, Algiers Navy 0.
San Diego N. 85, Compton Jr. 0.
Morris Field 45, Chatham Field 0.
Ottumwa A. B. 45, Camp Ellis 7.
Nevada C. G. 35, Nevada U. 0.

Grid Calendar

HIGH SCHOOL

TODAY

Freedom Res. at Rochester.

THURSDAY

*Freedom at Beaver, 8 p. m.

FRIDAY

*Aliquippa at Rochester, 8 p. m.
Shenango at Hopewell Twp.

SATURDAY

Ellwood City at Monaca, 2:30 p. m.
Midland at New Brighton, 2:30 p. m.
Beaver Falls at Butler, 2:30 p. m.

*Night games.

St. Louis Browns—American League Champions, 1944

Mike Kreevich

Chet Laabs

Don Gutteridge

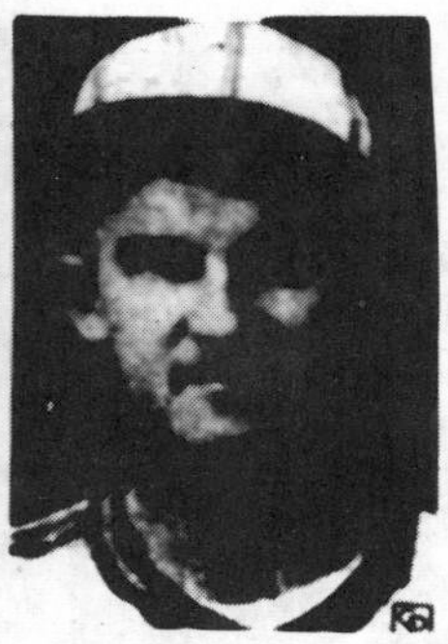
George McQuinn

Al Zarilla

Vernon Stephens

Mark Christman

Ray Hayworth

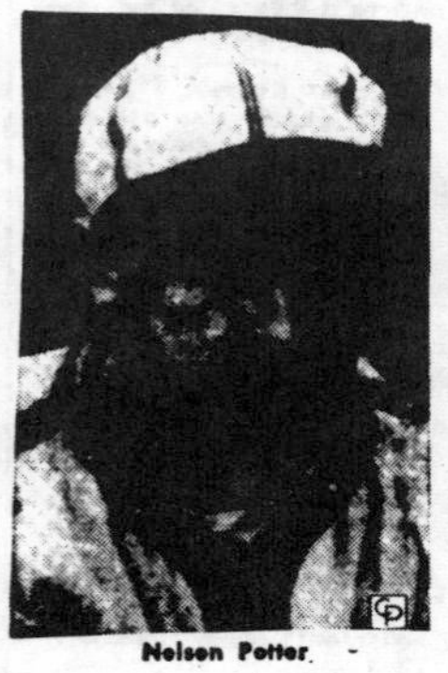
Nelson Potter

Sig Jakucki,

Bob Muncrief.

Denny Galehouse

SPORT SLANTS

By BILL ANDERSON

Major league club owners have been very cautious about Pete Gray, the sensational one-armed outfielder of the Memphis Chicks, who Southern Association sport writers and scouts are unanimously touting as a great big league prospect. Despite his physical handicap, Gray is one of the leading hitters in the circuit and an excellent outfielder. He rates a chance to move into big leagues, but so far there has been no bidding for his services. The owners, it is said, feel it woudn't be the best thing for baseball. Regardless of the reason, it now appears that Gray may not get the chance he so well deserves.

The Aliquippa Boys Club has organized a four-team ball league for boys of Junior high school age.

Pvt. Dan Karas, former gridder at Ambridge high school, is playing the fullback position on the Amarillo, Tex., Air Field football team this Fall. Week before last the Amarillo team flew by B-17 to New Mexico and defeated the Univ. of New Mexico eleven, 21-2. Karas tallied one point on a placement kick.

Freedom high school's game with Hopewell Township high, originally scheduled for Friday afternoon, November 3rd at Firemen's Field, New Sheffield, has been shifted to the Aliquippa high stadium and will be played on Saturday night, November 4th, starting at 8:15 o'clock.

A movement is underway in nearby Butler and Lawrence Counties to form a football conference among Class B high schools.

Mike Kozlina, Hopewell township high halfback, received a dislocated elbow in the Viking's game with Newell, W. Va.

Joe Rider, who until he was injured early in the 1943 season, was a prominent football and basketball official, handles the public address system at Ambridge high's home games this season.

GOOD WASTE PAPER is needed in our war effort. Save it.

Automatic Robot Developed To Set Up Bowling Pins

NEW YORK, Oct. 2 (UP) — Bowling's secret invention, the automatic pin-spotting machine which eliminates the pin-boy was revealed today in exhaustive demonstration by its inventor after nine years of ultra-secret development.

Perfected in 1940, and granted sanction of the American Bowling Congress, the machine will "revolutionize bowling as drastically as the sound-track did the motion picture industry," its manufacturers predicted.

Operating on the suction principal, electrically driven and automatically controlled, the machine can average nine and a half games per hour per alley as compared with a six-game average for pinboys.

"Not only can it spot pins faster than any bowler can bowl, but it performs to its perfect standard around the clock; human fatigue and temperament are eliminated entirely," its inventor said.

Requesting that his name and the manufacturer be withheld to avoid inquiries and orders which would interfere with the company's war production, the inventor provided demonstrations for the United Press.

Of steel construction, the pin setter is five feet wide and eight feet high above the alley bed. Pressing a button starts the motor and the operation thereafter is entirely automatic, with the bowling ball entering the pit setting up the cycle of pin-sweeping, score-registering, re-spotting and returning the balls.

"Experimentation in automatic machines has been going on for more than 40 years," the inventor said. "The first patent was taken out in 1888. One large firm spent more than $1,000,000 in experiments since 1913, and finally gave up."

An engineer with a large Brooklyn manufacturing company, the inventor drew the first blueprint in 1935, he said.

"Where others tried mechanics or electricity, I used the suction principle. In 1940, the machine was proven practical and thousands of games bowled by company employee teams gradually eliminated the "bugs."

Because of its high cost, the machine will never be sold, but rented to bowling establishments, he said, at rates comparable to usual pinsetting charges; ultimately, it may reduce the cost per line to bowlers. It can be operated by coin-boxes, and eventually may be supplemented by automatic score-boards.

Baseball Summary

NATIONAL LEAGUE
RESULTS SUNDAY

Pittsburgh 9, Philadelphia 1.
Philadelphia 7, Pittsburgh 1.
Brooklyn 6, Cincinnati 5.
Chicago 4, Boston 3.
Boston 7, Chicago 6.
*New York 6, St. Louis 5.
†St. Louis 10, New York 6.
†6 innings; called to permit St. Louis to catch train.
*13 innings.

FINAL TEAM STANDING

	W.	L.	Pct.	G.B.
St. Louis	105	49	.682	
Pittsburgh	90	63	.592	14½
Cincinnati	89	65	.578	16
Chicago	75	79	.487	30
New York	67	87	.435	38
Boston	65	89	.422	40
Brooklyn	63	91	.409	42
Philadelphia	61	92	.399	43½

AMERICAN LEAGUE
RESULTS SUNDAY

Washington 4, Detroit 1.
St. Louis 5, New York 2.
Philadelphia 5, Cleveland 2.
*Philadelphia 5, Cleveland 0.
Boston 3, Chicago 1.
Chicago 4, Boston 1.
*Ten innings.

FINAL TEAM STANDING

	W.	L.	Pct.	G.B.
St. Louis	89	65	.578	
Detroit	88	66	.571	1
New York	83	71	.539	6
Boston	77	77	.500	12
Cleveland	72	82	.468	17
Philadelphia	72	82	.468	17
Chicago	71	83	.461	18
Washington	64	90	.416	25

Beaver Man Home With Big Muskie

George H. Hamilton, Buffalo street, Beaver, president of the Hamilton Glove and Awning Company, returned home Saturday night from a two-week fishing trip in Canada, bringing with him the largest muskellonge ever taken at Port Severn, in the Georgian Bay district of Ontario. The muskie, about four feet long, weighed 32 pounds.

Hamilton also brought home a 9½ pound muskie and a pickerel weighing 5½ pounds, as well as other smaller fish, and James A. Phillips, Beaver Falls, secretary-treasurer of the Moltrup Steel Products Company, who was his fishing companion, hooked a big 20-pound muskie.

WANT TO BUY something? Tell what you want through the TIMES "wanted ads. In that way, perhaps you'll find what you want. The cost is small. Thousands of people read these small ads daily.

Pirates Clinch Second Place By Beating Phillies

NEW YORK, Oct. 2. (UP)—The 1944 baseball season was turned over to the record keepers today. In addition to the tightest American League pennant chase in history, the pencil-pushers recorded the winners of other hotly contested if lesser spots.

The Pittsburgh Pirates assured themselves of second place in the National League standings by winning one game of a double header from the Phillies while the Cincinnati Reds were losing to the Brooklyn Dodgers. The Bucs won 9-1 behind their ace, Truett (Rip) Sewell, who recorded his 21st win of the year. The Phillies won the nightcap 7-1.

The Dodgers 6-5 win clinched the seventh spot ahead of the Phillies.

The New York Giants, last place finishers a year ago, finished fifth by defeating the Cards 6-5 in the 13-inning opener. The Cards won the finale, 10-6 in a game called at the end of the sixth to ermit the champs to catch a train for home.

The fourth place Chicago Cubs split with sixth spot Boston, the Cubs winning the first 4-3 and the Braves the nightcap 7-6.

Connie Mack's Philadelphia Athletics tied with the Cleveland Indians for fifth place in the American League with a double victory over the tribe. They won the opened 5-2 and the 10-inning nightcap 5-0. Jittery Joe Berry got credit for both decisions in relief roles.

The fourth place Boston Red Sox split with the seventh spot finishers, 3-1 and 1-4.

The first air express service, inaugurated 17 years ago, reached 26 cities linked together by 4,508 route miles, while today 350 cities connected by 45,000 miles of airways enjoy the service. The compartment area of the first airplane express was but 25 sq. ft. and today is 250 sq. ft. The time for the flight across the continent has been reduced from 31 to 16 hours while the cost for shipping packages across the continent has been cut two-thirds.

The axolotl is one of several species of larval salamanders. They inhabit certain lakes of Mexico and the Rocky mountain region of the U. S. Their eggs resemble frogs' eggs, being laid in strings formed by viscous covering and attached to water plants. They hatch in two or three weeks.

New Brighton High Griddlers Down Rochester Rams For Third Victory

The Rochester high gridders experienced their second straight defeat of the current season on Saturday afternoon when they clashed with New Brighton's strong aggregation before nearly 4,000 fans at the Crimson's Oak Hill field. The score was 19 to 0.

Coach George Roark's fast-charging line and hard-running backs got the jump on the Rams in the early minutes of the first quarter and never eased the pressure, with the result that the Blue and White cleaters were cleanly outplayed and did not get into scoring position until the last minute of the game and time ran out before they could get a touchdown drive organized.

The Crimson and Gold tallied a touchdown in each of the first three periods. The first score came after an exchange of punts in the first period. The Rams received the opening kickoff, were held to six yards in three downs, and Frank Grdnic punted to the New Brighton 4..

The next few plays were enough to indicate that the Rams were in for a rough afternoon as the Crimson and Gold, operating smoothly from the T formation with Bill Edwards flipping accurate, perfectly timed laterals to Eddie Haddox and Al Peluso, quickly moved to the Rochester 35. There two penalties, one for 15 yards, set the Roarkmen back, but Haddox punted out of bounds on the Rochester four-yard line.

With their backs to their own goal line the Rams tried a couple of running plays, and Vic Rubbo, going into the line, attempted to toss a lateral pass, but the ball was fumbled and Quarterback Edwards of the Crimson recovered on the Rochester eight.

Haddox slammed over tackle for four yards and then over right guard for the first touchdown, and the score was 7 to 0 after Peluso converted the extra point from placement.

The Roarkmen made their second touchdown the hard way, marching 55 yards. Haddox and Claire Saunders each turned in nice runs around the ends after taking slick laterals from Edwards. Peluso scored the touchdown from the one-yard line.

Later in the second quarter the Crimson again threatened but was stopped on the Rochester 20-yard line after Dick McNutt had featured a drive from the home team's 35.

Haddox returned the second half kickoff to the New Brighton 35-yard line and the Crimson eleven was off to its third touchdown. This time the winners mixed a few forward passes with the rushing game. A pass, Edwards to John Ellis, left end, carried to the 50-yard line. After Haddox picked up five at right end, the same passing duo clicked again for a first and ten on the Ram 38. McNutt wheeled around left end behind sweeping interference for the next 20 yards and Haddox tossed an 18-yard pass to Ellis in the end zone for the touchdown.

Up to this point the Rams had not made one first down, but after Ed Supak returned the kickoff to the Rochester 35 they finally began to move and Rubbo made five yards at center, Wade Rall six at left end, Parelli two at tackle, and Supak plunged over center to the New Brighton 42. It looked like the Blue and White might generate a sustained march, but ill fortune struck on the next play when a bad pass was fumbled and Price, Brighton guard, recovered on the Brighton 47.

A little later the Rams put together two first downs and reached Brighton's 39-yard line, a 16-yard pass from Supak to Grdnic featuring, before the Crimson stiffened and held. On the punt New Brighton was penalized 15 yards for holding, which put the ball on the 14-yard line. An additional five-yard penalty set the Crimson back to its nine-yard line, but Haddox pulled the team out of the hole by making a beautiful quick kick to the Ram 36. The kick practically amounted to a 50-yard gain for the Crimson because Saunders intercepted a pass thrown by Supak on the Rochester 46.

In spite of a 15-yard penalty against them, the Roarkmen marched to the Ram 11, but were driven back to the 25, and finally lost the ball 35 yards from the goal line.

A number of Brighton subs were in the game in the last few minutes when a bad pass from center sailed high over Halfback Saunders' head and he was run out of bounds on the Brighton 18 after recovering the loose ball. The Rams took the ball 18 yards from a score, but there was time for only two plays.

First downs were 14 to 4 in favor of the New Brighton eleven. The victory was the third of the year for the Crimson, whose record is marred only by a tie with Ambridge, and it was Rochester's second setback in four starts. The lineups:

Rochester—0.		New Brighton—19.
LE	Grdnic	Ellis
LT	McDonald	Rawl
LG	Collins	Price
C	Clayton	F. Budiscak
RG	Gomory	Fortune
RT	Reynolds	Tucker
RE	Werthman	Garen
QB	Supak	Edwards
LH	Parelli	Haddox
RH	Rager	C. Saunders
FB	Rubbo	Peluso

Score by periods:
New Brighton .. 7 6 6 0—19

Touchdowns—Haddox, Peluso, Ellis.

Point after touchdown—Peluso (placement).

Missed points after touchdown—Peluso 2, (placement).

Substitutes — Rochester: Nocera, Mike, Leonberg, Carcaise, Burg, Farmer, Rall, McElhaney; New Brighton: Zettle, McNutt, Chogich, Wilson, Irwin, Crawford, J. Budiscak, Weber, Spratt.

Referee, Melman; Umpire, Rebele; Headlinesman, Gannon.

Detroit Fans Boo Leonard And Spence

DETROIT, Oct. 2. (UP)—Emil John Leonard and Stanley Orvil Spence are the two most unpopular men in this town.

Emil John, better known as "Dutch", is a pitcher for the Washington Senators. Stanley Orvil is an outfielder for the same team.

Dutch blew the Detroit Tigers right out of the World Series yesterday with a four-hit 4 to 1 triumph. Spence blasted a fourth-inning two-run homer that made his victory certain. Sentiment outweighed sportsmanship and 45,565 fans in Briggs Stadium booed them lustily.

It was a sad end for the Tigers who drove to the top of the league after trailing by 9 1-2 games on July 13 when they were in seventh place.

Card-Pitts Beat New York, 17 To 16

By UNITED PRESS

The Green Bay Packers maintained their unblemished record in the National Professional Football League by defeating the Detroit Lions 27-6 in Sunday's only schedule game.

In three exhibition games the Pittsburgh-Chicago combine defeated the New York Giants 17-16, the Cleveland Rams played a 7-7 tie with the Philadelphia Eagles, and the Chicago Bears beat the Washington Red Skins, 28-0.

Monday Roll Call Of Unbeaten Teams

NEW YORK, Oct. 2. (UP)—The Monday roll call of perfect record football teams, survivors of a welter of Saturday upsets, reads as follows:

East — Army, Cornell and Pennsylvania.

Midwest — Notre Dame, Wisconsin, Illinois, and Great Lakes Naval.

South — Georgia Tech and North Carolina Pre-Flight.

Rocky Mountain—Second Air Force Superbombers and Colorado College.

Missouri Valley—Tulsa and Oklahoma A. & M.

Southwest — Randolph Field, Texas, Texas Christian, Texas A. & M. and Southern Methodist.

Pacific Coast — Washington, California and Southern California.

There are other unbeaten teams in all sections, but they haven't met top-flight opposition as yet.

THE DAILY TIMES
1874—and WESTERN ARGUS—1803

ROCHESTER - BEAVER - MONACA - FREEDOM - BRIDGEWATER - CONWAY - VANPORT - MIDLAND

Established April 2, 1874 | Beaver and Rochester, Pa., Wednesday, December 6, 1944 | Single Copy 4 Cents — 24 Cents A Week

YANKS MAKE NEW SAAR CROSSINGS

U. S. TROOPS TIGHTEN TRAP ON JAPANESE

Yanks Closing In On Strong Enemy Force Pocketed On Leyte; Japanese Report Big Allied Convoy Sighted Off Mindanao; More Jap Vessels Sunk

By UNITED PRESS

American troops slogged forward over muddy, flooded trails to tighten their squeeze on the strong Japanese garrison pocketed on western Leyte Island today as unconfirmed Tokyo reports said a big Allied convoy had been sighted off Mindanao, in the Southern Philippines.

There was no confirmation of the enemy report on the new Allied convoy, which Tokyo said comprised 60 to 70 transports and supply ships and 20 escorting warships.

Tokyo said the fleet was sighted east of Mindanao yesterday and that Japanese planes still were attacking today.

JAP TANKS REPULSED

On Leyte, Gen. Douglas MacArthur's ground forces beat off a tank-led Japanese night attack on their road block below the Leyte river bridge some 18 miles north of Ormoc. The Americans chopped up a number of enemy pockets in that area and in the hills southwest of Dagami, east of Ormoc, but the torrential rains and mud made it slow going.

American and Allied planes, meanwhile, sank a Japanese destroyer and five merchant ships in Philippines and southern waters, and an American destroyer flotilla added two more enemy freighters to the toll during a night bombardment of Ormoc.

Other Allied planes continued their steady neutralization raids on Japanese airdromes in the Philippines and at Rabaul, New Britain.

REPAIR AIR STRIP

On the Burma front, American engineers began repairing the captured Japanese fighter strip outside Bhamo, 500 yards from the Chinese siege lines around the town itself. It also was dis-

Continued on Page Two

War Workers Being Recruited On Street

The special War Manpower Commission "recruiting crews" which have concentrated their efforts in the past few weeks in Harrisburg and other sections of this area today began to cover the Beaver County Area, it was announced today by Patrick T. Fagan, War Manpower Commission Area Director. This program will continue until December 12.

A serious shortage of labor in many of the essential plants in Beaver County was the reason for inaugurating the special recruiting program, George Barber, Manager of the Rochester U. S. E. S. office, explained.

Evidence of the effectiveness of having recruiters in the streets stopping men and women to urge them to take jobs in essential plants turning out needed material for war are shown by the War Manpower Commission records in Pittsburgh and McKeesport. The Rochester War Manpower Commission headquarters is at 101 Brighton avenue.

Brighton Taproom Damaged By Fire

An electric coil cooling unit in the basement of the Benjamin Balo taproom, 317 Fifth street, New Brighton, reportedly was the cause of a $2,000 fire there this morning at 5:25 o'clock, according to the proprietor. New Brighton firemen extinguished the blaze.

The old axiom, "where there's smoke, there's fire" was disproved late Tuesday afternoon when New Brighton firemen were called to the smoke-filled home of Edward West. Mr. West had been connecting a coal stove and misplaced the flue.

JESTING WITH ONLOOKERS, NAZIS MARCH TO REAR

GERMAN PRISONERS joke with smiling civilians in the Lutzelhouse area, France, as they are marched to the rear, where they will sit the war out in Allied prison enclosures. They seem to be little older than the children watching them. Note what appears to be a loaf of bread in one prisoner's hand. This is an official United States Army Signal Corps photo. *(International Soundphoto)*

Thirty To Leave Baden On Friday For Armed Forces

Thirty selectees will leave Baden Draft Board No. 1, Friday morning at 7:15 o'clock for Pittsburgh, for induction into the armed forces.

They are:

Frank J. Bendig, Jr., Zellenople; Frank J. Bierline, Freedom; Anthony J. Dosdor, Freedom; William Garbinsky, Ambridge; Floyd Ralph Wiley, Ellwood City; Joseph Ionta, Ellwood City; Anthony J. Yannachione, Freedom; Wayne J. Rhoades, Franklin; Elmer H. Otto, Freedom; Joseph W. Stoncak, Aliquippa.

James B. McMillen, Conway; John Korpash, Aliquippa; Ralph L. Tritt, Ellwood City; Donald J. Ayers, Conway; John J. Bruno, Conway; Thomas W. George, New Brighton; Patsy B. Ricci, Ambridge; Frank P. Schaffer, Harmony; Alvin L. Probst, Freedom; Harold J. Campbell, Aliquippa.

Harold L. Stang, Rochester; John Thomas Davidson, Aliquippa; Robert B. Markle, Ellwood City; Floyd L. Leonard, Sturgeon; Steve A. Ecimovic, Conway; Nick Pavlich, Clinton; Jack M. Hudson, Ellwood City; William C. Bennett, Ellwood City; James A. Taylor, Ellwood City; David L. Wiley, Ellwood City.

New Threat Made By Japs Against American Fliers

By UNITED PRESS

Japan, smarting under the impact of mounting Superfortress raids on Tokyo, uttered a veiled new threat today against the lives of captured American airmen.

Radio Tokyo said Japan, in formal replies to American and British inquiries about the treatment of Allied air prisoners, had made it clear that she would hold responsible "under international law those enemy airmen who are clearly found to have deliberately breached established practices of warfare."

It was on the self same grounds of "breaches of established practices of warfare" that Japan tried and executed several of the fliers who participated in the raid led by Lt. Gen. James H. Doolittle on Tokyo April 18, 1942.

A Tokyo broadcast by the official Japanese Domei agency said Japan had replied officially last Friday through the Swiss legation to inquiries received from the United States government September 26 and Britain September 6. No reason was given for the delay of nearly three months in answering the inquiries.

Two Local Soldiers In Casualty List

Sgt. Edward J. Kapusinski, Ninth avenue, Beaver Falls, and Pfc. Robert J. Marocco, Hopewell avenue, Aliquippa, were reported wounded in action in the European area in the casualty list issued today by the War Department.

Beaver Soldier In Hospital In Germany

Corp. Ray Stout, second son of the R. C. Stouts, Second street, Beaver, is in an army hospital in Germany. In the infantry, he has been with the Seventh U. S. Army and has seen plenty of action on the fighting front. In a V-mail letter to his parents, received today, he disclosed that he is in the hospital receiving excellent treatment. He did not disclose whether his hospitalization was caused by wounds, or from other causes. He did say that he was unable to walk because of the condition of his feet, that he and five buddies had been cut off from their main force for five days and nights without food, water, or blankets. He said "I am fortunate, since all but a few of my platoon were wiped out." The Stouts had received no word at noon today from the War Department regarding their son. An older son, Robert, is in the U. S. Navy in the Pacific.

Mother Of Two In Service Completes 2,000 Hours As Aide

While her son and daughter are serving with the armed forces overseas, a Beaver woman has been faithfully giving her services on the home front. She is Mrs. Mildred Honaker, Tuscarawas road, the first Beaver County Nurse's Aide to receive the coveted fourth stripe for completion of 2,000 hours of volunteer work.

Recognition of her untiring efforts was given at the monthly meeting of the Nurse's Aides of Providence hospital, in Seton Hall, Beaver Falls, Tuesday evening. Another Aide, Mrs. Margaret Wiegman, Beaver, was awarded her third stripe, having completed 1,000 hours of work.

Mrs. Honaker is a member of the first class of Nurse's Aides at Providence hospital capped in

Continued on Page Two

Monaca Soldier Home From India

Home from Burma and India where he served with the famous "Merrill's Marauders," Staff Sgt. Louis Kaiser has returned to his home in Monaca, having been given an honorable discharge.

With the exception of a broken left arm, received when he was thrown from a tree in which he took refuge as a hand grenade struck the ground nearby, he came through without a scratch.

Leaving Monaca high school before he graduated, he enlisted in the service and began his training at Arlington, Va., serving with the Infantry. From Arlington, he went to Jamaica, West Indies, and later to Burma and India.

He wears a Presidential unit citation ribbon, his unit having been the second to receive the award. He is a son of Mrs. Anna Rokic, Monaca, and the late Michael Kaiser, Monaca.

County Grand Jury Completes Work; 23 True Bills Returned

Thirteen persons were indicted by the December Grand Jury yesterday in 13 true bills returned to the court, along with four cases in which the grand jury refused to find indictments.

The grand jury completed its work Tuesday afternoon, but returned this morning to visit and inspect county institutions and buildings, including the court house, jail, county home and hospital and county sanatorium.

Altogether, in the two-day session of the Grand Jury, indictments were returned against defendants in 23 cases, and in nine cases the bills were returned marked "not true bills".

Jury trials will begin next Monday and continue until the list of cases is exhausted, probably within a week or ten days. Following are the returns made to the court by the grand jury late yesterday afternoon:

TRUE BILLS

Mary Colaluca, Aliquippa, larceny; Amelia Catroppa, Aliquippa, prosecutor.

Walter Kleemook, Baden, rape; R. W. Compton, prosecutor.

Andrew Mihalic, Midland, assault with intent to kill; Sam Bekich, prosecutor.

Thelma Shaw Price, Aliquippa, larceny; Eva Clark, prosecutor.

Robert Edward Smith, Beaver

Continued on Page Two

Officers Elected By School Boards

At a re-organization meeting of the East Rochester School Board, Tuesday evening, Miss Irma Romigh was elected secretary to succeed Miss Catherine Leffler. Other officers were re-elected. They are: President, Clifford Young, and vice-president Paul Reab.

John C. Irvin was re-elected president at the re-organization meeting of the Rochester Township school board Tuesday evening. Emmet L. Carney was re-elected vice-president.

War History

Halifax, Nova Scotia, was afire when an American ammunition ship exploded, December 6, 1917, news reports said.

GUARDS HELD BY PRISONERS AS HOSTAGES

Inmates Of Atlanta Penitentiary Threaten To Behead Four Guards; Prisoners Hold Out In One Section Of Prison After Attempted Break

ATLANTA, Ga., Dec. 6. (UP)—In watch towers overlooking the Atlanta Federal penitentiary sentries waited with machine guns today and kept constant watch on a segregation building where 25 desperate felons armed with knives and razors held four guards captive and threatened to behead them if officials tried to storm their prison within a prison.

The four guards, hostages in a revolt which flared Monday afternoon against confining Nazi saboteurs with other convicts, were alive and apparently unharmed last night. Early today official silence indicated that the situation was unchanged.

Warden Joseph W. Sanford and J. V. Bennett, director Federal Prisons, reported that the imprisoned guards were "seen through the windows of the segregation building" last night.

LOCKED IN CELL

A statement from the two officials confirmed that "the men have barricaded the doors of the five-storied segregation cell-block which houses the difficult cases as well as newly-admitted inmates.

"Apparently all but a small group of insubordinates in control are locked in their cells, the keys of which were captured by them," the statement continued. "The main body of inmates are cooperating as usual and the regular routine of the day is being followed."

A prison imposed "gag" kept reporters on the fringes of the penitentiary. Some sources believed that two Nazi saboteurs—Ernest Peter Burger and George John Dasch—were inmates of the institution and possibly were locked in with the hostages.

Burger and Dasch landed from a submarine on the East Coast in 1942 with six other enemy agents. The others were electrocuted. Burger was sentenced to life and Dasch got 30 years.

RAIDED BARBER SHOP

Sanford said last night that the revolt was "a sort of sit down strike," and disclaimed knowledge of what the prisoners wantey when they barricaded themselves with the guards after seizing the officials and raiding the prison barber shop of knives and razors. He said some prisoners had objected to German spies being housed in the same buildings with other prisoners.

Heat and water reportedly were cut off in the rebels' citadel where lights burned through the night in contrast with darkened buildings elsewhere in the yard.

The Atlanta penitentiary, built in 1902, is one of the nation's largest and claims that it's average prison population of 2,400 is the largest. Its physical plant is modern and its factories manufacture large quantities of war goods.

Railroad Worker Hurt At Aliquippa

H. B. Barthelow, 40, Aliquippa, conductor on the Aliquippa and Southern Railroad, Aliquippa, suffered a crushed right hand and broken arm when he fell beneath the wheels of a moving gondola car at 3:15 o'clock this morning. He was taken to South Side hospital, Pittsburgh.

The accident occurred when Barthelow attempted to cross between two gondolas of a moving train.

British Soldiers Go Into Action In Greek Revolt

ATHENS, Dec. 6. (UP)—British and Greek forces supporting the government of Premier George Papandreou opened a general assault today on rebellious EAM veterans and in the first onrush captured EAM headquarters and the central offices of the Communist party.

The government forces seized the Yannaro building in Constitution Square, the last center of resistance by the ELAS, the military arm of the EAM, in this part of the city. The buildings fell after a violent struggle in which an ELAS lieutenant-colonel and a major were arrested.

Intense fighting raged in a half-dozen sectors of Athens, with British and Greek government forces struggling to put down an uprising by the ELAS.

The showdown fight for control of the government appeared to have begun as the heavily-armed and reinforced Elas units pushed through the capital, overwhelming police posts and running head-on into the British tanks and infantry drawn up around the center of the city.

An Allied communique announced that the British were ordered into the fight after the insurrectionists had opened fire on their sentries.

"British and Greek regular forces have now gone into action to support the civil power," the communique said.

FIGHT IN STREETS

Fierce street fighting was resumed in the capital at dawn around Constitution Square and in the Hadjicosta and Psiro districts with British troops and tanks and regular Greek army units joining the government police against the Elas, military army of the EAM, (national liberation front.)

News of the approach of Elas reinforcements was disclosed in a communique from the headquarters of Lt. Gen. Ronald Scobie, British commander in Athens, who had ordered the Elas to quit Athens by midnight tonight under penalty of being dealt with as "enemy units."

British tanks already have intervened on a number of occasions to rescue besieged government forces and "in a few cases had to take action to prevent bloodshed," Scobie said.

The tanks fired several rounds of shells yesterday into houses from which leftists were attacking a civil prison, but up until

Continued on Page Two

Child Dies After Being Burned In Fire At Ambridge

Patricia Panela Roney, four-months-old daughter of Seaman First Class and Mrs. Alfred J. Rony, Ambridge, died Tuesday afternoon at 5:15 o'clock in Sewickley Valley hospital of burns received when the Roney apartment, 325 Thirteenth street, was destroyed by fire Tuesday at noon.

Mrs. Roney, with her 3½-year-old son, James, had gone to the adjoining house to telephone her mother-in-law and was notified of the fire by a neighbor. Rushing back to the home, she carried the child from the burning crib.

The interior of the apartment was completely destroyed, along with most of the family's clothing and other possessions. Caused by an overheated coal stove, it was reported today the stove was found on its side, indicating a possible explosion.

The body was removed to the Matter funeral home. Funeral arrangements will be made later pending the arrival of the child's father, a former TIMES employe, now serving with the Navy at Twentynine Palms, Calif. Mrs. Roney was the former Marguerite Dougherty, Ambridge.

CONWAY G. I. FIRST AMERICAN EVER SEEN BY NATIVES OF TROPICAL SO. PACIFIC ISLAND

SOMEWHERE IN THE SOUTHWEST PACIFIC—To several island villages, Corporal Frank Sochats, son of Mr. and Mrs. John Sochats, Conway, Pa., represented the entire Ground Forces of the United States Army. Corporal Sochats, a member of a regiment of the 31st Infantry Division, was on guard duty at an outpost commanded by First Lt. Francis T. O'Flaherty, son of Mrs. Mary E. O'Flaherty, Medford, Mass.

An island official asked the lieutenant to designate a soldier to be exhibited to the natives as a model American soldier. These island folk had never seen an American. Cpl. Sochats, the "typical" G. I. is blond, 25-years old, six feet in height and weighs 180 pounds.

With the officia. and a guide Frank set off in a large canoe rigged with two outriders and manned by a coxswain and six oarsmen. The three passengers sat in state under a thatched canopy. Two hours later, near their destination, they were met by a gaily-bedecked craft bearing the chief of the village. News of the impending arrival had been carried by jungle telegraph—the fabled tom-toms.

"It was all," Frank said, "just like the movies."

A coral reef prevented the visiting craft from going all the way to the shore. Frank was about to wade to the beach as he had done in other landings, but the chief forbade. The guest must be carried ashore. Frank made a triumphal entry on the shoulders of a native, who, though smaller than he, did not seem to find the burden

Continued on Page Two

Russians Only 50 Miles From Austria

Today's War Summary

By UNITED PRESS

WESTERN FRONT — American 3rd Army, striking along 50 mile front at central gateway to Rhineland, sweeps across Saar river at four and perhaps five points northwest of Saarlautern and crashes into German border fortress of Sarreguemines.

EASTERN FRONT — Russian armored columns roll through German defenses at Lake Balaton 50 miles from Austria as Moscow dispatches report Nazis are rushing reinforcements from Italy and Balkans.

PACIFIC—American troops repulse tank led Japanese night attack on north end of Ormoc pocket on Leyte while warships and planes add Japanese destroyer and seven other vessels to enemy shipping toll in Philippines waters.

AIR WAR—Hundreds of British bombers smash at Soest freight yards in Ruhr in wake of American attack that brought up luftwaffe over Berlin and cost Nazis 91 planes.

ITALY—British Eighth Army extends flanking drives north and south of Faenza after capture of Ravenna on Adriatic coast.

United States Third Army troops broke across the Saar river in four new places today, further breaching the last natural barrier before the Siegfried line in the Saar basin, and to the southeast reached the outskirts of the key border town of Sarreguemines, below Sarrbrucken.

On the eastern front, the Russians drove around both ends of Lake Balaton through cracking German defenses and Moscow reported the Nazis were drawing reserves from Italy and the Balkans in an effort to stem the Soviet sweep toward Austria, 50 miles away. Berlin said the Russians also had begun an enveloping movement on Budapest from the west, south and east.

About 800 Flying Fortresses and Liberators, accompanied by a like number of fighters, attacked the Leuna synthetic oil plant at Mersburg, rail yards at Bielefeld and other targets in Germany today.

The daylight attack followed the night raid by British heavy bombers on the Soest rail yards in the Ruhr Valley.

8TH ARMY ADVANCES

On the Italian front, Eighth Army forces pushing westward from Godo in the area of captured Ravenna were engaged in heavy fighting on the Lamone river line. South of Faenza, British and Polish troops crossed the Lamone on a wide front and established strong bridgeheads.

The Third Army's drive into the Saar dominated the news on the Western Front, where the First and Ninth Armies on the Cologne plain skirmished with the enemy as they consolidated for a new drive, and the American-French Sixth Army group in the south pushed to within seven miles of Colmar, chief remaining strong point of the German pocket on the Alsatian plain. American troops finally captured Selestat, 25 miles southwest of Strausbourg, after a three-day battle.

The fierce nature of the fighting on the Western Front was illustrated by a front line estimate that the Allies have knocked out 180,000 Germans in the first three weeks of the winter offensive.

The Third Army's new crossing of the Saar gave the Americans six to seven bridgeheads

Continued on Page Two

Monaca Board Calls 32 Selectees For Induction Dec. 11th

The following 32 selectees will leave Monaca on the 7:32 a. m. train for induction on December 11:

Edward Hollie, Midland; Mike Brdar, Ellwood City; Edgar John Rambo, Rochester; Peter Joseph Bernardi, Midland; Donald Francis Thomas, Aliquippa; Nick Steve Petkovich, near Aliquippa; David Leroy Johnston, near Monaca; Robert M. Moorhead, Monaca; Frederick Harry Vogt, Monaca; Sidney Charles Gibson, Monaca.

Frank Merle Eder, near Monaca; Daniel Richard Palucci, Monaca; Vincent Paul Fanferra Midland; John Alfred Weister, Kobuta; Eugene Tunney Adams, Monaca; Louis William Tipton, near Aliquippa; Walter Larry Zajac, Monaca; James Pilgrim Stoffel, Midland; Salvin Anthony Suffoletta, Midland; Thomas Wilson Tpoup, Smiths Ferry.

Donald LeRoy Parker, Monaca; Felix Madison Fullington, New Brighton; William Francis Dawson, near Hookstown; William James Baker, near Monaca; Robert Charles Eckles, near Industry; Darwin Kirk Mercer, near Georgetown; Orazio Petrella, Monaca; Paul Ursich, Monaca; Harley Berthel Coss, near Rochester; Nicholas Dawson Strouss, near Coraopolis; Walter Reasion Jenkins, Shippingport; Herman Culfo, Monaca.

Social Security Freeze Test Looms

WASHINGTON, Dec. 6. (UP)—Congress rushed head-on today toward its first test of strength with the White House since the election—on the question of freezing the Social Security payroll tax at one per cent for another year.

The House handed the Administration a thumping defeat on the issue late yesterday by passing a freeze bill, 262 to 72. The fight thus moved to the Senate where Chairman Walter F. George, D., Ga., of the Senate finance committee said he hoped to get the measure on the floor Friday.

Speedy action was endorsed by Sen. Arthur H. Vandenberg, R., Mich., who thrice previously has sponsored "freeze" legislation, because he wants congressional action out of the way in plenty of time for a chance to override a presidential veto before Congress takes its Christmas recess.

Eleven Killed In Truck Explosion

McALESTER, Okla., Dec. 6 —(UP)—Little hope was held today that any trace would be found of the four civilians and seven enlisted men who disappeared in the explosion of a truckload of torpedo warheads at the McAlester Naval Ammunition Depot, Navy authorities said.

The blast, which occurred yesterday while the men were making a routine transfer from a truck to a magazine, shattered windows in McAlester nine miles away and damaged one ammunition magazine. No trace has been found of the truck.

Weather Forecast

Western Pennsylvania: Cloudy and warmer today with rain beginning in the west portion this afternoon or evening. Occasional rain tonight and Thursday with mild temperature.

Freedom Soldier Wounded In Action

Word has been received by Mrs. Dorothy Sweeney Neuber, Fourth avenue, Freedom, that her husband, Pvt. Raymond R. Neuber, has been wounded in action.

Private Neuber enlisted in the Army, February 22, 1944, and received his basic training at Camp Wheeler, Ga., and was sent to Italy in August. From there he was transferred to France. He has been serving with the Infantry in the Seventh Army. The Neubers have a little daughter, Maria Rae.

Send the DAILY TIMES to your boy in the Army or Navy. "It's like a letter from home every day."

Amusements

Majestic Theatre

Dramatically, the history of Eddie Ballinger is recounted in the powerful screen drama, "My Buddy," starring Donald Barry, which comes to the screen of the Majestic Theatre on Friday.

"My Buddy," is Hollywood's first daring account of what might happen to the boy next door, if, when he comes marching home he finds himself considered excess baggage in a civilian world. Eddie Ballinger, whose embitterment leads him to forsake the love of his mother and his sweetheart to follow a career of crime, is conscious that things would have been different had he been given a chance to find security and happiness, by those whom he fought to protect.

Lest civilians forget, "My Buddy" is an appeal for understanding, and for preparation now, for the returning heroes.

The added feature for Friday and Saturday, "Bordertown Trail," stars Smiey Burnette.

Granada Theatre

The most revolutionary picture of its kind is due to arrive tonight at the Granada theatre when "The Hitler Gang" is to be flashed on the screen.

First, the black history of the Nazi regime is revealed in all its ugliness. Next, the cast chosen to portray the roles of Hitler, Himmler, Goering, Hess, Goebbels, to name a few, is a miracle of casting. Lastly, the film deals with the unknown aspects of the regime's rise to power. This feature alone provides the hair-raising scenes which should be witnessed by everyone.

Hitler's double-dealings with honorable nations is familiar to all but "The Hitler Gang" reveals how Hitler double-crossed his pals, too. In the early days, the deranged ex-corporal of Germany's defeated armies squealed to his superiors. It became his stepping-stone to power since the Prussian militarists rewarded their stool-pigeons well. The next rung on the ladder for Hitler was political activity and his hysterical oratory swayed enough greedy followers to form the Nazi party.

Rialto Theatre

"Something for the Boys" is tops; solid entertainment for all. The lightning of good fortune strikes thrice when three cousins who had never met before learn that they are the joint heirs to a Southern plantation—Magnolia Manor, near Masonville, Georgia. The cousins are Harry (Phil Silvers) a fast-talking sidewalk salesman of gadgets; Chiquita Hart (Carmen Miranda), a carborondum polisher, who makes with the hips to radio music no one else hears; and Blossom Hart (Vivian Blaine), a Brooklyn night club singer. The film's story revolves around the adventures, romantic and otherwise, of three cousins—who find themselves joint heirs to a real honest-to-goodness southern plantation, rich in tradition but on the Tobacco road side as far as everything else goes. When Michael O'Shea, a sergeant stationed in a nearby army camp, convinces them they'd be doing something for the boys if they'd convert their "mansion" into a hotel for army wives, the doors are thrown wide open to the fastest-moving, most hilarious series of sequences ever to be joy-packed into one film.

For Carmen Miranda devotees, "Something for the Boys" offers a real field day. The volatile Brazilian bombshell is at her bombastic best, singing, cavorting and committing mayhem on the King's English in her own rib-cracking way. And when it comes to romancing, Michael O'Shea is teamed with Vivian Blaine, the Cherry Blonde, who is something terrific. She sings, she dances, she's got looks—plus and the most bewitchingly vivacious personality to hit the screen in a long time. Keep your eye on her (as if we had to tell you). "Something for the Boys" is now playing at the Rialto in Beaver Falls.

The program is augmented by a Cartoon, Novelties, Sports, and the new "This Is America"—West Point.

SAME TO YOU, MISS ATWOOD.

Happy New Year

GLAMOR GAL of the ice, Donna Atwood, generally recognized as the national figure skating champion this year and star of the Ice Capades revue, gives you an early holiday greeting. *(International)*

Michael O'Shea, Vivian Blaine, Phil Silvers and Carmen Miranda make up the frolicsome foursome in the new Technicolor musical hit, "Something For The Boys," which opens today at the Oriental Theatre. An outstanding hit on Broadway, the song-and-dance-and-laugh-packed hit revolves about the adventures (romantic and otherwise) of three cousins who find themselves joint heirs of a broken-down southern "mansion," and who in an effort to "do something for the boys" open its doors to army wives, and one of the most hilarious series of sequences filmed.

Beaver Theatre

"Since You Went Away," David O. Selznick's first film since the Academy Award-winning "Gone With the Wind" and "Rebecca," starring Claudette Colbert, Joseph Cotten, Jennifer Jones, Shirley Temple, Monty Woolley, Lionel Barrymore and Robert Walker, opens tonight at the Beaver theatre.

Described as a "panorama of the home front," "Since You Went Away" is the first film to glorify America and the folks at home. In the simple story of the Hilton family, Selznick has delineated a portrait of all of the families of America. In this household composed of Anne Hilton and her two daughters, Janet and "Brig," the producer has captured all the laughter, warmth and pathos of the average American home whose man has gone to war.

Claudette Colbert, in the finest portrayal of her entire career, plays Anne Hilton, guardian angel and all-around protector of the morale and physical well-being of her family and friends. Miss Colbert, who has had a long and highly successful career in Hollywood, calls her role in "Since You Went Away" the best she has ever played.

Save KITCHEN FATS to win the war.

Rotary Club Here Sends Clothing To Bombed-Out Britons

Warm clothing collected recently by the Rochester Rotary Club with the co-operation of the public, will protect bombed-out men, women and children in England this winter.

Six cartons and four boxes weighing a total of 918 pounds have been shipped by the club. Much of the clothing will be distributed to victims of the recent German robot bombings.

Included in the shipment were 209 items of clothing for men, 399 for women and 133 for children. Four blankets, twenty-two pairs of gloves, and a ready-packed box containing seventy-five items completed the collection. A detailed inventory follows:

Men's garments — suits, 26; top coats, 33; trousers, 22; extra coats, 19; extra vests, 10; pairs of socks, 50; shirts, 10; sweaters, 10; underwear, 12; and shoes in pairs, 17.

Women's apparel — dresses, 92; slacks, 5; coats, 37; miscellaneous garments, 180; hats, 7; sweaters, 40; pairs of shoes, 38.

Children's wear — coats, 17; suits, 12; sweaters, 17; caps, 6; infants' garments, 81.

Postmaster General Not Santa Claus, But He Gets Letters

WASHINGTON, Dec. 7 (UP) —Frank C. Walker admits quite frankly that he is Postmaster General of the United States, but he wants the kiddies to know that no matter how strong the evidence, he definitely is not Santa Claus.

Walker's difficulties in being regarded either as Santa or his Washington representative began when he agreed to place his name on the bottom of a green and white leaflet urging people to mail Christmas packages in November.

It included illustrations of a letter carrier, a soldier manning a machine gun, three trains, a woman buying a necktie, a couple of Christmas trees and, just above Walker's signature, a package equipped with a pair of wings. Many children interpreted this as an invitation to send in their Christmas lists—to Walker.

Those with addresses will be forwarded to local postmasters for reply, the Post Office Department said. Those whose senders had supreme faith in the omniscience of the Postmaster General will have to be handed to Santa Claus himself.

Millions of housewives can't be wrong if they save FATS to help win the war.

SCOTT'S SCRAP BOOK By R. J. SCOTT

HEP, HEP, HUZZA, THE SHOUT OF THE CRUSADERS, BECAME THE "HIP, HIP, HURRAH" OF THE PRESENT DAY
SCRAPS
WHAT COMET IS SEEN ONLY ONCE IN AN ORDINARY LIFETIME?
HALLEY'S COMET
THIS KRISHNA DEVOTEE OF INDIA FOLLOWS THE ASCETIC PRACTICE OF WALKING ON HIS RIGHT HEEL
12-7

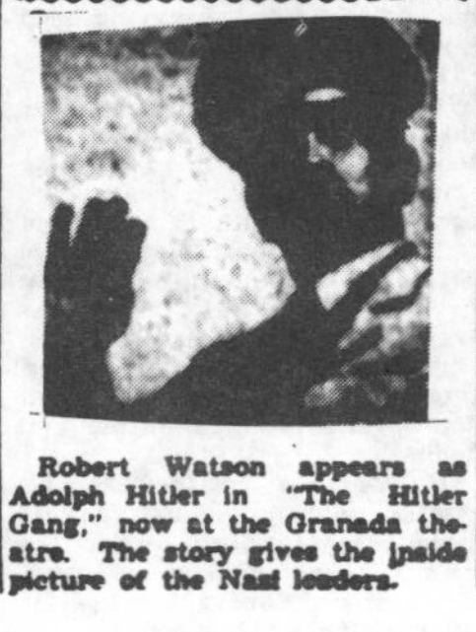

Robert Watson appears as Adolph Hitler in "The Hitler Gang," now at the Granada theatre. The story gives the inside picture of the Nazi leaders.

AS THE FIRST WAVE of American forces neared the shores of Mindoro Island, this rocket-firing LCI let go a powerful barrage of deadly projectiles to smother beach defenses. These rockets laid down a pattern of destruction at close range as the Yanks closed in. *(International Soundphoto)*

Inside WASHINGTON

U. S. Manpower Situation Entering Critical Phase | **Draft Boards Must Turn Toward Older Male Group**

Special to Central Press

● **WASHINGTON—Evidence piled up in Washington this week that the American manpower situation has again entered a critical phase as casualty lists reflect heavy fighting on all fronts.**

The War Department reported that Western Front casualties, exclusive of the air forces, from D-day through Dec. 1 totaled 258,124. This figure accounted for more than half the Army casualties since Pearl Harbor which added up to 483,957 as of Nov. 28.

Casualties Near Half Million

Close on the heels of the Selective Service announcement that the drafting of men between 27 and 38 would be resumed, the War Depastment stated it had become necessary to boost draft quotas from 60,000 to 80,000 per month.

For the past six months, the department explained, monthly quotas had been set at 60,000; because at the same time the Army was combing its ranks for men fit for active combat duty who were assigned to other jobs and to organizations no longer needed.

By this procedure, for example, 100 anti-aircraft battalions were retrained for infantry duty and other anti-aircraft men were retrained as individual infantry replacements. In addition, the air forces turned over 55,000 men to the ground forces, and 25,000 were transferred from the service forces, thus making up for the lowered quotas.

Now that it has scraped its own barrel, the Army has been forced to turn to the remaining civilian population for combat replacements.

• • • •

● DESPITE THE ARMED FORCES' demands for younger, physically fit soldiers and sailors, it looks as if more men from 26 through 37 will find themselves in uniform along about next February.

The need for more manpower by the military services was, of course, responsible for the new, tighter draft policy. And there is nowhere else to go except to the older group, since deferments were trimmed last summer on the 18-26 class.

Moreover, draft boards are going to be tough on men in the 26-37 category who obtained occupational deferments and then slipped off to peace-time jobs.

• • • •

● CONGRESS WILL NOT FACE the prospect of new tax legislation in the New Year. It will be the first time since the defense program got under way in 1940 that a major tax bill has not confronted that body.

The enactment last year of the Tax Simplification Bill ended war-time tax legislation. At least that was the intention of Congressional tax-bill writers. A major war catastrophe would be about the only thing capable of starting a movement to hike general tax rates further.

• • • •

● A BATTLE OVER POST-WAR COMPULSORY MILITARY TRAINING will swing into action soon after the new Congress convenes Jan. 5. The House military affairs committee already has arranged to hold hearings on the matter next month. The Senate military affairs committee plans similar hearings.

The controversy—which has strong support, also is bitterly opposed—is expected to rage into the spring, when major provisions of the selective service act expire May 15. Discussion of compulsory training is expected to tie-in with the argument over extension of these provisions.

• • • •

● A RECENT B-29 COMMUNIQUE said Superfortresses had attacked Iwo Jima, Jap base in the Bonin islands group. Six hours later a Navy communique said fleet forces, in cooperation with the B-29's, had raided Iwo Jima in the Volcano islands.

Where, Oh Where Is Iwo Jima?

Washington newsmen asked the two services to check, and went scurrying to war maps themselves.

Fact is, Iwo Jima is in the Volcanos; but the two groups are sometimes referred to as the "Volcano-Bonin Islands" and some maps list them as either the Volcanos or the Bonins.

Avery Cited For Failure To Cooperate With The Army

CHICAGO. — (A. P.) — Major General Joseph W. Byron reported today that Montgomery Ward & Company personnel who refused to cooperate in army operation of seized properties in seven cities was being replaced and made subject to selective service reclassification.

Specifically, the general named Sewell Avery, chairman of the board, "and other representatives" as having refused to operate the properties under his direction since the seizure under presidential order Thursday. Avery refused to recognize the seizure as constitutionally valid and said the company could not accept or obey it.

In a formal statement, Mr. Avery said:

"The order of the President of the United States to effect the seizure of the property and business of Montgomery Ward is a violation of the Constitution of the United States, which the President has sworn to uphold and defend. The Congress, which is the sole law-making authority under the Constitution, has given the President no power to seize the non-war business of Montgomery Ward.

"The purpose of the President's order is to enforce by an exercise of arbitrary power orders of the War Labor Board which the courts have declared to be merely advisory and unenforceable. The courts have held that any one who refuses to comply with orders of the War Labor Board is not defying a command of the government and that, since the orders are merely advisory, no government official has the right to impose punishments on those who do not comply.

"The President's order does not arise from any failure on Ward's part to pay fair wage rates. Ward's policy is, and has been, to pay wages as high or higher than those paid by other employers in the community for similar employment. Ward's only objection to any of the War Labor Board's wage recommendations has been in those instances where the board has arbitrarily demanded that Ward's substantially increase its rates above those of its competitors in the highly competitive retail field.

"The President has ordered the army to restrict the liberties of Ward's employees by imposing upon them the closed shop in the form of union maintenance. This is the final step in the coercion used by the administrative agencies of the government to force the closed shop upon employers and employees throughout the nation. Ward's has long believed that when the public awakens to the extent of this coercion, it will rise in indignation.

"Ward's defense of the freedom of its employees has not been prompted by any feeling of anti-unionism. All employees at Ward's are free to join or not join a union, as they wish. Ward's fully recognizes this privilege and has assured all employees that their opportunity with the company will be the same whether they are union members or not.

"Ward's cannot in good citizenship accept or obey the commands of those who have no legal power to give them and who are seeking to deprive Ward's of its constitutional rights and liberties. Ward's takes this position in defense of the constitutional rights and liberties of every citizen of the United States.

"The issues are now before the courts, where Ward's has sought for two years to have them decided. Ward's welcomes the opportunity to present its case to the courts."

General Byron also announced yesterday the army seized two warehouses in Detroit, "necessary for effective governmental operation of the four Ward's stores in the Detroit area." This made a total of 16 properties—10 retail stores, 3 mail order houses and 3 warehouses—now under army control.

Avery was in his office, near that being used by General Byron when the military manager's preliminary report to Secretary of War Stimson was released.

For more than 20 years the number of horses and mules in the United States has steadily declined.

PIN-UP ROUND THE CALENDAR

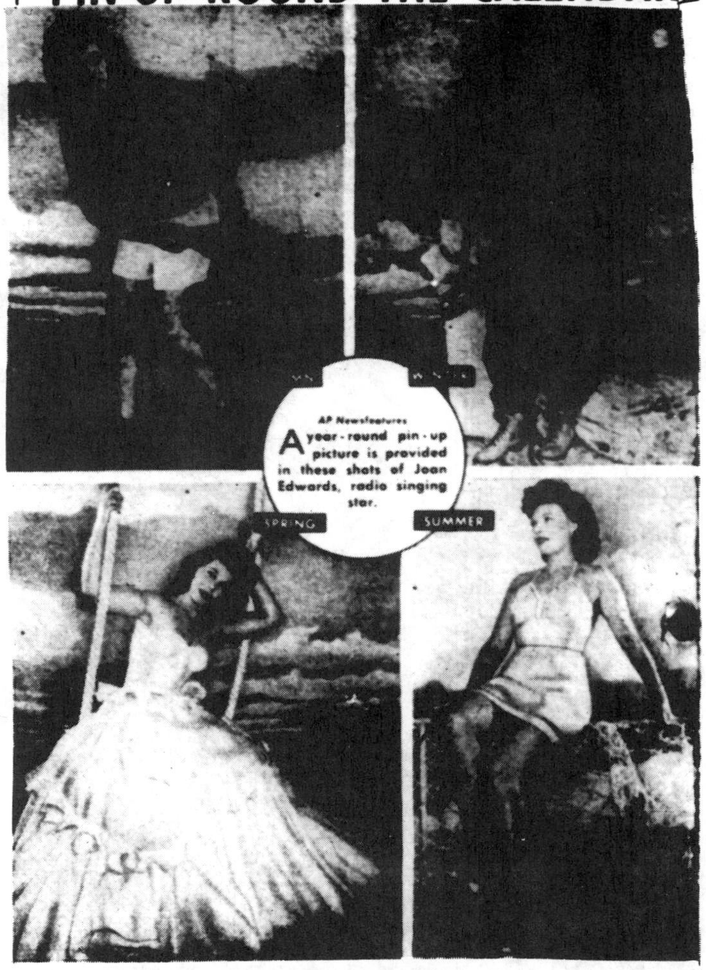
SPRING
SUMMER

AP Newsfeatures
A year-round pin-up picture is provided in these shots of Joan Edwards, radio singing star.

Monaca News

Rev. Simoleit Will Preach Tonight At Community Service

Rev. Hans O. F. Simoleit will preach on the theme, "Nevertheless or God's Way," at the closing service of the Week of Prayer in the Church of the Nazarene this evening at 7:30 o'clock. The offerings taken at the meetings will be used by the Monaca Ministerial Association for religious and educational purposes.

John Taormina, young son of Mr. and Mrs. Anthony Taormina, Indiana avenue, has been ill in his home since Monday. He is a student in the third grade.

Mrs. Leah Figley, Brodhead road, has returned from El Paso, Tex., where she spent three weeks with her husband, Pfc. Lawrence Figley, stationed at Ft. Bliss.

Mr. and Mrs. Paul Svhira, Washington avenue, have as their guest, Mrs. Svhira's sister, Miss Martha J. Markoski, New Castle, who is employed in Washington, D. C.

Mrs. Viola Beckman, Washington avenue, is visiting her brother-in-law and sister, Mr. and Mrs. Fred Dover, and family, Connellsville.

Mr. and Mrs. Michael Spisak and son, Eugene, have returned to their home in Ninth street following a one-week visit with Mrs. Spisak's mother, Mrs. Susan Dunchak, Spangler.

Pvt. John Borkovic, Jr., is spending eight days delay en route from Camp Croft, S. C., to Ft. Meade, Md., with his parents, Mr. and Mrs. John Borkovic, Walnut street. He is serving with an infantry unit.

Mrs. Jack Prosser, Brodhead road, is recovering in her home following a recent operation.

Mrs. Daniel O'Niell, Aliquippa, was a guest the past few days of Mr. and Mrs. Alex Skinner, Indiana avenue.

Mrs. Thomas Rowan, Speyerer avenue, is ill of pleurisy in her home.

Mrs. Sue Egger and daughter, Carole Sue, Washington avenue, have returned from Ft. Knox, Ky., where they visited Mrs. Egger's husband, Pvt. Allen J. Egger.

Lieut. Edward Ofcharka, Sebring, Fla., is spending a 15-day leave with his parents, Mr. and Mrs. Matthew Ofcharka, and family, Marshall road.

Mr. and Mrs. E. J. McClure, Potter Township, formerly of New Sewickley Township, have received word that their son, Cpl. James McClure, is ill in a hospital in France.

WLB STUDIES PROPOSAL

WASHINGTON, Jan. 11. (UP)—The shipping panel of the War Labor Board had under study today the question of whether to impose union maintenance of membership and dues check-off for the first time on barge lines operating between Pittsburgh and New Orleans to help relieve the manpower shortage on the rivers.

ALL COUNTY HOUSING PROJECTS HAVE WOMEN MANAGERS

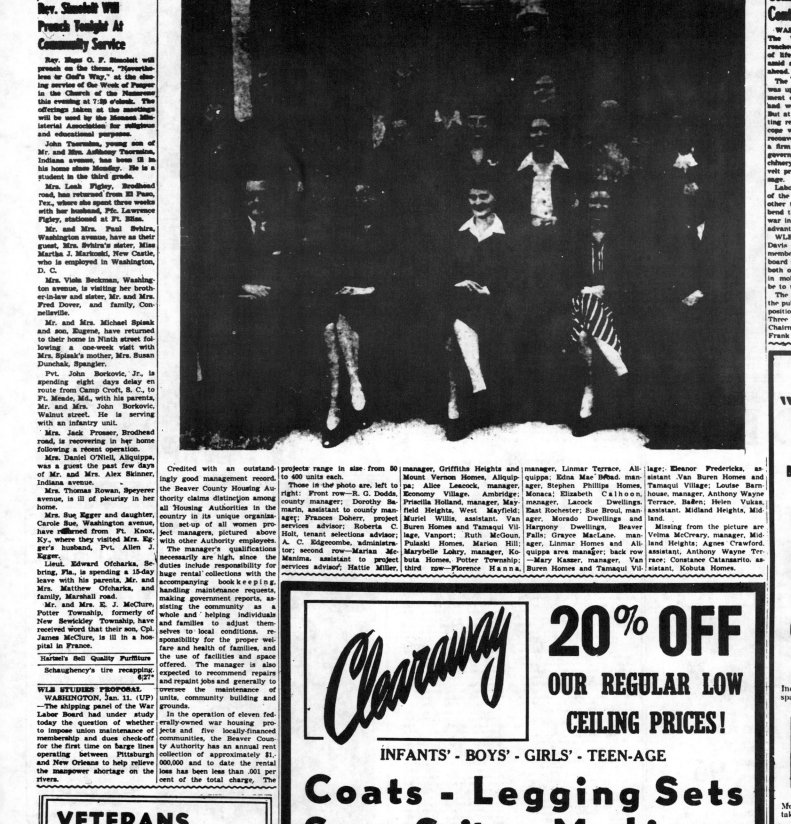

Credited with an outstandingly good management record, the Beaver County Housing Authority claims distinction among all Housing Authorities in the country in its unique organization set-up of all women project managers, pictured above with other Authority employees.

The manager's qualifications necessarily are high, since the duties include responsibility for huge rental collections with the accompanying bookkeeping, handling maintenance requests, making government reports, assisting the community as a whole and helping individuals and families to adjust themselves to local conditions, responsibility for the proper welfare and health of families, and the use of facilities and space offered. The manager is also expected to recommend repairs and repaint jobs and generally to oversee the maintenance of units, community building and grounds.

In the operation of eleven federally-owned war housing projects and five locally-financed communities, the Beaver County Authority has an annual rent collection of approximately $1,000,000 and to date the rental loss has been less than .001 per cent of the total charge. The projects range in size from 50 to 400 units each.

Those in the photo are, left to right: Front row—R. G. Dodds, county manager; Dorothy Samarin, assistant to county manager; Frances Doherr, project services advisor; Roberta C. Holt, tenant selections advisor; A. C. Edgecombe, administrator; second row—Marian McManima, assistant to project services advisor; Hattie Miller, manager, Griffiths Heights and Mount Vernon Homes, Aliquippa; Alice Leacock, manager, Economy Village, Ambridge; Priscilla Holland, manager, Mayfield Heights, West Mayfield; Muriel Willis, assistant, Van Buren Homes and Tamaqui Village, Vanport; Ruth McGoun, Pulaski Homes, Marion Hill; Marybelle Lohry, manager, Kobuta Homes, Potter Township; third row—Florence Hanna, manager, Linmar Terrace, Aliquippa; Edna Mae Broad, manager, Stephen Phillips Homes, Monaca; Elizabeth Calhoon, manager, Lacock Dwellings, East Rochester; Sue Broul, manager, Morado Dwellings and Harmony Dwellings, Beaver Falls; Grayce MacLane, manager, Linmar Homes and Aliquippa area manager; back row—Mary Kaszer, manager, Van Buren Homes and Tamaqui Village; Eleanor Fredericks, assistant Van Buren Homes and Tamaqui Village; Louise Barnhouse, manager, Anthony Wayne Terrace, Baden; Helen Vukas, assistant, Midland Heights, Midland.

Missing from the picture are Velma McCreary, manager, Midland Heights; Agnes Crawford, assistant, Anthony Wayne Terrace; Constance Catanzarito, assistant, Kobuta Homes.

War Labor Board Completes Three Controversial Years

WASHINGTON, Jan. 12 (AP). The War Labor Board has reached the end of its third year of life—all of them stormy—amid signs of bigger troubles ahead.

The board, figuratively, still was up to its neck in the settlement of wartime labor disputes and wage stabilization issues. But at the same time it was getting ready to shift its course to cope with the problems of the reconversion period and to lay a firm base for the long range governmental mediation machinery which President Roosevelt proposed in his budget message.

Labor and industry members of the WLB were battling each other tenaciously in efforts to bend this reconversion and post-war influence to their respective advantage.

WLB Chairman William H. Davis was leading the public members of the tri-partate board in a campaign to persuade both opponents that cooperation in molding the program would be to their mutual benefit.

The labor-industry conflict left the public members in their usual position of having to settle issues. Three of them—Davis, Vice Chairman George W. Taylor and Frank P. Graham—were frankly tired of being continually "on the spot" and were carrying on only because Mr. Roosevelt refused to accept their resignations.

Aside from its internal fight over future policy, the WLB was engaged in running battles with Sewell Avery, chairman of the board of Montgomery Ward and Company, and James C. Petrillo, president of the American Federation of Musicians (AFL), over their refusal to obey WLB directives.

Governmental seizure of private property for non-compliance with WLB directives, and often to end wartime strikes, has been the most spectacular corollary of the WLB's existence. There have been 31 cases of non-compliance referred to the White House, 25 of which resulted in seizure.

Putting rock salt on coal keeps it from freezing, so that railroad cars can be unloaded quickly and easily, several leading collieries have found.

DOC SYKE

By Ving Fuller

DOCTOR— I KEEP THINKING I'M A RARE 14TH CENTURY MASTERPIECE.
DR SYKE SIKKIATRIST
CHARMING! CHARMING! I SEE A SPEAKING LIKENESS ALL RIGHT!
THANK YOU.
BUT I THINK YOU'D BETTER GIVE ME THAT FRAME.
OH, NO, DOCTOR! I CAN'T—
I'M HANGING AT THE METROPOLITAN THIS AFTERNOON!
VING FULLER

Moose Increases Duckpin Margin

The Loyal Order of Moose Duckpin team added a full game to its lead astride the Community league last night at Orpheum alleys as it swept its match from the Croatians while the second place Drinkmore team was winning only two from Jacobson's.

The Celtic-Reds moved back into third place as a result of winning three games from MPIC. Sergi's copped the odd game from Sutherland's. Summaries:

Moose—2200

Cloud	125	127	153	
Haber ...	127	184	114	
McHaffie..	164	157	133	
Skiba	145	99	120	
Markovich.	132	114	138	
Lindman ..	124		87	
B. Staffalo	182	152	172	
Stalla		118		
Total ..	750	734	716	2200

Croatians—2038

Shetak ...	82	169	133	
Bianchi ...	148	142	135	
Agich	126	147	134	
Mativasic .	126	117	129	
Danvanic .	102	127	156	
Cikarb ...	108	114	125	
Thomas ..	115	117	155	
Totals ..	623	702	713	2038

Drinkmores—2511

Turby ...	145	147	98	
Scarcella .	138	166	147	
Frazier ..	134	146	147	
Malovich .	161	170	147	
Emert ...	155	186	171	
Anthony ..	144	230	180	
Homish ..	122	188	183	
Merges ...				
Totals ..	743	940	828	2511

Jacobson's—2238

Hurni	174	177	149	
Evans	132	151	145	
Leitschaft .	110		90	
Kowalski ..	121	116		
Hammitt ..	116	137	134	
Tho'shefsky	152	113	153	
Conrad ...	170	145	148	
Moreno ...		153	116	
Totals ..	748	763	729	2238

Celtic-Reds

Ender ...	134	113	161
Calabro ..	198	185	128
Montini ...	164	108	
Westman .	185	190	161
Prosper ..	129		130
Campbell .	139	137	150
Horvath ..	99		156
DePaul ...		108	
Ross		119	163
Totals ..	765	744	791

M.P.I.C.

D. Morelli .	129	165	104
S. Colonna.	102		
E. Salvati.	140	116	
L. Mansuetti	103		
S. Montini .	127	104	162
E. Mansuetti	159	110	168
Matz	174	103	171
N. Colonna			133
H. Frazan .		145	137
G. Turby ..		134	149
Totals ..	729	670	787

Sergi's—2311

Espey	185	195	140	
Marrone ..	107			
Yarosz ...	166	151	117	
Socarro ..	99	128	114	
Buffalin ..	124	99	140	
Patton ...	84	160	177	
Darkin ...	195	157	126	
Schomar ..		110	160	
Totals ..	777	791	743	2311

Sutherland's—2191

Opsatnik .	137	157	135	
Vest	123	161	150	
King	110		136	
Maiden ...	113			
Westlake .	71	164	175	
Sterbutcel	108	116		
Devae	157	148	160	
Zagar		141	109	
Henderson.		153	145	
Totals ..	640	785	766	2191

JUNIOR HIGH BASKETBALL
Standing Of Teams

	Won	Lost	Pct.
Franklin	6	0	1.000
Jones	4	2	.667
Hopewell	3	3	.500
Washington ...	3	3	.500
St. Titus	2	4	.333
St. Joseph	0	6	.000

Friday's scores: Franklin 16, Jones 14; St. Titus 17, St. Joseph 8; Washington 23, Hopewell 12.

Games this week: Monday, Washington at Jones; Tuesday, St. Titus at Hopewell, Franklin at St. Joseph. Thursday, St. Titus at Franklin; Friday, Jones at Hopewell, St. Joseph at Hopewell.

GRADE BASKETBALL
Standing Of Teams

	Won	Lost	Pct
Laughlin	4	0	1.000
Washington ...	3	0	1.000
Highland	2	2	.500
Jones	2	2	.500
Logstown	1	2	.333
St. Joseph	0	3	.000
McDonald Hts. .	0	3	.000

Friday's scores:

Laughlin 41, Logstown 11; Jones 27, Highland 18; Washington 17, St. Joseph 1.

Games this week: Monday, Laughlin at Washington, Logstown at Jones; Tuesday, McDonald Hts. at St. Joseph; Friday, Laughlin at St. Joseph, Highland vs. Logstown (at Laughlin), McDonald Hts. at Washington.

HIGH SCORER

By Jack Sords

WAIT 'TIL I GET WARMED UP!
BORYLA IS THE LEADING POINT MAKER OF THE HIGH-SCORING NOTRE DAME TEAM AND HAS ALREADY TIED AN ALL TIME IRISH RECORD FOR A SINGLE GAME WITH 26 POINTS AGAINST IOWA
VINCE BORYLA,
SIX FOOT FOUR INCH FRESHMAN CENTER OF NOTRE DAME, BEING COMPARED TO ED KRAUSE, IRISH CENTER WHO WON ALL-AMERICAN HONORS THREE TIMES

Metallurgical Duckpin Scores

Latest results in the Metallurgical Duckpin league were as follows:

Met. Office 1 —2100

Abson	124	95	119
Bradel	189	131	127
Coble	80	107	128
Fouse	141	130	160
H. Evans ..	197	140	111
Howel	152	131	124
Totals ...	803	639	658—2100

Met. Office 2—1633

Feigenbaum	128	107	112
Hazelwood .	85	65	131
Sadler	111	225	169
Totals ...	499	602	532—1633

Chem-Lab.

H. Kunzman	156	159	130
M. Kunzman	123	82	112
Keiser	158	151	107
Heck	112	98	110
Jukola	85	81	127
Frank	64	85	113
B. Evans ..	152	160	196
Lawton	127	152	132
Totals ...	716	720	698

Steel Works

Zutowsky ..	117	162	148
Bruno	149	113	127
Skiba	146	128	94
Demma ...	140	100	
Ludwico ...	108	107	82
Greer	97		136
Cochran ...	189	135	167
Wiehe	116	135	109
Long		136	112
Totals ...	691	696	690

Reds

Sicklesmith .	109	142	131
Reback	95	60	89
Francis	94	990	106
Totals ...	298	307	476

Blues

Martin	138	115	108
Schaffer ...	122	130	100
Totals ...	335	320	433

Wire Mill

Foore	97	108	107
Kreisberg .	154	163	129
Garrett	93	96	
Doty	133	122	99
Lang	80	63	101
Masquelier ..	88	131	121
Hurwitz ...	116	122	158
Barron	136	113	135
VanOmer ..			86
Totals ...	636	651	652

Tube Inv.

Best	135	131	162
G. Evans ...	123	82	102
Mathias	72	114	98
Hogan	161	92	96
Underwood .	181	145	137
Hartman ...			173
Totals ...	690	572	672

Baseball Scribes Honor McKechnie

NEW YORK, Jan. 22 (UP)—The New York Chapter of the Baseball Writers' Association today voted the Bill Slocum Memorial Award for meritorious service to baseball over a period of years to William B. McKechnie, manager of the Cincinnati Reds.

McKechnie will receive the award at the annual Baseball Writers' Dinner here Feb. 4. He became the 19th recipient of the plaque which first was awarded in 1929. Previous winners included Miller Huggins, William B. [illegible], na, Babe Ruth, Wilbert Robinson, John J. McGraw, Walter Johnson, Connie Mack, Walter (Rabbit) Maranville, Frank Frisch, Travis Jackson, K. M. Landis, William J. Klem, Joe McCarthy, Edward G. Barrow, J. Robert Quinn, Mel Ott, Sid Mercer and Branch Rickey.

LIPPEMEN - - - -

(Continued from Page Six)

steinmen tomorrow night.

Aliquippa—30

	FG	F	TP
Waters, f	0	5	5
Cable, f	3	1	7
Jones, c	2	1	5
Wright, g	1	1	3
Smisko, g	0	1	1
Turrizzianni, f	0	0	0
Prisuta, g	1	1	3
Ceravolo, f	3	0	6
Totals	10	10	30

Ellwood City—33

	FG	F	TP
Colavincenzo, f	5	3	13
Giovanni, f	2	0	4
Daugherty, c	6	1	13
Conti, g	0	0	0
Bellissimo, g	0	1	1
Ceretelli, g	1	0	2
Ford, f	0	0	0
Totals	14	5	33

Score by quarters:

Aliquippa	12	5	5	8—30
Ellwood City .	10	6	10	7—33

Fouls: Aliquippa, 10 out of 14; Ellwood City, 5 out of 11.

Monkeys Retain Duckpin Lead

Monkeys' lead in the Blast Furnace Duckpin league remained at 5½ games today after the pacesetters took two games from Tuyers Friday night at Orpheum alleys.

The second-place Coolers failed to capitalize on the loop leaders' slight lapse as they also could win only two games from Blow Pipes. Summaries:

Coolers

Puckett	126	76	131
Leviseur ...	129	129	154
Myers	140	150	123
Totals ...	595	555	608

Blow Pipes

Queener	95	127	95
Matthews ..	148	139	158
Cochran ...	81	124	122
Totals ...	522	590	575

Tuyers

Brittian	111	121	165
Tilly	146	96	
Seaman ...	122	116	130
Totals ...	472	427	576

Monkeys

Mayberry ..	93	94	101
Watson	134	141	131
Thomas ...	130	213	146
Fisher	147	109	120
Totals ...	504	527	498

BLAST FURNACE LEAGUE
Standing Of Teams

	W.	L.
Monkeys	32	16
Coolers	28	23
Tuyers	25	28
Blow Pipes	16	36

METALLURGICAL LEAGUE
Standing Of Teams

	W.	L.
Tube Inv.	13	5
Chem.-Lab	12	6
Steel Works	10	8
Reds	10	8
Wire Mill	9	9
Blues	8	10
Met. Office 1	6	12
Met. Office 2	4	14

TODAY'S Sport Parade

By JACK CUDDY

NEW YORK, Jan. 22 (UP)—A big-time operator in midwestern basketball betting, now visiting New York, denounces bitterly the "cheap chiselers and crooks" who are casting suspicions on the hoop sport with their "spread" quotations and their attempts to "fix" games.

He emphasized that "legitimate operators"—permanent bookmakers in most large cities who specialize in basketball and football wagers—are just as angry over the current situation as are college officials and promoters.

They are angry because activities of "small-time, fly-by-night bookies" and crooked gamblers cause regular clients of the "legitimates" to become suspicious of the sport, he explained. Moreover, sudden rumors of "fixes" (though usually unfounded) cause such lop-sided national betting on important games that the legits can not balance their books—can't lay-off to other bookies; and consequently wind up the day with "frozen" surpluses on artificially hot favorites. When these favorites win, the legits take it on the chin.

The operator from D— continued "The basis of income in legitimate bookmaking is the commission obtained from a balanced book; not from trying to outsmart or victimize the clients.

"In basketball, for example, I offer a point-handicap on a game—a handicap that has been set in the city of M— at noon on the day of the game by the smartest and best informed basketball handicappers in the country. Perhaps the handicappers have made team 'A' the 7-point favorite over team 'B'. The client bets on either team at odds of 6 to 5. If 'A' wins the game by more than 7 points, it's a fevorite victory. If the 'A' margin is exactly 7, neither bettor wins; and I get no commission. Yes, there are plenty of draws like that. If two men had bet $1,200 each—one on 'A' and the other on 'B'—my commission would have been $200, no matter which won.

"This is much different from spread betting—the kind that's causing most of the trouble at Madison Square Garden and other places. For the spread, bookies would take the handicap of 7 points and spread it to 6-7-8. The client, betting at even money, gives the bookie 8 points if he wagers on the favorite; but receives only 6 if he bets on the underdog. A favorite win of exactly 8 points means a draw for the winner bettor; a favorite margin of exactly 6 points means a draw for the underdog bettor. But—a favorite margin of 7 points means a loss for both bettors, with the bookie taking the entire pot.

"Frankly, spread betting is only for suckers. Every time a fan makes a spread bet, he is taking not only the normal chance of losing; but he is giving the bookie the advantage of the middle or handicap figure, which has been determined by experts. The fan is betting that those experts do not know their business; but they do. It is their business to determine the exact borderline of prowess between the two teams, in order to stimulate difference of opinion—and thus stimulate betting on both teams, giving the commission men action and a balanced book. It is remarkable how often the M— handicappers hit the margin of difference right on the nose. The consistency with which the middle figure arrives in important games is a major cause for the increasing yells of fix.

"No established bookmaker, with a respected clientele, will accept spread bets—in New York or anywhere else. Like the 'shell game,' spread betting is for suckers. But, worse than the shell game, it's a vicious, double-edged menace to basketball. The handicap break in favor of the bookie excites suspicion of dishonesty in games that are on the level; and sometimes it spurs unscrupulous bookies to attempt dishonest killings. No need to add shyster bookies to the ranks of the few crooked gamblers hovering about the fringes of basketball, like skulking wolves, trying to arrange for games to be thrown."

CAPTAIN YANK

By Frank Tinsley

WE ENTER THROUGH THIS GARDENER'S HUT, WHICH LEADS BY WAY OF A SECRET TUNNEL TO THE CELLARS OF LAO TEH'S HOUSE.
SLOPPY—C'MERE AN' TAKE A LOOK!... I T'INK WE'VE WALKED INTA A TRAP!
EYES OF THE DRAGON
LOCKED IN A CELLAR OF THE MYSTERIOUS HOUSE OF THE FOUR DRAGONS, YANK AND HIS FRIENDS MAKE A DISQUIETING DISCOVERY...

LEM AND OINIE

By Paul Fogarty and Bill Juhre

DOGGONIT, OINIE! KNOWIN' THAT PATULA'S HERE IN CIDER CITY AND ME NOT BEIN' ABLE T'REKONIZE HER ON ACCOUNTA SHE'S INNA DISGUISE FER SPYIN' PURPOSES IS GETTIN' MY GOAT!
NOPE
Y'SAID IT!
NOPE
NO— OH!—HELLO, MAW!
LEMUEL ZANESBORO PUDDLE! SHAME ON YOU—SCARING OLD LADIES THAT WAY!
LEM YOU T'INK YA'D REKKONIZE PATULER—NO MATTER HOW SHE WAS DISGUISED, HUH?
OINIE, GOTTA MATCH?
NOPE, AST DAT GUY!
MUCH OBLIGED, MISTER!
KEEP 'EM, PAL!

BIG SISTER

By Les Forgrave

WHAT MADE YOU SAY MRS. SODER'S HOUSE WASN'T THE SAME INSIDE AS IT USED TO BE?
I CAN'T JUST SAY, BUT OTHER TIMES IT'S BEEN SO COMFORTABLE AND CHEERY.
BUT THIS TIME THE CHEER AND COMFORT SEEMED TO BE GONE!
MAYBE THAT'S BECAUSE HER HUSBAND IS—
HOLD ON, BETH! HOLD ON! LOOK BACK THERE!
WHAT DO YOU SEE?
WHAT WAS IT? WHAT DID YOU SEE?
DOWN THERE! COMING UP THE STREET. SEE HIM?
IT'S THE FELLOW WHO GRABBED MRS. SODER'S POCKETBOOK!
WHAT IS HE DOING AROUND HERE? I THOUGHT THE POLICE HAD HIM!
BUDDY! HE'S TURNING IN AT MRS. SODER'S GATE!
I'LL BET HE'S AFTER REVENGE! WE'VE GOT TO GET BACK THERE!

VIC JORDAN

By Paine and Norris

I MET RAOUL CONDELLE NOT LONG BEFORE M'SIEU LAFONT WAS STRICKEN! RAOUL VISITED ME HERE NEARLY EVERY DAY... UNTIL LAST WEEK...
HE SAID HE HAD TO LEAVE TOWN, BUT THAT HE'D WRITE! HE HAS NOT WRITTEN YET BUT...
I'M AFRAID HE NEVER WILL, MARIE! DO YOU KNOW WHERE HE LIVED?
NO, M'SIEU JORDAN!
THERE'S ONLY ONE THING LEFT TO DO! PUT ON YOUR HAT AND COAT!
WHERE ARE WE GOING?
PARIS! MAYBE YOU'LL BE ABLE TO SPOT RAOUL'S PHOTOGRAPH IN THE ROGUES' GALLERY!
SO, M'SIEU JORDAN, YOU HAVE ESTABLISHED THAT LAFONT WAS POISONED! ANY CLUES?
I'VE HIS COOK HERE WITH ME TO LOOK THROUGH THE ROGUES' GALLERY! SHE WAS FRIENDLY WITH A STRANGER WHO DISAPPEARED JUST BEFORE LA FONT'S DEATH!
SEE YOUR BOY FRIEND, MARIE?
NOT YET!
M'SIEU JORDAN!
SO...THAT'S RAOUL!
NO! IT IS A FRIEND OF HIS!...I SAW THEM TOGETHER TWICE...OUTSIDE THE HOUSE!
NOW WE'RE MAKING PROGRESS!
BERNARD BAILY

McCreary To Head Red Cross Drive

March 1 marks the opening of a campaign to raise $290,000, Beaver County's share of the American Red Cross 1945 War Fund of the $200,000,000 to be sought nationally during March, 1945.

The Board of Directors of the local Red Cross Chapter have requested Judge R. E. McCreary to serve as campaign manager of the 1945 War Fund. This is the third consecutive year Judge McCreary has served in this capacity.

Working in close cooperation with Judge McCreary and Mr. R. C. Stout, Chapter chairman, is an Advisory committee comprised of T. C. Swarts, Aliquippa, Ralph Reed, New Brighton, and J. B. Jamison, Beaver Falls.

Preparations for the campaign have been under way for a period of weeks and hundreds of men and women have already volunteered their service. The County will be divided into nine areas under nine area chairmen. A fair quota will be fixed for each district and a quota assigned for industrial and other groups. Advanced gifts, all showing increased giving, are already arriving at campaign headquarters at the Chapter House, 1305 Third Avenue, New Brighton.

Judge McCreary declared today that Beaver County's quota was fixed after a careful and complete survey by the National Red Cross. The funds raised here will include an allotment to carry on the work of the local Chapter for the entire year as well as to assist with the national and international program of Red Cross.

Chairman McCreary declared, "Thousands of County families have come to know and depend upon the Red Cross in event of an emergency and this service is increasing daily with more and more men and women entering the Military service. Letters from soldiers in actual combat and in training camps reflect a depth of feeling towards the Red Cross. Beaver County parents know that the Red Cross is truly at the side of their sons and daughters no matter where they may be and this year's campaign slogan is rightfully 'Keep your Red Cross at His Side'."

End Of Racial Prejudices Urged

Calling upon the churches to furnish the leadership in eliminating racial discrimination, the Federal Council of the Churches of Christ in America declared today in a special race relations message that colored servicemen who have fought along with their white comrades "will not accept in peace that which in war they opposed unto the death."

"The war has made clear how false have been many of our racial attitudes," asserted the Message, an official statement of the national inter-church body. "Upon a hundred battlefields and in a thousand camps the tests of war have shown that there is no basic difference between men."

Acknowledging the "conspicuous" failure of American Christians to bring their racial actions into line with their professions, the message declared: "The non-white races who constitute the vast majority of the human race are rightly tired of the attitudes of superiority of those who through a racial minority, control the goverments of the world."

"It may be that for our land the testing ground of the vitality of the Christian faith will be in the area of race relations," the Message continued, "that test may come soon."

Describing the racial situation as "tense," the statement pointed out that Negroes are greatly concerned about jobs, about segregation in and out of the armed services and about equality of treatment after the war.

PT Boats Held Valuable Weapon

Marine engine builders of the Packard Motor Car Company today had the assurance that they are participating in production of "one of the most valuable weapons of the war."

The assurance came from Lieut. Iliff Richardson, 26-year-old Naval officer whose record in the South Pacific war zone includes duty aboard one of the two PT boats which took General MacArthur out of the Philippines in 1942, and nearly three years of guerilla activity on Leyte.

"The hard-hitting PT boats, powered by the engines you build, have been and will continue to be one of the most valuable weapons of this war," Lieut. Richardson told Packard workers during a tour of departments producing marine engines for all Navy PT boats and Army rescue craft.

"There is no ship that could replace those fast PT's for the kind of work they do, which at some points include the sinking of between five and ten Jap barges a night."

Mail "The Evening Times" to that boy or girl in armed service. They will enjoy reading it daily

SECOND GROUP OF ALIQUIPPA AND DISTRICT CHILDREN

HERE IS THE SECOND group of Aliquippa and district children. Left to right, top row, are Shirley Ann Pace, John Dean Propst, Sara Ann Schmidt, Andrew Dennis Babish, Jr., Marion Irene Norris, Stanford Rosen. Second row, Ronald Wayne Kuriak, Merrily Gallatin, Laurence Trbovich, Robert Cleveland, Marlene Mary Berman. Third row, Sandra Gruber, John Reddy, Sally Jean Buccini, Gregory Hamilton, Carol Ann Wimer, Edward Mihalik. Fourth row, Robert Lacour, Peggy Ruth Venable, Junior Simoni, April Elaine Benasutti, Harry Joseph Hartley, Jr., Joyce Ann Montini.

STAR AND BEAUTY DRINK A TOAST

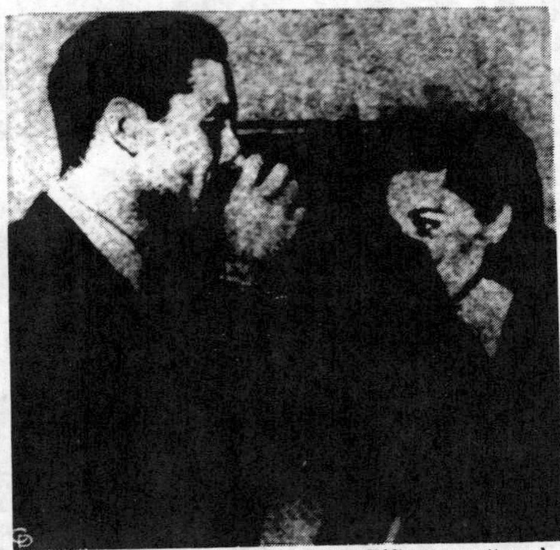

MOVIE STAR ERROL FLYNN and Nora Eddington, pretty and red-haired, are pictured toasting each other recently in a Hollywood, Calif., night club. Reports from Mexico City, Mex., indicate that they are the parents of a three-weeks-old daughter born at the American-British Hospital in that city. In the Federal Department of Vital Statistics in Mexico City the name of the child is entered as Deidre Flynn Eddington. (International Soundphoto)

AS HITLER AND QUISLING MET

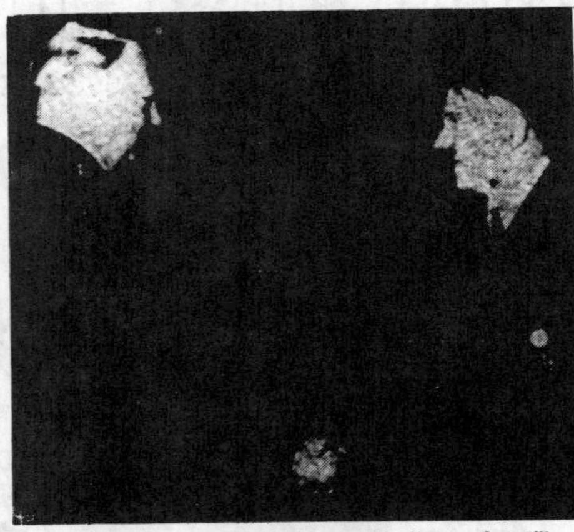

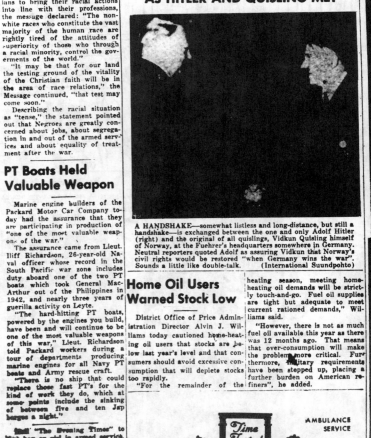

A HANDSHAKE—somewhat listless and long-distance, but still a handshake—is exchanged between the one and only Adolf Hitler (right) and the original of all quislings, Vidkun Quisling himself of Norway, at the Fuehrer's headquarters somewhere in Germany. Neutral reporters quoted Adolf as assuring Vidkun that Norway's civil rights would be restored "when Germany wins the war". Sounds a little like double-talk. (International Suundpohto)

Home Oil Users Warned Stock Low

District Office of Price Administration Director Alvin J. Williams today cautioned home-heating oil users that stocks are below last year's level and that consumers should avoid excessive consumption that will deplete stocks too rapidly.

"For the remainder of the heating season, meeting home-heating oil demands will be strictly touch-and-go. Fuel oil supplies are tight but adequate to meet current rationed demands," Williams said.

"However, there is not as much fuel oil available this year as there was 12 months ago. That means that over-consumption will make the problem more critical. Furthermore, military requirements have been stepped up, placing a further burden on American refiners", he added.

FOUR MILLION MUST PAY TWO YEARS' INCOME TAX ON OR BEFORE MAR. 15

WASHINGTON, Feb. 2.—(UP)—Some 4,000,000 Americans were being reminded today that they owe income taxes for 1942 or 1943 which must be paid up on or before March 15.

These are the persons who chose the instalment plan to meet the unforgiven portion of their 1942 or 1943 Income Tax bill. The Bureau of Internal Revenue reports that mailing of statements—"duns"—is being completed by the various collectors' offices.

In 1943, Congress decided that in connection with inauguration of the withholding tax system, taxpayers would be exempted from payment of 75 per cent of their 1942 or 1943 tax, whichever was smaller. In most cases the 1942 obligation was the smaller. Half of the unforgiven portion was due and payable last March 15, and the remainder on March 15, 1945.

Provision for payment of the final instalment was not made on the 1944 tax forms. This was principally because relatively few of the 50,000,000 taxpayers are affected. The Bureau said it wanted to keep its new simplified form as simple as possible and that to add to it would have caused too much confusion. So separate reminders—statements of amounts due—were sent to all who still owe.

Get In The Scrap — Save Paper!

UNTO OTHERS

When Trooper Albert H. Kimball's car radio blared orders from Connecticut State Police, he didn't know the call would land him in the pulpit of the Federated Church at Stafferdville.

Rev. Clayton B. Small, minister, lay ill in a hospital. With only eight minutes before the service, Mrs. Small telephoned police barracks for assistance. Lieut. H. J. Hurlbert radioed the trooper to proceed to the church in his patrol car. Trooper Kimball obeyed without question. In full uniform, he stepped into a pulpit for the first time in his life and began to preach. His subject: "Do Unto Others as You Would Have Them Do Unto You."

A Home Town Paper To a Soldier Is Like a Letter From Home

Beaver Falls Quintet Defeats Sharon To Win Section 3 Title; Meet Washington Friday Night

The Beaver Falls Tigers were back in the WPIAL Class A basketball championship tournament today after defeating Sharon high's cagers by the decisive score of 38 to 24 at Farrell in a game that broke a first place deadlock and gave the Orange and Black the Section 3 championship for the second straight year.

The Tigers, who have split even with the Sharon quintet in two regular season games, came from behind in the second half of the rubber match last night and roared to an easy victory. Sharon led 10 to 6 at the quarter and 16 to 14 at the half. In each of the last two periods the Tigers outscored Coach Dudey Moore's passers, 12 to 4.

There was no outstanding high scorer in the game. Big Chuck Kennedy led the winners with ten points and James followed with nine. "Admiral" Nemetz scored 10 points for Sharon.

As a result of last night's triumph the Tigers will move into the Class A championship tournament and will clash with the Washington high floormen, Section 2 champs, on the New Brighton high school court Friday night at eight o'clock in a quarter-final contest. Beaver Falls whipped the Washington team 63 to 18 early last December at Beaver Falls.

Two other Class A sectional playoffs were staged last night. Rankin high won the Section 7 crown by defeating Turtle Creek high, 31 to 30, and Brentwood became the Section 8 titlist after defeating Mt. Lebanon, 30 to 25.

The Class A tournament was launched last night when Connellsville high, beat Duquesne high 50 to 45, at McKeesport.

The first round of the Class B tournament was completed last night with South Union defeating Carmichaels at Washington, 34 to 32, in a game that required an extra period to decide.

The lineups:

BEAVER FALLS.	G.	F.	Pts.
Williford, f	2	2	6
Lupo, f	3	0	6
Kennedy, c	4	2	10
James, g	2	5	9
Boller, g	3	1	7
Totals	14	10	38

SHARON.	G.	F.	Pts.
Nemetz, f	5	0	10
Marshall, f	2	0	4
Butchko, c	1	4	6
Yarzag, g	1	0	2
Koss, g	1	0	2
Totals	10	4	24

Score by periods:

Beaver Falls	6	8	12	12—38
Sharon	10	6	4	4—24

Referee—Ketchell. Umpire—Klinzing.

St. Cecilia Beats Scout Team, 40-36

Led by Don Verrio, who counted 18 points, the St. Cecilia cagers defeated Scout Troop 421 by a 40 to 36 score on the St. Cecilia court. The lineups:

St. Cecilia	G.	F.	P.
Verrio, f	7	4	18
Colella, f	3	4	10
Gross, c	3	2	8
Mignanelli, g	1	0	2
Parker, g	0	0	0
Totals	15	10	40

Troop 421	G.	F.	P.
Heyman, f	2	2	6
Martino, f	6	2	14
Wick, c	6	1	13
Cumashot, g	0	0	0
Pander, g	1	1	3
Totals	15	6	36

Farley Leads For Commissioner Post

NEW YORK, Feb. 28—James Farley moved out front in the baseball commissioner race today as a bloc of clubowners was reported shifting support from President Ford Frick of the National League to the former postmaster general.

Although Farley never has said he is a candidate for the job it was believed he would be receptive.

McKeever Named Coach At Cornell

ITHACA, N. Y., Feb. 28 - Edward C. McKeever, acting athletic director and football coach, at Notre Dame, has been appointed head football coach at Cornell, succeeding Carl Snavely.

McKeever, who took over at Notre Dame when Frank Leahy joined the navy at the close of the 1943 football season, will begin his new duties April 1. His Notre Dame eleven won eight games last year while losing two to Army and Navy.

Jimmy Bivins Wins Over Johnny Flynn

CLEVELAND, Feb. 28. — Jimmy Bivins notched his eighteenth straight triumph last night with a unanimous 10-round decision over Johnny Flynn of Rochester, N. Y., before 9,037 at the Arena. The decision was loudly booed by Bivins' hometown crowd. Two rounds, the fourth and the tenth, were taken away from the Clevelander for low blows.

SECTION 11 FLOOR CHAMPIONS FOR 1945 SEASON

Pictured above is the Rochester High School basketball team which captured the Beaver County Class B honors by winning the WPIAL Section 11 championship. Members of the team in the photo are: Front row, left to right—Jack Werthman, Frank Grdnic, Jay McDonald, Eddie Supak, Robert Clayton; back row, left to right—Alfred Frank, Frank Pascuzzi, Pete Nocera, Coach William Peacock, Robert Fisher, Burdette Waddell, and Harold McElhaney.

After capturing the Section 11 crown, by winning 11 out of 12 league games, the Rams were eliminated from the WPIAL Class B tournament in the first round by Avalon by a 52 to 38 score.

Monday night's tournament game with Avalon high wound up the scholastic basketball careers of at least seven members of the Rochester squad, who are seniors. The seniors are Jack Werthman, guard, who was not with the team at the end of the season; Frank Grdnic; Jay McDonald; Supak, Bud Clayton, Frank, and Waddell. Juniors include Frank Pascuzzi, Robert Fisher, Harold McElhaney, and Ben Thomas and Charles Reader, who are not in the above squad picture. Pascuzzi, and Pete Nocera, the only sophomore on the varsity squad, it is said, are approaching 18 years of age and may be called for military service before the 1945-46 season. (Graule Photo)

SPORT SLANTS

By BILL ANDERSON

Although the New Wilmington high cage team has not shown before Valley basketball teams this season, many of them are picking the Greyhounds to beat the Avalon high passers, victors over Rochester, in their quarter-final Class B tourney game at New Brighton tomorrow night. The sentiment in favor of New Wilmington probably is due in part to the fact that the Greyhounds beat Wampum's Indians twice in the regular Section 21 season, and Wampum had little trouble beating Rochester in non-league games. Regardless of the outcome, the tournament game Thursday night promises to be a lively, interesting struggle.

..Avalon high's superiority over Rochester in their tournament game Monday night was chiefly in ball handling and passing. After the first few minutes of the first period the Avalon boys settled down to a forcing game and a dogged man-for-man defense. Interception of Rochester passes on several occasions not only messed-up the Rams' attack but turned into field goals for the Section 10 champions. Zeman, Avalon center, although he was not among the high scorers, was a valuable man for Coach Joe Gibson's club as he turned in excellent work under the hoops and his hard, accurate passes accounted for several field goals.

The New Cumberland Army cage team is going to play three games in this district next week, at Aliquippa, Ambridge, and the North Catholic high gym in Pittsburgh.. At North Catholic the New Cumberland team is to meet the Geneva College quintet on Thursday night, March 8th, it is said, and Monaca high will play North Catholic high in the preliminary game

After about 23 years in the major and minor leagues, Babe Herman has announced he is quitting baseball to devote all his time to raising turkeys and chickens on his California ranch. Herman, object of many jokes about hard-headed ball players, has been with the Hollywood Stars in the Pacific Coast League. In the majors he played the outfield for Brooklyn, Pittsburgh, Cincinnati, Chicago and Detroit.

Dr. H. C. Carlson, Pitt basketball coach has been quoted as declaring that the Westminster College cagers, on the occasion when they defeated the Panthers at Farrell a few weeks ago, were much better than was Army's once-defeated club when it tripped the Pitts. Carlson said the Titans' performance was one of the best he has ever seen.

Freedom Floormen Nosed Out By Butler In Last Minute Of Close Game, 21-20

Only players who will be eligible for varsity competition next season were used by the Freedom high and Butler high school teams in their game at Butler last night and the Butler cagers won in the last minute of play, 21 to 20.

Coach Mike Josephs started Winston, DePaolis and Love from the reserve squad and Dyminski and Mabin, who were varsity regulars all season. The Butler team was also made up of undergraduates.

Freedom held the lead throughout the game until near the end of the final period when the score was knotted at 20-20. Then, with only a few seconds remaining, McCune, Butler guard, stepped to the foul line and sank a free throw that gave his team its one-point victory. Freedom led 5 to 4 at the quarter, 12 to 8 at the half and 15 to 14 at the three-quarter mark.

Dyminski of Freedom led the scoring with 11 points, and Hepler counted ten for Butler. The game ended Freedom high's season. The lineups:

BUTLER	G.	F.	Pts.
Hepler, f	4	2-6	10
Shields, f	0	0-0	0
Showak, c	1	1-1	3
McCune, g	1	1-4	3
Leetch, g	0	0-2	0
Campbell, f	0	2-6	2
Duignan, c	0	1-2	1
Enright, g	1	0-1	2
Totals	7	7-22	21

FREEDOM	G.	F.	Pts.
Winston, f	0	2-2	2
Dyminski, f	4	3-5	11
DePaolis, c	1	1-3	3
Mabin, g	1	1-2	3
Love, g	0	1-4	1
Farls, f	0	0-0	0
Moss, g	0	0-0	0
Totals	6	8-16	20

Score by periods:

Butler	4	4	6	7—21
Freedom	5	7	3	5—20

Floor Calendar

HIGH SCHOOL

Thursday

(Class B Tourney)

Avalon vs. New Wilmington, New Brighton gym.

Bridgeville vs. Rostraver, Donora gym.

Youngwood vs. Etna, Homestead gym.

Friday

(Non-League)

Monaca at Chester.

(Class A Tourney)

Beaver Falls vs. Washington, New Brighton gym.

Ford City vs. Springdale, New Kensington gym.

Rankin vs. Donora, McKeesport gym.

Saturday

(Class B Tourney)

South Union vs. Ligonier, Donora gym.

(Class A Tourney)

Brentwood vs. Connellsville, McKeesport gym.

COLLEGE

Wednesday

Carnegie Tech at Allegheny.

Thursday

Westminster at Geneva.

Friday

Grove City at Allegheny

Saturday

Geneva at Wooster.

Akron at Westminster.

West Virginia at Carnegie Tech.

Beaver Team Paces Catholic Circuit

The SS. Peter and Paul bowlers of Beaver, continued their winning streak last week in the Men's Division of the Catholic Bowling League and remain in second half play. They were aided by Tony Taormina who turned in a 235 game, second highest single game of the season. Tony Fiorucci, league president, rolled a 567 series, the third high three-game total of the year.

St. Cyril dropped the Presentation team of Midland for a two game loss, while St. Marys No. 2 won two games from St. Josephs.

In the Ladies' Division St. Cyril No. 1, first round winner, now appears almost certain to add second round honors as well. Ruth Hoodnick posted a 488 for the second high three-game total of the season. She led the individual bowlers last week with a 182 game.

TEAM STANDINGS

(Men's Division)

	W.	L.
SS. Peter-Paul	6	0
St. Marys No. 1	3	0
St. Cyril	5	1
St. Marys No. 2	5	1
St. Felix	3	3
Presentation	1	2
St. Joseph	1	5
St. Cecilia	0	6

(Ladies Division)

	W.	L.
St. Cyril No. 1	19	5
St. Cecilia	16	8
Presentation	18	9
St. Joseph No. 2	14	10
St. Marys	17	10
St. Cyril No. 2	14	10
St. Cyril No. 3	14	10
St. Joseph No. 1	9	15
St. Joseph No. 3	6	18
St. Johns	2	22

Geneva-Titan Game Starts At 9 O'clock

Geneva College athletic officials announced today that the Covenanters' basketball game with Westminster College, on the Beaver Falls high school floor Thursday night has been scheduled to start at nine o'clock. A preliminary game between the Wyckoff Steel team of Ambridge and the Feikers of Northside, Pittsburgh, will get underway at 7:30 o'clock.

Plan Enforcement Of Dog Law In State

HARRISBURG, Feb. 28 (UP) —Strict enforcement of Pennsylvania's dog law during 1945 was promised today by the State Agriculture Department "to avoid another bad year for rabies."

Pointing out that last year's outbreak "was the worst ever experienced in Pennsylvania," Charles P. Bishop, director of the department's bureau of animal industry, said all unlicensed dogs running at large will be "killed on sight" and their owners if identified subjected to "immediate prosecution under the state dog law."

Stressing that the disease is not purely a "hot weather" problem, Bishop said peaks of 123 cases were reported in March and May and a low of 30 in October. The 1944 total of positive cases was 902, compared to 826 the previous year.

Basketball Scores

HIGH SCHOOL

(WPIAL Section Playoffs)

Beaver Falls 38, Sharon 24.

Brentwood 30, Mt. Lebanon 25.

Rankin 31, Turtle Creek 30.

(Class A Tourney)

Connellsville 50, Duquesne 45.

(Class B Tourney)

South Union 34, Carmich'ls 32.

(Jr. WPIAL Tourney)

Charleroi 33, Port Vue 32.

(Non-League)

Leetsdale 42, Edgewood 34.

N. Catholic 37, Avonworth 28.

Aliquippa 35, Monessen 32.

E. Liverpool 58, Toronto 32.

Butler 21, Freedom 20.

Shippingport

Memorial Service To Be Held For Soldier

A memorial service for Pfc. Robert F. Ewing, son of Mr. and Mrs. Henry F. Ewing, Shippingport, who was killed in action January 7 in Belgium, will be held Sunday at 4 o'clock in the Green Valley Methodist church, Shippingport. Private Ewing, who was a paratrooper in an airborne division, had been in the service nearly two years and had been overseas since last July. He received his training in North Carolina and Tennessee.

CHAMPION DIVERS of the ancient Olympics made their living diving for sponges.

Accumulated Pay Waits Liberated Army Nurses

SAN FRANCISCO, Feb. 28—Accumulated pay checks for the 68 army nurses held prisoner three years in the Philippines averaged $3,000 apiece, before allotments to families were subtracted, records showed today.

The highest ranking officer's check was for $12,000. But many of the nurses, besides contributing to families at home, also ordered subtractions for war bonds, which have piled up also.

A first group of 11 of the nurses, after health check at Letterman Hospital here, left by Army plane today for Washington and their homes in Eastern and Mid-Western States.

Bridgewater

Meeting Of Methodist Circle Is Postponed

The meeting of the Thelburn Circle of the Methodist church, which was to have been held Thursday night, has been postponed due to the death of Mrs. Frank Hopkins, Sr., an active member.

The American Legion Auxiliary will meet tonight at eight o'clock. Each member is to take a guest.

The Rochester Woman's club has invited members of the Bridgewater Woman's Club to be their guests Monday afternoon at 2:30 o'clock in the American Legion Home to hear a well-known news commentator.

Miss Eleanor Jean Kindelberger left Tuesday morning for Washington, D. C., where she is employed in the Post Office Department, following a ten-day visit with her parents, Mr. and Mrs. E. H. Kindelberger, and brother, Bob, Market street.

The trustees of the Presbyterian church will hold their monthly meeting in the church tonight at 8 o'clock.

Girl Scout News

TROOP PLANS BREAKFAST

Plans for a Sunday morning breakfast were made at the meeting of Girl Scout Troop 61, Rochester, at its weekly meeting Monday in St. Cecilia's school hall. Proper care of the flag was demonstrated.

Levy's Store To Become Irene's On March 1st

Elsewhere in today's paper announcement is made of the change in the name of the business now being conducted by Levy's, 1115 Seventh avenue, Beaver Falls. Effective March 1st this ladies apparel business will be known as Irene's and will continue to serve the Beaver Valley trade with the latest fashions in coats, suits and dresses.

IN TERRITORIAL DAYS, the name Arkansas was officially spelled Arkansaw.

Legal Notices

FICTITIOUS NAME

Notice is hereby given pursuant to the provisions of the Act of Assembly of June 28, 1917, P. L. 645, and its amendments and supplements, of intention to file in the office of the Secretary of the Commonwealth of Pennsylvania, at Harrisburg, and in the office of the Prothonotary of the Court of Common Pleas of Beaver County, Pennsylvania, on Wednesday, March 7, 1945, a Certificate for the conduct of a business in Beaver County, Pennsylvania, under the assumed or fictitious name, style or designation of White Motor Sales, with its principal place of business at Rear of 451 Deer Lane, Rochester, Pennsylvania. The character of said business is buying and selling used cars. The name and address of the person interested in said business is Grant C. White, 110 West Madison Street, Rochester, Pennsylvania. 2|28

MASTER'S NOTICE

Luigi Biancucci vs. Antonietta Biancucci. No. 66 September Term, 1944. In the Court of Common Pleas of Beaver County, Pennsylvania.

To Antonietta Biancucci, respondent above named:

You are hereby notified that the undersigned master duly appointed by the Court, will sit for the purpose of his appointment in Court Room No. 3, Court House, Beaver, Pennsylvania, on Wednesday, March 21, at 1:30 o'clock P. M. at which time and place you may appear and be heard if you so desire.

J. FRANK KELKER, JR., Master.

2|28&3|7

Boy Scout News

Area Meeting Held To Plan Monaca Scouting

Twenty-six men were present at a meeting Tuesday evening to form an organization to promote scouting in the Monaca area.

H. J. Chapy, area chairman, introduced Joseph S. Barnett, Fort McIntosh District Field Executive, who outlined the Scouting program and the activities planned for the next few months. Mr. Barnett introduced the new district chairman, Ralph Jewell, who described the duties of the Steering committee and its relation to the troop and to the district. George Day, district Advancement chairman, brought out the importance of the advancement program and offered assistance to the Monaca chairman of that activity. Eugene Geist, chairman of Organization and Extension in the Rochester area, will assist the new chairman of that activity in Monaca. Mr. Geist has been active in organizing one of the Monaca troops.

The Steering committee for the Monaca area was elected as follows: Advancement chairman, Christy Mangin; Organization and Extension, Frank Stake; Finance chairman, Arthur Wichert; Health and Safety chairman, Frank Dindinger; Camping and Activities, Sterling Lewis; Neighborhood Commissioners, Steve Balleck and Fred Allen, Jr.

Mr Lewis gave a report on the "camporee" to be held in May and outlined the part of each troop in Monaca at this activity.

Scoutmaster Paul Bland and Scoutmaster Henry Howells reported their troops ready to aid in case of flood emergency. Assistant Commissioner S. L. McNaugher reported that the new troop being organized at the Nazarene church was progressing rapidly. George Tew, now actively engaged in Cubbing in Rochester will play an important part in establishing Cubbing in Monaca.

Troop 454 was well represented, having the following Committeemen present: Henry Howells, Scoutmaster, Sterling Lewis, Eugene Suhrie, Louis Depner, Ray Patterson, and Mr Davis. Troop 426 was represented by Alex Bucsko; Troop 449 by Paul Bland and Dan Shaner; the new troop of the Nazarene church by Rev. D. P. Brickley. Other Scouters who will assist in the Monaca Scouting program who were present are: Arthur French, David Busang, and J. H. E. McMillan, chairman of the district finance drive.

Legal Notices

IN THE COURT OF COMMON PLEAS OF BEAVER COUNTY, PENNSYLVANIA

Paul Karasich, Libellant, vs. Katie Karasich, Respondent. No. 218 September Term, 1944. In Divorce.

MASTER'S NOTICE

To Katie Karasich, Respondent.

The undersigned has been appointed Master in the above entitled action in Divorce to take the testimony and report same to the Court together with his recommendation thereon, and will sit for the purpose of his appointment in Courtroom No. 3, Beaver County Courthouse, Beaver, Pennsylvania, on Tuesday, the 27th day of March, 1945, at 11:00 oclock A. M., Eastern War Time, at which time and place you may attend.

HAROLD E. CRAIG, Master.

2|28&3|7

ADMINISTRATOR'S NOTICE

Notice that letters of administration on the estate of Andrew Chury, alias Andreas Chury, alias Andreas Csury, deceased, late of the Borough of Conway, Beaver County, having been granted, all persons indebted to said estate will make payment and those having claims will present them to:

JOSEPH N. TOSH, Administrator.

c/o The Freedom National Bank, Freedom, Pennsylvania.

WAYNE S. LUCE, Attorney, Freedom, Penna.

1|31-2|7-14-21-28-3|7

EXECUTOR'S NOTICE

Notice that letters testamentary on the estate of Rebecca Breckenridge, deceased, late of the Borough of Rochester, Beaver County, having been granted, all persons indebted to said estate will make payment and those having claims will present them to:

Charles H. Breckenridge, Executor.

3405 Seventh Avenue, College Hill, Beaver Falls, Pa.

Wayne S. Luce, Attorney, Freedom, Penna.

1|31-2|7-14-21-28-3|7

PITTSBURGH MERCANTILE COMPANY

SAVE TIME SAVE MONEY SAVE POINTS

Sale of Cheese

Wis. White Cheddar

One year old - - - well cured. 10 points .... lb. 36c

Save Time—our handy "self-service" grocery department enables you to choose your items without having to wait in line for a serving clerk. Save Money—weekly, we offer special values that, many times cut your food budget quite a lot. Save Points—we realize the problems of shopping with points, thus we stock our food departments with many items that are tasty and nutritious, yet point-free. So, why not shop here and save 3 of your most important war-time possessions—Time, Money, Points.

Ration Reminders:

CANNED FOODS: C-2 through G-2 good through April 28; H-2 through M-2 good through June 2. N-2 through S-2 good through June 30. T-2 through X-2 good through July 31. (10 points each).

MEATS, BUTTER, etc.: T-5 through X-5 good through April 28; Y-5, Z-5 and A-2 through D-2 good through June 2; E-2 through J-2 good through June 30. K-2 through P-2 good through July 31 (10 points each).

SUGAR: Stamp 35 good for 5 pounds through June 2.

Fresh Sweet Cream Grade A Butter

lb. 50c

24 points. This Grade A Butter is nutritious and creamy and rich in vitamin B.

Oleomargarine ... 2 lbs. 45c
8 points.
Keyko Elgin

Champion Selected Large Grade A Eggs

2 doz. 97c

White shell Eggs ... packed in cartons.

Pitt Meat Eggs.....2 doz. 89c

Wisconsin Osaigo Cheddar Cheese

lb. 52c

10 points. This creamy white cheese is mild and delicious.

Wisconsin Swiss Cheese lb. 55c
10 points.

Fresh Munster Cheese . lb. 29c
10 points.

Cheese Spreads 2 lb. size 71c
Chee-Zee or Chateau. 20 points.

Borden ½-lb. pkgs...2 for 43c
5 points.

Hoffco Cheeses 2 6-oz. jars 43c
Sharp or Limburger. 4 points.

SWEET MILK Chocolate

lb. 55c

Below ceiling price.

Delicious coating chocolate in hunks as big as your fist. Buy several pounds for spring candy-making.

Chocolate Dandies . lb. 59c
Below ceiling price.

Mint Lozenges .... lb. 42c
Below ceiling price.

Bread Spread Special!

2-lb. jar Citrus Marmalade
and
2-lb. jar Grape Preserves
Both For 49c

Either may be bought separately.

Cotta Salami . . . . . lb. 38c
5 points

Skinless Weiners . . . lb. 35c
6 points

Meat Loaf . . Old Fashioned . . lb. 37c
4 points

Country Sausage . Smoked . lb. 42c
6 points

Perch Fillets . . . . . lb. 39c

Hershey Cocoa

2 ½ LB. PKGS. 19c

Below ceiling price offer!

Soon it will be time for home-made sodas and sundaes. Make your own chocolate syrup with Hershey Cocoa, sugar and water.

Cocomalt ...... 1-lb. can 43c

Dehydrated Noodle Soup

2 PKGS. 17c

Cooks in only 7 minutes. All you have to do is add water and boil. Betty Crocker brand.

Florida Oranges

doz. 59c

Large Florida oranges that are sweet and juicy. 126 size. Buy several dozen . . . The family eats more oranges in the Spring and Summer.

Rome Beauty
Apples .... 4 lbs. 39c

Yellow Onion Sets .... lb. 29c

Red Ripe Tomatoes .... lb. 29c

Home Grown
Spinach .... 2 lbs. 19c

Asparagus 69c
2½-lb. bunch

California Lemons .. doz. 49c
210 size.

All Purpose Lime

5 lb. bag 10c

General purpose lime to make your Victory Garden plot more fertile.

10-lb. bag 19c

25-lb. bag 39c

50-lb. bag 49c

No Points On These

FROZEN FOODS

Strawberries ...... 16-oz. pkg. 43c

Sliced Peaches .... 16-oz. pkg. 32c

Red Raspberries .. 10-oz. pkg. 32c

Peas .... 12-oz. pkg. 23c

Green Beans ..... 12-oz. pkg. 23c

Wax Beans .... 12-oz. pkg. 23c

Cut Corn .... 12-oz. pkg. 28c

Ford Hook Limas .. 12-oz. pkg. 36c

Fresh Assorted Layer Cakes

45c

Delicious layer cakes. Just like ones mother bakes! Assorted light and dark batters. Topped with maple, vanilla, strawberry or chocolate frostings.

Large Pecan Rolls ...32c

Round
Cinnamon Cakes 20c

Black Walnut Loaf 25c

Loaf Pound Cake 39c

Home-Made Bread ...13c

Round Rye Bread 13c

Raised Doughnuts doz. 27c

Glazed
Doughnuts ......doz. 32c

Loaf Pound Cake 43c
Iced.

NBC Snack Crackers

Ritz Crackers 25c
16-oz. pkg.

Skyflake Wafers 23c
Salted. 16-oz. pkg.

Graham Crackers 20c
Honey-Maid. 16-oz. pkg.

Pretzels 16c
Cellophane package.

SnoSheen Cake Flour

26c

44-oz. pkg. Below ceiling price offer.

So light and effective, this flour is a joy to use.

Calumet Baking Powder . 10c
8-oz. can.

Pancake Flour ......2 for 23c
Aunt Jemima. 20-oz. pkg.

Alaga Syrup 16c
1½-lb. bottle.

Libby Apple Sauce

Made from Western Apples.

22c

17-oz. jar. 10 points.

Apple Sauce is a low-point food that offers a variety of uses. As a dessert it can't be beat, baked as a side-dish it's delicious, and in casserole—sumptous.

Scott Peas and Carrots ...16c
16-oz. jar.

Walvet Paper Cleaner....29c
Non-crumbling.

Climax Paper Cleaner....23c
34-oz. pkg.

Flexo Softener 20c
32-oz. pkg.

Happyvale Sweet Corn...10c
20-oz. can. 20 points.

Get Off To The Right Start Each Morning With

Start O'Day Coffee

2 lbs. 63c

lb. 32c

You can be sure of a full-bodied, delicious coffee if you choose our own Start O'Day brand. This richly blended coffee is roasted and ground daily in our Coffee Roasting Plant. It's Fresh!

Fresh Golden Morn Coffee
2 lbs. 53c
lb. 27c

Asparagus Spears

43c

No. 2 can.

Val Vita Asparagus Spears are wonderfully tender. When cooked, these spears are temptingly delicious. 20 points.

Florida Orange Juice.....48c
Kistsweet. 46-oz. can.

Grapefruit Juice 33c
Floriland. 46-oz. can. 20 points.

Vegetable Cocktail 31c
V-8. 46-oz. can. 20 points.

Mother's Oats

27c

Below ceiling price offer.

Delicious Mother's Oats are so nutritious for growing children. Serve them each morning.

A-J Peach Preserves 32c
1-lb. jar.

A-J Apricot Preserves 32c
1-lb. jar.

Peanut Butter 37c
Radiant Ray. 24-oz. jar.

Cut Wax Beans...........16c
"Little Gem." 20-oz. tin. 10 points.

Camay Toilet Soap

2 cakes 15c

Below ceiling price offer!

A mild soap for both face and bath. Softly scented.

Ivory Soap..10-oz. bar 10c
6-oz. bar, 6c

Lava Soap....6-oz. bar 6c

Dutch Cleanser

2 cans 15c

Below ceiling price offer.

THE DAILY TIMES

1874—and WESTERN ARGUS—1803

ROCHESTER - BEAVER - MONACA - FREEDOM - BRIDGEWATER - CONWAY - VANPORT - MIDLAND

Established April 2, 1874 | Beaver and Rochester, Pa., Friday, April 13, 1945 | Single Copy 4 Cents — 24 Cents A Week

Americans Are Only Few Miles From Berlin

DEATH OF ROOSEVELT SHOCKS WORLD

County Mourns Death Of President

Tribute Paid To Roosevelt Here

Beaver County folk today joined the rest of the United States and the other Allied nations in mourning the sudden and shocking death of President Roosevelt, chief executive of the nation for more than 12 years.

News of the President's death in Warm Springs, Ga., stunned and shocked county residents Thursday evening and far into the night telephones buzzed as the news traveled over the district. Telephone operators in the Rochester exchange of the Bell Telephone Company were hard put to handle the great volume of calls.

"The President is dead!" was the startled word which passed swiftly through the Valley shortly before six o'clock last evening. But, so surprising was the news that most people who heard it thought at first it was some cruel hoax.

Five minutes after the word of Mr. Roosevelt's death was flashed to the nation a bulletin was placed in the window of the Rochester office of THE TIMES, but passersby who read the shocking news were disinclined to believe their own eyes.

Today schools and many public offices were closed and flags flew at halfstaff above government buildings throughout the county. Numerous meetings and other events were postponed in respect to Mr. Roosevelt.

PUPILS DISMISSED

All public and parochial schools throughout the county were closed today in respect for the late President Roosevelt. The students reported at the usual time and in most of the schools brief memorial services or devotional periods were conducted, and the students dismissed until Monday morning.

The Beaver County courts convened briefly this morning and on motion of District Attorney William Coghlan adjourned until Monday morning out of respect to the memory of President Roosevelt by President Judge Henry H. Wilson.

All offices at the court house, and the office of the county Juvenile Probation officers in the Detention Home, closed at noon today until Monday. Probation officers announced all appointments for the week end had been cancelled.

In opening today's brief session, of the Beaver County courts Judge Wilson said: "The King is dead; long live the King. One of the tests of democratic institutions is that there can be change without loss; but, when change comes suddenly and through death, it is wise for all of us to pause. Therefore, the Court will be in session, silently and with bowed heads, for one minute."

Continued on Page Four

Beaver Soldier Dies In Germany

Pfc. John Baker, 19, oldest son of Mr. and Mrs. James W. Baker, 420 College avenue, Beaver, died in Germany on April 3rd, according to a telegram received by his parents from the War Department today.

Pfc. Baker, who would have been 20 years of age on June 2nd, was a Browning automatic rifleman with the 297nd Infantry company of the 69th Division. He had been overseas since last October and in action on the Western Front for several months.

A graduate of Beaver high school, class of 1942, Pfc. Baker was inducted into the Army in July, 1942. After several months of service in the military police he was granted a transferral to the infantry, and received training for overseas combat duty.

In addition to the parents, he leaves one brother, Pvt. James W. Baker, Jr., who is receiving Army Air Forces training at Sheppard Field, Tex., and one sister, Vivian Jane Baker, a freshman in Beaver high school. His father is Secretary of Beaver Borough.

MEETING POSTPONED

The special meeting of the Rochester - Monaca - Freedom-Conway district, Girl Scouts, scheduled tomorrow in Rochester has been postponed one week.

Weather Forecast

Western Pennsylvania—Mostly cloudy and warm. Showers and scattered thunderstorms this afternoon and tonight. Saturday, mostly cloudy and cooler.

U. S. Warship Sunk, Others Damaged By Jap Aerial Attacks

By UNITED PRESS

Japanese "suicide" airmen sank a U. S. destroyer and damaged several other ships in raids yesterday on the American fleet off Okinawa, but lost 118 planes, Admiral Chester W. Nimitz announced today.

Radio Tokyo, however, admitted the loss of only two planes. The broadcast claimed the Japanese sunk or damaged 11 American vessels. The enemy broadcast said the raid was directed at eight separate groups of U. S. warships spread 100 miles off Okinawa's eastern coast.

Admiral Nimitz's communique said the damaged ships continued in operation.

The first attack was made yesterday morning when seven of the enemy planes were shot down off the west coast of Okinawa.

Several hundred of the planes, most of them obsolete and heavily armored, renewed the attack in the afternoon. Carrier planes and anti-aircraft fire from warships and ground batteries repulsed the attack.

YANKS STILL STALLED

The Japanese lost 111 planes in the second attack, either shot down or self-destroyed.

Formations of B-29 Superfortresses raided Tokyo beginning about midnight Friday, the Japanese radio reported.

The stalemated ground battle before Okinawa's capital, Naha, went into its fifth day.

American troops drove inland

Continued on Page Four

Plans Made Here For 7th War Loan

At a meeting of the Beaver County War Finance Committee, held at the Penn-Beaver hotel Thursday evening, county Chairman T. C. Swarts revealed that the Seventh War Loan quota for individual bond sales in Beaver county is $6,400,000. Of this amount, the E bond quota will be $4,700,000, and other types that may be purchased by individuals, $1,700,000. During the Sixth War Loan here, $4,622,900 worth of E bonds were sold in the county.

The payroll deduction plan of purchasing E bonds has already started and will continue until July 7. The Seventh War Loan campaign for general sales to individuals will run from May 14 to June 18, following which the drive for corporation sales will begin and continue to June 30.

CITIZENS OF ROCHESTER AND OF FREEDOM

Death of our Beloved President,

Franklin D. Roosevelt

has brought deep sorrow to all our people, and to all liberty-loving peoples throughout the world. In consequence, we respectfully proclaim that all business, commercial, and entertainment places in our respective towns be closed Saturday afternoon, from 3 to 5 o'clock, during the hours of the funeral services at the White House in Washington.

ALEX F. PEARSON,
Burgess of Rochester.

J. H. BOCKENSTEIN,
Burgess of Freedom.

Yank Spearheads May Be Only 16 Miles From Berlin

WAR SUMMARY

By UNITED PRESS

WESTERN FRONT — American columns roll across Berlin plain within 49 miles of German capital; unconfirmed reports say paratroops are within 16 miles of Berlin.

EASTERN FRONT— Zero hour appears near for Red Army march on Berlin.

PACIFIC — Japs lose 118 planes in suicidal attack on U. S. fleet off Okinawa; American invasion forces advance on Bohol, last major Philippines island held by Japanese.

ITALY—Three Fifth Army columns converge on La Spezia; Eighth Army widens Santerno bridgehead at eastern end of front.

Enemy military strategists admitted today that the west front has collapsed completely and the remnants of the Wehrmacht have been split, leaving two fronts, one in the Berlin area and the other in the south.

The west front was split in two by the smashing attacks of the American 1st, 3rd and 9th armies, a German commentator admitted. Those American armies had Berlin, Leipzig and Nuernberg as their immediate objectives. An American juncture with the Russian armies appeared possible within the next 72 hours.

The American Ninth Army spearhead was within 49 — and perhaps 16—miles of Berlin. Leipzig was less than 17 miles away, and at several points the American tanks were within 115 miles of the Red armies at Frankfort and Forst.

The Moscow radio reported that the Red Army was waging "fierce battles" from its bridgeheads across the Oder river, 30 miles east of Berlin, but gave no details. If the Americans maintain their same pace across the undefended Berlin plains, they will be nearer to Berlin than the Russians are by nightfall. The Autobahn down which the Ninth Army tanks are racing bypasses Berlin, to the south, and reaches the Russian front at Frankfurt. The eastern and western Allied armies thus could join without waiting to take Berlin.

WAR NOT NEAR END

The whole Allied strategy as it unfolds on the west front discloses a conviction that the war will not end with the fall of Berlin or even the juncture of the American and Russian armies somewhere near Berlin. The strategy appears to anticipate a continuation of hostilities on both of the two fronts into which Germany has been split by the American breakthrough in the west.

The war in the north would consist of the investiture of German and German-held ports from Rotterdam to Lubeck, on the Baltic. This would deprive Germany of communication with her U-boat bases and with the enemy forces locked up in Norway. In time it might bring a serious reduction of the submarine menace.

If the enemy loses its present submarine bases in the Scheldt Estuary, as well as Emden, Hamburg and Bremen, it may be necessary for the German navy to rely entirely upon its bases in the fjords of Norway. That, however, is complicated by the necessity of carrying fuel oil and ammunition from Germany to Norway through the Kattegat and Skaggerak which have been partially mined by the RAF.

German strategy may consist of creating a chain of "Dunkerques" all along the coast, in an effort to hold the ports just as the French ports of Dunkerque, Lorient, St. Nazaire and Bordeaux have been held to now.

ISOLATING BASES

The whole strength of the Canadian 1st Army and the

Continued on Page Four

LAST PHOTO OF FRANKLIN DELANO ROOSEVELT

Shown above is the last photograph of President Roosevelt taken before his death. (Pictures of the new chief executive, Harry S. Truman, appear on Page 8.)

TRUMAN TAKES OVER HEAVY BURDEN AS CHIEF EXECUTIVE

WASHINGTON, Apr. 13 (UP)—With a brisk step, President Harry S. Truman took over the heavy burden of his new office today, pledged to win the war which Franklin D. Roosevelt's leadership had carried to the verge of victory. Mr. Truman stepped from a black limousine under watchful secret service eyes and walked rapidly into the White House executive wing promptly at 9 a. m. He grinned at two dozen or more photographers who rushed forward to snap pictures.

One of Mr. Truman's first official acts was expected to be the signing of a formal proclamation announcing to the world that President Roosevelt had died and that the former Vice President had been installed as his successor.

Conferences with U. S. military leaders to discuss the vast responsibilities of the war were on the day's schedule.

Shocked as all others by news of Mr. Roosevelt's death, the new President spoke his promise to the world a few minutes after taking the oath of office last night.

"The world can be sure," he said, "that we will prosecute the war on both fronts, east and west, with all the vigor we possess to a successful conclusion."

TAKES OATH

The new President took the oath of office at 7:08 last night on word from Warm Springs, Ga., that Mr. Roosevelt was dead.

He asked Mr. Roosevelt's cabinet to "stay on" even before Chief Justice Harlan Fiske Stone administered the oath, which the new President took in the White House cabinet room, his family looking on.

Last night the Trumans slept in their five-room Connecticut avenue apartment in northwest Washington. There they will remain a little while before moving to the White House. But

Continued on Page Four

Tornado Leaves 100 Dead, 500 Injured In Oklahoma Towns

OKLAHOMA CITY, Okla., Apr. 13 (UP)—An estimated 100 persons were killed and more than 500 others were injured last night when a tornado ripped across Southeastern Oklahoma, causing extensive damage and casualties in a half a dozen communities.

There were at least 71 known dead and the toll was rising hourly as rescue workers recovered more bodies from the ruins of wrecked homes and buildings.

The greatest loss of life was reported at Antlers, a town of 3,200 population which was almost entirely laid waste by the terrific force of the tornado. At least 60 bodies were recovered and more were being found "every few minutes." More than 200 other persons were reported injured at Antlers.

Nine persons, including five students of the demolished Okla-

Continued on Page Four

Parents To Visit Schools At Monaca

Plans have been completed for the annual "Parent Night" in Monaca schools, Philip H. Petrie, supervising principal, announced today.

Thursday evening, April 19, from 6 to 8:30 o'clock has been set for the Junior-Senior high, and Friday evening, May 3, from 6 to 8:30, in the grades. Teachers of the respective classes will be in the receiving line.

INDOOR CARNIVAL

Rochester American Legion

Cancelled 'til Tues., Apr. 17

Due to death of the President.

Two Men Burned, One Fatally, By Electrical Wire

Two men were burned, one fatally, when a long ladder which they were moving in the sub-station area of the St. Joseph Lead Company plant, Potter Township, came in contact with a 66,000-volt high tension line, shortly after 10 o'clock this morning.

Herbert Mayberry, 51, Noss Plan, Rochester Township, died of burns about the back, feet and other parts of his body.

Arthur Laughner, 28, Potter Township, was taken to Rochester hospital and is expected to recover.

A Duquesne Light Company first aid crew, with inhalators, was called immediately after the accident and worked for some time in an effort to revive Mayberry, while a physician and company first aid crews gave assistance to both men.

Continued on Page Four

Husband Of Rochester Woman Missing In Action

Flight Officer Harold D. Roup, co-pilot of a B-24 Liberator bomber, has been reported missing in action over Hungary since March 26th, according to a War Department telegram received Thursday by his wife, Mrs. Helen White Roup, Reno street, Rochester.

Overseas since November, he is believed to have been on his ninth mission. He was stationed with the Fifteenth Air Force in Italy. The son of Mr. and Mrs. Harold O. Roup, Kittanning, he received his wings and appointment at Columbus, Miss. Mrs. Roup is making her home with her parents, Mr. and Mrs. John White, formerly of Meadville and Kittanning.

War History

The Germans hurled great masses of troops against British and Portuguese positions on the French-Belgian frontier, April 13, 1918.

Funeral Train Enroute To Capital Today

WARM SPRINGS, Ga., Apr. 13 (UP)—Franklin D. Roosevelt left at 11 a. m. (EWT) today on his last journey to the White House.

His body was placed in a copper-lined, mahogany casket. Four servicemen stood watch as a guard of honor over him as the special train that brought him here for a rest was prepared for the sad return as a general cortege.

The train will make a slow run to Washington. It is scheduled to arrive in the capital's Union Station at 10 a. m. tomorrow.

Mrs. Roosevelt, bearing her sorrow bravely, flew here to make the sad journey with the body back to Washington.

The President died at 4:35 p. m. EWT yesterday of a cerebral hemorrhage that struck him 2½ hours earlier. Death came to him in a small bedroom of "the Little White House" at the Warm Springs Foundation, his "other home." He was 63.

Funeral service will be held in the east room of the White House at 4 p. m. EWT tomorrow. At 10 p. m. the same day the funeral party will leave Washington by train for the ancestral Roosevelt estate on the Hudson at Hyde Park, N. Y. It will arrive there at 9 a. m. EWT Sunday.

The President will be buried at 10 a. m. Sunday in the sunlit garden between his Hyde Park home and the Franklin D. Roosevelt library—a garden bordered by a hemlock hedge and a profusion of rose bushes.

PATIENTS SAY GOODBYE

Those who arranged for the departure here made certain that the patients at Warm Springs—like him victims of infantile paralysis—would have a chance to say goodbye to the man who was their champion and inspiration.

They arranged it so the procession to the train would drive slowly past Georgia Hall, the main building of the Foundation and the first place the President always went when he came here. The patients will be lined up in their wheel chairs.

Mr. Roosevelt had been in slowly failing health for more than a year, but no one knew that he was suffering from any critical organic weakness. The first foreshadowing of death came at about 2 p. m., EWT, yesterday.

The President suddenly put his hand to the back of his head and said he had "a terrific headache." They were the last words he ever spoke. He fainted a few minutes later and never regained consciousness.

FAMILY SUMMONED

After the services in the White House on Saturday, the funeral party going to Hyde Park will include the Cabinet, heads of government agencies, a group of Representatives and Senators, Supreme Court Justices, members of the family, and some of the President's close friends.

The Roosevelt family was being summoned to Washington. Two sons now overseas will not be able to attend the funeral—Lt. John and Lt. Comdr. Franklin, Jr., both in the Navy—but their wives will be there. Other family members at the services will include Col. and Mrs. James Roosevelt and Brig. Gen. and Mrs. Elliott Roosevelt. Elliott is flying from Europe.

Until the burial, the Presi-

Continued on Page Four

People Of Britain Mourn Loss Of Good Friend, Roosevelt

LONDON, April 13. (UP)—Prime Minister Churchill called the British cabinet into special session today to consider the effect of President Roosevelt's death, which many diplomats feared might have grave repercussions on world security plans.

Foreign Secretary Anthony Eden will attend Mr. Roosevelt's funeral, it was announced officially.

Churchill and King George led the British in paying tribute to Mr. Roosevelt. For the first time in history the House of Commons adjourned in observance of the death of an American President.

Commons met for eight minutes, heard Churchill speak briefly but feelingly of the "immortal renown" of his good friend, and adjourned.

"BIG THREE" DEAD

Amid the mourning for Mr. Roosevelt, the realization persisted that the "Big Three" is dead with him. Saddened and bewildered diplomats, British and Allied, felt that the peculiar

Continued on Page Four

REQUIEM HIGH MASS

Will Be Celebrated

SATURDAY AT 10 A. M.

at S. S. Peter and Paul Church, Beaver, for the repose of the soul of our departed President and Commander-in-Chief. All children and adult members of the congregation are requested to attend. Special Memorial Service will be held Sunday evening at 7:45.

Frisco Conference To Be Conducted As Originally Planned

WASHINGTON, Apr. 13 (UP)—The United Nations will meet in San Francisco as scheduled on April 25, determined now to create as a memorial to Franklin D. Roosevelt a world organization capable of keeping the peace.

Mr. Roosevelt was one of the major architects of the new peace structure. His great collaborators — Premier Josef Stalin and Prime Minister Winston Churchill—described him on his death as the world leader in the cause of ensuring security for the whole world.

To Stalin he was "a great politician of world significance and a pioneer in the organization of peace and security after the war." To Churchill, whose friendship with Mr. Roosevelt began at the Atlantic Charter meeting in the summer of 1941, he was "the world leader in the cause of freedom."

PLANNED TO SPEAK

Mr. Roosevelt, who had done so much to prepare the United States this time to take its proper place in the new organization and to avoid the mistakes of 1920, had planned to address the opening session at San Francisco.

His sudden death will not delay the conference. His name and his thoughts still will dominate the opening meeting.

The first question which arose after the shock of Mr. Roosevelt's death had passed was: "Will the conference go on."

It was the first major decision President Truman had to make. And less than an hour after he had taken the Presidential oath he made it. Secretary of State Edward R. Stettinius, Jr., announced: "With the authority of President Truman, I wish to announce that the San Francisco conference will open on April 25 as planned."

WHERE THE PRESIDENT OF THE UNITED STATES DIED

This is an airview of the cottage at Warm Springs, Ga., where President Franklin D. Roosevelt Died.

NEW CHIEF EXECUTIVE

PRESIDENT HARRY S. TRUMAN

Truman Veteran Of First World War

WASHINGTON, April 13—President Harry S. Truman is the first Chief Executive of the United States who served as a combat soldier in modern warfare overseas.

Truman was a captain of artillery in the first World War and led his troops with distinction on the battlefields of France before returning to the story-book career from business obscurity through small state offices, the United States Senate, and the Vice Presidency to the highest office in the land.

The new President has long been active in the affairs of the American Legion, is an outspoken champion of the veterans of both World Wars and gained his knowledge of military affairs first hand in the trenches more than a quarter of a century ago.

The last soldier President of the United States was Theodore Roosevelt, who led his famous Rough Riders up Cuba's San Juan Hill in the Spanish-American War.

Pope Sends Condolences To Roosevelt Family

ROME, April 13.—Pope Pius XII received the news of President Roosevelt's death with visible sorrow early today and immediately telegraphed condolences to the President's family and the United States Government.

Italian Premier Ivanoe Bonomi, who was awakened after midnight to be given the news, expressed "profound sorrow" on behalf of the Italian people.

Hoover Says Nation To Drive Forward

NEW YORK, Apr. 13. Former President Herbert Hoover declared today that while the nation mourns the death of President Roosevelt, "we shall not hesitate" in the drive to victory. He issued the following statement in New York:

"The nation sorrows at the passing of its President. Whatever differences there may have been they end in the regrets of death.

"It is fortunate that in this great crisis of war our armies and navies are under such magnificent leadership that we shall not hesitate.

"The new President will have the backing of the country. While we mourn Mr. Roosevelt's death, we shall march forward."

THE INDIANA State Legislature of 1828 voted $14,000 to pay for all expenses for that session.

Sank Big Jap Ship

LT. WILLIAM E. DELANEY of Detroit, who scored four direct hits on the Jap super-battleship Yamoto, which was sunk during an engagement south of Kyushu, was shot down after he had unleashed four 500-pound bombs. Delaney crouched behind his tiny life raft almost in the middle of the enemy flotilla and watched the battered ships in their death throes. He was picked up four hours later by a U. S. flying boat. *(International)*

PRESIDENT TRUMAN; MOTHER

President Truman and mother, Mrs. Martha Truman, age 91

Hyde Park Mourns President's Death

HYDE PARK, N. Y., April 13—Neighbors of President Roosevelt, sorrowed by his death at Warm Springs, Ga., paid homage today to the man who made this village famous.

Dr. W. George W. Anthony, rector of St. James Episcopal church, of which the President was senior warden, said Sunday services would be dedicated to Roosevelt's memory.

The Hyde Park firehouse, where Roosevelt voted each year, will be draped in honor of the President, who was a life member of the Eagle Engine Company.

News of the death came as a shock to members of the Roosevelt Home Club, a group of neighbors who first organised to honor Roosevelt at the time he was Governor of New York.

Roosevelt Seventh To Die In Office

WASHINGTON, April 13—Harry S. Truman is the seventh Vice President to succeed to the Presidency on the death of the incumbent.

The others with the dates they took office:

John Tyler, 1840, on death of William Henry Harrison.

Millard Fillmore, 1850, on death of Zachary Taylor.

Andrew Johnson, 1865, on assassination of Abraham Lincoln.

Chester A. Arthur, 1881, on assassination of James A. Garfield.

Theodore Roosevelt, 1901, on assassination of William McKinley.

Calvin Coolidge, 1923, on death of Warren G. Harding.

Canadians Stunned By Roosevelt Death

OTTAWA, April 13.—Canadians received news of the death of President Roosevelt last night as a great personal loss.

The House of Commons, stilled by the word, paid moving tribute by standing for a minute of silence, and then adjourned until tomorrow afternoon. People in the streets read bulletins posted in newspaper office windows, almost too stunned to comment. One man said solemnly, "he was our friend."

Prime Minister W. L. MacKenzie King, a lifelong friend of the President whose close relationship had done much to bind the United States and Canada during the war years, was deeply affected by the news, his intimates disclosed.

NETHERLANDERS call oranges "sinaasappelen," or Messina apples.

Stettinius Next In Line For Presidency

WASHINGTON, April 13—Accession of Vice President Truman to the presidency moves Secretary of State Stettinius up to next in line for the office.

The vice presidency itself remains vacant, but Senator Kenneth D. McKellar, of Tennessee, president pro tempore, becomes permanent presiding officer of the Senate.

Congress long ago provided for a presidential succession ranging through seven cabinet positions.

In event of the death, removal or resignation of a vice president who has succeeded to the presidency, the line is this: Secretary of State, Secretary of the Treasury, Secretary of War, Attorney General, Postmaster General, Secretary of the Navy, Secretary of the Interior.

It never has been necessary in United States history to go beyond the vice president.

NEW FIRST LADY AND PRESIDENT'S DAUGHTER

Miss Margaret Truman Mrs. Harry S. Truman

TRUMAN SWORN IN AS PRESIDENT OF THE UNITED STATES

Vice President Harry S. Truman is shown above being sworn in as thirty-third president of the United States, succeeding the late Franklin D. Roosevelt. Left to right are Attorney General Francis Biddle, Secretary of State Edward R. Stettinius, Truman, Supreme Court Chief Justice Harlan F. Stone (administering the oath), War Mobilization Director Fred M. Vinson and Representative Joseph W. Martin of Massachusetts, minority leader in the House of Representatives. Note clock on mantel points to 7:10 p. m. Eastern War Time, exact moment Truman became president. Oath was taken in the White House. (International Soundphoto)

HOME-HEALTH HINTS

The Years Solve a Problem

By [illegible], Ph.D.

THE FOLLOWING letters were written ten years apart. After reading both [illegible] mothers should feel better.

1. "Dear Dr. [illegible]: Please read this letter [illegible] the letter on the back of the page. This was written [illegible] years ago. [illegible]

"[illegible] seems to care very little for her. She also is [illegible]. The younger ones don't try to [illegible] the older ones....

"The older boy (who is very bright) always [illegible]. He is nice away from home and loyal to his family.

"The girl, 15, does not do as much work as she should and is very mean to the rest of the family, and yet I am told is well-behaved away from home, never thinking of going out without my permission.

Adopted Boy

"The adopted boy is a general nuisance. He is always in trouble at school, away behind for his age, nearly always is annoying some one and yet is kind to animals, adores babies, is very generous and when I am alone with him, he is an angel.

"The baby boy, 12, small and very bright, seemed truthful and honest when younger but now thinks it is his business to be dishonest and quite disagreeable.

"I think one of the main things is they resent their father so much. He blames me for taking the children's part and they say I always take his side.

"Now for the good side of my husband. He is a good husband. We are still sweethearts. He pays me nice little compliments. We laugh at jokes [illegible] and when we are together we make silly rhymes. He really is good as gold and has a wonderful name with the neighbors [illegible] people. He never [illegible] to believe [illegible] I almost wish I had [illegible] and yet I do feel so [illegible]..."

I remember [illegible] that letter and pointing out to [illegible] the [illegible] letter:

Later Letter

2. "I know this is a crazy letter to send you but would like to tell you how things stand now.

"Boy No. 1 is married to a lovely girl, has a tiny daughter. He has a wonderful position with the [illegible] and is good to me.

"Boy No. 2 is in the navy somewhere. He writes often and I get money from him every month. The girl, now 24, has been married three years to a fine man and has a baby girl. She is very nice to us now, especially to her Dad. The youngest boy, 22, goes into the Air Corps this week. He attends college and is as polite to me as to strangers. I only wish I could let other mothers know what a change. My husband is 76 and I am 64. We both have fairly good health, get along better than when younger and are still considered sweethearts by our friends, and are we friends of our children! The adopted boy was drowned 5½ years ago. The day he went I had told him how good he was to me and he made the remark that day, 'I don't get into mischief any more.' Pardon me for taking your time but I have thought of sending this many times."

Solving Parent Problems

Q. Have you a bulletin on thumb-sucking?

A. Yes, to be had in the usual manner in a stamped envelope.

The Value of Vaccines and Other Treatment in Colds

By HERMAN N. BUNDESEN, M. D.

A GREAT deal of discussion has recently arisen because of the question as to whether or not vaccines are useful in the treatment of colds. The general concensus at present would seem to be that not a great deal is to be gained in most instances by the widespread use of such preparations, although they may be found of value in certain persons. In general, measures for preventing and treating colds have not been successful. The protection against colds which develops in the body during an attack does not last very long.

According to Doctor Anderson C. Hilding of Duluth, Minnesota, immunity against colds cannot be brought about by vaccines, nor is there any protection attained by spraying a vaccine into the nose and throat. The use of vitamin products, cold bath and exercise is thought by many to be equally ineffective. The administration of sulfonamide drugs has been suggested as a method of prevention, but because of the danger of reactions from these preparations, their widespread use in the prevention of colds would hardly appear advisable. They may help in the prevention of complications. In places where large groups of people get together, such as in a hospital or similar institution, disinfection of the air with antiseptic chemicals may be effective in preventing the spread of colds.

In the treatment of colds, the main efforts are directed toward relieving the symptoms. Drugs such as codeine and papaverine may be of help in shortening an attack if given early enough. These preparations must, of course, be given by a physician.

A person with a cold may well be isolated, not only for the protection of those around him, but also for his own protection, so that germs from other persons may not be transmitted to him. The breathing in of steam often will relieve the congestion in the nose and throat. A drug such as ephedrine in salt solution may be dropped into the nose, and this also may aid in opening the passageway.

The sulfonamide drugs have come into widespread use in the treatment of colds. Their chief value is in the prevention of complications such as ear infections, severe sore throat, or pneumonia. When any of these conditions threaten, the physician will prescribe the proper sulfonamide drug in the right dose.

Of course, a patient with a cold will do best if he remains at rest in bed so as to prevent chilling and fatigue. The complete answer to the problem of colds has, as yet, not been found.

• • •

Tomorrow, Dr. Bundesen will discuss "Hay Fever."

Christopher Hears a Voice

—It Could Have Been The Geranium Plant—

By MAX TRELL

OFTEN, late at night when everyone else in the house was fast asleep, Christopher Cricket would come out from the niche in the fireplace where he was spending the winter. Usually he sat himself down at the edge of the carpet, or under the leg of a chair, and tuned up his guitar. "A song," he would say aloud (although no one was in the room to hear him) "who would like to hear a song?"

He never received an answer to this question. That didn't bother him. "Very well," he would say, "I'll sing a pretty song. It won't be short and it won't be long."

Playing as He Sang

Then he would sing a song, strumming and plucking on his guitar as he sang. He didn't think anyone ever listened. But that didn't matter. He enjoyed doing it just the same.

Well, Christopher was singing a song about how the winter was nearly over and how one after another, the dry branches of the apple tree were telling each other that soon they would be filled with blossoms, when all at once he heard a voice saying:

"Pardon me, my friend. Is that a true song?"

Where Voice Comes From

"Of course it's true!" Christopher replied at once. Suddenly he realized that he didn't know where the voice was coming from. He had never heard it before. "Who said that?" he asked.

"I did!"

"Who are you, please?" Christopher demanded.

Instead of answering him, the voice said: "I've been living here all winter long. It has been very pleasant with the sun shining through the window. The wind has passed by but it hasn't blown on me. I haven't been cold. I haven't lost my leaves like the branches of the apple tree and yet—and yet I would be glad to know that the winter is nearly over."

"Who would like to hear a song?," asked Chris Cricket.

"It is nearly over," said Christopher.

Garden Come to Life

"Then soon the garden will come to life again. The flowers will stir in their beds. The vines on the garden-wall will start climbing again. The blades of grass will shoot up. And perhaps something wonderful will happen to me."

"What will happen to you?" Christopher asked, hoping to guess who the speaker was.

"I don't know exactly what. Perhaps I will be put out on the window-sill. Perhaps I will be put out on the porch. Best of all, perhaps I will be put out into the garden."

The voice stopped. Christopher had no way of finding out who had been speaking. All night long he wondered. And in the morning when it was light, he looked in the direction from which the voice had come and there, standing in the window, was the geranium plant. And Christopher wondered if it was the one who had talked to him the night before.

THE AVERAGE NAVY NURSE is 24 years old on entering the service.

THE STATE MOTTO of California is "Eureka," meaning "I have found it."

THE DAILY TIMES

1874—and WESTERN ARGUS—1803

ROCHESTER - BEAVER - MONACA - FREEDOM - BRIDGEWATER - CONWAY - VANPORT - MIDLAND

Established April 2, 1874 | Beaver and Rochester, Pa., Wednesday, April 18, 1945 | Single Copy 4 Cents — 24 Cents A Week

YANKS DRIVE INTO CZECHOSLOVAKIA

CAUTION TO BE EXERCISED BY PRESIDENT

Truman Outlines Pattern Of Administration In Broadcast To Troops On Battle Fronts Around World

WASHINGTON, Apr. 18 (UP)—President Truman's reports to Congress and the armed services outlined a cautious pattern today for the crucial 100 first days of an administration he promised to conduct in "the American tradition."

Plans were being made, as he broadcast last night, for a meeting of the Big Three foreign ministers here preliminary to the San Francisco conference. China and France may also be represented.

In his broadcast to the millions of uniformed Americans, the new President told of his shock at Franklin Delano Roosevelt's death. "He never faltered," he said, "nor shall we."

Mr. Truman spoke to the troops as a veteran who knows the mud, muck and danger of battle.

"I have done as you do in the field, when a commander falls," he said. "My duties and responsibilities are clear. I have assumed them. These duties will be carried on in keeping with the American tradition."

BRIEF BROADCAST

The five-minute broadcast was beamed from 32 short wave stations in this country. It was rebroadcast by Army and Navy stations. Amplified transcriptions reached those forward elements which couldn't get it otherwise. Some 8,000,000 armed Americans overseas heard the report to the services.

The first day of Truman administration routine left reporters gasping. The new President was a country boy. He goes to work around 8 a. m.

Mr. Roosevelt lay long abed and reached his office around 10 a. m., or later.

With his first press conference behind him, Mr. Truman named a World War I buddy to high office, ordered seizure of a Louisiana refinery and topped off a 14-hour day with his talk to the troops.

SILENT ON CHANGES

Most significant developments probably were his sharp refusal to discuss changes in government personnel and his nomination of John W. Snyder, St. Louis banker, to be Federal Loan Administrator. Mr. Truman's World War I pals will be much in the news henceforth. Snyder was in the 128th Field Artillery of the 35th Division. Mr. Truman served in the 129th.

Snyder also is a veteran of the Jesse H. Jones organization here. Jones was fired by Mr. Roosevelt as Loan Administrator and Secretary of Commerce to make room for Henry A. Wallace. Jones' jubilant approval of Snyder's nomination was proof enough that left wing hope of dominating the powerful lending agency had vanished. Wallace got the Commerce Department.

House Committee To Probe Prison Camps

WASHINGTON, Apr. 18 (UP)—Chairman Andrew J. May, D., Ky., announced today that his House Military Affairs committee will conduct a full-fledged investigation of the treatment of Axis prisoners of war in this country.

May said that the investigation would probably get under way a week from Thursday. Representatives of the State and War Departments will be asked in open hearings, he said, to tell the committee all the facts regarding U. S. treatment of prisoners of war.

The investigation is designed to "clear up a general public misunderstanding," May said. He added that there "has been too much mouthing about the prisoners of war situation by people who don't know what they're talking about."

IN BERLIN THURSDAY?

By UNITED PRESS

A Berlin broadcast heard by NBC in New York said that the Allies have set tomorrow for the Anglo-American-Russian entry into the Reich capital.

Lost And Found

LOST: Six Ration Books, Nos. 1, 2 and 3, in Caplan's store, Conway, about January 22nd. Martha Brown, Ellen Brown, R. F. D. No. 1, Freedom, Pa. 4'18

LOST: No. 3, No. 4 ration books. Ozella Simonson, R. D. I, Darlington. Return to DAILY TIMES, Rochester. 4'18-20 inc

LOST: Brown wallet in Rochester Post Office, contained gas stamps, identification, sum of money, social security and other cards. Ann Phillips, Allendale Rd., R. D. No. 2, New Brighton. Phone New Brighton 4291. Reward. 4'18-20 inc.

Jap Plane Bases Attacked Again By U. S. Bombers

By UNITED PRESS

American Superfortresses blasted Japanese suicide-plane bases on Kyushu again today, extending the crushing aerial offensive against the enemy's dwindling air power and homeland war industries.

The attack, the second within 12 hours, came on the third anniversary of Lt. Gen. James H. Doolittle's historic raid on Tokyo, which now is nearly one-tenth destroyed as the result of fire raids.

More than 100 big bombers struck at the six main airfields from which Japanese suicide pilots have been attacking American warships off Okinawa. Roaring out from the Marianas early today they passed some of the Superfortresses returning from yesterday afternoon's raids.

The 21st Bomber Command announced that the B-29 raid

Continued on Page Four

Demands Spurred For Punishment Of Axis War Criminals

WASHINGTON, Apr. 18 (UP)—New War Department disclosures of almost unbelievable Japanese atrocities today spurred demands in Congress for legislation to provide airtight guarantees of punishment for war criminals.

Sworn statements of American Army officers and enlisted men revealed yesterday that the Japanese tortured and massacred hundreds of men, women and children in Manila during the first two weeks of February.

As the War Department made these documents public, Brig. Gen. Carlos P. Romulo, resident commissioner of the Philippines in the United States, supplemented atrocity revelations with affidavits from priests, medical men and other civilians.

The new horror accounts came as the House Foreign Affairs committee prepared to consider war criminals legislation.

The State Department is reported to have endorsed one of the resolutions before the committee and to have frowned upon a second.

RESOLUTIONS DIFFER

The favored resolution, introduced by Rep. Cecil R. King, D., Calif., would authorize the United Nations to use "such means as may be necessary" to ferret out Axis officials seeking refuge

Continued on Page Four

Two Men Injured While At Work In Plants Here

Two district men were taken to Rochester hospital Tuesday afternoon when they were injured at work.

Howard Young, 57, 318 Maine avenue, Rochester, was treated for a chest injury reportedly suffered at the Welch-Bright Brick Company plant, Monaca. Anthony Sticanich, 55, 540 Ohio avenue, Midland, was burned about the face at the Pittsburgh Crucible Steel Company plant, Midland.

HELD BY NAZIS

Pfc. Joseph E. Anderson, Jr., (above) son of Mr. and Mrs. Joseph E. Anderson, Sr., Brown street, Rochester, is a German prisoner of war at Stalag 7-A, according to word received from him. Reported missing in action November 1, the family received word February 21 that he was safe and later received two cards written by him.

Overseas since last September, he has been in the armed forces two years, of which the first ten months were spent in the Army Specialized Training Program, from which he was transferred to the Infantry. He is a graduate of Rochester high school and before his induction was employed at the American Bridge Company plant, Ambridge. The Andersons have two other sons in the Armed Forces, First Lt. George M. with the Signal Corps in Paris and James P., seaman first class, a radioman with the Navy in the Pacific.

THIS IS A GERMAN CONCENTRATION CAMP--AND THOSE ARE BODIES

Row upon row of dead inmates fill the yard of the Lager Nordhausen, a Gestapo concentration camp near Nordhausen, Germany—an example of Nazi brutality. This is a U. S. Army Signal Corps Radiophoto.

State Health Dept. Civil Service Plan May Be Abandoned

HARRISBURG, Apr. 18 (UP)—The House had in position for final action today a bill giving the commonwealth an opportunity to disregard federal Hatch Act regulations, as another request was made for early sine die adjournment.

The proposal, sponsored by Rep. Adam T. Bower, R., Northumberland, would cost Pennsylvania taxpayers more than $3,000,000 every two years, but it would allow the state to scrap the Health Department's civil service system and ignore federal restrictions on political activity.

The bill would give the department $3,400,000 to carry out its health programs during the next biennium, which now are financed jointly by the state and federal governments. The department also would be prohibited from accepting federal funds when regulations on hiring or firing employes are involved.

STEWART INVOLVED

The innocent-looking proposal was a sequel to the U. S. Civil Service Commission's prosecution of Dr. A. H. Stewart, state health secretary, on charges of Hatch Act violations during the 1942 election campaign.

After a hearing, the commis-

Continued on Page Four

Ten County Soldiers Listed As Casualties

Names of one district soldier who has been killed, seven who have been wounded, one who is missing, and one who is a prisoner have been released for publication by the War Department today. Next of kin have been notified previously.

Sgt. James T. Rooney, Ambridge, was killed in action in the European area. The following men were wounded in Europe: Pfc. Walter J. Adriany, Pfc. Paul Hrynewich, Jr., Pvt. Andrew H. Karas, Jr., and Pvt. James A. Price, all of Ambridge; Pfc. John Popelia, Jr., Beaver Falls, and T/Sgt. William J. Shafer, New Brighton. Pfc. Ralph A. Avolis, West Aliquippa, is missing in action in the European area, and Sgt. Michael E. Zaritski, Aliquippa, is a prisoner of war in Germany. Pfc. Phillis G. Whipple, near Freedom, was wounded in the Pacific region.

Beaver Minister Named To Council Of Synod

At the afternoon session of the Beaver Presbytery, meeting in Magyar church, Beaver Falls, Tuesday, Dr. E. Conn Pires, Beaver, was elected to the General Council of synod for three years. The report of records was accepted and the North Branch Presbyterian church, near Monaca, was chosen as the site of the June meeting.

FREEDOM HIGH SCHOOL BAND TO PRESENT CONCERT FRIDAY

The Freedom High School Band will present its annual band concert Friday evening at eight o'clock in the auditorium, under the direction of Robert Carothers.

The program follows: National Anthem; "Invercargill," "Battle Mountain," "Columbia Fantasea Polka" (Jack Love, trumpet soloist) "Mignonnette Overture"; "Colleges on Parade"—Ohio State, Notre Dame, Wisconsin, featuring the twirlers.

"The Bells of St. Mary's," Mary Ellen Thompson, soloist; "I'm Falling in Love With Someone," soloist, Janice Arnold; "Begin the Beguine," "Bugle Call March," "New Colonial March," "Washington Post March," featuring the majorettes; marimbo solo, Shirley McKenna, accompanist, Catherine House; National Anthem.

Band members are: Janice Arnold, George Arbutina, Alan Boal, Dale Bott, Thomas Campbell, Joseph Catalano, Rudy Crispeno, Robert Faris, Fred Gutermuth, Marlin Hartman, Milan Kopac, Alan Love, Jack Love, Lillian Martin, Ruth Martin, Robert Matasick, Lillian Mihalow, George Noss, William Pfeiffer, Betty Peirsol, Joy Ann

Continued on Page Four

Noted Electrical Wizard To Speak At Beaver Apr. 23

New developments in electronics will be discussed by Dr. J. Owen Perrine, (above) Assistant Vice President of the American Telephone and Telegraph Company and a noted scientist, at a meeting sponsored by the Beaver Valley Foremen's Club the evening of April 23 in Beaver high

Continued on Page Four

Monaca Soldier Suffers Leg Wound In Germany

Pfc. Walter R. Shields, 21, younger son of Mr. and Mrs. Stewart Shields, Monaca, suffered leg wounds from a bullet somewhere in Germany April 2, according to a letter received by the parents. A telegram from the War Department was later received by the family. Pvt. Shields, with the Glider Infantry, has been in the service two years this month.

FORMER LOCAL MAN LEADS NAVY SQUADRON IN ATTACK ON JAPS

Lieutenant Commander Edward J. Pawka, formerly of Community Springs, Rochester Township, pilot of a Navy fighter plane and commanding officer of his squadron, led his unit in crushing strikes against industrial and military targets in Tokyo and Chichi Jima, according to a report just received from the Fleet.

Flying his Hellcat from a big Essex-class carrier, he pressed home his attacks through heavy weather and thick anti-aircraft fire. In the assault on the Jap capital he bagged an enemy plane in the air and damaged a hangar. All told he was in the air on three consecutive days carrying out his smashing raids in and around the Jap homeland.

A son of Mr. ad Mrs. F. M. Pawka, Rochester, he is married to the former Nancy Hall. They have one son, Michael Hall, five months.

Pawka, who has been in the Navy Air Force for several years is well-known in the local Valley.

The carrier on which he is based distinguished itself by taking part in the Tokyo strike only six weeks after its shake-down cruise, a feat that broke all previous records. In addition to the many military and industrial targets smashed during the two-day campaign, the Air Group's pilots shot down 44 planes and destroyed 46 others on the ground.

EDWARD J. PAWKA

Officers Installed By Interstate Group, Post Of British Vets

At a meeting of the Interstate Committee of the British Empire War Veterans Association in Tannous Hall, New Brighton, the following officers were elected and installed by Past Commander Alex M. Galbraith:

Commander, P. E. Henderson, Pittsburgh; first vice commander, T. Stanton, Youngstown, O.; second vice commander, William Burgess, New Brighton; Quartermaster, Fred Lummas, New Brighton; Adjutant, J. Hadley, Pittsburgh; Chaplain, J. Heppell, Beaver Falls; Service Officer, R. Gent, Youngstown, O.

After the installation one minute of silence was observed for the late President and appropriate remarks were made by Mr. MacLachlan, Pittsburgh. Consul Alex M. Galbraith, Pittsburgh, told some very interesting details of his trip to Britain and of the effect of "buzz bombs" on London. Capt. F. J. Collett, M. C. of the Lancashire Fusiliers, who recently returned from the C. B. I. front, told of the fighting in that sector and the terrible treatment prisoners received at the hands of the Japs.

POST INSTALLATION

After refreshments were served by the Edith Cavell Post Auxiliary, the following post officers were installed by Past Interstate

Continued on Page Four

Freedom Soldier's Feet Amputated In Europe

According to a letter received Tuesday by Mrs. Martha Hindman Ruckert, Eighth street, Freedom, her husband, Pvt. Allen Ruckert, is in an American hospital in France and both of his feet have been amputated. Although his feet and hands were badly frozen while serving with an Infantry unit in Germany, his hands are healing but he is still unable to write.

Reported missing in action January 11, he was later reported a prisoner of the Germans and in a recent letter revealed that he had been released by the Allies on Easter Sunday. He has been overseas since last October and in the armed forces since April 25, 1944. He is the son of Mr. and Mrs. George A. Ruckert, near Freedom and is the father of an 18-months-old daughter, Nina Jean.

Rochester Flier Safe Somewhere In Rumania

Mrs. Helen Roup, Reno street, Rochester, received a letter today from her husband, Flight Officer Harold D. Roup, co-pilot of a B-24 Liberator bomber, reported missing in action since March 28th, stating that he was somewhere in Rumania and was "safe and in friendly hands." Overseas since November, he was believed to be on his ninth mission when he was reported missing over Hungary.

Weather Forecast

Western Pennsylvania — Fair and colder today and tonight; frost tonight Thursday fair and not much change in temperature.

Soviet Troops In Sight Of Berlin

Today's War Summary

By UNITED PRESS

EASTERN FRONT—Soviet newspaper says Red Army is fighting within sight of Berlin.

WESTERN FRONT—Ninth Army battles for Elbe river crossing at Magdeburg; British tanks drive within 20 miles of Hamburg.

AIR WAR—Allied Air Forces resume assault on Germany after destroying 1,447 German planes in previous 18 hours.

PACIFIC—B-29's blast Japanese suicide-plane bases second time in 12 hours; Filipino guerrillas rescue 7,000 civilians from Baguio on Northern Luzon.

ITALY—Eighth Army drives within 10 miles of Bologna.

American armies rolled into Czechoslovakia and stormed the five keystone cities of Hitler's crumbling Third Reich today in a general offensive that Nazi spokesmen admitted had swept away their western front.

Flying columns of Lt. Gen. George S. Patton's American Third Army broke across the German frontier into Czechoslovakia early today on the final lap of a 200-mile dash from the Rhine that split the Reich in two.

The breakthrough was made at an undisclosed point near the northwestern tip of the enslaved Czechoslovak republic, barely 100 miles from Prague.

Patton's Third Army troops also fought their way into Chemnitz, about 50 miles northeast of their crossing point, and 80-odd miles west of the advancing Red Army.

Powerful tank and infantry forces of the American First, Seventh and Ninth armies, meanwhile, were storming the remaining four cornerstones of Germany's western line Leipzig, Halle, Nuernberg and Magdeburg.

American Ninth Army troops today cleared Magdeburg of German resistance up to the Elbe river line. Seventh Army troops broke in to Nuernberg at four different points today but encountered stiff resistance and heavy artillery fire.

BEYOND CITADELS

The Americans already had swept far beyond all five Nazi citadels to points as close as 70 miles from the Russians on the Berlin front and their fall appeared only a matter of days at most.

Die-hard German garrisons, most of them held in the fight only by the guns of Nazi elite guards, were battling desperately to hold the five strongholds and prevent a general breakthrough that might finish off the European war.

Nazi broadcasts reported that nine Soviet armies of perhaps 2,000,000 men were attacking on a 180-mile front from Stettin to Goerlitz and had linked their Oder river bridgeheads into a continuous 45-mile line east of Berlin. The Soviet newspaper Red Fleet said the Russians were fighting "within sight" of the ruined German capital.

The Allied Fifth and Eighth armies in Italy closed in slowly on Bologna in stiff fighting. Eighth Army forces were within 10 miles of the city on the southeast and another column outflanked it from the northeast.

Continued on Page Four

IN PACIFIC

Pfc. David Summerville, 22, (above) son of Mr. and Mrs. David Summerville, Sr., Monaca-Aliquippa road, is stationed with a telephone division of the Marines in the Pacific area. Enlisting in the Marines in December, 1942, he received his training at Parris Island, New River and Camp Pendleton and has been overseas one year. He is a veteran of the Leyte campaign and is at present at a rest camp. Before his enlistment he attended Monaca high school and was employed at the Colonial steel plant, Monaca.

Ernie Pyle Killed By Jap Bullet On Invaded Ie Island

WASHINGTON, Apr. 18 (UP)—Ernie Pyle, a peaceful little guy who became this war's greatest correspondent, has been killed in front line action.

Secretary of Navy James Forrestal announced that the 44-year-old Scripps-Howard Newspapers columnist was killed instantly by a Japanese machine gun bullet on Ie, a little island off Okinawa which was invaded a few days ago by American forces.

He was killed, Forrestal said, in the company of "the foot soldiers, the men for whom he had the greatest admiration."

It was because he always sought the company of the foot soldiers that Pyle became known as "the foxhole reporter."

Dispatches from Guam said Pyle was killed on the outskirts of the town of Ie at 10:15 a. m. today, Guam time (Tuesday night U. S. time). President Truman received the news in an already-bereaved White House while conferring with Forrestal, Secretary of War Henry L. Stimson and Secretary of State Edward R. Stettinius, Jr.

NATION SADDENED

The President immediately wrote out a statement in which he said the nation, sorrowing for its late President, was "saddened again by the death of Ernie Pyle."

Cabinet members, generals, admirals, members of Congress joined in mourning Pyle—joined with privates, sailors, sergeants and millions of every-day Americans to whom Pyle had described better than any other man what war was really like.

President Truman said "no man in this war has so well told the story of the American fighting man as America's fighting men wanted it told."

Pyle was killed instantly while standing beside the regimental commanding officer of Headquarters Troop, 77th Division, U. S. Army. At the time of his death he was with the foot soldiers, the men for whom he had the greatest admiration.

Before going to the Pacific area to cover the war there, Pyle had covered the war in Africa, Sicily, Italy, England and France. His father lives in Indiana and his wife lives in Albuquerque, N. M.

Monaca Soldier Missing In South Pacific Area

Pfc. Peter Brown, 21, Army Air Forces, elder son of Mr. and Mrs. Henry Brown, Brodhead road, has been missing in action in the South Pacific area, since March 14, his parents were informed by a War Department telegram Tuesday. In a letter received by the family, dated March 13, he stated he had received an Oak Leaf cluster in lieu of a second Bronze Star.

A graduate of Monaca high school in 1941, he entered the employ of the Pittsburgh and Lake Erie Railroad Company, as a signalman following his graduation and was stationed at Beaver Falls. He entered the service more than two years ago and has been overseas since last August. Pvt. Brown was a waist gunner on a B-24 Liberator. A younger son of the Browns, Roy Edward, 19, seaman, first class, in the service a year, also is in the South Pacific, on an LST.

SOLDIER COMING HOME

SAN FRANCISCO, Apr. 18 (UP)—The Army announced today that Pvt. John L. Peresnik, 846 Dues avenue, Ambridge, is one of a group of liberated prisoners of war from the Philippines who have left Letterman Hospital for their homes.

War History

The British line in Flanders was reported holding at every point, April 18, 1918.

NAZIS QUIT

TRUMAN PROCLAIMS VICTORY

V-E Day Quietly Observed Here

Fully aware of the difficult task that lies ahead in the war with Japan, Beaver County residents today thankfully received the news of victory over Germany and re-dedicated themselves to working for final victory.

Although jubilant and happy, people in most local communities gave little time to celebration of President Truman's official announcement that the armistice with Germany had been signed. Air raid sirens sounded and some church bells rang, but a holiday air was conspicuously absent.

Principal emphasis in the observance of V-E Day throughout Beaver county was placed on church services which will be held this evening in all communities. In some towns union services are scheduled, while in others services will be conducted in individual churches.

Although today was the day people all over America had hoped and prayed for during three and a half years of war with Germany, news of the armistice came as an anti-climax to the great struggle. German resistance in Europe had been dwindling away steadily for several weeks and the announcement of peace had been expected momentarily for many days.

County folks were sobered by the realization that a long and bloody struggle with Japan still remains before the final end of the war can be observed.

District war plants continued in operation and workers stayed on the job in response to President Truman's plea for "work, work, work." At the huge Curtiss-Wright Corporation propeller plant in Borough Township, a normal turnout of employees was reported both Monday and today. Workers gathered at the plant entrance to hear Truman's speech and short talks by E. C. Brandt, plant manager, and Capt. S. B. McIntyre, Air Forces representative, and then returned to their departments.

STREETS QUIET

Streets in most county communities were almost empty at nine o'clock this morning as President Truman made his announcement by radio. Schools continued in session in most localities, but closed in some. Many stores also closed to commemorate the day.

Governor Edward Martin ordered all state liquor stores

Continued on Page 27

Police Force At Rochester Cut As Economy Measure

A capacity crowd, including representatives of the Ministerial Association and Grace Lutheran Church Council was on hand Monday evening when Rochester Borough Council took action to reduce the police force as an economy measure in an effort to purchase a police car.

On the suggestion of Councilman Clifford Betz and a motion by Albert Heideger and Clifford Meredith, the position of Patrolman Charles St. Clair, the youngest policeman in point of service, was abolished; the job of assistant police chief, now held by Frank Craig ,was abolished, reducing him to a patrolman if he so desires the job, and the job of hill patrolman was restored to its former category, the salary being paid in part by the hill merchants and in part by the borough.

The voice vote carried nine to three as follows: For the motion — Walter Lehman, Louis Hartman, Walter Gordon, Gilbert Sohn, Curtis Meredith, Albert Heideger, Sam Brown, John Eakin and Cilfford Betz; dissenting—Paul Perkins, William Ketterer and Robert Cloughley .

ECONOMY URGED

In suggesting the action to the body, Mr. Betz stated that the police said they could not carry out their duties without the proper equipment.

"The police know and the citizens know the borough has no money to purchase a police car. The only way is to economize somewhere else in the public safety funds."

The action followed a heated discussion earlier in the meeting

Continued on Page 27.

Doenitz Probably Not To Be "War Criminal"

LONDON, May 8 (UP)—Grand Admiral Karl Doenitz, self-proclaimed successor to Adolf Hitler as fuehrer of Germany, probably will be treated as a defeated commander in chief. London sources said it was almost certain that he would not be tried as a war criminal since he had been a naval commander without political power throughout the war until its final days.

War History

A Russian army of 100,000 men was marching on Finland from Petrograd, May 8, 1918.

BLOODIEST WAR IN HISTORY ENDS AT 6:01 P. M. TODAY

PARIS, May 8 (UP)—The bloodiest war in European history will come to its official end at 12:01 a. m. tomorrow, European time, (6:01 p. m., EWT) today, with the formal end of hostilities on a continent desolated by more than five years of conflict. The agreement formalizing the unconditional surrender will be ratified in Berlin today, with Field Marshal Wilhelm Keitel, chief of the German high command, officially acknowledging that Germany is beaten.

To save lives, the cease fire order already has sounded. But the fighting went on today in some small and scattered sectors.

Fanatical Nazis, defying the high command's unconditional surrender, held out in some parts of Czechoslovakia, in French Atlantic ports, the channel islands, and some pinpoints in the Aegean.

And on the Russian front resistance continued in some considerable strength. But Prime Minister Churchill warned in London that if the Nazis held out after the 12:01 a. m. deadline, they would become outlaws under the rules of war, and would be attacked from all sides by the Allies.

(London reported that Marshal Stalin had announced in an order of the day that the Red Army has captured Olmuetz, a big Czechoslovak defense base.)

The British Admiralty announced today that all German and German-controlled ships of every type were being ordered to report their positions to the nearest Allied wireless station, receive orders to proceed to port and await further orders.

British warships steamed up the roadstead toward Oslo to accept the surrender of some 250,000 German troops in Norway.

What is left of the German

Continued on Page 27.

STANDING in a contemplative mood amidst tons of ticker tape and paper shreds at 42nd street and Broadway in Times Square, New York City, is Sgt. Arthur Moore of Buffalo, N. Y. Moore, who was wounded in Belgium, had watched New Yorkers celebrate the unconfirmed report of peace in Europe.

Greatest Armies In History Of World Lay Down Their Arms

WASHINGTON, May 8 (UP) Today the greatest array of fighting manpower the world has ever seen—fully 25,000,000 men—laid down their arms.

But some will pick them up again within a short time. It has been estimated that about 3,000,000 American soldiers now in Europe and an undetermined number of French, British and Dutch servicemen will journey to the South Pacific to wage war against the last remaining Axis power—Japan.

The army of the Soviet Union is the largest in Europe with an estimated 9,500,000 men under arms. The Geman army ranked second in size. As of last Autumn the Germans had about 9,000,000 men in their army, including about 1,000,000 non-Germans who were forced into service.

The United Sttes used 4,000,000 men to wage the battle against the Nazis on the continent. The British, used 1,000,000, while the French had an army by V-E Day of approximately 500,000. In addition to the regularly organized armies, partisan forces in all parts of Europe totalled about 1,000,000 men.

Rochester Minister Accepts New Post

Rev. Thurman McCracken, for five years pastor of the Rochester Wesleyan Methodist church, has accepted a call to the Wesleyan church at Indiana, Pa., and will assume his new pastorate June 12. His farewell sermon will be preached June 3. The McCrackens and their three children were former residents of Akron, O.

Rochesier Man Freed From Nazi Prison Camp

Mr. and Mrs. Ralph McGaffic, Lacock street, Rochester, received a letter Monday written by their son, Pvt. Wallace McGaffic, stating that he had been liberated April 13 from a German prison camp, 2-B, and would be home soon. Serving with the Rangers, he had been imprisoned 15 months and was formerly reported missing in action.

Weather Forecast

Western Pennsylvania Showers and cooler today followed by partly cloudy and cooler tonight and Wednesday.

Let's Keep Working And Praying

Today—V-E Day—is a day which has been long awaited by the people of the United States, along with our valiant Allies in the United Nations.

Today marks partial culmination of our all-out war effort which began with the infamous sneak attack on Pearl Harbor by the Japanese in the early morning of Sunday, December 7, 1941.

We emphasize that the day marks only partial culmination of victory—for the war against the treacherous Japanese continues unabated.

For England, France and Poland today marks the end of five years and eight months of "blood and sweat and tears," the end of the most horrible bloodshed, destruction and suffering in the history of the world, which began when the vaunted German army—the boastful, strutting, "invincible super race"—invaded Poland on September 1, 1939.

For Norway, Denmark, Holland, Belgium, Luxembourg and the other European countries taken over by the once-mighty Wehrmacht today means the end of oppression and persecution.

For the people of Russia, today means the end of bloodshed, destruction and hardship.

To the down-trodden, miserable, starving people of the countries which were occupied by the murdering, plundering, cruel Nazis today brings the dawn of new hope, a ray of light in a blacked-out world. To them it brings hope for the return of peace and justice and sanity to a world gone mad.

No longer must the people of the British Isles and Europe listen for the sound of approaching bombers, the wail of air raid sirens, the whistle of shells or the scream of V-bombs. No longer must they live in a world of darkness and fear.

We in the United States have escaped all that. Our cities, towns and farms are unmarked by bombs or bullets, by mountainous piles of rubble and the debris left in the wake of incendiary bombs. We have never known the terrible, clutching fear of imminent death, striking swiftly and horribly to snuff out the lives of men, women and children.

For that—if for nothing else—all of us should get down on our knees and give thanks to a kind and merciful God who has spared us the suffering, sorrow and affliction which has prevailed in the war-ravaged countries overseas.

Today is in reality a day of anti-climax, because it comes in fulfillment to what we have known from the beginning was inevitable—Victory!

Today is the day we have worked and prayed for since we entered the war against Germany and Italy.

In what more fitting way could we observe this day —V-E Day—than by continuing to work and pray for Victory in the gigantic task ahead, the war with Japan?

No Time Taken Out In Pacific War To Observe V-E Day

By UNITED PRESS

Allied fighting forces in the Pacific pressed unremitting warfare against the Japanese today with no time out for celebrating the end of the war in Europe.

Military authorities predicted that, even with reinforcements from the European theatre, it would require another year to beat the Japanese on the mainland. They conceded, however, that Japan might surrender sooner.

The "war as usual" brought new Allied blows in the land campaigns on Okinawa, the Philippines and Tarakan and another B-29 assault on Kyushu's suicide plane bases.

Marines led the general advance on southern Okinawa to drive within a mile of Naha, the capital. Troops of the 77th Division drove near Shuri, the island's second largest city, northeast of Naha. The Seventh Infantry Division made small gains down the east coast above Yonabaru.

TARAKAN TOWN TAKEN

Australian and Dutch troops were poised for a drive into the rich Paomesian oil fields east of

Continued on Page 27

People Of Europe Celebrate End Of Long, Costly War

LONDON, May 8. (UP) Londoners poured into the streets of this bomb-scarred capital today for what the Ministry of Information said would be regarded as "Victory in Europe Day."

They heard the news officially from the lips of Prime Minister Churchill broadcasting from the cabinet room at 10 Downing street at 3 p. m. (9 a. m. EWT). Paris announced that Gen. Charles De Gaulle also would broadcast an "official announcement of victory" at 3 p .m.

German Foreign Minister Count Ludwig Schwerin Von Krosigk reported over the German radio yesterday that all remaining German forces in Europe—estimated by the British war office at 1,635,000 men had capitulated.

Political and diplomatic correspondents of London morning newspapers attributed the delay in the official Allied announcement of the surrender to the insistence of President Truman and Premier Stalin .

STALIN HOLDS OUT

It generally was believed Stalin particularly balked at announcing victory until the diehard German forces in Czechoslovakia had agreed to the capitulation.

These forces yesterday denounced Schwerin Von Krosigk's surrender order and said they would fight on against the Red Army, though yielding in the west to the American Third Army.

The patriot radio at Prague said, however, that the German commander of the Czechoslovak garrison early today had accepted the unconditional surrender terms and at 1:30 a. m. issued orders to all German units in

Continued on Page 27.

President Urges Work, Prayer To Defeat Japanese

WASHINGTON, May 8 (UP)—President Truman today proclaimed victory in Europe but told the nation its fighting job would be finished only "when the last Japanese division has surrendered unconditionally."

He said "our victory is only half-won." He gave this counsel for the months to come:

"Work, work, work."

He gave this advice to the Japanese: Surrender.

Surrounded by his government leaders, Mr. Truman issued his proclamation of victory and his statement of the work yet to do at a historic news conference in the White House. Then he broadcast them to the nation.

The end of the war was proclaimed by President Truman, Prime Minister Churchill and Gen. Charles de Gaulle of France today, but Premier Stalin waited—presumably until Marshal Gregory K. Zhukov, conquerer of Berlin, sits down in the Reich capital and extracts assurance from German leaders that their troops will quit fighting the Red Army. Such fighting still was going on briskly in central Europe.

Outside, while the President spoke, a chill rain fell.

"This," the President said, "is a solemn but glorious hour."

He voiced the thought of millions by adding: "How I wish Franklin Roosevelt had lived to see this day."

The President reminded the nation in its flush of victory that it had not been fighting alone. And he proclaimed Sunday, May 13, a day of prayer.

"I call upon all the people of the United States whatever their faith, to unite in offering joyful thanks to God for the victory we have won and to pray that He will support us to the end of our present struggle and guide us into the way of peace.

"I also call upon my countrymen to dedicate this day of prayer to the memory of those who have given their lives to make possible our victory."

THANKS ALLIES

The President sent his congratulations and thanks to Prime Minister Winston Churchill, Premier Josef Stalin, Gen. Charles De Gaulle.

To Gen. Dwight D. Eisenhower he said: "All of us owe to you and to your men of many nations a debt beyond appraisal for their high contribution to the conquest of Naziism."

Mr. Truman counted the cost of victory. He did not forget "the terrible price we have paid to rid the world of Hitler and his evil band." But he also sounded a note of triumph and hope.

"United, the peace-loving nations," he said, "have demonstrated in the west that their arms are stronger by far than the might of dictators or the tyranny of military cliques that once called us soft and weak.

"The power of our peoples to defend themselves against all enemies will be proved in the Pacific war as it has been proved in Europe."

SEEKS ABIDING PEACE

And with victory, the President said, "we must work to bind up the wounds of a suffering world to build an abiding peace, a peace rooted in justice and in law."

For the Japanese, he said, the choice is between unconditional surrender and "utter destruction to Japan's industrial war production, to its shipping, and to everything that supports its military activity."

He gave Japan this promise, this invitation to survival: "Unconditional surrender does not mean the extermination or enslavement of the Japanese people."

He spelled out patiently the choice which is Japan's.

"The longer the war lasts," he said, "the greater will be the suffering and hardships which the people of Japan will undergo all in vain.

EXPLAINS TERMS

"Our blows will not cease until the Japanese military and naval forces lay down their arms in unconditional surrender.

"Just what does unconditional surrender of the armed forces mean for the Japanese people? It means the end of the war. It means the termination of the influence of the

Continued on Page 27.

SO PROUDLY WE HAIL our gallant Men and Women of Beaver who joined the colors in the cause of Freedom to achieve this Glorious Victory . . .

Stephen J. Ansio
John C. Searight
Robert A. Gibson
Edwin F. Heisley, Jr.
John K. Fink, Jr.
Robert V. Fink
Samuel H. Fisher
Richard C. Elstner
Daniel B. Dunning
Richard C. Dunning
Theodore Dunning
Herschel P. Ellis, Jr.
Joseph N. Beamer
Marion E. Hogsett
Ralph S. Hogsett
Homer L. Hogsett
L. Clyde Smith, Jr.
Victor L. Popp
William H. Reed
Charles E. Voeltzel
William J. Sloma
Jack L. Wright
Robert P. Thomas
John C. Reinhart
Robert H. Robinson
Paul R. Robinson
John L. Robinson
David W. Wycoff
James O. Sloss
Charles Riffle, Jr.
Russell D. Porter
Lynn B. Oppelt
Warren D. Morton
James E. Morton
F. Laroy Nulton
Gail M. Perault
Homer A. Suter, Jr.
Smith D. Hayward, Jr.
Ralph M. Rhinelander
Norman D. Patterson, Jr.
Raymond A. Holzworth
William H. Powers
Richard M. McDonald
Suzanne Doyle
John W. Porter
John J. Kohlman
Stephen B. Minton, Jr.
Arada C. Hall
Walter J. Rader
Howard W. Rader
Earl T. Rader
Donald H. Parsons
John W. McCullough
Lee J. Romigh
William E. Wolff
Earl Snodgrass
Ralph C. Tate
Jay E. Bechtel, Jr.
Kenneth E. Bechtel
George R. Wilson
Charles M. Wilson
Catherine R. Carnahan
Lawrence D. Mantz
Paul R. Schaff
Samuel McCaw, Jr.
Richard McClure
Arno H. Thompson, Jr.
Joseph L. Tomlinson
Lloyd L. Bebout
William R. Harris
Paul F. Irvin
Earl J. Morrow
Frank H. Morrow
Gilbert L. Morrow
Joseph G. Barnes
James E. Barnes
Robert J. Hage
Paul K. Wylie
Lloyd H. Shenefelt, Jr.
Jack S. Todd
Charles R. Eppers
Donald L. Eppers
Gerald L. Marshall
William R. Rowse
James Ferguson
Arthur L. Davis
Paul E. Davis
Donald R. Davis
Thomas Chantler
James W. Ashbrook
Robert C. Ashbrook
Chesley E. Deians
Clark H. Carroll
Gordon A. Carroll
Douglas E. Cowan
Martin S. Hunting
Richard K. Roosa
Lester A. Roosa
Donald P. Roosa
Howard E. Roosa
Hugh R. Nieman, Jr.
George W. Moorehead
Robert P. Hendrickson
Edward L. Hendrickson
Theodore H. Gulla
Annabelle Gulla
George B. Hartsuff
William H. Hartsuff
Floyd C. Graham
Herbert K. Anderson
William F. Irvin
Edward L. Irvin
John Stahl
Ralph H. Pauley, Jr.
William J. Pauley
Ray T. Stout
Robert C. Stout, Jr.
Albert D. Hill
William J. Umstead
William M. McClelland
Raymond J. Stoops
Richard R. Davidson
Paul C. Evans
Paul E. King
Richard C. Emery
Paul E. Emery
Robert B. Morris
Manuel Zentner
Horace W. Wanner
Ernest W. Fogel, Jr.
Ralph W. Franke
Thomas J. Craig
Robert F. Garvin
David M. Householder
Paul J. Huth
John J. Hays
James M. Allan
Thomas W. Bell
Charles A. Campbell
Robert V. Campbell
Elmer A. Duffy
Meyrick E. Green, Jr.
Paul D. McClintock
Donald E. Glass

George A. McCloskey
Richard C. McCloskey
Paul W. Schaughency
John T. Baker
Robert H. Stone
Charles D. Stone
Margaret Greesley
Donald W. Greesley, M. D.
Edward F. Swauger
Earl P. Worbs
David A. Worbs
Ralph F. Ziegler
Charles L. Zeigler
James D. Yohe
Hubert H. Washburn
Paul C. Washburn, M. D.
Lloyd S. Bennett
Paul Howe
Kenneth S. Leasure
Wernet M. Baker
Edward C. Brown
David H. Roll
Orin R. Roll
Lowell M. Smith

Paul A. Thompson
Robert R. Wheeler
Paul S. Wheeler
Wilson H. Wheeler
Donald R. Stephens
Edgar S. Funk
Richard A. Martsolf
Charles A. Munson, Jr.
James D. Large
Walter S. Bliss

Robert L. Haag
John R. Leech
William K. Leech
Robert S. Huffman
Richard A. Gaskin
John S. Gaskin
Vincent L. Campbell
Myles L. Campbell
Joseph J. Ezzo
James Conley
Carl N. Burtner
Robert W. Daumiller
Richard H. West
J. Eric Jones
William C. Emmerich
John Q. Campbell
Reed W. Campbell
Charles M. Ferrall
William C. Trushel
John V. C. Ewing
James P. Ewing
Alfred L. Ezzo
Colin McInnes, Jr.
James C. Donnelly
Robert D. Fleming III
Harold C. Scheel
Karl R. Knapp
Joseph K. Stone
Joseph A. Reiser
Glen K. Moorhead
Joseph I. Reno
Robert E. Snitger
James Cook
Clyde R. Anderson
Edward Giles, Jr.
Robert E. Bloom
Donald G. Portman
William R. Dunlap
Albert J. Guzzetti
Eugene H. Guzzetti
John W. Hites
Frank J. Boyde
Donald C. Boyde
William H. Thomas
James W. Reese
John H. Short, Jr.
Denis A. Duchene
Daniel F. Leary
Gerald J. Leary
Joseph L. Kennedy
Lawrence G. Bonnar
Homer D. Bonnar, Jr.
Wilson J. Rhodes, Jr.

Marian Rhodes
Victor M. Rhodes
Lee E. Koett, Sr.
Lee E. Koett, Jr.
John D. Smith
Robert T. Leech
James F. Kline
Robert J. Snapp
Lawrence G. Snapp
George H. Fesell
James E. Kolb
Steve B. Tusai
Jack B. Evans
Donald H. McLaughlin
Ralph H. McLaughlin
John R. Shearer
Eugene I. George
John A. Roth, Jr.
Joseph R. McMahon
John R. McDermott
Donald N. Morgan
Robert M. Morgan
Gaillard J. Worstell
Walter R. Fenterman
Raymond P. Rupple
Lewis F. Lovell
William A. Lovell
Howard C. Harris
Chester D. Harris
Robert S. Gordon
Marshall L. Frazier
Harold Bahm
Samuel Bahm
James A. Ray
Homer S. Portman
William K. Portman
Warren H. McConnell
Roy T. Casbourne

Charles A. Casbourne
Robert L. Bryan
Stanton O. Lyons
John H. LeSueur
Duwayne G. Jeffers
James T. Anderson
Gayle C. Gamble
Mary Jo Klanek
James O. Nelson
Frank W. Poe
William H. Snitger III
William E. Kaye, Jr.
Robert G. Bruehl
Charles C. Eaton
Francis S. Gratton
Thomas S. McConnell
Frank E. Schwartz
Albert F. Yost
Donald G. Wise
Helen A. Novak
Ralph Knowles
George P. Sherron
Clayton C. McConnaughy
Donald D. Leech
Hugh Fischer
J. Crawford Kennedy
Richard R. Kennedy
John E. Kennedy
Paul E. Kennedy
Phillip Martsolf, Jr.
Paul V. Bennett
Wilbert L. Stewart
Joseph R. Patterson, Jr.
John Henry Foster
Hugh Hazen Wilson
John Dean Wilson
Thomas E. Campbell
Ira Campbell
John D. Preston
Robert Thompson Oliphant
Richard Eugene Edwards
Robert Lee Edwards
John J. Bralkowski
Dewayne C. Schlosser
Paul L. Schlosser
Jack D. Schlosser
Robert E. Tallon
Charles W. Tallon
Louis D. Tallon
Wayne K. Tallon
George Harold Minton, Jr.
Walter C. Barnhart
George F. Sparhawk, Jr.
Robert Morrow McKee
William Charles McKee
Alfred D. Becken III
Findley Earl Bartley, Jr.
Sara A. McRoberts
John M. Snyder
William Donald Boyd
Leonard Eugene Boyd
Joseph G. McCaw, Jr.
Samuel Nesbit Craig
Lyle C. Kimple
James F. Scroggs
David J. Cooper, Jr.
Louis E. Braun
Stewart McIntyre
James L. Murray
Harold C. Steinfeld
George Richard Hamilton
James G. M. Weyand, M. D.
Frank J. Cascio
Charles J. Cascio

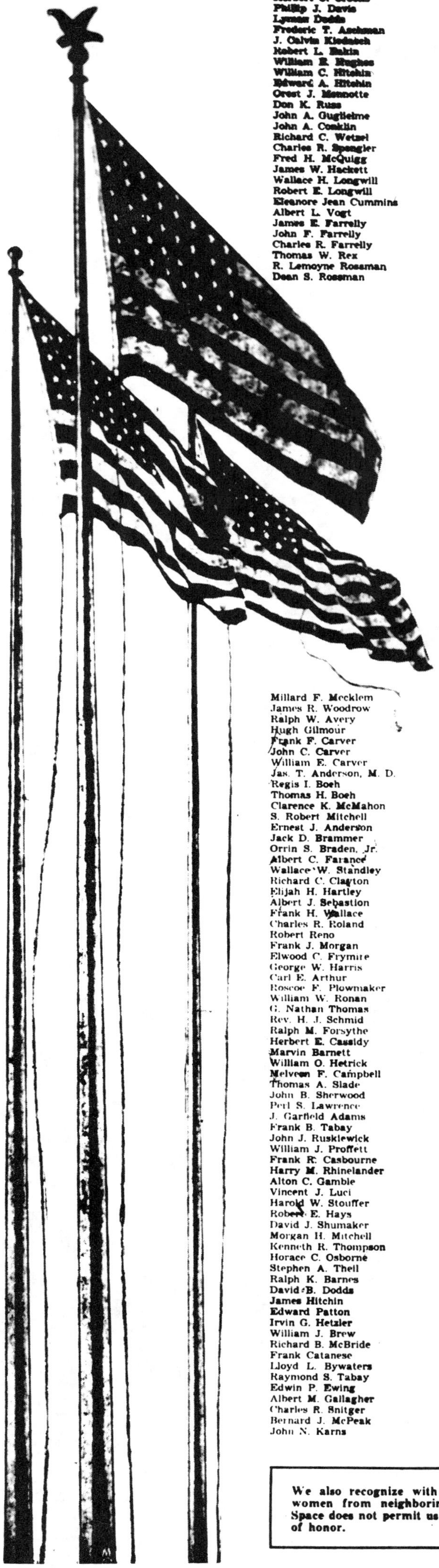

James H. Dilley
William R. Stewart
Herbert O. Crooks
Phillip J. Davis
Lyman Dodds
Frederic T. Aschman
J. Calvin Kiedaisch
Robert L. Eakin
William R. Hughes
William C. Hitchin
Edward A. Hitchin
Orest J. Mennotte
Don K. Russ
John A. Guglielme
John A. Conklin
Richard C. Wetzel
Charles R. Spengler
Fred H. McQuigg
James W. Hackett
Wallace H. Longwill
Robert E. Longwill
Eleanore Jean Cummins
Albert L. Vogt
James E. Farrelly
John F. Farrelly
Charles R. Farrelly
Thomas W. Rex
R. Lemoyne Rossman
Dean S. Rossman

Millard F. Mecklem
James R. Woodrow
Ralph W. Avery
Hugh Gilmour
Frank F. Carver
John C. Carver
William E. Carver
Jas. T. Anderson, M. D.
Regis I. Boeh
Thomas H. Boeh
Clarence K. McMahon
S. Robert Mitchell
Ernest J. Anderson
Jack D. Brammer
Orrin S. Braden, Jr.
Albert C. Farance
Wallace W. Standley
Richard C. Clayton
Elijah H. Hartley
Albert J. Sebastion
Frank H. Wallace
Charles R. Roland
Robert Reno
Frank J. Morgan
Elwood C. Frymire
George W. Harris
Carl E. Arthur
Roscoe F. Plowmaker
William W. Ronan
G. Nathan Thomas
Rev. H. J. Schmid
Ralph M. Forsythe
Herbert E. Cassidy
Marvin Barnett
William O. Hetrick
Melveen F. Campbell
Thomas A. Slade
John B. Sherwood
Perl S. Lawrence
J. Garfield Adams
Frank B. Tabay
John J. Ruskiewick
William J. Proffett
Frank R. Casbourne
Harry M. Rhinelander
Alton C. Gamble
Vincent J. Luci
Harold W. Stouffer
Robert E. Hays
David J. Shumaker
Morgan H. Mitchell
Kenneth R. Thompson
Horace C. Osborne
Stephen A. Theil
Ralph K. Barnes
David B. Dodds
James Hitchin
Edward Patton
Irvin G. Hetzler
William J. Brew
Richard B. McBride
Frank Catanese
Lloyd L. Bywaters
Raymond S. Tabay
Edwin P. Ewing
Albert M. Gallagher
Charles R. Snitger
Bernard J. McPeak
John N. Karns

Thomas R. Day
Ralph E. Spring
John W. Wise
Ward R. Heath
Charles H. Brown, Jr.
Kenneth H. Evans, Jr.
Laura P. Evans
James O. Evans, Jr.
W. Sutherland Campbell
Jacques H. LaPerriere
Audene H. Cooper
Donald C. Cooper
John R. Cooper, Jr.
Lawrence J. Conlon
George W. Dickinson
William E. McClarey
James A. Conrad
Robert J. Snyder
George S. Quay
Robert A. Quay
Frederick C. Armour
Walter J. Kountz
William M. Rhinehart, Jr.
Donald W. Barclay
William T. Bradshaw
Dominic C. Cascio
Paul C. Lloyd
Wayne W. Todd
Theodore G. Walton
Erskine E. Harton, Jr.
Paul B. Schmunk
Raymond C. Richards
Daniel E. Wilson
George E. Kirk, Jr.
Floyd W. Payne, Jr.
Boyd A. Howe
Charles D. Souders
Daniel P. Zamos
James G. Kelly
Robert B. Cunningham
Martha M. Stiffler
Erma J. Potter
William B. Wisner
William F. Kerr
George R. Gulland
Ben L. Rice, Jr.
Frank P. Hanna, Jr.
Charles Denny
Donald D. Sanderbeck
William D. Bartoe
Stanley Ziance
Steve Jurick
Lucy M. Stewart
Robert L. Reeder
John E. Wright
C. Dan Smith
Stephen M. Barnes
Lewis E. Bradshaw
Cramer K. Bradshaw
William R. Welty
John F. Hartwick
Alexander Stephani
William J. Eberhart
Francis J. Turner
Herman H. Schmid
Mary M. Brodigan
Carey J. Hughes
David M. Carver, Jr.
Richard D. Smith
Charles J. Staub, Jr.
Ernest J. Laney, Jr.
John C. Cool
Theodore E. Gooch
Frederick A. Cline, Jr.
John M. Copeland
Howard M. Wentley, Jr.
William P. Coghlan
Lawrence M. Osterman
William E. Osterman
George H. Adamson
Kelsey I. Harvey
Hiram C. Najarian
Jack B. Deeley
George P. Powell
Lloyd M. Thomas
Patricia S. Diesbach
Wm. L. Charlesworth
Glenn F. Jones
Richard E. Bauer
Lewis W. Patterson
Robert C. Boyd
James E. Barrett
John P. Barrett
Eric D. Meadows, Jr.
Richard E. Kronk
Charles E. Cook
Andrew J. Wright, Jr.
John W. Patterson
John G. Good, Jr.
David A. Nelson
Wm. F. Donaldson, Jr.
Lawrence E. Deemer
Thomas Fitzgerald
John A. Jordan
Howard L. Elstner
Paul T. Allebach
Donald D. Henderson
Robert D. Rhinelander
Warren E. Johnson
J. Harry Ferrall
Robert C. Boyd
Robert B. Carnahan
Thomas D. Carnahan
James W. Baker, Jr.
Laree Deeley
John E. Gibson
Connie Hall Funkhouser
Robert E. Dick
William M. Campbell
Robert L. Sitler
Frederick U. Rock
Frank W. Dittman
Robert J. Douglas
Howard S. Fleming
Jacob T. Leach
Edwin H. Goll
Jack Arthur Shaner
John Norman Cooke
Dean Dickson Berry
John T. Morgan, Jr.
John K. Jeffers
William O. Belloff
Harold L. Panner
Paul Vincent

We also recognize with sincere gratitude the men and women from neighboring towns in our armed forces. Space does not permit us to place their names on this roll of honor.

Here Is President Truman's Cabinet With Four New Members

Tom C. Clark, Attorney General — Clinton P. Anderson, Agriculture — Lewis B. Schwellenbach, Labor — Robert Hannegan, Postmaster-General — Edward R. Stettinius, State

Henry A. Wallace, Commerce — Henry Morgenthau, Treasury — Henry L. Stimson, War — Harold L. Ickes, Interior — James V. Forrestal, Navy

NEW GALILEE NEWS

Pfc. Helen L. Henry, S/T at Fitzsimmons General hospital, Denver, Colo., is home on a 15-day leave.

Mrs. Mary Altman of Hollywood, Calif., formerly of New Galilee, has announced the engagement of her daughter Virginia to Petty Officer Clyde Wiley, son of Mr. and Mrs. [illegible] Wiley, Blabon [illegible].

Miss Altman is a graduate of the Beaver Falls High school, class of '42, and a member of the [illegible] Sigma Phi national sorority. [illegible] fiance who has served in the [illegible] the past three years has recently been transferred to the [illegible] Pacific area, after being [illegible] on the west coast for a [illegible] date has been set for [illegible].

[illegible] Levy of Riverview [illegible]

Mrs. James I. Beck is ill with rheumatism.

Mrs. R. H. Welsh, who has been ill with pneumonia is improving.

Rev. C. Alexander and congregation of the First Baptist church of Wampum will be at the First Baptist church of New Galilee Sunday at 3 p. m. with Rev. Mr. Alexander guest speaker.

J. Elton Potter is seriously ill at his home on the New Galilee-Koppel road.

Mrs. C. C. Anderson and Carol Ann Hill were Pittsburgh visitors this week.

Mrs. Ralph Bodick visited at Wilkinsburg this week.

The local paper drive was very successful, the proceeds being 663.34. The amount of paper amounted to about four tons.

New Galilee public school will close the [illegible] of May. A basket picnic is being planned by the P. T. A. to be held Monday, May [illegible] at the [illegible].

[illegible] pupils of the eighth grade took the high school entrance tests last Saturday.

Homer M. Nesbit, former resident of this place, and Mrs. Nesbit left this week for California, where they expect to make their future home.

Chas. F. White is in Hartford, Conn., this week attending an engineers' conference.

Mrs. Mabel Wells and Mrs. Ruth Smith of New Brighton were callers at the W. C. Rhodes home this week.

Local firemen were called to the R. J. Beck garage Tuesday morning, which was damaged by a fire of undetermined origin.

The Tuesday Nite sewing club met with Mrs. Arthur Beatty, Maryland avenue, New Castle. The next meeting will be with Mrs. Ruth Brittain.

The New Galilee 4-H club has elected the following officers: President, Mary E. VanKirk; vice president, Janice McElvaney; secretary and treasurer, Barbara Shenafelt; [illegible] Miller, [illegible] Miller; news reporter, Shirley Brittain; Victory chairman, Phyllis J. Fry; song leader, Ruth Duncan. The next meeting will be Friday, June 1, 1945, at 1:30 o'clock in the city building.

Grace Miller was honored Tuesday evening in the home of Mr. and Mrs. Gus Miller, Sr., at a nicely appointed birthday dinner. Covers were laid for eight.

The Ruth Bible class of the U. P. church held their May meeting in the home of Mrs. Gladys Keane in Big Beaver township. During the business meeting officers were elected as follows: President, Mrs. George Walker; vice president, Miss Dorothy McAnlis; secretary, Mrs. Howard McConnell, and treasurer, Miss Marjorie McAnlis.

Mr. and Mrs. E. E. Ferrall have returned to their home in Carrollton, O., after a visit with friends here.

Big Beaver Grange met Tuesday evening. The Bell Telephone company arranged the presentation of an interesting program including a report of the company and its future plans. A social time followed and refreshments were served to the large crowd.

Big Beaver Grange Ladies' club met Tuesday afternoon with the program in charge of the music committee. Hostesses were Mrs. George Walker, Miss Elaine Gray, Mrs. Chester Leslie and Mrs. Chester Stewart.

BATAAN "JIVE"

SAN FRANCISCO — (AP) — Bobby-sox girls—the first they had seen—gathered around liberated heroes of Bataan and Corregidor.

One girl started jive-talking to Cpl. Marshal Stoutenburgh of Kelly's Corner, N. Y. He was baffled, but he retorted:

"This is wonderful — toxang yasame scocle shigota!"

The bobby-soxer retired in confusion.

"We'll call it a draw," laughed Cpl. Bill Peterson of Lake Park, Iowa. "All 'Marsh' told her was 'lots of rest and no work'—in Nip."

Looking At Life

Continued From Page Sixteen.

things than that to see if you and I will only, like Mrs. Ryan, "let our fancy have full sway."

• • •

No, I've never paid much attention to poetry. And maybe you haven't either.

I wonder whether most of us don't pay entirely too much attention to the music of the cash register and not nearly enough to the harmony in our hearts.

Falls were the greatest single cause of accidental deaths in 1943.

Local Nurse Applies For Overseas Duty

Mrs. Laura Mae [illegible] husband T/Sgt. Oren [illegible] was killed in Germany [illegible] has joined the [illegible] Corps and applied [illegible] duty.

The daughter [illegible] Harry Canon of [illegible], the young woman [illegible] next month for [illegible], Va.

She is a [illegible] Hospital [illegible] and recently [illegible] with the American Red Cross in the Pittsburgh blood bank. Her home was at 238 [illegible] avenue, Pittsburgh.

"I felt that the need was so great and I knew it is something I can do," said Mrs. Waters regarding her enlistment. "It means going in and sticking to it. That's what my husband did. [illegible]"

[illegible] Victim Is [illegible] To Hot Springs

[illegible] Lt. Robert M. Shannon, [illegible] of Clarence A. Shannon of R. [illegible] and a veteran of seven months' combat service as an infantry officer in France, has arrived at the Army and Navy General hospital, Hot Springs, Ark., after evacuation from overseas for treatment of arthritis.

Lt. Shannon was a platoon leader, executive officer and later company commander with the 7th Infantry Regiment of the Third Division. He wears the Bronze Star Medal for heroism in leading a patrol that knocked out a German machine gun nest which was holding up the advance of two rifle companies in southern France.

At Army and Navy General hospital, a rheumatism center of the army, Lt. Shannon will receive highly specialized medical care and the benefits of an extensive reconditioning program.

His wife resides at 535 Carbon street, Butler.

ARMY STATION HERE

A U. S. Army recruiting station has been located in Room 9 of the post office building at Beaver Falls. Sgt. Hallie Jolliffe is the officer in charge. She will be glad to be of service at all times as this is the only station in the county, Beaver Falls being the most centrally located. Enlistments for the W. A. C. will also be processed at this office.

Churchill's New Cabinet to Face Commons Tuesday

LONDON — (AP) — The new government of Prime Minister Churchill will face parliament for the first time Tuesday in what one political commentator said today would be "the fiercest baptism of any administration for a long time."

The Times of London lent support to the view of some observers that the "caretaker government," named last night to serve until Britain's general elections of July 5, was also Churchill's choice for his permanent administration, should the Conservative party retain its majority at the polls.

Praising the cabinet as a "carefully balanced team," the Times said its members, when they appear before the house, would "ask for a mandate to press on the Japanese war to its conclusion."

Churchill, who retained Anthony Eden as foreign secretary, chose mainly members of his own party to replace the 30 Labor and Liberal ministers leaving the government. Also there are a few from other parties, including the Liberal Maj. Gwilym Lloyd George, son of the late World War I prime minister David Lloyd George, as minister of fuel and power, and the Liberal National Ernest Brown, new minister of aircraft production. Cabinet members without definite party affiliation who were retained included Sir James Grigg, secretary of war.

The editorial reaction to the new government in the London press followed party lines.

Vacated key cabinet posts were filled largely by shifts to new positions of remaining Conservative cabinet members, whose old portfolios were taken by the newcomers.

Ben Friedman Ill

Suffering from pneumonia, Ben Friedman, well known local merchant, was taken to Providence hospital this morning. Mr. Friedman was taken ill at his room at the Brodhead hotel.

Jamaica has about one half the population of the British West Indies.

10 SENIORS GRADUATING WITH HONORS AT GENEVA

MILDRED HEIMLICH

BETTY HOLT

BETTY MAE MILLER

MARY JEAN MAYERS

MARJORIE MULDOON

HELEN REAGLE

ELAINE SUTTON

LORA SMITH

MARGARET RANSOM

Photos by Boylin News-Tribune Engraving

DIANA HERKOV

Ten seniors at Geneva college will be graduated with honors at commencement exercises to be held at 10 o'clock Monday morning in the college auditorium.

Graduating with highest honors are seven seniors who have pursued their course with especial merit. Miss Mildred Heimlich, Rochester, music and history; Miss Betty Holt, Negley, Ohio, biology; Miss Betty Mae Miller, Aliquippa, Spanish; Miss Mary Jean Mayers, Beaver Falls, Spanish and history; Miss Marjorie Muldoon, Butler, religious education; Mrs. Helen Reagle, Beaver Falls, religious education; and Miss Elaine Sutton, Ambridge, Spanish and Latin.

Receiving honors will be Miss Lora Smith, Youngstown, Ohio, business administration; Miss Margaret Ransom, Arlington, N. J., English, and Miss Diana Herkov, Aliquippa, business administration.

The honors system at Geneva is different from that found in many colleges because it stresses diversified readings with individual reports and discussions on the readings with professors in various fields. These readings, covering a wide range, are designed to foster in the student an appreciation and sound habits of good reading as well as the ability to discuss such reading with others. The various grades of honors depend upon the amount of reading and the quality of the work in courses. A thesis is written in the major field. This year the thesis subjects have been especially significant: several represent the expanding world-wide interests of America with emphasis on Latin America and Russia; some like Miss Heimlich's "American Music and the Civil War" and Mrs. Reagle's "The Teaching of Jesus and World Peace" reflect the emphasis on war and peace problems; other studies that are unusual are Miss Holt's "History and Catalogue of the Trees on the Geneva Campus" (there are more than 50 varieties), and Miss Ransom's study of "Shakespearean Productions of Broadway from 1930 to 1944."

These ten students have not only led the scholarship of the student body but have been active in most of the campus activities during their years in college. Miss Heimlich has adorned many an occasion with her playing and singing. There are four club presidents in this honors group: Miss Heimlich, English club; Miss Sutton, Spanish club; Miss Holt, French club, and Miss Miller, Mathematics club in 1945, English club in 1944.

Many parties and gatherings at the college have been entertained by Miss Mayers' playing. Miss Muldoon has been a leader among the group planning to devote their lives to religious activities. Mrs. Reagle has greatly endeared herself to all at Geneva. The mother of two college graduates, she has carried on the many obligations of a home and fitted graciously into the undergraduate life of her associates at Geneva. In her senior year she was vice president of the Woman's Student Association.

The editor of the Geneva Cabinet, the student paper, has been Miss Smith. Miss Herkov wrote for the Cabinet and during the time of the Air Corps groups at the college provided invaluable secretarial aid. The 1945 May Queen was Miss Ransom; in her court from this group were: Miss Miller, maid of honor; Misses Sutton and Smith, attendants.

Sunday, May 27, Is Annual Women's Day at the Second Baptist Church

This is an annual affair sponsored by the senior missionaries of the church. Mrs. M. L. Hicks, the president, who for years has presided over this group of women, has arranged an unusually interesting program. Beginning in the Bible School, the women will have the church programmed for mission activities. At 11 o'clock the pastor will bring the message to the women.

The three o'clock service will climax the day with an address by Mrs. W. S. Fitts, returned missionary from Africa. Mrs. Fitts spent more than 15 years in the heart of Africa and knows the conditions there first-hand. Hear her.

At 7:30 the program for the day will be brought to a close with a candle light service. Mrs. [illegible] Thomas, Mrs. Rosa Lee [illegible], Mrs. [illegible] Toliver and Mrs. Lucy Gordon, the program committee, have arranged a number of extra features for your benefit.

On Monday evening, the Beaver Valley Deacons and Trustees Association will meet at the church at 8 o'clock. Mr. W. H. [illegible], president. The deacons and trustees of the valley will [illegible] the round table [illegible] [illegible]

Stores Pushing Bonds Campaign

With store contests under way in a number of the city's retail establishments, interest in the selling of bonds during the Seventh War Loan campaign is at a high tempo. Howard Smart, Beaver Falls, is city chairman of this division and Harold Winkle, Beaver Falls, is county chairman.

Benson's has reported the highest record thus far of any drive. In first place at present in that store's bond sales is Grace Grimley, with Jessie Burroughs second and Lillian Shay and Dorothy Littell tied for third place. One girl sold $2,000 in "E" bonds yesterday.

J. C. Penney employes are competing in a nation-wide contest. High individuals to date are Zella Crider first, Janet Rose second and Mrs. Margaret Shanks, third. Sales here are also running far ahead of previous drives.

Employes of the G. C. Murphy company are competing for district awards, but names of leading contestants are not immediately available.

At the Woolworth store two groups are vying for honors. Purchases are being made through the Legion Auxiliary which has had a booth in the store continuously throughout the war. Mrs. Mildred Morgan is contest leader, Anna Mary Schweiger is in second place and Mrs. Anne McCarty, third. Much favorable comment has been heard regarding the store's bond window display of souvenirs and service photographs.

Other retail merchants are participating in the campaign through advertising, window and interior displays, and solicitation of employes and customers.

APPLICATIONS FOR MARRIAGE LICENSES

Richard M. Teall, Toledo, O., and Geraldine L. Ferner, New Castle.

John P. Moffett, Grove City, and Frances A. Mlack, New Brighton.

Richard F. Fulton, Beaver Falls, and Betty J. Wheeler, Beaver Falls.

11 Killed In Blast

EDGEWOOD, Md., (AP) — Eleven persons killed and 52 injured, three critically, was the toll today of an explosion and fire at historic Edgewood arsenal, the first major accident there since start of the war.

A special army board of inquiry is investigating the blast which rocked the station, headquarters of the Army's Chemical Warfare Service shortly after 3 P.M. yesterday. It occurred in a building filled with civilian workers assembling and loading two-pound igniter hand grenades.

WOUNDED IN ACTION

Mr. and Mrs. G. L. Sarver, Sr., of R. D. 1, have received word that their son, Sgt. George L. Sarver, Jr., 22, was wounded while on his last mission of the European War.

Sgt. Sarver has been serving with the Eighth Air Force in England. He has been awarded the Purple Heart.

Announced in casualty lists of Navy wounded today was Cpl. John Todorczuk, of the U. S. Marine Corps Reserve, a resident of 110 Ninth street, Conway. Todorczuk was wounded for the second time while in the service.

The Mail Box

The War Finance Committee of Beaver Falls wishes to extend to you its appreciation of your splendid cooperation in the inauguration of the Seventh War Loan Campaign.

The [illegible] your part [illegible] during the presentation of the Girl Marine Band concert was very desirable both from the standpoint of the audience and of the members of the Band. In addition to this particular favor on your part, you are well aware of the fact that the Seventh War Loan campaign is getting the type of publicity that will contribute largely to its success.

Yours very truly,
War Finance Committee of Beaver Falls
[illegible]

Arms Parley

[illegible]

A two-thirds affirmative vote is required to pass an amendment. If they succeed [illegible] down the proposals, the Big Four will then have to muster a full two-thirds of the committee to give affirmative approval to the Yalta formula. It remained to be seen whether the small nation opponents would throw the conference into a deadlock by blocking that approval.

Japan Admits

(Continued From Page One)

to be turned against Japan.

"More than two and a half times as many tons of bombs will be dropped on Japan" in the next 12 months "as the Allies dropped on Europe" in the closing year of the war against Germany said Rep. J. Buel Snyder (D-Pa) after hearing Gen. George C. Marshall outline the Army's plans. Even with Germany out of the war Congressmen expected war department expenditures to be cut by only 10 or 20 per cent.

McCreary, Reed

(Continued From Page One)

and his family have moved back to Beaver after having resided at Camp Hill, near Harrisburg, for a considerable portion of the period in which he was a member of the commission.

Attorney Sam B. Wilson, frequently a candidate, but never elected, for congress, and who in 1941 opposed Judge Frank E. Reader unsuccessfully as the Democratic nominee for the judgeship, has also filed on the Democratic ticket.

Thus two candidates are to be nominated on both the Republican and Democratic tickets on June 19. Should either or both of the candidates who have filed on both tickets receive both nominations, this will no doubt, be equivalent to their elections.

Persons who have followed county politics have been amazed at the extent of the personal activities throughout every voting precinct of the county by both Judge McCreary and Attorney Reed yet the two candidates are not campaigning together and have as yet failed to appear on the same program. Judge McCreary has been unable to fill many of the requests for public appearance due to the fact that his duties as judge confine him to his office.

B & W Tubing

(Continued From Page One)

Rock Island Arsenal in a completed state, with no provision for further construction in the field. This means that all the parts, including the tubing, must be in perfect working order with every detail accurate and to specifications ready for instant operation."

In order to meet these specifications the steel in the tubing must be capable of withstanding extreme shocks and very high pressures, and must meet the standard for machining at maximum rates. In 1940, the Company, working in conjunction with Rock Island Arsenal, began experimenting on lower alloy steels which would meet the specifications for physical soundness, and at the same time conserve the higher alloy steels which were on the critical list. A year later experiments showed that a tube could be made from national emergency steels (of lower alloy composition) which would meet all specifications, and at the same time be manufactured simply and easily on standard equipment. The tubing which is used for these recoil cylinders measures from two to seven inches in diameter, and has very thick walls. It is shipped in 25 foot lengths which are cut to individual pieces of between four and seven feet.

Obituary

DONALD H. PIFER

Donald Hays Pifer aged 25 years, of No. 1 Mayfield Heights apartments, died yesterday in Chicago. In that city on a visit with a friend he had been ill only since Wednesday.

Mr. Pifer was born in New Brighton and lived his entire life in the upper valley. He was a driver for the Beaver Valley Motor Coach company and a member of Central Methodist church.

He leaves his widow, Mrs. Dorothy Mae Pifer, and three sons, Richard Eugene, Ronald Gerard and Ralph Norman, all at home. Surviving also are his parents, Mr. and Mrs. Harry E. Pifer of Beaver Falls, and three sisters, Mrs. Alfred Taylor, Fallston; Mrs. Albert Timmins, Washington, D. C., and Mrs. Claude Lemley, Beaver Falls.

Friends will be received at the home beginning tomorrow.

FUNERAL NOTICES

PIFER: Funeral services for the late Donald Hays Pifer will be held in the family home, No. 1, Mayfield Heights, at 2:30 o'clock Tuesday afternoon. Burial will be made in Beaver cemetery. Lutton funeral home in charge.

ADDITIONAL CLASSIFIED ADS

FOR SALE

POULTRY EQUIPMENT—Oil and electric brooders, 250 and 500 capacity, shipment just in, $19.50 to $36.75; 50 gallon wood barrels, make good feed containers, $1.50 each. E. Frank Newell, R. D. No. 3, Beaver Falls. Phone 1813-R. 5-23-tf

LOOK! [illegible] One [illegible] foot floor type show case, one two pound computing scale, one gas heated combination barber's towel steamer and hot water tank, one Taylor electric freezemaster six quart ice cream freezer with attached mix storage compartment. Inquire one to six p. m. weekdays at 2317 8th Avenue, Beaver Falls. 5-23-6t

FOR SALE — Coffee grinder, paper baler, counters, (one marble top), paper racks, one show case and Edison Machine with records (official Laboratory size). Call New Brighton 4337-R. 5-24-6t

FOR SALE: Three rooms of furniture, bedroom, living room and kitchen. Phone Beaver Falls 4429. No dealers considered. 5-22-6t

FOR SALE—[illegible] weeks old red male Cocker Spaniel puppy, two red females, 10 months old, AKC registered. George "Doc" Graham, 14th Street, 20th Avenue, Pleasantview. 5-23-6x

FOR SALE: Four piece Circassian walnut bedroom suite, mahogany princess dresser, brass bed, complete, dining table, six chairs, china closet, buffet, two 9x12 rugs, long mirror, oak frame. Phone Beaver Falls 3789-J13. 5-24-3t

FOR SALE—Pekingese puppies, seven weeks old, male and female. Call at 1522 5th Avenue, New Brighton, or phone New Brighton 2298-J. 5-24-3t.

SPECIAL SALE— Just received more electric hotplates, one hole $4.95, two hole $8.95, No. 4 willow clothes baskets, $3.45, 9x12 congoleum rugs, $4.45; enamel combinets at $1.49; house paint, one gallon $1.39, quart 50c; four hour enamel, one gallon $2.50, quart 75c; Kem-tone, one gallon $2.98, quart 98c. Hostine & Co., 905 3rd Avenue, New Brighton. Phone 1244-J. 5-24-6t.

FOR SALE—One lot of berry crates and baskets. For information, call John Henderson, Beaver Falls, 650-R. 5-25-3x

FOR SALE — STORAGE TABLE FOR USE IN KITCHEN, $8.50; HIGH PEDESTAL STAND AND JARDINIERE, $4.00; RUSTIC FLOWER STAND AND JARDINIERE, $2.00; TWO 6x9 ANGLO PERSIAN RUGS, $30.00 EACH; OAK DOUBLE BED, $12.50; ROPE LEG LIBRARY TABLE, $10.00; WALNUT VANITY DRESSING TABLE COMPLETE WITH BENCH, $20.00; 8x10 AXMINSTER RUG, $12.50; OAK WASH STAND, $15.00; CAST IRON GAS RANGE, BOTTOM OVEN, 4 TOP BURNERS, EXCELLENT FOR BASEMENT USE FOR CANNING AND WASH DAYS, $7.50; TABLE FOR USE IN BASEMENT, $2.00; GOLD FRAME MIRROR 8"x27", $5.00; SHEETS; HAND AND BATH TOWELS; PILLOW CASES; FANCY WORK; LADY'S UMBRELLAS; SHOES; OVERSHOES; BEDROOM SLIPPERS, SIZE 5 AND 5½; ALL WOOL SWEATERS, SIZE 38; LADY'S EXCELLENT MAROON FLANNEL ROBE, SIZE 40, $10.00; 30 PIECES ROGERS HAMILTON SILVERWARE, $30.00 FOR THE SET; SILK GLOVES, SIZE 6; CARD TABLES; 2 DIAMOND RINGS, 1 DIAMOND BROOCH, BEST QUALITY DIAMONDS, PRICED RIGHT. SEE MR. CHARLES RONEY, 925 11TH STREET, BEAVER FALLS, PA., ANY TIME AFTER 10:30 A. M. TO 9:00 P. M. 5-25-3t

GARDEN SUPPLIES — BULK SEEDS, FERTILIZER, LIME, BONE MEAL, PEAT MOSS, SHEEP MANURE, CATTLE MANURE AND INSECTICIDES. J. H. BROOKS & SONS, 2326 8TH AVENUE, BEAVER FALLS, PHONE 2581. 5-16 to 6-6 inc.

FOR SALE—Studio couch and library table. Inquire 614-15th Street, Beaver Falls. 5-26-1x

FOR SALE—A Majestic electric sweeper, $6.00. Inquire 2503 8th avenue, Beaver Falls. 5-26-1t

HOUSES FOR RENT

FOR RENT: To couple without children, a furnished home on the outskirts of Beaver Falls for three months, beginning June 1. Write Box 300, % News-Tribune, Beaver Falls. 5-21-6t

FOR RENT— Five room house and bath, newly furnished, Chippewa township. Inquire Mean's Gas Station, near Beaver Falls. 5-25-2t.

REAL ESTATE FOR SALE

FOR SALE—Cabin, one acre of ground. Possession at once. Owner moved to Ohio. Price $400. Piper & Fullerton, Benson Building, Beaver Falls. 5-22-6t.

FOR SALE—Building lots and plots, with ashed streets and utilities. Excellent location, near Brighton-Rochester Road. Very reasonable. For appointment, call Beaver Falls 2319-J. 5-25-6x

LOST

LOST OR STRAYED—Pair of pigs in South Beaver Township. Finder please call Beaver Falls 3766-R-12, or notify Richard [illegible], R. D. No. 2, Beaver Falls. [illegible]

LOST—Seven No. [illegible] [illegible]

LOST—Lady's small Elgin watch, light leather band, between Puriton Drug and Post Office, New Brighton, Friday noon. Reward, call New Brighton 1325. 5-26-3x

News-Tribune Classified Ads bring results.

BABY CHICKS

FOR SALE—[illegible] Leghorn chicks, U. S. [illegible] Pullorum controlled. [illegible] Rossbury, New [illegible] Phone 6078, East Palestine [illegible] [illegible] Road.

APARTMENTS FOR RENT

FOR RENT—Three room apartment. Inquire 1515 8th [illegible] Beaver Falls. Phone 294[illegible] 5-[illegible]

FOR RENT—Three unfurnished rooms, private bath. Quiet home, adults only. Use of phone. Steam heat and water furnished. Possession June first. Inquire [illegible] 11th Avenue, New Brighton.

BUSINESS PLACES FOR SALE

FOR SALE — Rochester [illegible] Bar and Grill, formerly known as Custer's Hotel, 73 New York [illegible] nue. For further information call Rochester 1906-M. [illegible] Bange, Prop.

LEGAL NOTICES

ORDINANCE No.

AN ORDINANCE of the City of Beaver Falls, establishing a grade on Thirty-sixth Street east of College Avenue and Thirty-sixth Street Place both in the Seventh Ward of the said City.

Be it Ordained and Enacted by the Council of the City of Beaver Falls, County of Beaver, Commonwealth of Pennsylvania, and it is hereby Ordained and Enacted by the Authority of the same, that a grade be established on Thirty-sixth Street east of College Avenue and Thirty-sixth Street Place both in the Seventh Ward of the said City, and the same is hereby established as follows, to wit:

Section I. SOUTH CURB GRADE — THIRTY-SIXTH STREET:

Beginning at the east end of the curb return at the east side of College Avenue, elevation 889.[illegible]; thence eastwardly on a descending grade of a distance of 115 feet to the west line of Thirty-sixth Street Place, elevation 886.00; thence east a distance of 35 feet across Thirty-sixth Street Place on a level grade 886.00.

Section II. NORTH CURB GRADE:

Beginning at the east end of the curb return at the east side of College Avenue, elevation 890.30; thence eastwardly on a descending grade for a distance of 115 feet to the west line of Thirty-sixth Street Place, elevation 886.00.

Section III. GRADE—THIRTY-SIXTH STREET PLACE:

Beginning at the south line of Thirty-sixth Street at elevation 886.00; thence north across Thirty-sixth Street a distance of 5[illegible] feet on level grade, elevation 886.00; thence north on an ascending grade for a distance of 100 feet to elevation 890.00; thence north on [illegible] ascending grade for a distance of 140 feet to elevation 892.60; thence [illegible] on a descending grade for [illegible] tance of about 25 feet to [illegible] tion 892.40. This point [illegible] north line of Sunrise Gardens Plan of Lots and is the present grade of Craig Alley, a 15 foot alley running north to Thirty-eighth Street.

Section IV. That the City Engineer is hereby authorized and directed to draft the foregoing grade in the book known as the City Grade Book.

Section V. All ordinances or parts of ordinances, in so far as they conflict herewith, be and the same are hereby repealed.

Enacted by Council this ——— day of June, A. D., 1945.

——— Mayor and President of Council.

ATTEST:

——— City Clerk.

5:26-31; 6:[illegible]

EXECUTRIX NOTICE

Letters testamentary on the estate of William Herman Pe[illegible], deceased, late of New Brighton, Beaver County, Pa., having been granted to the undersigned, all persons indebted to said estate are requested to make payment, and those having claims to present the same without delay to

Margaret Butler Pe[illegible], Executrix

438 13th Ave., New Brighton, [illegible]

Richard P. Steward, Attorney.

5:5-12-19-26; 6:2

EXECUTORS' NOTICE

Notice is hereby given that Letters Testamentary have been issued on the estate of Mary [illegible] Acklin, late of the Borough of New Brighton, Beaver County, Pennsylvania, to the undersigned. All persons indebted to said estate will make payment and those having claim will present the same without delay.

JAMES A. COOK,
MARY E. COOK,
Executors
1403 Fifth Avenue,
Beaver Falls, Pa.

A. G. Helbling, Attorney
State Bank Building
Beaver Falls, Penna.

4-21-28; 5-5-12-19 & [illegible]

EXECUTORS' NOTICE

Notice that Letters Testamentary on the estate of Joseph [illegible] Marcus, deceased, late of [illegible] Falls, Beaver County, having been granted, all persons indebted to said estate will make payment and those having claims will present them to Ethel C. [illegible], John D. Ray, [illegible], 12th Street, Beaver Falls, [illegible]

4-21-28; [illegible]

EXECUTOR'S NOTICE

Letters testamentary on the estate of John J. Sch[illegible], deceased, late of Beaver Falls, Beaver County, Pa., having been granted to the undersigned, all persons indebted to said estate are requested to make payment, and those having claims to present the same without delay to

Rev. Stephen N. Schneider, Executor

814 9th St., New Brighton, Pa.

Richard P. Steward, Attorney.

5:5-12-19-26; 6:2

SOCIETY
news of clubs, classes and people
KATHLEEN M. PRIGG, Editor

Zorich-Petrick Engagement Told

Vivid Letters Of Yank To Mother Reviewed Here

"Robin of Delhi, India," a group of compiled letters from an American soldier to his mother, telling of the strange and exciting happenings to a stray boy in India who was befriended by a Yank doughboy, was reviewed last night before members of the Women's Missionary Society of the First Baptist church here by Mrs. James Kinkead when the group convened in the church social rooms.

The evening's devotionals were in charge of Mrs. Clair Kocher and the Society's president, Mrs. David Fowler announced a meeting of the Pittsburgh Baptist Association on June 7th and 8th at the First Baptist church, in Rochester. The afternoon session is slated between the hours of 1:30 p. m. and six oclock with Rev. George Merriam, the guest speaker.

During the evening's meeting, which begins at 7:30 o'clock, the group will be addressed by Rev Benj. Browne who will use as his topic "Healing For a Stricken World."

BLACK MENACE

MARY KELLY, 17, easily not the ugliest of the Kellys, shows the new Claire McCardell "Black Menace," a black, one-piece, Jelida jersey model at the annual Atlantic City showing of beachwear styles.

Women Attend May Festival

Mrs. Angeline Sylvester, Mrs. Frank Wilson, Mrs. Celeste Wagner, of Aliquippa, and Mrs. Carmella DeCarlo of Detroit, Mich., a guest here this week, attended the May Festival at Duquesne University of Pittsburgh Sunday.

Mrs. Sylvester's daughter, Miss Rita Sylvester, a junior student at the University, was one of a group of attendants forming the procession. Mary Virginia Walton of Pittsburgh was crowned Queen of the May.

Aliquippans At Graduation Party

Two Aliquippans were among the 15 guests who attended a post-commencement party Monday evening at Villa Madrid in Pittsburgh honoring Miss Grace Napoli of Rochester, who graduated this week from Rochester High school at ceremonies held in the Oriental Theatre there Monday at 10:30 a. m.

Special guests were Mrs. Angeline Sylvester and daughter, Rita, of 395 Franklin Ave.

Dinner was served in the early evening and the honored guest, daughter of Mr. and Mrs. Peter Napoli, was presented with a corsage of American Beauty roses.

Besides members of her family others attended from Pittsburgh and Ambridge.

The Mighty 7th Must Be Met! Buy YOUR Share!

Different Frock

9117
SIZES
12-20
30-42

A button-fronter that's different! Pattern 9117 is designed on lines to give a "bolero" effect; has draw-string waist (front only). So easy to make, to wear, to iron!

Pattern 9117 comes in sizes 12, 14, 16, 18, 20; 30, 32, 34, 36, 38, 40 42. Sizes 16, 2⅞ yards 39-inch.

Send Twenty cents in coins for this pattern to Evening Times, Pattern Dept., 232 West 18th St., New York 11, N. Y. Print plainly **size, name, address, style number.**

JUST OUT: The Marian Martin Summer Pattern Book, a collection of all that's new and smart in wearing apparel for the family. FREE Nightgown Pattern printed in book. Send Fifteen Cents for your copy.

No Definite Plans Made For Couple's Wedding

At a family dinner Monday evening at the home of Mr. and Mrs. Miter Baronisa of 112 Walnut St., here, announcement was made of the engagement of their daughter, Miss Alice Lou Zorich, to Petty Officer Third Class Michael J. Petrick, son of Mr. and Mrs. Andrew Petrick, 519 McKee Ave., West Aliquippa

Miss Zorich was graduated from Aliquippa High school and is employed as an inspector in the Seamless Tube department of the Jones and Laughlin Steel Corp.

Her fiance, here on several days' leave, will report to a base on the West Coast next week for further Naval assignment. A former employe of the local steel mill, he attended borough schools and left for the armed service more than two years ago. After undergoing 'boot' training at Sampson Naval Training Station, N. Y. he was sent into combat duty in the South Pacific where he remained for more than 22 months.

No definite plans have been made for the wedding.

Veterans Found Raising Level Of College Classes

IOWA CITY, Ia. (U.P.)—World War II veterans are showing a definite advancement of interest in educational achievement at the University of Iowa, according to William D. Coder, director of veterans service at the school.

"The veterans are more serious-minded than average undergraduate of prewar days," Coder said. "Their objectives are more clearly defined. They refuse to waste time and tend to raise the level of the classes for which they enroll.

"We have seen evidence of improved teaching techniques as a result of constructive criticism by veterans," he added.

Coder said returning veterans show a determination to be "mutually helpful." They assist newly arrived servicemen in orientation and provide volunteer tutoring. In cases of physical disability they help to solve transportation problems.

The veterans enter the life of the university readily, Coder said. He reported that "the residential and social patterns are exactly the same" as those of other students. A survey showed that veterans are represented in all the organized student activities .

Wounded Veteran Wants Mother To Get Medals

FORT DEVENS, Mass (U.P.)—A wounded soldier hospitalized at Fort Devens says his mother ought to get the Bronze and Silver Stars for which he has been recommended.

Sgt. Roland E. Tuttle of Kittery, Me., said his mother, Mrs. Evelyn M. Tuttle, ought to be honored because:

She is the mother of eleven children.

She works six days weekly at the Portsmouth Navy Yard as a painter's helper to support the family.

By working, she made it possible for two of her sons to enlist.

Two Brothers Hail Third On Iwo Jima

HOUSTON, Tex. (U.P.) — Two brothers "resting" in a convenient foxhole during the hardest battle of Iwo Jima spied a familiar figure strolling by at a fast trot.

"Hey," they called.

The other Marine stopped and the foxholed brothers recognized a third brother, Cpl. Weldon Haynie.

Weldon was in his first major battle and had no idea his other brothers, Sgts. Vastine and Orville, veterans of the Marianas, Saipan and Tinian, were on Iwo Jima.

Mid-Continent Airliners flew a total of 2.248.892 miles during 1944 as compared with 1,494,549 in 1943.

Mayo Arboretum Plans To Double Its Acreage

ROCHESTER, Minn. (U.P.)—Minnesota flora fanciers wanting to know what shrubs, flowers, orchard stock or other plants they may cultivate with best results probably can get the answer in time from the Mayo Arboretum.

The Arboretum, a joint enterprise of Mayo Properties Assn. and the University of Minnesota's school of agriculture, comprises 525 acres of testing ground near here. It is planned to double the acreage, making it the largest experimental area in the Middle West.

Currently, Prof. W.H. Alderman of the university farm school has under supervision 125 varieties of apples, and 40 each of raspberries and strawberries.

Superintendent of the Aboretum is Benjamin F. Dunn, agriculture instructor at Rochester high school who also owns and operates an orchard of his own.

Goat's Attack Fixes Farmer's Stiff Knee

Mexico, Mo (U.P.)—Farmer William Ware vouches for this story that proves an attack by a goat doesn't always make its victim the goat.

Some 17 years ago, Ware suffered an injury that left one of his legs stiff. All efforts to limber the joint failed, until—a couple of months ago he was rammed by one of his goats. He was hospitalized and now can bend the injured knee.

Today's Calendar

President's Day luncheon of the Aliquippa Chapter of Hadassah at the Roosevelt Hotel, Pittsburgh.

—o—

WAC Mothers' Club at the Aliquippa Service Canteen.

—o—

Mother and daughter banquet of Woodlawn Court No. 565 of Catholic Daughters of America at St. Titus parish hall at 7 p. m.

—o—

New Sheffield Parents and Teachers Association's final meeting of the year with special May Day program featured.

—o—

Card party at St. Catherine's R. C. church of Wireton sponsored by members of the Ladies' Guild.

—o—

Installation of officers and final meeting of the year of the Aliquippa Junior Woman's Club at Moose Temple, Aliquippa. Program to be presented under the auspices of Beaver County Girl Scouts.

Infant Baptized At Glenwillard

Wilma Collen, infant daughter of Mr. and Mrs. Joseph McCoy of Glenwillard, was baptized Sunday morning at St. Catherine's R. C. church, Wireton.

The baby's sponsors, Mr. and Mrs. Barney Hineman, also of McCoy Heights, were special guests at the christening dinner served at the Nicholas Grille at Ambridge.

The Mighty 7th Must Be Met!

Today's Needlework

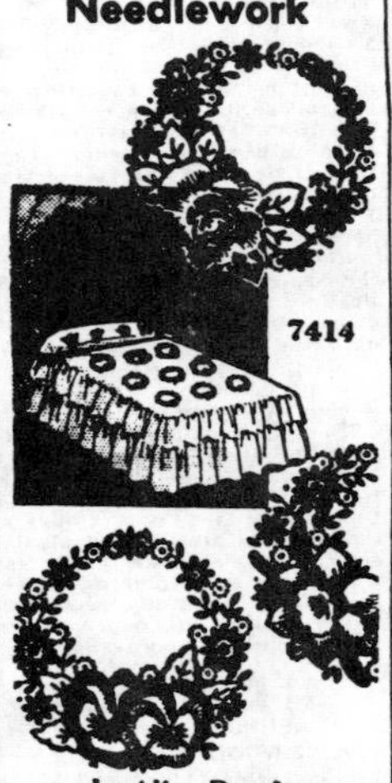
7414

by Alice Brooks

These are floral motifs that are just as adaptable for cloths and small linens as they are for bedspreads. A colorful variety!

It won't take long to turn a plain spread into a real beauty. Pattern 7414 has transfer of 17 motifs, 5x5 to 2½ x 2¾ inches.

Send **FIFTEEN CENTS** in coins for this pattern to The Evening Times, Household Arts Dept., 259 W. 14th St., New York 11, N. Y. Print plainly **NAME, ADDRESS and PATTERN NUMBER.**

Just out! Send fifteen cents more for our NEW 1945 Needlework Book—94 illustrations of designs; crocheting, knitting, embroidery, dolls, other toys, home decoration. Free Pattern for two crocheted handbags printed right in the book.

HOPEWELL'S MAY KING, QUEEN

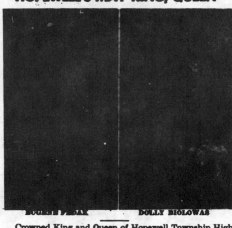

EUGENE FEDAK — DOLLY BIOLOWAS

Crowned King and Queen of Hopewell Township High school at impressive ceremonies held on the school lawn yesterday at 7 p. m. were Eugene Fedak and Miss Dolly Biolowas, both members of this year's graduating class.

Attendants to the Royal couple were Vera Williams, Jean John, Edith McCoy, Marian Morrow, Jack Lynn, Gordon Ahalt, George Brunton and Ray Feenstra.

Postwar Driving Seen Tough For Jeep Drivers

STATE COLLEGE, Pa. (U.P.)—The GI who drives a jeep in the Army will not make a good driver on America's highways after the war, according to Ames E. Neyhart, administrative head of the Institute of Public Safety at Pennsylvania State College.

Among the main differences between Army and civilian driving, Neyhart cited heavy two-way traffic limited parking space, and personal concern for the vehicle.

Even the terrain is different, Neyhart said. A congested public highway is not the same as a battlefield or the jungle, he added.

The truck driver faces different problems," Neyhart pointed out. "The large fleet owners have already learned that ex-servicemen must be re-tained regardless of previous Army experience."

Neyhart predicted there would be "an amazingly large number of people who must be taught safe driving practices after the war." He noted particularly the youths who have not learned to drive because of wartime restrictions on gasoline and tires.

Park Is Renamed For Cowboy-Artist

GREAT FALLS, Mont. (U.P.)—Margaret Park, named in 1895 for Margaret Harkness of St. Louis, who supposedly was the first white woman to see the upper falls of the Missouri River, has been renamed in honor of Charles M. Russell, Great Falls' famed cowboy-artist.

A memorial to Russell will be erected in the park to display and store the paintings, models and other items which have celebrated him as a renowned artist and philosopher of Montana.

His Spelling's Poor But Business Good

GREENVILLE, Miss. (U.P.) — Maybe John Lambrakis is a poor speller. And then again, maybe he's a good businessman.

The sign over Lambrakis' stand reads: "Hot Peauts."

Scores of people have stopped in to call his attention to the error, Lambrakis says. Most of them buy a sack of peanuts befor they leave.

3-Page Federal Form Needed For $1 Award

WEST MIFFLIN, Pa. (U.P.) — The Federal government owes West Mifflin the sum of one dollar but to get it the borough must apply on a form about three sheets in length.

The dollar was awarded West Mifflin in damages when unimproved streets were taken over by the government for construction of a housing project.

Squeeze Play

Visiting the East for the premiere of Columbia's "One Thousand And One Nights", in which she's a harem princess, Adele Jergens tends to her Vitamin C for beauty via the latest of the Florida valencia orange crop.

Brighton Woman Heads Medical Society Auxiliary

Miss Margaret Sutton of New Brighton was installed as president of the Women's Auxiliary to the Beaver County Medical Society when its members met here yesterday at luncheon in the First Methodist church at 1:30 o'clock.

Places were arranged for 28 at the festive table and the decorations, marking a color scheme of orchid and yellow, were accented with a centerpiece of iris and snapdragon.

During a brief business meeting conducted by the retiring president, Mrs. H. B. Jones, Sr., Green Garden road, here, the Auxiliary pledged $100 to the Medical Benevolent Fund.

Following the installation ceremony the afternoon's program featured Mrs. George Deurcshinger of Rochester in a review of the currently popular edition of "Anything Can Happen" and Mrs. J. W. Whitehill of Beaver who gave a resume of medical current events.

The group will convene again next September at a definite time and place to be announced later.

Paratrooper's Folks Get Telegram 6 Times

FORT WORTH, Tex. (U.P.)—Six times in the last year the N. W. Levels have received a telegram from the War Department "regretting to inform them . . ."

And six times they have learned that what the War Department regretted to inform them was that their son, S/Sgt. Newel W. Level Jr., had been wounded in action, not killed.

The much-battered paratrooper is now recuperating from his sixth wound in a French hospital.

Wilson Infant Christened Here

Mr. and Mrs. Lee DeCarlo, Detroit, Mich., were sponsors at the christening Sunday in St. Titus R. C. church of the infant daughter of Mr. and Mrs. Louis Wilson of 143 Oakwood Ave., here and were later special guests at a family dinner held at the home of the baby's paternal grandmother, Mrs. Frank Wilson.

Other guests attended from Coraopolis and Beaver Falls.

'No Smoking' Laws Jolt Councilmen

READING, Pa. (U.P.) — While checking to see if there were any city ordinances prohibiting smoking on streetcars and buses, local councilmen were surprised to find that they themselves were violating one.

Ordinance No. 19, adopted in 1913, reads: "There shall be no smoking in the council chamber during council sessions."

'BASKET CASE' STORIES UNFOUNDED, DESHON HOSPITAL HEAD SAYS

Dame Rumor has had lots of fertile ground whereon to sow her seeds during this war. Perhaps the most fertile spot she has been cultivating is the one whereon the weeds of "Basket Case" stories have been flourishing. Supposedly Deshon General hospital in Butler has been, on alternate days, the home of eleven, fourteen, and as high as fifty-six of these cases. The figure fifty-six gained such popular credence that it was repeated time and time again.

Let's look at the facts. A basket case is supposed to be a patient with both arms and both legs amputated. It is almost a complete physical impossibility for any soldier to be struck by such a terrific burst of shrapnel or shell fragments that the blow would necessitate the removal of all four of his limbs, without his being hit in a vital spot. The shell burst would have to form a circle around his trunk so that his heart or head would not be struck.

Your government has released the fact that there have been two triple amputees in this war. The same story also stated that there had been no quadruple amputees. That same day, personnel at Deshon General Hospital were hearing and re-hearing the rumor that there were a number of "basket cases" at the hospital.

The War Department wants the public to know that soldiers are being killed and wounded. The families of American soldiers have a right to know the truth. The cost of freedom runs high. But the unfounded stories that ill-advised persons are spreading in this and other communities all over America are demoralizing in the frightful impact that they make on the public mind. Army hospitals have no secret wards or locked rooms. No mother or father, no wife or sister has been, or ever will be, denied full and complete information about their loved ones.

In no manner is the War Department denying that some of our soldiers are returning to this country crippled and maimed, or that some of them are deaf and blind. But the War Department does say that all the medical skill of the Twentieth Century is being used for their recovery and convalescence, and that none of them are regarded as hopeless cases.

So well equipped and organized was the Army Medical Corps on D-Day in France that fully 85 per cent of all our casualties received medical attention within ten minutes after being wounded. One quarter of all the doctors in America are in the Army, performing operations and giving relief to our wounded, many of them almost under the guns of the enemy. Out of a group of 6,000 Americans wounded on D-Day, one died as a result of the wounds. The overall picture from our fighting fronts reveals that 97 out of every 100 wounded American soldiers will return to their homes as living proof of the Army Medical Corps' refusal to accept defeat.

Officials at Deshon General Hospital are calling on every public spirited American to help stop the spread of rumors about "basket cases". Families of wounded American soldiers should not be subjected to the additional mental torture that is caused by these vicious, unfounded rumors.

FOUR LOCAL BROTHERS SERVE, 2 OVERSEAS, 2 IN STATES

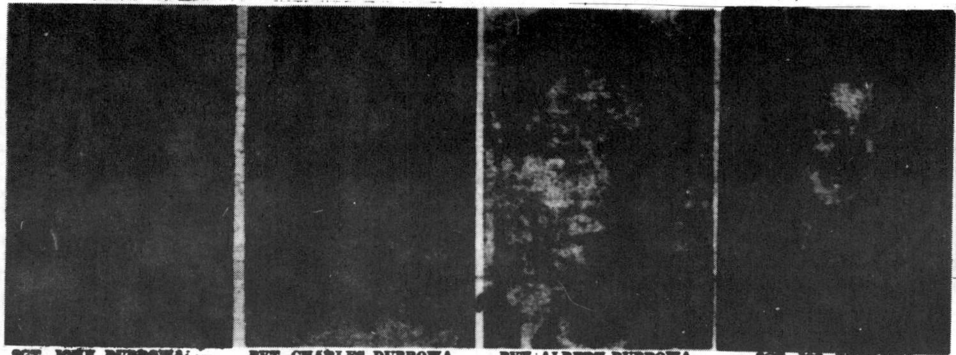

SGT. JOHN DUBROWA — PVT. CHARLES DUBROWA — PVT. ALBERT DUBROWA — SGT. JOS. DUBROWA

ALL SERVING IN THE U. S. ARMY are the four sons of Mr. and Mrs. John Dubrowa, Sr., of 218 Wykes St. John, Jr., is attending an AAF radar school in Florida. Joseph is with an infantry regiment somewhere in the Philippines. Charles is stationed at Camp Wheeler, Ga., with a detachment of infantry. Albert is somewhere on the European continent.

18-YEAR-OLD PRE-COMBAT BILL PUT INTO EFFECT BY ARMY

WASHINGTON, June 4.—(UP)—The Army has put into effect a congressional mandate requiring all replacements under 19 years of age to have a minimum of six months' training before entering combat by extending and expanding the training program insofar as it applies to these men.

The first step to extend replacement training was taken immediately after V-E Day when the period for individual training at Infantry replacement training centers was restored to 18 weeks. The Infantry training period had been reduced from 17 to 15 weeks shortly after the Germans attacked in the Ardennes last December.

In addition to the restored 17 week basic training, all armies are now initiating a nine weeks course of advanced replacement training for all replacements under 19 which will give them a total of 26 weeks of training as replacements, plus furlough time, before they are sent to replacement depots subject to shipment

These advanced courses will stress unit training similar to that received in the final two weeks of the bivouac period of the original 17 weeks training.

Camp Rucker, Ala., Camp Shelby, Miss., Camp Maxey, Tex., and Camp Howze, Tex., have been designated as Advanced Infantry Replacement training centers out of the 14 infantry replacement training centers in the country.

Fort Bragg, N. C., will give the first 17 weeks artillery training and Fort Sill, Okla., advanced artillery training in addition to the 17 weeks training.

For the other arms the full 26 weeks training will be provided at their respective replacement centers which are: Armored Units, Fort Knox, Ky.; Tank Destroyers, Camp Hood, Tex.; Paratroopers, Fort Benning, Ga.; Anti-aircraft Artillery, Fort Bliss, Tex.; and Cavalry, Fort Riley, Kan.

For the time being replacements over 19 will be sent to the replacement depots at Fort Meade, Md., and Ford Ord, Calif., after their 17 weeks individual training until those centers are filled to capacity.

At these centers replacements will receive such training as time and facilities permit until the men are sent overseas. It is anticipated they will be sent abroad as rapidly as shipping space is available in order to expedite the return of veterans under the rotation system or for discharge under the point system.

[illegible]

CHICAGO. (UP)—Chicago's record for hospitality to servicemen remained unscathed even when two bandits held up the tavern of Nick Van Hanxleden. The robbers took a three-carat diamond valued at $2,200 from the proprietor and $85 from Frank Curin, a patron. The thieves didn't even search four soldiers in the tavern.

STATE'S PUBLIC SCHOOLS FACE ACUTE TEACHER SHORTAGE

STATE COLLEGE, Pa., June [illegible].—(UP)—Pennsylvania faces an acute shortage of public school teachers in every field except English and history, Dr. M. R. Trabue, dean of the School of Education at Pennsylvania State College, said today.

"Wartime employment opportunities," explained Dr. Trabue, "have robbed the schools of their backlog of qualified teachers, the great majority of whom will undoubtedly prefer to remain in industry where salaries are higher."

An "immediate" need exists for agriculture teachers to satisfy the postwar demand for courses on modern farming methods, Dr. Trabue said. He also cited a need for science, mathematics, industrial arts, home economics, and trade teachers.

The shortage of health and physical education teachers has been increased by the war-inspired stress on physical fitness, according to Dr. Trabue, while "an inadequate number" of college students have been preparing to teach foreign languages.

ROBBED IN POLICE STATION

BOSTON. (UP)—Police at the Warren Ave. station were properly chagrined when Robert Shepard, a seaman, reported that his wallet containing $125 was missing from his clothing when he woke up after spending the night in the police dormitory for servicemen.

Doctor's Listing Cut 32 P.C.

CHICAGO. (UP)—Listings of physicians and surgeons have decreased 32.1 per cent in the Chicago classified telephone directory since March, 1941. In 1941 there were phones for 5,916 doctors. The 1945 directory shows 4,015. There are 179 fewer names in the last spring directory than in last September's edition.

Your Newsboy—

STUART SHANNON

14-year-old Stuart Shannon, 1110 Wade St., is another of the personable Evening Times delivery boys who serves readers on Plan 12.

An eighth grade student at Franklin Junior high school, Stuart says his favorite studies are mathematics and shop work.

Stuart tells us that many of his free hours are spent tinkering with automobile machinery.

The sports he likes best, he says, are football and basketball.

Freedom Airman Made Mercy Flight

Second Lieut. Robert H. Brandt, Jr., of Freedom, a navigator on a B-17 Flying Fortress of the 96th Bombardment Group flew on the initial Eighth Air Force "mercy mission" to the marooned Dutch civilians when Fortresses loaded with food supplies went in at tree top level to drop their life saving cargo on Ypenburgh airfield, south east of the Hague.

Lieut. Brandt's Fortress had a specially equipped bomb bay which ordnance and armament soldiers loaded with crates of food instead of explosives. Skimming over the North Sea the Forts dodged church steeples in the Hague area to "bomb" the waiting civilians who were perched atop houses and dikes waving the fliers on.

The veteran 96th Bomb. Group has flown more than 320 high altitude bombing attacks on Germanys' war industries and military installations in two years of combat flying. The group was cited by the President for its bombing of Focke Wulf aircraft plants at Posen, Poland. It is a unit of Third Air Division, itself cited by the President for its historic England to Africa shuttle bombing of Messerschmitt plane plants at Regensburg, Germany, in August, 1943.

A student before entering the Army Air Forces in February, 1943, Lieut. Brandt received his navigator's wings at Selman Field in November, 1944. He is the son of Mr. and Mrs. Robert H. Brandt, Sr., R. D. 1, Freedom.

More than 10,000 acres on battle-scarred islands in the Pacific have been planted in vegetable gardens to help supply the armed forces.

CHICAGO, June 4.—(UP)—Eggs, fish and grain products will be the main foods for U. S. civilians the rest of this year.

A United Press survey based on government and private sources show that pork and beef will be luxuries. Chicken will be only a little more abundant. Sugar will be available only for necessary uses—such as sweetening coffee, tea and cereals. And butter is rapidly approaching the status of a museum piece.

Chicken to some extent will help alleviate the meat shortage. But the Farm Bureau Federation said chicken raisers can't get enough feed. The Federation said the government would not grant needed manpower priorities to feed producers.

Main items on the family table, the government reported, will be: eggs, fluid milk, skim milk by-products, fresh and frozen fish, and grain products, with the [illegible]ception of rice in some areas.

Add to these items fresh vegetables from truck farms and victory gardens and the nation will [illegible] a well-balanced, if plain, diet.

Shortages of pork and beef are giving the housewife her biggest headache. Hog growers last fall followed the government's request to cut back production. But they reduced production by 40 per cent, leaving a big gap in the meat markets.

Housewives turned to beek to make up for the pork shortage. In a few weeks the beef supply had dwindled alarmingly. In many communities market owners and clerks had nothing to do.

Although output of beef and veal is expected to set a new record this year, less is finding its way into civilian homes.

The overall meat picture reflects the 30 per cent drop in pork [illegible]. Meat production in 1945, according to the government, will run approximately nine per cent less than last year. Civilian meat supplies will average 120 pounds per person for the whole year. For a family of three this will mean 360 pounds of meat, or less than a pound a day.

VET'S FARM LOANS DISCUSSED BY REGIONAL FARM SECURITY BOARD

A new $25,000,000 federal loan program exclusively for veterans was discussed recently by state directors of the Regional Farm Security administration in a two day session at Upper Darby, Pa.

The loans are a special extension of the Bankhead-Jones Farm Tenant Act, for which Congress has earmarked $25,000,000, Regional FSA Director J. H. Wood announced.

Wood said the loans will be made only to men with satisfactory farm training and experience who cannot secure the type of credit they require through any other sources. The administration's 220 local Farm Security Offices in the 11 northeastern states from Maine to Maryland will begin accepting applications July 1.

Under the Bankhead-Jones Act, 40-year, three per cent loans for the entire cost of a family type farm and necessary repairs can be made to men whose experience, character and ability indicate they will be able to manage and operate their own enterprises successfully, it was explained. More than 40,000 American farmers have secured these loans since the legislation was enacted seven years ago.

Big Housecleaning

CHICAGO (UP)—The new owners of Chicago's Congress hotel have what might be the biggest of all spring housecleaning jobs. They have started decorating and equipping the 1,000 rooms in the hotel—with no priorities on manpower or equipment.

Local GI Wins 'Boots And Wings'

Pvt. John T. Davidson, husband of Mrs. John T. Davidson, 108 Orchard St., has won the right to wear the "Boots and Wings" of the United States Army Parachute Corps. He has completed four weeks of jump training during which time he made five jumps, the last a tactical jump at night involving a combat problem on landing.

Jumping at the Parachute School has steadily developed to a recognized war science. American Paratroopers have been recognized throughout the world for their meritorious actions against the enemy.

In addition to producing jumpers, Parachute Specialist Training is given to qualified men in Communications, Demolition, Riggers and Parachute Maintenance, vital skills for Airborne Troops.

Wrap And Tie Frock

9035
SIZES 12-20

The sensational new wrap-and-tie frock, Pattern 9035, that's a beginner's dream for easy sewing. No armhole or side seams. . . just wrap, button and tie trimly at waist.

Pattern 9035 comes in sizes 12, 14, 16, 18 and 20. Size 16 takes 3⅜ yds. 39-inch fabric.

Send **Twenty cents** in coins for this pattern to Evening Times Pattern Dept., 232 West 18th St., New York 11, N. Y. Print plainly **size, name, address, style number.**

JUST OUT! The Marian Martin Summer Pattern Book, a collection of all that's new and smart in wearing apparel for the family. FREE Nightgown Pattern printed in book. Send Fifteen Cents for your copy.

CONTACT SOCIAL SECURITY BOARD, WORKERS OVER 65 URGED HERE

With cut-backs in ship and plane construction now being felt in some areas, James E. Marquis, manager of the Social Security Board Office in Ambridge urged all men and women over 65, who have been employed in offices, factories, shops or other places of business or industry to contact the nearest Social Security Board field office, whether or not they intend to retire.

"Suppose, for instance," Mr. Marquis said, "a worker 65 or older, who has worked long enough under the social security program to be fully insured, is laid off because of a cut-back in his employer's work, or his wages are reduced, or he becomes ill, it would be to his advantage to file immediately for retirement benefits. It might be several months before the unemployed or ill worker over 65 becomes re-employed, and if he does not apply immediately, he may lose several months of old-age and survivors insurance. Retirement benefits are not retroactive."

If a wife of a beneficiary is over 65, she too should make application for monthly retirement benefits when her husband files, Mr. Marquis added. Monthly benefits are due her and to any qualified children under 18, if they are dependent on their parents.

Federal old-age and suvivors insurance is not the same thing as State unemployment insurance benefits, Mr. Marquis explained. Unemployment insurance benefits come to the qualified worker from the State Unemployment Insurance Agency. Old-age benefits come to an insured worker 65 and over under the old-age and survivors insurance program. In both cases applications must be filed.

To make sure that a worker 65 or over gets all the retirement benefits that he may be entitled to, he should get in touch with the nearest Social Security Board office. The office which services Beaver County is located at 811 Merchant Street, Ambridge, Pa.

NEW POPS GET A BREAK

EVANSVILLE, Ind. (UP) — In the Deaconess hospital, both fathers and grandmothers-to-be have special accommodations on the maternity floor. A fathers' lounge and a grandmothers' lounge were built far away from the rest of the hospital so their pacing and worry wouldn't disturb the new mothers and nurses

More than 5,000 commercial fishermen caught a total of 14,460,000 pounds of fish in the upper Mississippi last year. The catch was valued at $1,073,200.

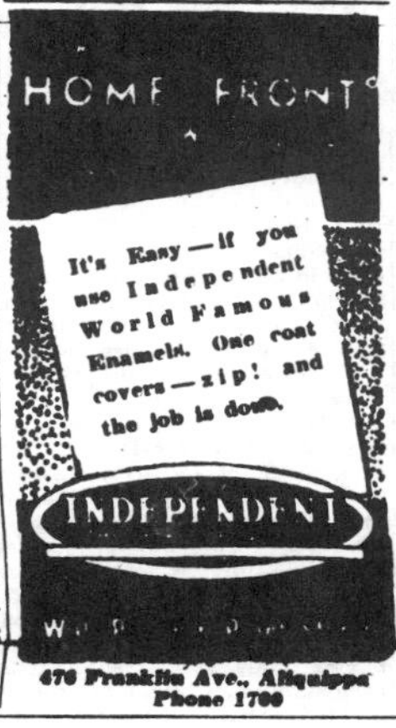
HOME FRONT
It's Easy—if you use Independent World Famous Enamels. One coat covers—zip! and the job is done.
INDEPENDENT
476 Franklin Ave., Aliquippa
Phone 1700

Yes, Dunhill Lighters $1.00
dunhill SERVICE LIGHTER
They're the famous Service Lighters that Dunhill designed for servicemen. Streamlined, windproof, hold a long supply of fuel. A Dunhill wartime achievement at $1.00.
We have them now— come in and get yours.
Eger's
LEADING JEWELER

Unfaltering Service Always
DAY or NIGHT
AMBULANCE SERVICE

MILK FOR HEALTH
HOMOGENIZED
SUTHERLAND'S MILK
PHONE 707

KNOW
It's the RIGHT HOME LOAN for YOU!
FINANCE with SPECIALISTS!
for low total-cost financing—
VISIT
Monaca Federal

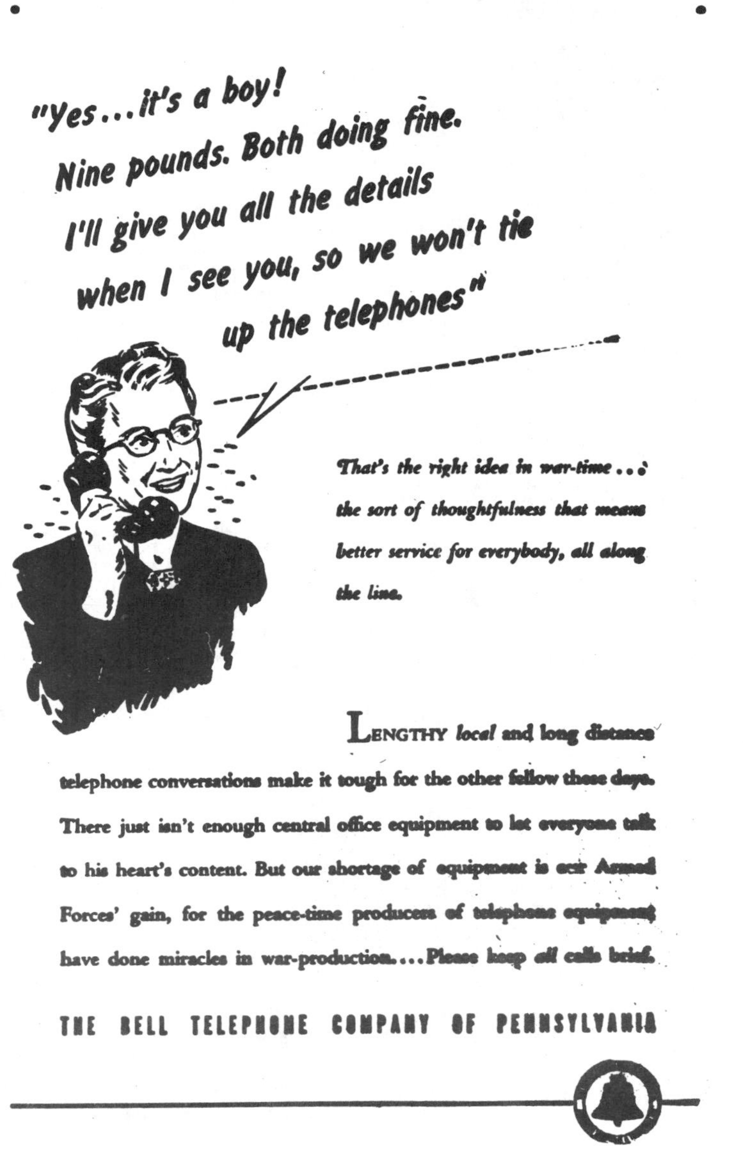
"yes... it's a boy!
Nine pounds. Both doing fine.
I'll give you all the details
when I see you, so we won't tie
up the telephones"
That's the right idea in war-time... the sort of thoughtfulness that means better service for everybody, all along the line.
LENGTHY local and long distance telephone conversations make it tough for the other fellow these days. There just isn't enough central office equipment to let everyone talk to his heart's content. But our shortage of equipment is our Armed Forces' gain, for the peace-time producers of telephone equipment have done miracles in war-production.... Please keep all calls brief.
THE BELL TELEPHONE COMPANY OF PENNSYLVANIA

Appeal Sounded For 6,000 Men

Redeployment Of Troops Threatened

A shortage of experienced cooks, butchers and other members of ship steward departments today seriously threatens to disrupt redeployment of troops home and to the South Pacifific. In renewing a nation-wide appeal for 6,000 immediately-needed men, the War Shipping Administration today disclosed that unless this quota is met homeward-bound soldiers will be delayed.

Despite intensive WSA recruiting drives through regular channels, Craig Vincent, Atlantic Coast WSA Recruiting and Manning Director declared the response had fallen short of requirements, complicated by the following:

1. Manning of 206 Liberty ships and 100 Victory ships converted to carry troops. This cnversion alone boosts steward's department complements from 12 to 28 aboard Libertys and from 15 to 45 on Victorys.

2. The rush job of redeployment has added an additional load on the normal recruiting of men for more than 4,000 WSA controlled vessels and for about 400 still to be launched this year.

3. Of the additional 6,000 men called for, 4,000 are immediately needed for ships along the Atlantic seaboard, where normally only 5,000 steward's department recruits are required annually.

4. The WSA planned "furlough-style" shipboard feeding of millions of troops.

Children's Home Gets $793.07

G. Harold Wagner, auditor general of Pennsylvania, has approved payment of $793.07 to the Beaver County Children's Home, New Brighton, for the quarter ending May 31, 1945.

The funds were appropriated by the Legislature for general maintenance.

Jiff-Made Mats

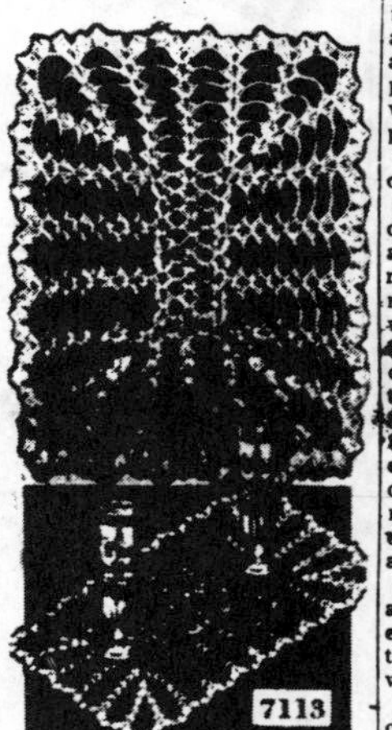
7113

By Alice Brooks

Dainty crocheted mats add so much to gracious living . . . save so much labor in laundering, too. Scarf may be made in any desired length.

Jiffy-made mats and scarfs are these in the easy shell-stitch. Useful and decorative, and take little thread. Pattern 7113 has directions.

Send **FIFTEEN CENTS** in coins for this pattern to The Evening Times, Household Arts., Dept., 259 W. 14th St., New York 11, N. Y. Print plainly **NAME, ADDRESS and PATTERN NUMBER.**

Just out! Send fifteen cents more for our NEW 1945 Needlework Book—94 illustrations of designs; crocheting, knitting, embroidery, dolls, other toys, home decoration. Free Pattern for two crocheted handbags printed right in the book.

BROTHERS SERVING U. S. ABROAD IN DIFFERENT FIGHTING UNITS

Two former Plan 12 boys, James and Kenneth Shoemaker who lived here for many years with their parents, Mr. and Mrs. Charles Shoemaker, Main St., are both serving Uncle Sam in different branches of the armed service and both on foreign assignments.

With the U.S. Navy in the South Pacific where he has participated in several major battles is Petty Officer First Class James Shoemaker, husband of the former Eleanore Campbell of Leetsdale; who is on duty aboard a U.S. destroyer.

A veteran of the invasions of France, Belgium, Luxembourg and Germany, Pfc. Kenneth Shoemaker, whose little daughter, Dianne, resides at Confluence, Pa., with his wife, the former Mary Parnell, is somewhere in Germany where he has served for nearly a year with a U.S. Tank Destroyer Battalion.

Bluejacket Shoemaker, former department manager for the Sears-Roebuck Co. at Ambridge and a graduate of St. Veronica's High school there, enlisted in the Navy more than three years ago.

Pfc. Kenneth entered the armed service 30 months ago while employed here by the Jones and Laughlin Steel Corp.

Their parents left last August for the West Coast and have permanently located at Chula Vista, Cal.

PFC. KENNETH SHOEMAKER

Legion Lists GI Bill Tips

The American Legion Auxiliary presents the following information based on the GI Bill of Rights for the benefit of returning veterans:

Q. Are Veterans of World War II entitled to burial benefits?

A. Yes, on the same basis as veterans of World War I.

Q. In the event of death in Service or after Service, as a direct result of a service connected disability, will a veteran's wife and children receive a pension?

A. If he has been granted service connection for a disability, disease or injury and death results from that disability, his widow and children under 18 years of age will be entitled to receive the pension until the age of 21 provided they are attending an approved institution of learning.

Q. How much will they receive?

A. A veteran's widow and children of World War II, who dies as a result of his service incurred disability, receives the same rates as those for World War I veterans. The widow receives $50.00 monthly; widow with one child, $65.00; $13.00 each additional child. No widow, one child, $25.00; no widow, two children $38.00, equally divided; $10:00 each additional child, total equally divided. Department father and mother, $45.00 or both $25.00 each, total not to exceed $100.00, as to widow and children.

Q. Would a veteran's mother and father, or both of them, be entitled to death pension in addition to the amounts payable to his wife and children?

A. Yes, if the veteran's parents can show that they were dependent on him, they would each be entitled to $25.00 mtonthly, or if only one parent, $45.00 monthly.

Conway GI Back From Pacific

Marine Cpl. John Todorczuk, 29, of Conway, recently arrived in the United States after serving 17 months in the Pacific. He will soon return home on a 30-day furlough.

Cpl. Todorczuk enlisted in the Marine Corps on November 17, 1942, at Pittsburgh. He saw action during the campaigns on Marshall Islands, Saipan, Tinian and Iwo Jima.

He was awarded the Purple Heart for wounds received in action on Saipan. He also wears the Presidential Unit Citation given the Fourth Marine Division.

Prior to his enlistment in the Marine Corps, Cpl. Todorczuk was employed as a steam derrick operator by the Pennsylvania Railpany.

He is the son of Mrs. Mary Todorczuk, 110 Ninth St.

BUY MORE BONDS TODAY

Geneva Offers Music Courses

During the present Geneva college summer session music of interest to academic students, professional students, and senior and junior high school students is offered. This is an opportunity for those interested in developing their talent in voice, piano, or violin.

For the beginners, Miss Elizabeth Johnston has a fine group now taking piano lessons. Ewart Reagan, of Pittsburgh, has an interesting group in advanced piano, including some of the outstanding piano students of the Valley. Andrew Calhoon is giving both individual and group lessons in violin.

Special work in voice, both individual and in groups of three, is offered by Miss Laura Jean Rice, who has charge of the Summer Session Music Program. Miss Rice, a former Geneva College music instructor, is well prepared to offer vocal lessons and will be glad to make appointments with those interested in improving their vocal talents. Group vocal lessons have the advantages, first of all, of being economical, and secondly, in that each member of the group of three may profit by the instruction and criticism given other members of the group.

A class in Music Appreciation and one in Public School Music will be offered during the second 4½ weeks of the summer session beginning July 12. One will also have the opportunity to enroll in in a rather lare number of other courses starting at that time. The College will welcome inquiries either by phone or letter.

Indiantown Gap, Officers Lauded

Major General Milton G. Baker, commanding general of the Pennsylvania Guard, today praised the facilities of the Indiantown Gap Military Reservation and the whole-hearted co-operation of its officers during the Guard's annual training period.

The 6,000 members of the Guard were assembled for the first time this year on a Division basis.

"Our assemblage on a Division basis," General Baker said, "Presented a greater problem for Brig. Gen. Malcolm F. Lindsey, the Commanding General of Indiantown Gap, in provding facilities for our training. He and his staff however, did a magnificient job and placed at our disposal everything the was needed for one of the most satisfactory training periods in the Guard's history."

General Baker pointed out that the training program this year was more elaborate than in the past.

The first telegraph line in the United States was constructed between Washington and Baltimore, Md.

Today's Pattern

9150
SIZES 34-50

Soft, feminine scallops impart 9150 is smart in any fabric; especially dainty in sheer cottons or cool rayons. Choice of 3 sleeve lengths.

Pattern 9150 comes in size 34, 36, 38, 40, 42, 44, 46, 48 and 50. Size 36 takes 2⅞ yards 30-inch fabric.

Send Twenty cents in coins for this pattern to Evening Times, Pattern Dept., 232 West 18th St., New York 11, N. Y. Print plainly size, name, address, style number.

JUST OUT! The Marian Martin Summer Pattern Book, a collection of all that's new and smart in wearing apparel for the family. FREE Nightgown Pattern printed in book. Send Fifteen Cents for your copy.

IN TRAINING

ANDREW RUPNICK

Andrew Rupnick, of 2809 Maple Ave., Aliquippa, is now in Merchant Marine training at the U.S. Maritime Service Training Station, Sheepshead Bay, N. Y., after having enlisted at the district Enrolling Office in Pittsburgh.

After an intensive course of first aid, seamanship, sea safety, physical training and nomenclature, he will be assigned to one of the ships of our great Merchant Marine. Men from 17 to 50½ are urgently needed to man ships carrying vital supplies from Europe to Pacific theatres of operation.

Rupnick is the son of Mr. and Mrs. John Rupnick. He attended Hopewell High School and prior to his enlisting worked for the National Electric Prod. Corp.

Navy Lists New Program For '17s'

The Navy today announced a new class for 17-year-old boys to enter the naval aviation preparatory training program on November 1, 1945, according to Commander C. McK. Lynch, USN (Ret.), Director, Office of Naval Officer Procurement, Keystone Hotel, Pittsburgh.

To qualify, young men can be enlisted during July, August, September and October provided such enlistment can be affected before they attain their 18th birthday. Former members of the Army Air Corps enlisted reserve on inactive duty are also eligible except that they must present a discharge from the Army before they can be enlisted. Eighteen-year-olds of this group must be enlisted within 15 days following their discharge from the Army.

All applicants must have been graduated from high school on or before October 1, 1945, or be in attendance at an accredited college or university. War diplomas from accredited high school will be accepted. It is desirable that candidates have had two years of high school mathematics, preferably elementary algebra and plain goemetry, and it is further desirable that candidates have had one year of high-school physics and a course in high-school trigonometry.

Local Soldier Cited In Pacific

Pfc. W. A. Tilly In Philippines

Pfc. William A. Tilly, son of Mr. and Mrs. Sam Tilly, of 1307 Irwin St., here, has earned the Phillippine Liberation Ribbon and a second battle star for his service in the Philippines.

Tilly is assigned to the 43rd Engineer Construction Battalion, one of the oldest engineer units in the Philippines.

Joining the Army Oct. 15, 1943, he embarked overseas July 8, 1944. In March he was promoted from private to private first class.

He holds the Good Conduct Medal and the Asiatic-Pacific Theatre Ribbon. He is entitled to wear also a Unit Presidential Citation Ribbon and a Meritorious Service Plaque, awarded to the 43rd Engrs. for its outstanding work in the Papuan and Dutch East Indies campaigns.

Tilly's wire lives at the same same address as his parents. He has a brother serving in the cavalry in France.

After attending Aliquippa High School, he worked as a pipe fitter and plumber for the Jones and Laughlin Steel Corp.

ALIQUPPAN WINS SILVER WINGS, APPOINTED FLYING OFFICER

Among the young "hell from heaven" men who won [illegible] wings June 27 at the Big Spring, Tex., Bombardier school was [illegible] Officer Leon F. Block, 19, of Aliquippa, who graduated [illegible] 126 and received his appointment as a flying officer in the [illegible] Forces.

F. O. LEON F. BLOCK

He is the son of Mr. and Mrs. Meyer Block, 402 Franklin Ave. A graduate of Aliquippa high school in 1943, F./O. Block also attended Riverside Military Academy in Gainsville, Ga., for a year before entering military service in 1944.

He is one of 16 Pennsylvania youths to graduate in this class at the Big Spring school, one of the largest in the AAF Training Command.

Already skilled aerial gunners before their training at Big Spring, these men have been thoroughly schooled in the use of the famous Norden bombsight and have mastered the art of precision bombing as well as the principles of dead reckoning and pilotage navigation. They are the real triple-threat airmen, these young bombardier-navigators.

Upon graduation these new Army Air Forces officers wear the silver wings of the rated bombardier. They have received the best training in the world and now leave the AAF Training Command, each to become that member of the combat crew known as the "hell from heaven" man.

The Chicago water system is one of the oldest, largest and most successful business enterprises in the world, representing an investment of over $184,800,000.

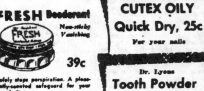

Weather Forecast
Western Pennsylvania: Moderately cool tonight and Thursday.

THE DAILY TIMES

1874—and WESTERN ARGUS—1863

ROCHESTER - BEAVER - MONACA - FREEDOM - BRIDGEWATER - CONWAY - VANPORT - MIDLAND

War History
British and French troops advanced three miles in a new Allied offensive at Amiens, August 8, 1918.

Established April 2, 1874 | Beaver and Rochester, Pa., Wednesday, August 8, 1945 | Single Copy 4 Cents — 24 Cents A Week

ATOM BOMB WRECKS HOROSHIMA

TRUMAN HOME, TO REPORT ON BIG 3 PARLEY

President To Report To Nation By Radio Thursday Evening On Potsdam Conference; Faces Pressing Problems

WASHINGTON, Aug. 8 (UP)—President Truman, back home after a historic 10,000 mile trip to Europe, devoted his full attention today to accumulated matters of state and his forthcoming report to the nation on the Potsdam conference.

The President will report to the nation on the Big Three conference Thursday evening at 10 o'clock. The White House said the address would be broadcast on all radio networks. Presidential Secretary Charles G. Ross said Mr. Truman would make a 30-minute address.

He scheduled no appointments for his first day back at the White House, planning to spend his time catching up with paper work and to put finishing touches on his address.

The President usually prefers short speeches. But he decided on a half hour address in this instance because of the momentous developments in the month he was away from the White House—the Potsdam conference, the surrender ultimatum to Japan and finally, the unveiling of the destructive new atomic bomb.

MAY WARN JAPS AGAIN

There was sharp speculation that the President might take occasion in his speech to warn Japan again that it must surrender now or see the entire country suffer the fate of Hiroshima.

In first announcing the existence of the bomb two days ago, Mr. Truman said that he would ask Congress to establish a commission to control the production and use of atomic power and that he would make recommendations himself on its employment.

The cruiser Augusta, which carried the President's party to and from Europe, docked at Newport News, Va., shortly before 5 o'clock yesterday afternoon. A special train awaited the President there and less than six hours later he was back in the White House.

He was met there by members of the cabinet and conferred with them briefly. A cabinet meeting was called for Friday.

FACES PROBLEMS

Awaiting the President were numerous pressing home front problems, most of them dealing with reconversion and preparation for peace.

The Senate war investigating committee, once known as the Truman committee, hopes to call on the President this week to urge that the Office of War Mobilization and Reconversion be given fuller authority over war agencies. The committee believes that lack of central control has muddled reconversion and threatens the country with mass unemployment in case of a sudden Japanese collapse.

The President also will be asked to support committee demands that the Army discharge experienced coal miners and railroad workers to keep the domestic economy going.

This is directly linked with other congressional requests that the Army reduce its size down to around 4,000,000 on grounds there is no need for the present strength of 7,000,000.

Senators also are looking to Mr. Truman to take the lead in promoting a definite full employment program for the post-war era.

Two Local Men Are Discharged By Army

Pfc. James E. Phillips, Harvey Run road, Freedom, and Pfc. Joseph F. Seman, Fourth street, Beaver Falls, were discharged from the Army Tuesday at Indiantown Gap.

The following twenty Beaver county soldiers arrived for redeployment and were to be given furloughs before reassignment:

T/4 James H. Davidson, Unionville; Pfc. John Danish, Conway; Cpl. Harry Nudi, Freedom; Cpl. John J. Grabner, Jr., and Pfc. Ford D. Weber, Rochester; Cpl. Theodore E. Braun, near Beaver, and T/5 Victor M. Rhodes, Beaver.

T/4 George H. Moore and Cpl. Blair E. Black, New Brighton; Sgt. George A. Foester, near Beaver Falls; T/5 George Firkaly and T/Sgt. Elmer R. Evanko, Ambridge; T/5 Fred R. McDowell, near Aliquippa, and six Aliquippa men, T/5 Steve Kulha, S/Sgt. Matthew J. Shetok, T/Sgt. Joseph Tisak, T/5 John J. Kuzma, T/5 George W. Walker and Pfc. Mike Guraly.

Lost And Found

Duquesne Light Sets Up Emergency Radio Network

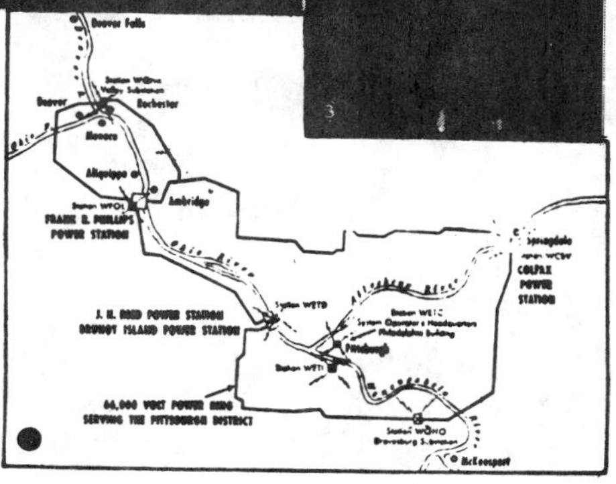
J. H. REED POWER STATION
BRUNOT ISLAND POWER STATION
66,000 VOLT POWER RING
SERVING THE PITTSBURGH DISTRICT
Station WQHO
Dravosburg Substation
McKeesport

1.—Serviceman Edward H. Klein of the Central Division, Distribution Department, Duquesne Light Company, using the 2-way radio unit in his truck for communication with his division office.

2.—Warren R. McMillen, dispatcher, Eastern Division, using his remote control of Station WQHO at Dravosburg Substation to dispatch an emergency trouble call to a mobile unit.

3.—The 175 ft.-high radio antenna tower at Station WQHR Valley Substation, near Rochester.

4.—Strategically located throughout Allegheny and Beaver Counties are the seven 2-way transmitting and receiving stations of the Duquesne Light Company shown on the above map. This emergency radio network was placed in operation to assure thousands of residential, commercial, and industrial electric customers the best possible electric service at all times. These stations, along with a number of trucks equipped with 2-way transmitting and receiving units, provide the company and its various operating divisions with additional communication links which it can utilize for emergency purposes when land telephone facilities are not available, or are temporarily disrupted or inadequate. It gives the company's System Operator, and its substations and Distribution Departments a fast, dependable and efficient communication system necessary during emergencies if electric service is to be quickly restored.

One Of Seven 2-Way Stations Located Near Rochester

To assure a fast, dependable and efficient system of communication during emergencies when land telephone facilities prove inadequate or are disrupted — and through this, to provide thousands of residential, commercial, and industrial customers with the best possible electric service during emergencies—the Duquesne Light Company has placed in operation an emergency radio communication system, E. C. Stone, vice president and general manager of the company, announced today.

This radio network covers the entire area served by the company (Allegheny and Beaver counties), and is in readiness at all times to supplement land telephone facilities in any part or all of the area, and to provide whatever communication might be necessary.

The radio network is comprised of seven 2-way radio transmitting and receiving stations, strategically located throughout the Duquesne Light Company territory, and a fleet of 2-way units installed in company trucks assigned to five operating divisions. All of the transmitting equipment is of the FM type, which pro-

Continued on Page Eight

Yugoslavia Moving To Left As Tito Seeks To Oust King

BELGRADE, Aug. 8. (UP)—Yugoslavia awaited King Peter's reaction today to Marshal Tito's declaration yesterday that the monarchy must give way to a liberal Republican government.

There was no immediate reply from the boy king, who is in London and who has steadfastly refused to surrender his claim to Yugoslavia's throne.

Tito, in a dramatic 25-minute speech to 1,100 tumultuously cheering delegates in the concluding session of the national liberation front, said:

"The monarchy is incompatible with democratic Yugoslavia. It is an out-moded, tyrannical institution that has been rejected by the vast majority of our people."

Tito urged that not only Peter, but all "reactionary em-

Continued on Page Four

Four County Men In Lists Of Casualties

The War Department released today the names of one Ambridge soldier who was killed in action and another who was wounded, both in the Pacific area. Pvt. Steve Pastyroryk was killed, and T/5 John Fetchin was wounded. The Navy department reported that two Ambridge Marines, Cpl. Noris McDonald Cook and Pfc. Charles Pukach, had been wounded in action. In all cases next of kin were notified previously.

TO WITHDRAW TROOPS

LONDON, Aug. 8. (UP)—Brig. Gen. E. F. Koenig, retiring commander of the United States Army's United Kingdom Base Section, said today that American forces will be "practically" withdrawn form Britain by next February 1. Approximately 175,000 U. S. troops, including 96,000 Air Forces personnel, remain in Britain.

Auto Industry To Spend Huge Sum For Expanding Plants

WASHINGTON, Aug. 8 (UP)—The War Production Board shortly will approve plans by the automobile industry to spend $150,000,000 for new plants and additions necessary for maximum production of civilian cars, it was learned today.

A high WPB official told the United Press that notification of the approval probably will go out to the industry some time next week.

He explained that the construction applications would be okayed on grounds the expansion program would provide for "additional insurance against unemployment next year."

Requests for construction authority have flowed in a steady stream to the WPB since it met with the automobile industry last July 11 and asked for prompt no-

Continued on Page Four

NEW PLANNING COMMISSION TO BE IMPORTANT FACTOR IN POST-WAR LIFE OF BEAVER COUNTY

(EDITOR'S NOTE: This is the first of two articles prepared by the Beaver County Planning Commission to acquaint the public with the basic purpose, principles and practices of community self-appraisal and development programing.)

POWERS AND PROCEDURES

Cities, boroughs and first class townships in Pennsylvania have had legislated planning and zoning authority for many years. Machinery for state planning, including the creation of a State Planning board with specified powers and duties, was set up by the State Legislature in 1936.

The 1937 State Legislature completed the picture of planning by extending planning and zoning powers to counties from the second to eighth classes, inclusive, to groups of counties or municipalities or individual corporations working through joint or regional commissions, and to townships of the second class, for zoning, only.

The Beaver County commissioners, after months of consideration and consultation with various interests throughout the county, adopted a resolution on May 19, 1945, establishing the Beaver County Planning Commission. The organization meeting of this commission was held June 6. The commissioners adopted a resolution dealing with zoning, and established the planning commission as the zoning commission for Beaver county in a resolution dated July 13.

The appointment of a planning and zoning commission for Beaver county is very timely. Indications are that the post-war period will bring great expansions both in industrial and residential building as soon as the green light is obtained from governmental agencies. During this development period the need for an over-all planning agency will be

Continued on Page Four

TOKYO PLANTS, YAWATA STEEL MILLS BOMBED

Aircraft Plant And Arsenal In Tokyo Blasted In Daylight Following Attack On Steel Center; Other Areas Also Bombed

GUAM, Aug. 8 (UP) — Two fleets of Superforts dropped demolition bombs on the Nakajima Musashino-Tama aircraft plant in Tokyo and on the once mighty Tokyo arsenal in today's second daylight B-29 attack on Japan, Gen. Carl A. Spaatz, commander of the U. S. Strategic Air Forces announced today.

A fleet of about 50 Superforts thundered bombs down on the Nakajima plant this afternoon, following a 1,000-ton daylight demolition raid on the great steel center of Yawata. A smaller force hit the Tokyo arsenal area for the first time since April 14. The Superforts met intense flak but no enemy aircraft.

Bombing on both of this afternoon's raids was visual.

(Radio Tokyo said about 65 Superforts raided the Tokyo district this afternoon, and that two were shot down, and 10 others heavily damaged "by Japanese interception.")

Nearly 100 Superfortresses, hitting the Japanese home islands for the fourth time in 24 hours, sent incendiaries crashing into the "death list" city of Fukuyama shortly before midnight yesterday, it was announced today.

AIRFIELDS HIT

While the bulk of the afternoon force of 65 B-29s attacked factories near Tanashi, Radio Tokyo said, the remainder feinted toward the Boso area and dropped a few bombs on Eastern Tokyo.

Still another force of 30 Superfortresses and 70 Mustangs and Thunderbolts attacked airfields and communications throughout the Central Army command area on the main Japanese home islands of Honshu, Radio Tokyo said.

More than 225 Superfortresses set fire to Yawata, the Pittsburgh of Japan, with demolition bombs in the morning attack.

Preliminary reports on the Yawata attack indicated it was so successful that the great steel center could be scratched from the list of Japanese cities doomed to destruction by the Superfortress command.

Large conflagrations were left burning among such major war plants as the Japan Iron and Steel Works, the Kokura Steel Company, Hitachi, Ltd., the Nippon Synthetic Industry and the Yasukawa Company.

P-47 Thunderbolts from Okinawa escorted the big bombers to Yawata, which lies at the north-

Continued on Page Four

Men 18 To 30 Now Deferred Face Draft

WASHINGTON, Aug. 8. (UP)—Selective Service warned today that greater numbers of men between 18 and 30 previously deferred for essential work will have to be drafted into the Armed Forces.

A report to the House military affairs committee said there was not a sufficient number of young men becoming 18 years of age each month to meet induction quotas.

Rep. John J. Sparkman, D., Ala., who received the report for the committee, said it also may mean that an additional number of men above 30 years of age will have to be drafted.

The report did not specify what occupational groups would be in line for induction. But it said that the 18 to 30 year deferred group included 65,000 members of the Merchant Marine, as well as "large numbers of men working in coal mines, railroads, ship repair yards and other essential war activities."

It listed in this group 449,457 who have been deferred to industry and 483,872 who have been deferred to agriculture, most of whom have not had induction physical examinations. The 18 to 30 group also includes 1,000,000 men who have been rejected for military service after taking physical examinations.

Nineteen Killed, Six Missing In Explosion

PORT ARTHUR, Ont., Aug. 8. (UP)—Officials feared today that the death toll in an explosion in a grain elevator may reach 25 after 19 bodies were taken from the wreckage.

Six men were reported missing and believed crushed under box cars which were smashed on tracks.

The explosion, caused by spontaneous combustion yesterday in the Saskatchewan pool elevator No. 5, blew out the four walls of the elevator. Most of the grain valued at $2,000,000 which was stored in the elevator was destroyed. The elevator's loss was estimated at $1,250,000.

Twenty Men To Be Inducted August 15 By Beaver Board

The following twenty registrants have been ordered to report at the Beaver Draft Board office in the Market street school building, at 7 a. m., August 15. They will entrain at the P. and L. E. Railroad station at 7:40 a. m. to go to Pittsburgh for induction:

Robert Leslie Albright, Beaver; Russell Stanley Bable, Darlington; Carl Albert Bashline, Beaver; Herbert Thomas Berbig, Bridgewater; Anthony Samuel Brognano, Racine; John George Czarnecky, New Brighton; Renzo John Ferrario, New Galilee; Clyde Allen Grimes, Beaver; Francis Majcher, Beaver Falls; Lawrence Malkoch, Bridgewater.

David Lyle McCall, Beaver Falls; Frank Lester Orend, Beaver; Jerald Lynne Parker, Darlington; Wilford Francis Pfeifer, Vanport; Raymond Cashious Ralston, Beaver; John Edward Roebuck, Detroit, Mich.; John Gilbert Snowden, Beaver Falls; William Gilleland Thomas, Beaver Falls; Jack Leroy Weir, Beaver Falls; John James Zentiska, Clinton, O.

Frankensteen Leads In Detroit Voting

DETROIT, Aug. 8. (UP)—Richard T. Frankensteen, United Automobile Workers International vice-president, emerged as No. 1 candidate for mayor today in a CIO sweep of yesterday's primary election.

Frankensteen gained one of two mayorality nominations in the non-partisan balloting, leading Mayor Edward J. Jeffries, Jr., and a field of five other contenders.

The powerful CIO registered a heavy labor vote as it backed its first official candidate for a major public office and succeeded in naming three candidates, one a minister, for the city's common council.

Frankensteen, 38-year-old head of CIO organization in the air craft industry, symbolized the union's first direct attempt to win ballot support. As a native of Detroit and a former automobile factory hand, he ran in the CIO's national stronghold. The city counts more than 400,000 dues-paying members.

Meantime, Frankensteen reiterated his statement that there would be "no strings attached" if he took office. He asserted that he would appoint a police commissioner who would not be tied to union labor.

Mulcahy Will Sign Phillies' Contract

NEWTON, Mass., Aug. 8 (UP) Pitcher Hugh Mudcahy, discharged after four and one-half years' Army service, will sign his contract with the Philadelphia Phillies Sunday and report for duty one week later, he disclosed today.

Mulcahy, first major league baseball player to enter the armed forces, made the announcement after talking by telephone with General Manager Herb Pennock of the Phillies. The big right-hander is visiting his parents' home here following his discharge at Fort Devens.

After signing the contract, he said, he will visit his wife and 4-months-old son, Hugh, Jr., at her parents' home in Beaver, Pa. He never has seen his son.

Italian War Relief Drive Planned Here

The Western Pennsylvania Relief for Italy Committee has announced a drive during the month of August to raise funds for the purchase of supplies for the war-torn people of Italy.

Volunteers of Italian descent will canvass Beaver County and funds raised will be converted into relief supplies such as milk, clothing and ambulances. Italians and Americans of Italian descent, along with Italian organizations and business concerns, will be asked to contribute. All funds raised will be sent to Italy through the American Relief for Italy, Inc.

The United War Fund of Allegheny County has approved the drive. The general headquarters will be in the Keystone Hotel, Pittsburgh, under the general chairmanship of Alderman Frank J. Zappala.

Attorney James B. Ceris, Ambridge, who has been appointed chairman for Beaver County for the drive, today stated: "Approximately 27 million people in liberated Italy are now suffering from the hardships of war. This is especially true of the undernourished children, orphans and aged people who are suffering from deprivation and a scarcity of food, clothing and the bare necessities of life."

SAVE THE FATS—Save your kitchen fats. They are needed to make bombs to beat the bums.

Sixty Per Cent Of City Ruined; Thousands Killed

PEARL HARBOR, Aug. 8 (UP)—Tokyo admitted today that America's single atomic bomb had completely destroyed most of Hiroshima leaving "seared" dead and wounded "too numerous to count."

The Japanese, shocked by the ruin, charged that the United States had violated international law by using the atomic explosive.

Radio Tokyo quoted authorized quarters in the capital as saying the United States was violating Article 22 of the Hague convention and showing disregard for humanity.

"The impact of the bomb was so terrific that practically all living things, human and animal, were literally seared to death by the tremendous heat and pressure engendered by the blast," one Japanese broadcast said.

American reconnaissance photographs confirmed that four and one-tenth square miles—60 per cent of the built-up area of Hiroshima had vanished.

Unofficial American sources believed Japanese dead and wounded might exceed 100,000.

Five major war plants and scores of smaller factories, office buildings and dwellings were known to have been levelled. Only a few skeletons of concrete buildings remained in the obliterated area. Additional damage outside the totally-destroyed section still was being assessed.

Radio Tokyo, breaking its silence of more than 60 hours after the raid, said the "indescribable destructive power" of the bomb had crushed big buildings and small dwellings alike in an unparalleled holocaust.

Inhabitants were killed by blast, fire and crumbling buildings, Tokyo said. Most bodies were so badly battered that it was impossible to distinguish between the men and the women.

CITY DEVASTATED

The Japanese, stunned by the destruction of Hiroshima, charged over the Tokyo radio that the United States was violating Article 22 of the Hague convention and showing disregard for humanity by attacking a non-military city with the atomic bomb.

Hiroshima actually was an important quartermaster depot and garrison city for the Japanese army.

"Those outdoors burned to death, while those indoors were killed by the indescribable pressure and heat," Tokyo said. It called the city a "disastrous ruin"

"With houses and buildings crushed, including the emergency medical facilities, the authorities are having their hands full in giving every available relief possible under the circumstances."

Radio Tokyo still referred to the atomic missile as merely a "new-type bomb." It said order gradually was being restored in the stricken city.

JAP CABINET MEETS

The Japanese cabinet was called into a special session at the official residence of Premier Kantaro Suzuki this morning to hear a report from its chief secretary, Hisatune Sekomizu, on the raid, Tokyo said.

The Japanese imperial household ministry announced that Prince Ri Gu, nephew of the head of the former ruling house of Korea, was killed in the raid, while fulfilling his duties as a lieutenant-colonel in the Japanese army.

Gen. Carl A. Spaatz, commander of the American Strategic Air Forces in the Pacific, said reconnaissance photographs revealed that fires touched off by the almost unbelievable heat of the bomb leaped block-wide streams and spread into the outskirts. The city appeared desolate in the photographs.

Strangely, the photographs showed no crater. However, Tokyo had reported that the bomb was dropped by parachute and exploded in the air. It was likely that the entire force of the blast was directed horizontally across the city below.

DEATH TOLL HEAVY

Although the built-up area of Hiroshima came to six and nine-tenths square miles, the city as a whole totalled 12 square miles with a population of 318,000—an average of 26,500 persons per square mile.

Few, if any, of the more than 100,000 persons in the totally devastated four square miles were believed to have escaped death or injury. The blast alone of the atomic bomb could kill persons within a four-mile range, and it was likely that there were many casualties outside the utterly-destroyed section.

Spaatz told newsmen that other Superfortresses were ready to carry more atomic bombs to Japan. Leaflets warning the enemy of his impending doom already were being prepared, he said.

Fukuoka, a city of approximately the same size as Hiroshima, was hit by almost 1,000 tons of bombs dropped by Superfortresses last June 20. The raid burned out one and three-tenths square miles of the city—approximately 20 per cent of it.

The single atomic bomb dropped on Hiroshima wiped out four and one-tenth square miles—69 per cent of the city and damaged a surrounding area.

Atomic Bomb Not To Bring Cut In Size Of U. S. Army

WASHINGTON, Aug. 8 (UP)—The U. S. Army still plans to land on the shores of Japan either with occupational troops or with full-scale invasion forces depending on what the atomic bomb does to the Japanese will and power to go on fighting.

For the Army to plan any other way, high officials believed today, would be to take unjustifiable risks. In the atomic bomb it has the deadliest weapon ever made. But it is just one weapon.

For that reason, the War Department has no intention despite scattered Congressional criticism—to cut the Army below the 7,000,000 men and women which it has felt all along are essential to the conquest of Japan.

Forty-eight hours after the historic announcements proclaiming the dawn of the atomic age, officials felt soberly constrained to point out that the new era has yet to reach its zenith. The new bomb certainly should shorten the Japanese war, they felt, but the only way it can end the conflict abruptly is for the Japanese themselves to decide to quit.

MAY GET NEW CHANCE

This, some observers believed, they will be given a second chance to do before the full fury of atomic bomb assault is unleashed against them. Certainly the Army is ready with plenty of the new bombs.

President Truman, now back from Germany, was thought by some to be considering a second ultimatum following up the surrender-or-be destroyed proclamation issued from Potsdam July 26. Or it may just take the form of more atom bombs. On Monday he reminded the Japanese of the Potsdam ultimatum and invited them, in the light of what the atomic bomb did to Hiroshima, to reconsider their ultimatum.

The alternative, he said, will be a rain of destruction "the like of which has never been seen on earth."

The Japanese military may feel they now have nothing to lose, and that national suicide is as acceptable to them personally as absolute defeat. In that event, it is not inconceivable to observers here that they would choose to drag the nation with them into utter and possibly final destruction.

Allies Agree Upon Control Of Austria

WASHINGTON, Aug. 8 (UP)—The Allies today set up control machinery for Austria similar to the German plan and announced the separation of Austria from Germany as one of their primary objectives.

The plans for four-nation control machinery, and the zones of Austria to be occupied by the United States, Britain, Russia and France, were released simultaneously in the four Allied capitals.

The control machinery provides that the city of Vienna will be directed by an inter-Allied governing authority to be composed of four commandants—one from each Allied nation.

In addition to separation of Austria from Germany, the primary tasks of the commission will be: "To secure establishment of a freely-elected Austrian government."

The Russians proposed at Potsdam that the provisional government headed by Karl Renner—now relegated to just Vienna—be extended to all of Austria. President Truman and the British insisted that the decision be postponed until American and British troops had moved into Vienna.

Highlights Of The War In The Pacific

VALIANT DEFENDERS at Corregidor in the Philippines are herded from their deep cave on the "Rock" after their surrender on May 6, 1942.

WHILE THE JAPS WERE BOASTING of their victories, a daring attack was made on Tokyo on April 18, 1942, under the command of Gen. "Jimmy" Doolittle. One of the bombers is shown taking off from the "Hornet."

THICK SMOKE POURS from the U.S.S. *West Virginia* as she burns at her anchorage after the Jap sneak attack on Pearl Harbor on Dec. 7, 1941. Other American warships also suffered very heavy damage.

MANY JAPS were killed in our campaign to take Saipan—future superfort base—in June, 1944. A bulldozer digs a grave here for the dead.

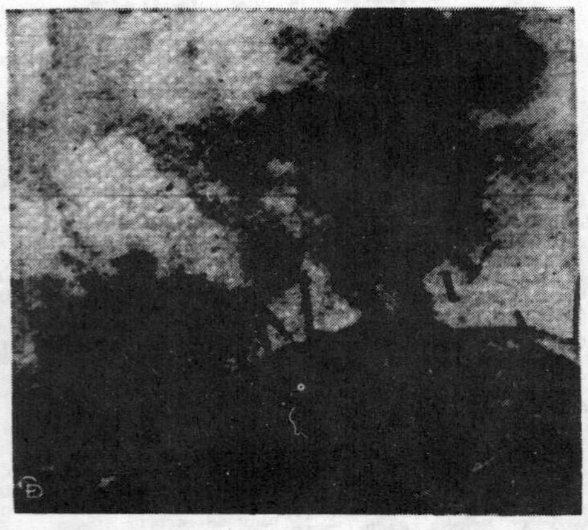

DEBRIS SHOOTS SKYWARD as U. S. Marines blast a Jap pillbox on Tarawa, Nov. 21, 1943. We paid a heavy toll in lives [illegible]

STORMING ASHORE on Guadalcanal on Aug. 7, 1942, U. S. Marines move inland to begin the battle for the first of many Jap-held island bases.

A STINGING DEFEAT was given the Japs in Midway battle, June 4, 1942. This Jap cruiser was one of nine big warships that were destroyed.

RIFLES READY, marines blast Japs from cave hideouts on Okinawa after landing on April 1, 1945. Organized enemy resistance ended June 22.

A HISTORIC MOMENT after the invasion of Iwo Jima, Feb. 19, 1945, as marines raise Old Glory on top of Mt. Suribachi following a bloody battle.

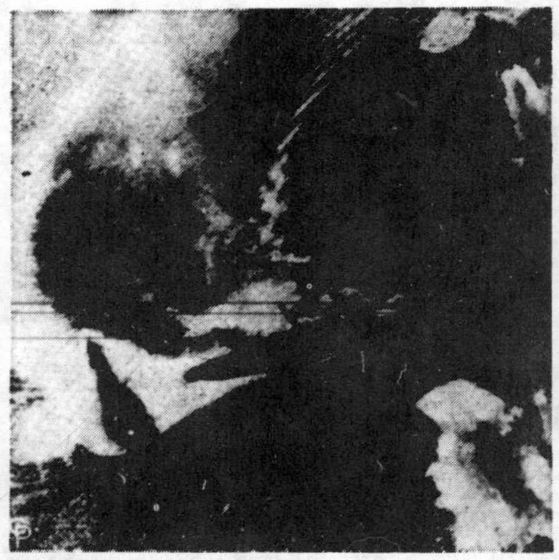

VAINLY TRYING to elude our bombers, one of about 40 enemy warships destroyed in the Philippine Sea in October, 1944, dashes about wildly.

GEN. MacARTHUR keeps his pledge to return to the Philippines. Splashing through the shallow surf, he lands on Leyte on October 20, 1944.

FALSE SURRENDER FLASH SETS OFF CAPITAL CROWDS

[illegible] FLASH that Japan had accepted the Allied surrender terms touched off the premature celebration outside the White House. Thousands of people jammed Pennsylvania avenue in front of the executive mansion and troops were called from nearby military posts to keep order. *(International)*

JAPS TRIED TO GET ATOMIC SECRETS

JAPAN HOPED TO DISCOVER the atomic bomb by [illegible] American secrets of atomic research, it is revealed in a story from the San Francisco Examiner. This picture, copyrighted by the San Francisco Examiner, shows three Japanese scientists who came to Berkeley, Cal., in 1940, for the purpose of learning what American scientists knew about [illegible] atomic energy. Left to right are Drs. [illegible], Yasuda, and Watanabe, all of Tokyo, and Dr. Edward McMillan, University of California physicist who fed them accurate but worthless information. In background is a blueprint of the atom-smashing cyclotron which Japs copied years ago. *(International)*

WHITE HOUSE VIGIL AWAITS JAP SURRENDER REPLY

RADIO, NEWSREEL MEN AND REPORTERS have [illegible] announcement that Jap surrender negotiations were under way. Above, the radio and [illegible] have their equipment set up, ready and waiting for President Truman's announcement that the war in the Pacific is ended. *(International Soundphoto)*

JAPS QUIT

Weather Forecast
Clearing and cooler today. Clear and cooler tonight; Thursday fair and cool.

THE DAILY TIMES
1874—and WESTERN ARGUS—1803
ROCHESTER - BEAVER - MONACA - FREEDOM - BRIDGEWATER - CONWAY - VANPORT - MIDLAND

War History
The Allies were steadily wiping out the German salient between Arras and the Oise river, August 15, 1918.

Established April 2, 1874 | Beaver and Rochester, Pa., Wednesday, August 15, 1945 | Single Copy 4 Cents — 24 Cents A Week

WAR IN PACIFIC OVER!

World Enters Era Of Peace; Long War Ends

WASHINGTON, Aug. 15 (UP)—The world today entered a bright new era of peace in which Gen. Douglas MacArthur summarily ordered Japan to send representatives to Manila to receive Allied surrender terms. He acted as supreme Allied commander.

MacArthur is expected to announce that Japan will sign on her home soil or in territorial waters—perhaps Tokyo Bay.

Radio Tokyo announced resignation of Premier Kantaro Suzuki's war cabinet shortly before MacArthur's order was dispatched. Suzuki's war minister already was a suicide.

American forces were ordered to cease offensive action last night. Tokyo broadcast to Japanese troops at midnight EWT (1 p. m., Wednesday Japanese time) the announcement of agreement to surrender.

MacArthur's message also "directed" the Japanese immediately to cease hostilities.

The victors at home already were on a two-day holiday binge and celebration of the peace—a peace beyond which lie the gravest conceivable dangers of reconstruction. But at long last there is peace in our time.

Italy, Germany and Japan were beaten. The Axis is dead.

President Truman announced Japan's agreement to unconditional surrender last night at 7 o'clock. There arose from the vast homelands of those who love democracy a shout heard 'round the world.

With the consent of the Allies, Mr. Truman named MacArthur supreme commander for the Allied powers. MacArthur, who fled in the night from Corregidor, will receive the surrender. He will command the forces which occupy designated areas in Japan. He will tell the Japanese Emperor what to do and say.

ORDERS SENT TO JAPAN

At the moment Mr. Truman was announcing Japan's surrender agreement and "full acceptance" of Potsdam declaration, Secretary of State James F. Byrnes was dispatching another note to Tokyo. It was handed to the Swiss legation

Continued on page Four

Jap Cabinet Quits; War Minister Ends Life By Hara-Kiri

SAN FRANCISCO, Aug. 15 — (UP)—The Japanese Cabinet resigned today and one member already has committed hara-kiri in the first of what may become a wave of suicides among Japan's beaten war lords.

The official Japanese Domei News Agency said War Minister Gen. Korechika Anami, 58, took his life at his official residence to "atone for his failure in accomplishing his duties as His Majesty's minister."

Domei said Premier Kantaro Suzuki tendered the resignation of his cabinet at 3:20 p. m. Tokyo time (2:20 a. m. EWT) because of "the new situation created by Japanese acceptance of the Potsdam declaration."

Japan's surrender required a new cabinet of men "with fresh

Continued on Page Four

Japanese Planes Attack 3rd Fleet After Surrender

GUAM, Aug. 10 (UP)—Japan sent planes against the Third Fleet today — as late as eight hours after her surrender was announced. At the same time, Tokyo warned Allied warships not to enter Japanese home waters pending an official Japanese "cease fire" order.

Admiral Chester W. Nimitz announced at 4 p. m. Tokyo time—eight hours after he had ordered his Pacific forces to cease offensive operations — that the Third Fleet had shot down five approaching Japanese planes off Honshu since noon.

The five planes—a bomber and four Zero fighters — were shot down during an "abortive enemy assault" that lasted 14 minutes, a fleet dispatch said. The Third Fleet was 110 miles off the Japanese coast at the time.

Nimitz said Gen. Douglas MacArthur, the new supreme Allied commander, had been asked to inform Japan that defense measures required American naval forces to destroy "any Japanese aircraft approaching our dispositions."

Almost simultaneously, Radio Tokyo broadcast that no imperial "cease fire" order had been issued to Japanese forces as yet, though one was expected "soon."

PLANES RECALLED

Nimitz' orders to all forces under his command to cease offensive operations was flashed

Continued on Page Four

Rationing Of Gas, Canned Vegetables, Fuel Oil Lifted

WASHINGTON, Aug. 15 (UP) —Gasoline rationing is ended, the Office of Price Administration announced today.

Nor will canned fruits and vegetables, fuel oil and oil stoves be rationed any longer, OPA said.

Rationing stop orders are effective immediately.

But rationing of meats, fats and oils, butter, sugar, shoes, tires and other commodities will continue indefinitely, OPA said, until military cutbacks and increased production can balance civilian supply and demand.

Price Administrator Chester Bowles said that "right now it's impossible" to say just when all civilian buying restrictions can be ended forever.

Industry, Business At Standstill Here

Streets in Beaver county communities were nearly empty and quiet today as war plants, stores, offices, banks and post offices closed for a one to two-day "Victory Holiday" after Tuesday evening's joyful celebration of the Japanese surrender.

Industry and business were at a standstill here, with war plants scheduled to remain closed today and Thursday while some stores will be closed only today and others both days.

County residents joined the nation in observing the two-day holiday proclaimed by President Truman. Only restaurants and motion picture theaters remained open today [illegible] this evening.

President Truman's and Governor Edward Martin's proclamations of a two-day holiday, today and Thursday, have been accepted by local business men, with the result that most Beaver Valley stores will remain closed until Friday, on which day normal business will be resumed.

V-J Day will come later, and it will not be a holiday. It will be proclaimed after the Japs have signed the surrender papers. The V-J proclamation will be largely a legal matter for the purpose of setting a date for the end of hostilities as required by various laws.

Bars and State liquor stores were closed immediately after the surrender announcement by

Continued on Page Four

Hirohito Blames Atomic Bomb For Defeat Of Japan

SAN FRANCISCO, Aug. 15 — (UP)—Emperor Hirohito, in the first broadcast ever made to his 100,000,000 subjects, said today that the atomic bomb forced Japan to accept the first military defeat in the 2,605 years of her history.

The bespectacled "Son of Heaven," speaking four hours after President Truman announced that the Pacific war was over, said that the atomic bomb, dropped for the first time only nine days before, was "new and cruel."

The Emperor spoke over the Japanese Broadcasting Corporation network at noon Tokyo time (11 p. m. Tuesday EWT). It was the first time, with the exception of a few government and military officials and members of the regal family, that any Japanese had heard the voice of the Emperor.

The Emperor, who soon must place himself under the direct command of Gen. Douglas Mac-

Continued on Page Four

One Injured, No Serious Damage In Celebration Here

One person was injured and a number of minor traffic accidents in which no one was reportedly injured occurred in the county Tuesday night as a result of the victory celebration.

No serious property damage or serious disorder was reported today in any of the Valley towns.

Robert Sheiar, 15, 2002 Fourteenth street, Beaver Falls, was admitted to Providence hospital at 9:30 o'clock Tuesday evening with a fractured leg sustained when the car on which he was riding the front fender, collided with another car at Sixteenth street and Seventh avenue, Beaver Falls.

Police reported four minor motor collisions during the celebration in Ambridge, with no damage resulting. Two torn store awnings were the only property

Continued on Page Four

MacArthur Takes Over Duties As Supreme Leader

MANILA, Aug. 15 (UP)—Gen. Douglas MacArthur, taking over as Allied supreme commander, ordered Japan today to cease hostilities immediately and send a "competent representative" to Manila to receive surrender terms.

MacArthur already has established radio communication with Emperor Hirohito and the Japanese government, a spokesman revealed.

Allied forces throughout the Pacific and Far East will be directed to cease hostilities only after the enemy has complied with similar orders, MacArthur said in a radio message to Tokyo.

Allied forces already have been ordered to cease offensive operations, but no formal order to cease all fire has been issued.

MacArthur ordered that, weather permitting, the Japanese representatives and advisers from the Japanese army, navy and air force fly from the southern tip of Kyushu to an Allied airfield on Ie Island, just west of Okinawa, on Frday between 8 and 11 a. m. Tokyo time (7 and 10 p. m. Thursday EWT).

He directed that Japan, in communicating with him regarding the flight, use the single code word, "Bataan"—a word that recalls MacArthur's worst defeat and one that spurred him to his greatest victory, the liberation of the Philippines.

The Japanese air force adviser accompanying the main surrender delegate must be thoroughly familiar with airdrome facilities in the Tokyo area, MacArthur said. This indicated that a high Allied representative would accompany the enemy delegation back to the Japanese capital.

ORDERS END OF FIGHTING

The order was MacArthur's second of the day to the Japanese. The first, addressed to Hirohito, the imperial government and imperial headquarters, called for cessation of hostilities at the earliest possible moment and asked that a radio station in the Tokyo area be designated for communication with his headquarters.

It was acknowledged within 20 minutes.

MacArthur moved swiftly to force Japan's formal surrender after being notified of his appointment. His office bustled with activity.

He revealed that he would is-

Continued on Page Four

County Wildly Celebrates End Of Pacific War

Beaver county had a gigantic hangover today—a hangover not induced by alcohol but one resulting from the wild and hilarious celebration of the end of the long and bloody war.

It was the greatest spontaneous celebration in the history of the county, the mightiest mass demonstration of delirious, unrestrained happiness and gayety over [illegible] here.

And the joyous celebration continued, but on a greatly reduced scale, today, the first of the two "Victory Holidays" proclaimed by President Truman—with more of the same expected Thursday, the second holiday declared by the President.

Today no one was making any attempt to return to normalcy. And no one cared.

This is it! The end of the war!

Peace!

In contrast to the noisy, teeming traffic and crowded sidewalks of last night, Valley streets were almost deserted this morning as industrial plants, stores, business officies and other places closed in observance of the end of the war.

Climaxing the more or less sporadic celebrating which had started before dawn Tuesday morning when the Tokyo radio flashed word that the Japanese acceptance of the Allied surrender terms was on its way, county residents went stark and raving wild—literally—at 7 o'clock last evening when President Truman announced Japan's full acceptance of the Potsdam Declaration.

Hardly had the President revealed the surrender of the Japanese than bedlam broke loose up and down the entire Beaver and Ohio valleys.

Fire sirens screamed, factory whistles shrieked, steamboat whistles and horns bellowed, automobile horns honked incessantly, guns were fired, children beat on pans and washtubs, men, women and children shouted for joy.

CACOPHONY OF SOUND

With the President's long-awaited announcement of the hoped-for surrender ending the bloodiest and most costly war in the history of the world a mighty cacophony of sound began which roared to a great crescendo through the valleys and over the hills as the evening wore on.

As the [illegible]

Continued on Page Four

Community Peace Services To Be Held In Valley

Although many folk assembled in churches throughout the Valley in the early hours after news of the Japanese surrender was received, to thank God for peace, others will attend services planned for tonight or on the official V-J Day.

ROCHESTER SERVICE

Rochester residents will gather for a union service of thanksgiving at 7:45 o'clock this evening in the Methodist church. Rev. Bernard Fetterly of the Passavant Memorial Homes, will preach and special music will be directed by Dr. John A. M. Stewart, Beaver.

Amid the noise and confusion

Continued on Page Four

LET US GIVE THANKS

Yesterday was the greatest day in the history of the world, the happiest day in the history of all mankind.

Yesterday marked the return to sanity of a world gone mad with killing, bloodshed and destruction.

Yesterday marked the end of the bloodiest, most costly war in the history of the world.

Surrender of the Japanese to the Allies ended a war which took the frightful toll of 55 million dead, wounded and missing, left millions of others homeless and destitute and put other millions behind the barbed wire of prisoner of war and concentration camps.

Acceptance of the terms of the Potsdam Declaration by the Japanese Empire ended a war which began nearly four years ago for the United States, nearly six years

Continued on Page Four

Peacelights In The Valley

Hundreds of pounds of soggy paper of all kinds and sizes littered the streets, sidewalks and doorways of main thoroughfares in Beaver Valley communities today in the wake of last night's wild celebration. Borough employes, storekeepers and other business men face a monumental task in cleaning up the debris left behind by the hilarious celebrants.

His curiosity aroused by the constant honking of passing automobiles, an "over-the-road" truck driver stopped his big tractor and trailer yesterday afternoon in Rochester.

"Is the war over, lady?" he asked a woman nearby.

"It sure is," she replied.

"Nuts to it, then," said the truck driver. "I'm knocking off work right now!"

High on a windy hill, just at dusk last evening, a minister stood in the center of a circle of men and women attending an outdoor church meeting giving thanks to God for the end of the war and praying for future peace—against a background of tooting auto horns and shrieking whistles, while beyond the distant hills a furnace in a mill which had mightily produced steel for the war cast a red glow over the sky.

Youngsters celebrating in Beaver Falls last night spied a truck loaded with cabbage parked in Seventh avenue. Whooping like commandos, the boys swarmed over the truck and began tossing heads of cabbage to passers-by. Within a few minutes the truck was empty.

Oblivious to the swirling traffic, two boys and two girls—carrying two large American flags—blithely marched along Brighton avenue in Rochester in their own little parade at the height of the celebration last evening.

Reckless driving and other violations of traffic laws were rampant last night as automobiles and trucks careened through Valley streets with horns blaring and occupants shouting, blowing horns, playing

Continued on Page Four

Beaver Falls Dollar Clearance Will Take Place On Friday

Dollar Clearance in Beaver Falls, originally planned for tomorrow, will be held Friday. This decision was reached this morning following a meeting of the Retail Committee of the Beaver Falls Board of Trade. Their action was in keeping with the two-day holiday proclamation issued by Governor Edward Martin for observance throughout the state. Today's paper carries the Dollar Clearance advertisements of many stores participating in the semi-annual bargain event. These values, which were to have been on sale Thursday, will be offered Friday, the new official Dollar Clearance. Read the ads tonight, keep your paper handy over Thursday, then plan to shop Friday at Beaver Falls' Dollar Clearance.

Draftees Leave Amid Smiles And Laughter

A marked contrast was noted in the attitudes of the families of selectees and the selectees themselves who left the Rochester Draft Board this morning for induction into the armed forces. Instead of the usual tears and a feeling of utter dejection, the families accompanying the group were waving and smiling as the boys marched sprightly to the Pennsylvania Railroad station.

SURRENDER SIDELIGHTS

PITTSBURGH, Aug. [illegible] —To celebrate [illegible] news, Heidenreich's drug store [illegible] night for the [illegible] 1936. But [illegible] night pharmacist, [illegible] all night, anyway. [illegible] has no lock.

In Philadelphia the [illegible] Bell rang out seven times [illegible] for each letter in the word [illegible] [illegible]ty."

On the day of [illegible] United States learned that [illegible] proud ship Indianapolis, [illegible] ship cruiser, had been [illegible] by a Japanese [illegible] 880 American dead or missing [illegible] 316 wounded. The [illegible] of the Indianapolis' [illegible] not among the dusk-to-dawn celebrants of victory.

WASHINGTON, Aug. 15. (UP) —Sure sign the war is over: A woman walked into a drug store loaded with 21 cartons of popular brand cigarettes.

"I bought these during the shortage," she told the clerk. "And now I'm afraid they'll go stale. Will you buy them back, please?"

The clerk said no, he wouldn't.

WASHINGTON, Aug. 15. (UP) —The date of Japan's final surrender—Aug. 14, 1945—was the fourth anniversary of the signing of the Atlantic Charter.

SAN FRANCISCO, Aug. 15. (UP)—Radio Tokyo broadcast an announcement of Japan's surrender to Japanese troops on the fighting fronts at 1 p. m. Tokyo time today.

LONDON, Aug. 11. (UP)—King George VI, speaking today from the throne at the state opening of Parliament, said that the atomic bomb had warned nations that they "must abolish recourse to war or perish by mutual destruction."

SAN FRANCISCO: Two nude beauties stepped a taxi near the civic center servicemen's dormitory, stepped out — unsteadily — and plunged into the center's lily pond. Servicemen tumbled hastily from the dormitory and cheered on the swimming girls. When the girls emerged, the servicemen offered towels which they accepted gratefully, stepped back into the taxi and sped off.

FAIRMONT, W. Va.: Servicemen and women will eat and drink free "as long as anything is left" in J. G. Papageorge's restaurant on the day following V-J Day.

LOUISVILLE, Ky.: A woman paraded through the heart of happy celebrants, passing out Kleenex by the hundreds. "The war's over," she shouted. "Have a Kleenex."

DENVER, Colo.: Six automobile accidents were reported within two hours after the surrender announcement. One celebrant, driving alone, drove his car directly into a brick wall.

SEATTLE: A gang of sailors barricaded one downtown street and kissed every female that came along - regardless of age.

CHICAGO: On Chicago's State street a small girl, astride her mother's shoulders, carried the sign: "My daddy's coming home - thank God!"

CHICAGO: Horns were blowing, bells ringing and people shouting on Roosevelt road in Chicago. But an elderly operator of a small magazine stand was absorbed in one of his periodicals. A sign on the stand read: "I am deaf."

WATERLOO, Ia., Aug. 15. (UP)—The news of the surrender of the Japanese was accepted with quiet calm in the home of Thomas Sullivans, parents of the five Iowa brothers who lost their lives in the sinking of the U. S. S. Juneau. Mrs. Sullivan wept softly when she heard the surrender news.

POWERFUL JAP

GENERAL JIRO MINAMI, a powerful figure behind the scenes at the end; perhaps the man who [illegible] the Jap Government to quit; president of the Political Association; powerful in politics; a [illegible] of the State; served as [illegible] of the Kwantung Army; [illegible] of Japan's oldest military [illegible]

[illegible] TO BUY something? [illegible]

WAR ENDS AS TRUMAN TELLS WORLD JAPAN ACCEPTS SURRENDER TERMS

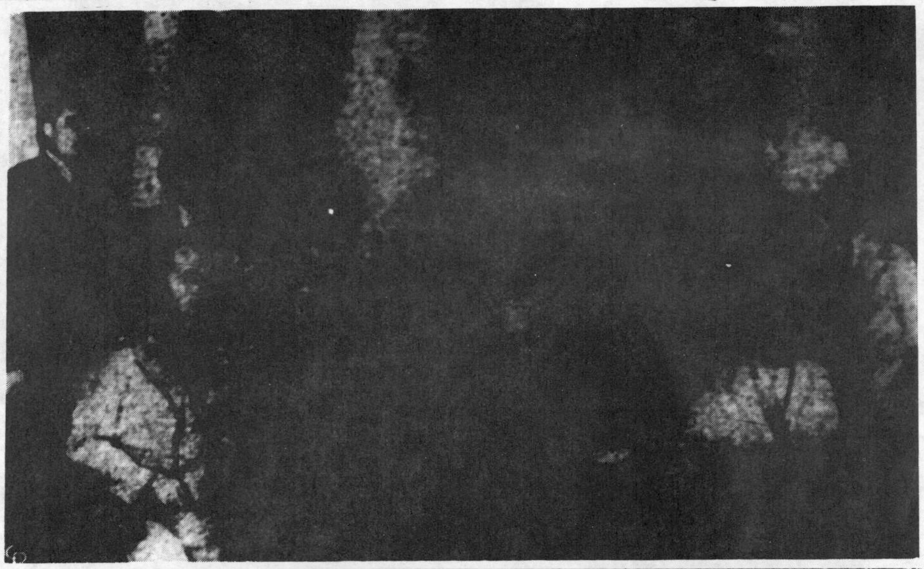

President [illegible] was received. Front row, left to right [illegible] Cordell Hull.

HIGHLIGHTS OF LONG AND BLOODY WAR IN PACIFIC

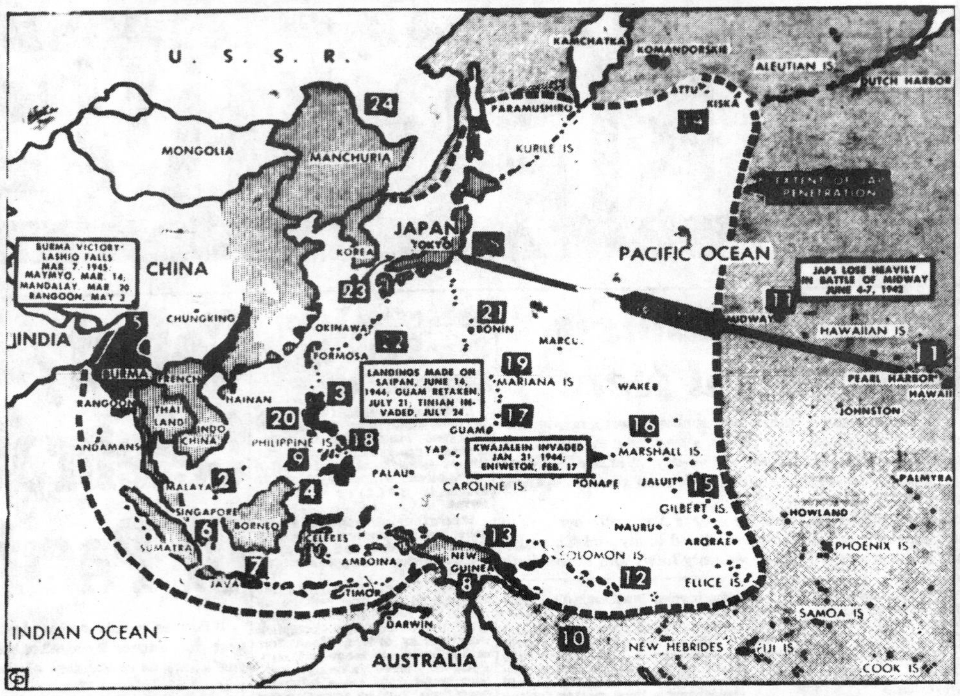
U. S. S. R.
KAMCHATKA
KOMANDORSKIE
ALEUTIAN IS.
DUTCH HARBOR
ATTU
KISKA
PARAMUSHIRO
MONGOLIA
MANCHURIA
KURILE IS.
EXTENT OF JAP PENETRATION
BURMA VICTORY: LASHIO FALLS MAR 7 1945 MAYMYO, MAR 14; MANDALAY MAR 20 RANGOON, MAY 3
CHINA
KOREA
JAPAN
TOKYO
PACIFIC OCEAN
JAPS LOSE HEAVILY IN BATTLE OF MIDWAY JUNE 4-7, 1942
CHUNGKING
INDIA
OKINAWA
BONIN
MARCUS
MIDWAY
HAWAIIAN IS.
FORMOSA
LANDINGS MADE ON SAIPAN, JUNE 14, 1944, GUAM RETAKEN, JULY 21, TINIAN INVADED, JULY 24
MARIANA IS.
WAKE
PEARL HARBOR
HAWAII
BURMA
HAINAN
GUAM
JOHNSTON
RANGOON
THAILAND
FRENCH INDO CHINA
PHILIPPINE IS.
YAP
KWAJALEIN INVADED JAN 31, 1944; ENIWETOK, FEB. 17
MARSHALL IS.
ANDAMANS
PALAU
CAROLINE IS.
PONAPE
JALUIT
PALMYRA
MALAYA
SINGAPORE
BORNEO
NAURU
GILBERT IS.
HOWLAND
SUMATRA
CELEBES
AMBOINA
NEW GUINEA
SOLOMON IS.
ARORAE
PHOENIX IS.
JAVA
TIMOR
ELLICE IS.
DARWIN
SAMOA IS.
INDIAN OCEAN
AUSTRALIA
NEW HEBRIDES
FIJI IS.
COOK IS.

THIS MAP covers the highlights of the Pacific war from the time of the treacherous attack on Pearl Harbor by the Japs on Dec. 7, 1941 until the day of the Nipponse peace offer. (1) Japs attack Pearl Harbor, Dec. 7, 1941; (2) Malay campaign started by the Japs, Dec. 8, 1941. (3) Landings made on Luzon, Dec. 10, 1941; (4) Borneo invasion started, Dec. 22, 1941; (5) Conquest of Burma begun, Jan. 10, 1942. (6) Singapore falls to Japs, Feb. 15, 1942; (7) Allies routed in Battle of Java Sea, Feb. 27, 1942; (8) First Japanese landing on New Guinea, March 8, 1942; (9) Surrender of Corregidor, May 6, 1942; (10) Japs defeated in Coral Sea Battle, May 4-7, 1942; (11) Japs lose battle of Midway, June 3-6, 1942. (12) Yanks land on Guadalcanal, Aug. 7, '42; (13) Japs routed in Bismarck Sea Battle, March 3, '43; (14) Allied forces retake Kiska, Aug. 15, '43; (15) Tarawa in the Gilberts retaken, Nov. 20-24, '43; (16) Jap territory invaded at Kwajalein, Jan. 31, '44. (17) Invade Marianas, June 14, '44; (18) Landings on Leyte, Oct. 20-26, '44; (19) First B-29 raids from Marianas bases, Nov. 24, '44; (20) Yanks land on Luzon, Jan. 9, '45; (21) Landings on Iwo Jima, Feb. 17, '45; (22) Okinawa invasion, April 1, '45; (23) Atomic bomb raid on Hiroshima, Aug. 6, '45. (24) Reds declare war on Japs, invade Manchuria, Aug. 9, 1945; (25) Tokyo gets Allied answer to surrender offer.

Take World Spotlight in Connection With Jap Surrender News

Session of Japanese Diet showing Hirohito on special throne.

Hirohito and horse

Imperial palace in Tokyo where emperor resides.

JAPANESE ARMED FORCES ARE STILL IN THESE AREAS

Sakhalin
Karafuto
Kuriles
CHINA
Tokyo
JAPAN
OKINAWA
FORMOSA
IWO
Hong Kong
Pacific
Wake
Marianas
Saipan
China Sea
GUAM
Ocean
Philippines
YAP
Carolines
Palau Is.
Marshalls
MALAY STATES
Singapore
Celebes
BORNEO
New Guinea
NEW BRITAIN
Solomons
SUMATRA
NETHERLANDS INDIES
Java
Timor
GUADALCANAL
Indian Ocean
AUSTRALIA

AS JAPANESE SURRENDER OFFER was received by Allied governments, here is the extent of territory still held by the Japs. Home islands and land taken by conquest or occupation are shown in black and shaded areas. Flags indicate bases retaken or wrested from Japan by U. S. (International)

THRONG WHITE HOUSE GROUNDS TO HEAR TRUMAN

M.P.'s and police hold back exuberant Washington throngs around the White House grounds as President Truman officially announces the end of the war with Japan.

CHEERING TIMES SQUARE MOB CELEBRATES VICTORY

View of Times Square, New York, as news of the official surrender of Japan reached the wild, cheering crowds.

SCENES LIKE THIS were going on all over the United States as the nation heard the news that the war was at an end. This picture was made in New York's famed Times Square as great crowds gathered in the early morning hours after the first news that Japan had surrendered was reported by the Tokyo radio and relayed here

(International Soundphoto)

"THANK GOD, IT'S OVER"

Yes, the war is over. Yes, it is natural that we should exult and celebrate. But it is also a time for soul-searching thinking.

. . . A time to think of the men who are beneath crosses at Anzio, St. Lo, along the Rhine, at Iwo Jima and Okinawa.

. . . A time to think of the men you won't see marching in the victory parades, the over 300,000 wounded who are still suffering . . . still struggling to recover what they gave up for us.

. . . a time to think of the 7,000,000 men — sons, husbands, brothers, fathers, who are still thousands of miles, and weeks, and months away from the ones they love.

We must — we will take care of our own — by buying another Victory Bond now — and continuing to buy them for as long as the need exists.

Surely you can see why the most important bonds you ever bought are the ones you buy now to complete the peace.

This is your biggest and greatest chance to salute the brave men who fought and won this war for you.

THIS ADVERTISEMENT IS A WEEKLY CONTRIBUTION TO AMERICA'S ALL-OUT WAR EFFORT BY THE FOLLOWING BEAVER COUNTY BUSINESS AND MANUFACTURING INSTITUTIONS.

Sahli's, Motor Car, Home Appliance, Furniture
The Farmers National Bank
Beaver Falls Paint & Glass Co.
Benson's Department Store
J. S. Gary Furniture
McDanel Refractory Porcelain Company
ABC Credit, Inc.
Walter H. Gross, Furniture, Home Appliances
Montgomery Ward & Co.
Ben Friedman, Men's and Boys' Wear
Ruben Furniture Co.
Shepperd's—Agency for Richman Bros.

Brierly & Brierly, Hardware
Dotre's Men's Shop
Baumgarten's Fruit Markets
Schoemer Pure Food Bakery
Wolfe Shoe Store
J. C. Penney Co.
Sun Drug Company, Inc.
The Regent Theatre
John T. Reeves & Co., Bankers
Stanley Studio
J. D. McAnlis & Son, Jeweler
Steiner's Home Store
John H. Brooks & Sons, Builders' Supplies

Ingram-Richardson Manufacturing Company
Michael Baker, Jr.
J. Orville Scott Funeral Home
G. C. Murphy Co.
Bell Telephone Co. of Pennsylvania
Curtiss-Wright Corp. Propeller Div. Beaver, Pa.
Falcon Equipment Company
Andalusia Dairy Co.
Gertelle Shop, Women's Ready-To-Wear
Gen. Brodhead Hotel
Corner Pharmacy
Saul's Men's and Boys' Wear
Annette Beauty Salon
First Federal Savings & Loan Association

Markson's—Furniture and Housefurnishings
Thos. F. Daquila—Buick-Studebaker Sales-Serv.
Miller's Shoe Store
Rosenblatt Furniture
R. W. McMullen—Chrysler-Plymouth
Gerson's, Your Jeweler
Eckerd's Drug Store
Beglin Stove & Furnace Co. Kalamazoo Dealers
McBeath Motor Co.
Sakraida's—Ladies' Ready-to-Wear
William A. Temple—Temple's Grocery
Jos. J. Spratt & Bro.—Homelike Funeral Parlor
Berkman's—Men's, Women's Ready-to-Wear
Loyal B. Young, Funeral Director
Martin's Market

SCHOOL EDITION

The News-Tribune

SCHOOL EDITION

BEAVER FALLS — NEW BRIGHTON, PA. WEDNESDAY, AUGUST 22, 1945

VALLEY SCHOOLS READY FOR BEGINNING OF NEW TERM

H. E. M'LAUGHLIN
President,
Garfield Business Institute

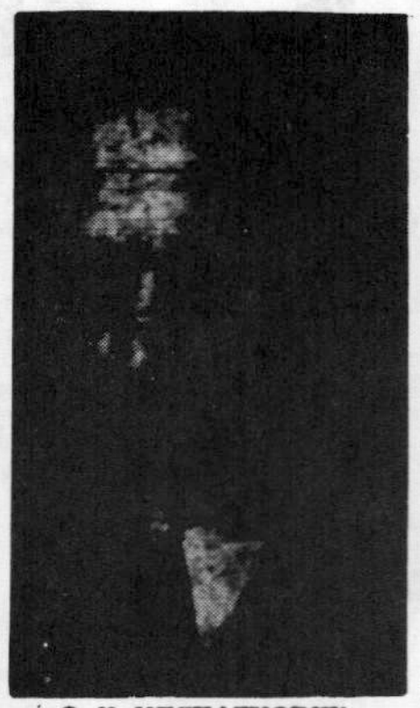

O. H. HECKATHORNE
Principal,
Beaver Falls Junior High Schools

L. D. SMITH
Principal,
Beaver Falls High School

ALF M. ASPER
Freedom High School Principal

FRANCIS E. MITCHELL
Supervisor of Elementary
Education, Beaver Falls Schools

PHILIP H. PETRIE
Supervising Principal,
Monaca School

ADA L. JACKSON
Supervising Principal, Freedom

E. D. DAVIDSON
Superintendent,
Beaver County Schools

FENTON FARLEY
Rochester High School Principal

Brighton Schools To Start Second Kindergarten Room With Beginning Of New Term

The schools of New Brighton will open Tuesday morning, September 4, with the high school convening at 8:30, the junior high at 8:40 and the elementary classes at 9:00.

A new kindergarten room is being opened this year at the third ward building. This will make two kindergarten rooms in New Brighton. The room in the Kenwood building will have class during the morning session of school beginning at 9:00 extending until 11:30. The third ward building will have afternoon classes beginning at 1:15 and extending to 3:30.

Registration for the kindergarten will the Tuesday and Wednesday, August 28, 29, and child who will be five years of age on or before February 1, 1946, will be eligible to enroll in the kindergarten. To be eligible to enroll in the first grade, a child must be six years old on or before February 1, 1946. Registration for first grade as well as any other new entrant in the schools will be Tuesday and Wednesday, August 28, 29. New entrants for the high school may report to the high school office for enrollment at the same time if the entrant so desires.

All of the buildings have been completely cleaned during the summer months; much painting has been done and the buildings are in first class condition for the opening of school.

Last year three were enrolled in the schools of New Brighton a total of 1,865 boys and girls. The enrollment for the 1945-1946 term is expected to be approximately the same.

A general teachers' meeting for all teachers in the system will be held prior to the opening of school. This meeting will be held on Monday September 3, in the auditorium at 8:00 a. m. Do to resignations there will be a number of new faces on the faculty this coming year. The following is a list of the teachers and their teaching assignments:

HIGH SCHOOL

Miriam Carter, English; Richard Hill, mathematics; Ethel Lytle, Latin; Constance Brant, science; Nancy Crocott, commercial; Melvin Miller, history; Mrs. Betty Johnson, English; J. Roger Hopkins, English; Anna Jane Garmen, history; Burton Painter, history; Virginia Moore, English; Virginia Couch, history; Elizabeth Shelar history; Mrs. Margaret Ripper, French; Betty Zittman, commercial; Margaret Halama, commercial; Mrs. Anne Geary, Spanish; Betty Breen, commercial; Eva Hickman, commercial; Anna Mary Campbell, science; Lois Shaffer, commercial; Juliette Dunham, English; Jeanne Thomas, English; Betty Miller, mathematics; Helen Hobbs, girls' physical education and science; Jean Tritschler, mathematics; George Roark, coach and science; Lloyd Taylor science, assistant principal; Paul Hamilton, principal; Mildred Thompson, secretary to superintendent; Mary Lou MacDonald, secretary to high school principal.

JUNIOR HIGH SCHOOL

Margaret Ann Twinem, seventh grade grammar; Mrs. Dorothy Whitmire, seventh grade geography; Lorna Johnston, seventh grade literature; Mary Elizabeth Pringle, seventh grade arithmetic; Mary Grimshaw, eighth grade geography; Nettie Thomas, eighth grade history; Dorothy Thomas, eighth grade literature; Nellie Beightol, eighth grade arithmetic; Margaret Dickey, eighth grade grammar; Richard Steinfeld principal, seventh grade history; Mae Evans school nurse; Ivan Coene shop; Mildred Pratt, art and home economics; Marian Templeton, music; Richard Fleming, music; Mary Heiser, librarian; Dr. P. F. Martsolf, school doctor; Dr. H. C. Coene, dental clinic; Mrs. Viola Mussey, attendance officer; Harry Garmen, tax collector; C. A. Douglass, delinquent tax collector.

CENTRAL

Mrs. Charles Wright, Edna McDanel, principal; Nellie Johnson, Grace Frishkorn, Isabelle Murphy and Miriam Meeder.

THIRD WARD

Florence Jones, principal; Mrs. Jane Evans, Mabel Hawthorne, Janet Thompson, Helen Sabol and Martha Irons.

FOURTH WARD

Helen Riddel, principal; Dorothy May Shaw, Isabelle Goettman, Mrs. Marian Duncan, Mrs. Catherine

(Continued on Page Thirteen)

Enrollment Of Some 3,300 Anticipated When Local Schools Open September 4th

An enrollment of approximately [illegible] when the Beaver Falls schools open Tuesday morning, September 4. Because of the war's end and the resultant decrease in jobs available for youth the enrollment is expected to show a small increase over the last several wartime years.

The grades will convene at 9:00 o'clock, the junior and senior high schools at 8:30 o'clock.

Listed as holidays on the school calendar are Armistice day, Monday, November 12; Thanksgiving, Thursday and Friday, November 22 and 23; and Christmas, Friday, December 21 at 3:00 o'clock to Wednesday morning, January 2.

Kindergartens for children who will be five years of age by February 1, 1946, will be opened at the Thirty-third and Eleventh street buildings.

New teachers this year will be: Helen Dice, kindergarten; Margaret Gardner kindergarten; Helen Fullerton Winsor, intermediate; Esther Daum, home economics; Mary Alice Hess, librarian; Pauline Goeddell commercial; Maxine Ellington, Spanish; Bernice Molt, English, and Robert L. Shoup, instrumental music.

The following persons have been elected as full-time substitutes for the school year 1945-46:

Muriel Phillips McCarl, vocal music; Violet McLaughlin, English; Annetta Doutt, English and art; Catherine Bell, English; Helen Treloar, general science, and Alice Fetterman, home economics.

Vacancies still exist in several positions: Social studies and art, vocational machine shop, vocational electric, commercial and general science.

The teacher assignment by buildings is as follows:

ELEMENTARY SCHOOLS

Francis Mitchell, supervisor; June Hornbecker, secretary.

Eleventh Street Building

Ethel J. Dunlap, principal

Ethel J. Dunlap, grade I; Helen McFadden, grade II; Gladys Hummel, grade III; Rozetta Huey, grade IV, history, music, art; Olive Hall, grade V, arithmetic and geography; Edna Wissinger, grade VI English and reading; Helen Dice, kindergarten.

Fifth Street Building

Helen Davidson, principal

Mabel Hardy, grade I; Ruth Whiteside, grade II; Florence Engle, grade III; Helen Jasper, grade IV, reading and English; Effie McCullough, grade V, arithmetic, music and art; Helen Davidson, grade VI, history and geography.

Eighth Avenue Building

Beatrice Hamilton, principal

Beatrice Hamilton, grade I; Mary Simpson, grade I; Wilda Roberts grade II; Edna Abraham, grade II; Ferndetta Caldwell, grade III; Mrs. Alberta McCullough, grade III; Marian Loos, grade IV, English and reading; Mrs. Marion Burtner, grade IV, health, physical education, music and art; Frances Scott, grade V, arithmetic, spelling, writing; Ethel Douds, grade VI, geography and history.

Thirty-eighth Street Building

Mabel Long, principal

Mabel Long, grade I; Viola Brooks, grade II; Gladys Fair, grade III; [illegible], grade IV, history, geography and reading; Rachel Cain, grade VI, English, arithmetic, music and art; Helen Winger, grade V.

Fifth Avenue Building

Dorothy Loeffler, principal

Grace Shoemaker, grade I; Dorothy Loeffler, grade I; Velma Metzger, grade II; Dorothy Freker, grade III; Catherine Ague, grade IV, history, music and art; Martha Anderson, grade V, reading and English; Helen Juhasz, grade VI, arithmetic and geography; Carolyn Jordan, orthogenic.

Thirty-third Street Building

Vesta Allen, principal

Viola E. Frishkorn, grade I; Florence Irons, grade II; Helen Massey, grade III; Vesta Allen, grade IV, history and geography; Inez Taggart, grade V, English and reading; Esther Smith, grade VI, arithmetic, music and art; Margaret Gardner, kindergarten.

JUNIOR HIGH SCHOOLS

College Hill

O. H. Heckathorne, principal

Esther Daum, home economics, science; Clara Mae Jannuzi, English; Thomas D. Mansell, social science; Howard S. Miller, mathematics and science; Hugh M. Miller, industrial arts; Muriel Phillips, ½ time music.

Seventh Avenue Building

O. H. Heckathorne, principal

Ruth Blinn, secretary

Leroy Angle, industrial arts; Violet McLaughlin, English; Paul Booth, physical education and health; Robert L. Shoup, instrumental music; Annetta Doutt, English and art; Lettie A. Davidson, social studies; Helen Louise Treloar, general science; Nellie Freed, social studies; Lyda Golden, mathematics; Frank F. Graham, commercial; John A. Griffiths, English; Vera Huey, vocal music; Ruth E. Hunter, English; Sidney Kane, mathematics; Jean Kuhn, orthogenic; Grace T. McGaughey, mathematics; Kathryn Ann Miller, instrumental music; Arthur G. Mitchell, mechanical drawing and mathematics; Bernice Molt, English; Jean Mowry, mathematics and science; Janet G. Pierce, librarian; U. C. Ramsey, science and mathematics; Grace D. Rodger, social studies; John Sahli, social studies; Ethel Scott, art; Alice Gourley Fetterman, home economics; Marie Taggart, English; Jean Turnbull, physical education and health; Ruth Walton, home economics; Muriel Phillips, vocational music.

SENIOR HIGH SCHOOL

Lawrence D. Smith, principal

Howard Mench, director of vocational education

Florence MacDonald, secretary

Ralph S. Axtell, mathematics; William R. Bilkey, history; Carl E. Blair, English; Helen Causey, home economics; Martha A. Cook, history; Mary Cook, history; Clara Behringer, English; Mary G. Dougherty, languages; Elizabeth Fullerton mathematics; Marion F. Groetzinger, commercial; Donald Grove, mechanical drawing; John L. Harr, biology; Norma Heinrich, physical education and health; Wendell Fiddler, retail selling; Ruth E. Hunter, music; Arthur eJrnberg, Mathematics and science; Regina Lutz, home economics; J. Neal Matthews, history; Irving R. Mayers, physics; Kathryn E. McDonald, commercial; Verna V. McKee, mathematics; Margaret M. Miller, English; Catherine Bell, English; Mary Alice Hess, librarian; Adolph J. Pletincks, instrumental music; Gladys E. Porter, art; Anna Toth, commercial; Lillie E. Redpath, English; Charlotte M. Rodey, languages; Leland Schachren, physical education and coach; E. Helen Sponcler, chemistry; June L. Stout, commercial; Harvey Fleischer, auto mechanics; Pauline Goeddel, commercial; Mary E. Thomas, English; George F. Troll, vocational woodwork; George Todd, general shop; Lewis Heeter, health and physical education; Joan Foss physical education and health; Maxine Ellington, Spanish and social studies.

Enrollment By Grades — — — Beaver Falls Public Schools

(NOTE DEPRESSION AND WARTIME EFFECT)

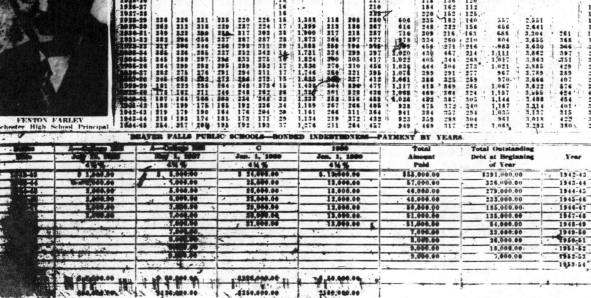

Year	1st Grade	2nd Grade	3rd Grade	4th Grade	5th Grade	6th Grade	Special Rooms	Total Elementary	7th Grade	8th Grade	9th Grade	Total Jr. High	10th Grade	11th Grade	12th Grade	Total Sr. High	Grand Total	9th Grade Promotions	High School Graduates
1921-22											204		136	101	99				66
1922-23											184		131	87	73				101
1923-24											185		153	105	73				78
1924-25											201		163	148	99				78
1925-26							18				217		178	136	120				93
1926-27							16				210		184	162	112				116
1927-28							16				223		220	152	125				107
1928-29	236	226	221	235	220	225	15	1,388	118	208	280	606	235	182	140	557	2,551		130
1929-30	262	212	218	229	237	224	17	1,399	213	136	267	616	248	222	156	656	2,641		125
1930-31	249	323	[illegible]	[illegible]	317	303	38	1,900	217	218	287	716	309	216	163	688	3,304	261	153
1931-32	382	296	256	337	287	287	28	1,873	304	297	377	978	334	260	210	804	3,655	368	198
1932-33	317	306	346	286	298	311	28	1,888	258	196	[illegible]	[illegible]	456	271	216	983	3,630	366	208
1933-34	385	326	285	227	212	342	14	1,731	324	299	397	1,020	430	467	214	1,111	3,862	397	212
1934-35	345	288	297	296	233	275	16	1,824	300	305	417	1,022	405	344	268	1,017	3,863	351	300
1935-36	284	299	292	295	289	352	17	1,828	270	310	456	1,036	444	304	273	1,021	3,885	429	255
1936-37	282	275	276	291	294	311	17	1,746	350	321	395	1,076	399	291	277	967	3,789	389	269
1937-38	265	253	[illegible]	272	296	272	15	1,625	[illegible]	327	412	1,061	386	325	259	970	3,666	407	257
1938-39	191	222	235	264	248	273	15	1,438	304	330	477	1,117	418	369	285	1,067	3,622	576	252
1939-40	178	162	211	246	248	262	26	[illegible]	301	328	436	[illegible]	469	364	324	1,157	3,555	424	422
1940-41	197	164	186	203	234	248	32	1,238	252	316	458	1,026	452	387	305	1,144	3,408	454	297
1941-42	188	199	175	165	192	236	34	1,189	267	266	405	938	475	372	340	1,187	3,314	401	331
1942-43	219	179	190	164	176	204	20	1,161	266	311	364	941	384	357	294	1,035	3,137	315	307
1943-44	218	193	174	181	173	171	29	1,134	219	272	432	923	359	298	304	961	3,018	422	315
1944-45	254	317	209	195	192	193	37	1,276	211	264	457	949	469	317	282	1,065	3,293	380	[illegible]

BEAVER FALLS PUBLIC SCHOOLS—BONDED INDEBTEDNESS—PAYMENT BY YEARS

[illegible]	A—College Hill [illegible] 4½%	A—College Hill May 1, 1927 4½%	C Jan. 1, 1930 4½%	1930 Jan. 1, 1930 4½%	Total Amount Paid	Total Outstanding Debt at Beginning of Year	Year
1942-43	$ [illegible]	$ 5,000.00	$ 24,000.00	$ 13,000.00	$55,000.00	$391,000.00	1942-43
[illegible]	[illegible]	5,000.00	25,000.00	13,000.00	57,000.00	336,000.00	1943-44
[illegible]	[illegible]	5,000.00	26,000.00	13,000.00	46,000.00	279,000.00	1944-45
[illegible]	[illegible]	6,000.00	28,000.00	12,000.00	48,000.00	233,000.00	1945-46
[illegible]	[illegible]	[illegible]	29,000.00	12,000.00	50,000.00	185,000.00	1946-47
[illegible]	[illegible]	7,000.00	30,000.00	13,000.00	51,000.00	135,000.00	1947-48
		7,000.00	31,000.00	13,000.00	51,000.00	84,000.00	1948-49
		7,000.00			7,000.00	33,000.00	1949-50
		8,000.00			8,000.00	26,000.00	1950-51
		[illegible]			9,000.00	18,000.00	1951-52
		9,000.00			9,000.00	7,000.00	1952-53
							1953-54
	$[illegible]	$ [illegible]	$[illegible]	$ 50,000.00			
	[illegible]	$[illegible]	$350,000.00	$100,000.00			

DR. J. R. MILLER
Superintendent,
Beaver Falls Schools

ERNEST B. McNITT
Superintendent,
New Brighton Schools

DR. M. M. PEARCE
President, Geneva College

ROBERT P. BARNER
Superintendent, Rochester Schools

E. G. GROLEAU
High School Principal, Monaca

G. A. McCORMICK
Superintendent, Beaver Schools

[illegible] A. BARKLEY
Assistant Superintendent,
Beaver County Schools.

Suggested Calendar For School Term Of 1945-1946

Realizing the need for a somewhat uniform school calendar throughout the county and acting on the suggestion of many of the teachers for a uniform calendar, the County Board of School Directors has approved the following calendar and recommended its adoption, so far as possible, by the several school districts of the county.

CALENDAR

1945

August 30-31—County Teachers Institute.
September 3—**National Labor Day.
September 4 (Tuesday)—School opens for 1945-1946 term of nine months.
September 17—*Constitution Day (158th Anniversary).
September 27 to October 3—Clean-Up and Fire Prevention Week.
September 28—*Frances E. Willard Day.
October 11—*General Casimir Pulaski Day.
October 12—*Columbus Day.
October 19—*Fall Arbor and Bird Day.
October 24—*William Penn Day.
November 5-11—*American Education Week.
November 11 (12)—**National Armistice Day.
November 22—**Thanksgiving Day and Weekend Vacation.
December 15 (14)—*National Bill of Rights Day.
December 21 to January 2—**Christmas Vacation.

1946

January 1—**New Year's Day.
January 2—Schools Re-Open.
January 13 (11)—*Stephen C. Foster Day
January 17-24—*National Thrift Week—Benjamin Franklin's Birthday.
February 12—*Lincoln's Birthday.
February 22—*Washington's Birthday.
April 1-10—*Free School Day—Day by Governor's Proclamation.
April 9-14—Conservation Week, *April 9, Spring Arbor and Bird Day—Unless it falls on Saturday, Sunday, or Good Friday, then during the Conservation Week. (Section 4001-A).
April 14 (15)—*Pan-American Day.
April 19—**Good Friday—Easter Vacation.
May 1—*Child Health and Festival Day.
May 18 (17)—*World Good Will Day.
May 30—**Memorial Day.
June 14—*National Flag Day.
*To be celebrated with programs in the school—made mandatory by law.
**Schools to be closed.
All other holidays optional.

CHARLES LINN
Principal, Beaver High School

Weather Forecast
Moderate temperature today. Clear and rather cool tonight. Tuesday, fair and warmer.

THE DAILY TIMES

1874—and WESTERN ARGUS—1803
ROCHESTER · BEAVER · MONACA · FREEDOM · BRIDGEWATER · CONWAY · VANPORT · MIDLAND

War History
British forces captured Lens, key to the German-held coal fields in Northern France, September 3 1918.

Established April 2, 1874 | Beaver and Rochester, Pa., Monday, September 3, 1945 | Single Copy 4 Cents — 24 Cents A Week

LABOR DAY - 1945

V-E Day
V-J Day

Local Plants Had Vital Part In War

Beaver County's many diversified industrial plants and their thousands of workers, along with other industries in the Pittsburgh Ordnance District, have played a vital part in the long and bloody war. The role of county war plants and workers will long be remembered for their contribution to the hard-won victory.

Since the fateful sneak attack on Pearl Harbor by the Japanese the Pittsburgh Ordnance District has produced almost 95 million tons of steel for the ships, shells, guns, tanks and other implements of war.

The district has manufactured 52,570,802 shells and bullets, along with millions of bomb casings and rocket casings.

It has provided bombers with 11,253,408 bombs, ranging from little four-pounders to 4000-pound "eggs."

Total weight of these bombs is 782,777 tons. They would load 600 B-29s for a daily trip over Tokyo for nearly seven months.

The enemy on all fronts has been punished by projectiles from 17,233 guns that were forged and rough bored here. In addition, this area turned out 2,443 finished 155 mm. "Long Toms."

This is part of the picture of the district's mighty aid to the nation, disclosed by Col. Robert C. Downie, chief of the Pittsburgh Ordnance District, on the eve of an anniversary.

On Thursday, it will be exactly five years since the Ordnance District was alerted for the procurement of weapons and equipment for World War II.

Looking back, the vast conversion that took place in this highly industrialized area is nothing short of amazing.

"You will find the story replete with examples of pioneering, aggressiveness, loyal and skillful labor and downright conversion ability," Col. Downie commented.

A cork company produced shells. A bath tub iron foundry turned out highest quality steel armored castings.

A glass company produced clay targets—part of a total of 73,775,350 such targets made in this district.

A mattress manufacturer became one of the country's best producers of metallic belt links for 50 caliber ammunition. It turned out 823,060,300 belt links.

A former tin plate mill was converted into the district's best producer of heavy artillery shells.

A producer of rods for oil wells turned out forged and rough turned gun tubes.

In a collection of old frame buildings, a company sprang up overnight to become the country's principal producer of hand grenade fuses. Here was developed a smokeless, flashless and noiseless grenade fuse which proved of tremendous value against the tricky Japs.

Since Pearl Harbor, the area covered by the Pittsburgh Ordnance District has yielded more than 19 billion dollars worth of material for War and Navy Departments and other Government agencies engaged in arming the nation for war.

The District covers Western Pennsylvania with the exception of Erie, Mercer and Crawford Counties; West Virginia, two counties of Ohio and two counties of Maryland.

Steel, of course, has been the district's greatest contribution to the war effort.

The steel produced in the area in the war years would make a one-inch round bar that would circle the earth at the equator 539 times.

Pittsburgh's mills produce more than twice as much steel as the Japanese Empire. One Pittsburgh plant alone produces half as much steel as all of Japan.

The steel industry's war products have ranged from huge structural sections for the Engineers, through the gamut of shell steel, down to steel wire only 5/1000 of an inch in diameter, or scarcely larger than a human hair.

But other industries played their part—and with notable contributions, Col. Downie pointed out.

The aluminum industry produced forgings, sheets and strips and fabricated light gauge metal parts for detonators and percussion caps.

Pittsburgh's chemical industry produced dynamite, trinitrotoluene, toluene and toluol, nitrate, synthetic resins and many other products.

Its glass industry broke a bottle neck in production of rolled optical glass.

One of the most valuable contributions of the District has been heavy caliber ammunition, Col. Downie said.

It has been the largest contributor to the artillery program in the entire United States. At one time, nearly 176,000 eight-inch rifle and howitzer shells a month were being produced.

Here's a summary of this

Continued on Page 26

Seven Persons Hurt Here In Week-End Traffic Accidents

Seven persons, one a pedestrian, were injured in district traffic accidents Saturday and Sunday. Five automobiles were badly damaged in wrecks.

Fred Lee Johnston, 35, 123 Sheffield avenue, Aliquippa, was taken to Rochester hospital for treatment of head and face lacerations suffered in a collision at Sheffield avenue and Brodhead road, Aliquippa, Saturday evening.

His brother, Elmer Johnston, Potter Township, was held by Aliquippa police pending the outcome of Fred's injuries. Donald Eheuvront, Chestnut street, Aliquippa, driver of the other car, was not injured. Each of the automobiles was damaged to the extent of $150.

FOUR HURT IN CRASH

Mrs. Geraldine Hagan, 46, Salem, O., a former nurse at Providence hospital, was injured along with her two daughters when the brakes on her car failed Saturday afternoon while driving down Steffin Hill.

Beaver Falls police said Mrs. Hagan's car collided head-on with another driven by Albert Park, 2339 College avenue, Beaver Falls, as she made the turn from Steffin Hill onto Twenty-fourth street. Park was treated in Providence hospital for lacerations of the head.

Mrs. Hagan suffered a nose injury, fractured ribs and knee injuries; her daughter, Geraldine, 10, a broken nose and eye injuries, and another daughter, Eileen, 18, lacerations of the nose and severe shock. All were treated in Providence hospital and then transferred to Salem hospital, where Mrs. Hagan is a nurse. The Hagan car was virtually demolished and the other badly damaged.

STRUCK BY AUTO

Norma Funkhouser, 17, Crescent Heights, suffered a head injury and lacerations of the face Sunday evening when she was struck by an automobile while walking in Mercer road a mile from New Brighton. The driver, Crawford Anderson, Ellwood City, took the injured girl to Beaver Valley hospital, where her condition was described as "fair."

WOMAN INJURED

Mrs. Otto Schaefer, 55, Pittsburgh, suffered fractured ribs and a broken wrist Sunday morning when a car driven by her husband left Darlington road at Locust Point and rolled into a deep ditch. She was taken to Providence hospital. Mr. Schaefer escaped uninjured.

NATIONAL TOLL LOW
By UNITED PRESS

At least 64 persons lost their lives over the Labor Day week end as excursionists swarmed over highways to celebrate the nation's first peacetime holiday since Pearl Harbor.

The National Safety Council predicted the biggest traffic toll in the history of American motoring—300 or more. Yet early reports bolstered hopes that drivers, traveling in old model cars with worn tires, might be exerting extra care.

Forty-six traffic fatalities were recorded for the first two days of the three-day Labor Day observance. There were 10 drownings and miscellaneous deaths.

Strikes To End At Three Plants

PITTSBURGH, Sept. 3. (UP)—Strikes will end in three Western Pennsylvania plants today or tomorrow, one of which had been in effect 11 weeks.

The Creighton plant of the Pittsburgh Plate Glass Co. was scheduled to resume operations today after 2,500 workers voted to return to work upon recommendation of officials of the Federation of Glass, Ceramic & Silica Sand Workers, (CIO).

Nearly 1,800 workers of the Oliver & Iron Steel Co., idle since Aug. 22, will return to work tomorrow ending a strike which arose in protest to the dismissal of a local CIO Steelworkers' president. The employes were notified by mail to return to their jobs by their union leaders.

At a special mass meeting held yesterday, 600 CIO steelworkers at the Coshocton Iron Works, division of the Combustion Engineering Co., voted to return to work tomorrow.

LABOR DAY, 1945, SEES ASSEMBLY LINES RECONVERT

THIS AUTOMOBILE which is being assembled in a Detroit plant where, just a few weeks ago, giant tanks crowded the assembly lines, is symbolic of the speed with which this Labor Day of 1945 ages American industry converting to peace-time civilian production.

Kobuta Employees Await Outcome Of Raw Rubber Survey

Employes of the Koppers Company plant at Kobuta will anxiously await the outcome of a survey to be made by a special rubber committee of the Office of War Mobilization to determine what to do with the nation's $700,000,000 synthetic rubber industry.

Members of the committee will be chosen from interested government agencies.

The new rubber committee is expected to make an immediate survey of the condition of rubber plantations which have been under Japanese control for three and one-half years.

According to rubber experts in the War Production Board, "no one knows" how much natural rubber will be immediately available for export when Allied troops move into Malaya.

NATURAL RUBBER NEEDED

Military personnel and representatives of the Foreign Economic Administration will appraise Japan's stores of both rubber and tin. Other U. S. representatives will go into the Southwest Pacific with British and Dutch groups to start production, survey equipment needs and estimate the time it will take to get supplies to U. S. manufacturers.

Natural rubber is badly needed because U. S. reserves are well

Continued on Page 24

Three Fire Departments Fight Brush Fire Here

Three fire departments—Beaver, Vanport and Midland—were called to Ohioview Saturday afternoon to fight a brush fire on the hillside above Montomery Island Dam. The firemen battled the stubborn blaze about 1 1-2 hours, during a high wind, and were successful in keeping the flames from reaching buildings.

Duration Of State Jobless Benefits May Be Extended

WASHINGTON, Sept. 3 (UP)—Senate finance committee members faced with the problem of writing a compromise unemployment compensation bill apparently were turning today toward a plan to extend the duration of state benefits with federal funds.

The committee plans to conclude hearings tomorrow on the bill, which would establish a $25-a-week standard for 26 weeks. Labor representatives testify today, with industry spokesmen scheduled for tomorrow.

The proposal to extend the length of time for state benefits with federal funds instead of attempting to raise all state funds to the $25-$26 week standard proposed in the bill was originally suggested by Sen. Ar-

Continued on Page 24

'Butcher Of Bataan' Finally Surrenders Philippines Forces

BAGUIO, The Philippines, Sept. 3 (UP)—Lt. Gen. Tomoyuki Yamashita, bullet-headed "Butcher of Bataan," was in Manila's Bilibid prison today after surrendering the last Japanese forces in the Philippines in a brief 11-minute ceremony.

Lt. Gen. Jonathan M. Wainwright and Lt. Gen. A. E. Percival, Great Britain's last-ditch defender of Singapore, watched grimly as the 59-year-old Yamashita affixed his signature to the eight-paragraph surrender document in a room of the high commissioner's building in Baguio, summer capital of the Philippines.

Yamashita, once called the "Tiger of Malaya" by his swaggering countrymen, probably faces charges as a war criminal. American military police escorted him from the room immediately after the ceremony, and he was led away to join 10,000 of his countrymen behind bars.

Maj. Gen. Edmond J. Leavey, deputy commander and chief of staff of the armed forces of the Western Pacific, signed for the Allied Nations. Using gold pens, he gave one to Wainwright who had defended Bataan and Corregidor in the dark days of the war. He gave another to Percival and a third to Lt. Gen. William D. Styer, commander of the

Continued on Page 24

Toll Of Dead, Wounded And Missing In War Totals 55 Million; 12 Million Prisoners

By UNITED PRESS

World War II has cost the peoples of this earth no fewer than 55,000,000 dead, wounded and missing by the most conservative but tentative and incomplete estimates from official statistics.

Behind barbed wire, as prisoners of war, are an additional 12,000,000 and they will be joined in the near future by the rest of the Japanese armed forces — an additional 4,000,000.

At the end, World War II had dragged to within a few days of a full six years. Great Britain had been in it actively for that whole time. The United States had been at war with the Axis for 3 years, 8 months, 6 days since Pearl Harbor. China, at war with Japan, continuously, since July 7, 1937, had been fighting over 8 years and 1 month.

This war, almost twice as costly as World War I in lives and money, has cost the people of the earth at least a trillion dollars in monies actually spent, plus many times that in lost work-hours and property destruction.

The United States alone has spent $300,000,000,000 so far and even if all war contracts are cancelled as soon as hostilities end, our total war bill will exceed $350,000,000,000 when all costs are paid.

It will be at least a year before the total cost of World War II can be known.

There is great variance between estimates by various departments of the same government. Hitler himself, last Feb. 24, estimated Germany's war losses at 12,500,000, of which 6,300,000 had been killed. Yet on July 29 a captured document which is now accepted as official and almost accurate lists Germany's war losses at 4,064,438 up to Nov. 30, 1944.

The casualties of all belligerents in World War I amounted to 29,750,000 of which Germany lost just under 7,000,000 dead and wounded. Nor do the German lists give the number of civilian casualties in air raids and invasions.

The following table shows the first available, minimum and conservative estimate of civilian and military dead, wounded or missing, exclusive of prisoners of war:

Soviet Russia, 21,000,000; Germany, 6,000,000 to 12,500,000; Poland Military, 900,000; Poland exterminated, 5,700,000; China, 3,000,000; Japan, 2,700,000; United States, 1,070,000; British Empire, 1,430,000; France, 1,000,000; Italy, 1,100,000.

Yugoslavia, 1,685,000; Austria, 700,000; Hungary, 600,000; Rumania, 700,000; Greece, 700,000; Holland, 275,000; Finland, 183,166; Belgium, 60,000; Czechoslovakia, 60,000; Philippines, 30,000; "Slaves" dead or missing, 350,000.

Number Of Points Needed For Army Discharge Lowered

WASHINGTON, Sept. 3 (UP)—Demobilization of America's 8,000,000-man World War II Army moved into high gear today as the formal surrender of Japan made it evident that the fighting was at last really over.

The War Department, in conformity with its announced intention last week, lowered the critical point discharge score to 80, allowed credit for points accumulated between V-E Day and V-J Day and permitted immediate release of men 35 years of age and over with at least two years honorable service. Point scores for WACS were lowered to 41.

At least 500,000 more Army personnel than were heretofore eligible to point discharge are expected to be eligible under the new plan. Point scores will have to be lowered still further, however, before enough men and women can be released to bring the Army down to the 2,500,000 level it expects to reach by next July 1.

As the Army reopened the demobilization gates wide, President Truman, promising to return soldiers and sailors to their homes "as soon as the ships and planes can get here," warned that for many service must continue for some time "to wipe out Japanese militarism just as we are cleaning out the militarism of Germany."

(Pacific dispatches said an occupation army of 1,500,000 men would move into Japan following the formal surrender. The Army listed occupation needs in the Pacific on next July 1 as 900,000.)

Army officials told the House military affairs committee last week that they would reduce the critical score from 85 to 80 and lower the automatic discharge age as soon as word was received from Gen. Douglas MacArthur that the bloodless occupation of Japan was assured.

The extension to V-J Day of the date for figuring point totals will add at least four to eight points to the score of every man and woman who has served continuously since May 12, the Army said.

"All points earned since the defeat of Germany for service, overseas duty, combat awards and parenthood thus will be added to the individual's original scores."

MORE POINTS ADDED

Under the revised system if a soldier now overseas had earned 72 points or more on V-E Day he would now be eligible for release since the four months since then (a month's credit is given if the better part of the final month is served) would give him 4 points for general service and another four for overseas duty.

If a soldier overseas acquired a child since V-E Day and he did not already have three children it would add another 12 points to his score, boosting a man with 60 or more points to the necessary 80. Similarly with combat badges, medals, etc.

Army officials last week said that when MacArthur's assurance came, in addition to dropping the point score to 80 no soldier with 60 points would be sent overseas. The War Department did not say in its announcement last night whether this policy is now in effect.

Authorization for discharge of men and women 35 and over with two years service does not in any way affect the present policy of permitting automatic discharges of personnel 38 and over regardless of length of service, the Army said.

TO CUT SCORE LATER

It said transportation is the vital factor in determining the speed of demobilization, and that when the number of men being brought home begins to slacken so that it appears there may be unused ship or plane space, "the critical score will again be reduced."

"There will be no vacant space on any homeward bound ship or plane," the Army promised.

The announcement said there were now only three highly technical skills so essential that men would have to stay in uniform regardless of their point scores: orthopedic mechanics, transmitter attendants at fixed stations and electroencephalographic (brain wave) specialists. Of these, it said, there are only a few in the entire Army.

The Navy released a 12-month discharge schedule under which 3,000,000 officers and men will be released by Sept. 1, 1946.

The Army and Navy ended all censorship of mail and telecommunications among members of the armed forces in all theatres.

BADEN SAILOR WOUNDED

A Navy Department casualty list released for publication today revealed that Seaman 1 c William H. Davis, State street, Baden, was wounded in action. Next of kin were notified previously.

More U. S. Troops Pour Into Japan

GENERAL MacARTHUR'S HEADQUARTERS, YOKOHAMA, Sept. 3 (UP)—The vanguard of a new Occupation Army flew into Southern Japan today as American troops in the Tokyo area expanded their foothold to more than 700 square miles.

Under an occupation program that ultimately will put 1,500,000 Allied troops in Japan, 20 American technicians landed in two transport planes at 1:30 p. m. (12:30 a. m. EWT) at Kanoya airfield on the southern tip of Kyushu, southernmost of the Japanese home islands.

They will set up communications facilities and otherwise prepare for large-scale American landings by air at Kanoya and by sea at Takasu, four miles southeast of Kanoya, beginning tomorrow.

The sea-borne forces will be landed under cover of Admiral Raymond A. Spruance's Fifth Fleet. Kanoya, site of the air-borne landings, formerly was a Japanese suicide-plane base for attacks on Okinawa.

(Radio Tokyo said 6,000 American troops also would be transferred from Atsugi airfield, 18 miles south of Tokyo, to Hiratsuka in northern Kyushu. The broadcast, reported by the FCC, said American authorities already had begun negotiations for the tansfer of the police chief and mayor of Hiratsuka.)

Japanese radio broadcasts said 3,000 troops of the Eighth Army began landing at the Tateyama naval and air base on the Chiba peninsula at the southeastern entrancne to Tokyo Bay at 9:20 a. m. (8:20 p. m. Sunday, EWT).

They will take over occupation of the area from an advance landing party of Marines.

Some 13,000 veterans of the Eighth Army's First Cavalry Division landed yesterday at Yokohama, Japan's fifth largest city and the main port for Tokyo, and took over its occupation from a handful of air-borne troops without incident.

The division which spearheaded MacArthur's drive from the Lingayen Gulf to Manila, has been selected to lead the Allied march into Tokyo, but the date for the formal Allied entry has not been announced.

TOKYO OUT OF BOUNDS

Tokyo was out of bounds to all Americans today, even including newsmen.

Despite an earlier announcement that 40,000 American troops had gone ashore in the area just south of Tokyo, authorities said the total number of troops brought in by both air and sea now totalled only 25,000.

But massed behind them at island bases where they had been training for a bloody invasion of Japan were nearly 1,500,000 other Allied troops who will pour into the enemy homeland in a steady stream to take over all key communications points and other strategic areas.

Gen. Douglas MacArthur, with Japan's surrender formally signed and sealed, disclosed that he will create a four-man advisory board to aid him in ruling the country through Emepror Hirohito and the Japanese government.

Admiral Chester W. Nimitz will represent the United States on the board, and other members will be drawn from the United Kingdom, Russia and China.

TO ENFORCE TERMS

At Guam, Nimitz' Pacific Fleet Headquarters issued a "guidance" order of the day to all naval occupatuion forces emphasizing that the terms signed by

Continued on Page 24

Million Japs On Pacific Islands Laying Down Arms

GUAM, Sept. 3. (UP)—The surrender of 1,000,000 or more Japanese troops from the Bonin Islands to New Guinea and from Penang to Wake was either under way or definitely in the works today as result of Japan's formal capitulation.

The only Japanese troops still fighting on the vast Pacific battlefronts were 10,000 holding out in the Shwegyin area of Burma. Cut off from radio communication with the outside world and unaware that Japan has capitulated, they raided a village 35 miles north of Rangoon Saturday night.

The situation, front by front, was:

PHILIPPINES—Lt. Gen. Tomoyuki Yamashita, the erstwhile "Butcher of Bataan" and "Tiger of Malaya," surrendered the last 40,000 survivors of his original army of 250,000 men in an 11-minute ceremony at the mountain resort city of Baguio north of Manila.

BONIN ISLANDS.—Lieutenant-General Tachibana, commander of the island group 650

Continued on Page 24

V-J DAY EDITION

Today's TIMES is crammed with V-J Day and Labor Day messages from Valley merchants, industries and other business places, along with stories pertaining to the war, both in the Pacific and in Europe.

In publishing this V-J edition, THE TIMES joins with its readers in giving thanks to God that the long and bloody war has ended after bringing so much suffering, bloodshed, sorrow and destruction to the world.

It is good to live again in a world which, once gone mad with greed and bloodshed, has returned to peace and sanity.

Now we must turn to the arduous task ahead—that of reconverting our lives, our industry and our business to peacetime pursuits. We must never forget the magnificent job our men and women in the armed forces have done in bringing victory and peace, nor must we forget those for whom the war will never end—those who must spend the rest of their lives in veterans' hospitals.

We must assure that those who gave their lives in the war did not die in vain, by preventing war — with its bloodshed and destruction — from ever again bringing suffering and misery to the world.

JAP ADMIRAL ENDS LIFE

SAN FRANCISCO, Sept. 3—(UP) Radio Tokyo said today that Vice Admiral Matsuo Morizumi, superintendent of shipbuilding and ordnance in the Osaka naval defense district, committed hari-kiri last night, presumably in a fit of despondency over Japan's surrender.

Water Pageant At Beaver Tonight

A large crowd is expected to witness the annual Laor Day water pageant at the Beaver swimming pool tonight at eight o'clock. The show will be presented under the direction of the pool manager, Jack Laney.

Mrs. John Beckert Dies At Rochester

Mrs. Katherine Beckert, 86, well-known Rochester woman, died late Sunday afternoon in her home.

The body was removed to the Hartzel funeral home and later to the home of her son, Henry Beckert, 619 Reno street, where the funeral service will be conducted Wednesday at 2:30 o'clock. Rev. Hans O. F. Simoleit, pastor of St. Paul's Lutheran church of which she was a member, will officiate. Burial will be in Oak Grove cemetery.

Born in Millheim, Germany, she had resided in Rochester forty-two years. Surviving are the husband, John Beckert; two other sons, Carl Beckert, Fallston, and Ernest Buchsenschutz, Portland, Me., and seven grandchildren.

COUNTY SERGEANT AWARDED BRONZE STAR MEDAL OVERSEAS

Tech. Sgt. Andrew L. Bingham, Jr., son of Mr. and Mrs. A. L. Bingham, Kennedy Place, New Brighton, recently was awarded the Bronze Star Medal for meritorious achievement in connection with military operations in North Africa and Italy from June 1, 1944 to July 31, 1945. He is chief clerk of the voucher audit section of the audit branch, Office of the Fiscal Director, MTOUSA.

His official citation read in part: "Sgt. Bingham exhibited exceptional ability, resourcefulness, and efficiency in the performance of his duties. His professional knowledge and constant devotion to duty proved invaluable to the operation of his section and his superior work was of great value to the fiscal director, and reflects great credit upon himself and the military service."

Overseas 16 months, Sgt. Bingham wears the Mediterranean Theater Ribbon with one Battle Participation Star and the Good Conduct Medal. A graduate of Washington and Jefferson College, Washington, Pennsylvania, class of 1929, he is married to Chief Petty Officer Ellamae M. Bingham, a Spar, stationed at the United States Coast Guard Training Station, Brooklyn.

5 Firms Pledge Sewage Disposal

HARRISBURG, Sept. 24—(U.P.)—The State Sanitary Water Board today had "direct and unequivocal promises" that five industrial firms will do all they can to meet waste treatment standards required by the commonwealth in its stream clearance campaign.

Although some of the companies which sent representatives to the Board meeting said they believe they had installed adequate treatment works, they agreed to improve disposal systems after the agency pointed out that they must meet certain standards.

Ursinus College, also ordered to appear at the meeting, did not send representatives, but notified the Board that it had employed an engineering firm to prepare sewage treatment plans.

The five industrial firms were Virginia Pulp and Paper Company, with plants at Williamsburg and Tyrone; Chemical Concentrates Corps., Whitemarsh Town Hip, Montgomery County; Hanover Canning, Hanover; Otto Chemical Company, Wetmore Township, McKean County, and Middleburg Tanning Corp., Middleburg.

Bearing acreage of California-Arizona navel oranges decreased slightly during the past 20 years; in the same period Valencia acreage showed a 90 per cent increase.

Child's Frock

9263 SIZES 2-8

Ummm, pretty! What a sweet, simple-to-make dress for your wee angel! Curved seams give Pattern 9263 a gay bolero effect, which you may accent by using contrast fabric.

Pattern 9263 comes in children's sizes 2, 4, 6, 8. Sizes 6, frock, takes 1⅛ yds. 35-in.; ⅝ yd. contrast.

Send TWENTY cents in coins for this pattern to Evening Times Pattern Dept., 232 West 18th St., New York 11, N. Y. Print plainly SIZE, NAME, ADDRESS, STYLE NUMBER.

NEW — the Marian Martin Fall and Winter Pattern Book is yours for Fifteen Cents more! All easy-to-make styles! ALSO printed right in the book is a page of complete directions for you — an accessories set: hat, jerkin and handbag.

Better Labor Relations Urged

Cited As Means To Raise Living Standards

PITTSBURGH, Sept. 24 (U.P.)—Improved management—employe relations could effect a standard of living ten times better than it is today, according to a Cleveland manufacturer.

James F. Lincoln, president of the Lincoln Electric Co., Cleveland, told members of the Smaller Manufacturers' Council here than an incentive plan for workers can produce 10 times as many goods at one-tenth the cost as under the present system.

Lincoln believes his policy of "incentive management," successful in his company for 15 years, can eliminate present labor agitation and enable post-war wages to be on a high level.

A change in the state of mind of the employe rather than a speed-up, is the key to the Lincoln plan. "Every man must be just as enthusiastic in doing work for which he gets paid as in taking part in a play for which he pays," Lincoln believes.

Latent abilities can only be brought about through an incentive program, Lincoln said, giving employes piece work pay, an annual bonus, and a role in the management.

Trade Schools License Ok Due

Committee's Approval Of Regulations Asked

HARRISBURG, Sept. 24 (U.P.)—An advisory committee representing business and labor today will be asked to approve regulations for licensing of Commonwealth trade schools, drafted by the State Public Instruction Department in accordance with a law passed by the last legislature.

Gov. Edward Martin appointed John O. Judge, Pittsburgh, as chief of the private trade school division, a new agency created in the department to carry out provisions of the act. The Post pays $4,200 annually.

Judge will meet with the Advisory Committee and the State Vocational Education Board to set up operating standards for the schools so they can obtain licenses by the Oct. 29 deadline.

The committee is composed of L. B. F. Raycroft, Philadelphia, manager of Public and Industry Relations for Electric Storage Battery Company; Hugh Smith and G. B. Ussery, managers of the Philadelphia and Pittsburgh Better Business Bureaus; James L. McDevitt, Pennsylvania Federation of Labor President, and John A. Phillips, Chairman of the State CIO Industrial Union Council.

The Department planned to expand membership on the Committee later.

Yank-German Wedlock Banned

BERLIN, Sept. 24 (U.P.)—The U. S. Group Council announced today that there was no intention of allowing marriages between service personnel and German civilians in the American occupation zone.

The announcement apparently blasted any hopes that any GIs might harbor for taking German wives. The Allied Control Council yesterday lifted all restrictions on such marriages, subject to the individual decision of each occupation zone commander.

It was understood that there was no prospect of lifting the marriage ban in the American zone, at least in the foreseeable future.

The relaxation of the fraternization rules yesterday becomes effective Oct. 1. The new decision also left to the zone commanders the matter of billeting troops with German families.

Instructions were being issued in the American zone today renewing the rule against marriages.

Texas has a 1945 cattle population of 7,590,000.

NYLON SALE AND NO CASUALTIES

ALTHOUGH YOU'RE PROBABLY INCLINED to doubt us, take our word for it—this is a nylon stocking sale and no one was trampled in the rush. A salesgirl in a McKeesport, Pa., store (top) waits on some of the fortunate customers who bought their hosiery at $2.25 a pair. At bottom can be seen the orderly line of women waiting to get into the store. Just to make certain that everything turned out O.K., only four customers at a time were permitted to enter the store. *(International)*

Devereaux Home

DISPLAYING a happy smile, Lt. Col. James P. Devereaux, hero of the defense of Wake Island, is shown as he arrived at Oakland Airport, Cal. He spent almost four years as a Jap prisoner after his capture on Wake. *(International Soundphoto)*

On the Way Back

AMONG the many war heroes heading home from imprisonment in Jap war camps is Sergt. Irving Strobing, Brooklyn, N. Y., pictured here as he arrived at Ft. Shafter, Hawaii. He was the "ghost voice" of Corregidor who sent the last message from the fortress before the "Rock" fell to overwhelming enemy forces. This is an official Signal Corps Radiophoto. *(International)*

Observe Pulaski Day, Martin Asks

HARRISBURG, Sept. 24 (U.P.)—Gov. Edward Martin has proclaimed Oct. 11 as General Pulaski Day and asks that appropriate ceremonies be held in all Commonwealth schools, churches and other appropriate places.

The proclamation, which also directed that flags be displayed from all public buildings, was in accordance with a 1931 Legislative act designed to "perpetuate the honored memory of General Pulaski."

Count Casimir Pulaski, a native of Poland, volunteered for service with George Washington's army during the Battle of Brandywine. He later was promoted to Brigadier General and commanded the Pulaski Legion of Cavalry which he organized. He was wounded during the siege of Savannah, Ga., Oct. 9, 1779, and died two days later.

First Harvard President

GREENVILLE, N. H. (U.P.)—Henry Duster, first president of Harvard College, is buried in an old cemetery in Greenville.

Vets, Ex-War Workers Can Learn Trade

HARRISBURG, Sept. 24 (U.P.)—Pennsylvania veterans and demobilized war workers have an opportunity to learn new trades—leading to "relatively secure, well-paid employment"—under a program mapped by the Pennsylvania Apprenticeship Council.

Frank K. Boal, Council secretary and deputy head of the State Labor and Industry Department, said 857 courses were organized through the cooperation of 1,800 employers in the commonwealth.

Apprenticeship training, he added, would be provided in building, manufacturing and automotive industries. He emphasized that the demand for skilled workers was increasing "despite the layoff of thousands of production workers and common laborers."

Marines Enlist Men 17 To 25

Two Sergeants Due Here Today, Tomorrow

Men 17 to 25 may now voluntarily enlist in the U. S. Marine Corps although they have not had previous military experience.

Two Marine sergeants, veterans of the fighting in the Pacific, will be in Aliquippa today and tomorrow to interview young men interested in joining the Marines.

Discharged men who are under 32 and who have not been separated from military service for more than a year will be accepted. Ex-Marines enlisting within 90 days after discharge will receive the remainder of the three month period as a reenlistment furlough.

No enlistments will be accepted in the U. S. Marine Corps Reserve. Marine veterans, regular, reserve or inductees, re-enlisting within 90 days following discharge will be appointed to their temporary rank held on the discharge date.

The island bases in the Pacific must be left in able hands, the Marine Corps believe. The Corps wants only the finest men to take over these bases from the war weary veterans who now await return home.

The new Marine will probably man former Japanese bases and outposts such as Truk, formidable enemy bastion in the Carolines. Men assigned to sea duty will find almost every port in the world open to them. The average length of duty overseas, with the fleet or on island bases, will be 18 months.

Plan 11 Snoopin'

By TEABABY

Local dance promotor Sib Green has booked Walter Harper's orchestra to provide music for dancing Friday night, Sept. 28, at the Fourth Ave. hall.

Nick Babich of Spaulding St., is now on leave from the Army. After many months of overseas duty, the likeable chap from the Hill wears the Purple Heart and upon his return to camp, he may be eligible for an honorable discharge.

Mrs. Etta Wilkens has recently returned from her trip to Florida.

Angelina Perich, 712 Davis St., was feted at a gala birthday party at her home this week. Present were Sophia and Ann Fechushak, Jenny Perich, Mildred Chervenka, Mrs. Turkovich and many out-of-towners. Topping the evening's entertainment was a solo by Ann Fechusak, whose number was from the operatic score, "Carmen." Miss Perich received numerous gifts from her many friends attending the party.

Pfc. Walter Reft is furloughing at home from the Army. He recently returned from a long stretch of overseas duty.

Seaman Alvin Unis is another fellow on a furlough. Seaman Unis has a brother, Charles, who is now overseas.

Marvin Morris will leave Sept. 26 for Riverside Military Academy in Georgia, accompanied by Marvin Neff, who is also enrolled at the Academy there.

SHOWS FOREIGN MOVIES

COLUMBIA, S.C.—The Laurel Street USO here has set up "The Laurel Street Filmarte," devoted to showing the best in foreign films. Every two weeks a French, Austrian, Russian, or English film of note is featured.

Nice on the Beach

PRETTY starlet Audrey Young models one of the newer bathing suits seen at the beaches about Hollywood. It's a two piece white diaper suit of jersey with a flower print design. *(International)*

State Employment Declines Only 1%

Wages Drop 7% From Preceding Month

PHILADELPHIA, Sept. 24 (U.P.)—Employment in Pennsylvania factories declined only one per cent during August despite the surrender of Japan, the Federal Reserve Bank of Philadelphia reported today.

Production workers employed in 2,800 reporting factories totaled 1,113,000, compared to 1,242,000 in August, 1944, the bank report showed.

The total amount of wages paid and hours worked were seven per cent less than in July. However, part of the decline was attributed to holidays following the surrender, the report said.

Average weekly earnings in reporting plants in August were $44.04, compared with a peak of $49.25 in March of this year. Average hourly earnings of $1.07 were two per cent lower than the March peak.

Delaware factories reported an increase of two per cent in employment during August, with increased activity in the canning industry responsible for the rise. Wages declined seven per cent and hours worked dropped four per cent.

Oklahoma Came Through

MUSKOGEE, Okla.—When the 3,000,000th guest of the Okmulgee Avenue USO appeared last month he received a $100 War Bond, an engraved identification bracelet, a telephone call home, and a miscellaneous supply of wearing apparel, all contributed by local groups.

EATING, DRINKING PERMIT ISSUANCE TO BEGIN WEEK

HARRISBURG, Sept. 24 (UP)—First licenses for Pennsylvania's rural eating and drinking establishments probably will be issued late this week, the State Department disclosed today.

The Department said it expects to mail sample copies of permits to local health officials in commonwealth cities, boroughs and first class townships sometime this week but would not begin licensing rural establishments until "at least a day after the samples are mailed."

Officials recommended that community authorities use licenses similar to those which will be used by the state in second class townships, but added that "there's no compulsion about this, we're just urging that the licenses be uniform."

Some permits already have been issued by local Health Boards. The State will handle enforcement of the new restaurant sanitation law only in second class townships.

The department said its sanitarians had recommended approval and licensing of between 200 and 300 rural eating and drinking places, but pointed out that all these recommendations must be reviewed by Secretary Harry W. Weest before permits would be granted.

The advisory health board drafted a list of stringent sanitary regulations which must be complied with by operators, even in localities where municipal officials will be charged with enforcement.

Found Dead In Car

QUAKER CITY police found the body of John B. Thayer (above), 50, financial vice president of the University of Pennsylvania, in his car near Fairmount Park, Philadelphia. His throat and wrists were slashed. It was said he was despondent ever since his son, Edward, was killed in combat in 1943. *(International)*

Unlabelled Ice Cream Being Sold

HARRISBURG, Sept. 24—(U.P.)—The State Agriculture Department issued another warning today that ice cream consumers should guard against purchases of inferior products.

Secretary Miles Horst said many retailers were selling unlabelled products, in some cases stocking them in cabinets of well-known, reliable manufacturers. Some of the ice cream does not meet state purity and weight requirements, Horst said.

Horst, who warned of this practice several weeks ago, said it had continued despite lifting of Government restrictions on manufacture of frozen foods.

A number of Philadelphia dealers already have been convicted of violations and fined an aggregate of more than $500.

Towns To Get Aid In Police Pensions

Due Half Of Taxes Paid By Insurance Firm

HARRISBURG, Sept. 24 (U.P.)—State Auditor General G. Harold Wagner today revealed that applications have been mailed to 61 Pennsylvania municipalities to determine eligibility for financial aid to their police pension funds.

Legislation passed by the 1945 General Assembly provides that one-half the amount of taxes paid by foreign casualty insurance companies shall be distributed to municipalities having organized police pension funds for use in such programs. The amount available this year is $761,018.

Wagner said that of some 3,000 questionnaires mailed to municipalities, 876 have been returned.

Included in the municipalities indicating they have police pension funds are:

Amridge, Midland, Beaver Falls, Butler and New Castle.

Texas ranks second in the nation in annual turkey production, trailing California.

Tax Structure Pleases Martin

HARRISBURG, Sept. 24—(U.P.)—Gov. Edward Martin was "well pleased" today with Pennsylvania's tax structure as compared with other states, but he awaited additional information before releasing full details.

The tax survey Martin ordered made several weeks ago by Dr. Edward B. Logan, budget secretary, and Floyd Chalfant, State Commerce Department head, was completed, but the chief executive said he wanted more information on rural areas.

Martin said several neighboring states appeared to be "in better shape than we are in certain respects," but generally Pennsylvania's tax structure was more favorable than the entire group included in the survey.

QUIPS, BRIDGERS IN 24TH GRID THRILLER

Year's Top Crowd Assured As Locals Bid For 'AA' Win

Rubenstein Blue; Aschman Expects 'Anything To Happen'

Aliquippa High spreads out its welcome mat to Ambridge High as the two rival football teams clash tonight at the local stadium in their 24th annual grid classic, which is tinged with more bitterness as the years roll on.

Carl Aschman's Red-and-Black eleven will enter the fray favorites to notch its third straight Class AA win, but Santa Claus may make an early appearance at the stadium tonight and place a victory in Moe Rubenstein's sock.

SEEKS UPSET

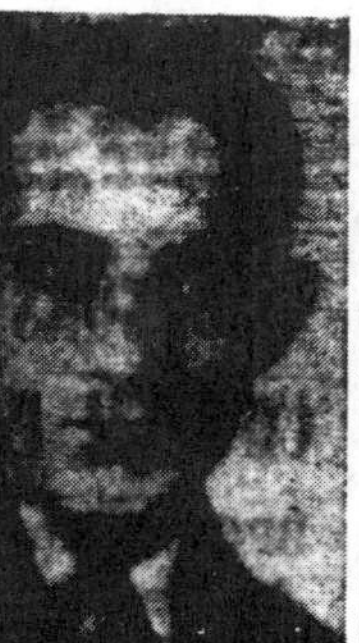

MOE RUBENSTEIN

The largest crowd of the season will jam the stadium to its full capacity as an additional five policemen squad from Ambridge will assist the Aliquippa police in handling the football throng expected to reach over 8,000 fans.

Game Is Sell-Out

The game is a sell-out as far as reserved seat tickets are concerned and 4,000 general admission tickets have been placed on sale downtown and at the Aliquippa schools. No student tickets will be sold at the game.

Having eliminated Butler and Rochester, 21-2 and 18-0 respectively, the Quips will have their hands full tonight as Rubenstein unfolds a few of his tricks. The Bridgers will stage a dog-fight battle to upset the Aschmanites, though they have lost their last three games. Victory-starved for so long has given the boys from across the bridge an appetite for a lusty win tonight over the favored and confident Quips.

Doubtful Starters

Rubenstein has announced that Ray Frangione and Mike Despines are doubtful starters. Alex Gozur may fill in for the latter at the left end position and Bob Hunt may replace Fragione at left guard.

Milan Maravich, veteran center,

(Continued on Page Seven)

RED PEPPERS

By NICK SVASOVICH

After messin' up on the World Series and the Aragon boxing opener last night, our average now limps at a wobbly .722.

It can't be any worse, so let's take another fling at calling 'em as we see 'em:

HIGH SCHOOL

Monaca, 12, Hopewell 7
Freedom 18, Leetsdale 6
Rochester 13, Beaver Falls 0
E. Liverpool 6, Midland 0
New Brighton 36, Trinity 6
Coraopolis 7, Neville 6

COLLEGE

Pitt 14, Michigan State 6
Navy 27, Penn State 13
Army 31, Michigan 14
Indiana 47, Nebraska 6
Ohio State 38, Wisconsin 6
Notre Dame 19, Dartmouth 6
California 18, UCLA 12
Purdue 48, Iowa 0
Duke 14, Wake Forest 7
Minnesota 68, Fort Warren 0
Penn 21, North Carolina 14
Syracuse 13, West Virginia 6
Columbia 7, Yale 0
Texas 34, Oklahoma 7
Temple 14, Bucknell 0

* * * *

Just messin' aroun' and talkin' it up down along the Wye sportsmen's beach, we came up with the following heterogeneous Ambridge-Aliquippa write-up:

"Hey, there. . . you. . . yeah. . . whatcher name?. . . Sam Urick . . . what's yours?. . . now let's not get funny, bub. . . whaddaya think of the game tonight? Who, why, and by how much? . . ."

Sam Urick: "We oughta take 'em by four touchdowns, providing Smisko is in the game. If he isn't, we'll still beat them, but by two touchdowns. The score? Aliquippa 28 Ambridge 0."

We whistled and the waitress gave us a dirty look from across the counter, but she had us figured wrong.

"Sue, whaddya say? . . . no date. . . . whaddaya say the outcome tonight will be?"

Sue Kmetz, downtown restaurant waitress: "Ambridge will win simply because of Aliquippa's jinx when the name of [illegible] They're [illegible] the name itself. Ambridge 6 Aliquippa 0."

Shufflin' down the street, we collided with Broadway Sam, who said: "Aliquippa will take them this time. Aliquippa 12 Ambridge 6."

Chuck Jurges, bartender downtown, said: "Aliquippa to wiggle out a victory over Rubenstein's team. Aliquippa 14 Ambridge 7."

Another Aliquippan, a war vet, who likes Ambridge to upset the Quips, is Miller Radich, who said: "Ambridge to down the Quips by passing, Ambridge 13 Aliquippa 6."

We hopped over to Ambridge and the first gent we saw we mistook for Rubenstein. . , "Hey. . . 'scuse me. . . er. . . ah. . . we thought you were. . . oh, the heck with it. . . who do you think will win the Ambridge-Aliquippa game?. . . . Are they playing this

(Continued on Page Seven)

Underdogs Eyeing WPIAL Grid Upsets

Host Of Unbeaten Contenders Are On The Spot Tonight

Quips, Duquesne, Monessen, Greensburg Face Elimination

Underdog teams will struggle tonight to dump highly-rated contenders out of the Class AA race in the WPIAL.

Aliquippa entertains Ambridge, Duquesne visits Scott, Norwin plays at Greensburg, and Monessen engages Johnstown at home.

Duquesne will try for its sixth straight victory, and its fourth in "AA", in visiting Scott at North Braddock Stadium. Powerful Duquesne has allowed opponents only 12 points, but Scott has improved in recent games and is determined to make a contest of it.

Greensburg Favored

Greensburg seeks a third win and its second straight in Class AA as host to Norwin of Irwin. Ace Wiley's Greensburgers defeated Connellsville, 26-0 last Friday night.

Unscored-on Johnstown Trojans are favored to win their fifth victory and their first AA match in battling the Greyhounds at Monessen. The Trojans beat Conemaugh Twp., Mt. Union, Perry and Glassport before deadlocking in a scoreless tie with Windber at Point Stadium last Saturday night.

Rams Meet Tigers

Some other games scheduled tonight present Rochester at Beaver Falls, Monongahela at Brownsville, Erie East at Clairton, Redstone at Connellsville, Farrell at New Castle, Penn at Har-Brack, Kittanning at Apollo, Sharon at Punxsutawney, Springdale at Arnold, Indiana at Blairsville, East Deer at Tarentum, Jefferson at Carmichaels, Claysburg at Bedford, Central Catholic at McKeesport, St. Vincent Prep against Johnstown Catholic at Point Stadium, Altoona Catholic at [illegible] daysburg, Weirton, W. Va. versus Linsly Academy at Wheeling, Lock Haven at Huntingdon, Hershey Industrial at Lewistown, Philipsburg at Tyrone, and Williamsburg at State College.

At Connellsville last night Armand Niccolai's Dunbar Township High scored in the third and fourth periods to topple South Union Township Blue Devils, 19-0, before 3,500 fans. Wee Willie Wright was the scoring ace with two touchdowns.

Other scores yesterday: Cecil 25, Findlay 6; Bellevue 27, Avalon 7; N. Braddock, Jr. 0, Swissvale Jr. 0; Wilkinsburg Jr. 14, Verona Jr. 0; Belle Vernon 7, Ellsworth 0; North Catholic 13, New Kensington 6; Somerset 27, Scottdale 0; Beaver 20, Mars 6; Masontown 41, Mapletown 0; Steubenville Central 82, Magnolia 0.

A katydid's ears are located in its forelegs.

"BIG THREE" OF TIGERS WHOOP IT UP AFTER WIN

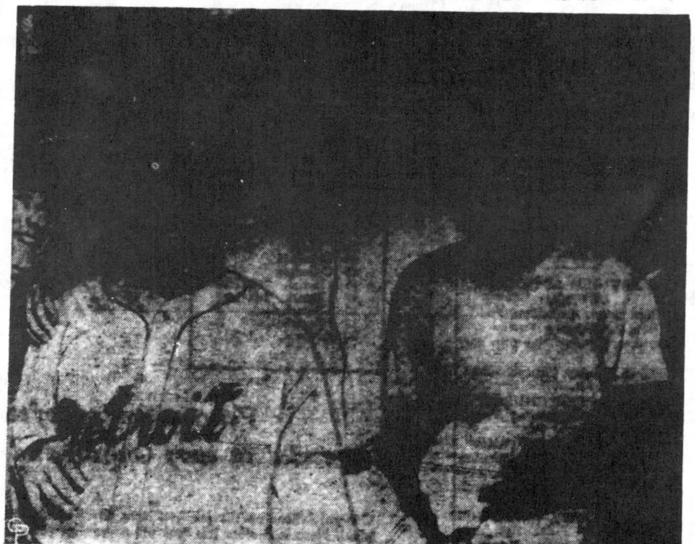

HAPPY STEVE O'NEILL, manager of the Detroit Tigers, with the winning battery of the club in the seventh and deciding game, Pitcher Hal Newhouser, center, and Catcher Paul Richards are shown after the 9-3 victory over the Cubs which gave the Tigers the world's championship. (International soundphoto)

Wary W&J Begins Grid Comeback

Prexies Oppose Fletcher Hospital

WASHINGTON, Pa., Oct. 12—Whether Washington and Jefferson College football teams will regain their prewar status will be answered tomorrow when the Presidents present their first team in three years against Fletcher General Army Hospital at Cambridge, O.

Coaches Wilbur (Fats) Henry and Furman Ness, after final pre-game drills yesterday, selected a probable starting lineup for the seasons inaugural.

William Keeler, 180, Greensburg, Pa., and John Love, 175, Smock, Pa. will start at ends. Terry Koval, 195, Marianna, Pa., and Carl Gillespie, 170, Washington, Pa. have won tackle berths.

Winning over heavier competition, Don Moore, 165, Cadiz, O., will be at center.

The backfield, deep in reserves, will operate from the "T" with 155-pound Carl Bucheit, Canonsburg, Pa., calling the signals. Bucheit fomerly played with Trinity College.

Harry Frazek, of Pittsburgh, and Preston Williams, of Homestead, Pa., each weighing 170, won halfback posts with their speedy showing in practice sessions.

Rudy Vujnovich, 190 of Pittsburgh, has been named fullback but his position is threatened by 210-pound Pete Shulin, Washington, Pa.

Zivic Matched

NEW YORK, Oct. 12. (UP)—Cpl. Fritzie Zivic, former welterweight champion, was signed today for a 10-round match with Joe Reddick of Paterson, N. J., at Ridgewood Grove Arena Oct. 20.

Series' Players In Exhibitions

NEW YORK, Oct. 12—(U.P.)—New York will get the last 1945 glimpse of baseball, it was revealed today with announcement that four Detroit Tiger stars and one Chicago Cub would play in exhibition games Sunday.

Hank Greenberg, Eddie Mayo and Doc Cramer of the Tigers will play with an all-star team against the Brooklyn Bushwicks at Dexter Park. Virgil Trucks of the Tigers and Bob Chipman of the Cubs will pitch for Chuck Dressen's all-stars against a Negro national league all-star team at Ebbets Field.

'46 Fish Seasons Same As This Year

Commission Lists Length, Limits

HARRISBURG, Oct. 12—(UP)—Pennsylvania anglers were advised today by the State Fish Commission that the various 1946 seasons would remain the same as this year's.

Charles A. French, State Fish Commissioner, said the agency approved these seasons which are identical to those followed this year both in length of time and creel limits:

TROUT—Brook, brown and rainbow, April 15-July 31, ten daily of combined species.

BASS—Small and large mouth, July 1-Nov. 30, six daily of combined species of not less than nine inches.

PIKE-PERCH—July 1-Nov. 30, six daily of not less than 12 inches.

PICKEREL—July 1-Nov. 30, six daily not less than 12 inches.

MUSKELLUNGE (Wester and Northern Pike)—July 1-Nov. 30, two daily of not less than 24 inches.

Fishermen also were reminded of the amendment to the motor boat law the 1945 legislature passed, which becomes effective next year.

The amendment provided that no boat of more than five horsepower may be operated on inland waters of the commonwealth in locations where the stream is not more than 150 feet wide. The restrictions, however, do not apply to motor boats or other watercraft engaged in commercial navigation.

The father of Albrecht Durer, German painter, designer and engraver, was a goldsmith. Albrecht was the third of a family of 18 children.

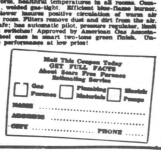

EVERY SONG RINGS THE GONG FOR ANOTHER ROUND OF LAUGHTER!

The News-Tribune

Sports Page

GABBY HARTNETT, former major league manager and catcher, is the new manager of the Buffalo team (International)

Army, Navy Clash Shaping Into First Rate Title Contest

By MURRAY ROSE

NEW YORK—(AP)—Now that Navy's intricate "T" machine finally has begun to click, the Middies' Dec. 1 clash with all-conquering Army begins to shape up as a first rate championship contest.

The Midshipmen served notice on the Cadets that they will be ready to roll in the Philadelphia fracas by the ease with which they bowled over a spunky Michigan club, 33-7, at Baltimore Saturday.

The Navy's harnessed power will be unleashed Saturday against poor little Wisconsin, beaten and battered 25-14 by Northwestern. This Baltimore tilt is Navy's last prep before the "big game."

Meanwhile, the Army, looking bigger and better than ever after their awesome 48-0 walloping of Notre Dame which made them the first Cadet corps in history to beat the Irish two straight, journeys to Philadelphia to take on potent Pennsylvania. The Quakers, beaten only by Navy, showed they were the class of the east, not counting the service teams of course, by knocking Columbia's light Lions from the ranks of the unbeaten and untied teams by a 32-7 count.

A third important eastern fray pits Holy Cross, one of the six major elevens left with unmarred records, against the deflated Temple Owls who were dropped from the all-conquering ranks 27-10 by Penn State. This is the last big obstacle in the way of a bowl bid for Stanley Koslowski and his Holy Cross mates who dumped the Coast Guard Academy 39-6 Sunday.

Along with Army, Oklahoma Aggies, Holy Cross and St. Mary's, Alabama and Virginia remain the only big time teams left with unblemished records.

HANK LUISETTI, one of the greatest of modern collegiate basketball players while at Stanford university and now in the service, is reported in line for Annapolis, where he will become assistant coach of the Navy basketball team (International)

Penn-Army Big Weekend Tilt

By LEE LINDER

PHILADELPHIA,—(A. P.)—There's no love for the Army mule on the University of Pennsylvania campus today as the echo of the Quakers 32-7 triumph over Columbia changed into a questioning "What will the Cadets do to Penn Saturday?"

The unbeaten, untied Columbia Lions were not as soft a touch as the lop-sided score might indicate. Columbia was seven points up on Penn 10 plays after the opening kickoff when Gene Rossides, 17-year-old all-America hopeful, pitched six aerial strikes to reach paydirt.

But here the Quaker line took over the Columbia offense was stopped cold—and the Penns cracked for touchdowns virtually at will.

So now comes the Army. Penn, beaten only by Navy, is going to need everything—maybe even a prayer—to upset an Army eleven that hasn't lost in 20 straight games.

"We'll try to work out some tricky defenses and do all we can to hold them," says Penn's George Munger. "I don't mean we aren't going to try to beat them."

Temple's Bowl dreams hit the ground with a sickening thud when the Owls checked in their first 1945 loss in seven starts, bowing 27-0 to Penn State at State College.

It wasn't too extraordinary an accomplishment for the Nittany Lions—like Penn only beaten by Navy—for State had been favored to knock the Templars for a loop. Penn State now is almost certain to get a Bowl bid.

Besides Penn and Penn State, three other Keystone state college football elevens won last Saturday; eight lost.

Villanova ended its season the same way it started it—with a triumph. The Wildcats smothered Boston College 41-0 at Philadelphia. The win gave Villanova an even split in an eight-game schedule.

West Chester Teachers college edged Swarthmore 12-7 to remain undefeated. A 6-6 tie with Delaware, however, mars the Teachers' unsullied record.

The University of Pittsburgh Panthers continued their losing ways for the fifth straight week, dropping a 14-0 decision to Ohio State.

For 50 minutes however, on a rain-swept field, the Panthers battled toe to toe with the Buckeyes hoping to score what would have been considered an upset with a deadlock. But the invading Ohioans were not to be denied—and two quick touchdowns were counted.

Rutgers took the brass cannon, symbolic of the Middle Three football title, away from Lafayette drubbing the Maroon 32-14 at Easton.

Slippery Rock Teachers edged Fairmont State Teacers 7-0 at Fairmont, W. Va.; Drexel Tech bowed 26-13 to Johns Hopkins at Baltimore; New York university whitewashed an invading Lehigh eleven 19-0; Haverford lost 32-20 to Delaware on the latter's gridiron, and Lincoln university was thumped 27-6 by Virginia State at Oxford, Pa., in other games.

Detroit, Cleveland Tie For Pro Lead; Steelers Top Cards

By JIMMY JORDAN

CHICAGO—(AP)—It will be at least two weeks before the principals in the National football league intersectional title playoff can be determined—and there isn't any surety today about which clubs will be named then.

Green Bay, the defending champion, is virtually out of any title consideration. Cleveland and Detroit are tied for the lead in the western section. Philadelphia, in second place in the eastern division, still has a chance to get into the playoffs although trailing Washington.

Detroit and Cleveland stayed on top of the western division standings yesterday by dumping over the teams given a chance to further upset the standings in an already crazy title chase. Detroit came from behind to beat the vastly improved Chicago Bears, 35 to 28, while Cleveland handed Green Bay a 20-7 beating, the third in seven starts for the champion packers.

Meanwhile, Washington was scoring 28 points in the last half to beat the Boston Yanks, 34 to 7. Philadelphia romped over New York, 38-17, with 17 points in the second quarter and 14 in the last period.

In the only other game, Pittsburgh dumped the Chicago Cardinals, 23-0, in what was the biggest upset in the league yesterday.

Baseball Leaders Look to Convention

By JACK HAND

NEW YORK—(A. P.)—Threats from the minor leagues that they would refuse to recognize Commissioner A. B. (Happy) Chandler unless the major loops were prepared to make concessions on draft prices and territorial protection appear to have dissolved today as baseball leaders turn their attention toward the National association convention in Columbus, December 5, 6 and 7.

Buried deep among the 51 proposed amendments to the code to be considered at Columbus, as forwarded from the office of Association President William G. Bramham, is a proposal that the major-minor agreement be extended to January 12, 1947 "to permit the revision committee to agree on changes and submit its proposals, presumably at the 1946 meetings."

Although this joint committee really did get to work on its problem during the summer, after four years of inactivity, and has prepared a compromise settlement, it is understood that most of the minors favor pigeon-holing the report for a year.

Eventually a showdown must come and a new pact must be drawn up but it probably will not happen at Columbus.

With baseball facing such reconversion problems as taking care of over 4,000 returning service players, most of its leaders are inclined to by-pass "family" quarrels.

An amendment permitting all classifications to pay bonuses to players for signing contracts, a privilege now enjoyed only by the Double A circuits except in the case of first year men, will certainly excite considerable debate. Many club owners are greatly concerned over the tendency to pay $10,000 and $15,000 bonuses to untried schoolboys. This amendment may bring the entire problem out into the open.

Still another proposal would set December 1, 1946, as the end of the "duration of the emergency" insofar as baseball is concerned. Leagues permitted to suspend because of the war would have to reorganize 90 days after that date or have their territory declared open.

Schoolboy Football Across Pennsylvania

By TOM SHRIVER

HARRISBURG—(AP)—There will be no armistice today in the war for scholastic football supremacy in Pennsylvania as more than 20 teams swing into action in holiday grid games.

Huntingdon, current pace-setter of the western conference seeks to keep its unbeaten streak intact against tail-end Ebensburg in one feature attraction, while Dunmore, Northern division leader of the Eastern Conference, invades Scranton Central for another big game.

Unbeaten State College High, tied by Tyrone, will wage its annual duel with Bellefonte, with the winner gaining possession of an antique iron kettle. Punxsutawney and Dubois clash for the new Beachuck trophy, named for the school mascots, the Beaver and Woodchuck.

Clearfield at Curwensville; Osceola Mills at Philipsburg, and Blakely at Jessup are other big games on the state program. In Pittsburgh the city championship is at stake as unbeaten Allegheny faces Westinghouse.

Huntingdon and Dunmore hope to remain in the thinning ranks of the unbeaten which now includes Donora, New Kensington, Williamsport, Bedford, and Kulpmong.

Lancaster was the latest to fall by the wayside, the Big Fifteen contenders bowing to John Harris, 21-7. In other conference frays Williamsport jolted William Penn of Harrisburg 18-7; Allentown defeated Easton, 19-7; York crushed Steelton 28-6, and Lebanon upset Reading 19-6.

Other games across the state found Donora rolling up a 41-0 score on Washington to end its regular season without a setback; Kulpmont beat Coal township 27-0 for its 20th straight win; Erie East nosed out Erie Tech 19-13; Johnstown edged McKeesport 7-0; Altoona crushed Braddock 34-0; Sharon tied Farrell 6-6; Warren, Ohio, nosed out New Castle 18-12, Hazleton blanked Shenandoah 14-0; and Pottsville jolted Tamaqua 27-14.

Hershey High clinched the South Penn Conference crown by beating Hanover 21-7; Northampton neared the Lehigh Valley crown by beating Stroudsburg 41-6; and Weynesburg ended an unbeaten season by jolting Swissvale, 19-6.

Hornets Trounce Loop Leading Caps, 7 to 3

Indianapolis finally knows today how it feels to lose a hockey game after winning eight and tying two of its first 10 American League starts.

The Pittsburgh Hornets gave the league-leading Caps a lesson in fancy stick handling right in their own back yard last night; 7 to 3.

"Hat tricks" were a dime a dozen, two of the Buffalo Bisons doing the stunt in their 10-3 romp over St. Louis.

Providence had the second largest turnout of its history, 6,401 fans, to watch the Rhode Island Reds bow to Hershey, 5-2, for their fifth straight loss.

New Haven also had a capacity house of 4,000 customers to watch Cleveland rack up its second victory in as many nights over the Eagles, 6-3.

Next league action is Wednesday night when Indianapolis will be at Buffalo and St. Louis at Hershey.

Weekly Football Schedule

Games for Saturday, Nov. 17, 1945

Home Team	1944 Score	Home Team	1944 Score
EAST		**SOUTH**	
		Southeastern Conference	
Dartmouth-Cornell	13-14	Auburn-Georgia	13-49
Drexel-Lehigh	13-6	Georgia Tech-Louis State	DNP
Holy Cross-Temple	30-0	Vanderbilt-Alabama	DNP
Penn-Army	7-62	**Other Games**	
Pittsburgh-Indiana	0-47	Catawba-V. M. I.	7-6
Princeton-Columbia	DNP	Maryland-Virginia	7-18
Rutgers-New York U	DNP	Miss. State-NW La. Inst.	DNP
Syracuse-Colgate	43-13	North Carolina-Wake Forest	0-7
Yale-Coast Guard	7-3	Presbyterian-Florida	DNP
WEST		Tulane-Clemson	36-20
Western Conference		V. P. I.-Richmond	DNP
Iowa-Minnesota	0-46	**SOUTHWEST**	
Michigan-Purdue	40-14	**Southwest Conference**	
Ohio State-Illinois	26-12	Rice-Texas A. & M.	0-19
Big Six Conference		So. Methodist-Arkansas	20-12
Kansas-Kansas State	14-18	**Other Games**	
Missouri-Oklahoma	21-21	Louis. Tech-SW La. Inst.	DNP
Other Games		Okla. A. & M.-Texas Tech	14-7
Baldwin-Wallace-Wooster	20-20	Tulsa-Baylor	DNP
Drake-Iowa State	0-0	**ROCKY MOUNTAINS**	
Earlham-Ball State	7-27	Brigham Young-Nevada	DNP
Great Lakes-Fort Warren	28-7	Colo. Coll-West Texas Coll	DNP
Ill. St. Norm.-Ill. Wesley	0-19	**PACIFIC COAST**	
Ill. Tr.-West Ill. Tr.	18-0	**Pacific Coast Conference**	
Northwestern-Notre Dame	0-21	California-Oregon	DNP
INTERSECTIONAL		Oregon State-Wash. State	DNP
		Other Games	
Michigan State-Penn State	DNP	U. C. L. A.-St. Mary's	20-0
Kentucky-Marquette	DNP	Washington-Idaho	DNP

DNP—Did not play each other (last) year.

Grid Calendar

HIGH SCHOOL

Today

Darlington at Newell, W. Va.
*Shadyside Academy at Beaver

Tuesday

*New Brighton at Beaver Falls, Reeves stadium, 8 p. m.
*Norwin at Rochester.

Thursday

*Zelienople at Monaca.

*Night games.

HAMLIE ACCEPTS BID TO DEPAUL BASKET TOURNEY

The six team field for DePaul university's invitational intercollegiate basketball tournament in the Chicago stadium December 12, 14 and 15 was within one of completion with the receipt yesterday of an acceptance from Hamline university of St. Paul, Minn. Other entrants are DePaul, Oregon, Washington and Bowling Green.

CUBS LEAVE FOR CAMP FEBRUARY 17

CHICAGO,—(A. P.)—The Chicago Cubs will leave for training at their Santa Catalina Island, California, camp February 17, James Gallagher, vice-president of the club, said today. Batterymen will comprise the first group. Infielders and outfielders will depart February 24. It will be the Cubs' first trip to their island camp since 1942.

RESUMES BASKETBALL

WASHINGTON, — (A. P.)—George Washington university will return to intercollegiate athletic competition in the approaching [illegible] after a layoff of [illegible]

Sport Briefs

By HUGH FULLERTON, JR.

NEW YORK (AP) Don't be too surprised if Louisiana turns up alongside Kansas and Indiana as a major basketball state one of these years. . . . That's partly behind the idea of building a 24-team court at L. S. U. . . . There's a big livestock show building that isn't used the rest of the year and Athletic Director T. P. Heard figures he can put in a hardwood floor and make it possible for as many as 100 teams to compete in the state high school tournament. . . .

MONDAY MATINEE

Football fans from the Rocky Mountain area are plugging Utah's Gay Adelt for "all" honors. . . . Gay hasn't been stopped twice in succession, writes one, and the offense can point for him on every play because he's the only one who can get to the line of scrimmage. . . . Madison Square Garden will stage 21 basketball doubleheaders this winter, which hardly looks as if the game was retreating to college gyms because of last winter's scandal. In Ned Irish's first year in the garden he put on eight twin bills.

CLEANING THE CUFF

In return for Joe Louis' appearance on Jack Benny's radio show, Rochester, Jack's stooge, will second Joe in an exhibition at San Francisco Thursday, both appearances strictly comedy. . . . The National Baseball Congress, which had over 200 radio stations giving baseball rule books, helpful hints and "how-to-play" books to kids last summer, plans to repeat the stunt next year.

Qu'p Bucktails Meet

The Aliquippa Bucktails are scheduled to meet Tuesday night, Nov. 13, at 8:00 o'clock in the evening at the club house. Following a short business meeting there will be refreshments, motion pictures and door awards.

Members are reminded not to forget the big turkey shoot scheduled for Sunday, Nov. 18 from 9:00 o'clock in the morning until dark, at the club house.

YALE COACH RETURNS

NEW HAVEN, Conn.—The return of John Skillman to his duties as coach of all racket sports at Yale University was announced recently. Skillman was on leave [illegible]

Tigers-Brighton Await Postponed Battle Tomorrow Night At Stadium

HERE ARE THE BEAVER FALLS TIGERS, undefeated in nine starts, and ready to go against the New Brighton [illegible] evening at 8 o'clock in Reeves Stadium. Shown from left to right are the following: First row—Chiappetta, Hornsell, [illegible] Leslie, Varga, McDanel, Brooks, Gumpf; middle row—Casey, Shumaker, Prellwitz, Bill James, Omogresso, McCandless, [illegible]; back row—Richter, Knapp, C. James, McCutcheon, Alderette, Mitchell, Midon, Britton, Mutscheller, John James. At [illegible] was taken, Bill Boller, quarterback and T-operator of the Tigers was missing. The game was postponed Friday [illegible] (News-Tribune Photostat)

WITH SIX WINS AND TWO DEFEATS, the above New Brighton Lions are set to go tomorrow night against the unbeaten Beaver Falls Tigers in the 31st annual renewal of their time-honored rivalry. Front row—Pontier, J. Budiscak, Powers, Demeter, [illegible], Crawford, Dwyer, Weber, C. Roser and Gillespie; back row—Chogich, Ramsey, Price, Wilson, Zettle, Holzworth, T. [illegible], Autenreith, Bowser. Coach George Roark is being assisted this year by Coleman Kopscak, former Carnegie Tech star. (New-Tribune Photostat)

Big Falls-Brighton Grid Game Carded Here For Tuesday Nite

Rochester Also To Close Season on Home Field With Norwin Hi

The big game of the year—a few days off its regular schedule—will be held tomorrow night at 8:00 o'clock in Reeves stadium with all the fanfare that would have accompanied the clash originally carded on Friday night, which was postponed due to rain in the morning and afternoon. The battle referred to is of course the Beaver Falls-New Brighton game that has been a treat for nearly a third of a century, marking the close of the season for both teams.

Postponed also from Friday night is the Rochester-Norwin game to be staged tomorrow evening on the Ram field in Rochester at 8:00 o'clock.

Holiday Game Tonight

Meanwhile, enthusiasts will be on hand from all over the county tonight when the Beaver Bobcats entertain the Shadyside academy eleven on the Beaver field following the parade in Beaver marking the annual Beaver county celebration of Armistice day.

In a game this afternoon at Newell, W. Va., the Darlington Hornets will seek their initial victory in three starts. It's the first season of football in Darlington high school history.

On Thursday evening, the final game in the county will be held at Monaca high's Memorial stadium with the Indians facing Zelienople high.

Teams Still Intact

The Beaver Falls-New Brighton game, expected to draw a capacity audience from miles around, will find both clubs still with the teams as intact as they would have been on Friday night.

All players injured in earlier season play have recovered and the usual battle royal is expected. The Beaver Falls band will stage a pre-game show in the darkened stadium, therefore holders of reserved seat ducats are instructed to come out early. New large numbers have been placed on the seats, making them easy for fans to pick out.

AUSTRALIA RECEIVES U. S. NET CHALLENGE

MELBOURNE, Australia, (A. P.) An official challenge from the United States for the Davis Cup, emblematic of international tennis supremacy, was received by the Australian Lawn Tennis association last week—nearly three months before the closing date for challenges, January 31, 1946.

ARMY QUINTET SWAMPS SWISS UNIVERSITY, 64 TO 12

GENEVA, Switzerland—(A. P.)—An all-star army basketball team, now touring Switzerland, defeated the University of Geneva recently, 64 to 12. Corporal Charles Edwards of Hammnod, Ind., former forward at Ohio State, was high man with 17 points. Second with 13 was Private First Class Davage Minor of Gary, Ind., former Toledo [illegible]

FOOTBALL Results

HIGH SCHOOL

Altoona 34; Braddock 0.
Andover 18; Exeter 7.
Central Catholic 6; Glassport 0.
Donora 41; Washington 0.
Greensburg 6; Wilkinsburg 6.
Hickory Township 21; Brookfield 12.
Johnstown 7; McKeesport 0.
Munhall 6; Homestead 0.

COLLEGE

Kentucky 19; West Virginia 6.
Ohio State 14; Pitt 0.
Penn State 27; Temple 0.
Slippery Rock 7; Fairmont 0.
Army 48; Notre Dame 0.
Brown 20; Yale 7.
Cornell 20; Colgate 6.
Harvard 28; Kings Point 7.
Navy 33; Michigan 7.
N. Y. U. 19; Lehigh 0.
Penn 32; Columbia 7.
Princeton 13; Dartmouth 13.
Villanova 41; Boston College 0.
Great Lakes 27; Michigan State 7.
Illinois 48; Iowa 7.
Indiana 49; Minnesota 0.
Northwestern 28; Wisconsin 14.
Ohio U. 33; Baldwin-Wallace 7.
Oklahoma 14; Iowa State 7.
Purdue 21; Miami (O.) 7.
Western Michigan 66; Wooster 0.
Auburn 52; Southwestern Louisiana 0.
Duke 26; North Carolina State 13.
Georgia 34; Florida 0.
Georgia Tech 41; Tulane 7.
Maryland 38; V. M. I. 0.
North Carolina 6; William & Mary 0.
Tennessee 34; Mississippi 0.
Oklahoma A. & M. 12; Tulsa 6.
Rice 26; Arkansas 7.
Texas 21; Baylor 14.
Texas A. & M. 3; Southern Methodist 0.
Texas Tech 12; Texas Christian 0.

SUNDAY SCORES

Holy Cross 39; Coast Guard Academy 6.
Loras 25; St. John's 7.
St. Louis 14; Fort Riley 7.

NATIONAL LEAGUE

Pittsburgh 23; Chicago Cards 0.
Washington 34; Boston 7.
Cleveland 20; Green Bay 7.
Philadelphia 38; New York 17.
Detroit 35; Chicago Bears 28.

SPORT SHORTS

STATE COLLEGE, Pa.—(AP)—Paul Campbell will resume his duties as Penn State wrestling coach following his recent discharge from the Navy.

Campbell, a lawyer and former Eastern intercollegiate champion, directs the wrestling squad only after a full day in his law office.

WILLIAMSPORT, Pa.—(AP)—The regular fall meeting of the Eastern Baseball league will be held at Utica on Sunday, Nov. 18. President Thomas H. [illegible]

[illegible] brought up [illegible]

PHILADELPHIA—(AP)—Villanova College Wildcats [illegible] their 1945 football season [illegible] night when they tackle the [illegible] ton College Eagles at Shibe Park, renewing a series interrupted [illegible] years ago.

Favored over the Boston College array, the Wildcats can complete their season with a [illegible] mark by [illegible] the New England [illegible] their 19-7 inaugural victory over Bucknell University and the contest with the Eagles are Wildcat wins over Marquette and Detroit, and losses to Navy, Holy Cross, Tennessee and Army.

PHILADELPHIA, (A. P.)—The University of Pennsylvania basketball team, defending Eastern Intercollegiate League champions, will play 17 games this season, director of athletics H. Jamison Swarts announces.

The schedule: Dec. 8, Dartmouth, away; 12, Swarthmore, away; 15, Cornell, home; [illegible] Princeton, away; Jan. 5, Dartmouth, home; 9, Valley Forge hospital, away; 12, Yale, away; [illegible] Army, away; 19, Columbia, home; 23, Muhlenberg, away; 26, St. Joseph's, home; 30, Navy Yard, away; Feb. 2, Cornell, away; 6, Coast Guard, away; 9, Princeton, home; 12, Columbia, away; 16, Navy, home.

PHILADELPHIA, (AP)—A 21-game court schedule has been scheduled for St. Joseph's College which opens its 45th season Dec. 5 against Washington University of Chestertown, Md., says Coach Billy Ferguson.

The schedule: Dec. 5, Washington College, home; 8, Utah, home; 12, Cathedral College, home; 15, Lafayette, away; [illegible], North Carolina, home; Jan. 1, Wyoming, home; 5, St. John's (Brooklyn), away; 9, Catholic University, away; 19, Rhode Island State, home; 23, Pennsylvania, home; 30, Elizabethtown College, home; Feb. 2, LaSalle, home; 6, Albright, home; 9, Juniata, home; 13, Brooklyn Polytech, home; 16, Rhode Island State, away; [illegible], Muhlenberg, away; 20, CCNY, home; March 2, Temple, home.

NEW PHYSICAL DIRECTOR

RIDGWAY, Pa.—(A. P.)—Captain Gerald R. Wiser of Port Matilda, will take over his new duties November 15 as director of physical education, basketball coach and assistant football for Ridgway public schools. He is a 1942 Penn State graduate and commanded an anti-tank company in the army for three years.

FAVORS MOVING SERVICE GAME

WASHINGTON, D. C.—(A. P.)—Secretary of War Patterson said that he thinks it would be a good idea to hold the Army-Navy football game in different parts of the country each year.

The annual service game usually is played in an eastern city. This year's game is scheduled for Philadelphia, December 1.

CARNERA WANTS TO COME BACK

ROME,—(A. P.)—Primo Carnera, former world heavyweight champoin who left boxing for movie acting and recently turned to wrestling, has applied to the Italian Boxing Federation for a permit to meet heavyweight Luigi Musina in Milan November 20 or 21. Carnera is now 38 years old.

Weather Forecast
Clearing tonight and continued rather cold Wednesday, cloudy and milder with occasional rain.

THE DAILY TIMES

1874—and WESTERN ARGUS—1803

ROCHESTER - BEAVER - MONACA - FREEDOM - BRIDGEWATER - CONWAY - VANPORT - MIDLAND

War History
Germany began turning its navy over to the Allies, November 20, 1918, with the surrender of 27 submarines to the British

Established April 2, 1874 | Beaver and Rochester, Pa., Tuesday, November 20, 1945 | Single Copy 4 Cents — 24 Cents A Week

HISTORIC TRIAL OF NAZIS OPENS TODAY

FDR BLAMED BY ADMIRAL FOR POLICIES

Pearl Harbor Probers Told How Kimmel's Predecessor Opposed Late President's Order Regarding Disposition Of Fleet

WASHINGTON, Nov. 20 (UP)—Adm. J. O. Richardson said today that Adm. Harold R. Stark, chief of naval operations, agreed with his argument against basing the fleet at Pearl Harbor in 1940, but that the late President Roosevelt overruled them.

Richardson was commander of the U. S. Fleet from January, 1940, until he was relieved on February 1, 1941, by Rear Admiral Husband E. Kimmell.

Richardson told the Pearl Harbor investigating committee he strongly opposed keeping the fleet in Hawaiian waters because it could not be effectively defended or supplied there.

He also testified that he never heard until today of a letter sent in January, 1941, by the late Secretary of Navy Frank Knox to former Secretary of War Henry L. Stimson in which Knox said it was "easily possible" that Japan might start hostilities with a surprise attack on Pearl Harbor.

The Knox letter was made public last August when results of the Army and Navy investigation of the Pearl Harbor attack were released by President Truman.

SAW ROOSEVELT TWICE

Richardson told the committee that he made two trips to Washington in 1940 to talk with President Roosevelt.

The investigating committee sought to learn today whether Richardson was relieved as commander of the U. S. Fleet because he opposed President Roosevelt's order to base the Pacific Fleet at Hawaii.

The admiral's testimony also developed that:

1. Mr. Roosevelt doubted in October, 1940 that we would go to war if the Japs attacked the Philippines but that he believed the Japs sooner or later would take some step that would lead us into war.

2. The President wanted the Fleet based at Hawaii as a restraining influence on the Japanese.

DIFFERED WITH F. D. R.

3. Richardson didn't think it had any restraining influence on the Japanese and involved distinct disadvantages if a war did come. He wanted the base maintained on the U. S. West Coast.

4. Richardson got the impression after a visit to the White House in October, 1940 that active open steps aimed at Japan were contemplated and he didn't think existing plans in event of war were adequate.

5. Adm. Harold R. Stark, then chief of Naval operations, expressed great concern over safety of the Fleet at Pearl Harbor and asked Richardson to take all necessary safety precautions. In December, 1940, he told Richardson war might come "any time after the next 90 days."

6. Richardson told Stark in January, 1941, of precautions taken but because of equipment shortages he still didn't think they were adequate to defend the Fleet and harbor against an air attack.

TELLS OF ARGUMENT

That was one of Richardson's last reports as Fleet commander. He gave a copy to his successor, Adm. Husband E. Kimmel, who was in command when the Japs delivered their sneak blow December 7, 1941.

Richardson told in detail of his argument with Mr. Roosevelt dur-

Continued on page Four

B-29 Sets New World Distance Record

WASHINGTON, Nov. 20 (UP)—A U. S. Superfortress enroute here from Guam broke the world's non-stop distance record today when it passed over La Crosse, Wis., at 9:30 a. m., the War Department announced.

When the plane reached La Crosse it had flown 7,368 miles, exceeding the previous record of 7,158 miles made in 1938 by British fliers who flew from Egypt to Australia.

The B-29 was expected here at 1:30 p. m. this afternoon.

Free Lecture on The Atomic Bomb

Under sponsorship of the Men's [Fell]owship organization of the Beaver United Presbyterian church, a free lecture on "Atomic Energy—the Atomic Bomb" will be given in Guild Hall at the church Wednesday evening, November 21, at 8:15 o'clock. Officers of the organization announced today that the public will be welcomed to this free discussion of a highly popular subject —11 20

Rochester Borough To Let Contract For Sewage Plans

Rochester Borough Council, meeting in semi-monthly session Monday evening in the municipal building, voted to enter into contract with the Baker Engineers for plans and specifications for a sewage disposal plant, required by the state, subject to approval of Borough Solicitor George A. Baldwin.

The frame house and shed located at the borough incinerator plant were sold to Nelson Dunlap, Rochester, for $50 to be razed and removed from the property.

TO PURCHASE SIGNS

A request by the public safety chairman, William Ketterer, for the purchase of a dozen stop signs and a dozen "no parking" signs was granted.

The finance committee was instructed to arrange a meeting between the tax collector and delinquent tax collectors to straighten out the delinquent tax collections.

An ordinance vacating a part of Railroad street in accordance with an agreement with the Pennsylvania Railroad Company was passed on first reading.

Fort McIntosh Boy Scout Officers Are Re-Elected For Year

Officers of the Fort McIntosh District, Boy Scouts of America, were all re-elected at the annual dinner-meeting of District Scouters, their wives, friends and other interested persons, Monday evening in Beaver.

The oficers, elected by balloting of representatives of Scout and Cub units during the dinner in the United Presbyterian church, are:

Ralph J. Jewell, Midland, chairman; Carl A. Swanson, Rochester Area vice-chairman; David G. Cameron, Beaver Area vice-chairman; Hugh J. Claspy, Monaca Area vice-chairman; Vance Thompson, Midland Area vice-chairman, and K. H. Jacobsen, Beaver, District commissioner.

District Committee members-at-large elected are:

Rochester—C. A. Berger, William Reid, William Moore, Louis Reese and Michael Baker, Jr.; Beaver—J. Ross Buchanan, Fred S. Schleiter, Charles E. Cole, Morris Shulgold and Jack Malone; Monaca—Fred Aiken, Jr., Alex Bucsko, J. H. E. McMillan, Frank T. Dindinger and Christy Mangin; Midland—Edward A. Robbins, Joseph Coughlin, Arthur Gittens, Edward W. Hopper and Merrill C. Wright.

AWARDS PRESENTED

George E. Day, Rochester, District advancement chairman, presented a plaque for the best attendance at the last District Court of Honor to Troop 478, of Brewer's school. D. I. Hutchinson, Rochester, District chairman of camping and activities, presented plaques to Troop 425, Grace Lutheran church, Rochester, for its camping record at Camp Umbstaetter last Summer, to Scoutmaster J. Bert Olsson, and plaques for the Beaver Area troops for winning the swimming meet and indoor track meet at Camp Umbstaetter, to Mr. Jacobsen.

Announcement was made by Mr. Jewell of the award of Scouters' keys to Eugene Geist, Rochester, and Mr. Olsson.

Rev. Edwin Siess, Freedom Scouter, asked the invocation and led group singing at the dinner, accompanied by Lucille Wilson Hutchinson, New Brighton.

MEETING FOLLOWS

A pageant in nine scenes, with special lighting effects and stage settings, highlighted the meeting in Beaver High school auditorium following the dinner. With Rev. Gerald O. Bishop, Freedom Scouter, as narrator, the pageant was given by a large cast of Scouts, Cubs, Scouters and a Den Mother and portrayed the various phases of Scouting and Cubbing.

Another feature was a colorful Court of Honor at which Mr. Olsson was presented his Eagle Scout badge by his small son. In addition, Star rank was conferred on several Scouts.

After announcement of results of the election by E. M. Wallover, Midland, the re-elected officers were escorted to the stage by a group of Scouts and were formally inducted by Scouts. District leaders and holders of the coveted Silver Beaver were introduced by Mr. Jewell.

A brief talk, entitled "Scouting and You", was given by Rev. Fr.

Continued on Page Four

Lost And Found

LOST: Lady's wallet, Monday evening, near Steinfield's store, Connecticut Ave., Rochester, containing $4.50, driver's and Social Security cards, etc. Finder please call Roch. 891-R. 11 20-21

LOST: Lady's Elgin wrist watch with gold chain bracelet, probably in Beaver or near Ludwig's store, New Brighton. Reward. Call Beaver 1731. 11 20-27 inc.

AUTO WORKERS AWAITING GM ANSWER TODAY

Company Given Until 4 O'Clock This Afternoon To Reply To Union Proposal For Arbitration Of Wage Demands, Inspect Books

By UNITED PRESS

CIO auto workers today awaited an answer from General Motors before calling a system-wide strike which an industry spokesman said might paralyze operations in every major automobile company except one.

General Motors, largest and strongest of the auto industry's Big Three, was given until 4 p. m. today to reply to a United Automobile Workers (CIO) proposal. This offered submission of wage demands to a three-man arbitration board.

UAW Vice-president Walter P. Reuther warned that the machinery was set for an immediate strike among 350,000 G-M employes should the company answer be unsatisfactory.

Almost simultaneously with the union's ultimatum, George Romney, director of the Automobile Manufacturers' Association, said that a strike against General Motors would be followed within a week by shutdowns in plants of all but one other major automobile manufacturer.

It was assumed that the unnamed manufacturer was the Ford Motor Co., traditionally an independent producer.

'PHONE STRIKE CONTINUES

In other labor disputes, the "voice with a smile" was stilled by a telephone strike in 116 Illinois communities, as UAW and Ford officials resumed conferences optimistically looked to for ending a 70-day strike in the company's Windsor, Ont., plant.

In all, strikes kept 330,500 U. S. workers away from their jobs, according to a United Press count.

A 28-day walkout at the Lafayette, Ind., plant of the Aluminum Company of America, ended today when 2,700 strikers returned to their jobs pending negotiation of a wage dispute. An additional 1,300 workers were idled by the strike.

In other new labor developments, Salt Lake City employes of Rio Grande Motorways, Inc., left their jobs in sympathy with striking Denver truck drivers, and four Chicago gear and machine shops were closed by strikes. A fifth work stoppage halted operations in a steel casting company in Chicago.

Seattle residents were without newspapers for the second day, with negotiations apparently stalemated between representatives of the city's three daily papers and the International Typographers' Union (AFL). Both sides protested willingness to negotiate but neither would take the initiative in efofrts to settle a wage dispute.

At St. Paul, Minn., Gov. Edward J. Thye appointed a three-man fact-finding commission to investigate a threatened strike of 1,000 Northland Greyhound bus employes. Under the State's Labor Dispute law, a 30-day waiting period automatically ensues.

THREE-POINT PLAN

In its ultimatum to General Motors, the UAW submitted a three-point proposal dependent on the company's willingness to open its books to a three-man arbitration board and providing that the Board's findings could

Continued on Page Four

GETS DISCHARGE

S/Sgt. Clifford E. Schnuth, Jr., (above) son of Mr. and Mrs. C. E. Schnuth, Orchard street, Vanport, is now home after receiving his honorable discharge from the Army Air Forces at Greensboro Army Air Base, N. C., He flew on 35 missions in the Pacific as a B-29 gunner, including nine raids over Tokyo. In service 25 months, he was awarded the Distinguished Flying Cross, the Air Medal with four Oak Leaf Clusters and three campaign stars.

FREED PRISONERS PASS THROUGH BLASTED NAGASAKI

ON THEIR WAY HOME, Australian prisoners of war, freed after the Jap surrender, pass through devastated Nagasaki, which was the second city to be hit by the atomic bomb.

Trustees Elected At Annual Meeting Of Home For Aged

Trustees were elected for three-year terms at the annual corporation meeting of the Beaver County Home for the Aged, New Brighton, Monday afternoon in the offices of Attorney Thompson Bradshaw, Beaver.

Those named as trustees were:

Mrs. W. R. Leigh, Monaca; Mrs. John W. Hunter, Rochester; Attorney Wayne Luce, Freedom, now in the Army; Edwin M. Wallover, Midland; Mrs. T. W. McConnell, New Brighton, and Chester A. Lewis, Beaver Falls.

Reports were submitted by the officers and auxiliaries.

Area Ahead Of State Average In Bond Drive

Today's Federal Reserve Bank reports show that the 19-county Fort Pitt Area has passed the state average in the sale of individual Victory bonds, including "E" bonds. In the all-important "E" bond sale, the district continued to trail the state.

Yesterday's report showed "E" bond sales amounting to $1,582,000 to bring the total to date to $11,961,000—this is 24.3 per cent of the drive quota.

In individual bonds, including "E's" $14,666,000 was sold yesterday to bring the total sales to $45,569,000 or 49.9 per cent of quota.

Jobless Payments Here $70,403 During Week

Unemployment compensation checks amounting to $70,403 were issued to Beaver County residents during the week ended November 15, State Treasurer Ramsey S. Black announced today. The state-wide total was $1,606,898.

During the same period, discharged county veterans of World War II received $5,478 under the Service Men's Readjustment Act. Pennsylvania veterans received a total of $711,502.

Rochester Hospital To Receive State Funds

G. Harold Wagner, Auditor General of Pennsylvania, has approved payment of $3,251.75 to the Rochester General Hospital, Beaver County, for the quarter ending August 31, 1944.

The funds are paid from appropriations authorized by the Legislature for the support of State-aided institutions, and are based upon the number of patients receiving free treatment, and general maintenance costs.

Boy Accidentally Kills Mother; Ends Own Life

BLUEFIELD, W. Va., Nov. 20 Donald Terry, 13, accidentally shot and killed his mother, Mrs. Laura Terry, 48, at their home Monday and after discovering what had happened ended his own life, Sheriff Perry Dye reported.

Employment Office To Close All Day Thursday

The U. S. Employment Office, Rochester, will be closed all day Thursday on account of Thanksgiving Day. All persons who have been signing claims for Unemployment Compensation on Thursday will report to the office Friday.

Truman's National Health Plan Faces Fight In Congress

WASHINGTON, Nov. 20 (UP)—President Truman's far-reaching health insurance program today faced a hard fight in Congress.

Even backers of the $3,000,000,000-a-year scheme conceded that strong opposition lies ahead. Similar proposals introduced a year ago died in committee.

Despite Mr. Truman's repeated statement that his program did not mean "socialized medicine," the Journal of the American Medical Association promptly asserted that this was "a peculiar interpretation of the term." The Journal charged editorially that the proposal would lead to "politically controlled medicine."

Sen. Robert A. Taft, R., O., also disputed Mr. Truman's denial that the program involved socialized medicine. AFL President William Green, however, telegraphed Mr. Truman congratulations on his "forward-looking" proposal which, Green said, "meets the most urgent human needs of our nation and merits universal support."

WOULD BOOST TAXES

Under the five-point program, the government would guarantee proper medical care for every American. This would cost $3,000,000,000 annually, according to its sponsors.

They favor collecting these funds through increasing Social Security taxes and, later, by taking monies from general tax collections.

One suggestion is to increase the Social Security tax for the employer and the employe an additional 1½ per cent each on annual salaries up to $3,600. The present Social Security tax is one per cent each for employer and employe on salaries up to $3,000.

In addition to providing for payment of medical bills, the measure would grant sickness compensation. A wage-earner during his illness would receive 80 per cent of his salary or $30 weekly, whichever is smaller. Other parts of the plan call for greater federal aid for construction of health centers and hospitals, and for professional education and research.

TO HOLD HEARINGS

The present proposal at least is assured speedy public hearings. In the Senate, the bill was referred to the education and labor committee which is headed by one of its sponsors, Sen James E. Murray, D., Mont., He plans to start hearings within 10 days. They will last at least two months, according to Sen. Robert R. Wagner, D., N. Y., another sponsor.

Murray and Wagner introduced their bill in the Senate and Rep. John D. Dingell, D., Mich., introduced an identical measure in the House soon after Mr. Truman outlined his proposals in a message to Congress.

While the individual would have to pay taxes for the health insurance, he would not necessarily have to accept its benefits. He could continue to use his own doctor, and pay the bill as he now does.

SIMILAR BILL KILLED

Neither would a doctor have to participate in the scheme, Wagner explained in a Senate speech. He said a physician could continue his normal private practice, or mix his private practice with patients whose bills would be

Continued on Page Four

Army Discharges 23 More Men At Indiantown Gap

Another twenty-three Beaver county soldiers have received their discharges at Indiantown Gap Military Reservation. They are:

Midland—Pvt. James J. Ancrile; Conway—Pfc. Michael R. Karnis; near Darlington—Pfc. Jeff C. Whan.

New Brighton—Sgt. Ray A. McQueen, Cpl. Richard O'Neil and T/4 Clair Radcliffe.

Beaver Falls—Pfc. Andrew Simon, Pfc. Henry Gnas, Cpl. Stephen Hartnett, T/4 David Starr and Pfc. Clarence Miller.

Ambridge—T/4 Nicholas Gaitanis, S/Sgt. Edward Sumrok, T/3 Edward Stolaski and T/5 Joseph Marzio.

Aliquippa—Sgt. Thomas Puskarich, Pvt. Mike Carmandi, T/5 Nick Maravich, Pfc. George Williams, T/5 William Arbogast and T/5 Walter Lovrich; West Aliquippa S Sgt. Robert Lasto.

Chinese To Take Over In Manchuria

CHUNGKING, Nov. 20 (UP)—Negotiations with Soviet Russia have resulted in permission for Gen. Chiang Kai Shek's government to take over Manchuria, Central Government sources said today.

Chinese Communists continued resisting the advance of two armies north of the Great Wall. The armies were striking north along the Mukden railroad.

The Soviet view was said to be one of upholding Russia's obligations under a treaty of last August 14 to permit the National Government to take over Manchuria, but that "actual military circumstances" there prevented the occupation.

It was reported that Russian negotiators insisted that Chinese airborne occupation forces be manned exclusively by Chinese.

HEADS 40 AND 8

CHICAGO, Nov. 20. (UP)—Ottis E. Mercer, Nashua, N. H., yesterday was elected president of the 40 and 8, American Legion fun organization. Mercer succeeded Spencer E. Eccles of Utah.

CIVILIAN AGAIN

T/Sgt. Harold C. Myers, Freedom, (above) returned to work at the Spang-Chalfant plant, Ambridge, Monday, after receiving his discharge from the Army Air Forces at Indiantown Gap. In service 42 months, he flew 60 missions as a B-25 engineer gunner with the famous "Skull and Wings" Squadron in India, Burma and China. He was overseas 14 months. He is the husband of Mrs. Helen Krehner Myers, formerly of Conway, and the son of Mr. and Mrs. William H. Myers, Tenth street, Freedom.

Indictment Read To Fallen Leaders

NUERNBERG, Nov. 20 (UP)—Twenty fallen leaders of the Nazi regime went on trial before a United Nations tribunal today and listened uneasily to a shocking indictment holding them directly responsible for the death and misery of World War II.

The portentous trial that for the first time in history sought to prove aggressive warfare a crime against all mankind opened in an atmosphere of grim, cold legality in Nuernberg's ancient Palace of Justice.

Twenty-two men were on trial, all top figures in the Nazi hierarchy that overawed Europe for a decade, but two were being judged in absentia—the ailing Ernst Kaltenbrunner and the missing Martin Bormann.

Sidney S. Alderman, Washington, D. C., of the American prosecuting staff, began the reading of the 25,000 word indictment shortly after the hearings opened at 10:30 a. m. (4:03 a. m. EST).

He spoke slowly and deliberately as he read off the first of the four principal accounts in the indictment — that charging the accused men of plunging the world into war.

He was followed to the dais by members of the British, French and Russian prosecution staffs, who intoned the succeeding passages of the indictment for the benefit of the four presiding justices and the jittery defendants.

Despite several recesses ordered by the court, the reading progressed more rapidly than had been expected and there was a strong possibility that the accused might enter their pleas before the end of today's session.

DEFENDANTS INTERESTED

The defendants themselves appeared to be the most interested men in the courtroom. They followed the reading of the indictment with rapt attention over their earphones attached to their bench.

Hermann Goering, the number-one defendant, twisted uneasily in his front row seat. From time to time he leaned over to whisper something to his benchmate, Rudolf Hess, and occasionally an inane grin twitched across his fat face.

He nodded several times as Alderman traced the illegal development of the German air force under his direction in the pre-Munich days when Nazi Germany was secretly arming for war against the world.

The yellow-faced Hess was impassive throughout, clinging stubbornly to his claim that he remembered nothing of the Hitler era in which he played so large a part.

HESS ALOOF

He spoke occasionally to Goering and Joachim von Ribbentrop, but for the most part he maintained an air of cold aloofness from his fellow-Nazis and his judges alike.

Hess stared grimly at the wall when the indictment enumerated the mass murders carried out by the Nazis in their bid for mastery of Europe. Goering's eyes dropped to the floor, and Franz von Papen merely cupped his chin in his hand in an academic manner.

Hjalmar Schacht, branded as the financial brains behind the Hitler facade, laughed derisively when the French prosecutor read off that section of the indictment dealing with the murders and mass deportations of the Nazi regime.

The shabby, fear-haunted men who now must answer to the world for the lives of more than 20,000,000 persons slaughtered on the battlefields and in the concentration camps of Europe rose to face their judges at 10:03 a. m. (4:03 a. m. EST.)

GOERING "NO. 1"

Goering, wearing a prominent "number one" across his ribbonless chest, was the first of the 20 present defendants to enter the court-room. He stepped in behind an American MP at 9:19 a. m. ,clad in a light-grey uniform wihout insignia.

Julius Streicher stalked in a few minutes later and sat down heavily. He leaned forward in his seat, one hand on his hip, and surveyed the courtroom arrogantly.

By 9:42 a. m., all the prisoners were in the dock and the room began filling up with members of the four-power prosecuting staffs and the black-robed, black-capped defense lawyers.

The trial was opened formally by the four presiding justices, Francis J. Biddle, American, Sir Geoffrey Lawrence, British, Maj. Gen. Iohann T. Nikitchenko, Russian, and Henri Donnedieu de Vabre, French.

Lawrence outlined the purposes of the tribunal and recited the history of this precedent-making case that for the first time in human annals establishes aggressive war as a crime against mankind.

"The tribunal has heard with satisfaction the steps taken by the prosecution to aid defense counsel make possible a just defense," Lawrence said.

"This tral is unique in the judicial history of the world. It is a solemn responsibility of all involved to discharge their duties

Continued on Page Four

Officers Re-Elected By Supervisors At Annual Meeting Here

E. Frank Newell, North Sewickley Township, was re-elected president of the Supervisors and Auditors Association of Beaver County at the cloing session of the organization's thirty-third annual meeting in the Court House, Monday.

Other officers of the Association also were re-eelcted. They are: Wm. Ziegler, New Sewickley Township, vice-president, and Norman P. McHattie, Big Beaver Township, secretary and treasurer.

The Association named Mr. Newell, Joe McCarthy, Brighton Township, and William Wright, Franklin Township, as delegates to the annual convention of the State Association of Road Supervisors. Fred Martin, Hopewell Township, and Clair Searight, Independence Township, were elected, as alternate delegates.

SPEAKERS HEARD

Inasmuch as the State Legislature is not scheduled to meet until after next year's meeting of the Supervisors Association, no resolutions relating to approval or disapproval of pending bills were presented.

Ernest Trimble, district township engineer of the State Highways Department, spoke of the appropriation of funds by boards of township supervisors at yesterday afternoon's session.

Other speakers were C. Roy Kerr, Ambridge, a member of the Beaver County Planning Commission, who urged the cooperation of the supervisors with the planning board in establishment of zoning regulations; H. A. Thompson, secretary of the State Association of Road Supervisors, who conducted a question box, and Judge-elect Morgan H. Sohn.

Recount Asked In Ambridge Election

Friends of Matthew P. Nussbaum, Ambridge tax collector, the Republican candidate for re-election at the November 6th election, today petitioned the Beaver County courts to have the ballot boxes of each of the borough's eight voting precincts opened and the vote cast for the office of tax collector re-counted.

On the basis of returns made by the election boards and the results of the tabulation of military ballots, Nussbaum received seven less votes than his Democratic opponent, Martin Skapik.

The County Return Board, which has just about completed its computation of the votes cast at the General Election on November 6th, was designated by the court today to make the recounts on November 26th.

Reorganization Bill Sent To Conference

WASHINGTON, Nov. 20 (UP)—The government reorganization bill headed today for a Senate-House conference for adjustment of differences in the Senate and House versions of the measure.

The bill, high on President Truman's list of "must" legislation, was passed by the Senate yesterday in basically the same form as it was approved by the House October 4.

Both bills provide that any executive reorganization plan will become effective unless both Houses vote to reject it within 60 days. The Senate turned down its judiciary committee's recommendation that any reorganization plan be subject to veto by either House.

Bridgewater School Water System Repaired

The monthly meeting of the Bridgewater board of school directors, Monday evening, was devoted to routine business. It was announced that the bill for repairs to the school furnace had been paid and that extensive repairs on the school's water system have been completed.

Weather Forecast
Fair and continued cold today, tonight and Saturday.

THE DAILY TIMES
1874—and WESTERN ARGUS—1803
ROCHESTER · BEAVER · MONACA · FREEDOM · BRIDGEWATER · CONWAY · VANPORT · MIDLAND

War History
Russia was to be represented unofficially at the Versailles peace conference, it was announced December 21, 1918.

Established April 2, 1874 | Beaver and Rochester, Pa., Friday, December 21, 1945 | Single Copy 4 Cents — 24 Cents A Week

GENERAL PATTON DIES OF AUTO INJURIES

Firms' Books To Be Examined By Fact Boards

By UNITED PRESS

Strikes at a glance:

A total of 431,000 U. S. workers were away from their jobs in labor disputes today, according to a United Press survey. The major highlights:

AUTOMOTIVE — The CIO auto workers' nationwide strike against General Motors entered its second month as company and union officials met in Washington to decide whether to resume collective bargaining on CIO demands for a 30-per-cent wage increase.

TRANSPORTATION—Government labor officials still awaited assurances from union and Greyhound bus officials that they would resume operations and allow a fact-finding board to study the wage issue which has curtailed service in 18 northeastern states.

OIL—A panel hearing the facts in the dispute between the CIO Oil Workers Union and 10 major refining companies was expected to reconvene next week.

UTILITIES—CIO United Electric Workers went ahead with plans to strike January 3 at 21 Western Electric plants in Northern New Jersey and New York to back up wage demands.

LUMBER — 30,000 AFL lumber workers remained away from their jobs in Pacific Northwest pine mills, pressing for an industrywide $1.10 minimum hourly wage.

STATEMENT ISSUED

The Administration gave Government fact-finding panels extensive authority to inquire into a company's ability to pay when recommending a wage boost for settlement of an industrial dispute.

General Motors Corporation and the United Automobile Workers (CIO) today agreed to meet in Detroit next Wednesday to discuss local plant union demands.

The administration announcement, outlining the jurisdiction of fact-finding boards, elaborated on President Truman's statement that such panels "unquestionably" should have the right to examine company records to determine their ability to pay wage increases.

The wage issue, involved in virtually every labor controversy in the country, accounted for the majority of the 431,000 strike-idled U. S. workers.

General Motors' opposition to opening its books was believed a major factor in today's meeting with the union.

BOTH SIDES FIRM

Walter P. Reuther, vice-president of the United Automobile Workers (CIO) heading the union's strike strategy against GM, told the fact-finding committee yesterday that the union didn't care about seeing the company's books so long as it got a satisfactory raise.

The union held out for a 30-per-cent pay boost, which it contends the company can meet without raising prices and still have record earnings for stockholders.

A similar demand against the

Continued on Page Six

Marine Corps League To Be Formed Here

An organization of ex-Marines to be known as the Marine Corps League will be formed in the County, members of the Beaver County American Legion Committee learned at their monthly meeting in the Freedom Legion Home, Thursday evening.

David Patton, Beaver, gave a report on the projected league and announced that all discharged Marines who are interested may acquaint themselves with its purposes and organization by contacting Russell McDanel, Beaver Falls.

Legion membership has shown an increase of approximately twenty per cent in all county posts, it was reported. County Commander Millard Mecklem, Beaver, presided. The January meeting will be held in Beaver Falls.

Lost and Found

Party who dropped $5 bill in Penn-Beaver Drug Store Thursday night may have same by presenting himself for identification. McCormick and Sheldon, proprietors. 12|21

LOST: Boy's yellow kid mitten, near Hetzel's Drug Store, Adams St., Rochester, Thursday evening. Return 480 Reno St., Rochester, or phone Rochester 2370-J. 12|21-22

LOST: Three keys in folder near Levine's Hardware Store, Rochester, by sailor boy. Needed badly. Finder please call Beaver Falls 2155-R. 12|21-22

LOST: Lower set ladies' false teeth in Adams St. and Connecticut Ave., Rochester, Monday evening. Reward if returned to office of Dr. Joseph G. Huth, 274 Connecticut Ave., Rochester. 12|21-24 inc.

LOST: Stethoscope. Dr. M. L. McClandless. Call Roch. 122. Reward. 12|21

Don't Forget Gifts For Your Newsboy, Mailman and Shut-Ins

In checking over your Christmas gift list for those whom you may have forgotten in the usual rush and confusion attendant to the Yuletide season, be sure that the names of your newsboys are included. Day after day, early and late, they go through sunshine or storm, rain or hail, sleet or snow to deliver your newspaper and your mail.

Also, don't forget "shut-ins" and those who must spend Christmas Day—traditionally the happiest holiday of the entire year—in hospitals, homes and institutions. Remember that they, unlike the rest of us, cannot spend the day surrounded by relatives and friends.

Forty-Eight More Soldiers, Sailors Receive Discharges

Forty-eight more Beaver county servicemen, including twenty-nine soldiers and nineteen sailors, have received their discharges. The following were released at Indiantown Gap:

Monaca—Sgt. Clark L. Dixon and Pfc. Felice DeVincentis.

Beaver — Sgt. Theodore Dunning, Pfc. Orin R. Roll and Pfc. Paul C. Evans.

Rochester—T/5 Milton L. Moscovitz; East Rochester — Sgt. Frank J. Markess and Pfc. Harold E. Cameron.

Freedom — Pfc. Arthur W. Pearl; Midland—Cpl. Samuel A. Rosatone; near Darlington—T/5 John Skolnik.

Conway—Cpl. James F. Collins, Pfc. Robert Kierdak and Pfc. Mike Curcia, Jr.

Baden—Pfc. John Denoble Jr., Pfc. Charles Trowbridge and Pfc. Orry Hertzog.

New Brighton — Sgt. Ernest Woodske, Pfc. Darrell J. Sheets, S/Sgt. Samuel Schaub and T/3 Russell Majors.

Beaver Falls—Pvt. Albert Blazak and Sgt. James Rexroad.

Fort Knox, Ky., discharged the following six soldiers:

Monaca—Pvt. Lee O. Anderson and T/5 Henry F. Schmuck.

Rochester—Pfc. Jack E. Leonard and T/5 Edward F. Mineard.

Beaver—Pfc. Robert L. Reeder; Midland— T/5 Joseph G. Kadilak.

Two Rochester sailors, MoMM 2/c Harry Lewis Cotters and Ens. Charles W. Chewning, were released at Nashville, Tenn., and Boston, Mass., while the following received their discharges at Sampson, N. Y.:

Near Beaver— S 2/c Martin J. Bishop; Rochester—S 1/c Anton Holy; Conway—PhM 3/c Peter V. Fanscich.

Monaca—MoMM 2/c Philip K. Folland, S 1/c Steve A. Turbish, S 1/c John E. McMillen and MoMM 3/c James J. Barber.

Beaver Falls—ARM 2/c Samuel Wolfson, MM 3/c William Dean and MoM 2/c Albert Maciose; near Beaver Falls—F 1/c James Weaver, CMoMM Daniel Chapman and F 1/c Louis Couch.

1,000 HOMELESS AS AMMUNITION TRUCK EXPLODES

THIS IS THE NAVY ammunition truck which exploded on the coast highway near LaJolla, Calif., leaving 1,000 persons homeless. Rockets, depth charges and shells ripped through Torrey Pines and Camp Callan housing centers, leaving every house uninhabitable. *(International Soundphoto)*

Great Expansion Of National Guard Planned in State

INDIANTOWN GAP, Pa., Dec. 21 (UP)—Spurred by a challenge from Maj. Gen. Norman D. Cota, overseas commander of the 28th Division, Pennsylvania went ahead today with plans to reorganize immediately its famed fighting unit as a National Guard outfit.

The plan came shortly after Gov. Edward Martin assured the division's officers, who gathered to consider the reorganization, that a headquarters office for the Pennsylvania National Guard will be opened January 7 in the State Military Affairs Department here.

While it was indicated previously that the guard could not be reorganized and returned to peacetime duty before 1947, Martin said activities may be started as early as July 1, 1946, because federal funds will be made available by that time.

The new organization will be expanded greatly. It will comprise an estimated 40,000 men, compared with 18,000 when it was federalized in February, 1941. It will have two divisions instead of one—the 28th and possibly an armored unit.

PLAN OUTLINED

Martin said the guard would be set up according to this plan:

The 28th Division, 11,391 men; one armored division, 8,669 men; one infantry combat team, 3,184; three air squadrons with ground echelons, 3,000; one anti-aircraft brigade, 3,181; one mechanized cavalry squadron, 736; one military police battalion, 458; one chemical mortar battalion, 545, or a total of 31,164.

In addition, there will be tank destroyer battalions, tank units, medical troops or service troops such as ordinance and quarter-

Continued on Page Six

J. & L. Plans River Wall at Aliquippa

The Jones and Laughlin Steel Corporation has asked Federal permission for a time extension on its permit to erect a slag wall at its Aliquippa plant, Ohio river. This wall will be 17,800 feet long.

Admiral Turner Blames Kimmel in Attack on Hawaii

WASHINGTON, Dec. 21. (UP)—Adm. Richmond Kelly Turner faced questioning by the Pearl Harbor committee today on his belief prior to Dec. 7, 1941, that there was a 50-50 chance of Japan attacking Hawaii.

Committee members wanted to know whether the war warnings he drafted in November, 1941, as Chief of Navy War Plans, adequately conveyed that belief to Adm. Husband E. Kimmel, commander of the Pacific Fleet based at Pearl Harbor.

Kimmel was relieved of his command after the Japanese raid caught him by surprise with most of his fleet anchored in the harbor.

Turner gave his 50-50 estimate late yesterday during examination by committee Counsel William D. Mitchell. He left no doubt that he felt Kimmel was to blame for the fact the fleet was caught by surprise.

CITES WARNING

Turner testified:

1. He thought a Nov. 27 war warning ordering Kimmel to "execute defensive deployment" preparatory to war with Japan "fully covered the situation."

2. Proper deployment under that order would have included air reconnaissance, submarine patrol and putting ships in position to resist a possible landing attempt.

Asked whether there was any consideration in the days before the attack of changing the fleet base from Hawaii to the West Coast, Turner said:

"I assumed that most or all of it would be at sea. That was the place for it under Kimmel's

Continued on Page Six

New Housing Rules To Be Told Today

WASHINGTON, Dec. 21. (UP)—The government will unveil today the new priorities regulations which will set aside 50 per cent of all construction material for homes costing less than $10,000.

Civilian Production Administrator John D. Small will outline the regulations at a press conference. They will contain a preference for veterans who are expected to get 75 to 80 per cent of all homes built under the program.

Faced with a critical shortage of building materials for low and medium priced homes, government housing experts have agreed that priorities are necessary to insure materials for this purpose. The bulk of building materials is now going into high cost housing and industrial construction.

Organized labor believes that $7,800 instead of $10,000 should be the ceiling for priority-built housing. It maintains that veterans can not pay $10,000 for a new home. A National Housing Agency official has stated that most veterans will not be able to buy new homes costing more than $6,000.

Providence Cadet Nurses to Receive Caps This Evening

The twenty-four members of the last Cadet Nurse class to train at Providence Hospital will receive their caps in a ceremony to be held in the third floor hall of the hospital's new building at eight o'clock this evening.

Sister Irenaeus, superintendent of the hospital, and Sister Mary Stephen, director of nurses will present caps to the following young women who have completed their pre-clinical training:

Sally Bralkowski, Rita Stenger and Patricia Porter, Beaver; Anna Hogan, Rochester; Josephine Riddei, Marian Figley, Mary Jane Burns and Lorraine Davenport, Monaca; Louise Mastrovich, Midland.

Catherine Frkuska, New Brighton; Margaret McLean, Caroline Miller, Ethelberta Smith, Marian Mackenstein, Olga Miklos and Margaret Bliss, Beaver Falls; Dona Lou Horstmann and Marjorie Early, Darlington; Helen Waugaman, Geraldine Vogel, Eleanor Sopko and Emma Flenner, Aliquippa; Jane Shaffer, Ellwood City, and Margaret Hagan, Salem, O.

PRIEST TO SPEAK

Rev. Fr. Sylvester Doyle, Providence hospital chaplain, will deliver the main address. Miss Mastrovich will make the "request" for the caps and Miss Vogel will pledge the class to allegiance to the hospital's nursing school.

After the capping ceremony, the young women will be classified as freshmen students in the Providence Hospital School of Nursing and will have two and a half years' more training to complete.

Before the ceremony, senior nursing students will present a Christmas playet entitled "The Unbidden Guest."

RATIONING OF TIRES ENDS JANUARY 1ST

Supply Not Yet Adequate to Meet All Demands; Spares on New Cars, White Sidewalls, Exports Banned

WASHINGTON, Dec. 21. (UP)—Tires come off the ration list Jan. 1 but it may still be some time before there'll be enough to allow all motorists to get a complete new set.

In announcing the end of rationing, OPA and the Civilian Production Administration said total production next year is expected to be about 66,000,000 passenger car tires, that's 13,000,000 more than ever produced in this country in a single year.

As of now, however, the supply is not enough to meet all possible requests. CPA therefore will continue to ban spares on new cars, production of white sidewall tires and tire export.

In addition, OPA asked tire dealers to do everything possible to take care of hardship cases first and to distribute tires to a maximum number of motorists. A complete set of new tires, it said, should be sold only to those who genuinely need them.

ONLY SUGAR LEFT

The end of tire rationing left sugar as the only commodity on a ration list which at one time included cars, shoes and almost all food items. Tire stocks were frozen the day after Pearl Harbor and rationing began Jan. 5, 1942.

During the rest of December, motorists who hold tire purchase certificates should turn them in to dealers so they can be supplied before rationing ends. After today, no additional certificates will be issued except in emergency cases.

OPA said quotas of truck tires almost equal demand and that there are no backlogs of unfilled truck tire applications. On Dec. 1 there were almost a million unfilled passenger car applications but this figure has been reduced, to a few hundred thousand.

About 14,000,000 truck tires are expected to be produced next year. Truck and bus tire production totalled 1,082,000 this month, a 138 per cent increase over July production.

Ships Rush To Aid LST in Pacific

SAN FRANCISCO, Dec. 21. (UP)—The landing craft LST 224, reported sinking in heavy seas 25 miles west of the Golden Gate, was in "no immediate danger," the Coast Guard said early today.

All ships in the area rushed to the scene, off the Farallon Islands, late last night when the vessel's ramp door jammed after it had been opened to rescue two men washed overboard.

The Coast Guard said that the door had been repaired. An attack transport was standing by while a Navy tug rushed to assist the landing ship into port.

Air-sea rescue teams spotted the two men swimming in the water. They were taken aboard the LST, apparently uninjured, the Coast Guard said.

Family of Four Asphyxiated in Pittsburgh Home

PITTSBURGH, Dec. 21 (UP)—A family of four, which had just moved into a crowded, one-room apartment, was wiped out by carbon monoxide fumes escaping from an old gas stove, police reported today.

The leaking stove brought death to Harrison Stewart Woy, 30; Mrs. Alice Woy, 22; and their children, Harrison, Jr., one-year-old, and Judith Ann, 2.

Woy died early today in Southside hospital after frantic efforts to pull him through by treatment under an oxygen tent had failed.

The rest of the family was found dead late yesterday in the crowded flat.

HAD JUST MOVED

Ironically, the Woys had moved into the apartment just two days before the tragedy. Their unpacked belongings, including the children's toys, were still scattered about the room. In the baby's crib was a single unwrapped Christmas present — a woolen snow suit.

The father's nude body was found sprawled grotesquely over the bed where his dead children lay. He apparently had been trying to carry them to a window. The body of Mrs. Woy, partially undressed, lay in a double bed. The children were in their night clothes.

The tragedy was discovered by Gus Muniz, who sublet the apartment. He had not seen the Woys since 11 p. m. Wednesday. A small, open-flame gas heater was still going full-blast when Muniz broke in. He later told a morgue official that the stove had never been defective —"it worked good for 18 years."

Ambridge Shipyard Offered for Sale By Federal Agency

The shipyard of the American Bridge Company at Ambridge, which turned out 143 Navy combat craft, was offered for sale by the Reconstruction Finance Corporation.

Built and operated for the Navy by the American Bridge Company, United States Steel subsidiary, the property includes 64 acres of land with 10 shipbuilding berths and five dockside fitting-out positions built to accommodate vessels 300 feet long.

Among the craft built at the plant were 119 LST's, four aviation repair vessels, first of their kind constructed in the country, and 20 lighters, ships used for shifting supplies in combat areas.

EMPLOYED 14,000

Peak employment was 14,000 at the yards, on which construction began late in 1942. The program tapered off last spring and was concluded before the end of the war.

Since then, the main building, one of 23, has been used for man-

Continued on Page Six

Increase Reported in Relief Cost in County

Ramsey S. Black, State Treasurer, reported that direct relief payments made to needy residents of Beaver County during the week ending today show an increase of $10 over those of the previous week. Payments for the week totaled $519, which was $43 higher than those of the comparable week of last year.

AUTO MISHAP PROVES FATAL TO WARRIOR

Famed Hero of Warfare in Europe Dies in Heidelberg Hospital After Condition Takes Sudden Turn For Worse

HEIDELBERG, Dec. 21 (UP)—Gen. George S. Patton, "Old Blood and Guts," died in the Army hospital here today.

Patton lost his fight against injuries suffered December 9 when his car collided with an Army truck as he was motoring to hunt pheasants not far from his headquarters.

The tough and stormy Army veteran suffered a broken neck in the accident and was partially paralyzed. But a little more than 48 hours after being rushed to the hospital, he was pronounced "out of danger" unless unforeseen complications set in.

WIFE AT SIDE

His wife Beatrice was sitting at his bedside in the hospital room around which an almost deadly silence prevailed. Nurses tiptoed through the corridor, and white-helmeted military police kept all visitors at a distance.

Doctors would not say definitely that Patton had pneumonia, but he appeared to be suffering from that or some related lung infection.

Complications began Wednesday night, when excessive bronchial secretions started and the General became very uncomfortable. They continued at an increasing rate during Thursday, and the evening bulletin reported the General's condition "not satisfactory."

INJURED DEC. 9

A team of famous international military surgeons had been attending Patton in his closely guarded first floor room in the Heidelberg Army hospital.

Patton was on a pheasant hunting expedition on Dec. 9, just before his scheduled return to the United States for possible retirement, when his Cadallic collided with a 2½ ton U. S. Army truck outside Manheim. Patton suffered deep head cuts and a broken neck. His third cervical vertebra was fractured, and the fourth was displaced.

Rushed to the Heidelberg hospital, he called in a chaplain and said "okay, let's get started." His condition remained critical about 48 hours, then improved steadily. He had begun to recover some of the sense of feeling in his paralyzed limbs.

Rochester Woman, 92, Claimed by Death

Mrs. Katherine Kindelberger, 92, died Thursday evening in the home of her daughter, Mrs. Leon Alleman, Virginia avenue extension, Rochester, where she had resided twenty-one years.

The body was removed to the Anderson funeral home, Beaver, and later returned to the Alleman residence, where friends are being received and where the funeral service will be held at 2:30 o'clock Sunday. Interment will take place in Beaver cemetery.

Mrs. Kindelberger came to Bridgewater from Germany in 1891 and was a member of St. Paul's Lutheran church, Rochester. In addition to Mrs. Alleman, she is survived by six other daughters, Mrs. Louise Musgrave, Mrs. Anna Zahn and Mrs. Caroline Hogan, Rochester; Mrs. Katherine Zehnder and Mrs. Minnie Mattern, Ambridge, and Mrs. Mary Striffler, Ingomar; three sons, Emil, Bridgewater, Martin, Rochester, and Fred, Lorain, O.; forty-four grandchildren, and numerous great-grandchildren and great-great grandchildren.

Westinghouse Workers Stage Brief "Sit-Down"

PITTSBURGH, Dec. 21 (UP)—A ten-minute sit-down strike was staged today by 10,600 employees of the Westinghouse Electric Corporation in a show of strength ordered by the United Electrical, Radio and Machine Workers (CIO). A general strike, which has been authorized by employees in a Smith-Connally Act vote, will not be called until after January 1, according to the union.

Yule Programs, Dinners Planned At Hospitals, Homes, Institutions

Although many persons in county hospitals and institutions will be unable to spend Christmas with their families and friends, many interesting activities have been planned to brighten the holiday season for them.

Carol singing, religious services, visits by Santa Claus and special dinners are among the holiday features scheduled for patients and residents in the hospitals and institutions. Corridors and rooms of the various buildings have been decorated in keeping with the Yuletide season.

Rochester Hospital will begin its observance of the Christmas season with a party this evening for the nurses in their gaily-decorated home. The hospital itself has Christmas trees in the dining room, the childrens' ward and the second and third floors, and wreaths in all the windows. Two groups of carol singers will sing Christmas Eve and Christmas morning. On Christmas Day there will be gifts for the children and special favors and decorations on each patient's tray.

"Santa Slaus" Edward J. Spratt, Beaver Falls, will visit Beaver Valley and Providence hospitals Christmas Eve for the 29th consecutive year. Both hospitals have brightly-lighted Christmas trees and other seasonal decorations. Student nurses of the two institutions will sing carols in the different wards. All three of the local hospitals will have turkey for Christmas dinner.

Christmas services will be conducted in the Beaver County Home by the Lutheran Inner Mission Society Sunday and by the Salvation Army Monday afternoon. Carol singers will be present Sunday evening. The home has three Christmas trees and several outside organizations are sending greeting cards, oranges and other gifts. A menu featuring stuffed pork chops will be served for Christmas dinner.

SANATORIUM

Beaver County Sanatorium will have its annual Christmas party Saturday evening. The program will include carols and entertainment and each patient will receive a gift and a box of candy from the Ladies Auxiliary to the Sanatorium. A turkey dinner will be served Christmas Day.

PASSAVANT HOMES

Each house at the Passavant Homes, Rochester, has its own Christmas tree in preparation for the Christmas Eve visit of Santa Claus, who will have a gift for each patient. After the church service Christmas morning, gifts sent by families and friends of

Continued on Page Six